EDUCATIONAL PSYCHOLOGY

THEORY AND PRACTICE

twelfth edition

ROBERT E. SLAVIN

Johns Hopkins University

Pearson

330 Hudson Street, NY, NY 10013

Director and Portfolio Manager: Kevin M. Davis
Content Producer: Janelle Rogers
Development Editor: Gail Gottfried
Content Project Manager: Pamela D. Bennett
Media Project Manager: Lauren Carlson
Portfolio Management Assistant: Anne McAlpine
Executive Field Marketing Manager: Krista Clark
Executive Product Marketing Manager: Christopher Barry

Procurement Specialist: Carol Melville
Cover Designer: Carie Keller
Cover Photo: Getty Images/Wealan Pollard
Full-Service Project Management: Kathy Smith,
     Cenveo® Publisher Services
Composition: Cenveo® Publisher Services
Printer/Binder: LSC Communications/Owensville
Cover Printer: Phoenix Color/Hagerstown
Text Font: Bembo MT Pro Regular

Cataloging-in-Publication Data is available on file at the Library of Congress.

1   18

ISBN 10:   0-13-489510-X
ISBN 13: 978-0-13-489510-9

ABOUT THE AUTHOR

ROBERT SLAVIN is director of the Center for Research and Reform in Education, Johns Hopkins University and chairman of the Success for All Foundation. He received his Ph.D. in Social Relations from Johns Hopkins in 1975, and since that time he has authored more than 300 articles and book chapters on such topics as cooperative learning, comprehensive school reform, ability grouping, school and classroom organization, desegregation, mainstreaming, research review, and evidence-based reform. Dr. Slavin is the author or coauthor of 20 books, including *Cooperative Learning, School and Classroom Organization, Effective Programs for Students at Risk, Preventing Early School Failure, Show Me the Evidence: Proven and Promising Programs for America's Schools, Two Million Children: Success for All, Effective Programs for Latino Students,* and *Educational Research in the Age of Accountability.* In 1985 Dr. Slavin received the Raymond Cattell Early Career Award for Programmatic Research from the American Educational Research Association. In 1988 he received the Palmer O. Johnson Award for the best article in an AERA journal. In 1994 he received the Charles A. Dana Award, in 1998 he received the James Bryant Conant Award from the Education Commission of the States, and in 2000 he received the Distinguished

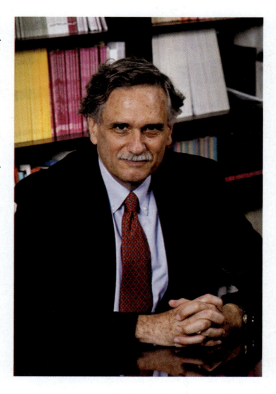

Services Award from the Council of Chief State School Officers. He again received the Palmer O. Johnson award for the best article in an AERA journal in 2008 and received the AERA Review of Research award in 2009. He was elected an AERA Fellow in 2010.

PREFACE

When I first set out to write *Educational Psychology: Theory and Practice,* I had a very clear purpose in mind. I wanted to give tomorrow's teachers the intellectual grounding and practical strategies they will need to be effective instructors. Most of the textbooks published then, I felt, fell into one of two categories: stuffy or lightweight. The stuffy books were full of research but were ponderously written, losing the flavor of the classroom and containing few guides to practice. The lightweight texts were breezy and easy to read but lacked the dilemmas and intellectual issues brought out by research. They contained suggestions of the "Try this!" variety, without considering evidence about the effectiveness of those strategies.

My objective was to write a text that:

- Presents information that is as complete and up to date as the most research-focused texts but is also readable, practical, and filled with examples and illustrations of key ideas.

- Includes suggestions for practice based directly on classroom research (tempered by common sense) so I can have confidence that when you try what I suggest, it will be likely to work.

- Helps you transfer what you learn in educational psychology to your own teaching by making explicit the connection between theory and practice through numerous realistic examples. Even though I have been doing educational research since the mid-1970s, I find that I never really understand theories or concepts in education until someone gives me a compelling classroom example; and I believe that most of my colleagues (and certainly teacher education students) feel the same way. As a result, the words *for example* or equivalents appear hundreds of times in this text.

- Appeals to readers; therefore, I have tried to write in such a way that you will almost hear students' voices and smell the lunch cooking in the school cafeteria as you read.

These have been my objectives for the book from the first edition to this, the twelfth edition. With every edition, I have made changes throughout the text, adding new examples, refining language, and deleting dated or unessential material. I am meticulous about keeping the text up to date, so this edition has more than 2,000 reference citations, 75 percent of which are from 2000 or later. The twelfth edition is updated with hundreds of new references (though essential classics are retained, of course). Although some readers may not care much about citations, I want you and your professors to know what research supports the statements I've made and where to find additional information.

The field of educational psychology and the practice of education have changed a great deal in recent years, and I have tried to reflect these changes in this edition. For example, today the Common Core State Standards and other college- and career-ready standards are increasing accountability pressures but also inviting more thoughtful teaching and learning, including writing, cooperative learning, and experimentation. I've tried to explain the new standards and show how they affect practice throughout the book, but do not discard the wisdom and research that came before them. In the earliest editions of this text, I said that we shouldn't entirely discard discovery learning and humanistic methods despite the popularity, then, of direct instruction. In the later editions, I made just the opposite plea: that we shouldn't completely discard direct instruction despite the popularity of active, student-centered teaching and constructivist methods of instruction. I continue to advocate a balanced approach to instruction. No matter what their philosophical orientations, experienced teachers know that they must be proficient in a wide range of methods and must use them thoughtfully and intentionally.

The twelfth edition presents new research and practical applications of many topics. Throughout, this edition reflects the "cognitive revolution" that has transformed educational psychology and teaching. No one can deny that teachers matter or that teachers' behaviors have a profound impact on student achievement. To make that impact positive, teachers must have both a deep understanding of the powerful principles of psychology as they apply to education and a clear sense of how these principles can be applied. The intentional teacher is one who constantly reflects on his or her practices and makes instructional decisions based on a clear conception of how these practices affect students. Effective teaching is neither a bag of tricks nor a set of abstract principles; rather, it is intelligent application of well-understood principles to address practical needs. I hope this edition will help you develop the intellectual and practical skills you need to do the most important job in the world—teaching.

NEW TO THIS EDITION

Among the many topics that receive new or expanded coverage in this edition are:

- Common Core State Standards and College- and Career-Ready Standards (throughout, but especially Chapters 1 and 14)
- The future of teaching (Chapter 1)
- More on Vygotsky's theories (Chapter 2)
- More on enhancing socioemotional development (Chapter 3)
- The development of reading from preschool onwards (Chapter 3)
- More on parent involvement (Chapter 4)
- Gay, lesbian, bisexual, and transgender students (Chapter 4)
- Updates of research on socioeconomic status, ethnicity, and English learners (Chapter 4)
- Emerging research in information processing and neuroscience (Chapter 6)
- Neuromyths and neuroclues (Chapter 6)
- The latest research on peer interaction and cooperative learning (Chapter 8)
- Project-based learning (Chapter 8)
- More on differentiated and personalized instruction (Chapter 9)
- A substantially updated section on technology applications (Chapter 9)
- A new "intentional teacher" section on technology applications
- New research on tutoring and small group remediation for struggling readers (Chapter 9)
- Research on mindset (Chapter 10)
- More on intrinsic incentives (Chapter 10)
- New sections on bullying and classroom management (Chapters 4 and 11)
- Expanded coverage of Response to Intervention (Chapter 12)
- Expanded coverage of autism spectrum disorder (Chapter 12)
- More on performance assessments (Chapter 13)
- Detailed coverage of the Common Core State Standards and college- and career-ready standards (throughout, but especially Chapter 14)
- Examples of test items and interpretation guides for Common Core assessments (Chapter 14)
- Additional coverage of value-added assessments (Chapter 14)
- More on data-informed teaching (Chapter 14)
- Description of policy changes in the Every Student Succeeds Act (Chapter 14)
- More on evidence-based reform (Chapter 14)
- More on computerized assessment (Chapter 14)
- Updated On the Web sections throughout

MYEDUCATIONLAB

One of the most visible changes in the twelfth edition, also one of the most significant, is the expansion of the digital learning and assessment resources embedded in the eText and the inclusion of MyEducationLab in the text. MyEducationLab is an online homework, tutorial, and assessment program designed to work with the text to engage learners and to improve learning. Within its structured environment, learners see key concepts demonstrated through real classroom video footage, practice what they learn, test their understanding, and receive feedback to guide their learning and to ensure their mastery of key learning outcomes. Designed to bring learners more directly into the world of K–12 classrooms and to help them see the real and powerful impact of educational psychology concepts covered in this book, the online resources in MyEducationLab with the Enhanced eText include:

- Video Examples. About 5 or 6 times per chapter, an embedded video provides an illustration of an educational psychology principle or concept in action. These video examples most often show students and teachers working in classrooms. Sometimes they show students or teachers describing their thinking or experiences.
- Self-Checks. In each chapter, self-check quizzes help assess how well learners have mastered the content. The self-checks are made up of self-grading multiple-choice items that not only provide feedback on whether questions are answered correctly or incorrectly, but also provide rationales for both correct and incorrect answers.
- Application Exercises. These scaffolded analysis exercises challenge learners to use chapter content to reflect on teaching and learning in real classrooms. The questions in these exercises are usually constructed-response. Once learners provide their own answers to the questions, they receive feedback in the form of model answers written by experts.

HOW THIS BOOK IS ORGANIZED

The chapters in this book address three principal themes: students, teaching, and learning. Each chapter discusses important theories and includes many examples of how these theories apply to classroom teaching.

This book emphasizes the intelligent use of theory and research to improve instruction. The chapters on teaching occupy about one-third of the total pages in the book, and the other chapters all relate to the meaning of theories and research practice. Whenever possible, the guides in this book present specific programs and strategies that have been evaluated and found to be effective, not just suggestions of things to try.

FEATURES

Licensure

This text has always had a very strong focus on helping its readers understand how educational psychology is used in teacher licensure tests like Praxis and the National Evaluation Series. And this edition has multiple tools to help you apply your learning to licensure and certification. In each chapter you can both identify and practice the appropriate knowledge and skills you have attained.

- To help you assess your own learning and prepare for licensure exams, Certification Pointers identify content likely to be on certification tests.
- A special marginal icon identifies content that correlates to InTASC standards. These correspond closely to Praxis, and many state assessments are patterned on Praxis. For those of you using the Pearson eText, when you click on the InTASC, you can read the appropriate standard without having to leave the page.

InTASC 8

Instructional Strategies

- In addition, Self-Assessment: Practicing for Licensure features at the end of each chapter are designed to resemble the types of questions and content typically encountered on state certification tests. Pearson eText users can answer these questions and receive immediate feedback.
- Finally, there is an appendix that maps the entire *Praxis II: Principles of Learning and Teaching* test to the book's content.

Embedded Video Examples and Explanations

MyEdLab
Video Example 1.1
Two first-grade teachers are interviewed about their instructional methods. Note how the interview process encourages the teachers to reflect on their own teaching. Teachers can ask themselves similar questions, leading to informed reflection.

In the Pearson eText, you will note that instead of photographs there are videos. The use of videos instead of photographs provides deeper and more complete examples.

In line with the emphasis on reflective, intentional practice, I've added a feature that is intended to bring a bit of myself from behind the curtain that usually divides author and readers. I've made available live interviews, called Personal Reflections, in which I reflect on my own experiences as a teacher, researcher, and parent to illuminate various aspects of the text. In these video podcasts, I offer examples and further explanations where I think I might be able to help you better understand a concept or an application. Readers of the eText can simply click on these videos to watch them without leaving their book.

The Intentional Teacher

One attribute seems to be a characteristic of all outstanding teachers: intentionality, or the ability to do things for a reason, purposefully. Intentional teachers constantly think about the outcomes they want for their students and how each decision they make moves students toward those outcomes. A key feature in each chapter, The Intentional Teacher is designed to help you develop and apply a set of strategies to carry out your intentionality.

The Intentional Teacher features will help you combine your increasing knowledge of principles of educational psychology, your growing experience with learners, and your creativity to make intentional instructional decisions that will help students become enthusiastic, effective learners. For those using the Pearson eText, you will be able to actually take the strategies described in each Intentional Teacher feature and observe and analyze their use in real classrooms. After answering a series of questions, you will be given feedback that allows you to compare your analysis with an expert's analysis.

Using Your Experience

Each chapter of the text opens with a vignette depicting a real-life situation that teachers encounter. Throughout the chapter narrative, I refer to the issues raised in the vignette. In addition, you have the opportunity to respond to the vignette in several related features, such as the Using Your Experience sections that follow each vignette. Each of these sections provides critical and creative thinking questions and cooperative learning activities that allow you to work with the issues brought up in the vignette, activate your prior knowledge, and begin thinking about the ideas the chapter will explore.

Common Core and 21st Century Learning

Throughout this book, a substantially revised feature presents information on 21st century learning and Common Core State Standards that relates to the topic of the chapter. Beyond this, 21st century learning skills and Common Core State Standards are discussed within the main parts of the text, as appropriate.

Educational policies and practices usually lag behind changes in society and the economy. The emphasis on 21st century learning is intended to help educators think more deeply about how each of the decisions they make about curriculum, teaching methods, use of technology, assessments, and so on contributes to helping students succeed not only by today's standards, but also in tomorrow's world.

Cartoons

Throughout the text is a series of cartoons created just for this book by my colleague, James Bravo, to illustrate key concepts in educational psychology. These are intended to be humorous and also to make you reflect.

Theory into Practice

The Theory into Practice sections in each chapter help you acquire and develop the tools you need to be an effective teacher. These sections present specific strategies to apply in your classroom. New Theory into Practice sections have been added throughout this edition.

INSTRUCTOR RESOURCES

- The **Instructor's Resource Manual** contains chapter overviews, suggested readings, answers to the textbook Self-Assessment features, and handout masters. The Instructor's Manual is available for download from the Instructor Resource Center at www.pearsonhighered.com/irc.

- The **PowerPoint® Presentation** highlights key concepts and summarizes text content. The PowerPoint Presentation is available for download from the Instructor Resource Center at www.pearsonhighered.com/irc.

- The **Online Test Bank**. The *Test Bank* that accompanies this text contains both multiple-choice and essay questions. There are also higher- and lower-level questions covering all of the content in the text.

- **TestGen**. TestGen is a powerful test generator available exclusively from Pearson Education publishers. You install TestGen on your personal computer (Windows or Macintosh) and create your own tests for classroom testing and for other specialized delivery options, such as over a local area network or on the web. A test bank, which is also called a Test Item File (TIF), typically contains a large set of test items, organized by chapter and ready for your use in creating a test, based on the associated textbook material. Assessments—including equations, graphs, and scientific notation—may be created for both print or testing online. The tests can be downloaded in the following formats:

  - TestGen Testbank file – PC
  - TestGen Testbank file – MAC
  - TestGen Testbank – Blackboard 9 TIF
  - TestGen Testbank – Blackboard CE/Vista (WebCT) TIF
  - Angel Test Bank (zip)

ACKNOWLEDGMENTS

In this edition, my assistant, Susan Davis, played a particularly important role. She created some new figures and tables, researched websites, obtained permissions, checked citations and references, and proofread drafts at all stages. I want to thank my editor at Pearson, Kevin Davis; my development editor, Gail Gottfried; my content manager, Janelle Rogers; my portfolio assistant, Anne McAlpine; and my full service agency project manager, Kathy Smith, who were extremely helpful throughout.

I would like to thank the reviewers of this edition: Rosaria Caporrimo, Montclair State University; Lori J. Flint, East Carolina University; Kimberly Kinsler, Hunter College of CUNY; Michelle Koussa, University of North Texas; Wilda Laija-Rodriguez, California State University Northridge; Claire J. McGauley, Wayne State University; and Elizabeth Pemberton, University of Delaware.

I also wish to thank my many colleagues who served as contributors and reviewers on previous editions.

Thomas Andre

Wallace Alexander, Thomas College

Patrick Allen, Graduate College of Union University

Ted Batson, Indiana Wesleyan University

Richard Battaglia, California Lutheran University

Elizabeth Anne Belford Horan, Methodist College

Sandra Billings, Fairfield University

Curtis Bonk, Indiana University

Silas Born, Bethany Lutheran College

Curtis Brant, Baldwin-Wallace College

Camille Branton, Delta State University

Joy Brown, University of North Alabama

Doris Burgert, Wichita State University

Mary Jane Caffey

Renee Cambiano, Northeastern State University

William Camp, Luzerne County Community College

Ann Caton, Rockford College

Bette Chambers, Johns Hopkins University

Kay Chick, Pennsylvania State University–Altoona

Martha Cook, Malone College

Faye Day, Bethel College

Sandra Damico

Melissa Dark

Christiane DeBauge, Indiana University

Donna Duellberg, Wayland Baptist University

Nick Elksnin, The Citadel

Joan Evensen, Towson University

E. Gail Everett, Bob Jones University

R. Joel Farrell, Faulkner University

Susan Frusher, Northeastern State University

Donna Gardner, William Jewell College

Shirlyn Garrett Wilson, Chicago State University

Michele Gill, University of Central Florida

Stacie Goffin

Gordon Greenwood

Chuck Greiner

Jennifer Gross Lara, Anne Arundel Community College

Carole Grove

Andrea Guillaume, California State University–Fullerton

Raphael Guillory, Eastern Washington University

Felicia A. B. Hanesworth, Medaille College

Millie Harris

Jan Hayes, Middle Tennessee State University

James Hedgebeth, Elizabeth City State University

Mark Hopkin, Wiley College

John Hummel, Valdosta State University

Margaret Hurd, Anne Arundel Community College

Daniel Hursh, West Virginia University

Kathryn Hutchinson, St. Thomas Aquinas College

Karen Huxtable-Jester, University of Texas at Dallas

Gretchen Jefferson, Eastern Washington University

Carolyn Jeffries, CSU Northridge

W. Y. Johnson, Wright State University

Jeffrey Kaplan, University of Central Florida

Jack Kaufman, Bluefield State College

Johanna Keirns

Pam Kidder-Ashley, Appalachian State University

Raye Lakey, Instructional Designer

Robert Landry, Winston-Salem State University

Dorothea Lerman, Louisiana State University

Jupian J. Leung, University of Wisconsin–Oshkosh

Judith Levine, Farmingdale State University

Judy Lewandowski, Indiana University South Bend

Judith Luckett, University of Central Florida

Betty Magjuka, Gloucester County College

Laurell Malone, North Carolina Central University

Lloyd McCraney, Towson University

Melanie J. McGill, Stephen F. Austin State University

Lienne Medford, Clemson University

Janet Medina, McDaniel College

DeAnn Miller-Boschert, North Dakota State University

Greg Morris, Grand Rapids Community College

Anne H. Nardi, West Virginia University

Pamela Nesselrodt, Dickinson College

Joe Nichols, Indiana University–Purdue University Fort Wayne

E. Michael Nussbaum, University of Nevada, Las Vegas

Kathryn Parr, University of Florida

Kathy Picchura-Couture, Steton University

Jonathan Plucker, Indiana University

Catherine Polydore, Eastern Illinois University

Dr. John L. Rausch, John Carroll University

Linda Robertello, Iona College

Steve Ross

Carrie Rothstein-Fisch, California State University–Northridge

Paul Rufino, Gloucester County College

Lisa Ruiz-Lee, University of Nevada, Las Vegas

Carol Scatena, Lewis University

Tom Scheft, North Carolina Central University

Diane Serafin, Luzerne County Community College–Shamokin

Joshua S. Smith, University of Albany

Donald Snead, Middle Tennessee State University

Louise Soares, University of New Haven

Elizabeth Sterling

Robert J. Stevens, Pennsylvania State University

Theresa Sullivan Stewart, University of Illinois at Springfield

Larry Templeton, Ferris State University

Leo Theriot, Central Bible College

Jane Thielmann-Downs, University of Houston Downtown

Melaine Timko, National University

Diana Treahy, Point Loma Nazarene University

Kathleen Waldron-Soler, Eastern Washington University

George Watson, Marshall University

Roger Webb, Southern Illinois University

Kathryn Wentzel, University of Maryland

Roberta Wiener, Pace University

Betty Wood, University of Arkansas at Little Rock

Priscilla Wright, Colorado Christian University

William Zangwill

Ronald Zigler, Pennsylvania State University–Abington

Wilkins-O'Riley Zinn, Southern Oregon University

BRIEF CONTENTS

CONTENTS

CHAPTER THREE
Social, Moral, and Emotional Development   44

CHAPTER FOUR
Student Diversity   64

CHAPTER FIVE
Behavioral and Social Theories of Learning   96

CHAPTER NINE
Grouping, Differentiation, and Technology   212

CHAPTER TWELVE
Learners with Exceptionalities   300

CHAPTER FOURTEEN
Standardized Tests and Accountability   382

LIST OF FEATURES

THEORY INTO PRACTICE

THE INTENTIONAL TEACHER

EDUCATIONAL PSYCHOLOGY

THEORY AND PRACTICE

WavebreakMediaMicro/Fotolia

CHAPTER ONE

Educational Psychology: A Foundation for Teaching

LEARNING OUTCOMES

At the end of this chapter, you should be able to:

1.1 Identify attributes of effective teachers

1.2 Describe the role of educational research in informing classroom practice

1.3 Discuss how you can become an intentional teacher

Ellen Mathis, a new teacher, is trying to teach creative writing to her third-grade class, but things are just not going the way she'd hoped. Her students are not producing much, and what they do write is not very imaginative and full of errors. For example, she recently assigned a composition on "My Summer Vacation," and all one of her students wrote was "On my summer vacation I got a dog and we went swimming and I got stinged by a bee."

Ellen wonders whether her students are just not ready for writing and need several months of work on such skills as capitalization, punctuation, and usage before she tries another writing assignment. However, one day Ellen notices some compositions in the hall outside of Leah Washington's class. Leah's third-graders are just like Ellen's, but their compositions are fabulous. The students wrote pages of interesting material on an astonishing array of topics. At the end of the day, Ellen catches Leah in the hall. "How do you get your kids to write such great compositions?" she asks.

Leah explains how she first got her children writing on topics they cared about and then gradually introduced "mini-lessons" to help them become better authors. She had the students work in small groups and help each other plan compositions. Then the students critiqued and helped edit one another's drafts, before finally "publishing" final versions.

"I'll tell you what," Leah offers. "I'll schedule my next writing class during your planning period. Come see what we're doing."

Ellen agrees. When the time comes, she walks into Leah's class and is overwhelmed by what she sees. Children are writing everywhere: on the floor, in groups, at tables. Many are talking with partners. Leah is conferencing with individual children. Ellen looks over the children's shoulders and sees one student writing about her pets, another writing a gory story about zombies, and another writing about a dream. Marta Delgado, a Hispanic student, is writing a funny story about her second-grade teacher's attempts to speak Spanish. One student is even writing a very good story about her summer vacation!

After school, Ellen meets with Leah, bursting with questions. "How did you get students to do all that writing? How can you manage all that noise and activity? How did you learn to do this?"

"I did go to a series of workshops on teaching writing," admits Leah. "But if you think about it, everything I'm doing is basic educational psychology."

Ellen is amazed. "Educational psychology? I took that course in college. I got an A in it! But I don't see what it has to do with your writing program."

"Well, let's see," said Leah. "To begin with, I'm using a lot of motivational strategies I learned in ed psych. For instance, when I started my writing instruction this year, I read students some funny and intriguing stories written by other classes, to arouse their curiosity. I got them motivated by letting them write about whatever they wanted, and also by having 'writing celebrations' in which students read their finished compositions to the class for applause and comments. My educational psychology professor was always talking about adapting to students' needs. I do this by conferencing with students and helping them with the specific problems they're having. I first learned about cooperative learning in ed psych, and later on I took some workshops on it. I use cooperative learning groups to let students give each other immediate feedback on their writing, to let them model effective writing for each other, and to get them to encourage each other to write. The groups also solve a lot of my management problems by keeping each other on task and dealing with many classroom routines. I remember that we learned about evaluation in ed psych. I use a flexible form of evaluation. Everybody eventually gets an A, but only when their composition meets a high standard, which may take many drafts."

Ellen is impressed. She and Leah arrange to visit each other's classes a few more times to exchange ideas and observations, and in time, Ellen's writers are almost as good as Leah's. But what most impresses her is the idea that educational psychology can be useful in her day-to-day teaching. She drags out her old textbook and finds that concepts that

(continued)

had seemed theoretical and abstract in her ed psych class actually help her think about current teaching challenges.

USING YOUR EXPERIENCE

CREATIVE THINKING Based on Leah's explanation of her writing instruction, brainstorm with one or more partners about educational psychology—what it is and what you will learn this semester. Guidelines: (1) The more ideas you generate, the better; (2) build on others' ideas as well as combining them; and (3) make no evaluation of ideas at this time. Take this list out a few times during the semester to review, evaluate, or even add ideas.

InTASC 3

Learning Environments

InTASC 8

Instructional Strategies

InTASC 10

Leadership and Collaboration

What is **educational psychology**? Educational psychology is the study of learners, learning, and teaching. However, for students who are or expect to be teachers, educational psychology is something more. It is the accumulated knowledge, wisdom, and seat-of-the-pants theory that every teacher should possess to intelligently solve the daily problems of teaching. Educational psychology cannot tell you as a teacher what to do, but it can give you the principles to use in making a good decision and a language to discuss your experiences and thinking (Ormrod, 2016; Woolfolk, Winne, & Perry, 2015). Consider the case of Ellen Mathis and Leah Washington. Nothing in this or any other educational psychology text will tell you exactly how to teach creative writing to a particular group of third-graders. However, Leah uses concepts of educational psychology to consider how she will teach writing and then to interpret and solve problems she runs into, as well as to explain to Ellen what she is doing. Educational psychologists carry out research on the nature of students and on effective methods of teaching in order to help educators understand principles of learning and give them the information they need to think critically about their craft and make teaching decisions that will work for their students.

WHAT MAKES A GOOD TEACHER?

Everyone knows that good teaching matters. One recent study found, for example, that a single year with an outstanding (top 5%) teacher adds $50,000 to a student's lifetime earnings! (Chetty, Friedman, & Rockoff, 2014). But what is it that makes a good teacher so effective? Is it warmth, humor, and the ability to care about students and value their diversity? Is it planning, hard work, and self-discipline? What about leadership, enthusiasm, a contagious love of learning, and speaking ability? Most people would agree that all of these qualities are needed to make a good teacher, and they would certainly be correct. But these qualities are not enough.

Knowing the Subject Matters (But So Does Teaching Skill)

There is an old joke that goes like this:

Question: What do you need to know to be able to teach a horse?

Answer: More than the horse!

InTASC 4

Content Knowledge

InTASC 5

Application of Content

This joke makes the obvious point that the first thing a teacher must have is some knowledge or skills that the learner does not have; you must know the subject matter you plan to teach. But if you think about teaching horses (or children), you will soon realize that although subject matter knowledge is necessary, it is not enough. A rancher may have a good idea of how a horse is supposed to act and what a horse is supposed to be able to do, but if he doesn't have the skills to make an untrained, scared, and unfriendly animal into a good saddle horse, he's going to end up with nothing but broken ribs and teeth marks for his trouble. Children are a lot smarter and a little more forgiving than horses, but teaching them has this in common with teaching horses: Knowledge of how to transmit information and skills is at least as important as knowledge of the information and skills themselves. We have all had teachers who were brilliant and thoroughly knowledgeable in their fields but who could not teach. Ellen Mathis may know as much as Leah Washington about what good writing should be, but she started off with a lot to learn about how to get third-graders to write well.

For effective teaching, subject matter knowledge is not a question of being a walking encyclopedia. Libraries of books and the magic of the Internet make vast amounts of knowledge readily available, so walking encyclopedias are not much in demand these days. What makes teachers effective is that they not only know their subjects, but also can communicate their knowledge to students. The celebrated high school math teacher Jaime Escalante taught the concept of positive and negative numbers to students in a Los Angeles barrio by explaining that when you dig a hole, you might call the pile of dirt +1, the hole −1. What do you get when you put the dirt back in the hole? Zero. Escalante's ability to relate the abstract concept of positive and negative numbers to everyday experience is one example of how the ability to communicate knowledge goes far beyond simply knowing the facts.

Mastering Teaching Skills

The link between what a teacher wants students to learn and students' actual learning is called *instruction*, or **pedagogy**. Effective instruction is not a simple matter of one person with more knowledge transmitting that knowledge to another (Baumert et al., 2010; Gess-Newsome, 2012). If telling were teaching, this book would be unnecessary. Rather, effective instruction demands the use of many strategies.

For example, suppose Paula Wilson wants to teach a lesson on statistics to a diverse class of fourth-graders. To do so, Paula must accomplish many related tasks. She must make sure that the class is orderly and that students know what behavior is expected of them. She must find out whether students have the prerequisite skills; for example, students need to be able to add and divide to find averages. If any do not, Paula must find a way to teach students those skills. She must engage students in activities that lead them toward an understanding of statistics, such as having students roll dice, play cards, or collect data from experiments; and she must use teaching strategies that help students remember what they have been taught. The lessons should also take into account the intellectual and social characteristics of students in the fourth grade and the intellectual, social, and cultural characteristics of these particular students. Paula must make sure that students are interested in the lesson and motivated to learn statistics. To see whether students are learning what is being taught, she may ask questions or use quizzes or have students demonstrate their understanding by setting up and interpreting experiments, and she must respond appropriately if these assessments show that students are having problems. After the series of lessons on statistics ends, Paula should review this topic from time to time to ensure that it is remembered.

These tasks—motivating students, managing the classroom, assessing prior knowledge, communicating ideas effectively, taking into account the characteristics of the learners, assessing learning outcomes, and reviewing information—must be attended to at all levels of education, in or out of schools. They apply as much to the training of astronauts as to the teaching of reading. How these tasks are accomplished, however, differs widely according to the ages of the students, the objectives of instruction, and other factors.

What makes a good teacher is the ability to carry out all the tasks involved in effective instruction. Warmth, enthusiasm, and caring are essential (Cornelius-White, 2007; Eisner, 2006; Marzano, 2011b), as are subject matter knowledge and understanding of how children learn (Baumert et al., 2010; Carlisle et al., 2011; Wiggins & McTighe, 2007). But it is the successful accomplishment of all the tasks of teaching that makes for instructional effectiveness.

Can Good Teaching Be Taught?

Some people think that good teachers are born that way. Outstanding teachers sometimes seem to have a magic, a charisma that mere mortals could never hope to achieve. Yet research has begun to identify the specific behaviors and skills that make a "magic" teacher (Borman & Kimball, 2005). An outstanding teacher does nothing that any other teacher cannot also do—it is just a question of knowing the principles of effective teaching and how to apply them. Take one small example: In a high school history class, two students in the back of the class are whispering to each other, and they are not discussing the Treaty of Paris! The teacher slowly walks toward them without looking, continuing his lesson as he walks. The students stop whispering and pay attention. If you didn't know what to look for, you might miss this brief but critical interchange and

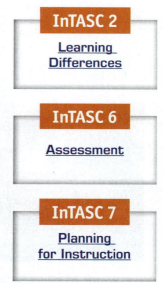

InTASC 2
Learning Differences

InTASC 6
Assessment

InTASC 7
Planning for Instruction

Connections 1.1
For more on effective instruction, see Chapter 7. Pedagogical strategies are also presented throughout the text in features titled The Intentional Teacher.

"If only I could get to my ed psych text . . ."

believe that the teacher just has a way with students, a knack for keeping their attention. But the teacher is simply applying principles of classroom management that anyone could learn: Maintain momentum in the lesson, deal with behavior problems by using the mildest intervention that will work, and resolve minor problems before they become major ones. When Jaime Escalante gave the example of digging a hole to illustrate the concept of positive and negative numbers, he was also applying several important principles of educational psychology: Make abstract ideas concrete by using many examples, relate the content of instruction to the students' backgrounds, state rules, give examples, and then restate rules.

Can good teaching be taught? The answer is definitely yes (Ball & Forzani, 2010). Good teaching has to be observed and practiced, but there are principles of good teaching that teachers need to know, which can then be applied in the classroom. The major components of effective instruction are summarized in Figure 1.1.

The Intentional Teacher

There is no formula for good teaching, no seven steps to Teacher of the Year. Teaching involves planning and preparation, and then dozens of decisions every hour. Yet one attribute seems to be characteristic of outstanding teachers: **intentionality**. Intentionality means doing things for a reason, on purpose. Intentional teachers constantly think about the outcomes they want for their students and about how each decision they make moves children toward those outcomes (Fisher & Frey, 2011). Intentional teachers know that maximum learning does not happen by chance.

FIGURE 1.1 • Components of Good Teaching

Yes, children do learn in unplanned ways all the time, and many will learn from even the most chaotic lesson. But to really challenge students, to get their best efforts, to help them make conceptual leaps and organize and retain new knowledge, teachers need to be intentional: purposeful, thoughtful, and flexible, without ever losing sight of their goals for every child.

The idea that teachers should always do things for a reason seems obvious. Yet in practice, it is difficult to constantly make certain that all students are engaged in activities that lead to important learning outcomes. Teachers very frequently fall into strategies that they themselves would recognize, on reflection, as being time fillers rather than instructionally essential activities. For example, an otherwise outstanding third-grade teacher once assigned seatwork to one of her reading groups. The children were given two sheets of paper with words in squares. Their task was to cut out the squares on one sheet and then paste them onto synonyms on the other. When all the words were pasted correctly, lines on the pasted squares formed an outline of a cat, which the children were then to color. Once the children pasted a few squares, the puzzle became clear, so they could paste the remainder without paying any attention to the words themselves. For almost an hour of precious class time, these children happily cut, pasted, and colored—not high-priority skills for third-graders. The teacher would have said that the objective was for children to learn or practice synonyms, of course; but in fact the activity could not possibly have moved the children forward on that skill. Similarly, many teachers have one child laboriously work a problem on a whiteboard while the rest of the class has nothing important to do. Some secondary teachers spend most of the class period going over homework and classwork and end up doing very little teaching of new content. Again, these may be excellent teachers in other ways, but they sometimes lose sight of what they are trying to achieve and how they are going to achieve it.

Intentional teachers are constantly asking themselves what goals they and their students are trying to accomplish. Is each portion of their lesson appropriate to students' background knowledge, skills, and needs? Is each activity or assignment clearly related to a valued outcome? Is each instructional minute used wisely and well? An intentional teacher trying to build students' synonym skills might have them work in pairs to master a set of synonyms in preparation for individual quizzes. An intentional teacher might have all children work a given problem while one works at the board, so that all can compare answers and strategies together. An intentional teacher might quickly give homework answers for students to check themselves, ask for a show of hands for correct answers, and then review and reteach only those exercises missed by many students to save time for teaching of new content. An intentional teacher uses a wide variety of instructional methods, experiences, assignments, and materials to be sure that children are achieving all sorts of cognitive objectives, from knowledge to application to creativity, and that at the same time children are learning important affective objectives, such as love of learning, respect for others, and personal responsibility. An intentional teacher constantly reflects on his or her practices and outcomes (Fisher & Frey, 2011; Marzano, 2011b).

Research finds that one of the most powerful predictors of a teacher's impact on students is the belief that what he or she does makes a difference. This belief, called **teacher efficacy** (Thurlings, Evers, & Vermeulen, 2015; Woolfolk-Hoy, Hoy, & Davis, 2009), is at the heart of what it means to be an intentional teacher. Teachers who believe that success in school is almost entirely due to children's inborn intelligence, home environment, or other factors that teachers cannot influence are unlikely to teach in the same way as those who believe that their own efforts are the key to children's learning. An intentional teacher, one who has a strong belief in her or his efficacy, is more likely to put forth consistent effort, to persist in the face of obstacles, and to keep trying relentlessly until every student succeeds (Farr, 2010). Intentional teachers achieve a sense of efficacy by constantly assessing the results of their instruction; trying new strategies if their initial instruction doesn't work; and continually seeking ideas from colleagues, books, online resources, magazines, workshops, and other sources to enrich and solidify their teaching skills (Corbett, Wilson, & Williams, 2005). Their sense of efficacy is one of the major factors behind teachers who are innovative and embrace change (Thurlings et al., 2015). Collective efficacy can have a particularly strong impact on student achievement (Woolfolk-Hoy et al., 2009). Groups of teachers, such as the entire faculty of an elementary school or all teachers in a secondary academic department, can attain collective efficacy by working together to examine their practices and outcomes, seeking professional development, and helping each other succeed (see Borko, 2004; Sachs, 2000; York-Barr, Sommerness, & Hur, 2008). Countries that are particularly successful in helping all children

InTASC 1

Learner Development

InTASC 2

Learning Differences

InTASC 5

Application of Content

MyEdLab
Video Example 1.1
Two first-grade teachers are interviewed about their instructional methods. Note how the interview process encourages the teachers to reflect on their own teaching. Teachers can ask themselves similar questions, leading to informed reflection.

succeed are ones that provide opportunities for teachers to work together and to take collective responsibility for their students (Sahlberg, 2012; Sawchuk, 2012; Stewart, 2010; Tucker, 2012).

The most important purpose of this book is to give you, tomorrow's teacher, the intellectual grounding in research, theory, and practical wisdom you will need in order to become an intentional, effective teacher. To plan and carry out effective lessons, discussions, projects, and other learning experiences, teachers need to know a great deal. Besides knowing your subjects, you need to understand the developmental levels and needs of your students. You need to understand how learning, memory, problem-solving skill, and creativity are acquired and how to promote their acquisition. You need to know how to set objectives, organize activities designed to help students attain those objectives, and assess students' progress toward them. You need to know how to motivate children, how to use class time effectively, and how to respond to individual differences among students. Intentional teachers are continually experimenting with strategies to solve problems of instruction and then observing the results of their actions to see if they were effective (Schunk, 2016). They pay attention to research on effective teaching and incorporate research findings in their daily teaching (Fleischman, 2006). Like Leah Washington in the vignette that opened this chapter, intentional teachers are constantly combining their knowledge of principles of educational psychology, their experience, and their creativity to make instructional decisions and help children become enthusiastic and effective learners.

This text highlights the ideas that are central to educational psychology and the related research. It also presents many examples of how these ideas apply in practice, emphasizing teaching practices, not only theory or suggestions, that have been evaluated and found to be effective. The text is designed to help you develop skills in **critical thinking** for teaching: a logical and systematic approach to the many dilemmas that are found in practice and research. No text can provide all the right answers for teaching, but this one tries to pose the right questions and to engage you by presenting realistic alternatives and the concepts and research behind them.

Many studies have looked at the differences between expert and novice teachers and between more and less effective teachers. One theme runs through these studies: Expert teachers are critical thinkers (Hogan, Rabinowitz, & Craven, 2003; Mosenthal, Lipson, Torncello, Russ, & Mekkelsen, 2004; Shulman, 2000). Intentional teachers are constantly upgrading and examining their own teaching practices, reading and attending conferences to learn new ideas, and using their own students' responses to guide their instructional decisions. There's an old saying to the effect that there are teachers with 20 years of experience and there are teachers with 1 year of experience 20 times. Teachers who get better each year are the ones who are open to new ideas and who look at their own teaching critically. Perhaps the most important goal of this book is to get you in the habit of using informed reflection to become one of tomorrow's expert teachers.

The importance of intentional teaching and critical thinking becomes even clearer when you reflect on the changes that will be taking place in teaching over the next 10–20 years. By 2030, the work of teachers will be utterly transformed (see Berry et al., 2011). During your teaching career, there will be dramatic changes in the role of technology, especially as access to the Internet becomes universal. New forms of schooling beyond the physical school, and forms of teaching that blend technological and traditional teaching, are already here and will be expanding. The role of research is certain to grow, and in coming years teachers will be able to choose from an array of programs, each of which has been scientifically evaluated and found to be effective (Slavin, 2013). New models of teacher preparation and inservice will become commonplace (Cochran-Smith & Power, 2010; Rose, 2010). Teachers are being held more and more accountable for their students' learning (Danielson, 2010; Darling-Hammond et al., 2012; David, 2010b; Schmoker, 2012; Stumbo & McWalters, 2010). All of these changes mean that teachers in 2030 will have to be flexible, resilient, and capable of using new approaches to new problems (Christenbury, 2010; Steele, 2010). For a long time, teachers could always fall back on their own experiences as students, and teach like their own teachers taught them. Those days are gone.

21st Century Skills

Back when I was growing up, the 21st century was expected to be totally different from the 20th. The Jetsons, for example, projected an image of flying cars, robots in every home, and all sorts of amazing technology. Serious futurologists expected more or less the same. The reality has turned out to be a little more down-to-earth, but nevertheless, developments in technology and globalization have dramatically changed key aspects of our economy and society. In particular, economic security, both for individuals and for nations, depends more than ever on innovation, creativity, and design. The ability to work cooperatively with others, to see many solutions to problems, and to be flexible and responsive to rapid change are all becoming keys to success, as traditional "strong back" jobs disappear to be replaced by "strong mind" careers.

All of these changes have profound significance for education. They lead educators to put a strong value on skills, attitudes, and ways of working that more closely resemble new workforce conditions. It should go without saying that students need extensive experience with technology, but that is not enough. They also need extensive experience working in groups, solving problems, and learning to read critically and think creatively (Beers, 2011; Marzano & Heflebower, 2012). Ironically, these kinds of experiences are at the core of the progressive philosophy of John Dewey and many others, which date back to the beginning of the 20th century (Rotherham & Willingham, 2009). What has changed is that these ideas are no longer optional, because they correspond so closely to today's needs. Moreover, these skills are now needed for everyone, from the executive office to the shop floor.

Consistent with this line of reasoning, a Partnership for 21st Century Skills has been created to promote policies defining and supporting student outcomes that align with today's needs (see P. Johnson, 2009; Partnership for 21st Century Skills, 2009). The Partnership has created a framework that organizes 21st century skills in four categories, synthesizing suggestions from dozens of stakeholder groups at all levels of education:

1. Core subjects and 21st century themes (such as language arts, mathematics, science, global awareness, and financial literacy) (see Cutshall, 2009; Hersh, 2009; Trefil & O'Brien-Trefil, 2009; Zhao, 2009)

2. Learning and innovation skills (such as creativity, critical thinking, and problem solving) (see Azzam, 2009; Graseck, 2009)

3. Information, media, and technology skills (see Barab, Gresalfi, & Arici, 2009; Ferriter, 2009a, b; Sprenger, 2009)

4. Life and career skills (such as initiative and self-direction) (see Gerdes & Ljung, 2009)

Common Core and College- and Career-Ready Standards

For many years, each state in the United States has had its own standards, which are expectations of what each child should know and be able to do in a given subject at a given age. Each state has also had its own assessments of attainment of those standards, generally using multiple-choice tests, and its own criteria for passing. These multiple-choice tests have been criticized in their own right for assessing only the most basic of skills, and the diversity of standards and assessments has led to wild differences between states in passing rates on state tests.

All of this is changing, and the changes will have a big impact on your life as a teacher. Many states have adopted **Common Core State Standards**, based in large part on the 21st century skills discussed earlier. Two large consortia of states have adopted specific measures aligned with the Common Core State Standards. These are called Smarter Balanced and PARCC (see Chapter 14 for descriptions). Other states have created their own college- and career-ready standards, which are often similar to Common Core assessments. These assessments are intended to indicate how students are moving toward success in college and careers, and to move teachers and schools toward innovative approaches to teaching in line with preparation for success in colleges and the workplace in the 21st century. The standards emphasize the following (see Kendall, 2011):

- Flexible, creative problem solving
- Ability to use technology
- Ability to participate in active discussions in one-to-one, small-group, and whole-class settings
- Focus on writing, speaking, and argumentation in groups
- Alignment of standards with college and career readiness

- Focus in reading on classic texts as well as new and multicultural texts
- Focus in math on problem solving in real-world contexts, mathematical reasoning, precision, and argumentation

The Common Core State Standards and other **college- and career-ready standards** are controversial, and they may or may not matter to your students' learning (see Barton, 2010; Loveless, 2012; and Schmidt & Huang, 2012 for opposing views), but they certainly matter to teachers and administrators, especially in states whose assessment systems are based on them. In preparation for Common Core and other college- and career-ready assessments, states and districts are doing a lot of professional development (Silver, Dewing, & Perini, 2012) and publishers are changing textbooks and software to match the standards. These changes are discussed in Chapter 14.

Most chapters of this text include a feature that presents information on Common Core and college- and career-ready standards and how they are related to the topic of the chapter. Beyond this, the Common Core and college- and career-ready standards are discussed throughout the main parts of the text, as appropriate.

All too often, educational policies and practices lag behind changes in society and the economy. The emphasis on the Common Core and college- and career-ready standards is intended to help you think more deeply about how each of the decisions you make about curriculum, teaching methods, use of technology, and assessments contributes to helping students succeed, not only by today's standards, but also in tomorrow's world.

ON THE WEB

For more on the Common Core, see ccsso.org, www.corestandards.org, www.nea.org, and engageny.org. For more on college and career-ready standards, see CCSSO (2015) and U.S. Department of Education (2015). Also, most state departments of education now discuss Common Core and/or college- and career-ready standards on their websites.

MyEdLab **Self-Check 1.1**

WHAT IS THE ROLE OF RESEARCH IN EDUCATIONAL PSYCHOLOGY?

Teachers who are intentional, critical thinkers are likely to enter classrooms equipped with knowledge about research in educational psychology. Every year, educational psychologists discover or refine principles of teaching and learning that are useful for practicing teachers. Some of these principles are just common sense backed up with evidence, but others are more surprising. One problem educational psychologists face is that almost everyone has ideas on the subject of educational psychology. Most adults have spent many years in schools watching what teachers do. Add to that a certain amount of knowledge of human nature, and *voila!* Everyone is an amateur educational psychologist. For this reason, professional educational psychologists are often accused of studying the obvious (see Ball & Forzani, 2007).

However, as we have painfully learned, the obvious is not always true. For example, most people assume that if students are assigned to classes according to their ability, the resulting narrower range of abilities in a class will let the teacher adapt instruction to the specific needs of the students and thereby increase student achievement. This assumption turns out to be false. Many teachers believe that scolding students for misbehavior will improve conduct. Many students will indeed respond to a scolding by behaving better, but for others, scolding may be a reward for misbehavior that actually increases it. Some "obvious" truths even conflict with one another. For example, most people would agree that students learn better from a teacher's

InTASC 1

Learner Development

InTASC 2

Learning Differences

instruction than by working alone. This belief supports teacher-centered direct instructional strategies, in which a teacher actively works with the class as a whole. However, most people would also agree that students often need instruction tailored to their individual needs. This belief, also correct, would demand that teachers divide their time among individuals, or at least among groups of students with differing needs, which would result in some students working independently while others receive your close attention. If schools could provide tutors for every student, there would be no conflict; direct instruction and individualization could coexist. In practice, however, classrooms typically have 20 to 30 students; as a result, more direct instruction (the first goal) almost always means less individualization (the second goal). Your task as an intentional teacher is to balance these competing goals according to the needs of particular students and situations.

The Goal of Research in Educational Psychology

The goal of research in educational psychology is to carefully examine "obvious" as well as less-than-obvious questions, using objective methods to test ideas about the factors that contribute to learning (Levin, O'Donnell, & Kratochwill, 2003; McComb & Scott-Little, 2003). The products of this research are principles, laws, and theories. A **principle** explains the relationship between factors, such as the effects of alternative grading systems on student motivation. **Laws** are simply principles that have been thoroughly tested and found to apply in a wide variety of situations. A **theory** is a set of related principles and laws that explains a broad aspect of learning, behavior, or another area of interest. Without theories, the facts and principles that are discovered would be like disorganized specks on a canvas. Theories tie together these facts and principles to give us the big picture. However, the same facts and principles may be interpreted in different ways by different theorists. As in any science, progress in educational psychology is slow and uneven. A single study is rarely a breakthrough, but over time, evidence accumulates on a subject and allows theorists to refine and extend their theories.

The Value of Research in Educational Psychology to You the Teacher

It is probably true that the most important knowledge teachers gain is learned on the job—in internships, while student teaching, or during their first years in the classroom. However, you as a teacher make hundreds of decisions every day, and each decision has a theory behind it, regardless of whether you are aware of it. The quality, accuracy, and usefulness of those theories ultimately determine your success. For example, one teacher may offer a prize to the student with the best attendance, on the theory that rewarding attendance will increase it. Another may reward the student whose attendance is most improved, on the theory that it is poor attenders who most need incentives to come to class. A third may not reward anyone for attendance but instead try to increase attendance by teaching more interesting lessons. Which teacher's plan is most likely to succeed? This depends in large part on the ability of each teacher to understand the unique combination of factors that shape the character of her or his classroom and therefore to apply the most appropriate theory.

Teaching as Decision Making

The aim of research in educational psychology is to test the various theories that guide the actions of teachers and others involved in education. There are many common situations, such as the following example, in which a teacher might use educational psychology.

Mr. Harris teaches an eighth-grade social studies class. He has a problem with Tom, who frequently misbehaves. Today, Tom makes a paper airplane and flies it across the room when Mr. Harris turns his back, to the delight of the entire class.

What should Mr. Harris do?

As an intentional teacher, Mr. Harris considers a range of options for solving this problem, each of which comes from a theory about why Tom is misbehaving and what will motivate him to behave more appropriately.

Connections 1.2

For more on effectively handling misbehavior, see Chapter 5.

Connections 1.3

For more on ability grouping, see Chapter 9.

MyEdLab

Video Example 1.2

Bob Slavin tells a story about his participation in a study that involved observing the behaviors of children with behavioral or emotional disorders. Why was his study ruined? What lesson can you learn from this example about using research to be an effective teacher?

Action	**Theory**
1. Reprimand Tom.	1. A reprimand is a form of punishment. Tom will behave to avoid punishment.
2. Ignore Tom.	2. Attention may be rewarding to Tom. Ignoring him would deprive him of this reward.
3. Send Tom to the office.	3. Being sent to the office is punishing. It also deprives Tom of the (apparent) support of his classmates.
4. Tell the class that it is everyone's responsibility to maintain a good learning environment and that if any student misbehaves, 5 minutes will be subtracted from recess.	4. Tom is misbehaving to get his classmates' attention. If the whole class loses out when he misbehaves, the class will keep him in line.
5. Explain to the class that Tom's behavior is interfering with lessons that all students need to know and that his behavior goes against the rules the class set for itself at the beginning of the year.	5. The class holds standards of behavior that conflict with both Tom's behavior in class and the class's reaction to it. By reminding the class of its own needs (to learn the lesson) and its own rules set at the beginning of the year, the teacher might make Tom see that the class does not really support his behavior.

Each of these actions is a common response to misbehavior. But which theory (and therefore which action) is correct?

The key might be in the fact that his classmates laugh when Tom misbehaves. This response is a clue that Tom is seeking their attention. If Mr. Harris scolds Tom, this might increase Tom's status in the eyes of his peers and thus reward his behavior. Ignoring misbehavior might be a good idea if a student were acting up to get your attention, but in this case it is apparently the class's attention that Tom is seeking. Sending Tom to the office does deprive him of his classmates' attention and therefore may be effective. But what if Tom is looking for a way to get out of class to avoid work? What if he struts out to confront the powers that be, to the obvious approval of his classmates? Making the entire class responsible for each student's behavior is likely to deprive Tom of his classmates' support and to improve his behavior; but some students may think that it is unfair to punish them for another student's misbehavior. Finally, reminding the class (and Tom) of its own interest in learning and its usual standards of behavior might work if the class does, in fact, value academic achievement and good behavior.

Research in education and psychology bears directly on the decision Mr. Harris must make. Developmental research indicates that as students enter adolescence, the peer group becomes all-important to them, and they try to establish their independence from adult control, often by flouting or ignoring rules. Basic research on behavioral learning theories shows that when a behavior is repeated many times, some reward must be encouraging the behavior, and that if the behavior is to be eliminated, the reward must first be identified and removed. This research would also suggest that Mr. Harris consider problems with the use of punishment (such as scolding) to stop undesirable behavior. Research on specific classroom management strategies has identified effective methods to use both to prevent a student like Tom from misbehaving in the first place and to deal with his misbehavior when it does occur. Finally, research on rule setting and classroom standards indicates that student participation in setting rules can help convince each student that the class as a whole values academic achievement and appropriate behavior, and that this belief can help keep individual students in line.

Armed with this information, Mr. Harris can choose a response to Tom's behavior based on an understanding of why Tom is doing what he is doing and what strategies are available to deal with the situation. He may or may not make the right choice, but because he knows several theories that could explain Tom's behavior, he will be able to observe the outcomes of his strategy and, if it is ineffective, to learn from that and try something else that will work. Research does not give Mr. Harris a specific solution; that requires his own experience and judgment. But research does give Mr. Harris basic concepts of human behavior to help him understand Tom's motivations and an array of proven methods that might solve the problem. And using research to help him make teaching decisions is one way Mr. Harris can achieve a sense of his own efficacy as a teacher.

Research + Common Sense = Effective Teaching

As the case of Mr. Harris illustrates, no theory, no research, no book can tell teachers what to do in a given situation. Making the right decisions depends on the context within which the problem arises, the objectives you have in mind, and many other factors, all of which must be assessed in the light of educated common sense. For example, research in mathematics instruction usually finds that a rapid pace of instruction increases achievement (Good, Grouws, & Ebmeier, 1983). Yet you may quite legitimately slow down and spend a lot of time on a concept that is particularly critical or may let students take time to discover a mathematical principle on their own. It is usually much more efficient (that is, it takes less time) to teach students skills or information directly than it is to let them make discoveries for themselves, but if you want students to gain a deeper understanding of a topic or to learn how to find information or to figure things out for themselves, then the research findings about pace can be temporarily shelved.

The point is that although research in educational psychology can sometimes be translated directly to the classroom, it is best to apply the principles with a hefty dose of common sense and a clear view of what is being taught to whom and for what purpose.

Research on Effective Programs

Research in educational psychology provides evidence not only about principles of effective practice but also about the effectiveness of particular programs or practices (Fleischman, 2006). For example, in the vignette at the beginning of this chapter, Leah Washington uses a specific approach to creative writing instruction that has been extensively evaluated as a whole (Harris, Graham, & Pressley, 2001). In other words, there is evidence that, on average, children whose teachers are using such methods learn to write better than those whose teachers use more traditional approaches. There is evidence on the effectiveness of dozens of widely used programs, from methods in particular subjects to strategies for reforming entire schools. The What Works Clearinghouse (http://ies.ed.gov/ncee/wwc/) and the Best Evidence Encyclopedia (www.bestevidence.org) review research in all subjects and grade levels. An intentional teacher should be aware of research on programs for his or her subject and grade level and should be willing to seek out professional development opportunities in methods known to make a difference for children.

InTASC 1

Learner
Development

THEORY INTO PRACTICE

Teaching as Decision Making

If there were no educational problems to solve, there would be no need for teachers to function as professionals. Professionals distinguish themselves from nonprofessionals in part by the fact that they must make decisions that influence the course of their work.

You must decide (1) how to recognize problems and issues, (2) how to consider situations from multiple perspectives, (3) how to call up relevant professional knowledge to formulate actions, (4) how to take the most appropriate action, and (5) how to judge the consequences (Silver, Strong, & Perini, 2007).

For example, Ms. O'Hara has a student named Shanika in her social studies class. Most of the time, Shanika is rather quiet and withdrawn. Her permanent record indicates considerable academic ability, but a casual observer would never know it. Ms. O'Hara asks herself the following questions:

(continued)

1. What problems do I perceive in this situation? Is Shanika bored, tired, uninterested, or shy, or might her participation be inhibited by something I or others are doing or not doing? What theories of educational psychology might I consider?
2. I wonder what Shanika thinks about being in this class. Does she feel excluded? Does she care about the subject matter? Is she concerned about what I or others think about her lack of participation? Why or why not? What theories of motivation will help me make a decision?
3. What do I know from theory, research, or practice that might guide my actions to involve Shanika more directly in class activities?
4. What might I actually do in this situation to enhance Shanika's involvement?
5. How would I know if I were successful with Shanika?

If Ms. O'Hara asks and tries to answer these questions—not only in the case of Shanika, of course, but for other students as well—she will improve her chances to learn about her work by doing her work. Philosopher John Dewey taught that the problems teachers face are the natural stimuli for reflective inquiry. Intentional teachers accept challenges and think productively about them (Marzano, 2011b).

ON THE WEB

For educator-friendly reviews of research on effective programs, see bestevidence.org and ies.ed.gov (type WWC into the search engine).

Impact of Research on Educational Practice

Many researchers and educators have bemoaned the limited impact of research in educational psychology on teachers' practices (see, for example, Kennedy, 2008). Indeed, research in education has nowhere near as great an impact on educational practice as research in medicine has on medical practice (Riehl, 2006). Yet research in education does have a profound *indirect* impact on educational practice, even if teachers are not aware of it. It affects educational policies, professional development programs, and teaching materials. For example, the Tennessee class size study (Finn, Pannozzo, & Achilles, 2003), which found important effects of class size in the early grades on student achievement, had a direct impact on state and federal proposals for class size reduction (Wasley, 2002). Research on beginning reading (National Reading Panel, 2000) dramatically transformed curriculum, instruction, and professional development for this subject. Research on the effects of career academies in high schools (Kemple, 1997) has led to a substantial increase in such programs.

It is important for you to become an intelligent consumer of research and not to take every finding or every expert's pronouncement as truth from Mount Olympus (Fleischman, 2006; Gibbs, 2009; Slavin, 2011). The following section briefly describes the methods of research that most often produce findings of use to educators.

"In light of research on class size, we're not cutting class, we're helping our classmates get a better education!"

THEORY INTO PRACTICE

How to Be an Intelligent Consumer of Educational Psychology Research

Let's say you're in the market for a new car. Before laying out your hard-earned money, you'll probably review the findings from various consumer research reports. You may want to know something about how various cars have performed in crash tests, which cars have the best gas mileage, or what the trade-in values of particular models are. Before embarking on this major investment, you want to feel as confident as you can about your decision. If you've been in this situation before, you probably remember that all of your research helped you make an informed decision.

Now that you are about to enter the profession of teaching, you should apply a similar consumer orientation in your decision making (Andrews, 2014; Fleischman, 2014). As a teacher, you will be called on to make hundreds of decisions each day. Your car-buying decision is influenced by a combination of sound research findings and common sense, and your decisions about teaching and learning should follow this same pattern. Teaching and learning are complex concepts subject to a wide variety of influences, so your knowledge of relevant research will serve to guide you in making informed choices.

How can knowing the simple formula *research + common sense = effective teaching* help you to be a more intelligent consumer of educational psychology research? The following recommendations show how you can put this formula into practice:

1. ***Be a consumer of relevant research.*** It's obvious you can't apply what you don't know. As a professional, you should maintain a working knowledge of relevant research. In addition to your course texts, which will be excellent resources for you in the future, you should become familiar with the professional journals in your field. Teacher-oriented journals such as *Educational Leadership* and *Phi Delta Kappan* contain easy-to-read summaries of research, for example. Websites such as bestevidence.org summarize program evaluations in a user-friendly way. In addition, check out *Annual Editions: Educational Psychology,* a yearly publication that reprints articles from various professional journals. Don't overlook the value of networking with other teachers, face to face or via the Internet. The example of Ellen Mathis and Leah Washington is an excellent illustration of how collaboration can expand your knowledge of what works.

2. ***Teach intentionally.*** As stated earlier in this chapter, there is no recipe for the ingredients that make up a commonsense approach to teaching. However, behaviors consistent with being an intentional teacher are about as close as we can get. Intentional teachers are thoughtful. Like Mr. Harris, you should consider multiple perspectives on classroom situations. When you take action, be purposeful and think about why you do what you do. Like other intentional teachers, you can follow your actions with careful reflection, evaluating whether your actions have resulted in the desired outcomes. You probably learned about the "scientific method" sometime during high school. Intentional teachers employ such a method in teaching, formulating a working hypothesis based on observations and background knowledge, collecting data to test the hypothesis, effectively organizing and analyzing the data, drawing sound conclusions based on the data, and taking a course of action based on the conclusions. For many experienced teachers, this cycle becomes automatic and internalized. When applied systematically, these practices can serve

(continued)

Certification Pointer

For teacher certification tests, you may need to show that you know how to access the professional literature, professional associations, and professional development activities to improve your teaching.

MyEdLab
Video Example 1.3
Bob Slavin describes one of his early experiences as a classroom teacher, working with an autistic boy. How is Bob's work with Mark a demonstration of critical thinking? Consider this experience, as well as that of Leah Washington in the Chapter One opening vignette. What can you learn from these experiences that will help you become an intentional teacher?

InTASC 7
Planning for Instruction

InTASC 9
Professional Learning and Ethical Practice

InTASC 10
Leadership and Collaboration

to validate research and theory and, as a result, increase your growing professional knowledge base (Schoenfeld, 2014).

3. ***Share your experiences.*** When you combine knowledge of research with your professional common sense, you will find yourself engaged in more effective practices. As you and your students experience success, share your findings. Avenues for dissemination are endless. In addition to publishing articles in traditional sources such as professional journals and organizational newsletters, don't overlook the importance of preparing schoolwide in-service demonstrations, papers for state and national professional conferences, and presentations to school boards. In addition, the Internet offers various newsgroups where teachers engage in ongoing discussions about their work.

MyEdLab Self-Check 1.2

HOW CAN I BECOME AN INTENTIONAL TEACHER?

Think about the best, most intentional teachers you ever had—the ones who seemed so confident, so caring, so skilled, so enthusiastic about their subject. Chances are, when they took educational psychology, they were as scared, uncertain, and overwhelmed about becoming a teacher as you might be today. Yet they kept at it and made themselves the great teachers you remember. You can do the same.

Teacher Certification

Before you can become an *intentional* teacher, you have to become a *certified* teacher. Each state, province, and country has its own requirements, but in most places you at least have to graduate from a 4-year college with a specified distribution of courses, although various alternative certification programs exist as well. You also will need to have a satisfactory student teaching experience. In most states, however, these are not enough. You also have to pass a teacher certification test, or licensure test. Many states base their requirements on the 10 principles of effective teaching shown in Figure 1.2. Developed by the Interstate Teacher Assessment and Support Consortium (InTASC), they form the basis for most teacher certification tests, whether developed by InTASC, by the Educational Testing Service (ETS), or by individual state departments of education (see Darling-Hammond, 2008).

The Praxis Series™ Professional Assessments for Beginning Teachers, developed by the Educational Testing Service, is the test most commonly used by states to certify teachers (ETS, 2012). The Praxis Series includes three categories of assessment that correlate with significant stages in teacher development. These are Praxis I: Academic Skills Assessment for entering a teacher training program, Praxis II: Subject Assessments for licensure for entering the profession, and Praxis III: Classroom Performance Assessments after the first year of teaching. Praxis II measures both general teaching skills and subject knowledge of over 120 topics ranging from agriculture to world literature. It is the test you take upon completing your teacher preparation program.

Detailed information about the Praxis series of tests can be found at ets.org. From this website you can access the tests-at-a-glance page, which includes test outlines, sample questions with explanations for the best answers, and test-taking strategies. There is also a list of state-by-state requirements to determine which Praxis tests each state uses, if any. Note that individual universities may also use Praxis, even if their states do not require it.

Each state, province, or institution that uses the Praxis tests sets its own passing requirements. The passing score for each test for each state is listed on the website and in a booklet you receive with your score report.

Connections 1.4

For additional help in preparing for licensure, see the appendix.

Standard #1: Learner Development

The teacher understands how learners grow and develop, recognizing that patterns of learning and development vary individually within and across the cognitive, linguistic, social, emotional, and physical areas, and designs and implements developmentally appropriate and challenging learning experiences.

Standard #2: Learning Differences

The teacher uses understanding of individual differences and diverse cultures and communities to ensure inclusive learning environments that enable each learner to meet high standards.

Standard #3: Learning Environments

The teacher works with others to create environments that support individual and collaborative learning, and that encourage positive social interaction, active engagement in learning, and self motivation.

Standard #4: Content Knowledge

The teacher understands the central concepts, tools of inquiry, and structures of the discipline(s) he or she teaches and creates learning experiences that make these aspects of the discipline accessible and meaningful for learners to ensure mastery of the content.

Standard #5: Application of Content

The teacher understands how to connect concepts and use differing perspectives to engage learners in critical thinking, creativity, and collaborative problem solving related to authentic local and global issues.

Standard #6: Assessment

The teacher understands and uses multiple methods of assessment to engage learners in their own growth, to monitor learner progress, and to guide the teacher's and learner's decision making.

Standard #7: Planning for Instruction

The teacher plans instruction that supports every student in meeting rigorous learning goals by drawing upon knowledge of content areas, curriculum, cross-disciplinary skills, and pedagogy, as well as knowledge of learners and the community context.

Standard #8: Instructional Strategies

The teacher understands and uses a variety of instructional strategies to encourage learners to develop deep understanding of content areas and their connections, and to build skills to apply knowledge in meaningful ways.

Standard #9: Professional Learning and Ethical Practice

The teacher engages in ongoing professional learning and uses evidence to continually evaluate his/her practice, particularly the effects of his/her choices and actions on others (learners, families, other professionals, and the community), and adapts practice to meet the needs of each learner.

Standard #10: Leadership and Collaboration

The teacher seeks appropriate leadership roles and opportunities to take responsibility for student learning, to collaborate with learners, families, colleagues, other school professionals, and community members to ensure learner growth, and to advance the profession.

FIGURE 1.2 • Interstate Teacher Assessment and Support Consortium (InTASC) Model Core Teaching Standards

Source: Council of Chief State School Officers. (2011). *The Interstate New Teacher Assessment and Support Consortium (InTASC) model core teaching standards: A resource for state dialogue.* Washington, DC: Author.

Many states, including California, Texas, Florida, and New York, have developed their own teacher certification tests. These usually include sections much like the Praxis Principles of Learning and Teaching.

Throughout this text you will find tips on topics likely to appear on teacher certification tests. These marginal notes, called *Certification Pointers*, highlight knowledge that is frequently required on state teacher licensure exams, including Praxis Principles of Learning and Teaching. Also see the appendix at the end of the text that correlates the content of each chapter to corresponding topics within the Praxis Principles of Learning and Teaching exam.

Certification Pointer

Teacher certification tests include a section on teacher professionalism. One aspect that is emphasized is being able to read and understand research on current ideas and debates about teaching practices.

Beyond Certification

Getting a teaching certificate is necessary but not sufficient to becoming an intentional teacher. Starting with your student teaching experience and continuing into your first job, you can create or take advantage of opportunities to develop your skills as an intentional teacher in a number of ways.

SEEK MENTORS Experienced teachers who are themselves intentional teachers are your best resource (Nieto, 2009). Not only are they highly effective, but they also understand and can describe what they're doing (and, ideally, can help you learn to do those things). Talk with experienced teachers in your school, observe them teaching, and ask them to observe you and share ideas, as Ellen Mathis did in the vignette at the beginning of this chapter. Many school systems provide induction programs to help new teachers develop in the crucial first years, but even if yours does not, you can create one for yourself by seeking out experienced and helpful mentors.

> **InTASC 9**
>
> **Professional Learning and Ethical Practice**

SEEK PROFESSIONAL DEVELOPMENT Districts, universities, state departments of education, and other institutions provide all sorts of professional development workshops for teachers on a wide range of topics. Take advantage of every opportunity to participate. The best professional development includes some sort of coaching or follow-up, in which someone who knows a given technique or program comes to your class to observe you implementing the program and gives you feedback (see Darling-Hammond & Richardson, 2009; Hirsh & Hord, 2008; Neufield & Roper, 2003). Workshops in which many teachers from your school participate together, and then have opportunities to discuss successes and challenges, can also be very effective (see Calderón, 1999).

> **InTASC 10**
>
> **Leadership and Collaboration**

TALK TEACHING Talk to your colleagues, your former classmates, your friends who teach, even your friends who don't teach. Share your successes, your failures, your questions. Teaching can be an isolating experience if it's just you and your students. Take every opportunity to share ideas and commiserate with sympathetic colleagues (Nieto, 2009). Join a book club to discuss articles and books on teaching (Hoerr, 2009).

ON THE WEB

When your friends and colleagues are worn out from your passion for teaching, try virtual colleagues on the Web. The following examples are just a few of the many teacher-oriented websites and blogs that offer opportunities to share advice, opinions, and observations.

Edublogs (edublogs.com)

The Knowledge Loom (knowledgeloom.org)

K–12 Practitioner's Circle (nces.ed.gov)

Typepad (typepad.com)

The Vent (proteacher.com)

There are websites for elementary teachers (elementary-teacher-resources.com), for middle school teachers (middleschool.net), and for teachers of various subjects, by topic (sitesforteachers.com). Resources for school librarians can be found at sldirectory.com. Resources for teachers using technology in their classrooms can be found at www.teachervision.com (search for educational technology).

PROFESSIONAL PUBLICATIONS AND ASSOCIATIONS Intentional teachers do a lot of reading. Your school may subscribe to teacher-oriented journals, or you might choose to do so. For example, look for *Teacher Magazine, Theory Into Practice, Learning, Young Children, Phi Delta Kappan, Educational Leadership,* or subject-specific journals such as *Reading Teacher* and *Mathematics Teacher.* Take a look at Edutopia (online at edutopia.org).

In addition, check out professional associations in your subject area or area of interest. The national teachers' unions—the American Federation of Teachers (AFT) and the National Education Association (NEA)—have publications, workshops, and other resources from which you can benefit greatly. Your state department of education, regional educational laboratory, or school district office may also have useful resources. Here are a few of the many useful websites:

American Educational Research Association: aera.net

American Federation of Teachers: aft.org

Canadian Educational Research Association: cea–ace.ca

Council for Exceptional Children: cec.sped.org

International Reading Association: reading.org

National Association for Bilingual Education: nabe.org

National Association for the Education of Young Children: naeyc.org

National Association of Black School Educators: nabse.org

National Council for the Social Studies: ncss.org

National Council of Teachers of English: ncte.org

National Council of Teachers of Mathematics: nctm.org

National Education Association: nea.org

National Institute for Literacy: nifl.gov

National Middle School Association: nmsa.org

National Science Teachers Association: nsta.org

Certification Pointer

The teacher professionalism section of Praxis II and other certification tests may ask you to identify the titles of several professional journals in your particular field of teaching (e.g., *Journal of Educational Psychology, Educational Leadership, Phi Delta Kappan*).

Certification Pointer

Teaching certification tests might expect you to know which professional associations offer meetings, publications, and dialogue with other teachers (e.g., American Educational Research Association, International Reading Association, American Federation of Teachers, National Education Association).

ON THE WEB

To find journals reporting research in education, try the following:

Educational Leadership: ascd.org

Phi Delta Kappan: pdkintl.org

Theory Into Practice: ehe.osu.edu

Journal of Teaching Writing: journals.iupui.edu

Education Week: edweek.org

Journal of Research in Childhood Education: tandfonline.com

Review of Educational Research: rer.sagepub.com

Better: Evidence-Based Education: bestevidence.org

MyEdLab **Self-Check 1.3**

SUMMARY

What Makes a Good Teacher?

Good teachers know their subject matter and have mastered pedagogical skills. They accomplish all the tasks involved in effective instruction with warmth, enthusiasm, and caring. They are intentional teachers, and they use principles of educational psychology in their decision making and teaching. They combine research and common sense.

What Is the Role of Research in Educational Psychology?

Educational psychology is the systematic study of learners, learning, and teaching. Research in educational psychology focuses on the processes by which information, skills, values, and attitudes are communicated between teachers and students in the classroom and on applications of the principles of psychology to instructional practices. Such research shapes educational policies, professional development programs, and teaching materials.

How Can I Become an Intentional Teacher?

Before you can become an intentional teacher, you have to become a certified teacher. Each state has its own requirements regarding education, student teaching, and licensure testing. These include the Test for Teaching Knowledge and the Praxis series. You can further develop your skills as an intentional teacher by seeking mentors, pursuing professional development, and talking to colleagues and friends about your experiences.

KEY TERMS

Review the following key terms from the chapter.

college and career-ready standards 10	law 11
Common Core State Standards 9	pedagogy 5
critical thinking 8	principle 11
educational psychology 4	teacher efficacy 7
intentionality 6	theory 11

SELF-ASSESSMENT: PRACTICING FOR LICENSURE

Directions: The chapter-opening vignette addresses indicators that are often assessed in state licensure exams. Reread the chapter-opening vignette and then respond to the following questions.

1. In the first paragraph, Ellen Mathis does not understand why her students are nonproductive and unimaginative in their writing. According to educational psychology research, which of the following teacher characteristics is Ellen most likely lacking?
   a. Classroom management skills
   b. Content knowledge
   c. Intentionality
   d. Common sense
2. Leah Washington talks with Ellen Mathis about getting students to write interesting compositions. Which of the following statements summarizes Leah's approach to teaching writing?
   a. Select teaching methods, learning activities, and instructional materials that are appropriate and motivating for students.
   b. Have students of similar abilities work together so the teacher can adapt instruction to meet the needs of each group.
   c. When working on writing activities, consider the teacher to be the instruction center.
   d. Individualization is the first goal of instruction; direct instruction is the second goal.
3. According to research on the development of expertise, what characteristic separates novice teachers from expert teachers?
   a. Novice teachers tend to rely on their pedagogical skills because their content knowledge is less complex than that of experts.
   b. Expert teachers do more short-term memory processing than novices because their thinking is more complex.

    c. Novice teachers have to constantly upgrade and examine their own teaching practices, whereas experts use a "best practices" approach.

    d. Expert teachers are critical thinkers.

4. Educational psychologists are often accused of studying the obvious. However, they have learned that the obvious is not always true. All of the following statements demonstrate this idea except one. Which one is obvious *and* supported by research?

    a. Student achievement is increased when students are assigned to classes according to their ability.

    b. Scolding students for misbehavior improves student behavior.

    c. Whole-class instruction is more effective than individualized instruction.

    d. Intentional teachers balance competing goals according to the needs of particular students and situations.

5. Leah Washington discusses many of her teaching strategies with Ellen Mathis. One can easily see that Leah views teaching as a decision-making process. She recognizes problems and issues, considers situations from multiple perspectives, calls on her professional knowledge to formulate action, and

    a. selects the most appropriate action and assesses the consequence.

    b. chooses a strategy that agrees with her individual beliefs about teaching.

    c. consults with expert teachers and administrators to assist with her plan of action.

    d. allows students to make instructional decisions based on their interests and needs.

6. The products of research are principles, laws, and theories. Leah Washington describes many principles and theories of educational psychology as she speaks with Ellen Mathis about teaching students to write compositions. First, describe an instruction action with which Ellen Mathis is having difficulties (e.g., Ellen assigns all students the same topic), and then describe principles and theories she can use to engage her students in exciting and meaningful lessons.

7. Intentional teachers are aware of resources available for professional learning. They continually refine their practices to address the needs of all students. List four actions you could take to find information to help you teach your students with limited English proficiency.

MyEdLab **Licensure Exam 1.1** Answer questions and receive instant feedback in your Pearson eText in MyEdLab.

GagliardiImages/Shutterstock

CHAPTER TWO

Cognitive Development

LEARNING OUTCOMES

At the end of this chapter, you should be able to:

2.1 Describe Piaget's theory of human development and discuss how it can apply in the classroom

2.2 Describe the theories of development presented by Vygotsky and by Bronfenbrenner and discuss how they apply in the classroom

2.3 Describe the distinct stages of language and literacy and explain how you can set up your classroom to promote literacy development

2.4 Describe how knowledge of social, moral, and emotional development informs intentional teaching

Patricia Wing is very proud of her third-grade class. Her students have done very well on state tests, and they are succeeding in all of their subjects, especially science, Patricia's own favorite. So she decides to give her students a challenge they'll really enjoy. "Class," she says, "I'm so excited to see the good work you've all done in science. Today, I'm going to give you a problem to solve in your teams that will stretch your minds, but I know you can solve it.

"At each of your tables you have a pendulum, several weights, and a stopwatch. You can change the weights on the pendulum, the length of the string, the push you give the weight to start it swinging, or anything you like. My question to you is this: What determines how many times the pendulum goes back and forth in a minute?"

The students get right to work with excitement. They try more weight and less weight, more push and less push, longer strings and shorter strings. Each team appoints a time keeper who writes down how many swings there are in a minute. The students argue with each other: "It's the weight!" "It's the push!" "It's the string!" The groups are working hard but haphazardly. None of them gets the right answer (which is that only the length of the string matters).

Patricia is astonished. The students know a lot about science, try hard, and work well together, yet they cannot solve the problem.

USING YOUR EXPERIENCE

CRITICAL THINKING Why do you think Patricia Wing's class cannot solve the pendulum problem? What does her experience suggest to you about why teachers should consider children's stages of development in their teaching?

Over the course of their first 18 years of life, children go through astounding changes. Most of these changes are obvious—children get bigger, smarter, and more socially adept, for example. However, many aspects of development are not so obvious. Individual children develop in different ways and at different rates, and development is influenced by biology, culture, parenting, education, and other factors. Every teacher needs to understand how children grow and develop to be able to understand how children learn and how best to teach them (Comer, 2005).

HOW DO CHILDREN DEVELOP COGNITIVELY?

The term **development** refers to how people grow, adapt, and change over the course of their lifetimes, through personality development, socioemotional development, cognitive development (thinking), and language development. This chapter begins with two major theorists of cognitive development whose ideas are widely accepted: Jean Piaget and Lev Vygotsky (see Bee & Boyd, 2010; Berk, 2013; Mahn & John-Steiner, 2013; McDevitt & Ormrod, 2016; Woolfolk & Perry, 2015).

Aspects of Development

Children are not miniature adults. They think differently and see the world differently. One of the first requirements of effective teaching is that you understand how students think and how they view the world. Effective teaching strategies must take into account students' ages and stages of development. A bright third-grader might appear to be able to learn any kind of mathematics but in fact may not have the cognitive maturity to do the abstract thinking required for algebra. In the opening vignette, Ms. Wing's class is smart and motivated, yet the pendulum task is a classic example of a kind of thinking that usually does not appear until adolescence, when most children gain the ability to think logically about problems of this kind and to proceed in a methodical way toward a solution.

InTASC 1

Learner Development

Issues of Development

Two central issues have been debated for decades among developmental psychologists: the degree to which development is affected by experience and whether development proceeds in stages.

NATURE–NURTURE CONTROVERSY Is development predetermined at birth, by heredity and biological factors, or is it affected by experience and other environmental factors? Today, most developmental psychologists (e.g., Bee & Boyd, 2010; Berk, 2013; Feldman, 2012; Woolfolk & Perry, 2015) believe that nature and nurture combine to influence development, with biological factors playing a stronger role in some aspects, such as physical development.

The argument about nature vs. nurture, heredity vs. environment, goes back to the Greeks (at least). The environmentalist philosopher John Watson (1930, p. 82) put his position this way:

> I'll guarantee to take any (child) at random and train him to become . . . a doctor, lawyer, artist, merchant-chief, and yes, even beggar-man and thief, regardless of his talents, penchants, tendencies, abilities, vocations, and race of his ancestors. I admit that I am going beyond my facts . . . but so have the advocates of the contrary . . . for thousands of years.

Source: From *Behaviorism* by John Broadus Watson. Published by W. W. Norton & Company, © 1930.

While few scientists today would go as far as Watson, there remains much debate about the relative influences of genes and environment. One problem is that the two interact. For example, if a child is a little better at sports than other children at a young age, he or she may receive a lot more practice, encouragement, and training in sports and therefore become an outstanding athlete. So was that outcome due to nature or nurture? Similarly, a child who shows promise in science at a young age may receive a lot of encouragement, leading him or her to develop motivation to learn science and seek science-related experiences. Nature or nurture? Obviously, nature and nurture are mixed up in any particular person or population. For educators, the key point is that while nothing can be done about a child's genes, a great deal can be done about his or her environment to build skill, motivation, and self-confidence. There is no question that teachers and parents make a huge difference in children's learning, over and above whatever the children's genetic predispositions may be.

CONTINUOUS AND DISCONTINUOUS THEORIES A second issue revolves around the notion of how change occurs. **Continuous theories of development**, such as information-processing models (Halford, Baker, McCredden, & Baine, 2005; Munakata, 2006), assume that development occurs in a smooth progression as skills develop and experiences are provided by caregivers and the environment. Continuous theories emphasize the importance of environment rather than heredity in determining development.

A second perspective assumes that children progress through a set of predictable and invariant stages of development. From this perspective, major changes happen when children advance to a new stage of development. All children are believed to acquire skills in the same sequence, although rates of progress differ from child to child. The abilities children gain in each subsequent stage are not simply "more of the same"; at each stage, children develop qualitatively different understandings, abilities, and beliefs. Skipping stages is rare or impossible, although at any given point the same child may exhibit behaviors characteristic of more than one stage (DeVries, 2008). In contrast to continuous theories, these **discontinuous theories of development** focus on inborn factors rather than environmental influences to explain change over time. Environmental conditions may have some influence on the pace of development, but the sequence of developmental steps is essentially fixed. According to this perspective, the 9-year-olds in Patricia Wing's class could not have solved the pendulum problem no matter how much they had been taught, because they had not reached a developmental stage that enables people to solve problems involving many factors at the same time.

Stage theorists, such as Piaget and Vygotsky, share the belief that distinct stages of development can be identified and described. However, their theories differ significantly in the number of stages and in their details (see DeVries, 2008).

HOW DID PIAGET VIEW COGNITIVE DEVELOPMENT?

Jean Piaget, born in Switzerland in 1896, is the most influential developmental psychologist in the history of psychology (see Wadsworth, 2004). After receiving his doctorate in biology, he became more interested in psychology, basing his earliest theories on careful observation of his own three children. Piaget thought of himself as applying biological principles and methods to the study of human development, and many of the terms he introduced to psychology were drawn directly from biology.

Piaget explored both why and how mental abilities change over time. For Piaget, development depends in large part on the child's manipulation of and active interaction with the environment. In Piaget's view, knowledge comes from action (see DeVries, 2008; Wadsworth, 2004). Piaget's theory of **cognitive development** proposes that a child's intellect, or cognitive ability, progresses through four distinct stages. Each stage is characterized by the emergence of new abilities and ways of processing information. Many of the specifics of Piaget's theories have been challenged in later research. In particular, many of the changes in cognitive functioning that he described are now known to take place earlier than he stated, at least under certain circumstances. Nevertheless, Piaget's work forms an essential basis for understanding child development.

How Development Occurs

SCHEMES Piaget believed that all children are born with an innate tendency to interact with and make sense of their environments. Young children demonstrate patterns of behavior or thinking, called **schemes**, that older children and adults also use in dealing with objects in the world. We use schemes to find out about and act in the world; each scheme treats all objects and events in the same way. When babies encounter a new object, how are they to know what this object is all about? According to Piaget, they will use the schemes they have developed and will find out whether the object makes a loud or a soft sound when banged, what it tastes like, whether it gives milk, and whether it goes thud when dropped (see Figure 2.1).

ASSIMILATION AND ACCOMMODATION According to Piaget, **adaptation** is the process of adjusting schemes in response to the environment by means of assimilation and accommodation. **Assimilation** is the process of understanding a new object or event in terms of an existing scheme. If you give young infants small objects that they have never seen before but that resemble familiar objects, they are likely to grasp them, bite them, and bang them. In other words, they will try to use existing schemes to learn about these unknown things (see Figure 2.1b). Similarly, a high school student may have a studying scheme that involves putting information on cards and memorizing the cards' contents. She may have had success with this in one subject and then applied the same scheme to many subjects.

Connections 2.1

For information on schema theory (a topic related to schemes) in connection with information processing and memory, see Chapter 6.

**FIGURE 2.1 •
Schemes**

Babies use patterns of behavior called *schemes* to learn about their world.

a. Banging is a favorite **scheme** used by babies to explore their world.

b. **Assimilation** occurs when they incorporate new objects into the scheme.

c. **Accommodation** occurs when a new object does not fit the existing scheme.

ON THE WEB

For more on Piaget's life and work, go to www.simplypsychology.org and enter Piaget into the search engine. For information on Piaget's theory applied to the classroom, visit piaget.weebly.com. The Jean Piaget Society's website can be found at piaget.org.

Certification Pointer

Most teacher certification tests will require you to know that a constructivist approach to learning emphasizes the active role that learners play in building their own understandings.

MyEdLab

Video Example 2.1

The children in this classroom, while studying tadpoles, are learning something new about growth. They can assimilate the idea that the tadpole grows legs, but they need to accommodate their concept of growth to understand why the tadpole's tail gets smaller.

Certification Pointer

When responding to the case studies in certification tests, you may be asked to identify appropriateness of instruction according to the students' Piagetian stage of development.

Sometimes, when old ways of dealing with the world simply don't work, a child might modify an existing scheme in light of new information or a new experience, a process called **accommodation**. For example, if you give an egg to a baby who has a banging scheme for small objects, what will happen to the egg is obvious (Figure 2.1c). Less obvious, however, is what will happen to the baby's banging scheme. Because of the unexpected consequences of banging the egg, the baby may change the scheme. In the future the baby might bang some objects hard and others softly. The high school student who studies only by means of memorization might learn to use a different strategy, such as discussing difficult concepts with a friend, to study subjects or topics in which memorization does not work very well.

The baby who banged the egg and the student who tried to memorize rather than comprehend had to deal with situations that could not be fully handled by existing schemes. This, in Piaget's theory, creates a state of disequilibrium, or an imbalance between what is understood and what is encountered. People naturally try to reduce such imbalances by focusing on the stimuli that cause the disequilibrium and developing new schemes, or adapting old ones, until equilibrium is restored. This process of restoring balance is called **equilibration**. According to Piaget, learning depends on this process. When equilibrium is upset, children have the opportunity to grow and develop. Eventually, qualitatively new ways of thinking about the world emerge, and children advance to a new stage of development. Piaget believed that physical experiences and manipulation of the environment are critical for developmental change to occur. However, he also believed that social interaction with peers, especially arguments and discussions, helps to clarify thinking and, eventually, to make it more logical. Research has stressed the importance of confronting students with experiences or data that do not fit into their current theories of how the world works as a means of advancing their cognitive development. Having students resolve disequilibrium working with peers is particularly effective (Slavin, 2014).

Piaget's theory of development represents **constructivism**, a view of cognitive development as a process in which children actively build systems of meaning and understandings of reality through their experiences and interactions (Berk, 2013; Schunk, 2016). In this view, children actively construct knowledge by continuously assimilating and accommodating new information.

Piaget's Stages of Development

Piaget divided the cognitive development of children and adolescents into four stages: sensorimotor, preoperational, concrete operational, and formal operational. He believed that all children pass through these stages in this order and that no child can skip a stage, although different children pass through the stages at somewhat different rates. The same individuals may perform tasks associated with different stages at the same time, particularly at points of transition into a new stage. Table 2.1 summarizes the approximate ages at which children and adolescents pass through Piaget's four stages. It also shows the major accomplishments of each stage.

SENSORIMOTOR STAGE (BIRTH TO AGE 2) The earliest stage is called **sensorimotor** because during this stage, babies and young children explore the world by using their senses and motor skills. Dramatic changes occur as infants progress through the sensorimotor period. Initially, all infants have inborn behaviors called **reflexes**. Touch a newborn's lips, and the baby will begin to suck; place your finger in the palm of an infant's hand, and the infant will grasp it. These and other innate behaviors are the building blocks from which the infant's first schemes form.

TABLE 2.1 • Piaget's Stages of Cognitive Development

People progress through four stages of cognitive development between birth and adulthood, according to Jean Piaget. Each stage is marked by the emergence of new intellectual abilities that enable people to understand the world in increasingly complex ways.

STAGE	APPROXIMATE AGES	MAJOR ACCOMPLISHMENTS
Sensorimotor	Birth to 2 years	Formation of concept of "object permanence" and gradual progression from reflexive behavior to goal-directed behavior.
Preoperational	2 to 7 years	Development of the ability to use symbols to represent objects in the world. Thinking remains egocentric and centered.
Concrete operational	7 to 11 years	Improvement in ability to think logically. New abilities include the use of operations that are reversible. Thinking is decentered, and problem solving is less restricted by egocentrism. Abstract thinking is not yet possible.
Formal operational	11 years to adulthood	Abstract and purely symbolic thinking is possible. Problems can be solved through the use of systematic experimentation.

Infants soon learn to use these reflexes to produce more interesting and intentional patterns of behavior. This learning occurs initially through accident and then through more intentional trial-and-error efforts. According to Piaget, by the end of the sensorimotor stage, children have progressed from their earlier trial-and-error approach to a more planned approach to problem solving. For the first time they can mentally represent objects and events. What most of us would call "thinking" appears now. This is a major advance because it means that the child can think through and plan behavior. For example, suppose a 2-year-old is in the kitchen watching his mother prepare dinner. If the child knows where the step stool is kept, he may ask to have it set up to afford a better view of the counter and a better chance for a nibble. The child did not stumble on this solution accidentally. Instead, he thought about the problem, figured out a possible solution that used the step stool, tried out the solution mentally, and only then tried the solution in practice (Trawick-Smith, 2014).

Another hallmark development of the sensorimotor period is the ability to grasp **object permanence**. Piaget argued that children must learn that objects are physically stable and exist even when the objects are not in the child's physical presence. For example, if you cover an infant's bottle with a towel, the child may not remove it, believing that the bottle is gone. By 2 years of age, children understand that objects exist even when they cannot be seen. Once they realize that things exist out of sight, children can start using symbols to represent these things in their minds so that they can think about them (Cohen & Cashon, 2003).

MyEdLab

Video Example 2.2

In this video, children participate in tasks that show their understanding of conservation of volume and conservation of number. Compare the responses, and identify each child's stage of cognitive development, according to Piaget's theory.

PREOPERATIONAL STAGE (AGES 2 TO 7) During the **preoperational stage**, children have greater ability to think about things and can use symbols to mentally represent objects (Massey, 2008; Ostroff, 2012). Their language and concepts develop at an incredible rate. Yet much of their thinking remains surprisingly primitive. One of Piaget's earliest and most important discoveries was that young children lack an understanding of the principle of **conservation**. For example, if you pour milk from a tall, narrow container into a shallow, wide one, and back again, in the presence of a preoperational child, the child will firmly believe that the tall glass has more milk (see Figure 2.2). Similarly, a preoperational child is likely to believe that a sandwich cut in four pieces is more sandwich or that a line of blocks that is spread out contains more blocks than a line that is compressed, even after being shown that the number of blocks is identical.

Several aspects of preoperational thinking help to explain the error on conservation tasks. One characteristic is **centration**: paying attention to only one aspect of a situation. In the example illustrated in Figure 2.2, children might have claimed that there was less milk after it was poured into the wide container because they centered on the height of the milk, ignoring its width. At the bottom of Figure 2.2, children focused on the length of the line of blocks and ignored its density (or the actual number of blocks).

Reversibility, the ability to change direction in one's thinking to return to a starting point, is another facet of thinking that is not yet developed in preoperational children. As adults, for

FIGURE 2.2 • Some Piagetian Conservation Tasks

Children at the preoperational stage cannot yet conserve. These tasks are mastered gradually over the concrete operational stage. Most children acquire conservation of number, mass, and liquid sometime between 6 and 7 years and of weight between 8 and 10 years.

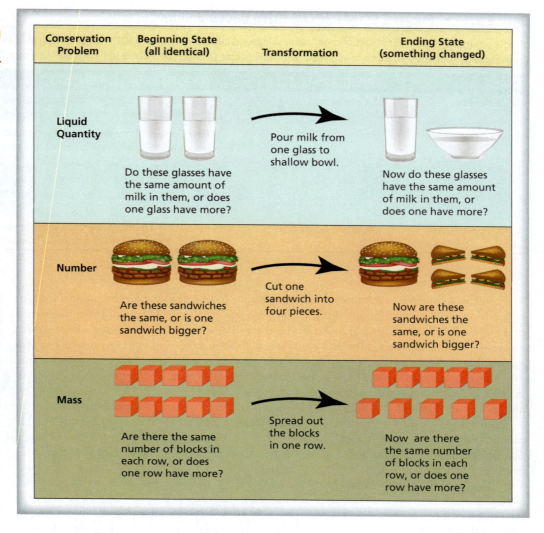

Conservation Problem	Beginning State (all identical)	Transformation	Ending State (something changed)
Liquid Quantity	Do these glasses have the same amount of milk in them, or does one glass have more?	Pour milk from one glass to shallow bowl.	Now do these glasses have the same amount of milk in them, or does one have more?
Number	Are these sandwiches the same, or is one sandwich bigger?	Cut one sandwich into four pieces.	Now are these sandwiches the same, or is one sandwich bigger?
Mass	Are there the same number of blocks in each row, or does one row have more?	Spread out the blocks in one row.	Now are there the same number of blocks in each row, or does one row have more?

MyEdLab

Video Example 2.3

Bob Slavin provides an example of developmental changes in children's egocentric thinking. How will your understanding of egocentrism help you as a teacher?

example, we know that if 7 + 5 = 12, then 12 − 5 = 7. If we add 5 items to 7 items and then take the 5 items away (reverse what we've done), we are left with 7 items again. If preoperational children could think this way, then they could mentally reverse the process of pouring the milk and realize that if the milk were poured back into the tall beaker, its quantity would not change.

Another characteristic of the preoperational child's thinking is a focus on states. In the milk problem the milk is poured from one container to another. Preschoolers ignore this pouring process and focus only on the beginning state (milk in a tall glass) and the end state (milk in a shallow dish). Unlike adults, the young preschooler forms concepts that vary in definition from situation to situation and are not always logical. How else can we explain the 2-year-old's ability to treat a stuffed animal as an inanimate object one minute and as an animate object the next? Eventually, though, the child's concepts become more consistent and less private. Children become increasingly concerned that their definitions match other people's. But they still lack the ability to coordinate one concept with another.

Finally, preoperational children are **egocentric** in their thinking. Children at this stage believe that everyone sees the world exactly as they do. For example, Piaget and Inhelder (1956) seated children on one side of a display of three mountains and asked them to describe how the scene looked to a doll seated on the other side. Children below the age of 6 or 7 described the doll's view as identical to their own, even though it was apparent to adults that this could not be so. Because preoperational children are unable to take the perspective of others, they often interpret events entirely in reference to themselves.

CONCRETE OPERATIONAL STAGE (AGES 7 TO 11) Although the differences between the mental abilities of preoperational preschoolers and concrete operational elementary school students are dramatic, concrete operational children still do not think like adults (Davis, 2008). They are very much rooted in the world as it is and have difficulty with abstract thought. Flavell describes the concrete operational child as taking "an earthbound, concrete, practical-minded sort of problem-solving approach, one that persistently fixates on the perceptible and inferable reality right there in front of him. A theorist the elementary-school child is not" (1986, p. 103). The term **concrete operational stage** reflects this earthbound approach. Children at this stage can form concepts, see relationships, and solve problems, but only as long as they involve objects and situations that are familiar.

During the elementary school years, children's cognitive abilities undergo dramatic changes. Elementary school children no longer have difficulties with conservation problems because they have acquired the concept of reversibility. For example, they can now see that the amount of milk in the short, wide container must be the same as that in the tall, narrow container, because if the milk were poured back into the tall container, it would be at the same level as before. Another fundamental difference between preoperational and concrete operational children is that the preoperational child responds to perceived appearances, whereas the older, concrete operational child responds to inferred reality. Flavell (1986) demonstrated this concept by showing children a red car and then, while they were still watching, covering it with a filter that made it appear black. When asked what color the car was, 3-year-olds responded "black," and 6-year-olds responded "red." The older, concrete operational child is able to respond to **inferred reality**, seeing things in the context of other meanings; preschoolers see what they see, with little ability to infer the meaning behind what they see.

One important task that children learn during the concrete operational stage is **seriation**, or arranging things in a logical progression—for example, lining up sticks from smallest to largest. To do this, they must be able to order or classify objects according to some criterion or dimension, in this case length. Once this ability is acquired, children can master a related skill known as **transitivity**, the ability to infer a relationship between two objects on the basis of knowledge of their respective relationships with a third object. For example, if you tell preoperational preschoolers that Tom is taller than Becky and that Becky is taller than Fred, they will not see that Tom is taller than Fred. Logical inferences such as this are not possible until the stage of concrete operations, during which school-age children develop the ability to make two mental transformations that require reversible thinking. The first of these is inversion (+A is reversed by −A), and the second is reciprocity (A < B is reciprocated by B > A). By the end of the concrete operational stage, children have the mental abilities to learn how to add, subtract, multiply, and divide; to place numbers in order by size; and to classify objects by any number of criteria. Children can think about what would happen if . . . , as long as the objects are in view—for example, "What would happen if I pulled this spring and then let it go?" Children can understand time and space well enough to draw a map from their home to school and are building an understanding of events in the past.

Children in the elementary grades also are moving from egocentric thought to decentered or objective thought. Decentered thought enables children to see that others can have different perceptions than they do. For example, children with decentered thought will be able to understand that different children may see different patterns in clouds. Children whose thought processes are decentered are able to learn that events can be governed by physical laws, such as the laws of gravity. These changes do not all happen at the same time. Rather, they occur gradually during the concrete operational stage.

FORMAL OPERATIONAL STAGE (AGE 11 TO ADULTHOOD) Sometime around the onset of puberty, children's thinking begins to develop into the form that is characteristic of adults (Horn, Drill, Hochberg, Heinze, & Frank, 2008; Packard & Babineau, 2008). The preadolescent begins to be able to think abstractly and to see possibilities beyond the here and now. These abilities continue to develop into adulthood. With the **formal operational stage** comes the ability to deal with potential or hypothetical situations; the form is now separate from the content.

Inhelder and Piaget (1958) described one task that is approached differently by elementary school students in the concrete operational stage than by adolescents in the formal operational

InTASC 1

Learner Development

FIGURE 2.3 • A Test of Problem-Solving Abilities

The pendulum problem uses a string, which can be shortened or lengthened, and a set of weights. When children in the concrete operational stage are asked what determines frequency (the number of times per minute that the pendulum swings back and forth), they will tackle the problem less systematically than will adolescents who have entered the stage of formal operations. (The answer is that only the string's length affects the frequency.)

stage—the pendulum problem that Patricia Wing gave to her third-graders. The children and adolescents were given a pendulum consisting of a string with a weight at the end. They could change the length of the string, the amount of weight, the height from which the pendulum was released, and the force with which the pendulum was pushed. They were asked which of these factors influenced the frequency (the number of swings per minute). Only the length of the string makes any difference in the frequency of the pendulum: The shorter the string, the more swings per minute. This experiment is illustrated in Figure 2.3. The adolescent who has reached the stage of formal operations is likely to proceed quite systematically, varying one factor at a time (e.g., leaving the string the same length and trying different weights). For example, in Inhelder and Piaget's (1958) experiment, one 15-year-old selected 100 grams with a long string and a medium-length string, then 20 grams with a long and a short string, and finally 200 grams with a long and a short string and concluded, "It's the length of the string that makes it go faster and slower; the weight doesn't play any role" (p. 75). In contrast, 10-year-olds (who can be assumed to be in the concrete operational stage) proceeded in a chaotic fashion, varying many factors at the same time and hanging on to preconceptions. One boy varied simultaneously the weight and the push; then the weight, the push, and the length; then the push, the weight, and the elevation; and so on. He first concluded, "It's by changing the weight and the push, certainly not the string."

The transitivity problem also illustrates the advances brought about by formal thought. Recall the concrete operational child who, when told that Tom was taller than Becky and that Becky was taller than Fred, understood that Tom was taller than Fred. However, if the problem had been phrased in the following way, only an older child who had entered the formal operational stage would have solved it: "Becky is shorter than Tom, and Becky is taller than Fred. Who is the tallest of the three?" Here the younger, concrete operational child might get lost in the combinations of greater-than and less-than relationships. Adolescents in the formal operational stage can imagine several different relationships among the heights of Becky, Tom, and Fred and can figure out the accuracy of each until they hit on the correct one. This example illustrates another ability of preadolescents and adolescents who have reached the formal operational stage: They can monitor, or think about, their own thinking.

Generating abstract relationships from available information and then comparing those abstract relationships to each other is a broadly applicable skill underlying many tasks in which adolescents' competence leaps forward. Piaget (1952a) described a task in which students in the concrete operational stage were given a set of 10 proverbs and a set of statements with the same meanings as the proverbs. They were asked to match each proverb to the equivalent statement. Again, concrete operational children can understand the task and choose answers. However, their answers are often incorrect because they often do not understand that a proverb describes a general

Connections 2.2

For more on thinking about one's own thinking, or metacognition, see Chapter 6.

principle. For example, asked to explain the proverb "Don't cry over spilled milk," a child might explain that once milk is spilled, there's nothing to cry about but might not see that the proverb has a broader meaning. The child is likely to respond to the concrete situation of spilled milk rather than understanding that the proverb means "Don't dwell on past events that can't be changed." Adolescents and adults have little difficulty with this type of task.

HYPOTHETICAL CONDITIONS Another ability that Piaget and others recognized in the young adolescent is an aptitude to reason about situations and conditions that have not been experienced. The adolescent can accept, for the sake of argument or discussion, conditions that are arbitrary, that are not known to exist, or even that are known to be contrary to fact. Adolescents are not bound to their own experiences of reality, so they can apply logic to any given set of conditions. One illustration of the ability to reason about hypothetical situations is found in formal debate, in which participants must be prepared to defend either side of an issue, regardless of their personal feelings or experience, and their success is judged on the basis of their documentation and logical consistency. For a dramatic illustration of the difference between children and adolescents in the ability to suspend their own opinions, compare the reactions of fourth- and ninth-graders when you ask them to present an argument in favor of the proposition that schools should be in session 6 days a week, 48 weeks a year. The adolescent is far more likely to be able to set aside her or his own opinions and think of reasons why more days of school might be beneficial. The abilities that make up formal operational thought—thinking abstractly, testing hypotheses, and forming concepts that are independent of physical reality—are critical to acquiring higher-order skills. For example, learning algebra or abstract geometry requires the use of formal operational thought, as does understanding complex concepts in science, social studies, and other subjects.

The thinking characteristics of the formal operations stage usually appear between ages 11 and 15, but there are many individuals who never reach this stage (Niaz, 1997; Packard & Babineau, 2008). As many as two-thirds of U.S. high school students do not succeed on Piaget's formal operations tasks (Meece & Daniels, 2008). Most individuals tend to use formal operational thinking in some situations but not others, and this remains true into adulthood.

HOW IS PIAGET'S WORK VIEWED TODAY?

Piaget's theory revolutionized, and in many ways still dominates, the study of human development. However, some of his central principles have been questioned in more recent research, and modern descriptions of development have revised many of his views (see Feldman, 2012; Schunk, 2016).

Criticisms and Revisions of Piaget's Theory

One important Piagetian principle is that development precedes learning. Piaget held that developmental stages were largely fixed and that such concepts as conservation could not be taught. However, research has established many cases in which Piagetian tasks can be taught to children at earlier developmental stages (Feldman, 2012). Several researchers have found that young children can be taught to succeed on simpler forms of Piaget's tasks before they reach the stage at which that task is usually achieved (Gelman, 2000; Kuhn, 2006; Siegler & Svetina, 2006). Piaget understood that children do not move, for example, from being nonconservers to being conservers all at once. Instead, they typically master conservation of number (blocks rearranged are still the same number of blocks) a year or two before they master conservation of weight (the weight of a ball of clay does not change when you flatten it). This observation makes the concept of set stages of development more difficult to justify (Miller, 2011). Similarly, in simple, practical contexts, children have been found to demonstrate their ability to consider the point of view of others (Siegler, 2006), and infants have been shown to demonstrate aspects of object permanence much earlier than Piaget predicted (Baillargeon, 2002).

The result of this research has been a recognition that children are more competent than Piaget originally thought, especially when their practical knowledge is being assessed, and that experience and direct teaching affect the pace of development (Feldman, 2012). Piaget (1964) responded to demonstrations of this kind by arguing that the children must have been on the verge of the next developmental stage already—but the fact remains that some of the Piagetian tasks can be taught to children well below the age at which they usually appear without instruction.

Certification Pointer

When responding to case studies in certification tests, you may be asked to design a lesson that would be considered developmentally appropriate for a group of adolescents.

Another point of criticism goes to the heart of Piaget's "stage" theory. Many researchers now doubt that there are broad stages of development affecting all types of cognitive tasks; instead, they argue that children's skills develop in different ways on different tasks and that their experience (including direct teaching in school or elsewhere) can have a strong influence on the pace of development (see Miller, 2011; Siegler, 2006; Trawick-Smith, 2014). The evidence is particularly strong that children can be taught to perform well on the Piagetian tasks assessing formal operations, such as the pendulum problem illustrated in Figure 2.3. Clearly, experience matters. Watch an intelligent adult learning to sail. Initially, he or she is likely to engage in a lot of concrete operational behavior, trying everything in a chaotic order, before systematically beginning to learn how to adjust the tiller and the sail to the wind and direction (as in formal operational thought).

Neo-Piagetian Views of Development

Connections 2.3

For more on information processing, see Chapter 6.

Neo-Piagetian theories are modifications of Piaget's theory that attempt to overcome its limitations and address problems that critics have identified. In particular, neo-Piagetians have demonstrated that children's abilities to operate at a particular stage depend a great deal on the specific tasks involved (Massey, 2008); that training and experience, including social interactions, can accelerate children's development (Birney, Citron-Pousiy, Lutz, & Sternberg, 2005; Flavell, 2004; Siegler, 2006); and that culture has an important impact on development (Gelman, 2000; Greenfield, 2004).

Neo-Piagetians see cognitive development in terms of specific types of tasks instead of overall stages. For example, different tasks described as indicators of concrete operational thinking appear at very different ages (Cohen & Cashon, 2003; Halford & Andrews, 2006). Neo-Piagetians refer to "dialectical thinking," the ability to see that real-life problems do not necessarily have a single solution (Sternberg, 2008). Influenced by Vygotsky (see the next section), Neo-Piagetians place a far greater emphasis than Piaget himself did on the impact of culture, social context, and education on the development process (Crisp & Turner, 2011; Maynard, 2008).

InTASC 1

Learner Development

InTASC 2

Learning Differences

THEORY INTO PRACTICE

Educational Implications of Piaget's Theory

Piaget's theories have had a major impact on the theory and practice of education (DeVries, 2008; Hustedt, Epstein, & Barnett, 2013; Ostroff, 2012; Schunk, 2016; Seifert, 2013). The theories focused attention on the idea of developmentally appropriate education—an education with environments, curriculum, materials, and instruction that are suitable for students in terms of their physical and cognitive abilities and their social and emotional needs. Piagetian theory has been influential in constructivist models of learning, which will be described in Chapter 8. Berk (2013) summarizes the main teaching implications drawn from Piaget as follows:

1. *A focus on the process of children's thinking, not only its products.* In addition to checking the correctness of children's answers, teachers must understand the processes children use to get to the answer. Appropriate learning experiences build on children's current level of cognitive functioning, and only when teachers appreciate children's methods of arriving at particular conclusions are they in a position to provide such experiences.

2. *Recognition of the crucial role of children's self-initiated, active involvement in learning activities.* In a Piagetian classroom the presentation of ready-made knowledge is deemphasized, and children are encouraged to discover for themselves through spontaneous interaction with the environment. Therefore, instead of teaching didactically, teachers provide a rich variety of activities that permit children to act directly on the physical world.

3. *A deemphasis on practices aimed at making children adultlike in their thinking.* Piaget referred to the question "How can we speed up development?" as "the American question." Among the many countries he visited, psychologists and educators in the United States seemed most interested in what techniques could be used to accelerate children's progress through the stages. Piagetian-based educational programs accept his firm belief that premature teaching could be worse than no teaching at all because it leads to superficial acceptance of adult formulas rather than to true cognitive understanding.

4. *Acceptance of individual differences in developmental progress.* Piaget's theory assumes that all children go through the same developmental sequence but that they do so at different rates. Therefore, teachers must make a special effort to arrange classroom activities for individuals and small groups of children rather than for the total class group. In addition, because individual differences are expected, children's educational progress should be assessed in terms of each child's own previous course of development rather than in terms of the performances of same-age peers.

MyEdLab **Self-Check 2.1**

HOW DID VYGOTSKY VIEW COGNITIVE DEVELOPMENT?

Lev Semionovich Vygotsky was a Russian psychologist who died in 1934. Although Piaget and Vygotsky never met, they were contemporaries who were aware of each other's early work (DeVries, 2008). Vygotsky's work was not widely read in English until the 1970s, however, and only since then have his theories become influential in North America. Vygotskian theory is now a powerful force in developmental psychology, and many of the critiques he made of the Piagetian perspective more than 70 years ago have come to the fore today (see Daniels, Cole, & Wertsch, 2007; Gredler & Shields, 2008; John-Steiner & Mahn, 2003; Winsler, 2003).

Vygotsky's work is based on two key ideas. First, he proposed that intellectual development can be understood only in terms of the historical and cultural contexts children experience. Second, he believed that development depends on the **sign systems** that individuals grow up with: the symbols that cultures create to help people think, communicate, and solve problems. Examples include a culture's language, its writing system, and its counting system. Focusing only on Western symbol systems, he argued, greatly underestimates cognitive development in diverse cultures (Mahn & John-Steiner, 2013; Trawick-Smith, 2014). In contrast to Piaget, Vygotsky proposed that cognitive development is strongly linked to input from others.

How Development Occurs

Recall that Piaget's theory suggests that development precedes learning. In other words, specific cognitive structures need to develop before certain types of learning can take place. Vygotsky's theory suggests that learning precedes development. For Vygotsky, learning involves the acquisition of signs by means of information from others and deliberate teaching. Development occurs as the child internalizes these signs so as to be able to think and solve problems without the help of others, an ability called **self-regulation**.

The first step in the development of self-regulation and independent thinking is learning that actions and sounds have a meaning. For example, a baby learns that the process of reaching toward an object is interpreted by others as a signal that the infant wants the object, and then reaches toward objects out of reach as a sign that he or she wants help getting the object. In the case of language acquisition, children learn to associate certain sounds with meaning. The second step in developing internal structures and self-regulation involves practice. The infant practices gestures that will get attention. The preschooler enters into conversations with others to master language.

Connections 2.4
For more on self-regulated learning, see Chapter 8.

MyEdLab
Video Example 2.4

Is organizing blocks in a pattern based on color a skill that is in the boy's zone of proximal development, or is it still too advanced for a child at his developmental level?

The final step is the use of signs to think and solve problems without the help of others. At this point, children become self-regulating, and the sign system has become internalized.

PRIVATE SPEECH Vygotsky proposed that children incorporate the speech of others and then use that speech to help themselves solve problems. **Private speech** is easy to see in young children, who frequently talk to themselves, especially when faced with difficult tasks (Corkum, Humphries, Mullane, & Theriault, 2008; Flavell, 2004). Later, private speech becomes silent but is still very important. Studies have found that children who make extensive use of private speech learn complex tasks more effectively than do other children (Al-Namlah, Fernyhough, & Meins, 2006; Emerson & Miyake, 2003; Schneider, 2002).

THE ZONE OF PROXIMAL DEVELOPMENT Vygotsky (1978) believed that learning takes place most effectively when children are working within their **zone of proximal development**. Tasks within the zone of proximal development are those that a child cannot yet accomplish alone but could accomplish with the assistance of more competent peers or adults. That is, the zone of proximal development describes tasks that a child has not yet learned but is capable of learning at a given time. Some educators refer to a "teachable moment" when a child or group of children is exactly at the point of readiness for a given concept (Berger, 2012). Vygotsky further believed that higher mental functioning usually exists in conversation and collaboration among individuals before it exists within the individual.

MEDIATION Vygotsky believed that complex skills, such as reasoning and problem solving, are developed via **mediation** with adults and higher-performing peers (Vygotsky, 1978; Wertsch, 2007). That is, older children and adults help learners by explaining, modeling, or breaking down complex skills, knowledge, or concepts. In this way they help learners obtain psychological tools, as when children are giving each other pointers on a computer game or modeling the use of debate strategies. The more knowledgeable peers or adults help the learner take the next learning step, but also add to the learner's "cultural tool kit." For example, imagine that two young friends are driving together and the driver (unintentionally) screeches around a corner. The passenger notes, "I always slow waaay down when I'm turning to keep that from happening." This advice, from a peer in the exact moment when it is likely to be meaningful, will not only help the driver corner better, but will add to the driver's "cultural tool kit" of solutions for driving problems and sense of mastery of a task of enormous cultural importance in Western societies. In a traditional culture, where young adolescents go through puberty rites, peers might share ideas about ways to prepare for a rite of passage, such as surviving alone in the jungle. Just as in the driving example, this sharing adds to the learner's "cultural tool kit"; it's just a different kit, designed for a different culture. Vygotsky's point is that each culture outfits each of its members with such a kit through a process of mediation, passing on knowledge, skills, and experience from older to younger members of the society.

"I'm sorry, Miss Scott, but this is outside of my zone of proximal development."

SCAFFOLDING A key idea derived from Vygotsky's notion of social learning is that of **scaffolding** (John-Steiner & Mahn, 2003; Rogoff, 2003): the assistance provided by more competent peers or adults. Typically, scaffolding means providing a child with a great deal of support during the early stages of learning and then diminishing that support and having the child take on increasing responsibility as soon as she or he is able. Scaffolding can be thought of as mediation on purpose, planfully helping a learner move from a current level of skill to independent capability to use a new skill. Parents use scaffolding when they teach their children to play a new game or to tie their shoes. A related concept is **cognitive apprenticeship**, which describes the entire process of modeling, coaching, scaffolding, and evaluation that is typically seen whenever one-to-one instruction takes place (John-Steiner & Mahn, 2003; Rogoff, 2003). For example, in *Life on the Mississippi*, Mark Twain describes how he was taught to be a steamboat pilot. At first the experienced pilot talked him through every bend in the river, but gradually he was left to figure things out for himself, with the pilot there to intervene only if the boat was about to run aground.

Connections 2.5

For more on scaffolding and cooperative learning, see Chapter 8.

COOPERATIVE LEARNING Vygotsky's theories support the use of cooperative learning strategies in which children work together to help one another learn (Slavin, 2014; Webb, 2008). Because peers are usually operating within each other's zones of proximal development, they often provide models for each other of slightly more advanced thinking (Gredler, 2009). In addition, cooperative learning makes children's inner speech available to others, so they can gain insight into one another's reasoning process. That is, children benefit from hearing each other "thinking out loud," especially when their groupmates talk themselves or each other through a problem.

ON THE WEB

To learn more about applications of Vygotsky's theories to education practice, visit mathforum.org. To learn more about Vygotsky and to compare his theories with Piaget's, visit www.simplypsychology.org and type Vygotsky into the search engine.

THEORY INTO PRACTICE

Classroom Applications of Vygotsky's Theory

Vygotsky's theories of education have major practical implications in the classroom (see Hustedt et al., 2013; Schunk, 2016; Seifert, 2013). The concept of a zone of proximal development implies that only instruction and activities that fall within this zone can be learned. Teaching content that is too easy or too difficult does not add to learning (see Figure 2.4). Also, according to a Vygotskian approach to instruction, teaching must emphasize scaffolding, with students taking more and more responsibility for their own learning (Berger, 2012; Daniels et al., 2007; Ostroff, 2012). Finally, students can benefit from cooperative learning arrangements among groups of learners with differing levels of ability. Tutoring by more competent peers can be effective in promoting growth within the zone of proximal development, as can interactions around complex tasks (Roth & Lee, 2007).

You can use information about Vygotsky's zone of proximal development in organizing classroom activities in the following ways:

- Instruction can be planned to provide practice within the zone of proximal development for individual children or for groups of children. For example, hints and prompts that helped children during a preassessment could form the basis of instructional activities.
- Scaffolding (John-Steiner & Mahn, 2003) provides hints and prompts at different levels. In scaffolding, the adult does not simplify the task, but the role of the learner is simplified "through the graduated intervention of the teacher."
- Cooperative learning activities can be planned with groups of children at different levels who can help each other learn (Slavin, 2014; Webb, 2008).

Scaffolding is directly related to the concept of a zone of proximal development. For example, a child might be shown pennies to represent each sound in a word (e.g., three pennies for the three sounds in "man"). To master this word, the child might be asked to place a penny on the table to show each sound in a word, and finally the child might identify the sounds without the pennies. The pennies provide a scaffold to help the child move from assisted to unassisted success at the task (Rogoff, 2003). In a high school laboratory science class, a teacher might provide scaffolding by first giving students detailed guides to carrying out experiments, then providing brief outlines that they might use to structure experiments, and finally asking them to set up experiments entirely on their own.

InTASC 1

Learner Development

InTASC 8

Instructional Strategies

Certification Pointer

Lev Vygotsky's work will probably be on your teacher certification test. You may be required to know that the zone of proximal development is the level of development just above where a student is presently functioning and why this is important for both teachers and students.

**FIGURE 2.4 •
Teaching Model Based
on Vygotsky's Theory**

In (a), the child performs a learned task; in (b), the child is assisted by a teacher or peer who interacts with the child to help him move into a new zone of proximal development (unlearned tasks at the limits of a learner's abilities) with a new learned task.

a. Learned task

b. Assisted learning at zone of proximal development

HOW DID BRONFENBRENNER VIEW DEVELOPMENT?

Urie Bronfenbrenner, a psychologist who was born in Russia but came as a child to the United States, described a "bioecological" model of human development (Bronfenbrenner & Morris, 2006). His model is summarized in Figure 2.5. The focus of his model is on the social and institutional influences on a child's development, from family, schools, places of worship, and neighborhoods, to broader social and political influences, such as mass media and government.

Bronfenbrenner's main contribution was in showing how development is influenced at each of the levels. Bronfenbrenner critiques the Piagetian view for its limited focus beyond the child (the microsystem). He notes the enormous influence of the home and family and the mutual influences between the child and the family. This *mesosystem* also binds children to parents, students to teachers, and friends to friends. The *exosystem* (e.g., community, local government, church) affects development directly and through its influence on families, and the *macrosystem*, including cultural and religious values as well as mass media, sets an important context for all of development. Finally, the *chronosystem* consists of the passage of time and those immediate historical events that change all of the factors surrounding the child. Bronfenbrenner emphasizes that all of these factors are constantly changing, and that the child him- or herself has an influence on many of them, especially the family.

The importance of the **bioecological approach** is in emphasizing the interconnectedness of the many factors that influence a child's development. A change in the family, such as a divorce or loss of a job, not only influences the child directly, but may also cause changes in the child's neighborhood, school, place of worship, and friends.

The bioecological approach is descriptive and philosophical, and does not have the extensive research support devoted to Piaget's or Vygotsky's perspectives. However, it builds out from Vygotsky's emphasis on sociocultural factors a more complete model of influences beyond biology on child development (see Bronfenbrenner & Evans, 2000).

MyEdLab **Self-Check 2.2**

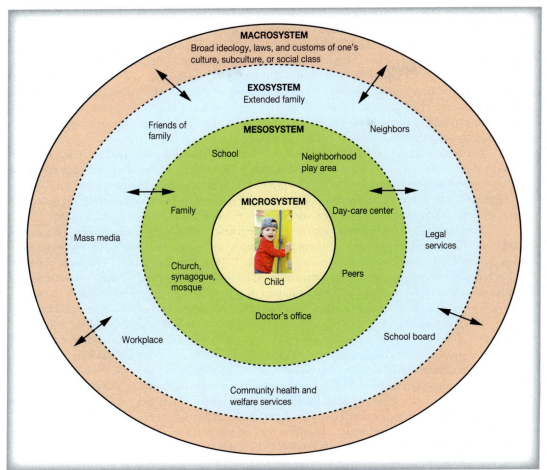

FIGURE 2.5 •
Bronfenbrenner's
Bioecological
Theory

Urie Bronfenbrenner
believed that a child's
development is affected
by social and institutional
influences.

Based on Bronfenbrenner,
U. (1999). Environments in
developmental perspective:
Theoretical and operational
models. In *Measuring
environment across the
lifespan: Emerging models and
concepts* (1st ed., pp. 3–28).
Washington, DC: American
Psychological Association.

HOW DO LANGUAGE AND LITERACY DEVELOP?

The aspects of development arguably of greatest concern to educators are language and literacy. Children who develop large vocabularies and become effective speakers, readers, and writers are likely to be successful in school and beyond (Owens, 2016). Development of language and literacy is a key objective of teaching, but there are also characteristic patterns of development over time seen in all cultures that are not the direct results of teaching.

Language and Literacy Development during the Preschool Years

Although there are individual differences in the rates at which children acquire language abilities, the sequence of accomplishments is similar for all children, no matter which language they are learning. Around age 1, children produce one-word utterances such as "bye-bye" and "Mommy." These words typically represent objects and events that are important to the child. Over the course of the second year of life, children begin to combine words into two-word sentences (e.g., "More milk"). During the preschool years, children's vocabulary increases, along with their knowledge of the rules of spoken language. By the time they start school, children have mastered most of the grammatical rules of language, and their vocabulary consists of thousands of words.

ORAL LANGUAGE Development of oral language, or spoken language, requires not only learning words but also learning the rules of word and sentence construction (Gleason & Ratner, 2009; Owens, 2016). For example, children learn the rules for forming plurals before they enter kindergarten. In a classic study, Berko (1985) showed preschoolers a picture of a made-up bird called a "Wug." She then showed them two such pictures and said, "Now there is another one. There are two of them. There are two _____." The children readily answered "Wugs," showing that they could apply general rules for forming plurals to a new situation. In a similar fashion, children learn to add *-ed* and *-ing* to verbs.

Interestingly, children often learn the correct forms of irregular verbs (such as "He broke the chair") and later replace them with incorrect but more rule-based constructions ("He breaked [or broked] the chair"). One 4-year-old said, "I flew my kite." He then thought for a moment and emphatically corrected himself, saying, "I *flewed* my kite!" These errors are a normal part of language development and should not be corrected.

Just as they learn rules for forming words, children learn rules for sentences. Their first sentences usually contain only two words ("Want milk," "See birdie," "Jessie outside"), but they soon learn to form more complex sentences and to vary their tone of voice to indicate questions ("Where doggie go?") or to indicate emphasis ("Want cookie!"). Three-year-olds can usually express rather complex thoughts, even though their sentences may still lack such words as *a, the,* and *did.*

Preschoolers often play with language or experiment with its patterns and rules. This experimentation frequently involves changing sounds, patterns, and meanings. One 3-year-old was told by his exasperated parent, "You're impossible!" He replied, "No, I'm impopsicle!" The same child said that his baby brother, Benjamin, was a man because he was a "Benja-man." Children often rearrange word sounds to create new words, rhymes, and funny sentences. The popularity of finger plays, nonsense rhymes, and Dr. Seuss storybooks shows how much young children enjoy playing with language.

Oral language development is heavily influenced by the amount and quality of the talking parents do with their children. A classic study by Hart and Risley (1995) found that middle-class parents talked far more to their children than did working-class parents, and that their children had substantially different numbers of words in their vocabularies. The amount of parent speech was as important as socioeconomic status; children of low-income parents who spoke to their children a great deal also had large vocabularies. Numerous studies have also shown that school programs directed at building vocabulary can be very effective (Hindman & Wasik, 2012; Marulis & Neuman, 2013).

While language development is similar for children who are speakers of all languages, children who speak languages other than English in U.S. schools have additional challenges. Teaching strategies to assist second language development are discussed in Chapter 4.

READING Learning to read in the early elementary grades is one of the most important of all developmental tasks, both because other subjects depend on reading and because in our society school success is so often equated with reading success. Children who do not learn to read well by third grade are at great risk for long-term problems (Lesnick, George, Smithgall, & Gwynne, 2010). Children often have complex language skills that are critical in reading, and the process of learning to read can begin quite early if children are read to (Giorgis & Glazer, 2009). Research on **emergent literacy**, or preschoolers' knowledge and skills related to reading (Morrow, Roskos, & Gambrell, 2015; National Institute for Literacy, 2008), has shown that children may enter school with a great deal of knowledge about reading and that this knowledge contributes to success in formal reading instruction. For example, young children have often learned concepts of print, such as that print is arranged from left to right, that spaces between words have meaning, and that books are read from front to back. Many preschoolers can "read" books from beginning to end by interpreting the pictures on each page. They understand about story plots and can often predict what will happen next in a simple story. They can recognize logos on familiar stores and products; for example, very young children often know that *M* is for *McDonald's.* Children who are read to and taught letters at home start off with an advantage in reading (Hood, Conlon, & Andrews, 2008), but all children can learn concepts of print, plot, and other prereading concepts if they attend preschools or kindergartens that emphasize reading and discussing books in class (Chambers, Cheung, & Slavin, in press; Diamond, Justice, Siegler, & Snyder, 2013; Hindman & Wasik, 2012; National Institute for Literacy, 2008). Similarly, young children can be taught to hear specific sounds within words (a skill called *phonemic awareness*), which contributes to later success in reading (Anthony & Lonigan, 2004; National Institute for Literacy, 2008). It is also important to take every possible opportunity to build children's vocabulary (Neuman, 2014) by pointing out new words in many contexts.

WRITING Children's writing also follows a developmental sequence (MacArthur, Graham, & Fitzgerald, 2015; Morrow et al., 2015; Tolchinsky, 2015). It emerges out of early scribbles and at

---

Certification Pointer

For teacher certification tests, you may be expected to know that children's over-generalizations of the rules of grammar are normal for young children and should not be corrected.

InTASC 2

Learning Differences

THEORY INTO PRACTICE

Promoting Literacy Development in Young Children

Many of the educational implications derived from research on children's literacy development transfer findings from two sources: parental and teacher behaviors that encourage oral language development and studies of young children who learn to read without formal classroom instruction. The most frequent recommendations include reading to children; surrounding them with books and other printed materials; making various writing materials available; encouraging reading and writing; and being responsive to children's questions about letters, words, and spellings (Casbergue & Strickland, 2015; Florez, 2008; Morrow, et al., 2015; National Institute for Literacy, 2008; Pianta et al., 2015).

You can use numerous props in the classroom, such as office space in a dramatic play area. Classrooms can have writing centers that make available computers with writing programs, magnetic letters, chalkboards, pencils, crayons, markers, and paper.

You can encourage children's involvement with print by reading in small groups, having volunteers read to children individually, and allowing children to choose books to read. Intimate reading experiences allow children to turn pages, pause to look at pictures or ask questions, and read along with an adult.

Predictable books such as *The Three Little Pigs* and *There Was an Old Lady Who Swallowed a Fly* allow beginning readers to rely on what they already know about literacy while learning sound–letter relationships. Stories are predictable if a child can remember what the author is going to say and how it will be stated. Repetitive structures, rhyme and rhythm, and a match between pictures and text increase predictability.

Children's understanding of literacy is enhanced when adults point out the important features of print. Statements such as "We start at the front, not at the back of the book"; "Move your finger; you're covering the words and I can't see to read them"; and "Point to each word as you say it, not to each letter, like this" help to clarify the reading process. You can indicate features in print that are significant and draw attention to patterns of letters, sounds, or phrases.

Programs that encourage parents to read with their preschoolers have shown that children benefit. One prominent example is Raising a Reader (Anthony et al., 2014), which helps parents read with young children.

MyEdLab
Video Example 2.5
The preschool child in this video has very clear ideas about literacy already. What types of activities would you expect that she and her family engage in regularly?

first is spread randomly across a page. This characteristic reflects an incomplete understanding of word boundaries, as well as an inability to mentally create a line for placing letters. Children invent spellings by making judgments about sounds and by relating the sounds they hear to the letters they know. In trying to represent what they hear, they typically use letter names rather than letter sounds; short vowels are frequently left out because they are not directly associated with letter names (Morrow, 2009). For example, one kindergartner labeled a picture of a dinosaur "DNSR."

Language and Literacy Development during the Elementary and Secondary Years

Language and literacy develop at a rapid rate for children in the elementary and secondary grades. For example, Graves (2007) estimates that the average student adds 3,000 words each year to his or her vocabulary. However, these words will vary, as a student's motivations, interest, culture, and peer group come to have a huge impact. For example, a girl who talks sports with her friends and family, plays sports, reads about sports, and watches sports on television builds up an enormous sports vocabulary. A girl who loves science and is in a family and peer group who talk about science builds up an equally enormous science vocabulary. But which of these—sports or science—will be on the SAT? Obviously, the girl immersed in science is at a great advantage in school because of her interests and social context.

Literacy also develops rapidly in the elementary and middle grades. Whereas the emphasis in the early elementary grades is primarily on decoding and fluency, students from second grade onward are increasingly focused on building comprehension, vocabulary, and study skills (Deshler, Palincsar, Biancarosa, & Nair, 2007; Kamil, Borman, Dole, Kral, & Salinger, 2008). Good readers use strategies such as predicting, reviewing, summarizing, and generating their own questions, and if these strategies are directly taught to elementary and secondary students, their comprehension improves (Biancarosa & Snow, 2006; Block & Duffy, 2008; Gersten, Chard, Jayanthi, & Baker, 2006).

THEORY INTO PRACTICE

Teaching Children to Read

There once was a saying in elementary education: "Math is taught, but reading is caught." Yet research over the past 20 years has shown that reading can and must be taught, explicitly, planfully, and systematically. Some students do "catch" reading no matter how it is taught, but for a very large number, perhaps the majority, it matters a great deal how reading is taught (Allington, 2011; Hunter, 2012; Schwanenflugel & Knapp, 2015).

An influential report by the National Reading Panel (2000) concluded that there were five key components to reading instruction, each of which must be successfully taught. These are as follows.

1. Phonemic awareness (or phonological awareness) is the ability to recognize sounds within words. For example, preschool and kindergarten children may learn to put the spoken words "tower," "tag," and "time" in the same category because they all start with the sound /t/. They might learn that without the /d/ sound, "dog" becomes "og." They might recognize that there are three sounds in the words "cat" and "pack," but four in "milk" and "child" (see, for example, Blachman et al, 1999; Center, 2005; Temple, Ogle, Crawford, & Freppon, 2016).

2. Phonics involves the ability to take letter sounds and form them into words, a process often called "decoding" (Blevins, 2011). This requires knowing the sounds letters make (sound–symbol correspondence) and then blending them into words. For example, children in kindergarten or first grade might learn the sounds made by the letters m, a, n. But can they put them together to make the word "man"? Sound blending can be taught and practiced so that students can quickly sound out words. This enables them to focus on meaning (see Center, 2005; Hunter, 2012; Rasinski & Zutell, 2010; Temple et al., 2016).

3. Comprehension, the meaning of text, is ultimately the whole purpose of reading. Students must be able to recognize words smoothly and quickly before comprehension can reach a high level. However, even students who are very good at decoding may struggle with comprehension. Beyond building decoding and fluency, students can become effective comprehenders by having many books read to them, by reading many books themselves, and by discussing books with peers and others (Duke & Carlisle, 2011). They may be taught to use "metacognitive strategies" such as predicting how a story will end, summarizing or stating the main idea of paragraphs, and learning strategies for dealing with unknown words or difficult content (Gambrell, Morrow, & Pressley, 2007; Guthrie, 2008). While decoding instruction is typically completed in the early grades, students need to grow in comprehension throughout their lives, especially

by reading books on many topics and in many genres. Students moving into upper elementary and secondary grades especially need to learn to read in content areas, such as science and social studies; to grow increasingly able to read and comprehend factual as well as narrative texts; to read critically, and to enjoy reading (Guthrie, 2008).

4. Our <u>vocabulary</u> consists of words for which we know the meanings. Much of one's vocabulary is built by daily life, exposure to media, and discussions with friends and family. However, there is a great deal of vocabulary that is unlikely to come up in daily life. Words specific to science, to math, to social studies, to art, to music, or to literature are all unlikely to be heard on the playground, but they are still extremely important. Vocabulary is built by giving students many opportunities to read about various topics and to discuss what they have read, especially in cooperative groups (Scott, Skobel, & Wells, 2008). In particular, giving students many opportunities to read about a wide variety of topics that greatly interest them builds vocabulary (Rasinski & Zutell, 2010). Teaching word meanings in context, ideally with pictures or actions to demonstrate meanings, can be very effective (Beck, McKeown, & Kucan, 2002; Blachowicz & Fisher, 2006; Graves, August, & Carlo, 2011; Hiebert & Reutzel, 2010).

   For English learners, learning English vocabulary imposes some added difficulties, but the basic strategies are not so different. English learners need a lot of opportunities to use their English in cooperative learning groups and other peer settings, to see words explained in context and with pictures, and to read in many genres (August & Shanahan, 2006a; Calderón & Minaya-Rowe, 2011). This is discussed further in Chapter 4.

5. <u>Fluency</u> is the speed at which students can decode and comprehend text. Reading fluency is important because slow readers lose comprehension and motivation (Temple et al., 2016). Reading fluency can be built by giving students many opportunities to read aloud, and by having students time each other's reading and try to improve their speeds. Fluency should never become more important than comprehension; students should not be asked to read fast while ignoring meaning. But rapid reading is a skill that can and should be taught (Center 2005; Temple et al., 2016).

MyEdLab **Self-Check 2.3**

THE INTENTIONAL TEACHER
Teaching in Light of Principles of Cognitive, Language, and Literacy Development

Intentional teachers use what they know about predictable patterns of cognitive, literacy, and language development to make instructional decisions.

- They are aware of what children of the age they teach are able to do now, and of the next steps in their development, and they help give their students opportunities to grow into new ways of thinking.
- They assess their children's thinking processes, using observation as well as formal measures, to understand their cognitive levels and barriers to their growth.
- They modify their instruction if they find that it is not challenging their students to make conceptual growth, or if they find that many students are struggling due to developmental unreadiness.

(continued)

- They give students many opportunities to work with diverse peers so that they can regularly experience how peers at slightly different cognitive levels proceed to solve problems.
- They give students many opportunities to solve complex, practical problems that force them to encounter cognitive issues appropriate to their developmental levels, such as puzzling science experiments and intriguing math problems.
- They take into account cultural, family, and community factors in their teaching without using these factors as excuses to demand less of certain students.
- They proactively invite parents and community members to be involved with their teaching, so that students can see a consistency of expectations among school, home, and community, and so that families and community members can better reinforce the school's goals for the children they share.

MyEdLab

Application Exercise 2.1

In the Pearson etext, watch a classroom video. Then use the guidelines in "The Intentional Teacher" to answer a set of questions that will help you reflect on and understand the teaching and learning presented in the video.

SUMMARY

How Do Children Develop Cognitively?

Most developmental psychologists believe that nature and nurture combine to influence cognitive development. Continuous theories of development focus on social experiences that a child goes through, whereas discontinuous theories emphasize inborn factors rather than environmental influence.

How Did Piaget View Cognitive Development?

Piaget postulated four stages of cognitive development through which people progress between birth and young adulthood. People adjust their schemes for dealing with the world through assimilation and accommodation. Piaget's developmental stages include the sensorimotor stage (birth to 2 years of age), the preoperational stage (2 to 7 years of age), and the concrete operational stage (ages 7 to 11). During the formal operational stage (age 11 to adulthood), young people develop the ability to deal with hypothetical situations and to monitor their own thinking.

How Is Piaget's Work Viewed Today?

Piaget's theory has been criticized for relying exclusively on broad, fixed, sequential stages through which all children progress, and for underestimating children's abilities. In contrast, neo-Piagetian theories place greater emphasis on social and environmental influences on cognitive development. Nevertheless, Piaget's theory has important implications for education. Piagetian principles are embedded in the curriculum and in effective teaching practices, and Piaget-influenced concepts such as cognitive constructivism and developmentally appropriate instruction have been important in education reform.

How Did Vygotsky View Cognitive Development?

Vygotsky viewed cognitive development as an outgrowth of social development through interaction with others and the environment. Mediated learning takes place in children's zones of proximal development, where they can do new tasks that are within their capabilities only with a teacher's or peer's assistance. Children internalize learning, develop self-regulation, and solve problems through vocal or silent private speech. Teachers provide interactional contexts, such as cooperative learning, mediation, and scaffolding, to help children build understanding of developmentally appropriate skills.

How Did Bronfenbrenner View Development?

Bronfenbrenner created a bioecological model to describe how family, school, community, and cultural factors impact a child's development.

How Do Language and Literacy Develop?

During the Preschool Years

Young children's language develops in predictable patterns as children use and play with language. Early literacy developments depend on children's experiences at home and on their learning about books and letters.

During the Elementary and Secondary Years

Students make rapid progress in vocabulary and reading comprehension. Motivation is a key to both, as are opportunities to use new words and reading skills with peers and in new forms.

KEY TERMS

Review the following key terms from the chapter.

accommodation 26	formal operational stage 29
adaptation 25	inferred reality 29
assimilation 25	mediation 33
bioecological approach 36	object permanence 27
centration 27	preoperational stage 27
cognitive apprenticeship 33	private speech 33
cognitive development 25	reflexes 26
concrete operational stage 29	reversibility 27
conservation 27	scaffolding 33
constructivism 26	schemes 25
continuous theories of development 24	self-regulation 33
development 23	sensorimotor stage 26
developmentally appropriate education 32	seriation 29
discontinuous theories of development 24	sign systems 33
egocentric 28	transitivity 29
emergent literacy 38	zone of proximal development 33
equilibration 26	

SELF-ASSESSMENT: PRACTICING FOR LICENSURE

Directions: This chapter addresses indicators that are often assessed in state licensure exams. Respond to the following questions.

1. According to Piaget, why do preoperational children think a cut-up sandwich is more sandwich than a whole one?
2. According to Vygotsky, why does cooperative work help children to learn?
3. According to Bronfenbrenner, how might a parents' divorce change a child's cognitive development?
4. Write a brief description of a typical student at one of the following grade levels: K–1, 2–5, 6–8, 9–12. Use the ideas of each theorist from this chapter to guide your description.
5. Make a list of developmentally appropriate teaching strategies for one of the following grade levels: K–1, 2–5, 6–8, 9–12.

> **MyEdLab** **Licensure Exam 2.1** Answer questions and receive instant feedback in your Pearson eText in MyEdLab.

Rawpixel.com/Shutterstock

CHAPTER THREE

Social, Moral, and Emotional Development

LEARNING OUTCOMES

At the end of this chapter, you should be able to:

3.1 Discuss differing views of social, emotional, and moral development

3.2 Identify the stages of children's social and emotional development

3.3 Apply knowledge of social, emotional, and moral development in considering how to solve problems in the classroom

3.4 Describe how knowledge of social, moral, and emotional development informs intentional teaching

At Parren Elementary/Middle School, eighth-graders are encouraged to become tutors for first-graders. They help them with reading, math, and other subjects. As part of this program, Sam Stevens has been working for about a month with Billy Ames.

"Hey, shorty!" says Sam one day when he meets Billy for a tutoring session.

"Hey, Sam!" As always, Billy is delighted to see his big buddy. But today his friendly greeting turns into a look of astonishment. "What have you got in your lip?"

"Haven't you ever seen a lip ring?"

Billy is impressed. "Awesome!"

"A lot of guys are wearing them."

"Didn't it hurt to get a hole in your lip?"

"A little, but I'm tough! Boy, was my mom mad, though. I have to take my lip ring off before I go home, but I put it back on while I'm walking to school."

"But didn't your mom . . ."

"Enough of that, squirt! You've got some math to do. Let's get to it!"

The interaction between Sam and Billy illustrates the enormous differences between the world of the adolescent and that of the child. Sam, at 13, is a classic young teen. His idealism and down-deep commitment to the positive are shown in his volunteering to serve as a tutor and in the caring, responsible relationship he has established with Billy. At the same time, Sam is asserting his independence by having his lip pierced and wearing a lip ring, against his mother's wishes. This independence is strongly supported by his peer group, however, so it is really only a shift of dependence from parents and teachers toward peers. His main purpose in wearing a lip ring is to demonstrate conformity to the styles and norms of his peers rather than to those of adults. Yet Sam does still depend on his parents and other adults for advice and support when making decisions that he knows have serious consequences for his future, and he does take off his lip ring at home to avoid a really serious battle with his parents.

Billy lives in a different world. He can admire Sam's audacity, but he would never go so far. Billy's world has simpler rules. He is shocked by Sam's daring to wear a lip ring. He is equally shocked by Sam's willingness to directly disobey his mother. Billy may misbehave, but within much narrower limits. He knows that rules are rules, and he fully expects to be punished if he breaks them.

USING YOUR EXPERIENCE

CRITICAL THINKING Teenagers assert their independence in ways that often are supported by their peer group, but not by their parents. In light of this, what kinds of clashes might you anticipate encountering in a secondary classroom, and how do you propose to handle them? What strategies could you use to prevent clashes in the first place?

WHAT ARE SOME VIEWS OF PERSONAL AND SOCIAL DEVELOPMENT?

As children improve their cognitive skills, they are also developing self-concepts, ways of interacting with others, and attitudes toward the world. Understanding personal and social development is critical to your ability to motivate, teach, and successfully interact with students at various ages (Berk, 2013; Boyd & Bee, 2012; Feldman, 2012; Squires, Pribble, Chen, & Pomes, 2013). Like cognitive development, personal development and social development are often described in terms of stages. We speak of the "terrible twos," not the "terrible ones" or the "terrible threes"; and when someone is reacting in an unreasonable, selfish way, we accuse that person of "behaving like a 2-year-old." The words *adolescent* and *teenager* are associated in Western culture with rebelliousness, identity crises, hero worship, and sexual awakening. These associations reflect stages of development that everyone goes through. This section focuses on a theory of personal and social development proposed by Erik Erikson, which is an adaptation of the developmental theories of the great psychiatrist Sigmund Freud. Erikson's work is often called a **psychosocial theory** because it relates principles of psychological and social development.

Erikson's Stages of Psychosocial Development

Like Piaget, Erikson had no formal training in psychology, but as a young man he was trained by Freud as a psychoanalyst. Erikson hypothesized that people pass through eight psychosocial stages in their lifetimes. At each stage, there are crises or critical issues to be resolved. Most people resolve each **psychosocial crisis** satisfactorily and put it behind them to take on new challenges, but some people do not completely resolve these crises and must continue to deal with them later in life. For example, many adults have yet to resolve the "identity crisis" of adolescence, and then they feel compelled to buy motorcycles in their 40s or 50s.

ERIKSON'S STAGES OF PERSONAL AND SOCIAL DEVELOPMENT As people grow, they face a series of psychosocial crises that shape personality, according to Erik Erikson. Each crisis focuses on a particular aspect of personality and involves the person's relationship with other people.

Stage I: Trust versus Mistrust (Birth to 18 Months) The goal of infancy is to develop a basic trust in the world. Erikson (1968, p. 96) defined basic trust as "an essential trustfulness of others as well as a fundamental sense of one's own trustworthiness." The mother, or maternal figure, is usually the first important person in the child's world. She is the one who must satisfy the infant's need for food and affection. If the mother is inconsistent or rejecting, she becomes a source of frustration for the infant rather than a source of pleasure (Cummings, Braungart-Rieker, & Du Rocher-Schudlich, 2003; Thompson, Easterbrooks, & Padilla-Walker, 2003). The mother's behavior creates in the infant a sense of mistrust for his or her world that may persist throughout childhood and into adulthood.

Stage II: Autonomy versus Doubt (18 Months to 3 Years) By the age of 2, most babies can walk and have learned enough about language to communicate with other people. Children in the "terrible twos" no longer want to depend totally on others. Instead, they strive toward autonomy, the ability to do things for themselves. The child's desires for power and independence often clash with the wishes of the parent. Erikson believed that children at this stage have the dual desire to hold on and to let go. Parents who are flexible enough to permit their children to explore freely and do things for themselves, but at the same time provide an ever-present guiding hand, encourage the establishment of a sense of autonomy. Parents who are overly restrictive and harsh give their children a sense of powerlessness and incompetence, which can lead to shame and doubt in one's abilities.

Stage III: Initiative versus Guilt (3 to 6 Years) During this period, children's continuously maturing motor and language skills permit them to be increasingly aggressive and vigorous in the exploration of both their social and physical environment. Three-year-olds have a growing sense of initiative, which can be encouraged by parents and other family members or caregivers who permit children to run, jump, play, slide, and throw. "Being firmly convinced that he is a person on his own, the child must now find out what kind of person he may become" (Erikson, 1968, p. 115). Parents who severely punish children's attempts at initiative will make the children feel guilty about their natural urges both during this stage and later in life.

Stage IV: Industry versus Inferiority (6 to 12 Years) Entry into school brings with it a huge expansion in the child's social world. Teachers and peers take on increasing importance for the child, while the influence of parents decreases. Children now want to make things. Success brings with it a sense of industry, a good feeling about oneself and one's abilities. Failure creates a negative self-image, a sense of inadequacy that may hinder future learning. And "failure" need not be real; it may be merely an inability to measure up to one's own standards or those of parents, teachers, or brothers and sisters.

Stage V: Identity versus Role Confusion (12 to 18 Years) The question "Who am I?" becomes important during adolescence. To answer it, adolescents increasingly turn away from parents and toward peer groups. Erikson believed that during adolescence the individual's rapidly changing physiology, coupled with pressures to make decisions about future education and career, creates the need to question and redefine the psychosocial identity established during the earlier stages. Adolescence is a time of change. Teenagers experiment with various sexual, occupational, and educational roles as they try to find out who they are and who they can be. This new sense of self, or "ego identity," is not simply the sum of the prior identifications. Rather, it is a reassembly or "an alignment of the individual's basic drives (ego) with his or her endowment (resolutions of the previous crises) and his or her opportunities (needs, skills, goals, and demands of adolescence and approaching adulthood)" (Erikson, 1980, p. 94).

Certification Pointer
For teacher certification tests you will probably be asked about Erik Erikson's stages of personal and social development. You should know that vigorous exploration of their physical and social behavior is a behavior typical of children in Stage III, initiative versus guilt.

Stage VI: Intimacy versus Isolation (Young Adulthood) Once young people know who they are and where they are going, the stage is set for the sharing of their life with another. The young adult is now ready to form a new relationship of trust and intimacy with another individual, a "partner in friendship, sex, competition, and cooperation." This relationship should enhance the identity of both partners without stifling the growth of either. The young adult who does not seek out such intimacy or whose repeated tries fail may retreat into isolation.

Stage VII: Generativity versus Self-Absorption (Middle Adulthood) Generativity is "the interest in establishing and guiding the next generation" (Erikson, 1980, p. 103). Typically, people attain generativity through raising their own children. However, the crisis of this stage can also be successfully resolved through other forms of productivity and creativity, such as teaching. During this stage, people should continue to grow; if they don't, a sense of "stagnation and interpersonal impoverishment" develops, leading to self-absorption or self-indulgence (Erikson, 1980, p. 103).

Stage VIII: Integrity versus Despair (Late Adulthood) In the final stage of psychosocial development, people look back over their lifetime and resolve their final identity crisis. Acceptance of accomplishments, failures, and ultimate limitations brings with it a sense of integrity, or wholeness, and a realization that one's life has been one's own responsibility. The finality of death must also be faced and accepted. Despair can occur in those who regret the way they have led their lives or how their lives have turned out.

Implications and Criticisms of Erikson's Theory

As with Piaget's stages, not all people experience Erikson's crises to the same degree or at the same time. The age ranges stated here may represent the best times for a crisis to be resolved, but they are not the only possible times. For example, children who were born into chaotic homes that failed to give them adequate security may develop trust after being adopted or otherwise brought into a more stable environment. People whose negative school experiences gave them a sense of inferiority may find, as they enter the work world, that they can learn and that they do have valuable skills—a realization that may help them finally to resolve the industry versus inferiority crisis that others resolved in their elementary school years. Erikson's theory emphasizes the role of the environment, both in causing the crises and in determining how they will be resolved. The stages of personal and social development are played out in constant interactions with others and with society as a whole. During the first three stages the interactions are primarily with parents and other family members, but the school plays a central role for most children in Stage IV (industry versus inferiority) and Stage V (identity versus role confusion).

Erikson's theory describes the basic issues that people confront as they go through life. However, his theory has been criticized because it does not explain how or why individuals progress from one stage to another and also because it is difficult to confirm through research (Miller, 2011).

WHAT ARE SOME VIEWS OF MORAL DEVELOPMENT?

Society could not function without rules that tell people how to communicate with one another, how to avoid hurting others, and how to get along in life generally. If you are around children much, you may have noticed that they are often rigid about rules. Things are either right or wrong; there is no in-between. If you think back to your own years in middle school or high school, you may recall being shocked to find that people sometimes break rules on purpose and that the rules that apply to some people may not apply to others. These experiences probably changed your concept of rules. Your idea of laws may also have changed when you learned how they are made. People meet and debate and vote; the laws that are made one year can be changed the next. The more complexity you can see, the more you find exists. Just as children differ from adults in cognitive and personal development, they also differ in their moral reasoning. First we will look at the two stages of moral reasoning described by Piaget, and then we will discuss related theories developed by Lawrence Kohlberg. Piaget proposed that there is a relationship between the cognitive stages of development and the ability to reason about moral issues. Kohlberg believed that the development of the logical structures proposed by Piaget is necessary to, although not sufficient for, advances in the area of moral judgment and reasoning.

Piaget's Theory of Moral Development

Piaget's theory of cognitive development includes a theory about the development of moral reasoning. Piaget believed that cognitive structures and abilities develop first. Cognitive abilities then determine children's abilities to reason about social situations. As with cognitive abilities, Piaget proposed that moral development progresses in predictable stages, in this case from a very egocentric type of moral reasoning to one that reflects a system of justice based on cooperation and reciprocity.

PIAGET'S STAGES OF PERSONAL AND MORAL DEVELOPMENT As people develop their cognitive abilities, their understanding of moral problems also becomes more sophisticated. Young children are more rigid in their views of right and wrong than older children and adults tend to be.

To explore moral development, Piaget posed two stories to older and younger children. In the first story, a boy broke 15 cups completely by accident. In the second story, a boy broke one cup while he was trying to steal a cookie. Piaget asked the children who was naughtier and should be punished more. Younger children of 5–10 years focused on the results of an action to make their judgments, regardless of each child's intentions—more cups broke so the first child was naughtier. This type of reasoning is called *heteronomous morality*. Older children in Piaget's experiment were able to make judgments based on the intent of an action—the second child was misbehaving, so he was naughtier. This type of reasoning is called *autonomous morality*. Piaget noted that these two phases overlap.

Recently, when presented with a similar story, one 5-year-old responded, "They are both mean because they broke cups," whereas a 10-year-old responded, "The first boy didn't do it on purpose." Table 3.1 summarizes the characteristics of heteronomous and autonomous morality, according to Piaget.

To understand children's moral reasoning, Piaget spent a great deal of time watching children play marbles and asking them about the rules of the game. The first thing he discovered was that before about the age of 6, children play by their own idiosyncratic, egocentric rules. Piaget believed that very young children were incapable of interacting in cooperative ways and therefore unable to engage in moral reasoning.

Piaget found that by age 6, children acknowledged the existence of rules, though they were inconsistent in following them. Frequently, several children who were supposedly playing the same game were observed to be playing by different sets of rules. Children at this age also had no understanding that game rules are arbitrary and something that a group can decide by itself. Instead, they saw rules as being imposed by some higher authority and unchangeable.

TABLE 3.1 • Piaget's Stages of Moral Development

HETERONOMOUS MORALITY	AUTONOMOUS MORALITY
Inflexible rules are made by authorities such as the police, parents, and teachers.	Intentions are more important than the results of one's behavior.
Rules are permanent, do not change, and must be followed.	There are times when it is ok to break rules.
Egocentrism in childhood results in children believing that others view their rule-following ideas in the same way that they do.	People may view "what is right" differently.
Degree of punishment should depend on how bad the results of one's actions were.	Degree of punishment should depend on intentions and the degree of misbehavior.
Misbehavior will always be punished. For example, if you do something bad, and then later on you fall and hurt your knee, it is because you misbehaved. This is called "immanent justice."	Coincidental bad outcomes are not seen as punishments for misbehavior.

Piaget (1964) labeled the first stage of moral development **heteronomous morality**; it has also been called the stage of "moral realism" or "morality of constraint." *Heteronomous* means being subject to rules imposed by others. During this period, young children are consistently faced with parents and other adults telling them what to do and what not to do. Violations of rules are believed to bring automatic punishment; people who are bad will eventually be punished. Piaget also described children at this stage as judging the morality of behavior on the basis of its consequences. They judge behavior as bad if it results in negative consequences, even if the actor's original intentions were good.

Piaget found that children did not conscientiously use and follow rules until the age of 10 or 12 years, when children are capable of formal operations. At this age, every child playing the game followed the same set of rules. Children understood that the rules existed to give the game direction and to minimize disputes between players. They understood that rules were something that everyone agreed on and that therefore, if everyone agreed to change them, they could be changed.

Piaget also observed that children at this age tend to base moral judgments on the intentions of the actor rather than on the consequences of the actions. Children often engage in discussions of hypothetical circumstances that might affect rules. This second stage is labeled **autonomous morality** or "morality of cooperation." It arises as the child's social world expands to include more and more peers. Through interaction and cooperation with other children, the child's ideas about rules and, therefore, morality begin to change. Rules are now what we make them. Punishment for transgressions is no longer automatic but must be administered by taking into account the transgressor's intentions and any extenuating circumstances.

According to Piaget, children progress from the stage of heteronomous morality to that of autonomous morality with the development of cognitive structures, but also because of interactions with equal-status peers. He believed that resolving conflicts with peers weakened children's reliance on adult authority and heightened their awareness that rules are changeable and should exist only as the result of mutual consent.

Research on elements of Piaget's theories generally supports his ideas, with one key exception. Piaget is felt to have underestimated the degree to which even very young children consider intentions in judging behavior. However, the progression from a focus on outcomes to a focus on intentions over the course of development has been documented many times.

Kohlberg's Stages of Moral Reasoning

Kohlberg's (1963, 1969) stage theory of moral reasoning is an elaboration and refinement of Piaget's. Like Piaget, Kohlberg studied how children (and adults) reason about rules that govern their behavior in certain situations. Kohlberg did not study children's game playing, but rather probed for their responses to a series of structured situations or **moral dilemmas**, the most famous of which is the following:

> In Europe a woman was near death from cancer. One drug might save her, a form of radium that a druggist in the same town had recently discovered. The druggist was charging $2,000, ten times what the drug cost him to make. The sick woman's husband, Heinz, went to everyone he knew to borrow the money, but he could only get together about half of what it cost. He told the druggist that his wife was dying and asked him to sell it cheaper or let him pay later. But the druggist said "No." The husband got desperate and broke into the man's store to steal the drug for his wife. Should the husband have done that? Why? (1969, p. 379)

> *Source*: From *Handbook of socialization theory and research in stage and sequence: The cognitive-developmental approach to socialization* by L. Kohlberg, D. A. Goslin. Published by Rand-McNally, © 1969.

On the basis of the answers he received, Kohlberg proposed that people pass through a series of six stages of moral judgment or reasoning. Kohlberg's levels and stages are summarized in Table 3.2. He grouped these six stages into three levels: preconventional, conventional, and postconventional. These three levels are distinguished by how the child or adult defines what he or she perceives as correct or moral behavior. As with other stage theories, each stage is more sophisticated and complex than the preceding one, and most individuals proceed through them in the same order (Colby & Kohlberg, 1984). Like Piaget, Kohlberg was concerned not so much with the child's answer as with the reasoning behind it. The ages at which children and adolescents

Certification Pointer

Teacher certification tests are likely to require you to know the theoretical contributions of Lawrence Kohlberg to the understanding of children's development of moral reasoning.

TABLE 3.2 • Kohlberg's Stages of Moral Reasoning

When people consider moral dilemmas, it is their reasoning that is important, not their final decision, according to Lawrence Kohlberg. He theorized that people progress through three levels as they develop abilities of moral reasoning.

I. PRECONVENTIONAL LEVEL	II. CONVENTIONAL LEVEL	III. POSTCONVENTIONAL LEVEL
Rules are set down by others. Stage 1: Punishment and Obedience Orientation. Physical consequences of action determine its goodness or badness. Stage 2: Instrumental Relativist Orientation. What is right is whatever satisfies one's own needs and occasionally the needs of others. Elements of fairness and reciprocity are present, but they are mostly interpreted in a "you scratch my back, I'll scratch yours" fashion.	Individual adopts rules and will sometimes subordinate own needs to those of the group. Expectations of family, group, or nation seen as valuable in own right, regardless of immediate and obvious consequences. Stage 3: "Good Boy–Good Girl" Orientation. Good behavior is whatever pleases or helps others and is approved of by them. One earns approval by being "nice." Stage 4: "Law and Order" Orientation. Right is doing one's duty, showing respect for authority, and maintaining the given social order for its own sake.	People define own values in terms of ethical principles they have chosen to follow. Stage 5: Social Contract Orientation. What is right is defined in terms of general individual rights and in terms of standards that have been agreed on by the whole society. In contrast to Stage 4, laws are not "frozen"—they can be changed for the good of society. Stage 6: Universal Ethical Principle Orientation. What is right is defined by decision of conscience according to self-chosen ethical principles. These principles are abstract and ethical (such as the Golden Rule), not specific moral prescriptions (such as the Ten Commandments).

Source: From *Handbook of socialization theory and research,* by L. Kohlberg and D. A. Goslin. By Rand McNally & Company (Chicago), Copyright © 1969 reprinted with permission of Rand McNally & Company (Chicago).

go through the stages in Table 3.2 vary considerably; in fact, the same individual may behave according to one stage at some times and according to another at other times. However, most children pass from the preconventional to the conventional level by the age of 9 (Kohlberg, 1969).

ON THE WEB

The Association for Moral Education (AME) provides an interdisciplinary forum for individuals interested in the moral dimensions of educational theory and practice at amenetwork.org. An overview of moral education theories, arranged by theorist, can be found at amenetwork.org. Also see the site for *The Journal of Moral Education*.

Stage 1, which is on the **preconventional level of morality**, is very similar in form and content to Piaget's stage of heteronomous morality. Children simply obey authority figures to avoid being punished. In Stage 2, children's own needs and desires become important, yet they are aware of the interests of other people. In a concrete sense they weigh the interests of all parties when making moral judgments, but they are still "looking out for number one." The **conventional level of morality** begins at Stage 3. Here morality is defined in terms of cooperation with peers, just as it was in Piaget's stage of autonomous morality. This is the stage at which children have an unquestioning belief that one should "do unto others as you would have them do unto you." Because of the decrease in egocentrism that accompanies concrete operations, children are cognitively capable of putting themselves in someone else's shoes. They can consider the feelings of others when making moral decisions. No longer do they simply do what will not get them punished (Stage 1) or what makes them feel good (Stage 2). At Stage 4, society's rules and laws replace those of the peer group. A desire for social approval no longer determines moral judgments. Laws are followed without question, and breaking the law can never be justified. Most adults are probably at this stage. Stage 5 signals entrance into the **postconventional level of morality**, a level of moral reasoning attained by fewer than 25 percent of adults, according to Kohlberg, in which there is a realization that the laws and values of a society are somewhat arbitrary and particular to that society. Laws are seen as necessary to preserve the social order and to ensure the basic rights of life and liberty. In Stage 6, one's ethical principles are self-chosen and based on abstract concepts such as justice and the equality and value of human rights. Laws that violate these principles can and should be disobeyed because "justice is above the law." Late in life, Kohlberg (1978, 1980) speculated that Stage 6 is not really separate from Stage 5 and suggested that the two be combined.

Kohlberg (1969) believed that moral dilemmas can be used to advance a child's level of moral reasoning, but only one stage at a time. He theorized that the way in which children progress from one stage to the next is by interacting with others whose reasoning is one or, at most, two stages above their own. Teachers can help students progress in moral reasoning by weaving discussions of justice and moral issues into lessons, particularly in response to events that occur in the classroom or in the broader society (see Sternberg, 2011).

Kohlberg found that his stages of moral reasoning ability occurred in the same order and at about the same ages in the United States, Mexico, Taiwan, and Turkey. Other research throughout the world has generally found the same sequence of stages, although there are clearly strong influences of culture on moral reasoning as well as on moral behavior (Nucci, 2009).

Criticisms of Kohlberg's Theory

Later research generally supports Kohlberg's main sequence of development (Boom et al., 2001; Dawson, 2002; Nucci, 2009), but there have also been many critiques. One limitation of Kohlberg's early work was that it mostly involved boys. Some research on girls' moral reasoning finds patterns that are somewhat different from those proposed by Kohlberg. Whereas boys' moral reasoning revolves primarily around issues of justice, girls are more concerned about issues of caring and responsibility for others (Gilligan, 1982; Gilligan & Attanucci, 1988; Haspe & Baddeley, 1991). Carol Gilligan argued, for example, that males and females use different moral criteria: Male moral reasoning is focused on people's individual rights, whereas female moral reasoning is focused more on individuals' responsibilities for other people. This is why, she argued, females tend to suggest altruism and self-sacrifice rather than rights and rules as solutions to moral dilemmas (Gilligan, 1982). Kohlberg (Levine, Kohlberg, & Hewer, 1985) revised his theory on the basis of these criticisms. However, most research has failed to find any male–female differences in moral maturity (Bee & Boyd, 2010; Jaffee & Hyde, 2000; Tangney & Dearing, 2002); nor is there convincing evidence that women are more caring, cooperative, or helpful than men (Turiel, 2006; Walker, 2004).

Another criticism of both Piaget's and Kohlberg's work is that young children can often reason about moral situations in more sophisticated ways than a stage theory would suggest (Arnold, 2000). For example, although young children often consider consequences to be more important than intentions when evaluating conduct, under certain circumstances children as young as 3 and 4 years of age use intentions to judge the behavior of others (Bussey, 1992). Also, 6- to 10-year-olds at the stage of heteronomous morality have been shown to make distinctions between rules that parents are justified in making and enforcing, and rules that are under personal or peer jurisdiction (Keenan & Evans, 2010). Finally, Turiel (2006) has suggested that young children make a distinction between moral rules, such as not lying and stealing, that are based on principles of justice, and social-conventional rules, such as not wearing pajamas to school, that are based on social consensus and etiquette. Research has supported this view, demonstrating that children as young as 2½ to 3 years make distinctions between moral and social-conventional rules.

The most important limitation of Kohlberg's theory is that it deals with moral reasoning rather than with actual behavior (Arnold, 2000). Many individuals at different stages behave in the same way, and individuals at the same stage often behave in different ways (Walker, 2004). In addition, the context of moral dilemmas matters. For example, a study by Einerson (1998) found that adolescents used much lower levels of moral reasoning when moral dilemmas involved celebrities than when they involved made-up characters. Similarly, the link between children's moral reasoning and their moral behavior may be unclear. For example, a study by Murdock, Hale, and Weber (2001) found that cheating among middle school students was affected by many factors, including motivation in school, success, and relationships with teachers, that have little to do with stages of moral development.

MyEdLab **Self-Check 3.1**

HOW DO CHILDREN DEVELOP SOCIALLY AND EMOTIONALLY?

As a teacher, you are responsible not just for the academic achievement of your children. You also strive to develop young people who are socially and emotionally healthy (see Comer, 2010; Hamre & Pianta, 2010; Parke & Clarke-Stewart, 2011; Squires, Pribble, Chen, & Pomes, 2013; Weissberg & Cascarino, 2013; Yoder, 2014). Like other aspects of development, social and emotional development depend on the experiences provided by schools and families, but they also follow predictable patterns. The following sections discuss these critical areas of development.

Socioemotional Development during the Preschool Years

A young child's social life evolves in relatively predictable ways (see Cummings et al., 2003; McHale, Dariotis, & Kauh, 2003). The social network grows from an intimate relationship with parents or other guardians to include other family members, nonrelated adults, and peers. Social interactions extend from home to neighborhood and from preschool or other child-care arrangements to formal school. Erik Erikson's theory of personal and social development suggests that during the preschool years, children must resolve the personality crisis of initiative versus guilt. The child's successful resolution of this stage results in a sense of initiative and ambition tempered by a reasonable understanding of the permissible. Early educators can encourage this resolution by giving children opportunities to take initiative, to be challenged, and to succeed (Denham, Zinsser, & Brown, 2013; Squires, Pribble, Chen, & Pomes, 2013). It is also important to emphasize self-regulation (Goodwin & Miller, 2013).

PEER RELATIONSHIPS During the preschool years, **peers** (other children who are a child's equal in age) begin to play an increasingly important role in children's social and cognitive development (Hay, Payne, & Chadwick, 2004; Ladd & Sechler, 2013). Children's relations with their peers differ in several ways from their interactions with adults. Peer play allows children to interact with other individuals whose level of development is similar to their own. When peers have disputes among themselves, they must make concessions and cooperate in resolving them if the play is to continue; unlike in adult–child disputes, in a peer dispute no one can claim to have ultimate authority. Peer conflicts also let children see that others have thoughts, feelings, and viewpoints that are different from their own. Conflicts also heighten children's sensitivity to the effects of their behavior on others. In this way, peer relationships help young children to overcome the egocentrism that Piaget described as being characteristic of preoperational thinking, helping them see that others have perspectives that are different from their own.

PROSOCIAL BEHAVIOR **Prosocial behaviors** are voluntary actions toward others such as caring, sharing, comforting, and cooperating. Research on the roots of prosocial behavior has contributed to our knowledge of children's moral as well as social development. Several factors seem to be associated with the development of prosocial behaviors (Eisenberg, 2001), including the following:

- Parental disciplinary techniques that stress the consequences of the child's behavior for others and that are applied within a warm, responsive parent–child relationship
- Contact with adults who indicate they expect concern for others, who let children know that aggressive solutions to problems are unacceptable, and who provide acceptable alternatives
- Contact with adults who attribute positive characteristics to children when they do well ("What a helpful boy you are!")

PLAY Most of a preschooler's interactions with peers occur during play (Hughes, 2010). However, the degree to which play involves other children increases over the preschool years. In a classic study of preschoolers, Mildred Parten (1932) identified four categories of play that reflect increasing levels of social interaction and sophistication. **Solitary play** is play that occurs alone, often with toys, and is independent of what other children are doing. **Parallel play** involves children engaged in the same activity side by side but with very little interaction or mutual influence. **Associative play** is much like parallel play but with increased levels of interaction in the form of sharing, turn-taking, and general interest in what others are doing. **Cooperative play** occurs when children join together to achieve a common goal, such as building a large castle with each child building a part of the structure. Children engage in more complex types of play as they grow

MyEdLab

Video Example 3.1

Watch as a preschool teacher steps in to help the children resolve a conflict on the playground. How does this experience help Caitlyn to develop new social and emotion regulation skills?

Connections 3.1

For suggested cooperative learning activities, see Chapter 8.

older, advancing from simple forms of parallel play to complex pretend play in which children cooperate in planning and carrying out activities (Berk, 2013; Hughes, 2010).

Play is important for children because it exercises their linguistic, cognitive, and social skills and contributes to their general personality development (Berk, 2013; Hughes, 2010; Johnson, Sevimli-Cellik, & Al-Mansour, 2013; Weisberg, Hirsh-Pasek, & Golinkoff, 2013). Children use their minds when playing because they are thinking and acting as if they were another person. When they make such a transformation, they are taking a step toward abstract thinking in that they are freeing their thoughts from a focus on concrete objects. Play is also associated with creativity, especially the ability to be less literal and more flexible in one's thinking. Play has an important role in Vygotsky's theories of development, because it allows children to freely explore ways of thinking and acting that are above their current level of functioning (Bodrova & Leong, 2007). Vygotsky (1978) wrote, "In play a child is always above his average age, above his daily behavior; in play it is as though he were a head taller than himself" (p. 102).

Preschoolers' play appears to be influenced by a variety of factors. For instance, preschoolers' interactions with peers are related to how they interact with their parents (Hughes, 2010). Three-year-olds who have warm and nurturing relationships with parents are more likely to engage in social pretend play and resolve conflicts with peers than are children who have less secure relationships with their parents. Children also play better with familiar peers and same-sex peers. Providing age-appropriate toys and play activities can support the development of play and peer interaction skills.

Connections 3.2
For more on Vygotsky, see Chapter 2.

Socioemotional Development during the Elementary Years

By the time children enter elementary school, they have developed skills for more complex thought, action, and social influence. Up to this point, children have been basically egocentric, and their world has been that of home, family, and possibly a preschool or day-care center. The early primary grades will normally be spent working through Erikson's (1963) fourth stage, industry versus inferiority. Assuming that a child has developed trust during infancy, autonomy during the early years, and initiative during the preschool years, that child's experiences in the primary grades can contribute to his or her sense of industry and accomplishment. During this stage, children start trying to prove that they are "grown up"; in fact, this is often described as the I-can-do-it-myself stage. Work becomes possible. As children's powers of concentration grow, they can spend more time on chosen tasks, and they often take pleasure in completing projects. This stage also includes the growth of independent action, cooperation with groups, and performing in socially acceptable ways with a concern for fair play (McHale et al., 2003).

Taken together, social-emotional factors make a significant difference in student achievement. For example, Miller, Connolly, & Macguire (2013) found an impact of psychological adjustment, school adjustment, and peer and family relationships on achievement among students ages 7–11 in Northern Ireland. Similarly, Banerjee, Weare, & Farr (2013) found that English students of teachers who fully implemented a program called Social and Emotional Aspects of Learning (SEAL) did better in achievement than students who were in classes with less of a focus on social-emotional learning.

SELF-CONCEPT AND SELF-ESTEEM Personal and social development for elementary school children also includes the important ideas of **self-concept** and **self-esteem** (Swann, Chang-Schneider, & McClarty, 2007). These aspects of children's development will be strongly influenced by experiences at home, at school, and with peers. Self-concept includes the way in which we perceive our strengths, weaknesses, abilities, attitudes, and values. Its development begins at birth and is continuously shaped by experience. Self-esteem reflects how we evaluate our skills and abilities.

ON THE WEB

For an article on how to strengthen children's self-esteem, go to askdrsears.com and type "self-confidence" into the search engine. Also see kidshealth.org and click on "Educators"; then type "self-esteem" into the search engine.

As children progress through middle childhood, their ways of thinking become less concrete and more abstract. This trend is also evident in the development of their self-concepts. Preschoolers think about themselves in terms of their physical and material characteristics, including size, gender, and possessions. In contrast, by the early elementary school years, children begin to focus

InTASC 2

Learning Differences

THEORY INTO PRACTICE

Promoting the Development of Self-Esteem

Our society promotes the idea that people, including students, are of equal worth. That is also the premise in a classroom. But students being of equal worth doesn't necessarily mean that they are equally competent. Some students are good in reading and others in math; some excel in sports and others in art.

Some classroom activities can give certain students the impression that they as individuals are of less value or worth than other students. Inappropriate competition or inflexible ability groups within the classroom may teach the wrong lesson to students (Battistich, 2010; Slavin, 2011).

This kind of research can help teachers avoid practices that may discourage children. However, it is not clear that improving self-esteem results in greater school achievement. In fact, research more strongly suggests that as a student grows more competent in school tasks, his or her self-esteem also improves, rather than the other way around (e.g., Chapman et al., 2000; Ellis, 2001b).

It is not necessary to bend the truth and say that all students are equally good in reading or math. You can, however, recognize progress rather than level of ability, focusing your praise on the student's effort and growing competence. As the student experiences success in school, a feeling of earned self-esteem will result (Roeser, Eccles, & Sameroff, 2000).

on more abstract, internal qualities such as intelligence and kindness when describing themselves. They can also make a distinction between their private or inner selves and their external, public selves. This becomes especially evident as they depend more on intentions and motives and less on objective behavior in their explanations of their own and others' actions.

During middle childhood, children also begin to evaluate themselves in comparison to others. A preschooler might describe herself by saying, "I like baseball," whereas several years later this same girl is likely to say, "I like baseball more than Sally does." The trend to use **social comparison** information to evaluate the self appears to correspond with developmental changes in academic self-esteem. Preschoolers and young children tend to evaluate themselves very positively, in ways that bear no relationship to their school performance or other objective factors. By second or third grade, however, children who are having difficulty in school tend to have poorer self-concepts (Chapman, Tunmer, & Prochnow, 2000). This begins a declining spiral. Students who perform poorly in elementary school are at risk for developing poor academic self-concepts and subsequent poor performance in upper elementary and secondary school (Guay, Marsh, & Boivin, 2003).

The primary grades give many children their first chance to compare themselves with others and to work and play under the guidance of adults outside their family. These adults must provide experiences that let children succeed, feel good about themselves, and maintain their enthusiasm and creativity (Battistich, 2010; Comer, 2010).

The key word regarding personal and social development is *acceptance*. The fact is, children do differ in their abilities; no matter what teachers do, students will have figured out by the end of the elementary years (and usually earlier) who is more able and who is less able. However, you can have a substantial impact on how students feel about these differences and on the value that low–achieving students place on learning even when they know they will never be class stars.

ON THE WEB

Dr. Robert Brooks has written some useful articles on promoting self-esteem in the classroom. See greatschools.org. Click on "Great Kids" and then type "teachers foster self-esteem" into the search box. The same website has information about promoting self-esteem in children with learning disabilities.

GROWING IMPORTANCE OF PEERS The influence of the child's family, the major force during the early childhood years, continues as parents provide role models in terms of attitudes and behaviors. In addition, relationships with brothers and sisters affect relationships with peers, and routines from home either are reinforced or must be overcome in school. However, the peer group takes on added importance. Speaking of the child's entrance into the world outside the family, Ira Gordon notes the importance of peers:

> If all the world's the stage that Shakespeare claimed, children and adolescents are playing primarily to an audience of their peers. Their peers sit in the front rows and the box seats; parents and teachers are now relegated to the back rows and the balcony. (Gordon, 1957, p. 166)
>
> *Source:* From *The social system of the high school: A study in the sociology of adolescence* by Calvin Wayne Gordon, Published by Free Press, © 1957.

In the lower elementary grades, peer groups usually consist of same-sex children who are around the same age. This preference may arise because of the variety of abilities and interests among young children. By the sixth grade, however, students often form groups that include both boys and girls. Whatever the composition of peer groups, they let children compare their abilities and skills to those of others. Members of peer groups also teach one another about their different worlds. Through this sharing of attitudes and values, children learn how to sort out and form their own.

FRIENDSHIPS IN MIDDLE CHILDHOOD During middle childhood, children's conceptions of friendship also mature. Friendship is the central social relationship between peers during childhood, and it undergoes a series of changes before adulthood (Scharf & Hertz-Lazarowitz, 2003). Children's understanding of friendship changes over the years (McHale et al., 2003). Between the ages of 3 and 7, children usually view friends as momentary playmates. Children of this age might come home from school exclaiming, "I made a new friend today! Jamie shared her doll with me," or "Bill's not my friend anymore 'cause he wouldn't play blocks with me." These comments reveal the child's view of friendship as a temporary relationship based on a certain situation rather than on shared interests or beliefs. As children enter middle childhood, friendships become more stable and reciprocal. At this age, friends are often described in terms of personal traits ("My friend Mary is nice"), and friendships are based on mutual support, caring, loyalty, and mutual give-and-take.

Friendships are important to children for several reasons. During the elementary school years, friends are companions with whom to have fun and do things. They also serve as important emotional resources by providing children with a sense of security in new situations and when family or other problems arise. Friends are also cognitive resources when they teach or model specific intellectual skills. Social norms for conduct, social interaction skills, and how to resolve conflicts successfully are also learned within the context of friendships (McHale et al., 2003).

PEER ACCEPTANCE One of the important aspects of peer relations in middle childhood is peer acceptance, or status within the peer group (Parke & Clarke-Stewart, 2011). A popular child is one who is named most often by peers as a person they like and least often as someone they dislike. In contrast, a rejected child is one named most often by peers as a person they dislike and least often as someone they like. A child may also be classified as neglected (not named frequently as either liked or disliked). On the other hand, a controversial child is frequently named as someone who is liked but is also frequently named as someone who is disliked. Average children are those who are named as being liked and as being disliked with moderate frequency.

Children who are not well accepted or are rejected by their peers in elementary school are at high risk (Ladd & Troop-Gordon, 2003; Wentzel, Barry, & Caldwell, 2004). These children are more likely to drop out of school, to engage in delinquent behavior, and to have emotional and psychological problems in adolescence and adulthood than are their peers who are more accepted (Ladd & Troop-Gordon, 2003). Some rejected children tend to be highly aggressive; others tend to be very passive and withdrawn, and these children may be victims of bullying (Pellegrini & Bartini, 2000). Children who are rejected, whether aggressive or withdrawn, seem to be at highest risk for difficulties (Wentzel et al., 2004).

Many characteristics seem to be related to peer acceptance, including physical attractiveness and cognitive abilities (Wentzel et al., 2004). Well-accepted and popular children tend to be cooperative, helpful, and caring and are rarely disruptive or aggressive. Children who are disliked by their peers tend to be highly aggressive and to lack prosocial and conflict resolution skills. Neglected and controversial children display less distinct behavioral styles and often change status over short periods of time (Parke & Clarke-Stewart, 2011).

Connections 3.3
For more on systematically reinforcing prosocial skills, see Chapter 5. For more on mindset, persistence, and effort, see Chapter 10.

THEORY INTO PRACTICE

Developing Social-Emotional Skills

There are numerous approaches to developing social-emotional skills among children and adolescents (Blazar & Kraft, 2015; Durlak et al., 2011). Many of these focus in particular on cooperative learning, teaching students strategies for effective interactions with peers and means of solving interpersonal problems. One such example is Communities That Care (Hawkins et al., 2008; Hawkins, Kuklinski, & Fagan, 2012), which focuses on cooperative learning, proactive classroom management, and development of social skills. A long-term follow-up study of this approach found that in their 20s, people who had been in this program in middle school had higher educational and academic attainment than did those who had been in a control group. Other successful programs that focus on social-emotional learning and direct teaching of SEL strategies include James Comer's School Development Program (Brown, Emmons, & Comer, 2010), PATHS (Domitrovich, Cortes, & Greenberg, 2007), and 4Rs (Aber et al., 2010).

Another approach to building social-emotional skills supportive of motivation to achieve is to help create "mindsets" among students that convince them that effort, not just intelligence, enables them to succeed. Several studies in which teachers focused on effort, and the availability of success to all who try, found positive effects on students' motivation and learning (Dweck, 2006, 2010, 2013; Snipes, Fancali, & Stoker, 2012). Another compelling approach emphasizes building students' persistence, or "grit," by teaching students to keep at difficult tasks until they find a way to complete them and learn the content (Duckworth, Gendler, & Gross, 2014; Duckworth & Steinberg, 2015).

Because peer acceptance is such a strong predictor of current and long-term adjustment, it is important to try to improve the social skills of children (Carney et al., 2015; Hamm & Zhang, 2010). This can be done by modeling and praising prosocial skills such as helping and sharing (Austin & Sciarra, 2010).

Socioemotional Development during the Middle School and High School Years

In adolescence, children undergo significant changes in their social and emotional lives as well (Rice & Dolgin, 2008). Partly as a result of their changing physical and cognitive structures, children in the upper elementary grades seek to be more grown-up. They want their parents to treat them differently, even though many parents are unwilling to see them in new ways. They also report that although they believe that their parents love them, they do not think their parents understand them. For both boys and girls in the upper elementary grades, membership in groups tends to promote feelings of self-worth. Not being accepted can bring serious emotional problems. Herein lies the major cause of the preadolescent's changing relationship with parents. It is not that preadolescents care less about their parents. It is just that their friends are more important than ever. This need for acceptance by peers helps to explain why preadolescents often dress alike. The story of Sam Stevens's lip ring at the beginning of this chapter illustrates how young adolescents express their belongingness with other peer group members through distinctive dress or behavior.

The middle school years often also bring changes in the relationship between children and their teachers. In primary school, children easily accept and depend on teachers. During the upper elementary years, this relationship becomes more complex (see Roeser et al., 2000). Sometimes students will tell teachers personal information they would not tell their parents. Some preadolescents even choose teachers as role models. At the same time, however, some preteens talk back to teachers in ways they would never have considered several years earlier, and some openly challenge teachers. Others become deeply alienated from school, starting a pattern that may lead to delinquency and dropping out (Austin & Sciarra, 2010).

MyEdLab
Video Example 3.2

Bob Slavin talks about a family interaction involving his teenage son. Does his story remind you of your own experiences in adolescence? What are some of the learning challenges that this time period poses for teachers and students?

IDENTITY DEVELOPMENT One of the first signs of early adolescence is the appearance of **reflectivity**, the tendency to think about what is going on in one's own mind and to study oneself. Adolescents begin to look more closely at themselves and to define themselves differently. They start to realize that there are differences between what they think and feel and how they behave. Using the developing intellectual skills that enable them to consider possibilities, adolescents are prone to be dissatisfied with themselves. They critique their personal characteristics, compare themselves to others, and try to change the way they are.

"School uniforms! That'll take away our individuality!"

Adolescents may also wonder whether other people see and think about the world in the same way they do. They become more aware of their separateness from other people and of their uniqueness. They learn that other people cannot fully know what they think and feel. The issue of who and what one "really" is dominates personality development in adolescence. According to Erikson, the stage is set during adolescence for a major concern with one's identity.

JAMES MARCIA'S FOUR IDENTITY STATUSES On the basis of Erikson's work, James Marcia (1991) identified from in-depth interviews with adolescents four identity statuses that reflect the degree to which adolescents have made firm commitments to religious and political values as well as to a future occupation.

1. *Foreclosure.* Individuals in a state of **foreclosure** have never experienced an identity crisis. Rather, they have prematurely established an identity on the basis of their parents' choices rather than their own. They have made occupational and ideological commitments, but these commitments reflect an assessment by parents or authority figures more than an autonomous process of self-assessment. Foreclosure indicates a kind of "pseudo-identity" that generally is too fixed and rigid to serve as a foundation for meeting life's future crises.

2. *Identity diffusion.* Adolescents experiencing **identity diffusion** have found neither an occupational direction nor an ideological commitment of any kind, and they have made little progress toward these ends. They may have experienced an identity crisis, but if so, they were unable to resolve it.

3. *Moratorium.* Adolescents in a state of **moratorium** have begun to experiment with occupational and ideological choices but have not yet made definitive commitments to either. These individuals are directly in the midst of an identity crisis and are currently examining alternative life choices.

4. *Identity achievement.* **Identity achievement** signifies a state of identity consolidation in which adolescents have made their own conscious, clear-cut decisions about occupation and ideology. The individual is convinced that these decisions have been autonomously and freely made and that they reflect his or her true nature and deep inner commitments.

By late adolescence (18 to 22 years of age), most individuals have developed a status of identity achievement. However, adolescents' emotional development seems to be linked to their identity status. For instance, levels of anxiety tend to be highest for adolescents in moratorium and lowest for those in foreclosure (Marcia, 1991). Self-esteem also varies; adolescents in identity achievement and moratorium report the highest levels and those in foreclosure and identity diffusion report the lowest levels (Marcia, 1991; Wallace-Broscious, Serafica, & Osipow, 1994).

In general, adolescents need to experiment and remain flexible if they are successfully to find their own identity. By trying out ways to be, then testing and modifying them, the adolescent can pick the characteristics that are most comfortable and drop the others. To do this, the adolescent must have the self-confidence to experiment and to declare an experiment over, to vary behavior, and to drop characteristics that don't fit, even if the characteristics are supported by others. It helps to have a stable and accepting set of parents, teachers, and peers who will respond positively to one's experimentation.

ON THE WEB

For explorations of many aspects of adolescent development, including identity development and self-esteem, search Nancy Darling's Lab at oberlin.edu.

ENHANCING SOCIAL-EMOTIONAL DEVELOPMENT There are many programs designed to improve the social-emotional development of children and adolescents. A review by Durlak et al. (2011) (also see Bandy & Moore, 2011; Hsueh et al., 2014; Terzian, Hamilton, & Ericson, 2011; Yoder, 2014) found that school-based social and emotional learning (SEL) programs can make a significant difference in SEL outcomes and, in some cases, improve academic achievement as well. These programs included school-day and after-school programs, and preventive programs for all students as well as those for students already experiencing difficulties. They covered all ages and all types of schools.

A focus on social-emotional learning can have long-lasting impacts on children. A study by Hawkins et al. (2008) (also see Kosterman, Haggerty, & Hawkins, 2010) found that children who received an SEL intervention focusing on proactive classroom management, interactive teaching, and cooperative learning, as well as child social skills development and parent training, had effects that were still important 15 years later, when the students were in their 20s. They reported higher levels of educational and economic attainment and higher levels of mental health, among other outcomes. Other SEL interventions, such as Communities That Care (Hawkins, Kuklinski, & Fagan, 2012), The Responsive Classroom (Rimm-Kaufman, 2010), PATHS (Domitrovich, Cortes, & Greenberg, 2007; Sheard & Ross, 2012), and 4Rs (Aber, Brown, Jones, & Roderick, 2010), also have shown positive effects on a variety of SEL and academic outcomes, and SEL is a central feature of James Comer's School Development Program (Brown, Emmons, & Comer, 2010).

SELF-CONCEPT AND SELF-ESTEEM Self-concept and self-esteem also change as children enter and go through adolescence. The shift toward more abstract portrayals that began in middle childhood continues, and adolescents' self-descriptions often include personal traits (friendly, obnoxious), emotions (depressed, psyched), and personal beliefs (liberal, conservative) (Harter, 1998). In addition, the self-concept becomes more differentiated. Susan Harter's work has identified eight distinct aspects of adolescent concept: scholastic competence, job competence, athletic competence, physical appearance, social acceptance, close friendships, romantic appeal, and conduct (Harter, 1998). Marsh (1993) identified five distinct self-concepts: academic verbal, academic mathematical, parent relations, same-sex, and opposite sex.

Self-esteem also undergoes fluctuations and changes during adolescence. Self-esteem is lowest as children enter middle school or junior high school and with the onset of **puberty** (Jacobs, Lanza, Osgood, Eccles, & Wigfield, 2002). Early-maturing girls tend to suffer the most dramatic and long-lasting decreases in self-esteem. In general, adolescent girls have lower self-esteem than boys (Jacobs et al., 2002). Global self-esteem or feelings of self-worth appear to be influenced most strongly by physical appearance and then by social acceptance from peers.

Improving self-esteem is mainly a matter of giving all students a sense that they are valued and successful (Goodwin, 2015; Yeager & Walton, 2011). It is also essential to avoid low expectations and comparisons to others who are more successful.

SOCIAL RELATIONSHIPS As children enter adolescence, changes in the nature of friendships take place. In general, the amount of time spent with friends increases dramatically; adolescents spend more time with their peers than with family members or by themselves. Adolescents who have satisfying and harmonious friendships also report higher levels of self-esteem, are less lonely, have more mature social skills, and do better in school than adolescents who lack supportive friendships (Kerr, Stattin, Biesecker, & Ferrer-Wreder, 2003).

During adolescence, the capacity for mutual understanding and the knowledge that others are unique individuals with feelings of their own also contribute to a dramatic increase in self-disclosure, intimacy, and loyalty among friends. As early adolescents strive to establish personal identities independent of their parents, they also look increasingly to their peers for security and social support. Whereas elementary school children look to parents for such support, by seventh grade same-sex friends are perceived to be as supportive as parents, and by 10th grade they are perceived to be the primary source of social support (Rice & Dolgin, 2008).

RELATIONSHIPS WITH PEERS In addition to their close friends, most adolescents also place high value on the larger peer group as a source of ideas and values as well as companionship and entertainment.

The nature of peer relationships in adolescence has been characterized in terms of social status and peer crowds. Social status, or levels of acceptance by peers, is studied with respect to the same status groups that are identified in middle childhood. As with elementary school-age children, popular and well-accepted

MyEdLab

Video Example 3.3

Adolescent students have no trouble identifying, naming, and characterizing the cliques and crowds in the school environment. Although cliques are often portrayed as negative or exclusive, membership in a clique has many positive benefits, including helping adolescents to explore values, personal identity, and social skills.

adolescents tend to display positive conflict resolution and academic skills, prosocial behavior, and leadership qualities, whereas rejected and poorly accepted children tend to display aggressive and antisocial behavior and low levels of academic performance (Frey & Nolen, 2010; Wentzel et al., 2004; Zettergren, 2003). These socially rejected children appear to be at great risk for later academic and social problems (Frey & Nolen, 2010). Wentzel et al. (2004) found, however, that rejected middle school children who were socially submissive did not display the same school-related problems as their rejected aggressive counterparts. These findings suggest that peer rejection and negative behavior together place these children at risk.

Peer relationships in adolescence have also been studied in terms of cliques and crowds with whom adolescents associate (Barber, Eccles, & Stone, 2001). A clique is a fairly small, intimate group that is defined by the common interests, activities, and friends of its members. In contrast, a crowd is a larger group defined by its reputation. Allegiance to a clique or crowd is common during adolescence but is not necessarily long-term or stable. Although the pressure to conform can be very powerful within these groups, only adolescents who are highly motivated to belong appear to be influenced by these norms in significant ways.

EMOTIONAL DEVELOPMENT Most adolescents experience emotional conflicts at some point. This is hardly surprising; they are going through rapid and dramatic changes in body image, expected roles, and peer relationships. The transitions from elementary to middle school or from junior high to high school can also be quite stressful (Anderman & Mueller, 2010; Sparks, 2011a). For most adolescents, emotional distress is temporary and is successfully handled, but for some the stresses lead to delinquency, drug abuse, or suicide attempts (Fisher, 2006). Emotional health is also a key factor in academic success in school (Lowe, 2011).

Emotional problems related to the physical, cognitive, and social development of upper elementary school-age children are common. Though preadolescents are generally happy and optimistic, they also have many fears, such as fear of not being accepted into a peer group, not having a best friend, being punished by their parents, having their parents get a divorce, or not doing well in school.

Other emotions of this age group include anger (and fear of being unable to control it), guilt, frustration, and jealousy. Preadolescents need help in realizing that these emotions and fears are a natural part of growing up. Adults must let them talk about these emotions and fears, even if they seem unrealistic to an adult. Feelings of guilt often arise when there is a conflict between children's actions (based on values of the peer group) and their parents' values. Anger is a common emotion at this age and is displayed with more intensity than many other emotions. Just as they often tell their preadolescents that they should not be afraid, parents often tell them that they should not get angry. Unfortunately, this is an unrealistic expectation, even for adults.

PROBLEMS OF ADOLESCENCE Adolescence can be a time of great risk for many, because teenagers are now able, for the first time, to engage in behaviors or make decisions that can have long-term negative consequences (Hamm & Zhang, 2010; Rice & Dolgin, 2008).

Emotional Disorders Secondary school teachers should be sensitive to the stresses that adolescents face and should realize that emotional disturbances are common (Galambos & Costigan, 2003). They should understand that depressed, hopeless, or unaccountably angry behavior can be a clue that the adolescent needs help, and they should try to put such students in touch with school counselors or other psychologically trained adults (Fisher, 2006). There are several proven approaches to improving emotional adjustment among adolescents (see Bywater & Sharples, 2012).

Bullying Taunting, harassment, and aggression toward weaker or friendless peers occur at all age levels, but they can become particularly serious as children enter early adolescence (Bluestein, 2011; Goodwin, 2011a; Lawner & Terzian, 2013; Rodkin, 2011). In fact, the amount of bullying that students think exists in their school is a key predictor of dropout (Cornell, Huang, Gregory, & Fan, 2013). For strategies for reducing bullying, see Chapter 11.

Dropping Out Dropping out of secondary school can put adolescents at considerable risk, as most dropouts condemn themselves to low-level occupations, unemployment, and poverty (Freeman & Simonsen, 2015; Rumberger, 2011). Of course, the factors that lead to dropping out begin early in students' school careers; school failure, retention (staying back), assignment to special education, poor attendance, and symptoms of depression all predict dropout (Quiroga, Janosz, Bisset, & Morin, 2013). Dropout rates have generally been declining, especially among African American and Hispanic students, although these students are still disproportionately at risk (Swanson, 2012).

Certification Pointer

Most teacher certification tests will require you to know how development in one domain, such as physical, may affect a student's performance in another domain, such as social.

Connections 3.4

For more on emotional disorders, see Chapter 12.

Dropout rates among students at risk can be greatly reduced by programs that give these students individual attention, high-status roles, and assistance with academic deficits (Battistich, 2010; Comer, 2010; Corrin et al., 2015; MacIver et al., 2010; What Works Clearinghouse (WWC), 2015). Students in smaller and more academically focused high schools tend to drop out at lower rates than other students (Lee & Burkam, 2003), and programs designed to engage students in prosocial activities can improve graduation rates (e.g., Balfanz, 2011; Porowski & Passa, 2011).

Drug and Alcohol Abuse Substance use continues to be widespread among adolescents. Eighty percent of high school seniors have tried alcohol (Jung, 2010), and 31 percent have tried marijuana (National Institute on Drug Abuse, 2005). Not surprisingly, drug and alcohol abuse are strongly connected to school failure, but social and academic success in school greatly reduces the likelihood of drug abuse (Fletcher, 2012).

Connections 3.5
To learn about prevention of delinquency, see Chapter 11.

Delinquency One of the most dangerous problems of adolescence is the beginning of serious delinquency. The problem is far more common among males than among females. Delinquents are usually low achievers who have been given little reason to believe that they can succeed by following the path laid out for them by the school (Hawkins et al., 2000; Thio, 2010; Tolan et al., 2013). Delinquency in adolescence is overwhelmingly a group phenomenon; most delinquent acts are done in groups or with the active support of a delinquent subgroup (Austin & Sciarra, 2010; Goode, 2011). For this reason, successful programs for preventing delinquency and violence among adolescents usually involve group interventions (Coren et al., 2013; Griffin & Botvin, 2012; Haggerty & Kosterman, 2012; Hawkins, Kuklinski, & Fagan, 2012; Silvia et al., 2011).

Risk of Pregnancy Pregnancy and childbirth are serious problems among all groups of female adolescents, but particularly among those from lower-income homes (Susman, Dorn, & Schiefelbein,

THE INTENTIONAL TEACHER
Taking Social, Moral, and Emotional Development into Account in Intentional Teaching

Intentional teachers are aware of the expected developmental characteristics of the students they teach, and are sensitive to the diversity among their students.

- They are aware of the key developmental tasks their students are trying to accomplish (in Erikson's scheme) and help their students toward successful resolution of these tasks.
- They are aware of their students' levels of moral development and give students opportunities to discuss and grapple with moral dilemmas appropriate to their ages.
- They work to create classroom practices that support positive socioemotional development and minimize unnecessary social comparisons or unhealthy competition.
- They help their students develop positive friendships by giving them many opportunities to work in productive groups and by reinforcing friendly, altruistic behavior.
- They find ways for parents to be involved in the school to link efforts between home and school to build positive socioemotional behaviors among all children.
- They watch for bullying and other negative interactions among students and intervene to establish classwide norms against this behavior.

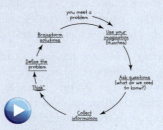

MyEdLab

Application Exercise 3.1

In the Pearson etext, watch a classroom video. Then use the guidelines in "The Intentional Teacher" to answer a set of questions that will help you reflect on and understand the teaching and learning presented in the video.

THEORY INTO PRACTICE

Preventing Adolescents' Problems

Not all adolescents experience serious problems, but among those who are at risk, it is far better to prevent problems before they arise. Many programs have demonstrated success with a wide range of problem behaviors by embedding preventive strategies into the regular curriculum. For example, a number of programs have reduced high-risk behaviors by introducing "life skills training," focusing on skills such as making good decisions and resisting peer pressure (Stipek, de la Sota, & Weishaupt, 1999); others focus on building norms of cooperation, altruism, and social responsibility (Battistich, Watson, Solomon, Lewis, & Schaps, 1999). Involving community agencies to engage children in prosocial behaviors is another frequently recommended practice (Kidron & Fleischman, 2006). Comprehensive whole-school reform models can have an impact on high-risk behaviors, especially truancy and dropping out, in middle school (Balfanz & MacIver, 2000) and high school (Bottoms, Feagin, & Han, 2005; Darling-Hammond, Ancess, & Ort, 2002; McPartland, Balfanz, Jordan, & Legters, 2002; MDRC, 2013; Stiefel, Schwartz, & Wiswall, 2015).

InTASC 3

Learning Environments

Certification Pointer

On your teacher certification test, you may be asked about the impact of students' physical, social, emotional, moral, and cognitive development on their learning.

2003). Just as many adolescents engage in delinquent behavior to try to establish their independence from adult control, adolescent females often engage in sex, and in many cases have children, to force the world to see them as adults. Because early childbearing makes it difficult for adolescent females to continue their schooling or get jobs, it is a primary cause of the continuation of the cycle of poverty into which many adolescent mothers were themselves born. Of course, the other side of teen pregnancy is teen fatherhood. Teen fathers also suffer behavioral and academic problems in school. Many programs intended to delay intercourse and reduce pregnancy exist. Research on these programs finds that sex education programs that emphasize both abstinence and the use of condoms and other birth control methods are more effective than those that emphasize abstinence only (Card & Benner, 2008).

Risk of Sexually Transmitted Diseases Compounding the traditional risks of early sexual activity is the rise in AIDS and other sexually transmitted diseases. AIDS is still rare during the adolescent years (National Institute of Allergy and Infectious Diseases, 2002). However, because full-blown AIDS can take 10 years to appear, unprotected sex, needle sharing, and other high-risk behaviors among teens contribute to the high rates of AIDS among young adults. The appearance of AIDS has made the need for early, explicit sex education a critical, potentially life-or-death matter. However, knowledge alone is not enough; sexually active adolescents must have access to condoms and realistic, psychologically sophisticated inducements to use them.

Sexual Identity It is during adolescence that people begin to explore their sexual identity, including young people who begin to identify with a gay or lesbian orientation. Gay, lesbian, bisexual, and transgendered adolescents can experience great stress and difficulties with their parents (Robinson & Espelage, 2011). They can especially have problems with peers, who might have strong norms against homosexuality and may engage in taunting, rejection, or even violent behavior toward gay or lesbian peers (GLSEN, 2009). Teachers need to model acceptance of gay and lesbian students and strictly enforce school rules forbidding disrespect toward anyone, gay or straight (Koppelman & Goodhart, 2008).

MyEdLab **Self-Check 3.2**

SUMMARY

What Are Some Views of Personal and Social Development?

Erikson proposed eight stages of psychosocial development, each dominated by a particular psychosocial crisis precipitated through interaction with the social environment. In Stage I, trust versus mistrust, the goal is to develop a sense of trust through interaction with caretakers. In Stage II, autonomy versus doubt (18 months to age 3), children have a dual desire to hold on and to let go. In Stage III, initiative versus guilt (3 to 6 years of age), children elaborate their sense of self through exploration of the environment. Children enter school during Stage IV, industry versus inferiority (6 to 12 years of age), when academic success or failure is central. In Stage V, identity versus role confusion (12 to 18 years), adolescents turn increasingly to their peer group and begin their searches for partners and careers. Adulthood brings Stage VI (intimacy versus isolation), Stage VII (generativity versus self-absorption), and Stage VIII (integrity versus despair).

What Are Some Views of Moral Development?

According to Piaget, children develop heteronomous morality (obedience to authority through moral realism) by around age 6 and later advance to autonomous morality (rational morality based on moral principles). Kohlberg's stages of moral reasoning reflect children's responses to moral dilemmas. In Stages 1 and 2 (the preconventional level), children obey rules set down by others while maximizing self-interest. In Stages 3 and 4 (the conventional level), the individual adopts rules, believes in law and order, and seeks the approval of others. In Stages 5 and 6 (the postconventional level), people define their own values in terms of abstract ethical principles they have chosen to follow.

How Do Children Develop Socially and Emotionally?

During the Preschool Years

Socioemotional development in early childhood can be partly described in terms of Erikson's psychosocial stage of initiative versus guilt. Peer relationships help children overcome the egocentrism that Piaget described as characteristic of preoperational thinking. Prosocial behavior includes caring, sharing, comforting, and cooperating. Parten identified four categories of play—solitary, parallel, associative, and cooperative—that reflect increasing levels of social interaction and sophistication. Play hones children's linguistic, cognitive, social, and creative skills.

During the Elementary Years

In middle childhood, children may be seen as resolving the psychosocial crisis that Erikson described as industry versus inferiority. School becomes a major influence on development, a place where the child develops a public self, builds social skills, and establishes self-esteem on the basis of academic and nonacademic competencies. In preadolescence, between ages 9 and 12, conformity in peer relations, mixed-sex peer groupings, and challenges to adult authority become more important.

During the Middle School and High School Years

Adolescents may be seen as resolving Erikson's psychosocial crisis of identity versus role confusion. They pay attention to how other people view them, search the past, experiment with roles, act on feelings and beliefs, and gradually seek greater autonomy and intimacy in peer relations. Foreclosure occurs when the individual chooses a role prematurely, but by late adolescence, most individuals have developed a state of identity achievement. Many factors, such as dropping out, substance abuse, and AIDS, place adolescents at risk.

KEY TERMS

Review the following key terms from the chapter.

associative play 52

autonomous morality 49

conventional level of morality 50

cooperative play 52

foreclosure 57

heteronomous morality 49

identity achievement 57

identity diffusion 57

moral dilemmas 49

moratorium 57

parallel play 52

peers 52

postconventional level of morality 50

preconventional level of morality 50

prosocial behaviors 52

psychosocial crisis 46

psychosocial theory 45

puberty 58

reflectivity 57

self-concept 53

self-esteem 53

social comparison 53

solitary play 52

SELF-ASSESSMENT: PRACTICING FOR LICENSURE

Directions: The chapter-opening vignette addresses indicators that are often assessed in state licensure exams. Reread the chapter-opening vignette, and then respond to the following questions.

1. As noted in the interaction between Sam and Billy, there are enormous differences between students several years apart. According to the information presented in the chapter, which of the following behaviors is more likely to be exhibited by Billy than by Sam?
   a. Obey parents
   b. Conform to peer demands
   c. Assert independence
   d. Be idealistic

2. According to the information presented in the chapter, which of the following behaviors is more likely to be exhibited by Sam than by Billy?
   a. Follow simple rules
   b. Defy convention
   c. Expect punishment for disobedience
   d. Be dependent on parents

3. Typically, a young child's social life evolves in relatively predictable ways. The social network grows from an intimate relationship with parents or other guardians to relationships with
   a. nonrelated adults, peers, and then other family members.
   b. peers, nonrelated adults, and then other family members.
   c. other family members, peers, and then nonrelated adults.
   d. other family members, nonrelated adults, and then peers.

4. For students like Sam Stevens, who is entering the stage of what Piaget terms "formal operations," which of the following instructional strategies would be considered developmentally appropriate?
   a. Teach Sam to hear specific sounds as he reads (phonemic awareness).
   b. Allow Sam to invent spellings by making judgments about sounds and by relating the sounds to the letters he knows.
   c. Help Sam to resolve the personality crisis of initiative versus guilt.
   d. Require Sam to write assignments that require debate (argue pro or con on an issue).

5. One of the first signs of early adolescence is the appearance of reflectivity. What is this?
   a. A return to egocentric thought
   b. The development of initiative
   c. The ability to think about one's own mind
   d. Joining others in working toward a common goal

6. Design a lesson that would be considered developmentally appropriate for someone Billy's age. Explain why you believe it would be appropriate.

7. Design a lesson that would be considered developmentally appropriate for someone Sam's age. Explain why you believe it would be appropriate.

8. One of the most serious problems of adolescence is delinquency. Delinquents are usually
   a. high achievers who turn to delinquency out of boredom.
   b. socially adept at leading others into crime.
   c. low achievers who feel they can't succeed in school.
   d. late-maturing adolescents.

9. According to Kohlberg's theory of moral development, how can a teacher help her third-graders move past their belief that "rules are rules with no exceptions"?
   a. Challenge the students' reasoning with explanations from the next higher stage.
   b. Discuss moral dilemmas.
   c. Read books to the class about moral behavior.
   d. Ask each student to write a story about someone who did not follow the rules.

MyEdLab **Licensure Exam 3.1** Answer questions and receive instant feedback in your Pearson eText in MyEdLab.

CHAPTER FOUR

Student Diversity

LEARNING OUTCOMES

At the end of this chapter, you should be able to:

4.1 Discuss how socioeconomic status can affect achievement, and identify ways schools can help children from low-income families succeed

4.2 Discuss how race, ethnicity, and language differences can each affect students' school experiences, and identify important principles for teaching in culturally diverse schools and also ways to help English learners succeed in English-speaking classrooms

4.3 Describe how gender bias can impact schooling, and identify ways to support all students with equality and respect

4.4 Describe common definitions of and theories about intelligence and learning styles

4.5 Describe how knowledge of student diversity informs intentional teaching

Marva Vance and John Rossi are first-year teachers at Emma Lazarus Elementary School. It's November, and Marva and John are meeting over coffee to discuss an event dreaded by many a first-year teacher: the upcoming Thanksgiving pageant.

"This is driving me crazy!" Marva starts. "Our classes are like the United Nations. How are we supposed to cast a Thanksgiving pageant? I have three Navajo children. Should I cast them as Native Americans, or would they be offended? My Vietnamese kids have probably never seen a turkey, and the idea of eating a big bird like that must be revolting to them. I wonder how meaningful this will be to my African Americans. I remember when I was in a Thanksgiving pageant and our teacher had us African American students be stagehands because she said there weren't any African American Pilgrims! Besides, what am I going to do about a narrator? Jose says he wants to be narrator, but his English isn't too good. Lakesha would be good, but she's often out for debate tournaments and would miss some rehearsals.

I've also been worrying about the hunters. Should they all be boys? Wouldn't it be gender stereotyping if the boys were hunters and the girls were cooks? What about Mark? He uses a wheelchair. Should I make him a hunter?"

John sighs and looks into his coffee. "I know what you're talking about. I just let my kids sign up for each part in the pageant. The boys signed up as hunters, the girls as cooks, the Native Americans . . . well, you get the idea. Maybe it's too late for us to do anything about stereotyping when the kids have already bought into their roles."

USING YOUR EXPERIENCE

CRITICAL THINKING Spend 4 or 5 minutes writing a plausible ending to the vignette. What did Marva Vance end up doing, and what were the results?

COOPERATIVE LEARNING In small groups of four students, role-play Marva and John's situation. Then discuss the issues they are raising. After 6 minutes, report your group's conclusions to the class.

Students differ. They differ in ethnicity, culture, social class, and home language. They differ in gender. Some have disabilities, and some are gifted or talented in one or more areas. They differ in performance level, learning rate, and learning style. Their differences can have important implications for instruction, curriculum, and school policies and practices. Marva and John are concerned with student diversity as it relates to the Thanksgiving pageants they are planning, but diversity and its meaning for education are important issues every day, not only on Thanksgiving. This chapter discusses some of the most important ways that North American students differ and some of the methods by which teachers can accept, accommodate, and celebrate student diversity in daily teaching. However, diversity is such an important theme that almost every chapter in this book touches on it. You are more than an instructor of students. Together with your students, you are one of the builders of tomorrow's society. A critical part of every teacher's role is to ensure that the equal opportunity we hold to be central to our nationhood is translated into equal opportunity in day-to-day life in the classroom.

WHAT IS THE IMPACT OF CULTURE ON TEACHING AND LEARNING?

If you have ever traveled to a foreign country, you noticed differences in behaviors, attitudes, dress, language, and food. In fact, part of the fun of traveling is discovering these differences in culture, or the shared norms, traditions, behaviors, language, and perceptions of a group (King, 2002). Though we usually think of cultural differences mostly as national differences, there is probably as much cultural diversity within the United States as between the United States and other industrialized nations. The life of a middle-class family in the United States or Canada may be more like that of a middle-class family in Italy, Ireland, or Israel than like that of a low-income family living a mile away. Yet although we value cultural differences between nations, differences within our own society are often less valued. The tendency is to value the characteristics of mainstream high-status groups and devalue those of other groups.

By the time children enter school, they have absorbed many aspects of the culture in which they were raised, such as language, beliefs, attitudes, ways of behaving, and food preferences. More accurately, most children are affected by several cultures, in that most are members of many overlapping groups. The cultural background of an individual child is affected by his or her ethnicity, socioeconomic status, religion, home language, gender, and other group identities and experiences (see Figure 4.1). Many of the behaviors associated with growing up in a particular culture have important consequences for classroom instruction (Banks, 2015; King & McInerney, 2014). For example, schools expect children to speak standard English. This is easy for students from homes in which standard English is spoken but difficult for those whose families speak other languages or significantly divergent dialects of English. Schools also expect students to be highly verbal, to spend most of their time working independently, and to compete with other students for grades and recognition. However, many cultures place a higher value on cooperation and peer orientation than on independence and competitiveness (Boykin & Noguera, 2011). Because the culture of the school reflects mainstream middle-class values, and because most teachers are from

FIGURE 4.1 • Cultural Diversity and Individual Identity

Source: Reprinted with the permission of James A. Banks from James A. Banks, *Cultural Diversity and Education: Foundations, Curriculum, and Teaching* (5th edition). Boston: Allyn and Bacon Pearson, Figure 4.3 (p. 77). Boston: Allyn and Bacon, 2006.

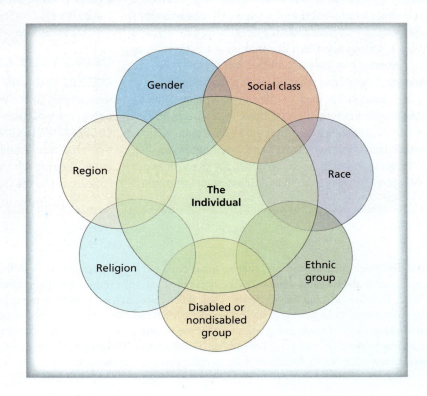

middle-class backgrounds, the child from a different culture is often at a disadvantage. Understanding students' backgrounds is critical for effectively teaching both academic material and the behaviors and expectations of the school (Asher, 2007).

HOW DOES SOCIOECONOMIC STATUS AFFECT STUDENT ACHIEVEMENT?

One important characteristic in which students differ is social class. Even in small rural towns where almost everyone is the same in ethnicity and religion, the children of the town's bankers, doctors, and teachers probably have a different upbringing from that experienced by the children of most farmhands or domestic workers.

Sociologists define social class, or **socioeconomic status (SES)**, in terms of an individual's income, occupation, education, and prestige in society (Duncan & Murnane, 2014a, b; Entwisle, Alexander, & Olson, 2010; Thompson & Hickey, 2011). These factors tend to go together, so SES is most often measured as a combination of the individual's income and years of education because these are most easily quantified. Table 4.1 shows the relation between typical social class groupings in the United States and family income.

In this book the term *upper middle class* or *upper class* is used to refer to families whose wage earners are in occupations requiring significant education past high school, *middle class* to those with good jobs that require some education past high school, *working class* to those who have relatively stable occupations not requiring higher education, and *lower class* to those in the urban or rural underclass who are often unemployed and might be living on government assistance.

However, social class indicates more than level of income and education. Along with social class goes a pervasive set of behaviors, expectations, and attitudes, which intersect with and are affected by other cultural factors. Students' social class origins are likely to have a profound effect on attitudes and behaviors in school. Students from working-class or lower-class backgrounds are less likely than middle-class students to enter school knowing how to count, name letters, cut with scissors, or name colors. They are less likely to perform well in school than are children from middle-class homes (Duncan & Murnane, 2014a, b; Entwisle et al., 2010; Sackett, Kuncel, Arneson, Cooper, & Waters, 2009; Sirin, 2005). Their parents are less likely to have close relationships with their children's teachers or to be extensively involved with the school (Nzinga-Johnson, Baker, & Aupperlee, 2009). Of course, these differences are true only on the average; many working-class and lower-class parents do an outstanding job of supporting their children's success in school, and many working-class and lower-class children achieve at a very high level (Erberber et al., 2015). Social class cuts across categories of race and ethnicity. Although it is true that Latino and African American families are, on average, lower in social class than white families, there is substantial overlap; the majority of all low-income families in the United States are white, and there are many middle-class nonwhite families (U.S. Census Bureau, 2013). Definitions of social class are based on such factors as income, occupation, and education, never on race or ethnicity.

Table 4.2 shows the reading performance of eighth-graders on the 2015 National Assessment of Educational Progress, or NAEP (National Center for Education Statistics [NCES], 2015). Note that children of more highly educated parents (a key component of social class) consistently

TABLE 4.1 • Social Class Groupings

	FAMILY INCOME
Top 5%	$186,000 or more
Upper class	$100,000 or more
Upper middle class	$63,000 to $100,000
Lower middle class	$40,000 to $63,000
Working class	$20,000 to $40,000
Lower class	$20,000 or less

Source: Based on data from U.S. Census Bureau, 2013 Annual Social and Economic Supplement to the Current Population Survey.

TABLE 4.2 • NAEP Reading Scores (2015) by Parents' Education: Grade 8

PARENTS' EDUCATION	PERCENTAGE SCORING AT OR ABOVE PROFICIENT
Graduated from college	51
Some education after high school	14
Graduated from high school	15
Did not finish high school	7

Source: Based on National Center for Education Statistics (NCES), 2015, *National Assessment of Educational Progress,* Washington, DC: Author.

scored higher than children of less educated parents. Similarly, among fourth-graders who qualified for free or reduced-price lunches, which the NAEP uses as an indicator of a child's family income, only 15 percent scored at or above "proficient" on the reading portion of the NAEP, in comparison to 42 percent of fourth-graders who did not qualify (NCES, 2015).

The Role of Child-Rearing Practices and Other Family Factors

Average differences between middle-class and lower-class parents in child-rearing practices are the main reason for differences in school achievement. As one indicator of this, there is much evidence that lower-class children adopted into middle-class homes achieve at much higher levels than their nonadopted (usually low-income) brothers and sisters, and at levels similar to those of their siblings born to their adoptive parents (van IJzendoorn, Juffer, & Klein Poelhuis, 2005).

Much research has focused on the differences in child-rearing practices between the average middle-class family and the average working-class or lower-class family (Alexander, Entwisle, & Olson, 2014; Dickerson & Popli, 2012; Holmes & Kiernan, 2013). Many children from low-income families receive an upbringing that is less consistent with expected school behavior than the upbringing middle-class children receive. By the time they enter school, middle-class children are likely to be good at following directions, explaining and understanding reasons, and comprehending and using complex language, whereas working-class or lower-class children may have less experience in all these areas (Parkay, 2006). Children from disadvantaged homes are more likely to have poor access to health care and may suffer from diseases of poverty such as lead poisoning (Murphey & Redd, 2014). They are more likely to be homeless and more likely to move often from school to school (Fantuzzo et al., 2012; Voight, Shinn, & Nation, 2012). Their mothers are less likely to have received good prenatal care (McLoyd, 1998). These factors can delay cognitive development, which also affects school readiness. Of course low-income families lack resources of all kinds to help their children succeed (Children's Defense Fund, 2009; Ryan, Fauth, & Brooks-Gunn, 2013). For example, children from disadvantaged families are far more likely to have uncorrected vision, hearing problems, asthma, or other health problems that may inhibit their success in school (Natriello, 2002; Rothstein, 2004). Children from very disadvantaged, chaotic homes may suffer from "toxic stress," which can have lifelong consequences (Johnson, Riley, Granger, & Riis, 2012; Shonkoff et al., 2012;).

Another important difference between middle-class and lower-class families is in the kinds of activities parents tend to do with their children. Middle-class parents are likely to express high expectations for their children and to reward them for intellectual development. They are likely to provide good models for language use, to talk and read to their children frequently, and to encourage reading and other learning activities. They are particularly apt to provide all sorts of learning materials for children at home, such as computers, books, and educational games (Entwisle et al., 2010; Yeung, Linver, & Brooks-Gunn, 2002). They are more likely to read to their children before they enter school (Hood et al., 2008). These parents are also likely to expose their children to learning experiences outside the home, such as museums, concerts, and zoos (Duke, 2000). They are more likely to be able to help their children succeed in school and to be involved in their education (Heymann & Earle, 2000). Middle-class parents are likely to expect and demand high achievement from their children; working-class and lower-class parents are more likely to demand good behavior and obedience (Knapp & Woolverton, 1995). Helping parents who are disadvantaged engage in more enriching interactions with their children can have a substantial impact on their children's cognitive performance. For example, the Parent–Child Home Program (PCHP) initiative provides mothers who are disadvantaged with toys for their toddlers and demonstrations of ways to play and talk with children to enhance their intellectual development. Studies have found strong and lasting effects of this simple intervention on children's cognitive skills and school success, in comparison to children whose parents did not receive PCHP services (Allen & Seth, 2004; Levenstein, Levenstein, & Oliver, 2002).

ON THE WEB
You can learn more about the Parent–Child Home Program (PCHP) by visiting parent-child.org.

The Link between Income and Summer Learning

Several studies have found that although low-SES and high-SES children make similar progress in academic achievement during the school year, the high-SES children continue to make progress over the summer, whereas low-SES children fall behind (Allington et al., 2010; Borman, Benson, & Overman, 2005; Heyns, 2002; Slates, Alexander, Entwisle, & Olson, 2012). These findings suggest that home environment influences not only academic readiness for school but also the level of achievement throughout students' careers in school. Middle-class children are more likely to be engaged in school-like activities during the summer and to have available more school-like materials. Working-class and lower-class children may be receiving less academically relevant stimulation at home and are more likely to be forgetting what they learned in school (Hill, 2001). The "summer slide" phenomenon has led many schools to offer summer school to at-risk students, and research reveals that this can be an effective strategy (Borman & Dowling, 2006; Kim & Quinn, 2013; Martin, Sharp, & Mehta, 2013; Zvoch & Stevens, 2013).

Connections 4.1
For more on summer school programs, see Chapter 9.

ON THE WEB
For information on summer learning, see summerlearning.org.

The Role of Schools as Middle-Class Institutions

Students from backgrounds other than the mainstream middle class may have difficulties in school in part because their upbringing emphasizes different behaviors from those valued in school. Two of these characteristically middle-class values are individuality and future time orientation (Jagers & Carroll, 2002). Most U.S. classrooms operate on the assumption that children should do their own work. Helping others is often defined as cheating. Students are expected to compete for grades, for their teachers' attention and praise, and for other rewards. Competition and individual work are values that are instilled early on in most middle-class homes. However, students from lower-class backgrounds are less willing to compete and are more interested in cooperating with their peers than are students from middle-class backgrounds (Boykin & Noguera, 2011). These students have often learned from an early age to rely on their communities, friends, and family and

Connections 4.2
For more on cooperative learning strategies, see Chapter 8.

Certification Pointer

Teacher certification tests may require that you identify the factors outside of school that can affect student learning. These include culture, family circumstances, community environments, health, and economic conditions.

have always helped and been helped by others. Not surprisingly, students who are most oriented toward cooperation with others learn best in cooperation with others, whereas those who prefer to compete learn best in competition with others (Slavin, 2011). Because of the mismatch between the cooperative orientation of many children who are minority group members or of lower SES and the competitive orientation of the school environment, many researchers (e.g., Boykin & Noguera, 2011; Howard, 2014) have argued that there is a structural bias in traditional classrooms that works against these children. They recommend using cooperative learning strategies at least part of the time with these students so that they receive instruction consistent with their cultural orientations (Slavin, 2011; Webb, 2008).

School and Community Factors

Often, children from low-income families are placed at risk for school failure by the characteristics of the communities they live in and the schools they attend (Aikens & Barbarin, 2008; Katz, 2015). For example, school funding in most areas of the United States is correlated with social class; middle-class children are likely to attend schools with greater resources, better-paid (and therefore better-qualified) teachers, and other advantages (Darling-Hammond, 2008). On top of these differences, schools serving low-income neighborhoods may have to spend much more on security, on services for children having difficulties, and on many other needs, leaving even less for regular education (Weissbourd & Dodge, 2012). This lack of resources can significantly affect student achievement (Land & Legters, 2002; Rothstein, 2004). In very impoverished neighborhoods, crime, a lack of positive role models, inadequate social and health services, and other factors can create an environment that undermines children's motivation, achievement, and mental health. Children in high-poverty communities tend to move a great deal and to have periods of homelessness, which of course have devastating effects on their learning (Murphy, 2011). In addition, teachers may hold low expectations for children who are disadvantaged, and this can affect their motivation and achievement (Becker & Luthar, 2002; Borman & Overman, 2004; Hauser-Cram, Sirin, & Stipek, 2003).

Promoting Resilience among Students Who Are Disadvantaged

Low socioeconomic status does not, of course, automatically doom children to failure. Many children at risk develop what is called *resilience,* the ability to succeed despite many risk factors (Borman & Overman, 2004; Erberber et al., 2015; Glantz, Johnson, & Huffman, 2002; Waxman, Gray, & Padron, 2002). Borman & Overman (2004), for example, used a large, national data set to look at students from disadvantaged homes who were succeeding in mathematics. At the individual level, resilient students were characterized by high self-esteem, positive attitudes toward school, and high motivation. More important, schools that produced resilient students were places that provided a supportive school community, a safe and orderly environment, and positive teacher–student relationships. For example, resilient students were more likely to report that "most of my teachers really listen to what I have to say" and disagree that "in class I feel put down by my teachers."

Other researchers have also identified characteristics of schools that promote resilience. These include high academic standards (Gorski, 2013; Jensen, 2014; Parrett & Budge, 2012), structured schools and classes with clear rules (Pressley, Raphael, & Gallagher, 2004), and widespread participation in after-school activities (Wigfield, Byrnes, & Eccles, 2006).

MyEdLab
Video Example 4.1

Watch as a school superintendent describes the challenges and rewards of working in urban schools. What does his experience suggest about the resilience of the students he works with?

InTASC 10

Leadership and Collaboration

ON THE WEB

For more on building resilience, see http://www.childtrends.org/what-can-schools-do-to-build-resilience-in-their-students/?utm_source=E-News%3A+Top+10+Most-Read+Research+of+2015&utm_campaign=E-news+1%2F7%2F16&utm_medium=email

School, Family, and Community Partnerships

If family background is a key factor for explaining differences in student achievement, then it follows that involving families in support of children's school success can be part of the solution. As a professional educator, you can reach out to families and other community members in a variety of ways to improve communication and respect between home and school and to give parents strategies to help their own children succeed. Epstein and colleagues (2002) describe six types of involvement that schools might emphasize in a comprehensive partnership with parents (also see Axford et al., 2012; Berger & Riojas-Cortez, 2016; See & Gorard, 2013; Walker & Hoover-Dempsey, 2008).

1. **Parenting.** Assist families with parenting and child-rearing skills, family support, understanding child and adolescent development, and setting home conditions to support learning at each age and grade level. Obtain information from families to help schools understand families' backgrounds, cultures, and goals for children.

2. **Communicating.** Inform families about school programs and student progress with school-to-home and home-to-school communications. Technology makes it easy to open up two-way communication with most families (Rideout, 2014), using email, Facebook, Twitter, and websites. Create two-way channels so that families can easily correspond with teachers and administrators.

"Mrs. Rogers, I think this is taking the idea of parent involvement a little too far!"

3. **Volunteering.** Improve recruitment, training, activities, and schedules to involve families as volunteers and audiences at the school or in other locations to support students and school programs.

4. **Learning at home.** Involve families with their children in academic learning activities at home, including homework, goal setting, and other curricular-linked activities and decisions. Encourage parents to read to children and to listen to them read.

5. **Decision making.** Include families as participants in school decisions, governance, and advocacy activities through PTA, committees, councils, and other parent organizations. Assist family representatives in obtaining information from, and giving information to, those they represent.

6. **Collaborating with the community.** Coordinate with community businesses, agencies, cultural and civic organizations, colleges or universities, and other groups (Price, 2008). Enable students to contribute service to the community.

Correlational research on parent involvement has clearly shown that parents who involve themselves in their children's educations have higher-achieving children than other parents (Flouri & Buchanan, 2004; Lee & Bowen, 2006; Van Voorhis et al., 2013). However, there has been more debate about the impacts of school programs to increase parent involvement. Many studies have shown positive effects of parent and community involvement programs, especially those that emphasize parents' roles as educators for their own children (see Comer, 2005; Epstein et al., 2002; Hood, Conlon, & Andrews, 2008; McElvany & Artelt, 2009; Patall, Cooper, & Robinson, 2008; Sanders, Allen-Jones, & Abel, 2002; Zigler, Pfannenstiel, & Seitz, 2008). However, many other studies have failed to find such benefits (Mattingly, Prisllin, McKenzie, Rodriguez, & Kayzar, 2002; Pomerantz, Moorman, & Litwak, 2007; Schutz, 2006). Providing very disadvantaged mothers with regular assistance from a trained nurse, especially in a program called The Nurse–Family Partnership, has been shown to improve many parent and child outcomes, including the child's achievement (Miller, 2015; Olds et al., 2007; Pinquart & Teubert, 2010; U.S. Administration for Children and Families, 2014).

A recent review of research on parents' reading with their grade K–3 children by Sénéchal and Young (2008) found that parents who explicitly taught their children to read had a much larger impact than those who only listened to their children reading. Another recent review by Jeynes (2012) compared the outcomes of various types of parent involvement programs for urban students. It found that the most effective programs for improving students' learning were those that emphasized shared reading between parents and children, as well as other partnerships between parents and teachers around

MyEdLab
Video Example 4.2

In this district, the partnership with the community is strong, allowing the students to have access to resources, such as computers, that they otherwise would not have been able to afford. How might you build strong and supportive long-term relationships with organizations within your own community?

academic and behavioral issues. Kim & Hill (2015) found that positive effects of parent involvement were equal for fathers and mothers. Programs that emphasized home–school communication and checking homework also had positive effects on learning. Another review on this topic by Mbwana, Terzian, and Moore (2009) found positive effects for parenting skills training programs and parent–child involvement programs, but programs without opportunities for parents to practice new skills with their children were less effective.

What the research suggests is that building positive relations with parents and giving parents practical means of helping their children succeed in school are important in improving the achievement and adjustment of all children.

Certification Pointer

Teacher certification tests may require you to outline specific actions that you might take as a teacher to connect the school and students' home environments to benefit your students' learning.

Supporting the Achievement of Children from Low-Income Groups

Schools can do a great deal to enable children from low-income families to succeed in school (Borman, 2002/2003; Carter & Darling-Hammond, 2016; Duncan & Murnane, 2014b; Gorski, 2013; Neuman, 2008; Parrett & Budge, 2012; Ryan, Fauth, & Brooks-Gunn, 2013; Slavin, 2002). A study by Aikens & Barbarin (2008) found that while social class was a strong predictor of children's starting point in kindergarten, their gains in reading from then on depended more on their schools and neighborhoods. Furthermore, there are now many intensive interventions designed to help develop children's cognitive skills early in life and to help their parents do a better job of preparing them for school (Chambers, de Botton, Cheung, & Slavin, 2013; Reynolds, Magnuson & Ou, 2010; Traylor, 2012). Studies of these programs have shown long-term positive effects for children growing up in very impoverished families, especially when the programs are continued into the early elementary grades (Conyers, Reynolds, & Ou, 2003; Duncan & Murnane, 2014b; Ramey & Ramey, 1998; Reynolds, Temple, Robertson, & Mann, 2002; Zimmerman, Rodriguez, Rewey, & Heidemann, 2008). One-to-one tutoring and small-group programs for struggling first-graders, for example, have shown substantial effects on the reading achievement of children who are at risk (Chambers et al., 2011; Slavin & Madden, 2015; May et al., 2015; Slavin, Lake, Davis, & Madden, 2011; Vernon-Feagans & Ginsberg, 2011; Wanzek et al., 2013). Small-group math programs also have been found to significantly increase achievement for children struggling in math (Fuchs et al., 2013; Gersten et al., 2015; Rolfhus et al., 2012). Success for All (Borman et al., 2007; Rowan, Correnti, Miller, & Camburn, 2009; Slavin, Madden, Chambers, & Haxby, 2009), which combines effective instructional programs, tutoring, and family support services, has demonstrated substantial and lasting impacts on the achievement of children in high-poverty schools. Other whole-school reform models, such as James Comer's (2010) School Development Program, America's Choice (Glazer, 2009), and the Talent Development High School (Balfanz, Jordan & Legters, 2004; MacIver et al., 2010), also have shown positive outcomes in high-poverty schools (see Cohen et al., 2014). Significant reductions in class size have been found to be particularly beneficial to children in high-poverty elementary schools, at least in the early grades (Finn et al., 2003), and these effects are long-lasting (Konstantopoulos & Chung, 2009). Small-group interventions for struggling students in secondary schools can also be effective (De Vivo, 2011; Slavin, Cheung, Groff, & Lake, 2008; Vaughn & Fletcher, 2011; Wanzek et al., 2013). High-quality summer school programs (Borman & Boulay, 2004; Borman, Goetz, & Dowling, 2009) can provide opportunities to move students who are at risk toward success. In fact, one large, randomized experiment found that disadvantaged students who were just given books to read during the summer gained significantly in reading performance (Allington et al., 2010), although other studies have not found benefits of this (e.g., Wilkins et al., 2012). These and other programs and practices demonstrate that low achievement by lower-class children is not inevitable. Achievement can be greatly improved by use of strategies that are readily available to schools (see Datnow, Lasky, Stringfield, & Teddlie, 2005; Jensen, 2013; Parrett & Budge, 2012), and researchers routinely find and describe high-poverty schools that produce high achievement (Center for Public Education, 2008; Chenoweth, 2009).

Nonschool Solutions to Achievement Problems of Children Who Are Disadvantaged

In a 2004 book, Richard Rothstein makes an important set of observations about the gaps in achievement between children who are middle-class and children who are disadvantaged. He

THEORY INTO PRACTICE

Parent Involvement

Parents and other family members have considerable influence over their children's success in school. If you establish positive relationships with parents, you can help them see the importance of supporting the school's educational objectives by, for instance, providing an uncluttered, quiet place for their children to do homework. The more clearly you communicate your expectations for their role in their children's learning, the more likely they will be to play that role. For example, if you expect children to practice reading every evening for homework, sending a form for parents to sign each night communicates the importance of the activity. Other strategies for involving parents in their children's learning include the following (see Berger & Riojas-Cortez, 2016; Kraft & Dougherty, 2013; Mendler, 2012; Ramirez & Soto-Hinman, 2009; Ridnouer, 2011; Walker & Hoover-Dempsey, 2008).

1. *Home visits.* At the beginning of the school year, it is useful to arrange for visits to your students' homes. Seeing where students come from gives you additional understanding of the supports and constraints that might affect their cognitive and emotional development.

2. *Frequent newsletters for families.* Informing families about what their children will be learning and how they might support that learning at home can increase student success. If you have English learners in your class, offering the newsletter in their first language is important both in improving communication and in showing respect.

3. *Family workshops.* Inviting parents and caregivers to your classroom so you can explain the program of study, along with your expectations, helps families understand how they can support their children's learning.

4. *Positive calls home.* Hearing good news about their children's schoolwork or behavior helps set up a productive cycle of positive reinforcement and increases the likelihood that the behavior will continue. This is especially helpful for family members whose own experiences with the school system were less than positive.

5. *Inviting family members to volunteer.* Asking family members to help out in your class by sharing their expertise, interests, or hobbies can make them feel valued. They can demonstrate their occupations, share cultural traditions, or help out with field trips or other special projects. Beyond providing extra assistance, this communicates to your students that you value the diversity of knowledge and expertise that their families bring to your class.

6. *Make family members your partners.* Communicating to parents and other family members that you are a team working together to promote their children's achievement makes your job easier and greatly improves parents' attitudes toward school and willingness to work with you in difficult situations as well as good times (Epstein et al., 2002; Mendler, 2012).

notes that major explanations for the difference in achievement come from problems not generally under the control of schools, which could be rectified by enlightened policies. Some of the examples he discusses include the following (also see Garcy, 2009; Joe, Joe, & Rowley, 2009; Ryan et al., 2013).

VISION Rothstein notes that poor children have severe vision impairment at twice the normal rate. Surprisingly, juvenile delinquents have extraordinarily high rates of vision problems. Rothstein cites data indicating that more than 50 percent of children who are minorities or from low-income backgrounds have vision problems that interfere with their academic work. Some require eyeglasses, and others need eye-exercise therapies. A study by Collins et al. (2015) found that second- and third-graders from disadvantaged homes who had vision problems but received free eyeglasses gained substantially in achievement relative to a control group. Even when children from low-income homes have prescriptions for glasses, they often do not obtain glasses. If they do have glasses, they may not wear them to school, or they may be lost or broken but not replaced (Collins et al., 2015).

HEARING Children who are disadvantaged have more hearing problems than middle-class children, in particular because of the failure to get medical care for ear infections (Rothstein, 2004).

LEAD EXPOSURE Children who are disadvantaged are far more likely to live in homes where dust from old lead paint is in the air, or where corroded pipes release lead into drinking water (Sanburn, 2016). Even small amounts of lead can result in loss of cognitive functioning and impaired hearing. Studies have found blood lead levels of poor children to be five times those of middle-class children (Brookes-Gunn & Duncan, 1997).

ASTHMA Poor urban children have remarkably high rates of asthma (Joe et al., 2009). Studies in New York and Chicago (Whitman, Williams, & Shah, 2004) found that one in four inner-city African American children had asthma, six times the national rate. In turn, asthma is a major cause of chronic school absence, and even in school, untreated asthma interferes with academic performance.

MEDICAL CARE Children who are disadvantaged are much less likely than middle-class children to receive adequate medical care. This leads to problems with absenteeism; poor motivation because of poor health; and the vision, hearing, and asthma problems mentioned earlier (Joe et al, 2009).

NUTRITION Although serious malnutrition is rare in the United States, unhealthy diets are common among children who are disadvantaged, and this affects academic performance (Joe et al., 2009). One study (Neisser et al., 1996) found that simply giving children vitamin and mineral supplements improved their test scores.

Rothstein's (2004) argument is that these and other problems associated with poverty could be addressed, and doing so could have a significant impact on the achievement of children from low-income families. Even though there are health agencies and social service agencies that are charged with solving these problems (see, for example, Wulczyn, Smithgall, & Chen, 2009), schools have the advantage that they see the children every day. Simple reforms, such as improving school lunches or providing free eyeglasses that stay at school, might be as effective as much more expensive interventions, such as tutoring or special education, which may not address the root causes of children's problems.

Implications of Socioeconomic Diversity for Teachers

Children enter school with varying degrees of preparation for the school behaviors that lead to success. Their conduct, attitudes, and values also vary. However, the mere fact that some children initially do not know what is expected of them and have fewer entry-level skills than others does not mean that they are destined for academic failure. Although there is a modest positive correlation between social class and achievement, it should not be assumed that this relationship holds for all children from lower-SES families. There are many exceptions. Many working-class and lower-class families can and do provide home environments that are supportive of their children's success in school. Autobiographies of people who have overcome poverty, such as *The Other Wes Moore* (Moore, 2010), often refer to the influence of strong parents and role models with high standards who expected nothing less than the best from their children and did what they could to help them achieve. Although you need to be aware of the struggles encountered by many pupils who are disadvantaged, you also need to avoid converting this knowledge into stereotypes (Jensen, 2009). In fact, there is evidence that middle-class teachers often have low expectations for working-class and lower-class students (Borman & Overman, 2004) and that these low expectations can become a self-fulfilling prophecy, causing students to perform less well than they could have (Becker & Luthar, 2002; Hauser-Cram et al., 2003).

MyEdLab **Self-Check 4.1**

HOW DO ETHNICITY AND RACE AFFECT STUDENTS' SCHOOL EXPERIENCES?

One major determinant of a student's cultural background is his or her ethnic origin. An **ethnic group** is made up of individuals who have a shared sense of identity, usually because of a common place of origin (such as Swedish, Polish, or Greek Americans), religion (such as Jewish or Catholic Americans), or race (such as African or Asian Americans). Note that **ethnicity** is not the same as race; **race** reflects only physical characteristics, such as skin color. The idea that races are distinct from each other even in physical characteristics is increasingly being questioned, and there are certainly no clear boundaries, especially as the number of multiracial people increases (Williams, 2009). Ethnic groups usually share a common culture, which may not be true of all people of a given race. African Americans who are recent immigrants from Nigeria or Jamaica, for example, are from ethnic backgrounds that are quite different from those of African Americans whose families have been in the United States for many generations, even if they share physical characteristics (King, 2002; Mickelson, 2002). Increasingly, Americans identify with multiple ethnic groups, and this has important consequences for their self-perceptions (Shih & Sanchez, 2005).

Most white Americans identify with one or more European ethnic groups, such as Polish, Italian, Irish, Greek, Scandinavian, or German. Identification with these groups might affect a family's traditions, holidays, food preferences, and, to some extent, outlook on the world. They may share a history of discrimination and hardship, but white ethnic groups are generally accepted today, and the differences among them have few implications for education.

The situation is quite different for other ethnic groups. In particular, African Americans (Loury, 2002), Latinos (Diaz-Rico & Weed, 2010), and Native Americans (Castagno & Brayboy, 2008; Lomawaima & McCarty, 2006) have yet to be fully accepted into mainstream U.S. society and (on average) have not yet attained the economic success or security that most European and many Asian ethnic groups have achieved. Students from these ethnic groups have been the focus of two of the most emotional issues in U.S. education since the mid-1960s: desegregation and bilingual education. The following sections discuss the situation of students of various ethnic backgrounds in schools today.

Racial and Ethnic Composition of the United States

The people who make up the United States come from many ethnic backgrounds, and every year the proportion of nonwhites and Hispanics is increasing. Table 4.3 shows estimates of U.S. population percentages according to ethnicity. Note that the proportion of non-Hispanic whites is declining; as recently as 1970, 83 percent of all Americans were in this category, but it is 62% in 2015 and predicted to be 46% in 2065. In contrast, the proportion of Hispanics and Asians has grown dramatically since 1990 and grew at an even more rapid rate from 2000 to 2010. The Pew Research Center (2015) predicts that by 2065, 13% of the U.S. population will be African American, 24% Hispanic, and 14% Asian. These trends, which are the result of immigration patterns and

TABLE 4.3 • Projected Percent of U.S. Population by Race and Hispanic Origin, 2015–2065

	2015	2025	2035	2045	2055	2065
Non-Hispanic White	62	58	55	51	48	46
African-American	12	13	13	13	13	13
Hispanic	18	19	21	22	23	24
Asian	6	7	9	10	12	14

Note: Asians include Pacific Islanders. Hispanics are of any race.

Source: Pew Research Center. (2015). *Modern immigration wave brings 59 million to U.S., driving population growth and change through 2065: Views of immigration's impact on U.S. society mixed.* Washington, D.C.: Author.

differences in birth rates, have profound implications for U.S. education. Our nation is becoming far more ethnically diverse (Hodgkinson, 2008; Lapkoff & Li, 2007).

Academic Achievement of Students from Underrepresented Groups

If students from all racial and ethnic groups scored at the same level as European and Asian Americans, there would probably be little concern about ethnic group differences in U.S. schools. Unfortunately, they don't. On virtually every test of academic achievement, African American, Latino, and Native American students, on average, score significantly lower than their European-American and Asian American classmates. Because members of these groups are less often in situations of economic security and power, they are sometimes referred to as **underrepresented groups**.

Table 4.4 shows reading scores on the 2015 National Assessment of Educational Progress (NAEP) according to students' race or ethnicity. African American, Hispanic, and American Indian children scored significantly lower than non-Hispanic white or Asian American children at all grade levels. In graduation rates, trends were similar: Whereas about 80 percent of White and Asian students graduate from high school, the rates are 63 percent for Latinos, 59 percent for African-Americans, and 53 percent for American Indian students (EPE Research Center, 2012). These differences correspond closely with differences among the groups in average socioeconomic status, which themselves translate into achievement differences (recall Table 4.2).

The achievement gap between African American, Latino, and white children may be narrowing, but not nearly rapidly enough. During the 1970s there was a substantial reduction, but since the early 1980s the gap has been diminishing slowly in both reading and math on the National Assessment of Educational Progress (NCES, 2015).

InTASC 6

Assessment

Barriers to the Achievement of Students from Underrepresented Groups

Why do many students from underrepresented groups score so far below European-American and Asian Americans on achievement tests? The reasons involve economics, society, families, and culture, as well as inadequate responses by schools (Carter & Darling-Hammond, 2016; Duncan & Murnane, 2014b; Ladson-Billings, 2006; O'Connor, Hill, & Robinson, 2009; Parkay, 2006; Rowley, Kurtz-Costes, & Cooper, 2010; Warikoo & Carter, 2009; Wiggan, 2007). The most important reason is that in our society, African Americans, Latinos (particularly Mexican Americans and Puerto Ricans), and Native Americans tend to occupy the lower rungs of the socioeconomic ladder. Consequently, many families in these groups are unable to provide their children with the stimulation and academic preparation that are typical of a middle-class upbringing. Neither ethnicity nor economics is destiny, of course. President Barack Obama is an African American raised by a single, working-class mother, and there are many very successful adults who overcome significant barriers. Yet those barriers do exist, and in spite of the many exceptions, it is still the case that children do not start off with equal resources, and this affects their life chances. In particular,

TABLE 4.4 • NAEP Reading Scores (NCES, 2015) by Race/Ethnicity: Grades 4 and 8

RACE/ETHNICITY	PERCENTAGE SCORING AT OR ABOVE PROFICIENT—GRADE 4	PERCENTAGE SCORING AT OR ABOVE PROFICIENT—GRADE 8
White	46	44
African American	18	16
Hispanic	21	21
Asian/Pacific Islander	57	54
American Indian/Alaska Native	21	22

Source: National Center for Education Statistics (NCES), 2015, *The Condition of Education,* Washington, DC: Author.

chronic unemployment, underemployment, and employment in very low-wage jobs, which are endemic in many communities of people from underrepresented groups, have a negative effect on family life, including contributing to high numbers of single-parent families in these communities (Duncan & Murnane, 2014a, b; U.S. Census Bureau, 2013).

Another important disadvantage that many students from underrepresented groups face is academically inferior, overcrowded schools (Barton, 2003; Tate, 2008). Middle-class and many working-class families of all ethnicities throughout the United States buy their way out of inner-city schools by moving to the suburbs or sending their children to private or parochial schools, leaving the public schools to serve people who lack the resources to afford alternatives. The remaining children, who are disproportionately members of ethnic minorities, are likely to attend the lowest-quality, worst-funded schools in the country (Biddle & Berliner, 2002; Ferguson & Mehta, 2004; Lee, 2004), where they often have the least-qualified and least- experienced teachers (Connor, Son, Hindman, & Morrison, 2004; Darling-Hammond, 2006; Haycock, 2001).

Often, students from minority groups perform poorly because the instruction they receive is inconsistent with their cultural background (Banks, 2015; Boykin & Noguera, 2011; Jagers & Carroll, 2002; Lee, 2008; Ogbu, 2004; Ryan & Ryan, 2005). Academic excellence itself may be seen as inconsistent with acceptance in a student's own community; for example, Ogbu (2004), Spencer, Noll, Stoltzfus, and Harpalani (2001), Stinson (2006), Tyson, Darity, and Castellino (2005), and others have noted the tendency of many African American students to accuse their peers of "acting white" if they strive to achieve. In contrast, Asian American parents may strongly stress academic excellence as an expectation, and as a result many (though not all) Asian subgroups do very well in school (Ng, Lee, & Park, 2007). African Americans (Boykin & Noguera, 2011; Jagers & Carroll, 2002; Lee, 2000, 2008), Native Americans (Castagno & Brayboy, 2008; Lomawaima & McCarty, 2002, 2006; Starnes, 2006), and Mexican Americans (Padrón, Waxman, & Rivera, 2002) generally prefer to work in collaboration with others and perform better in cooperative settings than in the competitive settings seen in most classrooms. Lack of respect for students' home languages and dialects can also lead to a diminishing of commitment to school. Low expectations for students who are minorities can contribute to their low achievement (Nasir & Hand, 2006; Ogbu, 2004; Tenenbaum & Ruck, 2007; Van Laar, 2001). This is especially true if, as often happens, low expectations lead well-meaning teachers or administrators to disproportionately place students from underrepresented groups in low-ability groups or tracks or in special education (O'Connor & Fernandez, 2006; Reid & Knight, 2006). It is important to note, however, that even though African American students often suffer from the low expectations of teachers and others, their expectations for themselves and their academic self-concepts tend to be at least as high as those of their white classmates (Eccles, Wigfield, & Byrnes, 2003; Van Laar, 2001).

Connections 4.3

To learn about motivational factors that affect some students who are members of minority groups and low achievers, including the role of teacher expectations and the phenomenon of learned helplessness, see Chapter 10.

Stereotype Threat

Imagine that you are left-handed and someone who looks authoritative tells you that research has shown that left-handed people are terrible at math problems involving money. Then you're given a sack of assorted pennies, nickels, dimes, and quarters, and asked to divide them into piles of equal value in 60 seconds.

How would you feel, and how would you do on the task? You might be very anxious, wanting to avoid confirming the stereotype about southpaws (which has no basis whatsoever in reality). You might try to sort the coins using your right hand. In the end, you might perform less well on this simple task than you would have if you hadn't been told that left-handers have difficulties with money problems.

This phenomenon, called *stereotype threat* (Aronson & Steele, 2005; Dee, 2015; Devonshire, Morris, & Fluck, 2013; Huguet & Régner, 2007; Kumar & Maehr, 2010), has been demonstrated to apply in many circumstances. Individuals who know of a stereotype associated with a group to which they belong are anxious about confirming the stereotype, and their anxiety causes them to perform below their real abilities. Obviously, stereotype threat is of greatest concern when members of a given ethnic, gender, or social group feel that they are not expected to do well on particular school tasks. Over time, a student might simply decide that a given activity is not for him or her, as when a girl decides that math is "not her thing" (Master, Cheryan, & Meltzoff, 2016).

To prevent or remedy stereotype threat, teachers must be careful never to express the belief that certain skills are easier or harder for certain people, and should give all students opportunities to shine and show leadership in all types of tasks. Individual students vary in skills and interests, of course, but teachers should never ascribe a student's success or failure on a given task to his or her membership in any group.

The low achievement of African American, Latino, and Native American children may well be a temporary problem. Gaps in achievement are slowly diminishing (NCES, 2013), and as African American and Hispanic families enter the middle class, their children's achievement will come to resemble that of other groups. In the 1920s it was widely believed that immigrants from southern and eastern Europe (such as Italians, Greeks, Poles, and Jews) were hopelessly backward and perhaps retarded (Oakes, 2005), yet the children and grandchildren of these immigrants now achieve at the same level as the descendants of the Pilgrims. However, we cannot simply wait for inequities to evaporate. The school is one institution that can break the cycle of poverty by giving children from impoverished backgrounds the opportunity to succeed. Most immediately, schools serving many African American, Latino, and Native American children can accelerate the achievement of these children by using effective instructional methods and by making a meaningful commitment to ensuring the success of all children.

Effects of School Desegregation

Before 1954, African American, white, and often Latino and Native American students were legally required to attend separate schools in 20 states and the District of Columbia, and segregated schools were common in the remaining states. Students from underrepresented groups were often bused miles away from their nearest public school to separate schools. In 1954, however, the Supreme Court struck down this practice in the landmark *Brown v. Board of Education of Topeka* case on the grounds that separate education was inherently unequal (Ancheta, 2006; Orfield, 2014; Welner, 2006). *Brown v. Board of Education* did away with legal segregation, but it was many years before large numbers of racially different students were attending school together. In the 1970s, a series of Supreme Court decisions found that the continued segregation of many schools throughout the United States was the result of past discriminatory practices, such as deliberately drawing neighborhood boundary lines to separate schools along racial lines. These decisions forced local school districts to desegregate their schools by any means necessary (Orfield, 2014).

Many districts were given specific standards for the proportions of students from underrepresented groups who could be assigned to any particular school. For example, a district in which 45 percent of the students were African American might be required to have an enrollment of 35 to 55 percent African Americans in each of its schools. To achieve desegregation, some school districts simply changed school attendance areas; others created special magnet schools (such as schools for the performing arts, for students who are talented and gifted, or for technology or science) to induce students to attend schools outside their own neighborhoods. However, in many large urban districts, segregation of neighborhoods is so extensive that districts would have to bus students to other neighborhoods to achieve racially balanced schools. School desegregation was supposed to increase the academic achievement of low-income students from underrepresented groups by giving them opportunities to interact with more middle-class, achievement-oriented peers. All too often, however, the schools to which students are bused are no better than the segregated schools they left behind, and the outflow of middle-class families from urban areas (which was well under way before busing began) often means that lower-class African American or Latino students are integrated with similarly lower-class whites (Orfield, 2014). Also, it is important to note that because of residential segregation and opposition to busing, most students from underrepresented groups still attend schools in which there are few, if any, whites, and in many areas segregation is once again on the increase (Orfield, Frankenberg, & Siegel-Hawley, 2010; Smith, 2002). Support for busing to achieve integration has greatly diminished among African American and Latino parents, and recent Supreme Court decisions have largely eliminated the judicial push for desegregation (Orfield, 2014; Orfield & Frankenberg, 2007; Superfine, 2010).

The overall effect of desegregation on the academic achievement of students from underrepresented groups has been small, though positive. However, when desegregation begins in elementary school, particularly when it involves busing children from underrepresented groups to

MyEdLab

Video Example 4.3

Bob Slavin describes some of his experiences with integrated high schools. Reflect on your experience with racial diversity. What was the racial or ethnic mix of your school, and what did the school do to encourage integration among students? How have your own experiences influenced your perspectives on classrooms and learning?

high-quality schools with substantially middle-class student bodies, desegregation can have a significant positive effect on the achievement of the students from underrepresented groups (Benner & Crosnoe, 2011; Goldsmith, 2011; Mickelson, 2015; Orfield, Frankenberg, & Siegel-Hawley, 2010; Orfield, 2014; Welner, 2006). This effect may result not from desegregation, but rather from attending a better school. One important outcome of desegregation is that African American and Latino students who attend desegregated schools are more likely to attend desegregated colleges, to work in integrated settings, and to attain higher incomes than their peers who attend segregated schools (Orfield, 2014).

THEORY INTO PRACTICE

Teaching in a Culturally Diverse School

Teachers can do a great deal to promote social harmony and equal opportunity among students in racially and ethnically diverse classrooms and schools (see Boykin & Noguera, 2011; Carter & Darling-Hammond, 2016; Curwin, 2010; Hawley & Nieto, 2010; Nieto & Bode, 2008; Oakes & Lipton, 2006; Parillo, 2008).

- Use fairness and balance in dealing with students. Students should never have any justification for believing that "people like me [whites, African Americans, Latinos, Vietnamese] don't get a fair chance" (Banks, 2015; Lee, 2014; Wessler, 2011).

- Choose texts and instructional materials that show all ethnic groups in equally positive and nonstereotypical roles. Make sure underrepresented groups are not misrepresented. Themes should be nonbiased, and individuals from underrepresented groups should appear in nonstereotypical high-status roles (Banks, 2015).

- Reach out to children's parents and families with information and activities appropriate to their language and culture (Lindeman, 2001). Avoid communicating bias, but discuss racial or ethnic relations openly and with empathy, rather than trying to pretend there are no differences (Polite & Saenger, 2003).

- Avoid stereotyping and emphasize the diversity of individuals, not groups (Koppelman & Goodhart, 2008).

- Let students know that racial or ethnic bias, including slurs, taunts, and jokes, will not be tolerated in the classroom or in the school. Institute consequences to enforce this standard (Wessler, 2011).

- Help all students to value their own and others' cultural heritages and contributions to history and civilization. At the same time, avoid trivializing or stereotyping cultures merely in terms of ethnic foods and holidays. Students need more than ever to value diversity and to acquire more knowledge and appreciation of other ways of life (Villegas & Lucas, 2007).

- Decorate classrooms, hallways, and the library/media center with murals, bulletin boards, posters, artifacts, and other materials that are representative of the students in the class or school or of the other cultures being studied (Manning & Baruth, 2009).

- Avoid resegregation. Tracking, or between-class ability grouping, tends to segregate high and low achievers, and because of historical and economic factors, students from underrepresented groups tend to be overrepresented in the ranks of low achievers. For this and other reasons, tracking should be avoided (Ferguson & Mehta, 2004; Hawley & Nieto, 2010; Oakes, 2005; Tyson et al., 2005).

InTASC 3

Learning Environments

InTASC 5

Application of Content

InTASC 8

Instructional Strategies

(continued)

- Be sure that assignments are not offensive or frustrating to students of diverse cultural groups. For example, asking students to write about their Christmas experiences is inappropriate for non-Christian students (Banks, 2015).

- Provide structure for intergroup interaction. Proximity alone does not lead to social harmony among racially and ethnically different groups. Students need opportunities to know one another as individuals and to work together toward common goals (Cooper & Slavin, 2004; Parillo, 2008).

- Use cooperative learning, which has been shown to improve relations across racial and ethnic lines (Cooper & Slavin, 2004; National Research Council, 2000). The positive effects of cooperative learning experiences often outlast the teams or groups themselves and may extend to relationships outside of school. Cooperative learning contributes to both achievement and social harmony (Slavin, 2013) and can increase the participation of children from underrepresented groups (Cohen, 2004).

MyEdLab

Video Example 4.4

As this teacher learned from a student, respecting a student's culture is very different from expecting a student to have particular interests, skills, or behaviors simply because he or she has a particular cultural background.

HOW DO LANGUAGE DIFFERENCES AND BILINGUAL PROGRAMS AFFECT STUDENT ACHIEVEMENT?

InTASC 7

Planning for Instruction

In 1979, only 9 percent of Americans aged 5 to 24 were from families in which the primary language spoken was not English. In 2007, this proportion had increased to 20 percent (Shin & Kominski, 2010), and projections forecast that by 2026, 25 percent of all students will come from homes in which the primary language is not English. Sixty-five percent of these students' families speak Spanish (NCES, 2004). However, many students speak any of dozens of Asian, African, or European languages (see Pang, Han, & Pang, 2011, for a discussion of issues with Asian-American students). The term **language minority** is used for all such students, and **limited English proficient (LEP)** and **English learner (EL)** are terms used for the much smaller number (about 9% of all U.S. students; Murphey, 2014) who have not yet attained an adequate level of English to succeed in an English-only program (Garcia, Jensen, & Scribner, 2009). These students are learning English as a second language and may attend classes for English learners in their schools. Language minority children who start kindergarten fully proficient in English generally keep up with national achievement norms (Kieffer, 2011), but those who are not fully English proficient tend, on average, to have long-term deficits in achievement.

Students with limited English proficiency present the educational system with a dilemma (August & Shanahan, 2006a; Hakuta, 2011; Li & Wang, 2008; Murphey, 2014). The ability to speak multiple languages in itself is an asset for students, both cognitively and practically (Adesope, Lavin, Thompson, & Ungerleider, 2009), yet those who have limited proficiency in English need to learn English to function effectively in U.S. society. However, until students are proficient in English, should they be taught math or social studies in their first language or in English? Should they be taught to read in their first language? These questions are not simply pedagogical—they have political and cultural significance that has provoked emotional debate. Many Latino parents want their children to be instructed in the Spanish language and culture to maintain their group identity and pride (Díaz-Rico & Weed, 2010). Other parents whose language is neither English nor Spanish often feel the same way (Arzubiaga, Noguerón, & Sullivan, 2009). Others, however, strongly prefer that their children be taught only in English.

ON THE WEB

For data and other information about the education of children in the Latino community, see childtrends.org's Hispanic Institute section.

Bilingual Education

The term **bilingual education** refers to programs for students who are acquiring English that teach the students in their first language part of the time while English is being learned. English learners are typically taught in one of four types of programs.

1. *English immersion.* The most common instructional placement for English learners is some form of English immersion, in which ELs are taught primarily or entirely in English. Typically, children with the lowest levels of English proficiency are placed in English as a Second Language (ESL) programs for English learners that build their oral English to help them succeed in their English-only curriculum (Callahan, Wilkinson, & Muller, 2010). English immersion programs may use carefully designed strategies to build students' vocabularies, simplify instructions, and help English learners succeed in learning the content (see, for example, Clark, 2009; Díaz-Rico & Weed, 2010; DiCerbo, Anstrom, Baker, & Rivera, 2014; Echevarría, Vogt, & Short, 2013; Gersten et al., 2007). Such models are often referred to as *structured English immersion.* Alternatively, ELs may simply be included in regular English instruction and be expected to do the best they can. This "sink or swim" approach is most common when the number of ELs is small and they speak languages other than Spanish.

2. *Transitional bilingual education.* A common but declining alternative for English learners is transitional bilingual education, programs in which children are taught reading or other subjects in their native language (most often Spanish) for a few years and then transition to English, usually in second, third, or fourth grade (Slama, 2014).

3. *Paired bilingual education.* In paired bilingual models, children are taught reading or other subjects in both their home language and English, usually at different times of the day.

4. *Two-way bilingual education.* Two-way, or dual language, models teach all students both in English and in another language, usually Spanish. That is, English-proficient students are expected to learn Spanish as Spanish-proficient students learn English (Calderón & Minaya-Rowe, 2003; Estrada, Gómez, & Ruiz-Escalante, 2009; Lessow-Hurley, 2005; Lindholm-Leary, 2004/2005). From the perspective of English learners, a two-way bilingual program is essentially a paired bilingual program, in that they are taught both in their native language and in English at different times.

Research on bilingual strategies for teaching reading generally supports paired bilingual methods (Greene, 1997; Reljic, Ferring, & Martin, 2014; Slavin & Cheung, 2005). This suggests that English learners need not spend many years building their oral English, but can learn English reading with a limited level of English speaking skills, and can then build their reading and speaking capabilities together (Slavin & Cheung, 2005). However, a five-year study comparing children randomly assigned either to receive all of their reading instruction in English or to receive instruction in Spanish in grades K–2 and then transition to English found no differences in English reading skills by fourth grade (Slavin, Madden, Calderón, Chamberlain, & Hennessey, 2011). The

Certification Pointer

In responding to a case study on a teacher certification test, you may be expected to know that conducting an assessment of students' oral language abilities both in their first language and in English would be a first step in helping English learners achieve.

language of instruction is only one factor in effective education for students who are EL, and the quality of instruction (whether in English only or in English and another language) is at least as important (August & Shanahan, 2006b; Calderón, 2011; Cheung & Slavin, 2012; Hakuta, 2011; Sparks, 2016; Valentino & Reardon, 2015).

ON THE WEB

The National Association for Bilingual Education provides support for the education of English learners at nabe.org. Resources for teachers of students who are ELs are presented at http://www.edutopia.org/blog/strategies-and-resources-supporting-ell-todd-finley, http://www.usingenglish.com/teachers/, and http://www.eslgold.com/. For a list of bilingual education organizations, see teach-nology.com and type "Bilingual education organizations" into its search engine. Other sites that contain useful information on teaching English learners and teaching foreign languages include the American Council on the Teaching of Foreign Languages (actfl.org), the International Association of Teachers of English as a Foreign Language (iatefl.org), the Center for Applied Linguistics (cal.org), Teachers of English to Speakers of Other Languages (tesol.org), and the California Department of Education (cde .ca.gov).

THEORY INTO PRACTICE

Teaching English Learners

Teachers in all parts of the United States and Canada are increasingly likely to have ELs in their classes. The following general principles can help these students succeed in the English curriculum (see August & Shanahan, 2006a; Calderón, 2011; Calderón & Minaya-Rowe, 2011; California Department of Education, 2012; Díaz-Rico & Weed, 2010; DiCerbo et al., 2014; Echevarría, Vogt, & Short, 2013; Farrell, 2009; Herrell & Jordan, 2016; Hill & Miller, 2013; Tong, Lara-Alecio, Irby, Mathes, & Kwok, 2008).

1. ***Don't just say it—show it.*** All students benefit from pictures, videos, concrete objects, gestures, and actions to illustrate difficult concepts, but ELs particularly benefit from teaching that includes visual as well as auditory cues (Calderón, 2007; Echevarría et al., 2013).

2. ***Use cooperative learning to provide safe opportunities to use academic English.*** Many ELs are shy in class, not wanting to use their English for fear of being laughed at. Yet the best way to learn a language is to use it. Structure opportunities for students to use English in academic contexts (Calderón, 2011). For example, when asking questions, first give students an opportunity to discuss answers with a partner, and then call on partner pairs. This and other forms of cooperative learning can be particularly beneficial for students learning English (August & Shanahan, 2006a; Bondie, Gaughrain, & Zusho, 2014; Calderón et al., 2004). Cooperative learning gives English learners constant opportunities to build confidence and facility in English.

InTASC 3

Learning Environments

InTASC 8

Instructional Strategies

3. ***Develop vocabulary.*** All children, but especially ELs, benefit from explicit teaching of new vocabulary. Give students many opportunities to hear new words in context and to use them in sentences they make up themselves. Learning dictionary definitions is not as useful as having opportunities to ask and answer questions, write new sentences, and discuss new words with partners (Calderón, 2011; Carlo et al., 2004; Echevarría et al., 2013; Fitzgerald & Graves, 2004/2005; Lesaux et al., 2014; Snow, 2006).

4. ***Keep instructions clear.*** English learners (and other students) often know the answers but get confused about what they are supposed to do. Take extra care to see that students understand assignments and instructions, for example, by asking students to restate instructions (Díaz-Rico & Weed, 2010).

5. ***Point out cognates.*** If you speak the home language of your ELs, point out cases in which a word they know is similar to an English word. For example, in a class with many students learning English, you might help them learn the word *amorous* by noting the similarity to the Spanish and Portuguese word *amor,* the French word *amour,* or the Italian word *amore,* depending on the students' languages (Carlo et al., 2004; Dong, 2009).

6. ***Never publicly embarrass children by correcting their English.*** Instead, praise their correct answer and restate it correctly. For example, Russian students often omit *a* and *the.* If a student says, "Mark Twain was famous author," you might respond, "Right! Mark Twain was a very famous author," without calling attention to your addition of the word *a.* To encourage students to use their English, establish a classwide norm of never teasing or laughing at English errors.

7. ***If students learning English are struggling in reading, provide small-group interventions.*** Numerous studies have found that ELs who are struggling to learn to read English benefit from intensive small-group tutorials (August & Shanahan, 2006a; Cheung & Slavin, 2005; Gersten et al., 2007; Huebner, 2009).

8. ***Engage parents.*** English learners are likely to benefit when their parents are supportive of their work in school. Engaging parents can help prevent problems and make families feel welcome and involved (Lawson & Alameda-Lawson, 2012).

Increasingly, research on bilingual education is focusing on the identification of effective forms of instruction for language-minority students, rather than on the question of which is the best language of instruction (Baker et al., 2014; Burr, Haas, & Ferriere, 2015; Calderón, Slavin, & Sanchez, 2011; Cheung & Slavin, 2012; Christian & Genesee, 2001; Janzen, 2008; Maxwell, 2012; U.S. Department of Education, 2000). Cooperative learning programs have been particularly effective both in improving the outcomes of Spanish reading instruction and in helping bilingual students make a successful transition to English-only instruction in the upper elementary grades (August & Shanahan, 2006a; Calderón et al., 2004, 2011; Cheung & Slavin, 2012). In California, which has the largest number of language-minority students in the United States, a referendum called Proposition 227, passed in 1998 (Merickel et al., 2003), mandated a maximum of one year for students with limited English proficiency to receive intensive assistance in learning English. After that, children were expected to be in mainstream English-only classes. This legislation reduced bilingual education in California, although parents could still apply for waivers to have their children taught in their first language. Massachusetts, Arizona, and other states have also passed legislation limiting bilingual education (Hakuta, Butler, & Witt, 2000), and even in states that do not ban it, bilingual education has been waning in popularity (Mora, 2009).

WHAT IS MULTICULTURAL EDUCATION?

In recent years, multicultural education has become a much-discussed topic in U.S. education. Definitions of **multicultural education** vary broadly. The simplest definitions emphasize including non-European perspectives in the curriculum—for example, the works of African, Latino, Asian, and Native American authors in English curricula; teaching about Columbus from the point of view of Native Americans; and teaching more about the cultures and contributions of non-Western societies (Banks, 2015; Bennett, 2015; Gollnick & Chinn, 2017; Manning & Baruth, 2009). Banks (2015) defines multicultural education as encompassing all policies and practices that schools might use to improve educational outcomes not only for students of different ethnic, social class, and religious backgrounds but also for students of different genders and exceptionalities (e.g., children who have mental retardation, hearing loss, or vision loss, or who are gifted).

ON THE WEB

For resources and discussions of multicultural education, visit the Multicultural Pavilion at edchange.org (click on the Projects tab). Also see the Center for Multilingual Multicultural Research (usc.edu), the National Association for Multicultural Education (nameorg.org), and the National Multicultural Institute (nmci.org).

Dimensions of Multicultural Education

Banks (2008) discusses five key dimensions of multicultural education.

Content integration involves your use of examples, data, and information from a variety of cultures. This is what most people think of as multicultural education: teaching about different cultures and about contributions made by individuals from diverse cultures, inclusion in the curriculum of works by members of underrepresented groups, including women, and the like (Bettmann & Friedman, 2004; Gollnick & Chinn, 2017; Hicks-Bartlett, 2004).

Knowledge construction consists of helping children understand how knowledge is created and how it is influenced by the racial, ethnic, and social class positions of individuals and groups (Banks, 2015). For example, students might be asked to write a history of the early colonization of America from the perspectives of Native Americans or African Americans to learn how the knowledge we take as given is in fact influenced by our own origins and points of view (Koppelman & Goodhart, 2008; Vavrus, 2008).

Prejudice reduction is a critical goal of multicultural education. It involves both advancement of positive relationships among students of different ethnic backgrounds (Cooper & Slavin, 2004; Stephan & Vogt, 2004) and development of more democratic and tolerant attitudes toward others (Banks, 2015; Gollnick & Chinn, 2017).

The term **equity pedagogy** refers to the use of teaching techniques that facilitate the academic success of students from different ethnic and social class groups. For example, there is evidence that members of some ethnic and racial groups, especially Mexican Americans and African Americans, learn best with active and cooperative methods (Boykin & Noguera, 2011).

An **empowering school culture** is one in which school organization and practices are conducive to the academic and emotional growth of all students. A school with such a culture might, for example, eliminate tracking or ability grouping, increase inclusion (and reduce labeling) of students with special needs, try to keep all students on a path leading to higher education, and consistently show high expectations. One example of an empowering school culture is the AVID project (Watt, Powell, & Mendiola, 2004), which places students from underrepresented groups who are at risk in college preparatory classes and provides them with tutors and other assistance to help them succeed in a demanding curriculum.

Certification Pointer

For your teacher certification test, you should recognize the importance of connecting your instruction to your students' cultural experiences.

MyEdLab **Self-Check 4.2**

HOW DO GENDER AND GENDER BIAS AFFECT STUDENTS' SCHOOL EXPERIENCES?

A child's sex is a visible, permanent attribute. Cross-cultural research indicates that gender roles are among the first that individuals learn and that all societies treat males differently from females. Therefore, gender-role or sex-role behavior is learned behavior. However, the range of roles occupied by males and females across cultures is broad. What is considered natural behavior for each gender is based more on cultural belief than on biological necessity. Nevertheless, the extent to which biological differences and gender socialization affect behavioral patterns and achievement is still a much-debated topic. The consensus of a large body of research is that despite the inherent biological differences, virtually all of the observed differences between males and females (beyond physical characteristics) can be clearly linked to differences in early socialization experiences (Eliot, 2012; Sadker, Zittleman, & Sadker, 2013).

Male and Female Thinking and Learning

Although there is much evidence of differences in temperament and personality between boys and girls (e.g., Else-Quest, Shibley, Goldsmith, & Van Hulle, 2006; Rose & Rudolph, 2006), there is considerable debate about differences in aptitude and achievement. The question of gender differences in intelligence or academic achievement has been debated for centuries, and the issue has taken on particular importance since the early 1970s. The most important point to keep in mind about this debate is that no responsible researcher has ever claimed that any male–female differences on any measure of intellectual ability are large in comparison to the amount of variability within each sex. In other words, even in areas in which true gender differences are suspected, these differences are so small and variable that they have few if any practical consequences (Eliot, 2012; Fine, 2010; Jordan-Young, 2010; Renzetti, Curran, & Maier, 2012; Sadker et al., 2013).

> **InTASC 1**
> **Learner Development**

A few differences are worthy of note. Twelfth-grade girls score significantly lower than boys on the quantitative section of the Scholastic Assessment Test (SAT) (Allspach & Breining, 2005) and on Advanced Placement tests in mathematics (Stumpf & Stanley, 1996). A summary of 20 major studies by Kim (2001) found that males scored better than females in math, whereas the opposite was true on English tests. A Program for International Student Assessment (PISA) study covering most developed countries found that girls' advantage over boys on reading was three times boys' advantage in math (Stoet & Geary, 2013). The most important cause is that females in our society have traditionally been discouraged from studying mathematics and, therefore, take many fewer math courses than males do (University of Wisconsin-Madison, 2009). In fact, as females have begun to take more math courses over the past two decades, the gender gap on the SAT and on other measures has been steadily diminishing (Allspach & Breining, 2005). A study by Hyde and Mertz (2009) found that there were no significant differences between boys and girls on state math assessments. The same is true on the National Assessment of Educational Progress (NCES, 2011; also see the Center on Educational Policy, 2010). However, despite the narrowing gap between boys and girls on tests of math and science, far fewer young women than young men enter careers in math and science, especially physics, engineering, and computer science (Ceci & Williams, 2009; Huebner, 2009; Warner, 2013).

Studies generally find that males score higher than females on tests of general knowledge, mechanical reasoning, and mental rotations; females score higher on language measures, including reading and writing assessments (Robinson & Lubienski, 2011; Strand, Deary, & Smith, 2006). There are no male–female differences in general verbal ability, arithmetic skills, abstract reasoning, spatial visualization, or memory span (Eliot, 2012). In school grades, females start out with an advantage over males and maintain this advantage into high school. Even in math and science, in which females score somewhat lower on tests, females still get better grades in class (Robinson & Lubienski, 2011). Young women are more likely than young men to earn a bachelor's degree (Beckwith & Murphey, 2016; Warner, 2013). Despite this, high school males tend to overestimate their skills in language and math (as measured by standardized tests), whereas females underestimate their skills (Herbert & Stipek, 2005; Pomerantz, Altermatt, & Saxon, 2002). In elementary school, males are much more likely than females to have reading problems (CEP, 2010; Lindsey, 2015) and are much more likely to have learning disabilities or emotional disorders (Smith, 2001).

Kindergarten girls have been found to be higher in self-regulation than boys, and this translates into better achievement in the early grades (Matthews, Ponitz, & Morrison, 2009).

The Boy Crisis

Although there has been a great deal written over the past 30 years about how girls are underserved in schools, in more recent years there has been more concern about the "boy crisis" (Beckwith & Murphey, 2016; Cleveland, 2011). It has long been the case that boys are more likely than girls to be assigned to special education, to be held back, to drop out, and to be in trouble with the law (Beckwith & Murphey, 2016). In fact, young men are ten times more likely than young women to be incarcerated. Girls have become much more likely to go to college and then to graduate, and many co-ed universities and colleges are 60 percent female or more. All of these differences exist despite the advantages that boys have on some aptitude tests.

Looking more closely at the data reveals that there is indeed a "boy crisis," but it does not apply across the board. African American boys are significantly more at risk than African American girls (Kafele, 2009; Noguera, 2012; Schott Foundation, 2010; Thomas & Stevenson, 2009), and learning disabilities and ADHD (attention deficit hyperactive disorder) are significantly more common (and damaging) among boys. These problems are serious and need to be attended to, but they do not justify panic about the entire gender (Mead, 2006). In fact, our perception of a "boy crisis" may simply be the result of the effects of changing practices that once discouraged girls from excelling in school (Warner, 2013).

Sex-Role Stereotyping and Gender Bias

If there are so few genetically based differences between males and females, why do so many behavioral differences exist? These behavioral differences originate from different experiences, including reinforcement by adults for different types of behavior (Eliot, 2012).

Male and female babies have traditionally been treated differently from the time they are born. The wrapping of the infant in either a pink or a blue blanket symbolizes the variations in experience that typically greet the child from birth onward. In early studies, adults described boy or girl babies wrapped in blue blankets as being more active than the same babies wrapped in pink. Other masculine traits were also ascribed to those wrapped in blue (Sadker, Zittleman, & Sadker, 2013). Recent research on the plasticity of the infant brain suggests that the different ways in which boy and girl babies are treated could actually cause brain differences (Eliot, 2012).

Although awareness of gender bias has begun to have some impact on child-rearing practices, children do begin to make gender distinctions and have gender preferences by around the age of 3 or 4. Thus, children enter school having been socialized into appropriate gender-role behavior for their age in relation to community expectations (Delamont, 2002). Differences in approved gender roles between boys and girls tend to be much stronger in low-SES families than in high-SES families (Sadker, Zittleman, & Sadker, 2013).

Socialization into this kind of approved **sex-role behavior** continues throughout life, and schools contribute to it. Interactions between socialization experiences and achievement are complex and it is difficult to make generalizations, but schools differentiate between the sexes in a number of ways. In general, males receive more attention from their teachers than females do (Jones & Dindia, 2004; Koch, 2003). Males receive more disapproval and blame from their teachers than do females, but they also engage in more interactions with teachers in such areas as approval, instruction giving, and being listened to (Jones & Dindia, 2004; Koch, 2003; Maher & Ward, 2002). Teachers tend to punish females more promptly and explicitly for aggressive behavior than males. Other differentiations are subtle, as when girls are directed to play in the house corner while boys are provided with blocks, or when boys are given drums to play in music class and girls are given the triangles.

Sexual Orientation and Gender Identity

I went to a high school of 2000 students. As far as I knew, not one of them was gay or lesbian. Of course, the important phrase is "as far as I knew." I later discovered that some of my classmates were gay or lesbian, or came out as gay or lesbian after high school. Those who knew or suspected they were gay or lesbian hid their orientation, because in those days such a label would have led to teasing, bullying, or worse.

THEORY INTO PRACTICE

Avoiding Gender Bias in Teaching

"In my science class the teacher never calls on me, and I feel like I don't exist. The other night I had a dream that I vanished" (Sadker et al., 2013). Unfortunately, the girl who complained of being ignored by her teacher is not alone. Schools shortchange female students in a variety of ways, from ignoring instances of sexual harassment to interacting less frequently with females than with males (American Association of University Women, 2002). Teachers tend to choose boys, boost the self-esteem of their male students, and select literature with male protagonists. The contributions and experiences of girls and women are still often ignored in textbooks, curricula, and standardized tests (Zittleman & Sadker, 2003).

Teachers, usually without being aware of it, exhibit **gender bias** in classroom teaching in three principal ways: reinforcing gender stereotypes, maintaining sex separation, and treating males and females differently as students (see Koch, 2003; Maher & Ward, 2002). These inequities can have negative consequences for boys as well as girls (Sadker et al., 2013; Weaver-Hightower, 2003).

AVOIDING STEREOTYPES: Avoid promoting sexual stereotypes. For example, you can assign jobs in the classroom without regard to gender, avoiding automatically appointing males as group leaders and females as secretaries, and asking both males and females to help in physical activities. You should also refrain from stating stereotypes, such as "Boys don't cry" and "Girls don't fight," and you should avoid labeling students with such terms as *tomboy*. Encourage students who show an interest in activities and careers that do not correspond to cultural stereotypes, such as a female student who likes math and science (King, Gurian, & Stevens, 2010). Girls can suffer from stereotype threat when they are led to believe that girls aren't good at a particular skill, such as math (Master et al., 2016). Never give any student any reason to believe that people like them are not good at one skill or another.

PROMOTING INTEGRATION: One factor that leads to gender stereotyping is the tendency for boys and girls (particularly in elementary school) to have few friends of the opposite sex and to engage mostly in activities with members of their own sex (Lindsey, 2015). Teachers sometimes encourage this by having boys and girls line up separately, assigning them to sex-segregated tables, and organizing separate sports activities for males and females. As a result, interaction in schools is less frequent between boys and girls than between students of the same sex. However, in classes in which cross-sex collaboration is encouraged, children have less stereotyped views of the abilities of males and females (Renzetti, Curran, & Maier, 2012).

TREATING FEMALES AND MALES EQUALLY: Too often, teachers do not treat males and females equally. Observational studies of classroom interactions have found that teachers interact more with boys than with girls and ask boys more questions, especially more abstract questions (Sadker & Zittleman, 2009). In one study, researchers showed teachers videotapes of classroom scenes and asked them whether boys or girls participated more. Most teachers responded that the girls talked more, even though in fact the boys participated more than the girls by a ratio of 3 to 1 (Sadker & Zittleman, 2009). The researchers interpreted this finding as indicating that teachers expect females to participate less and thus see low rates of participation as normal. You must be careful to give all students equal opportunities to participate in class, to take leadership roles, and to engage in all kinds of activities (Bernard-Powers, 2001; Stein, 2000). Use activities that are likely to engage the interest and perspectives of girls as well as boys (James, 2007, 2009). Encourage girls to study math and science, and make it clear that you expect and value excellence in these subjects from girls as well as boys (Halpern et al., 2007).

THEORY INTO PRACTICE

Supporting LGBT Students

Every secondary teacher, and many elementary teachers, will encounter LGBT students, and will need to be prepared to support them.

PREVENTING HARASSMENT AND BULLYING. LGBT students are frequent targets of taunting, bullying, and even physical violence (Robinson & Espelage, 2012). A survey by the Gay, Lesbian, and Straight Education Network (2011) found that 81.9 percent of LGBT students reported being verbally harassed, 38.3 percent physically harassed, and 18.3 percent physically assaulted at school as a consequence of their sexual orientation or gender identity.

Much harassment and bullying take place on social media, where anonymity allows for the expression of outrageous and hurtful insults, threats, and accusations. Some 63.5 percent of LGBT students reported feeling unsafe at school, and 71.3 percent reported hearing frequent homophobic remarks. Teachers and other educators need to express zero tolerance for all harassment and bullying, but especially for the targeting of LGBT students because they receive a disproportionate share. Teachers can help by creating a welcoming environment in their classrooms for all students, whatever their differences (Slesaransky-Poe, 2013). Speaking to students about their responsibility to stand up for classmates who are being bullied or harassed is one way of changing school norms. Avoiding the use of intense competition and not applying fear as a motivator also reduce the tendency of students to take out their frustrations on classmates.

According to the American Psychological Association (2016), sexual orientation is "an enduring pattern of emotional, romantic, and/or sexual attraction to men, women, or both sexes." *Transgender* means having behaviors or self-identification different from one's biological sex, and transgender individuals may choose to dress or behave in ways characteristic of that different sex (Savage & Harley, 2009). Collectively, people in any of these categories often refer to themselves as **LGBT (lesbian, gay, bisexual, transgender)** or as LGBTQ (adding Q for "questioning"), and roughly 3.5% of all Americans identify themselves as lesbian, gay, bisexual, or transgender (Keen, 2011). Sexual orientation is currently understood to be set at birth, and it is impossible to change (Bronski, Pellegrini, & Amico, 2013). However, sexual orientation exists on a continuum from completely straight to completely homosexual, and some adolescents may take on a given sexual identity for a time, whether straight or gay/lesbian.

Today, students are far more open about their sexual orientations, and society is far more accepting, up to a point. Bullying and harassment are still common for students who do not conform to behaviors expected of their gender (Gay, Lesbian, and Straight Education Network, 2011). As a teacher, your most important role with respect to sexual orientation is to accept students' differences, to model appropriate behavior, and to help students who may be struggling with their identities.

In sex education, students should be taught about sexual orientation and LGBT identity (McGarry, 2013). This serves to demystify the topic and to help students see that sexual orientation and gender identity are just two of many characteristics on which people differ. Teaching acceptance of differences is essential.

MyEdLab **Self-Check 4.3**

HOW DO STUDENTS DIFFER IN INTELLIGENCE AND LEARNING STYLES?

Intelligence is one of those words that people believe they understand until you ask them to define it. At one level, **intelligence** can be defined as a general aptitude for learning or an ability to

ON THE WEB

For more on LGBT students, see www.apa.org/topics/lgbt/transgender and www.glsen.org.

Numerous specific programs with evidence of effectiveness for preventing or dealing with bullying are available at www.childtrends.org/what-works.

acquire and use knowledge or skills. A consensus definition expressed by Sternberg (2008) is that intelligence is the ability to figure out how to get what you want out of life by purposefully using your strengths to compensate for your weaknesses.

The biggest problem comes when we ask whether there is any such thing as general aptitude (Plucker & Esping, 2014; Sternberg, 2008). Many people are terrific at calculus but couldn't write a good essay or paint a good picture if their lives depended on it. Some people can walk into a room full of strangers and immediately figure out the relationships and feelings among them; others may never learn this skill. As Will Rogers put it, "Everybody is ignorant, only on different topics." Clearly, individuals vary in their aptitude for learning any specific type of knowledge or skill taught in a specific way. A hundred students attending a lecture on a topic they knew nothing about beforehand will all walk away with different amounts and kinds of learning, and aptitude for that particular content and that particular teaching method is one important factor in explaining these differences. But would the students who learned the most in this class also learn the most if the lecture were on a different topic or if the same material were presented through hands-on experiences or in small groups?

The concept of intelligence has been discussed since before the time of the ancient Greeks, but the scientific study of this topic really began with the work of Alfred Binet, who devised the first measure of intelligence in 1904 (see Esping & Plucker, 2015). The French government asked Binet to find a way to identify children who were likely to need special help in their schooling. His measure assessed a broad range of skills and performances but produced a single score, called **intelligence quotient (IQ)**, which was set up so that the average French child would have an IQ of 100 (Hurn, 2002).

Definitions of Intelligence

Binet's work greatly advanced the science of intelligence assessment, but it also began to establish the idea that intelligence was a single thing—that there were "smart" people who could be expected to do well in a broad range of learning situations. Ever since Binet, debate has raged about this issue. In 1927 Charles Spearman claimed that although there were, of course, variations in a person's abilities from task to task, there was a general intelligence factor, or "g," that existed across all learning situations. Is there really one intelligence, as Spearman suggested, or are there many distinct intelligences?

The evidence in favor of "g" is that abilities are correlated with each other. Individuals who are good at learning one concept are likely, on the average, to be good at learning others. The correlations are consistent enough for us to say that there are not a thousand completely separate intelligences, but they are not nearly consistent enough for us to say that there is only one general intelligence (Sternberg, 2008). In recent years, much of the debate about intelligence has focused on deciding how many distinct types of intelligence there are and describing each. For example, Sternberg (2008) describes three types of intellectual abilities: analytical, practical, and creative. Moran, Kornhaber, and Gardner (2006) describe nine **multiple intelligences**. These are listed and defined in Figure 4.2.

In recent years, Gardner's (2004) multiple-intelligence (MI) theory has been very popular in education, but it has also been controversial. Waterhouse (2006), for example, notes that there is little evidence to support MI, citing findings both from brain research and from research on measurement of IQ to argue that although there are different cognitive strengths and personalities, this does not contradict the idea that there is such a thing as general intelligence (Watkins & Canivez, 2004). Chen (2004) and Gardner and Moran (2006) argue that intelligence is more than what can be measured on an IQ test but admit that the evidence for MI is indirect.

InTASC 8

Instructional Strategies

Connections 4.4
For more on the measurement of IQ, see Chapter 14.

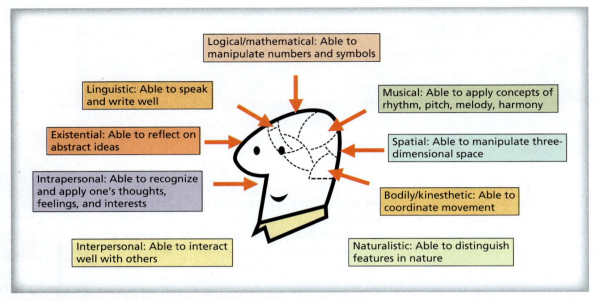

FIGURE 4.2 • Gardner's Multiple Intelligences

Moran, Kornhaber, and Gardner (2006) believe that intelligence is not to be thought of as a single entity, but rather as a combination of strengths. The types of intelligences that they described are shown above.
Source: Based on Moran, Kornhaber and Gardner (2006).

ON THE WEB

For a summary of Sternberg's work on intelligence, go to indiana.edu or wilderdom.com. For more on Gardner's multiple intelligences, visit tecweb.org (click on Learning Styles tab), thomasarmstrong.com, or howardgardner.com.

The precise number of intelligences is not important for you as an educator. What is important is the idea that good or poor performance in one area in no way guarantees similar performance in another. You should avoid thinking about children as smart or not smart, because there are many ways to be smart. Unfortunately, schools have traditionally recognized only a narrow set of performances, creating a neat hierarchy of students primarily in terms of what Gardner calls linguistic and logical/mathematical skills (only two of his nine intelligences). If schools want all children to be smart, they must use a broader range of activities and reward a broader range of performances than they have in the past.

Origins of Intelligence

The origins of intelligence have been debated for decades. Some psychologists (such as Toga & Thompson, 2005) hold that intelligence is overwhelmingly a product of heredity—that children's intelligence is largely determined by that of their parents and is set the day they are conceived. Others (such as Rifkin, 1998) just as vehemently hold that intelligence is shaped mostly by factors in a person's social environment, such as the amount a child is read to and talked to. Most investigators agree that both heredity and environment play an important part in intelligence (Petrill & Wilkerson, 2000; Plucker & Esping, 2004). It is clear that children of high-achieving parents are, on the average, more likely to be high achievers themselves, but this is as much because of the home environment created by high-achieving parents as it is because of genetics. As noted earlier in this chapter, there is evidence showing that lower-class children adopted into middle-class homes have much higher IQs than similar children who remain in lower-class homes (e.g., van IJzendoorn et al., 2005). One important piece of evidence in favor of the environmental view is

THEORY INTO PRACTICE

Multiple Intelligences

Gardner's theory of multiple intelligences implies that concepts should be taught in a variety of ways that call on many types of intelligence. Few lessons will contain parts that correspond to all types of intelligence, but a key recommendation of multiple-intelligence theory for the classroom is to include a variety of presentation modes in each lesson to expand the number of students who are likely to succeed (Armstrong, 2009; Campbell, Campbell, & Dickerson, 2004; Kornhaber, Fierros, & Veenema, 2004; Moran et al., 2006).

Intelligence, whether general or specific, is only one of many factors that influence the amount children are likely to learn in a given lesson or course. It is probably much less important than prior knowledge (the amount the student knew about the course beforehand), motivation, and the quality and nature of instruction. Intelligence does become important at the extremes; it is a critical issue in identifying students who have mental retardation and those who are gifted, but in the middle range, where most students fall, other factors are more important. IQ testing has very frequently been misused in education, especially when it has been used to assign students inappropriately to special education or to tracks or ability groups. Actual performance is far more important than IQ and is more directly susceptible to being influenced by teachers and schools (Sternberg, 2008). Boykin (2000) has argued that schools would do better to focus on developing talents rather than seeing them as fixed attributes of students.

that schooling itself clearly affects IQ scores. A review by Ceci (1991) found that the experience of being in school has a strong and systematic impact on IQ. For example, classic studies of Dutch children who entered school late because of World War II showed significant declines in IQ as a result, although their IQs increased when they finally entered school. A study of the children of mothers with mental retardation in inner-city Milwaukee (Garber, 1988) found that a program of infant stimulation and high-quality preschool could raise children's IQs substantially, and these gains were maintained at least through the end of elementary school. Studies of the Abecedarian program, which combined infant stimulation, child enrichment, and parent assistance, found lasting effects of early instruction on IQ (Ramey & Ramey, 1998). This and other evidence (see Kristof, 2009; Neuman, 2007) support the idea that IQ is not a fixed, unchangeable attribute of individuals but can change as individuals respond to changes in their environment.

Theories of Learning Styles

Just as students have different personalities, they also have different ways of learning. For example, think about how you learn the names of people you meet. Do you learn a name better if you see it written down? If so, you may be a visual learner, one who learns best by seeing or reading. If you learn a name better by hearing it, you may be an auditory learner. Of course, we all learn in many ways, but some of us learn better in some ways than in others (Swisher & Schoorman, 2001).

Aptitude–Treatment Interactions

Given the well-documented differences in learning styles and preferences, it would seem logical that different styles of teaching would have different impacts on different learners; yet this commonsense proposition has been difficult to demonstrate conclusively. Studies that have attempted to match teaching styles to learning styles have only inconsistently found any benefits for learning based on styles (Kirschner & van Merrienboer, 2013). However, the search for such aptitude–treatment interaction goes on. The commonsense conclusion from research in this area is that you should be alert to detecting and responding to the differences in the ways that children learn (see Ebeling, 2000).

Connections 4.5
For a description of studies indicating that IQ can be directly changed by certain programs, see Chapter 8.

Certification Pointer
Teacher certification tests may ask you to design a lesson that would accommodate students' various learning styles, in addition to their developmental needs.

InTASC 2
Learning Differences

InTASC 5
Application of Content

THEORY INTO PRACTICE

Understanding Diverse Thinkers

In his article "Celebrating Diverse Minds," Mel Levine (2004) of the University of North Carolina explores the importance of celebrating "all kinds of minds" as a way of making sure no child is left behind. He asks, "What becomes of students . . . who give up on themselves because they lack the kinds of minds needed to satisfy existing criteria for school success?"

Levine points out that learning differences can constitute daunting barriers, especially when they are not recognized and managed. Most important, these breakdowns can mislead us into undervaluing, unfairly accusing, and even undereducating students, thereby stifling their chances for success in school and life.

Many faltering students have specialized minds—brains exquisitely wired to perform certain kinds of tasks masterfully, but decidedly miswired when it comes to meeting other expectations. A student may be brilliant at visualizing, but embarrassingly inept at verbalizing. A classmate may reveal a remarkable understanding of people, but exhibit no insight about sentence structure.

Levine proposes addressing this problem in three ways:

- **Broaden student assessment.** Our understanding of learning differences often focuses on fixing deficits, rather than on identifying latent or blatant talents in struggling learners.
- **Reexamine the curriculum.** Explore new instructional practices and curricular choices in order to provide educational opportunities for diverse learners and to prepare them for a successful life.
- **Provide professional development for educators.** Provide teachers with training on the insights from brain research that will help them understand and support their students' diverse minds.

MyEdLab **Self-Check 4.4**

THE INTENTIONAL TEACHER

Teaching in Light of Socioeconomic, Ethnic, Language, Gender, and Intellectual Differences

Intentional teachers are aware of the diverse backgrounds and strengths of their children and take these into account in their teaching.

- They are aware of and respect student differences but do not use them as excuses to expect less of their students.
- They proactively seek professional development and other assistance to implement strategies known from research to improve outcomes for diverse students, such as cooperative learning, individual and small-group tutoring, and whole-school reform models.
- They involve parents and community members in school to connect their teaching with cultural and linguistic assets their students bring to school. They seek community volunteers to help individualize instruction for their students.

- They examine data on student achievement to inform their instructional decisions and make effective use of resources, including their own time.
- They make use of technology to individualize instruction for diverse learners who profit from this approach.
- They hold goals constant for all, while finding ways to help struggling students meet challenging standards.
- They insist on equal treatment for all, by themselves and all in the class.
- They learn about and use multicultural education methods to celebrate and build upon the assets of all of their students.

MyEdLab
Application Exercise 4.1

In the Pearson etext, watch a classroom video. Then use the guidelines in "The Intentional Teacher" to answer a set of questions that will help you reflect on and understand the teaching and learning presented in the video.

SUMMARY

What Is the Impact of Culture on Teaching and Learning?

Culture profoundly affects teaching and learning. Many aspects of culture contribute to a student's identity and self-concept and affect the student's beliefs and values, attitudes and expectations, social relations, language use, and other behaviors.

How Does Socioeconomic Status Affect Student Achievement?

Socioeconomic status—based on income, occupation, education, and social prestige—can profoundly influence students' attitudes toward school, background knowledge, school readiness, and academic achievement. The stress experienced by working-class and low-income families contributes to child-rearing practices, communication patterns, and lowered expectations that may challenge children when they enter school. Students from low-SES homes often learn a normative culture that is different from the middle-class culture of the school, which demands independence, competitiveness, and goal setting. However, low achievement is not an inevitable result of low socioeconomic status. Teachers can invite families to participate in their children's education, and this can improve students' achievement.

How Do Ethnicity and Race Affect Students' School Experiences?

Populations of underrepresented groups are growing dramatically as diversity in the United States and Canada increases. Students who are members of certain underrepresented groups— self-defined by race, religion, ethnicity, origins, history, language, and culture, such as African Americans, Native Americans, and Latinos—tend to have lower scores than European and Asian Americans on standardized tests of academic achievement. The lower scores correlate with lower socioeconomic status and reflect in part a legacy of discrimination against underrepresented groups and consequent poverty. School desegregation, long intended as a solution to educational inequities as a result of race and social class, has had mixed benefits. Continuing issues include ensuring fairness and equal opportunity, fostering racial harmony, and preventing segregation.

How Do Language Differences and Bilingual Programs Affect Student Achievement?

English learners are typically taught in one of four types of programs: English immersion, transitional bilingual, paired bilingual, and two-way bilingual. Bilingual programs teach students in their native language as well as in English. Research suggests that bilingual education, especially paired bilingual education, can have benefits for students. Recent legislation in states throughout the country has had a chilling effect on bilingual education.

What Is Multicultural Education?

Multicultural education calls for the celebration of cultural diversity and the promotion of educational equity and social harmony in the schools. Multicultural education includes content integration, knowledge construction, prejudice reduction, equity pedagogy, and an empowering school culture.

How Do Gender and Gender Bias Affect Students' School Experiences?

Many observed differences between males and females are clearly linked to differences in early socialization, when children learn sex-role behaviors regarded as appropriate. Ongoing research shows very few genetically based gender differences in thinking and abilities. However, gender bias in the classroom, including subtle differences in teacher behaviors toward male and female students and curriculum materials that contain sex-role stereotypes, has clearly affected student choices and achievement. One outcome is a gender gap in mathematics and science, though this gap is decreasing steadily. Lesbian, gay, bisexual, and transgender students experience much harassment and bullying, and schools need to create a climate of acceptance to help prevent this.

How Do Students Differ in Intelligence and Learning Styles?

Students differ in their abilities to deal with abstractions, to solve problems, and to learn. They also differ in any number of specific intelligences, so accurate estimations of intelligence should probably rely on broader performances than traditional IQ tests allow. Therefore, teachers should not base their expectations of students on IQ test scores. Binet, Spearman, Sternberg, and Gardner have contributed to theories and measures of intelligence. Both heredity and environment determine intelligence. Research shows that home environments, schooling, and life experiences can profoundly influence IQ.

Students differ in their prior learning and in their cognitive learning styles. Individual preferences in learning environments and conditions also affect student achievement.

KEY TERMS

Review the following key terms from the chapter.

aptitude–treatment interaction 91
bilingual education 81
content integration 84
culture 66
empowering school culture 84
English learners (EL) 80
equity pedagogy 84
ethnic group 75
ethnicity 75
gender bias 87
intelligence 88
intelligence quotient (IQ) 89

knowledge construction 84
language minority 80
LGBT (lesbian gay bisexual transgender) 88
limited English proficient (LEP) 80
multicultural education 84
multiple intelligences 89
prejudice reduction 84
race 75
sex-role behavior 86
socioeconomic status (SES) 67
underrepresented groups 76

SELF-ASSESSMENT: PRACTICING FOR LICENSURE

Directions: The chapter-opening vignette addresses indicators that are often assessed in state licensure exams. Reread the chapter-opening vignette, and then respond to the following questions.

1. Marva Vance and John Rossi discuss their students' diverse norms, traditions, behaviors, languages, and perceptions. Which of the following terms best describes the essence of their conversation?
   a. Race
   b. Socioeconomic status
   c. Intelligence
   d. Culture

2. Regarding the students of Marva Vance and John Rossi, which of the following statements on socioeconomic status is most likely true?
   a. Students from working-class or lower-class backgrounds perform academically as well as or better than students from middle-class homes.
   b. Students from disadvantaged homes are more likely to have inadequate access to health care.
   c. Students from middle-class and lower-class homes are equally likely to make academic progress over the summer.
   d. Schools overwhelmingly represent the values and expectations of the working class.

3. Marva Vance and John Rossi discuss their students' tendencies to accept the stereotypical roles assigned to them by society. According to research, what should the teachers do about this stereotyping?
   a. Allow students to select their own roles, even if they make stereotypical decisions.
   b. Tell the story of Thanksgiving as realistically as possible: Native American students play Native Americans, girls play cooks, and boys play hunters.
   c. Themes should be nonbiased, and individuals from underrepresented groups should appear in nonstereotypical high-status roles.
   d. Write a Thanksgiving play that includes the contributions of all underrepresented groups.

4. José, a student in Marva Vance's class, wants to be the narrator of the Thanksgiving pageant, even though he is not proficient in English. According to research on the effectiveness of bilingual programs, which strategy might Ms. Vance use to improve all her students' English speaking and writing skills?
   a. Ms. Vance should avoid bilingual programs because they have been found to be harmful to students in their English development.
   b. Ms. Vance should learn the languages of the students in her class.
   c. Ms. Vance should support bilingual education because studies have found that students in bilingual programs ultimately achieve in English as well as or better than students taught only in English.
   d. Ms. Vance should speak out about the detrimental effects of bilingual education on a student's self-esteem.

5. Marva Vance and John Rossi discuss stereotypical gender roles in the Thanksgiving pageant. From the research reported in this section, how should the teachers assign male and female students to the roles in the pageant?
   a. The teachers should encourage students to select roles in which they are interested, not roles that society expects them to play.
   b. The teachers should reduce the interactions of males and females in the pageant.
   c. The teachers should assign males and females to authentic roles: males are hunters, females are cooks.
   d. The teachers should assign all students to nontypical racial and gender roles.

6. What is multicultural education? What steps can teachers, administrators, and other school personnel take to reach their students from underrepresented groups?

7. Students differ in their prior learning and in their cognitive learning styles. What strategies can teachers use to reach all of their students?

8. List six strategies you could implement to involve parents or caregivers in helping students meet their potential.

MyEdLab **Licensure Exam 4.1** Answer questions and receive instant feedback in your Pearson eText in MyEdLab.

Blend Images/KidStock/Brand X Pictures/Getty Images

CHAPTER FIVE

Behavioral and Social Theories of Learning

LEARNING OUTCOMES

At the end of this chapter, you should be able to:

5.1 Define the concept of "learning" and describe the principles of behavioral learning theories and their implications for classroom practice

5.2 Describe social learning theories and their implications for classroom practice

5.3 Explain how behavioral and social theories of learning influence intentional teaching

CHAPTER OUTLINE (CONTINUED)

How Has Social Learning Theory Contributed to Our Understanding of Human Learning?

   Bandura: Modeling and Observational Learning

Meichenbaum's Model of Self-Regulated Learning

Strengths and Limitations of Behavioral Learning Theories

Julia Esteban, first-grade teacher at Tanner Elementary School, is trying to teach her students appropriate classroom behavior.

"Children," she says one day, "we are having a problem in this class that I'd like to discuss with you. Whenever I ask a question, many of you shout out your answers instead of raising your hand and waiting to be called on. Can anyone tell me what you should do when I ask the class a question?" Rebecca's hand shoots into the air. "I know, I know!" she says. "Raise your hand and wait quietly!"

Ms. Esteban sighs to herself. She tries to ignore Rebecca, who is doing exactly what she had just been told not to do, but Rebecca is the only student with her hand up, and the longer she delays, the more frantically Rebecca waves her hand and shouts her answer.

"All right, Rebecca. What are you supposed to do?"

"We're supposed to raise our hands and wait quietly for you to call on us."

"If you know the rule, why were you shouting out your answer before I called on you?"

"I guess I forgot."

"All right. Can anyone remind the class of our rule about talking out of turn?"

Four children raise their hands and shout together: "One at a time!"

"Take turns!"

"Don't talk when someone else is talking!"

Ms. Esteban calls for order. "You kids are going to drive me crazy!" she says. "Didn't we just talk about how to raise your hands and wait for me to call on you?"

"But Ms. Esteban," says Stephen without even raising his hand. "You called on Rebecca and she wasn't quiet!"

USING YOUR EXPERIENCE

CRITICAL AND CREATIVE THINKING Reflect on what Ms. Esteban might do differently in this situation to accomplish her goal.

COOPERATIVE LEARNING Discuss with another student what went wrong here. Also discuss similar ways in which you have seen inappropriate behavior reinforced in the past. Share some of these anecdotes with the class.

Children are excellent learners. What they learn, however, may not always be what we intend to teach. Ms. Esteban is trying to teach students how to behave in class, but by paying attention to Rebecca's outburst, she is actually teaching them the opposite of what she intends. Rebecca craves her teacher's attention, so being called on (even in an exasperated tone of voice) rewards her for calling out her answer. Not only does Ms. Esteban's response increase the chances that Rebecca will call out answers again, but also Rebecca now serves as a model for her classmates' own calling out. What Ms. Esteban says is less important than the actual response she makes to her students' behaviors.

The purpose of this chapter is to define learning and then present behavioral and social learning theories, explanations for learning that emphasize observable behaviors. **Behavioral learning theories** focus on the ways that pleasurable or unpleasant consequences of behavior change individuals' behavior over time and the ways individuals model their behavior on that of others. **Social learning theories** focus on the effects of thought on action and of action on thought. Later chapters present **cognitive learning theories**, which emphasize unobservable mental processes that people use to learn and remember new information or skills. In recent years, however, the boundaries between behavioral and cognitive learning theories have become increasingly indistinct as each school of thought has incorporated the findings of the other.

Connections 5.1

See Chapter 6 for more information about cognitive theories of learning.

WHAT IS LEARNING?

What is learning? This seems like a simple question until you begin to think about it. Consider the following four examples. Are they instances of learning?

1. A young child takes her first steps.
2. An adolescent male feels a strong attraction to certain females.
3. A child feels anxious when he sees the doctor coming with a needle.
4. Long after learning how to multiply, a girl realizes on her own that another way to multiply by 5 is to divide by 2 and multiply by 10 (e.g., 428×5 can be figured as follows: $428/2 = 214 \times 10 = 2,140$).

> **InTASC 1**
>
> **Learner Development**

Learning is usually defined as a change in an individual caused by experience (Schunk, 2012). Mayer (2008a) defines learning as "long-lasting change in the learner's knowledge as a result of the learner's experiences" (p. 171). Changes caused by development (such as growing taller) are not instances of learning. Neither are characteristics of individuals that are present at birth (such as reflexes and responses to hunger or pain). However, humans do so much learning from the day of their birth (and some say earlier) that learning and development are inseparably linked. Learning to walk (example 1 above) is mostly a developmental progression but also depends on experience with crawling and other activities. The adolescent sex drive (example 2) is not learned, but learning shapes individuals' choices of desirable partners.

A child's anxiety on seeing a doctor with a needle (example 3) is definitely learned behavior. The child has learned to associate the needle with pain, and his body reacts emotionally when he sees the needle. This reaction may be unconscious or involuntary, but it is learned nonetheless.

The fourth example, the girl's insight into the multiplication shortcut, is an instance of internally generated learning, better known as thinking. Some theorists would not call this learning, because it was not directly caused by the environment. But it might be considered a case of delayed learning, in which deliberate instruction in multiplication plus years of experience with numbers plus mental effort on the part of the girl produced an insight.

Learning takes place in many ways. Sometimes it is intentional, as when students acquire information presented in a classroom or when they look something up on the Internet. Sometimes it is unintentional, as in the case of the child's reaction to the needle. All sorts of learning are going on all the time. As you are reading this chapter, you are learning something about learning. However, you are also learning that educational psychology is interesting or dull, useful or useless. Without knowing it, you are probably learning about where on the page certain pieces of information are to be found. You might be learning to associate the content of this chapter with unimportant aspects of your surroundings as you read it, such as the smell of books in a library or the temperature of the room in which you are reading. The content of this chapter; the placement of words on the page; and the smells, sounds, and temperature of your surroundings are all **stimuli**. Your senses are usually wide open to all sorts of stimuli, or environmental events or conditions, but you are consciously aware of only a fraction of them at any one time.

The problem you face as a teacher is not how to get students to learn; students are already engaged in learning every waking moment. Rather, it is how to help students learn particular information, skills, and concepts that will be useful in their lives. How do we present students with the right stimuli on which to focus their attention and mental effort so that they will acquire important skills? That is the central challenge of instruction.

WHAT ARE BEHAVIORAL LEARNING THEORIES?

The systematic study of learning is relatively new. Not until the late 19th century was learning studied in a scientific manner. Using techniques borrowed from the physical sciences, researchers began conducting experiments to understand how people and animals learn. One of the most important early researchers was Ivan Pavlov. Among later researchers, B. F. Skinner was important for his studies of the relationship between behavior and consequences.

Pavlov: Classical Conditioning

In the late 1800s and early 1900s, Russian scientist Ivan Pavlov and his colleagues studied the digestive process in dogs (Borich, 2014; Ormrod, 2016). During their research, the scientists noticed changes in the timing and rate of salivation of these animals. Pavlov observed that if meat was placed in or near the mouth of a hungry dog, the dog would salivate. Because the meat provoked this response automatically, without any prior training or conditioning, the meat is referred to as an **unconditioned stimulus**. Similarly, because salivation occurred automatically in the presence of meat, also without the need for any training or experience, this response of salivating is referred to as an **unconditioned response**.

While the meat will produce salivation without any previous experience or training, other stimuli, such as the ringing of a bell, will not produce salivation. Because these stimuli have no effect on the response in question, they are referred to as **neutral stimuli**. Pavlov's experiments showed that if a previously neutral stimulus is presented at the same time as an unconditioned stimulus, the neutral stimulus becomes a **conditioned stimulus** and gains the power to prompt a response similar to that produced by the unconditioned stimulus. In other words, after the bell and the meat are presented together several times, the ringing of the bell alone causes the dog to salivate. This process is referred to as **classical conditioning**. A diagram of Pavlov's theory is shown in Figure 5.1. In experiments such as these, Pavlov and his colleagues showed how learning could affect what were once thought to be involuntary, reflexive behaviors, such as salivating.

Skinner: Operant Conditioning

Some human behaviors are clearly prompted by specific stimuli. Just like Pavlov's dogs, we salivate when we are hungry and see appetizing food. However, B. F. Skinner proposed that reflexive behavior accounts for only a small proportion of all actions. Skinner proposed another class of behavior, which he labeled *operant behaviors* because they operate on the environment in the apparent absence of any unconditioned stimuli, such as food. Skinner's work focused on the relation between behavior and its consequences (Borich, 2014; Ormrod, 2016). For example, if an individual's behavior is immediately followed by pleasurable consequences, the individual will engage in that behavior more frequently. The use of pleasant and unpleasant consequences to change behavior is often referred to as **operant conditioning**.

Skinner's work focused on placing subjects in controlled situations and observing the changes in their behavior produced by systematic changes in the consequences of their behavior (see Alberto & Troutman, 2013; Schunk, 2016; Walker, Shea, & Bauer, 2011). Skinner is famous for his development and use of the **Skinner box**, a device that contains a very simple apparatus for studying the behavior of animals, usually rats and pigeons. A Skinner box for rats consists of a bar that is easy for the rat to press, a food dispenser that can give the rat a pellet of food, and a water dispenser. The rat cannot see or hear anything outside of the box, so all stimuli are controlled by the experimenter.

In some of the earliest experiments involving Skinner boxes, the apparatus was first set up so that if the rat happened to press the bar, it would receive a food pellet. After a few accidental bar presses, the rat would start pressing the bar frequently, receiving a pellet each time. The food reward had conditioned the rat's behavior, strengthening bar pressing and weakening all other behaviors (such as wandering around the box). At this point, the experimenter might do any of several things. The food dispenser might be set up so that several bar presses were then required to obtain food, or so that some bar presses produced food but others did not, or so that bar presses no longer produced food. In each case the rat's behavior would be electronically recorded. One important advantage of the Skinner box is that it allows for careful scientific study of behavior in a controlled environment. Anyone with the same equipment can repeat Skinner's experiments.

Certification Pointer

Pavlov's work will probably be on your teacher certification test. Know that a ringing bell was the conditioned stimulus that he used to get dogs to salivate without the presence of meat. The bell became a conditioned stimulus because Pavlov first paired ringing with meat.

Certification Pointer

Most teacher certification tests will require you to know that when a teacher reinforces a student who raises her hand to speak, she is using operant conditioning.

ON THE WEB

The B. F. Skinner Foundation website at bfskinner.org aims to improve the understanding of human behavior through the work of B. F. Skinner.

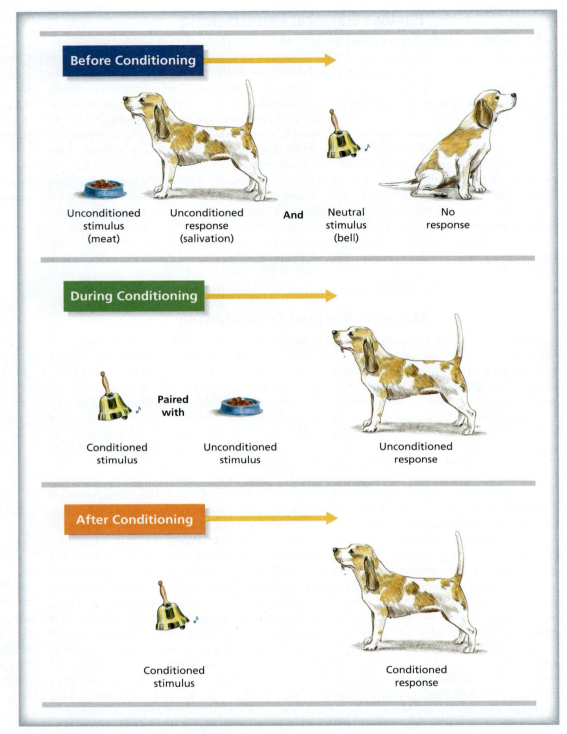

Before Conditioning

Unconditioned stimulus (meat) Unconditioned response (salivation) **And** Neutral stimulus (bell) No response

During Conditioning

Conditioned stimulus **Paired with** Unconditioned stimulus Unconditioned response

After Conditioning

Conditioned stimulus Conditioned response

FIGURE 5.1 • Classical Conditioning

In classical conditioning, a neutral stimulus (such as a bell) that at first prompts no response becomes paired with an unconditioned stimulus (such as meat) and gains the power of that stimulus to cause a response (such as salivation).

WHAT ARE SOME PRINCIPLES OF BEHAVIORAL LEARNING?

Behavioral learning theory has its own language to describe how consequences of behavior shape later behavior (also see Alberto & Troutman, 2013; Rappaport & Minahan, 2012; Sarafino, 2012; Schunk, 2016; Walker, Shea, & Bauer, 2011; Zirpoli, 2016).

The Role of Consequences

Skinner's pioneering work with rats and pigeons established a set of principles of behavior that have been supported in hundreds of studies involving humans as well as animals. Perhaps the most important principle of behavioral learning theories is that behavior changes according to its immediate **consequences**. Pleasurable consequences strengthen behavior; unpleasant consequences weaken it. In other words, pleasurable consequences increase the frequency with which an individual engages in a behavior, whereas unpleasant consequences reduce the frequency of a behavior. If students enjoy reading books, they will probably read more often. If they find stories boring or are unable to concentrate, they may read less often, choosing other activities instead. Pleasurable consequences are called *reinforcers;* unpleasant consequences are called *punishers.*

Reinforcers

A **reinforcer** is any consequence that strengthens (that is, increases the frequency of) a behavior. Note that the effectiveness of the reinforcer must be demonstrated. We cannot assume that a particular consequence is a reinforcer until we have evidence that it strengthens behavior for a particular individual. For example, candy might generally be considered a reinforcer for young children, but after a big meal a child might not find candy pleasurable, and some children do not like candy at all. A teacher who says, "I reinforced him with praise for staying in his seat during math time, but it didn't work," may be misusing the term *reinforced* if there is no evidence that praise is in fact a reinforcer for this particular student. No reward can be assumed to be a reinforcer for everyone under all conditions (Alberto & Troutman, 2013; Jones & Jones, 2016; Scheurmann & Hall, 2016; Zirpoli, 2016).

PRIMARY AND SECONDARY REINFORCERS Reinforcers fall into two broad categories: primary and secondary. **Primary reinforcers** satisfy basic human needs. Some examples are food, water, security, warmth, and sex. **Secondary reinforcers** are reinforcers that acquire their value by being associated with primary reinforcers or other well-established secondary reinforcers. For example, money has no value to a young child until the child learns that money can be used to buy things that are themselves primary or secondary reinforcers. Grades have little value to students unless their families notice and value good grades, and families' praise is of value because it is associated with love, warmth, security, and other reinforcers. There are three basic categories of secondary reinforcers. One is social reinforcers, such as praise, smiles, hugs, or attention. When Ms. Esteban recognized Rebecca, she was inadvertently giving Rebecca a social reinforcer: her own attention. Other types of secondary reinforcers are activity reinforcers (such as access to toys, games, or fun activities) and token (or symbolic) reinforcers (such as money, grades, stars, or points that individuals can exchange for other reinforcers).

POSITIVE AND NEGATIVE REINFORCERS Most often, the reinforcers used in schools are **positive reinforcers** that include praise, grades, and stars. However, a behavior is also strengthened if its consequence is an escape from an unpleasant situation or a way of preventing something unpleasant from occurring. For example, a parent might release a student from doing the dishes for completing homework. If doing the dishes is seen as an unpleasant task, release from it will be reinforcing. Escapes from unpleasant situations are called **negative reinforcers** (Sarafino, 2012; Scheuermann & Hall, 2016; Zirpoli, 2016).

The term *negative reinforcer* is often misinterpreted to mean punishment, as in "I negatively reinforced him for being late by having him stay in during recess" (Martella, Nelson, Marchand-Martella, & O'Reilly, 2012). One way to avoid this error in terminology is to remember that reinforcers (whether positive or negative) strengthen behavior, whereas punishment is designed to discourage or weaken behavior (see Table 5.1).

Connections 5.2
See Chapter 11 for classroom applications, including applied behavioral analysis.

MyEdLab
Video Example 5.1

In this special education class, students earn "money" for appropriate behaviors, and they can then spend it in an auction. Both the money and the auction items on which it is spent are secondary reinforcers.

TABLE 5.1 • Consequences in Behavioral Learning

STRENGTHENS BEHAVIOR	DISCOURAGES BEHAVIOR
Positive Reinforcement	No Reinforcement
Example: Rewarding or praising	Example: Ignoring
Negative Reinforcement	Removal Punishment
Example: Excusing from an undesirable task or situation	Example: Forbidding a desirable task or situation
	Presentation Punishment
	Example: Imposing an undesirable task or situation

Certification Pointer

Teacher certification tests are likely to require you to know that when a teacher says, "If you get an A on tomorrow's test, you won't have to do homework the rest of the week," she's using negative reinforcement (escape from an unpleasant consequence, assuming homework is unpleasant!).

InTASC 8

Instructional Strategies

InTASC 6

Assessment

THE PREMACK PRINCIPLE One important principle of behavior is that we can promote behaviors by making access to something desirable contingent on doing something less desirable. For example, a teacher might say, "As soon as you finish your work, you may go outside" or "Clean up your art project, and then I will read you a story." These are examples of the classic **Premack Principle** (Premack, 1965), sometimes called "Grandma's Rule" from the age-old statement "Eat

THEORY INTO PRACTICE

Classroom Uses of Reinforcement

The behavioral learning principle most useful for classroom practice is also the simplest: Reinforce behaviors you wish to see repeated. This principle may seem obvious, but in practice it is not as easy as it appears. For example, some teachers take the attitude that reinforcement is unnecessary, reasoning, "Why should I reinforce them? They're just doing what they're supposed to do!"

Guidelines for the use of reinforcement to increase desired behavior in the classroom follow (see Alberto & Troutman, 2013; Jones & Jones, 2016; Martella, Nelson, Marchand-Martella, & O'Reilley, 2012; Scheuermann & Hall, 2016; Walker et al., 2011; Wheeler & Richey, 2014).

1. *Decide what behaviors you want from students, and reinforce these behaviors when they occur.* For example, praise or reward good work. Do not praise or reward work that is not up to students' capabilities. As students begin a new task, they will need to be reinforced at every step along the way. Close approximations of what you hope to accomplish as a final product must receive positive feedback. Break down new behaviors (classroom assignments) into smaller parts and provide adequate rewards along the way.
2. *Tell students what behaviors you want; when they exhibit the desired behaviors and you reinforce them, tell them why.* Present students with a rubric that itemizes the criteria you will use when evaluating their work, and include the point value for each criterion. Students then will be able to discriminate their own strengths and weaknesses from the feedback they receive from you.
3. *Reinforce appropriate behavior as soon as possible after it occurs.* Delayed reinforcement is less effective than immediate reinforcement. When you are grading an assignment, present feedback to your students as soon as possible. It is important that students know how they are doing in class, so don't delay providing their grades. When constructing an assignment, you should always consider the grading scheme that you will use and how long it will take you to provide the intended feedback.

your vegetables, and then you may play." You can use the Premack Principle by alternating more enjoyable activities with less enjoyable ones and making participation in fun activities depend on successful completion of the less enjoyable ones. For example, in elementary school it may be a good idea to schedule music, which most students consider an enjoyable activity, after a difficult subject, so students will know not to fool around during the difficult subject and risk losing part of their desired music time (Borich, 2014; Martella et al., 2012; Wheeler & Richey, 2014).

INTRINSIC AND EXTRINSIC REINFORCERS Often, the most important reinforcer that maintains behavior is the pleasure inherent in engaging in the behavior. For example, most people have a hobby that they work on for extended periods without any reward. People like to draw, read, sing, play games, hike, or swim for no reason other than the fun of doing it. Reinforcers of this type are called **intrinsic reinforcers**, and people can be described as being intrinsically motivated to engage in a given activity. Intrinsic reinforcers are contrasted with **extrinsic reinforcers**, praise or rewards given to motivate people to engage in a behavior that they might not engage in without it. There is evidence that reinforcing children for certain behaviors they would have done anyway can undermine long-term intrinsic motivation (Deci & Ryan, 2002). Research on this topic finds that the undermining effect of extrinsic reinforcers occurs only in a limited set of circumstances, in which rewards are provided to children for engaging in an activity without any standard of performance, and only if the activity is one that children would have done on their own without any reward (Cameron & Pierce, 1994, 1996; Eisenberger, Pierce, & Cameron, 1999). Verbal praise and other types of feedback are extrinsic reinforcers that have been found to increase, not decrease, intrinsic interest. What this research suggests for practice is that you should be cautious about giving reinforcers to children for activities they would have done on their own. However, for most school tasks, which most students would not have done on their own, there is no basis for concern that use of extrinsic reinforcers will undermine intrinsic motivation, especially if those reinforcers are social and communicate recognition of students' growing mastery and independence. In fact, it has been argued that failure to use positive reinforcement when it would have been effective in increasing positive behaviors is unethical (e.g., Bailey & Burch, 2005; Maag, 2001). For example, consider a student who is at risk of being expelled due to fighting. If a program of positive reinforcement for avoiding fighting might have eliminated the student's fighting, then educators would be ethically bound to try such a plan (or others) before considering such a serious step as expulsion (Rappaport & Minahan, 2012a, b).

Connections 5.3

For more on intrinsic and extrinsic motivation, see Chapter 10.

ON THE WEB

For a debate on the issue of intrinsic versus extrinsic motivation, visit princeton.edu.

THEORY INTO PRACTICE

Practical Reinforcers

Anything that children like can be an effective reinforcer, but there are obvious practical limitations on what should be used in classrooms. One general principle of positive reinforcement is that it is best to use the least elaborate or tangible reinforcer that will work. In other words, if praise or self-reinforcement or feedback on progress will work, don't use certificates. If certificates will work, don't use small toys. If small toys will work, don't use food. One way to find out what reinforcers to use is to ask the students themselves, who are

(continued)

more likely to work for a reinforcer they have selected (Jones & Jones, 2016; Zirpoli, 2016). However, do not hesitate to use whatever practical reinforcer is necessary to motivate children to do important tasks. In particular, try all possible reinforcement strategies before even thinking of punishment (described next). A few categories of reinforcers and examples of each appear here (also see Alberto & Troutman, 2013; Martella et al., 2012; Scheuermann & Hall, 2016; Wheeler & Richey, 2014). These are arranged from least to most tangible.

1. *Self-reinforcement.* Students may be taught to praise themselves, give themselves a mental pat on the back, check off progress on a form, take a short break, or otherwise reinforce themselves for completing an assignment or staying on task (Schunk, 2016).

2. *Praise.* Phrases such as "Good job," "Way to go," "I knew you could do it," and other verbal praise can be effective, but the same message can often be delivered with a smile, a wink, a thumbs-up signal, or a pat on the back. In cooperative learning and peer tutoring, students can be encouraged to praise each other for appropriate behavior (Walker et al., 2011).

3. *Attention.* The attention of a valued adult or peer can be a very effective reinforcer for many children. Listening, nodding, or moving closer may provide a child with the positive attention she or he is seeking. For outstanding performance or for meeting goals over a longer time period, students might be allowed a special time to visit with the custodian, to help in the office, or to take a walk with the principal (Scheuermann & Hall, 2016; Wheeler & Richey, 2014; Zirpoli, 2016).

4. *Grades and recognition.* Good marks and other honors (e.g., certificates of accomplishment) can be effective both in giving students positive feedback on their efforts and in communicating progress to families, who are likely to reinforce good reports themselves. Public displays of good work, notes from the principal, and other commendations can have the same effect. Quiz scores, behavior ratings, and other feedback given frequently can be more effective than report card grades covering months of work.

5. *Call home.* Calling or sending a note to a child's caregivers to recognize success can be a powerful reinforcer.

6. *Home-based reinforcement.* Families can be effective partners in a reinforcement system. Teachers can work out an arrangement with families in which children receive special privileges at home when they meet well-specified standards of behavior or performance.

7. *Privileges.* Children can get free time, access to special equipment (such as soccer balls or games), or special roles (such as running errands or distributing papers). Children or groups who have behaved well can simply be allowed to line up first for recess or dismissal or enjoy other small privileges.

8. *Activity reinforcers.* After achieving preestablished standards, students can earn videos, games, or access to other fun activities. Activity reinforcers lend themselves particularly well to group contingencies, in which a whole class can earn free time or special activities if students collectively achieve a standard (Scheuermann & Hall, 2016; Wheeler & Richey, 2014).

9. *Tangible reinforcers.* Children can be rewarded for achievement or good behavior with points that they can exchange for small toys, erasers, pencils, marbles, comic books, stickers, and so on. Tangible reinforcers usually work better when children have a choice among several options (Jones & Jones, 2016; Zirpoli, 2016).

10. *Food.* Grapes, apples, carrots, yogurt, or other healthy snacks can be used as reinforcers.

Connections 5.4

For more on working with parents to reinforce behavior, see Chapter 11.

Connections 5.5

For more on the use of activity reinforcers, see Chapter 11.

Punishers

Consequences that weaken behavior are called *punishers*. Note that there is the same catch in the definition of **punishment** as in the definition of *reinforcement*: If an apparently unpleasant consequence does not reduce the frequency of the behavior it follows, it is not necessarily a punisher. For example, some students like being sent to the principal's office or out to the hall because it releases them from the classroom, which they see as an unpleasant situation (Rappaport & Minahan, 2012a, b; Scheuermann & Hall, 2016). Some students like to be scolded because it gains them your attention and perhaps enhances their status among their peers. As with reinforcers, the effectiveness of a punisher cannot be assumed but must be demonstrated. Punishment can take two primary forms.

PRESENTATION PUNISHMENT The use of unpleasant consequences, or **aversive stimuli**, characterizes **presentation punishment**, as when a student is scolded.

REMOVAL PUNISHMENT The withdrawal of a pleasant consequence describes **removal punishment**. Examples include loss of a privilege, having to stay in during recess, and receiving detention after school. Another example, called **response cost** (Landrum & McDuffie, 2008), involves charging a cost to students who are behaving inappropriately, such as a minute of detention after school for every minute off task. One frequently used form of removal punishment in classrooms is **time out**, in which a student who misbehaves is required to sit in the corner or in the hall for several minutes. Teachers often use time out when they believe that the attention of other students is serving to reinforce misbehavior; time out deprives the student who has misbehaved of this reinforcer. Using time out as a consequence for misbehavior has generally been found to reduce the misbehavior (Alberto & Troutman, 2013; Zirpoli, 2016).

In one classic study, White and Bailey (1990) evaluated use of a sit-and-watch consequence for physical education classes. Children who misbehaved were told what they had done wrong, were given a 3-minute sand timer, and were then asked to sit and watch until the sand ran out. The program was first tried in an alternative class for fourth- and fifth-graders with serious behavior problems. Figure 5.2 summarizes the findings. After a baseline of up to 343 disruptive behaviors in 10 minutes was observed, a behavioral checklist program was tried, in which teachers rated each child's behavior and sent poorly behaved children to the office or deprived them of a free period. This reduced misbehavior but did not eliminate it. However, when the sit-and-watch procedure was introduced, misbehavior virtually disappeared. The same sit-and-watch method was used in a regular fourth-grade physical education class, and the results were similar.

The issue of whether, when, and how to punish has been a source of considerable controversy among behavioral learning theorists. Some have claimed that the effects of punishment, especially presentation (aversive) punishment, are only temporary, that punishment produces aggression, and that it causes individuals to avoid settings in which it is used (Martin & Pear, 2011; Wheeler & Richey, 2014; Zirpoli, 2016). Even behavioral learning theorists who do support the use of punishment agree that it should be resorted to only when reinforcement for appropriate behavior has been tried and has failed; that when punishment is necessary, it should take the mildest possible form; and that punishment should always be used as part of a careful plan, never inconsistently or out of frustration. Physical punishment in schools (such as spanking) is illegal in most places (Jones & Jones, 2016; Walker et al., 2011) and is universally opposed by behavioral learning theorists on ethical as well as scientific grounds (see Alberto & Troutman, 2013; Bailey & Burch, 2005; Kazdin, 2001; Rappaport & Minahan, 2012a, b; Scheuermann & Hall, 2016; Wheeler & Richey, 2014).

Immediacy of Consequences

One very important principle of behavioral learning theories is that consequences that follow behaviors closely in time affect behavior far more than delayed consequences. Praising a student right away may be more effective than giving them a significant privilege later on. A smaller reinforcer that is given immediately generally has a much larger effect than a large reinforcer given later (Alberto & Troutman, 2013; Scheuermann & Hall, 2016; Wheeler & Richey, 2014). This concept explains much about human behavior. It suggests, for example, why people find it so difficult to give up smoking or overeating. Even though the benefits

Certification Pointer

For teacher certification tests you will probably need to know that unless an unpleasant consequence reduces the frequency of the behavior it follows, it may not be a punisher.

FIGURE 5.2 • Reducing Disruptive Behavior with Sit and Watch

The number of disruptive behaviors per 10-minute observation period is shown here.
Source: From *Reducing disruptive behaviors of elementary physical education students with Sit and Watch*, by A. G. White and J. S. Bailey. By University of Kansas, Copyright © 1990 reprinted with permission of University of Kansas.

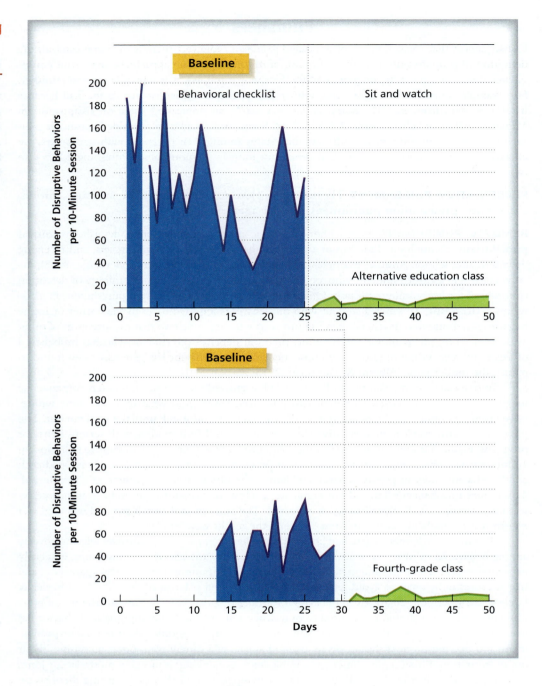

of giving up smoking or of losing weight are substantial and well known, the small but immediate reinforcement of just one cigarette or one doughnut often overcomes the behavioral effect of the large but delayed reinforcers. In the classroom the principle of immediacy of consequences is also very important. Moving close to a student who is misbehaving, touching his or her shoulder, or making a gesture (e.g., finger to lips to ask for silence) may be much more effective than a scolding or warning given at the end of class (Jones & Jones, 2016; Zirpoli, 2016).

Immediate feedback serves at least two purposes. First, it makes clear the connection between behavior and consequence. Second, it increases the informational value of the feedback. In dealing with misbehavior, you can apply the principle of immediacy of consequences by responding immediately and positively when students are not misbehaving—in effect, by catching them in the act of being good!

Shaping

Immediacy of reinforcement is important to teaching, but so is the decision of what to reinforce. Should a kindergarten teacher withhold reinforcement until a child knows the sounds of all 26 letters? Certainly not. It would be better to praise children for recognizing one letter, then for recognizing several, and finally for learning the sounds of all 26 letters. Should a music teacher withhold reinforcement until a young student has played a piano piece flawlessly? Or should the teacher praise the first halting run-through? Most students need reinforcement along the way. When you guide students toward goals by reinforcing the many steps that lead to success, you are using a technique called **shaping**.

The term *shaping* is used in behavioral learning theories to refer to the teaching of new skills or behaviors by reinforcing learners for approaching the desired final behavior (Alberto & Troutman, 2013; Scheuermann & Hall, 2016). For example, in teaching children to tie their shoelaces, we would not simply show them how it is done and then wait to reinforce them until they do the whole job themselves. Rather, we would first reinforce them for tying the first knot, then for making the loops, and so on, until they can do the entire task. In this way we would be shaping the children's behavior by reinforcing all those steps that lead toward the final goal.

Shaping is an important tool in classroom instruction. Let's say we want students to be able to write paragraphs with a topic sentence, three supporting details, and a concluding sentence. This task has many parts: being able to recognize and then produce topic sentences, supporting details, and concluding sentences; being able to write complete sentences using capitalization, punctuation, and grammar correctly; and being able to spell. If you taught a lesson on all these skills and then asked students to write paragraphs, scoring them on content, grammar, punctuation, and spelling, most students would fail and would probably learn little from the exercise.

Instead, you might teach the skills step by step, gradually shaping the final skill. Students might be taught how to write first topic sentences, then supporting details, then concluding sentences. Early on, they might be held responsible only for paragraph content. Later, the requirement for reinforcement might be increased to include grammar and punctuation. Finally, spelling might be added as a criterion for success. At each stage, students would have a good chance to be reinforced because the criterion for reinforcement would be within their grasp. The principle here is that students should be reinforced for behaviors that are within their current capabilities but that also stretch them toward new skills. (Recall from Chapter 2 that Vygotsky expressed the same idea as teaching in the proximal zone of development.)

MyEdLab
Video Example 5.2
This teacher effectively shapes students' paragraph-writing skills by breaking down the process into steps, modeling the first step, and engaging the students to help her complete the remaining steps. The students then have an opportunity to practice independently.

Extinction

By definition, reinforcers strengthen behavior. But what happens when reinforcers are withdrawn? Eventually, the behavior will be weakened, and ultimately it will disappear. This process is called **extinction** of a previously learned behavior (Borich, 2014).

Extinction is rarely a smooth process. When reinforcers are withdrawn, individuals often increase their rate of behavior for a while. For example, think of a door that you've used as a shortcut to somewhere you go frequently. Imagine that one day the door will not open. You may push even harder for a while, shake the door, turn the handle both ways, perhaps even kick the door. You are likely to feel frustrated and angry. However, after a short time you will realize that the door is locked and go away. If the door is permanently locked (without your knowing it), you may try it a few times over the next few days and then perhaps once after a month; only eventually will you give up on it.

Your behavior when confronted by the locked door illustrates a classic extinction pattern. Behavior intensifies when the reinforcer is first withdrawn and then rapidly weakens until the behavior disappears. Still, the behavior may return after much time has passed. For example, you could try the door again a year later to see whether it is still locked. If it is, you will probably leave it alone for a longer time, but perhaps not forever.

The characteristic **extinction burst**, the increase in levels of a behavior in the early stages of extinction, has important consequences for classroom management. For example, imagine that you have decided to extinguish a child's inappropriate calling out of answers (instead of raising her hand to be recognized) by ignoring her until she raises her hand quietly. At first, ignoring the child

A dinosaur goes through extinction.

is likely to increase her calling-out behavior, a classic extinction burst. You might then mistakenly conclude that ignoring isn't working, when in fact continuing to ignore inappropriate call-outs is exactly the right strategy if you keep it up (Martella et al., 2012; Walker et al., 2011). Worse, you might finally decide to give in and recognize the child after the third or fourth call-out. This would teach the worst possible message: that calling out works eventually if you keep doing it. This would probably result in an increase in the very behavior you were trying to reduce, as the child learns that "if at first you don't succeed, try, try again" (Rappaport & Minahan, 2012a, b; Scheuermann & Hall, 2016). This is the case in the vignette presented at the beginning of this chapter. Ms. Esteban at first ignores Rebecca's calling out, so she calls out even louder. Then the teacher calls on Rebecca, unintentionally communicating to her that only loud and persistent calling out will be reinforced.

Extinction of a previously learned behavior can be hastened when some stimulus or cue informs the individual that behaviors that were once encouraged will no longer be reinforced. In the case of the locked door, a sign saying, "Door permanently locked—use other entrance" would have greatly reduced the number of times you tried the door before giving up on it. Call-outs will be reduced much more quickly if Ms. Esteban tells her class, "I will no longer respond to children unless they are silent and are raising their hand," and then ignores all other attempts to get her attention.

Schedules of Reinforcement

The effects of reinforcement on behavior depend on many factors, one of the most important of which is the **schedule of reinforcement** (see Alberto & Troutman, 2013; Borich, 2014; Miltenberger, 2012; Wheeler & Richey, 2014). This term refers to the frequency with which reinforcers are given, the amount of time that elapses between opportunities for reinforcement, and the predictability of reinforcement.

FIXED RATIO (FR) One common schedule of reinforcement is the **fixed-ratio (FR) schedule**, in which a reinforcer is given after a fixed number of behaviors. For example, you might say, "As soon as you finish 10 problems, you may go outside." Regardless of the amount of time it takes, students are reinforced as soon as they finish 10 problems. This is an example of an FR10 schedule (10 behaviors for one reinforcer). One common form of fixed-ratio schedule gives reinforcement for each behavior. This is called *continuous reinforcement* (CRF), or FR1. Putting money in a soda machine is (usually) an example of continuous reinforcement because one behavior (inserting money) results in one reinforcer (a soda). Giving correct answers in class is also usually continuously reinforced. The student gives a good answer, and you say, "Right! Good answer!"

One important process in instruction is gradually increasing reinforcement ratios. Early in a sequence of lessons, it may be necessary to reinforce students for every correct answer, such as responding to every successful math problem. However, this is inefficient in the long run. As soon as students are answering math problems correctly, it may be possible to reinforce every 5 problems (FR5), every 10 (FR10), and so on. Thinning out the reinforcement schedule in this way enhances the students' ability to work independently without reinforcement and makes the behavior more resistant to extinction. Ultimately, students might be asked to do entire projects on their own, receiving no reinforcement until the projects are completed.

Fixed-ratio schedules are effective in motivating individuals to do a great deal of work—especially if the fixed ratio starts with continuous reinforcement (FR1) to get the individual going and then moves to higher requirements for reinforcement. One reason why high requirements for reinforcement produce higher levels of behavior than low requirements is that reinforcing too frequently can make the value of the reinforcer wear off. Students who are praised for every math problem will soon grow tired of being praised, and the reinforcer may lose its value.

VARIABLE RATIO (VR) A **variable-ratio (VR) schedule** of reinforcement is one in which the number of behaviors required for reinforcement is unpredictable, although it is certain that the behaviors will eventually be reinforced. For example, a slot machine is a variable-ratio reinforcer. It may pay off after 1 pull one time and after 200 pulls the next time, and there is no way to predict which pull will win. In the classroom, teachers often use a variable-ratio schedule when students raise their hands to answer questions. Although they never know when they will be reinforced by being able to give the correct answer, students may expect to be called on about 1 time in 20 in a class of 20 (a VR20 schedule) because, on the average, 20 behaviors are required for one reinforcer. Variable-ratio schedules tend to produce high and stable rates of behavior. In fact, almost all gambling games involve VR schedules, so they can be literally addicting. Similarly, use of frequent random checks of student work can help to motivate steady, careful work.

Variable-ratio schedules are highly resistant to extinction. Even after behaviors are no longer being reinforced, people may not give up working for a long time. Because they have learned that it may take a lot of work to be rewarded, they keep on working in the mistaken belief that the next effort might just pay off.

FIXED INTERVAL (FI) In **fixed-interval (FI) schedules**, reinforcement is available only at certain periodic times. The final examination is a classic example. Fixed-interval schedules create an interesting pattern of behavior. The individual may do very little until just before reinforcement is available and then expend a burst of effort as the time for reinforcement approaches. This pattern can be demonstrated with rats and pigeons on fixed-interval schedules, but it is even more apparent in students who cram at the last minute before a test or who write their monthly book reports the night before they are due. These characteristics of fixed-interval schedules suggest that frequent short quizzes may be better than infrequent major exams for encouraging students to do their best all the time, rather than pulling all-nighters before exams (Scheuermann & Hall, 2016; Wheeler & Richey, 2014).

VARIABLE INTERVAL (VI) In a **variable-interval (VI) schedule**, reinforcement is available at some times but not at others, and we have no idea when a behavior will be reinforced. An example of this is making spot checks of students who are doing assignments in class. Students are reinforced if they are working well at the particular moment you come by. Because they cannot predict when you will check them, students must be doing good work all the time. People may obey traffic laws out of respect for the law and civic responsibility, but it also helps that the police randomly check drivers' compliance with the law. Troopers using speed cameras often hide on overpasses or behind hills so that they can get a random sampling of drivers' behavior. If they were always in plain sight, their presence would be a signal to drive carefully, so the necessity for driving carefully at other times would be reduced.

Like variable-ratio schedules, variable-interval schedules are very effective for maintaining a high rate of behavior while being highly resistant to extinction. For example, let's say you have a policy of having students hand in their seatwork every day. Rather than checking every paper, you pull three papers at random and give these students extra credit if their seatwork is done well. This variable-interval schedule would probably motivate students to do their seatwork carefully. If you secretly stopped spot-checking halfway through the year, the students might never know it, figuring that their own paper just hadn't been pulled to be checked rather than realizing that reinforcement was no longer available for anyone.

Table 5.2 defines and gives additional examples of schedules of reinforcement.

TABLE 5.2 • Schedules of Reinforcement

Specific response patterns during reinforcement and extinction characterize each of the four types of schedules.

SCHEDULE	DEFINITION	RESPONSE PATTERNS DURING REINFORCEMENT	DURING EXTINCTION
Fixed ratio	Constant number of behaviors for required for reinforcement	Steady response rate; pause after reinforcement	Rapid drop in response rate after required number of responses passes without reinforcement
Variable ratio	Variable number of behaviors required for reinforcement	Steady, high response rate	Response rate stays high, then drops off
Fixed interval	Constant amount of time passes before reinforcement is available	Uneven rate, with rapid acceleration at the end of each interval	Rapid drop in response rate after interval passes with no reinforcement
Variable interval	Variable amount of time passes before reinforcement is available	Steady, high response rate	Slow decrease in response rate

Maintenance

The principle of extinction holds that when reinforcement for a previously learned behavior is withdrawn, the behavior fades away. Does this mean that teachers must reinforce students' behaviors forever?

Not necessarily. For rats in a Skinner box, the withdrawal of reinforcement for bar pressing will inevitably lead to extinction of bar pressing. However, humans live in a much more complex world that is full of natural reinforcers for most of the skills and behaviors that we learn in school. For example, students may initially require frequent reinforcement for behaviors that lead to reading. However, once they can read, they have a skill that unlocks the entire world of written language, a world that is highly reinforcing to most students. After a certain point, reinforcement for reading may no longer be necessary because the content of reading material itself maintains the behavior. Similarly, poorly behaved students may need careful, systematic reinforcement for doing schoolwork. After a while, however, they will find out that doing schoolwork pays off in grades, in family approval, in ability to understand what is going on in class, and in knowledge. These natural reinforcers for doing schoolwork were always available, but the students could not experience them until their schoolwork was improved by more systematic means.

The concept of resistance to extinction, discussed earlier (in the section on schedules of reinforcement), is central to an understanding of the **maintenance** of learned behavior. As was noted, when new behaviors are being introduced, reinforcement for correct responses should be frequent and predictable. However, once the behaviors are established, reinforcement for correct responses should become less frequent and less predictable. The reason for this is that variable schedules of reinforcement and schedules that require many behaviors before reinforcement is given are much more resistant to extinction than are fixed schedules or easy ones. For example, if you praise a student every time the student does a math problem, but then stop praising, the student may stop doing math problems. In contrast, if you gradually increase the number of math problems a student must do to be praised and praise the student at random intervals (a variable-ratio schedule), then the student is likely to continue to do math problems for a long time with little or no reinforcement from you.

The Role of Antecedents

We have seen that the consequences of behavior strongly influence behavior. Yet it is not only what follows a behavior that has influence. The stimuli that precede a behavior also play an important role (Borich, 2014; Schunk, 2016).

CUEING **Antecedent stimuli**, events that precede a behavior, are also known as cues because they inform us which behaviors will be reinforced and which will be ignored or punished. **Cues** come in many forms and give us hints about when we should change our behavior and when we should not. For example, during music class, a teacher might ask students to sing louder. At an activity in the library, the expectations are obviously different. The ability to behave one way in the presence of one stimulus—"Sing louder"—and a different way in the presence of another stimulus—"You're in the library—speak quietly"—is known as *stimulus discrimination*.

DISCRIMINATION When is the best time to ask your boss for a raise? When the company is doing well, the boss looks happy, and you have just done something especially good? Or when the company has just gotten a poor earnings report, the boss is glowering, and you have just made a costly error? Obviously, the first situation is more likely to lead to success. You know this because you have learned to discriminate between good and bad times to ask your boss to do something for you. **Discrimination** is the use of cues, signals, or information to determine when behavior is likely to be reinforced. The company's financial condition, the boss's mood, and your recent performance are discriminative stimuli with regard to the chances that your request for a raise will be successful. For example, if you say, "Answer in a complete sentence," you are establishing a discriminative stimulus: "Complete sentences with the right answer will be reinforced, other responses will not be." For students to learn discrimination, they must have feedback on the correctness or incorrectness of their responses. Studies of discrimination learning have generally found that students need to know when their responses are incorrect as well as when they are correct (Schunk, 2016).

Certification Pointer

Teacher certification tests may require you to know that holding up your hand to get students' attention is cueing, an antecedent stimulus that informs students which behaviors will be reinforced.

Learning is largely a matter of mastering more and more complex discriminations. For example, all letters, numbers, words, and mathematical symbols are discriminative stimuli. A young child learns to discriminate between the letters *b* and *d*. An older student learns the distinction between the words *effective* and *efficient*. An educational psychology student learns to discriminate *negative reinforcement* from *punishment*. A teacher learns to discriminate among facial and verbal cues indicating that students are bored or enthralled by a lecture, or somewhere in between.

Applying the concept of discriminative stimuli to classroom instruction and management is easy: You should tell students what behaviors will be reinforced. In theory, you could wait until students did something worthwhile and then reinforce it, but this would be incredibly inefficient. Rather, you should give students messages that say, in effect, "To be reinforced (e.g., with praise, grades, or stars), these are the things you must do." In this way, you can avoid having students spend time and effort on the wrong activities. When students know that what they are doing will pay off, they will usually work hard.

GENERALIZATION If students learn to stay in their seats and do careful work in math class, will their behavior also improve in science class? If students can subtract 3 apples from 7 apples, can they also subtract 3 oranges from 7 oranges? If students can interpret symbolism used by Shakespeare, can they also interpret symbolism used in African folktales? These are all questions of **generalization**, or transfer of behaviors learned under one set of conditions to other situations (Borich, 2014; Schunk, 2016). Generalization cannot be taken for granted. For example, when a classroom management program is successfully introduced in one setting, students' behaviors do not automatically improve in other settings. Instead, students learn to discriminate among settings. Even young children readily learn what is encouraged and what is forbidden in kindergarten, at home, and at various friends' houses. Their behavior may be quite different in each setting, according to the different rules and expectations.

For generalization to occur, it usually must be planned for. A successful classroom management program used in social studies class may be transferred to English class to ensure generalization to that setting. Students may need to study the use of symbolism by many authors in many cultures before they acquire the skill to interpret symbolism in general.

Obviously, generalization is most likely to occur across similar settings or similar concepts. A new behavior is more likely to generalize from reading class to social studies class than to recess or home settings. However, even in the most similar-appearing settings, generalizations may not occur. For example, many students may demonstrate complete mastery of spelling or language mechanics but fail to apply this knowledge to their own compositions. You should not assume that because students can perform effectively under one set of circumstances, they can also do so under a different set of circumstances.

TECHNIQUES FOR INCREASING GENERALIZATION There are many techniques for increasing the chances that a behavior learned in one setting, such as a given class, will generalize to other settings, such as other classes or, more important, real-life applications (see Alberto & Troutman, 2013; Martella et al., 2012; Walker et al., 2011. Some of these strategies involve teaching in a way that makes generalization easier. For example, arithmetic lessons involving money will probably transfer better to real life if they involve manipulating real or simulated coins and bills than if they involve only problems on paper. Another teaching strategy known to contribute to generalization is using many examples from different contexts. For example, students are more likely to be able to generalize the concept of supply and demand to new areas if they learn examples related to prices for groceries, prices for natural resources, values of collectibles (such as baseball cards), and wages for common and rare skills than if they learn only about grocery pricing. An obvious strategy for increasing generalization is "on-the-job training": teaching a given skill in the actual environment in which it will be used, or in a simulation of such an environment.

After initial instruction has taken place, there are many ways to increase generalization. One is to repeat instruction in a variety of settings. For example, after teaching students to use a given test-taking strategy in mathematics, such as "Skip difficult problems and go back to them after answering the easy ones," you might give students the opportunity to use this same strategy on a science test, a grammar test, and a health test. Another after-teaching technique is to help students make the link between a new skill and natural reinforcers in the environment so as to maintain that skill. For example, when children are learning to read, they can be given a regular homework assignment to read books or magazines that are of high interest to them, even if those materials are not "good literature." Initially, new reading skills may be better maintained by comic books than by literary classics, because for some children the comic books tie their new skill more immediately to the pleasure of reading, making generalization to nonschool settings more likely. Finally, you can increase generalization by directly reinforcing generalization—for example, by praising a student who connects a new idea to a different context or uses a skill in a new application.

MyEdLab **Self-Check 5.1**

HOW HAS SOCIAL LEARNING THEORY CONTRIBUTED TO OUR UNDERSTANDING OF HUMAN LEARNING?

Connections 5.6
For the relation of social learning theory to social construction of meaning, see Chapter 8.

Social learning theory is a major outgrowth of the behavioral learning theory tradition. Developed by Albert Bandura, social learning theory accepts most of the principles of behavioral theories but focuses to a much greater degree on the effects of cues on behavior and on internal mental processes, emphasizing the effects of thought on action and the effects of action on thought (Bandura, 1997, 2006; Schunk, 2016).

Bandura: Modeling and Observational Learning

Connections 5.7
For the relation of social learning theory to Vygotskian and neo-Piagetian views of development, see Chapter 2.

Bandura noted that the Skinnerian emphasis on the effects of the consequences of behavior largely ignored the phenomena of **modeling**—the imitation of others' behavior—and of vicarious experience—learning from others' successes or failures. He felt that much of human learning is not shaped by its consequences but is more efficiently learned directly from a model (Bandura, 1986; Schunk, 2016). The physical education teacher demonstrates jumping jacks, and students imitate. Bandura called this *no-trial learning* because students do not have to go through a shaping process but can reproduce the correct response immediately.

Bandura's (1997) analysis of **observational learning** involves four phases: the attentional, retention, reproduction, and motivational phases.

ON THE WEB

For more on social learning theory, go to http://www.learning-theories.com/social-learning-theory-bandura.html.

---

1. *Attentional phase.* The first phase in observational learning is paying attention to a model. In general, students pay attention to role models who are attractive, successful, interesting, and popular. This is why so many students copy the dress, hairstyle, and mannerisms of pop culture stars. In the classroom you gain the students' attention by presenting clear and interesting cues, by using novelty or surprise, and by motivating students.

2. *Retention phase.* Once teachers have students' attention, it is time to model the behavior they want students to imitate and then give students a chance to practice or rehearse. For example, you might show how to write the letter *A*. Then students would imitate your model by trying to write *A*'s themselves.

3. *Reproduction.* During the reproduction phase, students try to match their behavior to the model's. In the classroom the assessment of student learning takes place during this phase. For example, after seeing the letter *A* modeled and practicing it several times, can the student reproduce the letter so that it looks like your model?

4. *Motivational phase.* The final stage in the observational learning process is motivation. Students will imitate a model because they believe that doing so will increase their own chances

InTASC 1

Learner Development

to be reinforced. In the classroom the motivational phase of observational learning often entails praise or grades given for matching your model. Students pay attention to the model, practicing and reproducing it because they have learned that this is what you like, and they want to please you. When the child makes a recognizable *A,* you say, "Nice work!"

VICARIOUS LEARNING Although most observational learning is motivated by an expectation that correctly imitating the model will lead to reinforcement, it is also important to note that people learn by seeing others reinforced or punished for engaging in certain behaviors (Bandura, 1986; Schunk, 2016). This is why advertisers always include happy winners in their advertisements to induce people to enter promotional contests. We may consciously know that our chances of winning are one in several million, but seeing others so handsomely reinforced makes us want to imitate their contest-entering behavior.

Classroom teachers use the principle of **vicarious learning** all the time. When one student is fooling around, teachers often single out others who are working well and reinforce them for doing a good job. The misbehaving student sees that working is reinforced and (it is hoped) gets back to work. This technique was systematically examined in a classic study by Broden, Hall, Dunlap, and Clark (1970). Two disruptive second-graders, Edwin and Greg, sat next to each other. After a baseline period, the teacher began to notice and praise Edwin whenever he was paying attention and doing his classwork. Edwin's behavior improved markedly under this condition. Of greater interest, however, is that Greg's behavior also improved, even though no specific reinforcement for appropriate behavior was directed toward him. Apparently, Greg learned from Edwin's experience. In the case of Ms. Esteban and Rebecca at the opening of this chapter, other students saw Rebecca get Ms. Esteban's attention by calling out answers, so they modeled their behavior on Rebecca's.

One of the classic experiments in social learning theory is a study done by Bandura (1965) in which children were shown one of three films. In all three, an adult modeled aggressive behavior. In one film the model was severely punished. In another the model was praised and given treats. In a third the model received no consequences. After viewing one of the films, the children were observed playing with toys. The children who had seen the model punished engaged in significantly fewer aggressive acts in their own play than did the children who had seen the model rewarded or had viewed the film with no consequences.

Certification Pointer

Teacher certification tests may require you to know that learning vicariously means that you learn from observing or hearing about another's experiences.

Connections 5.8

For more on self-regulated learning, see Chapter 8.

THEORY INTO PRACTICE

Observational Learning

Have you ever tried to teach someone to tie his or her shoes? Imagine explaining this task to someone without the use of a model or imitation! Learning to tie our shoes is an example of how observational learning works.

Acquiring new skills by observing the behaviors of others is a common part of everyday life. In many situations children watch others talking and acting, and they witness the consequences of those activities as well. Such observations provide models that teach children strategies to use at other times and places.

Although the major focus of research on observational learning has been on specific behaviors, studies have also shown that attitudes, too, may be acquired through observation (Schunk, 2016). Teachers and parents alike are concerned with the models emulated by children. The value of these models goes beyond the specific abilities they possess and includes the attitudes they represent. In the classroom you must be certain to exemplify a standard of behavior consistent with the expectations you have for the students. For instance, if promptness and politeness are characteristics you want to foster in the students, then you must be certain to be prompt and polite.

MyEdLab

Video Example 5.3

In this class, students have different levels of skill at self-regulation, so the teacher has established policies that help students recognize their needs and take steps to develop these important skills.

MyEdLab

Video Example 5.4

Bob Slavin tells a story about a young girl who did not like to clean her room. Why do you think the charting strategy was so effective for Vanessa? What other sorts of modification strategies might be effective for grade-school children? For middle-school or high-school students?

Connections 5.9

For the related concept of teaching self-questioning strategies to develop metacognitive skills, see Chapter 6.

SELF-REGULATED LEARNING Another important concept in social learning theory is **self-regulation** (Bandura, 2006; Boekaerts, Pintrich, & Zeidner, 2000; Schunk, 2016). Bandura (1997) hypothesized that people observe their own behavior, judge it against their own standards, and reinforce or punish themselves. We have all had the experience of knowing we've done a job well and mentally patting ourselves on the back, regardless of what others have said. Similarly, we all know when we've done less than our best. To make these judgments, we have to have expectations for our own performance. One student might be delighted to get 90 percent correct on a test, whereas another might be quite disappointed.

Students can be taught to use self-regulation strategies, and they can be reminded to do so in a variety of contexts so that self-regulation becomes a habit. For example, students might be asked to set goals for the amount of time they expect to study each evening and to record whether they meet their goals. Children who are studying multiplication facts might be asked to time themselves on how quickly and accurately they can complete a 50-item facts test and then to try to beat their own record. Students might be asked to grade their own essays in terms of content, mechanics, and organization, and to see whether they can match your ratings. Gureasko-Moore, DuPaul, and White (2006) asked four 12-year-old boys who were frequently late and forgot materials and homework to keep a daily log of these behaviors. They met with each other daily, they jointly set goals for the group, and gradually all began coming to class on time and prepared. Each of these strategies puts students in control of their own learning goals, and each is likely to build a general strategy of setting and meeting personal goals and personal standards (Schunk, 2016).

As with any skill, self-regulated learning skills are likely to remain limited to one situation or context unless they are applied in many contexts. For example, children who learn to set study goals for themselves when working alone may not transfer these skills to situations in which they are working in groups or in your presence (Schunk, 2016), although they can readily learn to make these generalizations if they are taught or reminded to do so. Similarly, children may not transfer self-regulated learning strategies from English to math, or even from computations to problem solving (Schunk, 2016). For this reason, students need many opportunities to use goal-setting and self-evaluation strategies in a variety of contexts; to monitor and celebrate their progress; and to understand how, when, and why they should self-regulate.

Meichenbaum's Model of Self-Regulated Learning

Students can be taught to monitor and regulate their own behavior. Self-regulated learning strategies of this kind are often called **cognitive behavior modification** (Borich, 2014; Harris et al., 2001; Schunk, 2016). For example, Meichenbaum (1977) developed a strategy in which students are trained to say to themselves, "What is my problem? What is my plan? Am I using my plan? How did I do?" This strategy has been used to reduce disruptive behavior of students at many grade levels (Jones & Jones, 2016; Martella et al., 2012; Veenman, 2011). Manning (1988) taught disruptive third-graders self-statements to help them remember appropriate behavior and to reinforce it for themselves. As one instance, for appropriate hand-raising, students were taught to say to themselves while raising their hands, "If I scream out the answer, others will be disturbed. I will raise my hand and wait my turn. Good for me. See, I can wait!" (Manning, 1988, p. 197). Similar strategies have been successfully applied to help students monitor their own achievement. For example, poor readers have been taught to ask themselves questions as they read and to summarize paragraphs to make sure they comprehend text (Bornstein, 1985).

The steps involved in self-instruction are described by Meichenbaum (1977) as follows:

1. An adult model performs a task while talking to self out loud (cognitive modeling).

2. The child performs the same task under the direction of the model's instructions (overt, external guidance).

3. The child performs the task while instructing self aloud (overt self-guidance).

4. The child whispers the instructions to self as he or she goes through the task (faded, overt self-guidance).

5. The child performs the task while guiding his or her performance via private speech (covert self-instruction). (p. 32)

Encouraging self-regulated learning is a means of teaching students to think about their own thinking. Self-regulated learning strategies not only have been found to improve performance on the task students were taught but also have generalized to other tasks (Hadwin, 2008; Harris et al., 2001; Schunk, 2016; Veenman, 2011).

One example of a way to help children engage in self-regulated learning is providing students, when they are assigned a long or complex task, with a form for monitoring their progress. For example, a teacher who assigns students to write a report on the life of Martin Luther King, Jr., might hand out the following self-monitoring checklist:

TASK COMPLETION FORM

☐ Located material on Martin Luther King, Jr., in the library and online

☐ Read and took notes on material

☐ Wrote first draft of report

☐ Checked draft for sense

☐ Checked draft for mechanics:

    ☐ Spelling

    ☐ Grammar

    ☐ Punctuation

☐ Composed a typed or neatly handwritten final draft

The idea behind this form is that breaking down a complex task into smaller pieces encourages students to feel that they are making progress toward their larger goal. Checking off each step allows them to give themselves a mental pat on the back that reinforces their efforts. After seeing many checklists of this kind, students might be asked to make up their own to learn how to chart their progress toward a goal. For example, Reid and Lienemann (2006) taught a group of students with attention deficit disorders to list all of the tasks necessary to complete a writing assignment and then check these tasks off as they completed them. This increased the length and quality of their writing. Along similar lines, Trammel, Schloss, and Alper (1994) found that having children with learning disabilities keep records and make graphs of their homework completion significantly increased the amount of homework they did. A review by Robinson, Robinson, and Katayama (1999) found that cognitive behavior modification strategies can have a substantial impact, especially on reducing hyperactive, impulsive, and aggressive behaviors (e.g., Binder, Dixon, & Ghezi, 2000). Several of the studies reviewed found these effects to be long-lasting.

SELF-REINFORCEMENT In a classic study, Drabman, Spitalnik, and O'Leary (1973) designed and evaluated a procedure to teach students to regulate their own behavior. They asked teachers to rate student behaviors each day and reinforce students when they earned high ratings. Then they changed the program: They asked students to guess what rating the teacher had given them. The students were reinforced for guessing correctly. Finally, the reinforcers were gradually removed. The students' behavior improved under the reinforcement and guessing conditions, and it remained at its improved level long after the program ended. The authors explained that students who were taught to match the teacher's ratings developed their own standards for appropriate behavior and reinforced themselves for meeting those standards.

Information about one's own behavior has often been found to change behavior, even when that information is self-provided. For example, researchers have increased on-task behavior by having children mark down, every few minutes, whether they have been studying in the last few minutes (McCormick, Dimmit, & Sullivan, 2013). Many of us use this principle in studying, saying to ourselves that we will not take a break for lunch until we have finished reading a certain amount of material. Or we might buy ourselves chocolate if we've been conscientiously going to the gym.

Connections 5.10
For more on self-efficacy beliefs and student success, see Chapter 10.

Strengths and Limitations of Behavioral Learning Theories

The basic principles of behavioral learning theories are as firmly established as any in psychology and have been demonstrated under many different conditions. These principles are useful for explaining much of human behavior; they are even more useful in changing behavior in the classroom.

21ST CENTURY LEARNING

Self-Reliance

In the 21st century, success in high-paying jobs increasingly depends on the ability to work independently or with others for long periods without a superior closely monitoring the work. More than ever, students need to learn how to break assignments into bite-sized chunks and monitor (and reinforce) their own accomplishments. Students who learn how to motivate themselves have a skill that will help them succeed with any challenge that school or life brings. For this reason, assessments based on the Common Core State Standards are likely to emphasize larger tasks (rather than bite-sized multiple- choice questions) to ensure that students can organize complex content.

Students who feel confident in their ability to use metacognitive and self-motivational behaviors are likely to be high in self-efficacy—the belief that one's own efforts (rather than luck or other people or other external or uncontrollable factors) determine one's success or failure. Self-efficacy beliefs are perhaps the most important factor (after ability) in determining students' success in school (Bandura, 1997, 2006; Schunk & Zimmerman, 2013).

Certification Pointer

The idea that behavioral learning theories apply best to observable behavior (rather than to thinking, for example) may appear on teacher certification tests.

It is important to recognize, however, that behavioral learning theories are limited in scope. With the exception of social learning theorists, behavioral learning theorists focus almost exclusively on observable behavior. This is one reason why so many of the examples presented in this chapter involve the management of behavior (see Schunk, 2016). Less visible learning processes, such as concept formation, learning from text, problem solving, and thinking, are difficult to observe directly and have therefore been studied less often by behavioral learning theorists. These processes fall more into the domain of cognitive learning. Social learning theory, which is a direct outgrowth of behavioral learning theories, helps to bridge the gap between the behavioral and cognitive perspectives.

Behavioral and cognitive theories of learning are often posed as competing, opposite models. There are indeed specific areas in which these theories take contradictory positions. However, it is more accurate to see them as complementary rather than competitive—that is, as tackling different problems (Borich, 2014; Miltenberger, 2012; Schunk, 2016).

MyEdLab **Self-Check 5.2**

SUMMARY

What Is Learning?

Learning involves the acquisition of abilities that are not innate. Learning depends on experience, including feedback from the environment.

What Are Behavioral Learning Theories?

Early research into learning studied the effects of stimuli on reflexive behaviors. Ivan Pavlov contributed the idea of classical conditioning, in which neutral stimuli can acquire the capacity to evoke behavioral responses through their association with unconditioned stimuli that trigger reflexes. B. F. Skinner continued the study of the relationship between behavior and consequences. He described operant conditioning, in which reinforcers and punishers shape behavior.

THE INTENTIONAL TEACHER
Using Principles of Behavioral and Social Learning Theory to Improve Teaching and Learning

Intentional teachers are aware of principles of behavioral and social learning and use them flexibly to help students become productive and capable learners.

- They communicate clearly to their students which behaviors are expected and which should be avoided.
- They reinforce students for engaging in behaviors that lead toward learning success.
- They shape behaviors by breaking complex tasks down into smaller tasks and reinforce progress toward the complex goal.
- They avoid punishment whenever possible, never use physical punishment, and avoid using behavior modification to overcontrol students.
- They reinforce students' progress frequently in the early stages of learning a new skill, and less frequently and less predictably as new skills become established.
- They use many examples and real-life simulations to help students generalize from one situation to others and from school to practical application.
- They teach students to monitor and reinforce their own behaviors, with the intention of becoming self-motivated, self-regulated learners.
- They engage students in setting their own standards and in working out how to organize their work and break down complex tasks to meet these standards.

MyEdLab

Application Exercise 5.1

In the Pearson etext, watch a classroom video. Then use the guidelines in "The Intentional Teacher" to answer a set of questions that will help you reflect on and understand the teaching and learning presented in the video.

What Are Some Principles of Behavioral Learning?

Reinforcers increase the frequency of a behavior, and punishers decrease its frequency. Reinforcement can be primary or secondary, positive or negative. Intrinsic reinforcers are rewards inherent in a behavior itself. Extrinsic reinforcers are praise or rewards bestowed by others. Punishment involves weakening behavior by either introducing aversive consequences or removing reinforcers. The Premack Principle states that one way to increase less-enjoyed activities is to link them to more-enjoyed activities.

Shaping through timely feedback on each step of a task is an effective teaching practice based on behavioral learning theory. Extinction is the weakening and gradual disappearance of behavior as reinforcement is withdrawn.

Schedules of reinforcement are used to increase the probability, frequency, or persistence of desired behavior. Reinforcement schedules may be based on ratios or intervals and may be fixed or variable.

Antecedent stimuli serve as cues indicating which behaviors will be reinforced or punished. Discrimination involves using cues to detect differences between stimulus situations, whereas generalization involves responding to similarities between stimuli. Generalization involves the transfer or carryover of behaviors learned under one set of conditions to other situations.

How Has Social Learning Theory Contributed to Our Understanding of Human Learning?

Social learning theory is based on recognition of the importance of observational learning and self-regulated learning. Bandura noted that learning through modeling—directly or vicariously—involves four phases: paying attention, retaining the modeled behavior, reproducing the behavior, and being motivated to repeat the behavior. Bandura proposed that students should be taught to have expectations for their own performances and to reinforce themselves. Meichenbaum proposed steps for self-regulated learning that represent a form of cognitive behavior modification.

Behavioral learning theories are central to the application of educational psychology in classroom management, discipline, motivation, instructional models, and other areas. Behavioral learning theories are limited in scope, however, in that they describe only observable behavior that can be directly measured.

KEY TERMS

Review the following key terms from the chapter.

antecedent stimuli 110

aversive stimulus 105

behavioral learning theories 97

classical conditioning 99

cognitive behavior modification 114

cognitive learning theories 97

conditioned stimulus 99

consequences 101

cues 110

discrimination 110

extinction 107

extinction burst 107

extrinsic reinforcers 103

fixed-interval (FI) schedule 109

fixed-ratio (FR) schedule 108

generalization 111

intrinsic reinforcers 103

learning 98

maintenance 110

modeling 112

negative reinforcer 101

neutral stimuli 99

observational learning 112

operant conditioning 99

positive reinforcer 101

Premack Principle 102

presentation punishment 105

primary reinforcer 101

punishment 105

reinforcer 101

removal punishment 105

response cost 105

schedule of reinforcement 108

secondary reinforcer 101

self-regulation 114

shaping 107

Skinner box 99

social learning theories 97

stimuli (stimulus) 98

time out 105

unconditioned response 99

unconditioned stimulus 99

variable-interval (VI) schedule 109

variable-ratio (VR) schedule 108

vicarious learning 113

SELF-ASSESSMENT: PRACTICING FOR LICENSURE

Directions: The chapter-opening vignette addresses indicators that are often assessed in state licensure exams. Reread the chapter-opening vignette, and then respond to the following questions.

1. Julia Esteban, a first-grade teacher at Tanner Elementary School, calls on her students when they speak without raising their hands, a practice that goes against an established rule in the class. Which of the following types of conditioning can Ms. Esteban use to teach her students about appropriate hand-raising behaviors?

    a. Classical conditioning

    b. Operant conditioning

    c. Modeled conditioning

    d. Assisted conditioning

2. Which of the following explanations best summarizes Julia Esteban's problem with her students' failure to raise their hands prior to speaking?

    a. Ms. Esteban is using negative reinforcement rather than positive reinforcement.

    b. Ms. Esteban has failed to apply the Premack Principle when her students break the hand-raising rule.

    c. Ms. Esteban allows her students to make decisions about classroom rules, a practice that research studies have shown to be unsuccessful.

    d. Ms. Esteban should note that pleasurable consequences (rewarding appropriate behaviors) increase a behavior, whereas unpleasant consequences weaken the frequency of a behavior.

3. According to research on behavioral learning theories, which strategy might Ms. Esteban use to get her students to raise their hands prior to speaking?

    a. Reward those students who follow the rule.

    b. Punish those students who do not follow the rule.

    c. Ignore those students who follow the rule.

    d. Wait before administering any type of consequence for rule-breakers.

4. Imagine that Ms. Esteban's students have a difficult time breaking their habit of speaking out of turn. Which of the following techniques might she use to reinforce close approximations of the behaviors she wants her students to exhibit?

    a. Extinction

    b. Maintenance

    c. Shaping

    d. Discrimination

5. Which type of reinforcement schedule is Ms. Esteban using if she reinforces her students' appropriate behavior after a predetermined number of behaviors, but the students do not know when the reinforcement will be applied?

    a. Continuous

    b. Fixed-ratio schedule

    c. Fixed-interval schedule

    d. Variable-ratio schedule

6. Explain how classical conditioning and operant conditioning are alike and how they are different. Give at least one example of each.

7. Describe Albert Bandura's social learning theory. Bandura's analysis of observational learning involves four phases; describe each phase.

MyEdLab   **Licensure Exam 5.1** Answer questions and receive instant feedback in your Pearson eText in MyEdLab.

DGLimages/Shutterstock

CHAPTER SIX

Cognitive Theories of Learning

LEARNING OUTCOMES

At the end of this chapter, you should be able to:

6.1 Identify the processes and components of the information-processing model of human cognition

6.2 Explain how the brain works, and summarize what we have learned about education from research on the brain

6.3 Identify the factors that affect whether we remember or forget information, and describe strategies that students can use to remember class content

6.4 Discuss how metacognitive skills, study strategies, and cognitive teaching strategies help students learn

6.5 Describe how cognitive theories of learning inform intentional teaching

Verona Bishop's biology class is doing a unit on human learning. At the start of one lesson, Ms. Bishop does an experiment with her students. For 3 seconds, using an electronic whiteboard, she flashes a diagram of a model of information processing identical to the illustration in Figure 6.1. Then she asks students to recall what they notice. Some mention that they see boxes and arrows. Some see the words *memory* and *knowledge* and infer that the figure has something to do with learning. One student even sees the word *thinking*, though it isn't in the figure.

"Come now," says Ms. Bishop. "You noticed a lot more than that! You just may not have noticed what you noticed. For example, what did you smell?"

The whole class laughs. They all recall smelling the broccoli cooking in the cafeteria. The students catch on to the idea and begin to recall all the other details they noticed that had nothing to do with the diagram: the sounds of a truck going by, details of the classroom and the people in it, and so on.

After this discussion, Ms. Bishop says, "Isn't the brain amazing? In only 3 seconds you received an enormous amount of information. You didn't even know you were noticing the smell of the broccoli until I reminded you about it, but it was in your mind just the same. Also, in only 3 seconds your mind was already starting to make sense of the information in the figure." Cheryl thought she saw the word *thinking*, which wasn't there at all. But her mind leaped to that word because she saw words like *memory* that relate to *thinking*.

"Now imagine that you could keep in your mind, forever, everything that occurred in the 3 seconds you looked at the diagram: the arrows, the boxes, the words, the truck, the broccoli—everything. In fact, imagine that you could keep everything that ever entered your mind. What would that be like?"

"You'd be a genius!" ventures Samphan.

"You'd go crazy!" counters Jamal.

"I think Jamal is closer to the truth," says Ms. Bishop. "If your mind filled up with all that useless junk, you'd be in big trouble! One of the most important things we're going to learn about learning is that it is an active process of focusing in on important information, screening out unimportant information, and using what is already in our minds to decide which is which."

Ms. Bishop turns on the electronic whiteboard again.

"When we study this diagram in more detail, you'll use what you already know about learning, memory, forgetting, and diagrams to make sense of it. I hope you'll always remember the main ideas it's trying to show you. You'll soon forget the boxes and arrows, and even the smell of the broccoli will fade from your memory, but the parts of this diagram that make sense to you, and that answer questions you care about, may stay in your memory your whole life!"

USING YOUR EXPERIENCE

COOPERATIVE LEARNING Jot down two or three ways in which you try to memorize lists and study new concepts. Share with other students a strategy that you use to learn information better.

COOPERATIVE LEARNING What is your picture of learning, memory, and forgetting? After drafting your own picture, meet with four or five classmates to compose a summary illustration or diagram of human memory and cognition based on your individual ideas. After 10 minutes, share it with the class.

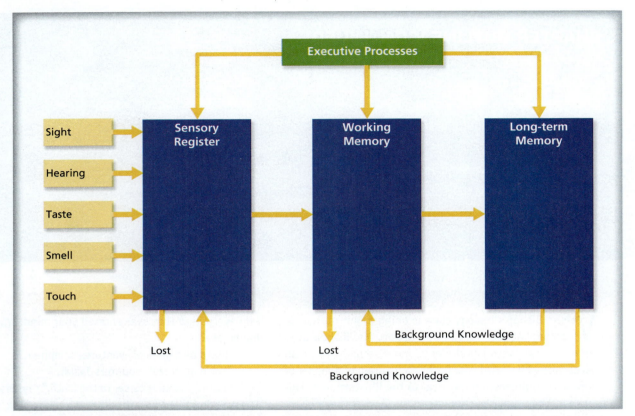

FIGURE 6.1 • An Updated Information-Processing Model of Learning and Memory

Information that is to be remembered must first reach a person's senses, then be attended to and transferred from the sensory register to the working memory, and then be processed again for transfer to long-term memory.

The human mind is a meaning maker. From the first microsecond you see, hear, taste, or feel something, you start a process of deciding what it is, how it relates to what you already know, and whether it is important to keep in your mind or should be discarded. This whole process may take place consciously, unconsciously, or both. This chapter describes how information is received and processed in the mind, how memory and forgetting work, and how you can help your students understand and remember critical information, skills, and ideas. This chapter also presents cognitive theories of learning, theories that relate to processes that go on within the minds of learners, and ways of helping students use their minds more effectively to learn, remember, and use knowledge and skills.

WHAT IS AN INFORMATION-PROCESSING MODEL?

Information constantly enters our minds through our senses. Most of this information is almost immediately discarded, and we may never even be aware of much of it. Some is held in our memories for a short time and then forgotten. For example, we may remember the seat number on a theater ticket until we find our seats, at which point we will forget the number. However, some information is retained much longer, perhaps for the rest of our lives. What is the process by which information is absorbed, and how can teachers take advantage of this process to help students retain critical information and skills? These questions have been addressed by cognitive learning theorists and have led to **information-processing theory**, a dominant theory of learning and memory since the mid-1970s.

Research on human memory (e.g., Ashcraft & Radvansky, 2010; Kolb & Whishaw, 2011; Nicholls et al., 2012; Ormrod, 2016; Purves, 2010; Scalise & Felde, 2017; Schunk, 2016; Sousa, 2011; Watson & Breedlove, 2012) has helped learning theorists to describe the process by which information is remembered (or forgotten). For many years, the dominant model of the learning process has been the *Atkinson–Shiffrin model of information processing* (Atkinson & Shiffrin, 1968). The model illustrated in Figure 6.1 is an update of that model.

How Information Processing Works

The model summarized in Figure 6.1 has three main components: the *sensory register, working memory* (sometimes called short-term memory), and *long-term memory*. Stimuli from the five senses come into the sensory register, where most are immediately forgotten. Those that matter to us for any reason are then passed on to working memory, where we evaluate the new stimuli in light of what is already in our long-term memories. Working memory is where "thinking" takes place. It is the most active part of the memory system, where we try to make sense of new stimuli and link them to what we already know. And then, if new information is determined to be useful, we store it in our long-term memories, possibly forever.

Executive Processing

The entire information-processing progression is not an automatic conveyor belt in which stimuli are made into knowledge. Quite the contrary. At each stage, the learning process is controlled by the learner. That control may be very conscious, as when a person tastes a new recipe for spaghetti sauce; focuses on taste, smell, and texture (in the stimulus registers); and brings these sensations into working memory, along with information from long-term memory on other spaghetti sauces or other information on spices, saltiness, or ingredients that help evaluate this sauce. Alternatively, the executive process may be less conscious, as when a person hears that her friend has the measles. Immediately, the person hearing this news is likely to decide to think about it, bringing the new stimulus (the news) into working memory, along with knowledge in long-term memory about measles, and emotions about the friend and about measles. All of this leads to long-term memories about this particular friend and this particular case of measles, which build on the knowledge base that was there before about measles (and this friend) in general.

Whether conscious or unconscious, willed or unwilled, the *executive process* is crucial (Ormrod, 2016; Schunk, 2016). It is what determines what a person is *interested* in putting into long-term memory, and then it determines how hard the person will think about the stimuli and information in long-term memory to form new and lasting memories. When a person studies for her driver's test the executive process is obvious; she uses the best study strategies she knows to learn the material by heart. But when a person accidentally trips and falls, every aspect of the experience is still processed under the control of the person falling. By the time he hits the ground, he has considered ways to minimize the pain, is remembering key aspects of previous falls, and is thinking of explanations or blame for this fall. Little of this executive process is automatic, although it takes place very fast without a lot of time for deliberation!

Learners approach each opportunity for learning with a set of motivations and orientations that determine the mental energy they are willing to devote to learning. Clearly, external incentives or punishers may increase motivation to use mental energy to learn how to get reinforcers and avoid punishments (Mazur, 2013). Intrinsic interests play a role; one learner is willing to devote mental energy to learn about cooking, while another is more interested in sports. The anticipated ease of learning is important. A person with a positive self-concept about learning foreign languages will put more mental energy into such learning than will someone who prides herself on learning math but not languages. Give these two people math to learn, and the opposite will happen. Someone who has a lot of background knowledge on a subject pays more attention to further information, because the new information is likely to be easy to learn.

Executive processes are almost like commands a person makes to his or her brain: "Brain, pay close attention to incoming stimuli of this type; look carefully in long-term memory for relevant information and skills already in there; put the new stimuli, knowledge, and skills together to create new knowledge; and file that knowledge in a place where I can easily access it whenever

I need it. Do it right now, and ignore pretty much everything else until you're done!" Not that anyone actually has such conversations with their own brain, but the executive process does consciously decide what is worth mental energy and then executes a plan to learn something the person considers useful.

The following sections describe the key elements and operations of information processing.

Sensory Register

The first component of the memory system that incoming information meets is the sensory register, shown at the left of Figure 6.1. Sensory registers receive large amounts of information from each of the senses (sight, hearing, touch, smell, taste) and hold it for a very short time, no more than a couple of seconds. If nothing happens to information held in a sensory register, it is rapidly lost. In fact, only a tiny proportion of what our senses receive is recalled even for an instant, because anything we do not consciously pay attention to is likely to be lost. As I'm writing this, I can see everything in my office, hear a heating fan and the murmur of voices in the hall, feel my glasses on my nose, and so on, none of which I would remember for a nanosecond if I were not writing about it. If I get an important phone call or e-mail, or if I get too many stimuli to attend to at once, my senses that are not involved in the immediate task at hand don't stop perceiving, but I no longer pay any attention to them at all.

The existence of sensory registers has two important educational implications. First, people must pay attention to information if they are to retain it. Second, it takes time to bring all the information seen in a moment into consciousness. For example, if students are bombarded with too much information at once and are not told or do not infer which aspects of the information they should pay attention to, they may have difficulty learning any of the information at all (Bawden & Robinson, 2009).

PERCEPTION When the senses receive stimuli, the mind immediately begins working on some of them. Therefore, the sensory images of which we are conscious are not exactly the same as what we saw, heard, or felt; they are what our senses perceived. Perception of stimuli is not as straightforward as reception of stimuli. Instead, it involves mental interpretation that is influenced by our mental state, our past experience, our knowledge, our motivations, and many other factors.

First, we perceive different stimuli according to rules that have nothing to do with the inherent characteristics of the stimuli. If you are sitting in a building, for example, you may not pay much attention to, or even hear, a distant fire engine's siren. If you are driving a car, you pay a great deal more attention. If you are standing outside a burning building waiting for the firefighters to arrive, you pay even more attention. Second, we do not perceive stimuli as we see or sense them but as we know (or assume) they really are. From across a room, a book on a bookshelf looks like a thin strip of paper, but we infer that it is a three-dimensional, rectangular form with many pages. You might see just the edge of a table and mentally infer the entire table. Your life experience (in long-term memory) tells you how to interpret stimuli and which stimuli to pay attention to. People are not born knowing what a fire engine sounds like, but they can quickly search their memories to identify that sound and react appropriately.

ATTENTION When you say to students, "Pay attention" or "Lend me your ears," you are using the words *pay* and *lend* appropriately. Like money, attention is a limited resource. When you ask students to spend their limited attention capacity on whatever you are saying, they must give up actively attending to other stimuli, shifting their priorities so that other stimuli are screened out (Gregory & Kaufeldt, 2015). For example, when people listen intently to an interesting speaker, they are unaware of minor body sensations (such as itches or hunger) and of other sounds or sights. An experienced speaker knows that when the audience looks restless, its attention is no longer focused on the lecture but might be turning toward considerations of lunch or other activities. Once your listeners are starting to check their iPhones, you know you're really in trouble. It is time to recapture the listeners' attention (Bunce, Flens, & Neiles, 2010).

GAINING ATTENTION How can you focus students' attention on the lesson at hand, and in particular on the most important aspects of what is being taught? How can you get students to tell their own brains, "OK, brain, this is important! It's interesting! It's worth knowing! Put mental energy into learning this content!"?

There are several ways to gain students' attention, all of which fall under the general heading of arousing student interest (Gregory & Kaufeldt, 2015). One way is to use cues that indicate "This is important." Some teachers raise or lower their voices to signal that they are about to impart critical information. Others use gestures, repetition, or body position to communicate the same message.

Another way to gain attention is to increase the emotional content of material (Armony, Chochol, Fecteau, & Belin, 2007). Attention and emotion activate some of the same parts of the brain (Vuilleumeir, 2005), which perhaps explains why people pay more attention to soap operas and reality shows (lots of emotion) than to typical classroom instruction (not so much). This is why newspaper headlines try to increase attention by saying "Senate Kills Mass Transit Proposal" rather than "Senate Votes against Mass Transit Proposal."

Unusual, inconsistent, or surprising stimuli also attract attention. For example, science teachers often introduce lessons with a demonstration or magic trick to pique student curiosity.

Finally, informing students that what follows is important to them will catch their attention. For example, you can ensure attention by telling students, "This will be on tomorrow's test." Of course, learners make their own decisions about what is important, and they learn more of what they think is important because they pay more attention to it.

Working (or Short-Term) Memory

Information that a person perceives and pays attention to is transferred to the second component of the memory system: **working memory** (Ashcraft & Radvansky, 2010; Kolb & Whishaw, 2011; Watson & Breedlove, 2012), a storage system that can hold a limited amount of information for a few seconds. It is the part of memory in which information that is currently being thought about is stored. The thoughts we are conscious of having at any given moment are being held in our **short-term memory**. When we stop thinking about something, it disappears from our short-term memory. Another term for short-term memory is *working memory* (Ashcraft & Radvansky, 2010; Schunk, 2016; Unsworth & Engle, 2007; Watson & Breedlove, 2012). This term emphasizes that the most important aspect of short-term memory is not its duration but the fact that it is active. Working memory is where the mind operates on information, organizes it for storage or discarding, and connects it to other information. Working memory is so important that many researchers consider working memory capacity to be essentially the same as intelligence (Ackerman, Beier, & Boyle, 2005; Kane, Hambrick, & Conway, 2005; Nicholls et al., 2012).

As you'll recall from Figure 6.1, information may enter working memory from sensory registers or from the third basic component of the memory system: long-term memory. Usually, both processes happen at the same time. When you see a robin, your sensory register transfers the image of the robin to your working memory. Meanwhile, you may (unconsciously) search your long-term memory for information about birds so that you can identify this particular one as a robin. Along with that recognition may come a lot of other information about robins, memories of past experiences with robins, or feelings about robins—all of which have been stored in long-term memory but are brought into consciousness (working memory) by your mental processing of the sight of the robin (Gathercole, Pickering, Ambridge, & Wearing, 2004; Mazur, 2013).

One way to hold information in working memory is to think about it or say it over and over. You have probably used this strategy to remember a phone number for a short time. This process of maintaining an item in working memory by repetition is called **rehearsal** (Purves, 2010). Rehearsal is important in learning because the longer an item remains in working memory, the greater the chance that it will be transferred to long-term memory (Greene, 2008). Recent research suggests that it is not the repeated study that makes the difference; rather, repeatedly trying to remember the information brings it into working memory and then strengthens it in long-term memory (Karpicke & Roediger, 2007; Schunk, 2016; Watson & Breedlove, 2012). Without rehearsal, items are not likely to stay in working memory for more than about 30 seconds. Because working memory has a limited capacity, information can also be lost from it by being crowded out by other information (Bawden & Robinson, 2009). You have probably had the experience of looking up a telephone number, being interrupted briefly, and finding that you have forgotten the number.

Teachers must allocate time for rehearsal during classroom lessons. Teaching too much information too rapidly is likely to be ineffective because, unless students are given time to mentally rehearse each new piece of information, later information will probably drive it out of their working

InTASC 1

Learner Development

"Mrs. Lee, can I be excused? My working memory capacity is full."

memories. When you stop a lesson to ask students whether they have any questions, you are also giving students a few moments to think over and mentally rehearse what they have just learned. This helps students to process information in working memory and thereby to establish it in long-term memory. This mental work is critical when students are learning new, difficult material.

WORKING MEMORY CAPACITY Working memory is believed to have a capacity of five to nine bits of information (Purves, 2010), although some research suggests that the average is more like four bits (Cowan, 2001; Maehara & Saito, 2007). That is, we can think about only five to nine distinct things (at most) at a time. However, any particular bit may itself contain a great deal of information. For example, think how difficult it would be to memorize the following shopping list:

flour	orange juice	pepper	mustard
soda pop	parsley	cake	butter
relish	mayonnaise	oregano	canned tomatoes
potatoes	milk	lettuce	syrup
hamburger	hot dogs	eggs	onions
tomato paste	apples	spaghetti	buns

This list has too many bits of information to remember easily. All 24 food items would not fit into working memory in random order. However, you could easily memorize the list by organizing it according to familiar patterns. As shown in Figure 6.2, you might mentally create three separate memory files: breakfast, lunch, and dinner. In each, you expect to find food and beverages; in the lunch and dinner files, you expect to find dessert as well. You can then think through the recipe for each item on the menus. In this way, you can recall what you have to buy, and you need maintain only a few bits of information in your working memory. When you enter the store, you are thinking, "I need food for breakfast, lunch, and dinner." First, you bring the breakfast file out of your long-term memory. It contains food (pancakes) and a beverage (orange juice). You might think through how you make pancakes step by step and buy each ingredient, plus orange juice as a beverage. When you have done this, you can discard breakfast from your working memory and replace it with the lunch file, and then the dinner file, going through the same processes. Note that all you did was replace 24 little bits of information with 3 big bits that you could then separate into their components.

FIGURE 6.2 • Example of Organization of Information to Facilitate Memory

A 24-item shopping list that would be very hard to remember in a random order can be organized into a smaller number of familiar categories, making the list easier to recall.

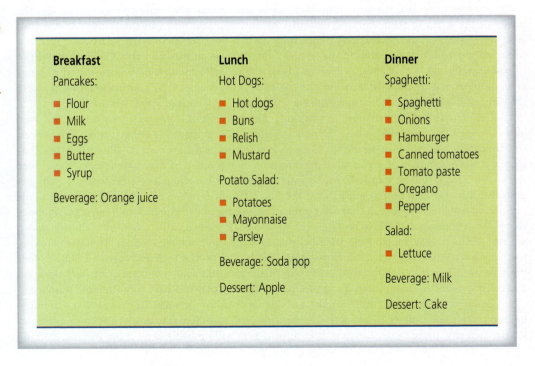

Breakfast

Pancakes:

- Flour
- Milk
- Eggs
- Butter
- Syrup

Beverage: Orange juice

Lunch

Hot Dogs:

- Hot dogs
- Buns
- Relish
- Mustard

Potato Salad:

- Potatoes
- Mayonnaise
- Parsley

Beverage: Soda pop

Dessert: Apple

Dinner

Spaghetti:

- Spaghetti
- Onions
- Hamburger
- Canned tomatoes
- Tomato paste
- Oregano
- Pepper

Salad:

- Lettuce

Beverage: Milk

Dessert: Cake

Working memory can be thought of as a bottleneck through which information from the environment reaches long-term memory (Maehara & Saito, 2007; Sousa, 2011; Watson & Breedlove, 2012). The limited capacity of working memory is one aspect of information processing that has important implications for the design and practice of instruction (Kolb & Whishaw, 2011; Schunk, 2016; Wolfe, 2010). For example, you cannot present students with many ideas at once unless the ideas are so well organized and so well connected to information already in the students' long-term memories that their working memories (with assistance from their long-term memories) can accommodate these ideas, as in the case of the shopping list just discussed.

As another illustration of the limited capacity of working memory, Mayer (2011a) compared a lesson on lightning storms that included a number of extraneous words, pictures, and music to a lesson without these elements. The simpler lesson produced higher performance on a transfer test. Apparently, the more coherent lesson used working memory capacity more effectively (see Mayer, 2009, 2011a).

INDIVIDUAL DIFFERENCES IN WORKING MEMORY Individuals differ, of course, in the capacities of their working memories to accomplish a given learning task. One of the main factors in enhancing this capacity is background knowledge. The more a person knows about something, the better able the person is to organize and absorb new information (Schunk, 2016; Sousa, 2011). However, prior knowledge is not the only factor. Individuals also differ in their ability to organize information and can be taught to consciously use strategies for making more efficient use of working memory capacity (Bailey & Pransky, 2014; Wyra, Lawson, & Hungi, 2007). Strategies of this kind are discussed later in this chapter.

Long-Term Memory

Long-term memory is that part of our memory system where we keep information for long periods of time. Long-term memory is thought to be a very large-capacity, very long-term memory store. In fact, many theorists believe that we may never forget information in long-term memory; rather, we might just lose the ability to find the information within our memory (Kolb & Whishaw, 2011; Sousa, 2011). We do not live long enough to fill up our long-term memory. The differences among sensory registers, working (short-term) memory, and long-term memory are summarized in Table 6.1.

People store not only information but also learning strategies in long-term memory for easy access (Kolb & Whishaw, 2011; Watson & Breedlove, 2012). This capacity, called *long-term working memory,* accounts for the extraordinary skills of experts (such as medical diagnosticians and educators) who must match current information with a vast array of patterns held in their long-term memories.

Theorists divide long-term memory into at least three parts: episodic memory, semantic memory, and procedural memory (Ashcraft & Radvansky, 2010; Nicholls et al., 2012; Ormrod, 2016; Sousa, 2011; Watson & Breedlove, 2012). **Episodic memory** is our memory of personal experiences, a mental movie of things we saw or heard. When you remember past events such as what you had for dinner last night or what happened at your high school prom, you are recalling information stored in your long-term episodic memory. Long-term **semantic memory** contains the facts and generalized information that we know; concepts, principles, or rules and how to use them; and our problem-solving skills and learning strategies. Most learning from class lessons is retained in semantic memory. **Procedural memory** refers to "knowing how" in contrast to "knowing that." The abilities to drive, keyboard, and ride a bicycle are examples of skills that are retained in procedural memory.

TABLE 6.1 • Characteristics of Memory Components

	FUNCTION	CAPACITY	DURATION
Sensory register	Receives initial stimuli; sight, sound, taste, smell, touch	Potentially huge	Very brief
Working (short-term) memory	Sorts through new stimuli and existing knowledge to find what is relevant; sorting and connecting new information with existing knowledge	5–9 items	About 12 seconds
Long-term memory	Stores knowledge, skills, and other memories and organizes them for easy retrieval	Virtually unlimited	Very long, perhaps forever

Certification Pointer

On a teacher certification test, you may be required to know that organizing material into familiar patterns can help students remember concepts and vocabulary. For example, to help young students remember the names of different animals, you could help students categorize them into pets, zoo animals, and farm animals.

Episodic, semantic, and procedural memory store and organize information in different ways. Information in episodic memory is stored in the form of images that are organized on the basis of when and where events happened. Information in semantic memory is organized in the form of networks of ideas. Information in procedural memory is stored as a complex of stimulus–response pairings (Kolb & Whishaw, 2011; Sousa, 2011). Brain studies (e.g., Elias & Saucier, 2006) have suggested that operations related to each of these types of long-term memory take place in different parts of the brain. Let's examine in detail what we mean by these three kinds of memory.

EPISODIC MEMORY Episodic memory contains images of experiences organized by when and where they happened (Ormrod, 2016; Watson & Breedlove, 2012). It consists of memories of personally experienced and remembered events, which combine sensory information, spatial knowledge, language, emotions, and motor information into a sort of personal story. For example, consider this question: What did you do on the night of your senior prom or dance? Most people answer this question by imagining themselves back on that night and describing the events. You might scan the dance floor in your mind's eye, recalling sights, sounds, and smells, and then think of the emotions you experienced, all of which are remembered together. One psychologist asked graduate students to come to a specific place for 1 hour a day and try to remember the names of their high school classmates. Over the course of a month, the students continued to recall new names. Interestingly, they used space and time cues, which are associated with episodic memory, to imagine incidents that enabled them to recall the names. For example, they might have recalled the day their social studies teacher came to school dressed as an Arctic explorer, and then mentally scanned their memory for the faces of the students who were there.

These demonstrations indicate that images are important in episodic memory and that cues related to space and time help us to retrieve information from this part of memory. You have probably taken an exam and said to yourself, "I should know this answer. I remember reading this section. It was right on the bottom left corner of the page with the diagram in the upper right."

Episodic memories are often difficult to retrieve because most episodes in our lives are repeated so often that later episodes get mixed up in memory with earlier ones, unless something happens during the episode to make it especially memorable. For example, few people remember what they had for lunch a week ago, much less years ago. However, there is a phenomenon called **flashbulb memory** in which the occurrence of an important event fixes mainly visual and auditory memories in a person's mind. For example, people who happened to be eating breakfast at the moment they first heard about the 2001 attack on the World Trade Center may well remember that particular meal (and other trivial aspects of the setting) forever. The reason for this is that the unforgettable event of that moment gives us access to the episodic (space and time) memories related to what would usually be forgotten details.

You can improve retention of concepts and information by explicitly creating memorable events involving visual or auditory images. For example, using projects, plays, simulations, and other forms of active learning can give students vivid images that they can remember and then employ to retrieve other information presented at about the same time. In support of this idea, there is much evidence that pictures illustrating text can help children to remember the text even when the pictures are no longer presented (Mayer, 2008b). The pictures presumably tie the semantic information to the child's episodic memory, making the information easier to retrieve. There is also evidence that students often create their own mental pictures, which then help them remember material they have studied (Mazur, 2013).

SEMANTIC MEMORY Semantic (or declarative) memory is organized in a very different way; it is mentally arranged in networks of connected ideas or relationships called **schemata** (singular: *schema*) (Mayer, 2011a, b). Recall that Piaget introduced the word *scheme* to describe a cognitive framework that individuals use to organize their perceptions and experiences. Cognitive processing theorists similarly use the terms *schema* and *schemata* to describe networks of concepts stored in individuals' memories that enable them to understand and incorporate new information. A schema is like an outline, with different concepts or ideas grouped under larger categories. Various aspects of schemata may be related by series of propositions, or relationships. For example, Figure 6.3 illustrates a simplified schema for the concept "bison," showing how this concept is related to other concepts in memory.

MyEdLab
Video Example 6.1
The Common Core and other career- and college-ready standards include writing about events at every grade, beginning in kindergarten. When students write personal narratives about events in their own lives, they're writing about episodic memories.

Connections 6.1
For more on the concept of schemes, see Chapter 2.

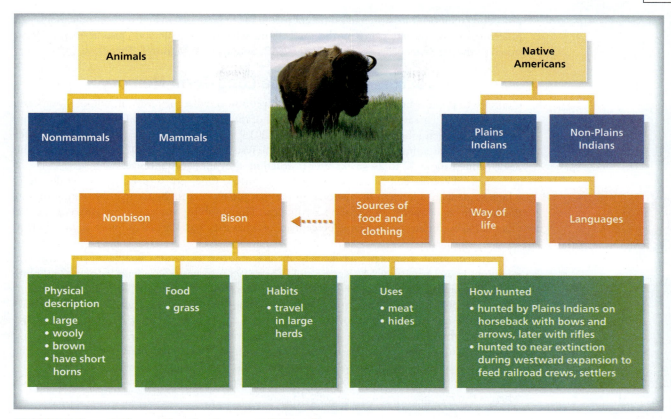

FIGURE 6.3 • Schema for the Concept "Bison"

Information in long-term semantic memory is organized in networks of related ideas. The concept "bison," for example, falls under the more general concepts "mammals" and "animals" and is related to many other ideas that help to differentiate it from other concepts in memory. *Source:* Olivier Le Queinec/Shutterstock.

In the figure, "bison" is linked to several other concepts. These may be linked to still more concepts (such as "How did Plains Indians hunt bison?") and to broader categories or concepts (such as "How have conservationists saved many species from extinction?"). Schema theory (Anderson, 2005) holds that we gain access to information held in our semantic long-term memory by mentally following paths like those illustrated in Figure 6.3. For example, you might have deep in your memory the idea that the Spanish introduction of the horse to North America revolutionized how the Plains Indians hunted bison. To get to that bit of information, you might start thinking about characteristics of bison, then think about how Plains Indians hunted bison on horseback, and then recall (or imagine) how they hunted bison before they had horses. Many pathways can be used to get at the same bit of information. In fact, the more pathways you have leading to a piece of information. and the better established those pathways are, the better access you will have to information in long-term semantic memory. Recall that the problem of long-term memory is not that information is lost but that we lose access to information.

One clear implication of schema theory is that new information that fits into a well-developed schema is retained far more readily than information that does not fit into a schema. Schema theory will be covered in more detail later in this chapter.

PROCEDURAL MEMORY Procedural memory is the ability to recall how to do something, especially a physical task. This type of memory is apparently stored in a series of stimulus–response pairings. For example, even if you have not ridden a bicycle for a long time, as soon as you get on one the stimuli begin to evoke responses. When the bike leans to the left (a stimulus), you "instinctively" shift your weight to the right to maintain balance (a response). Other examples of procedural memory include handwriting, typing, and running skills. Neurological studies show that

MyEdLab
Video Example 6.2

When students in this music class are tested, they're being assessed on their procedural memories. Students learn procedural skills in many other classes, too, such as lab sciences and mathematics.

procedural memories are stored in a different part of the brain than semantic and episodic memories; procedural memories are stored in the cerebellum, whereas semantic and episodic memories are stored in the cerebral cortex (Nicholls et al., 2012; Sousa, 2011; Watson & Breedlove, 2012).

Factors That Enhance Long-Term Memory

Contrary to popular belief, people retain a large portion of what they learn in school. Long-term retention varies a great deal according to the type of information, however. For example, concepts are retained much longer than names (Schunk, 2016). In general, retention drops rapidly in the first few weeks after instruction but then levels off (Watson & Breedlove, 2012). Whatever students have retained about 12 to 24 weeks after instruction, they may retain forever.

Several factors contribute to long-term retention. One, not surprisingly, is the degree to which students had learned the material in the first place (Purves, 2010). It is interesting to note that the effects of ability on retention are unclear. Higher-ability students score better at the end of a course but often lose the same percentage of what they had learned as lower-ability students do (Schunk, 2016).

Instructional strategies that actively involve students in lessons contribute to long-term retention. In a classic study, MacKenzie and White (1982) contrasted students in eighth and ninth grades learning geography under three conditions: traditional classroom instruction, traditional instruction plus fieldwork, and traditional instruction plus fieldwork plus active processing of information involved in fieldwork. Twelve weeks later (after summer vacation), the active processing group had lost only 10 percent of the information, whereas the other two groups had lost more than 40 percent. Similarly, Specht and Sandling (1991) contrasted undergraduates who learned accounting from traditional lectures with others who learned it through role playing. After 6 weeks, the traditionally taught students lost 54 percent of their problem-solving performance, whereas the role-playing group lost only 13 percent.

Other Information-Processing Models

Atkinson and Shiffrin's (1968) model of information processing, updated in Figure 6.1, is not the only one accepted by cognitive psychologists. Several alternative models do not challenge the basic assumptions of the Atkinson–Shiffrin model but elaborate aspects of it, particularly the factors that increase the chances that information will be retained in long-term memory.

LEVELS-OF-PROCESSING THEORY One widely accepted alternative model of information processing is called levels-of-processing theory (Craik, 2000; Tulving & Craik, 2000), which holds that people subject stimuli to different levels of mental processing and retain only the information that has been subjected to the most thorough processing. For example, you might perceive a tree but pay little attention to it. This is the lowest level of processing, and you are unlikely to remember the tree. Second, you might give the tree a name, such as *maple* or *oak*. Once named, the tree is somewhat more likely to be remembered. The highest level of processing, however, is giving meaning to the tree. For example, you might remember climbing the tree or commenting on its unusual shape, or you might have wondered whether the tree would fall on your house if it were struck by lightning. According to levels-of-processing theory, the more you attend to the details of a stimulus, the more mental processing you must do and the more likely you are to remember it. This was illustrated in a classic study by Bower and Karlin (1974), who had Stanford undergraduates look at yearbook pictures from Yale. Some of the students were told to classify the pictures as "male" or "female," and some were told to classify them as "very honest" or "less honest." The students who had to categorize the faces as "very honest" or "less honest" remembered them far better than did those who merely categorized them as "male" or "female." Presumably, the honesty raters had to do a much higher level of mental processing with the pictures than did the gender raters, and for this reason they remembered the faces better. Kapur and colleagues (1994), in another classic study, had students read a series of nouns. One group was asked to identify which words contained the letter *a*. Another group had to identify the nouns as "living" or "nonliving." As in the Bower and Karlin study and many others, the students who had to sort the words into "living" and "nonliving" recalled many more words. More interesting, however, was that brain imaging revealed that the "living/nonliving" students were activating a portion of their brains associated with enhanced memory performance, whereas the other students were not. This experiment adds important evidence to the idea that the brain treats "deep processing" and "shallow processing" differently (see Craik, 2000).

DUAL CODE THEORY A concept related to levels-of-processing theory is Paivio's dual code theory of memory, which hypothesizes that information is retained in long-term memory in two forms: visual and verbal (corresponding to episodic and semantic memory, respectively) (Clark & Paivio, 1991; Schunk, 2016). This theory predicts that information represented both visually and verbally is recalled better than information held in only one format. For example, you remember a face better if you also know a name, and you remember a name better if you can connect it to a face.

MyEdLab **Self-Check 6.1**

MyEdLab **Video Analysis Tool 6.1** Go to MyEdLab and click on the Video Analysis Tool to access the exercise "Teaching to encourage long-term retention: attention."

MyEdLab **Video Analysis Tool 6.2** Go to MyEdLab and click on the Video Analysis Tool to access the exercise "Teaching to encourage long-term retention: multiple representations."

WHAT DO WE KNOW FROM RESEARCH ON THE BRAIN?

In the past, research on learning, memory, and other cognitive functions took place using methods one step away from the brain itself. Scientists used ingenious experiments to learn about brain function from subjects' responses to particular stimuli or tests, examined individuals with unusual brain damage, or made inferences from experiments on animals. However, in recent years neuroscientists have developed the capacity to actually watch healthy brains in operation, using brain imaging methods such as functional magnetic resonance imaging (fMRI) (Mitchell & Johnson, 2009; Sousa, 2011). Scientists can now observe what parts of the brain are activated when an individual hears a symphony, reads a book, speaks a second language, or solves a math problem. This capability has led to an explosion of research on the brain (Elias & Saucier, 2006; Kolb & Whishaw, 2011; Ormrod, 2016; Schunk, 2016; Sousa, 2011; Watson & Breedlove, 2012).

It has long been known that specific mental functions are carried out in specific locations in the brain. For example, vision is localized in the visual cortex and hearing in the auditory cortex (see Figure 6.5). However, new research has revealed that the brain is even more specialized than was thought previously. When you think about a face, you activate a different part of the brain than when you think about a chair, a song, or a feeling. If you are bilingual in, say, Spanish and English, slightly different areas of your brain are activated when you speak each language. The two hemispheres of the brain have somewhat different functions; the left hemisphere is more involved in language, whereas the right is more involved in spatial and nonverbal information. However, despite the specialization within the brain, almost all tasks that we perform involve both hemispheres and many parts of the brain working together (Kolb & Whishaw, 2011; Nicholls et al., 2012; Purves, 2010).

How the Brain Works

The human brain is three pounds of mystery. It controls everything we do, everything we perceive and feel. Scientists and philosophers have been studying the brain for hundreds of years, yet only in recent years has real progress been made in understanding how the brain and the nervous system attached to it work. Brain research is a long way from giving educators specific suggestions for teaching. Yet we do understand a lot about how the brain operates, and we are learning more every year. Watch this space!

The most important components of the nervous system are neurons (Nicholls et al., 2012). A neuron is a long cell (see Figure 6.4). At one end are dendrites, which have thousands of tiny branches. The spaces between these branches are called synapses. Neurons receive stimuli from the environment, translate them into electrical impulses, and pass them on across the synapses to other neurons or to the brain. *Axons* at the end of the neuron pass information to other cells.

FIGURE 6.4 • Major Parts of the Neuron

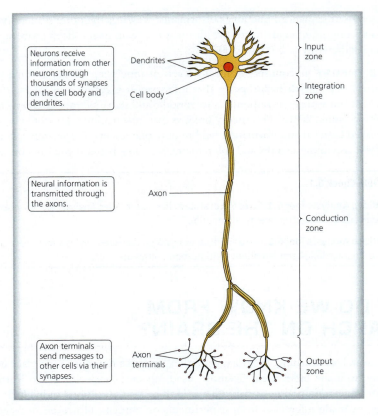

Neurons receive information from other neurons through thousands of synapses on the cell body and dendrites.

Dendrites

Cell body

Input zone

Integration zone

Neural information is transmitted through the axons.

Axon

Conduction zone

Axon terminals send messages to other cells via their synapses.

Axon terminals

Output zone

The brain receives stimuli from all the neurons in the body and has huge numbers of connections within itself. It is organized into two hemispheres, something like a walnut. Parts of the brain have specific functions, but almost any brain activity involves many parts of the brain and both hemispheres (Nicholls et al., 2012; Purves, 2010). Figure 6.5 shows areas of the brain that are particularly engaged in activities of various kinds. The human brain evolved from the inside out. The **brain stem** is the part of the brain that controls the most basic functions common to all animals. It maintains heartbeat, body temperature, and blood pressure, for example. The brain stem is sometimes called the "reptilian brain," because it does what a reptile's brain does.

The next layer above the brain stem is the **limbic system**. It has four important components. The **thalamus** is where information from the senses (except for smell) goes. That information is then passed on to the rest of the brain.

The **hypothalamus** controls the release of hormones to keep the body in balance. It controls functions such as sleep and intake of food and liquids.

The **hippocampus** is extremely important in learning. It controls the transfer of information from working memory to long-term memory (recall Figure 6.1). Patients with damage to their hippocampus can operate normally, but they cannot remember anything that happens to them after they lost their hippocampus.

The **amygdala** regulates basic emotions, such as fear, anger, and hunger.

The **cerebral cortex**, 80 percent of the brain's weight, is the part of the brain that is most unique to humans. It is wrinkled, with deep furrows. It carries out the highest mental functions, especially in its outermost layers. Within it, the **cerebellum** coordinates movement and also plays an important role in thinking.

The two hemispheres of the brain are connected by the **corpus callosum**, which helps to coordinate functions throughout the brain.

Figure 6.6 shows these main areas of the brain.

Brain Development

Brain development begins at conception. In its first four weeks of gestation, a fetus grows 200 billion neurons (Nicholls et al., 2012). Surprisingly, growth and development of the early brain are not straightforward, but are characterized by the forming of connections among neurons and

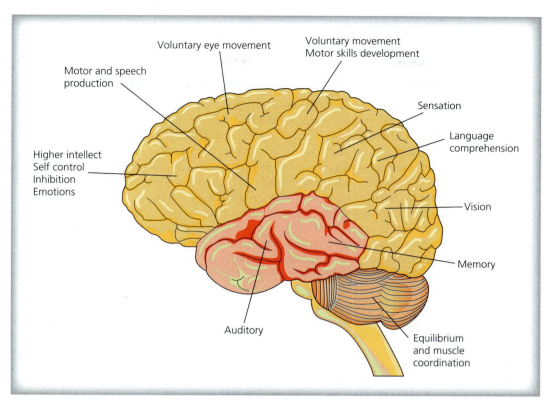

FIGURE 6.5 • Brain Physiology and Functions

Each part of the brain specializes in a particular category of functions.

the sloughing off of neurons that do not form connections. This process is affected by experience. For example, children who are deaf from birth have brains with far less development than other children in areas associated with hearing and far more development in areas associated with sight, touch, and so on. There is increasing evidence that children who are subjected to extremely deprived environments (e.g., where they are not spoken to or touched) suffer long-term loss of brain development (Sousa, 2011).

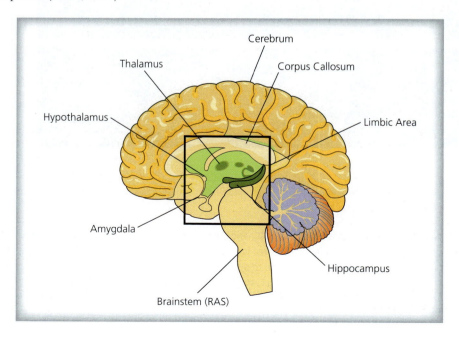

FIGURE 6.6 • Major Areas of the Brain

Most researchers believe that in most areas, the brain remains adaptable throughout life in the sense that engaging in activities that strengthen particular areas of the brain can have lasting impacts on brain function.

Implications of Brain Research for Education

Many findings from brain research have importance for education and child development. One has to do with early development, where studies find that the amount of stimulation early in a child's development relates to the number of neural connections, or synapses, which are the basis for higher learning and memory (Purves, 2010; Watson & Breedlove, 2012). The finding that the brain's capacity is not set at birth but is influenced by early experience has had an electrifying impact on the world of early childhood research and education policy. Further, some research suggests that extensive training can change brain structures, even into adulthood. For example, a study of London cabdrivers found that their training caused increased activity in a part of the brain that processes directions (Maguire et al., 2000), and that children who receive intensive tutoring in reading develop brain structures like those of proficient readers (Shaywitz, 2003; Shaywitz & Shaywitz, 2004; Temple et al., 2003; Turkeltaub, Gareau, Flowers, Zeffiro, & Eden, 2003). However, there is considerable debate about what this implies for instruction (Hruby & Hynd, 2006; Shaywitz & Shaywitz, 2007; Willis, 2007).

Another important finding of brain research is the discovery that as a person gains in knowledge and skill, his or her brain becomes more efficient. For example, Solso et al. (2007) compared the brain activation of an expert artist to that of novices. On a task familiar to the artist—drawing faces—only a small portion of his brain was active, whereas novices had activity in many parts of their brains (see Figure 6.7). Temple et al. (2003) and Turkeltaub et al. (2003) compared the brain activation of children with dyslexia to that of normal readers while they were reading. The children with dyslexia activated auditory as well as visual areas of their brains, as though they had to laboriously translate the letters into sounds and then the sounds into meaning. The proficient readers skipped the auditory step entirely. However, when the children were given tutoring and

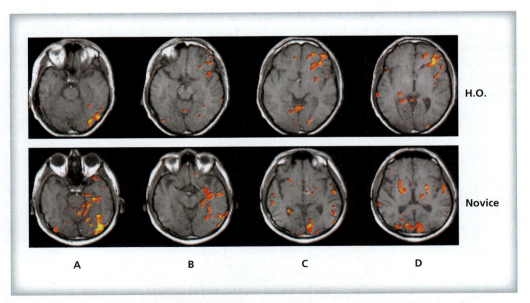

FIGURE 6.7 • Brain Activity of an Artist and a Nonartist While Drawing

fMRI scans made on an accomplished artist, H.O., and a nonartist control subject, showing right parietal activity for both people (see column A). This area is involved in facial perception, but it appears that the nonartist is demanding more energy than H.O. to process faces. In columns C and D, there is an increase in blood flow in the right frontal area of the artist, suggesting a higher-order abstraction of information.
Source: Solso Robert L., *Cognitive Psychology*, 6th Edition, ©2001. Reprinted by permission of Pearson Education, Inc., Upper Saddle River, NJ.

became adequate readers, their brain function changed to resemble that of children who had never had reading problems. Research long ago noted the importance of **automaticity**, or seemingly effortless performance made possible by extensive experience and practice, in the development of expertise. The brain studies show how automaticity can actually allow the brain to skip steps in solving problems.

Many studies (Shaywitz, 2003; Sousa, 2011) have found that proficient readers primarily activate three regions of the left brain. In contrast, dyslexics overactivate a region in the front of the brain called Broca's area, which controls speaking. In other words, poor readers seem to use an inefficient pathway (print to speech to understanding), whereas good readers use a more efficient pathway (print to understanding). More broadly, individuals with learning disabilities have been found to use less efficient brain processes than other learners (Blair, 2004; Halpern & Schulz, 2006; Worden, Hinton, & Fischer, 2011).

These and many other findings of brain research support the conclusion that the brain is not a filing cabinet for facts and skills but is engaged in a process of organizing information to make it efficiently accessible and usable. The process of discarding connections and selectively ignoring or excluding information and the process of making orderly connections among information are just as important as adding information, and perhaps even more so.

Applications of Brain Research to Classroom Teaching

The progress of brain research has quite naturally led to a call for applications to the practice of education. For example, Willis (2006), Sousa (2011), and Stansbury (2009) suggest that brain research justifies a shift away from linear, hierarchical teaching toward complex, thematic, and integrated activities. Gardner (2000) claims that brain research supports the importance of early stimulation, of activity in learning, and of music and emotions. All of these and other prescriptions may turn out to be valid, but at present the evidence for them, when it exists at all, comes from traditional cognitive psychology, not from brain research itself. Furthermore, the prescriptions from brain research are remarkably similar to the principles of progressive education described a century ago by John Dewey, without the benefit of modern brain research (see Ellis, 2001c). It may be that brain research will someday vindicate Dewey or lead to clear prescriptions for practice, but the rush to make grand claims for educational methods based on brain research has already led to a substantial body of cautionary literature (e.g., Coles, 2004; Jensen, 2000; Varma, McCandliss, & Schwartz, 2008).

Willingham (2006) argues that, although neuroscience has been moving forward "in leaps and bounds," significant help for classroom teachers from these advances is still well in the future. After all, he points out, although fMRI images might tell us which parts of a child's brain are active when she tries to read, this information doesn't really offer anything useful for that child's teacher. According to Willingham (2006), "very exciting research is being conducted. . . . Some of it is of interest to cognitive researchers trying to figure out how the brain works. And virtually all of it is far from being able to guide teachers" (p. 177).

Willingham (2006) cautions against trying to apply emerging neuroscientific data directly to the classroom. Rather, data should be considered as pieces of a very large cognitive puzzle. This caution is supported by the way in which such data have gotten into popular culture and into the literature about teaching during the past several decades. He points, for example, to research on left-brain versus right-brain functions that is often used to support a variety of instructional strategies, although brain-imaging data now confirm that both brain hemispheres participate in most cognitive tasks. He mentions as well the flurry of activity around providing stimulation for infants and young children, based on misinterpretation of data about stimulus–deprived subjects. Willingham does, however, see an immediate usefulness for neuroscientific findings in identifying children with learning disabilities, particularly dyslexia (Espy, Molfese, Molfese, & Modglin, 2004; Lyytinen et al., 2005).

Despite any reservations about finding direct correlations between neuroscience and classroom teaching, it is clear that psychological changes, behavioral changes, and changes in cognition as a consequence of learning are all correlated with changes in the operation of the brain (Worden, Hinton, & Fischer, 2011). We know something about *how* those changes occur, and we know something about *where* those changes occur. Neuroscience is on the cutting edge of behavioral science; it is supplying additional pieces of the cognitive puzzle all the time. A few consensus conclusions follow.

Certification Pointer
Teacher certification tests will require you to know that as individuals learn more, their brains become more efficient. This leads to automaticity, the effortless performance that comes with the development of expertise.

1. ***Not all learning is equally likely.*** Some types of learning are easier than others. For instance, humans readily acquire language and are attuned to social stimuli. Some learning seems more intuitive, or easy: For humans, this kind of learning appears to include language, understanding about objects and the behavior of objects in space, the geometry of three-dimensional space and the natural number system, and the distinction between living and nonliving things. Other learning can be counterintuitive or hard to learn, and this appears to include mastering fractions, algebra, and Newtonian physics, among other things (Mayer, 2011a).

   This is not news, of course, to classroom teachers, who are probably very much aware that language and spatial relationships come more easily to young learners than advanced math concepts.

2. ***Brain development constrains cognitive outcome.*** One cannot alter a brain that is not yet ready for incoming experience to affect it. That is a point made years ago by Jean Piaget, who studied children's cognition, not their brains, and we now know that there is a correspondence between changes in the brain and cognitive development (Kuhn, 2006). Whereas brain development takes place over a long time, *behavior change through learning cannot exceed the developmental status of the neural structure.*

   Developmental research also suggests that cognitive accomplishments in children and adolescents are probably best conceptualized as domain specific. Although the left and right hemispheres of the brain appear to participate together in most cognitive tasks, the brain is not entirely a general problem solver well adapted to all sorts of different challenges the person might encounter. It may be more accurate to envision the brain functioning as a series of specialized problem solvers with specific regions or circuits well adapted to handling limited kinds of problems, such as finding your way home (a geometric problem solver), figuring out language (a linguistic problem solver), or "reading" social information (a "people" problem solver).

   As Willingham (2006) suggests, the classroom applicability of this is not yet clear, but future findings may uncover implications for teachers in stimulating particular domains to achieve particular goals.

3. ***Some regions of the brain may be particularly important for cognitive outcomes and supporting certain sorts of neural activities related to learning and cognition.*** One region that has become a primary focus of much contemporary research is the prefrontal cortex. This region has been proposed as a mediator of behavioral planning and reasoning; attentional processes; impulsivity control; planning and executive cognitive functioning, and even the ability to use rules when engaged in cognitive tasks (Sousa, 2011). In short, this appears to be the seat of what we can term *deliberate cognitive activity,* which is what we try to encourage in the classroom.

   Interestingly enough, this region is structurally immature even in adolescence (Steinberg, 2011). Gray matter in the frontal cortex peaks at about age 11 in females and at 12 years in males (Giedd, 2004), whereas white matter volume in this region increases well into adulthood (Nicholls et al., 2012). This area is linked to the ability to inhibit impulses, to weigh consequences of decisions, to prioritize and strategize—in short, to act rationally. And it is still being remodeled well into early adulthood.

   What does all this mean to you when you are facing a classroom full of students? Given what we know about brain development and brain functioning, it means that those recipients of instruction are *not* empty, unformed boxes waiting to be "filled up" with information, directions, and skills. It means they are not even finished boxes—that the receptacle itself is still changing and re-forming. Learners are, in fact, neural works in progress, altering themselves with every new activity, every engagement, and every new skill acquired and fact learned. That remodeling is ongoing, protracted, and continuous. As neuroscience continues to provide a wealth of new data, and those data are woven together with the data provided by sociologists, behavioral scientists, psychologists, and educators, we may indeed find that brain research provides invaluable insights—and useful strategies—for us as teachers (see Katzir & Paré-Blagoev, 2006; Sousa, 2011; Wolfe, 2010).

Neuromyths and Neuroclues for Educators

Research on the brain is so exciting and is making such rapid progress that educators are impatient to put it to work in the classroom (Dubinsky, Roehrig, & Varma, 2013). Unfortunately, however, brain research is widely misunderstood and is often cited inaccurately. An entire industry of neuroscientists interested in education has sprung up to expose **neuromyths**, statements about educational implications of neuroscience that either are not yet justified or are flat-out untrue (see, for example, Dekker et al., 2012; Hook & Farah, 2012; Howard-Jones, 2014; Pasquinelli, 2012). Here are a few examples of prominent "neuromyths":

1. *Right brain, left brain.* For a long time, people have thought that the left hemisphere of the brain is responsible for analytical thinking (such as math), whereas the right brain specializes in creativity, music, and language. Not so. All parts of the brain are involved in all higher-order thinking and activity. The idea that there are "left brain" and "right brain" personalities is also not true. People do have greater or lesser skills in various areas, but these are not related to dominant hemispheres of their brains.

2. *People only use 10 percent of their brain capacity.* People use all of their brains all of the time. Could we learn more than we do? Sure. But there is no "unused capacity" in our brains.

3. *People have brain-based "learning styles" and learn best when taught according to that style.* The possibility that students will learn better if taught in their preferred learning style (auditory, visual, kinesthetic) has been tested in hundreds of experiments, and high-quality research fails to support it. Different students do learn in different ways, but the best way to deal with this is to use a variety of teaching methods, not to try to identify and then teach a particular learning style.

There is research going on trying to find out whether participating in art, music, and physical activity improves learning. There may be effective strategies of this kind, but it is not clear whether their effectiveness has anything to do with brain function (see Sousa, 2016).

We *do* know a lot that is supported by research and is at least consistent with our understanding of how the brain works (see Ormrod, 2016; Scalise & Felde, 2017; Schunk, 2016; Wolfe, 2010). Such "neuroclues" support the following guidelines for teachers.

1. *Give students opportunities to consolidate and rehearse new learning.* In light of the limited capacity of working memory, it makes sense to give students opportunities to practice, think about, and/or discuss new content with peers, so it can be transferred to long-term memory.

2. *Use simple graphics to reinforce learning.* Content learned in both visual and auditory ways is better retained than content learned in only one way. Use simple graphics that clearly illustrate key points to strengthen learning and retention (Mayer, 2011b).

3. *Allow students to enact concepts.* Especially for young children, acting out math concepts (e.g., hopping on a number line) seems to enhance learning (Howard-Jones, 2014a).

Some day we will understand a lot more about how to teach students in light of brain research, but we still have a lot to learn!

MyEdLab **Self-Check 6.2**

WHAT CAUSES PEOPLE TO REMEMBER OR FORGET?

Why do we remember some things and forget others? Why can we sometimes remember trivial things that happened years ago but not important things that happened yesterday? Most forgetting occurs because information in working memory was never transferred to long-term memory. However, it can also occur because we have lost our access to information in long-term memory.

Forgetting and Remembering

Over the years, researchers have identified several factors that make it easier or harder to remember information (see Bailey & Pransky, 2014; Ormrod, 2016; Schunk, 2016).

INTERFERENCE One important reason why people forget is **interference** (Bawden & Robinson, 2009; Dempster & Corkill, 1999), which happens when information gets mixed up with, or pushed aside by, other information. One form of interference occurs when people are prevented from mentally rehearsing newly learned information. In one classic experiment, Peterson and Peterson (1959) gave subjects a simple task: memorizing sets of three nonsense letters (such as FQB). The subjects were then immediately asked to count backward by 3s from a three-digit number (e.g., 287, 284, 281, etc.) for up to 18 seconds. At the end of that time the subjects were asked to recall the letters. They had forgotten far more of them than had subjects who learned the letters and then simply waited for 18 seconds to repeat them. The reason for this is that the subjects who were told to count backward were deprived of the opportunity to rehearse the letters mentally to establish them in their working memories. Nobel Prize–winning psychologist Daniel Kahneman (2011) gives dozens of similar examples from his research. As noted earlier in this chapter, you must take into account the limited capacity of working memory by allowing students time to absorb or practice (that is, mentally rehearse) new information before giving them additional instruction.

RETROACTIVE INHIBITION Another form of interference is called **retroactive inhibition**, which occurs when previously learned information is lost because it is mixed up with new and somewhat similar information. For example, young students may have no trouble recognizing the letter *b* until they are taught the letter *d*. Because these letters are similar, students often confuse them. Learning the letter *d* thus interferes with the previously learned recognition of *b*. In the same way, a traveler might know how to get around in a particular airport but then lose that skill to some extent after visiting many similar airports.

Of all the reasons for forgetting, retroactive inhibition is probably the most important. This phenomenon explains, for example, why we have trouble remembering frequently repeated episodes, such as what we had for dinner a week ago. Last night's dinner will be quickly forgotten because memories of dinners that come after it will interfere, unless something remarkable happens to clearly distinguish it from the dinners that follow.

PROACTIVE INHIBITION Sometimes previous knowledge interferes with learning later information. A classic case of **proactive inhibition** is that of a North American learning to drive on the left side of the road in England. It may be easier for a North American nondriver to learn to drive in England than for an experienced North American driver because the latter has so thoroughly learned to stay to the right—a potentially fatal error in England.

INDIVIDUAL DIFFERENCES IN RESISTANCE TO INTERFERENCE In a 1999 article, Dempster and Corkill raised the possibility that the ability to focus on key information and screen out interference is at the heart of cognitive performance. Reviewing research from many fields, including brain research, they noted strong relationships between measures of resistance to interference and school performance. For example, among children with similar IQs, those with learning disabilities perform much worse on measures of resistance to interference (see Forness & Kavale, 2000). Children with attention deficit hyperactivity disorders (ADHD) are very poor at screening out irrelevant stimuli. If you think about the stereotype of the "absent-minded professor," the ability to focus one's attention on a given problem to the exclusion of all else may be a hallmark of the kind of intellect a mathematician, scientist, or author should have to be productive.

FACILITATION It should also be noted that previous learning can often help a person learn similar information, in what is called **proactive facilitation**. For example, learning Spanish first may help an English-speaking student later learn Italian, a similar language. Learning a second language can also help with an already established language. It is often the case, for example, that English-speaking students find that the study of Latin helps them understand their native language better. This would be **retroactive facilitation**.

For another example, consider teaching. We often have the experience that learning to teach a subject helps us understand the subject better. Because later learning (e.g., learning to teach addition of fractions) increases our understanding of previously learned information (addition of fractions), this is a prime example of retroactive facilitation. Figure 6.2 summarizes the relationships among retroactive and proactive inhibition and facilitation.

THEORY INTO PRACTICE

Reducing Retroactive Inhibition

There are two ways to help reduce retroactive inhibition for students. The first is by not teaching similar and confusing concepts too closely in time. The second is to use different methods to teach similar concepts. When addressing several confusing or similar concepts, teach the first one thoroughly before introducing the next. For example, students should be completely able to recognize the letter *b* before the letter *d* is introduced. If these letters are introduced too closely together, learning one may interfere with learning the other. When the new letter is introduced, you must carefully point out the differences between *b* and *d,* and students must practice discriminating between the two until they can unerringly say which is which.

As another example, consider the following lists of Spanish and English word pairs:

A	B
llevar—to carry	*perro*—dog
llorar—to cry	*gato*—cat
llamar—to call	*caballo*—horse

List B is much easier to learn. The similarities among the Spanish words in list A (they are all verbs, start with *ll,* end with *ar,* and have the same number of letters and syllables) make them very difficult to tell apart. The English words in list A are also somewhat difficult to discriminate among because all are verbs that start with a *c.* In contrast, the words in list B are easy to discriminate from one another. Because of the problem of retroactive inhibition, presenting all the word pairs in list A in the same lesson would be a poor instructional strategy. Students would be likely to confuse the three Spanish words because of their similar spellings. Instead, students should be completely familiar with one word pair before the next is introduced.

Another way to reduce retroactive inhibition is to use different methods to teach similar concepts or to vary other aspects of instruction for each concept. For example, in social studies you might teach about Spain by using lectures and discussion, about France by using group projects, and about Italy by using videos. This would help students avoid confusing information about one country with that of another.

Most things that are forgotten were never firmly learned in the first place. The best way to ensure long-term retention of material taught in school is to make certain that students have mastered its essential features. This means assessing students' understanding frequently and reteaching if it turns out that students have not achieved adequate levels of understanding.

PRIMACY AND RECENCY EFFECTS One of the oldest findings in educational psychology is that when people are given a list of words to learn and then tested immediately afterward, they tend to learn the first few and the last few much better than those in the middle of the list. The tendency to learn the first items presented is called the **primacy effect**; the tendency to learn the last elements is called the **recency effect**. The most common explanation for the primacy effect is that we pay more attention and devote more mental effort to items presented first. As was noted earlier in this chapter, mental rehearsal is important in establishing new information in long-term memory. Usually, much more mental rehearsal is devoted to the first items presented than to later components (Anderson, 2005). Recency effects, in contrast, are based on the fact that little or no other information intervenes between the final items and the test.

TABLE 6.2 • Retroactive and Proactive Inhibition and Facilitation

Summary of the effects on memory of retroactive and proactive inhibition and facilitation.

	EFFECT ON MEMORY	
EFFECT ON LEARNING	**INHIBITION (NEGATIVE)**	**FACILITATION (POSITIVE)**
Later learning affects earlier learning	Retroactive inhibition (Example: Learning *d* interferes with learning *b*.)	Retroactive facilitation (Example: Learning to teach math helps with previously learned math skills.)
Earlier learning affects later learning	Proactive inhibition (*Example:* Learning to drive in the United States interferes with learning to drive in England.)	Proactive facilitation (*Example:* Learning Spanish helps with later learning of Italian.)

You should consider primacy and recency effects, which imply that material taught at the beginning or the end of the period is more likely to be retained than other information. To take advantage of this, you might organize your lessons to put the most essential new concepts early in the lesson and then to summarize at the end. Many teachers take roll, collect lunch money, check homework, and do other noninstructional activities at the beginning of the period. However, it is probably a better idea to postpone these activities and start the period right away with important concepts, waiting until later in the period to deal with necessary administrative tasks.

AUTOMATICITY Information or skills may exist in long-term memory but take so much time or so much mental effort to retrieve that they are of limited value when speed of access is essential. The classic case of this is reading. A child may be able to sound out every word on a page, but if he does so very slowly and laboriously, the child will lose comprehension and will be unlikely to read for pleasure (National Reading Panel, 2000). For reading and other skills in which speed and limited mental effort are necessary, long-term memory is not enough. *Automaticity* is required—that is, a level of rapidity and ease such that a task or skill involves little or no mental effort. For a proficient reader processing simple material, decoding requires almost no mental effort. As noted earlier, neurological studies show that the brain becomes more efficient as a person becomes a skilled reader (Temple et al., 2003; Turkeltaub, 2003). A beginning reader with serious learning disabilities uses both auditory and visual parts of the brain during reading, trying laboriously to sound out new words. In contrast, a skilled reader uses only a small, well-defined portion of the brain related to visual processing.

Automaticity is primarily gained through practice far beyond the amount needed to establish information or skills in long-term memory (Moors & De Houwer, 2006). A soccer player knows after 10 minutes of instruction how to kick a ball, but the player practices this skill thousands of times until it becomes automatic. A chess player quickly learns the rules of chess but spends a lifetime learning to quickly recognize patterns that suggest winning moves. Bloom (1986), who studied the role of automaticity in the performances of gifted pianists, mathematicians, athletes, and others, called automaticity "the hands and feet of genius."

Practice

The most common method for committing information to memory is also the most mundane: practice. Does practice make perfect?

Practice is important at several stages of learning. As was noted earlier in this chapter, information received in working memory must be mentally rehearsed if it is to be retained for more than a few seconds. The information in working memory must usually be practiced until it is established in long-term memory (Harmon & Marzano, 2015; Willingham, 2004).

MASSED AND DISTRIBUTED PRACTICE Is it better to practice newly learned information intensively until it is thoroughly learned, a technique called **massed practice**? Or is it more effective to practice a little each day over a period of time—**distributed practice**? Massed practice allows for faster initial learning, but for most kinds of learning, distributed practice is better for retention,

InTASC 5

Application of Content

InTASC 7

Planning for Instruction

even over short time periods (Cepeda, Pashler, Vul, Wixted, & Rohrer, 2006; Greene, 2008; Rohrer & Pashler, 2010). This is especially true of factual learning (Willingham, 2006); cramming factual information the night before could get you through a test, but the information probably won't be well integrated into your long-term memory. Long-term retention of all kinds of information and skills is greatly enhanced by distributed practice. This is the primary purpose of homework: to provide practice on newly learned skills over an extended period of time to increase the chances that the skills will be retained.

ENACTMENT Everyone knows that we learn by doing. It turns out that research on **enactment** supports this commonsense conclusion. That is, in learning how to perform tasks of many kinds, individuals learn much better if they are asked to enact the tasks (to physically carry them out) than if they simply read the instructions or watch a teacher enact the task (Engelkamp & Dehn, 2000). For example, students learn much more from a lesson on drawing geometric solids (such as cubes and spheres) if they have an opportunity to draw some rather than simply watching you do so.

GENERATION It has long been known that practice is more likely to lead to long-term retention when students create something using the new information, rather than merely rehearsing the existing information. Writing summaries, making concept maps, or teaching the content to a peer are more effective than simply reading or practicing content without creating something new from it (Bertsch, Pesta, Wiscott, & McDaniel, 2007; deWinstanley & Bjork, 2004; Sahadeo-Turner & Marzano, 2015). The generation principle is central to effective study strategies, discussed later in this chapter.

HOW CAN MEMORY STRATEGIES BE TAUGHT?

Much of what students learn in school are facts that must be remembered. These form the framework on which more complex concepts depend. Factual material must be learned as efficiently and effectively as possible to leave time and mental energy for meaningful learning, such as problem-solving, conceptual, and creative activities. If students can learn the routine parts more efficiently, they can free their minds for tasks that involve understanding and reasoning. Some learning involves memorization of facts or of arbitrary associations between terms. For example, *pomme,* the French word for apple, is an arbitrary term associated with an object. The capital of Iowa could just as well have been called *Iowapolis* as *Des Moines.* Students often learn ideas as facts before they understand them as concepts or skills. For instance, students may learn the formula for the volume of a cylinder as an arbitrary fact long before they understand why the formula is what it is.

> **InTASC 8**
>
> **Instructional Strategies**

> ## ON THE WEB
>
> For techniques and resources for improving memory, go to mindtools.com and click on Toolkit, then on Learning Skills, to find the memory items.

Verbal Learning

In many studies psychologists have examined **verbal learning** (Ashcraft & Radvansky, 2010; Bailey & Pransky, 2014; Schmidt & Marzano, 2015). For example, students might be asked to learn lists of words or symbols. Three types of verbal learning activities typically seen in the classroom have been identified and studied extensively: paired-associate, serial, and free-recall learning tasks.

1. **Paired-associate learning** involves learning to respond with one member of a pair when given the other member, usually from a list of pairs to be memorized. In typical experiments,

the pairs are arbitrary. Educational examples of paired-associate tasks include learning the state capitals, the names and dates of Civil War battles, the addition and multiplication tables, the atomic weights of the elements, and the spellings of words.

2. **Serial learning** involves learning a list of terms in a particular order. Memorization of the notes on the musical staff, the Pledge of Allegiance, the elements in order of atomic weight, and poetry and songs are serial learning tasks.

3. **Free-recall learning** tasks also involve memorizing a list, but not in a special order. Recalling the names of the 50 states, remembering the various types of reinforcement, memorizing the different genres of writing and recalling the organ systems in the body are examples of free-recall tasks.

PAIRED-ASSOCIATE LEARNING In paired-associate learning, the student must associate a response with each stimulus. For example, the student is given a picture of a bone (the stimulus) and must respond "tibia," or is given the symbol Au and must respond "gold." One important aspect in the learning of paired associates is the degree of familiarity the student already has with the stimuli and the responses. For example, it would be far easier to learn to associate foreign words with English words, such as *dog—chien* (French) or *dog—perro* (Spanish), than to learn to associate two foreign words, such as *chien—perro*.

Imagery Many powerful memory techniques are based on **imagery**, which consists of forming mental images to help remember associations. For example, the French word for fencing is *l'escrime,* pronounced "le scream." It is easy to remember this association (*fencing—l'escrime*) by forming a mental picture of a fencer screaming while being skewered by an opponent, as illustrated in Figure 6.8.

SERIAL AND FREE-RECALL LEARNING Serial learning involves comprehending facts in a particular order. Learning the events on a time line, learning the order of operations in long division, and learning the relative hardnesses of minerals are examples of serial learning. Free-recall learning involves assimilating a list of items that need not be remembered in order, such as the names of the Canadian provinces.

Loci Method A mnemonic device for serial learning that was used by the ancient Greeks employs imagery associated with a list of locations (see Anderson, 2005). In the **loci method** the student thinks of a very familiar set of locations, such as rooms in her own house, and then imagines each item on the list to be remembered in one specific location. Vivid or bizarre imagery can be used to place the item in the location. Once the connections between the item and the

FIGURE 6.8 •
Example of the Use of Images to Aid Recall

An English-speaking student learning French can easily remember that the French word for fencing is *l'escrime* by linking it to the English word *scream* and picturing a fencer screaming.

THEORY INTO PRACTICE

Keyword Mnemonics

One of the most extensively studied methods of using imagery and mnemonics (memory devices) to enhance paired-associate learning is the keyword method, which was originally developed for teaching foreign language vocabulary but was later applied to many other areas (Carney & Levin, 2002). Employing vivid imagery to recall the French word *l'escrime* is an illustration of the keyword method. In that case, the keyword was *scream*. It is called a keyword because it evokes the connection between the word *l'escrime* and the mental picture. The Russian word for building, *zdanie,* pronounced "zdan'-yeh," might be recalled by using the keyword *dawn* and imagining the sun coming up behind a building with an onion dome on top. A classic study by Atkinson and Raugh (1975) used this method to teach students a list of 120 Russian words over a 3-day period. Other students were given English translations of the Russian words and allowed to study as they wished. At the end of the experiment, the students who used the keyword method recalled 72 percent of the words, whereas the other students recalled only 46 percent. This result has been repeated dozens of times, using a wide variety of languages (e.g., Crutcher & Ericsson, 2003; Wyra et al., 2007), with students from preschoolers to adults. However, young children seem to require pictures of the mental images they are meant to form, whereas older children (starting in upper elementary school) learn equally well making their own mental images (Willoughby, Porter, Belsito, & Yearsley, 1999). Furthermore, having students work in pairs or cooperative groups has been found to enhance vocabulary learning via mnemonic strategies (Jones, Levin, Levin, & Beitzel, 2000).

The images that are used in the keyword method work best if they are vivid and active, preferably involving interaction. For example, the German word for room, *zimmer* (pronounced "tsimmer"), might be associated with the keyword *simmer*. Recall would probably be enhanced more by using an image of a distressed person immersed in a huge, steaming cauldron of water in a large bedroom than by using an image of a small pot of water simmering in the corner. The drama, action, and bizarreness of the first image make it memorable; the second is too commonplace to be easily recalled.

Similarly, Rummel, Levin, and Woodward (2002) showed students pictures to help them recall a link between various theorists of intelligence and their contributions. For example, to link Binet and measurement of higher mental processes, Rummel and colleagues showed students a race car driver protecting his *brain* with a *bonnet*. However, it should be noted that most of the research on mnemonic strategies has taken place under rather artificial, laboratory-like conditions, using materials that are thought to be especially appropriate for these strategies. Evaluations of actual classroom applications of these methods show more mixed results, and there are questions about the long-term retention of material learned by means of keywords (Carney & Levin, 1998; Wang & Thomas, 1995).

room or other location are established, the learner can recall each place and its contents in order. The same locations can be mentally cleared and used to memorize a different list. However, they should always be used in the same order to ensure that all items on the list have been remembered.

Pegword Method Another imagery method useful for serial learning is called the **pegword method** (Krinsky & Krinsky, 1996), in which a student memorizes a list of pegwords that rhyme with the numbers 1 to 10. To use this method, the student creates mental images related to items on the list to be learned with particular pegwords. For example, in learning the order of the first 10 U.S. presidents, you might picture George Washington eating a *bun* (1) with his wooden teeth, John Adams tying his *shoe* (2), Thomas Jefferson hanging by his *knees* from a branch of a *tree* (3), and so on.

Initial-Letter Strategies Another memory strategy involves a reorganization of information in which initial letters of a list to be memorized are arranged in a more easily remembered word or phrase. For example, many trigonometry classes have learned about the imaginary SOHCAHTOA tribe, whose letters help us recall that sine = opposite/hypotenuse, cosine = adjacent/hypotenuse, and tangent = opposite/adjacent. Many such **initial-letter strategies** exist for remembering the order of the planets by relative distance from the sun—Mercury, Venus, Earth, Mars, Jupiter, Saturn, Uranus, and Neptune. Students are taught a sentence in which the first letters of the words are the first letters of the planets in order, such as "My very educated monkey just served us nachos."

In a similar fashion, acronyms help people remember the names of organizations, such as NATO (North Atlantic Treaty Organization), and computer components, such as ROM (read-only memory). Initial-letter strategies may also help students remember procedural knowledge, such as steps in a process.

WHAT MAKES INFORMATION MEANINGFUL?

Consider the following sentences:

1. Enso flrs hmen matn snoi teha erso iakt siae otin tnes esna nrae.
2. Easier that nonsense information to makes than sense is learn.
3. Information that makes sense is easier to learn than nonsense.

Which sentence is easiest to learn and remember? Obviously, sentence 3. All three sentences have the same letters, and sentences 2 and 3 have the same words. Yet to learn sentence 1, you would have to memorize 52 separate letters, and to learn sentence 2, you would have to learn 10 separate words. Sentence 3 is easiest because to learn it, you need only learn one concept—a concept that readily fits your common sense and prior knowledge about how learning takes place. You know the individual words; you know the grammar that connects them; and you already have in your mind a vast store of information, experiences, and thoughts about the same topic. For these reasons, sentence 3 slides smoothly into your understanding.

The message in sentence 3 is what this chapter is all about. Most human learning, particularly school learning, involves making sense out of information, sorting it in our minds until it fits in a neat and orderly way, and using old information to help assimilate new learning. We have limited ability to recall rote information—how many telephone numbers can you remember for a month? However, we can retain meaningful information far more easily. Recall that most of the mnemonic strategies discussed in the previous section involve adding artificial meaning to arbitrary associations in order to take advantage of the much greater ease of learning meaningful information.

The message in sentence 3 has profound implications for instruction. One of your most important tasks as a teacher is to make information meaningful to students by presenting it in a clear, organized way; by relating it to information already in students' minds; and by making sure that students have truly understood the concepts being taught and can apply them to new situations.

Rote versus Meaningful Learning

Rote learning consists of the memorization of facts or associations, such as the multiplication tables, the chemical symbols for the elements, words in foreign languages, or the names of bones and muscles in the human body. Much of rote learning involves associations that are essentially arbitrary. For example, the chemical symbol for gold (Au) could just as well have been *Go* or *Gd*. In contrast, **meaningful learning** is not arbitrary, and it is related to information or concepts that learners already have. For example, if we learn that silver is an excellent conductor of electricity, this information is related to our existing information about silver and about electrical conductivity. Furthermore, the association between "silver" and "electrical conductivity" is not arbitrary. Silver really is an excellent conductor, and although we could state the same principle in many ways or in any language, the meaning of the statement "Silver is an excellent conductor of electricity" could not be arbitrarily changed.

InTASC 5

Application of Content

InTASC 7

Planning for Instruction

InTASC 8

Instructional Strategies

USES OF ROTE LEARNING We sometimes get the impression that rote learning is "bad" and meaningful learning is "good." This is not necessarily true. For example, when the doctor tells us we have a fractured tibia, we hope that the doctor has mastered the rote association between the word *tibia* and the leg bone it names. The mastery of foreign language vocabulary is an important case of rote learning. It is mainly due to overuse that rote learning has such a bad name in education. We can all remember being taught to parrot supposedly meaningful facts that we were forced to learn as rote, meaningless information. Long ago, William James (1912) gave an excellent example of this kind of false learning:

> A friend of mine, visiting a school, was asked to examine a young class in geography. Glancing at the book, she said: "Suppose you should dig a hole in the ground, hundreds of feet deep, how should you find it at the bottom—warmer or colder than on top?" None of the class replying, the teacher said: "I'm sure they know, but I think you don't ask the question quite rightly. Let me try." So, taking the book, she asked: "In what condition is the interior of the globe?" and received the immediate answer from half the class at once. "The interior of the globe is in a condition of igneous fusion." (p. 150)
>
> *Source:* From *Talks to teachers on psychology, and to students on some of life's ideals* by William James. Published by Cornell University Library, © 1912.

MyEdLab
Video Example 6.3
Bob Slavin describes visiting university students in China. Do you think the method for processing information that he witnessed is very effective? What have you found to be the best way for you to learn new information and retain it?

Clearly, the students had memorized the information without learning its meaning. "Igneous fusion" was probably gobbledegook to them. The information was useless because it did not tie in with other information they had.

INERT KNOWLEDGE The "igneous fusion" information that students had memorized is an example of what Bransford, Burns, Delclos, and Vye (1986) call **inert knowledge**. This is knowledge that could and should be applicable to a wide range of situations but is applied only to a restricted set of circumstances. Usually, inert knowledge consists of information or skills learned in school that we cannot apply in life. For example, you may know people who could pass an advanced French test but would be unable to communicate in Paris, or who can solve volume problems in math class but have no idea how much sand to order to fill a sandbox. Many problems in life arise not from a lack of knowledge but from an inability to use the knowledge we already have.

A classic experiment by Perfetto, Bransford, and Franks (1983) illustrates the concept of inert knowledge. In the experiment, college students were given problems such as the following: "Uriah Fuller, the famous Israeli superpsychic, can tell you the score of any baseball game before the game starts. What is his secret?"

Before seeing the problems, some of the students were given a list of sentences to memorize that were clearly useful in solving the problems; among the sentences was "Before it starts, the score of any game is 0 to 0." Students who were told to use the memorized sentences as clues performed much better on the problem-solving task than did other students, whereas students who memorized the clues *but were not told to use them* did no better than students who never saw the clues. What this experiment tells us is that having information in your memory does not guarantee that you can retrieve and use it when appropriate. Rather, you need to know how and when to use the information you have.

You can help students learn information in a way that will make it useful as well as meaningful to them. Effective teaching requires an understanding of how to make information accessible to students so that they can connect it to other information, think about it, and apply it outside of the classroom (Willingham, 2003).

Schema Theory

As noted earlier, meaningful information is stored in long-term memory in networks of connected facts or concepts called *schemata*. Recall the representation of the concept "bison" presented in Figure 6.3, showing how this one concept was linked to a wide range of other concepts. The most important principle of **schema theory** (Anderson, 2005; McVee, Dunsmore, & Gavelek, 2005) is that information that fits into an existing schema is more easily understood, learned, and retained than information that does not fit into an existing schema. The sentence "Bison calves can run soon after they are born" is an example of information that will be easily incorporated into your "bison" schema because you know that (1) bison rely on speed to escape from predators, and (2) more familiar animals (such as horses) that also rely on speed have babies that can run very early. Without all this prior knowledge, "Bison calves can run soon after they are born" would be more difficult to assimilate mentally and more easily forgotten.

HIERARCHIES OF KNOWLEDGE It is thought that most well-developed schemata are organized in hierarchies similar to outlines, with specific information grouped under general categories, which are grouped under still more general categories. Recall Figure 6.3. Note that in moving from the top to the bottom of the figure, you are going from general (animals and Native Americans) to specific (how Native Americans hunted bison). The concepts in the figure are well anchored in the schema. Any new information related to this schema will probably be learned and incorporated into the schema much more readily than information related to less established schemata or rote learning that does not attach to any schema (Schmidt & Marzano, 2015).

One important insight of schema theory is that meaningful learning requires the active involvement of the learner, who has a host of prior experiences and knowledge to bring to understanding and incorporating new information (Bailey & Pransky, 2014; Sahadeo-Turner & Marzano, 2015). What you learn from any experience depends in large part on the schema you apply to the experience.

THE IMPORTANCE OF BACKGROUND KNOWLEDGE One of the most important determinants of how much you can learn about something is how much you already know about it (Schmidt & Marzano, 2015). A classic study in Japan by Kuhara-Kojima and Hatano (1991) illustrates this clearly. College students were taught new information about baseball and music. Those who knew a great deal about baseball but not about music learned much more about baseball; the converse was true of those who knew a lot about music and little about baseball. In fact, background knowledge was much more important than general learning ability in predicting how much the students would learn. Learners who know a great deal about a subject have more well-developed schemata for incorporating new information. Not surprisingly, interest in a given subject contributes to background knowledge in it, as well as to depth of understanding and willingness to use background knowledge to solve new problems (Perfetti, 2003). However, learners often do not spontaneously use their prior understanding to help them learn new material. Teachers must purposefully link new learning to students' existing background knowledge (Bruning et al., 2004).

> **Connections 6.2**
> The term *modeling* is discussed in Chapter 5, in relation to Bandura's social learning theory.

> MyEdLab **Self-Check 6.3**
>
> MyEdLab **Video Analysis Tool 6.3** Go to MyEdLab and click on the Video Analysis Tool to access the exercise "Teaching to encourage long-term retention: meaningful content."

HOW DO METACOGNITIVE SKILLS HELP STUDENTS LEARN?

> **InTASC 7**
>
> **Planning for Instruction**

> **InTASC 8**
>
> **Instructional Strategies**

The term **metacognition** means knowledge about one's own learning (McCormick, Dimmit, & Sullivan, 2013; Ormrod, 2016; Schunk, 2016) or about how to learn. Thinking skills and study skills are examples of **metacognitive skills**. Students can be taught strategies for assessing their own understanding, figuring out how much time they will need to study something, and choosing an effective plan of attack to examine or solve problems (McCormick, Dimmit, & Sullivan, 2013). For example, in reading this book, you are bound to come across a paragraph that you don't understand on first reading. What do you do? Perhaps you reread the paragraph more slowly. Perhaps you look for other clues, such as pictures, graphs, or glossary terms to help you understand. Perhaps you read further back in the chapter to see whether your difficulty arose because you did not fully understand something that came earlier. These are all examples of metacognitive skills; you have learned how to recognize when you are not understanding and how to correct yourself (McCormick, Dimmitt, & Sullivan, 2013; Schunk, 2016). Another metacognitive strategy is the ability to predict what is likely to happen or to tell what is sensible and what is not. For example, when you first read the word *modeling* in Chapter 5, you knew right away that it did not refer to building models of ships or airplanes because you knew that this meaning would not fit in the context of this text.

ON THE WEB

For an overview of metacognition, visit brainfacts.org. For detailed research, see the *Journal of Metacognition and Learning*.

Although most students gradually develop adequate metacognitive skills, some do not. Teaching metacognitive strategies to students can lead to a marked improvement in their achievement (Schunk, 2016). Students can learn to think about their own thinking processes and apply specific learning strategies to think themselves through difficult tasks. **Self-questioning strategies** are particularly effective. In self-questioning, students look for common elements in a given type of task and ask themselves questions about these elements. Instructors start with specific questions and then let students find these critical elements on their own (Dunlosky et al., 2013). For example, Paris, Cross, and Lipson (1984) and King (1992) found that students comprehend better if they are taught to ask themselves *who, what, where,* and *how* questions as they read. Englert, Raphael, Anderson, Anthony, and Stevens (1991) gave students planning sheets with questions to ask themselves in planning their creative writing assignments. For whom am I writing? What is being explained? What are the steps? Essentially, students were taught to talk themselves through the activities they were engaged in, asking themselves or each other the questions a teacher would ask.

WHAT STUDY STRATEGIES HELP STUDENTS LEARN?

How are you reading this book? Are you underlining or highlighting key sentences? Are you taking notes or summarizing? Are you discussing the main ideas with a classmate? Are you putting the book under your pillow at night and hoping the information will somehow seep into your mind? Students have used these and many other strategies ever since the invention of reading, and such strategies have been studied almost as long. Even Aristotle wrote on the topic. Yet educational psychologists are still debating which study strategies are most effective.

Research on effective study strategies is confusing at best. Few forms of studying are found always to be effective, and fewer still are never effective. Clearly, the value of study strategies depends on their specifics and on the uses to which they are put (Schunk, 2016). A generalization about effective study strategies is that effective methods involve learners in reshaping the information, not just rereading (Callender & McDaniel, 2009) or highlighting without consciously choosing the most important information to highlight. Research on the most common study strategies is summarized in the following sections.

MyEdLab
Video Example 6.4
How effective are the study strategies that the students here describe?

Practice Tests

Perhaps the most effective study strategy is taking practice tests aligned with the real test to come. Test taking, especially when tests require constructed responses rather than multiple choice or fill-in-the-blank, causes test takers to engage in high-level processing of the content, thereby enhancing understanding and memory (Bailey & Pransky, 2014; Carpenter & Pashler, 2007; Harmon & Marzano, 2015; McDaniel, Roediger, & McDermott, 2007; Rohrer & Pashler, 2010). Furthermore, the practice test reminds you what you know and what you do not know, so that you can focus your studying most efficiently. Working in a study group in which the members make up practice tests for each other can be particularly effective (Ashcraft & Radvansky, 2010).

Note-Taking

A common study strategy used both in reading and in learning from lectures, **note-taking** can be effective for certain types of material because it requires mental processing of main ideas as one makes decisions about what to write. However, the effects of note-taking have been found to be inconsistent. Positive effects are most likely when note-taking is used for complex conceptual material in which the critical task is to identify the main ideas (Dunlosky et al., 2013; Kobayashi, 2005; Peverly et al., 2007). Also, note-taking that requires some mental processing is more effective than simply writing down what was read (Igo, Bruning, & McCrudden, 2005). For example, Bretzing and Kulhavy (1981) found that writing paraphrase notes (stating the main ideas in different words) and taking notes in preparation to teach others the material are effective note-taking strategies because they require a high degree of mental processing of the information.

One apparently effective means of increasing the value of students' note-taking is for you to provide partial notes before a lecture or reading, giving students categories to direct their own note-taking. Several studies have found that this practice, combined with student note-taking and review, increases student learning (Robinson, Katayama, Beth, Odom, & Hsieh, 2004).

Underlining

Perhaps the most common study strategy is underlining or highlighting. Yet despite the widespread use of this method, research on underlining generally finds few benefits (Gaddy, 1998). The problem is that most students fail to make decisions about what material is most critical and simply underline too much. When students are asked to underline the one sentence in each paragraph that is most important, they retain more, probably because deciding which is the most important sentence requires a higher level of processing (Harmon & Marzano, 2015).

Summarizing

Summarizing involves writing brief statements that represent the main ideas of the information being read. One effective way to use this strategy is to have students write one-sentence summaries after reading each paragraph (Marzano, 2010b). Another is to have students prepare summaries that are intended to help others learn the material—partly because this activity forces the summarizer to be brief and to consider seriously what is important and what is not (Bailey & Pransky, 2014).

Writing to Learn

A growing body of evidence supports the idea that having students explain in writing the content they are learning helps them understand and remember it (Klein, 1999). For example, Fellows (1994) had sixth-graders in a 12-week science unit on states of matter write about their understandings of the concepts at several points in the unit. A control group studied the same content without writing. The writing group retained substantially more of the content at post-test. This and other studies find that focused writing assignments help children learn the content about which they are writing. However, evidence on the effects of less focused "journal writing," in which students keep logs of their ideas and observations, is much more mixed.

Outlining and Concept Mapping

Certification Pointer

When responding to the case studies in certification tests, you may be asked to design a lesson that includes strategies for helping students learn relationships between ideas using concept mapping.

A related family of study strategies requires the student to represent the material studied in skeletal form. These strategies include outlining, networking, and concept mapping. **Outlining** presents the main points of the material in a hierarchical format, with each detail organized under a higher-level category. In networking and **concept mapping**, students identify main ideas and then diagram connections between them (Schmidt & Marzano, 2015). For example, the schematic representation of the concept "bison" shown in Figure 6.3 might have been produced by students themselves as a network to summarize factual material about bison and their importance to Plains Indians.

Research on outlining, networking, and concept mapping is limited and inconsistent but generally finds that these methods are helpful as study aids (Nesbit & Adesope, 2006).

The PQ4R Method

One of the best-known study techniques for helping students understand and remember what they read is the **PQ4R method** (Thomas & Robinson, 1972), which is based on an earlier version known as SQ3R, developed by F. P. Robinson (1961). The acronym stands for *preview, question, read, reflect, recite,* and *review.*

Research has shown the effectiveness of the PQ4R method for older children (Adams, Carnine, & Gersten, 1982), and the reasons seem clear. Following the PQ4R procedure focuses students on the meaningful organization of information and involves them in other effective strategies, such as question generation, elaboration, and distributed practice (opportunities to review information over a period of time).

THEORY INTO PRACTICE

Teaching the PQ4R Method

Explain and model the steps of the PQ4R method for your students, using the following guidelines:

1. *Preview.* Survey or scan the material quickly to get an idea of the general organization and the major topics and subtopics. Pay attention to headings and subheadings, and identify what you will be reading about and studying.

2. *Question.* Ask yourself questions about the material before you read it. Use headings to invent questions using the wh words: *who, what, why, where.*

3. *Read.* Read the material. Do not take extensive written notes. Try to answer the questions that you posed before reading.

4. *Reflect on the material.* Try to understand and make meaningful the presented information by (1) connecting it to what you already know, (2) relating the subtopics in the text to primary concepts or principles, (3) trying to resolve contradictions within the presented information, and (4) using the material to solve problems suggested by the material.

5. *Recite.* Practice remembering the information by stating points out loud and asking and answering questions. Use headings, highlighted words, and notes on major ideas to generate those questions.

6. *Review.* In the final step, actively review the material, focusing on asking yourself questions; reread the material only when you are not sure of the answers.

HOW DO COGNITIVE TEACHING STRATEGIES HELP STUDENTS LEARN?

In *Alice's Adventures in Wonderland,* the White Rabbit is unsure how to give his evidence in the trial of the Knave of Hearts. The King of Hearts gives him a bit of advice: "Begin at the beginning . . . and go on until you come to the end: then stop." The "King of Hearts method" is a common means of delivering lectures, especially at the secondary and college levels. However, you can do more to help your students understand lessons. You can prepare students to learn new material by reminding them of what they already know, asking questions, and helping students link and recall new information (Bailey & Pransky, 2014; Schmidt & Marzano, 2015; McCormick, 2003). Many aspects of effective lesson presentation are covered in Chapter 7, but the following sections discuss practices derived from cognitive psychology that can help students understand, recall, and apply essential information, concepts, and skills.

Making Learning Relevant and Activating Prior Knowledge

Read the following passage:

> With the hocked gems financing him our hero bravely defied all scornful laughter that tried to prevent his scheme. Your eyes deceive he had said. An egg, not a table, correctly typifies this unexplored planet. Now three sturdy sisters sought proof. Forging along, sometimes through calm vastness, yet more often through turbulent peaks and valleys, days became weeks as many doubters spread fearful rumors about the edge. At last, from nowhere, welcome winged creatures appeared signifying momentous success. (Dooling & Lachman, 1971, p. 217)
>
> *Source:* From *Effects of comprehension on retention of prose* by James D. Dooling and Roy Lachman. Published by Journal of Experimental Psychology, © 1971.

InTASC 2

Learning Differences

InTASC 8

Instructional Strategies

Connections 6.3

See, for example, "How Is a Direct Instruction Lesson Taught?" in Chapter 7.

MyEdLab

Video Example 6.5

In this class, the students are using already-learned information (the meaning of the prefix *super*) to figure out the meanings of new vocabulary words.

21ST CENTURY LEARNING

Learning How to Learn

Self-direction is a key skill in the 21st century, and it is emphasized in the Common Core State Standards. The Internet has made vast amounts of information easily available on Google, Wikipedia, and so on. The problem is that learners need to know how to organize their thinking to make effective use of all this information. They need to know how to identify what they already know about a topic, along with what they need to know, and they need to have a strategy for extracting the relevant information. Teaching students to take control of their own learning process helps them to use their time efficiently in reading for information, whether the material is on paper or online. In a world awash in data, knowing learning strategies such as the use of graphic organizers, outlining, and organizing information in hierarchies is essential.

Now read the paragraph again with the following information: The passage is about Christopher Columbus. Before you knew what the passage was about, it probably made little sense to you. You could understand the words and grammar and could probably infer that the story involved a voyage of discovery. However, once you learned that the story was about Columbus, you could bring all your prior knowledge about Columbus to bear on comprehending the paragraph, so that seemingly obscure references made sense. The "hocked gems" (Queen Isabella's jewelry), the egg (the shape of the earth), the three sturdy sisters (the *Niña, Pinta,* and *Santa Maria*), and the winged creatures (birds) become comprehensible when you know what the story is about.

In terms of schema theory, advance information that the story concerns Columbus activates your schema relating to Columbus. You are ready to receive and incorporate information relating to Columbus, to Isabella and Ferdinand, and to the ships. It is as though you had a filing cabinet with a drawer labeled "Columbus." When you know you are about to hear about Columbus, you mentally open the drawer, which contains files marked "Isabella," "ships," and "scoffers and doubters." You are now ready to file new information in the proper places. If you learned that the *Santa Maria* was wrecked in a storm, you would mentally file that information in the "ships" file. If you learned that most of the educated world agreed with Columbus that the Earth was round, you would file that information in the "scoffers and doubters" file. The file drawer analogy is not completely appropriate, however, because the files of a schema are all logically connected with one another. Also, you are actively using the information in your files to interpret and organize the new information.

ADVANCE ORGANIZERS David Ausubel (1963) developed a method called **advance organizers** to orient students to material they were about to learn and help them recall related information that could assist them in incorporating the new information. An advance organizer is an initial statement about a subject to be learned that provides a structure for the new information and relates it to knowledge that students already possess (Joyce, Weil, & Calhoun, 2000). For example, in one classic study (Ausubel & Youssef, 1963), college students were assigned to read a passage on Buddhism. Before reading the passage, some students were given an advance organizer comparing Buddhism to Christianity, whereas others read an unrelated passage. The students who were given the advance organizer retained much more of the material than the other students. Ausubel and Youssef maintain that the reason for this is because the advance organizer activates most students' knowledge of Christianity, and the students were able to use that knowledge to incorporate information about a less familiar religion.

Many studies have established that advance organizers increase students' understanding of certain kinds of material (see Schwartz, Ellsworth, Graham, & Knight, 1998). Advance organizers seem to be most useful for teaching content with a well-organized structure that might not be immediately apparent to students. However, they have not generally been found to help students learn factual information that does not lend itself to a clear organization or subjects that consist of a large number of separate topics (Corkill, 1992). In addition, methods designed to activate prior knowledge, such as advance organizers, can be counterproductive if the prior knowledge is weak or lacking (Schunk, 2016). If students know little about Christianity, relating Buddhism to Christianity may confuse rather than help them.

The use of advance organizers is a valuable strategy in its own right, but research on advance organizers also illustrates a broader principle that is extremely important: Activating prior knowledge enhances understanding and retention (Pressley, Harris, & Marks, 1992). Strategies other than advance organizers draw on this same principle. For example, having students discuss what they already know about a topic before they learn it (Pressley, Tannenbaum, McDaniel, & Wood, 1990) and having them make predictions about material to be learned (Fielding, Anderson, & Pearson, 1990) are additional ways to encourage students to make conscious use of prior knowledge.

Certification Pointer

On a teacher certification test, you may be asked to propose a strategy for stimulating the prior knowledge of students described in a particular case.

ANALOGIES Like advance organizers, explanatory analogies (comparisons or parallels) can contribute to understanding by linking new information to well-established background knowledge. For example, you could introduce a lesson on the human body's disease-fighting mechanisms by telling students to imagine a battle and to consider it as an analogy for the body's fight against infection. Similarly, you could preface a lesson on termite societies by asking students to think of the hierarchy of citizens within a kingdom, using that as an analogy for such insect societies. **Analogies** can help students learn new information by relating it to concepts they already know (Bulgren, Deshler, Schumaker, & Lenz, 2000).

One interesting classic study (Halpern, Hansen, & Riefer, 1990) found that analogies work best when they are most different from the process being explained. For example, college students' learning about the lymph system was aided more by describing it as analogous to the movement of water through a sponge than by comparing it to the movement of blood through veins. Apparently, it is more important that analogies be thoroughly familiar to the learner than that they relate in any direct way to the concepts being taught.

ELABORATION Cognitive psychologists use the term **elaboration** to refer to the process of thinking about material to be learned in a way that connects the material to information or ideas that are already in the learner's mind (Ormrod, 2016). As an example of the importance of elaboration, Stein, Littlefield, Bransford, and Persampieri (1984) conducted a series of experiments in which students were given lists of phrases to learn, such as "The gray-haired man carried the bottle." Some students were given the same phrases embedded in a more elaborate sentence, such as "The gray-haired man carried the bottle of hair dye." These latter students recalled the phrases much better than those who did not receive the elaboration, because the additional words tied the phrase to a well-developed schema that was already in the students' minds. The connection between *gray-haired man* and *bottle* is arbitrary until we give it meaning by linking these words with the *hair dye* idea.

You can apply this principle—that elaborated information is easier to understand and remember—to help students comprehend lessons. Students may be asked to think of connections between ideas or to relate new concepts to their own lives. For example, it may help students to understand the U.S. annexation of Texas and California if they consider these events from the perspective of Mexicans or if they compare the events to a situation in which a friend borrows a bicycle and then decides not to give it back. Elaboration can be taught as a skill to help students comprehend what they read (Schmidt & Marzano, 2015). In discussing a story or novel, you might ask students from time to time to stop and visualize what is happening or what's about to happen, as a means of helping them to elaborate their understanding of the material.

Organizing Information

Recall the shopping list discussed earlier in this chapter. When the list was presented in random order, it was very difficult to memorize, partly because it contained too many items to be held in working memory all at once. However, when the list was organized in a logical way, it was meaningful and therefore easy to learn and remember. The specific foods were grouped according to familiar recipes (e.g., flour, eggs, and milk were grouped under "pancakes"), and the recipes and other foods were grouped under "breakfast," "lunch," and "dinner."

Material that is well organized is much easier to learn and remember than material that is poorly organized (Schmidt & Marzano, 2015). Hierarchical organization, in which specific issues

THE INTENTIONAL TEACHER
Teaching in Light of Knowledge of Brain Function and Learning Strategies

Intentional teachers understand how learning takes place and planfully use effective strategies to help children learn and remember important knowledge and skills.

- They help students understand their own learning processes so they can learn more effectively.
- They understand how the limited capacity of working memory implies that students should not be bombarded with too much content at once and that students need time to process new concepts and skills.
- They use motivational strategies to encourage students to devote mental energy to learning.
- They teach to enhance long-term memory by teaching learning strategies and engaging students in active learning.
- They use methods to diminish mental interference, such as avoiding teaching easily confused topics at the same time.
- They use methods to enhance facilitation by pointing out commonalities among previously learned concepts and new ones.
- They provide extensive practice to help students gain automaticity in basic skills.
- They teach students effective study strategies and give them many opportunities to use them.
- They organize information to help students access new concepts.

MyEdLab

Application Exercise 6.1

In the Pearson etext, watch a classroom video. Then use the guidelines in "The Intentional Teacher" to answer a set of questions that will help you reflect on and understand the teaching and learning presented in the video.

---

are grouped under more general topics, seems particularly helpful for student understanding. For example, in a classic study by Bower, Clark, Lesgold, and Winzenz (1969), one group of students was taught 112 words related to minerals in random order (e.g., metals, alloys, limestone, steel, stones, rare, masonry). Another group was taught the same words organized into a four-level hierarchy. (The overarching category label "mineral" was considered level 1. Level 2 divided minerals into "metals" and "stones." Level 3 divided metals into "rare," "common," and "alloy" and stones into "precious" and "masonry." And level 4 provided more specific labels such as "platinum," "steel," "ruby," and "limestone.") The students were taught the words at levels 1 and 2 in the first of four sessions; those at levels 1, 2, and 3 in the second session; and those at levels 1 through 4 in the third and fourth sessions. The students in this second group recalled an average of 100 words, compared to only 65 for the group that received the random presentation—demonstrating the effectiveness of a coherent, organized presentation. In teaching complex concepts, not only is it necessary that material be well organized, but it is also important that the organizing framework itself be made clear to students (Kallison, 1986). For example, in teaching about minerals, you might present a diagram of the hierarchical framework, referring to it regularly and marking transitions from one part of it to another, as follows:

"Recall that alloys are combinations of two or more metals."

"Now that we've covered rare and common metals and alloys, let's move on to the second category of minerals: stones."

THEORY INTO PRACTICE

A Question-Exploration Routine (QER) for Complex Learning

Bulgren, Marquis, Lenz, Deshler, and Schumaker (2011) devised and successfully evaluated a method to help secondary students learn complex content that incorporates several proven study strategies. The method has three steps: Cue, Do, and Review.

Cue: The teacher introduces the topic of the lesson, informs students of the importance of learning the information, and distributes a one-page Question-Exploration Guide (QEG) to facilitate note-taking (see Figure 6.9).

Do: The teacher and students complete a guide following six thinking steps with the acronym ANSWER:

Ask a critical question

Note key terms and basic knowledge

Search for supporting questions and answer them

Work out a brief main-idea answer to the critical question

Explore the answer in a related area

Relate the answer to today's world

The key information is recorded on a Question-Exploration Guide, as in Figure 6.9.

Review: Students review all of the elements of the "Do" cycle to make sure they understand the critical content.

Bulgren et al. (2011) evaluated the QER procedure, comparing it to traditional lecture-discussion methods in teaching a brief unit on biological and chemical weapons. Students who experienced QER scored substantially better than those in the lecture–discussion group on all forms of assessment, especially when students had to construct their own responses.

USING QUESTIONING TECHNIQUES One strategy that helps students learn from written texts, lectures, and other sources of information is the insertion of questions requiring students to stop from time to time to assess their own understanding of what the text or teacher is saying (Schunk, 2016). Presenting questions before the introduction of the instructional material can also help students learn material related to the questions, as can having students generate their own questions (Dunlosky et al., 2013).

USING CONCEPTUAL MODELS Another means that you can use to help students comprehend complex topics is the introduction of conceptual models, or diagrams showing how elements of a process are related to one another. Figure 6.1, which illustrates information processing, is a classic example of a conceptual model. Use of such models organizes and integrates information. Examples of topics that lend themselves to using conceptual models are electricity, mechanics, computer programming, and the processes by which laws are passed. When models are part of a lesson, not only do students learn more but they also are better able to apply their learning to creatively solve problems (Mayer, 2008b). Knowledge maps, a variation on conceptual models, can be used to teach a wider variety of content. A knowledge map graphically shows the main concepts of a topic of study and the links between them. Giving students knowledge maps after a lesson has been shown to increase their retention of the lesson's content (Nesbit & Adesope, 2006; O'Donnell, Dansereau, & Hall, 2002).

Graphs, charts, tables, matrices, and other means of organizing information into a comprehensible, visual form have all been found to aid comprehension, memory, and transfer (Carney & Levin, 2002; Mayer, 2008a, b). However, these devices lose their effectiveness if they contain too much information that is not quickly communicated by the visuals (Butcher, 2006; Schnotz, 2002;

**FIGURE 6.9 •
Question-Exploration
Guide**

Source: From "The Effectiveness of
a Question-Exploration Routine for
Enhancing the Content Learning of
Secondary Students" by J. Bulgren,
J. Marquis, B. Lenz, D. Deshler,
and J. Schumaker in *Journal of
Educational Psychology*, Vol. 103
No. 03, pp. 578–593. Published by
Journal of Educational Psychology
(APA).

BULGREN ET AL.

Question Exploration Guide

Text Reference _Chapter 5, pp. 41-44_   Name: _David Cole_
Course
Unit   Critical   Title _Modern Warfare: Biological Weapons_
Lesson ___x___   Question #: ___2___   Date: _May 1, 2016_

① What is the Critical Question? Why are biological weapons such a great danger?

② What are the key Terms and explanations?
ORGANISM - A living thing   ANTIBODY - a body's own defense against infection
BIOLOGICAL WEAPON - An organism or its   ANTIBIOTIC - a man-made substance that kills harmful things
                    poisons that cause harm   VACCINE - a dead organism that gives protection

③ What are the Supporting Questions and answers? EXAMPLES & EFFECTS   TREATMENTS & PROBLEMS

What are examples & effects of each biological weapon?	VIRUS	Smallpox causes fever/blisters;	treated with vaccine (no longer made).
	BACTERIA	Anthrax harms lungs;	treated with vaccines/antibiotics (not enough).
What are treatments & problems with treatments for each biological weapon?	FUNGUS	Wilt kills crops;	treated with fungicides (can't cover large areas).
	TOXIN	Ricin poisons & kills;	no protection (must avoid).

④ What is the main Idea answer? Biological weapons can harm people and crops, and treatments are inadequate.

⑤ How can we use the main idea?
What are similarities between wilt & ricin?
(Both from plants.)
What are differences between wilt & ricin?
(Wilt is plants: ricin is a poison from plants.)

⑥ Is there an Overall Idea? Is there a real-world use?
Why must vaccines be given before exposure to biological
weapons? (Takes time to build immunity.)

Vekiri, 2002). Atkinson et al. (1999) described a method to confront this problem by combining
mnemonics with tables. To teach about the characteristics of various sharks, teachers made tables
in which humorous pictures linked the names of the sharks with their characteristics. For example,
dogfish sharks live near shore in moderate depth and have sawlike teeth, so the mnemonic showed
dogs emerging from a submarine in shallow water holding saws to cut down a "No Dogs Allowed"
sign on shore. Fifth-graders using this method retained much more about the characteristics of
nine sharks than did students who saw other kinds of displays.

MyEdLab **Self-Check 6.4**

MyEdLab **Video Analysis Tool 6.4**   Go to MyEdLab and click on the Video Analysis Tool to access the exercise
"Teaching to encourage long-term retention: metacognition."

SUMMARY

What Is an Information-Processing Model?

The three major components of memory are the sensory register, short-term or working memory,
and long-term memory. The sensory registers are very short-term memories linked to the senses.
Information received by the senses but not attended to is quickly forgotten. Once information is
received, it is processed by the mind in accord with our experiences and mental states. This activity is called *perception*.

Short-term or working memory is a storage system that holds five to nine bits of information at any one time. Information enters working memory from both the sensory register and
long-term memory. Rehearsal is the process of repeating information in order to hold it in working memory.

Long-term memory is the part of the memory system in which a large amount of information is stored for an indefinite time period. Cognitive theories of learning stress the importance of
helping students relate information being learned to information existing in long-term memory.

The three parts of long-term memory are episodic memory, which stores our memories
of personal experiences; semantic memory, which stores facts and generalized knowledge in the
form of schemata; and procedural memory, which stores knowledge of how to do things. Schemata are networks of related ideas that guide our understanding and action. Information that fits
into a well-developed schema is easier to learn than information that cannot be so accommodated.
Levels-of-processing theory suggests that learners remember only what they process. Students are

processing information when they manipulate it, look at it from different perspectives, and analyze it. Dual code theory further suggests the importance of using both visual and verbal coding to learn bits of information.

What Do We Know from Research on the Brain?

Technology that enables scientists to observe the brain in action has led to rapid advances in brain science. Findings have shown how specific parts of the brain process specific types of information in concert with other specific brain sites. As individuals gain expertise, their brain function becomes more efficient. Early brain development is a process of adding neural connections and then sloughing off those that are not used. Neuroscience is discovering much about how the brain operates, but this research does not yet have direct applications to teaching.

What Causes People to Remember or Forget?

Interference theory helps explain why people forget. It suggests that students can forget information when it gets mixed up with, or pushed aside by, other information. Interference theory states that two situations cause forgetting: retroactive inhibition, when learning a second task makes a person forget something that was learned previously, and proactive inhibition, when learning one thing interferes with the retention of things learned later. In accordance with the primacy and recency effects, people best remember information that is presented first and last in a series. Automaticity is gained by practicing information or skills far beyond the amount needed to establish them in long-term memory so that using such skills requires little or no mental effort. Practice strengthens associations of newly learned information in memory. Distributed practice, which involves practicing parts of a task over a period of time, is usually more effective than massed practice. Enactment also helps students to remember information.

How Can Memory Strategies Be Taught?

Teachers can help students remember facts by presenting lessons in an organized way and by teaching students to use memory strategies called *mnemonics*. Three types of verbal learning are paired-associate learning, serial learning, and free-recall learning. Paired-associate learning is learning to respond with one member of a pair when given the other member. Students can improve their learning of paired associates by using imagery techniques such as the keyword method. Serial learning involves recalling a list of items in a specified order. Free-recall learning involves recalling a list in any order. Helpful strategies include the loci method, the pegword method, rhyming, and initial-letter strategies.

What Makes Information Meaningful?

Information that makes sense and has significance to students is more meaningful than inert knowledge and information learned by rote. According to schema theory, individuals' meaningful knowledge is constructed of networks and hierarchies of schemata.

How Do Metacognitive Skills Help Students Learn?

Metacognition helps students learn by thinking about, controlling, and effectively using their own thinking processes.

What Study Strategies Help Students Learn?

Note-taking, selective directed underlining, summarizing, writing to learn, outlining, and mapping can effectively promote learning. The PQ4R method is an example of a strategy that focuses on the meaningful organization of information.

How Do Cognitive Teaching Strategies Help Students Learn?

Advance organizers help students process new information by activating background knowledge. Analogies, information elaboration, organizational schemes, questioning techniques, and conceptual models are other examples of teaching strategies that are based on cognitive learning theories.

KEY TERMS

Review the following key terms from the chapter.

advance organizers 150

amygdala 132

analogies 151

attention 124

automaticity 135

brain stem 131

cerebellum 132

cerebral cortex 132

concept mapping 148

corpus callosum 132

dendrites 131

distributed practice 140

dual code theory of memory 131

elaboration 151

enactment 141

episodic memory 127

flashbulb memory 128

free-recall learning 142

hippocampus 132

hypothalamus 132

imagery 142

inert knowledge 145

information-processing theory 122

initial-letter strategies 144

interference 138

keyword method 143

levels-of-processing theory 130

limbic system 132

loci method 142

long-term memory 127

massed practice 140

meaningful learning 144

metacognition 146

metacognitive skills 146

mnemonics 143

neuromyth 137

neurons 131

note-taking 147

outlining 148

paired-associate learning 141

pegword method 143

perception 124

PQ4R method 148

primacy effect 139

proactive facilitation 138

proactive inhibition 138

procedural memory 127

recency effect 139

rehearsal 124

retroactive facilitation 138

retroactive inhibition 138

rote learning 144

schemata 128

schema theory 145

self-questioning strategies 147

semantic memory 127

sensory registers 124

serial learning 142

short-term memory 124

summarizing 148

synapses 131

thalamus 132

verbal learning 141

working memory 124

SELF-ASSESSMENT: PRACTICING FOR LICENSURE

Directions: The chapter-opening vignette addresses indicators that are often assessed in state licensure exams. Reread the chapter-opening vignette, and then respond to the following questions.

1. According to information-processing theory, which component of the memory system did Verona Bishop's students first use during the 3-second experiment?
   a. Sensory register
   b. Short-term memory
   c. Working memory
   d. Long-term memory

2. Verona Bishop asks her students to "imagine that you could keep everything that ever entered your mind. What would that be like?" One student responds, "You'd be a genius!" Another responds, "You'd go crazy!" Why does Ms. Bishop side with the second student?
   a. Genius is an inherited trait not associated with memory.
   b. There is no correlation between genius and paying attention to environmental clues.
   c. Being bombarded with too much information all at once decreases learning.
   d. People with mental illness absorb more environmental information than people without mental illness.

3. During the 3-second memory experiment, Verona Bishop asks her students to recall information not associated with the overhead information she presented on the screen. What type of memory are students using when they recall smells, sounds, and details of the classroom and the people in it?
   a. Semantic memory
   b. Procedural memory
   c. Dual code memory
   d. Episodic memory

4. Cheryl, one of Verona Bishop's students, recalled seeing the word *thinking* on the overhead screen, even though it was not there. How does Ms. Bishop explain this phenomenon?
   a. Ms. Bishop actually said the word during the 3-second experiment, so Cheryl picked it up there.
   b. Humans have a tendency to learn the first and last bits of information presented, so Cheryl thought of the word *thinking* after the 3-second experiment.
   c. *Thinking* and *memory,* a word that was actually presented, are closely related and are probably stored close together in memory. When one is recalled, so is the other.
   d. Because the students had only 3 seconds to review the information, Cheryl's report of what she remembered contained guesses.

5. Consider that some of Verona Bishop's students attempted to memorize the information on the overhead screen in a random fashion. Which of the following learning strategies were they using?
   a. Free-recall learning
   b. Serial learning
   c. Paired-associate learning
   d. Process learning

6. Verona Bishop summarizes her experiment by telling her students that they will forget some details of the experiment but remember others. Why is this so?
   a. According to levels-of-processing theory, we tend to retain information that has been subject to thorough processing. If the students gave meaning to the information, it is likely to be remembered.
   b. According to dual code theory, visual information is more likely to be retained than verbal information. If the students saw the information, it is more likely to be remembered than if they heard it.

7. Describe several memory strategies that you can teach your students to help them remember the facts, concepts, and ideas presented in a lesson.

MyEdLab **Licensure Exam 6.1** Answer questions and receive instant feedback in your Pearson eText in MyEdLab.

Echo/Cultura/Getty Images

CHAPTER SEVEN

The Effective Lesson

LEARNING OUTCOMES

At the end of this chapter, you should be able to:

7.1 Define direct instruction and describe how to teach a lesson using direct instruction

7.2 Describe how best to teach for transfer of learning

7.3 Identify instructional situations in which discussion is most useful

7.4 Explain how knowledge of effective lessons informs intentional teaching

Jennifer Logan's eighth-grade physical science class is a happy mess. Students are working in small groups at lab stations, filling all sorts of bottles with water and then tapping them to see how various factors affect the sound. One group has set up a line of identical bottles and put different amounts of water in each one so that tapping the bottles in sequence makes a crude musical scale. "The amount of water in the bottle is all that matters," one group member tells Ms. Logan, and her groupmates nod in agreement. Another group has an odd assortment of bottles and has carefully measured the same amount of water into each. "It's the shape and thickness of the bottles that make the difference," says one group member. Other groups are working more chaotically, filling and tapping large and small, narrow and wide, and thick and thin bottles with different amounts of water. Their theories are wild and varied.

After half an hour of experimentation, Ms. Logan calls the class together and asks group members to describe what they did and what they concluded. Students loudly uphold their group's point of view. "It's the amount of water!" "It's the height of the bottles!" "It's the thickness of the bottles!" "No, it's their shape!" "It's how hard you tap the bottles!" Ms. Logan moderates the conversation but lets students confront each other's ideas and give their own arguments.

The next day, Ms. Logan teaches a lesson on sound. She explains how sound causes waves in the air and how the waves cause the eardrum to vibrate, transmitting sound information to the brain. She has two students come to the front of the class with a Slinky and uses the Slinky to illustrate how sound waves travel. She asks many questions of students, both to see whether they understand and to get them to take the next mental step. She then explains how sound waves in a tube become lower in pitch the longer the tube is. To illustrate this, she plays a flute and a piccolo. Lightbulbs are starting to click on in the students' minds, and Ms. Logan can tell from the responses to her questions that the students are starting to get the idea. At the end of the period, Ms. Logan lets the students get back into their groups to discuss what they have learned and to try to apply their new knowledge to the bottle problem.

When the students come into class on the third day of the sound lesson, they are buzzing with excitement. They rush to their lab stations and start filling and tapping bottles to test out the theories they came up with the day before. Ms. Logan walks among the groups, listening in on their conversations. "It's not the amount of water, it's the amount of air," she hears one student say. "It's not the bottle; it's the air," says a student in another group. She helps one group that is still floundering to get on track. Finally, Ms. Logan calls the class together to discuss their findings and conclusions. Representatives of some of the groups demonstrate the experiments they used to show how it was the amount of air in each bottle that determined the sound.

"How could we make one elegant demonstration to show that it's only the amount of air that controls the sound?" asks Ms. Logan.

The students buzz among themselves and then assemble all their bottles into one experiment. They make one line of identical bottles with different amounts of water. Then to demonstrate that it is the air, not the water, that matters, they put the same amount of water in bottles of different sizes. Sure enough, in each case, the more air space left in the bottle, the lower the sound.

Ms. Logan ends the period with a homework assignment: to read a chapter on sound in a textbook. She tells the students that they will have an opportunity to work in their groups to make certain that every group member understands everything in the sound lesson, and then there will be a quiz in which students will have to show individually that they can apply their new knowledge. She reminds them that their groups can be "superteams" only if everyone knows the material.

(continued)

The bell rings, and the students pour into the hallway, still talking excitedly about what they have learned. Some groupmates promise to call or text each other that evening to prepare for the group study the next day. Ms. Logan watches them file out. She's exhausted, but she knows that this group of students will never forget the lessons they've learned about sound, about experiments, and, most important, about their ability to use their minds to figure out difficult concepts.

USING YOUR EXPERIENCE

CREATIVE THINKING   Write the phrase *Effective Lesson* in the middle of a sheet of paper and circle it. Brainstorm all the types of instructional approaches you can think of that make an effective lesson. Now list the types of instructional approaches that Ms. Logan uses.

CRITICAL THINKING   How does Ms. Logan motivate the students? What strategies does she use to encourage retention of the material?

The lesson is where education takes place. All other aspects of schooling, from buildings to buses to administration, are designed to support teachers in delivering effective lessons; they do not educate in and of themselves. If you are like most teachers, you will spend most of your class time teaching lessons. The typical elementary or secondary school teacher may teach 800 to 1,000 class lessons each year!

Conducting effective lessons is at the heart of the teacher's craft. Some aspects of lesson presentation have to be learned on the job; good teachers get better at it every year. Yet educational psychologists have studied the elements that go into effective lessons, learning a great deal that is useful in day-to-day teaching at every grade level and in every subject (Antonetti & Garver, 2015; Dean, Hubbell, Pitler, & Stone, 2012; Fisher & Frey, 2013; Good & Brophy, 2008; Goodwin, 2011c; Rosenshine, 2008; Sahadeo-Turner & Marzano, 2015; Schmoker, 2011; Silver, Perini, & Dewing, 2012). This chapter and the four that follow it present the principal findings of this research and translate them into ways of thinking about the practical demands of everyday teaching.

As Ms. Logan's lesson illustrates, effective lessons incorporate many teaching methods. In four periods on one topic, she used direct instruction as well as discussion, cooperative learning, and other constructivist techniques. These methods are often posed as different philosophies, and the ideological wars over which is best go on incessantly (see Joyce, Weil, & Calhoun, 2004; Kirschner, Sweller, & Clark, 2006). Yet few experienced teachers would deny that teachers must be able to use all of them and to discern when each is appropriate.

This chapter focuses on the strategies that teachers apply to transmit information in ways that are most likely to help students understand, incorporate, and use new concepts and skills. Chapter 8 focuses on student-centered methods, in which students play an active role in structuring learning for themselves and for each other. However, the teaching strategies presented in these two chapters should be seen not as representing two sharply conflicting philosophies of education, but as complementary approaches to be used at different times for different purposes.

WHAT IS DIRECT INSTRUCTION?

At times, the most effective and efficient way to teach students is to present information, skills, or concepts in a direct fashion (Borich, 2014; Estes & Mintz, 2016; Good & Brophy, 2008; Hollingsworth & Ybarra, 2009; Jackson, 2011; Rosenshine, 2008; Schmoker, 2012a). The term **direct instruction** is used to describe lessons in which you transmit information directly to students, structuring class time to reach a clearly defined set of objectives as efficiently as possible. Direct instruction is particularly appropriate for teaching a well-defined body of information or skills that all students must master (Dean et al., 2012; Frontier & Rickabaugh, 2014). It is held to be less appropriate when deep conceptual change is an objective or when exploration, discovery, and open-ended objectives are the goals of instruction. However, recent research has supported the idea that direct instruction can be more efficient than discovery in conceptual development as well. Klahr and Nigam (2004) compared third-graders directly taught to do experiments that isolate the effects of one variable to those who carried out their own experiments without direct instruction. Those who received direct instruction performed much better in setting up new experiments.

Certification Pointer

You may be asked on your teacher certification test to describe techniques for planning instruction that incorporate learning theory, subject matter, and particular student developmental levels.

MyEdLab

Video Example 7.1

In this class period, students will be practicing their paragraph-writing skills. The teacher begins by reviewing the basic content knowledge—what makes a good paragraph? She then assesses their understanding by presenting examples of good and not-so-good paragraphs.

A great deal of research was done in the 1970s and 1980s to discover the elements of effective direct instruction lessons. Although different authors describe these elements differently (see Evertson & Poole, 2008; Good & Brophy, 2008; Rosenshine, 2008), researchers and teachers generally agree on the sequence of events that characterizes effective direct instruction lessons. First, you bring students up to date on any skills they might need for the lesson (e.g., you might briefly review yesterday's lesson if today's is a continuation) and tell students what they are going to learn. Then you devote most of the lesson time to teaching the skills or information, giving students opportunities to practice the skills or express the information, and questioning or quizzing students to determine whether they are learning the objectives. Lemov (2010) calls this progression "I/we/you." That is, I (the teacher) start the lesson. Then I do with your help (we #1). Then you do with my help (we #2). Then you do a little on your own (you #1), and finally, you do the whole thing on your own (you #2).

A brief description of the parts of a direct instruction lesson follows. The next section of this chapter will cover each part in detail.

1. *State learning objectives and orient students to the lesson.* Tell students what they will be learning and what performance will be expected of them. Whet students' appetites for the lesson by informing them how interesting, important, or personally relevant it will be to them. Give an astonishing or exciting opener that gets kids eager to learn the content (Lemov, 2010, calls this "the hook").

2. *Review prerequisites.* Go over any skills or concepts students need in order to understand the lesson.

3. *Present new material.* Teach the lesson, presenting information, giving examples, demonstrating concepts, and so on.

4. *Conduct learning probes.* Pose questions to students to assess their level of understanding and correct their misconceptions.

5. *Provide independent practice.* Give students an opportunity to practice new skills or use new information on their own.

6. *Assess performance and provide feedback.* Review independent practice work or give a quiz. Give feedback on correct answers, and reteach skills if necessary.

7. *Provide distributed practice and review.* Assign homework to provide distributed practice on the new material. In later lessons, review material and provide practice opportunities to increase the chances that students will remember what they learned and also be able to apply it in different circumstances.

HOW IS A DIRECT INSTRUCTION LESSON TAUGHT?

The general lesson structure takes vastly different forms in different subject areas and at different grade levels. Teachers of older students may take several days for each step of the process, ending with a formal test or quiz. Teachers of younger students may go through the entire cycle in a class period, using informal assessments at the end. Tables 7.1 and 7.2 present two quite different lessons to illustrate how direct instruction would be applied to different subjects and grade levels. The first lesson, "Subtraction with Regrouping," is an example of the first of a series of lessons directed at a basic math skill. In contrast, the second lesson, "The Origins of World War II," is an example of a lesson directed at higher-order understanding of critical events in history and their causes and interrelationships. Note that the first lesson (Table 7.1) proceeds step by step and emphasizes frequent learning probes and independent practice to help students thoroughly learn the concepts being taught, whereas the second lesson (Table 7.2) is characterized by an alternation among new information, discussion, and questions to assess comprehension of major concepts.

The sequence of activities outlined in these two lessons flows along a logical path, from arousing student interest to presenting new information to allowing students to practice their new knowledge or skills to assessment. This orderly progression is essential to direct instruction lessons at any grade level and in any subject, although the various components and how they are implemented would, of course, look different for different subjects and grades.

InTASC 4

Content Knowledge

InTASC 7

Planning for Instruction

Connections 7.1
For in-depth coverage of instructional objectives, writing lesson plans, and using taxonomies, see Chapter 13.

ON THE WEB

For tips on writing quality learning objectives, visit http://teachonline.asu .edu/, click on Course Design, then Writing Measurable Learning Objectives.

TABLE 7.1 • Sample Lesson for Basic Math: Subtraction with Regrouping

LESSON PART	TEACHER PRESENTATION

1. State learning objective and orient students to lesson.	"There are 32 students in this class. Let's say we were going to have a party, and I was going to get one cupcake for each student in the class. But 5 of you said you didn't like cupcakes. How many cupcakes would I need to get for the students who do like cupcakes? Let's set up the problem on the chalkboard the way we have before, and mark the tens and ones . . ."
	
	   tens ones
	     3 2 Students
	   − 5 Don't like cupcakes
	  ──────
	
	"All right, let's subtract: 2 take away 5 is . . . *hey!* We can't do that! Five is more than 2, so how can we take 5 away from 2? We can't!
	
	In this lesson we are going to learn how to subtract when we don't have enough ones. By the end of this lesson, you will be able to show how to rename tens as ones so that you can subtract."

2. Review prerequisites.	"Let's review subtraction when we have enough ones." Put on the chalkboard and have students solve: 47 56 89 −3 −23 −8 ─── ─── ─── How many tens are in 23? _____ How many are in 30? _____ Give answers, and discuss all items missed by many students.
3A. Present new material (first subskill).	Have table monitors help hand out five bundles of 10 popsicle sticks each and 10 individual sticks to each student. Using an overhead projector, explain how to use sticks to show 13, 27, and 30. Have students show each number at their own desks. Walk around to check.
4A. Conduct learning probes (first subskill).	Have students show 23 using their sticks. Check desks. Then have students show 40. Check desks. Continue until all students have the idea.
3B. Present new material (second subskill).	Using an overhead projector or electronic whiteboard, explain how to use sticks to show 6 minus 2 and 8 minus 5. Then show 13 and try to take away 5. Ask for suggestions on how this could be done. Show that by removing the rubber band from the tens bundle, we have a total of 13 ones and can remove 5. Have students show this at their desks. Walk around to check.
4B. Conduct learning probes (second subskill).	Have students show 12 (check) and then take away 4 by breaking apart the ten bundle. Then have students show 17 and take away 9. Continue until all students have the idea.
3C. Present new material (third subskill).	Give students worksheets showing tens bundles and single units. Explain how to show regrouping by crossing out a bundle of ten and rewriting it as 10 units and then subtracting by crossing out units.
4C. Conduct learning probes (third subskill).	Have students do the first items on the worksheet one at a time until all students have the idea.
5. Provide independent practice.	Have students continue, completing the worksheet on their own.
6. Assess performance and provide feedback.	Show correct answers to worksheet items on the overhead projector or electronic whiteboard. Have students mark their own papers. Ask how many got item 1, item 2, and so on, and discuss all items missed by more than a few students. Have students hand in papers.
7. Provide distributed practice and review.	Hand out homework, and explain how it is to be done. Review lesson content at start of following lesson and in later lessons.

TABLE 7.2 • Sample Lesson for History: The Origins of World War II

LESSON PART	TEACHER PRESENTATION
1. State learning objective and orient students to lesson.	"Today we will begin to discuss the origins and causes of World War II—perhaps the most important event in the 20th century. The political situation of the world today—the map of Europe, the political predominance of the United States, the problems of the Eastern European countries formerly under Russian domination, even the problems of the Middle East—all can be traced to the rise of Hitler and the bloody struggle that followed. I'm sure many of you have relatives who fought in the war or whose lives were deeply affected by it. Raise your hand if a relative or someone you know well fought in World War II." • "Germany today is peaceful and prosperous. How could a man like Hitler have come to power? To understand this, we must first understand what Germany was like in the years following its defeat in World War I and why an unemployed Austrian painter could come to lead one of the largest countries in Europe." • "By the end of this lesson you will understand the conditions in Germany that led up to the rise of Hitler, the reasons why he was successful, and the major events of his rise to power."
2. Review prerequisites.	Have students recall from the previous lesson: • The humiliating provisions of the Treaty of Versailles —Reparations —Demilitarization of the Ruhr —Loss of territory and colonies • The lack of experience with democracy in Germany
3. Present new material.	Discuss with students: • Conditions in Germany before the rise of Hitler —Failure of the Weimar Republic —Economic problems, inflation, and severe impact of the U.S. Depression —Belief that Germany lost World War I because of betrayal by politicians —Fear of communism • Events in Hitler's rise to power —Organization of National Socialist (Nazi) Party —Beer-Hall Putsch and Hitler's imprisonment —*Mein Kampf* —Organization of Brown Shirts (S.A.) —Election and appointment as chancellor
4. Conduct learning probes.	Questions to students throughout lesson should assess student comprehension of the main points.
5. Provide independent practice.	Have students independently write three reasons why the situation in Germany in the 1920s and early 1930s might have been favorable to Hitler's rise, and have students be prepared to defend their answers.
6. Assess performance and provide feedback.	Call on randomly selected students to read and justify their reasons for Hitler's success. Discuss well-justified and poorly justified reasons. Have students hand in papers.
7. Provide distributed practice and review.	Review lesson content at start of next lesson and in later lessons.

State Learning Objectives

The first step in presenting a lesson is planning it in such a way that the reasons for teaching and learning the lesson are clear. What do you want students to know or be able to do at the end of the lesson? Setting out objectives at the beginning of the lesson is an essential step in providing a framework into which information, instructional materials, and learning activities will fit (Gronlund & Brookhart, 2009).

Orient Students to the Lesson

At the beginning of a lesson, you need to establish a positive **mental set**, or attitude of readiness, in students: "I'm ready to get down to work. I'm eager to learn the important information or skills the teacher is about to present, and I have a rough idea of what we will be learning." This mental set can be established in many ways. First, you should require students to be on time to class and should start the lesson immediately when the period begins (Emmer & Evertson, 2012; Evertson,

Certification Pointer

For teacher certification tests, you may be asked to suggest techniques for building bridges between curriculum objectives and students' experiences.

THEORY INTO PRACTICE

Planning a Lesson

The first step of a lesson, stating learning objectives or outcomes, represents a condensation of much advance **lesson planning** (see Burden & Boyd, 2016; Dick, Carey, & Carey, 2015; Jackson, 2011; Reeves, 2011; Wiles & Bondi, 2015). As a teacher planning a lesson, you will need, at the least, to answer the following questions:

1. What will students know or be able to do after the lesson? What will be the outcomes of their learning? How will you know when and how well students have achieved these learning outcomes or objectives? (See Gronlund & Brookhart, 2009; Moss & Brookhart, 2012.)

2. What prerequisite skills are needed to learn this content? How will you make sure students have these skills?

3. What information, activities, and experiences will you provide to help students acquire the knowledge and skills they need in order to attain the learning outcomes? How much time will be required? How will you use in-class and out-of-class time? How will seatwork and homework assignments help students achieve the learning objectives? (See Dougherty, 2012.)

4. How will you arouse students' interest in the content? How will you motivate them to learn? How will you give them feedback on their learning?

5. What books and materials will you use to present the lesson? When will you preview or test all the materials and create guidelines for students' responses to them? Are all materials accurate, pedagogically sound, fair to different cultures, and appropriate in content and grade level?

6. What methods of teaching will you incorporate? For example, will you use reading, lecture, role playing, video viewing, demonstration, or writing assignments?

7. What participation structures will you use: whole-group or small-group discussions, cooperative learning groups, ability groups, or individual assignments? What learning tasks will groups and individuals perform? How will you organize, monitor, and evaluate groups?

"Dang. I'm not even ready for fifth period!"

Emmer, & Worsham, 2009). This establishes a sense of seriousness of purpose that is lost in a ragged start. Second, you need to arouse students' curiosity or interest in the lesson they are about to learn. The teacher in the first sample lesson (Table 7.1) does this by introducing subtraction with regrouping as a skill that would be necessary in connection with counting cupcakes for a class party, a situation of some relevance and interest to young students. In the second sample lesson (Table 7.2), the teacher advertises the importance of the lesson on the basis that understanding the origins and events of World War II will help students understand events today and makes the lesson personally relevant to students by having them think of a relative who either fought in World War II or was deeply affected by it. In the chapter-opening vignette, Ms. Logan piques her students' curiosity about sound by giving them an opportunity to experiment with it before the formal lesson.

A lesson on genetics might be introduced as follows:

Did you ever wonder why tall parents have taller-than-average children, and red-haired children usually have at least one red-haired parent? Think of your own family. If your father and mother are both taller than average, then you will probably be taller than average. Well, today we are going to have a lesson on the science called genetics, in which we will learn how characteristics of parents are passed on to their children.

THEORY INTO PRACTICE
Communicating Objectives to Students

Teacher education programs include training in creating lesson plans, beginning with a consideration of instructional objectives and learning outcomes. Sharing lesson plans with students is a good idea, because research suggests that knowledge of objectives can lead to improvements in student achievement. Use the following practical suggestions for sharing lesson objectives with your students (see Moss & Brookhart, 2012).

1. The objectives you communicate to students should be broad enough to encompass everything the lesson will teach. Research suggests that giving students too narrow a set of objectives may lead them to devalue or ignore other meaningful aspects of a lesson. In addition, broad objectives provide greater flexibility for adapting instruction as needed, once the lesson is under way.

2. The objectives you communicate should be specific enough in content to make clear to students what the outcomes of their learning will be—what they will know and be able to do, and how they will use their new knowledge and skills.

3. Consider stating objectives both orally and in writing and repeating them during the lesson to remind students why they are learning. Teachers often use verbal and written outlines or summaries of objectives. Providing demonstrations or models of learning products or outcomes is also effective. For example, an art teacher might show a student's drawing that demonstrates use of perspective to illustrate what students will be able to produce themselves, or a math teacher might show a math problem that students could not do at the beginning of a series of lessons but will be able to do at the end.

4. Consider using questioning techniques to elicit from students their own statements of objectives or outcomes. Their input will probably both reflect and inform your lesson plan. Some teachers ask students to express their ideas for meeting objectives or demonstrating outcomes, because research suggests that students who have a stake in the lesson plan and a sense of control over their learning will be more motivated to learn.

This introduction might be used to grab students' interest because it makes the subject personally relevant.

Humor or drama can also establish a positive mental set. An English teacher may use a top hat and a wand to capture student interest by "magically" transforming adjectives into adverbs (e.g., *sad* into *sadly*). Popular and instructionally effective children's television programs, such as "Sesame Street," use this kind of device constantly to get young children's attention and hold their interest in basic skills. Finally, in starting a lesson, you must give students a road map of where the lesson is going and what they will know at the end. Stating lesson objectives clearly has generally been found to enhance student achievement of those objectives (Gronlund & Brookhart, 2009; Marzano, 2011). Giving students an outline of the lesson in advance may also help them to incorporate new information (Bligh, 2000).

Connections 7.2
For more about the importance of activating students' prior knowledge, see Chapter 6.

Review Prerequisites

For the next major task in a lesson, you need to ensure that students have mastered prerequisite skills and to link information that is already in their minds with the information you are about to present. If today's lesson is a continuation of yesterday's and you are reasonably sure that students understood yesterday's lesson, then the review might simply remind them about the earlier lesson

Connections 7.3
See Chapter 6 for a definition of advance organizers.

and ask a few quick questions before beginning the new one. For instance, you might say, "Yesterday we learned how to add the suffix *-ed* to a word ending in *y*. Who will tell us how this is done?"

Because today's lesson—adding other suffixes to words ending in *y*—is a direct continuation of yesterday's, this brief reminder is adequate. However, if you are introducing a new skill or concept that depends on skills learned much earlier, then more elaborate discussion and assessment of prerequisite skills may be needed.

Sometimes you need to assess students on prerequisite skills before starting a lesson. In the first sample lesson (Table 7.1), the teacher briefly quizzes students on subtraction without regrouping and numeration skills in preparation for a lesson on subtraction with regrouping. If students show poor understanding of either prerequisite skill, the teacher will review those skills before going on to the new lesson.

Another reason you should review prerequisites is to provide advance organizers. As defined in Chapter 6, advance organizers are introductory statements by the teacher that remind students of what they already know and give them a framework for understanding the new material to be presented. In the second sample lesson (Table 7.2), the teacher sets the stage for the new content (Hitler's rise to power) by reviewing the economic, political, and social conditions in Germany that made Hitler's success possible.

Present New Material

Here begins the main body of the lesson, the point at which you present new information or skills.

Connections 7.4
See Chapter 6 for a discussion of the retention of well-organized information.

LESSON STRUCTURE   Lessons should be logically organized. Information that has a clear, well-organized structure is retained better than less clearly presented information (Good & Brophy, 2008; Rosenshine, 2008). A lesson on the legislative branch of the U.S. government might be presented as follows:

The Legislative Branch of the Federal Government (First Lesson)

    I. Functions and nature of the legislative branch (Congress)
        A. Passes laws
        B. Approves money for executive branch
        C. Has two houses—House of Representatives and Senate

   II. House of Representatives
        A. Designed to be closest to the people—representatives elected to two-year terms—proportional representation
        B. Responsible for originating money bills

 III. Senate
        A. Designed to give greater continuity to legislative branch—senators elected to six-year terms—each state has two senators
        B. Approves appointments and treaties made by executive branch

This would be a beginning lesson; subsequent lessons would discuss how laws are introduced and passed, checks and balances on legislative power, and so on. The lesson has a clear organization that you should point out to students. For example, you might pause at the beginning of the second topic and say, "Now we are going to learn about the lower house of Congress, the House of Representatives." This helps students form a mental outline that will help them remember the material. Research reveals that a clearly laid out structure and transitional statements about the structure of the lesson increase student understanding.

MyEdLab
Video Example 7.2

Watch as a teacher begins a phonics lesson, using direct instruction. What would you expect to be the next part of this lesson?

LESSON EMPHASIS   In addition to making clear the organization of a lesson by noting when the next subtopic is being introduced, instructionally effective teachers give clear indications about the most important elements of the lesson by saying, for example, "It is particularly important to note that. . . ." Repeat important points and bring them back into the lesson whenever appropriate. For example, in teaching about the presidential veto in the lesson on the legislative branch of government, you might say:

> Here again, we see the operation of the system of checks and balances we discussed earlier. The executive can veto legislation passed by the Congress, which in turn can withhold funds for actions of the executive. Remember, understanding how this system of checks and balances works is critical to an understanding of how the U.S. government works.

In this way, you emphasize one of the central concepts of the U.S. government—the system of checks and balances among the executive, legislative, and judicial branches—by bringing it up whenever possible and by labeling it as important.

LESSON CLARITY One consistent feature of effective lessons is clarity—the use of direct, simple, and well-organized language to present concepts (Borich, 2014; Burden & Boyd, 2016; Guillaume, 2016). Wandering off into digressions or irrelevant topics or otherwise interrupting the flow of the lesson detracts from clarity.

EXPLANATIONS Effective explanations are at the core of effective teaching. A review of research on explanations (Wittwer & Renkl, 2008) concluded that effective explanations take into account and link to what students already know (Bolhuis, 2003; Leinhardt & Steele, 2005) and emphasize concepts and principles, rather than just facts and skills. Effective explanations make use of strategies that help students visualize and organize complex ideas, such as embedded multimedia (Mayer, 2008a, b, 2009), and they give students opportunities to discuss their current understandings with peers in cooperative learning groups (Webb & Mastergeorge, 2003). Encouraging students to explain concepts to themselves can also enhance their learning (Fonesca & Chi, 2011).

Research finds that effective teachers also use many explanations and explanatory words (such as *because, in order to,* and *consequently*) and frequently use a pattern of **rule–example–rule** when presenting new concepts (Wittwer & Renkl, 2008), as in the following example:

> Matter may change forms, but it is never destroyed. If I were to burn a piece of paper, it would appear that the paper was gone, but in fact it would have been combined with oxygen atoms from the air and changed to a gas (mostly carbon dioxide) and ash. If I could count the atoms in the paper plus the atoms from the air before and after I burned the paper, we could see that the matter involved did not disappear, but merely changed forms.

Note that the teacher stated the rule ("Matter . . . is never destroyed"), next gave an example, and then restated the rule in the explanation of how the example illustrates the rule. Also note that a rule–example–rule sequence was used here to illustrate the rule–example–rule pattern!

WORKED EXAMPLES Worked examples are an established strategy for teaching certain kinds of problem solving, especially in mathematics (Atkinson, Derry, Renkl, & Wortham, 2000; Bokosmaty, Sweller, & Kalyuga, 2015; Renkl, 2011). For example, you might pose a problem and then work it out on a whiteboard or overhead, explaining your thinking at each step. In this way, you model the strategies an expert would use to solve the problem so that students can use similar strategies on their own. Research on worked examples generally finds that they are effective if they alternate with problems that students do on their own (e.g., one worked example followed by several problems of the same type) (Atkinson et al., 2000). Teaching students to stop during worked examples to explain to themselves or to a partner what is going on in each step enhances the effect of worked examples (Renkl, 2011). Worked examples are particularly effective for students tackling a new topic or skill (Bokosmaty et al., 2015).

DEMONSTRATIONS, MODELS, AND ILLUSTRATIONS Cognitive theorists emphasize the importance of students' seeing and, when appropriate, having hands-on experience with concepts and skills (Slavich & Zimbardo, 2012). Visual representations are maintained in long-term memory far more readily than information that is only heard (Schunk, 2016; Sousa, 2011). Showing, rather than simply telling, is particularly essential for children who are acquiring English (August & Shanahan, 2006b). Recall how Ms. Logan gave her students both hands-on experience (filling and tapping bottles) and a visual analogy (the Slinky representing sound waves) to give the students clear and lasting images of the main principles of sound. However, manipulatives (such as counting blocks) can be counterproductive to learning if they are not clearly related to the concept being taught (Campbell & Mayer, 2004).

EMBEDDED VIDEO Video, television, and DVDs have long been used in education. However, a new use is showing particular promise—video or DVD material that is embedded in on-screen text or class lessons used to illustrate key concepts. Research on embedded video finds that it helps

MyEdLab
Video Example 7.3
Bob Slavin describes his experience observing students participating in an innovative science lesson. What does his story tell us about discovery learning? As the teacher of this class, how could you turn this lesson around to teach them to arrive at the correct answer?

children learn and retain information to the degree that it is easy to understand and clearly linked to the main content (Mayer, 2008a, 2009). For example, two year-long studies by Chambers and colleagues (Chambers, Cheung, Madden, Slavin, & Gifford, 2006; Chambers et al., 2008) found that adding brief animations and puppet videos to illustrate letter sounds and sound blending significantly increased first-graders' progress in reading.

MAINTAINING ATTENTION Straight, dry lectures can be boring, and bored students soon stop paying attention to even the most carefully crafted lesson. For this reason you should introduce variety, activity, or humor to enliven the lecture and maintain student attention. For example, the use of humor has been found to increase student achievement (Badli & Dzulkifli, 2013; Jonas, 2010), and illustrating a lecture with easily understood graphics can help to hold students' attention (Mayer, 2008b). Although too much variation in mode of presentation can undermine achievement if it distracts students from the lesson content, several studies have established that students learn more from lessons that are presented with enthusiasm and expressiveness than from dry lectures (Cooper, 2014; Patrick, Hisley, & Kempler, 2000). In one sense, teaching is performing, and it appears that some of the qualities we look for in a performer are also helpful in increasing teachers' effectiveness.

CONTENT COVERAGE AND PACING One of the most important factors in effective teaching is the amount of content covered. In general, students whose teachers cover more material learn more than other students do (Jackson, 2011). This does not necessarily mean that you should teach faster; obviously, there is such a thing as going too fast and leaving students behind. Yet research on instructional pace does imply that most teachers could increase their pace of instruction (Good & Brophy, 2008), as long as degree of understanding is not sacrificed. In addition to increasing content coverage, a relatively rapid pace of instruction can also help with classroom management.

Conduct Learning Probes

Imagine an archer who shoots arrows at a target but never finds out how close to the bull's-eye the arrows fall. The archer wouldn't be very accurate to begin with and would certainly never improve in accuracy. Similarly, effective teaching requires you to be constantly aware of the effects of your instruction. All too often, teachers mistakenly believe that if they have covered a topic well and students appear to be paying attention, then instruction has been successful. Students often believe that if they have listened intently to an interesting lecture, they know the material presented. But this might not be true. If you do not regularly probe students' understanding of the material being presented, students might be left with serious misunderstandings or gaps in knowledge (Marzano, 2013; McMillan, 2011; Safer & Fleischman, 2005).

The term **learning probe** refers to any of a variety of ways of asking for brief student responses to lesson content. Learning probes give you feedback on students' levels of understanding and allow students to try out their understanding of a new idea to find out whether they have it right. Learning probes can take the form of questions to the class, as in the sample lesson on World War II presented in Table 7.2, or brief written or physical demonstrations of understanding, as in the sample subtraction lesson in Table 7.1.

CHECKS FOR UNDERSTANDING Whether the response to the learning probe is written, physical, or oral, the purpose of the probe is checking for understanding (Black, Harrison, Lee, Marshall, & Wiliam, 2004; Brookhart, Moss, & Long, 2008; Fisher & Frey, 2014a, c; Reeves, 2011; Stiggins & Chappuis, 2012). That is, use learning probes not so much to teach or to provide practice as to find out whether students have understood what they just heard. Use the probes to set the pace of instruction. If students are having trouble, you might slow down, discuss students' misunderstandings, help them learn from their errors, and provide additional explanation (Miller, 2013). If all students show understanding, you can move on to new topics. The following interchange shows how you might use learning probes to uncover student strengths and misunderstandings and then adjust instruction accordingly. The teacher, Mr. Swift, has written, on an interactive whiteboard, several sentences containing conversation, and students are learning the correct use of commas and quotation marks.

> *Mr. Swift:* Now we are ready to punctuate some conversation. Everyone get out a sheet of paper and copy this sentence, adding punctuation where needed: *Take the criminal downstairs Tom said condescendingly.* Is everyone ready? . . . Carl, how did you punctuate the sentence?

Connections 7.5
For more on the importance of attention in learning, see Chapter 6.

Connections 7.6
For more on the impact of time on learning, see Chapter 11.

InTASC 6

Assessment

Carl: Quote take the criminal downstairs quote comma Tom said condescendingly period.

Mr. Swift: Close, but you made the most common error people make with quotation marks. Maria, what did you write?

Maria: I think I made the same mistake Carl did, but I understand now. It should be: Quote take the criminal downstairs comma quote Tom said condescendingly period.

Mr. Swift: Good. How many got this right the first time? [Half of class raises hands.] OK, I see we still have some problems with this one. Remember, commas and periods go inside the quotation mark. I know that sometimes this doesn't make much sense, but if English always made sense, a lot of English teachers would be out of work! Think of quotation marks as wrappers for conversation, and the conversation, punctuation and all, goes inside the wrapper. Let's all try another. *Drive carefully Tom said recklessly.* Samphan?

Samphan: Quote drive carefully comma quote Tom said recklessly period.

Mr. Swift: Great! How many got it? [All but one or two raise hands.] Wonderful, I think you're all with me. The quotation marks "wrap up" the conversation, including its punctuation. Now let's all try one that's a little harder: *I wonder Tom said quizzically whether quotation marks will be on the test.*

This interchange contains several features worth noting. First, Mr. Swift had all students work out the punctuation, called on individuals for answers, and then asked all students whether they got the right answers. This is preferable to asking only one or two students to work (say, on the whiteboard) while the others watch, thus wasting the time of most of the class. When all students have to figure out the punctuation and no one knows whom Mr. Swift will call on to answer, all students actively participate and test their own knowledge, and Mr. Swift gets a quick reading on the level of understanding of the class as a whole.

Note also that when Mr. Swift found that half the class missed the first item, he took time to reteach the skill students were having trouble with, using a different explanation from the one he had used in his first presentation. By giving students the mental image of quotation marks as wrappers, he helped them to remember the order of punctuation in conversation. When almost all students got the second item, he moved to the next step, because the class had apparently mastered the first one.

Finally, note that Mr. Swift had plenty of sentences prepared on the interactive whiteboard, so he did not have to use class time to write out sentences. Learning probes should always be brief and should not be allowed to destroy the tempo of the lesson. By being prepared with sentences for learning probes, Mr. Swift was able to maintain student involvement and interest. In fact, he might have done even better if he had given students photocopies with unpunctuated sentences on them to reduce the time used in copying the sentences.

QUESTIONS Questions to students in the course of the lesson serve many purposes (Decristan et al., 2015; Fisher & Frey, 2014b; Marzano, 2013; Shute, 2008). You can use questions as Socrates used them, to prompt students to take the next mental step—for example, "Now that we've learned that heating a gas makes it expand, what do you suppose would happen if we cooled a gas?" You can also use questions to encourage students to think further about information they learned previously or to get a discussion started—for example, "We've learned that if we boil water, it becomes water vapor. Now, water vapor is a colorless, odorless, invisible gas. In that case, why do you suppose we can see steam coming out of a tea kettle?" With guidance, a class discussion would eventually arrive at the answer, which is that the water vapor recondenses when it hits the relatively cool air and that what is visible in steam is water droplets, not vapor (McTighe & Wiggins, 2013). You will often find it helpful to have students generate their own questions, either for themselves or for each other (Brookhart, 2007/2008). A great deal of evidence indicates that students gain from generating their own questions, especially questions that relate to their existing background knowledge about a topic they are studying (Good & Brophy, 2008; Schmoker, 2011; Stiggins & Chappuis, 2012).

Finally, you can use questions as learning probes (Fisher & Frey, 2007). In fact, any question is to some degree a learning probe, in that the quality of response will indicate how well students are learning the lesson. Research on the frequency of questions indicates that asking more questions related to the lesson at hand is more instructionally effective than asking relatively few questions (Good & Brophy, 2008). At all levels of schooling, factual questions generally help with factual skills, and questions that encourage students to think about concepts help with conceptual skills (Marzano, 2013).

THEORY INTO PRACTICE

Assessment for Learning

Formative assessment within class lessons is at the heart of an important movement called Assessment for Learning, established by two British researchers, Paul Black and Dylan Wiliam (Black, Harrison, Lee, Marshall, & Wiliam, 2003, 2004; Wiliam, 2007, 2007/2008, 2009; Wiliam & Leahy, 2015). Its authors emphasize the word *for* in the name; there is already too much assessment *of* learning, they argue, but not enough assessment during lessons that can inform teachers and students themselves of students' levels of understanding in ways that are both meaningful enough and timely enough to be useful in improving learning and teaching (Brookhart, 2010; Frey & Fisher, 2014; Lewin & Shoemaker, 2011). Assessment for Learning suggests dozens of strategies for helping students understand criteria for success, such as providing feedback, asking peers to provide feedback to each other, and letting students assess and report their own levels of understanding (Higgins, 2014; Wiliam & Leahy, 2015), as in the following list of examples.

1. In any class with a writing component, distribute anonymous writing products (e.g., essays, lab reports, book reports) from the previous year's class, and ask students to judge their quality before asking students to create their own writing products.

2. Ask "big questions" that are at the core of the learning objective, and give students time to talk among themselves and then share ideas with the class. For example, a math teacher might ask students to list fractions between one-half and one-fourth, both to understand students' grasp of fractional concepts and to spur their thinking (Fisher & Frey, 2014a, c). Students might be off the mark entirely, or they might think that three-eighths is the only possible answer, but with time and hints from the teacher, students might eventually realize that there are an infinite number of fractions between one-half and one-fourth. Similarly, you might ask why France supported Napoleon's wars throughout Europe, or why many plants have fruits surrounding seeds.

3. Avoid asking for volunteers to respond to questions (because it's always the same students who volunteer). Instead, put students' names on popsicle sticks or cards and call on them at random (Weinstein, 2007; Weinstein & Mignano, 2007). Lemov (2010) calls this "cold calling," calling on students whether or not their hands are raised, to ensure that all students are paying attention.

4. When appropriate, ask students to respond at once, perhaps by writing an answer on a small chalkboard and holding it up on cue, showing a letter card to answer a multiple-choice question, or giving a choral (unison) response.

5. Use "traffic lights": Ask students to assess their own understanding of a lesson and hold up a green card if they are solid, a yellow card if they are not sure, or a red card if they are not getting it. You can quickly scan the class, and move on if there is a sea of green, or stop and reteach if there's a lot of red and yellow (Wiliam & Leahy, 2015). Use cooperative learning strategies to let students work together to help each other master content, assess each other's learning, and lead each other toward productive lines of thinking.

WAIT TIME One issue related to questioning that has received much research attention is **wait time**, the length of time you wait for a student to answer a question before giving the answer or going on to another student. Research has found that teachers tend to give up too rapidly on students whom they perceive to be low achievers, a practice that tells those students that the teacher expects little from them (Miller, 2013).

Waiting approximately 3 seconds after asking a student a question yields better learning results than giving up more rapidly (Borich, 2014). Furthermore, following up with students who do not respond has been associated with higher achievement (Dean et al., 2012; Good & Brophy, 2008). Waiting for students to respond or staying with them when they do not communicates positive expectations for them. However, there is such a thing as waiting too long. A study by Duell (1994) found that a wait time as long as 6 seconds had a small negative effect on the achievement of university students.

CALLING ORDER In classroom questioning, **calling order** is a concern. Calling on volunteers is perhaps the most common method, but this allows some students to avoid participating in the lesson by keeping their hands down (Good & Brophy, 2008). Common sense would suggest that when the question is a problem to be worked (as in math), all students should attempt the problem before any individual is called on. For questions that are not problems to be worked, it is probably best to pose the question to the class as a whole and then ask a randomly chosen student (not necessarily a volunteer) to answer. Some teachers even carry around a class list on a clipboard and check off the students called on to make sure that all get frequent chances to respond, or put students' names on popsicle sticks and draw them at random from a can (Freiberg & Driscoll, 2005; Weinstein, 2007; Weinstein & Mignano, 2007). One teacher put her students' names on cards, shuffled them before class, and randomly selected cards to decide which students to call on. This system worked well until one student found the cards after class and removed his name from the deck!

In conducting learning probes, you might find it especially important to ask questions of students who usually perform above, at, and below the class average to be sure that all students understand the lesson.

ALL-PUPIL RESPONSE Many teachers ask students for **all-pupil responses** when there is only one possible correct answer. For example, you might say, "Class, in the words listed on the board [*write, wring, wrong*], what sound does the *wr* make?" To which the class responds together, "Rrrr!" This is called a **choral response**. Similarly, when appropriate, you can ask all students to use hand signals to indicate true or false, to hold up a certain number of fingers to indicate an answer in math, or to write a short answer on a small chalkboard and hold it up on cue (Wiliam & Leahy, 2015). Research shows that this type of all-pupil response has a positive effect on student learning (Good & Brophy, 2008; Rosenshine, 2008). In the subtraction with regrouping example used earlier in this chapter, recall that all students worked with popsicle sticks at their desks, and the teacher walked around to check their work. All-student responses give students many opportunities to respond, and they provide you with information on the entire class's level of knowledge and confidence.

MyEdLab
Video Example 7.4
Teachers often have established routines for choral responses. This teacher often cues her class by saying, "Get ready," and the children clap and move while responding.

Provide Independent Practice

The term **independent practice** refers to work students do in class on their own to practice or express newly learned skills or knowledge. For example, after hearing a lesson on solving equations in algebra, students need an opportunity to work several equations on their own without interruptions, both to crystallize their new knowledge and to help you assess their knowledge. Practice is an essential step in the process of transferring new information in working memory to long-term memory.

Independent practice is most critical when students are learning skills, such as mathematics, reading, grammar, composition, map interpretation, or a foreign language (Topping, Samuels, & Paul, 2007). Students can no more learn arithmetic, writing, or Spanish without practicing than they could learn to ride a bicycle from lectures alone. By contrast, independent practice is less necessary for certain concept lessons, such as the lesson on the origins of World War II outlined in Table 7.2 or a science lesson on the concept of magnetic attraction. In lessons of this kind, you can use independent practice to let students rehearse knowledge or concepts on their own, as the teacher did in the World War II lesson, but rehearsal is not as central to this type of lesson as practice of skills is to a subtraction lesson.

Connections 7.7
For more on working memory and long-term memory, see Chapter 6.

THEORY INTO PRACTICE

Questioning Strategies to Avoid

As a teacher, you ask a lot of questions, and it is easy for you to fall into bad habits, as demonstrated by the following common pitfalls (see Freiberg & Driscoll, 2005; Good & Brophy, 2008; Walsh & Sattes, 2005).

1. *Leading questions.* Your phrasing can give or strongly suggest the answer to a question, as in "You don't think the Pilgrims believed in religious toleration, do you?" Your tone of voice can easily give away the answer as well. If students know that they can tell the answer from your question, they do not need to pay attention to instruction to be prepared.

2. *Always asking the same students.* Many teachers ask questions only of the students who they believe will probably give right answers, avoiding those who might be slow to respond, unlikely to get the question right, or inclined to make trouble if questioned. Yet when students know it is unlikely that they will be called on, they may stop paying attention, so it is imperative that all students believe they could be selected at any moment. Using a random questioning pattern (by, for example, putting students' names on popsicle sticks and drawing them at random) ensures that all students are called on, *and* seeing the process of drawing names makes it clear to students that they must always be ready to respond.

3. *Asking questions all at one level.* Some teachers ask only factual questions. Others never ask factual questions. It is important to ask questions at all levels, simple and difficult, factual and conceptual.

4. *Engaging one student at length while others have nothing to do.* It's fine to ask complex questions that may take a while to answer, but avoid having nothing for the other students to do while one student is responding. You can avoid this by asking a question of the whole class, giving them time to work out their answers or discuss them with partners, and only then calling on students at random to give their answers. Following up on one student's answer with a question based on it helps ensure that students are paying attention to each other's answers, as in this example:

Teacher: Can anyone give me an example of a mammal that lives in the sea? Tony?

Tony: A dolphin?

Teacher: Thank you, Tony, that's a good example. Can anyone give another example besides the one Tony gave? . . . Natalia?

Natalia: A whale.

Teacher: Right again. Now class, if you saw an animal in the sea other than the ones Tony and Natalia mentioned, what facts about that animal would tell you that it's a mammal?

5. *Failing to correct wrong answers.* Some teachers, not wanting to embarrass students, do not correct wrong answers. It is important not to humiliate students who give wrong answers, but it is also important not to leave the class with the wrong impression, as in the following:

Teacher: Before the Russian Revolution, why do you think the Germans sent Lenin to Russia in a sealed train? . . . Marta?

Marta: They wanted to get him out of Germany.

Teacher: Perhaps, but remember, Germany and Russia were at war. Can anyone give me the main reason the Germans sent Lenin to Russia? Ahmed?

6. ***Ignoring answers.*** Every student who knows the answer to your question wants to say that answer. Calling on many students and being sure to acknowledge all answers give students a sense that it was beneficial to be prepared. In order to give all students a chance to share their answers, you can allow them a few moments to discuss answers with a partner. This ensures that even if you can't call on everyone, all students at least got to share their good answers with someone.

7. ***Asking too many yes–no questions.*** Questions that have only two possible answers are sometimes unavoidable, but they should not be overused. A guesser will be right 50 percent of the time, so a correct answer may or may not indicate knowledge. One way to avoid this problem is to ask a follow-up question after the correct answer to get at why the answer is correct, as in the following:

Teacher: If I multiply a fraction less than one by another fraction less than one, will the product be larger or smaller than the first fraction? . . . Louisa?

Louisa: Less.

Teacher: Class, raise your hand if you agree with Louisa (most do). All right, you're in the majority. Now Louisa, tell me why you think the product would be less.

8. ***Unclear questions.*** Sometimes, students do not know what they are being asked. For example, an English teacher might point to a sentence and ask, "What's wrong with this sentence?" without making it clear whether students are being asked to look at the grammar, the punctuation, the phrasing, or the meaning.

SEATWORK Research on seatwork, or in-class independent practice, suggests that it is typically both overused and misused (Good & Brophy, 2008; Weinstein, 2007; Weinstein & Mignano, 2007). Several researchers have found that student time spent receiving instruction directly from the teacher is more productive than time spent in seatwork (Burden & Boyd, 2016; Good & Brophy, 2008; Rosenshine, 2008). Time spent on seatwork is often wasted for students who lack the motivation, reading skills, or self-organization abilities to work well on their own. Yet a review of research on the teaching of reading to students with disabilities found that 40 percent of their time, on average, was spent on seatwork (Vaughn, Levy, Coleman, & Bos, 2002). Many students simply give up when they run into difficulties. Others fill out worksheets with little care for correctness, apparently interpreting the task as finishing the paper rather than as learning the material.

EFFECTIVE USE OF INDEPENDENT PRACTICE TIME The following recommendations for effective use of independent practice time are derived from the work of Evertson and colleagues (2009) and Good and Brophy (2008).

1. ***Do not assign independent practice until you are sure students can do it.*** This is probably the most important principle. Independent practice is practice, not instruction, and the students should already be able to do most of the items they are assigned to do on their own (Freiberg & Driscoll, 2005). In cognitive terms, practice serves as rehearsal for transferring information from working memory to long-term memory. For this to work, the information must first be established in students' working memories (Ashcraft & Radvansky, 2010).

   A high success rate on independent practice work can be accomplished in two ways. First, assignments should be clear and self-explanatory and should cover content on which all students can succeed. Second, students should rarely be given independent practice worksheets until they have indicated in learning probes that they can handle the material. For example, you might use the first items of a class assignment as learning probes, assigning them one at a time and discussing each one after students have attempted it until it is clear that all or almost all students have the right idea. You may prepare a series of questions on an overhead projector or interactive whiteboard and introduce them one at a time until most of the class is on the right track, only then revealing the rest of the items.

2. ***Keep independent practice assignments short.*** There is rarely a justification for long independent practice assignments. About 10 minutes of work is adequate for most objectives, but this is far less than most teachers usually assign (Rosenshine, 2008). Massed practice (e.g., many items at one sitting) has a limited effect on retention (Greene, 2008). Students are more likely to profit from relatively brief independent practice in class supplemented by distributed practice, such as homework (Cooper, Robinson, & Patall, 2006).

3. ***Give clear instructions.*** Make sure that all students understand the instructions and know what they are supposed to do. In the lower grades, ask students to read aloud or paraphrase the instructions to be sure that they have understood them.

4. ***Get students started, and then avoid interruptions.*** When students start on their independent practice work, circulate among them to be sure that everyone is under way before attending to the problems of individual students or other tasks. Once students have begun, avoid interrupting them.

5. ***Monitor independent work.*** It is important to monitor independent work—for example, by walking around the class while students are doing their assignments. This helps to keep students working and increases your availability for questions. You can also look in on students who may be struggling, to give them additional assistance.

6. ***Collect independent work and include it in student grades.*** Many students see no reason to do their best on seatwork because it usually has little or no bearing on their grades. Students should know that their seatwork will be collected and will count toward their grade. To this end, it is a good idea to save a few minutes at the end of each class period to briefly read answers to assigned questions and allow students to check their own papers or exchange papers with partners. Then students may pass in their papers for spot checking and recording. This procedure gives students immediate feedback on their seatwork and relieves you of having to check all papers every day. Make this checking time brief to avoid taking time from instruction.

Assess Performance and Provide Feedback

Every lesson should contain an assessment of the degree to which students have mastered the objectives that were set for the lesson (Chappuis, 2015; Duckor, 2014; Fisher & Frey, 2014; Marzano, 2010a; Mertler, 2014; Reeves, 2011; Tomlinson, 2014). Assessment can involve informally questioning students, using independent work as an assessment, using clickers or other electronic means of assessing student understanding, or giving a traditional quiz (Magaña & Marzano, 2014). One way or another, however, you should assess the effectiveness of the lesson and give the results of the assessment to students as soon as possible (Magaña & Marzano, 2014; Safer & Fleischman, 2005; Stiggins & Chappuis, 2012). There is evidence that testing itself improves students' retention of what they have learned, because the testing process makes it more likely that students will deeply process the information (Chappuis, 2015; Haynie & Haynie, 2008; Higgins, 2014). Students need to know when they are right and when they are wrong if they are to use feedback to improve their performance. Lemov (2010) suggests the use of "exit tickets" at the end of key lesson parts—a brief test of perhaps one to three questions, just to make sure all students are on track. In addition to assessing the results of each lesson, you need to test students from time to time on their learning of larger units of information. In general, more frequent testing results in greater achievement than less frequent testing, but any testing is much more effective than none at all (Good & Brophy, 2008). Feedback to students is important, but feedback to the teacher on student performance is probably even more important (Heritage, 2011, 2014). If students are learning everything they are taught, it may be possible to pick up the pace of instruction. However, if assessment reveals serious misunderstandings, you can reteach the lesson or take other steps to get students back on track.

Certification Pointer
Your teacher certification test may require you to choose the least effective teaching strategy to achieve a particular curriculum objective. You should know that one of the *least* effective strategies for practicing a skill that students have just learned is lengthy independent seatwork for which students do not receive feedback.

Connections 7.8
For in-depth coverage of assessment, see Chapter 13.

If some students have mastered the lesson and some have not, it may be appropriate to give more instruction only to the students who need it.

Provide Distributed Practice and Review

Practice or review, spaced out over time, increases retention of many kinds of knowledge (Greene, 2008). This has several implications for teaching. First, it implies that reviewing and recapitulating important information from earlier lessons enhances learning. Students particularly need to review important material at long intervals (e.g., monthly) to maintain previous skills. In addition, you should assign homework in most subjects, especially at the secondary level. Homework gives students a chance to practice skills learned in one setting at one time (school) in another setting at a different time (home). Homework can be used as formative assessment, providing both you and your students information on current levels of understanding of key concepts (Christopher, 2007/2008; Vatterott, 2014). Research on homework finds that it generally does increase achievement, particularly if teachers check it and give comments to students (Cooper, Robinson, & Patall, 2006; Trautwein, 2007). However, the effects of homework are not as clear in elementary school as they are at the secondary level (Cooper et al., 2006; Cooper & Valentine, 2001), and assigning excessively lengthy or boring homework can actually be detrimental to learning and motivation (Corno, 2000). Making homework interesting and worthwhile is critical to its value (Darling-Hammond & Ifill-Lynch, 2006; Marzano & Pickering, 2007; Vatterott, 2014). Good and Brophy (2008) recommend 5 to 10 minutes of homework per subject for fourth-graders, increasing to 30 minutes or more per subject for college-bound high school students. Homework can provide a means for parents to become constructively engaged in their children's schooling (Epstein & Van Voorhis, 2001; Xu & Corno, 2003), but it can also be a significant source of conflict in the home, especially for children having difficulty with the content (Walker & Hoover-Dempsey, 2001).

InTASC 5

Application of Content

InTASC 8

Instructional Strategies

21ST CENTURY LEARNING

Enhancing Classroom Lessons with Technology

Engaging students with technology to extend skills beyond the classroom is a focus of the Common Core State Standards, and using technology to integrate visual with auditory content is an excellent use of the power of technology. In the past, almost all teaching was directed to the same part of the brain. Both reading and hearing lectures address the same semantic processes, and through the 20th century, only the occasional picture or video addressed the equally important episodic learning processes. In the 21st century this is changing, as interactive whiteboards, DVDs, and other devices make it easy for teachers to incorporate brief bits of video or still pictures into their daily lessons, adding intrinsic motivation as well as strengthening learning by pairing pictures and spoken words or text (Mayer, 2009, 2011b). Pictures and videos should not be used if they distract attention from the instructional objective (in which case they are "seductive details"), but if they support the main objective they can be very useful. Students today are increasingly visual learners outside of school, and teachers can capitalize on these skills in school as well.

QUESTIONS

- What visual learning activities that students experience outside of school can be capitalized on in the classroom?

- Do you think it is ethical to give students extra credit for engaging in these kinds of activities if they enhance classroom learning?

HOW DOES RESEARCH ON DIRECT INSTRUCTION METHODS INFORM TEACHING?

Most of the principles of direct instruction discussed in this chapter have been derived from process–product studies, in which observers record the teaching practices of teachers whose students consistently achieve at a high level and compare them to the practices of teachers whose students make less progress (Good & Brophy, 2008; Rosenshine, 2008).

It is clear that direct instruction methods can improve the teaching of certain basic skills, but it is equally clear that much is yet to be learned about how and when they should be used. The prescriptions derived from studies of effective teachers cannot be applied uncritically in the classroom and expected to make a substantial difference in student achievement. Structured, systematic instructional programs based on these prescriptions can markedly improve student achievement in basic skills, but it is important to remember that the research on direct instruction has focused mostly on basic reading and mathematics, largely in the elementary grades. For other subjects and at other grade levels, we have less of a basis for believing that direct instruction methods will improve student learning (see Arends, 2004).

> MyEdLab Self-Check 7.1

HOW DO STUDENTS LEARN AND TRANSFER CONCEPTS?

InTASC 1
Learner Development

InTASC 2
Learning Differences

InTASC 8
Instructional Strategies

A very large proportion of all lessons focus on teaching concepts (Senn & Marzano, 2015). A concept is an abstract idea that is generalized from specific examples. For example, a red ball, a red pencil, and a red chair all illustrate the simple concept "red." A green book is not an instance of the concept "red." If you were shown the red ball, pencil, and chair and asked to say what they have in common, you would produce the concept "red objects." If the green book were also included, you would have to fall back on the much broader concept "objects."

Of course, many concepts are far more complex and less well defined than the concept "red." For example, the concept "justice" is one that people might spend a lifetime trying to understand. This book is engaged primarily in teaching concepts; in fact, at this very moment you are reading about the concept "concept"!

Concept Learning and Teaching

Concepts are generally learned in one of two ways. Most concepts that we learn outside of school we learn by observation. For example, a child learns the concept "car" by hearing certain vehicles referred to as "cars." Initially, the child might include trucks or motorcycles under the concept "car," but as time goes on, the concept is refined until the child can clearly differentiate "car" from "noncar." Similarly, the child learns the more difficult concepts "naughty," "clean," and "fun" by observation and experience.

Other concepts are typically learned by definition. For example, it is very difficult to learn the concepts "aunt" or "uncle" by observation alone. One could observe hundreds of "aunts" and "nonaunts" without deriving a clear concept of "aunt." In this case the concept is best learned by definition: To be an aunt, one must be a female whose brother or sister (or brother- or sister-in-law) has children. With this definition, instances and noninstances of "aunt" can be readily differentiated.

DEFINITIONS Just as children can learn concepts in two ways, instructors can teach them in two ways. You might give students instances and noninstances of a concept and later ask them to derive or infer a definition (Silver, 2010). Or you might give students a definition and then ask them to identify instances and noninstances. Some concepts lend themselves to the example–definition approach. For most concepts that are taught in school, it makes most sense to state a definition, present several instances (and noninstances, if appropriate), and then restate the definition, showing how the instances typify the definition. For example, we might define the concept "learning" as "a change in an individual caused by experience." Instances might include learning of skills, of information, of behaviors, and of emotions. Noninstances might include maturational changes, such as changes in behaviors or emotions caused by the onset of puberty. Finally, we might restate the definition and discuss it in light of the instances and noninstances.

EXAMPLES Teaching concepts involves extensive and skillful use of examples. Examples should first be ones that clearly illustrate the concept, then examples that test the limits of the concept and contrast examples to non-examples (Burden & Boyd, 2016).

Consider the concept "mammal." Easy examples are dogs, cats, and humans, and nonexamples are insects, reptiles, and fish. No problem so far. But what about dolphins? Bats? Snakes that bear live young? Kangaroos? Each of these is a more difficult example or nonexample of the concept "mammal"; each challenges the simplistic belief, based on experience, that terrestrial animals that bear live young are mammals and that aquatic animals, birds, and other egg-layers are not. The easy examples (dogs versus fish) establish the concept in general, but the more difficult examples (snakes versus whales) test the true boundaries of the concept. Students should thoroughly understand simple examples before tackling more complex cases.

Teaching for Transfer of Learning

Students often get so wrapped up in preparing for tests, and teachers in preparing students to take tests, that both forget the primary purpose of school: to give students the skills and knowledge necessary for them to function effectively as adults. If a student can fill in blanks on a language arts test but cannot write a clear letter to a friend or a prospective employer, or can multiply with decimals and percents on a math test but cannot figure sales tax, then that student's education has been sadly misdirected. Yet all too frequently, students who do very well in school or on tests are unable to transfer their knowledge or skills to real-life situations.

REAL-LIFE LEARNING **Transfer of learning** from one situation to another depends on the degree to which the information or skills were learned in the original situation and on the degree of similarity between the situation in which the skill or concept was learned and the situation to which it is to be applied (Day & Goldstone 2012; Hall & Greeno, 2008; Schunk, 2016). These principles, known since the beginning of the 20th century, have important implications for teaching. We cannot simply assume that students will be able to transfer their school learning to practical situations, so we must teach them to use skills in situations like those they are likely to encounter in real life or in other situations to which we expect learning to transfer. Students must receive specific instruction in how to use their skills and information to solve problems, and they must encounter a variety of problem-solving experiences if they are to be able to apply much of what they learned in school (Zmuda, 2010).

The most important thing to know about transfer of learning is that it cannot be assumed (Chi & VanLehn, 2012; Perkins & Salomon, 2012). The fact that a student has mastered a skill or concept in one setting or circumstance is no guarantee whatsoever that the student will be able to apply this skill or concept to a new setting, even if the setting seems (at least to the teacher) to be very similar (Schwartz, Chase, & Bransford, 2012). Classic examples are people who score well on tests of grammar and punctuation but cannot apply these skills in their own compositions, and people who can solve all sorts of math problems in school but do not apply their math knowledge in real life. As an example of this, Lave (1988) describes a man in a weight-loss program who was faced with the problem of measuring out a serving of cottage cheese that was three-quarters of the usual two-thirds cup allowance. The man, who had passed college calculus, measured out two-thirds of a cup of cottage cheese, dumped it out in a circle on a cutting board, marked a cross on it, and scooped away one quadrant. It never occurred to him to multiply $2/3 \times 3/4 = 1/2$, an operation that almost any sixth-grader could do on paper (but few might apply in a practical situation).

INITIAL LEARNING AND UNDERSTANDING Not surprisingly, one of the most important factors in transfer of a skill or concept from one situation to another is how well the skill or concept was learned in the first place. However, it also matters a great deal how well students understood the material and to what degree it was taught in a meaningful way (Perkins & Salomon, 2012). In other words, material that is memorized by rote is unlikely to transfer to new situations no matter how thoroughly it was mastered.

InTASC 5

Application of Content

InTASC 8

Instructional Strategies

LEARNING IN CONTEXT If transfer of learning depends in large part on similarity between the situation in which information is learned and that in which it is applied, then how can we teach in the school setting so that students will be able to apply their knowledge in the very different setting of real life?

One important principle of transfer is that the ability to apply knowledge in new circumstances depends in part on the variety of circumstances in which we have learned or practiced the information or skill (Schwartz et al., 2012). For example, a few weeks' experience as a parking attendant, driving all sorts of cars, would probably be better than years of experience driving one kind of car for enabling a person to drive a completely new and different car (at least in a parking lot!).

TEACHING OF CONCEPTS Research demonstrates that to teach a new concept, teachers should first present examples of the concept used in similar contexts and then offer examples in widely different contexts. This approach promotes the students' abilities to transfer the concept to new situations.

In teaching concepts, one way to increase the chance that students will appropriately apply the concepts to new situations is to give examples from a range of situations. A set of classic experiments by Nitsch (1977) illustrated this principle. Students were given definitions of words and then presented with examples to illustrate the concepts. Some received several examples in the same context; others received examples from mixed contexts. Students who received only the same-context examples could identify additional examples in the same context but were less successful in applying the concepts to new contexts. By contrast, the students who learned with the varied-context examples had some difficulties in learning the concept at first but, once they did, were able to apply it to new situations. The best strategy was a hybrid in which students received the same-context examples first and then the varied-context examples. Figure 7.1 shows an example for learning the word "flummoxed."

You can use many other methods to increase the probability that information or skills learned in one context will transfer to other contexts, particularly to real-life applications. For example, simulations can approximate real-life conditions, as when secondary students prepare for job interviews by role-playing with teachers or peers pretending to be interviewers. You can also facilitate transfer by introducing skills learned in one setting into a new setting. For example, a history teacher might do well to find out what writing or grammar skills are being taught in English classes and then remind students to use these same skills in history essays.

TRANSFER VERSUS INITIAL LEARNING What makes transfer tricky is that some of the most effective procedures for enhancing transfer are exactly the opposite of those for initial learning. As the Nitsch (1977) study illustrated, teaching a concept in many different contexts confuses students when done at the beginning of a sequence of instruction, but it enhances transfer if it occurs after

Concept to be taught: *flummoxed* Definition: *confused*	
SAME CONTEXT EXAMPLES	**VARIED CONTEXT EXAMPLES**
1. The magician's sudden disappearance flummoxed the crowd.	1. Rashandra was flummoxed by all the buttons and switches that operated her remote control car.
2. The crowd was flummoxed when the magician lifted the top of the pan and a bird flew out of it!	2. The two price tags on the same item flummoxed the shoppers.
3. When the magician appeared in the crowd instead of the stage, everyone was flummoxed. How did he get there?	3. Harold was flummoxed to find out that his friends had led him to a surprise birthday party.

FIGURE 7.1 • Same Context and Mixed-Context Examples to Introduce a New Word

students understand the concept in one setting. This principle holds important implications for teaching. In introducing a new concept, you should use similar examples until your students understand the concept, and then use diverse examples that still demonstrate the essential aspects of the concept (Perkins & Salomon, 2012).

As one example of this, consider a series of lessons on evolution. In introducing the concept, you should first use clear examples of how animals have evolved in ways that increase their chances of survival in their environments, using such examples as the evolution of flippers in seals or of humps in camels. Then you might present evolution in plants (e.g., evolution of a waxy skin on desert plants), somewhat broadening the concept. Next, you might discuss the evolution of social behaviors (such as cooperation in lions, baboons, and humans). Finally, you might explore phenomena that resemble the evolutionary process (such as the modification of businesses in response to selective pressures of free-market economies). In this way, you first establish the idea of evolution in one clear context (animals) and then gradually broaden the concept until your students can see how processes in quite different contexts demonstrate the principles of selective adaptation. If you had begun the lessons with a mixed discussion of animals, plants, societies, and businesses, it would have been too confusing. And if you had never moved beyond the evolution of animals, the concept would not have had much chance of transferring to different contexts. After learning about the concept of evolution in many different contexts, students are much more likely to be able to distinguish scientific and metaphorical uses and apply the concept to a completely new context, such as the evolution of art in response to changes in society (Day & Goldstone, 2012).

"I wasn't copying. I was transferring knowledge from one context to another!"

In teaching for transfer, it is important not only to provide many examples but also to point out in each example how the essential features of the concept are reflected (Chi & VanLehn, 2012). In the evolution lessons you might explain the central process as it applies to each particular case. The development of cooperation among lions, for instance, shows how a social trait evolved because groups of lions that cooperated were better able than others to catch game, to survive, and to ensure that their offspring would survive. Pointing out the essential elements in each example helps students apply a concept to new instances they have never encountered (Anderson et al., 1996). Similarly, comparing cases or situations illustrates a given concept, and pointing out similarities and differences between them can enhance transfer (Bulgren, Lenz, Schumaker, Deshler, & Marquis, 2002; Gentner, Loewenstein, & Thompson, 2002).

EXPLICIT TEACHING FOR TRANSFER Students can be explicitly taught to transfer skills to new circumstances (Silver, Dewing, & Perini, 2012). For example, Fuchs and colleagues (Fuchs, Fuchs, Finelli, Courey, & Hamlett, 2003) evaluated an "explicit transfer" technique in third-grade math classes. Children in the explicit transfer condition were taught what transfer means and given examples of how the same kind of story problems could be changed using different language, different contexts, and different numbers. The children were also taught to look at story problems to see if they resembled problems they had done before. For example, one problem asked how many packages of lemon drops (10 to a package) you'd have to buy to get 32 lemon drops. They then presented the same problem worded differently, with additional questions added, with different contexts, and so on. Teaching students how to look for commonalities among story problems significantly enhanced their success on transfer tasks.

MyEdLab **Self-Check 7.2**

HOW ARE DISCUSSIONS USED IN INSTRUCTION?

InTASC 8

Instructional Strategies

You can use discussions as part of instruction for many reasons. Discussions lend themselves to controversial topics, to questions for which there may be many right answers, and to affective or attitudinal objectives. They may be moderated by the teacher in the class as a whole or may take place in small student-led groups (Novak, 2014).

Subjective and Controversial Topics

Questions in many subjects do not have simple answers. There may be one right answer to an algebra problem or one right way to conjugate a German verb, but is there one right set of factors that explains what caused the Civil War? How were Shakespeare's writings influenced by the politics of his day? Should genetic engineering be banned as a danger to world health? These and many other questions have no clear-cut answers, so it is important for students to discuss and understand these issues instead of simply receiving and rehearsing information or skills. Such subjects as history, government, economics, literature, art, and music include many issues that lend themselves to discussion and to multiple and diverse explanations. Research finds that discussing controversial issues increases knowledge about the issues, while encouraging deeper understanding of the various sides of an issue (Johnson & Johnson, 1999).

Difficult and Novel Concepts

In addition to subjective and controversial subjects, discussions can clarify topics that do contain single right answers but involve difficult concepts that force students to see something in a different way. For example, a science teacher could simply give a lesson on buoyancy and specific gravity. However, because this lesson would challenge a simplistic view of why things float ("Things float because they are light"), students might understand buoyancy and specific gravity better if they had an opportunity to make and defend their own theories about why things float and if they faced such questions as "If things float because they are light, then why does a battleship float?" and "If you threw certain objects in a lake, they would sink part way but not to the bottom. Why would they stop sinking?" In searching together for theories to explain these phenomena, students might gain an appreciation for the meaning of buoyancy and specific gravity that a lecture alone could not provide.

Affective Objectives

You might also use discussions when affective objectives (objectives that are concerned with student attitudes and values) are of particular importance. For example, a course on civics or government contains much information about how our government works but also involves important values to be transmitted, such as civic duty and patriotism. You could teach "six reasons why it is important to vote," but the real objective here is not to teach reasons for voting, but rather to instill respect for the democratic process and a commitment to register and vote when the time comes. Similarly, a discussion of peer pressure might be directed at giving students the skills and the willingness to say no when classmates pressure them to engage in illegal, unhealthy, or undesirable behaviors. A long tradition of research in social psychology has established that group discussion, particularly when group members must publicly commit themselves, is far more effective at changing individuals' attitudes and behaviors than is even the most persuasive lecture.

Whole-Class Discussions

Discussions take two principal forms. In one, the entire class discusses an issue, with the teacher as moderator (Connolly & Smith, 2002; Gunter et al., 2003). In the other, students form small groups to examine a topic (Novak, 2014). A **whole-class discussion** differs from a usual lesson because the teacher plays a less dominant role. You may guide the discussion and help the class avoid dead ends, but you should encourage the students to come up with their own ideas. The following vignette illustrates an inquiry-oriented discussion led (but not dominated) by Ms. Wilson, who wants students to explore and develop their own ideas about the American Revolution using information they have recently learned.

MyEdLab
Video Example 7.5
Children learn that class discussion is part of teaching and learning as early as preschool.

> *Ms. Wilson:* In the past few weeks we've been learning about the events leading up to the American Revolution. Of course, because we are all Americans, we tend to take the side of the revolutionaries. We use the term *Patriots* to describe them; King George probably used a less favorable term. Yet many of the colonists were Loyalists, and at

times, the Loyalists outnumbered the Patriots. Let's think about how Loyalists would have argued against the idea of independence from Britain.

Beth: I think they'd say King George was a good king.

Vinnie: But what about all the things he did to the colonists?

Ms. Wilson: Give some examples.

Vinnie: Like the Intolerable Acts. The colonists had to put up British soldiers in their own houses, and they closed Boston Harbor.

Tanya: But those were to punish the colonists for the Boston Tea Party. The Loyalists would say that the Patriots caused all the trouble in the first place.

Ms. Wilson: Good point.

Frank: I think the Loyalists would say, "You may not like everything he does, but King George is still our king."

Richard: The Loyalists probably thought the Sons of Liberty were a bunch of thugs.

Ms. Wilson: Well, I wouldn't put it quite that way, but I think you're right. What did they do that makes you think that?

Ramon: They destroyed things and harassed the Loyalists and the British troops. Like they called them names and threw things at them.

Ms. Wilson: How do you think Loyalists would feel about the Boston Massacre?

Beth: They'd say those thugs got what they deserved. They'd think that it was Sam Adams's fault for getting everyone all stirred up.

Ms. Wilson: Let's think about it another way. We live in California. Our nation's capital, Washington, is three thousand miles away. We have to pay all kinds of taxes, and a lot of those taxes go to help people in Boston or Baltimore rather than people here. Many of the things our government does make people in California mad. We've got plenty of food, and we can make just about anything we want to right here. Why don't we have a California Revolution and have our own country?

Sara: But we're part of America!

Tanya: We can't do that! The army would come and put down the revolution!

Ms. Wilson: Don't you think that the Loyalists thought some of the same things?

Vinnie: But we can vote and they couldn't.

Ramon: Right. Taxation without representation!

Beth: I'll bet a lot of Loyalists thought the British would win the war and it would be better to stay on the side of the winners.

In this discussion Ms. Wilson was not looking for any particular facts about the American Revolution, but rather was trying to get students to use the information they had learned previously to discuss issues from a different perspective. Ms. Wilson let the students determine the direction of the discussion to a substantial degree. Her main tasks were to keep the discussion rolling, to get students to use specifics to defend their positions, to ensure that many students participated, and to help the students avoid dead ends or unproductive avenues.

ON THE WEB

For an example of how to conduct an effective class discussion, go to brighthubeducation.com, click on Teaching Tools, then on Teaching Methods, and type "classroom discussions" into the search engine.

Certification Pointer

For your teacher certification test you will need to demonstrate your understanding of the principles and techniques associated with a variety of instructional strategies. For example, you might be asked to identify the curricular goals for which whole-class discussion would be appropriate and how you would structure the discussion so it would be effective.

INFORMATION BEFORE DISCUSSION Before beginning a discussion, you must ensure that students have an adequate knowledge base. There is nothing so dreary as a discussion in which the participants don't know much about the topic. The American Revolution discussion depended on students' knowledge of the main events preceding the Revolution. Teachers can sometimes use a discussion before instruction as a means of generating interest in a topic, but at some point you must give students information. In the chapter-opening vignette, for example, Ms. Logan let students discuss and experiment not only before presenting a formal lesson but also after the lesson, when they had more information.

Small-Group Discussions

In a **small-group discussion**, students work in four- to six-member groups to discuss a particular topic, and the teacher moves from group to group, aiding the discussions (Cook & Tashlik, 2004; Spiegel, 2005). Because small-group discussions require that students work independently of the teacher most of the time, young or poorly organized students need a great deal of preparation and, in fact, might not be able to benefit from them at all. However, most students at or above the fourth-grade level can profit from small-group discussions.

Like any discussion, most small-group discussions should follow the presentation of information through teacher-directed lessons, books, or videos, or should take place after students have had an opportunity to find information for themselves in the library or online. When students know something about a subject, they might start to work in their groups, pulling their desks together if necessary to talk and hear one another more easily.

Each group should have a leader that you appoint. Leaders should be responsible, well-organized students but not necessarily the highest-achieving students. Groups may all discuss the same topic, or each may discuss a different subtopic of a larger topic that the whole class is studying. For example, in a unit on the Great Depression, one group might focus on causes of the Depression, another on the collapse of the banking system, a third on the social consequences of the Depression, and a fourth on the New Deal. You should give each group a series of questions to answer on the topic to be discussed. For example, if the topic were the collapse of the banking system, the questions might include the following:

1. What was the connection between the stock market crash of 1929 and the failures of so many banks?
2. What caused savers to lose confidence in the banks?
3. Why did the banks not have enough funds to pay savers who wanted to withdraw their money?
4. Why is a widespread run on banks unlikely today?

Certification Pointer

A certification test question may ask you to respond to a case study by identifying the strengths and weaknesses of the instructional strategies employed in the case.

The leader's role in each discussion group is to make sure that the group stays on the topic and questions assigned to it, and to ensure that all group members participate. A group recorder could be appointed to write down the group's ideas. At the end of the discussion, the group members prepare a report on their activities or conclusions to present to the rest of the class.

Research on small-group discussions indicates that these activities can increase student achievement more than traditional lessons if the students are well prepared to work in small groups and if the group task is well organized (Cohen & Lotan, 2014). Also, some research suggests that small-group discussions have greater effects on student achievement when students are encouraged to engage in controversy (Johnson & Johnson, 1999).

MyEdLab **Self-Check 7.3**

SUMMARY

What Is Direct Instruction?

Direct instruction is a teaching approach that emphasizes teacher control of most classroom events and the presentation of structured lessons. Direct instruction programs call for active teaching; clear lesson organization; step-by-step progression between subtopics; and the use of many examples, demonstrations, and visual prompts.

How Is a Direct Instruction Lesson Taught?

The first part of a lesson is stating learning objectives and orienting students to the lesson. The principal task is to establish both a mental set, so that students are ready to work and learn, and a "road map," so that students know where the lesson is going.

Part two of a lesson is to review prerequisites or pretests to ensure that students have mastered required knowledge and skills. The review might function as an advance organizer for the lesson.

Part three involves presenting the new material in an organized way, providing explanations and demonstrations and maintaining attention.

Part four, conducting learning probes, elicits students' responses to lesson content. This practice gives you feedback and lets students test their ideas. Questioning techniques are important, including the uses of wait time and calling order.

Part five of a lesson is independent practice, or seatwork, in which students apply their new skill. Research shows that independent practice should be given as short assignments with clear instructions and no interruptions, and that it should be given only when students can do the assignments. You should monitor work, collect it, and include it in assessments.

Part six is to assess performance and provide feedback. Every lesson should include an assessment of student mastery of the lesson objectives.

Part seven of a lesson is to provide distributed practice through homework and review. Information is retained better when practice is spaced out over a period of time.

THE INTENTIONAL TEACHER
Using What You Know about Direct Instruction to Improve Teaching and Learning

Intentional teachers select their instructional strategies with purpose. They understand the benefits and shortcomings of the strategies they select and then choose strategies based on their students, the content, and the context.

- They plan lessons appropriate to the objectives they have in mind, using (for example) direct instruction for well-defined objectives and discussions and using projects for less well-defined objectives.
- At the beginning of direct instruction lessons, they make students aware of lesson objectives, orient students to the lesson, and review prerequisites. They use feedback from these early stages of the lesson to modify their plans, if necessary, in light of what students already know.
- As they teach new concepts or skills, intentional teachers use humor, variety, examples, analogies, visuals, and technology to make their lessons engaging, easy to understand, and motivating.
- As they teach, intentional teachers constantly probe students' understanding, using formative assessments to see whether students are learning what they are teaching.
- After presenting main ideas, intentional teachers give students opportunities to practice what they have been taught in ways appropriate to the objectives.
- At the end of lessons, intentional teachers use formal or informal measures to find out whether students have attained lesson expectations. If not, they reteach key concepts.
- Intentional teachers provide appropriate, engaging, and interesting homework to give students opportunities to practice new skills or apply new concepts over time.

(continued)

- Intentional teachers are not satisfied with learning that is limited to a narrow, school-specific context. They teach to enhance transfer from topic to topic and from school to life.
- Intentional teachers use open-ended discussions to supplement direct instruction or to replace it when objectives are less well-defined, difficult, or affective.

MyEdLab
Application Exercise 7.1
In the Pearson etext, watch a classroom video. Then use the guidelines in "The Intentional Teacher" to answer a set of questions that will help you reflect on and understand the teaching and learning presented in the video.

KEY TERMS

Review the following key terms from the chapter.

all-pupil responses 171	mental set 163
calling order 171	process–product studies 176
choral response 171	rule–example–rule 167
concept 176	seatwork 173
direct instruction 160	small-group discussion 182
independent practice 171	transfer of learning 177
learning probe 168	wait time 171
lesson planning 164	whole-class discussion 180

SELF-ASSESSMENT: PRACTICING FOR LICENSURE

Directions: The chapter-opening vignette addresses indicators that are often assessed in state licensure exams. Reread the chapter-opening vignette, and then respond to the following questions.

1. In the chapter-opening vignette, Ms. Logan uses a variety of instructional strategies in the lesson on sound. Which of the following statements from the vignette is an example of Ms. Logan using direct instruction?
   a. Students are working in small groups at lab stations.
   b. After half an hour of experimentation, Ms. Logan calls the class together.
   c. Representatives from some of the groups demonstrate the experiment.
   d. Ms. Logan teaches a lesson on sound.
2. If Ms. Logan were to use a direct instruction approach to teach a science lesson on gravity, which of the following steps would come first?
   a. Conduct learning probes.
   b. State the learning objective.
   c. Present new material.
   d. Provide independent practice.

3. According to research on direct instruction, why should Ms. Logan conduct learning probes during her lesson on sound?
   a. To facilitate teaching the lesson
   b. To provide students practice with the concepts presented
   c. To give the teacher feedback on the students' level of understanding
   d. To catch students who are not paying attention

4. Ms. Logan plays a flute and a piccolo to demonstrate how sound waves travel through air. She hopes this demonstration will help her students understand the experiment with the bottles of water. What principle of instruction is she using?
   a. Reciprocal teaching
   b. Distributed practice
   c. Transfer of learning
   d. Alternative assessment

5. After Ms. Logan's students work in groups to finish the lesson on sound, she tells them they will be tested individually to demonstrate their knowledge; however, their group can be called a "superteam" only if everyone knows the material. What instructional strategy is the teacher using?
   a. Cooperative learning
   b. Small-group discussion
   c. Direct instruction
   d. Inquiry learning

6. Create a lesson using all of the steps of a direct instruction lesson.

7. What are some advantages and disadvantages of small-group discussions and whole-group discussions?

MyEdLab **Licensure Exam 7.1** Answer questions and receive instant feedback in your Pearson eText in MyEdLab.

Robert Kneschke/Shutterstock

CHAPTER EIGHT

Student-Centered and Constructivist Approaches to Instruction

LEARNING OUTCOMES

At the end of this chapter, you should be able to:

8.1 Identify key concepts of the constructivist view of learning and their implications for classroom practice

8.2 Discuss how to use cooperative learning most effectively in the classroom

8.3 Describe how you can teach your students problem-solving and thinking skills

8.4 Describe how student-centered and constructivist approaches to instruction influence intentional teaching

"You'll all recall," begins Mr. Dunbar, "how last week we figured out how to compute the area of a circle and the volume of a cube. Today you're going to have a chance to discover how to compute the volume of a cylinder. This time, you're really going to be on your own. At each of your lab stations you have five unmarked cylinders of different sizes. You also have a metric ruler and a calculator, and you may use water from your sink. The most important resources you'll have to use, however, are your minds and your partners. Remember, at the end of this activity, everyone in every group must be able to explain not only the formula for volume of a cylinder but also precisely how you derived it. Any questions? You may begin!"

The students in Mr. Dunbar's middle school math and science class get right to work. They are seated around lab tables in groups of four. One of the groups, the Master Minds, starts off by filling all its cylinders with water.

"OK," says Miguel, "we've filled all of our cylinders. What do we do next?"

"Let's measure them," suggests Margarite. She takes the ruler and asks Dave to record the measurements she dictates.

"The water in this little one is 36 millimeters high and . . . just a sec . . . 42 millimeters across the bottom."

"So what?" asks Yolanda. "We can't figure out the volume this way. Let's do a little thinking before we start measuring everything."

"Yolanda's right," says Dave. "We'd better work out a plan."

"I know," says Miguel, "let's make a hypo . . ., hypotha . . ., what's it called?"

"Hypothesis," says Yolanda. "Yeah! Let's guess what we think the solution is."

"Remember how Mr. Dunbar reminded us about the area of a circle and the volume of a cube? I'll bet that's an important clue."

"You're right, Miguel," says Mr. Dunbar, who happens to be passing by. "But what are you guys going to do with that information?"

The Master Minds are quiet for a few moments. "Let's try figuring out the area of the bottom of one of these cylinders," ventures Dave. "Remember that Margarite said the bottom of the little one was 42 millimeters? Give me the calculator . . . now how do we get the area?"

Yolanda says, "I think it was pi times the radius squared."

"That sounds right. So 42 squared—"

"Not 42; 21 squared," interrupts Margarite. "If the diameter is 42, the radius is 21."

"OK, OK, I would have remembered. Now, 21 squared is . . . 441, and pi is about 3.14, so my handy-dandy calculator says . . . 13,847."

"Can't be," says Miguel. "Four hundred times three is twelve hundred, so 441 times 3.14 can't be thirteen thousand. I think you did something wrong."

"Let me do it again . . . 441 times 3.14 . . . you're right. Now it's about 1,385."

"So what?" says Yolanda. "That doesn't tell us how to figure the volume!"

Margarite jumps in excitedly. "Just hang on for a minute, Yolanda. Now, I think we should multiply the area of the bottom by the height of the water."

"But why?" asks Miguel.

"Well," said Margarite, "when we did the volume of a cube, we multiplied length times width times height. Length times width is the area of the bottom. I'll bet we could do the same with a cylinder!"

"The girl's brilliant!" says Miguel. "Sounds good to me. But how could we prove it?"

"I've got an idea," says Yolanda. She empties the water out of all the cylinders and fills the smallest one to the top. "This is my idea. We don't know what the volume of the water in this cylinder is, but we do know that it's always the same. If we pour the same amounts of water into all four cylinders and use our formula, it should always come out to the same amount!"

"Let's try it!" says Miguel. He pours the water from the small cylinder into a larger one, refills it, and pours it into another of a different shape.

The Master Minds measure the bases and heights of the water in their cylinders, write down the measurements, and try out their formula. Sure enough, their formula always gives the same answer for the same volume of water. In great excitement they call Mr. Dunbar to come see what they are doing. Mr. Dunbar asks each of the students to explain what he or she has done.

"Terrific!" he says. "Not only did you figure out a solution, but everyone in the group participated and understood what you did. Now I'd like you to help me out. I've got a couple of groups that are really stumped. Do you suppose you could help them? Don't give them the answer, but help them get on track. How about Yolanda and Miguel help with the Brainiacs, and Dave and Margarite help with the Dream Team. OK? Thanks!"

(continued)

Learning is much more than memory. For students to really understand and be able to apply knowledge, they must work to solve problems, to discover things for themselves, to wrestle with ideas. Mr. Dunbar could have told his students that the formula for the volume of a cylinder is $\pi r^2 h$. With practice the students would have been able to feed numbers into this formula and grind out correct answers. But how much would it have meant to them, and how well could they have applied the ideas behind the formula to other problems? The task of education is not to pour information into students' heads, but to engage students' minds with powerful and useful concepts. The focus of this chapter is to examine ways of doing this.

WHAT IS THE CONSTRUCTIVIST VIEW OF LEARNING?

InTASC 8

Instructional Strategies

One of the most important principles of educational psychology is that teachers cannot simply give students knowledge. Students must construct knowledge in their own minds. You can facilitate this process by teaching in ways that make information meaningful and relevant to students, by giving students opportunities to discover or apply ideas themselves, and by teaching students to be aware of and consciously use their own strategies for learning. You can give students ladders that lead to higher understanding, but the students themselves must climb these ladders (Guskey & Anderman, 2008; McCombs, 2010).

Theories of learning based on these ideas are called **constructivist theories of learning**. The essence of constructivist theory is the idea that learners must individually discover and transform complex information if they are to make it their own (Anderson, Greeno, Reder, & Simon, 2000; Fosnot, 2005; Slavich & Zimbardo, 2012). Constructivist theory sees learners as constantly checking new information against old rules and then revising rules when they no longer work. This view has profound implications for teaching because it suggests a far more active role for students in their own learning than is typical in many classrooms. Because of the emphasis on students as active learners, constructivist strategies are often called *student-centered instruction* (Barnes, 2013b; Cornelius-White, 2007). In a student-centered classroom the teacher becomes the "guide on the side" instead of the "sage on the stage," helping students to discover their own meaning instead of lecturing and controlling all classroom activities (Noddings, 2008; Weinberger & McCombs, 2001; Zmuda, 2008).

Historical Roots of Constructivism

Connections 8.1

The work of Piaget and of Vygotsky is discussed in Chapter 2.

The constructivist revolution has deep roots in the history of education. It draws heavily on the work of Piaget and Vygotsky (recall Chapter 2), who both emphasized that cognitive change takes place only when previous conceptions go through a process of disequilibration in light of new information. Piaget and Vygotsky also stressed the social nature of learning, and both suggested the use of mixed-ability learning groups to promote conceptual change. Modern constructivist thought draws most heavily on Vygotsky's theories (Mahn & John-Steiner, 2013; Schunk, 2016; Seifert, 2013; Trawick-Smith, 2014), which have been used to support classroom instructional methods that emphasize cooperative learning, project-based learning, and discovery. Four key principles derived from Vygotsky's ideas have played an important role: social learning, the zone of proximal development, cognitive apprenticeship, and mediated learning.

SOCIAL LEARNING Vygotsky emphasized the social nature of learning (Daniels, Cole, & Wertsch, 2007; Gredler & Shields, 2008; Hall & Greeno, 2008). Children learn, he proposed, through joint interactions with adults and more capable peers. On cooperative projects, such as in Mr. Dunbar's class, children are exposed to their peers' thinking processes; this method not only makes the learning outcome available to all students, but also makes other students' thinking processes available to all. Vygotsky noted that successful problem-solvers talk themselves through difficult problems (Corkum et al., 2008; Flavell, 2004). In cooperative groups, children can hear this inner speech out loud and learn how successful problem-solvers are thinking through their approaches.

ZONE OF PROXIMAL DEVELOPMENT A second key concept is the idea that children learn best the concepts that are in their zones of proximal development (Berger, 2012). As discussed in Chapter 2, a child's zone of proximal development marks the range of tasks the child might not be able to do alone but can do with the assistance of peers or adults. For example, if a child cannot find the median of a set of numbers by herself but can do so with some assistance from her teacher, then finding medians is probably in her zone of proximal development. When children are working together, most of them will be performing on the given tasks at slightly higher or lower cognitive levels but still within each child's zone of proximal development.

COGNITIVE APPRENTICESHIP Another concept derived from Vygotsky that emphasizes both the social nature of learning and the zone of proximal development is **cognitive apprenticeship** (Wertsch, 2007). This term refers to the process by which a learner gradually acquires expertise through interaction with an expert, either an adult or an older or more advanced peer. In many occupations, new workers learn their jobs through a process of apprenticeship in which they work closely with experts who provide models, give feedback to less experienced workers, and gradually socialize new workers into the norms and behaviors of the profession. Student teaching is a form of apprenticeship. Constructivist theorists suggest that teachers transfer this long-standing and highly effective model of teaching and learning to day-to-day activities in classrooms, by engaging students in complex tasks and helping them through these tasks (as a master electrician would help an apprentice rewire a house) (Hamman, Berthelot, Saia, & Crowley, 2000) and also by engaging students in heterogeneous, cooperative learning groups in which more advanced students help less advanced peers through complex tasks (Slavin, 2011, 2013; Wentzel & Watkins, 2011).

Connections 8.2
For more on the zone of proximal development, see Chapter 2.

MyEdLab
Video Example 8.1

In this class, the teacher and the students work together in a cognitive apprenticeship, in which the teacher helps the students to engage in top-down processing and thus learn new practices for scientific reasoning.

ON THE WEB

To see an example of cognitive apprenticeship in a fourth-grade classroom, go to projects.coe.uga.edu.

MEDIATED LEARNING Finally, Vygotsky's emphasis on scaffolding, or mediated learning (Berger, 2012; Mahn & John-Steiner, 2013), is important in modern constructivist thought. Current interpretations of Vygotsky's ideas emphasize that students should be given complex, difficult, realistic tasks and then be provided enough help to achieve these tasks (rather than being taught little bits of knowledge that are expected someday to build up to complex tasks). This principle is used to support the classroom use of projects, simulations, explorations in the community, writing for real audiences, and other authentic tasks (Egan, 2008; Levy, 2008; Mahn & John-Steiner, 2013). The term *situated learning* (Anderson et al., 2000) is used to describe learning that takes place in real-life, authentic tasks. This perspective emphasizes learning in depth, rather than learning that is a mile wide and an inch deep.

Top-Down Processing

Constructivist approaches to teaching emphasize top-down rather than bottom-up instruction. The term *top-down* means that students begin with complex problems to solve and then work out or discover (with your guidance) the basic skills required. For example, students might be asked to write compositions and only later learn about spelling, grammar, and punctuation. This top-down processing approach is contrasted with the traditional bottom-up strategy, in which basic skills are gradually built into more complex skills. In top-down teaching, the tasks students begin with are complex, complete, and authentic, meaning that they are not parts or simplifications of the tasks that students are ultimately expected to perform but are the actual tasks. As one instance of a constructivist approach to mathematics teaching, consider an example from Lampert (1986). The traditional, bottom-up approach to teaching the multiplication of two-digit numbers by one-digit numbers (e.g., $4 \times 12 = 48$) is to teach students a step-by-step procedure to get the right answer. Only after students have mastered this basic skill are they given simple application problems, such as "Sondra saw some pencils that cost 12 cents each. How much money would she need to buy four of them?"

The constructivist approach works in exactly the opposite order, beginning with problems (often proposed by the students themselves) and then helping students figure out how to do the operations. Lampert's example of this appears in Figure 8.1. In the chapter-opening vignette, Mr. Dunbar used cooperative groups to help students derive a formula for the volume of a cylinder. Recall how the Master Minds bounced ideas off each other, tried out and discarded false leads, and ultimately came up with a solution and a way to prove that their solution was correct. None of the students could have solved the problem alone, so the groupwork was helpful in arriving at a solution. More important, the experience of hearing others' ideas, trying out and receiving immediate feedback on proposed solutions, and arguing about different ways to proceed gave the Master Minds the cognitive scaffolding that Vygotsky, Bruner, and other constructivists hold to be essential to higher-order learning (Fosnot, 2005).

Peer Interaction

InTASC 3

Learning Environments

Constructivist approaches to teaching typically make extensive use of interaction among students of the same age, on the theory that students will more easily discover and comprehend difficult concepts if they can talk with each other about the problems. Also, research finds that interest is strongly influenced by social factors (if your peers are interested in something or support your interest, you are likely to be interested) (Bergin, 2016). Again, the emphasis on the social nature of learning, and the use of groups of peers to model appropriate ways of thinking and to expose and challenge each other's misconceptions, are key elements of Piaget's and Vygotsky's conceptions of cognitive change (Barnes, 2013a; Senn & Marzano, 2015; Webb, 2008). Peer interaction methods, called *cooperative learning,* are described in more detail later in this chapter.

Discovery Learning

InTASC 5

Application of Content

InTASC 8

Instructional Strategies

Discovery learning is an important component of modern constructivist approaches that has a long history in education innovation. In **discovery learning** (Barnes, 2013a; Boss, 2015; Pahomov, 2014), students are encouraged to learn largely on their own through active involvement with concepts and principles, and teachers encourage students to have experiences and conduct experiments that permit them to discover principles for themselves. Jerome Bruner, a prominent advocate of discovery learning, put it this way: "We teach a subject not to produce little living libraries on that subject, but rather to get a student to think . . . for himself, to consider matters as an historian does, to take part in the process of knowledge-getting. Knowing is a process, not a product" (1966, p. 72). As one example of this, a study suggested that having high school students discover principles of physics increased their learning better than telling them the principles and then having them practice these principles (Schwartz, Chase, Oppezzo, & Chin, 2011).

Teacher: Can anyone give me a story that would go with the multiplication problem 12 × 4?

Student 1: There were 12 cups of hot chocolate, and each had 4 marshmallows in it.

Teacher: So if I did the multiplication about this story, what would I find out about the marshmallows?

Student 1: You'd know how many marshmallows you'd used in all.

Teacher: Wonderful! Let's draw a picture to help us understand the multiplication problem. Here are the 12 cups, and there are the 4 marshmallows in each. (Shows picture on whiteboard). As always, it is easier for us to count how many marshmallows there are altogether if we think of the cups in groups. What is our favorite number for thinking about groups?

Student 2: 10

Teacher: Right! Each of these 10 cups has 4 marshmallows in it (Draws a circle around 10 cups). Who can tell me how many marshmallows we have in the circled set?

Student 2: We have 40 marshmallows.

Teacher: How did you figure that out?

Student 2: Because 10 cups × 4 marshmallows = 40 marshmallows.

Teacher: And how many do we have left outside the circle?

Student 1: 8 more.

Teacher: So how many marshmallows did we use in all?

Student 1: 48, because you had the 40 marshmallows in the circle, plus the eight left over.

Teacher: What if I erase my circle and go back to looking at the 12 cups again? Is there any other way I could arrange the cups to count the marshmallows in a different way?

Student 2: You could do 3 sets of four.

Teacher: So if we circle the first group of 4 cups, each with 4 marshmallows in them, how many marshmallows do we have in this group?

Student 1: 16

Teacher: How did you figure that out?

Student 2: Because you had 4 cups of 4 marshmallows. 4 × 4 = 16.

Teacher: Who can tell me a multiplication problem that would go with our picture above?

Student 2: 16 × 3 = 48

Teacher: Yes! And how did you figure that out?

Student 2: Because there were 16 marshmallows in the first row, and there are three rows. That would be 16 × 3.

Teacher: Did we get the same number of marshmallows as we did the first time we grouped them?

Student 2: Yes, because we still have the same number of cups, and the same number of marshmallows.

FIGURE 8.1 • **Mathematical Stories for Teaching Multiplication**

Discovery learning has applications in many subjects. For example, some science museums make available a series of cylinders of different sizes and weights, some hollow and some solid. Students are encouraged to race the cylinders down a ramp. By careful experimentation, the students can discover the underlying principles that determine the cylinders' speed. Computer simulations can create environments in which students can discover scientific principles (De Jong, 2011). Innovative science programs (Singer, Marx, Krajcik, & Chambers, 2000) are particularly likely to be based on principles of discovery learning.

Discovery learning has several advantages. It arouses students' curiosity, motivating them to continue to work until they find answers. Students also learn independent problem-solving and critical-thinking skills, because they must analyze and manipulate information. However, discovery learning can also lead to errors and wasted time. For this reason, *guided* discovery learning is more common than pure discovery learning (Drapeau, 2014; Kirschner & van Merrienboer, 2008; Marzano, 2011). In guided discovery the teacher plays a more active role, giving clues, structuring portions of an activity, or providing outlines.

Self-Regulated Learning

A key concept of constructivist theories of learning is a vision of the ideal student as a **self-regulated learner** (Barnes, 2013a; Greene & Azevedo, 2007; Hadwin, 2008; Veenman, 2011), one who has knowledge of effective learning strategies and how and when to use them (Bandura, 2001; Dembo & Eaton, 2000; Hadwin, 2008; Zimmerman, 2013). For example, self-regulated learners know how to break complex problems into simpler steps or to test out alternative solutions (Hall & Greeno, 2008), they know how and when to skim and how and when to read for deep understanding, and they know how to write to persuade and how to write to inform (Graham, Harris, & Chambers, 2015; Zimmerman, 2013). Furthermore, self-regulated learners are motivated by learning itself, not only by grades or others' approval (Boekaerts, 2006), and they are able to stick to a long-term task until it is done. When students have both effective learning strategies and the motivation and persistence to apply these strategies until a job is done to their satisfaction, they are likely to be effective learners (Anderman & Dawson, 2011). Programs that teach children self-regulated learning strategies have been found to increase students' achievement (Cho & Bergin, 2009; Cleary & Zimmerman, 2004; Fuchs et al., 2003; Mason, 2004; Torrance, Fidalgo, & Garcia, 2007).

Connections 8.3
For more on the motivational aspects of self-regulated learning, see Chapter 10.

Scaffolding

As noted in Chapter 2, scaffolding is a practice based on Vygotsky's concept of assisted learning. According to Vygotsky, higher mental functions, including the ability to direct memory and attention in a purposeful way and to think in symbols, are mediated behaviors (DeVries, 2008; Mahn & John-Steiner, 2013). Mediated externally by culture, these and other behaviors become internalized in the learner's mind as psychological tools. In assisted learning, or **mediated learning**, the teacher is the cultural agent who guides instruction so that students will master and internalize the skills that permit higher cognitive functioning. This ability to internalize cultural tools is a function of the learner's age or stage of cognitive development. Once acquired, internal mediators allow greater self-mediated learning.

In practical terms, scaffolding might include giving students more structure at the beginning of a set of lessons and gradually turning responsibility over to them to operate on their own (Borich, 2014; Fisher & Frey, 2013; Jackson, 2009; Shepard, 2005; Wentzel & Brophy, 2014). For example, students can be taught to generate their own questions about material they are reading. Early on, you might suggest the questions, modeling the kinds of questions students might ask, but students later take over the question-generating task (Fisher & Frey, 2013). For another example of scaffolding, see Figure 8.2.

Connections 8.4
For more on scaffolding, see Chapter 2.

Constructivist Methods in the Content Areas

Constructivist and student-centered methods have come to dominate current thinking in all areas of curriculum (see Gabler & Schroeder, 2003; Henson, 2004; Loyens & Rikers, 2011; Pearson & Hiebert, 2015). The following sections describe constructivist approaches in reading, writing, mathematics, and science.

Nathan: This doesn't look like a "g." (Scribbles in frustration)

Adult: What shape do you see here at the top? (Points to a picture of the "g")
Nathan: A circle.
Adult: You're good at drawing circles. Let's see you do that. Nathan draws a circle.

Adult: Now what shape do you see here at the bottom?
Nathan: A hook.
Adult: Now add the hook to your circle. (Traces where it should go with her finger) Nathan adds hook and makes a lower-case "g."

Adult: So to make a "g" you start with a circle, and add a hook. Nathan tries writing again, saying to himself, "Start with a circle and add a hook" as he writes.

FIGURE 8.2 • Scaffolding

CONSTRUCTIVIST APPROACHES IN READING

Reciprocal Teaching One well-researched example of a constructivist approach based on principles of question generation is **reciprocal teaching** (Palincsar & Herrenkohl, 2002). This approach, designed primarily to help low achievers in elementary and middle schools learn reading comprehension, involves the teacher working with small groups of students. Initially, you model questions students might ask as they read, but students are soon appointed to act as "teacher" to generate questions for each other. Figure 8.3 presents an example of reciprocal teaching in use. Note in the example how the teacher directs the conversation about the book's subject at first but then turns the responsibility over to Marissa (who is about to turn it over to another student as the example ends). The teacher is modeling the behaviors she wants the students to be able to do on

Teacher: The title of this story is "Six-Dinner Sid." Let's have some predictions. I'm going to begin by guessing that this story is about a cat who eats a lot. Why do I say that?

First student: Because there is a cat on the cover.

Second student: And the title says he eats six dinners, and six dinners are a lot to eat!

Teacher: That's right. Most pets only eat once or twice a day. Let's predict now the kind of information you might read about Sid.

Third student: We might read about how he ends up eating so many dinners.

First student: And what he eats for dinner.

Teacher: What other information would you want to know? *(No response from students.)*

Teacher: I would like to know who is giving him all of this food. Any ideas?

Second student: Maybe his owner keeps feeding him a lot because he is hungry.

Third student: Or maybe a whole bunch of different people feed him.

Teacher: Those are interesting ideas, and either one could happen. Let's start reading the first four pages, and we'll see which of our predictions come true. I will be the teacher for this section. *(All read the section silently.)*

Teacher: So who is Six-Dinner Sid?

First student: A cat who eats six dinners.

Teacher: That's right. So we were correct in our prediction that Sid is a cat who eats a lot. What else did we predict that came true?

Second student: We predicted that we'd read about what he ate, and that different people were feeding him.

Teacher: We learned a lot about him so far. My summary of this first section would be that it describes how Sid the cat tricks six different people into feeding him each night. Let's continue. *(All read the next section)*

Teacher: Who will be the teacher for the next section? Marissa?

Marissa: Does anyone find out Sid is eating so much?

Teacher: Good question! And this goes back to our prediction that different people were feeding him. Who will you call on to answer your question?

Marissa: Jawohn.

Jawohn: The vet finds out that Sid has six different owners.

Marissa: The vet tells each of the owners about the other owners, who realize that they are each feeding Sid every night.

Teacher: Summarize now.

Marissa: This is how Sid's owners discover each other.

Teacher: That's right. The story goes on to tell us that the owners decide as a group that Sid will only get one dinner each night.

Marissa: The story tells us how much Sid likes to eat his six dinners. So I predict the next pages will tell us how he tries to eat six dinners again. I would like Dillon to be the next teacher.

Teacher: Excellent prediction.

FIGURE 8.3 • Example of a Reciprocal Teaching Lesson

their own, and then her role changes to that of facilitator and organizer as the students begin to generate the actual questions. Research on reciprocal teaching has generally found this strategy to increase the success of low achievers (Sporer, Brunstein, & Kieschke, 2009).

Questioning the Author Another constructivist approach for reading is Questioning the Author (Beck & McKeown, 2001; McKeown & Beck, 2004; Salinger & Fleischman, 2005).

In this method, children in grades 3–9 are taught to see the authors of factual material as real, fallible people and to then engage in simulated "dialogues" with the authors. As the students are reading a text, stop them from time to time to ask questions such as "What is the author trying to say, or what does she want us to know?" and then follow up with questions such as "How does that fit in with what she said before?" Ultimately, the students themselves take responsibility for formulating questions about the author's intent and meaning. A study of fifth- and sixth-graders found that students who experienced this technique recalled more from texts than did a comparison group, and were far more likely to describe the purpose of reading as *understanding* rather than simply memorizing the text (McKeown & Beck, 2004). A study of low-achieving kindergartners and first-graders also found positive effects of a similar strategy on vocabulary development (Beck & McKeown, 2007).

Concept-Oriented Reading Instruction Concept-Oriented Reading Instruction (CORI) (Wigfield & Guthrie, 2010) is a constructivist approach to teaching reading in the upper elementary grades. It emphasizes five key elements:

- Content goals. Students read material focused primarily on science goals.
- Giving students choices. Students are able to choose books and topics to read about in depth. This is intended to maximize intrinsic motivation to read.
- Hands-on activities in relation to text. Students explore science concepts in hands-on activities. This is intended to be beneficial to science learning, but from a reading perspective it puts reading in a meaningful and motivational context.
- A variety of expository (informational) texts.
- Collaboration among students. Students work in small groups to discuss what they are reading and to work together on science activities.

Numerous studies of CORI have found positive effects on children's reading comprehension and motivation (Wigfield & Guthrie, 2010).

CONSTRUCTIVIST APPROACHES TO WRITING A widely used set of constructivist approaches to the teaching of creative writing, writing process models (Graham, Harris, & Chambers, 2015; Murphy & Smith, 2015), engage students in small peer-response teams in which they work together to help one another plan, draft, revise, edit, and "publish" compositions. That is, children may review each other's drafts and offer helpful ideas for improvements in content as well as mechanics (e.g., spelling, punctuation), ultimately presenting compositions for some authentic purpose (such as a poetry reading or a literary review). In the process of responding to others' compositions, children gain insight into the process of writing and revision.

Research on writing process methods has found these strategies to have positive effects (De La Paz & McCutchen, 2011; Harris, Graham, & Mason, 2006). Strategies that provide specific scaffolding, such as instruction in graphic organizers to help children use metacognitive strategies for planning and evaluating their own work, have been particularly effective (De La Paz & Graham, 2002; Glaser & Brunstein, 2007; Graham, 2006; Harris, Graham, & Mason, 2006; Torrance & Fidalgo, 2011). There is also evidence that teaching writing in various content areas increases content learning in these subjects (Bangert-Drowns, Hurley, & Wilkinson, 2004; Headley, 2008; Rijlaarsdam, et al., 2010).

CONSTRUCTIVIST APPROACHES IN MATHEMATICS In constructivist approaches to elementary mathematics, students work together in small groups; teachers pose problems and then circulate among these groups to facilitate the discussion of strategies, join students in asking questions about strategies they have proposed, and occasionally offer alternative strategies when students appear to be stuck (Edwards, Esmonde, & Wagner, 2011). Constructivist approaches make extensive use of physical, pictorial, verbal, and symbolic presentations of mathematical ideas and give students opportunities to solve complex problems using these representations and to contrast different representations of the same concepts (Hiebert & Grouws, 2014). Cognitively Guided Instruction (CGI) (Carpenter, Fennema, Frank, Levi, & Empson, 2014) provides extensive professional development for teachers of primary mathematics, focusing on similar principles. There is good evidence that this program increases student achievement not only on measures related to higher-level thinking in mathematics, which is the program's focus, but also in computational skills.

MyEdLab
Video Example 8.2
Students in this elementary class construct their own approaches to solve math problems. How does encouraging constructivist problem solving in early grades lead to academic success in later grades?

THEORY INTO PRACTICE

Introducing Reciprocal Teaching

In introducing reciprocal teaching to students, you might begin as follows: "For the coming weeks we will be working together to improve your ability to understand what you read. Sometimes we are so busy figuring out what the words are that we fail to pay much attention to what the words and sentences mean. We will be learning a way to pay more attention to what we are reading. I will teach you to do the following activities as you read:

1. To think of important questions that might be asked about what is being read and to be sure that you can answer those questions
2. To summarize the most important information that you have read
3. To predict what the author might discuss next in the passage
4. To point out when something is unclear in the passage or doesn't make sense and then to see if we can make sense of it

"These activities will help you keep your attention on what you are reading and make sure that you are understanding it.

"The way in which you will learn these four activities is by taking turns in the role of teacher during our reading group sessions. When I am the teacher, I will show you how I read carefully by thinking of questions I have while reading, by summarizing the most important information I read, and by predicting what I think the author might discuss next. I will also tell you if I found anything I read to be unclear or confusing and how I made sense out of it.

"When you are the teacher, you will first ask the rest of us the questions you made up while reading. You will tell us if our answers are correct. You will summarize the most important information you learned while reading. You will also tell us if you found anything in the passage to be confusing. Several times throughout the story you will also be asked to predict what you think might be discussed next in the passage. When you are the teacher, the rest of us will answer your questions and comment on your summary.

"These are activities that we hope you will learn and use, not only when you are here in reading class but also whenever you want to understand and remember what you are reading—for example, in social studies, science, or history."

Daily Procedures

1. Pass out the passage for the day.
2. Explain that you will be the teacher for the first segment.
3. Instruct the students to read silently whatever portion of the passage you determine is appropriate. At the beginning, it will probably be easiest to work paragraph by paragraph.
4. When everyone has completed the first segment, model the following:
   - "The question that I thought a teacher might ask is . . ." Have the students answer your question. They may refer to the text if necessary.
   - "I would summarize the important information in this paragraph in the following way . . ."
   - "From the title of the passage, I would predict that the author will discuss . . ."
   - If appropriate, "When I read this part, I found the following to be unclear . . ."

5. Invite the students to make comments regarding your teaching and the passage with prompts such as the following:
   - "Was there more important information?"
   - "Does anyone have more to add to my prediction?"
   - "Did anyone find something else confusing?"
6. Assign the next segment to be read silently. Choose a student to act as teacher for this segment. Begin with the more verbal students who you think will have less difficulty with the activities.
7. Coach the student teacher through the activities as necessary. Encourage the other students to participate in the dialogue, but always give the student teacher for that segment the opportunity to go first and lead the dialogue. Be sure to give the student teacher plenty of feedback and praise for his or her participation.
8. As the training days go by, try to remove yourself more and more from the dialogue so that the student teacher initiates the activities, with students providing feedback. Your role will continue to be monitoring, keeping students on track, and helping them over obstacles. Throughout the training, however, continue to take your turn as teacher, modeling at least once a session.

In these and other constructivist approaches to mathematics, the emphasis is on beginning with real problems for students to solve intuitively and letting students use their existing knowledge of the world to solve problems any way they can (Edwards, Esmonde, & Wagner, 2011). The problem and solutions in Figure 8.1 (hot chocolate and marshmallows) illustrate this approach. Only at the end of the process, when students have achieved a firm conceptual understanding, are they taught formal, abstract representations of the mathematical processes they have been working with.

CONSTRUCTIVIST APPROACHES IN SCIENCE Discovery, groupwork, and conceptual change have long been emphasized in science education, so it is not surprising that many elementary and secondary science educators have embraced constructivist ideas (see Duschl & Hamilton, 2011; Harris & Marx, 2014; Olson & Mokhtari, 2010; Slavin, 2013; Slavin, Lake, Hanley, & Thurston, 2012; Thurston, 2014). In this subject, constructivism translates into an emphasis on hands-on, investigative laboratory activities (Hoachander & Yanofsky, 2011; Pine & Aschbacher, 2006; Singer et al., 2000), identifying misconceptions and using experimental approaches to correct these misconceptions (Harris & Marx, 2014), cooperative learning (Baines, Blatchford, & Chowne, 2007; Thurston, 2010, 2014), and teaching of metacognitive skills (Zohar & Peled, 2008).

Research on Constructivist Methods

Research comparing constructivist and traditional approaches to instruction is often difficult to interpret because constructivist methods are themselves very diverse and are usually intended to produce outcomes that are qualitatively different from those of traditional methods. For example, many researchers argue that acquisition of skills and basic information must be balanced against the deeper learning possible in constructivist approaches (Egan, 2008; Jensen & Nickelsen, 2008; Pahomov, 2014). But what is the appropriate balance, and for which objectives? Also, much of the research on constructivist methods is descriptive rather than comparative. However, there are studies showing positive effects of constructivist approaches on traditional achievement measures in mathematics (Edwards et al., 2011), science (Duschl & Hamilton, 2011), reading (Fox & Alexander, 2011; Pearson & Hiebert, 2015), and writing (De La Paz & McCutchen, 2011). However, other studies reported better results for explicit teaching than for constructivist approaches

Certification Pointer

For teacher certification tests, you may be expected to choose alternative teaching strategies to achieve particular instructional goals.

(Baker, Gersten, & Lee, 2002; Kirschner et al., 2006; Kirschner & van Merriënboer, 2013; Kroesbergen, Van Luit, & Maas, 2004). Much more research is needed to establish the conditions under which constructivist approaches are effective for enhancing student achievement. However, it is only reasonable to seek a balance between direct instruction and constructivist approaches and to use them to accomplish a wide range of objectives (Huebner, 2008).

> MyEdLab **Self-Check 8.1**
>
> MyEdLab **Video Analysis Tool 8.1** Go to MyEdLab and click on the Video Analysis Tool to access the exercise "Student-centered learning: scaffolding."

InTASC 3

Learning Environments

InTASC 8

Instructional Strategies

MyEdLab

Video Example 8.3

Textbook author Bob Slavin describes a seventh-grade math class that used cooperative learning activities. How might the math teacher have structured the lesson to ensure that all students would be involved and all would learn to solve similar problems?

Certification Pointer

On your teacher certification test, you may be required to suggest an appropriate way of assigning students in a case study to cooperative learning groups.

Connections 8.5

To learn about the benefits of cooperative learning methods for promoting harmony in culturally diverse classrooms, see Chapter 4.

HOW IS COOPERATIVE LEARNING USED IN INSTRUCTION?

In **cooperative learning** instructional methods, or peer-assisted learning (Rohrbeck, Ginsburg-Block, Fantuzzo, & Miller, 2003; Slavin, 2011, 2013; Webb, 2008), students work together in small groups to help each other learn. Many quite different approaches to cooperative learning are used. Most involve students in four-member mixed-ability groups (e.g., Slavin, 2011, 2013), but some methods use dyads (e.g., Fuchs, Fuchs, & Karnes, 2001) and some use varying group sizes (e.g., Cohen & Lotan, 2014; Johnson & Johnson, 1999; Kagan & Kagan, 2012). Typically, students are assigned to cooperative groups and stay together for many weeks or months. They are usually taught specific skills that will help them work well together, such as listening actively, giving good explanations, avoiding putdowns, and including other people.

Cooperative learning activities can play many roles in lessons (Slavin, 2011, 2013; Webb, 2008). Recall the chapter-opening vignette in Chapter 7: Ms. Logan used cooperative learning for three distinct purposes. At first, students worked as discovery groups, helping each other figure out how water in bottles could tell them about principles of sound. After the formal lesson, students worked as discussion groups. Finally, students had an opportunity to work together to make sure that all group members had learned everything in the lesson in preparation for a quiz, working in a group study format. In the vignette at the beginning of this chapter, Mr. Dunbar used cooperative groups to solve a complex problem.

ON THE WEB

For newsletters and resources for cooperative learning, visit the website of the International Association for the Study of Cooperation in Education at iasce.net. Information on cooperative learning methods developed at Johns Hopkins University is available at successforall.org. For the University of Minnesota Cooperative Learning Center, see serc.carleton.edu and co-operation.org. For PALS, see vanderbilt.edu. For Spencer Kagan's cooperative learning structures, see kaganonline.com.

Cooperative Learning Methods

Many quite different cooperative learning methods have been developed and researched. The most extensively evaluated cooperative learning methods are described in the following sections.

STUDENT TEAMS–ACHIEVEMENT DIVISIONS (STAD) Students are assigned to four-member learning teams in **Student Teams–Achievement Divisions (STAD)** (Slavin, 1995a). The groups are mixed in performance level, gender, and ethnicity. The teacher presents a lesson, and then students work within their teams to make sure that all team members have mastered the lesson. Finally, all students take individual quizzes on the material, at which time they may not help one another.

Students' quiz scores are compared to their own past averages, and points are awarded on the basis of the degree to which students meet or exceed their own earlier performances. These points are then summed to form team scores, and teams that meet certain criteria may earn certificates or other rewards. In a related method called Teams–Games–Tournaments (TGT), students play games with members of other teams to add points to their team scores.

STAD and TGT have been used in a wide variety of subjects, from mathematics to language arts to social studies, and have been used from second grade through college. The STAD method is most appropriate for teaching well-defined objectives, such as mathematical computations and applications, language usage and mechanics, geography and map skills, and science facts and concepts. However, it can easily be adapted for use with less well-defined objectives by incorporating more open-ended assessments, such as essays or performances. Many studies have found positive effects of STAD on learning of a variety of subjects (Slavin, 2013). STAD is described in more detail in the Theory into Practice feature below.

COOPERATIVE INTEGRATED READING AND COMPOSITION (CIRC) A comprehensive program for teaching reading and writing in the upper elementary grades, **Cooperative Integrated Reading and Composition (CIRC)** (Stevens & Slavin, 1995b) involves students working in four-member cooperative learning teams. They engage in a series of activities with one another, including reading to one another; making predictions about how narrative stories will come out; summarizing stories to one another; writing responses to stories; and practicing spelling, decoding, and vocabulary. They also work together to master main ideas and develop other comprehension skills. During language arts periods, students engage in writing drafts, revising and editing one another's work, and preparing for publication of team books. Several studies of the CIRC program have found positive effects on students' reading skills, including improved scores on standardized reading and language tests (Slavin, Lake, Chambers, Cheung, & Davis, 2009).

THEORY INTO PRACTICE

Student Teams—Achievement Divisions (STAD)

Student Teams–Achievement Divisions (Slavin, 1995a) is an effective cooperative learning method that consists of a regular cycle of teaching, cooperative study in mixed-ability teams, and quizzes, with recognition or other rewards provided to teams whose members excel.

STAD consists of a regular cycle of instructional activities:

- **Teach.** Present the lesson.
- **Team study.** Students work on worksheets in their teams to master the material.
- **Test.** Students take individual quizzes or other assessments (such as essays or performances).
- **Team recognition.** Team scores are computed on the basis of team members' scores, and certificates, a class newsletter, or bulletin board display recognizes high-scoring teams.

The following steps describe how to introduce students to STAD:

1. Assign students to teams of four or five members each. Groups of four are preferable; make five-member teams only if the class is not divisible by four. To assign the students, rank them from top to bottom on some measure of academic performance (e.g., past grades, test scores) and divide the ranked list into quarters, placing any extra students in the middle quarters. Then put one student from each quarter on each team, making sure that the teams are well balanced in gender and ethnicity. Extra (middle) students may become fifth members of teams.

(continued)

2. Make a worksheet and a short quiz for the lesson you plan to teach. Tell the class that during team study (one or two class periods), the team members' tasks are to master the material you have presented in your lesson and to help their teammates master the material. Inform students that they will have worksheets or other study materials that they can use to practice the skill being taught and to assess themselves and their teammates.

3. Have teammates move their desks together or move to team tables, and allow students about 10 minutes to decide on a team name. Then hand out worksheets or other study materials (two of each per team). Make sure students understand the following points before they begin:

   - Suggest that students on each team work in pairs or threes. If they are working problems (as in math), each student in a pair or threesome should work the problem and then check with his or her partner(s). If anyone misses a question, that student's teammates have a responsibility to explain it. If students are working on short-answer questions, they might quiz each other, with partners taking turns, alternately holding the answer sheet and then switching roles and attempting to answer the questions.
   - Emphasize to students that they have not finished studying until they are sure that all their teammates will make 100 percent on the quiz.
   - Make sure that students understand that the worksheets are for studying—not for filling out and handing in. That is why it is important for students to have the answer sheets, to check themselves and their teammates as they study.
   - Have students explain answers to one another instead of only checking each other against the answer sheet.
   - When students have questions, they should ask a teammate before asking you.

4. While students are working in teams, circulate through the class, praising teams that are working well and sitting in with each team to hear how the members are doing.

5. Distribute the quiz or other assessment, and give students adequate time to complete it. Do not let students work together on the quiz; at this point they must show what they have learned as individuals. Have students move their desks apart if this is possible. Either allow students to exchange papers with members of other teams or collect the quizzes to score after class.

6. Figure individual and team scores. Team scores in STAD are based on team members' improvements over their own past records. As soon as possible after each quiz, you should compute individual team scores and write a class newsletter (or prepare a class bulletin board) to announce the team scores. If at all possible, the announcement of team scores should be made in the first period after the quiz. This makes the connection between doing well and receiving recognition clear to students, increasing their motivation to do their best. Compute team scores by adding up the improvement points earned by the team members and dividing this sum by the number of team members who are present on the day of the quiz.

7. Recognize team accomplishments. As soon as you have calculated points for each student and figured team scores, you should provide some sort of recognition to any teams that average 20 improvement points or more. You might give certificates to team members or prepare a bulletin board display. It is important to help students value team success. Your own enthusiasm about team scores will help. If you give more than one quiz in a week, combine the quiz results into a single weekly score. After five or six weeks of STAD, reassign students to new teams. This allows students to work with other classmates and keeps the program fresh.

JIGSAW In classes using **Jigsaw** (Aronson, Blaney, Stephan, Sikes, & Snapp, 1978), students are assigned to six-member teams to work on academic material that has been broken down into sections. For example, a biography might be divided into early life, first accomplishments, major setbacks, later life, and impact on history. Each team member reads his or her section. Next, members of different teams who have studied the same sections meet in expert groups to discuss their parts. Then the students return to their teams and take turns teaching their teammates about their sections. Because the only way students can learn sections other than on their own is to listen carefully to their teammates, they are motivated to support and show interest in one another's work. In a modification of this approach called Jigsaw II (Slavin, 1995a), students work in four- or five-member teams, as in STAD. Instead of each student being assigned a unique section, all students read a common text, such as a book chapter, a short story, or a biography, and then each student receives a topic on which to become an expert. Students with the same topics meet in expert groups to discuss them, after which they return to their teams to teach what they have learned to their teammates. The students take individual quizzes, which result in team scores, as in STAD.

LEARNING TOGETHER A model of cooperative learning developed by David Johnson and Roger Johnson (1999), **Learning Together** involves students working in four- or five-member heterogeneous groups on assignments. The groups hand in a single completed assignment and receive praise and rewards based on the group product. This method emphasizes team-building activities before students begin working together and regular discussions within groups about how well they are working together.

PEER-ASSISTED LEARNING STRATEGIES (PALS) PALS is a structured cooperative learning method in which students work in pairs, taking turns as teacher and learner, using specific meta-cognitive strategies. Several studies of PALS have found positive effects of this approach in reading (e.g., Calhoon, Al Otaiba, Cihak, King, & Aralos, 2007; Mathes & Babyak, 2001) and math (e.g., Fuchs, Fuchs, & Karnes, 2001).

COOPERATIVE SCRIPTING Many students find it helpful to get together with classmates to discuss material they have read or heard in class. This age-old practice has been formalized in a method wherein students work in pairs and take turns summarizing sections of the material for one another. While one student summarizes, the other listens and corrects any errors or omissions. Then the two students switch roles, continuing in this manner until they have covered all the material to be learned. A series of studies of this **cooperative scripting** method has consistently found that students who study this way learn and retain far more than students who summarize on their own or simply read the material (O'Donnell, 2006). A related method, in which children take turns reading and summarizing to each other, was also found to be effective in studies by Van Keer and Vanderlinde (2013). It is interesting that although both participants in the cooperative pairs gain from the activity, the larger gains are seen in the sections that students teach to their partners, rather than those in the sections where they serve as listeners (Fuchs & Fuchs, 1997; Webb, 2008).

INFORMAL COOPERATIVE LEARNING STRUCTURES In addition to the methods described previously, there are numerous informal cooperative learning strategies that many teachers use as a regular part of their practice. These are summarized by Kagan & Kagan (2012). Some widely used informal structures follow.

Numbered Heads (or Random Reporter) Students in four-member teams are given secret numbers from 1 to 4. Students study together, trying to make sure that every team member knows the material. Then the teacher calls on, for example, all "number 2s" to respond. They may then be given a question or a problem to work without the help of their teammates. At a signal, they may all hold up an answer (e.g., on an erasable board), or individuals may be called on. The team gets points if the designated "random reporter" gives a correct answer. The idea is to motivate team members to teach each other and to focus on the learning of *all* team members, since they do not know who will represent them on a given problem.

Think-Pair-Share This simple activity asks students to sit in pairs. When teachers pose questions, they ask students to think, discuss with their partners, and then share their answers as a pair with the class. The idea is to get students to talk about their current understandings with a peer. It ensures that even very shy or hesitant learners have routine opportunities to discuss topics being taught.

Project-Based Learning   Project-based learning methods have long existed in education. John Dewey was a major advocate in the 1920s, for example. Today, project-based learning may be the most popular form of cooperative learning (see Cohen & Lotan, 2014; Larmer, 2014; Larmer, Mergendoller, & Boss, 2015; Senn & Marzano, 2015). Project-based learning is rarely used as the primary strategy for an entire course, but it is likely to be used from time to time for experiments, investigations, and reports.

The methods employed in **project-based learning** vary widely, but in general, they involve students working in self-chosen groups. Each group may work on its own task, which may also be self-chosen. For example, in a set of projects related to the environment, one group may choose to focus on water pollution, one on air pollution, one on global warming, one on alternative fuel sources, and one on diminishing habitat for animals. In each group a leader may be selected, or the leadership role may rotate among group members.

The group's task will be to produce a product that represents the group's learning. In the environment example, groups might be asked to prepare a briefing document for a government agency considering new policies to improve the environment. Group members might divide the task into parts. For example, one student might be responsible for an overview of the extent of the problem, another for writing about how environmental problems affect people, another for reviewing solutions that various countries or states have tried, and another for proposing practical solutions for the area in which their school is located. As group members research each part of the topic, they should discuss what they are finding out with their groupmates; share information they have found in books, on the Internet, or in interviewing experts; and then draft their parts of the report. Groupmates might provide each other with feedback on the content and form of their sections, and then all group members would make revisions and move toward a final product. As a final step, groups might create presentations to the class on their project conclusions, with all group members participating to argue for the urgent need for progress in their area, to advance ideas for solving environmental problems, and to offer facts and figures to back up their proposals. They might develop PowerPoints, show maps, diagrams, and physical artifacts, and even play recordings taken from interviews with experts.

The idea of a project is to go beyond learning facts and skills and learn something in depth, working closely with groupmates. Note that it is important in group projects to ensure that all groupmates have individual roles and products, to avoid just one or two students doing all the work (Brookhart, 2013b; Larmer, 2014)

Research on Cooperative Learning

Most research comparing cooperative learning to traditional teaching methods has evaluated group study methods such as STAD, Jigsaw II, CIRC, and Learning Together. More than 100 studies have compared achievement in classrooms using such methods to traditional classrooms over periods of at least four weeks (Slavin, 2013). The results have consistently favored cooperative learning as long as two essential conditions are met. First, some kind of recognition or small reward must be provided to groups that do well, so that group members can see that it is in their interest to help their groupmates learn. Second, there must be individual accountability. That is, the success of the group must depend on the individual learning of all group members, not on a single group product. For example, groups might be evaluated on the basis of the average of their members' scores on individual quizzes or essays (as in STAD). Without this individual accountability there is a danger that one student might do the work of others, or that some students might be shut out of group interaction because they were thought to have little to contribute (Chapman, 2001; Slavin, 2011, 2013; Webb, 2008).

Studies of cooperative learning methods that incorporate group goals and individual accountability show substantial positive effects on the achievement of students in grades 2 through 12 in all subjects and in all types of schools (Ellis, 2001b; Rohrbeck et al., 2003; Slavin, 1995a, 2010, 2013). A review of group learning with technology also found positive effects for well-structured methods (Lou, Abrami, & d'Apollonia, 2001). Effects are similar for all grade levels and for all types of content, from basic skills to problem solving. Cooperative learning methods are generally used for only a portion of a student's school day and school year (Antil, Jenkins, Wayne, & Vadasy, 1998), but one study found that students in schools using a variety of cooperative learning

Connections 8.6
For more on how cooperative learning methods benefit the social integration of students with special educational needs in the general education classroom, see Chapter 12.

Certification Pointer
On your teacher certification test, you may be asked to determine when you would *not* employ a particular cooperative learning strategy.

methods in almost all subjects for a two-year period achieved significantly better than students in traditionally organized schools (Stevens & Slavin, 1995a). Studies generally show equal effects of cooperative learning for high, average, and low achievers and for boys and girls (Roseth, Johnson, & Johnson, 2008; Slavin, 1995a). There is some evidence that these methods are particularly effective for African American and Latino students (Boykin & Noguera, 2011; Calderón et al., 1998; Hurley, 2000). A review of peer-assisted learning by Rohrbeck and colleagues (2003) reported that effects were strongest on younger, urban, and low-income students and/or students who are members of minority groups. More informal cooperative learning methods, lacking group goals and individual accountability, have not generally had positive effects on student achievement (Chapman, 2001; Klein & Schnackenberg, 2000; Slavin, 1995a, 2011, 2013).

In addition to group goals and individual accountability, a few classroom practices can contribute to the effectiveness of cooperative learning. For example, cooperative groups who are taught communication and helping skills (Kutnick, Ota, & Berdondini, 2008; Prichard, Bizo, & Stratford, 2006; Senn & Marzano, 2015; Webb & Mastergeorge, 2003) or are given specific structured ways of working with each other learn more than students in cooperative groups without these enhancements (Baker et al., 2002; Emmer & Gerwels, 2002; Mathes et al., 2003; Saleh, Lazonder, & De Jong, 2007). In addition, students who are taught metacognitive learning strategies (Friend, 2001; Jones et al., 2000; King, 1999; Kramarski & Mevarech, 2003) learn more than students in usual cooperative groups. For example, King (1999) taught students generic question forms to ask each other as they studied, such as "Compare and contrast _____ and _____," or "How does _____ affect _____?" Students who used these discourse patterns learned more than students who used other forms of cooperative learning. A great deal of research has shown that students who give extensive explanations to others learn more in cooperative groups than those who give or receive short answers or no answers (Webb, 2008).

21ST CENTURY LEARNING

Cooperative Learning

In the 21st century, teamwork and the ability to solve problems and learn in groups are increasingly important in the world of work, and every student should know how to work productively with others. Cooperative learning is strongly encouraged in writings about the Common Core State Standards and other college- and career-ready standards. A great deal of research, summarized in this chapter, has shown that working in cooperative groups with group goals and individual accountability increases students' learning of traditional academic content. Along the way, they are likely to acquire equally important teamwork skills, such as the ability to teach and learn with partners, to support and encourage partners' efforts, to disagree with dignity and hold to a reasoned opinion without putting others down, and to resolve interpersonal conflicts and create a positive working environment within teams. All of these common core skills will help young people thrive in today's workforce while also helping to create a more peaceful and prosocial environment.

QUESTIONS

- What kinds of problems might you encounter in the workplace in which the experience of working in groups in school could help participants find a good solution?

- Taking it a step further, looking at the clash of political factions, which skills gained in cooperative learning groups might be applicable to conflict resolution on a widespread scale?

There is less research on the effects of project-based forms of cooperative learning focused on ill-structured problems, but the studies that do exist generally show equally favorable results of cooperative methods designed for such problems (Blumenfeld et al., 1996; Cohen & Lotan, 2014; David, 2008; Thousand & Villa, 1994).

Methods incorporating "constructive conflict," in which students are taught positive ways to debate controversial issues, can also increase learning about the issues discussed (Lin & Anderson, 2008; Nussbaum, 2008; Roseth, Saltarelli, & Glass, 2011).

In addition to boosting achievement, cooperative learning methods have had positive effects on such outcomes as improved intergroup relations (Slavin, 1995b), self-esteem, attitudes toward school, and acceptance of children with special educational needs (Ginsburg-Block, Rohrbeck, & Fantuzzo, 2006; Roseth, Johnson, & Johnson, 2008; Slavin, 1995a). Studies find that cooperative learning is widely used (e.g., Antil et al., 1998), but the forms most often seen are informal methods lacking group goals and individual accountability, which research has found to be less effective than more structured methods.

> MyEdLab **Self-Check 8.2**

HOW ARE PROBLEM-SOLVING AND THINKING SKILLS TAUGHT?

InTASC 5

Application of Content

Students cannot be said to have learned anything useful unless they have acquired the ability to use information and skills to solve problems. For example, a student might be quite good at adding, subtracting, and multiplying but have little idea of how to solve this problem: "Sylvia bought four hamburgers at $1.25 each, two orders of french fries at 65 cents, and three large sodas at 75 cents. How much change did she get from a 10-dollar bill?"

Sylvia's situation is not unusual in real life, and the computations involved are not difficult. However, many students (and even some otherwise-competent adults) would have difficulty solving this problem. The difficulty of most application problems in mathematics lies not in the computations but in knowing how to set the problem up so that it can be solved. **Problem solving** is a skill that can be taught and learned (Fuchs et al., 2006).

The Problem-Solving Process

GENERAL PROBLEM-SOLVING STRATEGIES Students can be taught several well-researched strategies to use in solving problems (see, for example, Kirschner & van Merrienboer, 2008; Silver, 2010). Bransford and Stein (1993) developed and evaluated a five-step strategy called IDEAL:

I Identify problems and opportunities
D Define goals and represent the problem
E Explore possible strategies
A Anticipate outcomes and act
L Look back and learn

IDEAL and similar strategies begin with carefully identifying the problem that needs to be solved, defining the resources and information that are available, determining a way in which the problem can be represented (such as in a drawing, outline, or flowchart), and then breaking the process into steps that lead to a solution. For example, the first step is to identify the goal and figure out how to proceed.

In solving Sylvia's problem, the goal is to find out how much change she will receive from a 10-dollar bill after buying food and drinks. We might then break the problem into substeps, each with its own subgoal:

1. Figure how much Sylvia spent on hamburgers.
2. Figure how much Sylvia spent on french fries.
3. Figure how much Sylvia spent on sodas.
4. Figure how much Sylvia spent in total.
5. Figure how much change Sylvia gets from $10.00.

MEANS–ENDS ANALYSIS Deciding what the problem is and what needs to be done involves a **means–ends analysis**. Learning to solve problems requires a great deal of practice with different kinds of problems that demand thought. All too often, texts in mathematics and other subjects that include many problems fail to present examples that will make students think. They might give students a set of word problems whose solutions require the multiplication of two numbers. Students soon learn that they can solve such problems by looking for any two numbers and multiplying them. In real life, however, problems do not line themselves up neatly in categories. We might hear, "Joe Smith got a 5 percent raise last week, which amounted to $1,200." If we want to figure out how much Joe was making before his raise, the hard part is not doing the calculation, but knowing what calculation is called for. In real life this problem would not be on a page titled "Dividing by Percents." The more different kinds of problems students learn to solve, and the more they have to think to solve those problems, the greater the chance that, when faced with real-life problems, students will be able to transfer their skills or knowledge to the new situation.

EXTRACTING RELEVANT INFORMATION Realistic problems are rarely neat and tidy. Imagine that Sylvia's problem involved the following scenario:

> Sylvia walked into the fast-food restaurant at 6:18 with three friends. Between them, they bought four hamburgers at $1.25 each, two orders of french fries at 65 cents, and three large sodas at 75 cents. Onion rings were on sale for 55 cents. Sylvia's mother told her to be in by 9:00, but she was already 25 minutes late by the time she and her friends left the restaurant. Sylvia drove the 3 miles home at an average of 30 miles per hour. How long was Sylvia in the restaurant?

The first part of this task is to clear away all the extraneous information to get to the important facts. The means–ends analysis suggests that only time information is relevant, so all the money transactions and the speed of Sylvia's car can be ignored. Careful reading of the problem reveals that Sylvia left the restaurant at 9:25. This and her arrival time of 6:18 are all that matters for solving the problem. Once we know what is relevant and what isn't the solution is easy.

REPRESENTING THE PROBLEM For many kinds of problems, graphical representation might be an effective means of finding a solution. In a classic study, Adams (1974) provides an illustrative story.

> A Buddhist monk has to make a pilgrimage and stay overnight in a temple that is at the top of a high mountain. The road spirals around and around the mountain. The monk begins walking up the mountain at sunrise. He walks all day long and finally reaches the top at about sunset. He stays all night in the temple and performs his devotions. At sunrise the next day the monk begins walking down the mountain. It takes him much less time than walking up, and he is at the bottom shortly after noon. The question is: Is there a point on the road when he was coming down that he passed at the same time of day when he was coming up the mountain?
>
> *Source:* From *Conceptual blockbusting* by J. L. Adams. Published by Freeman, © 1974.

This can seem to be a difficult problem because people begin to reason in a variety of ways as they think about the man going up and down. Adams points out one representation that makes the problem easy: Suppose there were two monks, one leaving the top at sunrise and one starting up at sunrise. Would they meet? Of course they would.

In addition to drawings, there are many other ways of representing problems. Students may be taught to make diagrams, flowcharts, outlines, and other means of summarizing and depicting the critical components of a problem (Jitendra et al., 2009; Van Meter, 2001).

Teaching Creative Problem Solving

Most of the problems that students encounter in school require careful reading and some thought, but little creativity. However, many of the problems we face in life are not so cut-and-dried. Life is full of situations that call for creative problem solving, as in figuring out how to change or end a relationship without hurt feelings or how to repair a machine with a bent paper clip (Plucker, Beghetto, & Dow, 2004). The following strategies can help in teaching creative problem solving (Beghetto & Kaufman, 2013; Drapeau, 2014; Goodwin & Miller, 2013; Hetland, 2013; Senn & Marzano, 2015).

INCUBATION Creative problem solving is quite different from the analytical step-by-step process used to solve Sylvia's problems. In creative problem solving, one important principle is to avoid rushing to a solution; instead, it is useful to pause and reflect on the problem and think through, or incubate, several alternative solutions before choosing a course of action. Consider the following simple problem:

> Roger baked an apple pie in his oven in three-quarters of an hour. How long would it take him to bake three apple pies?

Many students would rush to multiply 45 minutes by 3. However, if they took some time to reflect, most would realize that baking three pies in the same oven would actually take about the same amount of time as baking one pie! In teaching this process, you must avoid putting time pressures on students. Instead of speed, they should value ingenuity and careful thought. A review of research on incubation (setting aside time to reflect on problems) by Sio and Ormerod (2009) found that time for incubation made the most difference on problems with many possible solutions, where creativity was most important.

SUSPENSION OF JUDGMENT In creative problem solving, students should be encouraged to suspend judgment and consider all possibilities before trying out a solution. One specific method based on this principle is called *brainstorming,* in which two or more individuals suggest as many solutions to a problem as they can think of, no matter how seemingly ridiculous. Only after they have thought of as many ideas as possible is any idea evaluated as a possible solution. The point of brainstorming is to avoid focusing on one solution too early and perhaps ignoring better ways to proceed.

APPROPRIATE CLIMATES Creative problem solving is enhanced by a relaxed, even playful environment (Beghetto & Kaufman, 2013; Senn & Marzano, 2015). Perhaps even more important, students who are engaged in creative problem solving must feel that their ideas will be accepted. People who do well on tests of creative problem solving seem to be less afraid of making mistakes and appearing foolish than those who do poorly. Successful problem solvers also seem to treat problem-solving situations more playfully (Drapeau, 2014), which suggests that a relaxed, fun atmosphere is important in the process. Students should certainly be encouraged to try different solutions and should not be criticized for taking a wrong turn.

ANALYSIS One frequently suggested method of creative problem solving is to analyze and juxtapose major characteristics or specific elements of a problem (Chen & Daehler, 2000). For example, careful analysis of the situation might help solve the following problem:

> A tennis tournament was set up with a series of rounds. The winner of each match advanced to the next round. If there were an odd number of players in a round, one player (chosen at random) would advance automatically to the next round. In a tournament with 147 players, how many matches would take place before a single winner would be declared?

We might solve this problem the hard way, making diagrams of the various matches. However, careful analysis of the situation would reveal that each match would produce exactly one loser. Therefore, it would take 146 matches to produce 146 losers (and one winner).

Certification Pointer
Teacher certification tests will require you to know appropriate strategies for engaging students in active learning to promote the development of creative problem-solving skills.

ENGAGING PROBLEMS One key to teaching problem solving is providing problems that intrigue and engage children. The same problem-solving skills can be presented to students in boring contexts or compelling scenarios, and this matters in the outcomes. For example, Bottge (2001) found that low-achieving secondary students, many with serious learning disabilities, could learn complex problem-solving skills related to building a cage for a pet or setting up a car racing track. Since John Dewey proposed it a hundred years ago, the motivational value of connecting problem solving to real life or simulations of real life has been demonstrated many times (Holt & Willard-Holt, 2000; Westwater & Wolfe, 2000). For example, many studies of garden-based learning have shown that situating science, math, and other subjects in real garden contexts enhances achievement (Williams & Dixon, 2013)

FEEDBACK Perhaps the most effective way to teach problem solving is to provide students with a great deal of practice on a wide variety of problem types, giving feedback not only on the correctness of their solutions but also on the process by which they arrived at the solutions (Fisher &

Frey, 2014a). The role of practice with feedback in solving complex problems cannot be overemphasized (Hetland, 2013). Mr. Dunbar's students, in the chapter-opening vignette, could not have arrived at the solution to their problem if they had not had months of practice and feedback on simpler problems.

Teaching Thinking Skills

One of the oldest dreams in education is finding a way to make students smarter—not only more knowledgeable or skillful but actually better able to learn new information of all kinds (Costa, 2008). Perhaps someday someone will come up with a "smart pill" that will have this effect; in the meantime, several groups of researchers have been developing and evaluating instructional programs designed to increase students' general thinking skills. One approach to teaching thinking skills is to incorporate them into daily lessons and classroom experiences—to create a "culture of thinking" (Costa, 2008; Ivey & Fisher, 2006; Ritchhart & Perkins, 2008; Sternberg, 2002; Swartz, 2009). As an example of integrating thinking skills into daily lessons, Tishman and colleagues (1995) describe an impromptu discussion in a class that has been taught a generic strategy for problem solving. Built around the four-step process (state, search, evaluate, and elaborate) summarized in Table 8.1, the strategy provides a framework for Ms. Mandly's sixth-graders to discuss why plants in terrariums that the class planted a month earlier are starting to die and what they might

TABLE 8.1 • Thinking Skills: Build a Strategy

Strategy Building Blocks

WHEN . . .	STRATEGY STEP	TACTICS
When you need to be clear about what you're doing or where you're going . . .	**State** . . . either the problem, the situation, or your goal(s).	• Identify the different dimensions of the situation. • Identify the parts of the situation you will focus on. • State precisely what you want to change or what you want your outcome to be. • Be specific!
When you need to think broadly about something . . .	**Search** . . . for ideas, options, possibilities, purposes, features, assumptions, causes, effects, questions, dimensions, hypotheses, facts, or interpretations.	• Brainstorm. • Look for different kinds of ideas. • Look at things from different points of view. • Look for hidden ideas. • Build on other people's ideas. • Use categories to help you search.
When you need to assess, rate, or decide something . . .	**Evaluate** . . . options, plans, ideas, theories, or objects.	• Look for lots of reasons. • Consider the immediate and long-term consequences. • List all the pros and cons, paying attention to both. • Try to be objective; avoid bias. • Use your imagination: How will it affect others?
When you need to think about the details of something . . .	**Elaborate** . . . possibilities, plans, options, hypotheses, or ideas.	• Make a detailed plan: Say what will happen at each step. • Visualize what it will look/feel/seem like *in detail*. • Ask yourself: What resources will be used? • How will it happen? • Who will be affected? • How long will it take? • Think about the different parts. • Draw a picture or write a description; imagine *telling* someone about it.

Source: Tishman, Shari; Perkins, David N.; Jay, Eileen, *The thinking classroom: Learning and teaching in a culture of thinking*, 1st Edition, © 1995. Reprinted by permission of Pearson Education, Inc., Upper Saddle River, NJ.

do about it. The class has learned the steps shown in Table 8.1 and can refer to a poster identical to it that is posted in the classroom.

> *Ms. Mandly:* Let's take a look at the poster. How can we build a strategy to deal with this situation? Which building blocks can we use?
>
> *Rory:* We should use the search step, to search for a solution to the problem.
>
> *Marc:* Yeah, but we're not even exactly sure what the problem is. We don't know if the plants in the terrarium are wilted because they have too much water or too little.
>
> *Ms. Mandly:* Are you suggesting we also need a state step, Marc?
>
> *Marc (after a moment of looking at the poster):* Yes. In two ways: I think we need to state the problem and we need to state our goal.
>
> *Ms. Mandly:* That sounds reasonable. Any other building blocks we can use?
>
> *Marc:* Yeah, that might not be enough. What if you take care of a terrarium, and it still wilts? Other people in your group will want to know what went wrong.
>
> *Ms. Mandly:* It sounds like we have two goals here. One, decide how to care for the terrarium. And two, make a plan for keeping track of the terrarium's care.

After more discussion, students agree on exactly which outcomes they want and move to the "search" step. Looking at the search tactics, they decided to brainstorm lots of different possible solutions. Ms. Mandly keeps track of their ideas on the blackboard and occasionally reminds them to keep in mind some key tactics: to look for hidden ideas and to look for different kinds of ideas. Among the students' ideas are the following:

1. Have a sign-up list.
2. Let the teacher decide who should water.
3. Have one person volunteer to do it all.
4. Make a rotating schedule for each group.
5. Make a rotating schedule, plus have weekly group meetings to discuss progress.

After students review and evaluate their brainstormed list, they unanimously agree that option 5—a rotating schedule plus weekly meetings—is best.

They then continue to step 4: Elaborate and make a plan. They design a rotating schedule for each terrarium group, and with Ms. Mandly's help they pick a time for weekly group meetings. Working through the "elaborate" step, they invent a detailed checklist for the designated weekly waterer to help track factors that might contribute to the terrarium's health, such as how much water has been given, the date of watering, and the temperature of the classroom (Tishman et al., 1995).

In the course of discussing the terrarium problem, the students are learning a broadly applicable strategy for approaching and solving complex problems. By calling on this and other strategies frequently, as they are appropriate in a classroom context, Ms. Mandly not only gives students useful strategies but also communicates the idea that strategy use is a normal and expected part of daily life.

Critical Thinking

Certification Pointer

When responding to the case studies in certification tests, you may be asked to design a lesson that includes strategies for teaching critical-thinking skills.

One key objective of schooling is enhancing students' abilities to think critically and make rational decisions about what to do or what to believe (Abrami et al., 2014; Bonney & Sternberg, 2011; Marzano et al., 2001). Examples of **critical thinking** include identifying misleading advertisements, weighing competing evidence, and identifying assumptions or fallacies in arguments. As with any other objective, learning to think critically requires practice; students can be given many dilemmas, logical and illogical arguments, valid and misleading advertisements, and so on. Effective teaching of critical thinking depends on setting a classroom tone that encourages the acceptance of divergent perspectives and free discussion (Epstein, 2008). There should be an emphasis on giving reasons for opinions rather than only giving correct answers. Skills in critical thinking are best acquired in relation to topics with which students are familiar. For example, students will learn more from a unit evaluating Nazi propaganda if they know a great deal about the history of Nazi Germany and the culture of the 1930s and 1940s. Perhaps most important, the goal of teaching critical thinking is to create a critical spirit, which encourages students to question what they hear and to examine their own thinking for logical inconsistencies or fallacies.

ON THE WEB

For articles and resources on critical thinking go to criticalthinking.org, the website of the Foundation for Critical Thinking.

MyEdLab **Self-Check 8.3**

THE INTENTIONAL TEACHER

Teaching Using Student-Centered and Constructivist Methods

- Intentional teachers know how to structure activities to enable students to learn using student-centered and constructivist methods.
- They give students frequent opportunities to create and discover new knowledge using projects, discussion, and open-ended experiments.
- They make extensive use of effective forms of cooperative learning, in which students work in small groups to achieve group goals based on the learning of all group members.
- They use specific methods such as reciprocal teaching, writing process, and inquiry in math and science to transfer responsibility for learning from themselves to their students.
- They teach problem-solving skills that are broadly applicable in their subject.
- They teach critical-thinking skills to help students approach various sources with an appropriate balance of openness and skepticism.

MyEdLab
Application Exercise 8.1

In the Pearson etext, watch a classroom video. Then use the guidelines in "The Intentional Teacher" to answer a set of questions that will help you reflect on and understand the teaching and learning presented in the video.

SUMMARY

What Is the Constructivist View of Learning?

Constructivists believe that knowing is a process and that learners must individually and actively discover and transform complex information to make it their own. Constructivist approaches emphasize top-down processing, in which students begin with complex problems or tasks and discover the basic knowledge and skills needed to solve the problems or perform the tasks. Constructivist approaches also emphasize cooperative learning, questioning or inquiry strategies, and other metacognitive skills.

Discovery learning and scaffolding are constructivist learning methods based on cognitive learning theories. Bruner's discovery learning highlights students' active self-learning, curiosity, and creative problem solving. Scaffolding, based on Vygotsky's views, calls for teachers to assist students at critical points in their learning.

How Is Cooperative Learning Used in Instruction?

In cooperative learning, small groups of students work together to help one another learn. Cooperative learning groups are used in discovery learning, discussion, and study for assessment. Cooperative learning programs such as Student Teams–Achievement Divisions (STAD) are successful because they reward both group and individual effort and improvement, and because groups are responsible for the individual learning of each group member.

How Are Problem-Solving and Thinking Skills Taught?

Problem-solving skills are taught through a series of steps, including, for example, means–ends analysis and problem representation. Creative problem solving requires incubation time, suspension of judgment, conducive climates, problem analysis, the application of thinking skills, and feedback. Thinking skills include, for example, planning, classifying, divergent thinking, identifying assumptions, recognizing misleading information, and generating questions. Thinking skills can be taught through structured programs; creating a culture of thinking in the classroom is another useful technique.

KEY TERMS

Review the following key terms from the chapter.

cognitive apprenticeship 189

constructivist theories of learning 188

Cooperative Integrated Reading and
  Composition (CIRC) 199

cooperative learning 198

cooperative scripting 201

critical thinking 208

discovery learning 190

Jigsaw 201

Learning Together 201

means–ends analysis 205

mediated learning 192

peer-assisted learning strategies
  (PALS) 201

problem solving 204

project-based learning 202

reciprocal teaching 193

self-regulated learners 192

Student Teams–Achievement Divisions
  (STAD) 198

SELF-ASSESSMENT: PRACTICING FOR LICENSURE

Directions: The chapter-opening vignette addresses indicators that are often assessed in state licensure exams. Reread the chapter-opening vignette, and then respond to the following questions.

1. Mr. Dunbar, in his lesson on the volume of a cylinder, asks his students to figure out how to measure volume through experimentation. What type of learning strategy is he using?
   a. Direct instruction
   b. Classical conditioning
   c. Discovery learning
   d. Teacher-mediated discussion

2. Why didn't Mr. Dunbar just tell his students that the formula for finding the volume of a cylinder is r^2h?
   a. He believes that students will gain deeper understanding if they work it out for themselves.
   b. He thought the lesson would take less time if the students could figure it out.

   c. He knows that discovery learning is superior to direct instruction.

   d. He is applying teaching strategies suggested by B. F. Skinner and other behaviorists.

3. In which of the following examples is Mr. Dunbar demonstrating Vygotsky's "zone of proximal development" concept?

   a. Mr. Dunbar says, "Today we are going to have a chance to discover how to compute the volume of a cylinder."

   b. Mr. Dunbar assigns his students to sit around the lab tables in groups of four.

   c. Mr. Dunbar, as he is passing by the Master Minds group, says, "You're right, Miguel, but what are you going to do with that information?"

   d. Mr. Dunbar praises the Master Minds group for figuring out the answer on its own.

4. Mr. Dunbar effectively uses cooperative learning strategies in his lesson on the volume of cylinders. He does all of the following except

   a. give recognition to the groups when they solve the problem.

   b. ensure that each group contains members who have similar abilities.

   c. make certain that each group member learns.

   d. mixes students in terms of race, ethnicity, gender, and special needs.

5. Which of the following cooperative learning strategies is Mr. Dunbar using?

   a. Project-based learning

   b. Learning Together

   c. Jigsaw

   d. STAD

6. Describe an example of discovery learning. What is the teacher's role in a discovery lesson? What strengths and limitations are found in discovery learning?

7. How can teachers improve students' problem-solving abilities?

MyEdLab **Licensure Exam 8.1** Answer questions and receive instant feedback in your Pearson eText in MyEdLab.

Vicki Kerr/UpperCut Images/Getty Images

CHAPTER NINE

Grouping, Differentiation, and Technology

LEARNING OUTCOMES

At the end of this chapter, you should be able to:

9.1 Describe different types of grouping used to accommodate achievement differences

9.2 List several ways to differentiate instruction for diverse learners

9.3 Identify types of programs for students placed at risk of academic difficulties

9.4 Describe how technology can be used effectively in education

9.5 Describe how grouping, differentiation, and technology influence intentional teaching

Mr. Arbuthnot is in fine form. He is presenting a lesson on long division to his fourth-grade class and feels that he's never been so clear, so interesting, and so well organized. When he asks questions, several students raise their hands; when he calls on them, they always know the answers. "Arbuthnot, old boy," he says to himself, "I think you're really getting to these kids!"

At the end of the period he passes out a short quiz to see how well his students have learned the long-division lesson. When the papers are scored, he finds, to his shock and disappointment, that only about a third of the class got every problem right. Another third missed every problem; the remaining students fell somewhere in between. "What went wrong?" he thinks. "Well, no matter, I'll set the situation right in tomorrow's lesson."

The next day, Mr. Arbuthnot is even better prepared, uses vivid examples and diagrams to show how to do long division, and gives an active, exciting lesson. He uses an interactive whiteboard to illustrate the key concepts. Even more hands than before go up when he asks questions, and the answers are usually correct. However, some of the students are beginning to look bored, particularly those who got perfect papers on the quiz and those who got none right.

Toward the end of the period, he gives another brief quiz. The scores are better this time, but there is still a group of students who got none of the problems correct. He is crestfallen. "I had them in the palm of my hand," he thinks. "How could they fail to learn?"

To try to find out what went wrong, Mr. Arbuthnot goes over the quiz papers of the students who missed all the problems. He immediately sees a pattern. By the second lesson, almost all students were proceeding correctly in setting up the long-division problems. However, some were making consistent errors in subtraction. Others had apparently forgotten their multiplication facts. Their problems were not with division at all; the students simply lacked the prerequisite skills.

"Well," thinks Mr. Arbuthnot, "at least I was doing great with some of the kids." It occurs to him that one of the students who got a perfect paper after the first lesson might be able to give him some idea how to teach the others better. He asks Teresa how she grasped long division so quickly.

"It was easy, "she says. "We learned long division last year!"

USING YOUR EXPERIENCE

CRITICAL THINKING List all of the ways in which Mr. Arbuthnot could be more effective in addressing student individual differences. Then list all of the ways in which he is effective in addressing student needs.

COOPERATIVE LEARNING Work with a group of four or five classmates. Pass a sheet of paper around the group, and ask each member to write down an idea to help Mr. Arbuthnot become more effective in addressing students' needs. After one idea is added, the sheet is passed to the next person in the group, who adds an idea and passes the sheet along, and so on. Share some of these ideas with the class.

WHAT ARE ELEMENTS OF EFFECTIVE INSTRUCTION BEYOND A GOOD LESSON?

InTASC 2

Learning Differences

InTASC 3

Learning Environments

InTASC 5

Application of Content

InTASC 7

Planning for Instruction

InTASC 8

Instructional Strategies

As Mr. Arbuthnot learned to his chagrin, effective instruction takes a lot more than good lectures. He gave a great lesson on long division, yet it was appropriate for only some of the students: those who had the needed prerequisites but had not already learned long division. To make his lesson effective for all of the students, he needed to adapt it to meet their diverse needs. Furthermore, the best lesson in the world won't work if students are not motivated to learn it or if inadequate time is allotted to enable all students to learn.

If high-quality lectures were all that mattered in effective instruction, we could probably just find the best lecturers in the world, record their lessons, and show the videos to students. But if you think about why video lessons would not work very well by themselves, you will realize how much more is involved in effective instruction than simply giving good lectures. First, the video teacher would have no idea what students already knew. A particular lesson might be too advanced or too easy for a particular group of students. Second, some students might be learning the lesson quite well, whereas others would be missing key concepts and falling behind. The video teacher would have no way of knowing which students needed additional help and, in any case, would have no way of providing it. There would be no way to question students to find out whether they were getting the main points and then to reteach any concept they had missed. Third, the video teacher would have no way of motivating students to pay attention to the lesson or to really try to learn it. If students failed to pay attention or misbehaved, the video teacher could not do anything about it. Finally, the video teacher would never know, at the end of a lesson, whether students had actually learned the main concepts or skills.

This analysis of video teaching illustrates why you must be concerned with many elements of instruction in addition to the presentation of information. You must know how to adapt your instruction to the students' levels of knowledge. You must motivate students to learn, manage student behavior, group students for instruction, and assess the students' learning.

To help make sense of all these elements of effective instruction, educational psychologists have proposed models of effective instruction. These models explain the critical features of high-quality lessons and how they interact to enhance learning.

Carroll's Model of School Learning and QAIT

One of the most influential articles ever published in the field of educational psychology was a paper by John Carroll titled "A Model of School Learning" (1963, 1989). In it, he describes teaching in terms of the management of time, resources, and activities to ensure student learning. Carroll proposes that learning is a function of (1) time actually spent on learning and (2) time needed to learn. Time needed is a product of aptitude, prior knowledge, and ability to learn; time spent depends on clock time available for learning, quality of instruction, and student perseverance.

Slavin (1995b) described a model focusing on the alterable elements of Carroll's model, those that the teacher or school can directly change. It is called the **QAIT model**, for quality, appropriateness, incentive, and time.

1. *Quality of instruction.* The degree to which the presentation of information or skills helps students easily learn the material. Quality of instruction is largely a product of the quality of the curriculum and of lesson presentation.

2. *Appropriate levels of instruction.* The degree to which the teacher makes sure that students are ready to learn a new lesson (that is, have the necessary skills and knowledge to learn it) but have not already learned the lesson. In other words, the level of instruction is appropriate when a lesson is neither too difficult nor too easy for students.

3. *Incentive.* The degree to which the teacher makes sure that students are motivated to work on instructional tasks and to learn the material being presented.

4. *Time.* The degree to which students are given enough time to learn the material being taught.

For instruction to be effective, each of these four elements must be adequate. No matter how high the quality of instruction, students will not learn a lesson if they lack the necessary prior

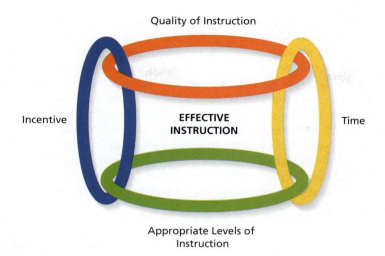

FIGURE 9.1 • The QAIT Model

Each of the elements of the QAIT model is like a link in a chain, and the chain is only as strong as the weakest link.

skills or information, if they lack the motivation, or if they lack the time they need to learn the lesson. However, if the quality of instruction is low, then it makes no difference how much students already know, how motivated they are, or how much time they have. Figure 9.1 illustrates the relationships among the elements in the QAIT model.

QUALITY OF INSTRUCTION Quality of instruction refers to the set of activities most people first picture when they think of teaching: lecturing, calling on students, discussing, helping students with seatwork, and so on. Involving peers as peer tutors or cooperative learning partners may add to quality of instruction. Technology (such as videos, computer graphics, interactive whiteboards, or other digital content) may contribute to the quality of instruction, as can hands-on experiences, laboratory exercises, or computer simulations. When instruction is high in quality, the information presented makes sense to students, interests them, and is easy to remember and apply.

The most important aspect of quality of instruction is the degree to which the lesson makes sense to students, which you ensure by presenting material in an orderly, organized way. You need to relate new information to what students already know. You need to use examples, demonstrations, pictures, and diagrams to make ideas vivid for students. You might use such cognitive strategies as advance organizers and memory strategies. Sometimes a concept will not make sense to students until they discover it or experience it themselves or until they discuss it with others. Engaging students with the content, through cooperative activities, creation of new products, simulations, games, or technology, can help make lesson concepts understandable and memorable for students.

APPROPRIATE LEVELS OF INSTRUCTION Perhaps the most difficult problem of classroom organization is the fact that students come into class with different levels of prior knowledge, skills, and motivation, as well as with different learning rates (Tomlinson, 2008). This was Mr. Arbuthnot's main dilemma. Student diversity requires teachers to provide appropriate levels of instruction. Teaching a class of 30 students (or even a class of 10) is fundamentally different from one-to-one tutoring because of the inevitability of differences among students that affect the success of instruction. You can always be sure that if you teach one lesson to the whole class, some students will learn the material much more quickly than others. In fact, some students might not learn the lesson at all; they might lack important prerequisite skills or adequate time (because to give them enough time would waste too much of the time of students who learn rapidly). Recognition of these instructionally important differences leads many teachers to search for ways of individualizing or differentiating instruction, adapting instruction to meet students' different needs, or grouping students according to their abilities. Some of the solutions typically used to accommodate individual differences in learning rates create problems of their own that could be more serious than the ones they are meant to solve (Willingham & Daniel, 2012). For example, you might give all students materials appropriate to their individual needs and allow students to work at their own rates, perhaps using computer-assisted instructional software designed for this purpose. This solves the problem of providing appropriate levels of instruction, but it creates serious new problems of managing the activities of 20 or 30 students doing 20 or 30 different things. Alternatively, you might group students within a relatively narrow range of abilities (e.g., Redbirds, Bluebirds, and Yellowbirds). However, this creates problems, too, because when you are working with the Redbirds, the Bluebirds and Yellowbirds must work without supervision or help, and students in the low groups may feel stigmatized and may lack positive behavioral models.

Adapting to individual needs may require adjusting the pace of instruction so that it is neither too fast nor too slow. For example, you should ask questions frequently to determine how much students have grasped. If the answers show that students are keeping up with the lesson, you might move along a little more rapidly. But if students' answers show that they are having trouble keeping up, you might review parts of the lesson and slow down the pace, or provide additional instruction at another time for students who are not keeping up.

INCENTIVE Thomas Edison wrote that "genius is one per cent inspiration and ninety-nine per cent perspiration." The same could probably be said of learning. Learning is work. This is not to say that learning isn't or can't be fun or stimulating—far from it. But it is true that students must exert themselves to pay attention, to conscientiously perform the tasks required of them, and to study; moreover, students must somehow be motivated to do these things. This incentive, or motivation, might come from characteristics of the tasks themselves (e.g., the interest value of the material being learned), from characteristics of students (such as their curiosity or positive orientation toward learning), or from rewards provided by the teacher or the school (such as praise, recognition, grades, or certificates).

If students want to know something, they will be motivated to exert the effort necessary to learn it. This is why there are students who can rattle off the names, batting averages, number of home runs, and all sorts of other information about every player of the Chicago Cubs but know little about science or history or math. To such students, baseball facts are of great interest, so they are willing to invest substantial effort to master them. Some information is naturally interesting to some or all students, but you can do much to create interest in a topic by arousing students' curiosity or by showing how knowledge gained in school can be useful outside of school. For example, baseball fans might be much more interested in learning about understanding proportions if they realized that this information is necessary for computing batting averages.

However, not every subject can be made fascinating to all students at all times. Most students need some kind of recognition or reward if they are to exert maximum effort to learn skills or concepts that might seem unimportant at the moment but will be critical for later learning. For this reason, schools use praise, feedback, grades, certificates, stars, prizes, access to fun activities, and other rewards to increase student motivation.

TIME The final element of the QAIT model is time. Instruction takes time. More time spent teaching something does not necessarily mean more learning; but if instructional quality, appropriateness of instruction, and incentive are all high, then spending more time on instruction will pay off in greater learning. The amount of time available for learning depends largely on two factors. The first is *allocated time*, the amount of time that you schedule for instruction and then actually use to teach. The other is *engaged time*, the amount of time students pay attention to the lesson. Both kinds of time are affected by classroom management and discipline strategies. If students are well behaved, are well motivated, and have a sense of purpose and direction, and if you are well prepared and well organized, then there is plenty of time for students to learn whatever you want to teach. However, many factors, such as interruptions, behavior problems, and poor transitions between activities, eat away at the time available for learning.

HOW ARE STUDENTS GROUPED TO ACCOMMODATE ACHIEVEMENT DIFFERENCES?

From the day they walk into school, students differ in their knowledge, skills, motivations, and predispositions toward what is about to be taught. Some students are already reading when they enter kindergarten; others need much time and support to learn to read well. When starting a new lesson, you can usually assume that some students already know a great deal about the lesson's

Connections 9.1
The rewards and general principles of motivation are discussed throughout Chapter 10.

Connections 9.2
Principles of classroom management and discipline are discussed throughout Chapter 11.

InTASC 2
Learning Differences

content, some know less but will master the content readily, and some might not be able to master the content at all within the time provided. Some have the prerequisite skills and knowledge to learn the lesson, whereas others do not. This was Mr. Arbuthnot's problem: Some of his students were not ready to learn long division, whereas others had already learned it before he began. Some of his students lacked the basic multiplication and subtraction skills crucial for long division. Others learned it during the first lesson and did not need the second. If Mr. Arbuthnot stopped to review multiplication and division, he would be wasting the time of the better-prepared students. If he set his pace of instruction according to the needs of his more able students, those with learning problems might never catch up. How can Mr. Arbuthnot teach a lesson that will work for all of his students, who are performing within the normal range but differ in prior knowledge, skills, and learning rates?

Accommodating instruction to student differences, or *heterogeneity*, is one of the most fundamental problems of education and often leads to politically and emotionally charged policies (Atkins & Ellsesser, 2003). One solution, which some advocate, is simply to retain more children in a grade until they meet grade-level requirements. Many states, for example, are now requiring that children who are not reading at grade level by third grade be required to repeat the grade (Robelen, 2012). Some countries outside of North America attempt to deal with the problem of student differences by testing children at around 10 to 12 years of age and assigning them to different types of schools, only one of which is meant to prepare students for higher education. In the United States, a similar function is sometimes carried out by assignment of secondary students to college preparatory, general, and vocational tracks, in which students are assigned to a specified curriculum sequence within which they take all their academic courses. This **tracking** rapidly diminished in the 1980s and 1990s, but instead, most secondary schools place students in ability-grouped classes by subject area. In theory, a student may be in a high-level math class but in a middle- or low-level English class (Lucas & Gamoran, 2002). Many secondary schools allow students, in consultation with counselors, to choose the level of each class, perhaps changing levels if a course turns out to be too difficult or too easy. All of these strategies, which result in students' attending classes that are more or less homogeneous in performance level, are forms of **between-class ability grouping**. The predominant form of ability grouping in middle, junior high, and high schools, it is also sometimes used in elementary schools.

Another common means of accommodating instruction to student differences in elementary schools is **within-class ability grouping**, as in the use of reading groups (Bluebirds, Redbirds, Yellowbirds) that divide students according to their reading performance. The problem of accommodating student differences is so important that many educators have suggested completely individualized instruction so that students can work at their own rates, which has led to the creation of individualized computer-assisted instructional programs.

Each of the many ways of accommodating differences among students has its own benefits, but each introduces its own problems, which sometimes outweigh the benefits. Some student differences can be easily accommodated (Jackson & Lambert, 2010; Pollock, Ford, & Black, 2012; Tomlinson, 2014). For example, you can support different learning styles by augmenting oral presentations with visual cues—perhaps writing on a whiteboard or showing pictures and diagrams to emphasize important concepts (Mayer, 2008a). You can accommodate other differences in learning styles by varying classroom activities, as in alternating active and quiet tasks or individual and group work. You can sometimes work with students on an individual basis and adapt instruction to their learning needs—for example, by reminding impulsive students to take their time or by teaching overly reflective students strategies for skipping problematic items so that they can complete tests on time.

Differences in prior knowledge and learning rates are more difficult to deal with. Sometimes the best way to deal with these differences is to ignore them and teach the whole class at a single pace, perhaps offering additional help to low-achieving students and giving extra extension or enrichment activities to students who tend to finish assignments rapidly (see Guskey, 2011; Tomlinson, 2014). You can consciously vary the examples and questions used to accommodate a range of students in each lesson (Small, 2010). You can let students who do poorly on tests or other assignments redo them until they achieve adequate performance (Wormeli, 2011). Appropriate use of cooperative learning methods, in which students of different performance levels help each other,

Connections 9.3
To learn more about student differences in general intelligence, specific aptitudes, and abilities and learning styles, see Chapter 4.

can be an effective means of helping all children learn (Cohen & Lotan, 2014; Slavin, 2013; Webb, 2008). Some subjects lend themselves more than others to a single pace of instruction for all. For example, it is probably less important to accommodate student achievement differences in social studies, science, and English than in mathematics, reading, and foreign languages. In the latter subjects, skills build directly on one another, so teaching a heterogeneous class at one set pace might do a disservice to both low and high achievers; low achievers might fail because they lack prerequisite skills, and high achievers might become bored at what is for them a slow pace of instruction.

Between-Class Ability Grouping

Connections 9.4
Programs for students who are gifted and those who have special needs are discussed in Chapter 12.

Probably the most common means of dealing with instructionally important differences is to assign students to classes according to their abilities. This between-class ability grouping can take many forms. In most middle and high schools, students are grouped separately by ability for each subject, so a student might be in a high-performing math class and an average-performing science class. In high schools, between-class ability grouping may be accomplished by course placements. For example, some seventh, eighth, and ninth graders take Algebra I, whereas others who do not qualify for Algebra I take general mathematics. Elementary schools use a wide range of strategies for grouping students, including many of the patterns found in secondary schools. Often, students in elementary schools are assigned to a mixed-ability class for homeroom, social studies, and science but regrouped by ability for reading and math (Lucas & Gamoran, 2002). Elementary schools are less likely than secondary schools to use ability grouping between classes but more likely to use ability grouping within classes, especially in reading (Chorzempa & Graham, 2006). At any level, however, the establishment of separate special-education programs for students with serious learning problems is one common form of between-class ability grouping, as is provision of separate programs for students who are academically gifted and talented.

Certification Pointer
For teacher certification tests, you may be asked to describe the strengths and weaknesses of between-class ability grouping. You should know that research does not support most forms of between-class ability grouping.

RESEARCH ON BETWEEN-CLASS ABILITY GROUPING Despite the widespread use of between-class ability grouping, research on this strategy does not support its use. Researchers have found that although ability grouping might have slight benefits for students assigned to high-track classes, these benefits are balanced by losses for students in low-track classes (Ireson & Hallam, 2001; Oakes, 2005; Slavin, 1987b, 1990).

ON THE WEB

The National Association for Gifted Children's position statement on ability grouping can be found at nagc.org. Also see NEA's Research Spotlight on Academic Ability Grouping (nea.org).

Why is between-class ability grouping so ineffective? Several researchers have explored this question. The primary purpose of ability grouping is to reduce the range of student performance levels that teachers must deal with so they can adapt instruction to the needs of a well-defined group. However, grouping is often done on the basis of standardized test scores or other measures of general ability, rather than according to performance in a particular subject. As a result, the reduction in the range of differences that are actually important for a specific class may be too small to make much difference (Oakes, 2005). Furthermore, concentrating low-achieving students in low-track classes seems to be harmful because it exposes them to too few positive role models. Many teachers do not like to teach such classes and might subtly (or not so subtly) communicate low expectations for students in them (Weinstein, 1996). Studies find that teachers actually do not make many adaptations to the needs of students in low-ability groups (Ross, Smith, Lohr, & McNelis, 1994). Several studies have found that the quality of instruction is lower in low-track classes than in middle- or high-track classes. For example, teachers of low-track classes are less enthusiastic and less well organized, teaching more facts and fewer concepts than teachers of high-track classes (Gamoran, Nystrand, Berends, & LePore, 1995; Oakes, 2005; Raudenbush, Rowan, & Cheong, 1993). Low-track classes are more likely to have novice teachers (Kalogrides & Loeb, 2013). Instruction in untracked mixed-ability classes more closely resembles teaching in high- and middle-track classes than that in low-track classes.

Perhaps the most damaging effect of tracking is its stigmatizing effect on students who are assigned to the low tracks; the message these students get is that academic success is not within their reach (Oakes, 2005). Students in lower-track classes are far more likely to become delinquent and truant and to drop out of school than are students of similar ability in middle-track or mixed placements (Oakes, 2005). Although these problems certainly exist in part because students in low-track classes are low in academic performance to begin with, this cannot be the whole story. For example, students who are assigned to the low track in middle or junior high school experience a rapid loss of self-esteem. Slavin and Karweit (1982) found that fifth- and sixth-graders in urban elementary schools were absent about 8 percent of the time. When these same students entered the tracked junior high school, absenteeism rose almost immediately to 26 percent, and the truancy was concentrated among students assigned to the bottom-track classes. The change happened too rapidly to be attributed entirely to characteristics of students. Something about the organization of the junior high school apparently convinced a substantial number of students that school was no longer a rewarding place to be.

One of the most insidious aspects of tracking is that low-track classes are often composed predominantly of students from lower socioeconomic backgrounds and from minority groups, whereas upper-track classes are more often composed of children from higher socioeconomic levels (Kalogrides & Loeb, 2013). A study by Yonezawa, Wells, and Serna (2002) found that even in high schools where students were theoretically given a "free choice" of academic levels, African American and Latino students disproportionately ended up in low-level classes. The creation of groupings that are so often associated with social class and race is impossible to justify in light of the lack of evidence that such groupings are educationally necessary.

Although individual teachers can rarely set policies on between-class ability grouping, it is useful for you to know that research does not support this practice at any grade level, and tracking should be avoided whenever possible. This does not mean that all forms of between-class grouping should be abandoned, however. For example, there is probably some justification for acceleration programs, such as offering Algebra I to mathematically talented seventh-graders or providing advanced placement or college classes in high school (see Chapter 12). Also, some between-class grouping is bound to occur in secondary schools, because some students choose to take advanced courses and others do not. However, the idea that having high, middle, and low sections of the same course enhances student achievement has not been supported by research. Mixed-ability classes can be successful at all grade levels, particularly if other, more effective means of accommodating student differences are used, such as within-class ability grouping, tutoring or other extra help for low achievers, and cooperative learning strategies, in which students work in mixed-ability groups.

Connections 9.5
Cooperative learning strategies are described in Chapter 8.

Untracking

For many years, educators and researchers have challenged between-class ability grouping at all levels. A number of guides to untracking and examples of successful untracking have been published (e.g., Burris, Heubert, & Levin, 2004; Fahey, 2000; Kugler & Albright, 2005; Oakes, Quartz, Ryan, & Lipton, 2000). Untracking recommendations focus on placing students in mixed-ability groups and holding them to high standards but providing many ways for them to reach those standards, including extra assistance for students who are having difficulty keeping up (Burris, Heubert, & Levin, 2006; Hubbard & Mehan, 1998). Appropriate forms of cooperative learning and project-based approaches have often been recommended as a means of opening up more avenues to high performance for all children (Slavin, 2013). Yet the road to untracking is far from easy, especially in middle and high schools (Cooper, 1998; Oakes et al., 2000; Rubin, 2003). In particular, untracking often runs into serious opposition from the parents of high achievers. Oakes and colleagues (2000) and Wells, Hirshberg, Lipton, and Oakes (1995) have pointed out that untracking requires changes in thinking about children's potentials, not only changes in school or classroom practices. Teachers, parents, and students themselves, these researchers claim, must come to see the goal of schooling as success for every child, not as sorting students into categories, if untracking is to take hold (Oakes et al., 2000). This change in perception is difficult to bring about; perhaps as a result, the move toward untracking is proceeding slowly at the secondary level (Hallinan, 2004).

Connections 9.6
Various forms of cooperative and project-based learning are described in Chapter 8.

Regrouping for Reading and Mathematics

Regrouping is a form of ability grouping often used in the elementary grades. In regrouping plans, students stay in mixed-ability classes most of the day but are assigned to reading and/or math classes on the basis of their performance in these subjects. For example, at 9:30 a.m. the fourth-graders in a school may move to different teachers so that they can receive reading instruction appropriate to their reading levels. One form of regrouping for reading, the **Joplin Plan**, regroups students across grade lines. For example, a reading class at the fourth grade, first semester reading level may contain third-, fourth-, and fifth-graders.

One major advantage of regrouping over all-day ability grouping is that students spend most of the day in a mixed-ability class. Thus, low achievers are not separated out as a class and potentially stigmatized. Perhaps for these reasons, regrouping plans, especially the Joplin Plan, have generally been found to increase student achievement (Gutiérrez & Slavin, 1992; Slavin, 1987b).

Within-Class Ability Grouping

Another way to adapt instruction to differences in student performance levels is to group students within classes, as is typical in elementary school reading classes. For example, a third-grade teacher might have the Rockets group using a 3–1 (third-grade, first-semester) text, the Stars group using a 3–2 (third-grade, second-semester) text, and the Planets group using a 4–1 (fourth-grade, first-semester) text.

Within-class ability grouping is very common in elementary reading classes (Chorzempa & Graham, 2006). Within-class ability grouping is rare in subjects other than reading or mathematics. In reading, teachers typically have each group working at a different point in a series of texts and allow each group to proceed at its own pace. In many math classes the teacher presents a lesson to the whole class and then meets with two or more ability groups, while other students are doing seatwork, to reinforce skills or provide enrichment as needed. In a strategy called mastery learning, teachers assemble a group for additional instruction after they have given a lesson, formatively assessed students, and identified those who are not meeting a mastery standard (typically, 80 percent correct) (Guskey, 2010). After "corrective instruction," teachers test again, hoping students will meet the mastery standards.

Certification Pointer

You may be asked on your teacher certification test to describe a technique for grouping students within a reading class to meet a wide range of student reading abilities.

RESEARCH ON WITHIN-CLASS ABILITY GROUPING Research on the achievement effects of within-class ability grouping has taken place largely in elementary mathematics classes. Most such studies have found that students in the ability-grouped classes learned more than students in classes without grouping (Slavin, 1987b). Students of high, average, and low achievement levels seem to benefit equally from within-class ability grouping. One study by Mason and Good (1993) found that teachers who flexibly grouped and regrouped students according to their needs had better math achievement outcomes than those who used permanent within-class groups. Surprisingly, there is little research on the effectiveness of reading groups, and that which does exist shows few benefits (Nomi, 2010).

The research suggests that small numbers of ability groups are better than large numbers (Slavin & Karweit, 1984). A smaller number of groups has the advantage of allowing more direct instruction from the teacher and using less seatwork time and transition time. With only three groups, seatwork time rises to at least two-thirds of class time. Teachers who try to teach more than three reading or math groups might also have problems with classroom management. Dividing the class into more than three groups does not decrease the magnitude or range of differences within each group enough to offset these problems (see Hiebert, 1983).

One interesting study by Chmielewski, Dumont, & Trautwein (2013) found that whereas top-track students had higher self-concepts than low-track students, the opposite was the case in within-class grouping, suggesting that within-class grouping does not have the stigmatization effect often seen in between-class grouping.

The main point to be drawn from research on within-class ability grouping is not that it is desirable but that if some form of grouping is thought to be necessary, grouping within the class is preferable to grouping between classes.

Retention

One of the most controversial issues in education is whether low-achieving students should be required to repeat grades. Approximately 3.5 percent of U.S. first-graders were retained in 2008–2009, and then 1 percent to 2 percent in each of grades 2 through 8 (Warren & Saliba, 2012). This means that about 14 percent of students are retained at some point before high school (Warren, Hoffman, & Andrew, 2014). Several states have recently passed highly controversial laws that require third-graders who are not reading at grade level to repeat a grade (Robelen, 2012), and this may be increasing retention rates in those states.

Proponents of holding back low-achieving students argue that this gives such students a "gift of time" to catch up and sets clear standards that they must strive to achieve. Students being considered for retention are usually given the opportunity to catch up in summer school or to receive other assistance leading to promotion, and it may be that the threat of retention brings many students into such services (March, Gershwin, Kirby, & Xia, 2009; McCombs, Kirby, & Mariano, 2009). Opponents note that students who are held back lose motivation; in fact, having been retained is one of the strongest predictors of dropping out (Allensworth, 2005; Jimerson, Anderson, & Whipple, 2002). Retention is disproportionately high among male students who are members of minority groups and/or come from disadvantaged homes (Beebe-Frankenberger, Bocian, MacMillan, & Gresham, 2004; Robelen, Adams, & Shah, 2012). There are also serious questions about whether tests used in many retention decisions are sufficiently reliable and valid (Penfield, 2010).

Is retention beneficial or harmful? In the short term, holding students back usually increases scores in a given school or district, not because students are learning more but because they are older when they take the test. For this reason, states and districts often report "dramatic gains" on state tests right after instituting a new policy of holding students back unless they meet a given test standard (Bali, Anagnostopoulos, & Roberts, 2005; McGill-Franzen, & Allington, 2006). In long-term studies, however, students who were retained typically end up learning less, or certainly no more, than similar low achievers of the same age who were not retained (Allensworth & Nagaoka, 2010; Burkam, Logerfo, Ready, & Lee, 2007; Hong & Raudenbush, 2005; Hong & Yu, 2007; Hughes, Kwock, & Im, 2013; Roderick & Nagaoka, 2005). The advantage that retained students initially have over their younger classmates tends to fade away within a few years (Allen, Chen, Willson, & Hughes, 2009; Moser, West, & Hughes, 2012).

The best solutions to the problems of low-achieving students involve neither retention nor "social promotion" (promoting students without regard to their levels of achievement). Instead, such children should be given special attention, diagnosis, and intensive interventions, such as tutoring, until their achievement falls within the normal range (Benson, 2014; Vaughn, Bos, & Schumm, 2014). An extra year of education is a very expensive intervention—for that amount of money, students can be given much more effective assistance (Reeves, 2006; Slavin, Lake, Davis, & Madden, 2011).

MyEdLab **Self-Check 9.1**

MyEdLab **Video Analysis Tool 9.1** Go to MyEdLab and click on the Video Analysis Tool to access the exercise "Differentiated instruction: grouping."

WHAT ARE SOME WAYS OF DIFFERENTIATING INSTRUCTION?

InTASC 2

Learning Differences

As alternatives to ability grouping, many proven strategies exist to improve the achievement of struggling students. This gets directly to the main problem that grouping is intended to solve. The array of proven approaches is particularly broad in reading, where many quite different approaches are known to be effective with struggling readers (Connor, Alberto, Compton, & O'Connor, 2014; Galuschka, Ise, Kreick & Schulte-Körne, 2014; Slavin, Lake, Davis, & Madden, 2011; Wanzek et al., 2013).

InTASC 8

Instructional Strategies

The problem of providing all students with appropriate levels of instruction could be completely solved if schools simply assigned each student his or her own teacher. Not surprisingly, studies of one-adult–one-student tutoring find substantial positive effects of tutoring on student achievement (Slavin, Lake, Davis, & Madden, 2011). One major reason for the effectiveness of tutoring is that the tutor can provide **differentiated instruction**, tailoring instruction precisely to a student's needs. If the student learns quickly, the tutor can move to other tasks; if not, the tutor can figure out what the problem is, try another explanation, or simply spend more time on the task.

There are situations in which tutoring by adults is feasible and necessary. Cross-age peer tutors (older students working with younger ones) can also be very effective (Thurston et al., 2012). In addition, educational innovators have long tried to simulate the one-to-one teaching situation by individualizing instruction. Teachers have found a variety of ways to informally accommodate the needs of different learners in heterogeneous classrooms (Tomlinson, 2014b; Tomlinson & Moon, 2013). Individualized instruction methods, in which students work at their own level and pace, were popular in the 1960s and 1970s, and this type of instruction continues in many forms of computer-based instruction. Differentiation strategies are discussed in the following sections.

Differentiated and Personalized Instruction

Differentiated instruction (Doubet & Hockett, 2015; Parsons, Dodman, & Burrowbridge, 2013; Silver, Jackson, & Moirao, 2011; Tomlinson, 2014b; Tomlinson & Moon, 2013) adapts the content, level, pace, and products of instruction to accommodate the different needs of diverse students in regular classes. The philosophy behind differentiated instruction emphasizes that all children can reach high standards, but some may need tailored assistance to do so. Recently, the related term *personalized instruction* has been widely used. It adds an emphasis on adapting to students' interests, values, and circumstances (Dobbertin, 2012; Powell & Kusuma-Powell, 2012; Richardson, 2012; Wolk, 2010). Computers are frequently central to personalized or differentiated instruction, as they can provide the same learning content in many ways and at many levels, and can help teachers keep track of all students' progress (Grant & Basye, 2014; Gura, 2016).

For an example of personalization, you might ask a diverse class to write a biography of Gandhi but to provide materials on Gandhi at different reading levels. Or you might create a common math test for a heterogeneous class but include a few "challenge questions" for students with stronger preparation in math. During seatwork, you might focus on students known to have difficulties with prerequisite skills or provide them preteaching on those skills before class; for example, before a unit on decimals, you might arrange an extra session to review fractions with students who are not solid with the fraction concepts central to decimals.

Part of the idea of differentiation is that even though all students need to reach the same goals, some will take more time and others less time to do so. Differentiated classes may give students opportunities to redo projects on which they have done poorly, rather than just receive low grades (Guskey, 2011; Tomlinson & Moon, 2013; Wormeli, 2011).

Differentiation and personalization are increasingly being provided by means of digital devices. This topic is discussed further later in this chapter .

Peer Tutoring

InTASC 3

Learning Environments

Students can help one another learn. In **peer tutoring**, one student teaches another. There are two principal types of peer tutoring: **cross-age tutoring**, in which the tutor is several years older than the student being taught, and same-age peer tutoring, in which a student tutors a classmate (Topping, Duran, & Van Keer, 2015). Cross-age tutoring is recommended by researchers more often than same-age tutoring—partly because older students are more likely to know the material, and partly because students might accept an older student as a tutor but resent having a classmate in that role. Sometimes peer tutoring is used with students who need special assistance, in which case a few older students might work with a few younger students. Other tutoring schemes have involved, for example, entire fifth-grade classes tutoring entire second-grade classes (Thurston, Tymms, Merrell, & Conlin, 2012). In these cases, half of the younger students might be sent to the older students' classroom, while half of the older students go to the younger students' classroom. Otherwise, peer tutoring may take place in the cafeteria, the library, or another school facility.

Peer tutoring among students of the same age can be easier to arrange and has also been found to be very effective (Rohrbeck et al., 2003). Among classmates of the same age and performance level, reciprocal peer tutoring, in which students take turns as tutors and tutees, can be both practical and effective (Fantuzzo, King, & Heller, 1992; Greenwood, Terry, Utley, Montagna, & Walker, 1993; Mathes, Torgeson, & Allor, 2001; Van Keer & Vanderlinde, 2013).

Adequate training and monitoring of tutors are essential. For a practical guide to peer tutoring, see Topping, Duran, & Van Keer, 2015. Some studies have found greater achievement gains for tutors than for tutees (Rekrut, 1992)! As many teachers have noted, the best way to learn something thoroughly is to teach it to someone else.

Connections 9.7
For more on reciprocal teaching, see Chapter 8.

ON THE WEB

For articles and resources on peer tutoring, visit the Peer Tutoring Resource Center at peertutoringresource.org and the Center for Effective Collaboration and Practice at cecp.air.org.

Tutoring by Teachers

One-to-one adult-to-child tutoring is one of the most effective instructional strategies known, and it essentially solves the problem of appropriate levels of instruction. The principal drawback to this method is cost. However, it is often possible to provide adult tutors for students who are having problems learning in the regular class setting. Tutoring is an excellent use of school aides (Brown et al., 2005; Madden & Slavin, 2015; Vadasy, Sanders, & Tudor, 2007); some school districts hire large numbers of paraprofessionals precisely for this purpose. In fact, research has found few achievement benefits of classroom aides unless they are doing one-to-one tutoring (see Slavin, 1994). Volunteers who are willing to work every day and who are carefully supervised and trained in phonetic approaches can also improve student learning, though not usually as much as paraprofessionals (Morrow-Howell et al., 2009; Roskosky, 2010; Tingley, 2001).

There are some circumstances in which one-to-one tutoring by teachers is particularly justifiable, despite the cost, such as for first-graders who are having difficulty learning to read. Failing to learn to read in the lower grades of elementary school is so detrimental to later school achievement that an investment in tutors who can prevent reading failure is worthwhile. A recent review of research on programs for struggling readers in the elementary grades found substantial positive effects of a variety of tutoring and small-group interventions (Slavin, Lake, Davis, & Madden, 2011).

A program called **Reading Recovery** (Lyons, Pinnell, & DeFord, 1993) provides one-to-one tutoring from specially trained teachers to first-graders who are not reading adequately. This program has been found to bring most children placed at risk to adequate levels of performance and can have long-lasting positive effects. Reading Recovery is used in thousands of elementary schools in the United States, Canada, the United Kingdom, and other countries. Although there is little disagreement that Reading Recovery has a positive effect on the reading success of first-graders who are at risk (see May et al., 2015; Pinnell et al., 1994; Slavin, Lake, Davis, & Madden, 2011), there are conflicting findings on the maintenance of these gains beyond first grade. A major long-term evaluation of Reading Recovery in London found strong immediate effects that had faded away by the time the children were 10 years old (Hurry & Sylva, 2007). There have also been questions about the cost-effectiveness of Reading Recovery (Hiebert, 1996; Shanahan, 1998) and about whether positive effects for small numbers of first-graders represent the best use of limited funds for an entire age group of children (see Hiebert, 1996; Schacter, 2000). However, if you see Reading Recovery as a starting point for a series of interventions designed to get at-risk children off to a good start, rather than as a cure that lasts forever, then there is no question that it greatly improves reading performance at a critical period in children's development.

In addition to Reading Recovery, several other programs have successfully used certified teachers, paraprofessionals, and even well-trained and well-supervised volunteers to improve the reading achievement of first-graders (Morris et al., 2000; Slavin, Lake, Davis, & Madden, 2011). A phonetic tutoring program called Reading Rescue has produced substantially better outcomes for first-graders than either a small-group remedial program or no intervention (Ehri, Dreyer,

THEORY INTO PRACTICE

Effectively Using Peer Tutoring Methods to Meet Individual Needs

Peer tutoring is an effective way to improve learning for both tutee and tutor, and no one doubts the value of this strategy for meeting individual needs within a classroom. However, it takes more than simply pairing off students for peer tutoring to result in improved learning.

To establish a tutoring program, recognize that specific skills need to be developed in both the tutors and the tutees. Whether the tutors are same-age peers, older students, or even adults, use care in selecting tutors. Consider not only the knowledge base of the tutors (i.e., their proven proficiency with the subject matter) but also their ability to convey knowledge clearly.

Typically, training will include basic instruction in modeling, prompting responses from tutees, using corrective feedback and praise/reinforcement, alternating teaching methods and materials (i.e., using multisensory methods), and recording and reporting progress. Students who receive tutoring need to be clear about their role in this process. It would be counterproductive to force any student into a tutorial relationship. Therefore, initially select only students who express a willingness to work with a tutor. Steadily make tutoring a part of the natural learning activities within a classroom or an entire school. Tutees and tutors should understand that the goal of the activity is to have each tutee reach a clear understanding of the concepts, not merely complete an assignment. To augment the preparation, you might want to use various role-playing activities during the training process. Demonstrate appropriate forms of instruction, feedback, reinforcement, and so on; then allow the participants to practice under supervised conditions. Corrective feedback within this controlled environment will allow you to feel more confident as the tutor–tutee pairs work together without your direct supervision.

Flugman, & Gross, 2007). An Australian program that used a combination of curricular reform, Reading Recovery tutoring, family support, and other elements showed significant effects on first-graders' reading performance (Crévola & Hill, 1998). A follow-up of a tutoring program for second- and third-graders found lasting effects on some reading measures eleven years later (Blachman et al., 2014).

One-to-one tutoring is nearly always very effective, and tutoring models that use structured phonetic methods are much more effective than other tutoring methods (Blachman et al., 2004; Brown, Morris, & Fields, 2005; Ehri et al., 2007; Slavin et al., 2011; Wanzek et al., 2013). Programs that supplement one-to-one or small-group tutoring by paraprofessionals with specially designed computerized content are particularly effective (Chambers et al., 2008, 2011; Madden & Slavin, 2015). Phonetic programs delivered by paraprofessionals with or without computers are almost as effective as tutoring given by certified teachers (Jenkins, Peyton, Sanders, & Vadasy, 2004; Markovitz et al., 2014; Vadasy, Sanders, & Tudor, 2007). Smaller positive effects have been found in studies of phonetic tutoring to groups of three to eight children (Hempenstall, 2008; Mathes et al., 2003, 2005).

Volunteers can be effective as tutors, but effects are smaller than those achieved with paraprofessionals (Jacob, Armstrong, & Willard, 2015; Morrow-Howell et al., 2009). A lot of time is required for the recruitment, training, and supervision of volunteers, but using them may help build community connections. Tutoring by adults, both individually and in groups of two or three, has also been found to be effective for primary-age students struggling in math (Fuchs et al., 2008).

Certification Pointer

For your teacher certification test, you will probably need to demonstrate your understanding of appropriate applications of cross-age tutoring. For example, you might be asked to identify the curricular goals for which cross-age tutoring would be appropriate, and how you would structure the tutoring so that it would be effective.

MyEdLab **Self-Check 9.2**

MyEdLab **Video Analysis Tool 9.2** Go to MyEdLab and click on the Video Analysis Tool to access the exercise "Differentiated instruction: materials."

WHAT EDUCATIONAL PROGRAMS EXIST FOR STUDENTS PLACED AT RISK?

Any child can succeed in school. Any child can fail. The difference between success and failure depends primarily on what the school, the parents, community agencies, and the child himself or herself do to create conditions that are favorable for learning (Thomas & Bainbridge, 2001). Before school entry we cannot predict very well which individual children will succeed or fail, but there are factors in a child's background that make success or failure more likely (on the average). For example, students who come from impoverished or chaotic homes, those who have marked developmental delays, and those who exhibit aggressive or withdrawn behavior are more likely to experience problems in school than are other students. These children are often referred to as **students at risk** (Boykin & Noguera, 2011). The term *at risk* is borrowed from medicine, in which it has long been used to describe individuals who do not have a given disease but are more likely than average to develop it. For example, a heavy smoker or a person with a family history of cancer might be at risk for lung cancer, even though not all heavy smokers or people with family histories of cancer actually get the disease. Similarly, a given child from an impoverished home might do well in school, but 100 such children are likely to perform significantly worse, on the average, than 100 children from middle-class homes. Boykin (2000) advocated using the term *placed at risk*, rather than *at risk*, to emphasize the fact that it is often an inadequate response to a child's needs by school, family, or community that places the child at risk. For example, a child who could have succeeded in reading if he or she had been given appropriate instruction, a reading tutor, or eyeglasses could be said to have been placed at risk by the lack of these services.

Before children enter school, the most predictive risk factors are related to their socioeconomic status and family structure. After they begin school, however, such risk factors as poor reading performance, grade repetition, and poor behavior become more important predictors of later school problems (such as dropping out) than family background factors (Hernandez, 2012).

Educational programs for students who are at risk fall into three major categories: compensatory education, early intervention programs, and special education. **Compensatory education** is the term used for programs designed to prevent or remediate learning problems among students who are from low-income families or who attend schools in low-income communities. Some intervention programs target infants and toddlers who are at risk to prevent possible later need for remediation. Other intervention programs are aimed at keeping children in school. Compensatory and early intervention programs are discussed in the following sections. Special education, discussed in Chapter 12, is designed to serve children who have more serious learning problems, as well as children with physical or psychological problems.

Compensatory Education Programs

Compensatory education programs are designed to overcome the problems associated with being brought up in low-income communities. Compensatory education supplements the education of students from disadvantaged backgrounds who are experiencing trouble in school or are thought to be in danger of having school problems. Head Start was designed to give preschool children from disadvantaged homes the skills they need for a good start in school. The largest compensatory education program, and the one that is most likely to affect regular classroom teachers, is **Title I**, a federally funded program that gives schools money to provide extra services for students from low-income families who are having trouble in school (see Borman, Stringfield, & Slavin, 2001; Manna, 2008).

Title I is not merely a transfer of money from the federal government to local school districts or schools. According to federal guidelines, these funds must be used to "supplement, not supplant" local educational efforts. This means that school districts cannot use the money to increase teachers' salaries or purchase ordinary supplies. Instead, funds must go directly toward increasing

InTASC 2
Learning Differences

InTASC 10
Leadership and Collaboration

Connections 9.8
For more on factors such as poverty and limited English proficiency that might place students at risk of school failure, see Chapter 4.

Connections 9.9
To learn about factors such as problems of childhood and adolescence that might place students at risk of school failure, see Chapter 3.

Connections 9.10
Special education is discussed in detail in Chapter 12.

the academic achievement of low achievers in schools that serve many students who are disadvantaged. Schools that serve very disadvantaged neighborhoods—neighborhoods in which at least 40 percent of the students qualify for free or reduced-cost lunch—can use Title I money to improve the school as a whole (but still not for basic costs, only for improving outcomes).

TITLE I PROGRAMS Title I programs can take many forms. Most often, a special Title I teacher provides remedial help to students who are experiencing difficulties in reading and, in many cases, in other subjects as well (Borman et al., 2001). However, Title I funds are also used to purchase technology, to provide professional development for teachers, and to hire paraprofessionals.

RESEARCH ON THE EFFECTS OF TITLE I Two major nationwide studies of the achievement effects of the programs offered under Title I were carried out in the 1980s and 1990s. The first, called the Sustaining Effects Study (Carter, 1984), found that Title I students did achieve better in reading and math than did similar low-achieving students who did not receive Title I services, but that these effects were not large enough to enable Title I students to close the gap with students performing at the national average. The greatest gains were for first-graders, whereas the benefits of Title I participation for students in fourth grade and above were slight.

The other major study of the effects of the compensatory services funded under Title I, called Prospects, also compared elementary and middle school children receiving compensatory education services both to similar children at risk who were not receiving services and to children who were never at risk. Prospects did not find any achievement benefits for children receiving Title I services (Puma, Jones, Rock, & Fernandez, 1993). A more detailed analysis by Borman, D'Agostino, Wong, and Hedges (1998) found similarly disappointing outcomes, although there were some positive effects for children who were less disadvantaged and for those who received services during some years but not others. However, the lowest-achieving students from the most disadvantaged backgrounds were not narrowing achievement gaps with agemates who were less disadvantaged.

Although the Prospects study did not find overall positive effects of receiving compensatory services, results were positive in some situations. One particularly influential factor was the degree to which Title I services were closely coordinated with other school services (Borman, 1997; Borman, D'Agostino, Wong, & Hedges, 1998). In other words, schools that closely integrated remedial or instructional Title I services with the school's main instructional program, and especially schools that used Title I dollars to enhance instruction for all students in schoolwide projects, obtained the best outcomes. This kind of integration contrasts with the traditional practice of sending low-achieving students to remedial classes where instruction is poorly coordinated with the classes they are leaving.

Although a review of many studies did find positive effects of Title I on average (Borman & D'Agostino, 2001; Borman, Hewes, Overman, & Brown, 2003), no one familiar with the data would argue that Title I impacts are large (Dynarski & Kaenz, 2015; Manna, 2008). However, the recent passage of the Every Student Succeeds Act (ESSA), which includes Title I, places far more emphasis than ever before on using Title I funds on proven programs and practices, such as comprehensive reforms, tutoring, and proven teaching methods. This may greatly improve the effectiveness of Title I (Slavin, 2013).

Early Intervention Programs

Connections 9.11

For more on prevention and early intervention, see Chapter 12.

Traditionally, Title I and other compensatory education programs have overwhelmingly emphasized remediation. That is, they typically provide services to children only after the children have already fallen behind. Such children might end up in special education or might be retained. It makes more sense to focus on prevention and **early intervention** than to focus on remediation in serving children placed at risk of school failure (see Chambers, Cheung, Slavin, Smith, & Laurenzano, 2010; Goodwin, 2012).

Programs that emphasize infant stimulation, parent training, and other services for children from birth to age 5 have been found to have long-term effects on the school success of students who are at risk. One example is Nurse-Family Partnerships, a program in which trained nurses visit impoverished new mothers to help them learn how to help their children develop physically, emotionally, and mentally (Miller, 2015). Another example is the Carolina Abecedarian program

(Campbell & Ramey, 1994), which found long-term achievement effects of an intensive program for children from low-income homes who receive services from infancy through school entry. The Perry Preschool program has also demonstrated long-term effects of an intensive program for 4-year-olds (Schweinhart & Weikart, 1998). Other programs have had similar effects (Chambers et al., 2010). In addition to such preventive programs, there is evidence that early intervention can keep children from falling behind in the early grades. For example, Whitehurst and colleagues (1999) found lasting effects of an early intervention program emphasizing phonemic awareness (knowledge of how sounds blend into words) and other preliteracy strategies.

Research on preventive strategies shows that children who are at risk can succeed if we are willing to give them high-quality instruction and intensive services early in their school careers (Slavin, 1997/1998). Early intervention also ensures that children who do turn out to need long-term services are identified early—and it ensures that those whose problems can be solved early are not needlessly assigned to special education (see Vellutino et al., 1996).

Comprehensive School Reform Programs

Comprehensive school reform (CSR) programs are schoolwide approaches that introduce research-based strategies into every aspect of school functions: curriculum, instruction, assessment, grouping, accommodations for children having difficulties, parent involvement, and other elements (Borman, Hewes, Overman, & Brown, 2003; Kidron & Darwin, 2007; Slavin, 2008a).

Many comprehensive school reform models were widespread in the 1990s and early 2000s, but by far the most widely used and extensively researched CSR program today is **Success for All** (Slavin, Madden, Chambers, & Haxby, 2009), a program that focuses on prevention and early intervention for elementary and middle schools serving disadvantaged communities. Success for All provides reading programs for preschool, kindergarten, and grades 1 through 8; one-to-one or small-group computer-assisted tutoring for struggling readers; family support services; and other changes in instruction, curriculum, and school organization designed to ensure that students do not fall behind in the early grades. Longitudinal studies of Success for All have shown that students in this program read substantially better than students in matched control schools throughout the elementary and middle grades, and that they are far less likely to be assigned to special education or to fail a grade (see Borman & Hewes, 2002; Borman et al., 2007; Muñoz, Dossett, & Judy-Gullans, 2004; Quint et al., 2015; Rowan & Correnti, 2009). In 2015–2016, Success for All was used in about 1,000 Title I schools in 46 states.

Other comprehensive reform programs focus on high schools. These include the Talent Development High School (Belfanz & Legters, 2011; MacIver et al., 2010), the Institute for Student Achievement (Academy for Educational Development, 2010; Bloom & Unterman, 2012; IMPAQ International, 2016), and Every Classroom, Every Day (Early et al., 2016).

After-School and Summer School Programs

Increasingly, Title I and other federal, state, and local education agencies are funding programs that extend learning time for students beyond the school day. Both after-school and summer school programs are expanding rapidly.

After-school programs typically combine some sort of academic activity, such as homework help, with sports, drama, and cultural activities (Cooper et al., 2000; Friedman, 2003; Neuman, 2010). Studies of after-school programs generally find that for such programs to enhance student achievement, they need to incorporate well-organized coursework, such as individual or small-group tutoring, to extend the academic day (Fashola, 2002; McComb & Scott-Little, 2003). However, reviews of research on the after-school remedial programs funded under supplemental educational services during the Bush administration did not show any consistent benefits of these programs (Chappell et al., 2011; Muñoz, Chang, & Ross, 2012).

Summer school sessions are also increasingly seen in schools, particularly as a last chance for students to avoid being retained in their grade. Summer school has long been advocated as a solution to the "summer loss" phenomenon, in which children from families that are low in socioeconomic status tend to lose ground over the summer, whereas middle-class students tend to gain (Cooper, Borman, & Fairchild, 2010). Research on summer school generally finds benefits for children's achievement (Borman & Boulay, 2004; David, 2010a; Smith, 2011/2012; Zvoch

THE INTENTIONAL TEACHER
Teaching in Light of Research on Grouping and Differentiation

Intentional teachers see students' needs, not texts, as the starting point for planning and providing instruction. They expect students to have varied areas of strength, and they plan instruction that meets the needs of individual students. They monitor student progress carefully and use resources beyond the classroom to meet the needs of students with varying capabilities.

- They consider how to balance the quality, appropriateness, motivation, and time factors in their lessons to maximize the success of all students.
- They use between-class ability grouping sparingly, if at all, and try to accommodate student differences in other ways.
- They orchestrate the use of tutoring, technology, and other supports to help struggling students succeed in the regular class, rather than counting on ability grouping, retention, or special education.
- They differentiate instruction to provide a variety of teaching styles, materials, and technologies to respond to the diverse needs of all students.
- They seek ways to use both cross-age and same-age peer tutoring to help all students learn.
- They seek ways to work with teachers, paraprofessionals, and volunteers to tutor struggling students so they can stay on track toward success.
- They make intelligent use of Title I and other compensatory education resources to prevent problems and improve teaching and learning.
- They promote the use of summer and after-school programs to extend learning time for all students, especially those having difficulties.

& Stevens, 2013). Studies by Kim (2006) and Allington et al. (2010) found that simply sending books home over the summer with fourth-graders, along with encouragement to read, increases their reading performance. However, larger, randomized evaluations of summer programs that just provide books to disadvantaged students do not find this outcome (Wilkins et al., 2012).

A review by Lauer and colleagues (2006) looked at the research on both types of out-of-school programs: summer school and after-school programs. They found small positive effects of out-of-school programs for reading and math when children who attended these programs were compared to those who did not. When the programs included tutoring, effects were much more positive. Effects were about the same for after-school as for summer school programs. The importance of these findings is the indication that struggling children can be helped by extending instructional time for them, especially if the additional time is used for targeted instructional activities.

MyEdLab **Self-Check 9.3**

HOW IS TECHNOLOGY USED IN EDUCATION?

Watch children of any age eagerly playing video games, sending text messages to their friends, or looking up information on the Internet. Adults who see this, or experience it themselves, ask themselves why the obvious power of technology, which is transforming every aspect of life, hasn't transformed education (Fisher, 2013; Maloy et al., 2014; Richardson, 2013; Roblyer, 2016;

TABLE 9.1 • Percent of U.S. Teens, Ages 13–17 Who Own Digital Devices

Desktop/laptop computer	87
Gaming console	81
Smartphone	73
Tablet	58
Basic cell phone	30

Source: Pew Research Center (2015). *Teen relationships survey*. Washington, DC: Author.

Rosen, 2011; Smaldino et al., 2015 Vander Ark, 2012). This is not to say that technology is not present in classrooms. Computers, interactive whiteboards, and all sorts of other technology are present to one degree or another in every school, and most middle-class children, at least, go home to an array of technology as well. Table 9.1 shows that as of 2015, 87 percent of all teens aged 13–17 had desktop or laptop computers, 73 percent had smartphones, and 58 percent had tablets (Pew Research Center, 2015). These numbers are going up rapidly, and as tablets and smartphones become more widespread, it is safe to say that universal access to the Internet is on its way. Digital devices are also becoming far more common in K–12 classrooms (Watson, Murin, Vashaw, Gemin, & Rapp, 2011). Yet only gradually is technology truly changing the core of teaching and learning in America's schools (Daccord & Reich, 2015; Lever-Duffy & McDonald, 2015; Pahomov, 2014; Pitler, Hubbell, & Kuhn, 2012; Roblyer, 2016; Sousa, 2016).

Not long ago, "technology in education" primarily meant computer-assisted instruction (CAI), methods in which students work on individualized, self-instructional content as a supplement to ordinary class instruction. CAI has been used for relatively short amounts of time each week, and perhaps not surprisingly, its impacts on student learning have been quite small (Dynarski et al., 2007; Cheung & Slavin, 2012b, 2013). However, there are now many quite different uses of technology in schools, and it no longer makes sense to ask, "What is the effect of technology on schools?" Instead, we have to look at what each application of technology makes possible, how it interacts with the burgeoning use of technology in homes and throughout society, and what the educational outcomes are for each type of application (Guernsey & Levine, 2015; Pitler, Hubbell, & Kuhn, 2012; Sousa, 2016). There is a tendency for school districts and government to invest in technology without a clear idea of how it will be used or what its outcomes are likely to be (Schneider, 2011). The remainder of this chapter discusses the main uses of technology in schools today, as well as the evidence on the learning outcomes found for each application).

InTASC 3

Learning Environments

InTASC 8

Instructional Strategies

MyEdLab
Video Example 9.1

Textbook author Bob Slavin discusses an experience visiting a school that served as a demonstration site for computers in education. Think about how computers were used in your classes when you were in grade school, and in high school. How do you see technology changing in schools, and what might you expect for the next 15 or 20 years?

ON THE WEB

The International Society for Technology in Education (ISTE) has developed standards for technology use in education. It provides guidance for teachers in the following areas:

- Facilitating and inspiring student learning and creativity
- Designing and developing digital-age learning experiences and assessments
- Modeling digital-age work and learning
- Promoting and modeling digital citizenship and responsibility
- Engaging in professional growth and leadership

There are widely respected ITSE standards for students (http://www.iste.org/standards/standards-for-students). See http://www.iste.org/standards/standards-for-teachers for ISTE National Educational Technology Standards for Teachers (NETS-T).

Useful information for students about computer etiquette can be found at ehow.com by typing "computer etiquette for kids" into the site's search engine.

There are now many types of technology applications in education. For example, teachers use technology in classroom teaching to plan instruction and present content to classes. Students use technology to learn and practice traditional subjects, explore, participate in simulations and games, communicate with others, and prepare papers and presentations. In addition, teachers and administrators use technology to accomplish administrative tasks, such as assessment, record keeping, reporting, and management (Gura, 2014; Roblyer & Doering, 2012; Thorsen, 2009). Examples of these three types of technology applications are described in the next sections.

Technology for Classroom Teaching

Teachers now routinely use digital technology to enhance their lessons to whole classes or groups of students.

COMPUTERS AND TABLETS Word processors, electronic spreadsheets, and presentation software are the most common electronic technologies utilized for preparing and delivering class lessons. You can use word processors for numerous traditional teaching tasks, such as preparing student worksheets, tests, rubrics, classroom signs, and posters. In addition, the "Review" tools in word processing enable you to provide individualized feedback through the use of "tracked changes" and "inserted comments." Simple desktop publishing features enable teachers to use color, graphics, and art to make texts appealing to students. The editing features of word processing programs make it easy for you to adapt documents to meet specific student needs.

Electronic spreadsheets organize and compute numerical data, producing charts and graphs to illustrate information. Spreadsheets are particularly helpful for teaching mathematics and science because they allow you to display numeric data visually, such as showing the impact of changes on variable values. They also make it easy to display students' work.

Teachers (and students) have available thousands of free and low-cost apps, for every imaginable purpose. For guidance on choosing good ones, see Ferlazzo, 2015. ISTE Standards for teachers: http://www.iste.org/standards/standards-for-teachers.

INTERACTIVE WHITEBOARDS AND ELECTRONIC RESPONSE DEVICES An **interactive whiteboard** is a large screen, visible to a whole class, on which it is possible to display anything that can be shown on a computer screen (Becker & Lee, 2009). Teachers or children can also write on the board and manipulate content that is already there, using either a finger or a special pen (depending on the brand). In addition, students can be provided with **electronic response devices**, or **clickers**, on which they can electronically answer your questions. You can then quickly assess which concepts your class has mastered and which concepts you need to spend more time teaching (Becker & Lee, 2009; Marzano, 2009).

Interactive whiteboards can help teachers solve the problems of orchestrating complex lessons. All lesson elements can be loaded into the computer and projected on the whiteboard, including PowerPoint slides, video clips, still pictures, letters, words, and other prepared content. Moreover, you can create, add to, or modify lessons using the vast digital resources available on the Internet. The whiteboard does not replace the teacher, but instead provides visual aids at the right time to facilitate teaching of exciting, varied, and effective lessons.

Studies of the impacts of the use of interactive whiteboards have found promising outcomes. Reviews by Pittard, Bannister, and Dunn (2003) and by Smith, Higgins, Wall, and Miller (2005) reported that research on interactive whiteboards shows positive effects of the approach on student learning.

A newer form of electronic response devices allows students to work on items at their own level and pace. For example, students in a math class who are working on decimal operations might be given on their handheld devices, problems focusing on fractions, fractional operations, and decimal place values. As they work through the problems, teachers get immediate information on the students' levels, progress, and errors, so they can target individual students or groups for additional help. Studies of this type of device have found positive effects on learning math (Sheard & Chambers, 2011) and grammar (Sheard, Chambers, Slavin, & Elliott, 2012).

Multimedia Teaching

Increasingly, technology is being used to combine text and visual content, such as animations or video. This multimedia approach has been found to enhance students' learning as long as the text and visuals directly support each other (Höffler & Leutner, 2006; Reed, 2006). For example, adding diagrams or animations to show how lightning works has been found to enhance the text, but adding motivational but nonexplanatory text (such as a picture of an airplane being hit by lightning) can actually detract from learning (Mayer, 2008b, 2009). Studies of first-grade reading found that adding video content on letter sounds, sound blending, and vocabulary to teacher-led reading lessons significantly increases students' learning (Chambers et al., 2006, 2008). A review on storybook reading found that incorporating music and animation added to learning, but games did not (Takacs et al., 2015).

Technology for Learning

Technology is used for a wide variety of purposes to help students learn. The applications of learning technology fall into the following categories: word processing and publishing, spreadsheets and databases, computer-assisted instruction, the Internet, multimedia, integrated learning systems, and computer programming (Fishman & Dede, 2016; Roblyer & Doering, 2012; Thorsen, 2009). See Chapter 12 for a discussion of uses of technology specific to special education and mainstreaming (Lever-Duffy & McDonald, 2015).

WORD PROCESSING AND DESKTOP PUBLISHING   One of the most common applications of computers, especially in grades 3 through 12, is **word processing** or **desktop publishing**. Increasingly, students are asked to write compositions on classroom computers. A key advantage of word processing over paper-and-pencil composition is the ease of revision (Hicks, 2015). In fact, there is evidence that automated feedback on compositions can improve writing and inquiry skills (Gerard et al., 2016; Roscoe & McNamara, 2013; VanLehn, 2011). Spell checkers and other utilities help students to worry less about mechanics and focus on the meaning and organization of their compositions. As writing instruction has moved toward an emphasis on the process of revision and editing, this capability has become very important. Word processing is probably the best-researched application of computers to instruction, and studies have shown that students who use computers write more, revise more, and take greater pride in their writing than do paper-and-pencil writers. Writing quality also tends to be somewhat better when students have access to word processors (Allen, Jacovina, & McNamara, 2015). This writing effect may be enhanced when each student has a laptop, instead of having to share a small number of computers (Lowther, Ross, & Morrison, 2003). Of course, word processing itself has become an essential skill in a vast range of occupations, so teaching students to use word processing programs (e.g., in high school business courses) has obvious value.

SPREADSHEETS   As with word processing, **spreadsheets** in education are extensions of software widely used by adults. Spreadsheets can convert raw data into graphs, charts, and other data summaries so that students can easily organize information and see the effects of various variables on outcomes (see Figure 9.2). For example, a student could enter data for the number of daily visitors to Wilbur the pig in a petting zoo. By assigning a formula to a given column, the student could customize the spreadsheet program to total the number of visits to Wilbur by day of the week, time of day, age of visitors, and so forth. Changing any number automatically changes row and column totals. The spreadsheet program could then show the data in raw numeric form or convert the data into a graph. Students are increasingly using spreadsheets to record data from science experiments and to reinforce mathematics skills.

DATABASES   A **database** is a computer program that keeps a lot of information available for reference or manipulation. Students can learn to search CD-ROM (ROM stands for read-only memory) databases such as encyclopedias, atlases, road maps, and catalogs to find information for a variety of instructional purposes. Databases of current information are readily available on the Internet. Databases of archived or current information can be particularly important in project-based learning because they may put a great deal of information within easy reach for open-ended reports and other projects.

In many databases, students can use **hypertext** and **hypermedia** to search a database (such as an encyclopedia) by clicking on a word or picture. This leads the student to related or more detailed information on a specific portion of the text (see Figure 9.3). Hypermedia can similarly provide pictures, music, video footage, or other information to illuminate and extend the information on a CD-ROM or online database. Hypermedia has exciting possibilities for allowing learners

Connections 9.12
To learn about the use of computers for students with disabilities, see Chapter 12.

**FIGURE 9.2 •
Example of a
Spreadsheet and
Resulting Graph**

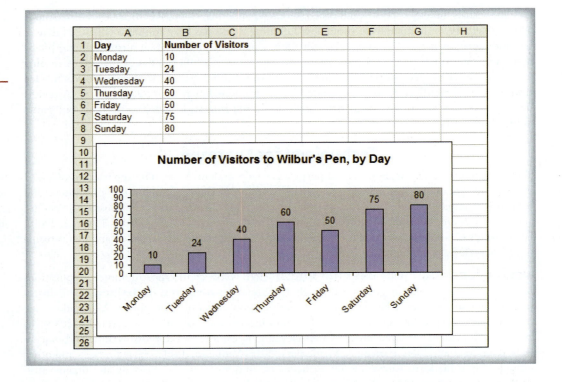

**FIGURE 9.3 •
Example of Hypertext**

Source: www.whitehouse.gov/
issues/technology.

to follow their interests or resolve gaps in understanding more efficiently than with traditional text, but so far, research on use of hypermedia finds limited and inconsistent effects on student learning that depend on both the type of material being studied and the nature of the learners (Kamil et al., 2000).

COMPUTER-ASSISTED INSTRUCTION Applications of **computer–assisted instruction (CAI)** range in complexity from simple drill and practice software to **complex problem–solving programs**.

DRILL AND PRACTICE One of the most common applications of computers in education is to furnish students with **drill and practice** on skills or knowledge. For example, many software programs provide students with practice on math facts or computations, geography, history facts, or science. Although computer experts often frown on drill and practice programs, calling them "electronic page turning," drill and practice programs used to replace independent seatwork have several major advantages, including immediate feedback, record keeping, appealing graphics, and variations in pace or level of items depending on the student's responses. This can increase students' motivation to do work that might otherwise be boring. Drill and practice programs should not be expected to teach by themselves, but they can reinforce skills or knowledge that students have learned elsewhere.

TUTORIAL PROGRAMS More sophisticated than drill and practice programs, **tutorial programs**, or "intelligent tutoring systems," are intended to teach new material and present appropriate correction and review based on the student's responses. The best tutorial programs come close to mimicking a patient human tutor. Increasingly, tutorial programs use speech and graphics to engage students' attention and present new information. Students are typically asked many questions, and the program branches in different directions depending on the answers, re-explaining if the student makes mistakes or moving on if the student responds correctly. Very sophisticated computer-managed programs that simulate the behaviors of expert human tutors are being developed and applied in a variety of settings (Roblyer, 2016), and several have shown positive outcomes in evaluations (e.g., Wijekumar et al., 2014). However, effects of intelligent tutorial programs on standardized tests have been quite small (Kulik & Fletcher, 2016).

INSTRUCTIONAL GAMES Most children are first introduced to computers through video games, and many educators (and parents) have wondered whether the same intensity, motivation, and perseverance that they see in children playing video games could be brought to the classroom (Ash, 2012b; Basye, Grant, Hausman, & Johnston, 2015; Carlson & Raphael, 2015; Gaydos, 2015; Goldman et al., 2013; Guernsey & Levine, 2015; Toppo, 2015). Many **instructional games** have been designed; most are simple extrapolations of drill and practice designs into a game format, but some are more creative. A review of research on digital games used in school found significant positive effects (Clark, Tanner-Smith, & Killingsworth, 2016), although another review, by Abdul Jabbar & Felicia (2015), emphasized that positive outcomes of gaming depend on integration with classroom goals and supports, and Takacs, Swart, & Bus (2015) found that games can be distracting in storybook reading.

The Internet for Students

Perhaps the fastest-growing technology applications in U.S. schools involve the **Internet** (Roblyer & Doering, 2012). As shown in Table 9.2, the number of people in the world with Internet access is rising dramatically, from 5.8 percent of the world in 2000 to 46.4 percent in 2015. Internet

TABLE 9.2 • Numbers of World Internet Users, 1995–2015

YEAR	USERS	PERCENT OF WORLD POPULATION
1995	16 million	0.4%
2000	361 million	5.8%
2005	1 billion	15.7%
2009	1.8 billion	26.6%
2010	1.9 billion	28.8%
2011	2.2 billion	32.7%
2012	2.4 billion	34.4%
2015	3.4 billion	46.4%

Source: www.internetworldstats.com

access for schools, which is becoming virtually universal (Watson et al., 2011), gives schools access to vast stores of information, including databases on every imaginable subject, libraries throughout the world, and other specialized information. This information can be used to help students become active, creative learners (Gutierrez, 2013; Jackson et al., 2012). For example, students can use the Internet to do WebQuests, in which they search the Internet on a given topic or theme. The Internet can also enable students to communicate with peers in other schools, regardless of distance. Through this capability students can create international projects or carry out cooperative projects with other schools (Roblyer & Doering, 2012). Most schools have set up their own Web pages, and many have created their own virtual museums or encyclopedias by collecting and synthesizing information from many sources. Students can contribute to **wikis** (online encyclopedias), podcasts, and other virtual publications that give them authentic opportunities to communicate their work (Dlott, 2007; Ohler, 2006).

EDUCATIONAL APPLICATIONS There are thousands of applications, or "apps," currently available on the Internet free or at low cost. These range from simple games to lesson ideas to whole courses. The problem for teachers, parents, and students who want to access these apps is in sifting through to find high-quality, appropriate content in the "digital Wild West." A guide to exploring the Internet for literacy programs was published by the Joan Ganz Cooney Center at Sesame Workshop (Guernsey & Levine, 2015).

SIMULATIONS As an interactive model of some sort of reality, **simulation software** allows students to operate within a simulated environment and, by doing so, to learn about that environment from the inside. For example, one of the earliest simulations, "Oregon Trail," gave students limited allocations of food, water, money, and horses. Students had to use these resources wisely to successfully move their wagon trains to the West. Modern simulations include Sim City Edu, Rise of Nations, Age of Mythology, Civilization, Zoo Tycoon, and Local Journey of the Zoominis (Gee & Levine, 2009). There is evidence that well-developed simulations can enhance learning (De Jong, 2011; Goldman et al., 2013).

WEBQUESTS A **WebQuest** is like a simulation, with the additional element of having users seek information on the Web to enhance their ability to play their role or contribute to a discussion or combined product. For example, Global Education (globaleducation.edna.edu.au) allows students to take any of a variety of roles related to the expansion of the desert in Mongolia. In order to participate meaningfully, students need to do research to understand issues from the perspective they have taken on. In Urban Science (epistemicgames.org), middle school students learn about urban planning, economics, and social policy to plan a new city.

MyEdLab
Video Example 9.2
Mr. Dunleavy uses a WebQuest in his lesson on Edgar Allan Poe. Note how he points out to the students that part of their task is to understand why the computer and the Internet are important resources for the lesson.

Certification Pointer
A teacher certification question may ask you to suggest a strategy for using technology to help students learn various instructional objectives.

ON THE WEB

Resources that can help you effectively use simulations, games, and lessons to engage students with technology include Universal Design for Learning (cast.org), and Edutopia (edutopia.org).

Resources to help students to make their own videos include Animoto (https://animoto.com/education) and Capzles (www.capzles.com).

WebQuest (www.webquest.org) helps teachers create challenging tasks for students to complete using the Web.

Sites such as Zoho Doc (www.zoho.com/docs) provide students with word processors, presentation tools, and spreadsheets, to help them do their own reports.

Several sites advise students and teachers about ethical and responsible uses of the Internet. These include Common Sense Education (www.commonsensemedia.org), and the Center for Digital Ethics and Policy (www.digitalethics.org).

THEORY INTO PRACTICE

Helping Students Judge Internet Sources

The easy availability of information (and misinformation) on the Internet means that students need to become critical readers, able to judge the truthfulness, impartiality, and usefulness of the information they find (Abilock, 2012; Badke, 2009; David, 2009; Richardson, 2009). In general, online content is more trustworthy if it is from a reliable source, has citations from other reliable sources, and shows signs of having been edited and reviewed by others (Abilock, 2012). Concerns about the reliability and completeness of information on the Internet has led many schools to pay for digital encyclopedias (such as the digital Encyclopaedia Britannica), even though Wikipedia and other online sources are free (Ash, 2012a). Table 9.3A and 9.3B show information for students to use in evaluating research sources.

TABLE 9.3A • Determining Reliability of Online Sources

Usually, popular topics are checked by many people, but less popular topics are not. A wiki about a person or company might be written by that person or company, so watch out! Use this checklist to help you determine whether a site is reliable.

Author

- The site has a .gov or .edu ending
- The author or organization is clearly stated
- I can easily find information about the author
- The author is known and respected
- A contact phone number or mailing address is given

Sources

- Sources of the information are given
- Sources of pictures or photographs are given

Content

- There are no ads or spam on the page
- The site has been updated within the past three to six months
- The purpose of the site is to give facts, not opinions
- The text has no misspellings or errors in punctuation
- The website links to other credible websites

TABLE 9.3B • Likely Reliability of Information Sources by Domains

HOW DOES IT END?	WHO OWNS IT?	IS IT RELIABLE
.gov	The government	Yes
.edu	A university or college	Yes
.org	A nonprofit organization or special interest group	Most likely
.com .net .biz	A company or business	It might be trustworthy, but you should be careful. Always verify information found on these sites.

ON THE WEB

For examples of websites that provide information for WebQuests, see edhelper.com and http://webquest.org/.

MULTIMEDIA PROJECTS Students can be encouraged to make their own **multimedia** projects—an update of the old-fashioned group report (Palmer, 2015). In project-based multimedia learning, students design, plan, and produce a product or performance, integrating media objects such as graphics, video, animation, and sound. For example, one seventh-grade class created a social studies and science multimedia presentation about the Black Plague, integrating animations of how the plague virus attacks and the perspectives of 14th-century farmers (Basye, Grant, Hausman, & Johnston, 2015; Gura, 2016).

Students can use a wide array of graphics tools to create their multimedia presentations, including CD-ROMs, digital photos, concept mapping, and graphic organizers. **CD-ROM** and online databases include clip art, photographs, illustrations, music, and sometimes video. Students can use them to create multimedia reports, projects, or explorations that combine audio, video, music, and pictures. **Digital video** and **photographs** can be used as a stimulus for writing or to illustrate projects. For example, students might take digital video or photographs of animals on a field trip to the zoo. Back in the classroom, these serve as a reminder to students of what they saw and also are used to illustrate their reports on the trip.

INTEGRATED LEARNING SYSTEMS Schools often purchase **integrated learning systems**—entire packages of hardware and software, including most of the types of software described previously. Integrated learning systems provide many terminals that are linked to each other and to computers that you can use to monitor individual student work (Lever-Duffy et al., 2003). Web versions of integrated learning systems are also available and add the benefit of providing online learning to students who need alternative schooling options. Research on the effectiveness of commercial integrated learning systems has found modest positive effects on mathematics achievement (Cheung & Slavin, 2013; Dynarski et al., 2007; Slavin & Lake, 2008; Slavin, Lake, & Groff, 2009; Texas Center for Educational Research, 2007), but few effects on reading achievement (Cheung & Slavin, 2012b; Slavin et al., 2008; Slavin et al., 2009).

Web 2.0

Web 2.0 denotes the modern use of the World Wide Web that incorporates free collaborative online communication using a template for users to enter their comments and responses (Dunn, 2011; Knobel & Wilber, 2009; Reeves, 2009). The groups of people who communicate this way are referred to as *virtual communities* or *social networkers*.

WEBLOGS (BLOGS) Weblogs, commonly called blogs, are like online diaries, where authors, or bloggers, post their thoughts and opinions. You can find a sample blog and a tutorial on how to start a blog on blogger.com. In education, blogs can be used as online storage for assignments and projects, for resources the students will need to download, as readers' guides for classroom books, or as a place where students can create and post content.

WIKIS A wiki is a website where visitors can add or change the information on the site. *Wiki* is a Hawaiian word meaning "quickly." The most widely known example is Wikipedia (wikipedia.org), a free online encyclopedia written (and constantly updated) by volunteers who submit whole articles or edit existing articles. In the classroom, wikis can be used during group projects for online collaboration and organizing a group's arsenal of information. A wiki, or a contribution to an existing wiki, can be the outcome of a group, class, or school project (Reich, Murnane, &

Willett, 2012). You can reference sites such as WikEd (wik.ed.uiuc.edu) to access a wide variety of educational resources.

RSS FEEDS **RSS** stands for Real Simple Syndication or Rich Site Summary. RSS lets users know when something new is posted on a blog, wiki, or RSS-capable website in which they're interested. For example, Education Week (edweek.org) provides educational RSS feeds from its publications, online discussion, and blogs on many topics.

PODCASTS Podcasts are multimedia files available on the Internet for playback on computers and mobile devices. There are podcasts on many topics, including TV newscasts and college lectures. You can use podcasts in the classroom to supplement lessons you are teaching. One source is the Education Podcast Network (podstock.ning.com), which lists podcasts by grade level and subject area.

SOCIAL NETWORKING Social networking is the use of websites to communicate with or to meet others who share the same interests. Facebook and LinkedIn are examples. Social networking consumes a huge amount of time for children and adolescents, with effects that are only dimly understood (Grimes & Fields, 2012). The most obvious negatives, the opportunities for cyberbullying and access to inappropriate content, are discussed later in this chapter.

Instructional Television and Embedded Multimedia

An old technology, educational television, is being used in new ways (see Guernsey & Levine, 2015; Shore, 2008). Research has long established the learning benefits of watching educational television shows such as *Sesame Street* (Fisch & Truglio, 2000; Mares & Pan, 2013) and *Between the Lions* (Linebarger, Kosanic, Greenwood, & Doku, 2004). Research suggests that children who watch a lot of educational television become better readers, whereas those who watch a lot of noneducational television become worse-than-average readers (Ennemoser & Schneider, 2007; Wright et al., 2001).

In **embedded multimedia** (Chambers, Cheung, Madden, Slavin, & Gifford, 2006), brief segments of video content are threaded into lessons. In two large experiments, Chambers and colleagues (2006, 2008) found that adding to daily reading instruction 5 minutes of animations and puppet skits illustrating letter sounds and sound blending significantly increases children's reading performance. A review of research contrasting the use of animations and of static pictures in lessons found that students learn better from animated content (Höffler & Leutner, 2006).

ASSISTIVE TECHNOLOGY Assistive technology helps students with physical disabilities such as hearing loss or deafness, speech disorders, vision impairment, or limited dexterity, as well as learning or cognitive delay that impairs performance of target skills (Carpenter, Johnston, & Beard, 2015; Marchez, Fischer, & Clark, 2015). Some examples of assistive technology are adaptive keyboards, screen readers, and screen magnifiers. Assistive technology is discussed further in Chapter 12.

MyEdLab
Video Example 9.3
ZoomText is an example of assistive technology that enlarges computer print for students with vision impairment.

COMPUTER-ASSISTED TUTORING Children who need intensive tutoring for reading problems in the early elementary grades are often given one-to-one or small-group tutoring by teachers to help them get on track to success by third grade. Studies by Chambers et al. (2008, 2012) and Madden & Slavin (2015) found that adding structured, closely aligned computer software with teaching by paraprofessionals improved the outcomes of tutoring, making one-to-six teaching with a computer as effective as one-to-one without a computer.

TECHNOLOGY APPLICATIONS WHEN ALL STUDENTS HAVE INTERNET ACCESS A major revolution is taking place in technology applications in education. Up to recent times, technology use was severely restricted because expensive computers were available in the school only for a small proportion of students at any one time, and few students had computers at home. Because of these concerns, the use of computers in most schools was limited to rotating students through computer labs or computers at the back of the class. It was impossible for teachers to assign work at home that required Internet access.

Universal access to the Internet is already here in schools serving primarily middle-class populations, and it is coming fast in all schools. Two trends are accelerating universal access.

21ST CENTURY LEARNING
Mindful Use of Technology

Today, it is hardly necessary to teach most students to use basic computer technology. They are likely to be comfortable and proficient with computers already. However, it is increasingly important for teachers to design and implement lessons requiring students to engage in the mindful use of technology to find useful information, to learn new skills, and to create documents, designs, and other products. Mindful use of technology implies using critical reading skills to decide what is likely to be true and useful in a body of information, and using learning-to-learn skills to plan a search for information, organize what is found, evaluate the information and select from it, summarize knowledge, and create reports or other new materials based on the summaries. Technology makes libraries of information easily available, but it also allows and even encourages aimless meandering and mindless entertainment. Helping students use technology as a tool rather than a toy gives them essential skills for our times (Daccord & Reich, 2015; Evans, 2015; McTighe & March, 2015).

QUESTION

- Do you think a classroom discussion of students' negative Internet experiences would serve as a warning of what not to do, or do you think it would encourage students to experiment with technology in ways they hadn't thought of and potentially place them in harm's way?

One is the rapid spread of digital devices, especially smartphones and tablets, and the dropping cost of entry-level tablets. Second, school districts are hoping to replace expensive paper texts with (potentially) much less expensive e-texts (see Larson, 2015; Tomassini, 2012). When e-texts become widely available and fall in price, it will be cost-effective for schools to give electronic tablets to children instead of giving them paper texts (Journell, 2012; Tomassini, 2012).

BRING YOUR OWN DEVICE Many schools are experimenting with "bring your own device" (BYOD) policies, in which students are asked to bring whatever devices they have to school every day: tablets, smartphones, laptops, or other devices with access to the Internet (such schools have loaners for students who lack devices) (Johnson, 2012; Schad, 2014). The students then take them home, making digital homework possible. Teaching strategies that take advantage of universal access to the Internet include the following:

Blended Learning The strategies employed in **blended learning** combine ordinary teaching with a broad range of Internet applications (Patterson, 2012). These may include computer-assisted instruction or any number of other applications, which students work on in class, at home, or both. Evidence is unclear about the benefits of this approach (Frey, Fisher, & Gonzalez, 2013; Kist, 2015; Means et al., 2010; Nolan, Preston, & Finkelstein, 2012; Smith, 2013; Staker & Horn, 2012). Initial evaluations are not finding positive effects (Goodwin & Miller, 2013), but this may change as teachers learn to use flipping effectively (Moran & Young, 2015).

Flipped Classroom One form of blended learning is the **flipped classroom** (Ash, 2012a; Fulton, 2012; Moran & Young, 2015; Sams & Bergmann, 2013). In this type of learning, teachers prepare digital lessons and make them available to students online. Students are expected to view the lessons at home and perhaps send answers to questions digitally. The class time is then free for use on cooperative learning, project-based learning, or other activities that require the presence of other students, as well as teachers. The school or home activities may also make extended use of technology for authoring reports, videos, or other productions, accessing information resources, or connecting with other students, perhaps far away (Bergmann & Sams, 2012). Experience with flipped classrooms, which are used largely in secondary schools, is revealing many problems. Not all students are able to learn traditional objectives on their own, so teachers still have to use class time to review and reinforce lessons. A major study of flipped learning in grades 5–6 math classes in England found no positive impacts of the approach (Villanueva, Rudd, Elliot, Chambers, & Blower, 2016).

Digital Homework When all students have Internet access at home, teachers can confidently assign homework that takes advantage of technology. This could be traditional homework that students send in to be automatically reviewed and corrected before class, or alternative types of homework, such as electronic reports and other creative activities. One growing application is called **Khan Academy** (Khan, 2012; Khan & Slavitt, 2013; Sparks, 2011b), a series of lessons in many subjects provided online at no cost. The lessons consist of explanations by a teacher, followed by exercises. Students proceed through the lessons at their own pace. An elaborate system of awards and badges rewards students' progress. Teachers may assign homework on Khan Academy or other programs to help students reinforce skills they may be weak on or as enrichment activities if they have mastered everything the class is currently doing.

Online homework facilitates diversity in students' assignments, not only by level (as in individualized programs such as Khan Academy) but also by interests. For example, students can select books for book reports from a much broader range of books than exists in their school, perhaps downloading books free from their local public library (Valenza & Stephens, 2012). Students can be asked to investigate science or social studies topics that interest them, using vast information resources throughout the world, and then to create multimedia reports.

Challenges of Integrating Technology

SETTING LIMITS

Cyberbullying Sad to say, bullying has always been a part of relationships among children. However, the advent of widespread access to technology has added to possibilities for bullying by making it easy to spread rumors, lies, embarrassing pictures, or insults about a schoolmate, while concealing their source. This behavior is called cyberbullying. **Cyberbullying** consists of threats or insults one person makes to another via instant or text messaging or over e-mail (Duggan, 2014; Englander, 2015; Hinduja & Patchin, 2011). For example, students may post insulting or damaging information about their victim(s) where others are sure to see it. In a study by Juvonen and Gross (2008), 72 percent of adolescents aged 12–17 reported experiencing cyberbullying. Students who are cyberbullied should be encouraged to print out the offensive messages as proof of their harassment and provide it to their teachers or principal. If possible, they should obtain the e-mail address of the bully. If students don't know who the bully is, it is recommended that they change their screen name and tell it only to trusted friends (Duggan, 2014; Englander, 2015; Hinduja & Patchin, 2011; Thorsen, 2009).

ON THE WEB

For information and resources to combat cyberbullying, see kidshealth.org's parent site, kids.usa.gov, cyberbullying.us, www.pewinternet.org/2014/10/22/online-harrassment, or stopcyberbullying.org.

Twenty-five percent of teens are abused digitally, which correlates to other kinds of dating abuse. For information on preventing digital sexual harassment during teen dating, see https://thatsnotcool.com/.

Cell Phones in Class The popularity of the cell phone for calling and sending text messages has had both positive and negative effects in the classroom (Trotter, 2009). On the positive side, the latest technology enables you to project instant messages onto a screen so the entire class can benefit from a teacher/student instant message exchange. Text messages can be archived, allowing students to later refer to links or to answers they've received. On the negative side, text messaging can be an in-class distraction, can transmit computer viruses, could potentially be used for cheating, and can be a forum for cyberbullying. Given these drawbacks, you need to set limits on the use of cell phones in the classroom.

Safety and Security of Students Students using the Internet can place themselves in harm's way, ranging from accidentally stumbling on inappropriate material to interacting with Internet predators. Simply by spending so much time on the Internet, many students inadvertently leave "digital footprints" that predators can use to contact them (Ferriter, 2011).

There are several ways to protect your students from viewing inappropriate material online (Online Safety and Technology Working Group, 2010). Although the best way to protect students is via responsible adult supervision, children can encounter objectionable material inadvertently, and Internet filtering software can help prevent many inappropriate sites from being viewed. In school applications involving the Internet, software can allow teachers to spot check students' messages and downloads, a good means of reducing students' access to inappropriate content and cyberbullying.

In addition, cybercrime, which is any illegal activity involving computers, is on the rise. Criminals now make more money via cybercrime than via drug-related crimes (Vamosi, 2005)! Even more frighteningly, studies have shown that one in five students received an online sexual solicitation in a one-year period, and that 29 percent of children provided their home address when asked (Bitter & Legacy, 2008).

Here are some general online safety guidelines that you can share with students to help them protect themselves from cybercrime and Internet predators:

- Never give out personal information to a person you've met online.
- Never, ever meet in person with someone you have met online.
- Never say anything you wouldn't want the world to hear, and never show any pictures online that you wouldn't want the world to see.
- Do not give out your user name or password, or any financial information whatsoever, in response to an e-mail, even if it appears to be initiated from a business whose name you recognize.
- Give out credit card or account information only over a secure website or telephone.

Table 9.4 lists some additional rules that students should follow to stay safe on the Internet.

TABLE 9.4 • Tips for Staying Safe on the Web

- Do not use your real name as your online screen or user name.
- Never share your passwords with anyone other than a parent or guardian.
- When you are finished, log out of any website that requires a password.
- Do not download anything from an unknown website.
- Never give out personal information, such as your full name, address, or phone number, or the name of your school.
- Don't know someone? Don't chat with them!
- Check the website's privacy settings before creating an online profile. An adult can help make sure your profile is secure and hidden from strangers.
- Never post pictures of yourself or others that you would not want your parents or teachers to see.

The Internet for Teachers

The Internet can provide rich resources for lesson planning. Teacher-related websites enable teachers to exchange information, support each other, share ideas, and problem-solve. Online resources for teachers include a variety of Web tools.

E-MAIL The advent of e-mail in the classroom has made it possible for teachers to communicate with each other and with parents quickly and easily. From an administrative perspective, e-mail can reduce the need for meetings because teachers can communicate via e-mail. Some schools use e-mail to take attendance.

DISCUSSION BOARDS A discussion board is similar to e-mail in that users respond to each other's comments, but on a discussion board an organizer provides topics for discussion on the initial screen, and then participants can choose the topic they wish to discuss. In this way, you can facilitate student debates on classroom-related issues and provide a forum for opinions.

WEB AUTHORING It is becoming common practice for teachers to post homework assignments, calendars, and general messages on a website for parents to access.

PROFESSIONAL DEVELOPMENT Technology is transforming professional development for teachers. PD content from one-hour inservices to year-long courses is now routinely offered online. Teachers participate in online chats and contribute to wikis as part of their professional growth (see Huber, 2010).

Technology for Administration

You can use a variety of technologies to accomplish the many administrative tasks associated with your work, such as grading, creating reports, writing class newsletters, extending invitations, and sending individual notes to parents. E-mail makes it easier for you to communicate with teaching assistants, administrators, parents, and others. Part of every teacher's job involves organizing, maintaining, and retrieving different types of data. This ranges from creating student rosters and logging students' contact information to tracking coverage of the district's language arts objectives (Archer, 2007). You can use portfolio assessment software to document student achievement. These programs allow you to collect and display the information when it comes time to report to parents.

As schools are being held more accountable for their students' achievements, school districts are using technology to monitor the progress of individual students, teachers, and schools via database management systems. In addition to tracking students' achievements, these management systems enable districts to monitor enrollment, attendance, and school expenditures. Data management software makes it easier for you to enter, retrieve, and update records and to create accurate, customized, professional reports for administrators or parents. You can track which students are mastering what content areas so that you can better target specific instruction to the students who need it most.

AUDIO AND VIDEO CONFERENCING Audio and video conferencing make it possible for groups of people, each in front of their respective computers, to see and hear each other anywhere in the world (Thorsen, 2009). This technology can eliminate the need for administrators to travel to as many meetings. In the classroom, conferencing allows students to witness historic moments or to discuss a topic they are studying with an expert who lives far away.

THE DIGITAL DIVIDE A persistent problem with technology in education is the "digital divide": the difference in technology access between advantaged and less advantaged students (Darling-Hammond, Zielezinski, & Goldman, 2014; Goodman, 2013; Johnson, 2015; Rideout & Katz, 2016). This difference exists both in access to digital devices (such as laptops, tablets, or smartphones), and in home subscriptions to broadband. Homework assignments that assume Internet access, flipped classrooms, and any other strategy that assumes Internet access run up against this problem. If only, say, 90 percent of students have Internet access, it might as well be 0 percent because teachers are unlikely to assign activities that 10 percent of students are not equipped to do.

Some schools deal with the broadband problem by sending home flashdrives containing content, but this limits the uses of the technology. Some schools allow students to use portable "hot spots." Others lend equipment to students who need it, or help parents contact organizations that help families gain access to high-speed, low-cost Internet service and computers. A national organization that does this is Connect2Compete (/cox.connect2compete.org). Another, called Everyone On, provides information on local sources (http://everyoneon.org).

> MyEdLab **Self-Check 9.4**

SUMMARY

What Are Elements of Effective Instruction beyond a Good Lesson?

Teachers must know how to adapt instruction to students' levels of knowledge. According to Carroll's Model of School Learning, effectiveness of instruction depends on time needed (a function of student aptitude and ability to understand instruction) and time actually spent learning (which depends on time available, quality of instruction, and student perseverance).

The QAIT model of effective instruction identifies four elements that are subject to the teacher's direct control: quality of instruction, appropriate level of instruction, incentive, and amount of time. The model proposes that instruction deficient in any of these elements will be ineffective.

How Are Students Grouped to Accommodate Achievement Differences?

Many schools manage student differences in ability and academic achievement through between-class ability grouping, tracking, or regrouping into separate classes for particular subjects during part of a school day. However, research shows that within-class groupings are more effective, especially in reading and math, and are clearly preferable to groupings that segregate or stigmatize low achievers. Untracking means placing students in mixed-ability groups. The students are held to high standards and provided with assistance in reaching those goals. Nongraded elementary schools combine children of different ages in the same classroom. Students are flexibly grouped according to their needs and performance levels.

What Are Some Ways of Differentiating Instruction?

Differentiation, peer tutoring, and tutoring by teachers are all methods for individualizing instruction. Research supports all of these solutions.

What Educational Programs Exist for Students Placed at Risk?

Students defined as at risk are any students who are likely to fail academically for any reason stemming from the student or from the student's environment. Such reasons are diverse and may include poverty.

Educational programs for students who are at risk include compensatory education, early intervention programs, and special education. Federally funded compensatory education programs include, for example, Head Start, which aims to help preschool-age children from low-income backgrounds achieve school readiness, and Title I, which mandates extra services to low-achieving students in schools that have many students from low-income families. Extra services include tutoring and continuous-progress plans.

Research supports the effectiveness of many prevention and intervention efforts such as Reading Recovery, and comprehensive school reform programs such as Success for All.

After-school and summer school arrangements are increasingly funded by federal, state, and local education agencies to extend students' learning time. Research is mixed regarding the effectiveness of compensatory education programs.

How Is Technology Used in Education?

Technology is used for many purposes in education. For example, teachers use technology, such as word processors, multimedia, and presentation software, for planning and presenting lessons.

Students use technology, such as word processing and CD-ROM reference software, for learning and preparing presentations. Computer-assisted instruction in the form of drill and practice, tutorials, instructional games, simulations, and the Internet is widespread. Teachers and administrators use technology for administrative tasks. Research on computer-assisted instruction demonstrates small to moderate positive effects on achievement.

THE INTENTIONAL TEACHER
Teaching with Technology

Intentional teachers use technology to accomplish well-defined goals that they cannot accomplish as well without technology. They recognize that there is no magic in the machine, but that technology can enhance their teaching, assessment, planning, and record keeping and can help link students to information, resources, and other students. The teacher's task is not to hand out digital devices and hope for the best, but to planfully use the capabilities that technology affords to improve student outcomes.

- They may use technology to prepare exciting, engaging lessons, incorporating various visual media that intrigue and enlighten students, provide visual content to reinforce verbal learning, and help organize concepts for students.
- They may use technology to replace traditional worksheets, giving students immediate feedback and remediation, as well as accommodating students' learning levels and pace.
- They may use technology to assess students' understanding, both to inform students and to learn quickly how individual students, and the class as a whole, are advancing toward class objectives.
- They may use technology to enable students to prepare multimedia projects or reports, working in groups or individually.
- They may use technology to engage students in simulations, such as doing science experiments that would be difficult or impossible to perform in class.
- They may use technology to facilitate planning of lessons, including seeking content for lessons on the Internet.
- They may use technology to connect with other teachers elsewhere and share lesson ideas, content, and advice.

MyEdLab
Application Exercise 9.1
In the Pearson etext, watch a classroom video. Then use the guidelines in "The Intentional Teacher" to answer a set of questions that will help you reflect on and understand the teaching and learning presented in the video.

KEY TERMS

Review the following key terms from the chapter.

between-class ability grouping 217

blended learning 238

CD-ROM 236

compensatory education 225

computer-assisted instruction (CAI) 232

cross-age tutoring 222

cyberbullying 239

databases 231

SELF-ASSESSMENT: PRACTICING FOR LICENSURE

Directions: The chapter-opening vignette addresses indicators that are often assessed in state licensure exams. Reread the chapter-opening vignette, and then respond to the following questions.

1. How does Mr. Arbuthnot, the fourth-grade teacher in the chapter-opening vignette, incorporate John Carroll's Model of School Learning into his lesson?
   a. Mr. Arbuthnot tries to match the time spent on learning with the time students need to learn.
   b. Mr. Arbuthnot groups students according to their ability level.
   c. Mr. Arbuthnot expects students to learn the concepts of long division through group discussion and inquiry.
   d. Mr. Arbuthnot equates quality of instruction with quantity of instruction.

2. Imagine that Mr. Arbuthnot decides to divide his class into three groups: those who know long division, those who know some long division, and those who do not know long division. What type of ability group would he be using?
   a. Tri-grade ability grouping
   b. High–low ability grouping
   c. Within-class ability grouping
   d. Between-class ability grouping

3. In the opening of the vignette, Mr. Arbuthnot teaches an engaging lesson on long division and then gives students a quiz on the content learned. What type of evaluation is this?
   a. Norm-referenced
   b. Standardized
   c. Minimum competency
   d. Formative

4. Mr. Arbuthnot decides that he cannot work individually with all the students who have not yet mastered long division. He decides that some sort of tutoring might solve his problem. If he selects the type of tutoring that is most effective, according to research, which of the following will he use?

    a. Cross–age peer tutoring

    b. Same–age peer tutoring

    c. Tutoring by certified teachers

    d. Computer tutoring

5. Describe programs that exist for students placed at risk.

6. Explain how Mr. Arbuthnot could integrate technology into his teaching. What does the research on computer-based instruction say?

MyEdLab **Licensure Exam 9.1** Answer questions and receive instant feedback in your Pearson eText in MyEdLab.

WavebreakMediaMicro/Fotolia

CHAPTER TEN

Motivating Students to Learn

LEARNING OUTCOMES

At the end of this chapter, you should be able to:

10.1 Describe theories of motivation

10.2 Describe how goals and attributions enhance achievement motivation

10.3 Discuss how teachers can increase their students' motivation to achieve

10.4 Describe how knowledge of motivation informs intentional teaching

The students in Cal Lewis's tenth-grade U.S. history class are all in their seats before the bell rings, eagerly awaiting the start of the period. After the bell, in he walks dressed as George Washington, complete with an 18th-century costume and powdered wig and carrying a gavel. He gravely takes his seat, raps the gavel, and says, "I now call to order this meeting of the Constitutional Convention."

The students have been preparing for this day for weeks. Each of them represents one of the 13 original states. In groups of two and three, they have been studying all about their states, the colonial era, the American Revolution, and the United States under the Articles of Confederation. Two days ago, Mr. Lewis gave each group secret instructions from their "governor" on the key interests of their state. For example, the New Jersey and Delaware delegations are to insist that small states be adequately represented in the government, whereas New York and Virginia are to demand strict representation by population.

In preparing for the debate, each delegation had to make certain that any member of the delegation could represent the delegation's views. To ensure this, Mr. Lewis assigned each student a number from one to three at random. When a delegation asks to be recognized, he will call out a number, and the student with that number will respond for the group.

Mr. Lewis, staying in character as George Washington, gives a speech on the importance of the task they are undertaking and then opens the floor for debate. First, he recognizes the delegation from Georgia. He randomly selects the number two, which turns out to be Beth Andrews. Beth is a shy girl, but she has been well prepared by her fellow delegates to represent Georgia, and she knows that they are rooting for her.

"The great state of Georgia wishes to raise the question of a Bill of Rights. We have experienced the tyranny of government, and we demand that the people have a guarantee of their liberties!"

Beth goes on to propose elements of the Bill of Rights that her delegation has drawn up. While she is talking, Mr. Lewis is rating her presentation on historical accuracy, appropriateness to the real interests of her state, organization, and delivery. He will use these ratings in evaluating each delegation at the end of the class period. The debate goes on. The North Carolina delegates argue in favor of the right of states to expand to the west; the New Jersey delegation wants western territories made into new states. Wealthy Massachusetts wants taxes to remain in the states where they are collected; poor Delaware wants national taxes. Between debates, the delegates have an opportunity to do some "horse trading," promising to vote for proposals important to other states in exchange for votes on issues important to them. At the end of the week, the class votes on 10 key issues. After the votes are taken and the bell rings, the students pour into the hall still arguing about issues of taxation, representation, and powers of the executive.

After school, Rikki Ingram, another social studies teacher, drops into Mr. Lewis's classroom. "I see you're doing your Constitutional Convention again this year. It looks great, but how can you cover all of U.S. history if you spend a month just on the Constitution?"

Cal smiles. "I know I'm sacrificing some coverage to do this unit, but look how motivated these kids are!" He picks up a huge sheaf of notes and position papers written by the South Carolina delegation. "These kids are working their tails off, and they're learning that history is fun and useful. They'll remember this experience for the rest of their lives!"

USING YOUR EXPERIENCE

CRITICAL THINKING Rikki Ingram seems concerned that Mr. Lewis's class is not covering the material well enough. What do you think are the advantages, disadvantages, and interesting or unclear aspects of Mr. Lewis's teaching strategy?

COOPERATIVE LEARNING With another student, relate stories of a social studies or other high school teacher who tried methods similar to Mr. Lewis's method of teaching. As a pair, retell your stories to a student from another pair.

Motivation is one of the most important ingredients of effective instruction. Students who want to learn can learn just about anything. But how can you ensure that every student wants to learn and will put in the effort needed to master complex material?

Mr. Lewis knows the value of motivation, so he has structured a unit that taps many aspects of motivation. By placing students in groups and evaluating them on the basis of presentations made by randomly selected group members, he has created a situation in which students are encouraging each other to excel. Social motivation of this kind is very powerful, especially for adolescents. Mr. Lewis is rating students' presentations according to clear, comprehensive standards and giving them feedback each day. He is tying an important period in history to students' daily lives by immersing them in active roles of debating and trading votes. These strategies are designed not only to make history fun but also to give students many sources of motivation to learn and re-member the history they have studied. Mr. Lewis is right. The students will probably never forget their experience in his class and are likely to approach new information about the American Rev-olution, the Constitution, and perhaps history in general with enthusiasm throughout their lives.

This chapter presents many of the ways in which you can enhance students' desire to learn academic material and the theories and research behind each method.

WHAT IS MOTIVATION?

One of the most critical components of learning, motivation is also one of the most difficult to measure. What makes a student want to learn? The willingness to put effort into learning is a product of many factors, ranging from the student's personality and abilities to the characteristics of particular learning tasks, incentives for learning, settings, and teacher behaviors.

All students are motivated. The question is: Motivated to do what? Some students are mo-tivated more to socialize or watch television than to do schoolwork. Your job is not to increase motivation per se but to discover, prompt, and sustain students' motivation to learn the knowledge and skills needed for success in school and in life, and to engage in activities that lead to this learn-ing. Imagine that Cal Lewis had come to class in 18th-century costume but had not structured tasks and evaluations to encourage students to study U.S. history. The students might have been amused and interested, but we cannot assume that they would have been motivated to do the work necessary to learn the material.

Psychologists define **motivation** as an internal process that activates, guides, and main-tains behavior over time (Anderman, Gray, & Chang, 2013; Pintrich, 2003; Schunk, Pintrich, & Meece, 2008; Zimmerman & Schunk, 2011). In plain language, motivation is what gets you go-ing, keeps you going, and determines where you're trying to go.

Motivation can vary in both intensity and direction (Ryan & Deci, 200; Zimmerman & Schunk, 2011). Two students might be motivated to play video games, but one of them might be more strongly motivated to do so than the other. Or one student might be strongly motivated to play video games, and the other equally strongly motivated to play football. Actually, though, the intensity and direction of motivations are often difficult to separate. The intensity of a motivation to engage in one activity might depend in large part on the intensity and direction of motivations to engage in alternative activities. If someone has only enough time and money to go to the movies or to play video games, but not both, motivation to engage in one of these activities is strongly influ-enced by the intensity of motivation to engage in the other (Fries, Dietz, & Schmid, 2008). Motiva-tion is important not only in getting students to engage in academic activities but also in determining how much students will learn from the activities they perform or from the information to which they are exposed. Students who are motivated to learn something use higher cognitive processes in learning about it and absorb and retain more from it (Driscoll, 2005; Jetton & Alexander, 2001; Pin-trich, 2003). They are more likely to transfer their learning to new situations (Pugh & Bergin, 2006).

Motivation to do something can come about in many ways (Stipek, 2002). Motivation can be a personality characteristic; individuals might have lasting, stable interests in participating in such broad categories of activities as academics, sports, or social activities. Motivation can come from intrinsic characteristics of a task: By making U.S. history fun, social, active, and engaging, Cal Lewis made students eager to learn it. Motivation can also come from sources extrinsic to the task, as it did when Cal Lewis rated students' performances in the Constitutional Convention simulation.

WHAT ARE SOME THEORIES OF MOTIVATION?

The first half of this chapter presents contemporary theories of motivation, which seek to explain why people are motivated to do what they do. The second half discusses the classroom use of incentives for learning and presents strategies for increasing students' motivations to learn and to do schoolwork.

Motivation and Behavioral Learning Theory

The concept of motivation is closely tied to the principle that behaviors that have been reinforced in the past are more likely to be repeated than are behaviors that have not been reinforced or that have been punished (see Bandura, 2006; Borich, 2014; Dick et al., 2015; Levitt, List, Neckermann, & Sadoff, 2012; Schunk, 2016). Why do some students persist in the face of failure whereas others give up? Why do some students work to please the teacher, others to make good grades, and still others out of interest in the material they are learning? Why do some students achieve far more than would be predicted on the basis of their ability and some achieve far less? Examination of reinforcement histories and schedules of reinforcement might provide answers to such questions, but it is usually easier to speak in terms of motivations to satisfy various needs.

Connections 10.1
For more on reinforcement of behaviors, see Chapter 5.

REWARDS AND REINFORCEMENT One reason why reinforcement history is an inadequate explanation for motivation is that human motivation is highly complex and context-bound. With very hungry animals we can predict that food will be an effective reinforcer. With humans, even hungry ones, we can't be sure what will be a reinforcer and what will not, because the reinforcing value of most potential reinforcers is largely determined by personal or situational factors. As an example of this, think about the value of $50 in exchange for one hour of light work. Most of us would view $50 as a powerful reinforcer, more than adequate to get us to do an hour of work. But consider these four situations:

1. Mr. Scrooge offers Bill $60 to paint his fence. Bill thinks this is more than enough for the job, so he does his best work. However, when he is finished, Mr. Scrooge says, "I don't think you did 60 dollars' worth of work. Here's 50."

2. Now consider the same situation, except that Mr. Scrooge originally offers Bill $40 and, when Bill is finished, praises him for an excellent job and gives him $50.

3. Dave and Barbara meet at a party, like each other immediately, and after the party take a long walk in the moonlight. When they get to Barbara's house, Dave says, "Barbara, I enjoyed spending time with you. Here's 50 dollars I'd like you to have."

4. Marta's aunt offers her $50 to give little Pepa a piano lesson next Saturday. However, if Marta agrees to do so, she will miss her chance to try out for the school baseball team.

In situations 1, 3, and 4, $50 is not a good reinforcer at all. In situation 1, Bill's expectations have been raised and then dashed by Mr. Scrooge. In situation 2, the amount of monetary reward is the same, but this situation is much more likely to make Bill want to paint Mr. Scrooge's fence again, because in this case, his reward exceeds his expectation. In situation 3, Dave's offer of $50 is insulting and would certainly not increase Barbara's interest in going out with him in the future. In situation 4, although Marta's aunt's offer would seem generous to Marta under most circumstances, it is insufficient reinforcement this particular Saturday because it interferes with a more highly valued activity.

DETERMINING THE VALUE OF AN INCENTIVE These situations illustrate an important point: The motivational value of an incentive cannot be assumed, because it might depend on many factors. When you say, "I want you all to be sure to hand in your book reports on time because they will count toward your grade," you might be assuming that grades are effective incentives for most students. However, some students might not care about grades, perhaps because their parents don't or because they have a history of failure in school and have decided that grades are unimportant. Saying to a student, "Good work! I knew you could do it if you tried!" might be motivating to a student who had just completed a task he or she thought was difficult, but insulting to one who thought the task was easy (because your praise implies that he or she had to work especially hard to complete the task). As in the case of Bill and Mr. Scrooge, students' expectations for rewards determine the motivational value of any particular reward. And it is often difficult to determine students' motivations from their behavior, because many different motivations can influence behavior. Sometimes, one type of motivation clearly determines behavior; at other times, several (perhaps conflicting) motivations are influential (Wentzel & Brophy, 2014).

Motivation and Human Needs

InTASC 1

Learner Development

Motivation can be thought of as a drive to satisfy needs, such as needs for food, shelter, love, and maintenance of positive self-esteem. People differ in the degree of importance they attach to each of these needs. Some need constant reaffirmation that they are loved or appreciated; others have a greater need for physical comfort and security. Also, the same person has different needs at different times. A drink of water would be appreciated much more after a 4-mile run than after a 4-course meal.

MASLOW'S HIERARCHY OF NEEDS Given that people have many needs, which will they try to satisfy at any given moment? To explain this, Maslow (1954) proposed a hierarchy of needs, which is illustrated in Figure 10.1. In Maslow's theory, needs that are lower in this hierarchy must be at least partially satisfied before a person will try to satisfy higher-level needs. For example, a hungry person or someone who is in physical danger will be less concerned about maintaining a positive self-image than about obtaining food or safety; but once that person is no longer hungry or afraid, self-esteem needs might become paramount. One critical concept that Maslow introduced is the distinction between deficiency needs and growth needs. **Deficiency needs** (physiological, safety, love, and esteem) are those that are critical to physical and psychological well-being. These needs must be satisfied, but once they are, a person's motivation to satisfy them diminishes. In contrast, **growth needs**, such as the need to know and understand things, to appreciate beauty, or to develop an appreciation of others, can never be satisfied completely. In fact, the more people are able to meet their need to know and understand the world around them, the greater their motivation may become to learn still more.

Certification Pointer

Teacher certification tests will require you to identify which needs Maslow identified as deficiency needs and which he identified as growth needs.

FIGURE 10.1 •
Maslow's Hierarchy of Needs

Maslow identifies two types of needs: deficiency needs and growth needs. People are motivated to satisfy needs at the bottom of the hierarchy before seeking to satisfy those at the top.

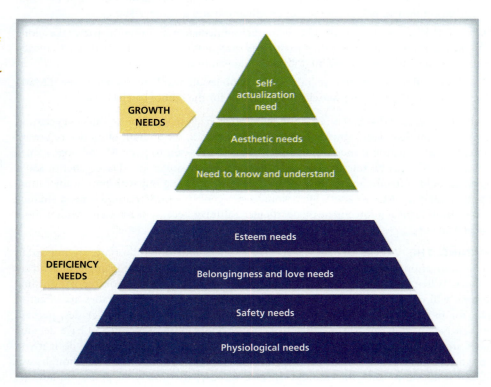

SELF-ACTUALIZATION   Maslow's theory includes the concept of **self-actualization**, which he defines as "the desire to become everything that one is capable of becoming" (Maslow, 1954, p. 92). Self-actualization is characterized by acceptance of self and others, spontaneity, openness, relatively deep but democratic relationships with others, creativity, humor, and independence—in essence, psychological health.

IMPLICATIONS OF MASLOW'S THEORY FOR EDUCATION   The importance of Maslow's theory for education is in the relationship between deficiency needs and growth needs. Obviously, students who are very hungry or in physical danger will have little psychological energy to put into learning. Schools and government agencies recognize that if students' basic needs are not met, learning will suffer. They have responded by providing free breakfast and lunch programs. The most important deficiency needs, however, are those for love and self-esteem. Students who do not feel that they are loved and that they are capable are unlikely to have a strong motivation to achieve the higher-level growth objectives (Bergin, 2016; Martin & Dowson, 2009; Stipek, 2002). A student who is unsure of his or her worth or capability will tend to make the safe choice: Go with the crowd, study for the test without interest in learning the ideas, write a predictable but uncreative essay, and so on. If you can put students at ease and make them feel accepted and respected as individuals, you are more likely (in Maslow's view) to help them become eager to learn for the sake of learning and willing to risk being creative and open to new ideas. A school that emphasizes social-emotional learning might, in this view, create an environment that is more conducive to academic as well as social-emotional learning (see Greenberg et al., 2003; Hoffman, 2009; Jennings & Greenberg, 2009).

Connections 10.2
Motivational factors affecting the academic performance of students who are at risk of school failure are discussed in Chapter 9.

Motivation and Attribution Theory

Teresa usually gets good grades, but she just received a D on her first quiz in a new class. The mark is inconsistent with her self-image and causes her discomfort. To resolve this discomfort, Teresa might decide to work harder to make certain that she never gets such a low grade again. However, she might try to rationalize her low grade: "The questions were tricky. I wasn't feeling well. The teacher didn't tell us the quiz was coming. I wasn't really trying. It was too hot." These excuses help Teresa account for one D—but suppose she gets several poor grades in a row. Now she might decide that she never did like this subject anyway or that the teacher shows favoritism to the boys in the class or is a hard grader. All of these changes in opinions and excuses are directed at avoiding an unpleasant pairing of inconsistent ideas: "I am a good student" and "I am doing poorly in this class, and it is my own fault."

Teresa is struggling to find a reason for her poor grades that does not require her to change her perception of herself as a good student. She attributes her poor performance to her teacher, to the subject matter, or to other students—external factors over which she has no control. Or, if she acknowledges that her poor performance is her own fault, she decides that it must be a short-term lapse based on a momentary (but reversible) lack of motivation or attention regarding this unit of instruction.

Attribution theory (see Hareli & Weiner, 2002; Weiner, 2000, 2010) seeks to understand just such explanations and excuses, particularly when applied to success or failure (wherein lies the theory's greatest importance for education, in which success and failure are recurrent themes). Weiner (2000) suggests that most explanations for success or failure have three characteristics. The first is whether the cause is seen as internal (within the person) or external. The second is whether it is seen as stable or unstable. The third is whether it is perceived as controllable. A central assumption of attribution theory is that people will attempt to maintain a positive self-image. Therefore, when they do well in an activity, they are likely to attribute their success to their own efforts or abilities; but when they do poorly, they will believe that their failure is based on factors over which they had no control (Weiner, 2010). In particular, students who experience failure will try to find an explanation that enables them to save face with their peers (Juvonen, 2000). It has been demonstrated that if groups of people are given a task and then told that they either failed or succeeded (even though all, in fact, were equally successful), those who are told that they failed will say their failure was because of bad luck, whereas those told that they succeeded will attribute their success to skill and intelligence (Weiner, 2000).

Attributions for others' behavior are also important. For example, students are more likely to respond to a classmate's request for help if they believe that the classmate needs help because of a temporary uncontrollable factor (such as getting hurt in a basketball game) than if they believe that help is needed because of a controllable factor (such as failure to study) (Weiner, 2010).

ATTRIBUTIONS FOR SUCCESS AND FAILURE   Attribution theory deals primarily with four explanations for success and failure in achievement situations: ability, effort, task difficulty, and luck. Ability and effort attributions are internal to the individual; task difficulty and luck attributions are external. Ability is taken to be a relatively stable, unalterable state. In contrast, effort can be altered. Similarly, task difficulty is essentially a stable characteristic, whereas luck is unstable and uncontrollable. These four attributions and representative explanations for success and failure are presented in Table 10.1.

Table 10.1 shows how students often seek to explain success and failure differently. When students succeed, they would like to believe that it was because they are smart (an internal, stable attribution), not because they were lucky or because the task was easy or even because they tried hard (because "trying hard" says little about their likelihood of success in the future). In contrast, students who fail would like to believe that they had bad luck (an external, unstable attribution), which allows for the possibility of succeeding next time (Weiner, 2010). Of course, over time, these attributions might be difficult to maintain. As in the case of Teresa, a student who gets one bad grade is likely to blame it on bad luck or some other external, unstable cause. After several bad grades, though, an unstable attribution becomes difficult to maintain; no one can be unlucky on tests week after week. Therefore, a student like Teresa might switch to a stable but still external attribution. For example, she could decide that the course is too difficult or the teacher is unfair or make some other stable, external attribution that lets her avoid making a stable, internal attribution that would shatter her self-esteem: "I failed because I don't have the ability" (Weiner, 2010). She might even reduce her level of effort so that she can maintain the belief that she could succeed if she really wanted to.

LOCUS OF CONTROL AND SELF-EFFICACY   One concept central to attribution theory is **locus of control** (Rotter, 1954). The word *locus* means "location." A person with an internal locus of control believes that success or failure is the result of his or her own efforts or abilities. Someone with an external locus of control is more likely to believe that other factors, such as luck, task difficulty, or other people's actions, cause success or failure. Internal locus of control is often called *self-efficacy,* the belief that one's behavior makes a difference (Bandura, 1997; Goddard, Hoy, & Woolfolk Hoy, 2004; Schunk & Pajares, 2004; Skinner & Greene, 2008). Locus of control or self-efficacy can be very important in explaining a student's school performance. For example, several researchers have found that students who are high in internal locus of control have better grades and test scores than students of the same intelligence who are low in internal locus of control (Cappella & Weinstein, 2001; Caprara et al., 2008; Zimmerman, 2013). Studies have found locus of control to be the second most important predictor (after ability) of a student's academic achievement (e.g., Dweck, 2007; Pietsch, Walker, & Chapman, 2003). The reason is easy to comprehend. Students who believe that success in school is due to luck, the teacher's whims, or other external

Connections 10.3
Attributions for success or failure that are related to the socioemotional factors of self-esteem and peer relations are discussed in Chapter 3.

TABLE 10.1 • Attributions for Success and Failure

Attribution theory describes and suggests the implications of people's explanations of their successes and failures.

		CAUSAL LOCUS		
		INTERNAL	**EXTERNAL**	
	Stable	Ability "I'm smart" "I'm stupid"	Task Difficulty "It was easy" "It was too hard"	
Causal Stability				Expectancy
	Unstable	Effort "I tried hard" "I didn't really try"	Luck "I lucked out" "I had bad luck"	
		Value (Pride)		

Source: From "The development of an attribution-based theory of motivation: A history of ideas" by Bernard Weiner in *Educational Psychologist.* Published by *Educational Psychologist,* © 2010.

factors are unlikely to work hard. They tend to procrastinate or avoid difficult tasks (Steel, 2007). In contrast, students who believe that success and failure are primarily due to their own efforts can be expected to work hard (Bandura, 2012; Joët, Usher, & Bressoux, 2011; Pressley et al., 2003). In reality, success in a particular class is a product of both students' efforts and abilities (internal factors) and luck, task difficulty, and teacher behaviors (external factors). But the most successful students will tend to overestimate the degree to which their own behavior produces success and failure. Some experiments have shown that even in situations in which success and failure are in fact completely based on luck, students who are high in internal locus of control will believe that it was their efforts that made them succeed or fail (see Weiner, 2010).

It is important to note that locus of control can change and depends somewhat on the specific activity or situation. One difficulty in studying the effects of locus of control on achievement is that achievement has a strong effect on locus of control (Bong & Skaalvik, 2003). For example, the same student might have an internal locus of control in academics (because of high academic ability) but an external locus of control in sports (because of low athletic ability). If this student discovered some unsuspected skill in a new sport, he or she might develop an internal locus of control in that sport (but probably still not in other sports).

IMPLICATIONS OF ATTRIBUTIONS AND SELF-EFFICACY FOR EDUCATION In the classroom, students receive constant information concerning their level of performance on academic tasks, either relative to others or relative to some norm of acceptability. This feedback ultimately influences students' self-perceptions (Bandura, 2006; Schunk, 2016). Attribution theory is important in helping you understand how students might interpret and use feedback on their academic performance and in suggesting how you might give feedback that has the greatest motivational value (see Tollefson, 2000). In particular, it suggests that you should always praise students for their effort (which is controlled by them) rather than their intelligence (which is not) (see Dweck, 2007).

Motivation and Mindset

The most important implication of attribution theory is that students have implicit theories, or **mindsets**, to explain success or failure. Carol Dweck (2006, 2010; Lin-Siegler, Dweck, & Cohen, 2016; Yeager & Dweck, 2012; Yeager et al., 2016) has taken this a step further by showing that existing mindsets can be changed and that this in turn can affect learning and other outcomes. In particular, Dweck and her colleagues describe experiments in which students were explicitly taught that intelligence is not a fixed, unchangeable characteristic of people, but a product of effort. For example, Blackwell, Trzesniewski, & Dweck (2007) reported an experiment with seventh graders. One group learned study skills in math along with an intervention designed to convince them that success in school is due to effort, not innate ability. Another group just learned study skills. Grades declined for the study-skills-only group, but increased for the "effort mindset" group. Several other experiments demonstrated similar outcomes among students of different ages (Yeager & Dweck, 2012).

The mindset experiments add a great deal to the claims of attribution theory, because they suggest that the positive relationship between effort attributions and achievement gains is not just due to people who perform well wanting to believe that they succeeded because they worked hard. If mindsets can be modified, and this affects achievement, then this provides strong evidence that mindsets cause achievement, not the other way around (see Lin-Siegler et al., 2016; Usher & Kober, 2012; Yeager, Walton, & Cohen, 2013).

Motivation and Self-Regulated Learning

Self-regulated learning, discussed in Chapter 5, refers to "learning that results from students' self-generated thoughts and behaviors that are systematically oriented toward the attainment of their learning goals" (Schunk & Zimmerman, 2013, p. 45). As this definition makes clear, self-regulated learning is closely related to students' goals. Students who are highly motivated to learn something are more likely than other students to consciously organize their learning, carry out a learning plan, and retain the information they obtain (Efklides, 2011; Schunk & Zimmerman, 2013). For example, students with high reading motivation are more likely to read on their own and to use effective comprehension strategies (Miller, Partelow, & Sen, 2004). This motivation can come from

MyEdLab
Video Example 10.1
Callie says she is not good in spelling but could get better with practice. She also says that when she has trouble, her parents encourage her to try herself before offering help. Would you describe her as having high self-efficacy?

Connections 10.4
For more on self-regulated learning, see Chapter 5.

Connections 10.5
For more on successful strategies for building self-determination, see Chapter 12.

many sources. Students can be taught specific self-regulation strategies, in which they learn to think strategically and evaluate their own efforts and outcomes. Such strategies have been shown to enhance learning (e.g., Germeroth & Day-Hess, 2013; Duckworth et al., 2016). Another source might be social modeling (Zimmerman, 2013), such as occurs when students see other students using self-regulated strategies. Another is goal-setting, in which students are encouraged to establish their own learning goals. A fourth is feedback that shows students that they are making good progress toward their learning goals, especially if the feedback emphasizes students' efforts and abilities (Zimmerman, 2013). Schunk and Zimmerman (2013) argue that motivation to engage in self-regulated learning is not the same as achievement motivation in general because self-regulated learning requires the learner to take independent responsibility for learning, not to simply comply with the teacher's demands. Fredricks, Blumenfeld, and Paris (2004) use the terms *engagement* and *investment* to describe motivation that leads students to engage in self-regulated learning, rather than simply doing the work and following the rules.

Motivation and Expectancy Theory

Expectancy theory is a theory of motivation based on the belief that people's efforts to achieve depend on their expectations of reward. Atkinson (1964) developed theories of motivation based on the following formula:

Motivation (M) = Perceived probability of success (Ps) $\times$ Incentive value of success (Is).

The formula is called an expectancy model, or **expectancy–valence model**, because it largely depends on the person's expectations of reward (see Pintrich, 2003; Stipek, 2002; Wentzel & Brophy, 2014; Wigfield, Tonks, & Klauda, 2009). What this theory implies is that people's motivation to achieve something depends on the product of their estimation of the chance of success (perceived probability of success, Ps) and the value they place on success (incentive value of success, Is). For example, if Mark says, "I think I can make the honor roll if I try, and it is very important to me to make the honor roll," then he will probably work hard to make the honor roll. However, one very important aspect of the $M = Ps \times Is$ formula is that it is multiplicative, meaning that if people either believe that their probability of success is zero or do not value success, then their motivation will be zero (Trautwein et al., 2012). If Mark would like very much to make the honor roll but believes that he hasn't a prayer of doing so, he will be unmotivated. If his chances are actually good but he doesn't care about making the honor roll, he will also be unmotivated. Wigfield and colleagues (2009) found that students' beliefs that they were capable and the degree to which they valued academic success were, taken together, more important than their actual ability in predicting their achievement.

Atkinson (1964) added an important aspect to expectancy theory in pointing out that under certain circumstances, an overly high probability of success can be detrimental to motivation. If Mark is very able, it might be so easy for him to make the honor roll that he does not need to do his best. Atkinson (1958) explained this by arguing that there is a relationship between probability of success and incentive value of success such that success in an easy task is not as valued as success in a difficult task. Therefore, motivation should be at a maximum at moderate levels of probability of success. For example, two evenly matched tennis players will probably play their hardest. Unevenly matched players will not play as hard; the poor player might want very much to win but will have too low a probability of success to try very hard, and the better player may not value winning enough to exert his or her best effort. Confirming Atkinson's theory, more recent research has shown that a person's motivation increases as task difficulty increases—up to a point at which the person decides that success is very unlikely or that the goal isn't worth the effort (DeBacker & Nelson, 1999). This and other research findings indicate that moderate to difficult (but not impossible) tasks are better than easy ones for learning and motivation (Wentzel & Brophy, 2014; Wigfield & Eccles, 2000).

IMPLICATIONS OF EXPECTANCY THEORY FOR EDUCATION The most important implication of expectancy theory is the commonsense proposition that tasks for students should be neither too easy nor too difficult. If some students believe that they are likely to get an A no matter what they do, then their motivation will not be at a maximum. Similarly, if some students feel certain they will fail no matter what they do, their motivation will be minimal. Therefore, grading systems

THEORY INTO PRACTICE

Giving Students Motivating Feedback

Students who attribute their past failures on tasks to lack of ability are unlikely to expect to succeed in similar tasks and are, therefore, unlikely to exert much effort (Juvonen, 2000; Weiner, 2010). Obviously, the belief that you will fail can be self-fulfilling. Students who believe that they will fail will be poorly motivated to do academic work, and this might in turn cause them to fail. Therefore, the most damaging idea you can communicate to a student is that the student cannot learn.

Few teachers would say such a thing directly to a student, but the idea can be communicated just as effectively in several other ways. One is to use a competitive grading system (e.g., grading on the curve) and to make grades public and emphasize relative student rankings. This practice can make small differences in achievement level seem large, and students who receive the poorest grades might decide that they can never learn.

Alternatively, deemphasizing grades and relative rankings but expressing the (almost always correct) expectation that all students in the class can learn is likely to help students see that their chances of success depend on their efforts—an internal but alterable attribution that lets students anticipate success in the future if they do their best.

A stable, internal attribution for success ("I succeed because I am smart") is also a poor motivator. Able students, too, need to believe that it is their effort, not their ability, that leads to academic success. Teachers who emphasize the amount of effort as the cause of success as well as failure and who reward effort rather than ability are more likely to motivate all their students to do their best than are teachers who emphasize ability alone (Goslin, 2003; Schunk, 2016; Yeager & Dweck, 2012). Some formal means of rewarding students for effort rather than ability are the use of rewards for improvement; the use of differentiated instruction, in which the basis of success is progress at the student's own level; and the inclusion of effort as a component of grading or as a separate grade.

Connections 10.6
For more on individualized instruction, see Chapter 9.

should be set up so that earning an A is difficult (but possible) for as many students as feasible, and so that earning a low grade is possible for students who exert little effort. Success must be within the reach, but not the easy reach, of all students.

MyEdLab **Self-Check 10.1**

WHAT FACTORS AFFECT STUDENTS' MOTIVATION?

One of the most important types of motivation for education is **achievement motivation**, or the generalized tendency to strive for success and to choose goal-oriented success/failure activities (Stipek, 2002; Schunk, 2016; Zimmerman & Schunk, 2011). Given a choice of work partners for a complex task, achievement-motivated students tend to choose a partner who is good at the task, whereas affiliation-motivated students (who express the need for love and acceptance) are more likely to choose a friendly partner. Even after they experience failure, achievement-motivated students will persist longer at a task than students who are lower in achievement motivation and thus attribute their failures to lack of effort (an internal but alterable condition), rather than to external factors such as task difficulty or luck. In short, achievement-motivated students want and expect to succeed; when they fail, they redouble their efforts until they do succeed (Wentzel & Wigfield, 2009). Journalist Paul Tough (2011) argued that students need "grit" to overcome life's many obstacles. **Grit** is a good synonym for *high achievement motivation* (see Hoerr, 2012, 2013; Usher & Kober, 2012).

InTASC 1
Learner Development

Connections 10.7

For more on grading student effort, see Chapter 13.

MyEdLab

Video Example 10.2

The students in this science class are learning to use a dichotomous key. The teacher fosters achievement motivation as he emphasizes that "success" in this activity is defined by actively engaging in the scientific thought process, not necessarily by finding a "correct" answer.

Not surprisingly, students who are high in achievement motivation tend to succeed at school tasks (Stipek, 2002; Wentzel & Brophy, 2014). However, it is unclear which causes which: Does high achievement motivation lead to success in school, or does success in school (based on ability or other factors) lead to high achievement motivation? Initially, achievement motivation is strongly affected by family experiences (Turner & Johnson, 2003), but after children have been in school for a few years, success and motivation cause each other. Success breeds the desire for more success, which in turn breeds success (Bandura, 2012; Dotterer, McHale, & Crouter, 2009; Wentzel & Wigfield, 2009). In contrast, students who do not experience success in achievement settings will tend to lose the motivation to succeed in such settings and will turn their interest elsewhere (perhaps to social activities, sports, or even delinquent activities in which they might succeed). Achievement motivation tends to diminish over the school years, but it appears that this trend is due both to the nature of children and to the nature of middle and high schools (Dotterer et al., 2009; Hidi & Harackiewicz, 2000; Stipek, 2002).

Motivation and Goal Orientations

Some students are motivationally oriented toward **learning goals** (also called *task* or *mastery goals*); others are oriented toward **performance goals** (Wentzel & Brophy, 2014; Rolland, 2012; Senko, Hulleman, & Harackiewicz, 2011). Students with learning goals see the purpose of schooling as gaining competence in the skills being taught, whereas students with performance goals primarily seek to gain positive judgments of their competence (and avoid negative judgments). Students who are striving toward learning goals are likely to take difficult courses and to seek challenges. In contrast, students with performance goals focus on getting good grades, taking easy courses, and avoiding challenging situations (Urdan & Mestas, 2006).

LEARNING VERSUS PERFORMANCE GOALS Students with learning goals and those with performance goals do not differ in overall intelligence, but their classroom performances can differ markedly. When they run into obstacles, performance-oriented students tend to become discouraged, and their performance is seriously hampered. In contrast, when learning-oriented students encounter obstacles, they tend to keep trying, and their motivation and performance might actually increase (Schunk, 2016; Sins, van Joolingen, Savelsbergh, & van Hout-Wolters, 2008). Learning-oriented students are more likely to use metacognitive or self-regulated learning strategies (Greene, Miller, Crowson, Duke, & Akey, 2004; Pajares, Britner, & Valiante, 2000; Senko et al., 2011; Usher & Kober, 2012). They are likely to learn more than performance-oriented students of the same abilities (Huang, 2012; Shih, 2005). On the other hand, they may not get grades that reflect their learning, because they may focus their studying on what interests them rather than on what gets them good grades (Hulleman, Durik, Schweigert, & Harackiewicz, 2008; Senko & Miles, 2008). Performance-oriented students who perceive their abilities as low are likely to fall into a pattern of helplessness, for they believe that they have little chance of earning good grades (Senko et al., 2011; Usher & Kober, 2012). There is some evidence that such students are more prone to cheat (Murdock & Anderman, 2006). Learning-oriented students who perceive their ability to be low are concerned with how much they themselves can learn without regard for the performance of others (Senko et al., 2011). Unfortunately, there is evidence that over their years in school, students tend to shift from learning or mastery goals to performance goals (Harackiewicz, Barron, Tauer, & Carter, 2000; Stipek, 2002). However, there is also evidence that teachers who emphasize learning and developing competence (rather than grades) as the goals of the class obtain better learning results from their students (Murayama & Elliot, 2009; Rolland, 2012; Usher & Kober, 2012).

The most important implication of research on learning goals versus performance goals is that you should try to convince students that learning, rather than grades, is the purpose of academic work (Wentzel & Brophy, 2014). This can be done by emphasizing the interest value and practical importance of the material that students are studying and by deemphasizing grades and other rewards. For example, you might say, "Today we're going to learn about events deep in the earth that cause the fiery eruptions of volcanoes!" rather than "Today we're going to learn about volcanoes. Pay attention so that you can do well on tomorrow's test." In particular, use of highly competitive grading or incentive systems should be avoided. When students perceive that there is

TABLE 10.2 • Learning Goals, Performance Goals, and Teaching to Develop Learning Goals

STUDENTS WITH LEARNING GOALS	STUDENTS WITH PERFORMANCE GOALS	TEACHING TO DEVELOP LEARNING GOALS
Value learning for its own sake	Value grades, praise, rank	Increase intrinsic interest; discuss value of knowing and being able to do new things, rather than value of grades
Motivated by challenge, interest	Motivated by doing better than others	Pose difficult, exciting challenges
Errors are part of the learning process	Errors lead to anxiety, loss of self-worth	Refer to honest errors as contributing to learning and growth
Evaluation against students' own standards and value of new knowledge and skills	Evaluation against performance levels of other students	Emphasize value of new knowledge and skills; encourage students to set their own high learning standards
Value process of getting new knowledge and skills, not just the right answer. Value creativity and multiple solutions	Value clear path to a single right answer	Emphasize the process of learning and multiple ways of arriving at good answers or products. Encourage creativity and playfulness in learning
Value working with others and exchanging ideas	Value doing better than others	Use cooperative learning; avoid highly competitive grading

only one standard of success in the classroom and that only a few people can achieve it, those who lack confidence in their ability will be likely to give up in advance (Summers, 2006). Table 10.2 summarizes the differences between the achievement goals of students with learning goals and those of students with performance goals, and summarizes strategies that you can use to promote learning or task goals among students. Studies indicate that the types of tasks that are used in classrooms have a strong influence on students' adoption of learning goals. Tasks that are challenging, meaningful, and related to real life are more likely to lead to learning goals than are other tasks (Cushman, 2006; Darling-Hammond & Ifill-Lynch, 2006; Gregory & Kaufeldt, 2015).

Learned Helplessness

An extreme form of the motive to avoid failure is called **learned helplessness**, which is a perception that no matter what one does, one is doomed to failure or ineffectuality: "Nothing I do matters." In academic settings, learned helplessness can be related to an internal, stable explanation for failure: "I fail because I'm stupid, and that means I will always fail." Students who experience repeated failures might develop a "defensive pessimism" to protect themselves from negative feedback (Martin, Marsh, & Debus, 2001).

Learned helplessness can arise from inconsistent, unpredictable use of rewards and punishments by parents or teachers—a pattern that can lead students to believe that there is little they can do to be successful. Students with learning disabilities, for example, are more likely than other students to respond to failure with helpless behavior (Pintrich & Schunk, 2002). You can prevent or alleviate learned helplessness by giving students (1) opportunities for success in small steps; (2) immediate feedback; and (3) most important, consistent expectations and follow-through.

Certification Pointer

For a case study on your teacher certification test, you may be required to suggest an appropriate strategy for improving student motivation by training students to attribute their successes to controllable causes, especially effort.

Teacher Expectations and Achievement

On the first day of class, Mr. Erhard called roll. Soon he got to a name that looked familiar. "Wayne Clements?"

"Here!"

"Do you have a brother named Victor?"

"Yes."

"I remember Victor. He was a terror. I'm going to keep my eye on you!"

As he neared the end of the roll, Mr. Erhard saw that several boys were starting to whisper to one another in the back of the room. "Wayne! I asked the class to remain silent while I read the roll. Didn't you hear me? I knew I'd have to watch out for you!"

InTASC 9

Professional Learning and Ethical Practice

InTASC 8

Instructional Strategies

THEORY INTO PRACTICE

Helping Students Overcome Learned Helplessness

The concept of learned helplessness derives from the theory that students might become academic failures through a conditioning process based on negative feedback from teachers, school experiences, peers, and students themselves. Numerous studies show that when students consistently fail, they eventually give up. They become conditioned to helplessness.

Teachers at both the elementary and secondary levels can help to counter this syndrome in a variety of ways, including attribution training, goal restructuring, self-esteem programs, success-guaranteed approaches, and positive feedback systems. The following general principles are helpful for all students, especially students who have shown a tendency to accept failure (see Jackson, 2011).

1. *Accentuate the positive.* Get to know the student's strengths and then use these as building blocks. Every student has something she or he does well. But be careful that the strength is authentic; don't make up a strength. For example, a student might like to talk a lot but write poorly. Have the student complete assignments by talking rather than writing. As confidence is restored, slowly introduce writing.

2. *Eliminate the negative.* Do not play down a student's weaknesses, but focus on an attainable path to success. In the preceding example, talk to the student about problems with writing. Then have the student develop a plan to improve on the aspects of his or her writing that are causing most trouble. Discuss the plan, and together make up a contract about how the plan will be completed.

3. *Go from the familiar to the new, using advance organizers or guided discovery.* Some students have difficulties with concepts, skills, or ideas with which they are not familiar. Also, students relate better to lessons that are linked to their own experiences. For example, a high school math teacher might begin a lesson with a math problem that students might face in the real world, such as calculating the sales tax when purchasing a digital tablet. Further, the teacher can ask students to bring to class math problems they have encountered outside of school. The whole class can become involved in solving a student's math problem.

4. *Create challenges in which students actively create problems and solve them using their own knowledge and skills.*

This dialogue illustrates how teachers can establish expectations for their students and how these expectations can be self-fulfilling. Mr. Erhard doesn't know it, but Wayne is generally a well-behaved, conscientious student, quite unlike his older brother, Victor. However, because of his experience with Victor, Mr. Erhard expects that he will have trouble with Wayne. When he sees several boys whispering, it is Wayne he singles out for blame, confirming for himself that Wayne is a troublemaker. After a few episodes of this treatment, we can expect Wayne to begin playing the role Mr. Erhard has assigned to him.

Research on teachers' expectations for their students has generally found that students live up (or down) to the expectations that their teachers have for them (Hinnant, O'Brien, & Ghazarian, 2009; Jussim & Harber, 2005; Rubie-Davies, 2007, 2008), particularly in the younger grades and when teachers know relatively little about their students' actual achievement levels. A Dutch study found that teachers' expectations for their 12-year-olds still had an effect on the students' achievement (controlling for their actual ability) five years later (de Boer, Bosker, & van der Werf, 2010). Furthermore, there is evidence that students in schools whose teachers have high expectations achieve more than those in other schools (Marks, Doane, & Secada, 1998). Of course, students' expectations for themselves are at least as important as those of their teachers. One study found that students whose self-perceptions exceeded their current performance later tended to improve in grades, whereas those whose self-perceptions were lower than their performance tended to drop in grades (Anderman, Anderman, & Griesinger, 1999).

COMMUNICATING POSITIVE EXPECTATIONS It is important to communicate to students the expectation that they can all learn (Marzano, 2010). Obviously, it is a bad idea to state the contrary—that a particular student cannot learn—and few teachers would explicitly do so. There are several implicit ways to communicate positive expectations of your students (or avoid negative ones).

1. *Wait for students to respond.* Teachers tend to wait longer for answers from students for whom they have high expectations than from other students. Longer wait times may communicate high expectations and increase student achievement (Stipek, 2002; Wentzel & Brophy, 2014).

2. *Avoid unnecessary achievement distinctions among students.* Assessment results and grades should be a private matter between students and their teacher, not public information. Students usually know who is good in school and who is not, but you can still successfully communicate the expectation that all students, not only the most able ones, are capable of learning (Weinstein, Madison, & Kuklinski, 1995).

3. *Treat all students equally.* Call on students at all achievement levels equally often, and spend equal amounts of time with them (Marzano, 2010). In particular, guard against bias.

Anxiety and Achievement

Anxiety is a constant companion of education. Every student feels some anxiety at some time while in school; but for certain students, anxiety seriously inhibits learning or performance, particularly on tests (Cassady & Johnson, 2002).

The main source of anxiety in school is the fear of failure and, with it, loss of self-esteem (Pintrich & Schunk, 2002). Low achievers are particularly likely to feel anxious in school, but they are by no means the only ones. We all know very able, high-achieving students who are also very anxious, maybe even terrified to be less than perfect at any school task.

Anxiety can block school performance in several ways. Anxious students might have difficulty learning in the first place, difficulty using or transferring knowledge they do have, and difficulty demonstrating their knowledge on tests (Bandalos, Yates, & Thorndike-Christ, 1995). Anxious students are likely to be overly self-conscious in performance settings, a feeling that distracts attention from the task at hand (Tobias, 1992). One particularly common form of debilitating anxiety is math anxiety. Many students (and adults) simply freeze up when given math problems, particularly word problems (Everson, Tobias, Hartman, & Gourgey, 1993).

You can apply many strategies to reduce the negative impact of anxiety on learning and performance. Clearly, creating a classroom climate that is accepting, comfortable, and noncompetitive helps. Giving students opportunities to correct errors or improve their work before handing it in also helps anxious children, as does providing clear, unambiguous instructions (Wigfield & Eccles, 1989). In testing situations, teachers have many ways to help anxious students do their best. You can avoid time pressure, giving students plenty of time to complete a test and check their work. Tests that begin with easy problems and only gradually introduce more difficult ones are better for anxious students, and tests with standard, consistent answer formats also help such students. Test-anxious children can be trained in test-taking skills and relaxation techniques, and these can have a positive impact on their test performance (Spielberger & Vagg, 1995).

MyEdLab **Self-Check 10.2**

Connections 10.8
For more on grouping students, see Chapter 9.

Connections 10.9
Programs designed to train test-anxious children in test-taking skills are discussed in Chapter 14.

MyEdLab
Video Example 10.3
Textbook author Bob Slavin tells a story about how expectations affected a student named Mary, who later became a teacher and sports coach. Why was Mary unable to use the same strategies with her students and athletes that her parents had used with her? What sorts of motivational strategies have been most effective in your own life, and which might you expect to use most frequently in your own career?

HOW CAN TEACHERS INCREASE STUDENTS' MOTIVATION TO LEARN?

Learning takes work. Euclid, a Greek mathematician who lived around 300 B.C. and wrote the first geometry text, was asked by his king whether there were any shortcuts he could use to learn geometry, as he was a very busy man. "I'm sorry," Euclid replied, "but there is no royal road to geometry." The same is true of every other subject: Students get out of any course of study only what they put into it.

Researchers have evaluated numerous strategies to improve motivation to learn based on the theories discussed above, such as methods to help students see that success is due to effort rather than intelligence (Dweck, 2006). Methods of this kind have generally been successful in increasing motivation and achievement (Lazowski & Hulleman, 2016).

The remainder of this chapter discusses the means by which students can be motivated to exert the effort that learning requires.

Intrinsic and Extrinsic Motivation

Sometimes a course of study is so fascinating and useful to students that they are willing to do the work required to learn the material with no incentive other than the interest level of the material itself. For example, many students would gladly take auto mechanics or photography courses and work hard in them, even if the courses offered no credit or grades. For these students the favorite subject itself has enough **intrinsic incentive** value to motivate them to learn. Other students love to learn about particular topics such as sports, insects, dinosaurs, or famous people in history and need little encouragement or reward to do so (Gottfried & Fleming, 2001; Schraw, Flowerday, & Lehman, 2001). Students who have a strong "future time perspective" (i.e., are willing to do things today that may benefit them in the future) are often particularly motivated to learn, even without immediate incentives (Husman & Lens, 1999).

However, much of what must be learned in school is not inherently interesting or useful to most students in the short run. Students receive about 900 hours of instruction every year, and intrinsic interest alone will not keep them enthusiastically working day in and day out. In particular, students' intrinsic motivation generally declines from early elementary school through secondary school (Gottfried & Fleming, 2001; Sethi, Drake, Dialdin, & Lepper, 1995). It also declines over the course of each school year (Corpus, McClintic-Gilbert, & Hayenga, 2009). For this reason, schools apply a variety of **extrinsic incentives**, rewards for learning that are not inherent in the material being learned (Wentzel & Brophy, 2014). Extrinsic rewards range from praise to grades to recognition to prizes or other rewards.

In the vignette at the beginning of this chapter, Cal Lewis tried to enhance both intrinsic and extrinsic motivation. His simulation of the Constitutional Convention was intended to arouse students' intrinsic interest in the subject, and his ratings of students' presentations and his feedback at the end of each period were intended to provide extrinsic motivation.

LEPPER'S EXPERIMENT ON THE IMPACT OF REWARDS ON MOTIVATION An important question in research on motivation concerns whether providing extrinsic rewards diminishes intrinsic interest in an activity. In a classic experiment exploring this topic, Lepper and colleagues (1973) gave preschoolers an opportunity to draw with felt-tip markers, which many of them did quite enthusiastically. Then the researchers randomly divided the children into three groups: One group was told that its members would receive a reward for drawing a picture for a visitor (a Good Player Award), one group was given the same reward as a surprise (not dependent on the children's drawing), and one group received no reward. Over the next 4 days, observers recorded the children's free-play activities. Children who had received a reward for drawing spent about half as much time drawing with felt-tip markers as did those who had received the surprise reward and those who got no reward. The authors suggested that promising extrinsic rewards for an activity that is intrinsically interesting might undermine intrinsic interest by inducing children to expect a reward for doing what they had previously done for nothing. A later study (Greene & Lepper, 1974) found that simply telling children that they would be watched (through a one-way mirror) had an undermining effect similar to that of a promised reward.

"The school board decided not to raise teachers' salaries. We didn't want to undermine their intrinsic motivation."

DO REWARDS DESTROY INTRINSIC MOTIVATION? In understanding the results of these studies, it is important to recall the conditions of the research. The students who were chosen for the studies showed an intrinsic interest in using marking pens. Those who did not were excluded from the experiments. Also, drawing with felt-tip pens does not resemble most school tasks. Many children love to draw at home, but few, even those who are most interested in school subjects, would independently study grammar and punctuation, work math problems, or learn the valences of chemical elements. Further, many of our most creative and self-motivated scientists (for example) were frequently rewarded as students with grades, science fair prizes, and scholarships for doing science, and virtually all successful artists have been rewarded at some point for their artistic creations. Research on older students doing more school-like tasks has generally failed to replicate the results of the Lepper and colleagues (1973) experiment (Cameron & Pierce, 1994, 1996; Eisenberger & Cameron, 1998). In fact, the use of rewards more often increases intrinsic motivation, especially when rewards are contingent on the quality of performance rather than on mere participation in an activity, when the rewards are seen as recognition of competence (Rosenfield, Folger, & Adelman, 1980), when the task in question is not very interesting, or when the rewards are social (e.g., praise) rather than material (Cameron, 2001; Cameron, Pierce, Banko, & Gear, 2005; Lepper, 1983; Ryan & Deci, 2000). Cameron (2001) summarizes the situation in which extrinsic rewards undermine intrinsic interest as follows: "A negative effect occurs when a task is of high interest, when the rewards are tangible and offered beforehand, and when the rewards are delivered without regard to success on the task or to any specified level of performance" (p. 40). This is a very narrow set of conditions, characterized by Bandura (1986, p. 246) as "of no great social import because rewards are rarely showered on people regardless of how they behave." However, Deci, Koestner, and Ryan (2001), while acknowledging that there are many forms of extrinsic rewards that have a positive or neutral impact on motivation, nevertheless argue that "the use of rewards as a motivational strategy is clearly a risky proposition, so we continue to argue for thinking about educational practices that will engage students' interest and support the development of their self-regulation" (2001, p. 50).

The research on the effects of extrinsic rewards on intrinsic motivation does counsel caution in the use of material rewards for engaging in tasks that students would do without rewards (see Lepper, 1998; Sansone & Harackiewicz, 2000). You should attempt to make everything you teach as intrinsically interesting as possible and should avoid handing out material rewards when they are unnecessary, but you should not refrain from using extrinsic rewards when they are needed. Often, extrinsic rewards may be necessary to get students started in a learning activity but may be phased out as students come to enjoy the activity and succeed at it (Goodwin, 2012a; Stipek, 2002; Wentzel & Brophy, 2014). Also, remember that in any given class, there are students who are intrinsically motivated to do a given activity and those who are not. To ensure that all students learn, strategic use of both intrinsic and extrinsic motivators is likely to be necessary.

Certification Pointer

On your teacher certification test, you should recognize the value of intrinsic motivation in promoting students' life-long growth and learning.

Enhancing Intrinsic Motivation

Classroom instruction should enhance intrinsic motivation as much as possible. Increasing intrinsic motivation is always helpful for learning, regardless of whether extrinsic incentives are also in use (Kafele, 2013; Vansteenkiste, Lens, & Deci, 2006). This means that you must try to get your students interested in the material you are presenting and then present it in an appealing way that both satisfies and increases students' curiosity about the material itself. A discussion of some means of doing this follows (see Wentzel & Brophy, 2014; Stipek, 2002).

CREATING A SUPPORTIVE CLASSROOM CLIMATE One way to build intrinsic motivation to learn is to create a classroom climate that is warm, accepting, and positive (Jackson & Zmuda, 2014; Marzano, 2011; Wentzel, 2010; Wormeli, 2014). In such classrooms, students work hard because they want to please a valued teacher, and they feel safe in trying out their ideas and taking intellectual risks. Classroom strategies that can be adapted to the needs of all students and communicate high expectations, with support for all students to reach high levels, may also add to intrinsic motivation (McCombs, 2010), as may classrooms that value cultural diversity and make all students feel welcome and provided for (Curwin, 2010; Kumar & Maehr, 2010). There is evidence that programs intended to improve social-emotional climate in the classroom also improve learning (e.g., Brown, Jones, LaRusso, & Aber, 2010).

AROUSING INTEREST It is important to convince students of the importance and interest level of the material that is about to be presented and to show (if possible) how the knowledge to be gained will be useful to students (Renninger & Hidi, 2011; Wentzel & Brophy, 2014). For example, intrinsic motivation to learn a lesson on percents might be increased by introducing the lesson as follows:

> Today we will begin a lesson on percents. Percents are important in our daily lives. For example, when you buy something at the store and a salesperson figures the sales tax, he or she is using percents. When we leave a tip for a waiter or waitress, we use percents. We often hear in the news things like "Prices rose seven percent last year." In a few years, many of you will have summer jobs, and if they involve handling money, you'll probably be using percents all the time.

Introducing lessons with examples relating the material to students' cultures can be particularly effective. For example, in introducing astronomy to a class with many Latino children, you could say, "Thousands of years ago, people in Mexico and Central America had calendars that accurately predicted the movement of the moon and stars for centuries into the future. How could they do this? Today we will learn about how planets, moons, and stars move in predictable paths." The purpose of these statements is to arouse student curiosity about the lesson to come, thereby enhancing intrinsic motivation to learn the material (Vacca, 2006).

Another way to enhance students' intrinsic interest is to give them some choice about what they will study or how they will study it (Stipek, 2002; Wentzel & Brophy, 2014). Choices need not be unlimited to be motivational. For example, students might be given a choice of writing about ancient Athens or Sparta, or a choice of working independently or in pairs.

MAINTAINING CURIOSITY A skillful teacher uses a variety of means to further arouse or maintain curiosity in the course of the lesson (Goodwin, 2014; Wormeli, 2014). Science teachers, for instance, often use demonstrations that surprise or baffle students and induce them to want to understand why. A floating dime makes students curious about the surface tension of liquids. "Burning" a dollar bill covered with an alcohol– water solution (without harming the dollar bill) certainly increases curiosity about the heat of combustion. Guthrie and Cox (2001) found that giving students hands-on experience with science activities greatly increased their learning from books on related topics. Encouraging students to be curious, and to ask themselves, their peers, and their teachers questions, adds to motivation (Engel, 2013).

Less dramatically, surprising or challenging students with a problem they can't solve with their current knowledge can arouse curiosity, and therefore intrinsic motivation (see Bottge, 2001). A seventh-grade teacher in England used this principle in a lesson on equivalent fractions. First, he had his students halve and then halve again $8/13$ and $12/20$. Working in pairs they instantly agreed on $4/13$ and $2/13$, and $6/20$ and $3/20$. Then he gave them $13/20$. After a moment of hesitation, students came back with 6 ½/20 and then 3 ¼/20! "Crikey!" he said. "All these fractions inside fractions are making me nervous! Isn't there some other way we can do this?" "Round off?" suggested one student. "Use decimals?" suggested another. Finally, after much discussion and argument, the students realized that they could use their knowledge about equivalent fractions to find the solutions: $13/40$ and $13/80$. Getting the students into a familiar pattern and then breaking that pattern excited the whole class, engaging them far more effectively than would have been possible by simply teaching the algorithm in the first place. The element of surprise, challenging the students' current understanding, made them intensely curious about an issue they'd never before considered.

SETTING CHALLENGING TASKS AND AMBITIOUS GOALS The U.S. Marines like to say, "The difficult we do immediately. The impossible takes a little longer."

This is the spirit you want to build in your students. No one is excited about doing routine or easy tasks, or attaining modest goals. Students can be highly motivated by scary-looking tasks, as long as you believe in them and guarantee that you and their peers will help when problems arise. They can be excited by impossible-looking goals, as long as they can see a step-by-step path to attaining them (Jackson & Zmuda, 2014; Kafele, 2013; Pink, 2009).

Never say, "This is easy." Instead, communicate that "this is tough but I know you can do it." There is a big difference!

Connections 10.10
The importance of student interest in creative problem solving and other constructivist approaches is discussed in Chapter 8.

Connections 10.11
The importance of student interest in lesson content and presentation is discussed in Chapter 7.

USING A VARIETY OF INTERESTING PRESENTATION MODES The intrinsic motivation to learn something is enhanced by the use of interesting materials, as well as by variety in mode of presentation. For example, you can maintain student interest in a subject by alternating use of videos, guest speakers, demonstrations, and so on, although the use of each resource must be carefully planned to be sure it focuses on the course objectives and complements the other activities. Use of computer games can enhance most students' intrinsic motivation to learn (Clark et al., 2013; Patterson, 2012). Among the things that make materials interesting are the use of emotional content (e.g., danger, love, money, heartbreak, disaster), concrete rather than abstract examples, cause-and-effect relationships, and clear organization (Jetton & Alexander, 2001; Schraw et al., 2001; Wade, 2001).

One excellent means of increasing interest in a subject is to use games or simulations (Clark et al., 2013; Phillips & Popovic, 2012; Marzano, 2010). A simulation, or role play, is an exercise in which students take on roles and engage in activities appropriate to those roles. Cal Lewis used a simulation to teach students about the Constitutional Convention. Programs exist that simulate many aspects of government; for example, students may take roles as legislators who must negotiate and trade votes to satisfy their constituents' interests or take the roles of economic actors (farmers, producers, consumers) who run a mini-economy. Creative teachers have long used simulations that they designed themselves. For example, you can have students write their own newspaper; design, manufacture, and market a product; or set up and run a bank. In particular, giving adolescents adult-like roles (in simulations) can increase their intrinsic motivation and engagement (Allen & Allen, 2010).

Nonsimulation games can also increase motivation to learn a given subject. The spelling bee is a popular example of a nonsimulation game. Teams–Games–Tournament, or TGT (Slavin, 1995a), uses games that can be adapted to any subject. Team games are usually better than individual games. A form of cooperative learning (recall Chapter 8), team games provide an opportunity for teammates to help one another and avoid one problem of individual games—that of more-able students consistently winning. If all students are put on mixed-ability teams, all have a good chance of success.

HELPING STUDENTS MAKE CHOICES AND SET THEIR OWN GOALS One fundamental principle of motivation is that people work harder for goals that they themselves set than for goals set for them by others (Anderman et al., 2013; Azzam, 2014; Ryan & Deci, 2000). For example, a student might set a minimum number of books she expects to read at home or a score she expects

InTASC 3
Learning Environments

InTASC 8
Instructional Strategies.

21ST CENTURY LEARNING

Intrinsic Motivation

In traditional teaching, it has long been necessary to use extrinsic incentives, such as grades and praise, to motivate students to do their best. Incentives are still likely to be important in the future, but new classroom teaching technologies can help increase intrinsic motivation for learning. Video clips, animations, demonstrations, and interactive technologies can add variety and fun to lessons and give students more active roles. This is not only useful for learning school subjects but also prepares students for a world in which they will increasingly need to take responsibility for motivation themselves and maintain high productivity in less structured, more flexible workplaces.

QUESTION

- Given what you now know about intrinsic and extrinsic motivation, what are some ways you might motivate students to learn about technology applications?

to attain on an upcoming quiz. At the next goal-setting conference you might discuss student attainment of (or failure to attain) goals and set new goals for the following week. During these meetings you might help students learn to set ambitious but realistic goals and should praise them for setting and then achieving their goals. Goal-setting strategies of this kind have been found to increase students' academic performance and self-efficacy (Page-Voth & Graham, 1999; Shih & Alexander, 2000). Similarly, there is much evidence that children are more highly motivated to engage in activities that they choose, even if the choice is just between two alternatives (Patall et al., 2008; Vokoun & Bigelow, 2008).

PRESENTATIONS Did you ever notice how hard students work to prepare for a play, a concert, or a science fair exhibit? They want to do their very best when there is an audience. You can use this in smaller ways (see Bergin, Bergin, Van Dover, & Murphy, 2013). For example, students might prepare and present group multimedia reports, brief plays, and other performances designed to inform and delight their audiences. These have to be designed carefully to avoid taking too much time. For example, groups might prepare a two-minute summary of a more elaborate report, with only one or two groups (chosen at random or chosen on the basis of the two-minute summary) getting a chance to show off their whole report. Alternatively, groups might each perform for another group rather than for the whole class, while you circulate among groups.

CAREER RELEVANCE Students are likely to work harder if they see a connection between course content and desirable careers, or other important life achievements (Fisher & Frey, 2014a). An evaluation of a program called CareerStart, an approach that emphasizes the career relevance of course content in middle school, found positive effects on math performance (Woolley et al., 2013).

Principles for Providing Extrinsic Incentives to Learn

Teachers should always try to enhance students' intrinsic motivation to learn academic materials, but at the same time, they should not hesitate to also use extrinsic incentives if these are needed (Borich, 2014; Levitt et al., 2012; Schunk, 2016; Wentzel & Brophy, 2014). Not every subject is intrinsically interesting to all students, and students must be motivated to do the hard work necessary to master difficult subjects. The following sections discuss a variety of incentives that can help motivate students to learn academic material.

EXPRESSING CLEAR EXPECTATIONS Students need to know exactly what they are supposed to do, how they will be evaluated, and what the consequences of success will be. Often, students' failures on particular tasks stem from confusion about what they are being asked to do (Jackson & Zmuda, 2014; Wentzel & Brophy, 2014). Communicating clear expectations is important. For example, you might introduce a writing assignment as follows:

> Today, I'd like you all to write a composition about what Thomas Jefferson would think of government in the United States today. I expect your compositions to be about six pages long, and I want them to compare and contrast the plan of government laid out by the nation's founders with the way government actually operates today. Your compositions will be graded on the basis of your ability to describe similarities and differences between the structure and function of the U.S. government in Thomas Jefferson's time and today, as well as on the originality and clarity of your writing. This will be an important part of your 6 weeks' grade, so I expect you to do your best!

Note that you are clear about what students are to write, how much material is expected, how the work will be evaluated, and how important the work will be for the students' grades. This clarity assures students that efforts directed at writing a good composition will pay off. If you had just said, "I'd like you all to write a composition about what Thomas Jefferson would think about government in the United States today," students might write the wrong thing, write too much or too little, or perhaps emphasize the if-Jefferson-were-alive-today aspect of the assignment rather than the comparative-government aspect. They would be unsure how much importance you intended to place on the mechanics of the composition as compared to its content. Finally, they would have no way of knowing how their efforts would pay off, lacking any indication of how much emphasis you would give to the compositions in computing grades.

A study by Graham, MacArthur, and Schwartz (1995) showed the importance of specificity. Low-achieving fifth- and sixth-graders were asked to revise compositions either to "make [your paper] better" or to "add at least three things that will add information to your paper." The students with the more specific instructions wrote higher-quality, longer revisions because they had a clearer idea of exactly what was being asked of them.

PROVIDING CLEAR FEEDBACK   The word **feedback** means information on the results of one's efforts. The term has been used throughout this text to refer both to information students receive on their performance and to information teachers obtain on the effects of their instruction. Feedback can serve as an incentive. Research on feedback has found that provision of information on the results of one's actions can be an adequate reward in many circumstances. However, to be an effective motivator, feedback must be clear, must be specific, and must be provided soon after performance (Schunk, 2016; Wentzel & Brophy, 2014). This is important for all students, but especially for young ones. For example, praise for a job well done should specify what the student did well:

- "Good work! I like the way you used the guide words in the dictionary to find your target words."

- "I like that answer. It shows you've been thinking about what I've been saying about freedom and responsibility."

- "This is an excellent essay. It started with a statement of the argument you were going to make and then supported the argument with relevant information. I also like the care you took with punctuation and word usage."

Specific feedback is both informative and motivational (Schunk et al., 2008). It tells students what they did right, so that they will know what to do in the future, and it helps give them an effort-based attribution for success ("You succeeded because you worked hard"). In contrast, if students are praised or receive a good grade without any explanation, they are unlikely to learn from the feedback what to do next time to be successful, and they might form an ability attribution ("I succeeded because I'm smart") or an external attribution ("I must have succeeded because the teacher likes me, the task was easy, or I lucked out"). As noted earlier in this chapter, effort attributions are most conducive to continuing motivation (Pintrich & Schunk, 2002). Similarly, feedback about mistakes or failures can add to motivation if it focuses only on the performance itself (not on students' general abilities) and if it is alternated with success feedback.

PROVIDING IMMEDIATE FEEDBACK   Immediacy of feedback is also very important (Curwin, 2014; Sparks, 2012; Zimmerman & Schunk, 2011). If students complete a project on Monday and don't receive any feedback on it until Friday, the informational and motivational value of the feedback will be diminished. First, if they made errors, they might continue all week making similar errors on related material, which might have been averted by feedback on the performance. Second, a long delay between behavior and consequence confuses the relationship between the two. Young students, especially, might have little idea why they received a particular grade if the performance on which the grade is based occurred several days earlier.

PROVIDING FREQUENT FEEDBACK   Feedback should be delivered frequently to students to maintain their best efforts (Perks & Middleton, 2014). For example, it is unrealistic to expect most students to work hard for 6 or 9 weeks in hopes of improving their grade unless they receive frequent feedback. Research in the behavioral learning theory tradition has established that no matter how powerful a reward is, it may have little impact on behavior if it is given infrequently; small, frequent rewards are more effective incentives than are large, infrequent ones. Research on frequency of testing has generally found that it is a good idea to give frequent brief quizzes to assess student progress, rather than infrequent long tests (Borich, 2014). Research also indicates the importance of asking many questions in class so that students can gain information about their own level of understanding and can receive reinforcement (such as praise and recognition) for paying attention to lessons.

INCREASING THE VALUE AND AVAILABILITY OF EXTRINSIC MOTIVATORS   Expectancy theories of motivation, discussed earlier in this chapter, hold that motivation is a product of the value an individual attaches to success and the individual's estimate of the likelihood of success (see Wigfield et al., 2009). One implication of this is that students must value incentives if they are to be effective motivators. Some students are not particularly interested in teacher praise or grades but might value notes sent home to their parents, a little extra recess time, or a special privilege in the classroom.

Connections 10.12
Feedback is also discussed in Chapter 7 and Chapter 13.

InTASC 6

Assessment

MyEdLab
Video Example 10.4
As this teacher helps his student develop an art portfolio for review by the College Board, he provides feedback indicating what the student has done well and then offers suggestions for making the portfolio better. He fosters intrinsic motivation as he encourages the student to reflect on his own performance and make an effort to improve.

Connections 10.13
For grading methods that recognize progress and effort, see Chapter 13.

Another implication of expectancy theory is that even though all students should have a chance to be rewarded if they do their best, no student should have an easy time achieving the maximum reward. This principle is violated by traditional grading practices, because some students find it easy to earn A's and B's, whereas others believe that they have little chance of academic success no matter what they do. In this circumstance, neither high achievers nor low achievers are likely to exert their best efforts. This is one reason why it is important to reward students for effort, for doing better than they have done in the past, or for making progress, rather than only for getting a high score. For example, students can build a portfolio of compositions, projects, reports, or other work and can then see how their work is improving over time. Not all students are equally capable of achieving high scores, but all are equally capable of exerting effort, exceeding their own past performance, or making progress, so these are often better, more equally available criteria on which to base reward (see Chapter 13).

Connections 10.14
For more on student portfolios, see Chapter 13.

Using Praise Effectively

Connections 10.15
For more on the use of praise as a reinforcer, see Chapter 11.

Praise serves many purposes in classroom instruction, but it is primarily used to reinforce appropriate behaviors and to give feedback to students on what they are doing right. Overall, it is a good idea to use praise frequently, especially with young children and in classrooms with many low-achieving students (Wentzel & Brophy, 2014). However, what is more important than the amount of praise given is the way it is given. Praise is effective as a classroom motivator to the extent that it is contingent, specific, and credible (Sutherland, Wehby, & Copeland, 2000). **Contingent praise** depends on student performance of well-defined behaviors. For example, if you say, "I'd like you all to open your books to page 92 and work problems one to ten," then give praise only to the students who follow directions. Praise should be given only for appropriate behaviors.

Specificity means to praise students for specific behaviors, not for general "goodness." For example, you might say, "Susan, I'm glad you followed my directions to start work on your composition," rather than "Susan, you're doing great!"

When praise is *credible*, it is given sincerely for good work. Wentzel and Brophy (2014) note that when praising low-achieving or disruptive students for good work, teachers often contradict their words with tone, posture, or other nonverbal cues. In addition to contingency, specificity, and credibility, Wentzel and Brophy's list includes several particularly important principles that reinforce topics discussed earlier in this chapter. For example, guidelines 7 and 8 emphasize that praise should be given for good performance relative to a student's usual level of performance. That is, students who usually do well should not be praised for a merely average performance, but students who usually do less well should be praised when they do better. This is related to the principle of accessibility of reward discussed earlier in this chapter; rewards should be neither too easy nor too difficult for students to obtain. Guideline 9 emphasizes the importance of praising effort, rather than intelligence or other factors that students do not control (see Dweck, 2007; Yeager & Dweck, 2012).

Certification Pointer
When responding to a case study on your certification test, you should know that providing praise that is contingent, specific, and credible can increase student motivation.

Teaching Students to Praise Themselves

There is increasing evidence that students can learn to praise themselves and that this increases their academic success. For example, children can learn to mentally give themselves a pat on the back when they finish a task or to stop at regular intervals to notice how much they have done. This strategy is a key component of self-regulated learning (Duckworth et al., 2016; Germeroth & Day-Hess, 2013; Zimmerman & Schunk, 2011; Zimmerman, 2013).

MyEdLab **Self-check 10.3**

MyEdLab **Video Analysis Tool 10.1** Go to MyEdLab and click on the Video Analysis Tool to access the exercise "Motivating students to pursue learning goals: attention."

MyEdLab **Video Analysis Tool 10.2** Go to MyEdLab and click on the Video Analysis Tool to access the exercise "Motivating students to pursue learning goals: achievement value."

MyEdLab **Video Analysis Tool 10.3** Go to MyEdLab and click on the Video Analysis Tool to access the exercise "Motivating students to pursue learning goals: expectancy."

MyEdLab **Video Analysis Tool 10.4** Go to MyEdLab and click on the Video Analysis Tool to access the exercise "Motivating students to pursue learning goals: control."

MyEdLab **Video Analysis Tool 10.5** Go to MyEdLab and click on the Video Analysis Tool to access the exercise "Motivating students to pursue learning goals: attribution."

SUMMARY

What Is Motivation?

Motivation is an internal process that activates, guides, and maintains behavior over time. There are different kinds, intensities, aims, and directions of motivation.

What Are Some Theories of Motivation?

In behavioral learning theory, motivation is a consequence of reinforcement. However, the value of a reinforcer depends on many factors, and the strength of motivation may be different in different students.

In Maslow's human needs theory, which is based on a hierarchy of needs, people must satisfy their lower-level (deficiency) needs before they will be motivated to try to satisfy their higher-level (growth) needs. Maslow's concept of the need for self-actualization, the highest need, is defined as the desire to become everything one is capable of becoming.

Attribution theory seeks to understand people's explanations for their success or failure. A central assumption is that people will attempt to maintain a positive self-image; when good things happen, people attribute them to their own abilities, whereas they tend to attribute negative events to factors beyond their control. Locus of control might be internal (success or failure is based on personal effort or ability) or external (success or failure is the result of luck or task difficulty). Students who are self-regulated learners perform better than those who are externally motivated. Self-regulated learners consciously plan and monitor their learning and thus retain more.

Expectancy theory holds that a person's motivation to achieve a goal depends on the product of that person's estimation of his or her chance of success and the value he or she places on success. Motivation should be at a maximum at moderate levels of probability of success. An important educational implication is that learning tasks should be neither too easy nor too difficult.

How Can Achievement Motivation Be Enhanced?

You can emphasize learning goals and positive or empowering attributions. Students with learning goals see the purpose of school as gaining knowledge and competence; these students tend to have higher motivation to learn than students whose performance goals are positive judgments and good grades. Use special programs such as attribution training to help students out of learned helplessness, in which students feel that they are doomed to fail despite their actions. Your expectations significantly affect students' motivation and achievement. You can communicate positive expectations for student learning and for reduced anxiety.

How Can Teachers Increase Students' Motivation to Learn?

An incentive is a reinforcer that people can expect to receive if they perform a specific behavior. Intrinsic incentives are aspects of certain tasks that in themselves have enough value to motivate students to do the tasks on their own. Extrinsic incentives include grades, gold stars, and other rewards. You can enhance intrinsic motivation by arousing students' interest, stoking curiosity, using a variety of presentation modes, and letting students set their own goals. Ways to offer extrinsic incentives include stating clear expectations; giving clear, immediate, and frequent feedback; and increasing the value and availability of rewards. Classroom rewards include praise, which is most effective when it is contingent, specific, and credible.

THE INTENTIONAL TEACHER
Using What You Know about Motivation to Improve Teaching and Learning

Intentional teachers know that, although students might be motivated by different incentives and to varying degrees, every student is motivated. They understand that many elements of motivation can be influenced by the teacher, and they capitalize on their ability to unearth and direct student motivation. They provide instruction that helps students find meaning in learning and in taking pride in their own accomplishments.

- They do what they can to ensure that students' basic needs for comfort and security are met so that they can devote their energies to learning.
- They constantly reinforce the idea that success in school and life is based on effort, which is under the students' own control, not on innate characteristics such as intelligence.
- They teach students to self-regulate by giving them opportunities to do work on their own and by teaching learning strategies such as goal-setting, self-evaluation, and self-reinforcement.
- They express positive expectations for all students and plan how they will help students who struggle to meet those expectations. They avoid making comparisons among students that communicate higher expectations for some than for others.
- They assign tasks that are difficult and challenging for all, but not impossibly so. They set tasks that students will feel proud to accomplish and that they believe are worth their efforts.
- They try to enhance intrinsic motivation to learn by making content interesting, relevant to students, useful, and engaging.
- They provide extrinsic incentives to learn when these are necessary, providing incentives that are symbolic rather than tangible whenever possible.
- They use praise to identify what students have done to deserve praise and to recognize effort. They teach students to recognize their own success and praise themselves, rather than depending on teachers or others to do so.

MyEdLab
Application Exercise 10.1

In the Pearson etext, watch a classroom video. Then use the guidelines in "The Intentional Teacher" to answer a set of questions that will help you reflect on and understand the teaching and learning presented in the video.

KEY TERMS

Review the following key terms from the chapter.

SELF-ASSESSMENT: PRACTICING FOR LICENSURE

Directions: The chapter-opening vignette addresses indicators that are often assessed in state licensure exams. Reread the chapter-opening vignette, and then respond to the following questions.

1. According to behavioral learning theorists, why are Cal Lewis's students motivated to learn about the Constitutional Convention?
   a. To obtain reinforcers
   b. To satisfy growth needs
   c. To eliminate deficiency needs
   d. To maximize expectancy effects

2. Mr. Lewis's students see the purpose of lessons about the Constitutional Convention gaining information about the history of the United States. What type of goal orientation is this?
   a. Performance goal
   b. Learning goal
   c. Expectancy goal
   d. Self-regulated goal

3. Beth Andrews, a shy girl in Mr. Lewis's class, proposes elements of the Bill of Rights to the convention members. If Beth has an internal locus of control, she is most likely to attribute her successful presentation to which of the following factors?
   a. The presentation requirements being easy
   b. Favoritism by the teacher
   c. Careful preparation
   d. Good luck

4. Mr. Lewis wants his students to work hard regardless of their ability level or the difficulty of the task. What type of attributions will he attempt to instill in his students?
   a. Internal–stable
   b. Internal–unstable
   c. External–stable
   d. External–unstable

5. Under what circumstances is it most important for Mr. Lewis to avoid the use of external incentives?
   a. When students are doing challenging work
   b. When the task communicates feedback about students' competence
   c. When students are motivated to do the work without extrinsic incentives
   d. When students have experienced a great deal of failure

6. Analyze Mr. Lewis's lesson and his students' willingness to participate from the perspective of each of the four theories of motivation presented in the chapter: behavioral, human needs, attribution, and expectancy.

7. Describe ways in which you can increase students' motivation to learn.

MyEdLab **Licensure Exam 10.1** Answer questions and receive instant feedback in your Pearson eText in MyEdLab.

Echo/Cultura/Getty Images

CHAPTER ELEVEN

Effective Learning Environments

LEARNING OUTCOMES

At the end of this chapter, you should be able to:

11.1 Understand the impact of time on learning

11.2 Discuss how to prevent and manage routine student misbehavior

11.3 Identify strategies to prevent and respond to student behavior problems

11.4 Describe how knowledge of effective learning environments informs intentional teaching

THE BELL RINGS OUTSIDE OF JULIA CAVALHO'S TENTH-GRADE ENGLISH CLASS. THE SOUND IS STILL ECHOING IN THE HALL WHEN MS. CAVALHO STARTS HER LESSON.

"Today," she begins, "you will become thieves. Worse than thieves. Thieves steal only your money or your property. You—" (she looks around the class and pauses for emphasis) "—will steal something far more valuable. You will steal an author's style. An author builds his or her style, word by word, sentence by sentence, over many years. Stealing an author's style is like stealing a work of art that someone took years to create. It's despicable, but you're going to do it."

During her speech the students sit in rapt attention. Two students, Mark and Gloria, slink in late. Mark makes a funny "Oops, I'm late" face and does an exaggerated tiptoe to his desk. Ms. Cavalho ignores both of them, as does the class. She continues her lesson.

"To whom are you going to do this dirty deed? Papa Hemingway, of course. Hemingway of the short, punchy sentence. Hemingway of the almost excessive attention to physical detail. You've read *The Old Man and the Sea*. You've read parts of *The Sun Also Rises* and *For Whom the Bell Tolls*."

While Ms. Cavalho talks, Mark makes an exaggerated show of getting out his books. He whispers to a neighboring student. Without stopping her lesson, Ms. Cavalho moves near Mark. He stops whispering and pays attention.

"Today you will become Hemingway. You will steal his words, his pace, his meter, his similes, his metaphors, and put them to work in your own stories."

Ms. Cavalho has students review elements of Hemingway's style, which the class has studied before.

"Everyone think for a moment. How would Hemingway describe an old woman going up the stairs at the end of a long day's work? Mai, what do you think?"

Mai gives her short description of the old woman.

"Sounds great to me. I like your use of very short sentences and physical description. Any other ideas? Kevin?"

Ms. Cavalho lets several students give Hemingway-style descriptions, using them as opportunities to reinforce her main points.

"In a moment," she says, "you're going to get your chance to become Ernest Hemingway. As usual, you'll be working in your writing response groups. Before we start, however, let's go over our rules about effective group work. Who can tell me what they are?"

The students volunteer several rules: Respect others, explain your ideas, be sure everyone participates, stand up for your opinion, keep voices low.

"All right," says Ms. Cavalho. "When I say begin, I'd like you to move your desks together and start planning your compositions. Ready? Begin."

The students move their desks together smoothly and quickly and get right to work. During the transition, Ms. Cavalho calls Mark and Gloria to her desk to discuss their lateness. Gloria has a good excuse, but Mark is developing a pattern of lateness and disruptiveness.

"Mark," says Ms. Cavalho, "I'm concerned about your lateness and your behavior in class. I've spoken to some

(continued)

of your other teachers, and they say you're behaving even worse in their classes than you do in mine. Please come here after school, and we'll see if we can come up with a solution to this problem."

Mark returns to his group and gets to work. Ms. Cavalho circulates among the groups, giving encouragement to students who are working well. When she sees two girls who are goofing off, she moves close to them and puts her hand on one girl's shoulder while looking at the plan for her composition. "Good start," she says. "Let's see how far you can get with this by the end of the period."

The students work in a controlled but excited way through the end of the period, thoroughly enjoying "stealing" from Hemingway. The classroom sounds like a beehive with busy, involved students sharing ideas, reading drafts to each other, and editing each other's compositions. At the end of the day, Mark returns to Ms. Cavalho's classroom.

"Mark," she says, "we need to do something about your lateness and your clowning in class. How would you suggest that we solve this problem?"

"Gloria was late, too," Mark protests.

"We're not talking about Gloria. We're talking about you. You are responsible for your own behavior."

"OK, OK, I promise I'll be on time."

"That's not good enough. We've had this conversation before. We need a different plan this time. I know you can succeed in this class, but you're making it hard on yourself as well as disrupting your classmates."

"Let's try an experiment," Ms. Cavalho goes on. "Each day, I'd like you to rate your own behavior. I'll do the same. If we both agree at the end of each week that you've been on time and appropriately behaved, fine. If not, I'll need to call your parents and see whether we can make a plan with them. Are you willing to give it a try?"

"OK, I guess so."

"Great. I'm expecting to see a new Mark starting tomorrow. I know you won't let me down!"

USING YOUR EXPERIENCE

CRITICAL THINKING What methods of classroom management does Ms. Cavalho use? What potential problems is she preventing?

CREATIVE THINKING Suppose Mark continues to be late for class. Plan a conference with his parents. What are the goals? How will they be implemented?

CRITICAL AND CREATIVE THINKING Analyze two variables, grade level and classroom management strategies, in a matrix. Using Ms. Cavalho's classroom as a starter, create this matrix with grade level on the horizontal row (e.g., elementary, middle, and high school), and then brainstorm classroom management strategies down the vertical column. Finally, check off which management strategies are influential at different grade levels.

WHAT IS AN EFFECTIVE LEARNING ENVIRONMENT?

InTASC 3

Learning Environments

InTASC 8

Instructional Strategies

There is no magic or charisma to make you an effective classroom manager. Setting up an effective learning environment is a matter of knowing a set of techniques that any teacher can learn and apply (Jones & Jones, 2016; Korpershoek et al., 2016; Poole & Evertson, 2012). Providing an effective learning environment includes strategies that teachers use to create a positive, productive classroom experience. Often called **classroom management**, strategies for providing effective learning environments include not only preventing and responding to misbehavior but also, and even more important, using class time well, creating an atmosphere that is conducive to interest and inquiry, and permitting activities that engage students' minds and imaginations (Cooper, 2014; Edwards, 2014; Levin, Nolan, Kerr, Elliott, & Bajovic, 2016). A class with no behavior problems can by no means be assumed to be a well-managed class.

The most effective approach to classroom management is effective instruction (Borich, 2014; Buffum, Mattos, Weber, & Hierck, 2014; Dean, Hubbell, Pitler, & Stone, 2012; Poole & Evertson, 2012; WWC, 2014a). Students who are participating in well-structured activities that engage their interests, who are highly motivated to learn, and who are working on tasks that are challenging yet within their capabilities rarely pose any serious management problems. The vignette involving Ms. Cavalho illustrates this. She has a well-managed class not because she behaves like a drill sergeant, but because she teaches interesting lessons, engages students' imaginations and energies, makes efficient use of time, and communicates a sense of purpose, high expectations, and contagious enthusiasm. However, even a well-managed class is sure to contain individual students who will misbehave. Although Ms. Cavalho's focus is on preventing behavior problems, she is also ready to intervene when necessary to see that students' behaviors are within acceptable limits (see Emmer & Stough, 2008). For some students, a glance, physical proximity, or a hand on the shoulder is enough. For others, consequences might be necessary. Even in these cases, Ms. Cavalho does not let behavior issues disrupt her lesson or her students' learning activities.

This chapter focuses on effective use of time, the creation of effective learning environments, classroom management, and discipline. Creating an effective learning environment involves organizing classroom activities, instruction, and materials to provide for effective use of time; to create a happy, productive classroom; and to minimize disruptions (Bluestein, 2014; Borich, 2014; Jones & Jones, 2016). **Discipline** consists of methods used to prevent behavior problems or to respond to existing behavior problems so as to reduce their occurrence in the future (see Bender, 2015; Charles, Senter, & Charles, 2014; Levin, Nolan, Kerr, Elliott, & Bajovic, 2016; Losen, 2015).

WHAT IS THE IMPACT OF TIME ON LEARNING?

Obviously, if no time is spent teaching a subject, students will not learn it. However, within the usual range of time allocated to instruction, how much difference does time make? This has been a focus of considerable research (see Farbman, 2012; Gabrieli, 2010; Kolbe, Partridge, & O'Reilly, 2013; Redd et al., 2012). Although it is clear that more time devoted to instruction has a positive impact on student achievement, the effects of additional time are often modest or inconsistent (Kidron & Lindsay, 2014; Midkife & Cohen-Vogel, 2015). Programs that extend time for learning beyond the ordinary school day, such as after-school and summer school programs, or even providing double math or reading periods, have mixed effects and are usually beneficial only if they provide targeted, intensive instruction to struggling children (Berry & Hess, 2013; Kim & Quinn, 2013; Meyer & Van Klaveren, 2013; Nomi & Allensworth, 2013; Patall, Cooper, & Allen, 2010; Redd et al., 2012; Taylor, 2014).

What seems to be more important than total clock hours is how time is used in class. **Engaged time**, or **time on task**, the number of minutes actually spent learning, is the time that is most frequently found to contribute to learning (e.g., Bodovski & Farkas, 2007; Rowan, Correnti, & Miller, 2002). In other words, the most important aspect of time is the one that is under your direct control as the teacher: the organization and use of time in the classroom (Barnes, 2013b; Dean, Hubbell, Pitler, & Stone, 2012; Edwards, 2014; Jones & Jones, 2016; Manning & Bucher, 2013).

InTASC 3
Learning Environments

InTASC 7
Planning for Instruction

Using Allocated Time for Instruction

Time is a limited resource in schools. A typical U.S. school is in session about 6 hours a day for 180 days each year (Kolbe et al., 2013). Time for educational activities can be expanded by means of homework assignments or (for some students) participation in after-school activities or summer school, but the total time available for instruction is essentially set. Out of these 6 hours (or so) must come time for teaching a variety of subjects plus time for lunch, recess, and physical education; transitions between classes; announcements; and so on. Over a 40- to 60-minute period in a particular subject, many quite different factors reduce the time available for instruction. Figure 11.1 illustrates how time scheduled for mathematics instruction in 12 second- to fifth-grade classes observed by Karweit and Slavin (1981) was whittled away.

The classes that Karweit and Slavin (1981) observed were in schools in and around a rural Maryland town. Overall, the classes were well organized and businesslike, with dedicated and hardworking teachers. Students were generally well behaved and respectful of authority. However, even in these very good schools, the average student spent only 60 percent of the time scheduled for mathematics instruction actually learning mathematics. First of all, about 20 class days were lost to such activities as standardized testing, school events, field trips, and teacher absences. On days when instruction was given, class time was lost because of late starts and noninstructional activities such as discussing upcoming events, making announcements, passing out materials, and disciplining students. Finally, even when math was being taught, many students were not actually engaged in the instructional activity. Some were daydreaming during lecture or seatwork times, goofing

**FIGURE 11.1 •
Where Does the Time
Go?**

Observations of elementary
school mathematics classes
showed that the time students
actually spend learning in
class is only about 60 percent
of the time allocated for
instruction.
Source: Based on data from
N. L. Karweit and R. E. Slavin,
"Measurement and Modeling
Choices in Studies of Time and
Learning," *American Educational
Research Journal, 18*(2).

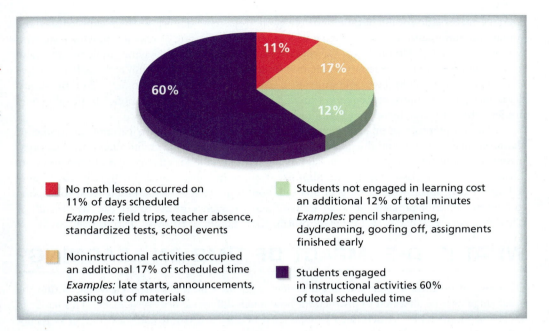

■ No math lesson occurred on
11% of days scheduled
Examples: field trips, teacher absence,
standardized tests, school events

■ Noninstructional activities occupied
an additional 17% of scheduled time
Examples: late starts, announcements,
passing out of materials

■ Students not engaged in learning cost
an additional 12% of total minutes
Examples: pencil sharpening,
daydreaming, goofing off, assignments
finished early

■ Students engaged
in instructional activities 60%
of total scheduled time

off, or sharpening pencils; others had nothing to do, either because they were finished with their assigned work or because they had not yet been assigned a task. The 60 percent figure estimated by Karweit and Slavin is, if anything, a high estimate. In a much larger study, Weinstein and Mignano (1993) found that elementary school students spent only about one-third of their time engaged in learning tasks (see also Hong, 2001; Meek, 2003).

Available instructional time is called **allocated time**, the time during which students have an opportunity to learn. When you are lecturing, students can learn by paying attention. When students have written assignments or other tasks, they can learn by doing them. There are several ways that allocated time can be maximized (see Emmer & Evertson, 2012; Evertson & Emmer, 2013; Jones & Jones, 2016; Oliver, 2012).

PREVENTING LOST TIME One way that instructional time disappears is through losses of entire days or periods. Many of these losses are inevitable because of events such as standardized testing days and snow days, and we certainly would not want to abolish important field trips or school assemblies simply to get in a few more periods of instruction. However, frequent losses of instructional periods interrupt the flow of instruction and can ultimately deprive students of sufficient time to master the curriculum.

Making good use of all classroom time is less a matter of squeezing out a few more minutes or hours of instruction each year than of communicating to students that learning is an important business that is worth their time and effort. If you find excuses not to teach, students may learn that learning is not a serious enterprise. In studying an outstandingly effective inner-city Baltimore elementary school, Salganik (1980) describes a third-grade teacher who took her class to the school library, which she found locked. She sent a student for the key, and while the class waited, the teacher whispered to her students, "Let's work on our doubles. Nine plus nine? Six plus six?" The class whispered the answers back in unison. Did a couple of minutes working on addition facts increase the students' achievement? Of course not. But it probably did help to develop a perception that school is for learning, not for marking time.

PREVENTING LATE STARTS AND EARLY FINISHES A surprising amount of allocated instructional time is lost because you may not start teaching at the beginning of the period. A crisp, on-time start to a lesson is important for setting a purposive tone to instruction. If students know that you do not start on time, they may be lackadaisical about getting to class on time; this attitude makes future on-time starts increasingly difficult. In Ms. Cavalho's class, students know that if they are late, they will miss something interesting, fun, and important. As a result, nearly all of them are in class and ready to learn when the bell rings.

You can also shortchange students by not teaching until the end of the period. This is less damaging than a ragged or late start, but it is still worth avoiding by planning more instruction than you think you'll need, in case you finish the lesson early.

PREVENTING INTERRUPTIONS One important cause of the loss of time allocated for instruction is interruptions, which may be externally imposed, such as announcements or the need to sign forms sent from the principal's office, or may be caused by teachers or students themselves. Interruptions not only directly cut into the time for instruction but also break the momentum of the lesson, which reduces students' attention to the task at hand.

Avoiding interruptions takes planning. For example, some teachers put a "Do not disturb—learning in progress!" sign on the door to inform would-be interrupters to come back later. One teacher wore a special hat during small-group lessons to remind her other second-graders not to interrupt her during that time. Rather than signing forms or dealing with other "administrivia" at once, some teachers keep a box where students and others can deposit any forms for attention later, while students are doing independent or group work or after the lesson is over.

Anything you can postpone doing until after a lesson should be postponed. For example, if you have started a lesson and a student walks in late, go on with the lesson and deal with the tardiness later.

HANDLING ROUTINE PROCEDURES You can spend too much time on simple classroom routines. For example, some elementary teachers spend many minutes getting students ready for lunch or dismissal because they call students to line up by name, one at a time. This is unnecessary. Early in the school year, many teachers establish the practice of calling students to line up only when the entire table (or row) is quiet and ready to go. Lining up for lunch then takes seconds, not minutes.

Other procedures should also become routine for students. They must know, for example, when they may go to the washroom or sharpen a pencil, and they should not ask to do these things at other times. You may collect papers by having students pass them to the front or to the left or by having table monitors collect the table's papers. Distribution of materials must also be planned for. Exactly how these tasks are done is less important than the students knowing clearly what they are to do. Many teachers assign regular classroom helpers to take care of distribution and collection of papers, taking messages to the office, erasing the blackboard, and other routine tasks that are annoying interruptions for teachers but that students love to do. Use student power as much as possible.

MAINTAINING A RAPID PACE OF INSTRUCTION Research finds that students learn more from teachers who cover a lot of content in each lesson (Wentzel & Brophy, 2014). A rapid pace also contributes to students' interest and time on task.

MINIMIZING TIME SPENT ON DISCIPLINE Methods of disciplining students are discussed at length later in this chapter. However, one aspect of disciplining should be mentioned at this point. Whenever possible—which is almost always—disciplinary statements or actions should not interrupt the flow of the lesson. A sharp glance, silently moving close to an offending student, or a hand signal, such as putting finger to lips to remind a student to be silent, is usually effective for the kind of minor behavior problems that you must constantly deal with, and these signals allow the lesson to proceed without interruption. For example, Ms. Cavalho could have interrupted her lesson to scold Mark and Gloria, but that would have wasted time and disrupted the concentration and focus of the whole class. If students need talking to about discipline problems, the time to do it is after the lesson or after school, not in the middle of a lesson. If Diana and Martin are talking during a quiet reading time instead of working, it would be better to say, "Diana and Martin, see me at three o'clock" rather than to launch into an on-the-spot speech about the importance of being on task during seatwork times.

Using Engaged Time Effectively

Engaged time (or time on task) is the time individual students actually spend doing assigned work. It differs from allocated time, in which the entire class has an opportunity to engage in learning activities, because engaged time may be different for each student, depending on individual attentiveness and willingness to work. Strategies for maximizing student time on task are discussed in the following sections. Several studies have found that teacher training programs based on

MyEdLab
Video Example 11.1
Ms. Kazecki describes some of the routines and procedures that her students know and follow. Notice how the routines help to maximize instructional time and maintain discipline.

Connections 11.1
For more information about the importance of time use and time management in effective teaching, see Chapter 9.

Connections 11.2

For more information about arousing student interest and focusing student attention, see Chapter 7 and Chapter 6.

Connections 11.3

For more information about active learning, see Chapter 8.

Certification Pointer

You may be asked on your teacher certification test to discuss why it is important for a teacher to plan carefully for transitions and describe what can happen when transitions are not implemented with care.

principles presented in the following sections increase student engagement and, in some cases, learning (Epstein, 2008; Good & Brophy, 2014; Jones & Jones, 2016).

TEACHING ENGAGING LESSONS The best way to increase students' time on task is to teach lessons that are so interesting, engaging, and relevant to their interests that students will pay attention and eagerly do what is asked of them (Borich, 2014; Dean et al., 2012; Emmer & Evertson, 2012; Evertson & Emmer, 2013; Hardin, 2012; Kauffman et al., 2011; Kratochwill, 2012). Part of this strategy calls for you to emphasize active, rapidly paced instruction with varied modes of presentation and frequent opportunities for student participation and to deemphasize independent seatwork, especially unsupervised seatwork (as in follow-up time in elementary reading classes). Research has shown that student engagement is much higher when you are teaching than during individual seatwork (Evertson & Emmer, 2013). Engaged time is also much higher in well-structured cooperative learning programs than in independent seatwork (Slavin, 2013), and giving students many opportunities to participate actively in lessons is associated with greater learning as well (What Works Clearinghouse (WWC), 2014a, b).

MANAGING TRANSITIONS Transitions are changes from one activity to another—for example, from lecture to seatwork, from subject to subject, or from lesson to lunch. Elementary school classes have been found to average 31 major transitions a day, occupying 15 percent of class time (Burns, 1984). Transitions are the seams of class management at which classroom order is most likely to come apart.

Following are three rules for the management of transitions:

1. When making a transition, you should give a clear signal to which your students have been taught to respond. For example, in the elementary grades, some teachers use a bell or a hand signal to indicate to students that they should immediately be quiet and listen to instructions.

2. Before the transition is made, students must be certain about what they are to do when the signal is given. For example, you might say, "When I say 'Go,' I want you all to put your books away and get out the compositions you started yesterday. Is everyone ready? All right, go!"

3. Make transitions all at once. Students should be taught to make transitions as a group, rather than one student at a time (Evertson & Emmer, 2013). You should give directions to the class as a whole or to well-defined groups: "Class, I want you all to put away your laboratory materials and prepare for dismissal as quickly and quietly as you can. . . . I see that Table Three is quiet and ready. Table Three, please line up quietly. Table Six, line up. Table One . . . Table Four. Everyone else may line up quietly. Let's go!"

MAINTAINING GROUP FOCUS DURING LESSONS Maintaining group focus means using classroom organization strategies and questioning techniques to ensure that all students in the class stay involved in the lesson, even when only one student is called on by the teacher.

Examples of tactics for increasing the involvement of all include using choral responses, having all students hold up their work so you can see it, circulating among the students to see what they are doing, and drawing other children into the performance of one child (e.g., "I want you all to watch what Suzanne is doing so you can tell me whether you agree or disagree with her answer"). Ms. Cavalho increased involvement and **accountability** by having all students prepare a Hemingway-like description and *only then* asking for a few of them to be read.

The idea behind these tactics is to maintain the involvement of all students in all parts of the lesson. You should be concerned not only about drawing all students into class activities but also about avoiding activities that relegate most students to the role of spectator for long periods. For example, a very common teaching error is asking one or two students to work out a lengthy problem on the chalkboard or electronic whiteboard, or to read an extended passage, while the rest of the class has nothing to do. Such methods waste the time of much of the class, break the momentum of the lesson, and leave the door open for misbehavior (Wentzel & Brophy, 2014).

Group alerting comprises questioning strategies that are designed to keep all students on their toes during a lecture or discussion. One example of group alerting is creating suspense before calling on a student by saying, "Given triangle *ABC*, if we know the measures of sides *A* and *B* and of angle *AB*, what else can we find out about the triangle? . . . [Pause] . . . Maria?" Note that this keeps the whole class thinking until Maria's name is called. The opposite effect would have been created by saying, "Maria, given triangle *ABC* . . . ," because then only Maria would have been alerted. Calling on students in random order is another example of group alerting, as is letting students know that they may be asked questions about the preceding reciter's answers. For example, you might follow up Maria's answer with "What is the name of the postulate that Maria used? . . . Ralph?"

MAINTAINING GROUP FOCUS DURING SEATWORK When students are doing seatwork and you are available to work with them, it is important to monitor activities and to informally check individual students' work. That is, you should circulate among your students to see how they are doing. This enables you to identify any problems students are having before they waste seatwork time practicing errors or giving up in frustration. If students are engaged in cooperative group work, students can check each other's work, but you still need to check frequently with each group to see that students are on the right track.

Seatwork times are excellent opportunities for providing individual help to students who are struggling to keep up with the class, but you should resist the temptation to work too long with an individual student. Interactions with students during seatwork should be as brief as possible because if you get tied down with any one student, the rest of the class may drift off-task or run into problems of their own.

OVERLAPPING A teacher's ability to attend to interruptions or behavior problems while continuing a lesson or other instructional activity is known as **overlapping**. For example, while teaching a lesson on reading comprehension, a teacher sees a student looking at a book unrelated to the lesson. Without interrupting his lesson, the teacher walks over to the student, takes her book, closes it, and puts it on her desk, all while continuing to speak to the class. This takes care of the student's misbehavior without slowing the momentum of the lesson, and the rest of the class hardly notices that the event occurred. Similarly, Ms. Cavalho squelched a whispering incident just by moving closer to the whispering students while continuing her lesson.

Interruptions are sometimes unavoidable, but the ability to keep the main activity going while handling them is strongly related to overall classroom order and to achievement (Wentzel & Brophy, 2014).

Certification Pointer

For your teacher certification test, you may be asked to make suggestions for helping students stay on task in a particular case.

Overdoing Time on Task

A class that is rarely on task is certainly not a well-managed class. However, it is possible to go too far in the other direction, emphasizing time on task to the exclusion of all other considerations. For example, in a study of time on task in elementary mathematics (Karweit & Slavin, 1981), one teacher's class was found to be engaged essentially 100 percent of the time. The teacher accomplished this by walking up and down the rows of desks looking for the slightest flicker of inattention. This class learned very little math over the course of the year.

Several studies have found that increasing time on task in classrooms where students were already reasonably well behaved did not increase student achievement (Slavin, 1986; Stallings & Krasavage, 1986). Overemphasizing time on task can be detrimental to learning in several ways. For example, complex tasks that involve creativity and uncertainty tend to produce lower levels of time on task than simple, cut-and-dried tasks (Evertson & Randolph, 1995; Weinstein & Mignano, 2007). Yet it would clearly be a poor instructional strategy to avoid complex or uncertain tasks just to keep time on task high. Maintaining classroom order is an important goal of teaching, but it is only one of many (see Charles et al., 2014; Levin et al., 2016).

Classroom Management in the Student-Centered Classroom

It is important to note that most research on classroom management has taken place in traditionally organized classrooms, in which students have few choices about what they do and few interactions with each other. In more student-centered classrooms, children are likely to be spending much of their time working with each other, doing open-ended projects, writing, and experimenting. Bluestein (2014), Evertson and Randolph (1995), and Freiberg (2014) have discussed the shift that must take place in thinking about classroom management for such classrooms. Clearly, classroom management is more participatory in a student-centered classroom, with students involved in setting standards of behavior. Equally clearly, the type of behavior to be expected will be different. It is impossible to imagine a student-centered classroom that is silent, for example. Yet in other respects the requirements for managing student-centered classrooms are not so different from those for managing traditional ones. Rules are still needed and must be consistently communicated to students and consistently enforced (Freiberg, Connell, & Lorentz, 2001; Freiberg & Lamb, 2009). If students in student-centered classrooms are deeply involved and motivated by the variety, activity, and social nature of classroom activities, then disciplinary actions will be less necessary (Weinstein & Mignano, 2007). Inevitably, however, certain students' misbehavior will disrupt others' learning, and you must have strategies to help students live up to norms to which all members of the class have agreed.

MyEdLab Self-Check 11.1

MyEdLab Video Analysis Tool 11.1 Go to MyEdLab and click on the Video Analysis Tool to access the exercise "Effective learning environments: maximizing instructional time."

MyEdLab Video Analysis Tool 11.2 Go to MyEdLab and click on the Video Analysis Tool to access the exercise "Effective learning environments: maximizing engaged time."

WHAT PRACTICES CONTRIBUTE TO EFFECTIVE CLASSROOM MANAGEMENT?

InTASC 7

Planning for Instruction

Research has consistently shown that basic commonsense planning and groundwork go a long way toward preventing discipline problems from ever developing. Simple measures include starting the year properly, arranging the classroom for effective instruction, setting class rules and procedures, and making expectations of conduct clear to students (Curwin, 2013; Emmer & Evertson, 2012; Evertson & Emmer, 2013; Wentzel & Brophy, 2014). Further, establishing caring connections between teachers and students helps establish a cooperative tone in the classroom that reduces discipline problems (Borich, 2014; Freiberg & Lamb, 2009; Hardin, 2012; Kauffman et al., 2011; Manning & Bucher, 2013).

Different grade levels and student groups present different management concerns. For instance, with younger students, teachers need to be concerned about acquainting students with the norms and behaviors that are expected in school (Evertson & Emmer, 2013; Weinstein & Mignano, 2007). Programs focusing on establishing consistent schoolwide behavior expectations and on building positive relationships and school success through the use of cooperative learning have been effective in improving the behavior of elementary school children (Burke et al., 2011; Freiberg et al., 2001; O'Donnell, Hawkins, Catalano, Abbott, & Day, 1995).

In middle school and high school, students can grasp the principles that underlie rules and procedures and can rationally agree to observe them (Emmer & Evertson, 2012; Savage & Savage, 2010; Weinstein & Mignano, 2007). At the same time, some adolescents resist authority and place greater importance on peer norms. Aggressive behavior, truancy, and delinquency also increase as students enter adolescence. In the upper grades, departmentalization, tracking, and class promotion might become management issues, especially with students who have established patterns of learned helplessness or academic failure. Teachers of older students need to be concerned with motivating them toward more self-regulation in observing rules and procedures and in learning the course material. Programs that increase the clarity of rules, consistency of rule enforcement, and frequency of communication with the home have been very effective in improving adolescents' behavior (Hawkins, Kuklinski, & Fagan, 2012).

Starting Out the Year Right

InTASC 3

Learning Environments

Research has revealed that the first days of school are critical in establishing classroom order for the whole year. Teachers whose classes were mostly on task over the course of the school year, compared to teachers whose classes were less consistently on task, were more likely to engage in the following activities during the first days of school (Curwin, 2013; Evertson & Emmer, 2013; Weinstein & Mignano, 2007; Wong & Wong, 2004).

1. More-effective managers have a clear, specific plan for introducing students to classroom rules and procedures, and they spend as many days as necessary carrying out their plan until students know how to line up, ask for help, and so on.

2. More-effective managers work with the whole class initially (even if they plan to group students later). They remain involved with the whole class at all times, rarely leaving any students without something to do or without supervision. For example, more-effective managers seldom work with an individual student unless the rest of the class is productively occupied.

3. More-effective managers spend extra time during the first days of school introducing procedures and discussing class rules (often encouraging students to suggest rules themselves). These teachers usually remind students of class rules every day for at least the first week of school.

4. More-effective managers teach students specific procedures. For example, some have students practice lining up quickly and quietly; others teach students to respond to a signal such as a bell, a flick of the light switch, or a call for attention.

5. More-effective managers use simple, enjoyable tasks as first activities. Materials for the first lessons are well prepared, clearly presented, and varied. These teachers ask students to get right to work on the first day of school and give them instructions on procedures gradually, to avoid overloading them with too much information at a time.

6. More-effective managers respond immediately to stop any misbehavior.

Setting Class Rules

One of the first management-related tasks at the start of the year is setting class rules. Three principles govern this process. First, class rules should be few in number. Second, they should make sense and be seen as fair by students. Third, they should be clearly explained and deliberately taught to students (Curwin, 2013). A major purpose of clearly explaining general class rules is to give a moral authority for specific procedures (Kagan, Kyle, & Scott, 2004). For example, all students will understand and support a rule such as "Respect others' property." This simple rule can be invoked to cover such obvious misbehaviors as stealing or destroying materials, but it also serves as a reason for putting materials away, cleaning up litter, and refraining from marking up textbooks. Students may be asked to help set the rules, or they may be given a set of rules and asked to give examples of these rules. Class discussions give students a feeling of participation in setting rational rules that everyone can live by (Brasof, 2011; Freiberg, 2012; Strout, 2005). When the class as a whole has agreed on a set of rules, offenders know that they are transgressing community norms, not the teacher's arbitrary regulations, as in the following all-purpose set of class rules.

1. ***Be courteous to others.*** This rule forbids interrupting others or speaking out of turn, teasing or laughing at others, bullying, fighting, and so on.

2. ***Respect others' property.***

3. ***Be on task.*** This includes listening when the teacher or other students are talking, working on seatwork, continuing to work during any interruptions, staying in one's seat, being at one's seat and ready to work when the bell rings, and following directions.

4. ***Raise hands to be recognized.*** This is a rule against calling out or getting out of one's seat for assistance without permission.

MyEdLab
Video Example 11.2
At the start of the school year, Ms. Zeiler establishes the rules for her kindergarten classroom. Her routines and her classroom environment reinforce students' awareness of the rules throughout the year.

21ST CENTURY LEARNING

Effective Use of Time

New technologies are making it easier for teachers to create productive learning environments (Bluestein, 2014; Budhai & Taddei, 2015). In addition to adding intrinsic motivation through the use of brief videos, interactive devices, and other means of making lessons fun and engaging, it is now becoming possible to use electronic response devices to constantly obtain feedback on students' levels of learning, so that you can target lessons to the exact needs of your students, and students can immediately see their own levels of learning. Using these devices, all students can quickly answer a question or enter an opinion at the same time. You can display the answers or the percentage of answers that were correct on a chart or graph to display to the class. You can immediately find out what students know or what they are thinking, so you can adjust your lessons in light of student learning. Students know that their knowledge will always be assessed, instead of hoping that someone else will be called on. These and other technologies can focus classroom

(continued)

activities on the most productive content and tasks, such as those now being emphasized in the Common Core State Standards and other college- and career-ready standards, and motivate students to pay attention and work enthusiastically individually and in groups.

QUESTION

- Think of as many ways as possible of using electronic response devices in teaching students at the age level and subject you expect to teach. Which of these seem most likely, and which least likely, to increase learning?

WHAT ARE SOME STRATEGIES FOR MANAGING ROUTINE MISBEHAVIOR?

The preceding sections of this chapter discussed means of organizing classroom activities to maximize time for instruction and minimize the time required for dealing with such minor disturbances as students talking out of turn, getting out of their seats without permission, and not paying attention. Interesting lessons, efficient use of class time, and careful structuring of instructional activities will prevent most such minor behavior problems—and many more serious ones as well (Freiberg & Lapointe, 2006; Wentzel & Brophy, 2014). Time off task can lead to more serious problems; many behavior issues arise because students are frustrated or bored in school. Instructional programs that actively involve students and provide all of them with opportunities for success can help prevent such problems.

However, effective lessons and good use of class time are not the only means of preventing or dealing with inappropriate behavior. Besides structuring classes to reduce the frequency of misconduct, teachers must have strategies for dealing with such problems when they do occur (Bender, 2015; Charles, Senter, & Charles, 2014; Korpershoek et al., 2016; Losen, 2015; WWC, 2014b).

Before considering disciplinary strategies, it is important to reflect on their purpose. Students should learn much more in school than the "three Rs." They should learn that they are competent learners and that learning is enjoyable and satisfying. A classroom environment that is warm, supportive, and accepting fosters these attitudes. Furthermore, there is a strong link between attentive, nondisruptive behavior and student achievement (Wentzel & Brophy, 2014).

A healthy classroom environment cannot be created if students do not respect teachers or teachers do not respect students (Curwin, 2013; Lemov, 2010; Mendler & Mendler, 2011). Although you should involve students in setting class rules and take student needs or input into account in organizing the classroom, you are ultimately the leader who establishes and enforces rules by which students must live. These class rules and procedures should become second nature to students. If you have not established your authority in the classroom, you are likely to spend too much time dealing with behavior problems, or yelling at students, to be instructionally effective. Furthermore, the clearer the structure and routine procedures in the classroom, the more freedom you can allow students. The following sections discuss strategies for dealing with typical discipline problems.

The Principle of Least Intervention

MyEdLab

Video Example 11.3

Textbook author Bob Slavin tells a story about a teacher who effectively handles one student's minor misbehavior without disrupting the lesson. Why is this type of subtle discipline so valuable?

In dealing with routine classroom behavior problems, the most important principle is that you should correct misbehaviors by using the simplest intervention that will work (Jones & Jones, 2016; Kyle & Rogien, 2004). Many studies have found that the amount of time spent disciplining students is negatively related to student achievement. Your main goal in dealing with routine misbehavior is to do so in a way that both is effective and avoids unnecessarily disrupting the lesson (Charles et al., 2014; Jones & Jones, 2016; Poole & Evertson, 2012). If at all possible, the lesson must go on while any behavior problems are dealt with. A continuum of strategies for dealing with minor misbehaviors, from least disruptive to most, is presented in Table 11.1 and discussed in the following sections.

TABLE 11.1 • Principle of Least Intervention

STEP	PROCEDURE	EXAMPLE
1	Prevention	Teacher displays enthusiasm, varies activities, keeps students interested.
2	Nonverbal cues	Tanya turns in paper late; teacher frowns.
3	Praise of correct behavior that is incompatible with misbehavior	"Tanya, I hear you completed your science fair project on time for the judging. That's great!"
4	Praise for other students	"I see most of you turned your papers in on time today. I really appreciate that."
5	Verbal reminders	"Tanya, please turn in your next paper on time."
6	Repeated reminders	"Tanya, it's important to turn your paper in on time."
7	Consequences	Tanya spends 10 minutes after class starting on the next paper assignment.

Prevention

The easiest behavior problems to deal with are those that never occur in the first place. As illustrated earlier in this chapter, teachers can prevent behavior problems by presenting interesting and lively lessons, making class rules and procedures clear, keeping students busy on meaningful tasks, and using other effective techniques of basic classroom management (Jones & Jones, 2016; Landrum, Scott, & Lingo, 2011; Levin et al., 2016). Ms. Cavalho's class is an excellent example of this. Her students rarely misbehave because they are interested and engaged. Creating a spirit in an entire school that is friendly, inviting, and comfortable also reduces motivations to misbehave (Cross, Thompson, & Erceg, 2014).

Varying the content of lessons, using a variety of materials and approaches, displaying humor and enthusiasm, and instituting cooperative learning or project-based learning can all reduce boredom-induced behavior problems. You can avert frustration caused by material that is too difficult or assignments that are unrealistically long by breaking assignments into smaller steps and doing a better job of preparing students to work on their own. Fatigue can be reduced if short breaks or physical activities (such as stretching) are allowed, activities are varied, and difficult subjects are scheduled in the morning, when students are fresh.

ON THE WEB

To learn more about classroom management, check out the website of the Center for the Prevention of School Violence. To see a teacher-created website, go to theteachersguide.com. Also see educationworld.com. Information for new and future teachers can be found at adprima.com and nea.org.

Nonverbal Cues

You can eliminate much routine classroom misbehavior without breaking the momentum of the lesson by using simple **nonverbal cues** (Levin et al., 2016; Poole & Evertson, 2012). Making eye contact with a misbehaving student might be enough to stop misbehavior. For example, if two students are whispering, you might simply catch the eye of one or both of them. Moving close to a student who is misbehaving also usually alerts the student to shape up. If these techniques fail, a light hand on the student's shoulder is likely to be effective (although touch should be used cautiously with adolescents, who may be sensitive about being touched). These nonverbal strategies all clearly convey the same message: "I see what you are doing and don't like it. Please get back to work." The advantage of communicating this message nonverbally is that the lesson need not be interrupted. In contrast, verbal reprimands can cause a ripple effect; many students stop working while one is being reprimanded (Wentzel & Brophy, 2014). Instead of interrupting the flow of concentration for many, nonverbal cues usually have an effect only on the student who is misbehaving, as illustrated earlier in this chapter by the example of the teacher who continued his lesson while silently closing and putting away a book one student was reading. That student was the only one in the class who paid much attention to the whole episode.

THEORY INTO PRACTICE

Consistency Management and Cooperative Discipline

One of the most extensively evaluated schoolwide approaches to classroom management is Consistency Management and Cooperative Discipline (CMCD) (Freiberg, Huzinec, & Templeton, 2009; Freiberg & Lapointe, 2006; Freiberg et al., 2001). CMCD focuses on preventing behavior problems by engaging all students in leadership roles within the class, using timers to ensure that transitional activities are quickly dealt with, and establishing predictable routines. Students have opportunities to share opinions and resolve disputes in classroom meetings. Teachers randomly draw students' names on popsicle sticks to ensure fairness in questioning during lessons. Several studies of CMCD have found that the program improves not only students' behaviors but also their learning of reading and math skills (Freiberg et al., 2009; Freiberg et al., 2001).

Praising Behavior That Is Incompatible with Misbehavior

Praise can be a powerful motivator for many students. One strategy for reducing misbehavior in class is to make sure to praise students for behaviors that are incompatible with the misbehavior you want to reduce. That is, catch students in the act of doing right. For example, if students often get out of their seats without permission, praise them on the occasions when they get to work right away and stay focused (Jones & Jones, 2016).

Praising Other Students

It is often possible to get one student to behave by praising others for behaving appropriately. For example, if Polly is goofing off, you might say, "I'm glad to see so many students working so well—Jake is doing a good job, Carol is doing well, and José and Michelle are also working nicely." When Polly finally does get to work, you should praise her, too, without dwelling on her past inattention: "I see James and Walter and Polly doing such good work."

Verbal Reminders

If a nonverbal cue is impossible or ineffective, a simple verbal reminder may help to bring a student into line. The reminder should be given immediately after the student misbehaves; delayed reminders are usually ineffective. If possible, the reminder should state what students are supposed to be doing rather than dwelling on what they are doing wrong. For example, it is better to say, "John, please attend to your own work" than "John, stop copying from Alfredo's paper." Stating the reminder positively communicates more positive expectations for future behavior than making a negative statement (Evertson & Emmer, 2013). Also, the reminder should focus on the behavior, not on the student. Although a particular student behavior may be intolerable, the student himself or herself is always accepted and welcome in the classroom.

Repeated Reminders

Most often a nonverbal cue, praising of other students, or a simple reminder will be enough to end minor misbehavior. However, sometimes students test your resolve by failing to do what has been asked of them or by arguing or giving excuses. This testing will diminish over time if students learn that you mean what you say and will use appropriate measures to ensure an orderly, productive classroom environment.

When a student refuses to comply with a simple reminder, one strategy to attempt first is a repetition of the reminder, ignoring any irrelevant excuse or argument. Canter (2014) calls this strategy the *broken record*. If a student has a legitimate issue to discuss, you might deal with it, but all too often students' arguments and excuses are nothing more than a means of drawing out an interaction with you to avoid getting down to work (see Walker & Gresham, 2013). Recall, for example, how Ms. Cavalho refused to be drawn into a discussion of Gloria's lateness when it was Mark's behavior that was at issue.

Applying Consequences

When all previous steps have been ineffective in getting the student to comply with a clearly stated and reasonable request, the final step is to pose a choice to the student: Either comply or suffer the consequences (Benson, 2014; Bender, 2015; Levin et al., 2016; Losen, 2015). Examples of consequences are sending the student to a "time out" area, making the student miss a few minutes of recess or some other privilege, keeping the student after school, or calling the student's parents. A consequence for not complying with the teacher's request should be mildly unpleasant, short in duration, and applied as soon as possible after the behavior occurs. Certainty is far more important than severity; students must know that consequences follow misbehavior as night follows day. One disadvantage of using severe or long-lasting punishment (e.g., no recess for a week) is that it can create resentment in the student and a defiant attitude. Also, it might be difficult to follow through on severe or long-lasting consequences. Mild but certain consequences communicate, "I cannot tolerate that sort of behavior, but I care about you and want you to rejoin the class as soon as you are ready."

Before presenting a student with a consequence for noncompliance, you must be absolutely certain that you can and will follow through if necessary. When you say, "You may choose to get to work right away, or you may choose to spend 5 minutes of your recess doing your work here," you must be certain that you or someone will be available to monitor the student in the classroom during recess. Vague or empty threats ("You stop that or I'll make you wish you had!" or "You get to work or I'll have you suspended for a month!") are worse than useless. If you are not prepared to follow through with consequences, students will learn to shrug them off. Further, uncertainty about consequences can invite power struggles (Mendler & Mendler, 2011). Keep the rules simple and certain.

After a consequence has been applied, you should avoid referring to the incident. For example, when the student returns from a 10-minute exclusion from class, you should accept her or him back without any sarcasm or recriminations. The student now deserves a fresh start.

MyEdLab **Self-Check 11.2**

MyEdLab **Video Analysis Tool 11.3** Go to MyEdLab and click on the Video Analysis Tool to access the exercise "Effective learning environments: minimizing misbehavior."

HOW IS APPLIED BEHAVIOR ANALYSIS USED TO MANAGE MORE SERIOUS BEHAVIOR PROBLEMS?

The previous section discussed how to deal with behaviors that might be appropriate on the playing field but are out of line in the classroom. Some other behaviors are not appropriate anywhere, such as fighting, stealing, destruction of property, and gross disrespect for teachers or other school staff. These are far less common than routine classroom misbehavior but far more serious. Behavioral learning theories, described in Chapter 5, have direct application to effective responses to serious misbehavior. Simply put, behavioral learning theories hold that behaviors that are not reinforced or are punished will diminish in frequency. The following sections present **applied behavior analysis**, an analysis of classroom behavior in terms of behavioral concepts, and give specific strategies for preventing and dealing with misbehavior (Alberto & Troutman, 2013; Axelrod, 2012; Rappaport & Minahan, 2012a, b; Scott, Anderson, & Alter, 2012; Walker & Graham, 2013).

ON THE WEB

For articles on applied behavior analysis, visit the website for the Cambridge Center for Behavioral Studies at behavior.org.

How Student Misbehavior Is Maintained

A basic principle of behavioral learning theories is that if any behavior persists over time, it is being maintained by some reinforcer. To reduce misbehavior in the classroom, we must understand which reinforcers maintain that misbehavior in the first place (Alberto & Troutman, 2013; Axelrod, 2012; Rappaport & Minahan, 2012a, b).

The most common reinforcer for classroom misbehavior is attention—from the teacher, the peer group, or both. Students receiving one-to-one tutoring rarely misbehave, both because they already have the undivided attention of an adult and because no classmates are present to attend to any negative behavior. In the typical classroom, however, students have to go out of their way to get the teacher's personal attention, and they have an audience of peers who might encourage or applaud their misdeeds.

TEACHER'S ATTENTION Sometimes students misbehave because they want the teacher's attention, even if it is negative. This is a more common reason for misbehavior than many teachers think. A puzzled teacher might say, "I don't know what is wrong with Nathan. I have to stay with him all day to keep him working! Sometimes I get exasperated and yell at him. My words fall off him like water off a duck's back. He even smiles when I'm scolding him!"

When students appear to misbehave to gain your attention, the solution is relatively easy: Pay attention to these students when they are doing well, and ignore them (as much as possible) when they misbehave. When ignoring their actions is impossible, imposing time out (e.g., sending these students to a quiet corner) may be effective.

InTASC 8

Instructional Strategies

Connections 11.4
For more information about behavioral theory, see Chapter 5.

PEERS' ATTENTION Another very common reason why students misbehave is to get the attention and approval of their peers. The classic instance of this is the class clown, who is obviously performing for the amusement of his or her classmates. However, many other forms of misbehavior are motivated primarily by peer attention and approval—in fact, few students completely disregard the potential impact of their behavior on their classmates. For example, students who refuse to do what you ask are consciously or unconsciously weighing the effect of their defiance on their standing among classmates (Hartup, 2005).

Even preschoolers and early elementary school students misbehave to gain peer attention, but beginning around the third grade, and especially during the middle and high school years, it is particularly likely that student misbehavior is linked to peer attention and support. As students enter adolescence, the peer group takes on extreme importance, and peer norms begin to favor independence from authority. When older children and teenagers engage in serious delinquent acts (such as vandalism, theft, bullying, and assault), they are usually supported by a delinquent peer group.

Strategies for reducing peer-supported misbehavior are quite different from those for dealing with misbehavior that is meant to capture the teacher's attention. Ignoring misbehavior will be ineffective if the misbehavior is reinforced by peers. For example, if a student is balancing a book on his head and the class is laughing, the behavior can hardly be ignored because it will continue as long as the class is interested (and will encourage others to behave likewise). Furthermore, scolding might only attract more attention from classmates or, worse, enhance the student's standing among peers. Similarly, when two students are whispering or talking to each other, they are reinforcing each other for misbehaving, and ignoring their behavior will only encourage more of it.

If simple reminders (such as moving close to the student) are not working, the two primary responses to peer-supported misbehavior are to remove the offender from the classroom to deprive her of peer attention or to use **group contingencies**, strategies in which the entire class (or groups of students within the class) is rewarded on the basis of everyone's good behavior. Under group contingencies, all students benefit from their classmates' good behavior, so peer support for misbehavior is removed. Group contingencies and other behavior management strategies for peer-supported misbehavior are described in more detail later in this chapter.

RELEASE FROM UNPLEASANT STATES OR ACTIVITIES A third important reinforcer for misbehavior is release from boredom, frustration, fatigue, or unpleasant activities (Caine & McClintic, 2014). As noted in Chapter 5, escaping from or avoiding an unpleasant stimulus is a reinforcer. Some students see much of what happens in school as unpleasant, boring, frustrating, or tiring. This is particularly true of students who experience repeated failure in school (Fisher, Frey, & Lapp, 2011). But even the most able and motivated students feel bored or frustrated at times.

Students often misbehave simply to escape from unpleasant activities. This can be clearly seen with students who frequently ask permission to get a drink of water, go to the washroom, or sharpen their pencils. Such students are more likely to make these requests during independent seatwork than during cooperative learning activities or even a lecture, because seatwork can be frustrating or anxiety-provoking for students who have little confidence in their academic abilities. More serious misbehaviors can also be partially or completely motivated by a desire for release from boredom, frustration, or fatigue. A student might misbehave just to stir things up. Sometimes students misbehave precisely so that they will be sent out of the classroom. Obviously, sending such a student to the hall or the principal's office can be counterproductive.

The best solution for misbehaviors arising from boredom, frustration, or fatigue is prevention. Students rarely misbehave during interesting, varied, engaging lessons (Borich, 2014). Actively involving students in lessons can head off misbehaviors that are the result of boredom or fatigue. Use of cooperative learning methods or other means of involving students in an active way can be helpful. You can prevent frustration by using materials that ensure a high success rate for all, thus making sure that all students are challenged but none are overwhelmed. Changing instruction and assessments to help students succeed can be an effective means of resolving frustration-related behavior problems.

Principles of Applied Behavior Analysis

The behavior management strategies outlined earlier (e.g., nonverbal cues, reminders, mild but certain punishment) might be described as informal applications of behavioral learning theories. These practices, plus the prevention of misbehavior by the use of efficient class management and engaging lessons, will be sufficient to create a good learning environment in most classrooms.

Connections 11.5
For more information about the problems of tracking, see Chapter 9.

However, more systematic behavior modification methods are sometimes needed. **Behavior modification** is the systematic application of antecedents and consequences to change behavior (Alberto & Troutman, 2013; Mazur, 2013; Miltenberger, 2012; Shea & Bauer, 2012). For example, one widely used approach called Positive Behavioral Interventions and Supports (PBIS) has been found to enable schools to improve schoolwide behavior and other outcomes using these strategies (Bradshaw et al., 2009; Bradshaw, Waasdorp, & Leaf, 2015; Horner, Sugai, & Anderson, 2010; Scott, Anderson, & Alter, 2012; Walker & Gresham, 2013). In classrooms in which most students are well behaved but a few have persistent behavior problems, individual behavior management strategies can be effective. In classrooms in which many students exhibit behavior problems, particularly when there is peer support for misbehavior, whole-class strategies or group contingencies may be needed (Bradshaw, 2012). Such strategies are most often required when many low-achieving students or students who lack motivation are put in one class, as often happens in special-education classes and in schools that use tracking or other between-class ability grouping methods.

Setting up and using any applied behavior analysis program requires following a series of steps proceeding from the observation of the behavior through program implementation to program evaluation (see Alberto & Troutman, 2013; Jones & Jones, 2016; Rappaport & Minahan, 2012a, b; Sarafino, 2012; Shea & Bauer, 2012; Walker & Gresham, 2013; Zirpoli, 2016). The steps listed here are, to a greater or lesser extent, part of all applied behavior analysis programs:

1. Identify target behavior(s) and reinforcer(s).

2. Establish a baseline for the target behavior.

3. Choose a reinforcer and criteria for reinforcement.

4. If necessary, choose a punisher and criteria for punishment.

5. Observe behavior during program implementation, and compare it to baseline.

6. When the behavior management program is working, reduce the frequency of reinforcement.

Individual behavior management strategies are useful for coping with individual students who have persistent behavior problems in school.

IDENTIFY TARGET BEHAVIORS AND REINFORCERS The first step in implementing a behavior management program is to observe the misbehaving student: Identify one behavior or a small number of behaviors to target first and see which reinforcers maintain the behavior(s). Another purpose of this observation is to establish a baseline against which to compare improvements. A structured individual behavior management program should aim to change only one behavior or a small set of closely related behaviors. Tackling too many behaviors at a time risks failure with all of them, because the student might not clearly see what he or she must do to be reinforced.

The first behavior targeted should be one that is serious, easy to observe, and (most important) occurs frequently. For example, if a child gets into fights on the playground every few days but gets out of his or her seat without permission several times per hour, you might start with the out-of-seat behavior and deal with the fighting later. Ironically, the more frequent and persistent a behavior, the easier it is to get rid of. This is because positive or negative consequences can be applied frequently, making the connection between behavior and consequence clear to the student.

In observing a student, try to determine what reinforcer(s) are maintaining the target behavior. If a student misbehaves with others (e.g., talks without permission, swears, or teases) or if a student's misbehavior usually attracts the attention of others (e.g., clowning), then you might guess that the behavior is peer supported. If the behavior does not attract much peer attention but always requires teacher attention (e.g., getting out of seat without permission), then you might guess that the behavior is supported by your own attention.

ESTABLISH BASELINE Observe the student to see how often the target behavior occurs. Before you do this, you will need to clearly define exactly what constitutes the behavior. For example, if the target behavior is "bothering classmates," you will have to decide what specific behaviors constitute "bothering" (perhaps teasing, interrupting, and taking materials).

SELECT REINFORCERS AND CRITERIA FOR REINFORCEMENT Typical classroom reinforcers include praise, privileges, and tangible rewards. Praise is especially effective for students who misbehave to get your attention. It is often a good idea to start a behavior management program by using attention and praise for appropriate behavior to see whether this is sufficient. However, be prepared to use stronger reinforcers if praise is not enough (see Alberto & Troutman, 2013; Walker & Gresham, 2013). In addition to praise, you may find it useful to give stars, "smilies," or other small rewards when students behave appropriately. Some teachers use a rubber stamp to mark students' papers with a symbol indicating good work. These small rewards make your praise more concrete and visible and let students take their work home and receive praise from their parents. Figure 11.2 provides suggestions for social reinforcers and preferred activities to encourage positive behavior.

SELECT PUNISHERS AND CRITERIA FOR PUNISHMENT, IF NECESSARY Behavioral learning theories strongly favor the use of reinforcers for appropriate behavior rather than punishers for inappropriate behavior. The reasons for this are practical as well as ethical. Punishment often creates resentment; so even if it solves one problem, it could create others. Even if punishment would work as well as reinforcement, it should be avoided whenever possible because it is not conducive to the creation of a happy, healthy classroom environment (Dueck, 2014; Walker & Gresham, 2013). Alternatives to punishment may include restitution for any harm a student has done (Smith, Fisher, & Frey, 2015).

However, punishment of one kind or another is necessary in some circumstances, and it should be used without qualms when reinforcement strategies are impossible or ineffective (Losen, 2015). A program of punishment for misbehavior (e.g., depriving a student of privileges) should always be the last option considered, never the first, and physical punishment should never be applied.

A punisher is any unpleasant stimulus that an individual will try to avoid. Common punishers used in schools are reprimands, being sent out of class or to the principal's office, and detention or missed recess. Corporal punishment (e.g., spanking) is illegal in most states and districts and highly restricted in others, but regardless of laws or policies, it should never be used in schools. It is neither a necessary nor an effective response to misbehavior (Jones & Jones, 2016).

Long ago, O'Leary and O'Leary (1972) listed seven principles for the effective and humane use of punishment:

1. Use punishment sparingly.
2. Make it clear to the child why he or she is being punished.
3. Provide the child with an alternative means of obtaining positive reinforcement.
4. Reinforce the child for behaviors that are incompatible with those you wish to weaken (e.g., if you punish for being off task, also reinforce for being on task).
5. Never use physical punishment.

FIGURE 11.2 •
**Social Reinforcers
and Preferred
Activities**

Social Reinforcers
Praise
"You're really working hard!"
"Good for you for not giving up."
"I'm proud of you for figuring this out yourself."
"What a nice straight line!"
"I see a student who is following directions well."
"You've done a nice job of comparing and contrasting here."
"Your understanding of chemical formulas is really improving!"

Proximity
Sitting next to teacher
Helping teacher do task
Getting to sit with a friend during an informal activity

Non-verbal Expression
Smile and nod
Thumbs up
High five
Wink

Preferred Activities
Extra time at recess
Extra time with desired equipment or technology
Being line leader
Picking out book for class at story time
Earning a special event, like Pajama Day or class party

---

6. Never punish when you are in a very angry or emotional state.

7. Punish when a behavior starts rather than when it ends.

Source: From *Classroom management: The successful use of behavior modification* by K. D. O'Leary and
S. G. O'Leary. published by Wiley, © 1992.

One effective punisher is called **time out**. The teacher tells a misbehaving student to go to a
separate part of the classroom, the hall, the principal's or vice principal's office, or another teacher's
class. If possible, the place where the student is sent should be uninteresting and out of view of
classmates. One advantage of time-out procedures is that they remove the student from the attention of classmates. Therefore, time out may be especially effective for students whose misbehavior
is motivated primarily by peer attention. The sit-and-watch procedure described in Chapter 5 is a
good example of the use of time out. Students who misbehaved in a physical education class were
given a sand timer and asked to sit and watch the timer for 3 minutes. This consequence, applied
immediately and consistently, soon virtually eliminated misbehavior (White & Bailey, 1990).

Assign time outs infrequently. When you do assign them, do so calmly and surely. The student is to go straight to the time-out area and stay there until the prescribed time is up. Time-out
assignments should be brief; about 5 minutes is usually adequate. However, timing should begin
only after the student settles down; if the student yells or argues, that time should not count. During time out, no one should speak to the student. Do not scold the student before, during, or after
time out. Students should be told why they are being given time out but should not otherwise be
lectured. If the principal's office is used, the principal should be asked not to speak to the student.

REDUCE THE FREQUENCY OF REINFORCEMENT Once a reinforcement program has been in
operation for a while and the student's behavior has improved and stabilized at a new level, the frequency of reinforcement can be reduced. Initially, reinforcers might be applied to every instance of
appropriate behavior; as time goes on, every other instance and then every several instances might

Connections 11.6

For more information about
sit and watch as a punishment
for misbehavior, see Chapter 5.

Certification Pointer

For your teacher
certification test you will
need to demonstrate your
understanding of appropriate
applications of applied
behavioral analysis.

be reinforced. Reducing the frequency of reinforcement helps to maintain the new behaviors over the long run and aids in extending the behaviors to other settings.

Applied Behavior Analysis Programs

Home-based reinforcement strategies and daily report card programs are examples of behavior modification plans involving individual students. A group contingency program is an example of behavior modification in which the whole class is involved.

HOME-BASED REINFORCEMENT Some of the most practical and effective classroom management methods are **home-based reinforcement strategies** (Alberto & Troutman, 2013; Scott et al., 2012; Walker & Gresham, 2013). Teachers give students a daily or weekly report card to take home, and parents are instructed to provide special privileges or rewards to students on the basis of these teacher reports. Home-based reinforcement is not a new idea; a one-room schoolhouse museum in Vermont displays weekly report cards from the 1860s!

Home-based reinforcement has several advantages over other equally effective behavior management strategies. First, parents can give much more potent rewards and privileges than schools can. For example, parents control access to such activities as television, computers, video games, trips to the store, and going out with friends. Parents also know what their own children like and, therefore, can provide more individualized privileges than the school can. Second, home-based reinforcement gives parents frequent good news about their children. Parents of disruptive children usually hear from the school only when their child has done something wrong. This is bad for parent–school relations and can lead to much blame and finger-pointing. Third, home-based reinforcement is easy to administer. You can involve any adults who deal with the child (other teachers, bus drivers, playground or lunch monitors) in the program by having the student carry a daily report card all day. Finally, over time, daily report cards can be replaced by weekly report cards and then biweekly report cards without loss in effectiveness, until just the school's usual 6- or 9-week report cards are used.

DAILY REPORT CARDS Figure 11.3 presents a daily report card for an elementary school student. His teacher rates his behavior and schoolwork at the end of each day. The student is responsible for carrying his report card with him at all times and for making sure that it is marked at the end of each day. Whenever he makes at least 3 stars, his parents have agreed to give him a special privilege: His father is to read him an extra story before bedtime and let him stay up 15 minutes longer than usual. Whenever he forgets to bring home his report card, his parents are to assume that he did not meet the criterion. If this were a middle or high school student or a student in a departmentalized

FIGURE 11.3 •
Example of a Daily Report Card

	Monday	Tuesday	Wednesday	Thursday	Friday
Followed directions	☆	☆			
Completed assignments	☆	☆			
Kept hands and feet to self	☆				
Asked for help	☆	☆			
Parent Initials	*LM*	*LM*			

elementary school (where he changes classes for each subject), he would carry his report card to every class, and each teacher would mark it. Obviously, this approach requires some coordination among teachers, but the effort is certainly worthwhile if the daily report card dramatically reduces a student's misbehaviors and increases his or her academic output, as it has in dozens of studies evaluating this method (Barth, 1979). For example, a study by Fabiano et al. (2010) found substantial positive effects of daily report cards for sixth-graders with attention deficit hyperactivity disorders.

GROUP CONTINGENCY PROGRAMS A reinforcement system in which an entire group is rewarded on the basis of the behavior of the group members is called a **group contingency program**. Teachers have always used group contingencies, as in "We'll go to lunch as soon as all students have put their work away and are quiet." When the teacher says this, any one student can cause the entire class to be late to lunch. Or you might say, "If the class averages at least 90 on tomorrow's quiz, then you'll all be excused from homework for the rest of the week." This group contingency will depend on the average performance of all group members, rather than on any single student's performance.

THEORY INTO PRACTICE

Using a Daily Report Card System

Setting up and implementing a daily report card system requires the following steps:

1. Decide which behaviors to include in the daily report card. Choose a behavior or set of behaviors on which the daily report card is to be based. Devise a rating scheme for each behavior, and construct a standard report card form. Your daily report card might be more or less elaborate than the one in Figure 11.3. For example, you might break behavior down into more precise categories, such as getting along with others, staying on task, and following class rules.

2. Explain the program to parents. Home-based reinforcement programs depend on parent participation, so it is critical to inform parents about the program and to obtain their cooperation. Parents should be told what the daily report card means and asked to reward their children whenever they bring home a good report card. In presenting the program to parents, teachers should explain what parents might do to reward their children. Communications with parents should be brief, positive, and informal and should generate a feeling that "we're going to solve this together." The program should focus on rewarding good behavior rather than on punishing bad behavior. The following examples demonstrate rewards that parents might use at home:

- Special activities with a parent (e.g., reading, flying a kite, building a model, shopping, playing a game, going to the zoo)
- Special foods
- Baking cookies or cooking
- Operating equipment that is usually reserved for adults (e.g., the dishwasher or vacuum cleaner)
- Access to special games, toys, technology, or equipment
- Small rewards (such as coloring books, paper, comic books, erasers, or stickers)
- Additional play time, television time, video game time, and the like
- Having a friend spend the night
- Later bedtime or curfew

Parents should be encouraged to choose rewards that they can give every day (that is, nothing too expensive or difficult).

(continued)

The best rewards are those that build closeness between parent and child, such as doing special activities together. Many children who have behavior problems in school also have problems at home and might have relationships with their parents that are less than ideal. Home-based reinforcement programs provide an opportunity for parents to show their love for their child at a time when the child has something to be proud of. A special fun, relaxed time with Dad or Mom can be especially valuable as a reward for good behavior in school and for building the parent–child relationship.

3. *When behavior improves, reduce the frequency of the report.* When home-based reinforcement works, it often works dramatically. Once the student's behavior has improved and stabilized, it is time to decrease the frequency of the reports to parents (of course, discuss any changes with the parents). Special report cards might then be issued only weekly (for larger but less frequent rewards). As noted in Chapter 5, the best way to ensure maintenance is to thin out the reinforcement schedule—that is, to increase the interval between reinforcers.

One important advantage of group contingencies is that they are relatively easy to administer. Most often, the whole class is either rewarded or not rewarded, freeing you from applying different contingencies with different students. For example, suppose you say, "If the whole class follows the class rules this morning, we will have 5 extra minutes of recess." If the class does earn the extra recess, they all get it together; you do not have to arrange to have some students stay out longer while others are called inside.

Certification Pointer

Your teacher certification test may require you to describe types of classroom management procedures that would tend to make class discussions more productive.

The theory behind group contingencies is that when a group is rewarded on the basis of its members' behavior, the group members will encourage one another to do whatever helps the group gain the reward. Group contingencies can turn the same peer pressure that often supports misbehaviors into pressure opposing misbehavior. When the class can earn extra recess only if all students are well behaved all morning, no one is likely to find it funny when Joan makes silly faces or Quinn speaks disrespectfully to the teacher.

Group contingencies have been used successfully in many forms and for many purposes (Epstein, 2008; Kauffman et al., 2006). For example, in a strategy called The Good Behavior Game, the class is divided into two teams. When the teacher sees any member of a team disobeying class rules, the whole team receives a check mark displayed on the whiteboard. If a team has five or fewer check marks at the end of a period, all team members get to take part in a free-time activity at the end of the day. If both teams get more than five check marks, the one with fewer check marks receives the free time. Not only has this strategy been found to be effective right away, but long-term follow-up studies of first-graders who experienced this approach have found lasting impacts on children's lives (Bradshaw, Zmuda, Kellam, & Ialongo, 2009; Bradshaw, Waasdorp & Leaf, 2015; Flower, McKenna, Bunuan, Muething, & Vega, 2014; Ialongo, Poduska, Wethamer, & Keller, 2001).

Ethics of Behavioral Methods

The behavior analysis strategies described in this chapter can be powerful. Properly applied, they will usually bring the behavior of even the most disruptive students to manageable levels. However, there is a danger that teachers might use such techniques to overcontrol students. They could be so concerned about getting students to sit down, stay quiet, and look productive that they lose sight of the fact that school is for learning, not for social control. Behavior management systems can increase time for learning, but unless the quality of instruction, appropriate levels of instruction, and incentives for learning are also adequate, the additional time might be wasted.

Some people object to applied behavior analysis on the basis that it constitutes bribing students to do what they ought to do anyway. However, all classrooms use rewards and punishers (such as grades, praise, scolding, and suspension). Applied behavior analysis strategies simply apply these rewards in a more systematic way and avoid punishers as much as possible.

InTASC 3
Learning
Environments

THEORY INTO PRACTICE

Establishing a Group Contingency Program

As noted earlier, a group contingency behavior management program can be as simple as the statement "Class, if you are all in your seats, on task, and quiet this morning, you may have 5 extra minutes of recess." However, having a little more structure can increase the effectiveness of the group contingency.

1. *Decide which behaviors will be reinforced.* As in any whole-class behavior modification program, the first step in instituting a group contingency is to establish a set of class rules.

2. *Set up a developmentally appropriate point system.* There are essentially three ways to implement a group contingency behavior management program. One is simply to rate class behavior each period or during each activity. That is, an elementary school class might receive 0 to 5 points during each individual instructional period such as reading, language arts, and math. A secondary school class might receive one overall rating each period or separate ratings for behavior and completed assignments. The class would then be rewarded each day or week if they exceeded a preestablished number of points.

Another way to set up a group contingency program is to rate the class at various times during the day. For example, you might set a timer to ring an average of once every 10 minutes (but varying randomly from 1 to 20 minutes). If the whole class is conforming to class rules when the timer rings, then the class earns a point. The same program can be used without the timer by giving the class a point every 10 minutes or so if all students are conforming to class rules. Some teachers put a marble into a jar from time to time whenever the class is following rules. Each marble is then worth 30 seconds of extra recess. The sound of marbles going into the jar tells the students they are doing well. In secondary schools, where extra recess is not possible, each marble might represent 30 seconds of break time held at the end of the period on Friday.

3. *Consider deducting points for serious misbehavior.* The group contingency reward system by itself should help to improve student behavior. However, it might still be necessary to react to occasional serious misbehavior. For example, you might deduct 10 points for any instance of fighting or of serious disrespect for the teacher. When points must be deducted, do not negotiate with students about it. Simply deduct them, explaining why they must be deducted and reminding students that they may earn them back if they follow class rules.

4. *When behavior improves, reduce the frequency of the points and reinforcers.* Initially, the group contingency should be applied every day. When the class's behavior improves and stabilizes at a new level for about a week, you may change to giving rewards once a week. Ultimately, the class may graduate from the point-and-reward system entirely, although feedback and praise based on class behavior should continue.

5. *Combine group and individual contingencies if necessary.* The use of group contingencies need not rule out individual contingencies for students who need them. For example, students who continue to have problems in a class where a group contingency is being used might still receive daily or weekly report cards to take home to their parents.

Applied behavior analysis methods should be instituted only when it is clear that preventive or informal methods of improving classroom management are not enough to create a positive environment for learning. It is unethical to overapply these methods, but it might be equally unethical to fail to apply them when they could avert serious problems. For example, it might be unethical to refer a child to special education or to suspend, expel, or retain a child on the basis of a pattern of behavior problems before using positive behavior management methods long enough to see whether they can resolve the problem without more draconian measures.

HOW CAN SERIOUS BEHAVIOR PROBLEMS BE PREVENTED?

Everyone misbehaves. There is hardly a person on Earth who has not at some time done something he or she knew to be wrong or even illegal. However, some people's misbehavior is far more frequent or serious than others', and students in this category cause their teachers and school administrators (not to mention their parents and themselves) a disproportionate amount of trouble and concern (Goode, 2011; Osher, Bear, Sprague, & Doyle, 2010; Thio, 2010).

Serious behavior problems are not evenly distributed among students or schools. Most students who are identified as having severe behavior problems are male; from three to eight times as many boys as girls are estimated to have serious conduct problems (Perkins & Borden, 2003). Serious delinquency is far more common among students from impoverished backgrounds, particularly in urban locations. Students with poor family relationships are also much more likely than other students to become involved in serious misbehavior and delinquency, as are students who are low in achievement and those who have attendance problems (see Hawkins et al., 2000; Herrenkohl, Maguin, Hill, Hawkins, & Abbott, 2001; Perkins & Borden, 2003).

The school has an important role to play in preventing or managing serious misbehavior and delinquency, but the student and the school are only one part of the story. Delinquent behavior often involves the police, courts, and social service agencies, as well as students' parents and peers (Fowler, 2011). However, there are some guidelines for prevention of delinquency and serious misbehaviors.

Preventive Programs

As noted earlier in this chapter, the easiest behavior problems to deal with are those that never occur. There are many approaches that have promise for preventing serious behavior problems. One is simply creating safe and prosocial classroom environments and openly discussing risky behaviors and ways to avoid them (Learning First Alliance, 2001; Osher, Dwyer, & Jackson, 2004). Another is giving students opportunities to play prosocial roles as volunteers, tutors, or leaders in activities that benefit their school and community (Allen, 2003; Freiberg & Lapointe, 2006; Goodwin, 2012b). Creating democratic, participatory classrooms can give students ways of achieving recognition and control in a positive environment, reducing the need to act out (Greene, 2011; Hyman & Snook, 2000). Smaller, less impersonal schools have been found to reduce bullying and violence (Pellegrini, 2002). Programs that improve academic achievement also often affect behavior as well (Barr & Parrett, 2001; Greene, 2011). These kinds of strategies embed preventive activities in the day-to-day lives of students, rather than singling them out for special treatment.

Identifying Causes of Misbehavior

Even though some types of students are more prone to misbehavior than others, these characteristics do not cause misbehavior. Some students misbehave because they perceive that the rewards for misbehavior outweigh the rewards for good behavior. For example, students who do not experience success in school might perceive that the potential rewards for hard work and good behavior are small, so they turn to other sources of rewards. Some, particularly those who are failing in many different domains, find their niche in groups that hold norms that devalue achievement and other prosocial behavior (Wentzel, 2003). The role of the delinquent peer group in maintaining delinquent behavior cannot be overstated. Delinquent acts among adolescents and preadolescents are usually done in groups and are supported by antisocial peer norms (Gardner & Steinberg, 2005; Perkins & Borden, 2003).

Enforcing Rules and Practices

Expectations that students will conform to school rules must be consistently expressed. For example, graffiti or other vandalism must be repaired at once so that other students do not get the idea that misbehavior is common or accepted. However, rules should be enforced firmly but fairly; rigid applications of "zero tolerance" policies have often been found to be counterproductive (Browne-Dianis, 2011; Freiberg & Reyes, 2008).

Enforcing School Attendance

Truancy and delinquency are strongly related. When students are out of school, they are often in the community making trouble. Further, unexcused absences are a strong predictor of low achievement (Gottfried, 2009). There are many effective means of reducing truancy (Casoli-Reardon et al., 2012; Fisher, Frey, & Lapp, 2011; Lehr, Hansen, Sinclair, & Christenson, 2003; Snyder et al., 2010). In a classic study, Brooks (1975) had high school students with serious attendance problems carry cards to be signed by their teachers at the end of each period they attended. Students received a ticket for each period attended, plus bonus tickets for good behavior in class and for going 5 days without missing a class. The tickets were used in a drawing for a variety of prizes. Before the program began, the target students were absent 60 percent of all school days. During the program, absences dropped to 19 percent of school days. Over the same period, truancy among other students with attendance problems who were not in the program increased from 59 percent to 79 percent.

Barber and Kagey (1977) markedly increased attendance in an entire elementary school by making full participation in once-a-month parties dependent on student attendance. Several activities were provided during the parties, and students could earn access to some or all of them according to the number of days they attended class.

Fiordaliso, Lordeman, Filipczak, and Friedman (1977) increased attendance among chronically truant junior high school students by having the school call their parents whenever the students were present several days in a row. The number of days before calling depended on how severe the student's truancy had been. Parents of the most often truant students, who had been absent 6 or more days per month, were called after the student attended for only 3 consecutive days.

THEORY INTO PRACTICE

Check and Connect

Check and Connect is a model in which school-based "monitors" work with students, families, and school personnel to improve the attendance and engagement of students in schools. The program has documented significant gains on attendance in elementary schools (Lehr, Sinclair, & Christenson, 2004) and on dropout reduction and overall school success in middle schools (Sinclair, Christenson, Evelo, & Hurley, 1998). Check and Connect includes the following elements (Lehr et al., 2004; Pohl & Storm, 2014; Stout & Pohl, 2012):

- **Relationship building.** Fostering mutual trust and open communication, nurtured through a long-term commitment that is focused on students' educational success
- **Routine monitoring of alterable indicators.** Systemically checking warning signs of withdrawal (attendance, academic performance, behavior) that are readily available to school personnel and that can be altered through intervention
- **Individualized and timely intervention.** Providing support that is tailored to individual student needs, based on level of engagement with school, associated influences of home and school, and the leveraging of local resources
- **Long-term commitment.** Committing to stay with students and families for at least 2 years, including following students during transitions across school levels and following highly mobile youth from school to school and program to program

(continued)

- **Persistence plus.** Maintaining a persistent source of academic motivation, continuity of familiarity with the youth and family, and consistency in the message that "education is important for your future"
- **Problem solving.** Promoting the acquisition of skills to resolve conflict constructively and to look for solutions rather than a target of blame
- **Affiliation with school and learning.** Facilitating students' access to and active participation in school-related activities and events.

Practicing Intervention

Classroom management strategies should be used to reduce inappropriate behavior before it escalates into delinquency. Improving students' behavior and success in school can prevent delinquency (Bender, 2015; Benson, 2014; Campbell Collaboration, 2016; Losen, 2015; Walker & Gresham, 2013). For example, Hawkins, Guo, Hill, Battin-Pearson, and Abbott (2001) used preventive classroom management methods such as those emphasized in this chapter, along with interactive teaching and cooperative learning, to help low-achieving seventh-graders. In comparison with control-group students, the students in the program were suspended and expelled less often, had better attitudes toward school, and were more likely to expect to complete high school. Freiberg and Lapointe (2006) reviewed research on several promising preventive approaches of this kind. A set of related programs for home and school, called The Incredible Years, teaches social-emotional regulation strategies, and has been found to improve student behavior in many studies (Hutchings, 2012; Webster-Stratton, 2012). Use of applied behavior analysis programs for misbehavior in class can also contribute to the prevention of delinquency (Bradshaw, 2012; Walker & Gresham, 2003). Group contingencies can be especially effective with predelinquent students, because this strategy can deprive students of peer support for misbehavior.

Certification Pointer

A teacher certification question may ask you to respond to a case study by suggesting ways of helping students develop the social skills that would help resolve conflicts presented in the case.

Requesting Family Involvement

Involve the student's home in any response to serious misbehavior. When misbehavior occurs, parents should be notified. If misbehavior persists, parents should be involved in establishing a program, such as a home-based reinforcement program, to coordinate home and school responses to misbehavior (Berger & Riojas-Cortez, 2016; Feil, Frey, & Golly, 2012; Gettinger, Brodhagen, Butler, & Schienebeck, 2013). There are well-developed programs, such as Guiding Good Choices (Haggerty & Kosterman, 2012) and the Incredible Years (Webster-Stratton, 2012), that have been found to help parents improve positive behaviors and reduce negative ones in their teenagers (Terzian, Hamilton, & Ericson, 2011).

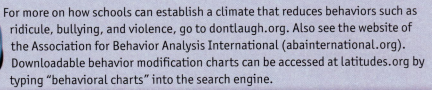

ON THE WEB

For more on how schools can establish a climate that reduces behaviors such as ridicule, bullying, and violence, go to dontlaugh.org. Also see the website of the Association for Behavior Analysis International (abainternational.org). Downloadable behavior modification charts can be accessed at latitudes.org by typing "behavioral charts" into the search engine.

Using Peer Mediation

Students can be trained to serve as peer mediators, particularly to resolve conflicts between fellow students. Students who are having problems with other students might be asked to take these problems to peer mediators rather than to adults for resolution, and the peer mediators themselves might actively look for interpersonal problems among their classmates and offer help when such problems occur. Peer mediators have been found to be effective in resolving a variety of interpersonal problems, from insults and perceptions of unfairness among students to stealing to physical

1. Introduce yourselves: "Hi, my name is _____. I'm a conflict manager and this is my partner _____."
2. Ask the parties: "Do you want to solve the problem with us or with a teacher?" If necessary, move to a quiet place to solve the problem.
3. Explain to the parties: "First you have to agree to four rules":
   a. Agree to solve the problem.
   b. No name-calling.
   c. Do not interrupt.
   d. Tell the truth.
4. Conflict Manager 1 asks Person 1: "What happened? How do you feel?" Conflict Manager 1 repeats what Person 1 said, using active listening: "So, what you're saying is . . ."
5. Conflict Manager 2 asks Person 2: "What happened? How do you feel?" Conflict Manager 2 repeats what Person 2 said, using active listening: "So, what you're saying is . . ."
6. Ask Person 1: "Do you have a solution?" Ask Person 2: "Do you agree with the solution?" If no: "Do you have another solution?" and so on until disputants have reached a solution agreeable to both of them.
7. Have disputants tell each other what they have just agreed to: "So will you tell each other what you've just agreed to?"
8. Congratulate them both: "Thank you for working so hard to solve your problem. Congratulations."
9. Fill out Conflict Manager Report Form.

FIGURE 11.4 • Peer Conflict Management?

Source: Classroom Law Project, Portland, OR.

aggression (Frey & Nolen, 2010). Peer mediators need to be carefully trained and monitored if they are to be effective. Figure 11.4 shows a guide for peer mediators that is used in one conflict management program.

Confronting Bullying

A widespread problem in schools at all levels is bullying, where students repeatedly torment weaker peers. Among students in grades 6 to 10, 30 percent have reported involvement in bullying (Espelage, Holt, & Poteat, 2010).

Bullying is particularly common among boys; a 1998 survey by the National Institute of Child Health and Human Development (Nansel, Overpeck, Pilla, Ruan, Simons-Morton, & Scheidti, 2001). found that boys were more likely to report being bullies (26%) or victims (21%). Rates for girls were 14 percent for both categories (Levin & Nolan, 2010). Rates were much higher in middle and high school than in elementary school (Sampson, 2002). In a recent survey, 50 percent of high school students admitted participating in bullying and 47 percent said they had been bullied (Goodwin, 2011a). Bullying can have serious negative effects on both the bully and the victim, leading to escalating violence as well as to depression and anxiety (Espelage et al., 2010). Recently, bullying online, or cyberbullying, has become increasingly common; it may include put-downs, nasty rumors, and humiliating pictures posted on social networking sites (Lawner & Terzian, 2013).

Interviews with students who have experienced bullying suggest that few could solve the problem on their own. Stopping bullying required telling adults or peers (Davis & Nixon, 2011). This highlights the importance of creating a school environment in which reporting bullying is encouraged, not seen as "tattling."

Effective approaches to prevent bullying in schools include the following components (see Ansary, Greene, & Green, 2015; Emmer & Evertson, 2012; Farrington & Ttofi, 2009; Lawner & Terzian, 2013; Levin et al, 2016; Murawski, Lockwood, Khalili, & Johnston, 2010; Swearer, Espelage, Vaillancourt, & Hymel, 2010; Weissbourd & Jones, 2012).

1. Develop and publicize a schoolwide antibullying policy (Cross, Thompson, & Erceg, 2014).
2. Educate all students about bullying and its negative effects on the whole school, and engage peers in schoolwide efforts to eliminate bullying (Lawner & Terzian, 2013; Rodkin, 2011).

Connections 11.7
For more on cyberbullying, see Chapter 9.

MyEdLab
Video Example 11.4
Ms. Salazar leads a discussion about bullying in her middle-school classroom. Why would this activity be particularly effective for children in this age group?

3. Provide training in social skills and recognize students who engage in prosocial activities. Particularly important skills are empathy, impulse control, and anger management (Frey, Hirschstein, & Guzzo, 2000).

4. Monitor locations and activities in which bullying occurs.

5. Establish consequences for bullying behavior.

6. Engage parents in discussions of bullying and in finding solutions (Lawner & Terzian, 2013).

ON THE WEB

For information on programs to confront bullying in school, see stopbullyingnow .com, clemson.edu, and cfchildren.org.

Judiciously Applying Consequences

Avoid the use of suspension (or expulsion) as punishment for all but the most serious misbehavior. Suspension often exacerbates truancy, both because it makes students fall behind in their work and because it gives them experience with time out of school. In-school suspension, detention, and other penalties are more effective (Benson, 2014; Bender, 2015). If a student has harmed anyone else, he or she should have an opportunity to make restitution in some form (Mirsky, 2011; Smith, Fisher, & Frey, 2015).

When students misbehave, they should be punished; but when punishment is applied, it should be brief. Being sent to a time-out area or detention room is a common punishment that is effective for most students. Loss of privileges may also be used. However, any punishment should not last too long. It is better to make a misbehaving student miss 2 days of football practice than to throw him off the team, in part because once the student is off the team, the school would have little else of value to offer or withhold. Every child has within himself or herself the capacity for good behavior as well as for misbehavior. *The school must be the ally of the good in each child at the same time that it is the enemy of misbehavior.* Overly harsh penalties and penalties that do not allow the student to reenter the classroom on an equal footing with others risk pushing students into the antisocial, delinquent subculture. When a student has paid her or his debt by losing privileges, experiencing detention, or whatever the punishment might be, he or she must be fully reaccepted as a member of the class.

MyEdLab **Self-Check 11.3**

SUMMARY

What Is an Effective Learning Environment?

Creating effective learning environments involves strategies that teachers use to maintain appropriate behavior and to respond to misbehavior in the classroom. Keeping students interested and engaged and showing enthusiasm are important in preventing misbehavior. Creating an effective learning environment is a matter of knowing a set of techniques that teachers can learn and apply.

What Is the Impact of Time on Learning?

Methods of maximizing allocated time include preventing late starts and early finishes, preventing interruptions, handling routine procedures smoothly and quickly, minimizing time spent on discipline, and using engaged time effectively. Engaged time, or time on task, is the time that individual students spend actually doing assigned work. Teachers can maximize engaged time by teaching engaging lessons, sustaining momentum, establishing smoothness of instruction, managing transitions, maintaining group focus, and overlapping. In a student-centered classroom, classroom management is more participatory, with students involved in setting standards of behavior; however, rules are still needed and must be consistently communicated and enforced.

What Practices Contribute to Effective Classroom Management?

Practices that contribute to effective classroom management include starting the year properly and developing rules and procedures. Class rules and procedures should be explicitly presented to students and applied promptly and fairly.

What Are Some Strategies for Managing Routine Misbehavior?

One principle of classroom discipline is good management of routine misbehavior. The principle of least intervention means using the simplest methods that will work. There is a continuum of strategies from least to most disruptive: prevention of misbehavior; nonverbal cues such as eye contact, which can discourage a minor misbehavior; praise of incompatible, correct behavior; praise of other students who are behaving; simple verbal reminders given immediately after students misbehave; repetition of verbal reminders; and application of consequences when students refuse to comply. For serious behavior problems, swift and certain consequences must be applied. A call to the student's parents can be effective.

How Is Applied Behavior Analysis Used to Manage More Serious Behavior Problems?

The most common reinforcer for both routine and serious misbehavior is attention from teachers or peers. When the student misbehaves to get the teacher's attention, one effective strategy is to pay attention to correct behavior while ignoring misbehavior as much as possible; scolding often acts as a reinforcer of misbehavior.

Individual behavior management strategies are useful for students with persistent behavior problems in school. After establishing baseline behavior, select reinforcers such as verbal praise or small, tangible rewards and punishers such as time outs (removing a child from a situation that reinforces misbehavior). Also establish criteria for applying reinforcement and punishment.

THE INTENTIONAL TEACHER
Using What You Know about Effective Learning Environments to Improve Teaching and Learning

Intentional teachers are leaders in their classrooms who take responsibility for managing time, activities, and behaviors. At the core of their success as classroom managers is high-interest, meaningful instruction. Intentional teachers use instructional time to its fullest by structuring a positive, consistent environment with reasonable rules and time-conscious procedures. They proactively prevent misbehavior and have a planned range of responses to misbehavior should it occur despite efforts at prevention. Intentional teachers' actions reflect their understanding that effective learning environments result from careful planning and vigilant monitoring.

- They carefully plan instructional time to ensure that there is adequate time for high-quality teaching.
- They minimize interruptions and time-wasting activities.
- They focus on increasing engaged time by teaching fast-paced, challenging, engaging lessons, rather than relying on disciplinary strategies to maintain high time on task.
- They start out the year right, engaging students in setting class rules and establishing efficient procedures for dealing with daily management.
- They manage routine misbehavior by using the least intrusive intervention that will work.

(continued)

- They use classroom management methods that are positive and do not disrupt teaching, such as preventing misbehavior by using engaging methods, using nonverbal cues to remind students of expectations, and praising students who are doing what is expected.
- If necessary, they apply proven, practical behavior modification methods to improve students' behavior. These methods should emphasize reinforcement rather than punishment and must never include physical punishment.
- They may use proven methods such as group contingencies and home-based reinforcement to solve behavior problems.
- They prevent more serious behavior problems by involving parents, using peer mediation, and improving attendance.
- They are prepared to apply mild but certain consequences if behavior problems continue.

Home-based reinforcement strategies might involve giving students daily or weekly report cards to take home and instructing parents to provide rewards on the basis of these reports. The steps to setting up such a program include deciding on behaviors to use for the daily report card and explaining the program to parents.

Group contingency programs are those in which an entire group is rewarded on the basis of the behavior of the group members.

One objection to behavior management techniques is that they can be used to overcontrol students. Behavior management strategies should always emphasize praise and reinforcement, reserving punishment as a last resort.

How can Serious Behavior Problems Be Prevented? There are few sure methods of preventing delinquency, but some general principles include clearly expressing and consistently enforcing classroom rules, reducing truancy however possible, avoiding the use of between-class ability grouping, instituting preventive classroom management strategies, involving parents in any response to serious misbehavior, using peer mediation, refraining from the use of suspension, applying only brief punishment, and reintegrating students after punishment. Check and Connect is one program that incorporates many of these principles.

MyEdLab

Application Exercise 11.1

In the Pearson etext, watch a classroom video. Then use the guidelines in "The Intentional Teacher" to answer a set of questions that will help you reflect on and understand the teaching and learning presented in the video.

KEY TERMS

Review the following key terms from the chapter.

accountability 276

allocated time 274

applied behavior analysis 283

behavior modification 285

classroom management 272

discipline 273

engaged time 273

group alerting 276

group contingencies 284

group contingency program 289

home-based reinforcement strategies 288

nonverbal cues 281

overlapping 277

time on task 273

time out 287

SELF-ASSESSMENT: PRACTICING FOR LICENSURE

Directions: The chapter-opening vignette addresses indicators that are often assessed in state licensure exams. Reread the chapter-opening vignette, and then respond to the following questions.

1. Ms. Cavalho works hard to prevent behavior problems and disruption in her classroom. Which of the following terms refers to her interaction with Mark?
   a. Management
   b. Discipline
   c. Learning environment
   d. Instruction

2. According to research, how could Ms. Cavalho increase student achievement in her classroom?
   a. Increase allocated time for instruction by 10 percent above what is normal.
   b. Increase engaged time to 100 percent of the allocated classroom time.
   c. Increase engaged time by 10 percent above what is normal.
   d. Decrease allocated time by starting late and finishing early.

3. Ms. Cavalho continues her lesson on writing style even as Mark attempts to interrupt. This is called
   a. engaged time.
   b. allocated time.
   c. momentum.
   d. overlapping.

4. Ms. Cavalho uses the principle of least intervention in her classroom. She works to prevent inappropriate behavior first, and if that does not work, she gives nonverbal cues and verbal reminders about how to act. She has used these strategies with Mark. Assume that Mark's behavior does not change after their discussion. What should she do next?
   a. Apply consequences.
   b. Give praise for appropriate behavior.
   c. Ask students to solve the problem.
   d. Ignore the behavior.

5. Daily report cards, group contingency programs, home-based reinforcement programs, and individual behavior management programs are all based on
   a. assertive discipline practices.
   b. delinquency prevention.
   c. behavioral learning theory.
   d. the principle of least intervention.

6. Discuss ethical considerations in the use of individual and group behavior management programs.

7. Explain how you would prevent the following misbehaviors: speaking out of turn, teasing, physical fighting.

MyEdLab **Licensure Exam 11.1** Answer questions and receive instant feedback in your Pearson eText in MyEdLab.

BSIP SA/Alamy Stock Photo

CHAPTER TWELVE

Learners with Exceptionalities

LEARNING OUTCOMES

At the end of this chapter section, you should be able to:

12.1 Identify the most common exceptionalities that entitle students to special educational services

12.2 Describe the laws and policies that define special education

12.3 Discuss effective educational strategies for students with exceptionalities, including response to intervention and inclusion

12.4 Describe how learners with exceptionalities influence intentional teaching

Elaine Wagner, assistant principal at Dover Elementary School, comes in to work one day and is stopped by the school secretary.

"Good morning," the secretary says. "There's a Helen Ross here to see you. She is interested in enrolling her children. She's waiting in your office. Looks nervous—I gave her some coffee and settled her down."

"Thanks, Beth," says Ms. Wagner. She goes into her office and introduces herself to Ms. Ross.

"I appreciate your seeing me," says Ms. Ross. "We're planning to move to Dover next fall, and I wanted to look at the schools before we move. We have one child, Tommy, going into second grade, and Annie is going into kindergarten. I'm really concerned about Tommy. In the school he's in now, he's not doing very well. It's spring, and he's hardly reading at all. His teacher says he might have a learning disability, and the school wants to put him in special education. I don't like that idea. He's a normal, happy kid at home, and it would crush him to find out he's 'different,' but I want to do what's best for him. I guess the main thing I want to see is what you do for kids like Tommy."

"Well," says Ms. Wagner, "the most important thing I can tell you about our school is that our philosophy is that every child can learn, and it is our job to find out how to reach each one. I can't tell you exactly what we'd do with Tommy, of course, because I don't know him, but I can assure you of a few things. First, we'll attend to his reading problem right away. We believe in preventing problems if we can, and if problems still show up despite our best efforts, we use the most intensive help there is as early as possible. If Tommy is having serious reading problems, we'll probably arrange to give him one-to-one tutoring so that he can catch up quickly with the other second-graders. Second, we'll try to keep him in his regular classroom if we possibly can. If he needs special-education services, he'll get them, but in this school we try everything to solve a child's learning problems before we refer him or her for testing that might lead to special-education placement. Even if Tommy does qualify for special education, we'll structure his program so that he is with his regular class as much as possible. We will develop an individualized education plan for him. Finally, I want to assure you that you will be very much involved in all decisions that have to do with Tommy and that we'll talk with you frequently about his progress and ask for your help at home to make sure that Tommy is doing well."

"Ms. Wagner, that all sounds great. But how can you give Tommy the help he needs and still let him stay in his regular class?"

"Why don't I take you to see some of our classes in operation right now?" says Ms. Wagner. "I think you'll see what I mean."

Ms. Wagner leads the way through the brightly lit corridors lined with student projects, artwork, and compositions. She turns in at Mr. Esposito's second-grade class. There, she and Ms. Ross are met by a happy, excited buzz of activity. The children are working in small groups, measuring each other's heights and the lengths of fingers and feet. Some children are trying to figure out how to measure the distance around each other's heads. Another teacher, Ms. Park, is working with some of the groups.

Ms. Wagner and Ms. Ross step back into the hall. "What I wanted to show you," says Ms. Wagner, "is how we

(continued)

integrate our students with special needs into the general education classroom. Could you tell which students were students with special needs?"

"No," admits Ms. Ross.

"That's what we hope to create—a classroom in which children with special needs are so well integrated that you can't pick them out. Ms. Park is the special-education teacher for the younger grades, and she teams with Mr. Esposito during math and reading periods to serve all of the second-graders who need special services. Ms. Park will help any child who is having difficulty, not only students with special needs, because a large part of her job is to prevent students from ever needing special education. Sometimes she'll work with individual kids or small groups that need help. She often teaches skills that children will be learning in advance, so they will be better prepared in class. For example, she might have gone over measurement with some of the kids before this lesson so that they'd have a leg up on the concept."

Ms. Wagner leads the way to a small room near the library room. She points through a window at a teacher working with one child. "What you see there is a tutor working with a first-grader who is having difficulty in reading. If your Tommy were here, he might do this as well. We try to do anything we can to keep kids from falling behind in the first place so that they can stay out of special education and make progress along with their classmates."

Ms. Wagner shows Ms. Ross all over the school. In one class a child with a visual disability is reading text from a computer that has inch-high letters. In another they see a child with Down syndrome working in a cooperative learning group on a science project. In a third classroom a child using a wheelchair is leading a class discussion.

Ms. Ross is fascinated.

"I had no idea a school could be like this. I'm so excited that we're moving to Dover. This looks like the perfect school for both of my children. I only wish we could have moved here two years ago!"

USING YOUR EXPERIENCE

COOPERATIVE LEARNING In groups of five, discuss Tommy Ross and students like him. One person assumes the role of Ms. Wagner; one is his future homeroom teacher, Mr. Esposito; one is Ms. Ross; one is the special-education teacher, Ms. Park; and one is the special-education director for the district. Discuss how Tommy will be screened for a potential learning disability in reading, and list some strategies that his teachers might use if, in fact, he does have a learning disability.

COOPERATIVE LEARNING Divide groups of four classmates into pairs. Ask each student to interview his or her partner about what a learning disability in reading might look like (i.e., how a reading disability might be identified) and what a teacher might do to address this situation. Ask the two interviewers to share what they have learned within their group. Then reverse the roles. The two new interviewers should tell their group what they have learned about reading disabilities.

InTASC 1

Learner Development

InTASC 2

Learning Differences

InTASC 3

Learning Environments

Dover Elementary School is organized around two key ideas: first, that all children can learn, and second, that it is the school's responsibility to find ways to meet each child's needs in the general education classroom to the greatest extent possible. Dover Elementary is committed to identifying children's strengths as well as their problems and to provide the best program it can for each child. Every school has children with exceptionalities who can do well in school when they are given the specific supports they need to learn. This chapter describes children with exceptionalities and programs that are designed to help them achieve their full potential.

WHO ARE LEARNERS WITH EXCEPTIONALITIES?

In one sense, every child is exceptional. No two children are exactly alike in their ways of learning and behaving, in their activities and preferences, in their skills and motivations. All students would benefit from programs uniquely tailored to their individual needs.

However, schools cannot practically meet the precise needs of every student. For the sake of efficiency, students are grouped into classes and given common instructional experiences designed to provide the greatest benefit to the largest number at a moderate cost. This system works reasonably well for the great majority of students. However, some students do not fit easily into this mold. Some students have sensory or physical disabilities, such as hearing or vision loss or orthopedic disabilities, that restrict their ability to participate in the general education classroom program without special assistance. Other students have intellectual disabilities, emotional or behavioral disorders, or learning disabilities that make it difficult for them to learn in the general education classroom without assistance. Finally, some students have such outstanding talents that the general education classroom teacher finds it difficult to meet their unique needs without help.

To receive special-education services, a student must have one of a few designated categories of disabilities or disorders. These general labels, such as "specific learning disabilities," "intellectual disabilities," and "orthopedic impairments," cover a wide variety of problems.

Labels tend to stick, making change difficult, and the labels themselves can become handicaps for the student. Education professionals must avoid using labels in a way that unintentionally stigmatizes students, dehumanizes them, segregates them socially from their peers, or encourages discrimination against them in any form (Hehir, 2007). The term **learners with exceptionalities** may be used to describe any individuals whose physical, mental, or behavioral performance is so different from the norm—either higher or lower—that additional services are required to meet their needs.

The terms *disability* and *handicap* are not interchangeable. A **disability** is a functional limitation a person has that interferes with the person's physical or cognitive abilities. A **handicap** is a condition imposed on a person with disabilities by society, the physical environment, or the person's attitude. For example, a student who uses a wheelchair is handicapped by a lack of access ramps (Friend & Bursuck, 2016; Hallahan, Kauffman, & Pullen, 2015; Turnbull, Turnbull, Wehmeyer, & Shogren, 2016).

"People-First" Language

It is important to ensure that our language and choice of vocabulary and terminology in referring to people with disabilities convey the appropriate message of respect. There are two basic principles to keep in mind. The first is to *put people first*. An example of this would be to refer to Frankie as a student with a learning disability, not as a "learning disabled child." He is a student first; the fact that he has a learning disability is secondary. The second principle is to *avoid making the person equal the disability* (Smith et al., 2016). Each student has many characteristics, and the disability is only one of them. To define the child in terms of the disability does him or her an injustice. The following sections discuss characteristics of students with the types of exceptionalities that are most commonly seen in schools.

Types of Exceptionalities and the Numbers of Students Served

Some exceptionalities, such as loss of vision and hearing, are relatively easy to define and measure. Others, such as intellectual disabilities, learning disabilities, autism spectrum disorders, and emotional disorders, are much harder to define, and their definitions have evolved over time. In fact, recent decades have seen dramatic changes in these categories (Hallahan et al., 2015). Since the mid-1970s, the numbers of children in categories of disabilities that are most easily defined, such as physical impairments, have remained fairly stable. However, the number of students categorized as learning disabled has steadily increased, the number identified as having autism spectrum disorders has skyrocketed, and the use of the category "intellectual disability" has diminished.

Figure 12.1 (U.S. Department of Education, 2014) shows the percentages of all students, ages 3 to 21, receiving special-education services in 2013–2014. There are several important pieces of information in this figure. First, notice that the overall percentage of students ages 3 to 21 currently receiving special education is about 12.9 percent; that is, about 1 out of 8 students, ages 3 to 21, is categorized as exceptional. Of these, the largest proportion is categorized as having specific learning disabilities (4.6 percent of all students) or speech or language disabilities (2.7 percent). Since 1980–1981, the proportion of children categorized as having intellectual disabilities has diminished from 2.0 percent to 0.9 percent, while children with specific learning disabilities have risen from 3.6 percent to 4.6 percent. This is probably due to different definitions, not necessarily to changes in the children.

Certification Pointer

Teacher certification tests will require you to identify areas of **exceptionality** in learning, including learning disabilities, visual and perceptual difficulties, and specific physical challenges.

FIGURE 12.1 •
Percentage of Children Ages 3–21 Receiving Special-Education Services 2013–2014 as a Percentage of Total Public School Enrollment

All disabilities	12.9
Specific learning disabilities	4.5
Speech or language impairments	2.7
Intellectual disability	0.9
Emotional disturbance	0.7
Hearing impairments	0.2
Orthopedic impairments	0.1
Other health impairments	1.6
Visual impairments	0.1
Multiple disabilities	0.3
Autism	1.1
Traumatic brain injury	0.1
Developmental delay	0.8

Source: U.S. Department of Education, Office of Special Education Programs, Individuals with Disabilities Education Act (IDEA) (2015). *Digest of Education Statistics table 204.30.* Washington, DC: Author.

FIGURE 12.2 •
Percentage of Children Ages 3–21 Receiving Special-Education Services 2013–2014 as a Percentage of All Students with Disabilities

All disabilities	100
Specific learning disabilities	35
Speech or language impairments	20.6
Intellectual disability	6.6
Emotional disturbance	5.5
Hearing impairments	1.2
Orthopedic impairments	0.9
Other health impairments	12
Multiple disabilities	2.0
Autism	8.3
Developmental delay	6.3

Source: U.S. Department of Education, Office of Special Education Programs, Individuals with Disabilities Education Act (IDEA) (2015). *Digest of Education Statistics table 204.30.* Washington, DC: Author.

Figure 12.2 shows the percentages of students ages 3 to 21 receiving special-education services who had various disabilities in 2013–2014 (U.S. Department of Education, 2014). Specific learning disabilities (35 percent of all students with disabilities), speech and language impairments (21 percent), and intellectual disabilities (7 percent) are far more common than physical or sensory disabilities. In a class of 25, a teacher might, on the average, have one or two students with learning disabilities and one with a speech impairment. In contrast, only about 1 class in 40 is likely to have a student who has hearing or vision loss or a physical disability.

Students with Intellectual Disabilities

According to the American Association on Intellectual and Developmental Disabilities (AAIDD, 2010), people with intellectual disabilities have significant limitations in both intellectual functioning and adaptive behavior. They typically have low scores on tests of intelligence and also have difficulty in maintaining the standards of personal independence and social responsibility that would be expected based on age (Hallahan et al., 2015; Turnbull et al., 2016). These impairments in intelligence and adaptive behavior become apparent sometime between conception and age 18.

CAUSES OF INTELLECTUAL DISABILITIES Among the many causes of intellectual disabilities are genetic inheritance; chromosomal abnormalities, such as Down syndrome (Turner & Alborz, 2003); diseases passed from mother to fetus in utero, such as rubella (German measles) and syphilis; fetal chemical dependency syndromes caused by a mother's abuse of alcohol or cocaine during pregnancy; birth accidents that result in oxygen deprivation; childhood diseases and accidents, such as encephalitis or traumatic brain injury; and toxic contamination from the environment, such as lead poisoning (Hallahan et al., 2015). Many of these, especially lead poisoning, are particularly likely in impoverished, underserved areas (Murphey & Redd, 2014).

INTELLIGENCE QUOTIENT (IQ) To understand how severity of impairment in children with intellectual disabilities is classified, it is first important to recall from Chapter 4 the concept of **intelligence quotient (IQ)**, derived from scores on standardized tests. Students with IQs above 70 are generally regarded as being in the normal range. Slightly more than 2 percent of students have IQs below this range. However, education professionals do not use IQ alone to determine the severity of cognitive impairment. They take into account a student's school and home performance, scores on other tests, and cultural background.

CLASSIFICATIONS OF INTELLECTUAL DISABILITIES Children and adolescents with intellectual disabilities are often categorized on the basis of their intellectual functioning and adaptive skills, and on the basis of the supports they need (AAIDD, 2010 Turnbull et al., 2016). Table 12.1 defines four categories of services that people with intellectual disabilities might need and gives examples of these services.

However the categories are defined, children with mild intellectual disabilities, who need intermittent or limited support, are rarely identified before they enter school (Hallahan et al., 2015; Heward, 2013). This is by far the largest category of intellectual disabilities, and children in this category may appear entirely normal at home.

There is increasing evidence that as many as 50 percent of all cases of intellectual disabilities could have been prevented by improving prenatal care; ensuring proper nutrition; preventing accidents, diseases, and ingestion of poisons (such as lead paint) among children; and providing children with safe, supportive, and stimulating environments in early childhood (Heward, 2013). Studies of intensive early intervention programs emphasizing infant stimulation, effective preschool programs, parent support programs, and other services have shown lasting impacts on the performance of children who are at risk for intellectual disabilities (Bradley et al., 1994; Campbell & Ramey, 1994; Noonan & McCormick, 1993; Ramey & Ramey, 1992). Even children with more pervasive intellectual disabilities benefit substantially from intensive prevention programs in their early childhood years. A recent experiment found that giving children with IQs in the range of 40–80 frequent one-to-one or small-group tutoring over a 4-year period made a significant difference in their reading performance (Allor, Mathes, Roberts, Cheatham, & Al Otaiba, 2014).

Connections 12.1
For more on IQ, see Chapter 4.

Connections 12.2
For more about IQ testing, see Chapter 14.

TABLE 12.1 • Intensities of Supports for Children and Adolescents with Intellectual Disabilities

TYPE OF SUPPORT	DEFINITION AND EXAMPLES
Intermittent	Supports on an as-needed basis. Characterized by episodic nature, person not always needing the support(s), or short-term supports needed during life span transitions (e.g., job loss or an acute medical crisis). Intermittent supports may be high-intensity or low-intensity when provided.
Limited	An intensity of supports characterized by consistency over time, time-limited but not of an intermittent nature, might require fewer staff members and less cost than more intense levels of support (e.g., time-limited employment training or transitional supports during the school-to-adult period).
Extensive	Supports characterized by regular involvement (e.g., daily) in at least some environments (such as work at home) and not time-limited (e.g., long-term support and long-term home living support).
Pervasive	Supports characterized by their constancy, high intensity; provided across environments; potential life-sustaining nature. Pervasive supports typically involve more staff members and greater intrusiveness than extensive or time-limited supports.

Source: Adapted from AAMR, *Intellectual disabilities: Definitions, Classification, and Systems of Supports*, p. 26. Copyright 2002 by American Association on Mental Retardation. Reprinted by permission.

THEORY INTO PRACTICE

Teaching Adaptive Behavior Skills

Instructional objectives for helping students who have intellectual disabilities to acquire adaptive behavior skills are not very different from those that are valuable for all students. Every student needs to cope with the demands of school, develop interpersonal relationships, learn language skills, grow emotionally, and take care of personal needs. The difference is that students who have intellectual disabilities may need explicit instruction in these skills. Teachers can help students by directly instructing or supporting students in the following areas (Cook & Tankersley, 2013; Friend & Bursuck, 2016; Hallahan, Kauffman, & Pullen, 2015; Heward, 2013):

1. *Coping with the demands of school.* Attending to learning tasks, organizing work, following directions, managing time, and asking questions.

2. *Developing interpersonal relationships.* Learning to work cooperatively with others, responding to social cues in the environment, using socially acceptable language, responding appropriately to teacher directions and cues, and enhancing social awareness.

3. *Developing language skills.* Understanding directions, communicating needs and wants, expressing ideas, listening attentively, and using appropriate voice modulation and inflection.

4. *Socioemotional development.* Seeking out social participation and interaction (decreasing social withdrawal) and being motivated to work (decreasing work avoidance, tardiness, and idleness).

5. *Personal care.* Practicing appropriate personal hygiene, dressing independently, taking care of personal property, and moving successfully from one location to another.

The preceding Theory into Practice section suggests ways in which general education classroom teachers can help students who have intellectual disabilities to acquire adaptive behavior skills. Specific ways of modifying instruction for students with special needs are discussed later in this chapter.

Students with Learning Disabilities

Learning disabilities (LD) are not a single condition but a wide variety of specific disabilities that are presumed to stem from some dysfunction of the brain or central nervous system. The following definition is adapted from the National Joint Committee on Learning Disabilities (1988, p. 1).

> Learning disabilities is a general term for a diverse group of disorders characterized by significant difficulties in the acquisition and use of listening, speaking, reading, writing, reasoning, or computing. These disorders stem from the individual and may occur across the life span. Problems in self-regulatory behaviors, social perception, and social interaction may exist with learning disabilities but do not by themselves constitute a learning disability. Learning disabilities may occur with other handicapping conditions but are not the result of those conditions.
>
> *Source:* Based on "Learning Disabilities: Issues on Definition." Published by National Joint Committee on Learning Disabilities © 1988.

InTASC 2

Learning Differences

IDENTIFYING STUDENTS WITH LEARNING DISABILITIES Different interpretations of the many definitions of *learning disability* have led state and local school districts to vary widely in their eligibility requirements and provisions for students with learning disabilities (Bender, 2012). In 2013, for example, 35 percent of all students ages 3 to 21 with disabilities were identified as having specific learning disabilities (U.S. Department of Education, 2015).

In some school districts a student who falls more than two grade levels behind expectations and has an IQ in the normal range is likely to be called *learning disabled*. Students with learning disabilities have some or all of the following characteristics:

- Normal intelligence or even giftedness
- Discrepancy between intelligence and performance
- Delays in achievement in one or more major areas (such as reading or math)
- Attention deficit or high distractibility
- Hyperactivity or impulsiveness
- Poor motor coordination and spatial relations ability
- Difficulty solving problems
- Perceptual anomalies, such as reversing letters, words, or numbers
- Difficulty with self-motivated, self-regulated activities
- Overreliance on teacher and peers for assignments
- Specific disorders of memory, thinking, or language
- Immature social skills
- Disorganized approach to learning

Definitions of learning disabilities once required evidence of a serious discrepancy between actual performance and the performance that might have been predicted on the basis of one or more tests of cognitive functioning, such as an IQ test (Meyer & Rose, 2000; Siegel, 2003). In practice, many children were identified as having a learning disability as a result of having substantial differences between some subscales of an IQ test and others or between one ability test and another. This emphasis on discrepancies came under attack in the 1990s, however. For example, Fletcher and colleagues (1994) studied children ages 7.5 to 9.5 who were failing in reading. Some of these children had major discrepancies between their IQs and their performance; others had (low) IQ scores consistent with poor performance. On an extensive battery of assessments, the discrepant and "nondiscrepant" children were nearly identical. In either case, what they lacked were skills closely related to reading. A similar pattern has been found for students with mathematics disabilities (Swanson & Jerman, 2006). These studies have undermined the idea that there is a sharp-edged definition of learning disabilities distinct from low achievement (Mercer & Pullen, 2009; Stuebing et al., 2002; Wong & Butler, 2013).

Based on this research, the 2004 reauthorization of the main U.S. special-education law, IDEA, eliminated the use of discrepancy as part of the definition of learning disabilities and asked that states develop new definitions defining learning disabilities as a failure to respond to high-quality instruction based on well-validated principles.

CHARACTERISTICS OF STUDENTS WITH LEARNING DISABILITIES On average, students with learning disabilities tend to have lower academic self-esteem than students who have no such disabilities, although in nonacademic arenas their self-esteem levels are like those of other children (Elbaum & Vaughn, 2001; Kelly & Norwich, 2004; Manning, Bear, & Minke, 2001). On most social dimensions, children with learning disabilities resemble other low achievers (Bender, 2015). Boys are more likely than girls to be labeled as learning disabled. African Americans, Latinos, and children from families in which the head of the household has not attended college tend to be overrepresented in special-education classes, whereas female students are underrepresented (Harry & Klingner, 2014; O'Connor & Fernandez, 2006; Waitoller, Artiles, & Cheney, 2010). The 2004 reauthorization of IDEA requires states and the federal government to monitor ethnic group differences in special-education placements and to change policies that perpetuate them.

MyEdLab
Video Example 12.1
Bridget eloquently articulates some of the challenges of having dyslexia. It's important for parents and teachers to recognize and address the academic and the social needs of students with learning disabilities.

Students with Attention Deficit Hyperactivity Disorder

Students with **attention deficit hyperactivity disorder (ADHD)** have difficulties maintaining attention because of a limited ability to concentrate (Mash & Wolfe, 2003). ADHD includes impulsive actions, attention deficits, and sometimes hyperactive behavior. These characteristics differentiate students with ADHD from students with learning disabilities, who have attention

InTASC 7

Planning for
Instruction

InTASC 8

Instructional
Strategies

THEORY INTO PRACTICE

TEACHING STUDENTS WITH LEARNING DISABILITIES

There are many types of learning disabilities, and issues in teaching students with learning disabilities differ by age level. In general, effective teaching for students with learning disabilities uses the same strategies that are effective with other students, except that there might be less margin for error. In other words, a student with learning disabilities is less likely than other students to learn from poorly organized instruction. The following general concepts apply to effective teaching for students with learning disabilities (see Bender, 2015; Brooks, 2005; Cook & Tankersley, 2013; Connor, Alberto, Compton, & O'Connor, 2014; Gersten et al., 2009; Mercer & Pullen, 2009).

1. *Emphasize prevention.* Many of the learning deficits that cause a child to be categorized as having learning disabilities can be prevented. For example, high-quality early childhood programs and primary-grades teaching significantly reduce the number of children identified with learning disabilities (Conyers et al., 2003; Snow et al., 1998). Structured one-to-one or small-group tutoring for first-graders struggling with reading can be particularly effective in preventing reading disabilities (Blachman et al., 2014; May et al., 2015; Slavin, Lake, Davis, & Madden, 2011; Temple, Ogle, Crawford, & Freppon, 2016). Early reading strategies emphasizing phonics, which benefit most children, are essential to a large proportion of children at risk for reading disabilities (Cavanaugh et al., 2004; Galuschka, Ise, Krick, & Schutte-Korne, 2014). Clearly, the easiest learning disabilities to deal with are those that never appear in the first place.

Recognizing that the great majority of children labeled as having learning disabilities experience problems in reading, the 2004 reauthorization of IDEA encourages schools to provide scientifically validated reading programs to students who are at risk, and it allows schools to spend up to 15 percent of their IDEA funding for prevention and early intervention to help struggling students before they fall far enough behind to warrant a disability diagnosis.

2. *Teach learning-to-learn skills.* Many students with learning disabilities lack good strategies for studying, test taking, and so on. These skills can be taught. Many studies have shown that students with learning disabilities who are directly taught study strategies and other cognitive strategies perform significantly better in school (Gersten, Fuchs, Williams, & Baker, 2001; Harris et al., 2001; Jackson & Lambert, 2010; Jitendra, Edwards, Sacks, & Jacobson, 2004; Swanson, 2001).

3. *Give frequent feedback.* Students with learning disabilities are less likely than other students to be able to work productively for long periods of time with little or no feedback. They do better in situations in which they get frequent feedback on their efforts, particularly feedback about how they have improved or how they have worked hard to achieve something. For example, children with learning disabilities are likely to do better with brief, concrete assignments that are immediately scored than with long-term assignments. If long-term projects or reports are assigned, the students should have many intermediate goals and get feedback on each (Schunk, 2016).

4. *Use teaching strategies that engage students actively in lessons.* Students with learning disabilities are particularly unlikely to learn from long lectures. They tend

to do best when they are actively involved. This implies that teachers who have such students in their classes should make extensive use of hands-on projects, cooperative learning, and other active learning methods, although it is important that these activities be well structured and have clear goals and roles (see Slavin, Lake, Davis, & Madden, 2011).

5. *Use effective classroom management methods.* Because of their difficulties with information processing and language, many students with learning disabilities experience a great deal of frustration in school and respond by engaging in minor (or major) misbehavior. Effective classroom management methods can greatly reduce this misbehavior, especially strategies that emphasize prevention. For example, students with learning disabilities are likely to respond well to a rapid pace of instruction with much variety and many opportunities to participate and respond successfully (Bender, 2015; Charles et al., 2014; Jones & Jones, 2016).

6. *Coordinate supplementary services with classroom instruction.* Many students with learning disabilities need some sort of supplementary services, such as small-group tutorials, resource teachers, one-to-one tutoring, or computer-assisted instruction. Whatever these services are, they should be closely aligned with the instruction being given in academic classes (Vaughn, Bos, & Schumm, 2014). For example, if a student is working on *Treasure Island* in class, a tutor should also work on *Treasure Island*. If a student's math class is working on fractions, so should the resource teacher. Of course, there are times when supplementary services cannot be coordinated fully with classroom instruction, such as when a student needs work on study strategies or prerequisite skills. However, every effort should be made to create as much linkage as possible, so that the student can see an immediate learning payoff in the general education classroom for his or her efforts in the supplementary program. The students who are having the greatest difficulties in learning should not have to balance two completely different kinds of teaching on different topics.

InTASC 2

Learning Differences

InTASC 7

Planning for Instruction

deficits for other unknown reasons (American Psychiatric Association, 2011). Children with ADHD do not qualify for special education unless they also have some other disability condition that is defined in the law (Friend & Bursuck, 2016; Hallahan et al., 2015; Heward, 2013). There is much debate about whether ADHD exists as a distinct diagnostic category (APA, 2011). About 7.8 percent of children ages 4 to 17 have been diagnosed with ADHD (Brown, 2007). Research indicates that males with ADHD outnumber females in ratios varying from 4:1 to 9:1 (Kauffman & Landrum, 2009). Children with ADHD may be impulsive, acting before they think or without regard for the situation they are in, and they often can be inattentive and may find it hard to sit still. Medications for ADHD are widely prescribed, and a variety of drugs have been found to make hyperactive children more manageable and improve their academic performance (Brown, 2007; Evans et al., 2000). They can also have side effects, such as insomnia, weight loss, and blood pressure changes, and they should not be prescribed unless other strategies for helping children focus their attention have been tried.

Students with Speech or Language Impairments

Some of the most common disabilities are problems with speech and language. About 1 in every 30 to 40 students has a communication disorder serious enough to warrant speech therapy or other special-education services.

Although the terms *speech* and *language* are often used interchangeably, they are not the same. Language is the communication of ideas using symbols and includes written language, sign

MyEdLab
Video Example 12.2

Children with attention deficit hyperactivity disorder can present behaviors that challenge teachers' classroom management skills. How can the adults in Eric's life help him to set goals and learn to engage in self-regulation?

THEORY INTO PRACTICE

Students with ADHD: The Role of the Teacher

Attention deficit hyperactivity disorder (ADHD) is usually associated with inattention, impulsivity, and hyperactivity. Educational implications of ADHD for students can include significant academic, behavior, and social problems stemming from the inability to pay attention. Specific suggestions for the general education classroom teacher who has students with ADHD include the following (see Brown, 2007; Kauffman & Landrum, 2009; Rosenberg, Westling, & McLeskey, 2011):

- Make sure students understand all classroom rules and procedures.
- Consider carefully the seating arrangements of students with ADHD to prevent distractions and to keep these students in proximity to the teacher.
- Adhere to the principles of effective classroom management described in Chapter 11.
- Understand that certain behaviors, although not desirable, are not meant to be noncompliant—students might not be able to control their behaviors.
- Allow students who are hyperactive to have many opportunities to be active.
- Minimize the use of punishment or threats to manage students' behavior, but instead emphasize recognition for good behavior. Daily report cards (see Chapter 11) have been very effective with students with ADHD.
- Group students with ADHD wisely, taking into consideration the purpose of the group and the other students who will be members of the group.
- Teach students to manage their own behaviors—including self-monitoring, self-evaluation, self-reinforcement, and self-instruction (Binder et al., 2000; Schunk, 2016).
- Maintain ongoing communication with the students' homes by using daily report cards or other instruments to convey information (see Chapter 11).
- Collaborate with special-education personnel to develop behavioral and instructional plans for dealing with attention problems.

Certification Pointer

For a case study on your teacher certification test, you may be asked to suggest how to help a student with a very limited attention span to focus on a lecture and organize the concepts.

language, gesture, and other modes of communication in addition to oral speech. Speech is the formation and sequencing of sounds. It is quite possible to have a speech disorder without a language disorder or to have a language disorder without a speech disorder (Bernstein & Tiegerman-Farber, 2009).

STUDENTS WITH SPEECH DISORDERS There are many kinds of **speech disorders** (Bernthal, Bankson, & Flipsen, 2013; Fogle, 2013). The most common are articulation (or phonological) disorders, such as omissions, distortions, or substitutions of sounds. For example, some students have difficulty pronouncing *r*'s, saying "sowee" for "sorry." Others have lisps, substituting *th* for *s*, saying "thnake" for "snake."

Misarticulated words are common and developmentally normal for many children in kindergarten and first grade, but they drop off rapidly through the school years. Moderate and extreme deviations in articulation diminish over the school years with or without speech therapy. For this reason, speech therapists often decide not to work with a child who has a mild articulation problem. However, speech therapy is called for if a student cannot be understood or if the problem is causing the student psychological or social difficulties (such as being teased).

Speech disorders of all kinds are diagnosed and treated by speech pathologists or speech therapists. The classroom teacher's role is less important here than with other disability areas.

However, the classroom teacher does have one crucial role to play: displaying acceptance of students with speech disorders. Most speech disorders eventually resolve themselves. The lasting damage is more often psychological than phonological; students with speech disorders often are subjected to a great deal of teasing and social rejection. Teachers can model acceptance of the child with speech disorders in several ways. First, teachers should be patient with students who are stuttering or having trouble producing words, and they should never finish a student's sentence or allow others to do so. Second, teachers should avoid putting students who have speech problems into high-pressure situations that require quick verbal responses. Third, teachers should refrain from correcting students' articulation in class.

STUDENTS WITH LANGUAGE DISORDERS Impairments of the ability to understand language or to express ideas in one's native language constitute **language disorders** (Bernstein & Tiegerman-Farber, 2009; Kamhi & Catts, 2012; Vinson, 2012). Problems that result from limited English-speaking proficiency (LEP) of students whose first language is not English are not considered language disorders.

Difficulties in understanding language (receptive language disorders) or in communicating (expressive language disorders) might result from such physical problems as hearing or speech impairment. If not, they are likely to indicate intellectual disabilities or learning disabilities. Many students come to school with what appear to be receptive or expressive language disorders but that in fact result from a lack of experience with standard English because they speak either a language other than English or a dialect of English (Maxwell & Shah, 2012). Preschool programs that are rich in verbal experience and direct instruction in the fundamentals of standard English have been found effective in overcoming language problems that are characteristic of children from disadvantaged homes (Vinson, 2012).

Students with Emotional and Behavioral Disorders

All students are likely to have emotional problems at some point in their school careers, but about 1 percent have such serious, long-lasting, and pervasive emotional or psychiatric disorders that they require special education. As in the case of learning disabilities, students with serious emotional and behavioral disorders are far more likely to be boys than girls, by a ratio of more than 3 to 1 (Kauffman & Landrum, 2013; U.S. Department of Education, 2005).

Students with **emotional and behavioral disorders** have been defined as those whose educational performance is adversely affected over a long period of time and to a marked degree by any of the following conditions:

1. An inability to learn that cannot be explained by intellectual, sensory, or health factors
2. An inability to build or maintain satisfactory interpersonal relationships with peers and teachers
3. Inappropriate types of behavior or feelings under normal circumstances
4. A general, pervasive mood of unhappiness or depression
5. A tendency to develop physical symptoms, pains, or fears associated with personal or school problems

CAUSES OF EMOTIONAL AND BEHAVIORAL DISORDERS Serious and long-term emotional and behavioral disorders may be the result of numerous factors (Hallahan et al., 2015; Kauffman & Landrum, 2013; Yell, Meadows, Drasgow, & Shriner, 2014). Neurological functioning, psychological processes, a history of maladaptations, self-concept, and lack of social acceptance may all play a role (Friend & Bursuck, 2016; Rosenberg, Westling, & McLeskey, 2011). Children who are aggressive or bullying were often abused at home (Lereya, Samara, & Wolke, 2013). Some of the same factors, including family dysfunction and maltreatment, also play a role in disturbances that may temporarily affect a child's school performance.

Many factors that affect families can disrupt a student's sense of security and self-worth for a period of time. Changes in the family structure, for example, might leave a child depressed, angry, insecure, defensive, and lonely, especially in the case of divorce, relocation to a new community, a parent's unemployment, the addition of a new sibling, the addition of a stepparent, or the death or

Connections 12.3
Problems that result from limited English proficiency are discussed in Chapter 4.

Connections 12.4
For more on preschool and primary programs that help overcome problems of children from disadvantaged homes, see Chapter 9.

MyEdLab
Video Example 12.3
Children with behavioral disorders may need extra attention and support to act appropriately in the classroom (Bender, 2015; Borich, 2014; Harrison, Bunford, Evans, & Owens, 2013). However, teachers need to ensure that the attention they pay to the child's behavior does not detract from their focus on the student's academic needs and strengths.

Connections 12.5
Behavior management programs for students exhibiting aggressive behavior are described in Chapter 11.

serious illness of a family member. Physical, mental, or sexual abuse by family members or others can also lead to serious emotional and behavioral problems. This can include bullying or cyberbullying in school (Lawner & Terzian, 2013).

One problem in identifying serious emotional and behavioral disorders is that the term covers a wide range of behaviors, including aggression, hyperactivity, withdrawal, inability to make friends, anxiety, and phobias (Kauffman & Landrum, 2013; Yell et al., 2014). Also, children with emotional disorders quite frequently have other disabilities, such as intellectual disabilities or learning disabilities, and it is often hard to tell whether an emotional problem is causing the diminished academic performance or school failure is causing the emotional problem, since academic struggles cause frustration that can lead to anxiety and aggression (Caine & McClintic, 2014).

CHARACTERISTICS OF STUDENTS WITH EMOTIONAL AND BEHAVIORAL DISORDERS

Scores of characteristics are associated with emotional and behavioral disorders (Kauffman & Landrum, 2013; Losen, 2015; Rosenberg et al., 2011; Yell et al., 2014). The important issue is the degree of the behavior problem. Virtually any behavior that is exhibited excessively over a long period of time might be considered an indication of emotional disturbance. However, most students who have been identified as having emotional and behavioral disorders share some general characteristics. These include poor academic achievement, poor interpersonal relationships, and poor self-esteem. The inclusion of **conduct disorders**, or serious and sustained misbehaviors, in classifications of emotional and behavioral disorders is controversial. By law, students with conduct disorders must also have some other recognized disability or disorder to receive special-education services. IDEA has long protected children who have emotional and behavioral disorders from ordinary punishments (such as suspension) for disruptive behavior. The 2004 reauthorization maintains this protection for behaviors related to the child's disability, but not for unrelated behaviors.

STUDENTS EXHIBITING AGGRESSIVE BEHAVIOR Students with conduct disorders and socialized–aggressive behaviors might frequently fight, steal, destroy property, and refuse to obey teachers. These students tend to be disliked by their peers, their teachers, and sometimes their parents. They typically do not respond to punishment or threats, although they may be skilled at avoiding punishment. Aggressive children not only pose a threat to the school and to their peers but also put themselves in grave danger. Aggressive children, particularly boys, often develop serious emotional problems later in life, have difficulty holding jobs, and get involved in criminal behavior (van Goozen, Fairchild, Snoek, & Harold, 2007). Effective approaches for these children include behavior management strategies such as those described in Chapter 11 (Jones & Jones, 2016; Levin et al., 2016; Yell et al., 2014). For all forms of emotional and behavioral disorders, the best approach to start with is prevention, creating happy, emotionally supportive classes in which students feel welcome and successful (Page & Page, 2011). However, there are effective strategies for students with serious problems (see Coren et al., 2013); these include mentoring (Tolan et al., 2013), home-based reinforcement for appropriate behavior, and restorative practices, in which students who harm others are required to make it up to them in concrete ways (Smith, Fisher, & Frey, 2015).

STUDENTS WITH WITHDRAWN AND IMMATURE BEHAVIOR Children who are withdrawn, immature, low in self-esteem, or depressed typically have few friends or play with children much younger than themselves. They often have elaborate fantasies or daydreams and either very poor or grandiose self-images. Some might be overly anxious about their health and feel genuinely ill when under stress. Some students exhibit school phobia by refusing to attend or by running away from school.

Unlike children who are aggressive, who can appear quite normal when they are not being aggressive, children who are withdrawn and immature often appear odd or awkward at all times. They almost always suffer from a lack of social skills. Many children in this category have come to be recognized as having Asperger syndrome, discussed in the following section (Hall, 2013).

Students with Autism Spectrum Disorder

The U.S. Department of Education defines **autism** as a developmental disability that significantly affects social interaction and verbal and nonverbal communication. It is usually evident before age 3 and has an adverse affect on educational performance. Children with autism are typically extremely withdrawn and have such severe difficulties with language that they might be entirely mute. They often engage in self-stimulation activities such as rocking, twirling objects, or flapping their hands. However, they may have normal or even outstanding abilities in certain areas.

The term **autism spectrum disorder** describes a much broader range of severity, including a mild form of autism called **Asperger syndrome** (Boutot & Myles, 2011; Hall, 2013; National Research Council, 2001). Children with Asperger syndrome may be able to function in society and can be successful in school, but they have significant problems with social relations, perhaps avoiding eye contact, misinterpreting social cues, and behaving in odd ways. The numbers of children being identified as autistic has quadrupled since 2000–2001, and the numbers being diagnosed across the whole autism spectrum have increased even more than this, but most or all of this increase is due to expanded definitions, not to an autism epidemic. For unknown reasons, autism is far more prevalent among boys than among girls (Friend, 2011; Hall, 2013). It is thought to be caused by brain damage or other brain dysfunction (Volkmar & Pauls, 2003).

There is no cure for autism, and appropriate interventions depend on the child's level of functioning (see Burns, 2013; Hall, 2013; Robison, 2012; Wheeler, Mayton, & Carter, 2015). Early behavioral intervention has been found to be effective (Reichow, Barton, Boyd, & Hume, 2014). The main focus should be on teaching these children social skills that might be taken for granted in other children, such as making eye contact, smiling, and greeting others. The National Research Council (2001), in a review of the literature, concluded that successful strategies include systematic teaching of communication skills, social skills, and cognitive skills in a step-by-step progression. A review by de Bruin, Deppeler, Moore, & Diamond (2013) emphasized self-management interventions, such as those described in Chapter 5. Children with autism spectrum disorders who are in general education classes may benefit from teaching that uses more visuals and a more predictable structure (Boutot & Myles, 2011; Gunn, 2013; Hall, 2013; Palm, 2013). Also, children with autism spectrum disorders often have restricted interest, but addressing those interests in classroom teaching has been found to be beneficial to learning (Gunn & Delafield-Butt, 2016).

MyEdLab
Video Example 12.4

For some teachers, working with a child with autism is a positive and life-changing experience. The most effective teachers focus on each child's needs and strengths.

THEORY INTO PRACTICE

Interventions for Children with Autism Spectrum Disorder

The National Council for Special Education in Ireland has published a systematic literature review of the research evidence available on educational interventions for children with autism spectrum disorder (ASD) (Bond, Symes, Hebron, Humphrey, & Morewood, 2016).

Among other questions, the review considered what works best in the provision of education for people with ASD. The literature review included 85 best-evidence studies published between 2008 and 2013. These studies were considered to be of at least medium standard for the quality of evidence, methodological appropriateness, and effectiveness of the intervention. Most studies focused on preschool children and children aged 5 to 8 years.

For preschool children, two interventions were rated as having the most supporting evidence:

- Interventions designed to increase joint attention skills, usually involving one-to-one delivery of a play-based/turn-taking intervention by a teacher or parent
- Comprehensive preschool intervention programs that offered a comprehensive educational experience for the child, targeting areas such as behavior, social skills, communication, and learning

For school-aged children, three interventions were rated as having the most supporting evidence:

(continued)

- Peer-mediated interventions: group interventions with peers to support the development of social skills in children with ASD and/or help peers to interact more successfully with children with ASD
- Multi-component social skills interventions, which included several elements, such as social skills training, peer support in school, and the involvement of parents in supporting the child's social skills
- Use of behavioral interventions based on behavioral principles to target challenging/interfering behaviors in children with ASD, often on the basis of an initial functional assessment followed by specific interventions

ON THE WEB

More information on autism spectrum disorders can be found at autism-society .org. Also see the CDC website, cdc.gov, and the CEC website https://www.cec .sped.org/.

Students with Sensory, Physical, and Health Impairments

Sensory impairments are problems with the ability to see or hear or otherwise receive information through the body's senses. Physical disorders include conditions such as cerebral palsy, spina bifida, spinal cord injury, and muscular dystrophy. Health disorders include, for example, acquired immune deficiency syndrome (AIDS); seizure disorders; diabetes; cystic fibrosis; sickle-cell anemia; and bodily damage from chemical addictions, child abuse, or attempted suicide.

STUDENTS WITH VISUAL DISABILITIES Most students' visual problems are correctable by glasses or other types of corrective lenses. A **vision loss** is considered a disability only if it is not correctable. It is estimated that approximately 1 out of every 1,000 children has a visual disability. Such disabilities are usually referred to as *blindness* or *visual impairment*. A child defined as legally blind is one whose vision is judged to be 20/200 or worse in the better eye, even with correction, or whose field of vision is significantly narrower than that of a person with normal vision. Persons with partial sight, according to this classification system, are those whose vision is between 20/70 and 20/200 in the better eye with correction.

It is a misconception to assume that individuals who are legally blind have no sight. More than 80 percent of students who are legally blind can read large- or regular-print books. Assistive technology that is used to enlarge and clarify text has further expanded the numbers of students who can participate normally in class (Boone & Higgins, 2007). This implies that many students with vision loss can be taught by means of a modification of usual teaching materials. Classroom teachers should be aware of the signs indicating that a child has a vision problem. Undoubtedly, children who have difficulty seeing also have difficulty in many areas of learning, because classroom lessons typically use a tremendous amount of visual material. Here are several possible signs of vision loss: (1) child often tilts head; (2) child rubs eyes often; (3) child's eyes are red, inflamed, or crusty or may water excessively; (4) child has difficulty reading small print or can't discriminate letters; (5) child complains of dizziness or headaches after a reading assignment (Sornson, 2001). If you notice any of these problems, you should refer the student for appropriate vision screening. It is crucial to catch vision problems early, before they adversely affect students' learning and motivation.

STUDENTS WHO ARE DEAF OR HARD OF HEARING **Hearing disabilities** range from complete deafness to problems that can be alleviated with a hearing aid (Paul & Whitelaw, 2011). The appropriate classification of an individual with hearing loss depends on the measures required to compensate for the problem. Simply having a student sit at the front of the classroom might be enough to compensate for a mild hearing loss. Many children can communicate adequately by listening to your voice and watching your lips. Others may need a hearing aid, and those with more severe problems will need to use a nonverbal form of communication such as sign language (Scheetz, 2012). Approaches to reading instruction also need to be modified (Schirmer & Mc-Gough, 2005). Many children, not just those with hearing disabilities, can benefit from amplification of the teacher's voice or the use of assistive technology on computers to amplify and clarify speech (Boone & Higgins, 2007). Following are several suggestions to keep in mind:

1. Seat children with hearing problems in the front of the room, slightly off center toward the windows. This will allow them to see your face in the best light.

2. If the hearing problem is predominantly in one ear, students should sit in a front corner seat so that their better ear is toward you.

3. Speak at the student's eye level whenever possible.

4. Give important information and instructions while facing the class. Avoid talking while facing away from the class.

5. Do not use exaggerated lip movements when speaking.

6. Learn how to assist a child who has a hearing aid.

ON THE WEB

There are many web-based resources for special needs educators. Family Friendly Fun with Special Needs (family-friendly-fun.com) offers a great collection of resources for use with children with special needs on a variety of topics. The Special Needs Resource site (snrproject.com) showcases international students, assistive technologies, and other resources for the parents of special learners. Internet Resources for Special Children is an organization dedicated to providing information, activities, and support for learners with special needs. Visit Special Needs Opportunity Windows (snow.idrc.ocad.ca) for professional development, student activities, and parent resource materials. DREAMMS for Kids, Inc. (dreamms.org) is created by a nonprofit parent and professional service agency that specializes in assistive technology (AT)–related research, development, and information dissemination. CAST (Center for Applied Special Technology) (cast.org) is an educational not-for-profit organization that uses technology to expand opportunities for all people, including those with disabilities. The National Center on Universal Design for Learning (udlcenter.org) promotes the use of materials and strategies that meet the needs of all learners. The National Center to Improve Practice in Special Education through Technology, Media, and Materials (http://cecp.air.org/teams/stratpart/ncip.asp) works to improve educational outcomes for students with disabilities by promoting the effective use of assistive and instructional technologies among educators and related personnel serving these students. Closing the Gap (closingthegap.com) is a rich source for information on innovative applications of computer technology for persons with disabilities. This site provides a comprehensive examination of the most current uses of technology by persons with disabilities and the professionals who work with them. Internet Special Education Resources (iser.com) is a nationwide directory of professionals who serve the learning disabilities and special-education communities. ISER helps parents and caregivers find local special-education professionals to help with learning disabilities and attention deficit hyperactivity disorder assessment, therapy, advocacy, and other special needs. The University of Washington's Adaptive Technologies site (washington.edu) has an extensive collection of publications and videos about technologies to help people with disabilities.

Students Who Are Gifted and Talented

MyEdLab

Video Example 12.5

Many schools offer advanced-placement (AP) classes to provide accelerated work for students who are gifted. In what ways does this class encourage the students to think creatively or solve challenging problems?

Who are the gifted and talented? Almost all children, according to their proud parents; and in fact, many students do have outstanding talents or skills in some area. **Giftedness** was once defined almost entirely in terms of superior IQ or demonstrated ability, such as outstanding performance in mathematics or chess, but the definition now encompasses students with superior abilities in a wide range of activities, including the arts (Colangelo & Davis, 2009; Olszewski-Kubilius & Thomson, 2013; Plucker & Callahan, 2014; Sternberg, 2007). High IQ is still considered part of the definition of gifted and talented (Steiner & Carr, 2003), and most students who are so categorized have IQs above 130. However, the members of some groups are underidentified as gifted and talented; these groups include females, students with disabilities, underachievers, and students who are members of racial or ethnic minority groups (Sternberg, 2007). Approximately 3 to 5 percent of students are considered gifted or talented (Plucker & Callahan, 2014).

CHARACTERISTICS OF STUDENTS WHO ARE GIFTED AND TALENTED Children who are intellectually gifted typically have strong motivation (Colangelo & Davis, 2009; Gottfried & Gottfried, 2004). They also are academically superior, usually learn to read early, and generally do excellent work in most school areas (Olszewski-Kubilius & Thomson, 2013). One of the most important studies of children with intellectual gifts, begun by Lewis Terman in 1926, followed 1,528 individuals who had IQs higher than 140 as children. Terman's research exploded the myth that high-IQ individuals were brainy but physically and socially inept. In fact, Terman found that children with outstanding IQs were larger, stronger, and better coordinated than other children and became better adjusted and more emotionally stable adults (Terman & Oden, 1959). Yet many people still assume that gifted students, especially males, are likely to have socioemotional problems (Preckel, Baudson, Krolak-Schwerdt, & Glock, 2015).

EDUCATION OF STUDENTS WHO ARE GIFTED How to educate students who are gifted is a matter of debate (see Davis, Rimm, & Siegle, 2011; Plucker & Callahan, 2014). Some programs for those with gifts and talents involve special secondary schools for students who are gifted in science or in the arts. Others include special classes for high achievers in regular schools (see Olszewski-Kubilius & Thomson, 2013). One debate in this area concerns acceleration versus enrichment. Advocates of acceleration (e.g., Colangelo, Assouline, & Gross, 2005) argue that students with intellectual gifts should be encouraged to move through the school curriculum rapidly, perhaps skipping grades and going to college at an early age. Others (e.g., Callahan, Moon, Oh, Azano, & Hailey, 2015; Renzulli & Reis, 2000; VanTassel-Baska & Brown 2007) maintain that rather than merely moving students through school more rapidly, programs for those who are gifted should engage them in more creative and problem-solving activities.

Research on programs for students who are gifted provides more support (in terms of student achievement gains) for acceleration than for enrichment (Rogers, 2009). However, this could be because the outcomes of enrichment, such as creativity or problem-solving skills, are difficult to measure. **Acceleration programs** for students who are gifted often involve the teaching of advanced mathematics or other subjects to students at early ages. A variation on the acceleration theme is a technique called curriculum compacting, in which teachers may skip over portions of the curriculum that the students who are very able do not need (Brulles & Winebrenner, 2012).

Enrichment programs take many forms. Renzulli and Reis (2000) suggest an emphasis on three types of activities: general exploratory activities, such as projects that allow students to find out about topics on their own; group training activities, such as games and simulations to promote creativity and problem-solving skills; and individual and small-group investigations of real problems, such as writing books or newspapers, interviewing elderly people to write oral histories, and conducting geological or archaeological investigations.

One problem with enrichment programs for students who are gifted and talented is simply that most of the activities suggested for these students would benefit all students (Borland, 2008; Tomlinson & Javius, 2012). In recognition of this, many schools are now incorporating activities that are characteristic of enrichment programs into the curriculum for all students, thereby meeting the needs of students who are gifted and talented without physically separating them from their peers (Colangelo & Davis, 2009; Davis et al., 2011; Rakow, 2012). Examples of such activities include increased use of projects, experiments, independent study, and cooperative learning. Also, many high schools are making advanced-placement courses broadly available, although the benefits of this for college access or performance are unclear (Roderick & Stoker, 2010).

> MyEdLab **Self-Check 12.1**

WHAT IS SPECIAL EDUCATION?

Special education is any program provided for children with disabilities instead of, or in addition to, the general education classroom program. The practice of special education has changed dramatically in recent years and is still evolving (see Hallahan et al., 2015; Heward, 2013; Smith et al., 2016; Turnbull, Turnbull, Wehmeyer, & Shogren, 2016). Federal legislation has been critical in setting standards for special-education services administered by states and local districts.

Public Law 94-142 and IDEA

In 1975, Congress revolutionized the education of children with exceptionalities by enacting Public Law 94-142, the Education for the Handicapped Act, which profoundly affected both special and general education throughout the United States (Hallahan et al., 2015; Heward, 2013; Hulett, 2009). It prescribed the services that all children who had disabilities must receive, and gave the children and their parents legal rights that had not previously been affirmed. A basic tenet of P.L. 94-142 is that every child who is disabled is entitled to special education appropriate to the child's needs at public expense. This means, for example, that school districts or states must provide special education to children who have severe intellectual or physical disabilities.

MyEdLab

Video Example 12.6
Federal legislation specifies that every child with a disability is entitled to special education. Many teachers find that the laws help them to plan appropriately and remain accountable.

P.L. 94-142 was extended beyond its original focus in two major pieces of legislation. In 1986, Public Law 99-457 extended the entitlement to free, appropriate education to children ages 3 to 5. It also added programs for infants and toddlers who are seriously disabled. Public Law 101-476, which passed in 1990 and changed the name of the special-education law to the Individuals with Disabilities Education Act (IDEA), required that schools plan for the transition of adolescents with disabilities into further education or employment starting at age 16. It also replaced the term *handicapped children* with the term *children with disabilities.*

In 1997, Public Law 105-17, the Individuals with Disabilities Education Act Amendments of 1997, or IDEA '97, was passed to reauthorize and strengthen the original act (Heward, 2013; Hulett, 2009; National Information Center for Children and Youth with Disabilities, 1998). Among the goals of this law were raising educational expectations for children with disabilities; increasing the role of parents in the education of their children with disabilities; ensuring that regular classroom teachers are involved in planning for and assessing these children, including students with disabilities in local and state assessments; and supporting professional development for all who educate children with disabilities (U.S. Department of Education, 1998).

IDEA was further updated in 2004 under Public Law 108-446, known as the Individuals with Disabilities Education Improvement Act. This revision emphasized prevention and early intervention, allowing schools to spend special-education funds to prevent children from needing special-education services. It changed the definition of learning disabilities to eliminate from it the concept of discrepancy between IQ and achievement, asked states to monitor and correct racial disparities in assignment to special education, and coordinated IDEA with other reforms, especially No Child Left Behind. The major provisions of IDEA 2004 are summarized in Table 12.2.

LEAST RESTRICTIVE ENVIRONMENT The provision of IDEA that is of greatest importance to general education classroom teachers is that students with disabilities must be assigned to the least restrictive environment that is appropriate to their needs. This provision gives a legal basis for the practice of mainstreaming, a term that has now been replaced by the term inclusion (Friend, 2011; McLeskey, Rosenberg, & Westling, 2013; Mastropieri, 2016; Salend, 2016; Smith, Polloway, Doughty, Patton, & Dowdy, 2016). This means that general education classroom teachers are likely to have in their classes students with mild disabilities (such as learning disabilities, mild intellectual disabilities, physical disabilities, or speech problems) who might leave class for special instruction part of the day. It also means that classes for students with more serious disabilities are

Certification Pointer
On your teacher certification test, you should know that the mandate to place students in the least restrictive educational environment possible developed as a result of efforts to normalize the lives of children with disabilities.

TABLE 12.2 • Key Components of the Individuals with Disabilities Education Act (IDEA) (2012)

PROVISIONS	DESCRIPTION
Least restrictive environment	Children with disabilities are educated with children who do not have disabilities as much as possible.
Individualized Education Program	All children served in special education must have an Individualized Education Program.
Due-process rights	Children and their parents must be involved in decisions about special education.
Due-process hearing	Parents and schools can request an impartial hearing if there is a conflict over special-education services.
Nondiscriminatory assessment	Students must be given a comprehensive assessment that is nondiscriminatory in nature.
Related services	Schools must provide related services, such as physical therapy, counseling, and transportation, if needed.
Free, appropriate public education	The primary requirement of IDEA is the provision of a free, appropriate public education to all school-age children with disabilities.
Mediation/resolution	Parents have a right, if they choose, to mediation or a resolution session to resolve differences with the school. Using mediation should not deny or delay a parent's request for a due-process hearing.
Transfer of rights	When the student reaches the age of majority, as defined by the state, the school shall notify both the parents and the student and transfer all rights of the parents to the child.
Discipline	A child with a disability cannot be expelled or suspended for 10 or more cumulative days in a school year without a manifest determination as to whether the child's disability is related to the inappropriate behavior.
State assessments	Children with disabilities must be included in districtwide and statewide assessment programs with appropriate accommodations. Alternative assessment programs must be developed for children who cannot participate in districtwide or statewide assessment programs.
Transition	Transition planning and programming must begin when students with disabilities reach age 16.

Source: Smith, Tom E.; Polloway. Edward A.; Patton, James R.; Dowdy, Carol A., *Teaching students with special needs in inclusive settings,* 5th Edition © 2008. Reprinted by permission of Pearson Education, Inc., Upper Saddle River, NJ.

likely to be located in general education school facilities and that these students will probably attend some activities with their peers without disabilities.

INDIVIDUALIZED EDUCATION PROGRAM (IEP) Another important requirement of IDEA is that every student with a disability must have an **Individualized Education Program (IEP)** that guides the services the student receives. The IEP describes a student's problems and delineates a specific course of action to address these problems. Generally, it is prepared by a special services committee composed of school professionals such as special-education teachers, special-education supervisors, school psychologists, the principal, counselors, and/or classroom teachers. Special services teams go by different names in different states; for example, they may be called child study teams or appraisal and review teams. The student's parent must consent to the IEP. The idea behind the use of IEPs is to give everyone concerned with the education of a child with a disability an opportunity to help formulate the child's instructional program. The requirement that a parent sign the IEP is designed to ensure parental awareness of and approval of what the school proposes to do for the child. A parent might hold the school accountable if the child does not receive the promised services.

The law requires that evaluations of students for possible placement in special-education programs be done by qualified professionals. Although general education classroom and special-education teachers will typically be involved in the evaluation process, teachers are not generally allowed to administer the psychological tests (such as IQ tests) that are used for placement decisions.

IDEA gives children with disabilities and their parents legal safeguards with regard to special-education placement and programs. For example, if parents believe that a child has been diagnosed incorrectly or assigned to the wrong program, or if they are not satisfied with the services a child is receiving, they may bring a grievance against the school district. Also, the law directs that parents be notified about all placement decisions, conferences, and changes in program.

For children with special needs who are under the age of 3, a specialized plan focusing on the child and his or her family is typically prepared; it is called an Individualized Family Service Plan (IFSP). At the other end of the education system, an Individualized Transition Plan (ITP) is often written for adolescents with special needs before their 17th birthday. The ITP anticipates the student's needs as he or she makes the transition from school to work and to adult life.

An Array of Special-Education Services

An important aspect of an IEP is a special-education program that is appropriate to the student's needs (Rix et al., 2015; Smith et al., 2016). Every school district offers children with special needs an array of services intended to be flexible enough to meet the unique needs of all. In practice, these services are often organized as a continuum going from least to most restrictive, as follows:

1. Direct or indirect consultation and support for general education teacher

2. Special education up to 1 hour per day

3. Special education 1 to 3 hours per day; resource program

4. Special education more than 3 hours per day; self-contained special education

5. Special day school

6. Special residential school

7. Home/hospital

In general, students with more severe disabilities receive more restrictive services than those with less severe disabilities. For example, a student with severe intellectual disabilities is unlikely to be placed in a general education classroom during academic periods, whereas a student with a speech problem or a mild learning disability is likely to be in a general education classroom for most or all of the school day. However, severity of disability is not the sole criterion for placement; also considered is the appropriateness of the various settings for an individual student's needs. For example, a student in a wheelchair with a severe orthopedic disability but no learning problems could easily attend and profit from general education classes, whereas a student with a hearing deficit might not.

With the exception of students who have physical or sensory disabilities, few students receive special education outside of the school building. The great majority of students who have learning disabilities or speech impairments attend general education classes part or most of the day, usually supplemented by 1 or more hours per day in a special-education resource room. This is also true for the majority of students with physical disabilities and almost half of all students with emotional disorders. Most other students with special needs attend special classes located in their school buildings. The continuum of services available to students with disabilities, from least to most restrictive, is described in the following sections.

GENERAL EDUCATION CLASSROOM PLACEMENT The needs of many students with disabilities can be met in the general education classroom with little or no outside assistance. For example, students who have mild vision or hearing loss may simply be seated near the front of the room. Students with mild to moderate learning disabilities may have their needs met in the general education classroom if the teacher uses strategies for accommodating instruction to student differences. For example, the use of instructional aides, tutors, or parent volunteers can allow exceptional students to remain in the general education classroom. You can often adapt your instruction to make it easier for students to succeed. For example, one teacher noticed that a student with perceptual problems was having difficulties with arithmetic because he could not line up his numbers. She solved the problem by giving him graph paper to work on.

Research generally shows that the most effective strategies for dealing with students who have learning and behavior problems are those used in the general education classroom. Special-education options should usually be explored only after serious efforts have been made to meet students' needs in the general education classroom (see Salend, 2016; Smith et al., 2016; Vaughn, Bos, & Schumm, 2014).

COLLABORATION WITH CONSULTING TEACHERS AND OTHER PROFESSIONALS In **collaboration**, several professionals work cooperatively to provide educational services. Students with disabilities who are included in the general education classroom benefit from professionals such as the consulting resource room teacher, school psychologist, speech and language specialists, and other professionals who collaborate with the general education teacher to develop and implement appropriate educational experiences for the students.

Many school districts provide classroom teachers with consultants to help them adapt their instruction to the needs of students with disabilities. Consulting teachers typically are trained in

Connections 12.6
Strategies for accommodating instruction to student differences are discussed in Chapter 9.

InTASC 10
Leadership and Collaboration

special education as well as general education. They might come into the classroom to observe the behavior of a student, but most often they suggest solutions to the general education teacher rather than working directly with students. Research finds that well-designed consulting models can be effective in helping teachers to maintain students with mild disabilities, particularly those with learning disabilities, in the general education classroom (Friend & Bursuck, 2016; Mastropieri, 2016).

For some types of disabilities, itinerant (traveling) teachers provide special services to students a few times a week. This pattern of service is typical of programs for students with speech and language disorders.

RESOURCE ROOM PLACEMENT Many students with disabilities are assigned to general education classes for most of their school day but participate in resource programs at other times. Most often, resource programs focus on teaching reading, language arts, mathematics, and occasionally other subjects. A resource room program usually involves a small number of students working with a special-education teacher. Ideally, the resource teacher meets regularly with the classroom teacher to coordinate programs for students and to suggest ways in which the general education classroom teacher can adapt instruction when the students are in the general education class (Salend, 2016; Smith et al., 2016; Vaughn et al., 2014).

Sometimes resource teachers work in the general education classroom. For example, a resource teacher might work with one reading group while the general education classroom teacher works with another. This arrangement avoids pulling students out of class—which is both inefficient (because of the transition time required) and potentially demeaning because the students are excluded from class for some period of time. Team teaching involving general education and special-education teachers also enhances communication between the teachers (Friend & Bursuck, 2014; McLeskey et al., 2013; Smith et al., 2016).

SPECIAL-EDUCATION CLASS PLACEMENT WITH PART-TIME INCLUSION Many students with disabilities are assigned to special classes taught by a special-education teacher but are integrated alongside students without disabilities part of the school day. These students join other students most often for music, art, and physical education; somewhat less often for social studies, science, and mathematics; and least often for reading. One important difference between this category of special services and the resource room model is that in the resource room, the student's primary placement is in the general education class; the classroom teacher is the homeroom teacher and generally takes responsibility for the student's program, with the resource teacher providing extra support. In the case of a student who is assigned to special education and is integrated part of the day, the situation is reversed. The special-education teacher generally serves as the homeroom teacher and takes primary responsibility.

InTASC 6

Assessment

THEORY INTO PRACTICE

Preparing IEPs

INITIAL REFERRAL The process of preparing an Individualized Education Program begins when a student is referred for assessment. Referrals for special-education assessment can be made by parents, physicians, principals, or teachers. Classroom teachers most often initiate referrals for children with suspected learning disabilities, intellectual disabilities, speech impairment, or emotional disturbance. Most other disabilities are diagnosed before students enter school. In most schools, initial referrals are made to the building principal, who contacts the relevant school district staff.

SCREENING AND ASSESSMENT As soon as the student is referred for assessment, an initial determination is made to accept or reject the referral. In practice, almost all referrals are accepted. The evaluation and placement team may look at the student's school records and interview classroom teachers and others who know the student. If the team members decide to accept the referral, they must obtain parental permission to do a comprehensive assessment.

Members of the special services team include professionals designated by the school district plus the parents of the referred student and, if appropriate, the referred student. If the referral has to do with learning or emotional problems, a school psychologist or guidance counselor will usually be involved. If the referral has to do with speech or language problems, a speech pathologist or speech teacher will typically serve on the team. The building principal usually chairs the team but may designate a special-education teacher or other professional to do so.

The referred student is then given tests to assess strengths and weaknesses. For learning and emotional problems, these tests are usually given by a school psychologist. Specific achievement tests (such as reading or mathematics assessments) are often given by special-education or reading teachers. Parents must give permission for any specialized assessments. Increasingly, portfolios of student work, teacher evaluations, and other information collected over extended time periods are becoming important parts of the assessment process (Smith & Tyler, 2010).

If appropriate, the school may try a prereferral intervention before deciding on placement in special education. For example, a child having serious reading problems might be given a tutor for a period of time before being determined to have a reading disability. For a child with a behavior problem, a home-based reinforcement program or other behavior management program might be set up. If these interventions work, the child might not be assigned to special education but could be served within the general education program. Even if a child does need special-education services, the prereferral intervention is likely to provide important information about the kind of services most likely to work. Prereferral interventions are becoming far more common under current policies favoring Response to Intervention, which is discussed later in this chapter.

WRITING THE IEP When the comprehensive assessment is complete, the special services team members meet to consider the best placement for the student. If they determine that special education is necessary, they will prepare an IEP. In Figure 12.3 a flowchart shows how the IEP process operates. Figure 12.4 is an example of an IEP. Usually, the special-education teacher and/or the classroom teacher prepares the IEP. The student's parent(s) must sign a consent form regarding the placement decision, and in many school districts a parent must also sign the IEP. This means that parents can (and in some cases do) refuse to have their children placed in special-education programs. At a minimum, the IEP must contain the following information (Smith et al., 2016).

1. ***Statements indicating the child's present level of performance.*** Statements typically include the results of specific tests as well as descriptions of classroom functioning. Behavior-rating checklists, work samples, or other observation forms may be used to clarify a student's strengths and weaknesses.

2. ***Goals indicating anticipated progress during the year.*** For example, a student might have a goal of reading at a fourth-grade level as measured by a standardized test, of improving classroom behavior so that disciplinary referrals are reduced to zero, or of completing a bricklaying course in a vocational education program.

MyEdLab
Video Example 12.7

Developing and teaching from an IEP requires that educators, parents, and the students themselves cooperate successfully with a clear focus on the child's needs.

(continued)

3. *Intermediate (shorter-term) instructional objectives.* A student who is having difficulties in reading might be given a short-term objective (STO) of completing a certain number of individualized reading comprehension units per month, or a student with emotional and behavior problems might be expected to get along with peers better and avoid fights.

4. *A statement of the specific special-education and related services to be provided, as well as the extent to which the student will participate in general education programs.* The IEP might specify, for example, that a student would receive two 30-minute sessions with a speech therapist each week. An IEP for a student with a learning disability might specify 45 minutes per day of instruction from a resource teacher in reading, plus consultation between the resource teacher and the classroom teacher on ways to adapt instruction in the general education classroom. A student with an intellectual handicap might be assigned to a self-contained special-education class, but the IEP might specify that the student participate in the general physical education program. The IEP would specify any adaptations necessary to accommodate the student in the general education class, such as wheelchair ramps, large-type books, or CDs.

5. *The projected date for the initiation of services and the anticipated duration of services.* Once the IEP has been written, the student must receive services within a reasonable time period. Students may not be put on a waiting list; the school district must provide or contract for the indicated services.

6. *Evaluation criteria and procedures for measuring progress toward goals on at least an annual basis.* The IEP should specify a strategy for remediating the student's deficits. In particular, the IEP should state the objectives the student is to achieve and how those objectives are to be attained and measured. It is critical to direct special-education services toward a well-specified set of learning or behavior objectives rather than simply deciding that a student falls into some category and, therefore, should receive some service. Ideally, special education for students with mild disabilities should be a short-term, intensive treatment to give students the skills needed in a general education classroom. All too often, a student who is assigned to special education remains there indefinitely, even after the problem for which the student was initially referred has been remediated.

IEPs must be updated at least once a year. The updating provides an opportunity for the team to change programs that are not working or to reduce or terminate special-education services when the student no longer needs them.

Developing and teaching from an IEP requires that educators, parents, and the students themselves cooperate successfully with a clear focus on the child's needs.

Connections 12.7

For more on home-based reinforcement strategies, see Chapter 11.

SELF-CONTAINED SPECIAL EDUCATION A self-contained special-education program is a class located in a school separately from the general education instructional program. Until the mainstreaming movement began in the early 1970s, this (along with separate schools for children with intellectual disabilities) was the typical placement for students with disabilities. Students in self-contained programs are taught by special-education teachers and have relatively few contacts with the general education instructional program.

Some students attend separate special day schools. These are typically students with severe disabilities, such as severe retardation or physical disabilities, or students whose presence might be

**FIGURE 12.3 •
Flowchart for the IEP
Process**

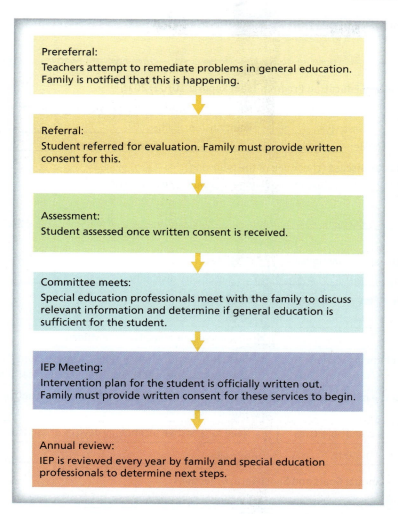

Prereferral:
Teachers attempt to remediate problems in general education.
Family is notified that this is happening.

Referral:
Student referred for evaluation. Family must provide written
consent for this.

Assessment:
Student assessed once written consent is received.

Committee meets:
Special education professionals meet with the family to discuss
relevant information and determine if general education is
sufficient for the student.

IEP Meeting:
Intervention plan for the student is officially written out.
Family must provide written consent for these services to begin.

Annual review:
IEP is reviewed every year by family and special education
professionals to determine next steps.

disruptive to the general education school, such as those with serious emotional disturbances. In addition, small numbers of students with disabilities attend special residential schools for students with profound disabilities who require special treatment.

RELATED SERVICES IDEA 2004 guarantees "related services" for children with disabilities; these are services that a child with a disability requires to benefit from general or special education. For example, school psychologists are often involved in the process of diagnosing students with disabilities and sometimes participate in the preparation of IEPs (Reschly, 2003). In addition, they may counsel the student or consult with the teacher about behavioral and learning problems. Speech and language therapists generally work with students on a one-to-one basis, although they may provide some small-group instruction for students with similar problems. These therapists also consult with teachers about ways to address student difficulties. Physical and occupational therapists treat motor difficulties under the direction of a physician. School social workers and pupil personnel workers serve as a major link between the school and the family and are likely to become involved when problems at home are affecting students' school performance or behavior.

Classroom teachers have important roles in the education of children with disabilities. They are important in referring students to receive special services, in participating in the assessment of students, and in preparing and implementing IEPs. The Theory into Practice section on pages 320–322 describes the process by which classroom teachers seek special-education services for students (see Gettinger, Brodhagen, Butler, & Schienebeck, 2013; Hallahan et al., 2015; Smith et al., 2016).

MyEdLab **Self-Check 12.2**

FIGURE 12. 4 • Sample Individualized Education Program

Individualized Education Program Team Report: 10/01/2016

Student's Last Name: ___Smith___ First: ___Joe___ MI: _____ DOB: ___04/18/2007___ Grade: ___4___

Parent's Last Name: ___Smith___ First: _Juan___ Relationship: _Father_____

Native Language or Other Communication Mode: ___None_____ Interpreter Needed: _____No_____

The Purpose of This IEP Team Meeting is to Discuss (check one of the following):

__ Initial Eligibility _X_ Review/Revise IEP __ Reevaluation __ Change of Disability Reevaluation

Parent Invitations and Contacts:

Method of contact: ___Phone___ by: _____Principal_____ Date: ___09/20/2016___ Result: ___Contacted___

Eligibility for Special Education:

The IEP Team determined this student to be: __ Ineligible   _X_ Eligible

Primary disability: ___Learning disability/dyslexia_____ Secondary disability: ___none_____

Factors to Consider in Order to Provide a Free and Appropriate Public Education (FAPE)

Consider (check) each of the following:

_X_ Strengths of the student	_X_ Communication needs of the student
_X_ Parent input and concerns for enhancing student's education	_n/a_ Positive behavior interventions, supports, and strategies for students whose behavior impedes learning
_X_ Results of an initial evaluation or the most recent re-evaluation of the student	_n/a_ Language needs for students with limited English proficiency
_n/a_ Progress on the current IEP annual goals and objectives	_n/a_ Need for assistive technology devices or services
_X_ Student's anticipated needs or other matters	

Annual Goals and Short-Term Objectives

Data used to determine present level of academic achievement and functional performance:

Evaluation	Criterion	Schedule	Status of Progress on Objectives
S: Student's Daily Work	__% Accuracy	Weekly	**1** Achieved/Maintained
D: Documented Observation	__ of __ Rate	Daily	**2** Progressing at a rate sufficient to meet the annual goal
R: Rating Scale	__ Achievement Level	Monthly	
T: Standardized Test	Other (specify above)	Other	**3** Progressing below a rate sufficient to meet the annual goal
O: Other (specify above)		(specify above)	**4** Not applicable
			5 Other (specify above)

Annual Goal: Joe will read short stories at a third-grade level independently to demonstrate improved decoding and reading comprehension skills.			
Short-Term Objectives (at least two per goal)	Evaluation	Criterion	Schedule
1. Joe will demonstrate comprehension of reading strategies by utilizing them independently 80% of the time when reading single paragraphs and short reading items from daily living (e.g., ads, jokes, etc.).	S, D, O (informal reading inventory)	80% accuracy independently	M

2. Joe will answer questions about a paragraph he reads with 80% accuracy independently	S, O (informal reading inventory)	80% accuracy independently	M
3. Joe will answer questions about a 3-paragraph story with 80% accuracy given minimal cues.	S, O (informal reading inventory)	80% accuracy, minimal cues	M

Date	Status Obj 1	Status Obj 2	Status Obj 3	Comments/Data on Progress
10/01/2016	1	1	2	Joe is able to use his strategies independently at the 1–2 paragraph level. Needs prompts on longer passages.

Reporting Progress

_X_ Parents will be informed in writing of progress on goals and objectives of this IEP at the regular reporting periods applicable to general education students.

Additional Reporting: How: _____ When: _____

Supplementary Aids/Services/Personnel Supports

_X_ The IEP Team has considered supplementary aids/services and supports. Needed services are listed below.

Supplementary Aids/Services/Supports	Amount of Time/Frequency/Conditions	Location
Tutoring by paraprofessional	3 times per week for 20 minutes	Room 3

Special Education Programs/Related Services

Is there a need for a teacher with a particular endorsement? Y / N   If yes, please specify:_____

Special Education Program/Services Rule No.	Frequency and Duration	Initiation Date and Location

Special Transportation

X No __ Yes, specifics: _____

Commitment Signatures

_____
Student

_____
Parent

_____
Parent

_____
Public Education Agency Representative/Designee

_____
General Education Teacher

_____
Special Education Teacher/Provider

WHAT IS RESPONSE TO INTERVENTION?

The emphasis in IDEA 2004 for students with learning disabilities is on **Response to Intervention**, an approach in which students are identified for special-education services not primarily on the basis of tests, but rather on their ability to profit from increasingly intensive instruction (Addison & Warger, 2011; Brown-Chidsey & Bickford, 2015; Fisher & Frey, 2014; Fuchs & Fuchs, 2006; Gettinger, Brodhagen, Butler, & Schienebeck, 2013; Johnston, 2011; Wixson, 2011).

In particular, children who are struggling in reading might be given small-group remediation, one-to-one tutoring, computer-assisted instruction, or other assistance to help them get on track. Only if intensive and long-term interventions have been consistently applied and found to be ineffective might a child be evaluated for potential learning disabilities, and even at this stage, the child's response to the additional assistance would be as diagnostically important as any test scores (Buffum, Mattos, & Weber, 2010, 2011; Burke & Depka, 2011; Fisher & Frey, 2010).

Response to Intervention is intended to replace the longstanding emphasis on discrepancy between IQ and performance, which has been found to be a poor predictor of actual performance (Fuchs, Fuchs, & Compton, 2004), with a criterion that focuses directly on the reading problems that cause most referrals in the first place. It also emphasizes immediate preventive services rather than waiting until children are far behind.

Response to Intervention often involves a three-tier model of services to struggling students. Figure 12.5 illustrates the concept, and the following sections describe each of the tiers.

Tier 1: Prevention

Tier 1 consists of whole-class strategies designed to help all children succeed. Examples of Tier 1 strategies include giving clear, simple directions to ensure that all students know what to do, teaching study strategies and metacognitive skills, using cooperative learning in small groups, and applying effective classroom management strategies (see Fuchs & Fuchs, 2006; Heward, 2013). The idea behind Tier 1 is to use effective teaching methods and to broaden the range of students who can succeed without any special interventions. Perhaps 80 percent of students never need anything more than such preventive strategies.

Tier 2: Immediate Intervention

Even with the best preventive efforts, some students still fall behind and need assistance. The idea in Response to Intervention is to provide such students with assistance targeted to their needs, rather than considering special education. Tier 2 interventions may involve adding time (such as after-school or summer school programs), assigning students to computer-assisted instruction, or other means of solving the immediate problem. For example, a student who is struggling in reading might receive individual or small-group tutoring from teachers, aides, or volunteers, so that the problem is resolved as quickly as possible and the student can continue in the regular class

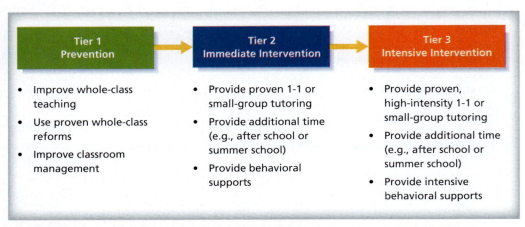

FIGURE 12.5 • Response to Intervention: Three-Tier Model of Support

(Gelzheiser et al., 2011; Slavin et al., 2011; Steubing et al., 2015; Wonder-McDowell, Reutzel, & Smith, 2011). Giving students structured, step-by-step procedures to help them succeed at computer tasks, such as writing (Lane et al., 2011), or math problem solving (Slavin & Lake, 2008) can be effective Tier 2 interventions. Perhaps 15 percent of students ever need Tier 2 assistance.

Tier 3: Intensive Intervention

Tier 3 consists of more intensive interventions for students who have not made sufficient progress in Tiers 1 and 2, perhaps 5 percent of struggling students. These individuals are at risk for special education or retention, both of which are very expensive and disruptive interventions, so Tier 3 strategies should be as intensive and long-lasting as necessary to keep students on track. Tier 3 strategies differ from Tier 2 strategies only in intensity and duration. They might include one-to-one tutoring by teachers or aides, extended small-group tutoring, or extra time (see Slavin et al., 2011). Outcomes of these services should be carefully monitored to see that students are making good progress, so that any problems are identified and resolved right away.

In concept, Tier 3 services could be provided indefinitely, as an alternative to assessing students for possible placement in special education. Only when every plausible service has been tried and has failed to resolve the student's problems might special education be considered.

WHAT IS INCLUSION?

The least restrictive environment clause of P.L. 94-142 revolutionized the practice of special education as well as general education. As has already been noted, it requires that students who are exceptional be assigned to the least restrictive environment that is appropriate to their needs (Friend & Bursuck, 2016; Karten, 2016; Salend, 2016). Refer to Figure 12.6 for definitions of least restrictive environment and inclusion. This provision has resulted in greatly increased contact between students with disabilities and students without disabilities. In general, students with all types of disabilities have moved one or two notches up the continuum of special-education services. Students who were once placed in special schools are now generally accommodated in separate classrooms in general education schools. Students who were once placed in separate classrooms in general education schools, particularly students with mild retardation and learning disabilities, are now most often assigned to general education classes for most of their instruction.

InTASC 2
Learning Differences

InTASC 3
Learning Environments

InTASC 7
Planning for Instruction

InTASC 8
Instructional Strategies

Mainstreaming:

"The temporal, instructional, and social integration of eligible exceptional children with normal peers based on an ongoing, individually determined educational planning and programming process" (Kaufman et al., 1975, pp. 40–41).

Least restrictive environment:

The provision in Public Law 94-142 (renamed the Individuals with Disabilities Education Act, or IDEA) that requires students with disabilities to be educated to the greatest extent appropriate alongside their peers without disabilities.

Inclusive education:

"Students attend their home school with their age and grade peers. It requires that the proportion of students labeled for special services is relatively uniform for all of the schools within a particular district. . . . Included students are not isolated into special classes or wings within the school" (National Association of State Boards of Education, 1992, p. 12).

Full inclusion:

Students who are disabled or at risk receive all their instruction in a general education setting; support services come to the student.

Partial inclusion:

Students receive most of their instruction in general education settings, but the student may be pulled out to another instructional setting when such a setting is deemed appropriate to the student's individual needs.

FIGURE 12.6 • Terminology: Inclusive Education

MyEdLab
Video Example 12.8
Textbook author Bob Slavin discusses an experience visiting a special education class. What are the possible positive benefits this teacher's children might realize as a result of her belief? What are the potential negative ramifications of her approach?

A movement for **full inclusion** calls for including all children in general education classes, with appropriate assistance (see Artiles, Kozleski, Dorn, & Christensen, 2006). Proponents of full inclusion argue that pull-out programs discourage effective partnerships between general and special educators in implementing IEPs and that students in pull-out programs are stigmatized when they are segregated from other students. These proponents suggest that special-education teachers or paraprofessionals team with classroom teachers and provide services in the general education classroom (Karten, 2016; McLeskey et al., 2013; Vaughn et al., 2014).

Many (perhaps most) classroom teachers have students with disabilities, who are usually receiving some type of special-education services part of the day. Most of these integrated students are categorized as having learning disabilities, speech impairments, mild retardation, or emotional disorders. High-quality inclusion models can improve the achievement and self-confidence of these students. Inclusion also enables students with disabilities to interact with peers and to learn conventional behavior. However, inclusion also creates challenges. When integrated students are performing below the level of the rest of the class, some teachers struggle to adapt instruction to these students' needs. It can also be challenging to cope with the often negative attitudes of students without disabilities toward their classmates who have disabilities (McLeskey et al., 2013; Smith et al., 2015), which might defeat attempts at social integration. Unfortunately, some classroom teachers are uncomfortable about having students with disabilities in their classes, and many feel poorly prepared to accommodate these students' needs (Vaughn et al., 2014). Inclusion provides an opportunity for more effective services but is by no means a guarantee that better services will actually be provided (see Kauffman, McGee, & Brigham, 2004; Riehl, 2000).

Research on Inclusion

Research on inclusion, which is often referred to as *mainstreaming,* has focused on students with learning disabilities, mild intellectual disabilities, and mild emotional disorders, whose deficits can be termed "mild academic disabilities" (Holloway, 2001; Klingner et al., 2016; McLeskey et al., 2013; Salend, 2016; Smith et al., 2016). Several studies have compared students with mild academic disabilities in special-education classes to such students in general education classes. When the general education teacher uses an instructional method that is designed to accommodate a wide range of student abilities, students with mild disabilities generally learn much better in the general education classroom than in special-education classes. One classic study on this topic was done by Calhoun and Elliott (1977), who compared students with mild intellectual disabilities and emotional disorders in general education classes to students with the same disabilities in special-education classes. The general education classes and the special-education classes used the same individualized materials, and the teachers (trained in special education) were rotated across classes to ensure that the only difference between the general and special programs was the presence of classmates without disabilities in the general education classes. The results of the Calhoun and Elliott (1977) study were that mainstreamed children learned more and had higher self-esteem than similar students taught in separate special education classes. A study by Roach and Elliott (2006) found that, controlling for many factors, access to the central curriculum was strongly correlated with achievement for students with cognitive disabilities. Other studies (e.g., Gottlieb & Weinberg, 1999; Reynolds & Wolfe, 1999; Saleno & Garrick-Duhaney, 1999) have yielded more mixed results.

A key element in effective inclusion is maintaining close coordination between classroom and special-education teachers (Friend & Bursuck, 2016; McLeskey et al., 2013; Smith et al., 2016). An experiment by Fuchs, Fuchs, and Fernstrom (1993) shows how coordination can improve student performance and accomplish full integration of all students with learning disabilities into general education classes over a period of time. In this study, children in pull-out math programs were given frequent curriculum-based measures assessing their progress relative to the school's math program. Special-education teachers examined the requirements for success in the general education class and prepared children specifically to succeed in that setting. As the children reached a criterion level of skills in math, they were transitioned into the general education class and then followed up to ensure that they were succeeding there. Over the course of a school year, all 21 students involved in the study were successfully transitioned to full-time general education class placement and learned significantly more than matched control students did.

InTASC 10

Leadership and Collaboration

There is very little research on the outcomes of full inclusion programs that integrate children who generally would not have been integrated into traditional mainstreaming models. There are descriptions of outstanding full inclusion programs (e.g., Villa & Thousand, 2003), but there have also been reports of full inclusion disasters (e.g., Baines, Baines, & Masterson, 1994). However, the goals of including students with even the most profound disabilities in general education classrooms are difficult to measure (see McLeskey et al., 2013). Full inclusion is a goal worth striving toward with care, caution, and flexibility (Capper, Kampschroer, & Keyes, 2000; Downing, 2001).

WHAT ARE EFFECTIVE STRATEGIES FOR STUDENTS WITH DISABILITIES IN GENERAL EDUCATION?

The great majority of students with disabilities attend general education classes for part or all of the day. You can help these students succeed by using the strategies described in the following sections: adapting their instruction to accommodate individual needs, teaching learning strategies, using preventive methods to keep students from running into trouble in the first place, and providing intensive early interventions when learning problems first appear.

Adapting Instruction

Teacher behaviors that are associated with effective teaching for students with disabilities in the general education classroom are essentially the same as those that improve achievement for all students (Armstrong, 2012; Bender, 2012; Benson, 2014; Klingner et al., 2016). Nevertheless, some adaptations in instructional strategies will help you better meet the needs of students with disabilities. When students have difficulty with instruction or materials in learning situations, the recommendation is frequently to adapt or modify the instruction or the materials (see Carolan & Guinn, 2007; Giangreco, 2007). The particular adaptation that is required depends on the student's needs and could be anything from format adaptation to the rewriting of text materials. The following Theory into Practice describes four common types of adaptations for accommodating integrated students (also see Heward, 2013; McLeskey et al., 2013; Salend, 2016; Smith et al., 2016; Vaughn et al., 2014).

> **InTASC 8**
>
> Instructional Strategies

THEORY INTO PRACTICE

Adapting Instruction for Students with Special Needs

FORMAT ADAPTATIONS FOR WRITTEN ASSIGNMENTS You can change the format in which a task is presented without changing the actual task. Such a change might be needed for a variety of reasons: (1) An assignment is too long; (2) the spacing on the page is too close to allow the student to focus on individual items; (3) the directions for the task are insufficient or confusing; or (4) the models or examples for the task are absent, misleading, or insufficient. The critical concept here is that even though task and response remain the same, you can make adaptations in the way the material is presented (Kleinert & Kearns, 2001).

Occasionally, the directions for a task or assignment must be simplified. For example, you might substitute in a set of directions the word *circle* for *draw a ring around*. You could also teach students the words that are commonly found in directions (Bender, 2012). By teaching students how to understand such words, you will help them become more independent learners. Models or examples presented with a task may also be changed to more closely resemble the task.

(continued)

CONTENT ADAPTATIONS In some instances, students might require an adaptation in the content being presented, such as when so much new information is presented that the student cannot process it quickly or when the student lacks a prerequisite skill or concept necessary to complete a task.

One way to adapt the amount of content being presented is to isolate each concept (Bryant, Smith, & Bryant, 2008) and require mastery of each concept as a separate unit before teaching the next concept. Although this type of adaptation involves smaller units of material, the same content will be covered in the end.

Adaptations that are required because students lack essential prerequisites might be as simple as explaining vocabulary or concepts before teaching a lesson. More complex adaptations are required when students lack prerequisite skills or concepts that cannot be explained easily or when students do not have a skill they need to learn the lesson. For example, if the math lesson involves multiplying fractions and a student has not yet learned how to multiply fractions, this skill will have to be taught before the student can address the word problems.

ADAPTATIONS IN MODES OF COMMUNICATION Some students require adaptations in either the way they receive information or the way they demonstrate their knowledge of specific information (Bender, 2015; Schultz, 2012). Many students cannot learn information when their only means of getting it is through reading but *can* learn it if the information is made available in other forms. Be creative in considering the possibilities. You might have students watch a demonstration, video, or computer game. Or you might have them listen to an audio recording, lecture/discussion, or debate. The Internet has thousands of lessons and demonstrations available on every conceivable subject, and you or your students can find many ways to learn a given concept.

A different type of adaptation might be required if a student cannot respond as the task directs. If a student has a writing problem, for example, you might ask the student to tell you about the concept in a private conversation and record the student's response with an audio recorder, or ask the student to present an oral report to the class. Or you might let the student represent the knowledge by drawing a picture or diagram or by making a video or multimedia report.

EXTENDING TIME Extending time for students to complete activities and take tests may be all that is necessary for many students, who may simply be slow workers or may be anxious in testing circumstances (Lovett, 2010; Overton, 2016).

UNIVERSAL DESIGN FOR LEARNING An important movement in facilitating inclusion is called Universal Design for Learning (National Center on Universal Design for Learning, 2011; Rose & Rappolt-Schlichtmann, 2008; Steinfeld & Maisel, 2011). The idea of UDL is to create materials and instructional strategies designed to meet the needs of the broadest possible range of learners. UDL may use multiple means of presentation, including print, audio, video, and computer-delivered content. It may use multiple means of letting learners show what they know, including speaking and writing, but also voice recognition or other electronic devices. It may use multiple means of letting learners engage with each other and multiple means of motivating students. As education technology advances, it is likely that adaptations to the needs of learners with exceptionalities of all kinds will become more and more commonplace and will make it easier for teachers to effectively teach a broad range of students in one class.

Teaching Learning Strategies and Metacognitive Awareness

Many students do poorly in school because they have failed to learn how to learn. Programs that are directed at helping students learn such strategies as note-taking, summarization, and memorization methods have been very successful with children and adolescents who have learning disabilities (Deshler, 2005; Jackson & Lambert, 2010; Mastropieri, 2016). Increasingly, research is identifying a variety of ways to teach students with learning disabilities to use metacognitive strategies to comprehend what they read (Gersten et al., 2001, 2009) and to build "self-determination" skills, such as the ability to work independently (Algozzine et al., 2009).

InTASC 8

Instructional Strategies

Prevention and Early Intervention

The debate over inclusion versus special education for children with learning problems revolves around concerns about children whose academic performance is far below that of their agemates. However, many of these children could have succeeded in school in the first place if effective prevention and early intervention programs had been available to them.

There is strong evidence that a substantial portion of students who are now in the special-education system could have been kept out of it if they had had effective early intervention. Studies of high-quality early childhood programs such as the Perry Preschool (Berrueta-Clement et al., 1984), the Abecedarian Project (Ramey & Ramey, 1992), and the Milwaukee Project (Garber, 1988) all showed substantial reductions in special-education placements for students with learning disabilities and mild intellectual disabilities (Siegel, 2003). Programs that provide one-to-one tutoring to first-graders who are struggling in reading have also shown reductions in the need for special-education services for students with learning disabilities (see the following section). Success for All, which combines effective early childhood programs, curriculum reform, and one-to-one tutoring, has reduced special-education placement by more than half (Borman & Hewes, 2003; Slavin & Madden, 2001) and has substantially increased the reading achievement of children who have already been identified as needing special-education services (Ross, Smith, Casey, & Slavin, 1995; Smith, Ross, & Casey, 1994). These and other findings suggest that the number of children who need special-education services could be greatly reduced if prevention and early intervention programs were more widely applied.

Connections 12.8

For more on the Success for All approach, see Chapter 9.

Tutoring and Small-Group Interventions for Struggling Readers

Because reading difficulties are nearly always involved in assignments to special education for learning disabilities, preventing reading failure and helping children who are already behind in reading is essential. Research on a variety of one-to-one and small-group tutoring models, reviewed in Chapter 9, has shown substantial positive effects on the reading performance of struggling readers (see Amendum, Vernon-Feagans, & Ginsberg, 2011; Gelzheiser et al., 2011; Harn et al., 2012; Slavin, Lake, Davis, & Madden, 2011). Tutoring should almost always be tried before a child is assessed for a possible reading disability.

Computers and Students with Disabilities

Computers provide opportunities to individualize instruction for students with disabilities. The use of computers to help children with exceptionalities has four major advantages (Carpenter, Johnston, & Beard, 2015; Marchez, Fischer, & Clark, 2015). First, computers can help to individualize instruction in terms of method of delivery, type and frequency of reinforcement, rate of presentation, and level of instruction (Anderson-Inman & Horney, 2007; McKenna & Walpole, 2007). Second, computers can give immediate corrective feedback and emphasize the active role of the child in learning (Boone & Higgins, 2007). Third, computers can hold the attention of children who are easily distractible. Fourth, computer instruction is motivating and patient. Computer software that encourages interaction among students, including simulations, games, and projects, can provide motivation and give students ways to succeed (Darling-Hammond, Zielezinski, & Goldman, 2014). For students with physical disabilities, computers can offer greater ease in learning and communicating information. For example, computers can enlarge text or read text aloud for children with visual disabilities (Poel, 2007).

FIGURE 12.7 • Adaptive Technologies for Students with Disabilities

For Students with Limited Motor Control

- Cursor and mouse enhancements allow students who do not have sufficient fine motor control to use a keyboard. Mouse enhancement utilities can be trained to recognize gestures made with mouse commands. Other features include high visibility, color, and animated cursors.
- Key definition programs allow students to define function keys on their keyboard to complete common tasks with fewer keystrokes.
- Virtual keyboard software displays a picture of a computer keyboard on the screen. Students can "type" on this virtual keyboard using a mouse, trackball, or similar pointing device, instead of pushing keys on a real keyboard.

For Students with Visual Impairments

- Magnification software programs ease reading on a computer monitor by displaying text in large fonts (from 2 to 16 times the normal view) and with foreground and background colors of the user's choice.
- Scanners allow students to scan documents that are then converted into editable word processing and spreadsheet documents. These can be magnified and edited on the screen or read aloud by a speech synthesizer.
- Speech synthesizers read aloud what is displayed on the screen—the contents of the active window, menu options, or text that has been typed. They can save documents in audio format as well. There are speaking calendars and talking calculators that read out every operation, as well as mathematical results.
- Braille readers and writers permit students to access the Internet, send and receive e-mail, and create documents by converting text into Braille.

For Students with Hearing Impairments

- Voice recognition software converts spoken words into written text. It can be programmed to execute particular commands—for example, taking a user to favorite websites with a single voice command.

For Students with Learning Disabilities

- Some word processing programs have a word prediction and abbreviation-expansion program that makes writing faster and easier for those with physical or learning disabilities who use a keyboard to write. Both features help reduce the number of keystrokes needed for typing and can make writing more productive.
- Concept-mapping software helps students understand the relationship between concepts by constructing, navigating, sharing, and criticizing knowledge models represented as concept maps.

Connections 12.9

For more on computer-based instruction, see Chapter 9.

Certification Pointer

When responding to a case study on your certification test, you should be familiar with adaptive technologies for assisting students with disabilities.

Most children in special-education programs seem to like learning from computers. Computers may make students who lack motivation more enthusiastic about their studies. They feel more in control because they are being taught in a context that is positive, reinforcing, and nonthreatening. However, findings on the actual learning benefits of computer-assisted instruction for students with disabilities have been inconsistent (MacArthur, Ferretti, Okolo, & Cavalier, 2001).

One valuable approach using computers is to provide children who are academically disabled with activities in which they can explore, construct, and communicate. Word processors serve this purpose (Bender, 2012), and other programs have been specifically designed for children with disabilities (Meyer & Rose, 2000; Wagmeister & Shifrin, 2000). Refer to Figure 12.7 for examples of computers and other technology for students with disabilities. Chapter 9 describes many additional applications of technology in education.

Buddy Systems and Peer Tutoring

InTASC 3

Learning Environments

One way to help meet the needs of students with disabilities in the general education classroom is to provide these students with assistance from classmates without disabilities, using either a buddy system for noninstructional needs or peer tutoring to help with learning problems (Mastropieri, 2016).

A student who volunteers to be a special-education student's buddy can help that student cope with the routine tasks of classroom life. For example, a buddy can guide a student with vision loss, help a student who is academically disabled to understand directions, or deliver cues or prompts as needed in some classes. In middle school and high school settings, a buddy can take notes for a student with hearing loss or learning disabilities or can make photocopies of his or her own notes. The buddy can also ensure that the student with a disability has located the correct text page during a lesson and has the materials necessary for a class. The buddy's primary responsibilities are to help the student with special needs adjust to the general education classroom, to answer questions, and to provide direction for activities. Use of this resource allows the general education classroom teacher to address more important questions related to instructional activities.

Another way of helping students within the general education classroom is peer tutoring (Topping et al., 2015; Watkins & Wentzel, 2008). Teachers who use peers to tutor in the classroom should ensure that they are carefully trained. This means that the peer tutor must be taught how to provide assistance by modeling and explaining, how to give specific positive and corrective feedback, and when to allow the student to work alone. Peer tutors and tutees may both benefit: the special-education student by acquiring academic concepts and the tutor by gaining a better acceptance and understanding of students with disabilities. Sometimes, older students with disabilities tutor younger ones; this generally benefits both students.

Special-Education Teams

When a student with disabilities is integrated into the general education classroom, the classroom teacher often works with one or more special educators to ensure success (Friend & Barron, 2014; Friend & Bursuck, 2016; Kampwirth & Powers, 2016; McLeskey et al., 2013; Salend, 2016; Smith et al., 2016). The classroom teacher might participate in conferences with special-education personnel, a special educator might at times be present in the classroom, or the classroom teacher might consult with a special educator at regular intervals. Whatever the arrangement, classroom teachers and special educators must recognize that each has expertise crucial to the student's success. The classroom teacher is the expert on classroom organization and operation on a day-to-day basis, the curriculum of the classroom, and the expectations placed on students for performance. The special educator is the expert on the characteristics of a particular group of students with disabilities, the learning and behavioral strengths and deficits of the mainstreamed student, and instructional techniques for a particular kind of disability. All this information is important to the successful integration of students, which is why communication between general education and special-education teachers is indispensable (McLeskey et al., 2013; Wilson & Blednick, 2011).

Connections 12.10

For more on peer tutoring, see Chapter 9.

Certification Pointer

For teacher certification tests you may be expected to suggest ways of structuring peer tutoring to help meet the needs of students with disabilities.

InTASC 10

Leadership and Collaboration

21ST CENTURY LEARNING

Including All Learners

Advances in assistive technologies are revolutionizing the educational possibilities for students with disabilities (Klingner et al., 2016). Computer programs able to enlarge text have long existed to help students with visual impairments, but the increasing use of interactive whiteboards and other whole-class lesson technologies now make it easy to provide enlarged text and pictures that enable students with visual impairments to follow regular class lessons. Similarly, the opportunity to make far greater use of visual and interactive content to supplement lessons is likely to provide alternative pathways to success in school for students with learning disabilities and other special needs. In the 21st century, standards for educational attainment will rise, but there will be a greater variety of ways in which students can meet these standards. There is a strong focus on universal designs for learning in the Common Core Standards now being adopted in most states, to make a demanding curriculum accessible to the broadest possible range of learners (Karten, 2016).

QUESTION

- Make a chart showing the types of disabilities your students may have. Which technologies seem particularly appropriate for each?

Communication should begin before students are placed in the general education classroom and should continue throughout the placement. Both teachers must have up-to-date information about the student's performance in each setting to plan and coordinate an effective program. Only then can instruction targeted at improving the student's performance in the general education classroom be designed and presented. In addition, generalization of skills and behaviors from one setting to the other will be enhanced.

Social Integration of Students with Disabilities

Connections 12.11

For more on teaching adaptive skills to help students in their socioemotional development, see Chapter 3.

Placement of students in the general education classroom is only one part of their integration into that environment. These students must be integrated socially as well as instructionally (see Wilkins, 2000). As the classroom teacher, you play a critical role in this process. Much has been written about the effects of teacher expectations on student achievement and behavior. In the case of students with disabilities, your attitude toward these students is important not only for teacher–student interactions but also as a model for the students without disabilities in the classroom. The research on attitudes toward individuals with disabilities provides several strategies that might be useful to the general education classroom teacher who wants to promote successful social integration by influencing the attitudes of students without disabilities. One strategy is to use cooperative learning methods (Nevin, 1998; Stevens & Slavin, 1995b). Social skills training has also been found to improve the social acceptance of children with disabilities (Troop & Asher, 1999).

MyEdLab **Self-Check 12.3**

SUMMARY

Who Are Learners with Exceptionalities?

Learners with exceptionalities are students who have special-education needs in relation to societal or school norms. An inability to perform appropriate academic tasks for any reason inherent in the learner makes that learner exceptional. A handicap is a condition or barrier imposed by the environment or the self; a disability is a functional limitation that interferes with a person's mental, physical, or sensory abilities. The often arbitrary classification systems for learners with exceptionalities are widely debated, and the use of labels may lead to inappropriate treatment or damage students' self-concepts.

About 13 percent of students ages 3 to 21 in the United States receive special-education services. Examples of learners with exceptionalities are students with intellectual disabilities, specific learning disabilities, speech or language disorders, emotional and behavioral disorders, autism spectrum disorders, and vision or hearing loss. Students who are gifted and talented are also regarded as exceptional and may be eligible for special accelerated or enrichment programs. Clearly identifying learners with exceptionalities and accommodating instruction to meet their needs are continuing challenges.

What Is Special Education?

Special-education programs serve children with disabilities instead of, or in addition to, the general education classroom program.

Public Law 94-142 (1975), which was amended by P.L. 99-457 (1986) to include preschool children and infants with serious disabilities, is now called the Individuals with Disabilities Education Act (IDEA). It articulates the principle that every child with a disability is entitled to appropriate special education at public expense. The current version of the law, IDEA 2004, calls for greater involvement of parents and classroom teachers in the education of children with disabilities. The least restrictive environment clause means that students with special needs must be mainstreamed into general education classes as much as possible. IDEA mandates that an Individualized Education Program (IEP) be prepared for every student with a disability. The principle behind the use of IEPs is to give everyone concerned with the education of a child with a disability an opportunity to help formulate the child's instruction program. An array of services is available for students who are exceptional, including support for the general education teacher, special education for part of the day in a resource room, special education for more than 3 hours per day in a special-education classroom, special day schools, special residential schools, and homes/hospitals.

THE INTENTIONAL TEACHER

Using What You Know about Learners with Exceptionalities to Improve Teaching and Learning

Intentional teachers creatively seek ways to reach each of their students. They create inclusive environments and commit themselves to fostering learning for all. Intentional teachers serve as members of professional teams in order to collaborate to meet the needs of students with special needs.

- They plan how to prevent learning, behavioral, and emotional problems in their classes, applying effective teaching methods, classroom management methods, and means of meeting individual needs.
- They strategically coordinate with special-education teachers, counselors, and other professionals working with their children to ensure coordination in addressing students' needs.
- They keep close track of students' progress so they can identify leaning problems as early as possible and intervene right away.
- They plan their lessons and class activities with the needs of all students in mind.
- They use resources such as paraprofessionals, resource teachers, and computers to solve any learning problems identified in children who need assistance.
- They use Response to Intervention strategies to try to solve learning problems without involving special education.
- They cooperate with others to create and then implement Individualized Education Programs (IEPs) that will help students with disabilities succeed in general education, if possible.
- They use strategies such as small-group and individualized tutoring, computer- assisted instruction, and other applications of technology to bring struggling students to the achievement level of their general education class.
- They teach all students "learning to learn" skills, such as study strategies, to help them become independent learners.
- They organize cooperative learning and peer tutoring to help diverse students help each other learn.
- They help gifted and talented students achieve their full potential using acceleration and enrichment strategies.
- They find ways to integrate socially isolated students into their classes.

MyEdLab

Application Exercise 12.1

In the Pearson etext, watch a classroom video. Then use the guidelines in "The Intentional Teacher" to answer a set of questions that will help you reflect on and understand the teaching and learning presented in the video.

What Is Response to Intervention?

Response to Intervention (RTI) means using modifications to instruction or intensive services in the general education classroom before referring a struggling student for special education. RTI approaches generally provide struggling students with three tiers of intervention: prevention (whole class), immediate assistance (small group or individual), and intensive, extended assistance.

What Is Inclusion?

Inclusion means placing students with special needs in general education classrooms for at least part of the time. Full inclusion of all children in general education classes with appropriate assistance is a widely held goal. Research has shown that inclusion is effective in raising many students' performance levels, especially when cooperative learning, buddy systems, peer tutoring, computer instruction, modifications in lesson presentation, and training in social skills are regular parts of classroom learning. Research has also shown that some disabilities, especially reading disabilities, can be prevented through programs of prevention and early intervention.

What Are Effective Strategies for Students with Disabilities in General Education?

Teachers in inclusive classrooms can help their students with disabilities succeed by adapting instruction and modifying materials, teaching students specific learning strategies, and providing tutoring and computer practice.

KEY TERMS

Review the following key terms from the chapter.

acceleration programs 316
Asperger syndrome 313
attention deficit hyperactivity disorder
   (ADHD) 307
autism 312
autism spectrum disorder 313
collaboration 319
conduct disorders 312
disability 303
emotional and behavioral disorders 311
enrichment programs 316
exceptionality 303
full inclusion 328
giftedness 316
handicap 303
hearing disabilities 314
inclusion 317

Individualized Education Program
   (IEP) 318
Individuals with Disabilities Education
   Act (IDEA) 317
intellectual disability 304
intelligence quotient (IQ) 305
language disorders 311
learners with exceptionalities 303
learning disabilities (LD) 306
least restrictive environment 317
mainstreaming 317
Public Law 94-142 317
Response to Intervention 326
sensory impairments 314
special education 317
speech disorders 310
vision loss 314

SELF-ASSESSMENT: PRACTICING FOR LICENSURE

Directions: The chapter-opening vignette addresses indicators that are often assessed in state licensure exams. Reread the chapter-opening vignette, and then respond to the following questions.

1. Elaine Wagner, assistant principal at Dover Elementary School, meets with Helen Ross about her son, Tommy, who is having a difficult time in another school. She explains to Ms. Ross that Tommy would need to meet certain criteria to receive special-education services. Which of the following examples is an indication that a student needs special-education services?
   a. The student must have an IQ at or below 120.
   b. The student must have at least one of a few designated categories of disabilities.
   c. The student must be below the 50th percentile in his or her academic work.
   d. All parents who request special-education services for their children must receive them.

2. Suppose you are going to be Tommy's new teacher. If his mother were to ask you about the difference between a handicap and a disability, what would you say?

   a. A disability is a condition in which a person has difficulty with cognitive functioning, whereas a handicap is a condition in which a person has difficulty with physical functioning.

   b. A disability is a condition in which a person has barriers placed on him or her by society, whereas a handicap is the disabling condition.

   c. A disability is a functional limitation a person has that interferes with her or his physical or cognitive abilities, whereas a handicap is a condition imposed on a person with disabilities by society, the physical environment, or the person's attitude.

   d. The terms *disability* and *handicap* are synonymous.

3. Which of the following public laws gave parents like Helen Ross an increased role in making decisions about the education of their children?

   a. Public Law 94–142, the Education for the Handicapped Act

   b. Public Law 99–457, the amendment to P.L. 94–142

   c. Public Law 101–476, the Individuals with Disabilities Education Act

   d. Public Law 105–17, the Individuals with Disabilities Education Act Amendments

4. Assistant Principal Elaine Wagner tells Helen Ross that even if Tommy needs special-education services, he will be placed in the "least restrictive environment." What does this mean for Tommy?

   a. Tommy will be placed in the general education classes as much as possible and removed for special-education services only if necessary.

   b. Tommy will be placed in a special-education room that does not restrict his movements or academic choices.

   c. Tommy will be eligible for any and all special-education services.

   d. Tommy will receive public funds to pay for his private special-education services.

5. Helen Ross, Tommy's mother, asks Elaine Wagner, "Your school's philosophy on inclusion sounds just right for Tommy. Why don't all schools adopt it? What disadvantages are there?" Ms. Wagner, who is current on her knowledge about inclusion, would most likely make which of the following responses?

   a. Data show that students enrolled in inclusion programs do not do as well academically as those who are enrolled in special-education classrooms.

   b. General education classroom teachers sometimes lack appropriate training and materials and are already overburdened with large class sizes and inadequate support services.

   c. Special-education experts are not convinced that there is such a thing as a learning disability. They believe that all students should be in a general education classroom.

   d. Many parents of general education students do not feel it is fair to adapt instruction to meet the needs of students with disabilities.

6. How would you go about developing an Individualized Education Program (IEP) for Tommy if it is determined that he has a reading disability?

7. Describe the advantages and disadvantages of enrolling students with special needs in the general education classroom.

MyEdLab **Licensure Exam 12.1** Answer questions and receive instant feedback in your Pearson eText in MyEdLab.

Guerilla/Alamy Stock Photo

CHAPTER THIRTEEN

Assessing Student Learning

LEARNING OUTCOMES

At the end of this chapter, you should be able to:

13.1 Identify well-constructed instructional objectives and explain how they are used effectively

13.2 Differentiate among types of evaluations based on their purposes

13.3 Describe how to write fair, effective tests and a variety of types of test items

13.4 Explain how to evaluate student work using authentic, portfolio, and performance assessment

13.5 Describe how assessment of student learning influences intentional teaching

CHAPTER OUTLINE (CONTINUED)

Mr. Sullivan is having a great time teaching about the Civil War, and his eleventh-grade U.S. history class is having fun, too. Mr. Sullivan is relating all kinds of anecdotes about the war. He describes a battle fought in the nude (a group of Confederates were caught fording a river), the time Stonewall Jackson lost a battle because he took a nap in the middle of it, and several stories about women who disguised their gender to fight as soldiers. He tells the story of a Confederate raid (from Canada) on a Vermont bank. He passes around real minié balls and grapeshot, and wondered if they had killed anyone. In fact, Mr. Sullivan has gone on for weeks about the battles, the songs, and the personalities and foibles of the generals. Finally, after an interesting math activity in which students have to figure out how much Confederate money they would need to buy a loaf of bread, Mr. Sullivan has students put away all their materials to take a test.

The students are shocked. The only question is: What were the main causes, events, and consequences of the Civil War?

Mr. Sullivan's lessons are fun. They are engaging. They use varied presentation modes. They integrate skills from other disciplines. They are clearly accomplishing one important objective of social studies: building enjoyment of the topic. However, as engaging as Mr. Sullivan's lessons are, there is little correspondence between what he is teaching and what he is testing. He and his students are on a happy trip, but where are they going?

USING YOUR EXPERIENCE

COOPERATIVE LEARNING In a group of four or five students, draw a value line from 1 to 100, with 1 representing poor teaching and 100 representing great teaching. Take turns marking where you would place Mr. Sullivan on this scale. Let each person explain his or her rating. Now review the ratings and change them as appropriate. Discuss better methods that Mr. Sullivan might use to teach and then assess his students.

In teaching lessons, units, and courses, how do you know where you are going and whether or not you and your students are getting there? This chapter discusses objectives and assessments, as well as the goals of teaching and ways of determining whether goals are being achieved. Objectives are the learning plan for what students should know and be able to do at the end of a course of study; lessons must be designed to accomplish these objectives. Evaluations of students must indicate the extent to which each student has actually mastered those objectives by the end of the course (Banks, 2012; McMillan, 2011; Spinelli, 2011). Every teacher should have a clear idea of where the class is going, how it will get there, and how to know whether it has arrived.

WHAT ARE INSTRUCTIONAL OBJECTIVES AND HOW ARE THEY USED?

InTASC 7

Planning for Instruction

What do you want your students to know or be able to do at the end of today's lesson? What should they know at the end of a series of lessons on a particular subject? What should they know at the end of the course? Knowing the answers to these questions is one of the most important prerequisites for intentional, high-quality instruction (Burke, 2009; Moss & Brookhart, 2012). A teacher is like a wilderness guide with a troop of tenderfeet. If you do not have a map or a plan for getting the group where it needs to go, the whole group will surely be lost. Mr. Sullivan's students are having a lot of fun, but because their teacher has no plan for how his lessons will give them essential concepts related to the Civil War, they are unlikely to learn those concepts.

Setting out objectives at the beginning of a course is an essential step in providing a framework into which individual lessons will fit (Moss, Brookhart, & Long, 2011; Reeves, 2011). Without such a framework it is easy to wander off the track, to spend too much time on topics that are not central to the course. One high school biology teacher spent most of the year teaching biochemistry; her students knew all about the chemical makeup of DNA, red blood cells, chlorophyll, and starch, but little about zoology, botany, anatomy, or other topics that are usually central to high school biology. Then in late May the teacher panicked because she realized that the class had to do a series of laboratory exercises before the end of the year. On successive days they dissected a frog, a sheep eye, a sheep brain, and a pig fetus! Needless to say, the students learned little from those hurried labs and little about biology in general. This teacher did not have a master plan and was deciding week by week (or perhaps day by day) what to teach, thereby losing sight of the big picture—the scope of knowledge that is generally agreed to be important for a high school student to learn in biology class. Few teachers follow a plan rigidly once they make it, but the process of making it is still very helpful.

An **instructional objective**, sometimes called a *behavioral objective,* is a statement of skills or concepts that students are expected to know at the end of some period of instruction. Typically, an instructional objective is stated in such a way as to make it clear how the objective will be measured (see Mager, 1997). Some examples of instructional objectives are as follows:

- Given 100 division facts (such as 27 divided by 3), students will give correct answers to all 100 in 3 minutes.
- When asked, students will name at least five functions that characterize all living organisms (respiration, reproduction, etc.).
- In an essay, students will be able to compare and contrast the artistic styles of van Gogh and Gauguin.
- Given the statement "Resolved: The United States should not have entered World War I," students will be able to argue persuasively either for or against the proposition.

Connections 13.1

For more on lesson planning and lesson objectives as components of effective instruction, see Chapter 7.

Note that despite varying enormously in the type of learning involved and the performance levels they address, these objectives have several things in common. Mager (1997), whose work launched the behavioral objectives movement, described objectives as having three parts: performance, conditions, and criteria. Explanations and examples are given in Table 13.1.

TABLE 13.1 • Parts of a Behavioral Objectives Statement

	PERFORMANCE	CONDITIONS	CRITERION
Definition	An objective always says what a learner is expected to do.	An objective always describes the conditions under which the performance is to occur.	Whenever possible, an objective describes the criterion for acceptable performance.
Question Answered	What should the learner be able to do?	Under what conditions do you want the learner to be able to do it?	How well must it be done?
Example	Correctly use adjectives and adverbs.	Given 10 sentences with missing modifiers, . . .	. . . the student will correctly choose an adjective or adverb in at least 9 of the 10 sentences.

Planning Lesson Objectives

In practice, the skeleton of a behavioral objective is condition–performance–criterion. First, state the conditions under which learning will be assessed, as in the following:

- Given a 10-item test, students will be able to . . .
- In an essay, the student will be able to . . .
- Using a compass and protractor, the student will be able to . . .

The second part of an objective is usually an action verb that indicates what students will be able to do. For example (from Gronlund & Brookhart, 2009):

- Write
- Distinguish between
- Identify
- Match
- Compare and contrast

Finally, a behavioral objective generally states a criterion for success, such as the following:

- . . . all 100 multiplication facts in 3 minutes.
- . . . at least five of the nations that sent explorers to the New World.
- . . . at least three similarities and three differences between the U.S. government under the Constitution and under the Articles of Confederation.

Sometimes a criterion for success cannot be specified as the number correct. Even so, success should be specified as clearly as possible:

- The student will write a two-page essay describing the social situation of women as portrayed in *A Doll's House*.
- The student will think of at least six possible uses for an eggbeater other than beating eggs.

WRITING SPECIFIC OBJECTIVES   Instructional objectives must be adapted to the subject matter being taught. When students must learn well-defined skills or information with a single right answer, specific instructional objectives can be written as follows:

- Given 10 problems involving addition of two fractions with like denominators, students will solve at least 9 correctly.
- Given 10 sentences lacking verbs, students will correctly choose verbs that agree in number in at least 8 sentences. Examples: My cat and I [has, have] birthdays in May. Each of us [want, wants] to go to college.
- Given a 4-meter rope attached to the ceiling, students will be able to climb to the top in less than 20 seconds.

Some material, of course, does not lend itself to such specific instructional objectives, and it would be a mistake in such cases to adhere to objectives that have numerical criteria. For example, the following objective could be written:

- The student will list at least five similarities and five differences between the situation of immigrants to the United States in the early 1900s and that of immigrants today.

Note that this objective asks for lists, which might not demonstrate any real understanding of the topic. A less specific but more meaningful objective might be the following:

- In an essay, the student will compare and contrast the situation of immigrants to the United States in the early 1900s and that of immigrants today.

This general instructional objective would allow students more flexibility in expressing their understanding of the topic and promote comprehension rather than memorization of lists of similarities and differences.

WRITING CLEAR OBJECTIVES Instructional objectives should be specific enough to be meaningful. For example, consider the following objective concerning immigrants:

- Students will develop a full appreciation for the diversity of peoples who have contributed to the development of U.S. society.

This sounds nice, but what does "full appreciation" mean? Such an objective neither helps you prepare lessons nor helps students understand what is to be taught and how they will be assessed.

PERFORMING A TASK ANALYSIS In planning lessons, it is important to consider the skills required in the tasks to be taught or assigned. For example, you might ask students to use the Internet to write a brief report on a topic of interest. The task seems straightforward enough, but consider the separate skills involved:

- Knowing how to find information on the Internet
- Knowing how to judge sources on the Internet according to their objectivity and accuracy
- Getting the main idea from expository material
- Planning or outlining a brief report
- Writing expository paragraphs
- Understanding language mechanics skills (such as capitalization, punctuation, and usage)

MyEdLab

Video Example 13.1

Two teachers discuss plans for a unit on civilizations and their impact on history. Can you identify the prerequisites that they expect the students to know and the component skills they expect students to use and develop during the unit?

These skills could themselves be broken down into subskills. You must be aware of the subskills involved in any learning task to be certain that students know what they need to know to succeed. Before assigning the Internet report task, you would need to be sure that students knew how to use Internet resources and that they could comprehend and write expository material. You might teach or review these skills before sending students to their computers.

In teaching any new skill, it is important to consider all the subskills that go into it. Think of all the separate steps involved in adding fractions, in writing chemical formulas, or in identifying topic sentences and supporting details. For that matter, consider the skills that go into writing a business letter on MS Word, as illustrated in Figure 13.1.

This process of breaking tasks or objectives down into their simpler components is called **task analysis**. In planning a lesson, a three-step process for task analysis may be used.

1. *Identify prerequisite skills.* What should students already know before you teach the lesson? For example, for a lesson on adding fractions with unlike denominators, students need to know how to find least common multiples, how to multiply to find equivalent fractions, how to add fractions with like denominators, and how to simplify fractions.

2. *Identify component skills.* In the actual lesson, what subskills must students be taught before they can learn to achieve the larger objective? To return to the adding-fractions example, each of the steps must be planned for, taught, and assessed during the lesson.

3. *Plan how component skills will be assembled into the final skill.* The final step in task analysis is to reassemble the subskills into the complete process being taught. For example, students might be able to do each of the skills needed to add fractions with unlike denominators, but this does not necessarily mean they can put them all together to do the whole task. The subskills must be integrated into a complete process that students can understand and practice.

BACKWARD PLANNING Just as lesson objectives are more than the sum of specific task objectives, the objectives of a course of study are more than the sum of specific lesson objectives. For this reason it makes sense to start by writing broad objectives for the course as a whole, then objectives for large units, and only then specific behavioral objectives (see Gronlund & Brookhart, 2009). This is known as **backward planning**. For example, Mr. Sullivan would have done well to identify the objective of his Civil War unit as follows:

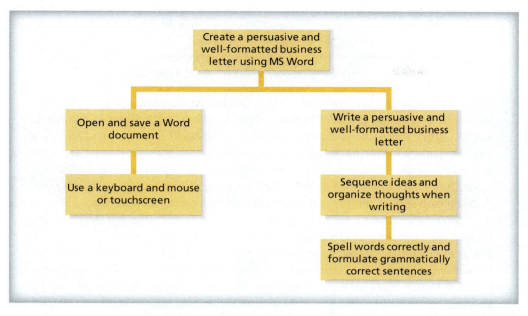

FIGURE 13.1 •
Example of a Skill Hierarchy

Before students can practice the main skill (writing a business letter on MS Word), they must be able to use a computer and compose a letter. These skills must all be learned before the main skill can be mastered. They are independent of one another and can be learned in any order. Before composing a letter, students must be able to spell words and organize written ideas. Finally, to use a computer, the learner first has to learn how to use a mouse/touchscreen and how to open and save documents.

"Students will understand the major causes, events, and consequences of the Civil War." Next he might have written more detailed objectives related to causes, events, and consequences and then planned units and individual lessons around these objectives. A detailed example of the backward planning process is illustrated in Table 13.2 and described in the next Theory into Practice.

TABLE 13.2 • Example of Objectives for a Course in Language Arts

Teachers can allocate instructional time for a course by (a) deciding what topics to cover during the year or semester, (b) deciding how many weeks to spend on each topic, (c) choosing units within each topic, (d) deciding how many days to spend on each, and (e) deciding what each day's lesson should be.

COURSE OBJECTIVES (WEEKS ALLOCATED)	UNIT OBJECTIVES (DAYS ALLOCATED)	LESSONS
Writing fictional stories: 3	Parts of a story: 2	Lesson 1: Parts of a Story—Overview
Writing nonfiction: 3	Details and elaboration: 3	Introduction
Writing persuasive essays: 2	Writing, revision, and the creative process: 3	Setting
. . . etc.	. . . etc.	Protagonist
		Antagonist
		Plot
		Conclusion
		Lesson 2: Parts of a Story–Identification from Examples
		Introduction
		Setting
		Protagonist
		Antagonist
		Plot
		Conclusion

THEORY INTO PRACTICE

Planning Courses, Units, and Lessons

In planning a course, it is important to set long-term, middle-term, and short-term objectives before starting to teach (Diamond, 2008; Dougherty, 2012; Fisher & Frey, 2014c; Reeves, 2015). Before the students arrive for the first day of class, you need to have a general plan of what will be covered all year, a more specific plan for what will be in the first unit (a connected set of lessons), and a very specific plan for the content of the first lessons (as shown in Table 13.2). All states and many districts have established standards for each subject, and these standards should help guide your planning.

Table 13.2 implies a backward planning process. First, the course objectives are established. Then unit objectives are designated. Finally, specific lessons are planned. The course objectives list all the topics to be covered during the year. You might divide the number of weeks in the school year by the number of major topics to determine what each will require. More or less time could be reserved for any particular topic, as long as adequate time is allowed for the others. A whole semester could be spent on any one of the topics in Table 13.2, but this would be inappropriate in a survey course on life science. You must make hard choices before the first day of class about how much time to spend on each topic to avoid spending too much time on early topics and not having enough time left to do a good job with later ones. Some history teachers always seem to find themselves still on World War I in mid-May and have to compress most of the 20th century into a couple of weeks!

Table 13.2 shows approximate allocations of weeks to each of the topics to be covered. These are only rough estimates to be modified as time goes on.

Unit Objectives and Unit Tests After course objectives have been laid out, the next task is to establish objectives for the first unit and to estimate the number of class periods to spend on each objective (Diamond, 2008). It is a good idea to write a unit test as part of the planning process. Writing a test in advance helps you focus on the important issues to be covered. For example, in a 4-week unit on the Civil War, Mr. Sullivan might have decided that the most important concepts students should learn are the causes of the war, a few major points about the military campaigns, the importance of the Emancipation Proclamation, Lincoln's assassination, and the history of the Reconstruction period. These topics would be central to the unit test on the Civil War. Writing this test could have helped him put into proper perspective the importance of the various issues that should be covered. It's not that he shouldn't have shared anecdotes and shown students Civil War weapons, but preparing the unit test would have helped him keep the big picture in mind.

The test that you prepare as part of your course planning might not be exactly the test that you give at the end of the unit. You may decide to change, add, or delete items to reflect the content you actually covered. But this does not diminish the importance of having decided in advance exactly what objectives you wanted to achieve and how you were going to assess them.

Many texts provide unit tests and objectives, making your task easier. Sample objectives and test items are available from state and local departments of education, and they can be found on the Internet. However, even if you have ready-made objectives and tests, it is still important to review their content and change them as necessary to match what you expect to teach.

Certification Pointer

For your teacher certification test, you may be asked to take a goal from a state curriculum standard and write a behavioral objective to meet that standard.

If you prepare unit tests from scratch, use the guide to test construction presented later in this chapter. Be sure that the test items cover the various objectives in proportion to their importance to the course as a whole (that is, the more important objectives are covered by more items), and include items that assess higher-level thinking as well as factual knowledge.

Lesson Plans and Lesson Assessments The final step in backward planning is to plan daily lessons. Table 13.2 shows how a given unit objective might be broken down into daily lessons. The next step is to plan the content of each lesson. A lesson plan consists of an objective, a plan for presenting information, a plan for giving students practice (if appropriate), a plan for assessing student understanding, and, if necessary, a plan for reteaching students (or whole classes) if their understanding is inadequate.

Aligning Objectives and Assessment

Because instructional objectives are stated in terms of how they will be measured, it is clear that objectives are closely aligned with **assessment**, which consists of measuring the degree to which students have learned the objectives set out for them. Most assessments in schools are tests or quizzes or informal verbal assessments such as questions in class. However, students can also show their learning by writing an essay, creating a multimedia presentation, painting a picture, doing a car tune-up, or baking a pineapple upside-down cake.

One critical principle of assessment is that assessments and objectives must be clearly linked (Martone & Sireci, 2009; McAfee, Leong, & Bodrova, 2016). Students learn some proportion of what they are taught; the greater the overlap between what was taught and what is tested, the better students will score on the test and the more accurately any need for additional instruction can be determined (Lloyd et al., 2013; Popham, 2014a; Russell & Airasian, 2012; Squires, 2009). Teaching should be closely linked to instructional objectives, and both should clearly relate to assessment (Buhle & Blachowicz, 2008/2009). If any objective is worth teaching, it is worth testing, and vice versa.

As noted earlier, one way to specify objectives for a course is to actually prepare test questions before the course begins (see Waugh & Gronlund, 2013). This allows you to write general **teaching objectives** (clear statements of what students are expected to learn through instruction) and then to clarify them with very specific **learning objectives** (specific behaviors students are expected to exhibit at the end of a series of lessons), as in the following examples.

InTASC 6

Assessment

Teaching Objective	Specific Learning Objective (Test Questions)
a. Ability to subtract three-digit numbers regrouping once or twice	a1. 237 a2. 412 a3. 596 -184 -298 -448
b. Understanding use of language to set mood in Edgar Allan Poe's "The Raven"	b1. How does Poe reinforce the mood of "The Raven" after setting it in the first stanza?
c. Ability to identify the chemical formulas for common substances	Write the chemical formulas for the following: c1. Water _____ c2. Carbon dioxide _____ c3. Coal _____ c4. Table salt _____

Using Taxonomies of Instructional Objectives

Connections 13.2
For information on thinking skills and critical thinking, see Chapter 8.

INTASC 5

Application of Content

MyEdLab
Video Example 13.2
In a lesson intended to encourage students to see relationships between geography and economy, Ms. Holmquest encourages her class to analyze information. It's clear from this lesson, as well as from the chart on the board, that previous lessons focused on knowledge and comprehension.

In writing objectives and assessments, it is important to consider different skills and different levels of understanding. For example, in a science lesson on insects for second-graders, you might want to impart both information (the names of various insects) and a set of attitudes (such as an appreciation of the importance of insects to the ecosystem and the idea that science is fun). In other subjects you might try to convey facts and concepts that differ by type. For example, in teaching a lesson on topic sentences in reading, you might have students first recall the definition of topic sentences, then identify topic sentences in paragraphs, and finally write their own topic sentences for original paragraphs. Each of these activities demonstrates a different kind of understanding of the concept "topic sentence," and this concept has not been adequately taught if students can do only one of these activities. These various lesson goals can be classified by type and degree of complexity. A taxonomy, or system of classification, helps you to categorize instructional activities.

BLOOM'S TAXONOMY In 1956, Benjamin Bloom and some fellow researchers (Bloom, Englehart, Furst, Hill, & Krathwohl, 1956) published a **taxonomy of educational objectives** that has been influential in the research and practice of education ever since. Bloom and his colleagues categorized objectives from simple to complex or from factual to conceptual. The following key elements (from simple to complex) constitute what is commonly called Bloom's taxonomy for the cognitive domain (Badgett & Christmann, 2009; Marzano & Kendall, 2007).

1. *Knowledge (recalling information).* The lowest level of objectives in Bloom's hierarchy, knowledge comprises objectives such as memorizing math facts or formulas, scientific principles, or verb conjugations.

2. *Comprehension (translating, interpreting, or extrapolating information).* Comprehension objectives require that students show an understanding of information as well as the ability to use it. Examples include interpreting the meaning of a diagram, graph, or parable; inferring the principle underlying a science experiment; or predicting what might happen next in a story.

3. *Application (using principles or abstractions to solve novel or real-life problems).* Application objectives require students to use knowledge or principles to solve practical problems. Examples include using geometric principles to figure out how many gallons of water to put into a swimming pool of given dimensions, or using knowledge of the relationship between temperature and pressure to explain why a balloon is larger on a hot day than on a cold day.

4. *Analysis (breaking down complex information or ideas into simpler parts to understand how the parts relate or are organized).* Analysis objectives require students to see the underlying structure of complex information or ideas. Examples of analysis objectives include contrasting schooling in the United States with education in Japan, or identifying the main idea of a short story.

5. *Synthesis (creation of something that did not exist before).* Synthesis objectives involve using skills to create completely new products. Examples include writing a composition, deriving a mathematical rule, designing a science experiment to solve a problem, or making up a new sentence in a foreign language.

6. *Evaluation (judging something against a given standard).* Evaluation objectives require making value judgments against some criterion or standard. For example, students might be asked to compare the strengths and weaknesses of two tablet computers in terms of flexibility, power, and available software.

Because Bloom's taxonomy is organized from simple to complex, some people interpret it as a ranking of objectives from trivial (knowledge) to important (synthesis, evaluation). However, this is not the intent of the taxonomy. Different levels of objectives are appropriate for different purposes and for students at different stages of development (Marzano & Kendall, 2007). For example, you want your physician to have a deep understanding of how the human body works, but you also hope she knows the names of all the body parts, medicines, and devices in her area of specialization, all knowledge-level objectives!

TABLE 13.3 • Examples of Objectives in a Behavior Content Matrix

A behavior content matrix can remind teachers to develop instructional objectives that address skills at various cognitive levels.

TYPE OF OBJECTIVE	EXAMPLE 1: THE AREA OF A CIRCLE	EXAMPLE 2: MAIN IDEA OF A STORY	EXAMPLE 3: THE COLONIZATION OF AFRICA
Knowledge	Give the formula for area of a circle.	Define *main idea*.	Make a time line showing how Europeans divided Africa into colonies.
Comprehension		Give examples of ways to find the main idea of a story.	Interpret a map of Africa showing its colonization by European nations.
Application	Apply the formula for area of a circle to real-life problems.		
Analysis		Identify the main idea of a story.	Contrast the goals and methods used in colonizing Africa by the different European nations.
Synthesis	Use knowledge about the areas of circles and volumes of cubes to derive a formula for the volume of a cylinder.	Write a new story based on the main idea of the story read.	Write an essay on the European colonization of Africa from the perspective of a Bantu chief.
Evaluation		Evaluate the story.	

The primary importance of Bloom's taxonomy is in its reminder that we want students to have many levels of skills. All too often, teachers focus on measurable knowledge and comprehension objectives and forget that students cannot be considered proficient in many skills until they can apply or synthesize those skills (see Iran-Nejad & Stewart, 2007). On the other side of the coin, some teachers fail to make certain that students are well rooted in the basics before heading off into higher-order objectives.

USING A BEHAVIOR CONTENT MATRIX One way to be sure that your objectives cover many levels is to write a **behavior content matrix**. This is simply a chart that shows how a particular concept or skill will be taught and assessed at different cognitive levels. Examples of objectives in a behavior content matrix appear in Table 13.3. Note that for each topic, objectives are listed for some but not all levels of Bloom's taxonomy. Some topics do not lend themselves to some levels of the taxonomy, and there is no reason why every level should be covered for every topic. However, using a behavior content matrix in setting objectives forces you to consider objectives above the knowledge and comprehension levels.

OBJECTIVES BEYOND THE BASICS Learning facts and skills is not the only important goal of instruction. Sometimes the feelings that students have about a subject or about their own skills are at least as important as how much information they learn. Instructional goals related to attitudes and values are called **affective objectives**. Many people would argue that a principal purpose of a U.S. history or civics course is to promote values of patriotism and civic responsibility, and that one purpose of any mathematics course is to give students confidence in their ability to use mathematics. In planning instruction, it is important to consider affective as well as cognitive objectives. Love of learning, confidence in learning, and development of prosocial, cooperative attitudes are among the most important objectives you should have for your students. Sternberg (2008) suggests that schools supplement objectives related to the 3R's (reading, 'riting, and 'rithmetic) with three more R's: reasoning, resilience, and responsibility (also see Rothstein & Jacobsen, 2009; Stiggins & Chappuis, 2012). In addition, creativity is an objective worth pursuing, even if measuring it is not straightforward (Brookhart, 2013a).

Research on Instructional Objectives

Three principal reasons are given for writing instructional objectives. One is that this exercise helps to organize your planning. As Mager (1997) puts it, if you're not sure where you're going, you're liable to end up someplace else and not even know it. Another is that establishing instructional objectives helps to guide evaluation. Finally, it is hypothesized that development of instructional objectives improves student achievement.

Although it would be a mistake to overplan or adhere rigidly to an inflexible plan, most experienced teachers create, use, and value objectives and assessments that are planned in advance. Perhaps the most convincing support for the establishment of clear instructional objectives is indirect. Cooley and Leinhardt (1980) found that the strongest single factor predicting student reading and math scores was the degree to which students were actually taught the skills that were tested. This implies that instruction is effective to the degree to which objectives, teaching, and assessment are coordinated with one another. Specification of clear instructional objectives is the first step in ensuring that classroom instruction is directed toward giving students critical skills, those that are important enough to test.

It is important to make sure that instructional objectives that are communicated to students are broad enough to encompass everything the lesson or course is supposed to teach. There is some danger that giving students too narrow a set of objectives might focus them on some information to the exclusion of other facts and concepts.

WHY IS EVALUATION IMPORTANT?

InTASC 6

Assessment

Evaluation, or assessment, consists of all the means used in schools to formally measure student performance (Lloyd et al., 2013; McMillan, 2011; Popham, 2014; Waugh & Gronlund, 2013). These include quizzes and tests, written evaluations, and grades. Student evaluation usually focuses on academic achievement, but many schools also assess behaviors and attitudes. Many elementary schools provide descriptions of student behaviors (such as "follows directions," "listens attentively," "works with others," "uses time wisely"). In upper elementary, middle, and high school the prevalence of behavior reports diminishes successively, but even many high schools rate students on such criteria as "works up to ability," "is prepared," and "is responsible."

Why do teachers use tests and grades? You use them because, one way or another, you must periodically check and communicate about students' learning. Tests and grades tell teachers, students, and parents how students are doing in school. You can use tests to determine whether your instruction was effective and to find out which students need additional help. Students can use tests to find out whether their studying strategies are paying off. Parents need grades to learn how their children are doing in school; grades usually serve as the one consistent form of communication between school and home. Schools sometimes need grades and tests to make student placements. States and school districts need tests to evaluate schools and, in some cases, teachers. Ultimately, colleges use grades and standardized test scores to decide whom to admit, and employers use grade-based evidence of attainment, such as diplomas and other credentials, in hiring decisions. Teachers must therefore evaluate student learning; few would argue otherwise. Research on the use of tests finds that students learn more in courses that test students than in those that do not (Dempster, 1991; Haynie & Haynie, 2008).

Student evaluations serve six primary purposes (see Waugh & Gronlund, 2013):

1. Feedback to students
2. Feedback to teachers
3. Information to parents
4. Information for selection and certification
5. Information for accountability
6. Incentives to increase student effort

Evaluation as Feedback

Connections 13.3

For more on feedback as a component of effective teaching, see Chapter 7.

Imagine that a store owner tried several strategies to increase business—first advertising in the newspaper, then sending fliers to homes near the store, and finally holding a sale. However, suppose that after trying each strategy, the store owner failed to record and compare the store's revenue. Without taking stock this way, the owner would learn little about the effectiveness of any of the strategies and might well be wasting time and money. The same is true of teachers and students. They need to know as soon as possible whether their investments of time and energy in a given activity are paying off in increased learning.

FEEDBACK FOR STUDENTS Like the store owner, students need to know the results of their efforts (Fisher & Frey, 2014c; Marzano, Yanoski, Hoegh, & Simms, 2013). Regular evaluation gives them feedback on their strengths and weaknesses. For example, suppose you had students write compositions and then gave back written evaluations. Some students might find out that they needed to work more on content, others on the use of modifiers, and still others on language mechanics. This information would help students to improve their writing much more than would a grade with no explanation (Brookhart & Nitko, 2015; Chappuis, Stiggins, Chappuis, & Arter, 2012).

To be useful as feedback, evaluations should be as specific as possible (Quinn, 2012). For example, Cross and Cross (1980/1981) found that students who received written feedback in addition to letter grades were more likely than other students to believe that their efforts, rather than luck or other external factors, determined their success in school.

FEEDBACK TO TEACHERS One of the most important (and often overlooked) functions of evaluating student learning is to provide feedback to teachers on the effectiveness of their instruction. You cannot expect to be optimally effective if you do not know whether students have grasped the main points of your lessons. Asking questions in class and observing students as they work gives you some idea of how well students have learned; but in many subjects brief but frequent quizzes, writing assignments, and other student products are necessary to provide more detailed indications of students' progress. Well-crafted questions can help you understand students' thinking and uncover misconceptions (Brookhart, 2014; McTighe & Wiggins, 2013; Salend, 2016; Wiliam & Leahy, 2015). Evaluations also give information to the principal and the school as a whole, which can be used to guide overall reform efforts by identifying where schools or subgroups within schools are in need of improvement (McTighe & Curtis, 2015; Mertler, 2014; Schimmer, 2016). Electronic whiteboards with digital response devices can provide teachers with immediate information on how many students have understood each objective the teachers have taught and assessed (Magaño & Marzano, 2014).

Evaluation as Information

A report card is called a report card because it reports information on student progress. This reporting function of evaluation is important for several reasons.

INFORMATION TO PARENTS First, routine school evaluations of many kinds (test scores, stars, and certificates as well as report card grades) keep parents informed about their children's schoolwork. For example, if a student's grades are dropping, the parents might know why and may be able to help the student get back on track. Second, grades and other evaluations set up informal home–based reinforcement systems. Recall from Chapter 11 that many studies have found that reporting regularly to parents when students do good work and asking parents to reinforce good reports improve student behavior and achievement. Without much prompting, most parents naturally reinforce their children for bringing home good grades, thereby making grades important and effective as incentives.

INFORMATION FOR SELECTION Some sociologists see the sorting of students into societal roles as a primary purpose of schools: If schools do not actually determine who will be a butcher, a baker, or a candlestick maker, they do substantially influence who will be a laborer, a skilled worker, a white-collar worker, or a professional. This sorting function takes place gradually over years of schooling. In the early grades, students are sorted into reading groups. Later some eighth-graders take algebra, whereas others take prealgebra or general mathematics. In high school, students are often steered toward advanced, basic, or remedial levels of particular courses, and a major sorting takes place when students are accepted into various colleges and training programs. Moreover, throughout the school years, some students are selected into special-education programs, into programs for the gifted and talented, or into other special programs with limited enrollments.

Closely related to selection is certification, the use of tests to qualify students for promotion or for access to various occupations. For example, many states and local districts have tests that students must pass to advance from grade to grade or to graduate from high school. Bar exams for lawyers, board examinations for medical students, and tests for teachers such as the National Teachers' Examination are examples of certification tests that control access to professions.

INFORMATION FOR ACCOUNTABILITY Often, evaluations of students serve as data for the evaluation of teachers, schools, districts, or even states. Every state has some form of statewide testing program that allows the states to rank every school in terms of student performance (Banks, 2012;

Connections 13.4
For more on information for parents, see Chapter 11.

MyEdLab
Video Example 13.3
This teacher provides evaluative feedback individually to the student and then later to his mother. In both conferences, she asks how they can work together to help support the student's learning.

Connections 13.5

For more information on ability grouping, see Chapter 9.

Miller, Linn, & Gronlund, 2013). These test scores are also often used in evaluations of principals, teachers, and superintendents. Consequently, these tests are taken very seriously.

Evaluation as Incentive

One important use of evaluations is to motivate students to give their best efforts (Dueck, 2014; Vagle, 2014). In essence, high grades, stars, and prizes are given as rewards for good work. Students value grades and prizes primarily because their parents value them. Some high school students also value grades because they are important for getting into selective colleges.

MyEdLab **Self-Check 13.1**

InTASC 6

Assessment

HOW IS STUDENT LEARNING EVALUATED?

Evaluation strategies must be appropriate for the uses that are made of them (McMillan, 2011; Penuel & Shepard, 2016; Salend, 2016). To understand how assessments can be used most effectively in classroom instruction, it is important to know the differences between formative and summative evaluations and between norm-referenced and criterion-referenced interpretations.

Formative and Summative Evaluations

Certification Pointer

For your teacher certification test, you may be given a case illustrating an evaluation of student performance, and you will need to categorize that evaluation as formative or summative.

Assessments can be divided into two categories: formative and summative. Essentially, a formative evaluation asks, "How well are you doing and how can you be doing better?" A summative evaluation asks, "How well did you do?" A **formative evaluation** is designed to tell teachers whether additional instruction is needed and to tell students whether additional learning is needed (Gewertz, 2015; Heritage, 2011; Higgins, 2014; Marzano et al., 2013; Tomlinson & Moon, 2013). Formative, or diagnostic, tests are given to discover strengths and weaknesses in learning and to make midcourse corrections in pace or content of instruction (Fisher & Frey, 2014a). Formative evaluations might even be made "on the fly" during instruction, through oral or brief written learning probes, or by listening to students during groupwork. Increasingly, computerized exercises and games are being used to give teachers and students immediate feedback on students' learning (Phillips & Popović, 2012). Formative evaluation is useful to the degree that it is informative, closely tied to the curriculum being taught, timely, and frequent (Dunn & Mulvenon, 2009; Fogarty & Kerns, 2009; McMillan, 2011; Popham, 2014a; Spinelli, 2011). For example, frequent quizzes that are given and scored immediately after specific lessons might serve as formative evaluations, providing feedback to help both teachers and students improve students' learning. Effective uses of formative assessments in lessons were discussed in Chapter 7.

In contrast, **summative evaluation** refers to tests of student knowledge at the end of instructional units (such as final exams). Summative evaluations may or may not be frequent, but they must be reliable and (in general) should allow for comparisons among students. Summative evaluations should also be closely tied to formative evaluations and to course objectives (Gronlund & Brookhart, 2009; Schimmer, 2016).

Connections 13.6

For more on standardized testing, see Chapter 14.

Norm-Referenced and Criterion-Referenced Evaluations

Certification Pointer

Your teacher certification test may require you to evaluate when it would be more appropriate to use a criterion-referenced test and when to use a norm-referenced test.

Interpretation in order to attach a degree of value to a student's performance is an important step in an evaluation. The distinction between norm referencing and criterion referencing is based on the way students' scores are interpreted.

Norm-referenced interpretations focus on comparisons of a student's scores with those of other students. Within a classroom, for example, grades commonly are used to give teachers an idea of how well a student has performed in comparison with classmates. A student might also have a grade-level or school rank (Guskey, 2014); and in standardized testing, student scores might be compared with those of a nationally representative norm group.

Criterion-referenced interpretations focus on assessing students' mastery of specific skills, regardless of how other students did on the same skills. Criterion-referenced evaluations are best if they are closely tied to specific objectives or well-specified domains of the curriculum being taught. Table 13.4 compares the principal features and purposes of criterion-referenced and norm-referenced testing (see also Waugh & Gronlund, 2013; Popham, 2014b; Thorndike & Thorndike-Christ, 2010).

TABLE 13.4 • Comparison of Two Approaches to Achievement Testing

Norm-referenced tests and criterion-referenced tests serve different purposes and have different features.

FEATURE	NORM-REFERENCED TESTING	CRITERION-REFERENCED TESTING
Principal use	Survey testing	Mastery testing
Major emphasis	Measures individual differences in achievement	Describes tasks students can perform
Interpretation of results	Compares performance to that of other individuals	Compares performance to a clearly specified achievement domain
Content coverage	Typically covers a broad area of achievement	Typically focuses on a limited set of learning tasks
Nature of test plan	Table of specifications is commonly used	Detailed domain specifications are favored
Item selection procedures	Items selected to provide maximum discrimination between individuals (to obtain high score variability); easy items typically eliminated from the test	Includes all items needed to adequately describe performance; no attempt is made to alter item difficulty or to eliminate easy items to increase score variability
Performance standards	Level of performance determined by *relative* position in some known group (e.g., student ranks fifth in a group of 20)	Level of performance commonly determined by *absolute* standards (e.g., student demonstrates mastery by defining 90 percent of the technical terms)

Source: Gronlund, Norman E., *How to make achievement tests and assessment,* 5th Edition, © 1993. Reprinted by permission of Pearson Education, Inc., Upper Saddle River, NJ.

Formative evaluation is almost always criterion referenced. In formative testing, teachers want to know, for example, who is having trouble with Newton's laws of thermodynamics, not which student is first, fifteenth, or thirtieth in the class in physics knowledge. Summative testing, in contrast, can be either criterion referenced or norm referenced. Even if it is criterion referenced, however, teachers usually want to know, on a summative test, how each student did in comparison with other students.

Matching Evaluation Strategies with Goals

Considering all the factors discussed up to this point, what is the best strategy for evaluating students? The first answer is that there is no one best strategy (Penuel & Shepard, 2016; Popham, 2014a, b). The best means of accomplishing any one objective of evaluation might be inappropriate for other objectives. Therefore, you should choose different types of evaluation for different purposes. At a minimum, two types of evaluation should be used: one directed at providing incentive and feedback, and the other directed at ranking individual students relative to the larger group.

EVALUATION FOR INCENTIVE AND FEEDBACK Traditional grades are often inadequate as incentives to encourage students to give their best efforts and as feedback to teachers and students (Tomlinson & Moon, 2014; Wiliam, 2014). The principal problems are that grades are given too infrequently, are too far removed in time from student performance, and are poorly tied to specific student behaviors. Research has found that achievement is higher in classrooms where students receive immediate feedback on their quizzes than in classrooms where feedback is delayed (Duckor, 2014; Tomlinson, 2014a; Wiggins, 2012).

Another reason why grades are less than ideal as incentives is that they are usually based on comparative standards. In effect, it is relatively easy for high-ability students to achieve A's and B's but very difficult for low achievers to do so. As a result, some high achievers do less work than they are capable of doing, and some low achievers give up. As was noted in Chapter 10, a reward that is too easy or too difficult to attain, or one that is felt to be a result of ability rather than of effort, is a poor motivator (Chapman & King, 2005; Wigfield & Eccles, 2000).

For these reasons, traditional grades should be supplemented by evaluations that are better designed for incentive and feedback. For example, teachers might give daily quizzes of 5 or 10 items that are scored in class immediately after completion, or they might have students write daily "mini-essays" on a topic the class is studying. These give both students and teachers the information they need to adjust their teaching and learning strategies and to rectify any deficiencies revealed by the evaluations (Shepard, 2005). If teachers make quiz results important by having them count toward course grades or by giving students with perfect papers

Connections 13.7

Rewards and motivation are discussed in Chapter 5.

Connections 13.8

For more on which rewards make poor motivators, see Chapter 10.

special recognition or certificates, then quiz scores also serve as effective incentives, rewarding effective studying behavior soon after it occurs. It is important to have a clear and objective set of criteria that student work is compared with so students can see exactly why they scored as they did. If the criteria are illustrated using a rubric that has descriptions of different levels of achievement (scores) as well as examples of student work that is at the highest levels of achievement (or better yet, that is typical of each possible score students might receive according to the rubric), then students can see exactly how their achievement compares with the criteria (Stiggins & Chappuis, 2012).

Connections 13.9

For more on rewards that are too easy to attain, see Chapter 10.

Evaluation for Comparison with Others

There are times when you need to know and to communicate how well students are doing in comparison to others. This information is important to give parents (and students themselves) a realistic picture of student performance. For example, students who have outstanding skills in science ought to know that they are exceptional, not only in the context of their class or school, but also in a broader state or national context. In general, students need to form accurate perceptions of their strengths and weaknesses to guide their decisions about their futures.

Comparative evaluations are traditionally provided by grades and by standardized tests. Unlike incentive/feedback evaluations, comparative evaluations need not be conducted frequently. Rather, the emphasis in comparative evaluations must be on fair, unbiased, reliable assessment of student performance.

To be fair, comparative evaluations and other summative assessments of student performance must be firmly based on the objectives established at the beginning of the course and consistent with the formative incentive/feedback evaluations in format as well. No teacher wants a situation in which students do well on week-to-week assessments but then fail the summative evaluations because there is a lack of correspondence between the two forms of evaluation. For example, if the summative test uses essay questions, then the formative tests leading up to it should also include essay questions (Tileston & Darling, 2008).

There are two keys to reliable summative assessment. First, you should use multiple assessment opportunities (Brookhart & Nitko, 2015; Popham, 2014a). No student should receive a grade based

Connections 13.10

For more on grades and standardized tests, see Chapter 14.

21ST CENTURY LEARNING

The advent of the Common Core State Standards, discussed in detail in Chapter 14, has profound implications for classroom assessment. Assessments based on the Common Core will be used for accountability in most states. To be fair to students (and teachers), students should have regular opportunities to practice activities and assessments based on Common Core State Standards. The English/Language Arts standards emphasize analysis and integration of content, writing, use of technology, and collaboration, all of which can and should affect classroom assessments as well. The Mathematics standards emphasize problem solving, reasoning, constructing arguments, and collaboration. These would be valuable parts of regular assessment even if the Common Core didn't exist, but the widespread adoption of the Common Core gives teachers one more good reason to focus on deeper learning, integration of diverse content, technology use, and collaboration (Marzano et al., 2013; Zhao, 2015).

Creativity and Authentic Problem Solving
Since the progressive era began a hundred years ago, educators have advocated creativity and authentic problem-solving skills as key outcomes of education. Yet because these outcomes are difficult and time-consuming to measure reliably, they are often downplayed in comparison to relatively easy-to-assess facts and skills. New assessment software, especially adaptive testing, is beginning to make regular assessment of creativity and authentic problem solving more practical, as when computers are employed to

InTASC 5

Application of Content

pose complex, open-ended problems at the student's precise level of functioning. Such solutions, used as frequent benchmark assessments as well as summative assessments, may soon help teachers both to focus more on these essential 21st century skills and to monitor students' development as creative problem-solvers.

QUESTION

- What are the potential difficulties in judging creativity?
- Do you think it is ethical to penalize a student based on what is judged to be a lack of creativity?
- Do you think creativity should count toward grades?
- Is creativity a necessary life skill?
- How might a lack of creativity be a problem in the workplace?

on only one test, because too much can go wrong with only one assessment. Second, you should test learning when it is completed, not as it is developing. It is better to collect summative evaluation information as students complete instructional units, as well as to use major unit and final tests.

MyEdLab Self-Check 13.2

MyEdLab Video Analysis Tool 13.1 Go to MyEdLab and click on the Video Analysis Tool to access the exercise "Formative assessment: teacher's perspective."

MyEdLab Video Analysis Tool 13.2 Go to MyEdLab and click on the Video Analysis Tool to access the exercise "Formative assessment: revision and practice."

HOW ARE TESTS CONSTRUCTED?

Once you know the concept domains to be assessed in a test of student learning, it is time to write test items. Writing good achievement tests is a critical skill for effective teaching. This section presents some basic principles of achievement testing and some practical tools for test construction (see Chappuis, 2015; Miller et al., 2013; Popham, 2014; Salend, 2016; Witte, 2012). Achievement testing is taken up again in Chapter 14 in relation to standardized tests.

Connections 13.11
For more on achievement testing in relation to standardized tests, see Chapter 14.

Principles of Achievement Testing

Gronlund and Brookhart (2009) listed six principles to keep in mind in preparing achievement tests, paraphrased as follows:

1. *Achievement tests should measure clearly defined learning objectives that are in harmony with in-structional objectives.* Perhaps the most important principle of achievement testing is that the tests should correspond with the course objectives and with the instruction that is actually provided (Lloyd et al., 2013; Squires, 2009; Thorndike & Thorndike-Christ, 2010; Waugh & Gronlund, 2013). An achievement test should never be a surprise for students; rather, it should assess the students' grasp of the most important concepts or skills the lesson or course is supposed to teach.

2. *Achievement tests should measure a representative sample of the learning tasks included in the instruction.* With rare exceptions (such as multiplication facts), achievement tests do not assess every skill or fact students are supposed to have learned. Rather, they sample from among all the learning objectives. If students do not know in advance what questions will be on a test, then they must study the entire course content to do well. However, the test items must be representative of all the objectives (contents and skills) that were covered. For example, if an English literature course spent 8 weeks on Shakespeare and 2 weeks on other Elizabethan authors, the test should have about four times as many items related to Shakespeare as to the others. Items that are chosen to represent a particular objective must be central to that objective. There is no place in achievement testing for tricky or obscure questions. For example, a unit test on the American Revolution should ask questions related

Connections 13.12
For more on the characteristics and uses of standardized achievement tests, see Chapter 14.

to the causes, principal events, and outcomes of that struggle, not about who rowed George Washington across the Delaware. (*Answer:* John Glover and his Marblehead Marines.)

3. ***Achievement tests should include the types of test items that are most appropriate for measuring the desired learning outcomes.*** Items on achievement tests should correspond as closely as possible to the ultimate instructional objectives (Banks, 2012; Schimmer, 2014; Witte, 2012). For example, in mathematics problem solving, one of your goals might be to enable students to solve problems like the ones they will encounter outside of school. Matching items or multiple-choice questions might be inappropriate for this kind of exam, because in real life we do not select from a menu of possible solutions to a problem.

4. ***Achievement tests should fit the particular uses that will be made of the results.*** Each type of achievement test has its own requirements. For example, a test that is used for diagnosis would focus on particular skills with which students might need help. A diagnostic test of elementary arithmetic might contain items on subtraction involving zeros in the minuend (e.g., 307 minus 127), a skill with which many students have trouble. In contrast, a test that is used to predict future performance might assess a student's general abilities and breadth of knowledge. Formative tests should be very closely tied to material that has recently been presented, whereas summative tests should survey broader areas of knowledge or skills.

5. ***Achievement tests should be as reliable as possible but should nevertheless be interpreted with caution.*** A test is reliable to the degree that students who are tested a second time fall in the same rank order. In general, writers of achievement tests increase test reliability by using relatively large numbers of items and by including few items that nearly all students get right or that nearly all students miss (O'Connor, 2009). The use of clearly written items that focus directly on the objectives that are actually taught also enhances test reliability. Still, no matter how rigorously reliability is built into a test, there will always be some error of measurement. Students have good and bad days or can be lucky or unlucky guessers. Some students are test-wise and usually test well; others are test-anxious and test far below their actual knowledge or potential. Therefore, no single test score should be viewed with excessive confidence. Any test score is only an approximation of a student's true knowledge or skills and should be interpreted as such.

6. ***Achievement tests should improve learning.*** Achievement tests of all kinds, particularly formative tests, provide important information on students' learning progress (Dueck, 2014; Sousa, 2016). Stiggins and Chappuis (2012), for example, urge that assessments *for* learning are more important than assessments *of* learning. Achievement testing should be seen as part of the instructional process and used to improve instruction and guide student learning (Chappuis, 2015; Russell & Airasian, 2012). This means that achievement test results should be clearly communicated to students soon after the test is taken; in the case of formative testing, students should be given the results immediately. Teachers should use the results of formative and summative tests to guide instruction, to locate strong and weak points in students' understandings, and to set an appropriate pace of instruction.

Connections 13.13

For more on the reliability of achievement tests, see Chapter 14.

InTASC 6

Assessment

THEORY INTO PRACTICE

Making Assessments Fair

Although fairness in assessment is something everyone believes in, defining fairness in assessment is not straightforward. Indeed, the latest edition of the *Standards for Educational and Psychological Testing* gives four definitions and acknowledges that many more appear in the literature (AERA/APA/NCME, 1999). Fairness means being honest, impartial, and free from discrimination. Besides being ethical, fairness makes good instructional sense. Fair testing encourages students to expend more effort on learning because they come to see that success depends only on what they know and can do (Oosterhof, 2009).

Fairness in assessment arises from good practice in four phases of testing: writing, administering, scoring, and interpreting assessments. Practices that lead to fairness in these areas are considered separately below.

Writing Assessments Base assessments on course objectives. Students expect a test to cover what they have been learning. They also have a right to a test that neither "tricks" them into wrong answers nor rewards them with a high score for guessing or bluffing.

Avoid contexts and expressions that are more familiar or intriguing to some students than to others. One challenge in writing tests is to make sure none of your students are advantaged or disadvantaged because of their different backgrounds. For example, music, sports, or celebrity-related examples might be appealing to some students but not others. Language choices and specific topics should not be used if they are more well known or interesting to some students than to others. If avoiding such choices proves impossible, then at least make sure the items that favor some students are balanced by others that favor the rest.

Giving Assessments Make sure students have had equal opportunities to learn the material on the assessment. Regardless of whether students have learned as much as they can, at least they should have had equal chances to do so. If some students are given extra time or materials that are withheld from others, those others probably will not feel they have been treated fairly.

Make sure students are familiar with the formats they will be using to respond. If some students are not comfortable with the types of questions on an assessment, they will not have an equal chance to show what they can do. If that might be the case, provide some practice with the format beforehand to help them succeed.

Give plenty of time. Most tests in education do not cover content that will eventually be used under time pressure. Thus, most assessments should reward quality instead of speed. Only by allowing enough time so that virtually all students have an opportunity to answer every question can you prevent haste from being a barrier to performance.

Scoring Assessments Make sure the rubric used to score responses awards full credit to an answer that is responsive to the question asked, as opposed to requiring more information than requested for full credit. If the question does not prompt the knowledgeable student to write an answer that receives full credit, then it should be changed. It is unfair to reward some students for doing more than has been requested in the item; not all students will understand the real (and hidden) directions because they have not been told.

Interpreting Assessments Base grades on summative end-of-unit assessments rather than formative assessments that are used to make decisions about learning as it is progressing. The latter are intended to be diagnostic and are used to help accomplish learning. Because grades certify attainment, they should be determined on the basis of assessments made after learning has taken place.

Base grades on several assessment formats (McTighe & Wiggins, 2013). Because students differ in their preferred formats, some are advantaged by selected-response tests, others by essay tests, others by performance assessments, and still others by papers and projects. Also, base grades on multiple assessments taken at different times. Make appropriate accommodations for English learners and for students with disabilities, such as giving more time on tests if they need it (Herrera, Cabral, & Murray, 2013; Voltz, Sims, & Nelson, 2010). Finally, make sure factors that might result in atypical performance for a student are recognized to minimize the importance of the student's score on that assessment. If it is known that a student has not done her or his best, then basing a grade or other important decision on that assessment is not only unfair but also inaccurate.

ON THE WEB

DiscoverySchool.com has rubrics for every kind of assessment imaginable, as well as lesson plans and other useful information for educators. For student project assessment rubrics, see eduscapes.com. For a website on creating a rubric, see http://rubistar.4teachers.org/ and http://elearningindustry.com/the-5-best-free-rubric-making-tools-for-teachers.

Using a Table of Specifications

Achievement tests should measure well-specified objectives. The first step in the test development process is to decide which concept domains the test will measure and how many test items will be allocated to each concept. Waugh & Gronlund (2013) suggest that teachers make up a **table of specifications** for each instructional unit, listing the various objectives taught and the different levels of understanding to be assessed (also see Guskey, 2005). The levels of understanding might correspond to Bloom's taxonomy of educational objectives (Bloom et al., 1956; Marzano & Kendall, 2009). Bloom, Hastings, and Madaus (1971) recommend classifying test items for each objective according to six categories, as shown in Table 13.5, a table of specifications for a social studies unit.

The table of specifications varies for each type of course and is nearly identical to behavior content matrixes, discussed earlier in this chapter. This is as it should be; a behavior content matrix is used to lay out objectives for a course, and the table of specifications tests those objectives.

Once you have written items corresponding to your table of specifications, look over the test in its entirety and evaluate it against the following standards:

1. Do the items emphasize the same concepts you have emphasized in day-to-day instruction? (Recall how Mr. Sullivan, in the chapter-opening vignette, ignored this commonsense rule.)

2. Has an important area of content or any objective been overlooked or underemphasized?

3. Does the test cover all levels of instructional objectives included in the lessons?

4. Does the language of the items correspond to the language and reading level you used in the lessons?

5. Are the instructions clear, even for students who have difficulty with instructions?

6. Is there a reasonable balance between what the items measure and the amount of time that will be required for students to develop a response?

7. Did you write model answers or essential component outlines for the short essay items? Does the weighting of each item reflect its relative value among all the other items?

Evaluation that is restricted to information acquired from paper-and-pencil tests provides only certain kinds of information about students' progress in school. Other sources and strategies for appraisal of student work must be used, including checklists, interviews, classroom simulations, role-playing activities, and anecdotal records. To do this systematically, you may keep a journal or log to record concise and cogent evaluative information on each student throughout the school year.

Writing Selected-Response Test Items

Test items that can be scored correct or incorrect without the need for interpretation are referred to as **selected-response items**. Multiple-choice, true–false, and matching items are the most common forms. Note that the correct answer appears on the test and the student's task is to select it. There is no ambiguity about whether the student has or has not selected the correct answer. Each type, however, has its own advantages and disadvantages.

MULTIPLE-CHOICE ITEMS Considered by some educators to be the most useful and flexible of all test forms (Badgett & Christmann, 2009; Waugh & Gronlund, 2013), **multiple-choice items** can be used in tests for most school subjects. The basic form of the multiple-choice item is a **stem** followed by choices, or alternatives. The stem may be a question or a partial statement that is completed by one of several choices. No perfect number of choices exists, but using four or five is most common—one correct response and wrong but plausible answers that are referred to as **distractors** or **foils**.

TABLE 13.5 • Table of Specifications for a Social Studies Unit on the Suffragists

This table of specification classifies test items and objectives according to six categories ranging from knowledge of terms to ability to apply knowledge.

A. KNOWLEDGE OF TERMS	B. KNOWLEDGE OF FACTS	C. KNOWLEDGE OF RULES AND PRINCIPLES	D. SKILL IN USING PROCESSES AND PROCEDURES	E. ABILITY TO MAKE TRANSLATIONS	F. ABILITY TO MAKE APPLICATIONS
Suffrage	Make a timeline of important events in the suffrage movement	What laws did the suffragists break?		Make a Venn diagram to compare and contrast the suffragists with other groups in America who were denied their right to vote.	Write a diary entry from the point of view of a teenage girl whose mother was put in jail during a suffragists rally.
Equality	Give three examples of ways women were not given rights that were equal to those given to men	Compare the rights of women in the United States in 1920 to the rights of women in ancient Athens.	How were the principles stated in the Declaration of Independence not in line with the laws for women, and especially for African-American women?	The class will form two teams who will debate about whether equality exists among all students within our school.	Research and write a report on gender inequality today. Contrast it to the gender inequalities that existed during the American suffrage movement. What do you think about the term "equality"—can there be degrees of equality?
Ballot	Write a short paragraph on what a ballot is	Pretend you are in charge of a ballot box in 1916. Make a list of rules you would post on it.	Name a situation where you'd use a ballot even now	After voters cast ballots, how are they used to determine who wins an election?	In many countries, people cannot vote. If we could not vote in our country, how might this change our government and people's lives?
Civic	Define civic	What does it mean to be civic-minded?	What actions can you take to be civic-minded?	Identify five people in history who are/were civic minded and explain what they did	Develop a hypothetical civic-improvement project.
Picket	Explain what it means to picket	Is it legal to picket?	Make a picket sign about something serious you'd like to protest	Find a newspaper article about a situation where picketing was involved. Write a 1-2 paragraph opinion about whether you think that was the most effective way to protest in that situation.	Why is the right to picket an important part of our democracy?

The following examples demonstrate two types of multiple-choice items, one with a question stem and the other with a completion stem:

1. What color results from the mixture of equal parts of yellow and blue paint?
   a. Black
   b. Gray
   c. Green [*correct choice*]
   d. Red
2. U.S. presidents are actually elected to office by
   a. all registered voters.
   b. our congressional representatives.

c. the Electoral College. [*correct choice*]

d. the Supreme Court.

When writing a multiple-choice item, keep two goals in mind. First, a capable student should be able to choose the correct answer and not be distracted by the wrong alternatives. Second, you should minimize the chance that a student who is ignorant of the subject matter can guess the correct answer. To achieve this, the distractors must look possible to the uninformed; their wording and form must not identify them readily as bad answers. Hence, one of the tasks in writing a good multiple-choice item is to identify two, three, or four plausible, but not tricky, distractors.

THEORY INTO PRACTICE

Writing Multiple-Choice Tests (Format Suggestions)

The following guidelines are useful resources for constructing effective multiple-choice items (see Badgett & Christmann, 2009; McMillan, 2011).

1. Make the stem sufficiently specific to stand on its own without qualification. In other words, the stem should contain enough information to set the context for the concepts in it. The following example shows a stem for which insufficient context has been established:

Applied behavior analysis can be
a. classical conditioning.
b. punishment.
c. reinforcement contingencies.
d. self-actualization.

An improved version of this stem is the following:

What is the main emphasis of modern classroom use of applied behavior analysis?
a. Classical conditioning
b. Punishment
c. Reinforcement contingencies [*correct choice*]
d. Self-actualization

2. Avoid long and complicated stems unless the purpose of the item is to measure a student's ability to deal with new information or to interpret a paragraph. The stem should not be too wordy; a test is not the place to incorporate instruction that should have been given in the lessons.

3. The stem and every choice in the list of potential answers ought to fit grammatically. In addition, avoid repeating phrases or words to begin each of the alternatives; instead, these should be part of the stem. It is also a sound idea to have the same grammatical form (say, a verb) at the beginning of each choice, as in the following example.

The task of statistics is to
a. *make* the investigation of human beings more precise and rigorous.
b. *promote* the social sciences to a status of being as respectable as the physical sciences.
c. *predict* human behavior.
d. *reduce* large masses of data to an interpretable form. [correct choice]

4. Take special care in using no-exception words such as *never, all, none,* and *always.* These words are most commonly found in incorrect statements because the requirement of no exceptions usually makes statements wrong. In multiple-choice items these words often give clues to the test-wise but concept-ignorant student. Words allowing qualification, such as *often, sometimes, seldom, usually, typically, generally,* and *ordinarily,* are most often found in correct statements (or responses that are true) and, along with no-exception words, such specific determiners should be avoided whenever possible, or at least distributed among both correct answers and distractors.

5. Avoid making the correct choice the only one that is qualified (e.g., by an "if" clause). Also, it should be neither the longest nor the shortest of the alternatives (the longest can otherwise be guessed to be right because absolutely correct answers often require qualification and precision). These features make a choice stand out.

6. Do not use an item that can be answered on the basis of information contained in another item on the same test.

7. Avoid overly inclusive options that contain other options. For example, the choices "dogs" and "setters" should not be in the same item because a setter is a type of dog. Similarly, be cautious in using "all of the above" as an alternative, because it often reduces the possible correct choices to one or two alternatives. The following example illustrates how a student might know very little and get the correct answer. By knowing that only one of the choices is incorrect, a student will reduce the number of plausible choices from four to two.

What type of research is best for investigating the effects of a new instructional program on mathematics achievement?

    a. Correlational
    b. Experimental [*correct choice*]
    c. Historical
    d. All of the above

The student who knows that "Historical" is not a good choice also knows that item d must be incorrect, so the answer must be a or b.

8. After a test, discuss the items with students, and note their interpretations of the wording of each. Students often understand certain phrases quite differently from the way you may have intended. Such feedback will help you revise items for the next test, as well as inform you about students' understandings.

9. Do not include a choice that is transparently absurd. All choices should seem plausible to a student who has not studied.

Besides these guidelines for writing multiple-choice items, here are some suggestions about format:

- List the choices vertically rather than side by side.
- Use letters rather than numerals to label the choices, especially on scientific and mathematical tests.
- Use word structures that make the stem agree with the choices according to acceptable grammatical practice. For example, a completion-type stem would require that each of the choices begin with a lowercase letter (unless it begins with a proper noun).
- Avoid repeating the same word or phrase in the stem and in only one alternative.
- Avoid overusing one letter position as the correct choice, as well as any patterns in the correct answers. Instead, correct choices should appear in random letter positions.

As an illustration of how test "wiseness" rather than knowledge can help students pass an exam, take the brief test in Figure 13.2.

**FIGURE 13.2 •
A Test of "Test
Wiseness"**

The following test is about a made-up country, Quizzerland. Use your test wiseness to guess the answers to these very bad items.

1. What is the main currency used in Quizzerland?
   a. Dollar
   b. Peso
   c. Quark
   d. Pound
2. Describe the pattern of annual rainfall in Quizzerland.
   a. Mostly rainy in the highlands, dry in the lowlands
   b. Rainy
   c. Dry
   d. Snowy
3. How many children are there in Quizzerlandian families?
   a. Never more than 2
   b. Usually 2–3
   c. Always at least 3
   d. None
4. What would be the correct response to any question asked here?
   a.
   b.
   c.
   d.

Answers:
1. c (process of elimination)
2. a (longer item with qualifications is usually correct)
3. b ("always" and "never" items are usually wrong)
4. d (this response hasn't been used yet)

TRUE–FALSE ITEMS Another type of multiple-choice question is the **true–false item**. The main drawback of the true–false format is that students have a 50 percent chance of guessing correctly. For this reason, it should rarely be used.

MATCHING ITEMS As commonly presented, **matching items** usually take the form of two lists, say *A* and *B*. For each item in list *A,* the student has to select one item in list *B*. The basis for choosing must be clearly explained in the directions. Matching items can be used to cover a large amount of content; that is, a large (but not unmanageably large) number of concepts should appear in the two lists. Each list should cover related content (use more than one set of matching items for different types of material). The primary cognitive skill that matching exercises test is recall.

Matching items can often be answered by elimination because many teachers maintain a one-to-one correspondence between the two lists. To engage students in the content, not the format, teachers should either include more items in list *B* than in list *A* or allow reuse of the items in list *B*.

Writing Constructed-Response Items

Constructed-response items require the student to supply rather than select the answer. The simplest form is fill-in-the-blank items, which can often be written to reduce or eliminate ambiguity in scoring. Still, unanticipated responses might lead to ambiguous answers, raising questions in the mind of the instructor on how to score them. Constructed-response items also come in short essay and long essay forms.

FILL-IN-THE-BLANK ITEMS When there is clearly only one possible correct answer, an attractive format is completion, or "fill in the blank," as in the following examples.

1. The largest city in Germany is _____.

2. What is 15 percent of $198.00? _____

3. The measure of electric resistance is the _____.

The advantage of these **completion items** is that they can reduce the element of test-wiseness to near zero. For example, compare the following items:

1. The capital of Maine is _____.

2. The capital of Maine is

   a. Sacramento

   b. Augusta

   c. Juneau

   d. Boston

A student who has no idea what the capital of Maine is could pick Augusta from the list in item 2 because it is easy to rule out the other three cities. In item 1, however, the student has to know the answer. Completion items are especially useful in math, because multiple-choice items may help to give the answer away or reward guessing, as in the following example

$$\begin{array}{r} 4037 \\ -\ 159 \end{array}$$

   a. 4196

   b. 4122

   c. 3878 [*correct answer*]

   d. 3978

If students subtract and get an answer other than any of those listed, they know that they have to keep trying. In some cases they can narrow the alternatives by estimating rather than knowing how to compute the answer.

It is critical to avoid ambiguity in completion items. In some subject areas this can be difficult because two or more answers can reasonably fit a fragment that does not specify the context, as in the next two examples.

1. The Battle of Hastings was in _____. [Date or place?]

2. "H_2O" represents_____. [Water or two parts hydrogen and one part oxygen?]

If there is any ambiguity possible, it is probably best to move to a selection type of item such as multiple choice.

Writing and Evaluating Essay Tests

Short essay questions allow students to respond in their own words. The most common form for a **short essay item** provides a question for the student to answer. The answer may range from a sentence or two to a page of, say, 100 to 150 words. A **long essay item** requires more length and more time, allowing greater opportunity for students to demonstrate organization and development of ideas. Although they differ in length, the methods available to write and score them are similar.

The essay form can elicit a wide variety of responses, from giving definitions of terms to comparing and contrasting important concepts or events. These items are especially suited for assessing students' ability to analyze, synthesize, and evaluate. Hence, you might use them to appraise students' progress in organizing data and applying concepts at the highest levels of instructional objectives. Of course, these items depend heavily on writing skills and the ability to phrase ideas, so exclusive use of essays might cause the teacher to underestimate the knowledge and effort of a student who has learned the material but is a poor writer.

One of the crucial mistakes teachers make in writing essay items is failing to specify clearly the approximate detail required in the response and its expected length. Stating how much weight an item has relative to the entire test is generally not sufficient to tell students how much detail must be incorporated in a response. The following example illustrates this point.

Poor Essay Item

Discuss the role of the prime minister in Canadian politics.

Improvement

In five paragraphs or less, identify three ways in which the Canadian prime minister and the U.S. president differ in their obligations to their respective constituencies. For each of the three, explain how the obligations are different.

Note that the improved version expresses a length (five paragraphs or less), the aspect to be treated (differences between the prime minister and the president), the number of points to be covered (three; if you write "at least three," that would introduce ambiguity into the task), how the points should be selected (differ in their obligations to their respective constituencies), and the direction and degree of elaboration needed (explain how the obligations are different). This item points the student toward the desired response and gives you a greater opportunity to explain the criteria by which student responses will be judged.

An essay item should contain specific information that students are to address. Some teachers are reluctant to name the particulars they want students to discuss, because they believe that supplying a word or phrase in the instructions is giving away too much information. But if an item is ambiguous, different students will interpret it differently. Consequently, they will be responding to different questions, and the test will almost surely not be fair to all of them.

Essay items have a number of advantages in addition to letting students state ideas in their own words. For example, essay items are not susceptible to correct guesses. They can promote efficient assessment by requiring students to combine several concepts in one response. They can also be used to measure creative abilities, such as writing talent or imagination in constructing hypothetical events, as well as assessing organization and fluency.

On the negative side is the problem of reliability in scoring essay responses. Some studies demonstrate that independent marking of the same essay response by different teachers can result in appraisals ranging from excellent to a failing grade (Popham, 2014a). A second drawback is that essay responses take considerable time to evaluate. The time you save by writing one essay item instead of several other kinds of items must be paid back when grading the essays. Third, essay items in general take considerable response time from students. Consequently, they typically cannot be used to cover broad ranges of content. Nevertheless, essay items enable teachers to see how well students can use the material they have been taught. Breadth is sacrificed for depth.

The following suggestions provide additional guidelines for writing effective essay items.

1. As with any item format, match the items with the instructional objectives.

2. Do not use such general directives in an item as "discuss," "give your opinion about," or "tell all you know about." Rather, carefully choose specific response verbs such as "compare," "contrast," "identify," "list and define," and "explain the difference."

3. Write a response to the item before you give the test to estimate the time students will need to respond. About four times your response time is a fair estimate.

4. Rewrite the item to point students clearly toward the desired response.

5. Require all students to answer all items. Even though it seems attractive to allow student choice in which items to answer, that is fundamentally an unfair practice. First, students differ in their ability to make the best selections. Second, the items will not be of equivalent difficulty. And third, students who know they will have a choice can increase their score by studying very carefully only part of the material.

After writing an essay item—and clearly specifying the content that is to be included in the response—you must have a clear idea of how you will score various elements of a student's response. The first step is to write a model response or a detailed outline of the essential elements students are being directed to include in their responses to which you can compare students' responses. If you intend to use evaluative comments but not letter grades, your outline or model will serve as a guide for pointing out to students any omissions and errors in their responses, as well as the good points of their answers. If you are using letter grades to score the essays, you should compare elements of students' responses with the contents of your model and give suitable credit to responses that match the relative weights of elements in the model.

If possible, you should ask a colleague to assess the validity of the elements and their weights in your model response. Going a bit further and having the colleague apply the model criteria to one or more student responses will increase the reliability of your scoring (see Langer & Colton, 2005). Be sure to offer to do the same for them!

One issue related to essay tests is whether and how much to count grammar, spelling, and other technical features. If you do count these factors, give students separate grades in content and in mechanics so that they will know the basis on which their work is being evaluated.

A powerful use of assessment in instruction is to generate one or more scoring rubrics that can be shared with students well in advance of the test. The rubrics, like the example, should be generic, in that they can be applied to a broad range of essays. Students can see which aspects of their achievement will contribute to a positive evaluation and can practice to make sure their work illustrates those critical elements. You might show students (anonymous) essays from previous years to illustrate the rubric. One rubric for high school math problem solving appears in Figure 13.3.

Level 3

The response indicates application of a reasonable strategy that leads to a correct solution in the context of the problem. The representations are essentially correct. The explanation and/or justification is logically sound, clearly presented, fully developed, and supports the solution, and does not contain significant mathematical errors. The response demonstrates a complete understanding and analysis of the problem.

Level 2

The response indicates application of a reasonable strategy that may be incomplete or undeveloped. It may or may not lead to a correct solution. The representations are fundamentally correct. The explanation and/or justification supports the solution and is plausible, although it may not be well developed or complete. The response demonstrates a conceptual understanding and analysis of the problem.

Level 1

The response indicates little or no attempt to apply a reasonable strategy or applies an inappropriate strategy. It may or may not have the correct answer. The representations are incomplete or missing. The explanation and/or justification reveals serious flaws in reasoning. The explanation and/or justification may be incomplete or missing. The response demonstrates a minimal understanding and analysis of the problem.

Level 0

The response is completely incorrect or irrelevant. There may be no response, or the response may state, "I don't know."

FIGURE 13.3 • Generic Rubric for Brief Constructed-Response Items in High School Mathematics in Maryland

Source: W. D. Schafer, G. Swanson, N. Bené, & G. Newberry, "Effects of Teacher Knowledge of Rubrics on Student Achievement in Four Content Areas," *Applied Measurement in Education, 14,* 2001, pp. 151–170.

THEORY INTO PRACTICE

Detecting Bluffing in Students' Essays

Students who are not well prepared for essay tests are likely to try to bluff their way through. Credit should not be given unless the question is specifically answered. Here are some common types of bluffing:

1. ***Student repeats the question in statement form (slightly paraphrased) and tells how important the topic is.*** ("The role of assessment in teaching is extremely important. It is hard to imagine effective instruction without it.")

2. ***Student writes on a topic he or she knows about and fits it to the question.*** (A student who knows testing well but knows little about performance assessment, and is asked to compare testing and performance assessment, might describe testing in considerable detail and frequently state that performance assessment is much superior for evaluating the type of learning measured by the test.)

3. ***Student liberally sprinkles the answer with basic concepts whether they are understood or not.*** (Asked to write about any assessment technique, a student responds by frequently mentioning the importance of "validity" and "reliability.")

4. ***Student includes the teacher's basic beliefs wherever possible.*** ("The intended learning outcomes must be stated in performance terms before this type of test is constructed or selected.")

Writing and Evaluating Problem-Solving Items

Connections 13.14
For more on problem solving, see Chapter 8.

In many subjects, such as mathematics and the physical and social sciences, instructional objectives include the development of skills in problem solving, so it is important to assess students' performance in solving problems (Badgett & Christmann, 2009; McMillan, 2011). A **problem-solving assessment** requires students to organize, select, and apply complex procedures that have at least several important steps or components. It is important to appraise the students' work in each of these steps or components.

The following example shows a seventh-grade-level mathematical problem and a seventh-grader's response to it. The discussion of evaluating problem solving that follows can be applied to any discipline.

InTASC 5

Application of Content

InTASC 6

Assessment

PROBLEM

Suppose two gamblers are playing a game in which the loser must pay an amount equal to what the other gambler has at the time. If Player A won the first and third games, and Player B won the second game, and they finished the three games with $12 each, with how much money did each begin the first game? How did you get your answer?

A student's response:

After game	A had	B had
3	$12.00	$12.00
2	6.00	18.00
1	15.00	9.00
In the beginning	$ 7.50	$16.50

When I started with Game 1, I guessed and guessed, but I couldn't make it come out to 12 and 12.

Then I decided to start at Game 3 and work backward. It worked!

How will you objectively evaluate such a response? As in evaluating short essay items, you should begin your preparation for appraising problem-solving responses by writing either a model response or, perhaps more practically, an outline of the essential components or procedures that are involved in problem solving. As with essays, problem solving may take several different yet valid approaches. The outline must be flexible enough to accommodate all valid possibilities.

THEORY INTO PRACTICE

Peer Evaluations

An evaluation technique often used in cooperative learning, especially in creative writing and (less often) mathematics problem solving, is to have students rate each other's work on a specific set of criteria before the teacher rates them on the same criteria (Brookhart, 2013a; Erkens, 2015; Reynolds, 2009; Smith, 2009). The peer evaluation does not contribute to a student's score or grade but gives the student feedback to use in revising the composition or product. Figure 13.4 shows a peer response guide that might be used for a comparison–contrast writing assignment. The partner, and then the teacher, enters a check mark for each category in which the student has done an adequate job. The partner and the teacher also mark the student's paper to make suggestions for improvement. Peer evaluation provides a formative evaluation for the writer, but it also gives the evaluator an invaluable opportunity to take the teacher's perspective and gain insight into what constitutes good writing.

EVALUATING PROBLEM-SOLVING ITEMS Problem solving involves several important components that fit most disciplines, including understanding the problem to be solved, attacking the problem systematically, and arriving at a reasonable answer. Following is a detailed checklist of elements common to most problem solving that can guide the weighting of elements in your evaluation of a student's problem-solving abilities.

Problem-Solving Evaluation Elements

- ☐ **1.** Problem organization
    - ☐ a. Representation made by table, graph, chart, etc.
    - ☐ b. Representation shown fits the problem.
    - ☐ c. Global understanding of the problem demonstrated.
- ☐ **2.** Procedures (mathematical: trial and error, working backward, experimental process, empirical induction)
    - ☐ a. A viable procedure was attempted.
    - ☐ b. The procedure was carried to a final solution.
    - ☐ c. Computation (if any) was correct.
- ☐ **3.** Solution (mathematical: a table, number, figure, graph, etc.)
    - ☐ a. Answer was reasonable.
    - ☐ b. Answer was checked.
    - ☐ c. Answer was correct.
- ☐ **4.** Logic specific to the detail or application of the given information was sound.

If you wish to give partial credit for an answer that contains correct elements, or if you want to inform students about the value of their responses, you must devise ways to do this consistently. The following points offer some guidance.

(continued)

1. Write model responses before giving partial credit for such work as essay writing, mathematical problem solving, laboratory assignments, and any work that you evaluate according to the quality of its various stages.

2. Explain to students in sufficient detail the meaning of the grades you give to communicate the value of the work.

The following examples illustrate outlines of exemplary student work from mathematics and social studies or literature.

FROM MATHEMATICS Students are given the following problem:

In a single-elimination tennis tournament, 40 players are to play for the singles championship. Determine how many matches must be played.

Evaluation

☐ a. Evidence that the student understood the problem, demonstrated by depiction of the problem with a graph, table, chart, equation, etc. (*3 points*)

☐ b. Use of a method for solving the problem that had potential for yielding a correct solution—for example, systematic trial and error, empirical induction, elimination, working backward. (*5 points*)

☐ c. Arrival at a correct solution. (*3 points*)

The three components in the evaluation were assigned points according to the weight the teacher judged each to be worth in the context of the course of study and the purpose of the test. You can give full credit for a correct answer even if all the work is not shown in the response, provided that you know that students can do the work in their heads. But it is important to guard against the halo effect, which occurs when you know which student wrote which response and you alter the grading of the paper in accordance with your opinion of the student. The same response should receive the same score no matter who wrote it. Use of a detailed rubric, or scoring guide, in evaluation is a way to make scoring more objective and thus to avoid any halo effects.

FROM SOCIAL STUDIES OR LITERATURE Students are asked to respond with a 100-word essay to the following item:

Compare and contrast the development of Inuit and Navajo tools on the basis of the climates in which these two peoples live.

Evaluation

☐ a. The response gives evidence of specific and accurate recall of the climates in which the Inuit and Navajos live (*1 point*) and of Inuit and Navajo tools. (*1 point*)

☐ b. The essay develops with continuity of thought and logic. (*3 points*)

☐ c. An accurate rationale is provided for the use of the various tools in the respective climates. (*3 points*)

☐ d. An analysis comparing and contrasting the similarities and differences between the two groups and their tool development is given. (*8 points*)

☐ e. The response concludes with a summary and closure. (*1 point*)

These two examples should suggest ways to evaluate items in other subject areas as well. Giving partial credit for much of the work students do certainly results in a more thorough evaluation of student progress than does scoring the work as merely right or wrong. The examples show how to organize objective assessments for evaluating work that does not lend itself to the simple forms of multiple-choice, true–false, completion, and matching items. Points do not have to be used to evaluate components of the responses. In many situations, some kind of evaluative descriptors might be more meaningful. **Evaluative descriptors** are statements describing strong and weak features of a response to an item, a question, or a project. In the mathematics example, a teacher's evaluative descriptor for item a might read, "You have drawn an excellent chart showing that you understand the meaning of the problem, and that is very good, but it seems you were careless when you entered several important numbers in your chart."

Note that each of these examples is much like a rubric and can be generalized to broad ranges of topics. If teachers and students discuss these during instruction, students will have a device that helps them understand what they are working toward, and both teachers and students will have a common language that they can use during instruction and in their formative assessments.

Criterion	Partner	Teacher
Content		
1. Shows how concepts are similar		
2. Shows how concepts are different		
3. Well organized		
4. Good opening sentence		
5. Good concluding sentence		
Mechanics		
1. Spelling correct		
2. Grammar correct		
3. Punctuation correct		
4. At least 2 pages		

**FIGURE 13.4 •
Example of a Partner
Response Form for a
Comparison–Contrast
Assignment**

MyEdLab **Self-Check 13.3**

WHAT ARE AUTHENTIC, PORTFOLIO, AND PERFORMANCE ASSESSMENTS?

After much criticism of traditional testing (e.g., Beers, 2011; McTighe & Curtis, 2015; Shepard, 2000; Zhao, 2015), critics have developed and implemented alternative assessment systems that are designed to avoid the problems raised by typical multiple-choice tests. The key idea behind the testing alternatives is that students should be asked to document their learning or demonstrate that they can actually do something real with the information and skills they have learned in school (Brookhart, 2015; Greenstein, 2012; Lewin & Schoemaker, 2011; McTighe & Wiggins, 2013). For example, students might be asked to keep a portfolio, design a method of measuring wind speed, draw a scale model of a racing car, or write something for a real audience. Such tests are referred to as *authentic assessments* or *performance assessments* (McTighe & Wiggins, 2013). One goal of these "alternative assessments" is to demonstrate achievement in realistic contexts. In reading, for example, the authentic assessment movement has led to the development of tests in which students are asked to read and interpret longer sections of text and show a deep understanding.

InTASC 6

Assessment

In science, authentic assessments might involve having students set up and carry out an experiment. In writing, students might be asked to write real letters or newspaper articles. In math, students might solve complex physical problems that require insight and creativity. Authentic tests sometimes require students to integrate knowledge from different domains—for example, to use algebra in the context of reading about and performing a science experiment and to write up the results.

Portfolio Assessment

One popular form of alternative assessment is **portfolio assessment**: the collection and evaluation of samples of student work over an extended period (Brookhart, 2015; Greenstein, 2012; McMillan, 2011). You may collect student compositions, projects, and other evidence of higher-order functioning and use this evidence to evaluate student progress over time. For example, many teachers have students maintain portfolios of their writings that show the development of a composition from first draft to final product; portfolios can also be used for journal entries, book reports, artwork, computer printouts, or papers showing development in problem solving (Brookhart, 2015). Portfolios are increasingly being maintained on computers to supplement paper files (Diehm, 2004; Niguidula, 2005). Refer to Figure 13.5 for sample criteria in evaluating student writing portfolios.

**FIGURE 13.5 •
Sample of Criteria for Evaluating Students' Writing Ability through Portfolio Assessment**

Portfolio Evaluation Form				
Name:	**Improvement Needed** **1**	**2**	**3**	**Excellent** **4**
1. All assigned work is included				
2. Log sheet is completed				
3. Final reflection is completed				
4. Work demonstrates improvement on previous areas of weakness				
5. Writing incorporates teacher's feedback from earlier work				
6. Portfolio demonstrates improved writing overall				
Additional Criteria				
7.				
8.				
9.				
10.				
Teacher Comments:				

Portfolio assessment has important uses when you want to evaluate students for reports to parents or other within-school purposes. When combined with on-demand assessments and used with consistent and public rubrics, portfolios showing improvement over time can provide powerful evidence of change to parents and to students themselves (Burke, 2009).

Certification Pointer
A teacher certification question may ask you to respond to a case study by suggesting a way to implement portfolio assessment that would be appropriate for the case.

ON THE WEB

For reports, newsletters, and other publications about assessment, particularly performance and portfolio assessment, visit cresst.org, the National Center for Research on Evaluation, Standards, and Student Testing (CRESST), located at UCLA. To view articles and multimedia related to assessment and other topics in education, go to the website of the George Lucas Educational Foundation at edutopia.org. Also visit the Education Commission of the States website, which contains a list of assessment-related sites, at ecs.org.

THEORY INTO PRACTICE

Using Portfolios in the Classroom

PLANNING AND ORGANIZATION

- Develop an overall flexible plan for student portfolios. What purposes will the portfolios serve? What items will be required? When and how will they be obtained? What criteria will be applied for reflection and evaluation?
- Plan sufficient time for students to prepare and discuss portfolio items. Assessing portfolios takes more time and thought than correcting paper-and-pencil tests.
- Begin with one aspect of student learning and achievement, and gradually include others as you and the students learn about portfolio procedures. The writing process, for instance, is particularly well suited to documentation through portfolios.
- Choose items to be included in portfolios that will show developing proficiency on important goals and objectives. Items that address multiple objectives help to make portfolio assessments more efficient.
- Collect at least two types of items: required indicators (Arter & McTighe, 2001; Murphy & Underwood, 2000) or core items and optional work samples. Required or core indicators are items collected for every child that will show how each is progressing. Optional work samples show individual students' unique approaches, interests, and strengths.
- Place a list of goals and objectives in the front of each portfolio along with a list of required indicators, and also include a place for recording optional items, so that you and the students can keep track of contents.

IMPLEMENTATION

- In order to save time, to ensure that portfolio items are representative of students' work, and to increase authenticity, embed the development of portfolio items into ongoing classroom activities.

(continued)

- Give students responsibility for preparing, selecting, evaluating, and filing portfolio items and keeping portfolios up to date. Young children will need guidance with this.
- For selected portfolio items, model reflection and self-assessment for students to help them become aware of the processes they used, what they learned, what they have yet to learn, and what they might need to do differently next time.
- Be selective. A portfolio is not a haphazard collection of work samples, audio or video recordings, pictures, websites, and other products. It is a thoughtful selection of items that exemplify children's learning. Random inclusion of items quickly becomes overwhelming.
- Use information in portfolios to place learners on a sequence of developing skills.
- Analyze portfolio items for insight into students' knowledge and skills. As you do this, you will understand more of the students' strengths and needs, thinking processes, preconceptions, misconceptions, error patterns, and developmental benchmarks.
- Use portfolio information to document and celebrate students' learning, to share students' accomplishments with parents and other school personnel, and to improve and target classroom instruction. If portfolios are not linked to improving instruction, they are not working. (For guides to portfolio evaluation, see Brookhart, 2013; McTighe & Wiggins, 2013; Stiggins & Chappuis, 2012.)

Performance Assessment

Tests that involve actual demonstrations of knowledge or skills in real life are called **performance assessments** (Brookhart, 2015; McMillan, 2011; Popham, 2014a; Shavelson, 2013). For example, ninth-graders might be asked to conduct an oral history project, reading about a significant recent event and then interviewing the individuals involved. The quality of the oral histories, done over a period of weeks, indicates the degree of the students' mastery of the social studies concepts involved. Wiggins (1993) describes assessments used in the last 2 weeks of school in which students must apply everything they have learned all year to analyze a sludge that mixes a variety of solids and liquids. Some schools are requiring elaborate "exhibitions," such as projects developed over many months, as demonstrations of competence. More time-limited performance assessments might ask students to set up experiments, respond to extended text, write in various genres, or solve realistic math problems. Technology enables students to set up complex experiments that require deep understanding of and insight into science or math, for example (Clarke-Midura, 2014).

Effectiveness of Performance Assessments

One of the most important criticisms of traditional standardized tests is that they can focus teachers on teaching only a narrow range of skills that happen to be on the test (see Popham, 2004). How might performance assessments be better? At least in theory, it should be possible to create tests that would require such a broad understanding of subject matter that the test would be worth teaching to.

For example, consider the performance test in math shown in Figure 13.6. Imagine that your students will have to demonstrate their time-telling skills. The only way to teach to such a test will be to expose students to the various ways to tell time.

Beyond all the practical problems and expense of administering and scoring performance tests, it is not yet clear whether performance tests will solve all the problems of standardized testing. For example, Shavelson, Baxter, and Pine (1992) studied performance assessments in science.

Capability to Be Assessed

- *Goal to be assessed:* Establishes the time using a clock
- *Type of capability involved:* Rule

Performance to Be Observed

- *Domain of tasks associated with goal being assessed*
  - Tells time using a digital or analog clock
  - With an analog clock, tells time with numbers or other markings on the face
  - With digital or analog clock, tells time with or without seconds indicated
  - With digital or analog clock, tells time with different shapes, sizes, and colors used for the clock face
- *Description of task to be performed:* Student views the face of an analog clock and states the displayed time
  - *Focus on process or product?* Product
  - *Prerequisite skills to be verified: The student can read numbers.*
- *Required materials*
  - Clock face with movable hour and minute hands. The face should contain numbers to designate hours. The clock should not have a second hand.
- *Guidelines for administration*
  - Use eight different time settings, with the minute hand twice within each of the quarter hours.
  - Vary the hour hand through its full range.
  - The minute and hour hands should be distinctly visible in all settings.
- *Instructions to students*
  - Say to the student, "What time does this clock show?"

Scoring Plan

  Time stated by student is correct within 1 minute.

FIGURE 13.6 • Example of a Performance Assessment Activity: Telling Time

Source: Oosterhof, Albert. *Developing and using classroom assessments* (4th ed.) (c) 2009, p. 186. Reprinted and electronically reproduced by permission of Pearson Education Inc., Upper Saddle River, NJ.

They found that student performance on such assessments could be reliably rated, but different performance assessments produced very different patterns of scores, and student scores were still related more closely to student aptitude than to what students were actually taught. Similar findings were reported in studies by the Educational Testing Service (1995), Linn (1994), and Supovitz and Brennan (1997).

Scoring Rubrics for Performance Assessments

Performance assessments are typically scored according to rubrics that specify in advance the type of performance that is expected for each activity (Brookhart, 2013; Burke, 2009; Popham, 2014; Vagle, 2014). Figure 13.7 shows one rubric (from Taylor, 1994) that was developed for an essay on character development in stories that students had read.

Performance assessment tasks are similar to essay items in that students might approach them in multiple ways. It is, therefore, also important for performance assessments that students understand the criteria for scoring. One way to ensure this is to write a few generic rubrics that are flexible enough to apply to the full range of student performance. Figure 13.3 gave an example of a generic rubric that has been applied to outcomes in high school mathematics. It has been suggested that using rubrics such as this in classroom instruction can enhance student achievement (Schafer, Swanson, Bené, & Newberry, 2001).

Planning for performance assessments takes time, and avoiding the pitfalls of subjectivity in rating performances takes practice. However, a few well-thought-out, well-written items for a performance assessment could serve, for example, as a summative evaluation for all or most of your educational objectives for an entire unit (see Figure 13.8).

Certification Pointer

You may be asked on your teacher certification test to give an example of a performance goal and then to write a behavioral objective, an activity, and an assessment of student learning that would accomplish the goal.

FIGURE 13.7 •
Sample Scoring Rubric: Targeted Performance, Performance Criteria, and a Description of Performances at Different Score Points

Source: Catherine Taylor, "Assessment for Measurement or Standards," *American Educational Research Journal, 31*(2), pp. 231–262, 1994.

Performance

Essay on Character Development in Literature

Performance Criteria

- Character is identified.
- At least three aspects of the character's development during the course of the story are described.
- Appropriate support for each character aspect is given, using excerpts from the story.
- Character's contribution to the story's plot is described.
- At least three excerpts from the story are given as support for the writer's ideas about the character's contribution to the story.
- Text references used for support are appropriate.

Scoring Rubric

4 points	Essay is complete, thorough, and insightful in describing the character's development and contribution to the story. Adequate support is given to encourage us to consider the writer's point of view. All excerpts from the text enhance our understanding of the writer's view of the character.
3 points	Essay is complete in describing the character's development and contribution to the story. Adequate support is given to encourage us to consider the writer's point of view. Most excerpts from the text enhance our understanding of the writer's view of the character.
2 points	Essay is complete in its description of either the character's development or the character's contribution to the story. Some support is given to help us consider the writer's point of view. Most excerpts from the text enhance our understanding of the writer's view of the character for the element described.
1 point	Essay is mostly complete in its description of either the character's development or the character's contribution to the story. Support is given for the writer's point of view, but it is not always convincing. Few excerpts from the text enhance our understanding of the writer's view of the character for the element described.
0 points	The written essay was not completed, is significantly lacking in performance of all criteria, or is off task.

Assessment through Digital Games and Simulations

Computers have long been used to assess students' learning, but until recently they have only provided easy, rapid scoring and recordkeeping. Today, however, computers are beginning to be used to assess students' performance as they participate in games, simulations, and other activities (Schaaf, 2015). For example, students working together on a simulated lab exercise in science might be assessed digitally on the basis of their personal contributions to the lab (Erkens, 2015). Students playing games against the computer might have fun and learn, but at the same time their responses can be recorded and evaluated against standards. Some day, perhaps students will no longer take tests that are separate from the learning activities they do every day (McTighe & Curtis, 2015).

Psychology Fair Rubric

✓ **Our Psychology Project . . .**

☐ (25 pts) Provides background information—it cites other studies, explains our interest in the topic, and presents a rationale for the topic. [The better the background information, the more detailed it is, and the more it "fits," the more points you earn.]

   Brief example: "We are interested in how dress affects behavior. We always felt better when we were dressed up and also thought that less violence occurs between people who 'dress up.' Cohen and Cohen (1987) found that students who wore uniforms performed 10 percent better on exams and were cited for fewer office referrals. Thus we wanted to look into this topic further."

☐ (25 pts) Gives a description of the study (an abstract—a *general* statement in 100 words or fewer about your project).

   Brief example: "This study investigates the relationship between academic performance and the use of uniforms in schools. Three schools in Derry County, Pennsylvania, were surveyed on issues of academic performance and office referrals. The use of uniforms showed an increase in achievement and decreased behavioral problems."

☐ (40 pts) Has a measurable hypothesis with specific variables defined and identified.

☐ (25 pts) Includes at least one graph, chart, or other visual aid that *summarizes the data*. Someone should be able to look at your graph/chart and clearly see what the variables and results were.

☐ (10 pts) Includes a clean copy of any survey or other scale that was used to gather data.

☐ (40 pts) Includes a written procedure that tells the observer *exactly* what we did.

   Brief example: "We took 3 days to survey 100 students and 30 teachers."

☐ (30 pts) Includes a section that explains the data and tells whether the hypothesis was accurate.

   Brief example: "Our data reflect that our hypothesis was correct: The 30 percent increase in scores reflects the improved achievement of students while . . ." [Again, develop your explanation. If you say only, "We were right" or "Our hypothesis is correct/wrong," you will not receive more than half the points.]

☐ (30 pts) Includes a section explaining the significance of the study—why it is important.

   Brief example: "This is an important study because it reflects a bias that many people may not be aware of, as well as a way in which students can improve scores and reduce their own behavioral problems. It further . . ."

☐ (50 pts) Is interactive. That is, observers can take the test, view the screen, do the quiz, and so on. [This can be done in a variety of ways. For instance, if the test is long, have observers do part of it or show a video of your procedure.]

Total Points Possible: 275

FIGURE 13.8 • Semester-Long Assessment

Source: Mr. Charles Greiner, Lusher Charter School. New Orleans/Tulane University.

HOW ARE GRADES DETERMINED?

One of the most perplexing and often controversial tasks you face is grading student work (Brookhart & Nitko, 2015; Reeves, 2015; Quinn, 2012; Schimmer, 2016; Scriffiny, 2008). Is grading necessary? It is clear that some form of summative student evaluation is necessary, and grading of one kind or another is the form predominantly used in most schools.

Establishing Grading Criteria

Many sets of grading criteria exist, but regardless of the level of school that teachers teach in, they generally agree on the need to explain the meaning of grades they give (Brookhart & Nitko, 2015; Stiggins & Chappuis, 2012; Vatterott, 2015). Grades should communicate at least the relative value of a student's work in a class. They should also help students to understand better what is expected of them and how they might improve. They can also serve as a basis for a productive conversation with students and parents (Webber & Wilson, 2012).

Teachers and schools that use letter grades attach the following general meanings to the letters:

A = superior; exceptional; outstanding attainment

B = very good, but not superior; above average

C = competent, but not remarkable work or performance; average

D = minimum passing, but serious weaknesses are indicated; below average

E = failure to pass; serious weaknesses demonstrated

Assigning Letter Grades

All school districts have a policy or common practice for assigning report card grades. Most use A-B-C-D-F letter grades, but many (particularly at the elementary school level) use various versions of outstanding–satisfactory–unsatisfactory (Brookhart & Nitko, 2015; Reeves, 2015; Schimmer, 2016). Some simply report percentage grades. The criteria on which grades are based vary enormously from district to district. Secondary schools usually give one grade for each subject taken, but most elementary schools and some secondary schools include ratings on effort or behavior as well as on performance.

The criteria for giving letter grades might be specified by a school administration, but grading criteria are most often set by individual teachers using very broad guidelines. In practice, few teachers could get away with giving half their students A's or with failing too many students; but between these two extremes, teachers may have considerable leeway (see Guskey, 2014; Tomlinson & Moon, 2013).

ABSOLUTE GRADING STANDARDS Grades may be given according to absolute or relative standards. Absolute grading standards might consist of preestablished percentage scores required for a given grade, as in the following example:

Grade	Percentage Correct
A	90–100 percent
B	80–89 percent
C	70–79 percent
D	60–69 percent
F	Less than 60 percent

In another form of absolute standards, called *criterion-referenced grading,* you decide in advance which performances constitute outstanding (A), above-average (B), average (C), below-average (D), and inadequate (F) mastery of the instructional objective.

Absolute percentage standards have one important disadvantage: Student scores might depend on the difficulty of the tests they are given. For example, a student can pass a true–false test (if a passing grade is 60 percent) by knowing only 20 percent of the answers and guessing on the rest (getting half of the remaining 80 percent of the items correct by chance). On a difficult test where guessing is impossible, however, 60 percent could be a very high score. For this reason, use of absolute percentage criteria should be tempered with criterion-referenced standards. That is, you might use a 60–70–80–90 percent standard in most circumstances but establish (and announce to students) higher standards for tests that students are likely to find easy and lower standards for more difficult tests.

Another disadvantage is that the ranges of the grades are typically different, especially for F's. A student who receives an F may be very close to a D or may be hopelessly far from "passing." This is true for the other grades, too, but the large range of F (0 to 60 percent) emphasizes the uncertainty. Moreover, the consequences of an F are often quite severe.

RELATIVE GRADING STANDARDS A relative grading standard is a system whereby a teacher gives grades according to the students' rank in their class or grade. The classic form of relative grading is specifying what percentage of students will be given A's, B's, and so on. A form of this practice is called *grading on the curve* because students are given grades on the basis of their position on a predetermined distribution of scores.

Relative grading standards have the advantage of placing students' scores in relation to one another without regard to the difficulty of a particular test. However, relative grading standards also have serious drawbacks (see Guskey, 2014; O'Connor, 2009). One is that because they hold the number of A's and B's constant, students in a class of high achievers must get much higher scores to earn A's or B's than students in low-achieving classes—a situation that is likely to be seen as unfair. Teachers often deal with this problem by giving relatively more A's and B's in high-achieving classes than in others. Another disadvantage of relative grading is that it creates competition among students; when one student earns an A, this diminishes the chances that others may do so. Competition can inhibit students from helping one another and hurt social relations among classmates (Guskey, 2014).

Strict grading on the curve and guidelines for numbers of A's and B's have been disappearing in recent years. For one thing, there has been a general grade inflation; more A's and B's are given now than in the past, and C is no longer the expected average grade but often indicates below-average performance (Goodwin, 2011; Pattison, Grodsky, & Muller, 2013). Anderson (1994) summarized a national survey of eighth-graders who were asked to report their English grades since sixth grade. The results were as follows:

Mostly A's: 31 percent

Mostly B's: 38 percent

Mostly C's: 23 percent

Mostly D's: 6 percent

Mostly less than D's: 2 percent

Results were similar in mathematics, and grades were only slightly lower in high-poverty schools than in middle-class schools. It is likely that these self-reported grades are somewhat higher than those students actually received, but it is nevertheless likely that the average grade today is B, not C.

The most common approach to grading involves looking at student scores on a test, taking into account test difficulty and the overall performance of the class, and assigning grades in such a way that about the "right number" of students earn A's and B's and the "right number" fail. Teachers vary considerably in their estimates of what these right numbers should be, but schools often have unspoken norms about how many students should be given A's and how many should fail.

Performance Grading

One of the most important limitations of traditional grades is that although they may give some indication of how students are doing in comparison to others, they provide no information about what students know and can do. A student who gets a B in English might be disappointed or breathe a sigh of relief, depending on what she expected. However, this grade does not tell her or her parents or teachers what she can do, what she needs to do to progress, or where her strengths or weaknesses lie (Marzano & Heflebower, 2011; Quinn, 2012). Furthermore, giving a single grade in each subject can reinforce the idea that students are more able or less able, or perhaps more motivated or less motivated, rather than the idea that all students are growing.

Some schools have responded to these limitations with an alternative approach to grading called *performance grading* (Guskey, 2014), in which teachers determine what children know and can do and then report this in a way that is easy for parents and students to understand (Guskey, 2014). Figure 13.9 (from Wiggins, 1994) shows one page of a language arts assessment keyed to fifth-grade exit standards, or expectations of what a fifth-grader should know. A parent who receives a form like this can see how the student is progressing toward the kind of performance the school district has defined as essential. Note that although the form does provide information on how the student is doing in comparison to other students, the emphasis is on growth over time.

Cherry Creek School District
Polton Community Elementary
School Fairplay Progress Report
(Language Arts Section)

Student Name _____   Grade 3 _____ 4 _____
Teacher _____   School Year _____

Performance-based graduation requirements focus on student mastery of the proficiencies. The curriculum and written progress report are geared toward preparing students for this task. A date (for example, 3/12) indicates where a student is performing on a continuum of progress based on the fifth-grade exit standards.

	Basic	Proficient	Advanced
Language Arts Proficiency 1 Listens, interpreting verbal and nonverbal cues to construct meaning.	Actively listens, demonstrates understanding, and clarifies with questions and paraphrasing.	Actively listens for purpose, demonstrates understanding, and clarifies with questions and paraphrasing.	Actively listens for purpose, demonstrates understanding, clarifies with questions and paraphrasing, classifies, analyzes, and applies information.
Language Arts Proficiency 2 ◄———————————————————————————————————► Conveys meaning clearly and coherently through speech in both formal and informal situations.	Appropriately speaks to inform, explain, demonstrate, or persuade. Organizes a speech and uses vocabulary to convey a message.	Appropriately speaks to inform, explain, demonstrate, or persuade. Organizes a formal speech and uses vocabulary to convey a message.	Appropriately speaks to inform, explain, demonstrate, or persuade. Organizes a formal speech with details and transitions adapting subject and vocabulary. Uses eye contact, gestures, and suitable expression for an audience and topic.
Language Arts Proficiency 3 ◄———————————————————————————————————► Reads to construct meaning by interacting with the text, by recognizing the different requirements of a variety of printed materials, and by using appropriate strategies to increase comprehension.	Reads varied material, comprehends at a literal level. Recalls and builds knowledge through related information. Begins to use strategies to develop fluency, adjusting rate when reading different material.	Reads varied material, comprehends literally and interpretively. Synthesizes and explores information, drawing inferences. Critiques author's intent, analyzes material for meaning and value. Applies strategies to increase fluency, adjusting rate when reading different material.	Reads varied material, comprehends and draws inferences, recalls and builds knowledge through related information. Applies strategies to increase fluency, adjusting rate when reading different material.
Language Arts Proficiency 4 ◄———————————————————————————————————► Produces writing that conveys purpose and meaning, uses effective writing strategies, and incorporates the conventions of written language to communicate clearly.	Appropriately writes on assigned or self-selected topics. Clear main ideas, few details. Weak elements in the beginning, middle, end. Sentence structure lacks variety and contains errors.	Appropriately writes on assigned or self-selected topics. Clear main ideas, interesting details, clear organization, sequencing, varied sentence structure, edits to reduce errors. Appropriate voice and word choice.	Appropriately writes on assigned or self-selected topics. Connects opinions, details, and examples. Effective organization and sequencing, meaningful sentence structure, edits to eliminate most errors. Appropriate voice and word choice.

As compared to the class in the area of Language Arts, your child
Note: The teacher places a check in one box per marking period to indicate child's status in language arts.

1	2	3	Marking Periods
			Displays strong performance
			Demonstrates appropriate development
			Needs practice and support

FIGURE 13.9 • Sample Performance Grading Criteria

SCORING RUBRICS FOR PERFORMANCE GRADING A key requirement for the use of performance grading is collection of work samples from students that indicate their level of performance on a developmental sequence. Collecting and evaluating work that students are already doing in class (such as compositions, lab reports, or projects) is called *portfolio assessment* (Brookhart, 2013, 2014, 2015; McTighe & Wiggins, 2013), discussed earlier in this chapter. An alternative is to give students tests in which they can show their abilities to apply and integrate knowledge, skills, and judgment. Most performance grading schemes use some combination of portfolios and on-demand performance tests. In either case, student performance is usually evaluated against rubrics, which describe, for example, partially proficient, proficient, and advanced performance, or which indicate a student's position on a developmental sequence.

Other Alternative Grading Systems

Several other approaches to grading are used in conjunction with innovative instructional approaches. In the system called *contract grading,* students negotiate a particular amount of work or level of performance that they will achieve to receive a certain grade. For example, a student might agree to complete five book reports of a given length in a marking period to receive an A. **Mastery grading** involves establishing a standard of mastery, such as 80 or 90 percent correct on a test. All students who achieve that standard receive an A; students who do not achieve it the first time receive corrective instruction and then retake the test to try to achieve the mastery criterion (Fisher, Frey, & Pumpian, 2011; Guskey, 2014). Finally, many teachers give grades based on improvement or effort, usually in combination with traditional grades. In this way a student who is performing at a low level relative to others can nevertheless receive feedback indicating that he or she is on a path leading to higher performance (see Tomlinson & Moon, 2013).

LETTING STUDENTS RETAKE TESTS Many teachers allow students to retake tests, especially if they failed the first time (Dueck, 2011; Wormeli, 2011). This can be a good idea if it gives students an opportunity to do additional studying and master the material the class is studying. For example, a student might be given 2 days to study the content that was tested and then take an alternative form of the test. (Giving the same test to the student is not recommended because that would allow the student to study only the questions that were asked.) The student might then be given a grade that is one letter grade lower than he or she scored on the second test, because the student had an advantage in having an extra opportunity to study. There is some danger that if students know they can retake tests, they might not study until after attempting the first test, but in general, giving students a second chance is a good way to allow those who are willing to put in extra effort to improve a poor grade. Some schools give grades of A, B, C, or incomplete, permitting additional time and support until all students are able to earn at least a C (Kenkel, Hoelscher, & West, 2006).

Assigning Report Card Grades

Most schools give report cards four or six times per year—that is, every 6 or 9 weeks. Report card grades are most often derived from some combination of the following factors (Brookhart & Nitko, 2015; Reeves, 2015):

- Scores on quizzes and tests
- Scores on papers and projects
- Scores on homework
- Scores on seatwork
- Class participation (academic behaviors in class, answers to class questions, and so on)
- Deportment (classroom behavior, tardiness, attitude)
- Effort

   These are listed in order from the most formal and reliable measures of achievement to those considered least valid as a learning indicator. The first two factors listed are summative assessments, and virtually everyone would consider them appropriate for grading. The next two are typically formative and thus indicate how learning is progressing when it is still incomplete. They are less appropriate because they do not convey information about status at the end of instructional units.

MyEdLab
Video Example 13.5
Textbook author Bob Slavin presents a story about his first experience grading students' papers. Why do you think a teacher might feel he or she "failed" when a student fails a class? What can you do to make sure you can always justify the grades you give students?

The final three might contribute to achievement, but they are not achievement. Basing grades on them could communicate misinformation to others about students (Guskey, 2014). Teachers often give different weights to various factors, stating (for example) that grades will be based 30 percent on quizzes, 30 percent on a final test, 20 percent on homework, and 20 percent on class participation. This helps communicate to students what is most important to the teacher.

One important issue arises when scores are to be combined for grading—how to treat missing work, such as homework assignments (O'Connor, 2009; Reeves, 2006, 2015). Some teachers assign a "zero" to missing work. Similarly, they may assign a zero to tests for other reasons. But a zero can be devastating (it is so far from even a passing grade that it is virtually impossible for the student to recover). This practice can only be viewed as punitive. A better strategy might be to use a system whereby grades are converted to a reasonable set of numerical grades (e.g., A = 4, B = 3, etc.), with 0 given for any missing work. To illustrate the difference in these two strategies, consider a student who misses one assignment out of five. If she were given a zero for the missing work and her scores for the assignments were 92, 86, 0, 73, and 91, her average score would be 68.4, or a D in a 60–70–80–90 grading scheme. Converting the scores using the letter grades, on the other hand, would give her a mean of 2.6, which would be a solid C. Another solution used in some schools is to award a minimum grade of 50 on a 100-point scale, to avoid having a single zero make success impossible. A study of this in high schools found that a minimum grade did not cause grade inflation and had benefits in terms of course passing (Carey & Carifio, 2012).

Sometimes a student's performance on a test or a quiz seems unusually poor for him or her. Such atypical assessments might occur for nonacademic reasons, such as a disruption at home or in school. A private conversation with the student about the test or quiz might uncover a problem that should be looked into, and the student might be given an opportunity to retake the test. Some teachers drop the lowest score a student receives on quizzes to avoid penalizing the student for one unusual slippage.

THE INTENTIONAL TEACHER
Using What You Know about Assessing Student Learning to Improve Teaching and Learning

Intentional teachers assess student learning in ways that align with both their goals and their instruction. They use assessment results to adjust their instruction and to provide important feedback to students, families, and communities. Intentional teachers know that no one measure is ideal for every circumstance, and they implement a range of assessments that fits their purposes and circumstances.

- They plan courses, units, and lessons around essential objectives.
- They carefully align their assessments of students' learning with these objectives.
- They use taxonomies of instructional objectives to be sure that they teach all types of objectives, not just knowledge and comprehension.
- They use formative assessments continually to find out what students have learned so far, and then use that information both to inform students and to adjust the level and pace of their teaching.
- They create tests and quizzes that touch on all types of learning and focus on key unit objectives.
- They create assessments that reliably determine whether students have or have not mastered essential concepts and skills.
- They use a variety of response formats in tests, including constructed-response as well as multiple-choice and fill-in-the-blanks questions.
- They assess higher-order skills, such as problem solving and creativity.

- For appropriate content, they collect and evaluate portfolios of student work so they can determine how students are progressing on authentic tasks. Examples include compositions, problem solving, art projects, and music performances.
- They give grades fairly and reliably based on students' achievement of standards, and explain to students and their parents what the grades were based on and what needs to be done to improve them.
- They proactively engage students and parents in discussions about grading, with an emphasis on what has been accomplished and what remains to be accomplished.
- They give students opportunities to improve their grades by retaking similar tests after doing additional studying, or use a mastery grading system in which students have multiple opportunities to meet standards.

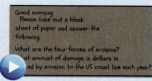

MyEdLab

Application Exercise 13.1

In the Pearson etext, watch a classroom video. Then use the guidelines in "The Intentional Teacher" to answer a set of questions that will help you reflect on and understand the teaching and learning presented in the video.

One important principle in report card grading is that grades should never be a surprise. Students should always know how their grades will be computed, whether classwork and homework are included, and whether class participation and effort are taken into account. Being clear about standards for grading helps you avert many complaints about unexpectedly low grades and, more important, lets students know exactly what they must do to improve their grades (Guskey, 2014; O'Connor & Wormeli, 2011; Reeves, 2015).

Many schools give an "interim" grade in the middle of a marking period, which gives students an early idea of how they are doing and a warning if they seem headed for trouble. A variation on this practice is to provide an interim grade only if students are heading for a D or F. Adding comments to the grade to explain what the student needs to do to earn a higher grade can be very helpful in maintaining motivation and improving performance (Dueck, 2014).

Another important principle is that grades should be private. There is no need for students to know one another's grades; making grades public only invites invidious comparisons among students. Finally, it is important to restate that grades are only one method of student evaluation. Written evaluations can provide useful information to parents and students (Marzano, Yanoski, Hoegh, & Simms, 2013). Computerized gradebooks are now widely available and widely used. Guskey (2014), however, warns that you should be careful when using this time-saving software and avoid letting the program make decisions that you should make yourself (Mertler, 2014).

MyEdLab Self-Check 13.4

SUMMARY

What Are Instructional Objectives and How Are They Used?

Research supports the use of instructional, or behavioral, objectives, which are clear statements about what students should know and be able to do at the end of a lesson, unit, or course. These statements also specify the conditions of performance and the criteria for assessment. In lesson planning, task analysis contributes to the formulation of objectives, and backward planning facilitates the development of specific objectives from general objectives in a course of study. Objectives are closely linked to assessment. Bloom's taxonomy of educational objectives classifies educational objectives from simple to complex, including knowledge, comprehension, application, analysis, synthesis, and evaluation. A behavior content matrix helps to ensure that objectives cover many levels.

Why Is Evaluation Important?

Formal measures of student performance or learning are important as feedback for students and teachers, as information for parents, as guidance for selection and certification, as data for assessing school accountability, and as incentives for increasing student effort.

How Is Student Learning Evaluated?

Strategies for evaluation include formative evaluation; summative evaluation; norm-referenced evaluation, in which a student's scores are compared with other students' scores; and criterion-referenced evaluation, in which students' scores are compared to a standard of mastery. Students are evaluated through tests or performances. The appropriate method of evaluation depends on the goal of evaluation. For example, if the goal of testing is to find out whether students have mastered a key concept in a lesson, a criterion-referenced formative quiz or a performance would be the most appropriate.

How Are Tests Constructed?

Tests are constructed to elicit evidence of student learning in relation to the instructional objectives. Achievement tests should be constructed in keeping with six principles: They should (1) measure clearly defined learning objectives, (2) examine a representative sample of the learning tasks included in instruction, (3) include the types of test items most appropriate for measuring the desired learning outcomes, (4) fit the uses that will be made of the results, (5) be as reliable as possible and interpreted with caution, and (6) improve learning. A table of specifications helps in the planning of tests that correspond to instructional objectives. Types of test items include multiple-choice, true–false, completion, matching, short essay, and problem-solving items. Each type of test item has optimal uses, along with advantages and disadvantages. For example, if you want to learn how students think about, analyze, synthesize, or evaluate some aspect of course content, a short essay test might be most appropriate, provided that you have time to administer it and evaluate students' responses.

What Are Authentic, Portfolio, and Performance Assessments?

Portfolio assessment and performance assessment avoid the negative aspects of pencil-and-paper multiple-choice tests by requiring students to demonstrate their learning through work samples or direct real-world applications. Performance assessments are usually scored according to rubrics that specify in advance the type of performance expected.

How Are Grades Determined?

Grading systems differ in elementary and secondary education. For example, informal assessments might be more appropriate at the elementary level, whereas letter grades become increasingly important at the secondary level. Grading standards might be absolute or relative (grading on the curve). Performance grading is a way for teachers to determine what children know and can do. A key requirement for performance grading is judicious collection of work samples from students that indicate level of performance. Another approach is to give students tests in which they can show their abilities. Other systems include contract grading and mastery grading. Report card grades typically average scores on tests, homework, seatwork, class participation, deportment, and effort.

KEY TERMS

Review the following key terms from the chapter.

affective objectives 347

assessment 345

backward planning 343

behavior content matrix 347

completion items 361

criterion-referenced interpretations 350

distractors 357

evaluation 348

evaluative descriptors 367

foils 357

formative evaluations 350

halo effect 366

instructional objective 340

learning objectives 345

SELF-ASSESSMENT: PRACTICING FOR LICENSURE

Directions: The chapter-opening vignette addresses indicators that are often assessed in state licensure exams. Reread the chapter-opening vignette and then respond to the following questions.

1. Mr. Sullivan is having a difficult time connecting what he is teaching and what he is testing. Which of the following evaluation tools is most likely to help Mr. Sullivan make the connection?
   a. Multiple-choice test
   b. Instructional objectives
   c. Traditional teaching strategies
   d. Open-book testing

2. Mr. Sullivan might use a chart showing how a concept or skill will be taught at different cognitive levels in relation to an instructional objective. What is this chart called?
   a. Task analysis
   b. Backward planning
   c. Behavior content matrix
   d. Table of specifications

3. Mr. Sullivan might improve the connection between what he teaches and what he tests by following which of the following pieces of advice?
   a. Include all instructional content in the test.
   b. Make a test that includes all item types: true–false, multiple-choice, matching, short answer, essay, and problem-solving items.
   c. Be free from the confines of instructional objectives.
   d. Design a test that fits the particular uses that will be made of the results.

4. Which of the following types of evaluation is Mr. Sullivan using?
   a. Summative
   b. Aptitude
   c. Affective
   d. Task analysis

5. Why would Mr. Sullivan choose to construct a table of specifications?
   a. To indicate the type of learning to be assessed for different instructional objectives
   b. To measure a student's performance against a specified standard
   c. To make comparisons among students
   d. To identify conditions of mastery

6. In a brief essay, explain why evaluation is important.

7. Write instructional objectives, create a table of specifications using Bloom's taxonomy, develop a lesson plan, and write a short test for a topic of study.

MyEdLab **Licensure Exam 13.1** Answer questions and receive instant feedback in your Pearson eText in MyEdLab.

Highwaystarz/Fotolia

CHAPTER FOURTEEN

Standardized Tests and Accountability

LEARNING OUTCOMES

At the end of this chapter, you should be able to:

14.1 Identify different types of standardized tests and their uses

14.2 Address issues related to standardized testing and in-class testing

14.3 Discuss how teachers are held accountable for their students' achievement

14.4 Describe how knowledge of standardized tests and accountability informs intentional teaching

Jennifer Tranh is a fifth-grade teacher at Lincoln Elementary School. She is meeting with the parents of one of her students, Anita McKay.

"Hello, Mr. and Mrs. McKay," says Ms. Tranh when Anita's parents arrive. "I'm so glad you could come. Please take a seat, and we'll start right in. First, I wanted to tell you what a delight it is to have Anita in my class. She is always so cheerful, so willing to help others. Her work is coming along very well in most subjects, although there are a few areas I'm a bit concerned about. Before I start, though, do you have any questions for me?"

Mr. and Mrs. McKay say to Ms. Tranh that they think Anita is having a good year and that they are eager to hear how she is doing.

"All right. First of all, I know you've seen the results of Anita's California Achievement Tests. We call those 'CATs' for short. Most parents don't understand these test scores, so I'll try to explain them to you. First, let's look at math. As you know, Anita has always been a good math student, and her scores and grades reflect this. She got an A on her last report card and a percentile score of 90 on math computations. That means that she scored better than 90 percent of all fifth-graders in the country. She did almost as well on math concepts and applications—her score is in the 85th percentile."

"What does this 'grade equivalent' mean?" asks Mrs. McKay.

"That's a score that's supposed to tell how a child is achieving in relation to his or her grade level. For example, Anita's grade equivalent of 6.9 means that she is scoring more than a year ahead of the fifth-grade level."

"Does this mean she could skip sixth-grade math?" asks Mr. McKay.

Ms. Tranh smiles. "I'm afraid not. It's hard to explain, but a grade equivalent score of 6.9 is supposed to be what a student at the end of sixth grade would score on a fifth-grade test. It doesn't mean that Anita already knows sixth-grade material. Besides, we take any student's testing information with a grain of salt. We rely much more on day-to-day performance and classroom tests to tell how each student is doing. In this case the standardized CAT scores are pretty consistent with what we see Anita doing in class. But let me show you another example that shows less consistency. I'm sure you noticed that even though Anita's reading grades have been pretty good, her scores in reading comprehension were much lower than her scores in most other areas. She got a percentile score of only 30. This is almost a year below grade level. I think Anita is a pretty good reader, so I was surprised. I gave her another test, the Gray Oral Reading Test. This test is given one-on-one, so it provides a much better indication of how well students are reading. On the Gray, Anita scored at grade level. This score is more indicative of where I see her reading in class, so I'm not concerned about her in this area.

"On the other hand, there is a concern I have about Anita that is not reflected in her standardized tests. She scored near the 70th percentile in both language mechanics and language expression. This might make you think Anita's doing great in language arts, and she is doing well in many ways. However, I'm concerned about Anita's writing. I keep a portfolio of student writing over the course of the year. This is Anita's here. She's showing some development in writing, but I think she could do a lot better. As you can see, her spelling, punctuation, and grammar are excellent, but her stories are very short and factual. As you know, we don't give grades

(continued)

in writing. We use a rating form that shows the student's development toward proficient writing. Based on her portfolio I rated her at proficient, but to go to advanced, I'd like to see her write more and really let her imagination loose. She tells great stories orally, but I think she's so concerned about making a mistake in mechanics that she writes very conservatively. On vacation you might encourage her to write a journal or to do other writing wherever it makes sense."

"But if her standardized test scores are good in language," says Mrs. McKay, "doesn't that mean that she's doing well?"

"Test scores tell us some things, but not everything," says Ms. Tranh. "The CAT is good on simple things such as math computations and language mechanics, but it is not so good at telling us what children can actually do. That's why I keep portfolios of student work in writing, in math problem solving, and in science. I want to see how children are actually developing in their ability to apply their skills to doing real things and solving real problems. In fact, now that we've gone over Anita's grades and standardized tests, let's look at her portfolios, and I think you'll get a much better idea of what she's doing here in school."

USING YOUR EXPERIENCE

COOPERATIVE LEARNING AND CREATIVE THINKING Act out this parent–teacher conference about test scores. Have volunteers take the roles of Mrs. McKay, Mr. McKay, and Ms. Tranh. One volunteer can act as moderator to clarify any miscommunications and to keep the conference moving.

CRITICAL THINKING What do you know from reading this case? What do you still want to know? And what did you learn here? Has Ms. Tranh told us everything we need to know about Anita's standardized test scores and portfolio assessments in writing, math, and science?

InTASC 10

Leadership and Collaboration

Jennifer Tranh's conversation with the McKays illustrates some of the uses and limitations of grades and standardized tests. The CATs and the Gray Oral Reading Test give Ms. Tranh information that relates Anita's performance in some areas to national norms, and Anita's grades give Ms. Tranh some idea how Anita is doing relative to her classmates, but neither standardized tests nor grades provide the detail or comprehensiveness reflected in the portfolios of work and other observations of Anita's performance. Taken together, cautiously interpreted standardized tests, grades, portfolios of work, and other classroom assessments provide a good picture of Anita's performance. Each has value, and all the information should be evaluated in making educational decisions.

WHAT ARE STANDARDIZED TESTS AND HOW ARE THEY USED?

InTASC 6

Assessment

Do you remember taking SATs, ACTs, or other college entrance examinations? Did you ever wonder how those tests were constructed, what the scores meant, and to what extent your scores represented what you really knew or could really do? The SATs and other college entrance examinations are **standardized tests**. Unlike the teacher-made tests discussed in Chapter 13, a standardized test is typically given under the same "standardized" conditions to thousands of similar students for whom the test is designed, which enables the test publisher to establish norms to which any individual score can be compared. For example, if a representative national sample of fourth-graders had an average score of 37 items correct on a 50-item standardized test, then 37 would be the fourth-grade "national norm" on this test, the score dividing those above and those below "the norm."

Traditional standardized tests have been subjected to a great deal of criticism and controversy, and today a wide variety of alternative assessments are used. However, standardized tests of many kinds continue to be given for a wide range of purposes at all levels of education. This chapter explains how and why standardized tests are implemented and how scores on these tests can be interpreted and applied to important educational decisions. It discusses why standardized tests are used to hold districts, schools, and teachers accountable for student performance, and how federal and state policies focusing on accountability have increased the stakes. It also includes information on criticisms of standardized testing and on alternatives that are being developed, debated, and applied.

Standardized tests are usually meant to offer a yardstick that teacher-made tests cannot provide, against which to compare individuals or groups of students. For example, suppose a child's parents ask you how their daughter is doing in math. You say, "Fine, she got a score of 81 percent on her latest math test." For some purposes this information would be adequate. But for other purposes the parents might want to know much more. How does 81 percent compare to the scores of other students in this class? How about other students in the school, the district, the state, or the whole country? In some contexts the score of 81 percent might help to qualify the girl for a special program for students with mathematical gifts; in others it might suggest the need for remedial instruction. Suppose you found that the class averaged 85 percent correct on the math test. How is this class doing compared to other math classes or to students nationwide? A teacher-made test cannot yield this information.

Standardized tests are typically carefully constructed to provide accurate information about students' levels of performance. Most often, curriculum experts establish what students at a particular age should know and be able to do in a particular subject. Then questions are written to assess the various skills or information that students are expected to possess. The questions are tried out on various groups of students. Items that nearly all students get right or nearly all miss are usually dropped, as are items that students find unclear or confusing. Patterns of scores are carefully examined. If students who score well on most items do no better than lower-scoring students on a particular item, then that item is likely to be dropped.

Eventually, a final test is developed and given to a large selected group of students from all over the country. Attempts are usually made to ensure that this group resembles the larger population of students who will ultimately use the test. For example, a test of geometry for eleventh-graders might be given to a sampling of eleventh-graders in urban, rural, and suburban locations; in different regions of the country; in private as well as public schools; and to students with different levels of preparation in mathematics. Care is taken to include students of all socioeconomic and ethnic backgrounds. This step establishes the **norms** for the test, which provide an indication of how an average student will score (Brookhart & Nitko, 2015; Kaplan & Saccuzzo, 2013; Kubiszyn & Borich, 2010; Popham, 2014a). Scores on the new test might be compared to those on existing tests. Finally, a testing manual is prepared, explaining how the test is to be given, scored, and interpreted. The test is now ready for general use. The test development process has created a test whose scores have meaning outside the confines of a particular classroom or school and can be used in a variety of ways. Important functions of standardized testing include placement, diagnosis, evaluation, and school improvement.

Selection and Placement

Standardized tests are often used to select students for entry or placement in specific programs. For example, the SAT (Scholastic Assessment Test) or ACT (American College Testing Program) that you probably took in high school may have been considered by your college admissions board in deciding whether to accept you as a student. Similarly, admission to special programs for students who are gifted and talented might depend in part on standardized test scores. Along with other information, standardized tests can provide information to help you decide whether to place students in special-education programs. Elementary schools may apply standardized reading scores for placing students in reading groups. Some colleges base prerequisites for certain courses on making certain scores. Standardized tests are sometimes used to determine eligibility for grade-to-grade promotion, graduation from high school, or entry into an occupation. For example, most states make standardized test scores part of the teacher certification process. Some states and districts use students' test scores, along with other information, to evaluate teachers.

Diagnosis

Standardized tests are often used to diagnose individual students' learning problems or strengths (Nicoll, Lu, Pignone, & McPhee, 2012). For example, a student who is performing poorly in school might be given a battery of tests to determine whether he or she has a learning disability. At the same time, the testing might identify specific deficits that need remediation. Teachers frequently employ diagnostic tests of reading skills, such as the Gray Oral Reading Test that Ms. Tranh used, to identify a student's particular reading problem. For example, a diagnostic test

Connections 14.1
For discussions of between-class and within-class ability grouping, see Chapter 9.

might indicate that a student's decoding skills are fine but that reading comprehension is poor; or that a student has good computation skills but lacks problem-solving skills. More fine-grained diagnostic tests might tell a teacher that a physics student is doing well in states of matter but not scientific measurement, or that a foreign language student has a good understanding of grammar but lacks competence in expression. Sophisticated assessments can help you determine the depth of students' understanding of complex concepts.

Evaluation and Accountability

Perhaps the most common application of standardized testing is to evaluate students' progress and teachers' and schools' effectiveness. For example, districts and states use tests to hold educators accountable for the achievement of their students by evaluating the gains that schools make in overall student performance. Parents often want to know how their children are doing in comparison with the typical achievement of children at their grade level. For individual students, standardized test scores are meaningful in evaluation only if you use them along with other information, such as the students' actual performance in school and in other contexts, as Ms. Tranh did. Many students who score poorly on standardized tests often excel in school, college, or occupations; either they have trouble taking tests or they have important skills that are not measured by such tests. However, some students demonstrate their achievement best on standardized tests. For an extended discussion of accountability and related educational policies, see the section "How Are Educators Held Accountable for Student Achievement?" later in this chapter.

School Improvement

Standardized tests can contribute to improving the schooling process. The results of some standardized tests provide information about appropriate student placement and diagnostic information that is important in remediation. In addition, achievement tests can guide curriculum development and revision when areas of weakness appear (see Kallick & Colosimo, 2009). Standardized tests can play a role in guidance and counseling as well. This is true not only for achievement and aptitude testing but also for more specialized types of measures, such as vocational interest inventories and other psychological scales employed for counseling students.

Schools often turn to academic achievement tests to evaluate the relative success of competing educational programs or strategies. For example, if a teacher or school tries out an innovative teaching strategy, tests can help reveal whether it was more successful than previous methods. Statewide and districtwide test results often serve as a yardstick by which citizens can judge the success of their local schools. However, educating students is a complex process, and standardized tests can provide only a small portion of the information necessary for evaluating teachers, programs, or schools. Problems arise when standardized test scores are over-emphasized or used for purposes other than those for which they were designed.

Certification Pointer
You may be asked on your teacher certification test to define standardized tests and discuss their purposes.

WHAT TYPES OF STANDARDIZED TESTS ARE GIVEN?

Three kinds of standardized tests are commonly used in school settings: aptitude tests, norm-referenced achievement tests, and criterion-referenced achievement tests (Kaplan & Saccuzzo, 2013; Popham, 2014a, b; Reynolds & Livingston, 2012; Salkind, 2013). An **aptitude test** is designed to assess students' abilities. It is meant to predict the ability of students to learn or to perform particular types of tasks, rather than to measure how much the students have already learned. The most widely used aptitude tests measure general intellectual aptitude, but many other, more specific tests measure particular aptitudes, such as mechanical or perceptual abilities or reading readiness. The SAT, for example, is meant to predict a student's aptitude for college studies. An aptitude test is successful to the degree that it predicts performance. For example, a reading readiness test given to kindergartners that did not accurately predict how well the students would read when they reached first or second grade would be of little use.

Achievement tests are used to (1) predict students' future performance in a course of study, (2) diagnose students' difficulties, (3) serve as formative tests of students' progress, and (4) serve as summative tests of learning.

Norm-referenced achievement tests are assessments of a student's knowledge of a particular content area, such as mathematics, reading, or French as a foreign language. The norms that are referenced are the results from a representative group of students to which scores can be compared. The tests are purposely constructed to reveal differences among students. Those differences are expected to be the result of quality of instruction and student learning, rather than differences from school to school in curricula, so they assess some but not all of the skills that are taught in any one school. A norm-referenced achievement test cannot range too broadly because it is designed for nationwide use, and the curricula for any given subject vary from district to district. For example, if some seventh-graders learn about base-2 arithmetic or Venn diagrams but others do not, then these topics are unlikely to appear on a national mathematics test.

A criterion-referenced achievement test also assesses a student's knowledge of subject matter, but rather than comparing the achievement of an individual student against national norms, it is designed to measure the degree to which the student has mastered certain well-specified skills. The information that a criterion-referenced test produces is quite specific: "Thirty-seven percent of Ontario fifth-graders can fill in the names of the major Western European nations on an outline map" or "Ninety-three percent of twelfth-graders at Alexander Hamilton High School know that increasing the temperature of a gas in a closed container increases the gas's pressure." Sometimes criterion-referenced test scores are used in comparisons between schools or between districts, but typically no representative norming group is used. If a group of curriculum experts decides that every fifth-grader in Illinois should be able to fill in an outline map of South America, then the expectation for that item is 100 percent; it is of less interest whether Illinois fifth-graders score better or worse on this item than students in other states. What is more important is that, overall, students improve each year on this item.

Aptitude Tests

Although aptitude tests, norm-referenced achievement tests, and criterion-referenced tests are distinct from one another in theory, there is in fact considerable overlap among them. For example, aptitudes are usually measured by evaluating achievement over a very broadly defined domain. School learning can thus affect students' aptitude test scores, and a student who scores well on one type of test will usually score well on another (Popham, 2014a).

GENERAL INTELLIGENCE TESTS The most common aptitude tests given in school are tests of **intelligence**, or general aptitude for school learning (Kaplan & Saccuzzo, 2013; Reynolds & Livingston, 2012). The intelligence quotient, or IQ, is the score that is most often associated with intelligence testing, but other types of scores are also calculated.

Intelligence tests are designed to provide a general indication of individuals' aptitudes in many areas of intellectual functioning. Intelligence itself is seen as the ability to deal with abstractions, to learn, and to solve problems (Sternberg, Jarvin, & Grigorenko, 2009), and tests of intelligence focus on these skills. Intelligence tests give students a wide variety of questions to answer and problems to solve.

THE MEASUREMENT OF IQ The measurement of the intelligence quotient (IQ) was introduced in the early 1900s by Alfred Binet, a French psychologist, to identify children with such serious learning difficulties that they were unlikely to profit from regular classroom instruction (Esping & Plucker, 2015). The scale that Binet developed to measure intelligence assessed a wide range of mental characteristics and skills, such as memory, knowledge, vocabulary, and problem solving. Binet tested a large number of students of various ages to establish norms (expectations) for overall performance on his tests. He then expressed IQ as a ratio of **mental age** (the average test scores of students at a particular age) to **chronological age**, multiplied by 100. For example, 6-year-olds (chronological age [CA] = 6) who scored at the average for all 6-year-olds (mental age [MA] = 6) would have an IQ of 100 (6/6 × 100 = 100). Any 6-year-olds who scored at a level typical of 7-year-olds (MA = 7) would have IQs of about 117 (7/6 × 100 = 117).

Over the years the mental age/chronological age ratio has been dropped, and IQ is now defined as having a mean of 100 and a standard deviation of 15 (a standard deviation is a measure of how

Connections 14.2
To learn more about student differences in general intelligence, specific aptitudes, and abilities and learning styles, see Chapter 4.

spread out scores are, defined later in this chapter) at any age. Most scores fall near the mean, with small numbers of scores extending well above and below the mean, forming a "bell curve." In theory, about 68 percent of all individuals will have IQs within one standard deviation of the mean; that is, from 85 (one standard deviation below the mean) to 115 (one standard deviation above), and 95 percent will be found in the range up to two standard deviations from the mean (between 70 and 130).

Intelligence tests are designed to provide a general indication of an individual's aptitudes in many areas of intellectual functioning. The most widely used tests contain many different scales. Each scale measures a different component of intelligence. Most often, a person who scores well on one scale also does well on others, but this is not always so. The same person might do very well on general comprehension and similarities, less well on arithmetic reasoning, and poorly on block design, for example.

Intelligence tests are administered either to individuals or to groups. Tests such as the Otis–Lennon Mental Ability Tests, the Lorge–Thorndike Intelligence Tests, and the California Test of Mental Maturity, are often given to large groups of students as general assessments of intellectual aptitude. These tests are not as accurate or detailed as intelligence tests administered individually to people by trained psychologists, such as the Wechsler Intelligence Test for Children–Fourth Edition (WISC-IV) or the Stanford–Binet test. For example, students who are being assessed for possible placement in special education for learning difficulties usually take an individually administered test (most often the WISC-IV), along with other tests.

IQ scores are important because they are correlated with school performance. That is, students who have higher IQs tend, on the average, to get better grades, score higher on achievement tests, and so on. These educational attainments then translate into success in employment and income, on average (Hauser, 2010). By the time a child is about age 6, IQ estimates tend to become relatively stable, and most people's IQs remain about the same into adulthood. However, some people experience substantial changes in their estimated IQ, often because of schooling or other environmental influences (Ceci, 1991).

Connections 14.3
For a discussion of the use of IQ scores in the classification of learners with exceptionalities or for special-education services, see Chapter 12.

MULTIFACTOR APTITUDE TESTS Another form of aptitude test that provides a breakdown of more specific skills is the **multifactor aptitude battery**. Many such tests are available, with a range of content and emphases. They include scholastic abilities tests such as the SAT; elementary and secondary school tests, such as the Differential Aptitude Test, the Cognitive Abilities Test, and the Test of Cognitive Skills; reading readiness tests, such as the Metropolitan Reading Readiness Test; and various developmental scales for preschool children. At a minimum, most of these tests provide not only overall aptitude scores but also subscores for verbal and nonverbal aptitudes. Often, subscores are even more finely divided to describe more specific abilities.

Norm-Referenced Achievement Tests

Whereas aptitude tests focus on general learning potential and knowledge acquired both in school and out, achievement tests focus on skills or abilities that are traditionally taught in schools. In general, standardized achievement tests fall into one of four categories: achievement batteries, diagnostic tests, single-subject achievement measures, and criterion-referenced achievement measures (Popham, 2014; Salkind, 2013).

ACHIEVEMENT BATTERIES Standardized **achievement batteries**, such as the California Achievement Test, the Iowa Tests of Basic Skills, the Comprehensive Test of Basic Skills, the Stanford Achievement Test, and the Metropolitan Achievement Tests, are used to measure individual or group achievement in a variety of subject areas. These survey batteries include several small tests, each in a different subject area, and are usually administered to a group over a period of several days. Many of the achievement batteries available for use in schools are similar in construction and content. However, because of slight differences among the tests in the instructional objectives and subject matter sampled within the subtests, it is important before selecting a particular test to examine it carefully for its match with a specific school curriculum and for its appropriateness relative to school goals. Achievement batteries usually have several forms for various age or grade levels so that achievement can be monitored over a period of several years (Kubiszyn & Borich, 2010; Salkind, 2013).

NATIONAL ASSESSMENT OF EDUCATIONAL PROGRESS (NAEP) The National Assessment of Educational Progress is a very important test given by the U. S. Department of Education to a selection of students in all states. It is like other achievement tests but is used to measure growth of all students in the United States on reading, math, science, and writing. NAEP is given only every two years in math and reading, and less frequently in science and writing. In addition to indicating gains over time,

NAEP enables the U.S. government to compare the performance of states and also certain large cities. NAEP scores are not used for accountability but, rather, are designed to provide a fair measure for the whole country, because state test scores are not designed to remain stable or to be comparable to tests given in other states. In fact, states scoring highest in the country in percent passing their own state tests often score at the bottom on NAEP, and vice versa. For NAEP scores over time and in different states and cities, visit the website of the National Center for Educational Statistics (www.nces.gov).

DIAGNOSTIC TESTS Differing from achievement batteries in that they generally focus on a specific content area and emphasize the skills that are thought to be important for mastery of that subject matter, **diagnostic tests** produce much more detailed information than other achievement tests (Nicoll et al., 2012). For example, a standardized mathematics test often produces scores for math computations, concepts, and applications, whereas a diagnostic test would give scores on more specific skills, such as adding decimals or solving two-step word problems. Diagnostic tests are available mostly for reading and mathematics and are intended to show specific areas of strength and weakness in these skills. The results can be used to guide remedial instruction or to structure learning experiences for students who are expected to learn the skill.

SUBJECT AREA ACHIEVEMENT TESTS Teachers make up most classroom tests for assessing skills in specific subjects. However, school districts can purchase specific achievement tests for almost any subject. A problem with such tests is that unless they are tied to the particular curriculum and instructional strategies used in the classroom, they may not adequately represent the content that has been taught. If standardized achievement tests are considered for evaluating learning in specific areas, the content of the test should be closely examined for its match with the district curriculum, the instruction the students have received, and the district's or state's standards and assessments.

Criterion-Referenced Achievement Tests

Criterion-referenced tests differ from norm-referenced standardized tests in several ways (McMillan, 2011; Popham, 2014). Such tests can take the form of a survey battery, a diagnostic test, or a single-subject test. In contrast to norm-referenced tests, which are designed for schools with varying curricula, criterion-referenced tests are most meaningful when constructed around a well-defined set of objectives. For many tests, these objectives can be chosen by the school district, building administrator, or teacher. The items on the test are selected to match specific instructional objectives, often with three to five items measuring each objective. Therefore, the tests can indicate which objectives individual students or the class as a whole have mastered. Test results can be used to guide future instruction or remedial activities. For this reason these tests are sometimes referred to as objective-referenced tests.

Criterion-referenced tests differ from other achievement tests in the way they are scored and how the results are interpreted. On criterion-referenced tests, it is generally the score for each objective that is important. Results could show, for example, how many students can multiply two digits by two digits or how many can write a business letter correctly. Moreover, students' scores on the total test or on specific objectives are interpreted with respect to some criterion of adequate performance independent of group performance. Examples of criterion-referenced tests include tests for drivers and pilots, which are designed to determine who can drive or fly, not who is in the top 20 percent of drivers or pilots. Tests for teachers are also criterion referenced.

Scores on criterion-referenced tests are frequently reported in the form of the number of items that the student got correct on each objective. From these data you can gauge whether the student has mastered the objective.

Standard Setting

When tests are used for making decisions about mastery of a subject or topic, some procedure must be employed to determine the test cutoff scores that indicate various proficiency levels (Kubiszyn & Borich, 2010; McClarty, Way, Porter, Beinters, & Miles, 2013; Popham, 2014a). Most methods of establishing a **cutoff score** rely on the professional judgment of representative groups of teachers and other educators. Qualified professionals might examine each item in a test and judge the probability that a student with a given level of proficiency would get the item correct. They then base the cutoff score for mastery or proficiency on these probabilities. Standards set using procedures like this are common in licensing exams as well as in many state and district accountability programs.

MyEdLab
Video Example 14.1
An expert in education, Gerald Bracey described both norm-referenced and criterion-referenced tests and discussed some limitations of each.

Connections 14.4
For more on norm-referenced and criterion-referenced testing, see Chapter 13.

Certification Pointer
On your teacher certification test you may need to know that a criterion-referenced test would give you better information than a norm-referenced test about how much each student has learned about a particular aspect of the curriculum.

HOW ARE STANDARDIZED TESTS INTERPRETED?

After students take a standardized test, the tests are usually sent for computer scoring to the central office or the test publisher. The students' raw scores (the number correct on each subtest) are translated into one or more **derived scores**, such as percentiles, grade equivalents, or normal curve equivalents, which relate the students' scores to those of the group on which the test was normed. These statistics are described in the following sections (see McMillan, 2011; Popham, 2014a).

Percentile Scores

A **percentile score**, or percentile rank (sometimes abbreviated in test reports as % ILE), indicates what percentage of students in the norming group scored lower than a particular score. For example, if a student achieved at the median for the norming group (that is, if equal numbers of students scored better than and worse than that student), the student would have a percentile rank of 50 because his or her scores exceeded those of 50 percent of the others in the norming group. If you ranked a group of 30 students from bottom to top on test scores, the 25th student from the bottom would score in the 83rd percentile ($25/30 \times 100$ 83.3).

Grade-Equivalent Scores

Grade-equivalent scores relate students' scores to the average scores obtained by students at a particular grade level. Let's say a norming group achieved an average raw score of 70 on a reading test at the beginning of fifth grade. This score would be established as a grade equivalent of 5.0. If a sixth-grade norming group achieved a test score of 80 in September, this would be established as a grade equivalent of 6.0. Now let's say that a fifth-grader achieved a raw score of 75. This is halfway between the score for 5.0 and that for 6.0, so this student would be assigned a grade equivalent of 5.5. The number after the decimal point is referred to as "months," so a grade equivalent of 5.5 would be read "five years, five months." In theory, a student in the third month of fifth grade should have a score of 5.3 (five years, three months), and so on. Only the 10 months of the regular academic year, September to June, are counted.

The advantage of grade equivalents is that they are easy to interpret and make some intuitive sense. For example, if an average student gains one grade equivalent each year, we call this progressing at expected levels. If we know that a student is performing 2 years below grade level (say, a ninth-grader is scoring at a level typical of seventh-graders), this gives us some understanding of how poorly the student is doing.

However, grade-equivalent scores should be interpreted as only a rough approximation (McMillan, 2011). For one thing, students do not gain steadily in achievement from month to month. For another, scores that are far from the expected grade level do not mean what they appear to mean. A fourth-grader who scores at, say, the 7.4 grade equivalent is by no means ready for seventh-grade work; this score simply means that the fourth-grader has thoroughly mastered fourth-grade work and has scored as well as a seventh-grader might on the fourth-grade test. Obviously, the average seventh-grader knows a great deal more than what is assessed on a fourth-grade test, so there is no real comparison between a fourth-grader who scores at a 7.4 grade equivalent and a seventh-grader who does so. The two tests they took are very different.

Shifting definitions of grade-level expectations can also complicate the interpretation of scores. On state accountability tests, far more than 50 percent of students often meet standards, even if the state average is low on national tests. This "test inflation" is sometimes called the "Lake Wobegon Effect." (In humorist Garrison Keillor's mythical town of Lake Wobegon, "All the children are above average.") Because the norms vary from test to test, statements about how many students are at a given level should always be taken with a grain of salt. What is more meaningful is how students are changing over time, or how one district, school, or subgroup compares to another on the same test (Popham, 2014a). State test scores tend to rise over time, as students and teachers get used to test formats and emphases. When this happens, states often change tests, and scores drop a long way all in one year. Then, for the next several years, scores improve again on the new test.

Standard Scores

Several kinds of scores describe test results according to their positions on the normal curve. A normal curve describes a distribution of scores in which most fall near the mean, or average, with a symmetrically smaller number of scores appearing the farther we go above or below the mean (Salkind, 2013). A frequency plot of a **normal distribution** produces a bell-shaped curve. For example, Figure 14.1 shows a frequency distribution from a test with a mean score of 50. Each × indicates one student who got a particular score; there are 10 ×'s at 50, so we know that 10 students got this score. Nine students got 49s and nine got 51s, and so on, and very few students made scores above 60 or below 40. Normal distributions like the one shown in Figure 14.2 are common in nature; for example, height and weight are normally distributed throughout the general adult population. Standardized tests are designed so that extremely few students will get every item or no item correct, so scores on them are typically normally distributed.

STANDARD DEVIATION One important concept related to normal distributions is the **standard deviation**, a measure of the dispersion of scores. The standard deviation is, roughly speaking, the average amount by which scores differ from the mean. For example, consider these two sets of scores:

Set A		Set B
85		70
70		68
65	< Mean >	65
60		62
45		60
Standard deviation: 14.6		Standard deviation: 4.1

Note that both sets have the same mean (65) but that otherwise they are quite different, Set A being more spread out than Set B. This is reflected in the fact that Set A has a much larger standard deviation (14.6) than Set B (4.1). The standard deviation of a set of scores indicates how spread out the distribution is. When scores or other data are normally distributed, we can predict how many scores will fall a given number of standard deviations from the mean. This is illustrated in Figure 14.2, which shows that in any normal distribution, about 34 percent of all scores fall between the mean and one standard deviation above the mean (+1 SD), and a similar number fall between the mean and one standard deviation below the mean (−1 SD). If you go out two standard deviations from the mean, about 95 percent of the scores are included.

Scores on standardized tests are often reported in terms of how far they lie from the mean as measured in standard deviation units. For example, IQ scores are normed so that there are a mean of 100 and a standard deviation of 15. This means that the average person will score 100, someone

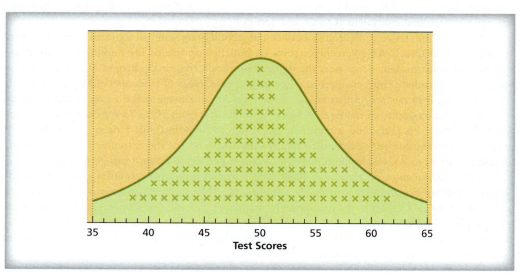

Test Scores

**FIGURE 14.1 •
Frequency of Scores
Forming a Normal
Curve**

If 100 people take a test and the score for each is marked by an *x* on a graph, the result could suggest a normal curve. In a normal distribution, most scores are at or near the mean (in this case, 50), and the number of scores progressively decreases farther from the mean.

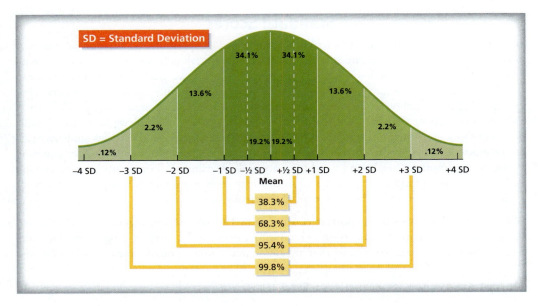

scoring one standard deviation above the mean will score 115, someone scoring one standard deviation below will score 85, and so on. Therefore, in theory about 68 percent of all IQ scores (that is, a little more than two-thirds) fall between 85 (−1 SD) and 115 (+1 SD). SAT scores are also normed according to standard deviations, with the mean for each scale set at 500 and a standard deviation of 100. That puts more than two-thirds of all scores between 400 and 600. For IQ, 95 percent will be between 70 (−2 SD) and 130 (+2 SD).

STANINES A standard score that is sometimes used is the **stanine score** (from the words <u>sta</u>ndard <u>nine</u>). Stanines have a mean of 5 and a standard deviation of 2, so each stanine represents a 0.5 standard deviation. Stanine scores are reported as whole numbers, so a person who earned a stanine score of 7 (+1 SD) actually fell somewhere between 0.75 SD and 1.25 SD above the mean.

NORMAL CURVE EQUIVALENTS Another type of standard score that is sometimes used is the **normal curve equivalent** (NCE). A normal curve equivalent can range from 1 to 99, with a mean of 50 and a standard deviation of approximately 21. NCE scores are similar to percentiles, except that intervals between NCE scores are equal (which is not the case with percentile scores). Another standard score, used more often in statistics than in reporting standardized test results, is the *z*-score, which sets the mean of a distribution at 0 and the standard deviation at 1. Figure 14.3 shows how a set of normally distributed raw scores with a mean percent correct of 70 percent and a standard deviation of 5 would be represented in *z*-scores, stanines, normal curve equivalents, percentile scores, and equivalent IQ and SAT scores.

Note the difference in the figure between percentile scores and all standard scores (*z*-score, stanine, NCE, IQ, and SAT). Percentile scores are bunched up around the middle of the distribution because most students score near the mean. This means that small changes in raw scores near the mean can produce large changes in percentiles (percentages of students below the score). In contrast, changes in raw scores that are far above or below the mean make a smaller difference in percentiles. For example, an increase of 5 points on the test from 70 to 75 moves a student from the 50th to the 84th percentile, an increase of 34 percentile points; but 5 more points (from 75 to 80) increases the student's percentile rank by only 14 points. At the extreme, the same 5-point increase, from 80 to 85, results in an increase of only 1 percentile point, from 98 to 99.

This characteristic of percentile ranks means that changes in percentiles should be interpreted cautiously. For example, one teacher might brag, "My average kids increased 23 percentile points [from 50 to 73], while your supposedly smart kids gained only 15 percentile points [from 84 to 99]. I really did a great job with them!" In fact, the bragging teacher's students gained only 3 points in raw score, or 0.6 standard deviation, whereas the other teacher's students gained 10 points in raw score, or 2 standard deviations!

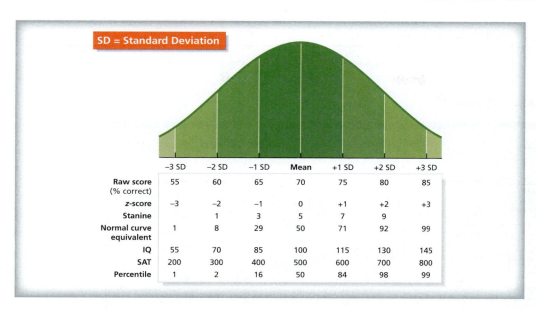

SD = Standard Deviation							
	−3 SD	−2 SD	−1 SD	Mean	+1 SD	+2 SD	+3 SD
Raw score (% correct)	55	60	65	70	75	80	85
z-score	−3	−2	−1	0	+1	+2	+3
Stanine		1	3	5	7	9	
Normal curve equivalent	1	8	29	50	71	92	99
IQ	55	70	85	100	115	130	145
SAT	200	300	400	500	600	700	800
Percentile	1	2	16	50	84	98	99

**FIGURE 14.3 •
Relationships
among Various Types
of Scores**

Raw scores that are normally distributed can be reported in a variety of ways. Each reporting method is characterized by its mean, by the range between high and low scores, and by the standard deviation interval.

THEORY INTO PRACTICE

Interpreting Standardized Test Scores

This section presents a guide to interpreting test reports for one widely used standardized test of academic performance, the Terra Nova, published by CTB/McGraw-Hill (2008). Other widely used nationally standardized tests (such as the CAT, the Iowa, and the Stanford) use similar report formats.

CLASS RECORD SHEET Figure 14.4 shows portions of a Terra Nova class record sheet for children in a Title I sixth-grade reading class.

Identification Data

Look first at the top of the form. The grade (6.7) indicates that at the time of post-testing, students were in month 7 of sixth grade (April; September is month 0). Information at the bottom left shows testing dates, school, district, test norm, and "quarter month" (i.e., weeks since school began).

Scores

Under each column, test scores are shown in two metrics: norm-references scores, and national percentiles. Section A at the far right shows us what the group score range was (for example, 54–90 in Reading). Section C highlights the average scores in the nation and charts the scores of Mrs. Jones's class in relation to that.

INDIVIDUAL PROFILE REPORT Like most standardized tests, the Terra Nova provides a detailed analysis of the test performance of each child. Figure 14.5 shows an example for a third-grader, Gary Jones (a real report, but not his real name).

At the top of the report is a list of Gary's scores in five subjects. In Reading, for example, Gary's Basic Understanding score is 91. The National Objectives Performance Index indicates that he could be expected to answer 79 questions correctly if he'd been tested on 100 such types of questions, a difference of 12 points, as indicated in the next box. The next box shows his mastery range as 48–70. Gary has done much better than this at 91. All of this information is interpreted visually in Section B.

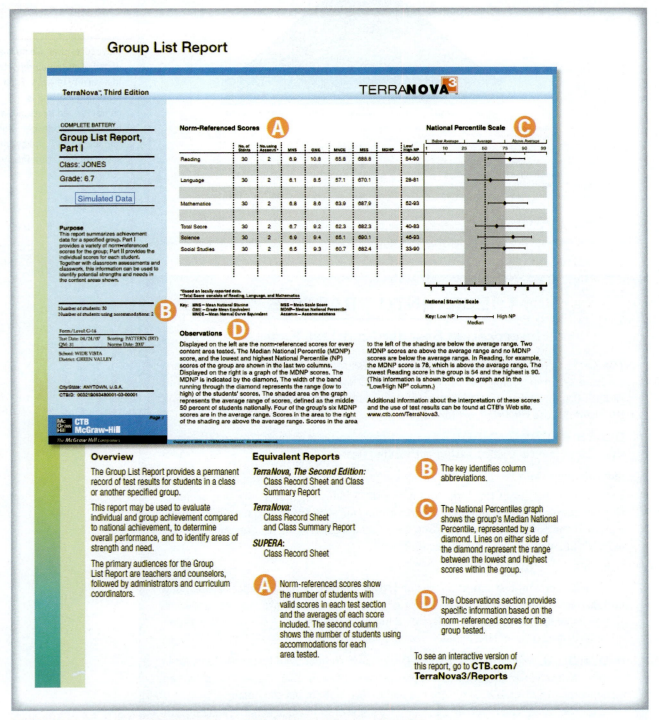

FIGURE 14.4 • Sample Class Record Sheet for a Standardized Test

When a class of students takes a standardized test, the results may be compared by means of a form similar to the one shown here.
Source: CTB-McGraw Hill (2008). *Introducing Terra Nova, 3rd edition: The new standard in achievement* (p. 4). Reproduced with permission of CTB/McGraw-Hill LLC. Terra Nova and CAT are registered trademarks of the McGraw-Hill Companies, Inc.

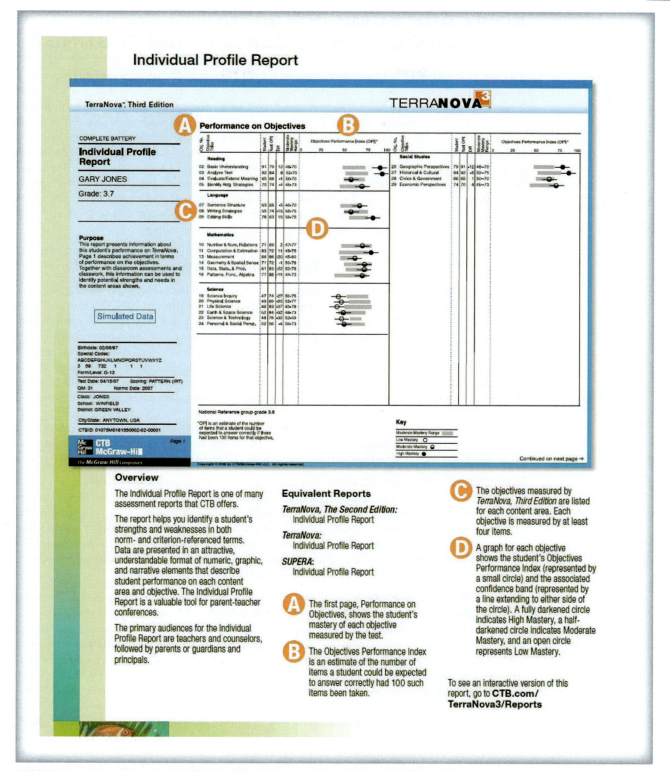

FIGURE 14.5 • Sample Individual Test Record for a Standardized Test

Reports for individuals who take standardized tests may include overall scores and scores on specific content objectives.

Source: CTB-McGraw Hill (2008). *Introducing Terra Nova, 3rd edition: The new standard in achievement* (p. 3). Reproduced with permission of CTB/McGraw-Hill LLC. Terra Nova and CAT are registered trademarks of the McGraw-Hill Companies, Inc.

WHAT ARE SOME ISSUES CONCERNING STANDARDIZED AND CLASSROOM TESTING?

The use of standardized tests to assess teachers, schools, and districts has increased dramatically in recent years. All states now have statewide testing programs in which students at selected grade levels take state tests. **No Child Left Behind (NCLB)**, the federal education law introduced in the Bush administration, required annual testing of reading and math in grades 3–8 and one grade in high school (usually 11). This is still true under the 2015 Every Student Succeeds Act (ESSA). State education departments analyze scores on these tests to evaluate the state's educational program as a whole and to compare the performance of individual school districts, schools, and teachers as part of accountability programs. Accountability is one of several issues related to uses and abuses of standardized tests. Issues concerning testing, standards, and related topics are among the most hotly debated questions in U.S. education (Brookhart & Nitko, 2015). In recent years there have been many developments and proposals for changes in testing.

Test Validity

We use test scores to make inferences about the students we are measuring. The **validity** of a test is the extent to which those inferences are justified (Kubiszyn & Borich, 2010; McMillan, 2011). The types of evidence that are used to evaluate the validity of a test vary according to the test's purpose. For example, if a test is being selected to help teachers and administrators determine which students are likely to have some difficulty with one or more aspects of instruction, primary interest will be in how well the test predicts future academic performance. However, if the aim is to describe the current achievement levels of a group of students, primary interest will focus on the accuracy of that description. In short, validity deals with the relevance of a test for its intended purpose.

Because of the various roles that tests are expected to play in schools and in the education process, three classes of evidence of validity are of concern to test users: content, criterion, and consequential evidence (Popham, 2014; Reynolds & Livingston, 2012; Salkind, 2013).

CONTENT EVIDENCE OF VALIDITY The most important criterion for the usefulness of a test—especially an achievement test—is whether it assesses what the user wants it to assess. The criterion called **content evidence** is an assessment of the degree of overlap between what is taught (or what should be taught) and what is tested. It is determined by content experts through careful comparison of the content of a test with state or district standards or with the objectives of a course or program. For example, a test that emphasizes dates and facts in history, while curricula and state or local standards emphasize key ideas of history, could not be considered valid.

CRITERION-RELATED EVIDENCE OF VALIDITY Gathered by looking at relationships between scores on the test and other sets of scores, **criterion–related evidence** compares test results with expectations based on understandings about these various assessments. For example, **predictive evidence** of a test's validity might be a measure of its ability to help predict future behavior. If we are using a test to predict students' future school performance, one way to examine the test's validity is to relate the test scores to some measure of students' subsequent performance. If an appropriate level of correspondence exists between the test and later performance, then the test can be used to provide predictive information for students. For example, test scores on SATs and ACTs have been shown to relate reasonably well to performance in college; many college admissions officers therefore use these scores (along with high school grades and other information) in deciding which applicants to accept.

Another criterion-related form called **concurrent evidence** of validity determines whether the test measures the same domain as another test. For example, if a group IQ test were to be substituted for an individual IQ test, one would first want to know whether they yielded comparable scores. By giving both tests to the same students in a study, one could evaluate the relationship between their scores.

Another form of concurrent evidence is called **discriminant evidence**. Achievement tests, for example, might be expected to show a relative *lack* of relationship with some variables. For example, a test of mechanical aptitude should be correlated with a test taker's ability to assemble a machine, but it should *not* correlate too well with verbal aptitude, which is a different skill, or with gender, which has nothing to do with the skill being measured.

Test Reliability

Whereas validity relates to the skills and knowledge measured by a test, the **reliability** of a test relates to the accuracy with which these skills and knowledge are measured (Kaplan & Saccuzzo, 2013; McMillan, 2011; Popham, 2014). Test scores are supposed to result from the knowledge and skill of the students being measured. But when a test is administered, aspects related to both the test itself and the circumstances surrounding its administration could cause the results to be inaccurate. In theory, if a student were to take equivalent tests twice, he or she should obtain the same score both times. The extent to which this would not occur involves the subject of reliability. Random features of the assessment (such as ambiguous test items, differences in specific item content, lucky or unlucky guessing, inconsistent motivation, and anxiety) all affect test scores and could cause results for different administrations of equivalent tests to differ. In addition, on essays or other performance measures, differences between raters reduce reliability. If it can be shown that individuals receive similar scores on two administrations of the same test, then some confidence can be placed in the test's reliability. If the scores are greatly inconsistent, it is difficult to put much faith in a particular test score. Generally, the longer the test and the more similar the items are to each other, the greater is the reliability.

Reliability is commonly measured using a coefficient that has a theoretical range from 0 to 1. The higher the number, the more reliable the test. In general, good standardized achievement tests should have coefficients of 0.90 or higher. Reliability might be thought of as reflecting how consistently a test measures something about students. Validity reflects how meaningful a test score is for something we care about. Thus a test cannot have validity without reliability, but a test can be reliable without being valid. As an example of reliability without validity, consider your reaction if your instructor assigned course grades on the basis of student height. He or she would have a highly reliable assessment (height can be determined quite accurately), but the scores would not be valid indicators of your knowledge or skill. Now imagine a test of creativity in which students were asked to describe innovative uses for a can opener. If raters could not agree on how to score students' responses, or if scores varied a great deal when students took the same test 6 months later, then the scale would lack reliability and therefore could not be considered valid.

Taken together, reliability and validity are most important when tests are being used for particularly important purposes, such as assigning students to special education or retaining them, or evaluating teachers or schools. For such purposes, multiple measures, all with high reliability and validity, are essential (Penfield, 2010).

Test Bias

Some major criticisms of traditional standardized tests involve issues of validity and reliability (see Linn, 2000). Critics argue that such tests

- Provide false information about the status of learning in the nation's schools (Bracey, 2003)
- Are unfair to (or biased against) some kinds of students (e.g., students from diverse backgrounds, those with limited proficiency in English, females, and students from low-income families) (see Lissitz & Schafer, 2002; Orfield & Kornhaber, 2001; Scheurich, Skrla, & Johnson, 2000; Suzuki, Ponterotto, & Meller, 2000)
- Tend to corrupt the processes of teaching and learning, often reducing teaching to mere preparation for testing
- Focus time, energy, and attention on the simpler skills that are easily tested, and away from higher-order thinking skills and creative endeavors (Campbell, 2000; Popham, 2014)

One major issue in the interpretation of standardized test scores is the possibility of **bias** against students from low-income or diverse backgrounds. In one sense, this is a question of test validity: A test that gives an unfair advantage to one or another category of student cannot be

Certification Pointer
Your teacher certification test is likely to require you to understand assessment-related issues such as test validity, test reliability, bias, and scoring concerns.

considered valid. Of greatest concern is the possibility that tests could be biased because their items assess knowledge or skills that are common to one group or culture but not to another. For example, a test that includes a reading comprehension passage about a trip to the beach could be biased against students who live far from a beach or cannot afford to travel to a beach. A passage about Halloween could be unfair to Jehovah's Witnesses, who do not celebrate Halloween.

Test publishers routinely assess bias in test items (called *item bias*). Items that exhibit lower (or higher) scores for student demographic groups (e.g., gender or race groups) than expected on the basis of the test as a whole are flagged for evaluation. These items are usually referred to a committee with representatives from a broad range of demographic groups, which is likely to exclude the item. A related issue is sensitivity. It should go without saying that test items with any kind of overt cultural or gender stereotyping should be rejected. For example, a test whose items always refer to doctors as "he" or give Hispanic names only to menial workers should never be used.

Computerized Test Administration

The use of computers to administer tests is becoming more common. In its simplest form, students are presented with the same multiple-choice items in the same order in which students would take them if they sat for the typical paper-and-pencil test. However, the computer makes it possible to tailor the selection of items to the performance of the student. In **computer-adaptive** administration (Olson, 2005), follow-up to any single item depends on the student's success in answering, with harder items following correct responses and easier items presented after wrong answers. As the test progresses, a running estimate of the student's performance over the entire test is continually updated. This can result in real time savings; students can commonly take tests in less than one-third the time for a paper-and-pencil administration, with the same degree of accuracy. Also, computer-adaptive testing can zero in on a particular set of skills at the forward edge of what a student knows, giving more accurate information on those skills while avoiding the waste of time on items that are either very easy or impossible for the student. On the other hand, recent studies comparing test scores taken on computers to the scores on the same tests given on paper are finding that, at least in the first year, students in many states are performing much better on the paper tests (Herold, 2016). In Rhode Island, for example, 42.5 percent of students scored "proficient" in English/Language Arts on a paper version of the Common Core PARCC test, while only 34 percent scored this well on the computer version. In other states, however, no difference between paper administration and computer administration was found.

Testing Accommodations for Students with Disabilities

How should students with disabilities participate in standardized testing? Some kinds of accommodations, such as enlarging text for students with vision problems, are not controversial. Far more controversial are accommodations for students with learning disabilities, such as extending testing time and reading items to students (Lovett, 2010; Voltz, Sims, & Nelson, 2010). A review of many studies by Sireci and colleagues (2005) examined the effects of various accommodations. They found that extending testing time increases scores for all students (not only those with disabilities), although students with disabilities benefit more than other students. Reading items to students, however, is primarily beneficial to students with disabilities. Given these findings, it is important for policymakers to establish clear guidelines in accountability systems for when accommodations may and may not be used, to avoid biasing scores one way or the other.

Testing Accommodations for English Learners

The national accountability movement has heightened concern about the testing of English learners. Obviously, students who speak no English cannot respond meaningfully on tests given in English, but if English learners are excused from testing, there is a danger that their needs will not be adequately addressed (Kieffer, Lesaux, Rivera, & Francis, 2009). State accountability systems (as in Texas) have used tests in Spanish in the early grades. Other accommodations include rewriting tests to simplify the instructions or the items themselves, providing extra time, or presenting tests in two languages at the same time (English and the native language) and letting students choose which to answer.

ON THE WEB

For more on issues related to the principles of educational assessment, go to the website of the National Council on Measurement in Education (NCME) (ncme .org) and the website of James McMillan of Virginia Commonwealth University on Fundamental Assessment Principles for Teachers and Administrators (pareonline.net). Also see the National Center for the Improvement of Educational Assessment (nciea.org) and the National Board on Educational Testing and Public Policy (bc.edu, then Research, then Research Centers and Institutes).

MyEdLab **Self-Check 14.2**

HOW ARE EDUCATORS HELD ACCOUNTABLE FOR STUDENT ACHIEVEMENT?

A growing trend in recent years has been the effort to hold teachers, schools, and districts accountable for what students learn (Klein, 2016). All U.S. states, most Canadian provinces, and England (among many other countries) have implemented regular standardized testing programs and publish the results on a school-by-school basis. Many districts supplement these state tests with additional tests, including "benchmark assessments" that are given several times each year to help guide instruction toward meeting state standards. Not surprisingly, principals and other administrators watch these scores the way business owners watch their profit sheets. Standardized tests have become "high-stakes" tests, which means that their results have serious consequences for educators and (increasingly) for students themselves. For example, many states and districts now require that students score at a given level on state tests in order to be promoted from grade to grade or to graduate from high school. Many states and districts issue school report cards listing such data as test scores, attendance, retentions, and suspensions; these might be reported in newspapers or otherwise publicized. Test scores are frequently used in decisions about hiring, firing, promotion, and transfer of principals and superintendents, and sometimes teachers.

ON THE WEB

To learn more about accountability and state-level assessment issues, visit the website for the Council of Chief State School Officers (CCSSO) at ccsso.org. CCSSO is an organization of public officials who lead K–12 education in the 50 states. For information on accountability for charter schools, see charterschoolcenter.org. For accountability and assessment issues for students with disabilities, see cehd.umn.edu.

The accountability movement stems in part from the public's loss of confidence in education. Legislators (among others), upset by examples of students graduating from high school unable to read or compute, have demanded that schools establish higher standards and that students achieve them (McDermott, 2007).

The accountability movement has many critics, however (Hamilton, Stecher, & Yuan, 2008; Rotberg, 2001; Ryan & Shepard, 2008; Schlechty, 2011). Many argue that accountability assessment tempts schools to teach only what is tested, emphasizing reading and mathematics at the expense of, for instance, science and social studies (David, 2011; Marx & Harris, 2006), and emphasizing easily measured objectives (such as punctuation) over more important but hard-to-measure objectives (such as composition) (Gallagher, 2010). Many educators point out that

MyEdLab

Video Example 14.2

Textbook author Bob Slavin describes a controversial decision by a school district to reduce the time students spend at recess. Consider the potential negative ramifications of cutbacks to noncore-curricular programs. How can educators best address the growing need to prepare all students to meet more rigorous academic standards?

accountability assessments fail to take into account differences in the challenges faced by schools (Barton, 2007/2008; Darling-Hammond et al., 2012). A school or classroom might test poorly because the students are from disadvantaged backgrounds or do not yet speak English well, rather than because they were given poor instruction. Students in high-poverty schools may have fewer opportunities to learn because their funding is often lower than that of other schools (Orfield & Kornhaber, 2001; Starratt, 2003). High student mobility, especially prevalent in low-SES urban areas, might mean that schools are held accountable for students they have only had with them for a few weeks or months. School performance from year to year is unstable, and schools may be rewarded or punished based on minor variations of no statistical importance (Fuller, Wright, Gesicki, & Kang, 2007; Kelly & Monczunski, 2007). High-stakes testing can lead schools and districts to try to "game the system" by adopting policies that artificially inflate scores by removing potentially low-scoring students from the testing pool, such as assigning more children to special education, categorizing more students as limited English proficient, or retaining more students (Booher-Jennings & Beveridge, 2007; Heilig & Darling-Hammond, 2008). Many observers have noted that teachers, under extraordinary pressure, sometimes use unethical strategies to increase students' scores (Hamilton et al., 2008; Popham, 2014a), and there have been many cheating scandals due to intense pressures on teachers and administrators to increase scores (Starnes, 2011).

Several researchers (e.g., Amrein & Berliner, 2003; Ellmore & Fuhrman, 2001; Neill, 2003) have questioned whether increased accountability actually leads to higher achievement. The federal government regularly gives tests to a national sample of students. Scores on this National Assessment of Educational Progress (NAEP) can be compared with state test scores. Carnoy and Loeb (2002) found only slight differences in NAEP score gains between states with strong accountability systems and other states, whereas Neill and Gaylor (2001) and Amrein and Berliner (2003) found that states with strong accountability systems had *lower* gains on NAEP than other states. A blue-ribbon National Research Council panel reviewed a variety of studies of high-stakes accountability strategies and found few benefits for learning (Sparks, 2011a). On the other hand, a study in the U.K. found that when England kept standardized testing but Wales dropped it, scores on international tests in Wales began to drop behind those of England (McNally, 2014).

Regardless of the criticisms, the demand for accountability is here to stay (Popham, 2014a). One advantage of accountability is that it increases the pressure on schools and teachers to pay attention to students who might otherwise fall through the cracks and to help those who need help the most. States are required to report "disaggregated" scores, meaning that they are separately held accountable for gains of students of each ethnicity, limited English proficient students, and so on. This can focus school leaders on finding ways to ensure that all groups are making progress (Scheurich et al., 2000). Another advantage is that accountability encourages schools to search out improved instructional methods and guarantees routine evaluation of any innovations that schools try (Wiliam, 2010).

State accountability tests are based on state standards. In most states today, these standards are aligned with the Common Core State Standards (CCSS) or other "college- and career-ready standards" similar to CCSS. These are discussed later in this chapter.

Whether or not states have adopted CCSS or other college- and career-ready standards, their standards are usually at least supplemented with items chosen or developed by diverse groups of stakeholders (including teachers, parents, employers, and researchers), who express their judgments about what should be taught and learned. Through a consensus-building process, a state pools the thinking of educators and noneducators in defining the content domains it demands through its assessments. This process forces education leaders and policymakers to make clear what it is they want children to learn, which can then help them set policies in line with these objectives.

Every Student Succeeds Act (ESSA)

In December 2015, the U.S. Congress passed an update of the main law that governs the federal role in education. This law, which was known as No Child Left Behind (NCLB) from 2002 to 2015, is now called the Every Student Succeeds Act, or ESSA (Klein, 2016). The federal government provides only about 7 percent of funding for public education (the rest comes from state and local taxes), but that 7 percent is very influential, especially for schools that serve numerous disadvantaged students, English learners, and students who receive special-education services.

As a teacher, you will probably encounter policies that exist because of ESSA or are affected by it. Here are some key issues addressed by ESSA that are likely to matter to you (see Education Week, 2015).

1. *Accountability.* Perhaps the most universal impact of ESSA is on accountability (Chenowith, 2016; Rothman & Marion, 2016). As was the case in NCLB, students will be tested in reading and math in each of grades 3 through 8, plus one grade in high school (usually grade 11). However, in contrast to NCLB, the federal government will not pressure states to use particular tests and will not mandate specific consequences for schools that do not meet state standards. States will be given more autonomy to set up their own assessment and accountability systems.

2. *Accountability Goals.* Instead of just measuring achievement outcomes, states will be required to set "challenging" standards and monitor progress on additional criteria. These include English language proficiency, high school graduation, and at least one additional indicator chosen by the state, such as student engagement, access to advanced coursework, or school climate/safety (see Blad, 2016).

3. *Low-Performing Schools.* Under NCLB, schools scoring in the lowest 5 percent of their state could apply for School Improvement Grants, which provided schools with substantial funding but required major changes, such as transferring or firing the principal and half the staff. ESSA maintains special funding for low-performing schools but leaves it up to states, districts, and schools to design their own programs. However, evidence of the effectiveness of these programs must exist. (Evidence-based reform is discussed later in this chapter.)

4. *Title I Funding.* Under NCLB, schools serving many disadvantaged students received extra funding to help them improve outcomes for these students. (Title I is described in Chapter 4.) ESSA will continue Title I funding with just a few minor changes.

Connections 14.5
See Chapter 4 for a description of the achievement gap between majority and minority students.

THEORY INTO PRACTICE

Teaching Test-Taking Skills

As standardized testing has taken on increasing importance in the evaluation of students, teachers, and schools, so too has the preparation of students to take these tests. Of course, the best way to get students ready for tests is to do a good job of teaching them the material (Salend, 2011; Schmidt & Cogan, 2009; Tileston & Darling, 2008). However, schools also need to help many students to become test-savvy so they can show what they really know on standardized tests and get the highest scores possible.

Many ethical issues are involved in helping students do well on standardized tests (Popham, 2014a; Salend, 2016). For example, one way to help students score well would be to know the test items in advance and teach students the answers. Clearly, this would be cheating. A much more ethically ambiguous case arises when teachers know what subjects will be on the test and teach only material that they know will be tested. For example, if a standardized test does not assess acquaintance with Roman numerals, a math teacher might skip this topic to spend more time on an objective that will be tested. This practice is criticized as "teaching to the test." However, it could also be argued that it is unfair to test students on material that they have not been taught and that instruction, therefore, should be closely aligned with tests (Popham, 2014a; Tileston & Darling, 2008). The issue is that a standardized test can assess only a small sample of all objectives that are taught in school, and gearing instruction toward the objectives that will be on the test, to the exclusion of all

Connections 14.6
For more on teaching test-taking skills in the context of teaching metacognitive awareness and study skills, see Chapter 6.

(continued)

others, would produce a very narrow curriculum. Because of this temptation to limit instruction to the content of upcoming tests, it is important to maintain test security. Specific items on a test should never be shared with teachers in advance of the administration date.

Beyond matching instructional content with general test objectives, there are many ways to help students learn to do well on tests in general. Research has found that students can be taught to be test-wise and that this increases their standardized test scores (Bangert-Drowns, Kulik, Kulik, & Morgan, 1991). Students can also be taught coping strategies to deal with their anxiety about testing. These strategies can sometimes help children approach tests with more confidence and less stress (Flippo, 2008).

Questions have been raised about the effectiveness of programs that prepare students for the SAT. Because the SAT measures cognitive skills, it is perhaps to be expected that instructional programs can improve scores. The consensus among researchers is that coaching (especially long-term coaching) is effective for the SAT, particularly for low-achieving students (Becker, 1990), when it focuses on the skills the SAT measures.

Some ways of helping students to prepare for standardized tests include the following (see Flippo, 2008; Tileston & Darling, 2008).

1. Give students practice with similar item formats. For example, if a test will use multiple-choice formats, give students practice with similar formats in routine classroom quizzes and tests. If a test will use an unusual format such as verbal analogies (e.g., Big:Small::Honest: _____), give students practice with this type of item.

2. Suggest that students skip over difficult or time-consuming items and return to them later.

3. If there is no penalty for guessing on a test, suggest to students that they always fill in some answer. If there is a penalty for guessing, students should be encouraged to guess only if they can narrow down the options by eliminating one or more choices.

4. Suggest that students read all options on a multiple-choice test before choosing one. Sometimes more than one answer is correct, but one of them should always be the better answer.

5. Suggest to students that they use all available time. If they finish early, they should go back over their answers.

MyEdLab

Video Example 14.3

In this classroom, the teacher is preparing her students to take statewide standardized tests later in the year. How can she best prepare them without compromising the validity of the test?

Common Core State Standards

A big change in testing and accountability is taking place in many states. This involves the widespread adoption of the **Common Core State Standards** (CCSS) starting in 2010, and state assessments based on the Common Core. The standards were developed by the National Governor's Association and the Council of Chief State School Officers with encouragement from the Obama administration (see U.S. Department of Education, 2015). Originally, 46 states signed up to adopt the standards and one of two assessments aligned with them, the **Smarter Balanced** assessment or **PARCC (Partnership for Assessment of Readiness for College and Career)**. However, in recent years, many states have dropped these assessments and made their own, while others have dropped the standards entirely.

The purpose of the Common Core Standards was to have all American students and schools working toward similar objectives, as is common in European and Asian countries that routinely score better than the United States does on international assessments. Part of the focus was eliminating the substantial differences from state to state in standards and in criteria for proficiency on state tests. Before Common Core, a score that would be considered proficient in one state might be judged far from proficient in a neighboring state (Schneider, 2015). However, with so many states dropping the Common Core State Standards, this situation has not changed as much as many had hoped. Still, most states do subscribe to the broader concept of "**college- and career-ready standards**," which may or may not use assessments based on the Common Core State Standards (U.S. Department of Education, 2015).

The biggest change brought about by the CCSS is in the nature of the standards and the assessments based on them. The Common Core strongly emphasizes writing, argumentation, reasoning, and use of technology (Doorey, 2014; Herman & Linn, 2014). Although the standards apply only to English/language arts and mathematics, schools are encouraged to focus on reading and math throughout the day, teaching (for example) reading strategies for factual text in social studies and teaching relevant mathematics in science. The English/language arts and mathematics standards are summarized in Table 14.1.

In the time between the issuing of the standards and the transition to the tests based on them, many guides to teaching based on the standards have appeared (see, for example, Allyn, 2013; Cawn, 2015; Evenson et al., 2013a, b; Pearson & Hiebert, 2015; Tomlinson & Imbeau, 2014). Publishers and staff development organizations now provide schools with materials and training aligned with the Common Core (e.g., Davis, 2014; Jensen & Nickelsen, 2013; Marzano, Yanoski, Hoegh, & Simms, 2013; Tibbals & Bernhardt, 2015; Udelhofen, 2014).

As is to be expected, the Common Core standards have come in for some criticism. Porter, McMaken, Hwang, and Yang (2011) compared the Common Core State Standards to those of high-performing countries and U.S. states and found little overlap, and only small improvements in emphasis on higher-order skills. Others have agreed or disagreed with this judgment (e.g., Beach, 2011; Chandler, Fortune, Lovett, & Scherrer, 2016; Cobb & Jackson, 2011; Dingman, Teuscher, Newton, & Kasmer, 2013; Ohler, 2013). Calfee and Wilson (2016) strongly criticized the Common Core literacy standards. Dietel (2011), noting the intention of Common Core assessments to use performance assessments, notes the disappointing history of performance assessments in state accountability programs. Problems have been noted in adapting the Common Core to students with special needs (Karten, 2016; Shah, 2012). Loveless (2012) and Hess and McShane (2013) wonder whether all the fiddling with state and (now) national standards that have dominated education policy since the 1980s has made any difference, and predict a dismal fate for Common Core.

TABLE 14.1 • Focus of the Common Core State Standards

Mathematics Standards

1. Make sense of problems and persevere in solving them.
2. Reason abstractly and quantitatively.
3. Construct viable arguments and critique the reasoning of others.
4. Model with mathematics.
5. Use appropriate tools strategically.
6. Attend to precision.
7. Look for and make use of structure.
8. Look for and express regularity in repeated reasoning.

English/Language Arts Standards

1. Analyze how and why individuals, events, and ideas develop and interact over the course of a text.
2. Integrate and evaluate content presented in diverse formats and media, including visually and quantitatively, as well as in words.
3. Read and comprehend complex literary and informational texts independently and proficiently.
4. Develop and strengthen writing as needed by planning, revising, editing, rewriting, or trying a new approach.
5. Use technology, including the Internet, to produce and publish writing and to interact and collaborate with others.
6. Conduct short as well as more sustained research projects based on focused questions, demonstrating understanding of the subject matter under investigation.

Computerized testing, used in PARCC tests, has also been criticized by many (Gullen, 2014), and students have been found to score lower on computerized tests than on the same tests administered on paper (Herold, 2016).

Whatever the validity of these concerns, Common Core is already stimulating a national conversation about what is worth teaching and about how to get teachers beyond the age-old "I do, we do, you do" form of instruction (Ferguson, 2013; Phillips & Wong, 2012). CCSS assessments tend to be long (up to 10 hours) and difficult (Doorey, 2014; Gewirtz, 2013; Herman & Linn, 2014), and PARCC tests require use of computers in the testing itself. It may be some time before we know whether the new standards and assessments will improve outcomes for students, but they are certainly shaking things up!

THEORY INTO PRACTICE

Smarter Balanced and PARCC Tests

In the national movement toward college- and career-ready standards, some states adopted one of two Common Core assessments (Smarter Balanced or PARCC), and others modeled their state assessments on these. Figures 14.6 and 14.7 show examples illustrating mathematics and English/language arts items respectively, from the Smarter Balanced tests.

Grade 4 Mathematics

Item	Claim	Domain	Target	DOK	CCSS-MC	CCSS-MP
#1	1	OA	A	1	4.OA.A, 4.NBT.B.4	N/A

A baker has 159 cups of brown sugar and 264 cups of white sugar. How many total cups of sugar does the baker have?

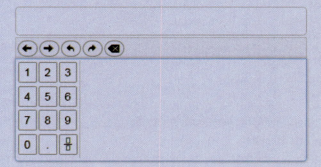

Key: 423

Rubric: (1 point) The student enters the correct number of cups.

FIGURE 14.6 • Sample Smarter Balanced Math Question

Source: Used by Permission of Smarter Balanced Assessment Consortium, UCLA

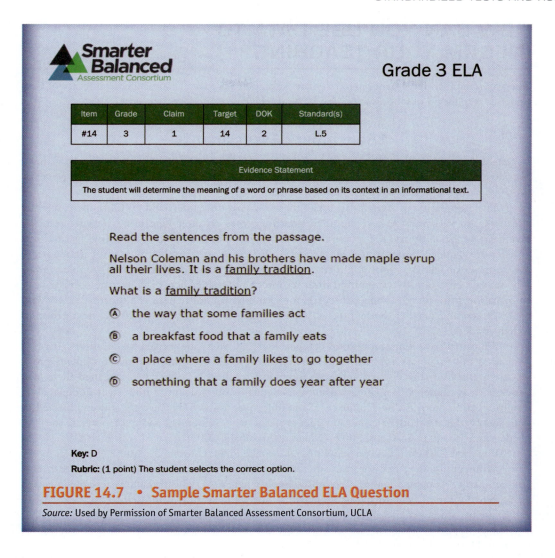

FIGURE 14.7 • Sample Smarter Balanced ELA Question

Source: Used by Permission of Smarter Balanced Assessment Consortium, UCLA

Evidence-Based Reform

Research in education has always produced insights and suggestions for practice, but in recent years, the research-to-practice pipeline has been greatly enriched. Specific programs in every subject and grade level are increasingly being evaluated in large experiments that compare schools using those programs to those continuing with traditional practices. Often schools, teachers, or students are assigned at random either to receive the experimental treatment or to serve as a control group.

Evidence-based reform is producing many programs that schools can adopt with confidence. These include programs in elementary and secondary reading, math, and science; programs for struggling readers; programs for English language learners; technology applications; and much more. Educators can find out about proven programs in education at a government website, http://ies.ed.gov/ncee/wwc/, ot at a Johns Hopkins University site, www.bestevidence.org. These clearinghouses are like *Consumer Reports* for educators. They help educators make wise choices for their children, so that they can increase students' chances of meeting the ambitious standards of the Common Core and other college- and career-ready standards.

ESSA is encouraging the use of programs with "strong," "moderate," or "promising" evidence of effectiveness. In particular, programs used in schools that receive grants because of very low achievement must have evidence of effectiveness, and proposals for funding from several federal sources qualify for extra points if they propose to use proven programs.

HOW CAN YOU USE DATA TO INFORM YOUR TEACHING?

The accountability movement has led to many attempts to use data to inform educators about how students, teachers, and schools are doing beyond what is required by each state.

Benchmark Assessments

In test-obsessed American schools, you'd think the last thing we'd need is more tests. Yet many districts and states are administering **benchmark assessments** that assess children three, five, or even eight times a year, usually in reading and math.

The popularity of benchmark assessments is easy to understand. NCLB increased the already substantial pressure on schools to improve scores on their state tests. Yet state tests are given too infrequently and the scores arrive too late to be of much use in adjusting instructional policies or practices. For example, most states test in the spring. By the time scores are reported, it is summer or fall. A school might find out in July that its math scores are in trouble. Yet by July, schools have already committed their resources and made their plans for the coming year. Information from fourth-grade test scores, for example, cannot benefit the fourth-graders who took the test and may be too late to be of much value to fifth-graders or to the next group of fourth-graders.

Educators have long understood this problem and have long looked for solutions. Today, a wide array of benchmark assessments designed to yield useful early information on students' progress are available. Many districts and even individual teachers have designed and used their own benchmark assessments. Benchmark assessments enable you to identify how each student, class, subgroup, and school is doing on each of the objectives assessed by the state and emphasized in state and district standards, so you can target professional development and reform where they are needed most (Fogarty & Kerns, 2009; Odden & Archibald, 2009).

Benchmark assessments can allow schools to take their achievement "pulse," but as in medicine, taking a pulse does not constitute a cure. It's what the doctor and patient do next that matters. Similarly, a benchmark assessment tells schools where they're headed and where they need to focus, but the use of benchmark assessments has not yet been shown in itself to increase student achievement. Studies of providing benchmark assessment information to schools find positive but very small impacts on student learning (Konstantopoulos, Miller, & VanderPloeg, 2013; Slavin, Cheung, Holmes, Madden, & Chamberlain, 2013).

Benchmark assessments are useful tools in the hands of enlightened educators, but they are nothing more than indicators of children's current achievement. As part of a comprehensive strategy for district and school reform, benchmark assessments can play a key supporting role, but only a supporting role (Chappuis & Chappuis, 2007/2008). If we're going to take even more of our children's precious class time for testing, we must use the results intelligently and proactively to improve core teaching and learning.

Data-Driven Reform

The movement toward the use of benchmark assessments is part of a broader trend toward using data to drive reforms in schools and districts (James-Ward, Fisher, Frey, & Lapp, 2013; Mandinach & Gummer, 2016; Mertler, 2014; Sykes & Wilson, 2016; Venables, 2014). **Data-driven reform** goes beyond simply looking at scores on state tests. School leaders involved in such reforms organize information from state tests and benchmark assessments by subskill, subgroup, grade level, and other categories, adding information on attendance, dropout programs in use in schools, and so on to find "root causes" for the school's problems (Datnow & Park, 2015; Hamilton et al., 2008, 2009; Hess & Mehta, 2013; Mandinach & Gummer, 2016; Smith, Johnson, & Thompson, 2012). They next carefully consider potential solutions to their problems, ideally programs with strong evidence of effectiveness (see Coalition for Evidence-Based Policy, 2003; Odden, 2009; Slavin et al., 2012; Towne, Wise, & Winters, 2005); implement those solutions; and then continue to monitor benchmark and test data to see that they are working.

THEORY INTO PRACTICE

Data-Driven Reform

Heritage and Chen (2005) discuss an approach to data-driven reform that uses a Web-based tool called the Quality School Portfolio (QSP) to help school leaders organize and make sense of data. They then describe a process for using data to guide school reform:

1. ***Determine what you want to know.*** Data-based reform should begin with a problem that the educators involved want to solve or a question they want answered. No one pays attention to data that do not tell them something they want to know.

2. ***Collect data.*** Educators involved in data-based reform organize existing data and collect new data to answer the questions they have posed. The data could include state and benchmark tests, additional assessments (such as writing or math problem-solving assessments not part of the state test), information on materials and programs being used by teachers, teachers' and students' attitudes, or whatever else might affect decisions about reforms being considered (Bernhardt, 2005; Depascale, 2012).

3. ***Analyze results.*** The next step is to organize the data, first simply computing averages and then using the data to test ideas about what is causing the problems the school is trying to solve. For example, imagine that a school has lower math scores than it likes. A school committee reviews the state test scores and quarterly benchmark scores, and they all tell the same story: Scores are low and are not improving. Could it be that the teachers are not focusing on all skills tested? The committee looks at scores on portions of the test (e.g., fractions, geometry, word problems) and finds that the scores are low across the board. Could the problem be isolated to certain subgroups? The committee looks at scores for boys and girls, African Americans, Hispanics, and whites. They see one surprising pattern: Girls seem to be doing particularly poorly. The committee arranges to visit classes and see what is happening. When they return to discuss their findings, they have a whole new perspective on the data. Teachers throughout the school are making extensive use of traditional lectures and problem solving, as suggested by their texts. In many classes, an aggressive group of boys dominates the discussions, whereas most girls are bored and feel left out of the class activities. They found classes in which most girls never participated and did not say a single thing in a 50-minute lesson. Linking their quantitative data with their observations, the committee decides the problem may be that teaching methods are not engaging all students.

4. ***Set priorities and goals.*** In data-based reform, it is not enough simply to know the data. The school must take action based on the data. This begins with setting priorities and goals for solutions the school might try. The goals should be measurable, focused on student achievement, realistic, and attainable (Bernhardt, 2005). In the case of the school with the math problem, the committee sets a goal of improving the math performance of all students, with a particular focus on the girls, and organizes a plan to closely monitor quarterly benchmark data.

5. ***Develop strategies.*** The most important step in data-driven reform is to develop specific strategies to solve identified problems. School leaders need to consider potential solutions for the problems they have observed. For example, to solve an achievement problem, the school might look at the federal What Works Clearinghouse (ies.ed.gov) or the *Best Evidence Encyclopedia* (bestevidence.org), both of which summarize scientific reviews of research on educational programs for grades pre-K to 12.

(continued)

In the case of the school with the math problem, committee members look at the *Best Evidence Encyclopedia* and find that there is good evidence for cooperative learning in elementary math. They reason that this could increase the participation of all students. They find a local trainer to prepare the teachers in using cooperative learning in math, and over time, they begin to see their math benchmark scores improve. Later, when the state test scores came back, the committee is glad to see that math scores have improved for all students, but especially for girls, who are now fully engaged with math in all classrooms.

Allan Odden and his colleagues (Odden, 2009; Odden & Archibald, 2009) have done studies of schools and districts that make exceptional gains on state accountability tests. They found that successful schools and districts follow a path like the one just laid out. They look carefully at their own data, identify areas of need, select and carefully implement proven programs, and continuously use data to track their success in implementing new strategies. The Johns Hopkins University Center for Research and Reform in Education (CRRE) evaluated a district reform program of this kind in 59 high-poverty districts in seven states and found significant gains, especially in reading (Slavin et al., 2012). However, the gains appeared not when data analysis tools began to be used, but when schools in the districts began to select and implement proven reading and math programs.

Value-Added Assessment Systems

A key issue in all assessment for accountability is dealing with the fact that schools are not equal in their student inputs. Those serving areas with many students who are disadvantaged or English learners face greater difficulties in reaching standards than do schools serving middle-class areas. One solution to this problem adopted by several states is to focus on what are called *value-added assessments,* determinations of how much learning a school has added to its students. The most widely known of these is the Educational Value-Added Assessment System (EVAAS), which was first used in Tennessee (as TVAAS) and later extended to several other states. The idea is that even though schools do not all face the same challenges in getting their students to pass state tests, they can be more legitimately compared on the degree to which they can move students forward from *whatever* baseline level of learning they start with (Jorgenson, 2012; Wiliam, 2010). As appealing as this idea is, value-added models have been criticized on technical grounds (e.g., Amrein-Beardsley, 2008, 2009; Darling-Hammond et al., 2012; McCaffrey, Lockwood, Koretz, Louis, & Hamilton, 2004) as being potentially inaccurate, failing to account for student risk factors, and exhibiting other problems. A study comparing teacher ratings by principals and value-added models found almost no correlation (Harris, Ingle, & Rutledge, 2014). The concern is that using value-added scores as a basis for accountability will not solve the problem of inequalities in starting points, because schools in low-SES communities are still less likely to score well on value-added measures. Recently, value-added scores have begun to be used as part of teacher evaluations, not just school evaluations, and this has raised even more technical as well as political concerns (Darling-Hammond, 2012; Scherrer, 2012; Wolk, 2010). The American Educational Research Association (2015) recently issued a statement on value-added models (VAM) that established technical requirements for their use. Unfortunately, few if any states using value-added models meet these standards, according to AERA.

ON THE WEB

For more on data-driven reform, visit the What Works Clearinghouse (ies.ed.gov), the Best Evidence Encyclopedia (bestevidence.org), the Center for Research and Reform in Education (education.jhu.edu), the National Center for Research on Evaluation, Standards, and Student Testing (CRESST) (cse.ucla.edu), The Education Trust (edtrust.org), or the Consortium for Policy Research in Education (cpre.wceruw.org).

SUMMARY

What Are Standardized Tests and How Are They Used?

The term *standardized* describes tests that are uniform in content, administration, and scoring and, therefore, allow for the comparison of results across classrooms, schools, and school districts. Standardized tests such as the SAT and CTBS measure individual performance or ability against standards, or norms, that have been established for many other students in the school district, state, or nation for which each test is designed. Standardized test scores are used for selection and placement, such as grade promotion or college admission; for diagnosis and remediation; for evaluation of student proficiency or progress in content areas; and for evaluation of teaching strategies, teachers, and schools.

What Types of Standardized Tests Are Given?

Aptitude tests, such as tests of general intelligence and multifactor batteries, predict students' general abilities and preparation to learn. IQ tests administered to individuals or groups attempt to measure individual aptitude in the cognitive domain. Achievement tests assess student proficiency in various subject areas. Diagnostic tests focus on specific subject matter to discover strengths or weaknesses in mastery. Norm-referenced testing interprets scores in comparison with the scores of other people who took the test, and criterion-referenced testing interprets scores based on fixed performance criteria.

How Are Standardized Tests Interpreted?

Scores that are derived from raw scores include percentiles, the percentage of scores in the norming group that fall below a particular score; grade equivalents, the grade and month at which a particular score is thought to represent typical performance; and standard scores, the students' performance in relation to the normal distribution of scores. Standard scores include stanines (based on the standard deviation of scores), normal curve equivalents (based on a comparison of scores with the normal distribution), and z-scores (the location of scores above or below the mean).

What Are Some Issues Concerning Standardized and Classroom Testing?

Tests and test items must have validity, the quality of testing what is intended to be tested. Predictive validity means that the test accurately predicts future performance. Reliability means that test results are consistent when the test is administered at different places or times. Test bias in any form compromises validity. Other issues related to standardized testing include ethics in the content of tests, student preparation for testing, the uses of test scores, the relationship of tests to the curriculum, and computer administration of tests.

How Are Educators Held Accountable for Student Achievement?

Educators are increasingly held accountable for student achievement. Test scores are often used in decisions about hiring, firing, and promoting educators. Critics say that holding teachers accountable for student gains (1) is unfair because of different student starting points and (2) may encourage teaching to the test or adopting policies that artificially inflate standardized scores. An advantage of accountability is that it increases pressure on schools to pay attention to students who might otherwise fall through the cracks. Because accountability tests are based on standards about what should be learned, they can help clarify learning objectives.

THE INTENTIONAL TEACHER
Using What You Know about Standardized Tests to Improve Teaching and Learning

Intentional teachers know that standardized tests can provide some—albeit limited—information about how teachers, schools, and students are performing. They can interpret standardized scores and use results from standardized tests for decision making. Intentional teachers rely on other assessment measures to complete the complicated picture of student learning.

- They understand how and why standardized tests are made and know their uses and limitations.
- They understand how different types of standardized tests are used for different purposes.
- They can interpret the reports provided with standardized test results.
- They understand how tests can be reliable and valid, and how to avoid bias in test construction.
- They understand how national and state policies affect accountability testing.
- They know how to help students prepare for standardized testing without letting this responsibility dominate their teaching.
- They know how accommodations are made for testing students with disabilities and English learners.
- They know how to use benchmark data to inform their teaching and school planning.

MyEdLab

Application Exercise 14.1

In the Pearson etext, watch a classroom video. Then use the guidelines in "The Intentional Teacher" to answer a set of questions that will help you reflect on and understand the teaching and learning presented in the video.

KEY TERMS

Review the following key terms from the chapter.

SELF-ASSESSMENT:
PRACTICING FOR LICENSURE

Directions: The chapter-opening vignette addresses indicators that are often assessed in state licensure exams. Reread the chapter-opening vignette and then respond to the following questions.

1. Ms. Tranh speaks to Anita's parents about the many measures of achievement available to assess Anita's academic ability. Which of the following types of assessment would Ms. Tranh use to predict Anita's future performance?
    a. Placement test
    b. Achievement test
    c. Aptitude test
    d. Diagnostic test
2. Which of the following interpretations would Ms. Tranh make if Anita were to score at the mean of a standardized test?
    a. percentile = 90, stanine = 0, $z = 20$
    b. NCE = 50, $z = 0$, percentile = 50
    c. GE = 7.2, stanine = 5, NCE = 45
    d. $z = 1$, NCE = 60, percentile = 50
3. Ms. Tranh tells Mr. and Mrs. McKay that Anita's grade-equivalent score on the CAT is 6.9. What does this mean?
    a. Anita is almost ready for seventh-grade work.
    b. Anita found the test very easy.
    c. Anita has done as well as an end-of-year sixth-grader.
    d. Anita scored at the 6.9 percentile.
4. Ms. Tranh compares her students' scores on a math test with those of another class. She finds that the students' average score in both classes is 75, but the students in her class have scores that are much more spread out. This means that Ms. Tranh's results will have a larger
    a. mean.
    b. median.
    c. standard deviation.
    d. normal curve.
5. If Anita scored consistently on the CAT over multiple applications, it can be said that the test has
    a. predictive validity.
    b. content validity.
    c. construct validity.
    d. reliability.
6. Write a short essay describing the advantages and major criticisms of standardized tests.

MyEdLab **Licensure Exam 14.1** Answer questions and receive instant feedback in your Pearson eText in MyEdLab.

Using This Text to Prepare for the Praxis™ Principles of Learning and Teaching Exam

Topics Covered on the Praxis™ Exam for the Principles of Learning and Teaching (PLT Tests)	Chapter Content Aligned with Praxis™ Topics
I. Students as Learners (22.5% of total test)	
A. Student Development and the Learning Process	
1. **Understands the theoretical foundations of how students learn** a. **Knows how knowledge is constructed** b. **Knows a variety of means by which skills are acquired** c. **Understands a variety of cognitive process and how they are developed**	**Chapter 2: Cognitive, Language, and Literacy Development** • How Do Children Develop Cognitively? (pp. 23–24) • How Did Piaget View Cognitive Development? (pp. 24–31) • How Did Vygotsky View Cognitive Development? (pp. 33–36) **Chapter 3: Social, Moral, and Emotional Development (Entire Chapter)** **Chapter 5: Behavioral and Social Theories of Learning (Entire Chapter)** **Chapter 6: Cognitive Theories of Learning (Entire Chapter)** **Chapter 8: Student-Centered and Constructivist Approaches to Instruction (Entire Chapter)** *Important terms related to learning theory:* Chapter 2 Key Terms (p. 42) Chapter 5 Key Terms (p. 118) Chapter 6 Key Terms (p. 156) Chapter 8 Key Terms (p. 210)
2. **Knows the major contributions of foundational theorists to education. Relates the work of theorists to educational contexts** • **Bandura** • **Bruner** • **Dewey** • **Piaget** • **Vygotsky** • **Kohlberg** • **Bloom**	**Chapter 2: Cognitive, Language, and Literacy Development (Entire Chapter)** **Chapter 3: Social, Moral, and Emotional Development** • What Are Some Views of Personal and Social Development? • Erickson's Stages of Psychosocial Development (pp. 45–47) • What Are Some Views of Moral Development? • Piaget's Theory of Moral Development (pp. 48–49) • Kohlberg's Stages of Moral Reasoning (pp. 49–51) • How Do Children Develop Socially and Emotionally? (pp. 52–61) **Chapter 5: Behavioral and Social Theories of Learning** • What Are Behavioral Learning Theories? • Pavlov: Classical Conditioning (p. 99) • Skinner: Operant Conditioning (p. 99) • How Has Social Learning Theory Contributed to Our Understanding of Human Learning? • Bandura: Modeling and Observational Learning (pp. 112–114) • Meichenbaum's Model of Self-Regulated Learning (pp. 114–115) **Chapter 6: Cognitive Theories of Learning** • What Do We Know from Research on the Brain? (pp. 131–137) • Applications of Brain Research to Classroom Teaching (pp. 135–136) • What Makes Information Meaningful? • Schema Theory (pp. 144–145) • How Do Cognitive Teaching Strategies Help Students Learn? • Making Learning Relevant and Activating Prior Knowledge (pp. 148–151) **Chapter 8: Student-Centered and Constructivist Approaches to Instruction** • What Is the Constructivist View of Learning? • Discovery Learning (p. 180) • Self-Regulated Learning (p. 192) • How is Cooperative Learning Used in Instruction? (pp. 198–204)

Topics Covered on the Praxis™ Exam for the Principles of Learning and Teaching (PLT Tests)	Chapter Content Aligned with Praxis™ Topics
I. Students as Learners (22.5% of total test) *(continued)*	
A. Student Development and the Learning Process *(continued)*	

<table>
<tr><td></td><td>

Chapter 13: Assessing Student Learning
- Using Taxonomies of Instructional Objectives (pp. 346–347)

</td></tr>
<tr><td>

3. Understands the concepts and terms related to a variety of learning theories: metacognition, schema, transfer, self-efficacy, self-regulation, zone of proximal development, and classical and operant conditioning

</td><td>

Chapter 2: Cognitive, Language, and Literacy Development
- How Do Children Develop Cognitively? (pp. 23–24)
- How Did Piaget View Cognitive Development? (pp. 24–31)
- How Is Piaget's Work Viewed Today? (pp. 31–33)
- How Did Vygotsky View Cognitive Development? (pp. 33–36)

Theory into Practice: Classroom Applications of Vygotsky's Theory (p. 35)

Chapter 5: Behavioral and Social Theories of Learning
- What Are Behavioral Learning Theories?
  - Pavlov: Classical Conditioning (p. 99)
  - Skinner: Operant Conditioning (p. 99)
- What Are Some Principles of Behavioral Learning?
  - The Role of Consequences (p. 101)
  - Reinforcers (pp. 101–103)
  - Punishers (p. 105)
  - Immediacy of Consequences (pp. 105–106)
  - Shaping (p. 107)
  - Extinction (pp. 107–108)
  - Schedules of Reinforcement (pp. 108–109)
  - Maintenance (pp. 110)
  - The Role of Antecedents (pp. 110–112)
- How Has Social Learning Theory Contributed to Our Understanding of Human Learning?
  - Bandura: Modeling and Observational Learning (pp. 112–114)
  - Meichenbaum's Model of Self-Regulated Learning (pp. 114–115)
  - Strengths and Limitations of Behavioral Learning Theories (pp. 115–116)

Theory into Practice: Classroom Uses of Reinforcement (p. 102)
Theory into Practice: Practical Reinforcers (pp. 103–104)
Chapter 2 Key Terms (p. 42)
Chapter 5 Key Terms (p. 118)

</td></tr>
<tr><td>

4. Knows the distinguishing characteristics of the stages in each domain of human development (i.e., cognitive, physical, social, and moral)
  a. Describes the characteristics of a typical child in each stage and each domain
  b. Recognizes typical and atypical variance within each stage and each domain

</td><td>

Chapter 2: Cognitive, Language, and Literacy Development
- How Do Children Develop Cognitively? (pp. 23–24)

Chapter 3: Social, Moral, and Emotional Development
- What Are Some Views of Personal and Social Development?
  - Erikson's Stages of Psychosocial Development (pp. 45–47)
  - Implications and Criticisms of Erikson's Theory (p. 47)
- What Are Some Views of Moral Development?
  - Piaget's Theory of Moral Development (pp. 48–49)
  - Kohlberg's Stages of Moral Reasoning (pp. 49–51)
  - Criticisms of Kohlberg's Theory (p. 51)
- How Do Children Develop Socially and Emotionally?
  - Socioemotional Development during the Preschool Years (pp. 52–53)
  - Socioemotional Development during the Elementary Years (pp. 53–56)
  - Socioemotional Development during the Middle School and High School Years (pp. 56–57)
  - Enhancing Socioemotional Development (p. 58)

</td></tr>
</table>

Topics Covered on the Praxis™ Exam for the Principles of Learning and Teaching (PLT Tests)	Chapter Content Aligned with Praxis™ Topics

I. Students as Learners (22.5% of total test) *(continued)*

A. Student Development and the Learning Process *(continued)*

5. **Understands how learning theory and human development impact the instructional process**
   a. **Defines the relationship between learning theory and human development**
   b. **Provides examples of how learning theory is impacted by human development**
   c. **Uses knowledge of learning theory to solve educational problems**
   d. **Uses knowledge of human development to solve educational problems**
	Chapter 2: Cognitive, Language, and Literacy Development
	● How Do Children Develop Cognitively?
	 • Aspects of Development (p. 22)
	 • Issues of Development (pp. 22–24)
	● How Did Piaget View Cognitive Development?
	 • How Development Occurs (pp. 25–26)
	 • Piaget's Stages of Development (pp. 26–31)
	● How Is Piaget's Work Viewed Today?
	 • Criticisms and Revisions of Piaget's Theory (pp. 31–32)
	 • Neo-Piagetian Views of Development (p. 32)
	● How Did Vygotsky View Cognitive Development?
	 • How Development Occurs (pp. 33–36)
	● How Do Language and Literacy Develop?
	 • Language and Literacy Development during the Preschool Years (pp. 36–39)
	 • Language and Literacy Development during the Elementary and Secondary Years (pp. 39–40)
	Theory into Practice: Educational Implications of Piaget's Theory (pp. 32–33)
	Theory into Practice: Classroom Applications of Vygotsky's Theory (p. 35)
	
	Chapter 5: Behavioral and Social Theories of Learning
	● What Are Behavioral Learning Theories?
	 • Pavlov: Classical Conditioning (p. 99)
	 • Skinner: Operant Conditioning (p. 99)
	Theory into Practice: Classroom Uses of Reinforcement (p. 102)
	● What Are Some Principles of Behavioral Learning?
	 • The Role of Consequences (p. 201)
	 • Reinforcers (pp. 101–103)
	 • Punishers (p. 105)
	 • Immediacy of Consequences (pp. 105–106)
	 • Shaping (p. 107)
	 • Extinction (pp. 107–108)
	 • Schedules of Reinforcement (pp. 108–109)
	 • Maintenance (pp. 110)
	 • The Role of Antecedents (pp. 110–112)
	● How Has Social Learning Theory Contributed to Our Understanding of Human Learning?
	 • Bandura: Modeling and Observational Learning (pp. 112–114)
	 • Meichenbaum's Model of Self-Regulated Learning (pp. 114–115)
	 • Strengths and Limitations of Behavioral Learning Theories (pp. 115–116)
	
	Chapter 6: Cognitive Theories of Learning
	● What Is an Information-Processing Model?
	 • How Information Processing Works (p. 123)
	 • Executive Processing (pp. 123–124)
	 • Sensory Register (pp. 124–125)
	 • Working (or Short-Term) Memory (pp. 125–127)
	 • Long-Term Memory (pp. 127–130)
	 • Factors That Enhance Long-Term Memory (p. 130)
	 • Other Information-Processing Models (pp. 130–131)
	● What Do We Know from Research on the Brain? (pp. 131–137)
	 • How the Brain Works (pp. 131–132)
	 • Brain Development (pp. 132–134)
	 • Implications of Brain Research for Education (pp. 134–135)
	 • Applications of Brain Research to Classroom Teaching (pp. 135–136)
	 • Neuromyths and Neuroclues for Educators (p. 137)

Topics Covered on the Praxis™ Exam for the Principles of Learning and Teaching (PLT Tests)	Chapter Content Aligned with Praxis™ Topics

I. Students as Learners (22.5% of total test) *(continued)*

A. Student Development and the Learning Process *(continued)*

- What Causes People to Remember or Forget?
  - Forgetting and Remembering (pp. 137–140)
  - Practice (pp. 140–141)
- How Can Memory Strategies Be Taught?
  - Verbal Learning (pp. 141–144)
- What Makes Information Meaningful?
  - Rote versus Meaningful Learning (pp. 144–145)
  - Schema Theory (pp. 145–146)
- How Do Metacognitive Skills Help Students Learn? (pp. 146–147)
- What Study Strategies Help Students Learn?
  - Practice Tests (p. 147)
  - Note-Taking (pp. 147–148)
  - Underlining (p. 148)
  - Summarizing (p. 148)
  - Writing to Learn (p. 148)
  - Outlining and Concept Mapping (p. 148)
  - The PQ4R Method (p. 147)
- How Do Cognitive Teaching Strategies Help Students Learn?
  - Making Learning Relevant and Activating Prior Knowledge (pp. 148–151)
  - Organizing Information (pp. 151–154)

Chapter 10: Motivating Students to Learn
- What Are Some Theories of Motivation?
  - Motivation and Behavioral Learning Theory (pp. 249–250)
  - Motivation and Human Needs (pp. 250–251)
  - Motivation and Attribution Theory (pp. 251–253)
  - Motivation and Mindset (p. 253)
  - Motivation and Self-Regulated Learning (pp. 253–254)
  - Motivation and Expectancy Theory (pp. 254–255)
- What Factors Affect Students' Motivation?
  - Motivation and Goal Orientations (pp. 256–257)
  - Learned Helplessness (p. 257)
  - Teacher Expectations and Achievement (pp. 257–259)
  - Anxiety and Achievement (p. 259)
- How Can Teachers Increase Students' Motivation to Learn?
  - Intrinsic and Extrinsic Motivation (pp. 260–261)
  - Enhancing Intrinsic Motivation (pp. 261–264)
  - Principles for Providing Extrinsic Incentives to Learn (pp. 264–266)
  - Using Praise Effectively (p. 266)
  - Teaching Students to Praise Themselves (p. 266)

B. Students as Diverse Learners

1. **Understands that a number of variables affect how individual students learn and perform.**
   a. **Identifies a number of variables that affect how students learn and perform: Learning style, gender, culture, SES, prior knowledge and experience, motivation,**

Chapter 2: Cognitive, Language, and Literacy Development
- How Did Piaget View Cognitive Development?
  - Piaget's Stages of Development (pp. 26–31)
- How Did Vygotsky View Cognitive Development? (pp. 33–36)

Chapter 3: Social, Moral, and Emotional Development
- Socioemotional Development during the Elementary Years (pp. 53–56)
  - Self-Concept and Self-Esteem (pp. 53–54)
  - Promoting the Development of Self-Esteem (p. 54)

Chapter 4: Student Diversity
- How Does Socioeconomic Status Affect Student Achievement? (pp. 67–74)
- How Do Ethnicity and Race Affect Students' School Experiences? (pp. 75–80)
- How Do Language Differences and Bilingual Programs Affect Student Achievement? (pp. 80–83)

Topics Covered on the Praxis™ Exam for the Principles of Learning and Teaching (PLT Tests)	Chapter Content Aligned with Praxis™ Topics

I. Students as Learners (22.5% of total test) *(continued)*

B. Students as Diverse Learners *(continued)*

self-confidence/self-esteem, cognitive development, maturity, language
b. **Provides examples of how variables might affect how students learn and perform**
	Theory into Practice: Teaching English Learners (pp. 83–84)
	● How Do Gender and Gender Bias Affect Students' School Experiences? (pp. 85–88)
	● How Do Students Differ in Intelligence and Learning Styles?
	  • Definitions of Intelligence (pp. 89–90)
	  • Theories of Learning Styles (p. 91)
	Theory into Practice: Multiple Intelligences (p. 91)
	
	Chapter 6: Information Processing and Cognitive Theories of Learning
	● What Is an Information-Processing Model?
	  • How Information Processing Works (p. 123)
	● How Can Memory Strategies Be Taught?
	  • Verbal Learning (pp. 141–144)
	● Applications of Brain Research to Classroom Teaching (pp. 135–136)
	  • Neuromyths and Neuroclues for Educators (p. 137)
	
	Chapter 9: Grouping, Differentiation, and Technology
	● How Are Students Grouped to Accommodate Achievement Differences? (pp. 216–221)
	
	Chapter 10: Motivating Students to Learn
	● What Are Some Theories of Motivation? (pp. 249–255)
	● What Factors Affect Students' Motivation? (pp. 255–259)
	● How Can Teachers Increase Students' Motivation to Learn? (pp. 260–266)
	
	Chapter 12: Learners with Exceptionalities
	● What Are Effective Strategies for Students with Disabilities in General Education?
	  • Teaching Learning Strategies and Metacognitive Awareness (p. 331)

2. **Recognizes areas of exceptionality in students' learning**
a. **Identifies areas of exceptionality**
  • cognitive
  • auditory
  • visual
  • motor/physical
  • speech-language
  • behavioral
b. **Explains a variety of ways exceptionalities may impact student learning**
	Chapter 12: Learners with Exceptionalities
	● Who Are Learners with Exceptionalities?
	  • Types of Exceptionalities and the Numbers of Students Served (pp. 303–304)
	  • Students with Intellectual Disabilities (pp. 304–306)
	  • Students with Learning Disabilities (pp. 306–307)
	  • Students with Attention Deficit Hyperactivity Disorder (pp. 307–309)
	  • Students with Speech or Language Impairments (pp. 309–311)
	  • Students with Emotional and Behavioral Disorders (pp. 311–312)
	  • Students with Autism Spectrum Disorder (p. 312)
	  • Students with Sensory, Physical, and Health Impairments (pp. 314–315)
	  • Students Who Are Gifted and Talented (pp. 316–317)

3. **Understands the implications and application of legislation relating to students with exceptionalities on classroom practice.**
a. **Identifies the provisions of legislation relevant to students with exceptionalities**
  • **Americans with Disabilities Act (ADA)**
  • **Individuals with Disabilities in Education Act (IDEA)**
  • **Section 504, Rehabilitation Act (504)**
	Chapter 12: Learners with Exceptionalities
	● What Is Special Education?
	  • Public Law 94-142 and IDEA (pp. 317–318)
	  • An Array of Special-Education Services (pp. 319–325)
	● What Is Response to Intervention? (pp. 326–327)
	● What Is Inclusion? (pp. 327–329)
	
	Chapter 14: Standardized Tests and Accountability
	● How Are Educators Held Accountable for Student Achievement?
	  • Every Student Succeeds Act (ESSA) (pp. 400–401)
	  • Common Core State Standards (pp. 402–404)

Topics Covered on the Praxis™ Exam for the Principles of Learning and Teaching (PLT Tests)	Chapter Content Aligned with Praxis™ Topics

I. Students as Learners (22.5% of total test) *(continued)*

B. Students as Diverse Learners *(continued)*

b. Explains how the provisions of legislation relating to students with exceptionalities affect classroom practice	
4. Recognizes the traits, behaviors, and needs of intellectually gifted students	**Chapter 12: Learners with Exceptionalities** • Who Are Learners with Exceptionalities? • Students Who Are Gifted and Talented (pp. 316–317)
5. Recognizes that the process of English language acquisition affects the educational experience of English language learners	**Chapter 2: Cognitive, Language, and Literacy Development** • How Do Language and Literacy Develop? (pp. 37–39) **Chapter 4: Student Diversity** • How Do Language Differences and Bilingual Programs Affect Student Achievement? • Bilingual Education (pp. 80–83) *Theory into Practice: Teaching English Learners (pp. 82–83)*

6. Knows a variety of approaches for accommodating students with exceptionalities in each phase of the education process
a. Recognizes students with exceptionalities require particular accommodation
b. Knows how to modify instruction, assessment, and communication methods to meet a recognized need
	Chapter 4: Student Diversity
	• How Do Language Differences and Bilingual Programs Affect Student Achievement?
	  • Bilingual Education (pp. 80–83)
	Theory into Practice: Teaching English Learners (pp. 81–82)
	Chapter 9: Grouping, Differentiation, and Technology
	• What Educational Programs Exist for Students Placed at Risk?
	  • Compensatory Education Programs (pp. 225–226)
	  • Early Intervention Programs (pp. 226–227)
	  • Comprehensive School Reform Programs (p. 227)
	  • After-School and Summer School Programs (pp. 227–228)
	Chapter 12: Learners with Exceptionalities (Entire Chapter)

C. Student Motivation and Learning Environment

1. Knows the major contributions of foundational behavioral theorists to education
a. Relates the work of behavioral theorists to educational contexts
• Thorndike
• Watson
• Maslow
• Skinner
• Erikson
	Chapter 2: Cognitive, Language, and Literacy Development
	• Issues of Development
	• Nature-Nurture Controversy (pp. 23–24)
	Chapter 3: Social, Moral, and Emotional Development
	• What Are Some Views of Personal and Social Development?
	• Erickson's Stages of Psychosocial Development (pp. 45–47)
	• How Do Children Develop Socially and Emotionally? (pp. 52–61)
	Chapter 5: Behavioral and Social Theories of Learning
	• What Are Behavioral Learning Theories?
	  • Pavlov: Classical Conditioning (p. 99)
	  • Skinner: Operant Conditioning (p. 99)
	Chapter 10: Motivating Students to Learn
	• What Is Motivation? (p. 248)
	• What Are Some Theories of Motivation?
	  • Motivation and Behavioral Learning Theory (pp. 249–250)
	  • Motivation and Human Needs (pp. 250–251)
	  • Motivation and Attribution Theory (pp. 251–253)
	  • Motivation and Mindset (p. 253)
	  • Motivation and Self-Regulated Learning (pp. 253–254)
	  • Motivation and Expectancy Theory (pp. 254–255)
	• Theory into Practice: Giving Students Motivating Feedback (p. 254)

Topics Covered on the Praxis™ Exam for the Principles of Learning and Teaching (PLT Tests)	Chapter Content Aligned with Praxis™ Topics

I. Students as Learners (22.5% of total test) *(continued)*

C. Student Motivation and Learning Environment *(continued)*

2. **Understands the implications of foundational motivation theories for instruction, learning, and classroom management**
   a. **Defines terms related to foundational motivation theory**
   - self-determination
   - attribution
   - extrinsic/intrinsic motivation
   - cognitive dissonance
   - classic and operant conditioning
   - positive and negative reinforcement
   b. **Relates motivation theory to instruction, learning, and classroom management**

Chapter 5: Behavioral and Social Theories of Learning
- What Are Behavioral Learning Theories?
  - Pavlov: Classical Conditioning (p. 99)
  - Skinner: Operant Conditioning (p. 99)
- What Are Some Principles of Behavioral Learning?
  - Reinforcers (pp. 101–103)

Chapter 10: Motivating Students to Learn
- Motivation and Attribution Theory
- How Can Achievement Motivation Be Enhanced? (p. 266)
- How Can Teachers Increase Students' Motivation to Learn? (pp. 259–266)

3. **Knows principles and strategies for classroom management**
   a. **Knows how to develop classroom routines and procedures**
   b. **Knows how to maintain accurate records**
   c. **Knows how to establish standards of conduct**
   d. **Knows how to arrange classroom space**
   e. **Recognizes ways of promoting a positive learning environment**

Chapter 1: Educational Psychology: A Foundation for Teaching
Theory into Practice: Teaching as Decision Making (p. 13)

Chapter 11: Effective Learning Environments
- What Practices Contribute to Effective Classroom Management?
  - Starting Out the Year Right (p. 278)
  - Setting Class Rules (p. 279)
- What Are Some Strategies for Managing Routine Misbehavior?
  - The Principle of Least Intervention (p. 280)
  - Prevention (pp. 280–281)
  - Nonverbal Cues (p. 281)
  - Praising Behavior That Is Incompatible with Misbehavior (p. 282)
  - Praising Other Students (p. 282)
  - Verbal Reminders (p. 282)
  - Repeated Reminders (pp. 282–283)
  - Applying Consequences (p. 283)
- How Is Applied Behavior Analysis Used to Manage More Serious Behavior Problems?
  - How Student Misbehavior Is Maintained (pp. 284–285)
  - Principles of Applied Behavior Analysis (pp. 285–288)
  - Applied Behavior Analysis Programs (pp. 288–290)
  - Ethics of Behavioral Methods (pp. 290–292)
- How Can Serious Behavior Problems Be Prevented?
  - Preventive Programs (p. 292)
  - Identifying Causes of Misbehavior (p. 292)
  - Enforcing Rules and Practices (p. 293)
  - Enforcing School Attendance (p. 293)
  - Practicing Intervention (p. 294)
  - Requesting Family Involvement (p. 294)
  - Using Peer Mediation (p. 294)
  - Confronting Bullying (pp. 295–296)
  - Judiciously Applying Consequences (p. 296)

Topics Covered on the Praxis™ Exam for the Principles of Learning and Teaching (PLT Tests)	Chapter Content Aligned with Praxis™ Topics

I. Students as Learners (22.5% of total test) *(continued)*

C. Student Motivation and Learning Environment *(continued)*

4. Knows a variety of strategies for helping students develop self-motivation
   a. Assigning valuable tasks
   b. Providing frequent positive feedback
   c. Including students in instructional decisions
   d. De-emphasizing grades

Chapter 10: Motivating Students to Learn
- How Can Teachers Increase Students' Motivation to Learn?
  - Intrinsic and Extrinsic Motivation (pp. 260–261)
  - Enhancing Intrinsic Motivation (pp. 261–264)
  - Principles for Providing Extrinsic Incentives to Learn (pp. 264–266)
  - Using Praise Effectively (p. 266)
  - Teaching Students to Praise Themselves (p. 266)

The Intentional Teacher: Using What You Know About Motivation to Improve Teaching and Learning (p. 268)

Theory into Practice: Helping Students Overcome Learned Helplessness (p. 258)

II. Instructional Process (22.5% of total test)

A. Planning Instruction

1. Understands the role of district, state, and national standards and frameworks in instructional planning
   a. Understands the theoretical basis of standards-based instruction
   b. Knows resources for accessing district, state, and national standards and frameworks
   c. Understands how standards and frameworks apply to instructional planning

Chapter 1: What Makes a Good Teacher?
- Common Core State Standards (pp. 9–10)

Chapter 12: Learners with Exceptionalities
- What is Special Education?
  - PL 94–142 and IDEA (pp. 317–318)
- What Is Response to Intervention?
  - Tier 1: Prevention (p. 326)
  - Tier 2: Immediate Intervention (pp. 326–327)
  - Tier 3: Intensive Intervention (p. 327)

Chapter 14: Standardized Tests and Accountability
- Every Student Succeeds Act (ESSA) (pp. 400–401)
- Common Core State Standards (pp. 402–404)

2. Knows how to apply the basic concepts of predominant educational theories to instructional contexts
   a. Understands the basic concepts of cognitivism
      - schema
      - information processing
      - mapping
   b. Understands the basic concepts of social learning theory
      - modeling
      - reciprocal determinism
      - vicarious learning
   c. Understands the basic concepts of constructivism
      - learning as experience
      - problem-based learning
      - zone of proximal development
      - scaffolding
      - inquiry/discovery learning

Chapter 1: Educational Psychology: A Foundation for Teaching
- What Makes a Good Teacher?
  - Common Core Standards (pp. 9–10)

Chapter 2: Cognitive, Language, and Literacy Development
- How Development Occurs (pp. 25–26)
  - Zone of Proximal Development (p. 34)
  - Scaffolding (p. 34)

Theory into Practice: Educational Implications of Piaget's Theory (pp. 32–33)
Theory into Practice: Classroom Applications of Vygotsky's Theory (p. 35)

Chapter 5: Behavioral and Social Theories of Learning
- What Are Behavioral Learning Theories?
  - Pavlov: Classical Conditioning (p. 99)
  - Skinner: Operant Conditioning (p. 99)
- What Are Some Principles of Behavioral Learning?
  - Reinforcers (pp. 101–103)
  - Intrinsic and extrinsic reinforcers (p. 103)
  - Punishers (p. 105)
- How Has Social Learning Theory Contributed to Our Understanding of Human Learning?
  - Bandura: Modeling and Observational Learning (pp. 112–114)

Topics Covered on the Praxis™ Exam for the Principles of Learning and Teaching (PLT Tests)	Chapter Content Aligned with Praxis™ Topics

II. Instructional Process (22.5% of total test) *(continued)*

A. Planning Instruction *(continued)*

d. Understands the basic concepts of behaviorism
• conditioning
• intrinsic and extrinsic rewards
• reinforcement
• punishment
e. Knows how to apply the basic concepts of behaviorism, constructivism, social learning theory, and cognitivism to instructional contexts
	Chapter 6: Cognitive Theories of Learning
	● What Is An Information Processing Model?
	  • Long-term memory (p. 127–130)
	● What Study Strategies Help Students Learn?
	  • Outlining and Concept Mapping (p. 148)
	The Intentional Teacher: Teaching in Light of Knowledge of Brain Function and Learning Strategies (p. 152)
	
	Chapter 7: The Effective Lesson
	● What Is Direct Instruction? (pp. 160–161)
	● How Is a Direct Instruction Lesson Taught? (p. 161)
	● How Do Students Learn and Transfer Concepts? (pp. 176–179)
	● How Are Discussions Used in Instruction?
	  • Whole-Class Discussions (pp. 180–182)
	  • Small-Group Discussions (p. 182)
	
	Chapter 8: Student-Centered and Constructivist Approaches to Instruction
	● What Is the Constructivist View of Learning?
	  • Historical Roots of Constructivism (pp. 188–189)
	  • Zone of proximal development (p. 189)
	  • Discovery learning (pp. 190–192)
	  • Scaffolding (p. 192)
	  • Constructivist Methods in the Content Areas (pp. 191–197)
	● How Are Problem Solving and Thinking Skills Taught? (pp. 204–209)

3. Understands how scope and sequence affect instructional planning
a. Defines and provides examples of scope
b. Defines and provides examples of sequence
c. Understands the relationship between scope and sequence and standards of learning
d. Understands the role of scope and sequence in curriculum planning
	Chapter 7: The Effective Lesson
	● What Is Direct Instruction? (pp. 160–161)
	● How Is a Direct Instruction Lesson Taught? (pp. 161–175)
	● How Do Students Learn and Transfer Concepts? (pp. 176–179)
	● How Are Discussions Used in Instruction?
	  • Whole-Class Discussions (pp. 180–182)
	  • Small-Group Discussions (p. 182)
	The Intentional Teacher: Using What You Know about Direct Instruction to Improve Teaching and Learning (pp. 183–184)
	
	Chapter 8: Student-Centered and Constructivist Approaches to Instruction
	● What Is the Constructivist View of Learning?
	  • Constructivist Methods in the Content Areas (pp. 192–197)
	● How Is Cooperative Learning Used in Instruction? (pp. 198–204)
	The Intentional Teacher: Teaching Using Student-Centered and Constructivist Methods (p. 209)

4. Knows how to select content to achieve lesson and unit objectives	**Chapter 2: Cognitive, Language, and Literacy Development** *Theory into Practice: Educational Implications of Piaget's Theory* (pp. 32–33) *Theory into Practice: Classroom Applications of Vygotsky's Theory* (p. 35) *Theory into Practice: Teaching Children to Read* (p. 40) *The Intentional Teacher:* Teaching in Light of Principles of Cognitive, Language, and Literacy Development (pp. 41–42) **Chapter 7: The Effective Lesson** *The Intentional Teacher:* Using What You Know about Direct Instruction to Improve Teaching and Learning (pp. 185–186) **Chapter 8: Student-Centered and Constructivist Approaches to Instruction** *The Intentional Teacher:* Teaching Using Student-Centered and Constructivist Methods (p. 211)

Topics Covered on the Praxis™ Exam for the Principles of Learning and Teaching (PLT Tests)	Chapter Content Aligned with Praxis™ Topics

II. Instructional Process (22.5% of total test) *(continued)*

A. Planning Instruction *(continued)*

	Chapter 9: Grouping, Differentiation, and Technology ● How Is Technology Used in Education? • Technology for Classroom Teaching (pp. 231–232) • The Internet for Teachers (pp. 234–237) • Technology for Learning (pp. 232–234) • The Internet for Students (pp. 234–237) • Web 2.0 (pp. 237–238) • Instructional Television and Embedded Multimedia (pp. 238–240) **Chapter 12: Learners with Exceptionalities** ● What Are Effective Strategies for Students with Disabilities in General Education? • Computers and Students with Disabilities (pp. 330–331)
5. Knows how to develop observable and measureable instructional objectives in the cognitive, affective, and psychomotor domains **a. Distinguishes among the different learning domains** **b. Knows how to apply Bloom's Taxonomy to the development of instructional objectives** **c. Knows how to describe observable behavior** **d. Knows how to describe measureable outcomes**	**Chapter 7: The Effective Lesson** *Theory into Practice: Planning a Lesson* (p. 164) *Theory into Practice: Communicating Objectives to Students* (p. 165) **Chapter 12: Learners with Exceptionalities** *Theory into Practice: Preparing IEPs* (pp. 320–321) **Chapter 13: Assessing Student Learning** ● What Are Instructional Objectives and How Are They Used? • Planning Lesson Objectives (pp. 341–343) • Aligning Objectives and Assessment (p. 345) • Using Taxonomies of Instructional Objectives (pp. 346–347) • Research on Instructional Objectives (pp. 347–348) *Theory into Practice: Planning Courses, Units, and Lessons* (pp. 344–345)
6. Is aware of the need for and is able to identify various resources for planning enrichment and remediation **a. Identifies when remediation is appropriate** **b. Identifies when enrichment is appropriate** **c. Identifies a variety of resources for locating, adapting, or creating enrichment and remediation activities**	**Chapter 9: Grouping, Differentiation, and Technology** ● How Are Students Grouped to Accommodate Achievement Differences? • Between-Class Ability Grouping (pp. 218–219) • Untracking (p. 219) • Regrouping for Reading and Mathematics (p. 220) • Within-Class Ability Grouping (pp. 220–221) • Retention (p. 221) ● What Are Some Ways of Differentiating Instruction? • Differentiated and Personalized Instruction (p. 222) • Peer Tutoring (pp. 222–223) • Tutoring by Teachers (pp. 223–225) ● What Educational Programs Exist for Students Placed at Risk? • Compensatory Education Programs (pp. 225–226) • Early Intervention Programs (pp. 226–227) • Comprehensive School Reform Programs (p. 227) • After-School and Summer School Programs (pp. 227–228) **Chapter 11: Effective Learning Environments (whole chapter)** **Chapter 12: Learners with Exceptionalities** ● Who are Learners with Exceptionalities? • Students Who are Gifted and Talented (pp. 316–317) ● What Is Inclusion? • Research on Inclusion (pp. 328–329)

Topics Covered on the Praxis™ Exam for the Principles of Learning and Teaching (PLT Tests)	Chapter Content Aligned with Praxis™ Topics

II. Instructional Process (22.5% of total test) *(continued)*

A. Planning Instruction *(continued)*

- What Are Effective Strategies for Students with Disabilities in General Education?
  - Adapting Instruction (p. 329)
  - Universal Design for Learning (p. 330)
  - Teaching Learning Strategies and Metacognitive Awareness (p. 331)
  - Prevention and Early Intervention (p. 331)
  - Tutoring and Small-Group Interventions for Struggling Readers (p. 331)
  - Computers and Students with Disabilities (pp. 331–332)
  - Buddy Systems and Peer Tutoring (pp. 332–333)
  - Special-Education Teams (pp. 333–334)
  - Social Integration of Students with Disabilities (p. 334)

---

7. **Understands the role of resources and materials in supporting student learning**
   a. **Identifies and explains the uses of a variety of resources and materials that support student learning**
      - **computers, the Internet, and other electronic resources**
      - **library collection**
      - **videos, DVDs**
      - **artifacts, models, manipulatives**
      - **guest speakers and community members**
   b. **Knows how to develop lessons as part of thematic and/or interdisciplinary units**
   c. **Understands the basic concepts of thematic instruction**
   d. **Understands the components of thematic units**
      - **selecting a theme**
      - **designing integrated learning activities**
      - **selecting resources**
      - **designing assessments**
   e. **Understands the basic concepts of interdisciplinary instruction**
   f. **Understands the components of interdisciplinary units**
      - **collaborating**
      - **generating applicable topics**
      - **developing an integrative framework**
      - **planning instruction for each discipline**

Chapter 7: The Effective Lesson
- How Do Students Learn and Transfer Concepts?
  - Concept Learning and Teaching (pp. 176–177)
  - Teaching for Transfer of Learning (pp. 177–179)
- How Are Discussions Used in Instruction?
  - Subjective and Controversial Topics (p. 180)
  - Difficult and Novel Concepts (p. 180)
  - Affective Objectives (p. 180)
  - Whole-Class Discussions (pp. 180–182)
  - Small-Group Discussions (p. 182)

Chapter 9: Grouping, Differentiation, and Technology
- How Is Technology Used in Education?
  - Technology for Classroom Teaching (p. 230)
  - Multimedia Teaching (pp. 230–231)
  - Technology for Learning (pp. 231–233)
  - The Internet for Students (pp. 233–236)
  - Web 2.0 (pp. 236–237)
  - Instructional Television and Embedded Multimedia (pp. 237–239)
  - Technology Applications When All Students Have Internet Access (pp. 237–238)
- *Theory into Practice: Helping Students Judge Internet Sources* (p. 235)

Chapter 11: Effective Learning Environments
- What Is an Effective Learning Environment? (pp. 272–273)
- What Is the Impact of Time on Learning? (pp. 273–277)

Chapter 13: Assessing Student Learning
- What Are Instructional Objectives and How Are They Used?
  - Planning Lesson Objectives (pp. 341–343)
  - Aligning Objectives and Assessment (p. 345)
  - Using Taxonomies of Instructional Objectives (pp. 346–347)
  - Research on Instructional Objectives (pp. 347–348)

Topics Covered on the Praxis™ Exam for the Principles of Learning and Teaching (PLT Tests)	Chapter Content Aligned with Praxis™ Topics

II. Instructional Process (22.5% of total test) *(continued)*

A. Planning Instruction *(continued)*

- designing integrative assessment
- recognizes their role in collaborating with instructional partners in instructional planning
g. Identifies a variety of instructional planning partners
  - special education teachers
  - library media specialists
  - teachers of the gifted and talented
  - IEP team members
  - para educators
h. Describes the roles each partner plays in collaborative activities

B. Instructional Strategies

1. Understands the cognitive processes associated with learning
   a. Critical thinking
   b. Creative thinking
   c. Questioning
   d. Inductive and deductive reasoning
   e. Problem solving
   f. Planning
   g. Memory
   h. Recall

Chapter 2: Cognitive, Language, and Literacy Development (Entire Chapter)
Theory into Practice: Educational Implications of Piaget's Theory (pp. 32–33)
Theory into Practice: Classroom Applications of Vygotsky's Theory (p. 35)
Theory into Practice: Promoting Literacy Development in Young Children (p. 39)

Chapter 5: Behavioral and Social Theories of Learning
- How Has Social Learning Theory Contributed to Our Understanding of Human Learning? (pp. 112–116)

Chapter 6: Cognitive Theories of Learning
- What Is an Information-Processing Model? (pp. 122–131)
- What Do We Know from Research on the Brain? (pp. 131–137)
  - How the Brain Works (pp. 131–132)
  - Brain Development (pp. 132–134)
  - Implications for Education (pp. 134–135)
  - Applications of Brain Research to Classroom Teaching (pp. 135–136)
  - Neuromyths and Neuroclues for Educators (p. 137)
- What Causes People to Remember or Forget? (pp. 137–141)
- How Can Memory Strategies Be Taught? (pp. 141–144)
- What Makes Information Meaningful?
  - Rote versus Meaningful Learning (pp. 144–145)
  - Schema Theory (pp. 145–146)
- How Do Metacognitive Skills Help Students Learn? (pp. 146–147)
- What Study Strategies Help Students Learn? (pp. 147–148)
- How Do Cognitive Teaching Strategies Help Students Learn?
  - Making Learning Relevant and Activating Prior Knowledge (pp. 149–151)
  - Organizing Information (pp. 151–154)
The Intentional Teacher: Teaching in Light of Knowledge of Brain Function and Learning Strategies (p. 152)

Chapter 8: Student-Centered and Constructivist Approaches to Instruction
- How Are Problem-Solving and Thinking Skills Taught? (pp. 204–209)
The Intentional Teacher: Teaching Using Student-Centered and Constructivist Methods (p. 209)

Topics Covered on the Praxis™ Exam for the Principles of Learning and Teaching (PLT Tests)	Chapter Content Aligned with Praxis™ Topics
II. Instructional Process (22.5% of total test) *(continued)*	
B. Instructional Strategies *(continued)*	

<table>
<tr>
<td>

2. **Understands the distinguishing features of different instructional models**
   a. **Describes a variety of instructional models**
      - direct
      - indirect
      - independent
      - experiential
      - interactive

</td>
<td>

Chapter 5: Behavioral and Social Theories of Learning
- What Are Some Principles of Behavioral Learning? (pp. 101–112)
- How Has Social Learning Theory Contributed to Our Understanding of Human Learning?
  - Bandura: Modeling and Observational Learning (pp. 112–114)
  - Meichenbaum's Model of Self-Regulated Learning (pp. 114–115)
  - Strengths and Limitations of Behavioral Learning Theories (pp. 115–116)

Chapter 6: Cognitive Theories of Learning
- What Is an Information-Processing Model? (pp. 122–131)
- What Do We Know From Research on the Brain? (pp. 131–137)

Chapter 7: The Effective Lesson
Theory into Practice: Planning a Lesson (p. 164)
- How Is a Direct Instruction Lesson Taught? (pp. 161–175)
The Intentional Teacher: Using What You Know about Direct Instruction to Improve Teaching and Learning (pp. 183–184)

Chapter 8: Student–Centered and Constructivist Approaches to Instruction
- What Is the Constructivist View of Learning? (pp. 188–193)
- How Is Cooperative Learning Used in Instruction? (pp. 193–204)
- How Are Problem Solving and Thinking Skills Taught? (pp. 204–209)

Chapter 10: Motivating Students to Learn
- What Are Some Theories of Motivation? (pp. 249–255)

</td>
</tr>
<tr>
<td>

3. **Knows a variety of instructional strategies associated with each instructional model**
   a. **Identifies instructional strategies associated with direct instruction**
      - explicit teaching
      - drill and practice
      - lecture
      - demonstrations
      - guides for reading, listening, viewing
   b. **Identifies instruction strategies associated with indirect instruction**
      - problem solving
      - inquiry
      - case studies
      - concept mapping
      - reading for meaning
      - cloze procedures
   c. **Identifies instructional strategies associated with independent instruction**
      - learning contracts
      - research projects
      - learning centers
      - computer mediated instruction
      - distance learning

</td>
<td>

Chapter 5: Behavioral and Social Theories of Learning
- What Are Some Principles of Behavioral Learning? (pp. 101–112)
- How Has Social Learning Theory Contributed to Our Understanding of Human Learning? (pp. 112–116)
Theory into Practice: Classroom Uses of Reinforcement (p. 102)

Chapter 6: Cognitive Theories of Learning
- What Do We Know from Research on the Brain? (pp. 131–137)
  - Implications of Brain Research for Education (pp. 134–135)
  - Applications of Brain Research to Classroom Teaching (pp. 135–136)
- How Can Memory Strategies Be Taught? (pp. 141–144)
- How Do Metacognitive Skills Help Students Learn? (pp. 146–147)
- What Study Strategies Help Students Learn?
  - Note-Taking (p. 147)
  - Underlining (p. 148)
  - Summarizing (p. 148)
  - Writing to Learn (p. 148)
  - Outlining and Concept Mapping (p. 148)
  - PQ4R Method (p. 148)
- How Do Cognitive Teaching Strategies Help Students Learn? (pp. 149–154)
Theory into Practice: A Question-Exploration Routine (QER) for Complex Learning (p. 153)

Chapter 7: The Effective Lesson
Theory into Practice: Planning a Lesson (p. 164)
- How Is a Direct Instruction Lesson Taught? (pp. 161–175)
- How Are Discussions Used in Instruction?
  - Whole-Class Discussions (pp. 180–182)
  - Small-Group Discussions (p. 182)
The Intentional Teacher: Using What You Know about Direct Instruction to Improve Teaching and Learning (pp. 183–184)

</td>
</tr>
</table>

Topics Covered on the Praxis™ Exam for the Principles of Learning and Teaching (PLT Tests)	Chapter Content Aligned with Praxis™ Topics
II. Instruction and Assessment (22.5% of total test) *(continued)*	
C. Questioning Techniques *(continued)*	

Chapter 13: Assessing Student Learning
- Why Is Evaluation Important?
  - Evaluation as Feedback (pp. 348–349)
  - Evaluation as Information (pp. 349–350)
  - Evaluation as Incentive (p. 350)

---

2. Understands the uses of questioning
  a. Explains and provides examples of different purposes of questioning
  - developing interest and motivating students
  - evaluating students' preparation
  - reviewing previous lessons
  - helping students to set realistic expectations
  - engaging students in discussion
  - determining prior knowledge
  - preparing students for what is to be learned
  - guiding thinking
  - developing critical and creative thinking skills
  - checking for comprehension or level of understanding
  - summarizing information
  - stimulating students to pursue knowledge on their own

Chapter 7: The Effective Lesson
- How Is a Direct Instruction Lesson Taught?
  - Conduct Learning Probes (pp. 168–171)
  - Assess Performance and Provide Feedback (pp. 174–175)
  - Questions (p. 169)
Theory into Practice: Assessment for Learning (p. 170)

Chapter 13: Assessing Student Learning
- What Are Instructional Objectives and How Are They Used?
  - Planning Lesson Objectives (pp. 341–343)
  - Aligning Objectives and Assessment (p. 345)
  - Using Taxonomies of Instructional Objectives (pp. 346–347)
  - Research on Instructional Objectives (pp. 347–348)
- Why Is Evaluation Important?
  - Evaluation as Feedback (pp. 348–349)
  - Evaluation as Information (pp. 349–350)
  - Evaluation as Incentive (p. 350)
- How Is Student Learning Evaluated?
  - Matching Evaluation Strategies with Goals (pp. 351–352)

---

3. Knows strategies for supporting students in articulating their ideas
  a. Explains and provides examples of strategies for supporting students in articulating their ideas
  - verbal and non-verbal prompting
  - restatement
  - reflective listening statements
  - wait time

Chapter 7: The Effective Lesson
- How Is a Direct Instruction Lesson Taught?
  - Assess Performance and Provide Feedback (pp. 174–175)
  - Questions (p. 169)
  - Wait Time (p. 171)

Chapter 13: Assessing Student Learning
- How Are Tests Constructed?
  - Using a Table of Specifications (p. 355)
- What Are Authentic, Portfolio, and Performance Assessments?
  - Portfolio Assessment (pp. 368–369)
  - Performance Assessment (p. 370)
  - Effectiveness of Performance Assessments (pp. 370–371)
  - Scoring Rubrics for Performance Assessments (p. 371)
Theory into Practice: Using Portfolios in the Classroom (pp. 369–370)

Topics Covered on the Praxis™ Exam for the Principles of Learning and Teaching (PLT Tests)	Chapter Content Aligned with Praxis™ Topics

II. Instruction and Assessment (22.5% of total test) *(continued)*

C. Questioning Techniques *(continued)*

4. Knows methods for encouraging higher levels of thinking
  a. Explains and provides examples of methods for encouraging students' higher levels of thinking, thereby guiding students to
   • reflect
   • challenge assumptions
   • find relationships
   • determine relevancy and validity of information
   • design alternate solutions
   • draw conclusions
   • transfer knowledge
	Chapter 6: Cognitive Theories of Learning
	• What Study Strategies Help Students Learn? (pp. 1147–148)
	• How Do Cognitive Teaching Strategies Help Students Learn? (pp. 149–154)
	
	Chapter 7: The Effective Lesson
	• How Do Students Learn and Transfer Concepts? (pp. 176–179)
	
	Chapter 8: Student-Centered and Constructivist Approaches to Instruction
	• What Is the Constructivist View of Learning?
	  • Peer Interaction (p. 190)
	  • Discovery Learning (p. 190)
	  • Scaffolding (p. 192)
	• How Are Problem-Solving and Thinking Skills Taught?
	  • The Problem-Solving Process (pp. 204–205)
	  • Teaching Creative Problem Solving (pp. 205–207)
	  • Teaching Thinking Skills (pp. 207–208)
	  • Critical Thinking (pp. 208–209)

5. Knows strategies for promoting a safe and open forum for discussion
  a. Knows basic techniques for establishing and maintaining standards of conduct for discussions
   • engaging all learners
   • creating a collaborative environment
   • respecting diverse opinions
   • supporting risk taking
	Chapter 5: Behavioral and Social Theories of Learning
	• What Are Some Principles of Behavioral Learning? (pp. 101–112)
	
	Chapter 7: The Effective Lesson
	• How Are Discussions Used in Instruction? (pp. 179–182)
	
	Chapter 8: Student-Centered and Constructivist Approaches to Instruction
	• How Is Cooperative Learning Used in Instruction? (pp. 198–204)
	
	Chapter 11: Effective Learning Environments
	• What Practices Contribute to Effective Classroom Management? (pp. 278–280)
	• What Are Some Strategies for Managing Routine Misbehavior? (pp. 280–283)
	• How Can Serious Behavior Problems Be Prevented? (pp. 292–296)

D. Communication Techniques

1. Understands various verbal and nonverbal communication modes
  a. Explains and provides examples of
   • body language
   • gesture
   • tone, stress, and inflection
   • eye contact
   • facial expression
   • personal space
	Chapter 2: Cognitive, Language, and Literacy Development (Entire Chapter)
	• How Do Language and Literacy Develop? (pp. 37–40)
	Theory into Practice: Promoting Literacy Development in Young Children (p. 39)
	
	Chapter 3: Social, Moral, and Emotional Development
	• How Do Children Develop Socially and Emotionally? (pp. 52–61)
	Theory into Practice: Developing Social-Emotional Skills (p. 56)
	
	Chapter 7: The Effective Lesson
	• How Are Discussions Used in Instruction? (pp. 179–182)
	The Intentional Teacher: Using What You Know about Direct Instruction to Improve Teaching and Learning (pp. 183–184)
	
	Chapter 8: Student-Centered and Constructivist Approaches to Instruction
	• What Is the Constructivist View of Learning? (pp. 188–198)
	The Intentional Teacher: Teaching Using Student-Centered and Constructivist Methods (p. 208)
	
	Chapter 11: Effective Learning Environments
	• What Practices Contribute to Effective Classroom Management? (pp. 278–279)
	• What Are Some Strategies for Managing Routine Misbehavior?
	  • Prevention (pp. 280–281)
	  • Nonverbal Cues (p. 281)
	  • Praising Behavior That Is Incompatible with Misbehavior (p. 282)
	  • Praising Other Students (p. 282)
	  • Verbal Reminders (p. 282)

Topics Covered on the Praxis™ Exam for the Principles of Learning and Teaching (PLT Tests)	Chapter Content Aligned with Praxis™ Topics

II. Instruction and Assessment (22.5% of total test) *(continued)*

D. Communication Techniques *(continued)*

2. Is aware of how culture and gender can affect communication	**Chapter 4: Student Diversity** • What Is the Impact of Culture on Teaching and Learning? (pp. 66–67) • How Does Socioeconomic Status Affect Student Achievement? (pp. 67–74) • How Do Ethnicity and Race Affect Students' School Experiences? (pp. 75–79) • How Do Language Differences and Bilingual Programs Affect Student Achievement? (pp. 80–83) • How Do Gender and Gender Bias Affect Students' School Experiences? (pp. 85–88) *Theory into Practice: Avoiding Gender Bias in Teaching (p. 87)* *Theory into Practice: Teaching in a Culturally Diverse School (pp. 79–80)*

3. Knows how to use various communication tools that enrich the learning environment
  a. Audio and visual aids
  b. Text and digital resources
  c. Internet and other computer-based tools
	Chapter 9: Grouping, Differentiation, and Technology
	• How Is Technology Used in Education?
	  • Technology for Class Teaching (p. 230)
	  • Multimedia Teaching (pp. 230–231)
	  • Technology for Learning (pp. 231–233)
	  • The Internet for Students (pp. 233–236)
	  • Web 2.0 (pp. 236–237)
	  • Instructional Television and Embedded Multimedia (pp. 237–239)
	Theory into Practice: Helping Students Judge Internet Sources (p. 235)
	
	Chapter 12: Learners with Exceptionalities
	• What Are Effective Strategies for Students with Disabilities in General Education? (pp. 329–334)

4. Understands effective listening strategies
  a. Explains and provides examples of active listening strategies:
    • attending to speaker
    • restating key points
    • asking questions
    • interpreting information
    • providing supportive feedback
    • being respectful
	Chapter 10: Motivating Students to Learn
	• How Can Teachers Increase Students' Motivation to Learn? (pp. 260–266)
	The Intentional Teacher: Using what You Know about Motivation to Improve Teaching and Learning (p. 268)

III. Assessment (approximately 15% of total test)

A. Assessment and Evaluation Strategies

1. Understands the role of formal and informal assessment in informing the instructional process
  a. Defines and provides uses and examples of formal and informal assessment modes
  b. Explains a variety of ways the results of formal and informal assessment are used to make educational decisions.
	Chapter 13: Assessing Student Learning
	• What Are Instructional Objectives and How Are They Used?
	  • Aligning Objectives and Assessment (p. 345)
	  • Using Taxonomies of Instructional Objectives (pp. 346–347)
	• Why Is Evaluation Important?
	  • Evaluation as Feedback (pp. 348–349)
	  • Evaluation as Information (pp. 349–350)
	  • Evaluation as Incentive (p. 350)
	• How Is Student Learning Evaluated?
	  • Formative and Summative Evaluations (p. 350)
	  • Norm-Referenced and Criterion-Referenced Evaluations (pp. 350–351)
	  • Matching Evaluation Strategies with Goals (pp. 351–352)

Topics Covered on the Praxis™ Exam for the Principles of Learning and Teaching (PLT Tests)	Chapter Content Aligned with Praxis™ Topics

III. Assessment (approximately 15% of total test) *(continued)*

A. Assessment and Evaluation Strategies *(continued)*

	● What Are Authentic, Portfolio, and Performance Assessments?
	  • Portfolio Assessment (pp. 368–369)
	  • Performance Assessment (p. 370)
	  • Effectiveness of Performance Assessments (pp. 370–371)
	  • Scoring Rubrics for Performance Assessments (p. 371)
	
	Chapter 14: Standardized Tests and Accountability
	● What Are Standardized Tests and How Are They Used?
	  • Selection and Placement (p. 385)
	  • Diagnosis (pp. 385–386)
	  • Evaluation and Accountability (p. 386)
	  • School Improvement (p. 386)
	The Intentional Teacher: Using What You Know about Standardized Tests to Improve Teaching and Learning (p. 410)

2. **Understands the distinctions among the different types of assessment**
• **Defines and provides uses and examples of formative, summative, and diagnostic assessment**
	Chapter 13: Assessing Student Learning
	● How Is Student Learning Evaluated?
	  • Formative and Summative Evaluations (p. 350)
	  • Norm-Referenced and Criterion-Referenced Evaluations (pp. 350–351)
	  • Matching Evaluation Strategies with Goals (pp. 351–352)
	● How Are Tests Constructed?
	  • Principles of Achievement Testing (pp. 353–354)
	  • Using a Table of Specifications (p. 356)
	  • Writing Selected-Response Test Items (pp. 356–360)
	  • Writing Constructed-Response Items (pp. 360–361)
	  • Writing and Evaluating Essay Tests (pp. 361–363)
	  • Writing and Evaluating Problem-Solving Items (pp. 364–365)
	● What Are Authentic, Portfolio, and Performance Assessments?
	  • Portfolio Assessment (pp. 368–369)
	  • Performance Assessment (p. 370)
	  • Effectiveness of Performance Assessments (pp. 370–371)
	  • Scoring Rubrics for Performance Assessments (p. 371)
	Theory into Practice: Making Assessments Fair (pp. 354–355)
	Theory into Practice: Peer Evaluations (pp. 365–367)
	Theory into Practice: Using Portfolios in the Classroom (pp. 369–370)
	
	Chapter 14: Standardized Tests and Accountability
	● How Are You as an Educator Held Accountable for Student Achievement?
	  • Benchmark Assessments (p. 406)
	  • Data-Driven Reform (p. 406)
	  • Value-Added Assessment Systems (p. 408)
	● What Types of Standardized Tests Are Given?
	  • Aptitude Tests (pp. 387–388)
	  • Norm-Referenced Achievement Tests (pp. 388–389)
	  • Criterion-Referenced Achievement Tests (p. 389)
	  • Standard Setting (p. 389)

Topics Covered on the Praxis™ Exam for the Principles of Learning and Teaching (PLT Tests)	Chapter Content Aligned with Praxis™ Topics

III. Assessment (approximately 15% of total test) *(continued)*

A. Assessment and Evaluation Strategies *(continued)*

3. **Knows how to create and select appropriate assessment format to meet a specific instructional objective**
   - **Knows how to create assessments in a variety of formats**
   - **Is able to select an assessment format to meet a specific instructional objective**

Chapter 13: Assessing Student Learning
- What Are Instructional Objectives and How Are They Used?
  - Aligning Objectives and Assessment (p. 345)
- How Is Student Learning Evaluated?
  - Formative and Summative Evaluations (p. 350)
  - Norm-Referenced and Criterion-Referenced Evaluations (pp. 350–351)
  - Matching Evaluation Strategies with Goals (pp. 351–352)
- How Are Tests Constructed?
  - Principles of Achievement Testing (pp. 353–354)
  - Using a Table of Specifications (p. 256)
  - Writing Selected-Response Test Items (pp. 356–360)
  - Writing Constructed-Response Items (pp. 360–361)
  - Writing and Evaluating Essay Tests (pp. 361–363)
  - Writing and Evaluating Problem-Solving Items (pp. 364–365)
- What Are Authentic, Portfolio, and Performance Assessments?
  - Portfolio Assessment (pp. 368–369)
  - Performance Assessment (p. 370)
  - Effectiveness of Performance Assessments (pp. 370–371)
  - Scoring Rubrics for Performance Assessments (p. 371)

Theory into Practice: Making Assessments Fair (pp. 354–355)
Theory into Practice: Writing Multiple-Choice Tests (pp. 358–359)
Theory into Practice: Peer Evaluations (pp. 365–367)
Theory into Practice: Using Portfolios in the Classroom (pp. 369–370)

4. **Knows how to select from a variety of assessment tools to evaluate student performance**
   a. **Knows a variety of assessment tools, their uses, strengths, and limitations**
      - **rubrics**
      - **analytical checklists**
      - **scoring guides**
      - **anecdotal notes**
      - **continuums**
   b. **Is able to select an assessment tool appropriate for quantifying the results of a specific assessment**

Chapter 13: Assessing Student Learning
- What Are Instructional Objectives and How Are They Used?
  - Aligning Objectives and Assessment (p. 345)
- How Is Student Learning Evaluated?
  - Formative and Summative Evaluations (p. 350)
  - Norm-Referenced and Criterion-Referenced Evaluations (pp. 350–351)
  - Matching Evaluation Strategies with Goals (pp. 351–352)
- How Are Tests Constructed?
  - Principles of Achievement Testing (pp. 353–354)
  - Using a Table of Specifications (p. 356)
  - Writing Selected-Response Test Items (pp. 356–360)
  - Writing Constructed-Response Items (pp. 360–361)
  - Writing and Evaluating Essay Tests (pp. 361–363)
  - Writing and Evaluating Problem-Solving Items (pp. 364–365)
- What Are Authentic, Portfolio, and Performance Assessments?
  - Portfolio Assessment (pp. 368–369)
  - Performance Assessment (p. 370)
  - Effectiveness of Performance Assessments (pp. 370–371)
  - Scoring Rubrics for Performance Assessments (p. 371)

Topics Covered on the Praxis™ Exam for the Principles of Learning and Teaching (PLT Tests)	Chapter Content Aligned with Praxis™ Topics

III. Assessment (approximately 15% of total test) *(continued)*

A. Assessment and Evaluation Strategies *(continued)*

5. **Understands the rationale behind and uses of students' self and peer assessment**
   a. **Defines and provides uses and examples of student self-assessment modes**
   b. **Defines and provides uses and examples of peer assessment modes**
   c. **Explains the strengths and limitations of self and peer assessment modes**

Chapter 8: Student-Centered and Constructivist Views of Learning
- How Is Cooperative Learning Used in Instruction? (pp. 198–204)

Chapter 10: Motivating Students to Learn
- Enhancing Intrinsic Motivation
- Helping Students Make Choices and Set Their Own Goals (pp. 263–264)

Chapter 13: Assessing Student Learning
- What Are Instructional Objectives and How Are They Used?
  - Aligning Objectives and Assessment (p. 345)
- What Are Authentic, Portfolio, and Performance Assessments?
  - Portfolio Assessment (pp. 368–369)
  - Performance Assessment (p. 370)
  - Effectiveness of Performance Assessments (pp. 370–371)
  - Scoring Rubrics for Performance Assessments (p. 371)

Theory into Practice: Peer Evaluations (p. 365)

6. **Knows how to use a variety of assessment formats**
   a. **Describes and provides uses, strengths, and limitations of a variety of assessment formats**
      - essay
      - selected response
      - portfolio
      - conference
      - observation
      - performance
   b. **Is able to select an assessment format appropriate to a specific educational context**

Chapter 13: Assessing Student Learning
- What Are Instructional Objectives and How Are They Used?
  - Aligning Objectives and Assessment (p. 345)
- How Is Student Learning Evaluated?
  - Formative and Summative Evaluations (p. 350)
  - Norm-Referenced and Criterion-Referenced Evaluations (pp. 350–351)
  - Matching Evaluation Strategies with Goals (pp. 351–352)
- How Are Tests Constructed?
  - Principles of Achievement Testing (pp. 353–354)
  - Using a Table of Specifications (p. 356)
  - Writing Selected-Response Test Items (pp. 356–360)
  - Writing Constructed-Response Items (pp. 360–361)
  - Writing and Evaluating Essay Tests (pp. 361–363)
  - Writing and Evaluating Problem-Solving Items (pp. 364–365)
- What Are Authentic, Portfolio, and Performance Assessments?
  - Portfolio Assessment (pp. 368–369)
  - Performance Assessment (p. 370)
  - Effectiveness of Performance Assessments (pp. 370–371)
  - Scoring Rubrics for Performance Assessments (p. 371)

Theory into Practice: Detecting Bluffing in Student Essays (p. 364)

B. Assessment Tools

1. **Understands the types and purposes of standardized tests**
   a. **Explains the uses of the different types of standardized tests**
      - achievement
      - aptitude
      - ability
   b. **Recognizes the data provided by the different types of standardized tests**

Chapter 14: Standardized Tests and Accountability
- What Are Standardized Tests and How Are They Used?
  - Selection and Placement (p. 385)
  - Diagnosis (pp. 385–386)
  - Evaluation and Accountability (p. 386)
  - School Improvement (p. 386)
- What Types of Standardized Tests Are Given?
  - Aptitude Tests (pp. 387–388)
  - Norm-Referenced Achievement Tests (pp. 388–389)
  - Criterion-Referenced Achievement Tests (p. 389)
  - Standard Setting (p. 389)
- How Are Standardized Tests Interpreted?
  - Percentile Scores (p. 390)
  - Grade-Equivalent Scores (p. 390)
  - Standard Scores (pp. 391–392)
- How Can You Use Data to Inform Your Teaching? (pp. 406–408)

Topics Covered on the Praxis™ Exam for the Principles of Learning and Teaching (PLT Tests)	Chapter Content Aligned with Praxis™ Topics

III. Assessment (approximately 15% of total test) *(continued)*

B. Assessment Tools *(continued)*

2. Understands the distinction between norm-referenced and criterion-referenced scoring
• explains the uses of norm-referenced and criterion-referenced tests
• explains data provided by a norm-referenced and a criterion-referenced test
	Chapter 13: Assessing Student Learning
	● How Is Student Learning Evaluated?
	  • Norm-Referenced and Criterion-Referenced Evaluations (pp. 350–351)
	
	Chapter 14: Standardized Tests and Accountability
	● What Types of Standardized Tests Are Given?
	  • Norm-Referenced Achievement Tests (pp. 388–389)
	  • Criterion-Referenced Achievement Tests (p. 389)

3. Understands the terminology related to testing and scoring a. Defines and explains terms related to testing and scoring • validity • reliability • raw score • scaled score • percentile • standard deviation • mean, mode, and median • grade-equivalent scores • age-equivalent scores	● Key Terms: Chapters 13 and 14

4. Understands the distinction between holistic and analytical scoring
a. Describes holistic scoring and analytical scoring
b. Identifies an educational context for each
	Chapter 13: Assessing Student Learning
	● How Is Student Learning Evaluated?
	  • Formative and Summative Evaluations (p. 350)
	  • Norm-Referenced and Criterion-Referenced Evaluations (pp. 350–351)
	  • Matching Evaluation Strategies with Goals (pp. 351–352)
	● How Are Tests Constructed?
	  • Principles of Achievement Testing (pp. 353–354)
	  • Using a Table of Specifications (p. 356)
	  • Writing Selected-Response Test Items (pp. 356–360)
	  • Writing Constructed-Response Items (pp. 360–361)
	  • Writing and Evaluating Essay Tests (pp. 361–363)
	  • Writing and Evaluating Problem-Solving Items (pp. 364–365)
	● What Are Authentic, Portfolio, and Performance Assessments?
	  • Portfolio Assessment (pp. 368–369)
	  • Performance Assessment (p. 370)
	  • Effectiveness of Performance Assessments (pp. 370–371)
	  • Scoring Rubrics for Performance Assessments (p. 371)
	● How Are Grades Determined?
	  • Establishing Grading Criteria (pp. 73–374)
	  • Assigning Letter Grades (pp. 374–375)
	  • Performance Grading (pp. 375–377)
	  • Other Alternative Grading Systems (p. 377)
	  • Assigning Report Card Grades (pp. 377–379)

Topics Covered on the Praxis™ Exam for the Principles of Learning and Teaching (PLT Tests)	Chapter Content Aligned with Praxis™ Topics
III. Assessment (approximately 15% of total test) *(continued)*	
B. Assessment Tools *(continued)*	

	Chapter 14: Standardized Tests and Accountability
	● What Are Standardized Tests and How Are They Used?
	  • Selection and Placement (p. 385)
	  • Diagnosis (pp. 385–386)
	  • Evaluation and Accountability (p. 386)
	  • School Improvement (p. 386)
	● What Types of Standardized Tests Are Given?
	  • Aptitude Tests (pp. 387–388)
	  • Norm-Referenced Achievement Tests (pp. 388–389)
	  • Criterion-Referenced Achievement Tests (p. 389)
	  • Standard Setting (p. 389)
	● How Are Standardized Tests Interpreted?
	  • Percentile Scores (p. 390)
	  • Grade-Equivalent Scores (p. 390)
	  • Standard Scores (pp. 391–392)

5. Knows how to interpret assessment results and communicate their meaning to students, their caregivers, and school personnel
a. Understands what scores and testing data indicate about a student's ability, aptitude, or performance
b. Is able to explain results of assessments using language appropriate for the audience
	Chapter 13: Assessing Student Learning
	● How Are Grades Determined?
	  • Establishing Grading Criteria (pp. 372–373)
	  • Assigning Letter Grades (pp. 374–375)
	  • Performance Grading (p. 375)
	  • Other Alternative Grading Systems (p. 377)
	  • Assigning Report Card Grades (pp. 377–379)
	
	Chapter 14: Standardized Tests and Accountability
	● How Are Standardized Tests Interpreted?
	  • Percentile Scores (p. 390)
	  • Grade-Equivalent Scores (p. 390)
	  • Standard Scores (pp. 391–392)
	Theory into Practice: Smarter Balanced and PARCC Tests (pp. 404–405)

IV. Professional Development, Leadership, and Community (approximately 15% of total test)	

1. Is aware of professional development practices and resources
• **professional literature**
• **professional associations**
• **workshops**
• **conferences**
• **learning communities**
• **graduate courses**
• **independent research**
• **internships**
• **mentors**
• **study groups**
	Chapter 1: Educational Psychology: A Foundation for Teaching
	  • Beyond Certification (pp. 18–19)
	  • Seek Mentors (p. 18)
	  • Seek Professional Development (p. 18)
	  • Talk Teaching (p. 18)
	  • Professional Publications and Associations (p. 18)
	On The Web: Virtual Colleagues (p. 17)
	On The Web: Professional Journals (p. 18)

Topics Covered on the Praxis™ Exam for the Principles of Learning and Teaching (PLT Tests)	Chapter Content Aligned with Praxis™ Topics
IV. Professional Development, Leadership, and Community (approximately 15% of total test) *(continued)*	

2. **Understands the implications of research, views, ideas, and debates on teaching practices**
   a. **Knows resources for accessing research, views, ideas, and debates on teaching practices**
   b. **Interprets data, results, and conclusions from research on teaching practices**
   c. **Is able to relate data, results, and conclusions from research and/or views, ideas, and debates to a variety of educational situations**

Chapter 1: Educational Psychology: A Foundation for Teaching
- What Makes a Good Teacher?
  - Common Core State Standards (pp. 9–10)
- What Is the Role of Research in Educational Psychology? (pp. 10–15)

Chapter 12: Learners with Exceptionalities
- What Is Special Education? (pp. 317–325)

Chapter 14: Standardized Tests and Accountability
- How Are Educators Held Accountable for Student Achievement?
  - Every Student Succeeds Act (ESSA) (pp. 400–401)
  - Common Core State Standards (pp. 402–404)
  - Evidence-Based Reform (pp. 405)

The Intentional Teacher (all)

---

3. **Recognizes the role of reflective practice for professional growth**
   a. **Defines the purposes of reflective practice**
   b. **Knows a variety of activities that support reflective practice**
   - reflective journal
   - self and peer assessment
   - incident analysis
   - portfolio
   - peer observation
   - critical friend

Chapter 1: Educational Psychology: A Foundation for Teaching
- Beyond Certification (pp. 18–19)
  - Seek Mentors (p. 18)
  - Seek Professional Development (p. 18)
  - Talk Teaching (p. 18)
  - Professional Publications and Associations (p. 18)

On The Web: Virtual Colleagues (p. 18)
On The Web: Professional Journals (p. 19)

Chapter 13: Assessing Student Learning
- What Are Instructional Objectives and How Are They Used?
  - Planning Lesson Objectives (pp. 341–343)
  - Aligning Objectives and Assessment (p. 345)
  - Using Taxonomies of Instructional Objectives (pp. 346–347)
  - Research on Instructional Objectives (pp. 347–348)
- Why Is Evaluation Important?
  - Evaluation as Feedback (pp. 348–349)
  - Evaluation as Information (pp. 349–350)
  - Evaluation as Incentive (p. 350)
- How Is Student Learning Evaluated? (pp. 350–353)
- Vignettes Throughout the Book Discuss Peer Mentoring

---

4. **Is aware of school support personnel who assist students, teachers, and families**
   a. **Guidance counselors**
   b. **IEP team members**
   c. **Special education teachers**
   d. **Speech, physical, and occupational therapists**
   e. **Library media specialists**
   f. **Teachers of the gifted and talented**
   g. **Para educators**

Chapter 1: Educational Psychology: A Foundation for Teaching
- How Can I Become an Intentional Teacher?
  - Beyond Certification (pp. 18–19)

On The Web: Virtual Colleagues (p. 19)

Chapter 12: Learners with Exceptionalities
- What is Special Education? (pp. 317–325)
  - An Array of Special-Education Services (pp. 319–320)

Topics Covered on the Praxis™ Exam for the Principles of Learning and Teaching (PLT Tests)	Chapter Content Aligned with Praxis™ Topics
IV. Professional Development, Leadership, and Community (approximately 15% of total test) *(continued)*	

5. **Understands the role of teachers and schools as educational leaders in the greater community**
   - **role of teachers in shaping and advocating for the profession**
   - **perceptions of teachers**
   - **partnerships with parents and family members**
   - **partnerships with the community**

Chapter 4: Student Diversity
- How Does Socioeconomic Status Affect Student Achievement?
  - School and Community Factors (p. 70)
  - Promoting Resilience among Students Who Are Disadvantaged (p. 70)
  - School, Family, and Community Partnerships (pp. 71–72)
  - Supporting the Achievement of Children from Low-Income Groups (pp. 72)
  - Nonschool Solutions to Achievement Problems of Children Who Are Disadvantaged (pp. 72–74)

Theory into Practice: Parent Involvement (p. 72)

6. **Knows basic strategies for developing collaborative relationships with colleagues, administrators, other school personnel, parents/caregivers, and the community to support the educational process**
   a. **Knows the elements of successful collaboration**
      - **developing an action plan**
      - **identifying the stakeholders**
      - **identifying the purpose of collaboration**
      - **supporting effective communication**
      - **seeking support**

Chapter 4: Student Diversity
- How Does Socioeconomic Status Affect Student Achievement?
  - School and Community Factors (p. 70)
  - Promoting Resilience among Students Who Are Disadvantaged (p. 70)
  - School, Family, and Community Partnerships (pp. 71–72)
  - Supporting the Achievement of Children from Low-Income Groups (pp. 72)
  - Nonschool Solutions to Achievement Problems of Children Who Are Disadvantaged (pp. 72–74)

Theory into Practice: Parent Involvement (p. 73)

Chapter 12: Learners with Exceptionalities
- What Is Special Education? (pp. 317–325)
  - An Array of Special-Education Services (pp. 319–323)
  - Collaboration with Consulting Teachers (pp. 319–320)
- What Are Effective Strategies for Students with Disabilities in General Education? (pp. 329–334)
  - Special-Education Teams (pp. 333–334)

Theory Into Practice: Preparing IEPs (pp. 320–322)

7. **Understands the implications of major legislation and court decisions relating to students and teachers**
   - **equal access**
   - **privacy and confidentiality**
   - **First Amendment issues**
   - **Intellectual freedom**
   - **Mandated reporting of child neglect/abuse**
   - **due process**
   - **liability**

Chapter 12: Learners with Exceptionalities
- What Is Special Education?
  - Public Law 94–142 and IDEA (pp. 317–318)
  - An Array of Special-Education Services (pp. 319–323)
- What Is Response to Intervention?
  - Tier 1: Prevention (p. 326)
  - Tier 2: Immediate Intervention (pp. 326–327)
  - Tier 3: Intensive Intervention (p. 327)
- What Is Inclusion?
  - Research on Inclusion (pp. 328–329)

Chapter 14: Standardized Tests and Accountability
- How Are Educators Held Responsible for Student Achievement?
  - Every Student Succeeds Act (ESSA) (pp. 400–401)
  - Common Core State Standards (pp. 402–404)

GLOSSARY

acceleration programs Rapid promotion through advanced studies for students who are gifted or talented.

accommodation Modifying existing schemes to fit new situations.

achievement batteries Standardized tests that include several subtests designed to measure knowledge of particular subjects.

achievement motivation The desire to experience success and to participate in activities in which success depends on personal effort and abilities.

achievement tests Standardized tests measuring how much students have learned in a given context.

accountability The degree to which people are held responsible for their task performances or decision outcomes.

adaptation The process of adjusting schemes in response to the environment by means of assimilation and accommodation.

advance organizers Activities and techniques that orient students to the material before reading or class presentation.

affective objectives Objectives that have to do with student attitudes and values.

allocated time Time during which students have the opportunity to learn.

all-pupil responses Responses made by the entire class.

amygdala The part of the brain that regulates basic emotions.

analogies Images, concepts, or narratives that compare new material to information students already understand.

antecedent stimuli Events that precede behaviors.

applied behavior analysis The application of behavioral learning principles to understanding and changing behavior.

aptitude test A test designed to measure general abilities and to predict future performance.

aptitude–treatment interaction Interaction of individual differences in learning with particular teaching methods.

Asperger syndrome A mild disorder of social and communication skills.

assessment A measure of the degree to which instructional objectives have been attained.

assimilation Understanding new experiences in terms of existing schemes.

associative play Play that is much like parallel play but with increased levels of interaction in the form of sharing, turn-taking, and general interest in what others are doing.

attention Active focus on certain stimuli to the exclusion of others.

attention deficit hyperactivity disorder (ADHD) A disorder characterized by difficulties maintaining attention because of a limited ability to concentrate; includes impulsive actions and hyperactive behavior.

attribution theory A theory of motivation that focuses on how people explain the causes of their own successes and failures.

autism A category of disability that significantly affects social interaction, verbal and nonverbal communication, and educational performance.

autism spectrum disorder Any of a continuum of disorders involving social and communication difficulties.

automaticity A level of rapidity and ease such that tasks can be performed or skills utilized with little mental effort.

autonomous morality In Piaget's theory of moral development, the stage at which a person understands that people make rules and that punishments are not automatic.

aversive stimulus An unpleasant consequence that a person tries to avoid or escape.

backward planning Planning instruction by first setting long-range goals, then setting unit objectives, and finally planning daily lessons.

behavior content matrix A chart that classifies lesson objectives according to cognitive level.

behavior modification Systematic application of antecedents and consequences to change behavior.

behavioral learning theories Explanations of learning that emphasize observable changes in behavior.

benchmark assessments Brief tests given every few months to help a teacher know whether students are on track toward success on state standards.

between-class ability grouping The practice of grouping students in separate classes according to ability level.

bias An undesirable characteristic of tests in which item content discriminates against certain students.

bilingual education Instructional program for students who speak little or no English in which some instruction is provided in the native language.

bioecological approach A model of human development proposed by Urie Bronfenbrenner, who focuses on the social and institutional influences on a child's development, from family, schools, places of worship, and neighborhoods, to broader social and political influences, such as mass media and government.

blended learning Strategies wherein ordinary teaching is combined with a wide range of digital applications.

brain stem The part of the brain that controls basic functions common to all animals.

calling order The order in which students are called on by the teacher to answer questions during the course of a lesson.

CD-ROM A computer database designed for "read-only memory" that provides massive amounts of information, including pictures and audio; it can be of particular importance to students doing projects and research activities.

centration Paying attention to only one aspect of an object or situation.

cerebellum The part of the brain that controls smooth, coordinated movement.

cerebral cortex The main part of the brain, which carries out the highest mental functions.

choral responses Responses spoken by an entire class in unison.

chronological age The age of an individual in years.

classical conditioning The process of repeatedly associating a previously neutral stimulus with an unconditioned stimulus in order to evoke a conditioned response.

classroom management Methods used to organize classroom activities, instruction, physical structure, and other features to make effective use of time; to create a happy and productive learning environment; and to minimize behavior problems and other disruptions.

cognitive apprenticeship The process by which a learner gradually acquires expertise through interaction with an expert, either an adult or an older or more advanced peer.

cognitive behavior modification Procedures based on both behavioral and cognitive principles for changing one's own behavior by means of self-talk and self-instruction.

cognitive development Gradual, orderly changes by which mental processes become more complex and sophisticated.

cognitive learning theories Explanations of learning that focus on mental processes.

collaboration Process in which professionals work cooperatively to provide educational services.

College- and Career-Ready Standards Assessments intended to indicate how students are moving toward success in college and careers, and to move teachers and schools toward innovative approaches to teaching in line with the needs of colleges and the workplace in the 21st century.

Common Core State Standards A set of academic performance standards being adopted by most U.S. states.

compensatory education Programs designed to prevent or remediate learning problems among students from communities where lower socioeconomic status predominates.

completion items Fill-in-the-blank test items.

computer-adaptive An approach to assessment in which a computer is used to present items, and each item presented is chosen to yield the best new information about the examinee based on prior responses to earlier items.

computer-assisted instruction (CAI) Individualized instruction administered by computer.

concept An abstract idea that is generalized from specific examples.

concept mapping Diagramming main ideas and the connections between them.

concrete operational stage Stage at which children develop the capacity for logical reasoning and understanding of conservation but can use these skills only in dealing with familiar situations.

concurrent evidence A type of criterion-related evidence of validity that exists when scores on a test are related to scores from another measure of the same or a very similar trait.

conditioned stimulus A previously neutral stimulus that evokes a particular response after having been paired with an unconditioned stimulus.

conduct disorders Socioemotional and behavioral disorders that are indicated in individuals who, for example, are chronically disobedient or disruptive.

consequences Pleasant or unpleasant conditions that follow behaviors and affect the frequency of future behaviors.

conservation The concept that certain properties of an object (such as weight) remain the same regardless of changes in other properties (such as length).

constructivism View of cognitive development that emphasizes the active role of learners in building their own understanding of reality.

constructivist theories of learning Theories that state learners must individually discover and transform complex information, checking new information against old rules and revising rules when they no longer work.

content evidence A measure of the match between the content of a test and the content of the instruction that preceded it.

content integration Teachers' use of examples, data, and other information from a variety of sources.

contingent praise Praise that is effective because it refers directly to specific task performances.

continuous theories of development Theories based on the belief that human development progresses smoothly and gradually from infancy to adulthood.

control group Group that receives no special treatment during an experiment.

conventional level of morality Stages 3 and 4 in Kohlberg's model of moral reasoning, in which individuals make moral judgments in consideration of others.

Cooperative Integrated Reading and Composition (CIRC) A comprehensive program for teaching reading and writing in the upper elementary grades; students work in four-member cooperative learning teams.

cooperative learning Instructional approaches in which students work in small mixed-ability groups.

cooperative play Play in which children join together to achieve a common goal.

cooperative scripting A study method in which students work in pairs and take turns orally summarizing sections of material to be learned.

corpus callosum Structure that connects the two hemispheres of the brain and coordinates their functioning.

correlational study Research into the relationships between variables as they naturally occur.

criterion-referenced interpretations Assessments that rate how thoroughly students have mastered specific skills or areas of knowledge.

criterion-related evidence A type of evidence of validity that exists when scores on a test are related to scores from another measure of an associated trait.

critical thinking The ability to make rational decisions about what to do or what to believe.

cross-age tutoring Tutoring of a younger student by an older one.

cues Signals about which behavior(s) will be reinforced or punished.

culture The language, attitudes, ways of behaving, and other aspects of life that characterize a group of people.

cutoff score The score designated as the minimum necessary to demonstrate mastery of a subject.

cyberbullying Threats or insults that one person directs at another via instant or text messaging or over e-mail.

databases Computer programs that contain large volumes of information, such as encyclopedias and atlases.

data-driven reform School reform strategies emphasizing careful analysis of data and implementation of proven programs to strengthen areas of need.

deficiency needs Basic requirements for physical and psychological well-being as identified by Maslow.

dendrites Branched projections at the end of a neuron that help conduct information in a brain cell.

derived scores Values computed from raw scores that relate students' performances to those of a norming group (e.g., percentiles and grade equivalents).

descriptive research Research study aimed at identifying and gathering detailed information about a topic of interest.

desktop publishing A computer application for writing compositions that lends itself to revising and editing. *See* word processing.

development Orderly and lasting growth, adaptation, and change over the course of a lifetime.

developmentally appropriate education Instruction adapted to the current developmental status of children (rather than to their age alone).

diagnostic tests Tests of specific skills used to identify students' needs and to guide instruction.

differentiated instruction An approach to teaching that adapts the content, level, pace, and products of instruction in regular classes to accommodate different needs of diverse students.

disability The limitation of a function, such as cognitive processing or physical or sensory abilities.

discipline Methods used to prevent behavior problems from occurring or to respond to behavior problems so as to reduce their occurrence in the future.

digital video and photographs Video and photographs that can be loaded into a computer and shared electronically.

direct instruction Approach to teaching in which the teacher transmits information directly to the students; lessons are goal oriented and structured by the teacher.

discontinuous theories of development Theories describing human development as occurring through a fixed sequence of distinct, predictable stages governed by inborn factors.

discovery learning A constructivist approach to teaching in which students are encouraged to discover principles for themselves.

discriminant validity A type of evidence of validity shown when scores on a test are related or unrelated to scores from one or more measures of other traits when educational or psychological theory about these traits predicts they should be related or unrelated.

discrimination Perception of and response to differences in stimuli.

distractors Incorrect responses that are offered as alternative answers to a multiple-choice question. *See* foils.

distributed practice Technique in which items to be learned are repeated at intervals over a period of time.

drill and practice Application of computer technology to provide students with practice of skills and knowledge.

dual code theory of memory Theory suggesting that information coded both visually and verbally is remembered better than information coded in only one of those two ways.

early intervention Programs that target infants and toddlers who are at risk to prevent possible later need for remediation.

educational psychology The study of learning and teaching.

egocentric Believing that everyone views the world as one views it oneself.

elaboration The process of connecting new material to information or ideas already in the learner's mind.

electronic response devices (clickers) Electronic devices on which students enter answers to questions and have them registered on a computer or interactive whiteboard.

embedded multimedia Video content woven into teachers' lessons.

emergent literacy Knowledge and skills related to reading that children usually develop from experience with books and other print media before the beginning of formal reading instruction in school.

emotional and behavioral disorders Exceptionalities characterized by problems with learning, interpersonal relationships, and control of feelings and behavior.

empowering school culture A school culture in which the institution's organization and practices are conducive to the academic and emotional growth of all students.

enactment A learning process in which individuals physically carry out tasks.

engaged time or time on task Time students spend actively engaged in learning the task at hand.

English learners (EL) Students in U.S. schools who are not native speakers of English.

enrichment programs Programs in which assignments or activities are designed to broaden or deepen the knowledge of students who master classroom lessons quickly.

episodic memory A part of long-term memory that stores images of our personal experiences.

equilibration The process of restoring balance between present understanding and new experiences.

equity pedagogy Teaching techniques that facilitate the academic success of students from different ethnic and social class groups.

ethnic group A group within a larger society that sees itself as having a common history, social and cultural heritage, and traditions, often based on race, religion, language, or national identity.

ethnicity A history, culture, and sense of identity shared by a group of people.

evaluation Measurement of student performance in academic and, sometimes, other areas; used to determine appropriate teaching strategies.

evaluative descriptors Statements describing strong and weak features of a response to an item, question, or project.

Every Student Succeeds Act (ESSA) Main federal education law, which replaced No Child Left Behind in December, 2015. Specifies federal testing and accountability policies, funding for Title I, special education, and other purposes, and much more.

exceptionality A student's physical, mental, or behavioral performance that is so different from the norm—either higher or lower—that additional services are required to meet their needs.

expectancy theory A theory of motivation based on the belief that people's efforts to achieve depend on their expectations of reward.

expectancy–valence model A theory that relates the probability and the incentive value of success to motivation.

experiment Procedure used to test the effect of a treatment.

experimental group Group that receives treatment during an experiment.

external validity Degree to which results of an experiment can be applied to real-life situations.

extinction The weakening and eventual elimination of a learned behavior as reinforcement is withdrawn.

extinction burst The increase in levels of a behavior in the early stages of extinction.

extrinsic incentive A reward that is external to the activity, such as recognition or a good grade.

extrinsic reinforcers Praise or rewards given to motivate people to engage in behavior that they might not engage in otherwise.

feedback Information on the results of one's efforts.

fixed-interval (FI) schedule Reinforcement schedule in which desired behavior is rewarded following a constant amount of time.

fixed-ratio (FR) schedule Reinforcement schedule in which desired behavior is rewarded following a fixed number of behaviors.

flashbulb memory Important events that are fixed mainly in visual and auditory memory.

flipped classroom A classroom where class time is free for use on cooperative learning, project-based learning, or other activities that require the presence of other students and teachers. Teachers prepare digital lessons and make them available to students online. Students are expected to view the lessons at home and perhaps send answers to questions digitally.

foils Incorrect responses that are offered as alternative answers to a multiple-choice question. *See* distractors.

foreclosure An adolescent's premature establishment of an identity based on parental choices, rather than on his or her own desires.

formal operational stage Stage at which one can deal abstractly with hypothetical situations and reason logically.

formative evaluations Evaluations designed to determine whether additional instruction is needed.

free-recall learning Learning of a list of items in any order.

full inclusion Arrangement whereby students who have disabilities or are at risk receive all their instruction in a general education setting; support services are brought to the student.

gender bias Stereotypical views and differential treatment of males and females, often favoring one gender over the other.

generalization Carryover of behaviors, skills, or concepts from one setting or task to another.

giftedness Exceptional intellectual ability, creativity, or talent.

grade-equivalent scores Standard scores that relate students' raw scores to the average scores obtained by norming groups at different grade levels.

grit High achievement motivation.

group alerting Questioning strategies that encourage all students to pay attention during lectures and discussions.

group contingencies Class rewards that depend on the behavior of all students.

group contingency program A program in which rewards (or punishments) are given to a class as a whole for adhering to (or violating) rules of conduct.

Group Investigation A cooperative learning model in which students work in small groups using cooperative inquiry, group discussion, and cooperative planning and projects, and then afterward make presentations to the whole class on their findings.

growth needs Needs for knowing, appreciating, and understanding, which people try to satisfy after their basic needs are met.

halo effect Bias due to carryover of a general attitude about a respondent, as when a teacher knows which student wrote which response, and his or her opinion of the student affects grading.

handicap A condition imposed on a person with disabilities by society, the physical environment, or the person's attitude.

hearing disabilities Degree of deafness; uncorrectable inability to hear well.

heteronomous morality In Piaget's theory of moral development, the stage at which children think that rules are unchangeable and that breaking them leads automatically to punishment.

hippocampus Part of the brain that controls transfer of information from short-term to long-term memory.

home-based reinforcement strategies Behavior modification strategies in which a student's school behavior is reported to parents, who supply rewards.

hypertext and hypermedia Related information that appears when a computer user clicks on a word or picture.

hypothalamus The portion of the brain that controls the release of hormones, and functions such as sleep, hunger, and thirst.

identity achievement A state of consolidation reflecting conscious, clear-cut decisions about occupation and ideology.

identity diffusion Inability to develop a clear direction or sense of self.

imagery Mental visualization of images to improve memory.

inclusion The temporal, instructional, and social integration of eligible children who have exceptionalities with peers who do not have exceptionalities based on an ongoing, individually determined educational planning and programming process. *See* mainstreaming.

independent practice Component of instruction in which students work by themselves to demonstrate and rehearse new knowledge.

Individualized Education Program (IEP) A program tailored to the needs of a learner with exceptionalities.

Individuals with Disabilities Education Act (IDEA) The main federal law concerning the education of all children and adolescents with disabilities.

inert knowledge Learned information that could be applied to a wide range of situations but whose use is limited to restricted, often artificial, applications.

inferred reality The meaning of stimuli in the context of relevant information.

information-processing theory Cognitive theory of learning that describes the processing, storage, and retrieval of knowledge in the mind.

initial-letter strategies Strategies for learning in which initial letters of items to be memorized are made into a more easily remembered word or phrase.

instructional games Drill and practice exercises presented in a game format.

instructional objective A statement of skills or concepts that students should master after a given period of instruction.

integrated learning systems Entire packages of hardware and software that schools purchase. They can form many links and teachers can monitor individual student work this way, and also connect to students who have to learn in distant locations.

intellectual disabilities Disorders, usually present at birth, that result in below-average intellectual skills and poor adaptive behavior.

intelligence General aptitude for learning, often measured by the ability to deal with abstractions and solve problems.

intelligence quotient (IQ) An intelligence test score that for people of average intelligence should be near 100.

intentionality Doing things for a purpose; teachers who practice intentionality plan their actions on the basis of the outcomes they want to achieve.

interactive whiteboard Large touchscreen that teachers can use to display and modify digital content for an entire class.

interference Inhibition of recall of certain information by the presence of other information in memory.

internal validity The degree to which an experiment's results can be attributed to the treatment in question, rather than to other factors.

Internet A large and growing telecommunications network of computers around the world that communicate electronically.

intrinsic incentive An aspect of an activity that people enjoy and therefore find motivating.

intrinsic reinforcers Behaviors that a person enjoys engaging in for his or her own sake, without any other reward.

Jigsaw A cooperative learning model in which students are assigned to six-member teams to work on academic material that has been broken down into sections for each member.

Joplin Plan A regrouping method in which students are grouped across grade lines for reading instruction.

keyword method A strategy for improving memory by using images to link pairs of items.

Khan Academy A series of lessons in many subjects provided online at no cost. The lessons consist of explanations by a teacher, followed by exercises. Students proceed through the lessons at their own pace. An elaborate system of awards and badges rewards students' progress.

knowledge construction Helping students understand how the knowledge we take in is influenced by our origins and points of view.

laboratory experiment Experiment in which conditions are highly controlled.

language disorders Impairments in one's ability to understand language or to express ideas in one's native language.

language minority In the United States, native speakers of any language other than English.

laws Principles that have been thoroughly tested and found to apply in a wide variety of situations.

learned helplessness The expectation, based on experience, that one's actions will ultimately lead to failure.

learners with exceptionalities Individuals whose physical, mental, or behavioral performance is so different from the norm—either higher or lower—that additional services are required to meet their needs.

learning A change in an individual that results from experience.

learning disabilities (LD) Disorders that impede academic progress of people who are not mentally retarded or emotionally disturbed.

learning goals The goals of students who are motivated primarily by desire for knowledge acquisition and self-improvement. Also called *mastery goals.*

learning objectives Specific behaviors that students are expected to exhibit at the end of a series of lessons.

learning probe A method, such as questioning, that helps teachers find out whether students understand a lesson.

Learning Together A cooperative learning model in which students in four- or five-member heterogeneous groups work together on assignments.

least restrictive environment Provision in IDEA that requires students with disabilities to be educated alongside peers without disabilities to the greatest extent appropriate.

lesson planning Procedure that includes stating learning objectives, such as what the students should know or be able to do after the lesson; what information, activities, and experiences the teacher will provide; how much time will be needed to reach the objective; what books, materials, and media support the teacher will provide; and what instructional method(s) and participation structures will be used.

levels-of-processing theory Explanation of memory that links recall of a stimulus to the amount of mental processing it receives.

LGBT (lesbian/gay/bisexual/transgender) Collectively, people in any of these categories. Q (to denote "questioning") is sometimes added, for LGBTQ.

limbic system Layer immediately above the brainstem, composed of the thalamus, hypothalamus, hippocampus, and amygdala.

limited English proficient (LEP) Possessing limited mastery of English.

loci method A strategy for remembering lists by picturing items in familiar locations.

locus of control A personality trait that determines whether people attribute responsibility for their own failure or success to internal or external factors.

long essay item A test question requiring an answer of more than a page.

long-term memory The components of memory in which large amounts of information can be stored for long periods of time.

mainstreaming The temporal, instructional, and social integration of eligible children who have exceptionalities with peers who do not have exceptionalities based on an ongoing, individually determined educational planning and programming process. *See* inclusion.

maintenance Continuation (of behavior).

massed practice Technique in which facts or skills to be learned are repeated often over a concentrated period of time.

mastery grading Grading that requires an established standard of mastery, such as 80 or 90 percent correct on a test. Students who do not meet that standard the first time may receive corrective instruction and then retake the test to try to achieve mastery.

matching items Test items that are presented in two lists, each item in one list matching one or more items in the other list.

meaningful learning Mental processing of new information that relates to previously learned knowledge.

means–ends analysis A problem-solving technique that encourages identifying the goal (ends) to be attained, the current situation, and what needs to be done (means) to reduce the difference between the two conditions.

mediated learning Assisted learning; an approach in which the teacher guides instruction by means of scaffolding to help students master and internalize the skills that permit higher cognitive functioning.

mediation Exposing learners to more advanced ways of thinking and solving problems.

mental age The average test score received by individuals of a given chronological age.

mental set Students' attitude of readiness to begin a lesson.

metacognition Knowledge about one's own learning or about how to learn ("thinking about thinking").

metacognitive skills Methods for learning, studying, or solving problems.

mindset Student theories about their successes and failures.

mnemonics Devices or strategies for aiding the memory.

modeling Imitation of others' behavior.

moral dilemmas In Kohlberg's theory of moral reasoning, hypothetical situations that require a person to consider values of right and wrong.

moratorium Experimentation with occupational and ideological choices without definite commitment.

motivation The influence of needs and desires on the intensity and direction of behavior.

multicultural education Education that teaches the value of cultural diversity.

multifactor aptitude battery A test that predicts ability to learn a variety of specific skills and types of knowledge.

multimedia Electronic material such as graphics, video, animation, and sound, which can be integrated into classroom projects.

multiple-choice items Test items that usually consist of a stem followed by choices or alternatives.

multiple intelligences In Gardner's theory of intelligence, a person's nine separate abilities: logical/mathematical, linguistic, musical, naturalist, spatial, bodily/kinesthetic, interpersonal, intrapersonal, and existential.

negative correlation Relationship in which high levels of one variable correspond to low levels of another.

negative reinforcer Release from an unpleasant situation, given to strengthen behavior.

neuromyth Statements about educational implications of neuroscience that either are not yet justified or are untrue.

neuron A long cell in the brain that helps transmit information.

neutral stimuli Stimuli that have no effect on a particular response.

No Child Left Behind (NCLB) *See* Every Student Succeeds Act (ESSA).

nonverbal cues Eye contact, gestures, physical proximity, or touching that a teacher uses to communicate without interrupting verbal discourse.

normal curve equivalent A set of standard scores ranging from 1 to 99, having a mean of 50 and a standard deviation of about 21.

normal distribution A bell-shaped symmetrical distribution of scores in which most scores fall near the mean, with progressively fewer occurring as the distance from the mean increases.

norm-referenced interpretations Assessments that compare the performance of one student against the performance of others.

norms Standards that are derived from the test scores of a sample of people who are similar to those who will take the test and that can be used to interpret scores of future test takers.

note-taking A study strategy that requires decisions about what to write.

object permanence Understanding that an object exists even when it is out of sight.

observational learning Learning by observation and imitation of others.

operant conditioning The use of pleasant or unpleasant consequences to control the occurrence of behavior.

overlapping A teacher's ability to respond to behavior problems without interrupting a classroom lesson.

outlining Representing the main points of material in hierarchical format.

paired-associate learning Learning of items in linked pairs so that when one member of a pair is presented, the other can be recalled.

parallel play Play in which children engage in the same activity side by side but with very little interaction or mutual influence.

PARCC (Partnership for Assessment of Readiness for College and Career) A state assessment aligned with the Common Core State Standards.

pedagogy The study of teaching and learning with applications to the instructional process.

peer-assisted learning strategies (PALS) A structured cooperative learning method in which students work in pairs, taking turns as teacher and learner, using specific metacognitive strategies.

peers People who are equal in age or status.

peer tutoring Tutoring of one student by another.

pegword method A strategy for memorization in which images are used to link lists of facts to a familiar set of words or numbers.

percentile score A derived score that designates what percentage of the norming group earned raw scores lower than a particular score.

perception A person's interpretation of stimuli.

performance assessments Assessments of students' ability to perform tasks in real-life contexts rather than just showing knowledge. Also called *authentic assessments*.

performance goals The goals of students who are motivated primarily by a desire to gain recognition from others and to earn good grades.

portfolio assessment Assessment of a collection of a student's work to show growth, self-reflection, and achievement.

positive correlation Relationship in which high levels of one variable correspond to high levels of another.

positive reinforcer Pleasurable consequence given to strengthen behavior.

postconventional level of morality Stages 5 and 6 in Kohlberg's model of moral reasoning, in which individuals make moral judgments in relation to abstract principles.

PQ4R method A study strategy that has students preview, question, read, reflect, recite, and review material.

preconventional level of morality Stages 1 and 2 in Kohlberg's model of moral reasoning, in which individuals make moral judgments in their own interests.

predictive evidence A type of criterion-related evidence of validity demonstrated when scores on a test are related to scores from a measure of a trait that the test could be used to predict.

prejudice reduction A critical goal of multicultural education; involves development of positive relationships and tolerant attitudes among students of different backgrounds.

Premack Principle Rule stating that enjoyable activities can be used to reinforce participation in less enjoyable activities.

preoperational stage Stage at which children learn to represent things in the mind.

presentation punishment An aversive stimulus following a behavior, used to decrease the chances that the behavior will occur again.

primacy effect The tendency for items at the beginning of a list to be recalled more easily than other items.

primary reinforcer Food, water, or other consequence that satisfies a basic need.

principle Explanation of the influences of various factors on student outcomes, guided by theory.

private speech Children's self-talk, which guides their thinking and action; eventually internalized as silent inner speech.

proactive facilitation Increased ability to learn new information based on the presence of previously acquired information.

proactive inhibition Decreased ability to learn new information, caused by interference from existing knowledge.

problem solving The application of knowledge and skills to achieve certain goals.

problem-solving assessment Test that calls for organizing, selecting, and applying complex procedures that have at least several important steps or components.

problem-solving program Program designed specifically to develop students' critical-thinking skills.

procedural memory A part of long-term memory that stores information about how to do things.

process–product studies Research approach in which the teaching practices of effective teachers are recorded through classroom observation.

project-based learning When students work in groups to produce a product that represents their learning.

prosocial behaviors Actions that show respect and caring for others.

psychosocial crisis According to Erikson, the set of critical issues that individuals must address as they pass through each of the eight life stages.

psychosocial theory A set of principles that relates social environment to psychological development.

puberty Developmental stage at which a person becomes capable of reproduction.

Public Law 94-142 Federal law enacted in 1975 requiring provision of special-education services to eligible students.

punishment Unpleasant consequences used to weaken behavior.

QAIT model A model of effective instruction that focuses on elements that teachers can directly control: quality, appropriateness, incentive, and time.

race Visible genetic characteristics of individuals that cause them to be seen as members of the same broad group (e.g., African, Asian, Caucasian).

random assignment Selection by chance into different treatment groups; intended to ensure equivalence of the groups.

randomized field experiment Experiment conducted under realistic conditions in which individuals are assigned by chance to receive different practical treatments or programs.

Reading Recovery A program in which specially trained teachers provide one-to-one tutoring to first-graders who are not reading adequately.

recency effect The tendency for items at the end of a list to be recalled more easily than other items.

reciprocal teaching A small-group teaching method based on principles of question generation; through instruction and modeling, teachers foster metacognitive skills primarily to improve the reading performance of students who have poor comprehension.

reflectivity The tendency to analyze oneself and one's own thoughts.

reflexes Inborn automatic responses to stimuli (e.g., eye blinking in response to bright light).

regrouping A method of ability grouping in which students in mixed-ability classes are assigned to reading or math classes on the basis of their performance levels.

rehearsal Mental repetition of information, which can improve its retention.

reinforcer A pleasurable consequence that maintains or increases a behavior.

relative grading standard Grades given according to a student's rank in his or her class or grade.

reliability A measure of the consistency of test scores obtained from the same students at different times.

removal punishment Withdrawal of a pleasant consequence that may be reinforcing a behavior, designed to decrease the chances that the behavior will recur.

response cost Procedure of charging misbehaving students against their free time or other privileges.

Response to Intervention Policies in which struggling children are given increasing levels of assistance and evaluated for possible special-education services only if they fail to respond.

retroactive facilitation Increased comprehension of previously learned information because of the acquisition of new information.

retroactive inhibition Decreased ability to recall previously learned information, caused by learning of new information.

reversibility The ability to perform a mental operation and then reverse one's thinking to return to the starting point.

rote learning Memorization of facts or associations that might be essentially arbitrary.

RSS (Real Simple Syndication or Rich Site Summary) RSS lets users know when something new is posted on a blog, wiki, or RSS-capable website in which they're interested.

rule–example–rule Patterned teaching of concepts that involves first presenting a rule or definition, then giving examples, and finally showing how examples illustrate the rule.

scaffolding Support for learning and problem solving; might include clues, reminders, encouragement, breaking the problem down into steps, providing an example, or anything else that allows the student to grow in independence as a learner.

schedule of reinforcement The frequency and predictability of reinforcement.

schemata Mental networks of related concepts that influence understanding of new information; the singular is *schema*.

schema theory Theory stating that information is stored in long-term memory in schemata (networks of connected facts and concepts), which provide a structure for making sense of new information.

schemes Mental patterns that guide behavior.

seatwork Work that students are assigned to do independently during class.

secondary reinforcer A consequence that people learn to value through its association with a primary reinforcer.

selected-response items Test items in which respondents can select from one or more possible answers, such that the scorer is not required to interpret their response.

self-actualization A person's ability to develop his or her full potential.

self-concept A person's perception of his or her own strengths, weaknesses, abilities, attitudes, and values.

self-esteem The value each of us places on our own characteristics, abilities, and behaviors.

self-questioning strategies Learning strategies that call on students to ask themselves *who, what, where,* and *how* questions as they read material.

self-regulated learners Students who have knowledge of effective learning strategies and how and when to use them.

self-regulation The ability to think and solve problems without the help of others.

semantic memory A part of long-term memory that stores facts and general knowledge.

sensorimotor stage Stage during which infants learn about their surroundings by using their senses and motor skills.

sensory impairments Problems with the ability to receive information through the body's senses.

sensory register Component of the memory system in which information is received and held for very short periods of time.

serial learning Memorization of a series of items in a particular order.

seriation Arranging objects in sequential order according to one aspect, such as size, weight, or volume.

sex-role behavior Socially approved behavior associated with one gender as opposed to the other.

shaping The teaching of a new skill or behavior by means of reinforcement for small steps toward the desired goal.

short essay item A test question the answer to which may range from a sentence or two to a page of 100 to 150 words.

short-term memory The component of memory in which limited amounts of information can be stored for a few seconds. Sometimes called *working memory*.

sign systems Symbols that cultures create to help people think, communicate, and solve problems.

simulation software Computer programs that model real-life phenomena to promote problem-solving abilities and motivate interest in the areas concerned.

single-case experiment Experiment that studies a treatment's effect on one person or one group by contrasting behavior before, during, and after application of the treatment.

Skinner box An apparatus developed by B. F. Skinner for observing animal behavior in experiments that involved operant conditioning.

small-group discussion A discussion among four to six students in a group working independently of a teacher.

Smarter Balanced A state assessment aligned with the Common Core State Standards.

social comparison The process of comparing oneself to others to gather information and to evaluate and judge one's abilities, attitudes, and conduct.

social learning theories Learning theories that emphasize not only reinforcement but also the effects of cues on thought and of thought on action.

socioeconomic status (SES) A measure of prestige within a social group that is most often based on income and education.

solitary play Play that occurs alone.

special education Programs that address the needs of students with mental, emotional, or physical disabilities.

speech disorders Oral articulation problems, occurring most frequently among children in the early elementary school grades.

spreadsheets Computer programs that convert data into tables, charts, and graphs.

standard deviation A statistical measure of the degree of dispersion in a distribution of scores.

standardized tests Tests that are usually commercially prepared for nationwide use and designed to provide accurate and meaningful information on students' performance relative to that of others at their age or grade level.

stanine score A type of standardized score ranging from 1 to 9, having a mean of 5 and a standard deviation of 2.

stem A question or partial statement in a test item that is completed by one of several choices.

stimuli Environmental conditions that activate the senses; the singular is *stimulus*.

Student Teams–Achievement Divisions (STAD) A cooperative learning method for mixed-ability groupings that involves team recognition and group responsibility for individual learning.

students at risk Students who are subject to school failure because of their own characteristics and/or because of inadequate responses to their needs by school, family, or community.

Success for All A comprehensive approach to instruction and supportive services for preschool, kindergarten, and grades 1 through 8, with one-to-one tutoring, family support services, and changes in instruction designed to prevent students from falling behind.

summarizing Writing brief statements that represent the main idea of the information being read.

summative evaluations Final evaluations of students' achievement of an objective.

synapses Tiny branches on the end of a dendrite that receive stimuli and pass them on to other neurons or to the brain.

table of specifications A list of instructional objectives and expected levels of understanding that guides test development.

task analysis Breaking tasks down into fundamental subskills.

taxonomy of educational objectives Bloom's ordering of objectives from simple learning tasks to more complex ones.

teacher efficacy The degree to which teachers feel that their own efforts determine the success of their students.

teaching objectives Clear statements of what students are intended to learn through instruction.

thalamus Structure that receives information from all senses except smell and passes the information on to the rest of the brain.

theory A set of principles that explains and relates certain phenomena.

time on task The time a student is actually engaged in learning.

time out Removal of a student from a situation in which misbehavior was being reinforced.

Title I Federal funding provided to schools that serve many children from low-income homes to help them improve their academic achievement.

tracks Curriculum sequences to which students of specified achievement or ability level are assigned.

transfer of learning The application of knowledge acquired in one situation to new situations.

transitivity A skill learned during the concrete operational stage of cognitive development whereby individuals can mentally arrange and compare objects.

treatment A special program that is the subject of an experiment.

true–false items A form of multiple-choice test items, most useful when a comparison of two alternatives is called for.

tutorial programs Computer programs that teach new material, varying their content and pace according to the student's responses.

unconditioned response A behavior that is prompted automatically by a stimulus.

unconditioned stimulus A stimulus that naturally evokes a particular response.

uncorrelated variables Variables for which there is no relationship between levels of one compared to another.

underrepresented group An ethnic or social group whose members are less likely than the members of other groups to experience economic security or power.

untracking A focus on teaching students in mixed-ability groups and holding them to high standards, but also providing many ways for students to reach those standards.

validity A measure of the degree to which a test is appropriate for its intended use.

variable Something that can have more than one value.

variable-interval (VI) schedule Reinforcement schedule in which desired behavior is rewarded following an unpredictable amount of time.

variable-ratio (VR) schedule Reinforcement schedule in which desired behavior is rewarded following an unpredictable number of behaviors.

verbal learning Learning of words (or facts expressed in words).

vicarious learning Learning based on observation of the consequences of others' behavior.

vision loss Degree of uncorrectable inability to see well.

wait time Length of time that a teacher waits for a student to answer a question.

Web 2.0 Web 2.0 denotes the modern use of the World Wide Web that incorporates free collaborative online communication using a template for users to enter their comments and responses.

whole-class discussion A discussion among all the students in the class with the teacher as moderator.

wiki A website, such as Wikipedia, containing content to which the user can add or make modifications.

within-class ability grouping A system of accommodating student differences by dividing a class of students into two or more ability groups for instruction in certain subjects.

word processing A computer application for writing compositions that lends itself to revising and editing. *See* desktop publishing.

working (or short-term) memory The component of memory in which limited amounts of information can be stored for a few seconds.

zone of proximal development Level of development immediately above a person's present level.

z-score A standard score having a mean of 0 and a standard deviation of 1.

REFERENCES

Abdul Jabbar, A., & Felicia, P. (2015). Gameplay engagement and learning in game-based learning: A systematic review. *Review of Educational Research, 85*(4), 740–779.

Aber, L., Brown, J., Jones, S., & Roderick, T. (2010). SEL: The history of a research–practice partnership. *Better: Evidence-based Education, 2*(2), 14–15.

Abilock, D. (2012). True—or not? *Reading: The core skill, 6*(69), 70–74.

Abrami, P., Bernard, R., Borokhovski, E., Waddington, D., Wade, C., & Persson, T. (2014). Strategies for teaching students to think critically: A meta-analysis. *Review of Educational Research, 85*(2), 275–314.

Academy for Educational Development. (2010). *ISA outcome evaluation: Final report.* New York: Author.

Ackerman, P., Beier, M., & Boyle, M. (2005). Working memory and intelligence: The same or different constructs? *Psychological Bulletin, 131*(1), 30–60.

Adams, A., Carnine, D., & Gersten, R. (1982). Instructional strategies for studying content area texts in the intermediate grades. *Reading Research Quarterly, 18,* 27–53.

Adams, J. L. (1974). *Conceptual blockbusting.* San Francisco, CA: Freeman.

Addison, P., & Warger, C. (2011). *Building your school's capacity to implement RTI: An ASCD action tool.* Alexandria, VA: ASCD.

Adesope, O., Lavin, T., Thompson, T., & Ungerleider, C. (2009, April). *A systematic review and meta-analysis on the cognitive benefits of bilingualism.* Paper presented at the annual meeting of the American Educational Research Association, San Diego, CA.

AERA (2015). AERA statement on use of value-added models (VAM) for the evaluation of educators and educator preparation programs. *Educational Researcher, 44*(8), 448–452.

AERA/APA/NCME. (1999). *Standards for educational and psychological testing.* Washington, DC: American Educational Research Association.

Aikens, N., & Barbarin, O. (2008). Socioeconomic differences in reading trajectories: The contribution of family, neighborhood, and school contexts. *Journal of Educational Psychology, 100*(2), 235–251.

Alberto, P. A., & Troutman, A. C. (2013). *Applied behavior analysis for teachers* (9th ed.). Upper Saddle River, NJ: Pearson.

Alexander, K., Entwisle, D., & Olson, L. (2014). *The long shadow: Family, background, disadvantaged urban youth, and the transition to adulthood.* New York, NY: The Russell Sage Foundation.

Algozzine, B., Marr, M., Kavel, R., & Dugan, K. (2009). Using peer coaches to build oral reading fluency. *Journal of Education for Students Placed at Risk, 14*(3), 256–270.

Allen, C., Chen, Q., Willson, V., & Hughes, J. (2009). Quality of research design moderates effects of grade retention on achievement: A meta-analytic, multilevel analysis. *Educational Evaluation and Policy Analysis, 31*(4), 480–499.

Allen, J., & Allen, C. (2010). The big wait. *Educational Leadership, 68*(1), 22–26.

Allen, L. K., Jacovina, M. E., & McNamara, D. S. (2015). Computer-based writing instruction. In C. A. MacArthur, S. Graham, & J. Fitzgerald (Eds.), *Handbook of writing research* (2nd ed.). New York: Guilford Press.

Allen, L., & Seth, A. (2004). Bridging the gap between poor and privileged. *American Educator, 28*(2), 34–42.

Allen, R. (2003). The democratic aims of service learning. *Educational Leadership, 60*(6), 51–54.

Allensworth, E. (2005). Dropout rates after high-stakes testing in elementary school: A study of the contradictory effects of Chicago's efforts to end social promotion. *Evaluation and Policy Analysis, 27*(4), 341–364.

Allensworth, E., & Nagaoka, J. (2010). Issues in studying the effects of retaining students with high-stakes promotion tests: Findings from Chicago. In J. Meece & J. Eccles (Eds.), *Handbook of research on schools, schooling, and human development* (pp. 327–341). New York, NY: Routledge.

Allington, R. (2011). *What really matters for struggling readers* (3rd ed.). New York: Addison-Wesley.

Allington, R., McGill-Franzen, A., Camilli, G., Williams, L., Graff, J., Zeig, J., Zmach, C., & Nowak, R. (2010). Addressing summer reading setback among economically disadvantaged elementary students. *Reading Psychology, 31*(5), 411–427.

Allor, J., Mathes, P., Roberts, J., Cheatham, J., & Al-Otaiba, S. (2014). Is scientifically-based reading instruction effective for students with below-average IQs? *Exceptional Children, 80*(3), 287–306.

Allspach, J., & Breining, K. (2005). *Gender differences and trends over time for the SAT reasoning test.* Princeton, NJ: Educational Testing Service.

Allyn, P. (2013). *Before ready: Powerful effective steps to implementing and achieving the Common Core State Standards.* Upper Saddle River, NJ: Pearson.

Al-Namlah, A. S., Fernyhough, C., & Meins, E. (2006). Sociocultural influences on the development of verbal mediation: Private speech and phonological decoding in Saudi Arabian and British samples. *Developmental Psychology, 42,* 117–131.

Amendum, S., Vernon-Feagans, L., & Ginsberg, M. (2011). The effectiveness of a technologically facilitated classroom-based early reading intervention. *The Elementary School Journal, 112*(1), 107–131.

American Association of University Women. (2002). *Harrassment-free hallways: How to stop sexual harassment in schools.* Washington, DC: Author.

American Association on Intellectual and Developmental Disabilities (AAIDD). (2010). *Intellectual disability: Definition, classification, and systems of support* (11th ed.). Washington, DC: Author.

American Psychiatric Association. (2011). *DSM-V development: Attention deficit/hyperactivity disorder.* Washington, DC: Author.

American Psychological Association. (2016). *Answers to your questions about transgender people, gender identity, and gender expressions.* Retrieved January 20, 2016 from http://www.apa.org/topics/lgbt/transgender.pdf

Amrein, A., & Berliner, D. (2003). The effects of high-stakes testing on student motivation and learning. *Educational Leadership, 60*(5), 32–38.

Amrein-Beardsley, A. (2008). Methodological concerns about the education value-added assessment system. *Educational Researcher, 37*(2), 65–75.

Amrein-Beardsley, A. (2009). The unintended, pernicious consequences of staying the course. *International Journal of Education Policy and Leadership, 4*(6), 1–13.

Ancheta, A. (2006). Civil rights, education research, and the courts. *Educational Researcher, 35*(1), 26–29.

Anderman, E. M., Anderman, L. H., & Griesinger, T. (1999). The relation of present and possible academic selves during early adolescence to grade point average and achievement goals. *The Elementary School Journal, 100*(1), 3–18.

Anderman, E., & Dawson, H. (2011). Learning with motivation. In R. Mayer & P. Alexander (Eds.), *Handbook of research on learning and instruction* (pp. 219–242). New York, NY: Routledge.

Anderman, E., & Mueller, C. (2010). Middle school transitions and adolescent development. In J. Meece & J. Eccles (Eds.), *Handbook of research on schools, schooling, and human development* (pp. 198–215). New York, NY: Routledge.

Anderman, E., Gray, D., & Chang, Y. (2013). Motivation and classroom learning. In W. Reynolds, G. Miller, & I. Weiner (Eds.) *Handbook of psychology* (Vol. 7, 2nd ed., pp. 99–116). Hoboken, NJ: Wiley.

Anderson, J. (1994). *What do student grades mean? Differences across schools.* Washington, DC: U.S. Department of Education, Office of Educational Research and Improvement.

Anderson, J. R. (2005). *Cognitive psychology and its implications* (6th ed.). New York: Worth.

Anderson, J. R., Greeno, J. G., Reder, L. M., & Simon, H. (2000). Perspectives on learning, thinking, and activity. *Educational Researcher, 29*(4), 11–13.

Anderson, J. R., Reder, L. M., & Simon, H. A. (1996). Situated learning and education. *Educational Researcher, 25*(4), 5–11.

Anderson-Inman, L., & Horney, M. (2007). Supported eText: Assistive technology through text transformations. *Reading Research Quarterly, 42*(1), 153–160.

Andrews, D. (2014). In search of feasible fidelity. In R. E. Slavin (Ed.), *Classroom management and assessment* (pp. 50–55). Thousand Oaks, CA: Corwin.

Ansary, N., Elias, M., Greene, M., & Green, S. (2015). Guidance for schools selecting antibullying approaches: Translating evidence-based strategies to contemporary implementation realities. *Educational Researcher, 44*(1), 27–36.

Anthony, J. L., & Lonigan, C. J. (2004). The nature of phonological awareness: Converging evidence from four studies of preschool and early grade school children. *Journal of Educational Psychology, 96*(1), 43–55.

Anthony, J., Williams, J., Zhang, Z., Landry, S., & Dunkelberger, M. (2014). Experiential evaluation of the value added by Raising a Reader and supplemental parent training in shared reading. *Early Education and Development, 25*(4), 493–514.

Antil, L., Jenkins, J., Wayne, S., & Vadasy, P. (1998). Cooperative learning: Prevalence, conceptualizations, and the relation between research and practice. *American Educational Research Journal, 35*(3), 419–454.

Antonetti, J. V., & Garver, J. R. (2015). *17,000 classroom visits can't be wrong: Strategies that engage students, promote active learning, and boost achievement.* Alexandria, VA: ASCD.

Archer, J. (2007). Information exchange. *Technology counts 2007, 37–41.* Retrieved June 1, 2007, from www.edweek/go/tc07

Arends, R. I. (2004). *Learning to teach* (6th ed.). New York, NY: Worth.

Armony, J., Chochol, C., Fecteau, S., & Belin, P. (2007). Laugh (or cry) and you will be remembered. *Psychological Science, 18,* 1027–1029.

Armstrong, T. (2009). *Multiple intelligences in the classroom* (3rd ed.). Alexandria, VA: ASCD.

Armstrong, T. (2012). *Neurodiversity in the classroom: Strength-based strategies to help students with special needs succeed in school and life.* Alexandria, VA: ASCD.

Arnold, M. L. (2000). Stage, sequence, and sequels: Changing conceptions of morality, post-Kohlberg. *Educational Psychology Review, 12,* 365–383.

Aronson, E., Blaney, N., Stephan, C., Sikes, J., & Snapp, M. (1978). *The jigsaw classroom.* Beverly Hills, CA: Sage.

Aronson, J., & Steele, C. (2005). Stereotypes and the fragility of human competence, motivation, and self-concept. In C. Dweck & E. Elliot (Eds.), *Handbook of competence and motivation.* New York, NY: Guilford Press.

Arter, J., & McTighe, J. (2001). *Scoring rubrics in the classroom.* Thousand Oaks, CA: Corwin.

Artiles, A., Kozleski, E., Dorn, S., & Christensen, C. (2006). Chapter 3: Learning in inclusive education research—Re-mediating theory and methods with a transformative agenda. *Review of Research in Education, 30*(1), 65–108.

Arzubiaga, A., Noguerón, S., & Sullivan, A. (2009). The education of children in immigrant families. *Review of Research in Education, 33,* 246–271.

Ash, K. (2012a, August 29). Educators evaluate "flipped classrooms." *Education Week, 32*(2), s6–s8.

Ash, K. (2012b, May 9). Growing use of digital games in K–8 fueled by teachers, survey finds. *Education Week,* 12–13.

Ashcraft, M. H., & Radvansky, G. A. (Eds.). (2010). *Cognition* (5th ed.). Boston, MA: Prentice Hall.

Asher, N. (2007). Made in the (multicultural) U.S.A.: Unpacking tensions of race, culture, gender, and sexuality in education. *Educational Researcher, 36*(2), 65–73.

Atkins, J., & Ellsesser, J. (2003). Tracking: The good, the bad, and the questions. *Educational Leadership, 61*(2), 44–47.

Atkinson, J. W. (1958). Towards experimental analysis of human motivation in terms of motive, expectancies and incentives. In J. W. Atkinson (Ed.), *Motives in fantasy, action, and society.* Princeton, NJ: Van Nostrand.

Atkinson, J. W. (1964). *An introduction to motivation.* Princeton, NJ: Van Nostrand.

Atkinson, R. C., & Raugh, M. R. (1975). An application of the mnemonic keyword method to the acquisition of Russian vocabulary. *Journal of Experimental Psychology: Human Learning and Memory, 104,* 126–133.

Atkinson, R. C., & Shiffrin, R. M. (1968). Human memory: A proposed system and its component processes. In K. Spence & J. Spence (Eds.), *The psychology of learning and motivation* (Vol. 2). New York, NY: Academic Press.

Atkinson, R. K., Derry, S. J., Renkl, A., & Wortham, D. (2000). Learning from examples: Instructional principles from the worked examples research. *Review of Educational Research, 70*(2), 181–214.

Atkinson, R., Levin, J., Atkinson, L., Kiewra, K., Meyers, T., Kim, S., Renandya, W., & Hwang, Y. (1999). Matrix and mnemonic text-processing adjuncts: Comparing and combining their components. *Journal of Educational Psychology, 91*(2), 342–357.

August, D., & Shanahan, T. (Eds.). (2006a). *Developing literacy in second-language learners.* Mahwah, NJ: Erlbaum.

August, D., & Shanahan, T. (2006b). Synthesis: Instruction and professional development. In D. August & T. Shanahan (Eds.), *Developing literacy in second-language learners* (pp. 351–364). Mahwah, NJ: Erlbaum.

Austin, V. L., & Sciarra, D. T. (2010). *Children and adolescents with emotional and behavioral disorders.* Upper Saddle River, NJ: Pearson.

Ausubel, D. P. (1963). *The psychology of meaningful verbal learning.* New York, NY: Grune & Stratton.

Ausubel, D. P., & Youssef, M. (1963). Role of discriminability in meaningful parallel learning. *Journal of Educational Psychology, 54,* 331–336.

Axelrod, S. (2012). Dealing with classroom management problems. *Better: Evidence-based Education, 5*(1), 16–17.

Axford, N., Lehtonen, M., Kaoukji, D., Tobin, K., & Berry, V. (2012). Engaging parents in parenting programs: Lessons from research and practice. *Children and Youth Services Review, 34*(10), 2061–2071.

Azzam, A. (2009). Why creativity now? A conversation with Sir Ken Robinson. *Educational Leadership, 67,* 22–26.

Azzam, A. (2014). Motivated to learn: A conversation with Daniel Pink. *Educational Leadership, 72*(1), 12–17.

Badgett, J., & Christmann, E. (2009). *Designing elementary instruction and assessment.* Thousand Oaks, CA: Corwin.

Badke, W. (2009). Stepping beyond Wikipedia. *Educational Leadership, 66*(6), 54–58.

Badli, T., & Dzulkifli, M. A. (2013). The effect of humour and mood on memory recall. *Procedia-Social and Behavioral Sciences, 97,* 252–257.

Bailey, F., & Pransky, K. (2014). *Memory at work in the classroom: Strategies to help underachieving students.* Alexandria, VA: ASCD.

Bailey, J., & Burch, M. (2005). *Ethics for behavior analysis.* Mahwah, NJ: Erlbaum.

Baillargeon, R. (2002). The acquisition of physical knowledge in infancy: A summary in eight lessons. In U. Goswami (Ed.), *Blackwell handbook of childhood cognitive development* (pp. 47–83). Malden, MA: Blackwell.

Baines, E., Blatchford, P., & Chowne, A. (2007). Improving the effectiveness of collaborative groupwork in primary schools: Effects on science attainment. *British Educational Research Journal, 33*(5), 663–680.

Baines, L., Baines, C., & Masterson, C. (1994). Mainstreaming: One school's reality. *Phi Delta Kappan, 76*(1), 39–40, 57–64.

Baker, S., Gersten, R., & Lee, D. S. (2002). A synthesis of empirical research on teaching mathematics to low-achieving students. *The Elementary School Journal, 103*(1), 51–73.

Baker, S., Lesnaux, N., Jayantahi, M., Dimino, J., Proctor, C., Morris, J., Gersten, R., ... & Neweman-Conchar, R. (2014). *Teaching academic content and literacy to English learners in elementary and middle school. (NCEE 2014-4012).* Washington, DC: IES, USDOE.

Balfanz, R. (2011). Back on track to graduate. *Educational Leadership, 68*(7), 54–58.

Balfanz, R., Jordan, W., & Legters, N. (2004). *Catching Up: Impact of the Talent Development ninth grade instructional interventions in reading and mathematics in high-poverty high schools.* Center for Research on the Education of Students Placed at Risk, Johns Hopkins University.

Balfanz, R., & MacIver, D. (2000). Transforming high-poverty urban middle schools into strong learning institutions: Lessons from the first five years of the Talent Development Middle School. *Journal of Education for Students Placed at Risk, 5*(1 & 2), 137–158.

Bali, V., Anagnostopoulos, D., & Roberts, R. (2005). Toward a political explanation of grade retention. *Evaluation and Policy Analysis, 27*(3), 133–155.

Ball, D., & Forzani, F. (2007). What makes education research "educational"? *Educational Researcher, 36*(9), 529–540.

Ball, D., & Forzani, F. (2010). Teaching skillful learning. *Educational Leadership, 68*(4), 40–45.

Bandalos, D. L., Yates, K., & Thorndike-Christ, T. (1995). Effects of math self-concept, perceived self-efficacy, and attributions for failure and success on test anxiety. *Journal of Educational Psychology, 87*(4), 611–623.

Bandura, A. (1965). Influence of models' reinforcement contingencies on the acquisition of imitative responses. *Journal of Personality and Social Psychology, 28*(2), 117–148.

Bandura, A. (1986). *Social foundations of thought and action: A social-cognitive theory.* Englewood Cliffs, NJ: Prentice-Hall.

Bandura, A. (1997). *Self-efficacy: The exercise of control.* New York, NY: Freeman.

Bandura, A. (2001). Social cognitive theory: An agentic perspective. *Annual Review of Psychology, 52,* 1–26.

Bandura, A. (2006). Toward a psychology of human agency. *Perspectives on Psychological Science, 1,* 2–10.

Bandura, A. (2012). On the functional properties of perceived self-efficacy revisited. *Journal of Management, 38,* 9–44.

Bandy, T., & Moore, K. (2011). What works for promoting and enhancing positive social skills: Lessons from experimental evaluations of programs and interventions. Retrieved from www.childtrends .org/Files//Child_Trends_2011_03_02_RB_WWSocialSkills.pdf

Banerjee, R., Weare, K., & Farr, W. (2013). Working with "Social and Emotional Aspects of Learning" (SEAL): Associations with school ethos, pupil social experiences, attendance, and attainment. *British Educational Research Journal, 40*(4), 718–742.

Bangert-Drowns, R. L., Hurley, M., & Wilkinson, B. (2004). The effects of school-based writing-to-learn interventions on academic achievement: A meta-analysis. *Review of Educational Research, 74*(1), 29–58.

Bangert-Drowns, R. L., Kulik, C. C., Kulik, J. A., & Morgan, M. (1991). The instructional effect of feedback in test-like events. *Review of Educational Research, 61*(2), 213–238.

Banks, J. (2015). *Cultural diversity and education: Foundations, curriculum, and teaching.* Boston, MA: Pearson.

Banks, J. A. (2008). *An introduction to multicultural education* (4th ed.). Boston, MA: Pearson.

Banks, S. (2012). *Classroom assessment: Issues and practices* (2nd ed.). Long Grove, IL: Waveland.

Barab, S., Gresalfi, M., & Arici, A. (2009). Why educators should care about games. *Educational Leadership, 67*(1), 76.

Barber, B., Eccles, J., & Stone, M. (2001). Whatever happened to the jock, the brain, and the princess? Young adult pathways linked to adolescent activity involvement and social identity. *Journal of Adolescent Research, 16,* 429–455.

Barber, R. M., & Kagey, J. R. (1977). Modification of school attendance for an elementary population. *Journal of Applied Behavior Analysis, 10,* 41–48.

Barnes, M. (2013a). *Role reversal: Achieving uncommonly excellent results in the student-centered classroom.* Alexandria, VA: ASCD.

Barnes, M. (2013b). *The five-minute teacher: How do I maximize time for learning in my classroom?* Alexandria, VA: ASCD.

Barr, R. D., & Parrett, W. H. (2001). *Hope fulfilled for at-risk and violent youth* (2nd ed.). Boston, MA: Allyn & Bacon.

Barth, R. (1979). Home-based reinforcement of school behavior: A review and analysis. *Review of Educational Research, 49,* 436–458.

Barton, P. (2003). *Parsing the achievement gap: Baselines for tracking progress.* Princeton, NJ: Educational Testing Service.

Barton, P. (2007/2008). The right way to measure growth. *Educational Leadership, 65*(4), 70–73.

Barton, P. (2010). National education standards: To be or not to be? *Educational Leadership, 67*(7), 22–29.

Basye, D., Grant, P., Hausman, S., & Johnston, T. (2015). *Get active: Reimagining learning spaces for student success.* Arlington, VA: ISTE.

Battistich, V. (2010). School contexts that promote students' positive development. In J. Meece & J. Eccles (Eds.), *Handbook of research on schools, schooling, and human development* (pp. 111–127). New York, NY: Routledge.

Battistich, V., Watson, M., Solomon, D., Lewis, C., & Schaps, E. (1999). Beyond the three R's: A broader agenda for school reform. *The Elementary School Journal, 99*(5), 415–432.

Baumert, J., Kunter, M., Blum, W., Brunner, M., Voss, T., Jordan, A., . . . Tsai, Y. (2010). Teachers' mathematical knowledge, cognitive activation in the classroom, and student progress. *American Educational Research Journal, 47*(1), 133–180.

Bawden, D., & Robinson, L. (2009). The dark side of information: Overload, anxiety, and other paradoxes and pathologies. *Journal of Information Science, 35*(2), 180–191.

Beach, R. (2011). Issues in analyzing alignment of language arts Common Core Standards with state standards. *Educational Researcher, 40*(4), 179–182.

Beck, I., & McKeown, M. (2001). Inviting students into the pursuit of meaning. *Educational Psychology Review, 13*(3), 225–242.

Beck, I., & McKeown, M. (2007). Increasing young low-income children's oral vocabulary repertoires through rich and focused instruction. *The Elementary School Journal, 107*(3), 251–272.

Beck, I., McKeown, M., & Kucan, L. (2002). *Bringing words to life: Robust vocabulary instruction.* New York, NY: Guilford Press.

Becker, B. E., & Luthar, S. S. (2002). Social-emotional factors affecting achievement outcomes among disadvantaged students: Closing the achievement gap. *Educational Psychologist, 37*(4), 197–214.

Becker, C., & Lee, M. (2009). *The interactive whiteboard revolution: Teaching with IWBs.* Victoria, Australia: ACER Press.

Becker, H. J. (1990). Coaching for the scholastic aptitude test: Further synthesis and appraisal. *Review of Educational Research, 60*(3), 373–417.

Beckwith, S., & Murphey, D. (2016). *5 things to know about boys.* Washington, DC: ChildTrends.

Bee, H., & Boyd, D. (Eds.). (2010). *The developing child* (12th ed.). Boston, MA: Allyn & Bacon.

Beebe-Frankenberger, M., Bocian, K. L., MacMillan, D. L., & Gresham, F. M. (2004). Sorting second grade students with academic deficiencies: Characteristics differentiating those retained in grade from those promoted to third grade. *Journal of Educational Psychology, 96*, 204–215.

Beers, S. (2011). *Teaching 21st century skills: An ASCD action tool.* Alexandria, VA: ASCD.

Beghetto, R., & Kaufman, J. (2013). Fundamentals of creativity. *Educational Leadership, 70*(5), 11–15.

Bender, W. (2015). *20 disciplinary strategies for working with challenging students.* West Palm Beach, FL: Learning Sciences International.

Bender, W. N. (2012). *Differentiating instruction for students with learning disabilities* (3rd ed.). Thousand Oaks, CA: Corwin.

Benner, A., & Crosnoe, R. (2011). The racial/ethnic composition of elementary schools and young children's academic and socioemotional functioning. *American Educational Research Journal, 48*(3), 621–646.

Bennett, C. I. (2015). *Comprehensive multicultural education* (8th ed). Boston, MA: Pearson.

Benson, J. (2014). *Hanging in: Strategies for teaching the students who challenge us most.* Alexandria, VA: ASCD.

Berger, E. H., & Riojas-Cortez, M. (2016). *Parents as partners in education* (9th ed). Boston, MA: Pearson.

Berger, K. (2012). *The developing person through childhood and adolescence* (8th ed.). New York, NY: Worth.

Bergin, D. (2016). Social influences on interest. *Educational Psychologist, 51* (1), 7-22.

Bergin, D., Bergin, C., Van Dover, T., & Murphy, B. (2013). Learn more: Show what you know. *Phi Delta Kappan, 95*(1), 54–60.

Bergmann, J., & Sams, A. (2012). *Flip your classroom: Reach every student in every class every day.* Alexandria, VA: ASCD.

Berk, L. (2013). *Development through the lifespan* (6th ed.). Upper Saddle River, NJ: Pearson.

Berko, J. (1985). The child's learning of English morphology. *Word, 14*, 150–177.

Bernard-Powers, J. (2001). Gender effects in schooling. In C. F. Diaz (Ed.), *Multicultural education for the 21st century.* New York, NY: Longman.

Bernhardt, V. (2005). Data tools for school improvement. *Educational Leadership, 62*(5), 66–69.

Bernstein, D. K., & Tiegerman-Farber, E. (Eds.) (2009). *Language and communication disorders in children* (6th ed.). Boston, MA: Allyn & Bacon.

Bernthal, J. E., Bankson, N. W., & Flipsen, P. (2013). *Articulation and phonological disorders: Speech sound disorders in children* (7th ed.). Upper Saddle River, NJ: Pearson.

Berrueta-Clement, J. R., Schweinhart, L. J., Barnett, W. S., Epstein, A. S., & Weikart, D. P. (1984). *Changed lives.* Ypsilanti, MI: High/Scope.

Berry, B., & Hess, F. (2013). Expanded learning, expansive teacher leadership. *Phi Delta Kappan, 94*(5), 58–61.

Berry, B., Bernett, J., Betlach, K., C'de Baca, S., Highley, S., Holland, J., … Wasserman, L. (2011). *Teaching 2030.* New York, NY: Teachers College Press.

Bertsch, S., Pesta, B. J., Wiscott, R., & McDaniel, M. A. (2007). The generation effect: A meta-analytic review. *Memory & Cognition, 35*, 201–210.

Bettmann, E. H., & Friedman, L. J. (2004). The Anti-Defamation League's A Word of Difference Institute. In W. G. Stephan & W. P. Vogt (Eds.), *Education programs for improving intergroup relations.* New York, NY: Teachers College Press.

Biancarosa, C., & Snow, C. E. (2006). *Reading next—A vision for action and research in middle and high school literacy: A report to Carnegie Corporation of New York* (2nd ed.). Washington, DC: Alliance for Excellent Education.

Biddle, B., & Berliner, D. (2002). Unequal school funding in the United States. *Educational Leadership, 59*(8), 48–59.

Binder, L. M., Dixon, M. R., & Ghezi, P. M. (2000). A procedure to teach self-control to children with attention deficit hyper-activity disorder. *Journal of Applied Behavior Analysis, 33*, 233–237.

Birney, D., Citron-Pousiy, J., Lutz, D., & Sternberg, R. (2005). The development of cognitive and intellectual abilities. In M. Borstein & M. Lamb (Eds.), *Developmental science: An advanced textbook* (5th ed., pp. 327–358). Hillsdale, NJ: Erlbaum.

Bitter, G. G., & Legacy, J. M. (2008). *Using technology in the classroom* (7th ed.). Boston, MA: Pearson.

Blachman, B. A., Tangel, D. M., Ball, E. W., Black, R. S., McGraw, C. (1999). Developing phonological awareness and word recognition skills: A two-year intervention with low-income, inner-city children. *Reading and Writing: An Interdisciplinary Journal, 11*, 239-273.

Blachman, B., Fletcher, J., Minger, K., Schatschneider, C., Murray, M., & Vaughn, M. (2014). Intensive reading remediation in grade 2 or 3: Are there effects a decade later? *Journal of Educational Psychology, 106*(1), 46–57.

Blachman, B., Schatschneider, C., Fletcher, J., Francis, D., Clonan, S., Shaywitz, B., & Shaywitz, C. (2004). Effects of intensive reading remediation for second and third graders and a one year follow-up. *Journal of Educational Psychology, 96*(3), 444–461.

Blachowicz, C. L. Z., & Fisher, P. J. (2006). *Teaching vocabulary in all classrooms* (3rd ed.). Boston, MA: Pearson.

Black, P., Harrison, C., Lee, C., Marshall, B., & Wiliam, D. (2003). Working inside the black box: Assessment for learning in the classroom. *Phi Delta Kappan, 86*(1), 8–21.

Black, P., Harrison, C., Lee, C., Marshall, B., & Wiliam, D. (2004). *Assessment for learning.* New York, NY: Open University Press.

Blackwell, L., Trzesniewski, K., & Dweck, C. (2007). Theories of intelligence and achievement across the junior high school transition: A longitudinal study and an intervention. *Child Development, 78*, 246–263.

Blad, E. (2016). Moving beyond just academics as a way to assess effectiveness. *Education Week, 35*(16), 16–17.

Blair, C. (2004). Learning disability, intelligence, and fluid cognitive functions of the prefrontal cortex: A developmental neuroscience approach. *Learning Disabilities: A Contemporary Journal, 2*(1), 22–29.

Blazar, D., & Kraft, M. A. (2015). *Teacher and teaching effects on students' academic behaviors and mindsets (Working paper #41)*. Washington, DC: Mathematica Policy Reesarch.

Blevins, W. (2011). *Teaching phonics*. New York, NY: Scholastic.

Bligh, D. (2000). *What's the use of lectures?* San Francisco: Jossey-Bass.

Block, C., & Duffy, G. (2008). Research on teaching comprehension. In C. Block & S. Parris (Eds.), *Comprehension instruction: Research-based best practices* (2nd ed., pp. 19–37). New York, NY: Guilford Press.

Bloom, B. S. (1986). Automaticity: The hands and feet of genius. *Educational Leadership, 43,* 70–77.

Bloom, B. S., Englehart, M. B., Furst, E. J., Hill, W. H., & Krathwohl, O. R. (1956). *Taxonomy of educational objectives: The classification of educational goals. Handbook 1: The cognitive domain.* New York, NY: Longman.

Bloom, B. S., Hastings, J. T., & Madaus, G. F. (1971). *Handbook on formative and summative evaluation of student learning.* New York, NY: McGraw-Hill.

Bloom, H. S., & Unterman, R. (2012). *Sustained positive effects on graduation rates produced by New York City's Small Public High Schools of Choice.* New York, NY: MDRC.

Bluestein, J. (2011). What's so hard about win-win? *Educational Leadership, 69*(1), 30–34.

Bluestein, J. (2014). *Managing 21st century classrooms: How do I avoid ineffective classroom management practices?* Alexandria, VA: ASCD.

Blumenfeld, P. C., Marx, R. W., Soloway, E., & Krajcik, J. (1996). Learning with peers: From small group cooperation to collaborative communities. *Educational Researcher, 25*(8), 37–40.

Bodovski, L., & Farkas, G. (2007). Mathematics growth in early elementary school: The roles of beginning knowledge, student engagement, and instruction. *The Elementary School Journal, 108*(2), 115–131.

Bodrova, E., & Leong, D. J. (2007). *Tools of the mind: The Vygotskian approach to early childhood education* (2nd ed.). Columbus, OH: Merrill/Prentice Hall.

Boekaerts, M. (2006). Self-regulation and effort investment. In E. Sigel & K. A. Renninger (Eds.), *A handbook of child psychology: Vol. 4. Child psychology in practice* (pp. 345–377). Hoboken, NJ: Wiley.

Boekaerts, M., Pintrich, P. R., & Zeidner, M. (Eds.). (2000). *Handbook of self-regulation.* San Diego, CA: Academic Press.

Bokosmaty, S., Sweller, J., & Kalyuga, S. (2015). Learning geometry problem solving by studying worked examples: Effects of learner guidance and expertise. *American Educational Research Journal, 52*(2), 307–333.

Bolhuis, S. (2003). Towards process-oriented teaching for self-directed life-long learning: A multidimensional perspective. *Learning and Instruction, 13,* 327–347.

Boom, J., Brugman, D., & van der Heijden, P. G. M. (2001). Hierarchical structure of moral stages assessed by a sorting task. *Child Development, 72,* 535–548.

Bond, C., Symes, W., Hebron, J., Humphrey, N., & Morewood, G. (2016). *Educating persons with Autism Spectrum Disorder: A systematic literature review.* Ireland: National Council for Special Education.

Bondie, R., Gaughran, L., & Zusho, A. (2014). Fostering English learners' confidence. *Educational Leadership, 72*(3), 42–43.

Bong, M., & Skaalvik, E. (2003). Academic self-concept and self-efficacy: How different are they really? *Educational Psychology Review, 15*(1), 1–40.

Bonney, C., & Sternberg, R. (2011). Learning to think critically. In R. Mayer & P. Alexander (Eds.), *Handbook of research on learning and instruction* (pp. 166–196). New York, NY: Routledge.

Booher-Jennings, J., & Beveridge, A. (2007). Who counts for accountability? High-stakes test exemptions in a large urban school district.

In A. Sadovnik, J. O'Day, G. Bohrnstedt, & K. Borman (Eds.), *No Child Left Behind and the reduction of the achievement gap: Sociological perspectives on federal education policy.* New York, NY: Routledge.

Boone, R., & Higgins, K. (2007). The role of instructional design in assistive technology research and development. *Reading Research Quarterly, 42*(1), 134–160.

Borich, G. D. (2014). *Effective teaching methods: Research-based practice* (8th ed). Boston, MA: Pearson.

Borko, H. (2004). Professional development and teacher learning: Mapping the terrain. *Educational Researcher, 33*(8), 3–15.

Borland, J. H. (2008). Gifted students. In T. L. Good (Ed.), *21st century learning* (Vol. 2, pp. 141–149). Thousand Oaks, CA: Sage.

Borman, G. (2002/2003). How can Title I improve achievement? *Educational Leadership, 60*(4), 49–53.

Borman, G. D. (1997). *A holistic model of the organization of categorical program students' total educational opportunities.* Unpublished doctoral dissertation, University of Chicago.

Borman, G. D., & Boulay, M. (2004). *Summer learning: Research, policies, and programs.* Mahwah, NJ: Erlbaum.

Borman, G. D., & D'Agostino, J. V. (2001). Title I and student achievement: A quantitative synthesis. In G. D. Borman, S. C. Stringfield, & R. E. Slavin (Eds.), *Title I: Compensatory education at the crossroads* (pp. 25–57). Mahwah, NJ: Erlbaum.

Borman, G. D., & Overman, L. T. (2004). Academic resilience in mathematics among poor and minority students. *The Elementary School Journal, 104*(3), 177–195.

Borman, G. D., D'Agostino, J. V., Wong, K. K., & Hedges, L. V. (1998). The longitudinal achievement of Chapter I students: Preliminary evidence from the Prospects study. *Journal of Education for Students Placed at Risk, 3*(4), 363–399.

Borman, G. D., Goetz, M., & Dowling, N. (2009). Halting the summer achievement slide: A randomized field trial of the kindergARTen summer camp. *Journal of Education for Students Placed at Risk, 14*(2), 133–147.

Borman, G. D., Hewes, G. M., Overman, L. T., & Brown, S. (2003). Comprehensive school reform and achievement: A meta-analysis. *Review of Educational Research, 73*(2), 125–230.

Borman, G. D., Slavin, R. E., Cheung, A., Chamberlain, A., Madden, N. A., & Chambers, B. (2007). Final reading outcomes of the national randomized field trial of Success for All. *American Educational Research Journal, 44*(3), 701–731.

Borman, G., & Dowling, N. M. (2006). Longitudinal achievement effects of multiyear summer school: Evidence from the Teach Baltimore randomized field trial. *Educational Evaluation and Policy Analysis, 28*(1), 25–48.

Borman, G., & Hewes, G. (2002). Long-term effects and cost effectiveness of Success for All. *Educational Evaluation and Policy Analysis, 24*(2), 243–266.

Borman, G., & Kimball, S. (2005). Teacher quality and educational quality: Do teachers with higher standards-based evaluation ratings close student achievement gaps? *The Elementary School Journal, 106*(1), 3–20.

Borman, G., Benson, J., & Overman, L. (2005). Families, schools, and summer learning. *The Elementary School Journal, 106*(2), 131–150.

Borman, G., Stringfield, S., & Slavin, R. (Eds.). (2001). *Title I: Compensatory education at the crossroads.* Mahwah, NJ: Erlbaum.

Bornstein, P. H. (1985). Self-instructional training: A commentary and state-of-the-art. *Journal of Applied Behavior Analysis, 18,* 69–72.

Boss, S. (2015). *Real-world projects: How do I avoid ineffective classroom management practices?* Alexandria, VA: ASCD.

Bottge, B. A. (2001). Using intriguing problems to improve math skills. *Educational Leadership, 58*(6), 68–72.

Bottoms, J. E., Feagin, C. H., & Han, L. (2005). *Making high schools and middle grades schools work.* Atlanta, GA: Southern Regional Education Board.

Boutot, E. A., & Myles, B. S. (2011). *Autism spectrum disorders: Foundations, characteristics, and effective strategies.* Upper Saddle River, NJ: Pearson.

Bower, G. H., & Karlin, M. B. (1974). Depth of processing pictures of faces and recognition memory. *Journal of Experimental Psychology, 103,* 751–757.

Bower, G. H., Clark, M. C., Lesgold, A. M., & Winzenz, D. (1969). Hierarchical retrieval schemes in recall of categorized word lists. *Journal of Verbal Learning and Verbal Behavior, 8,* 323–343.

Boyd, B. (2012). Five myths about student discipline. *Educational Leadership, 70*(2), 62–66.

Boyd, D., & Bee, H. (2012). *Lifespan development* (6th ed.). Boston, MA: Allyn & Bacon.

Boykin, A. W. (2000). The talent development model of schooling: Placing students at promise for academic success. *Journal of Education for Students Placed at Risk, 5*(1 & 2), 3–25.

Boykin, A., & Noguera, P. (2011). *Creating the opportunity to learn: Moving from research to practice to close the achievement gap.* Alexandria, VA: ASCD.

Bracey, G. (2003). The 13th Bracey report on the condition of education. *Phi Delta Kappan, 84*(8), 616–621.

Bradley, R. H., Whiteside, L., Mundfrom, D. J., Casey, P. H., Caldwell, B. M., & Barrett, K. (1994). Impact of the Infant Health and Development Program (IHDP) on the home environments of infants born prematurely and with low birthweight. *Journal of Educational Psychology, 80,* 531–541.

Bradshaw, C. (2012). Positive behavioral interventions and supports. *Better: Evidence-based education, 5*(1), 20–21.

Bradshaw, C., Waasdorp, T., & Leaf, P. (2015). Examining variation in the impact of school-wide positive behavioral interventions and supports: Findings from a randomized controlled effectiveness trial. *Journal of Educational Psychology, 107*(2), 546–557.

Bradshaw, C., Zmuda, J., Kellam, S., & Ialongo, N. (2009). Longitudinal impact of two universal preventive interventions in first grade on educational outcomes in high school. *Journal of Educational Psychology, 101*(4), 926–937.

Bransford, J. D., & Stein, B. S. (1993). *The ideal problem solver* (2nd ed.). New York, NY: Freeman.

Bransford, J. D., Burns, M. S., Delclos, V. R., & Vye, N. J. (1986). Teaching thinking: Evaluating evaluations and broadening the data base. *Educational Leadership, 44*(2), 68–70.

Brasof, M. (2011). Student input improves behavior, fosters leadership. *Phi Delta Kappan, 93*(2), 20–24.

Bretzing, B. B., & Kulhavy, R. W. (1981). Note taking and passage style. *Journal of Educational Psychology, 73,* 242–250.

Broden, M., Hall, R. V., Dunlap, A., & Clark, R. (1970). Effects of teacher attention and a token reinforcement system in a junior high school special education class. *Exceptional Children, 36,* 341–349.

Bronfenbrenner, U. (1999). Environments in development perspective: Theoretical and operational models. In *Measuring environment across the lifespan: Emerging models and concepts* (1st ed., pp. 3–28). Washington, DC: American Psychological Association.

Bronfenbrenner, U., & Evans, G. (2000). Developmental science in the 21st century: Emerging questions, theoretical models, research designs and empirical findings. *Social Development, 9*(1), 115–125.

Bronfenbrenner, U., & Morris, P. A. (2006). The bioecological model of human development. In W. Damon & R. M. Lerner (Eds.), *Handbook of child psychology, Vol. 1: Theoretical models of human development* (6th ed., pp. 793–828). New York: Wiley.

Bronski, M., Pellegrini, A., & Amico, M. (2013). *You can tell by looking and 20 other myths about LGBT life and people.* Boston, MA: Beacon Press.

Brookes-Gunn, J., & Duncan, G. (1997). The effects of poverty on children. *Children and Poverty, 7*(2), 55–71.

Brookhart, S. (2007/2008). Feedback that fits. *Educational Leadership, 65*(4), 54–59.

Brookhart, S. (2010). *How to assess higher-order thinking skills in your classroom.* Alexandria, VA: ASCD.

Brookhart, S. (2013a). Assessing creativity. *Educational Leadership, 70*(5), 28–34.

Brookhart, S. (2013b). *Grading and group work: How do I assess individual learning when students work together?* Alexandria, VA: ASCD.

Brookhart, S. (2013c). *How to create and use rubrics for formative assessment and grading.* Alexandria, VA: ASCD.

Brookhart, S. (2014). *How to design questions and tasks to assess student thinking.* Alexandria, VA: ASCD.

Brookhart, S. (2015). Performance assessment: Showing what students know and can do. West Palm Beach, FL: Learning Sciences International.

Brookhart, S., & Nitko, A. (2015). *Educational assessment of students.* Boston, MA: Pearson.

Brookhart, S., Moss, C., & Long, B. (2008). Formative assessment that empowers. *Educational Leadership, 66*(3), 52–57.

Brooks, B. D. (1975). Contingency management as a means of reducing school truancy. *Education, 95,* 206–211.

Brooks, R. (2005). Creating a positive school climate for students with learning disabilities: The power of mindsets. In G. Sideritis & T. Citro (Eds.), *Research to practice: Effective interventions in learning disabilities* (pp. 1–20). Weston, MA: Learning Disabilities Worldwide.

Brown, F., Emmons, C., & Comer, J. (2010). The broader picture. *Better: Evidence-based Education, 2*(2), 18–19.

Brown, J., Jones, S., LaRusso, M., & Aber, J. L. (2010). Improving classroom quality: Teacher influences and experimental impacts of the 4Rs program. *Journal of Educational Psychology, 102*(1), 153–167.

Brown, K., Morris, D., & Fields, M. (2005). Intervention after grade 1: Serving increased numbers of struggling readers effectively. *Journal of Literacy Research, 37*(1), 61–94.

Brown, T. (2007). A new approach to attention deficit disorder. *Educational Leadership, 64*(5), 22–28.

Brown-Chidsey, R., & Bickford, K. (2015). *Practical handbook of multi-tiered systems of support.* New York, NY: Guilford Press.

Browne-Dianis, J. (2011). Stepping back from zero tolerance. *Educational Leadership, 69*(1), 24–28.

Brulles, D. & Winebrenner, S. (2012). Clustered for success. *Educational Leadership, 69*(5), 41–45.

Bruner, J. S. (1966). *Toward a theory of instruction.* New York, NY: Norton.

Bruning, R. H., Schraw, G. J., Norby, M. M., & Ronning, R. R. (2004). *Cognitive psychology and instruction* (4th ed.). Columbus, OH: Merrill.

Bryant, D. P., Smith, D. D., & Bryant, B. R. (2008). *Teaching students with special needs in inclusive classrooms.* Boston, MA: Allyn & Bacon.

Budhai, S., & Taddei, L. (2015). *Teacing the 4Cs with technology: How do I use 21st century tools to teach 21st century skills?* Alexandria, VA: ASCD.

Buffum, A., Mattos, M., & Weber, C. (2010). The why behind RTI. *Educational Leadership, 68*(2), 10–16.

Buffum, A., Mattos, M., & Weber, C. (2011). *Simplifying response to intervention.* Bloomington, IN: Solution Tree.

Buffum, A., Mattos, M., Weber, E., & Hierck, T. (2014). *Uniting academic and behavior interventions.* Bloomington, IN: Solution Tree.

Buhle, R., & Blachowicz, C. (2008/2009). The assessment double play. *Educational Leadership, 66*(4), 42–47.

Bulgren, J. A., Lenz, B. K., Schumaker, J. B., Deshler, D. D., & Marquis, J. G. (2002). The use and effectiveness of a comparison routine in diverse secondary content classrooms. *Journal of Educational Psychology, 94*(2), 356–371.

Bulgren, J., Deshler, D., Schumaker, J., & Lenz, B. (2000). The use and effectiveness of analogical instruction in diverse secondary content classrooms. *Journal of Educational Psychology, 92*(3), 426–441.

Bulgren, J., Marquis, J., Lenz, B., Deshler, D., & Schumaker, J. (2011). The effectiveness of a question-exploration routine for enhancing the content learning of secondary students. *Journal of Educational Psychology, 103*(3), 578–593.

Bunce, D. M., Flens, E. A., & Neiles, K. Y. (2010). How long can students pay attention? A study of student attention decline using clickers. *Journal of Chemical Education, 87*(2), 1438–1443.

Burden, P., & Boyd, D. (2016). *Methods for effective teaching* (7th ed.). Boston, MA: Pearson.

Burkam, D., LoGerfo, L., Ready, D., & Lee, V. (2007). The differential effects of repeating kindergarten. *Journal of Education for Students Placed at Risk, 12*(2), 103–136.

Burke, K. (2009). How to assess authentic learning (5th ed.). Thousand Oaks, CA: Corwin.

Burke, R., Oats, R., Ringle, J., Fichtner, L., & DelGaudio, M. (2011). Implementation of a classroom management program with urban elementary schools in low-income neighborhoods: Does program fidelity affect student behavior and academic outcomes? *Journal of Education for Students Placed at Risk, 16*(3), 201–218.

Burkee, K., & Depka, E. (2011). *Using formative assessment in the RTI framework*. Bloomington, IN: Solution Tree.

Burns, M. (2013). New views into the science of educating children with autism. *Phi Delta Kappan, 94*(4), 8–12.

Burns, R. B. (1984). How time is used in elementary schools: The activity structure of classrooms. In L. W. Anderson (Ed.), *Time and school learning: Theory, research, and practice*. London, England: Croom Helm.

Burr, E., Haas, E., & Ferriere, K. (2015). *Identifying and supporting English learner students with learning disabilities: Key issues in the literature and practice*. Washington, DC: USDOE.

Burris, C., Heubert, J., & Levin, H. (2004). Math acceleration for all. *Educational Leadership, 61*(5), 68–71.

Burris, C., Heubert, J., & Levin, H. (2006). Accelerating mathematics achievement using heterogeneous grouping. *American Educational Research Journal, 43*(1), 105–136.

Bussey, K. (1992). Lying and truthfulness: Children's definitions, standards, and evaluative reactions. *Child Development, 63,* 129–137.

Butcher, K. (2006). Learning from text with diagrams: Promoting mental model development and inference generation. *Journal of Educational Psychology, 98*(1), 182–197.

Bywater, T., & Sharples, J. (2012). Effective evidence-based interventions for emotional well-being: Lessons for policy and practice. *Research Papers in Education, 27*(4), 389–408.

Caine, R., & McClintic, C. (2014). *Handling student frustrations: How do I help students manage emotions in the classroom?* Alexandria, VA: ASCD.

Calderón, M. (1999). Teacher learning communities for cooperation in diverse settings. *Theory into Practice, 38*(2), 94–99.

Calderón, M. (2007). *Teaching reading to English language learners, grades 6–12*. Thousand Oaks, CA: Corwin.

Calderón, M. (2011). *Teaching reading and comprehension to English learners, K-5*. Bloomington, IN: Solution Tree.

Calderón, M. E., & Minaya-Rowe, L. (2003). *Designing and implementing two-way bilingual programs*. Thousand Oaks, CA: Corwin.

Calderón, M., & Minaya-Rowe, L. (2011). *Preventing long-term ELs: Transforming schools to meet core standards*. Thousand Oaks, CA: Corwin.

Calderón, M., August, D., Slavin, R. E., Durán, D., Madden, N. A., & Cheung, A. (2004). *The evaluation of a bilingual transition program for Success for All*. Baltimore, MD: Johns Hopkins University, Center for Research on the Education of Students Placed at Risk.

Calderón, M., Hertz-Lazarowitz, R., & Slavin, R. E. (1998). Effects of bilingual cooperative integrated reading and composition on students making the transition from Spanish to English reading. *Elementary School Journal, 99*(2), 153–165.

Calderón, M., Slavin, R., & Sanchez, M. (2011). Effective instruction for English learners. *The future of children, 21*(1), 103–127.

Calfee, R. C., & Wilson, K. M. (2016). *Assessing the Common Core: What's gone wrong—and how to get back on track*. New York, NY: Guilford Press.

Calhoon, M., Al Otaiba, S., Cihak, D., King, A., & Avalos, A. (2007). The effects of a peer-mediated program on reading skill acquisition for two-way bilingual first-grade classrooms. *Learning Disability Quarterly, 30*(3), 169–184.

Calhoun, G., & Elliott, R. (1977). Self-concept and academic achievement of educable retarded and emotionally disturbed children. *Exceptional Children, 44,* 379–380.

California Department of Education. (2012). *Improving education for English learners: Research-based approaches*. Sacramento, CA: CDE Press (at www.cde.ca.gov/re/pn).

Callahan, C., Moon, T., Oh, S., Azano, A., & Hailey, E. (2015). What works in gifted education: Documenting the effects of an integrated curricular/instructional model for gifted students. *American Educational Research Journal, 52*(1), 137–167.

Callahan, R., Wilkinson, L., & Muller, C. (2010). Academic achievement and course taking among language minority youth in U.S. schools: Effects of ESL placement. *Educational Evaluation and Policy Analysis, 32*(1), 84–117.

Callender, A., & McDaniel, M. (2009). The limited benefits of rereading educational texts. *Contemporary Educational Psychology, 34*(1), 30–41.

Cameron, J. (2001). Negative effects of reward on intrinsic motivation—a limited phenomenon: Comment on Deci, Koestner, and Ryan (2001). *Review of Educational Research, 71*(1), 29–42.

Cameron, J., & Pierce, W. D. (1994). Reinforcement, reward, and intrinsic motivation: A meta-analysis. *Review of Educational Research, 64,* 363–423.

Cameron, J., & Pierce, W. D. (1996). The debate about rewards and intrinsic motivation: Protests and accusations do not alter the results. *Review of Educational Research, 66*(1), 39–51.

Cameron, J., Pierce, W. D., Banko, K., & Gear, A. (2005). Achievement-based rewards and intrinsic motivation: A test of cognitive mediators. *Journal of Educational Psychology, 97*(4), 641–655.

Campbell Collaboration. (2016). *Effects of school-based interventions to improve student behavior: A review of six Campbell systematic reviews*. Oslo, Norway: Author.

Campbell, D. (2000). Authentic assessment and authentic standards. *Phi Delta Kappan, 81*(5), 405–407.

Campbell, F. A., & Ramey, C. T. (1994). Effects of early intervention on intellectual and academic achievement: A follow-up study of children from low-income families. *Child Development, 65,* 684–698.

Campbell, J., & Mayer, R. E. (2004, April). *Concrete manipulatives: For whom are they beneficial?* Paper presented at the annual meeting of the American Educational Research Association, San Diego, CA.

Campbell, L., Campbell, B., & Dickerson, D. (2004). *Teaching and learning through multiple intelligences*. Boston, MA: Pearson.

Canter, L. (2014). *Classroom management for academic success.* Bloomington, IN: Solution Tree.

Cappella, E., & Weinstein, R. (2001). Turning around reading achievement: Predictors of high school students' academic resilience. *Journal of Educational Psychology, 93*(4), 758–771.

Capper, C. A., Kampschroer, E. F., & Keyes, M. W. (2000). *Meeting the needs of students of all abilities: How leaders go beyond inclusion.* Bloomington, IN: Phi Delta Kappan.

Caprara, G., Fida, R., Vecchione, M., Del Bove, G., Vecchio, G., Barbaranelli, C., & Bandura, A. (2008). Longitudinal analysis of the role of perceived self-efficacy for self-regulated learning in academic continuance and achievement. *Journal of Educational Psychology, 100*(3), 525–534.

Card, J. J., & Benner, T. A. (2008). *Programs for adolescent sexual health.* New York, NY: Springer.

Carey, T., & Carifio, J. (2012). The minimum grading controversy: Results of a quantitative study of seven years of grading data from an urban high school. *Educational Researcher, 41*(6), 201–208.

Carlisle, J., Kelcey, B., Rowan, B., & Phelpa, G. (2011). Teachers' knowledge about early reading: Effects on students' gains in reading achievement. *Journal of Research on Educational Effectiveness, 4*(4), 289–321.

Carlo, M. S., August, D., McLaughlin, B., Snow, C. E., Dressler, C., Lippman, D., Lively, T., & White, C. (2004). Closing the gap: Addressing the vocabulary needs of English language learners in bilingual and mainstream classrooms. *Reading Research Quarterly, 39*(2), 188–215.

Carlson, G., & Raphael, R. (2015). *Let's get social.* Arlington, VA: ISTE.

Carney, R. N., & Levin, J. R. (1998). Do mnemonic memories fade as time goes by? Here's looking anew! *Contemporary Educational Psychology, 23*(3), 276–297.

Carney, R. N., & Levin, J. R. (2002). Pictorial illustrations still improve students' learning from text. *Educational Psychology Review, 14*(1), 5–26.

Carney, R., Stratford, B., Anderson, K., Rojas, A., & Daneri, M. (2015). *What works for reducing problem behaviors in early childhood: Lessons from experimental evaluations.* Bethesda, MD: ChildTrends.

Carnoy, M., & Loeb, S. (2002). Does external accountability affect student outcomes? A cross-state analysis. *Educational Evaluation and Policy Analysis, 24*(4), 305–331.

Carolan, J., & Guinn, A. (2007). Differentiation: Lessons from master teachers. *Educational Leadership, 64*(5), 44–47.

Carpenter, L. B., Johnston, L. B., & Beard, L. A. (2015). *Assistive technology: Access for all students.* Boston, MA: Pearson.

Carpenter, S., & Pashler, H. (2007). Testing beyond words: Using tests to enhance visuospatial map learning. *Psychonomic Bulletin & Review, 14*, 474–478.

Carpenter, T., Fennema, E., Frank, M., Levi, L., & Empson, S. (2014). *Children's mathematics: Cognitively Guided Instruction.* Heinemann.

Carroll, J. B. (1963). A model of school learning. *Teachers College Record, 64*, 723–733.

Carroll, J. B. (1989). The Carroll model: A 25-year retrospective and prospective view. *Educational Researcher, 18*, 26–31.

Carter, L. F. (1984). The sustaining effects study of compensatory and elementary education. *Educational Researcher, 13*(7), 4–13.

Carter, P., & Darling-Hammond, L. (2016). Teaching diverse learners. In D. Gitomer & C. Bell (Eds.), *Handbook of research on teaching* (5th ed.). (pp. 593–638). Washington, DC: AERA.

Casbergue, R. M., & Strickland, D. (2015). *Reading and writing in preschool.* New York, NY: Guilford Press.

Casoli-Reardon, M., Rappaport, N., Kulick, D., & Reinfeld, S. (2012). Ending school avoidance. *Educational Leadership, 70*(2), 50–55.

Cassady, J. C., & Johnson, R. E. (2002). Cognitive anxiety and academic performance. *Contemporary Educational Psychology, 27,* 270–295.

Castagno, A., & Brayboy, B. (2008). Culturally responsive schooling for indigenous youth: A review of the literature. *Review of Educational Research, 78*(4), 941–993.

Cavanaugh, C., Kim, A.-H., Wanzek, J., & Vaughn, S. (2004). Kindergarten reading interventions for at-risk students: Twenty years of research. *Learning Disabilities: A Contemporary Journal, 2*(1), 1–8.

Cawn, B. (2015). *Texts, tasks, and talk: Instruction to meet the Common Core in grades 9–12.* Bloomington, IN: Solution Tree.

Ceci, S. J. (1991). How much does schooling influence general intelligence and its cognitive components? A reassessment of the evidence. *Developmental Psychology, 27,* 703–722.

Ceci, S., & Williams, W. (Eds.). (2009). *Why aren't more women in science? Top researchers debate the evidence* (pp. 47–55). Washington, DC: American Psychological Association.

Center for Public Education. (2008). *High-performing, high-poverty schools: Research review.* Fairfax, VA: Caliber Associates.

Center on Education Policy. (2010). *Are there differences in achievement between boys and girls?* Washington, DC: Author.

Center, Y. (2005). *Beginning reading.* New South Wales, Australia: Allen & Unwin.

Cepeda, N. J., Pashler, H., Vul, E., Wixted, J. T., & Rohrer, D. (2006). Distributed practice in verbal recall tasks: A review and quantitative synthesis. *Psychological Bulletin, 132,* 354–380.

Chambers, B., Cheung, A., & Slavin, R. (in press). Literacy and language outcomes of balanced and developmental-constructivist approaches to early childhood education: A systematic review. *Educational Research Review.*

Chambers, B., Cheung, A., Madden, N., Slavin, R. E., & Gifford, R. (2006). Achievement effects of embedded multimedia in a Success for All reading program. *Journal of Educational Psychology, 98*(1), 232–237.

Chambers, B., Cheung, A., Slavin, R., Smith, D., & Laurenzano, M. (2010). *Effective early childhood programmes: A best-evidence synthesis.* York, England: Institute for Effective Education, University of York.

Chambers, B., de Botton, O., Cheung, A., & Slavin, R. (2013). Effective early childhood education programs for disadvantaged children: A systematic review and case studies. *Handbook of research on the education of young children* (pp. 322–331). New York, NY: Routledge.

Chambers, B., de Botton, O., Cheung, A., Slavin, R. E. (2012). Effective early childhood programs for children at risk of school failure. In O. N. Saracho & B. Spodek (Eds.), *Handbook of research on the education of young children* (3rd ed., pp. 322–331). New York, NY: Routledge.

Chambers, B., Slavin, R. E., Madden, N. A., Abrami, P. C., Tucker, B. J., Cheung, A., & Gifford, R. (2008). Technology infusion in Success for All: Reading outcomes for first graders. *Elementary School Journal, 109*(1), 1–15.

Chambers, B., Slavin, R., Madden, N., Abrami, P., Logan, M., & Gifford, R. (2011). Small-group, computer-assisted tutoring to improve reading outcomes for struggling first and second graders. *The Elementary School Journal, 111*(4), 625–640.

Chander, K., Fortune, N., Lovett, J., & Scherrer, J. (2016). What should Common Core assessments measure? *Phi Delta Kappan, 97*(5), 60–65.

Chapman, C., & King, R. (2005). *Differentiated assessment strategies.* Thousand Oaks, CA: Corwin.

Chapman, E. (2001, April). *More on moderations in cooperative learning outcomes.* Paper presented at the annual meeting of the American Educational Research Association, Montreal, Canada.

Chapman, J., Tunmer, W., & Prochnow, J. (2000). Early reading-related skills and performance, reading self-concept, and the development of academic self-concept: A longitudinal study. *Journal of Educational Psychology, 92*(4), 703–708.

Chappell, S., Nunnery, J., Pribesh, S., & Hager, J. (2011). A meta-analysis of supplemental education services provider effects on student achievement. *Journal of Education for Students Placed at Risk, 16*(1), 1–23.

Chappuis, J. (2015). *Seven strategies of assessment for learning.* Boston, MA: Pearson.

Chappuis, J., Stiggins, R., Chappuis, S., & Arter, J. (2012). Classroom assessment for student learning: Doing it right—doing it well (2nd ed.). Upper Saddle River, NJ: Pearson.

Chappuis, S., & Chappuis, J. (2007/2008). The best value in formative assessment. *Educational Leadership, 65*(4), 14–19.

Charles, C. M., Senter, G., & Charles, M. (2014). *Building classroom discipline* (11th ed.). Upper Saddle River, NJ: Pearson.

Chatterji, M. (2006). Reading achievement gaps, correlates, and moderators of early reading achievement: Evidence from the Early Childhood Longitudinal Study (ECLS) kindergarten to first grade sample. *Journal of Educational Psychology, 98*(3), 489–507.

Chen, J.-Q. (2004). Theory of multiple intelligences: Is it a scientific theory? *Teachers College Record, 106,* 17–23.

Chen, Z., & Daehler, M. (2000). External and internal instantiation of abstract information facilitates transfer in insight problem solving. *Contemporary Educational Psychology, 25*(4), 423–449.

Chenoweth, K. (2009). *How it's being done: Urgent lessons from unexpected schools.* Cambridge, MA: Harvard Education Press.

Chetty, R., Friedman, J. N., & Rockoff, J. E. (2014). Measuring the impact of teachers II: Teacher value-added and student outcomes in adulthood. *American Economic Review, 104*(9), 2633–2679. Retrieved from http://dx.doi.org/10.1257/aer.104.9.2633

Cheung, A., & Slavin, R. (2012a). Effective reading programs for Spanish-dominant English language learners in the elementary grades: A best-evidence synthesis. *Review of Educational Resarch, 82*(4), 351–395.

Cheung, A., & Slavin, R. (2012b). How features of educational technology programs affect student reading outcomes: A meta-analysis. *Educational Research Review, 7*(3), 198–215.

Cheung, A., & Slavin, R. (2013). The effectiveness of educational technology applications for enhancing mathematics achievement in K–12 classrooms. *Educational Research Review, 9,* 88–113.

Cheung, A., & Slavin, R. E. (2005). Effective reading programs for English language learners and other language-minority students. *Bilingual Research Journal, 29*(2), 241–267.

Chi, M., & VanLehn, K. (2012). Seeing deep structure from the interactions of surface features. *Educational Psychologist, 47*(3), 177–188.

Children's Defense Fund. (2009). *Child poverty.* Washington, DC: Author. Also available at www.childrensdefense.org

Chmielewski, A., Dumont, H., & Trautwein, U. (2013). Tracking effects depend on tracking type: An international comparison of students' mathematics self-concept. *American Educational Research Journal, 50*(5), 925–957.

Cho, M.-H., & Bergin, D. (2009, April). *Review of self-regulated learning models and implications for theory development.* Paper presented at the annual meeting of the American Educational Research Association, San Diego, CA.

Chorzempa, B., & Graham, S. (2006). Primary-grade teachers' use of within-class ability grouping in reading. *Journal of Educational Psychology, 98*(3), 529–541.

Christenbury, L. (2010). The flexible teacher. *Educational Leadership, 68*(4), 46–50.

Christian, D., & Genesee, F. (Eds.). (2001). *Bilingual education.* Alexandria, VA: TESOL.

Christopher, S. (2007/2008). Homework: A few practice arrows. *Educational Leadership, 65*(4), 74.

Clark, D., Tanner-Smith, E., & Killingsworth, S. (2016). Digital games, design, and learning: A systematic review and meta-analysis. *Educational Evaluation and Policy Analysis, 37* (4), 79–122.

Clark, D., Tanner-Smith, E., Killingsworth, S., & Bellamy, S. (2013). *Digital games for learning: A systematic review and meta-anlaysis.* Menlo Park, CA: SRI International.

Clark, J. M., & Paivio, A. (1991). Dual coding theory and education. *Educational Psychology Review, 3*(3), 149–210.

Clark, K. (2009). The case for structured English immersion. *Educational Leadership, 66*(7), 42–47.

Clarke, J. (2012). Invested in inquiry. *Educational Leadership, 69*(5), 60–64.

Clarke-Midura, J. (2014). The role of technology in science assessments. In R. E. Slavin (Ed.), *Science, technology, & mathematics (STEM)* (pp. 48–51). Thousand Oaks, CA: Corwin.

Cleary, T. J., & Zimmerman, B. J. (2004). Self-regulation empowerment program: A school-based program to enhance self-regulated and self-motivated cycles of student learning. *Psychology in the Schools, 41,* 537–550.

Cleveland, K. (2011). *Teaching boys who struggle in school: Strategies that turn underachievers into successful learners.* Alexandria, VA: ASCD.

Coalition for Evidence-Based Policy. (2003). *Identifying and implementing educational practices supported by rigorous evidence: A user friendly guide.* Washington, DC: U.S. Department of Education.

Cobb, P., & Jackson, K. (2011). Assessing the quality of the Common Core State Standards for mathematics. *Educational Researcher, 40*(4), 183–185.

Cochran-Smith, M., & Power, C. (2010). New directions for teacher preparation. *Educational Leadership, 67*(5), 7–13.

Cohen, D., Peurach, D., Glazer, J., Gates, K., & Goldin, S. (2014). *Improvement by design: The promise of better schools.* Chicago, IL: The University of Chicago Press.

Cohen, E. G. (2004). Producing equal-status interaction amidst classroom diversity. In W. G. Stephan & W. P. Vogt (Eds.), *Education programs for improving intergroup relations.* New York, NY: Teachers College Press.

Cohen, E., & Lotan, R. (2014). *Designing groupwork: Strategies for the heterogeneous classroom* (3rd ed.). New York, NY: Teachers College Press.

Cohen, L. B., & Cashon, C. H. (2003). Infant perception and cognition. In R. M. Lerner, M. A. Easterbrooks, & J. Mistry (Eds.), *Handbook of psychology: Vol. 6. Developmental psychology* (pp. 65–89). Hoboken, NJ: Wiley.

Colangelo, N., & Davis, G. A. (Eds.). (2009). *Handbook of gifted education* (3rd ed.). Boston, MA: Allyn & Bacon.

Colangelo, N., Assouline, S., & Gross, M. U. M. (2005). *A nation deceived: How schools hold back America's brightest students.* Iowa City, IA: International Center for Gifted Education and Talent Development.

Colby, C., & Kohlberg, L. (1984). Invariant sequence and internal consistency in moral judgment stages. In W. Kurtines & J. Gewirts (Eds.), *Morality, moral behavior, and moral development.* New York, NY: Wiley-Interscience.

Coles, G. (2004). Danger in the classroom: "Brain Glitch" research and learning to read. *Phi Delta Kappan, 85*(5), 344–357.

Collins, M., Friedman, D., Repka, M., Owoeye, J., Mudie, L., Anglemeyer, K., Slavin, R., & Corcoran R. (2015, May). *Preliminary results from the Baltimore Reading and Eye Disease Study (BREDS).* Paper presented at the annual meeting of the Association for Research in Vision and Ophthalmology, Seattle, WA.

Comer, J. (2005). Child and adolescent development: The critical missing focus in school reform. *Phi Delta Kappan, 86*(10), 757–763.

Comer, J. (2010). The Yale Child Study Center school development program. In J. Meece & J. Eccles (Eds.), *Handbook of research on schools, schooling, and human development* (pp. 419–433). New York, NY: Routledge.

Connolly, B., & Smith, M. W. (2002). Teachers and students talk about talk: Class discussions and the way it should be. *Journal of Adolescent and Adult Literacy, 46*(1), 16–26.

Connor, C. M., Son, S. H., Hindman, A. H., & Morrison, F. J. (2004). *Teacher qualifications, classroom practices, and family characteristics: Complex effects on first-graders' vocabulary and early reading outcomes.* Ann Arbor, MI: University of Michigan, Department of Psychology.

Connor, C., Alberto, P., Compton, D., & O'Connor, R. (2014). *Improving reading outcomes for students with or at risk of reading disabilities: A synthesis of the contributions from the IES Research Centers.* Washington, DC: IES, USDOE.

Conyers, L., Reynolds, A., & Ou, S. (2003). The effect of early childhood intervention and subsequent special education services: Findings from the Chicago child–parent centers. *Educational Evaluation and Policy Analysis, 25*(1), 75–95.

Cook, A., & Tashlik, P. (2004). *Talk, talk, talk: Discussion based classrooms.* New York, NY: Teachers College Press.

Cook, B. G., & Tankersley, M. (2013). *Research-based practices in special education.* Upper Saddle River, NJ: Pearson.

Cooley, W. W., & Leinhardt, G. (1980). The instructional dimensions study. *Educational Evaluation and Policy Analysis, 2,* 7–26.

Cooper, H., & Valentine, J. C. (2001). Using research to answer practical questions about homework. *Educational Psychologist, 36*(3), 143–153.

Cooper, H., Borman, G., & Fairchild, R. (2010). School calendars and academic achievement. In J. Meece & J. Eccles (Eds.), *Handbook of research on schools, schooling, and human development* (pp. 342–355). New York, NY: Routledge.

Cooper, H., Charlton, K., Valentine, J. C., & Muhlenbruck, L. (2000). Making the most of summer school: A meta-analytic and narrative review. *Monographs of the Society for Research in Child Development, 65*(1, Serial No. 260), 1–118.

Cooper, H., Robinson, J. C., & Patall, E. (2006). Does homework improve academic achievement? *Review of Educational Research, 76*(1), 1–62.

Cooper, K. (2014). Eliciting engagement in the high school classroom: A mixed-methods examination of teaching practices. *American Educational Research Journal, 51*(2), 363–402.

Cooper, R. (1998). Urban school reform: Student responses to detracking in a racially mixed high school. *Journal of Education for Students Placed at Risk, 4*(3), 259–275.

Cooper, R., & Slavin, R. E. (2004). Cooperative learning: An instructional strategy to improve intergroup relations. In W. G. Stephan & W. P. Vogt (Eds.), *Education programs for improving intergroup relations.* New York, NY: Teachers College Press.

Corbett, D., Wilson, B., & Williams, B. (2005). No choice but success. *Educational Leadership, 62*(6), 8–13.

Coren, E., Hossain, R., Pardo, J., Veras, M., Chakrabordy, K., Harris, H., & Martin, A. (2013). Interventions for promoting reintegration and reducing harmful behavior and lifestyles in street-connected children and young people: A systematic review. *Campbell Systematic Reviews.* doi:10.4073/csr.2013.6

Corkill, A. J. (1992). Advance organizers: Facilitators of recall. *Educational Psychology Review, 4,* 33–67.

Corkum, P., Humphries, K., Mullane, J., & Theriault, F. (2008). Private speech in children with ADHD and their typically developing peers during problem-solving and inhibition tasks. *Contemporary Educational Psychology, 33*(1), 97–115.

Cornelius-White, J. (2007). Learner-centered teacher-student relationships are effective: A meta-analysis. *Review of Educational Research, 77*(1), 113–143.

Cornell, D., Gregory, A., Huang, F., & Fan, X. (2013). Perceived prevalence of teasing and bullying predicts high school dropout rates. *Journal of Educational Psychology, 105*(1), 138–149.

Corno, L. (2000). Looking at homework differently. *The Elementary School Journal, 100*(5), 529–548.

Corpus, J., McClintic-Gilbert, M., & Hayenga, A. (2009). Within-year changes in children's intrinsic and extrinsic motivational orientations: Contextual predictors and academic outcomes. *Contemporary Educational Psychology, 34*(2), 154–166.

Corrin, W., Parise, L., Cerna, O., Haider, Z., & Somers, M. (2015). *Case management for students at risk of dropping out.* New York, NY: MDRC.

Costa, A. (2008). The thought-filled curriculum. *Educational Leadership, 65*(5), 20–25.

Council of Chief State School Officers. (2011). *The Interstate New Teacher Assessment and Support Consortium (INTASC) model core teaching standards: A resource for state dialogue.* Washington, DC: Author.

Council of Chief State School Officers (2015). *College- and career-ready standards.* Retrieved July 28, 2016 from http://www.ccsso.org/Resources/Programs/College-_and_Career-Ready_Standards.html.

Cowan, N. (2001). The magical number 4 in short-term memory: A reconsideration of mental storage capacity. *Behavioral and Brain Sciences, 24,* 87–185.

Craik, F. I. M. (2000). Memory: Coding processes. In A. Kazdin (Ed.), *Encyclopedia of psychology.* Washington, DC: American Psychological Association.

Crévola, C. A., & Hill, P. W. (1998). Evaluation of a whole-school approach to prevention and intervention in early literacy. *Journal of Education for Students Placed at Risk, 3*(2), 133–157.

Crisp, R. J., & Turner, R. N. (2011). Cognitive adaptation to the experience of social and cultural diversity. *Psychological Bulletin, 137,* 242–266.

Cross, D., Thompson, S., & Erceg, E. (2014). *Friendly schools plus evidence for practice: Whole-school strategies to enhance students' social skills and reduce bullying.* Bloomington, IN: Solution Tree.

Cross, L. H., & Cross, G. M. (1980/1981). Teachers' evaluative comments and pupil perception of control. *Journal of Experimental Education, 49,* 68–71.

Crutcher, R. J., & Ericsson, K. A. (2003). The effects of practice on mnemonic encodings involving prior knowledge and semantic memory. *Journal of Experimental Psychology: Learning Memory and Cognition, 29*(6), 1387–1389.

Cummings, E. M., Braungart-Rieker, J. M., & Du Rocher-Schudlich, T. (2003). Emotion and personality development in childhood. In R. M. Lerner, M. A. Easterbrooks, & J. Mistry (Eds.), *Handbook of psychology: Vol. 6. Developmental psychology* (pp. 211–239). Hoboken, NJ: Wiley.

Curwin, R. (2010). *Meeting students where they live: Motivation in urban schools.* Alexandria, VA: ASCD.

Curwin, R. (2013). *Affirmative classroom management: How do I develop effective rules and consequences in my school?* Alexandria, VA: ASCD.

Curwin, R. (2014). Can assessments motivate? *Educational Leadership, 72*(1), 38–40.

Cushman, K. (2006). Help us care enough to learn. *Educational Leadership, 63*(5), 34–37.

Cutshall, S. (2009). Clicking across cultures. *Educational Leadership, 67*(1), 40–44.

Daccord, T., & Reich, J. (2015). How to transform teaching with tablets. *Educational Leadership, 72*(8), 18–23.

Daniels, H., Cole, M., & Wertsch, J. V. (Eds.) (2007). *The Cambridge companion to Vygotsky.* New York, NY: Cambridge University Press.

Danielson, C. (2010). Evaluations that help teachers learn. *Educational Leadership, 68*(4), 35–39.

Darling-Hammond, L. (2006). Securing the right to learn: Policy and practice for powerful teaching and learning. *Educational Researcher, 35*(7), 13–24.

Darling-Hammond, L. (2008). Teacher quality definition debates: What is an effective teacher? In T. L. Good (Ed.), *21st century learning* (Vol. 2, pp. 12–22). Thousand Oaks, CA: Sage.

Darling-Hammond, L. (2012, March 14). Value-added teacher evaluation: The harm behind the hype. *Education Week, 32.*

Darling-Hammond, L., & Ifill-Lynch, O. (2006). If they'd only do their work! *Educational Leadership, 63*(5), 8–13.

Darling-Hammond, L., & Richardson, N. (2009). Teacher learning: What matters? *Educational Leadership, 66*(5), 46–55.

Darling-Hammond, L., Amrein-Beardsley, A., Haertel, E., & Rothstein, J. (2012). Evaluating teacher evaluation. *Phi Delta Kappan, 93*(6), 8–15.

Darling-Hammond, L., Ancess, J., & Ort, S. W. (2002). Reinventing high school: Outcomes of the Coalition Campus Schools Project. *American Educational Research Journal, 39*(3), 639–673.

Darling-Hammond, L., Zielezinski, M., & Goldman, S. (2014). *Using technology to support at-risk students' learning.* Washington, DC: Alliance for Excellent Education.

Datnow, A., & Park, V. (2015). Data use for equity. *Educational Leadership, 72*(5), 48–54.

Datnow, A., Lasky, S., Stringfield, S., & Teddlie, C. (2005). Systemic integration for educational reform in racially and linguistically diverse contexts: A summary of the evidence. *Journal of Education for Students Placed at Risk, 10*(4), 441–453.

David, J. (2008). Project-based learning. *Educational Leadership, 65*(5), 80–84.

David, J. (2009). Teaching media literacy. *Educational Leadership, 66*(6), 84–86.

David, J. (2010a). Some summer programs narrow learning gaps. *Educational Leadership, 68*(3), 78–80.

David, J. (2010b). Using value-added measures to evaluate teachers. *Educational Leadership, 67*(8), 81–82.

David, J. (2011). High-stakes testing narrows the curriculum. *Educational Leadership, 68*(6), 78–80.

Davis, B. M. (2014). *Cultural literacy for the Common Core.* Bloomington, IN: Solution Tree.

Davis, G. A., Rimm, S. B., & Siegle, D. (2011). *Education of the gifted and talented* (6th ed.). Upper Saddle River, NJ: Pearson.

Davis, H. (2008). Development: 3–5. In T. L. Good (Ed.), *21st century learning* (Vol. 1, pp. 82–92). Thousand Oaks, CA: Sage.

Davis, S., & Nixon, C. (2011). What students say about bullying. *Educational Leadership, 69*(1), 18–23.

Dawson, T. L. (2002). New tools, new insights: Kohlberg's moral judgment stages revisited. *International Journal of Behavioral Development, 26,* 154–166.

Day, S., & Goldstone, R. (2012). The import of knowledge export: Connecting findings and theories of transfer of learning. *Educational Psychologist, 47*(3), 153–176.

de Boer, H., Bosker, R., & van der Werf, M. (2010). Sustainability of teacher expectation bias effects on long-term student performance. *Journal of Educational Psychology, 102*(1), 168–179.

de Bruin, C. L., Deppeler, J. M., Moore, D. W., & Diamond, N. T. (2013). Public school-based interventions for adolescents and young adults with an autism spectrum disorder: A meta-analysis *Review of Educational Research, 83*(4), 521–550.

De Jong, T. (2011). Instruction based on computer simulations. In R. Mayer & P. Alexander (Eds.), *Handbook of research on learning and instruction* (pp. 446–466). New York, NY: Routledge.

De La Paz, S., & Graham, S. (2002). Explicitly teaching strategies, skills, and knowledge: Writing instruction in middle school classrooms. *Journal of Educational Psychology, 94*(2), 687–698.

De La Paz, S., & McCutchen, D. (2011). Learning to write. In R. Mayer & P. Alexander (Eds.), *Handbook of research on learning and instruction* (pp. 32–54). New York, NY: Routledge.

De Vivo, K. (2011). A comprehensive approach to adolescent literacy intervention. *Better: Evidence-based Education, 4*(1), 20–21.

Dean, C., Hubbell, E., Pitler, H., & Stone, B. (2012). *Classroom instruction that works: Research-based strategies for increasing student achievement* (2nd ed.). Alexandria, VA: ASCD.

DeBacker, T., & Nelson, R. M. (1999). Variations on an expectancy-value model of motivation in science. *Contemporary Educational Psychology, 24*(2), 71–94.

Deci, E. L., & Ryan, R. M. (Eds.). (2002). *Handbook of self-determination research.* Rochester, NY: University of Rochester Press.

Deci, E., Koestner, R., & Ryan, R. (2001). Extrinsic rewards and intrinsic motivation in education: Reconsidered once again. *Review of Educational Research, 71*(1), 1–27.

Decristan, J., Klieme, E., Kunter, M., Hochweber, J., Buttner, G., Fauth. B…& Hardy, I. (2015). Embedded formative assessment and classroom process quality: How do they interact in promoting science understanding? *American Educational Research Journal, 52*(6), 1133–1159.

Dee, T. (2015). Social identity and achievement gaps: Evidence from an affirmative intervention. *Journal of Research on Educational Effectiveness, 8*(2), 149–168.

Dekker, S., Lee, N., Howard-Jones, P., & Jolles, J. (2012). Neuromyths in education: Prevalance and predictors of misconceptions among teachers. *Frontiers of Psychology, 18,* 429.

Delamont, S. (2002). Gender and education. In D. L. Levinson, P. W. Cookson, Jr., & A. R. Sadovnik (Eds.), *Education and sociology: An encyclopedia* (pp. 273–279). New York, NY: Routledge.

Dembo, M., & Eaton, M. (2000). Self-regulation of academic learning in middle-level schools. *The Elementary School Journal, 100*(5), 472–490.

Dempster, F. N. (1991). Synthesis of research on reviews and tests. *Educational Leadership, 72*(8), 71–76.

Dempster, F. N., & Corkill, A. J. (1999). Interference and inhibition in cognition and behavior: Unifying themes for educational psychology. *Educational Psychology Review, 11*(1), 1–74.

Denham, S., Zinsser, K., & Brown, C. (2013). The emotional basis of learning and development in early childhood education. *Handbook of research on the education of young children* (pp. 67–88). New York, NY: Routledge.

Denton, C. A., Anthony, J. L., Parker, R., & Hasbrouck, J. E. (2004). Effects of two tutoring programs on the English reading development of Spanish–English bilingual students. *The Elementary School Journal, 104*(4), 289–305.

Depascale, C. (2012). Managing multiple measures. *Principal, 91*(5), 6–10.

Deshler, D. D. (2005). Adolescents with learning disabilities. *Learning Disabilities Quarterly, 28*(2), 122–123.

Deshler, D., Palincsar, A., Biancarosa, G., & Nair, M. (2007). *Informed choices for struggling adolescent readers.* Newark, DE: International Reading Association.

Devonshire, V., Morris, P., & Fluck, M. (2013). Spelling and reading development: The effect of teaching children multiple levels of representation in their orthography. *Learning and Instruction, 25,* 85–94.

DeVries, R. (2008). Piaget and Vygotsky: Theory and practice in early education. In T. L. Good (Ed.), *21st century learning* (Vol. 1, pp. 184–193). Thousand Oaks, CA: Sage.

deWinstanley, P. A., & Bjork, E. L. (2004). Processing strategies and the generation effect: Implications for making a better reader. *Memory & Cognition, 32*(6), 945–955.

Diamond, K., Justice, L., Siegler, R., & Snyder, P. (2013). *Synthesis of IES research on early intervention and early childhood education.* Washington, DC: USDOE.

Diamond, R. M. (2008). *Designing and assessing courses and curricula: A practical guide* (3rd ed.). New York, NY: Wiley.

Díaz-Rico, L. T., & Weed, K. Z. (2010). *The crosscultural, language, and academic development handbook: A complete K–12 reference guide* (4th ed.). Boston, MA: Allyn & Bacon.

DiCerbo, P. A., Anstrom, K. A., Baker, L. L., & Rivera, C. (2014). A review of the literature on teaching academic English to English language learners. *Review of Educational Research, 84*(3), 446.

Dick, W., Carey, L., & Carey, J. (2015). *The systematic design of instruction.* Boston, MA: Pearson.

Dickerson, A., & Popli, G. (2012). *Pesistent poverty and children's cognitive development: Evidence from the UK Millennium Cohort Study.* London, England: CLS.

Diehm, C. (2004). From worn-out to web-based: Better student portfolios. *Phi Delta Kappan, 85*(10), 792–795.

Dietel, R. (2011). Testing to the top. *Phi Delta Kappan, 92*(8), 32–36.

Dingman, S., Teuscher, D., Newton, J., & Kasmer, L. (2013). Common mathematics standards in the United States. *The Elementary School Journal, 113*(4), 541–565.

Dlott, A. (2007). A (pod)cast of thousands. *Educational Leadership, 64*(7), 80–82.

Dobbertin, C. (2012). "Just how I need to learn it." *Educational Leadership, 69*(5), 66–70.

Domitrovich, C. E., Cortes, R., & Greenberg, M. T. (2007). Improving young children's social and emotional competence: A randomized trial of the preschool PATHS program. *Journal of Primary Prevention, 28*(2), 67–91.

Dong, Y. (2009). Linking to prior learning. *Educational Leadership, 66*(7), 26–31.

Dooling, D. J., & Lachman, R. (1971). Effects of comprehension on retention of prose. *Journal of Experimental Psychology, 8,* 216–222.

Doorey, N. (2014). The Common Core assessments: What you need to know. *Educational Leadership, 71*(6), 57–61.

Dotterer, A., McHale, S., & Crouter, A. (2009). The development and correlates of academic interests from childhood through adolescence. *Journal of Educational Psychology, 101*(2), 509–519.

Doubet, K., & Hockett, J. (2015). *Differentiation in middle and high school: Strategies to engage all learners.* Alexandria, VA: ASCD.

Dougherty, E. (2012). *Assignments matter: Making the connections that help students meet standards.* Arlington, VA: ASCD.

Downing, J. E. (2001). *Including students with severe and multiple disabilities in typical classrooms.* Baltimore, MD: Brookes.

Drabman, R., Spitalnik, R., & O'Leary, K. (1973). Teaching self-control to disruptive children. *Journal of Abnormal Psychology, 82,* 10–16.

Drapeau, P. (2014). *Sparing student creativity: Practical ways to promote innovative thinking and problem solving.* Alexandria, VA: ASCD.

Driscoll, M. P. (2005). *Psychology of learning for instruction* (3rd ed.). Boston, MA: Allyn & Bacon.

Dubinsky, J., Roehrig, G., & Varma, S. (2013). Infusing neuroscience into teacher professional development. *Educational Researcher, 42*(6), 317–329.

Duckor, B. (2014). Formative assessment in seven good moves. *Educational Leadership, 71*(6), 28–33.

Duckworth, A. L., Gendler, T. S., & Gross, J. J. (2014). Self-control in school-age children. *Educational Psychologist, 49*(3), 199–217.

Duckworth, A. L., & Steinberg, L. (2015). Understanding and cultivating self-control in children and adolescents. *Child Development Perspectives, 9*(1), 32–37.

Duckworth, A., White, R., Gross, J., Matteucci, A., & Shearer, A. (2016). A stitch in time: Strategic self-control in high school and college students. *Educational Psychology, 108*(3), 329–341.

Dueck, M. (2011). How I broke my own rule and learned to give retests. *Educational Leadership, 69*(3), 72–75.

Dueck, M. (2014). *Grading smarter, not harder: Assessment strategies that motivate kids and help them learn.* Alexandria, VA: ASCD.

Duell, O. K. (1994). Extended wait time and university student achievement. *American Educational Research Journal, 31*(2), 397–414.

Duggan, M. (2014). *Online harassment.* At www.pewinternet .org/2014/10/22/online-harrassment

Duke, N. K. (2000). For the rich it's richer: Print experiences and environments offered to children in very low- and very high-socioeconomic status first-grade classrooms. *American Educational Research Journal, 37*(2), 441–478.

Duke, N. K., & Carlisle, J. F. (2011). The development of comprehension. In M. L. Kamil, P. D. Pearson, E. B. Moje, & P. Afflerbach (Eds.), *Handbook of Reading Research* (Vol. IV, pp. 199–228). London, England: Routledge.

Duncan, G., & Murnane, R. (2014a). Growing income inequality threatens American education. *Phi Delta Kappan, 95*(6), 8–14.

Duncan, G., & Murnane, R. (2014b). *Restoring opportunity: The crisis of inequality and the challenge for American education.* Cambridge, MA: Harvard University Press.

Dunlosky, J., Rawson, K., Marsh, E., Nathan, M., & Willingham, D. (2013). Improving students' learning with effective learning techniques: Promising directions from cognitive and educational psychology. *Psychological Science in the Public Interest, 14*(1), 4–58.

Dunn, K., & Mulvenon, S. (2009). A critical review of research on formative assessment: The limited scientific evidence of the impact of formative assessment in education. *Practical Assessment, Research & Evaluation, 14*(7), 1–11.

Dunn, L. (2011). Making the most of your class website. *Educational Leadership, 68*(5), 60–62.

Durlak, J., Weissberg, R., Dymnicki, A., Taylor, R., & Schellinger, K. (2011). The impact of enhancing students' social and emotional learning: A meta-analysis of school-based universal interventions. *Child Development, 82*(1), 405–432.

Duschl, R., & Hamilton, R. (2011). Learning science. In R. Mayer & P. Alexander (Eds.), *Handbook of research on learning and instruction* (pp. 78–107). New York, NY: Routledge.

Dweck, C. (2007). The perils and promises of praise. *Educational Leadership, 65*(2), 34–39.

Dweck, C. S. (2006). *Mindset: The new psychology of success.* New York, NY: Random House.

Dweck, C. S. (2010). Even geniuses work hard. *Educational Leadership, 68*(1), 16–20.

Dweck, C.S. (2013). Social development. In P. Zelazo (Ed.), *Oxford handbook of developmental psychology.* New York, NY: Oxford University Press.

Dynarski, M., & Kaenz, K. (2015). *Why federal spending on disadvantaged students (Title I) doesn't work.* Washington, DC: Brookings.

Dynarski, M., Agodini, R., Heaviside, S., Novak, T., Carey, N., Campuzzano, L., … Sussex, W. (2007). *Effectiveness of reading and mathematics software products: Findings from the first student cohort.* Washington, DC: Institute of Education Sciences.

Early, D. M., Berg, J. K., Alicea, S., Si, Y., Aber, L., Ryan, R. M., & Deci, E. L. (2016). The impact of Every Classroom, Every Day on high school student achievement: Results from a school-random-ized trial. *Journal of Research on Educational Effectiveness, 9*(1), 3–29.

Ebeling, D. G. (2000). Adapting your teaching to any learning style. *Phi Delta Kappan, 82*(3), 247–248.

Eccles, J. S., Wigfield, A., & Byrnes, J. (2003). Cognitive develop-ment in adolescence. In R. M. Lerner, M. A. Easterbrooks, & J. Mistry (Eds.), *Handbook of psychology: Vol. 6. Developmental psychol-ogy* (pp. 325–350). Hoboken, NJ: Wiley.

Echevarria, J., Vogt, M. E., & Short, D. (Eds.). (2013). *Making content comprehensible for elementary English learners: The SIOP model* (2nd ed.). Columbus, OH: Pearson.

Education Week. (2015). *The Every Student Succeeds Act: Explained.* Retrieved August 26, 2016 from http://www.edweek.org/ew/articles/2015/12/07/the-every-student-succeeds-act-explained.html?intc=highsearch

Educational Testing Service. (1995). *Performance assessment: Different needs, difficult answers.* Princeton, NJ: Author.

Educational Testing Service. (2012). *Praxis II overview.* Retrieved from www.ets.org/praxis/about/praxisii

Edwards, A., Esmonde, I., & Wagner, J. (2011). Learning mathemat-ics. In R. Mayer & P. Alexander (Eds.), *Handbook of research on learning and instruction* (pp. 55–77). New York, NY: Routledge.

Edwards, J. (2014). *Time to teach: How do I get organized and work smarter?* Alexandria, VA: ASCD.

Efklides, A. (2011). Interactions of metacognition with motivation and affect in self-regulated learning: The MASRL model. *Educa-tional Psychologist, 46*(1), 6–25.

Egan, K. (2008). Learning in depth. *Educational Leadership, 66*(3), 58–64.

Ehri, L. C., Dreyer, L. G., Flugman, B., & Gross, A. (2007). Reading Rescue: An effective tutoring intervention model for language-minority students who are struggling readers in first grade. *Ameri-can Educational Research Journal, 44*, 414–448.

Einerson, M. (1998). Fame, fortune, and failure: Young girls' moral language surrounding popular culture. *Youth and Society, 30*, 241–257.

Eisenberg, N. (2001). The core and correlates of affective social com-petence. *Social Development, 10*, 120–124.

Eisenberger, R., & Cameron, J. (1998). Reward, intrinsic interest, and creativity: New findings. *American Psychologist, 53*(6), 676–679.

Eisenberger, R., Pierce, W. D., & Cameron, J. (1999). Effects of rewards on intrinsic motivation—negative, neutral, and positive: Comment on Deci, Koestner, and Ryan (1999). *Psychological Bul-letin, 125*, 677–691.

Eisner, E. (2006). The satisfactions of teaching. *Educational Leadership, 63*(6), 44–47.

Elbaum, B., & Vaughn, S. (2001). School-based interventions to enhance the self-concept of students with learning disabilities: A meta-analysis. *The Elementary School Journal, 101*(3), 303–330.

Elias, L. J., & Saucier, D. M. (2006). *Neuropsychology: Clinical and experimental foundations.* Boston, MA: Allyn & Bacon.

Eliot, L. (2012). *Pink brain, blue brain: How small differences grow into troublesome gaps—and what we can do about it.* Oxford, UK: One World Publications.

Ellis, A. K. (2001b). Cooperative learning. In A. K. Ellis (Ed.), *Re-search on educational innovations.* Larchmont, NY: Eye on Education.

Ellis, A. K. (2001c). Innovations from brain research. In A. K. Ellis (Ed.), *Research on educational innovations.* Larchmont, NY: Eye on Education.

Ellmore, R. F., & Fuhrman, S. H. (2001). Holding schools account-able: Is it working? *Phi Delta Kappan, 83*(1), 67–72.

Else-Quest, N., Shibley, J., Goldsmith, H., & Van Hulle, C. (2006). Gender differences in temperament: A meta-analysis. *Psychological Bulletin, 132*(1), 33–72.

Emerson, M. J., & Miyake, A. (2003). The role of inner speech in task switching: A dual-task investigation. *Journal of Memory and Language, 48*, 148–168.

Emmer, E. T., & Evertson, C. M. (2012). *Classroom management for middle and high school teachers* (9th ed.). Upper Saddle River, NJ: Pearson.

Emmer, E. T., & Gerwels, M. C. (2002). Cooperative learning in el-ementary classrooms: Teaching practices and lesson characteristics. *The Elementary School Journal, 103*(1), 75–91.

Emmer, E. T., & Stough, L. M. (2008). Responsive classroom man-agement. In T. L. Good (Ed.), *21st century learning* (Vol. 1, pp. 140–148). Thousand Oaks, CA: Sage.

Engel, S. (2013). The case for curiosity. *Educational Leadership, 70*(5), 36–40.

Engelkamp, J., & Dehn, D. M. (2000). Item and order information in subject-performed tasks and experimenter-performed tasks. *Jour-nal of Experimental Psychology: Learning, Memory, & Cognition, 26*, 671–682.

Englander, E. (2015). What's behind bad behavior on the web? *Edu-cational Leadership, 72*(8), 30–34.

Englert, C. S., Raphael, T. E., Anderson, L. M., Anthony, H. M., & Stevens, D. D. (1991). Making strategies and self-talk visible: Writing instruction in regular and special education classrooms. *American Educational Research Journal, 28*, 337–372.

Ennemoser, M., & Schneider, W. (2007). Relations of television viewing and reading: Findings from a 4-year longitudinal study. *Journal of Educational Psychology, 99*(2), 349–368.

Entwisle, D., Alexander, K., & Olson, L. (2010). Socioeconomic sta-tus: Its broad sweep and long reach in education. In J. Meece & J. Eccles (Eds.), *Handbook of research on schools, schooling, and human development* (pp. 237–255). New York, NY: Routledge.

EPE Research Center. (2012). Graduation rates in the United States. *Education Week, 31*(4), p. 26.

Epstein, A. (2008). An early start on thinking. *Educational Leadership, 65*(5), 38–43.

Epstein, J. L., & Van Voorhis, F. L. (2001). More than minutes: Teachers' roles in designing homework. *Educational Psychologist, 36*(3), 181–193.

Epstein, J. L., Sanders, M. G., Salinas, K., Simon, B., Van Voorhis, F., & Jansorn, N. (2002). *School, family and community partnerships: Your handbook for action* (2nd ed.). Thousand Oaks, CA: Corwin.

Erberber, E., Stephens, M., Memedova, S., Ferguson, S., & Kroeger, T. (2015, March). Socioeconomically disadvantaged students who are academically successful: Examining academic resilience cross-nationally. *IEA's Policy Brief Series, No. 5.* Amsterdam: IEA.

Erikson, E. H. (1963). *Childhood and society* (2nd ed.). New York, NY: Norton.

Erikson, E. H. (1968). *Identity, youth and crisis.* New York, NY: Norton.

Erikson, E. H. (1980). *Identity and the life cycle* (2nd ed.). New York, NY: Norton.

Erkens, C. (2015). *Collaborative common assessments.* Bloomington, IL: Solution Tree.

Espelage, D., Holt, M., & Poteat, P. (2010). Individual and contex-tual influences on bullying: Perpetration and victimization. In J. Meece & J. Eccles (Eds.), *Handbook of research on schools, schooling, and human development* (pp. 146–160). New York, NY: Routledge.

Esping, A., & Plucker, J. (2015). Alfred Binet and the children of Paris. In S. Goldstein, D. Princiotta, & J. A. Naglieri (Eds.). *Hand-book of Intelligence.* New York: Springer.

Espy, K. A., Molfese, D. L., Molfese, V. J., & Modglin, A. (2004). Development of auditory event-related potentials in young children and relations to word-level reading abilities at age 8 years. *Annals of Dyslexia, 54*(1), 9–38.

Estes, T., & Mintz, S. (2016). *Instruction: A models approach.* Boston, MA: Pearson.

Estrada, V., Gómez, L., & Ruiz-Escalante, J. (2009). Let's make dual language the norm. *Educational Leadership, 66*(7), 54–58.

Evans, J. (2015). More verbs, fewer nouns: SpeakUp surveys give insight into how students want to learn. *Educational Leadership, 72*(8), 10–12.

Evans, S. W., Pelham, W. E., Smith, B. H., Bukstein, O., Gnagy, E. M., Greiner, A. R., Altenderfer, L., & Baron-Myak, C. (2000). Dose-response effect of methylphenidate on ecologically valid measures of academic performance and classroom behavior in adolescents with ADHD. *Experimental and Clinical Psychopharmacology, 9*(2), 163–175.

Evenson, A., McIver, M., Ryan, S., Schwols, A., & Kendall, J. (2013a). *Common Core standards for elementary grades K–2 math and English language arts: A quick-start guide.* Arlington, VA: ASCD.

Evenson, A., McIver, M., Ryan, S., Schwols, A., & Kendall, J. (2013b). *Common Core standards for elementary grades 3–5 math and English language arts: A quick-start guide.* Arlington, VA: ASCD.

Everson, H., Tobias, S., Hartman, H., & Gourgey, A. (1993). Test anxiety and the curriculum: The subject matters. *Anxiety, Stress, and Coping, 6,* 1–8.

Evertson, C. M., & Poole, I. R. (2008). Proactive classroom management. In T. L. Good (Ed.), *21st century learning* (Vol. 1, pp. 131–139). Thousand Oaks, CA: Sage.

Evertson, C. M., & Randolph, C. H. (1995). Classroom management in the learning-centered classroom. In A. C. Ornstein (Ed.), *Teaching: Theory into practice.* Boston, MA: Allyn & Bacon.

Evertson, C. M., & Emmer, E. T. (2013). *Classroom management for elementary teachers* (9th ed.). Saddle River, NJ: Pearson.

Evertson, E., Emmer, E., & Worsham, M. (2009). *Classroom management for middle and high school teachers.* Boston, MA: Allyn & Bacon.

Fabiano, G., Vujnovic, R., Pelham, W., Waschbusch, D., Massetti, G., Pariseau, M., … Volker, M. (2010). Enhancing the effectiveness of special education programming for children with attention deficit hyperactivity disorder using a daily report card. *School Psychology Review, 3*(2), 219–230.

Fahey, J. A. (2000). Who wants to differentiate instruction? We did. … *Educational Leadership, 58*(1), 70–72.

Fantuzzo, J. W., King, J. A., & Heller, L. R. (1992). Effects of reciprocal peer tutoring on mathematics and school adjustment: A component analysis. *Journal of Educational Psychology, 84,* 33–39.

Fantuzzo, J., LeBoeuf, W., Chen, C., Rouse, H., & Culhane, D. (2012). The unique and combined effects of homelessness and school mobility on the educational outcomes of young children. *Educational Researcher, 41*(9), 393–402.

Farbman, D. (2012). *The case for improving and expanding time in school.* Retrieved from www.timeandlearning.org

Farr, S. (2010). Leadership: Not magic. *Educational Leadership, 68*(4), 28–33.

Farrell, T. (2009). *Teaching reading to English language learners: A reflective guide.* Thousand Oaks, CA: Corwin.

Farrington, D., & Ttofi, M. (2009). School-based programs to reduce bullying and victimization. *Campbell Systematic Reviews,* 10.4073/csr.2009.6.

Fashola, O. S. (2002). *Building effective after school programs.* Thousand Oaks, CA: Corwin.

Feil, E., Frey, A., & Golly, A. (2012). First Step to Success for preschool children. *Better: Evidence-based Education, 5*(1), 22–23.

Feldman, R. S. (2012). *Understanding psychology.* New York, NY: McGraw-Hill.

Fellows, N. J. (1994). A window into thinking: Using student writing to understand conceptual changes in science learning. *Journal of Science Teaching, 31,* 985–1001.

Ferguson, M. (2013). When the (education) revolution comes . . . *Phi Delta Kappan, 95*(2), 68–69.

Ferguson, R., & Mehta, J. (2004). An unfinished journey: The legacy of Brown and the narrowing of the achievement gap. *Phi Delta Kappan, 85*(9), 656–669.

Ferlazzo, L. (2015). Apps, apps everywhere. Are any good, you think? *Educational Leadership, 72*(8), 67–69.

Ferriter, B. (2009a). Learning with blogs and wikis. *Educational Leadership, 66*(5), 34–39.

Ferriter, B. (2009b). Taking the digital plunge. *Educational Leadership, 67*(1), 85.

Ferriter, W. (2011). A pen that remembers. *Educational Leadership, 68*(8), 88–89.

Fielding, L. G., Anderson, R. C., & Pearson, P. D. (1990). *How discussion questions influence children's story understanding* (Tech. Rep. No. 490). Champaign, IL: University of Illinois, Center for the Study of Reading.

Fine, C. (2010). *Delusions of gender: How our minds, society, and neurosexism create sex differences.* New York, NY: Norton.

Finn, J. D., Pannozzo, G. M., & Achilles, C. M. (2003). The "whys" of class size: Student behavior in small classes. *Review of Educational Research, 73*(3), 321–368.

Fiordaliso, R., Lordeman, A., Filipczak, J., & Friedman, R. M. (1977). Effects of feedback on absenteeism in the junior high school. *Journal of Educational Research, 70,* 188–192.

Fisch, S., & Truglio, R. (2000). *G is for growing: 30 years of research on Sesame Street.* Mahwah, NJ: Erlbaum.

Fisher, D. (2006). Keeping adolescents "alive and kickin'" it: Addressing suicide in schools. *Phi Delta Kappan, 87*(10), 784–786.

Fisher, D., & Frey, N. (2007). Checking for understanding: Formative assessment techniques for your classroom. Alexandria, VA: ASCD.

Fisher, D., & Frey, N. (2010). *Enhancing RTI: How to ensure success with effective classroom instruction and intervention.* Alexandria, VA: ASCD.

Fisher, D., & Frey, N. (2011). *The purposeful classroom: How to structure lessons with learning goals in mind.* Alexandria, VA: ASCD.

Fisher, D., & Frey, N. (2013). *Better learning through structured teaching: A framework for the gradual release of responsibility* (2nd ed.). Alexandria, VA: ASCD.

Fisher, D., & Frey, N. (2014a). *Checking for understanding: Formative assessment techniques for your classroom* (2nd ed.). Arlington, VA: ASCD.

Fisher, D., & Frey, N. (2014b). Conversational moves. *Educational Leadership, 72*(3), 84–85.

Fisher, D., & Frey, N. (2014c). Midcourse corrections. *Educational Leadership, 72*(2), 80–81.

Fisher, D., Frey, N., & Lapp, D. (2011). Focusing on the participation and engagement gap: A case study on closing the achievement gap. *Journal of Education for Students Placed at Risk, 16*(1), 56–64.

Fisher, D., Frey, N., & Pumpian, I. (2011). No penalties for practice. *Educational Leadership, 69*(3), 46–51.

Fisher, M. (2013). *Digital learning strategies: How do I assign and assess 21st century work?* Alexandria, VA: ASCD.

Fishman, B., & Dede, C. (2016). Teaching and technology: New tools for new times. In D. Gitomer & C. Bell (Eds.), *Handbook of research on teaching* (5th ed.). (pp. 1335–1388). Washington, DC: AERA.

Fitzgerald, J., & Graves, M. (2004/2005). Reading supports for all. *Educational Leadership, 62*(4), 68–71.

Flavell, J. (2004). Theory-of-mind development: Retrospect and prospect. *Merrill-Palmer Quarterly, 50,* 21–45.

Flavell, J. H. (1986, January). Really and truly. *Psychology Today, 20*(1), 38–44.

Fleischman, S. (2006). Moving to evidence-based professional practice. *Educational Leadership, 63*(6), 87–90.

Fleischman, S. (2014). Before choosing, ask three questions. In R. E. Slavin (Ed.), *Classroom management and assessment* (pp. 55–59). Thousand Oaks, CA: Corwin.

Fletcher, A. (2012). Addressing school effects on drug use. *Better: Evidence-based Education, 4*(3), 16–17.

Fletcher, J. M., Shaywitz, S. E., Shankweiler, D. P., Katz, L., Liberman, I. Y., Stvebing, K. K., … Shaywitz, B. A. (1994). Cognitive profiles of reading disability: Comparisons of discrepancy and low achievement definitions. *Journal of Educational Psychology, 86,* 6–23.

Flippo, R. (2008). *Preparing students for testing and doing better in school.* Thousand Oaks, CA: Corwin.

Florez, I. R. (2008). Early childhood education: The developmentally appropriate practice debate. In T. L. Good (Ed.), *21st century learning* (Vol. 1, pp. 396–404). Thousand Oaks, CA: Sage.

Flouri, E., & Buchanan, A. (2004). Early father's and mother's involvement and child's later educational outcomes. *British Journal of Educational Psychology, 74*(2), 141–153.

Flower, A., McKenna, J., Bunuan, R., Muething, C., & Vega, R. (2014). Effects of the Good Behavior Game on challenging behavior in school settings. *Review of Educational Research, 84*(4), 546–571.

Fogarty, R., & Kerns, G. (2009). *inFormative assessment: When it's not about a grade.* Thousand Oaks, CA: Corwin.

Fogle, P. E. (2013). *Essentials of communication sciences and disorders.* Stamford, CT: Cengage.

Fonesca, B., & Chi, M. (2011). Instruction based on self-explanation. In R. Mayer & P. Alexander (Eds.), *Handbook of research on learning and instruction* (pp. 296–321). New York, NY: Routledge.

Forness, S. R., & Kavale, K. A. (2000). What definitions of disabilities say and don't say: A critical analysis. *Journal of Learning Disabilities, 33*(3), 239–256.

Fosnot, C. (Ed.). (2005). *Constructivism: Theory, perspectives, and practice* (2nd ed.). New York, NY: Teachers College Press.

Fowler, D. (2011). School discipline feeds the "pipeline to prison." *Phi Delta Kappan, 93*(2), 14–19.

Fox, E., & Alexander, P. (2011). Learning to read. In R. Mayer & P. Alexander (Eds.), *Handbook of research on learning and instruction* (pp. 7–31). New York, NY: Routledge.

Fredricks, J. A., Blumenfeld, P. C., & Paris, A. H. (2004). School engagement: Potential of the concept, state of the evidence. *Review of Educational Research, 74*(1), 59–109.

Freeman, J., & Simonsen, B. (2015). Examining the impact of policy and practice interventions on high school dropout and school completion rates: A systematic review of the literature. *Review of Educational Research, 85*(2), 205–248.

Freiberg, H. J., & Driscoll, A. (Eds.). (2005). *Universal teaching strategies* (4th ed.). Boston, MA: Pearson.

Freiberg, H. J., & Reyes, A. (2008). Zero tolerance: A reconsideration of practice and policy. In T. L. Good (Ed.), *21st century learning* (Vol. 1, pp. 149–160). Thousand Oaks, CA: Sage.

Freiberg, H. J., Connell, M. L., & Lorentz, J. (2001). Effects of consistency management on student mathematics achievement in seven Chapter I elementary schools. *Journal of Education for Students Placed at Risk, 6*(3), 249–270.

Freiberg, H., & Lamb, S. (2009). Dimensions of person-centered classroom management. *Theory into Practice, 48,* 99–105.

Freiberg, H., & Lapointe, J. (2006). Research-based programs for preventing and solving disciplinary problems. In C. Evertson & C. Weinstein (Eds.), *Handbook of classroom management: Research, practice, and contemporary issues.* Mahwah, NJ: Erlbaum.

Freiberg, H., Huzinec, C., & Templeton, S. (2009). Classroom management—a pathway to student achievement: A study of fourteen inner-city elementary schools. *The Elementary School Journal, 110*(1), 63–80.

Freiberg, J. (2012). From tourists to citizens. *Better: Evidence-based education, 5*(1), 12–13.

Freiberg, J. (2014). From tourists to citizens. In R. E. Slavin (Ed.), *Classroom management and assessment* (pp. 80–84). Thousand Oaks, CA: Corwin.

Frey, K., & Nolen, S. (2010). Taking "steps" toward positive social relationships: A transactional model of intervention. In J. Meece & J. Eccles (Eds.), *Handbook of research on schools, schooling, and human development* (pp. 478–496). New York, NY: Routledge.

Frey, K., Hirschstein, M., & Guzzo, B. (2000). Second step: Preventing aggression by promoting social competence. *Journal of Emotional and Behavioral Disorders, 8,* 102–112.

Frey, N., & Fisher, D. (2014). Implementing response to instruction and intervention with older students. In R. E. Slavin (Ed.), *Classroom management and assessment* (pp. 126–130). Thousand Oaks, CA: Corwin.

Frey, N., Fisher, D., & Gonzalez, A. (2013). *Teaching with tablets: How do I integrate tablets with effective instruction?* Alexandria, VA: ASCD.

Friedman, L. (2003). Promoting opportunity after school. *Educational Leadership, 60*(4), 79–82.

Friend, M. (2011). *Special education: Contemporary perspectives for school professionals* (3rd ed.). Columbus, OH: Merrill.

Friend, M., & Barron, T. (2014). Co-teaching: Inclusion and increased student achievement. In R. E. Slavin (Ed.), *Classroom management and assessment* (pp. 121–125). Thousand Oaks, CA: Corwin.

Friend, M., & Bursuck, W. D. (2016). *Including students with special needs* (7th ed.). Boston, MA: Pearson.

Friend, R. (2001). Effects of strategy instruction on summary writing of college students. *Contemporary Educational Psychology, 26*(1), 3–24.

Fries, S., Dietz, F., & Schmid, S. (2008). Motivational interference in learning: The impact of leisure alternatives on subsequent self-regulation. *Contemporary Educational Psychology, 33*(2), 119–133.

Frontier, T., & Rickabaugh, J. (2014). *Five letters to improve learning: How to prioritize for powerful results in your school.* Alexandria, VA: ASCD.

Fuchs, D., & Fuchs, L. (2006). Introduction to response to intervention: What, why, and how valid is it? *Reading Research Quarterly, 41*(1), 92–128.

Fuchs, D., & Fuchs, L. S. (1997). Peer-assisted learning strategies: Making classrooms more responsive to diversity. *American Educational Research Journal, 34*(1), 174–206.

Fuchs, D., Fuchs, L. S., & Compton, D. L. (2004). Identifying reading disability by responsiveness to instruction: Specifying measures and criteria. *Learning Disability Quarterly, 27,* 216–227.

Fuchs, D., Fuchs, L. S., & Fernstrom, P. (1993). A conservative approach to special education reform: Mainstreaming through transenvironmental programming and curriculum-based measurement. *American Educational Research Journal, 30,* 149–177.

Fuchs, L. S., Fuchs, D., & Karnes, K. (2001). Enhancing kindergartners' mathematical development: Effects of peer-assisted learning strategies. *The Elementary School Journal, 101*(5), 495–510.

Fuchs, L., Compton, D., Fuchs, D., Hamlett, C., DeSelms, J., Seethaler, P., … & Changas, P. (2013). Effects of first-grade number knowledge tutoring with contrasting forms of practice. *Journal of Educational Psychology, 105*(1), 58–77.

Fuchs, L., Fuchs, D., Finelli, R., Courey, S., & Hamlett, C. (2003). Expanding schema-based transfer instruction to help third graders solve real-life mathematical problems. *American Educational Research Journal, 41*(2), 419–445.

Fuchs, L., Fuchs, D., Finelli, R., Courey, S., Hamlett, C., Sones, E., & Hope, S. (2006). Teaching third graders about real-life mathematical problem solving: A randomized controlled study. *The Elementary School Journal, 106*(4), 293–312.

Fuchs, L., Powell, S., Hamlett, C., Fuchs, D., Cirino, P., & Fletcher, J. (2008). Remediating computational deficits at third grade: A randomized field trial. *Journal of Research on Educational Effectiveness, 1*(1), 2–32.

Fuller, B., Wright, J., Gesicki, K., & Kang, E. (2007). Gauging growth: How to judge NCLB? *Educational Researcher, 36*(5), 268–278.

Fulton, K. (2012). 10 reasons to flip. *Phi Delta Kappan, 94*(2), 20–24.

Gabler, I. C., & Schroeder, M. (2003). *Constructivist methods for the secondary classroom.* Boston, MA: Allyn & Bacon.

Gabrieli, C. (2010). More time, more learning. *Educational Leadership, 67*(7), 38–44.

Gaddy, M. L. (1998, April). *Reading and studying from highlighted text: Memory for information highlighted by others.* Paper presented at the annual meeting of the American Educational Research Association, San Diego, CA.

Galambos, N. L., & Costigan, C. L. (2003). Emotional and personality development in adolescence. In R. M. Lerner, M. A. Easterbrooks, & J. Mistry (Eds.), *Handbook of psychology: Vol. 6. Developmental psychology* (pp. 351–372). Hoboken, NJ: Wiley.

Gallagher, K. (2010, November 17). Why I will not teach to the test. *Education Week, 36.*

Galuschka, K., Ise, E., Krick, K., & Schulte-Korne, G. (2014). Effectiveness of treatment approaches for children and adolescents with reading disabilities: A meta-analysis of randomized controlled trials. *PLoS ONE, 9*(2), e899000.

Gambrell, L., Morrow, L. M., & Pressley, M. (Eds.) (2007). *Best practices in literacy instruction.* New York, NY: Guilford Press.

Gamoran, A., Nystrand, M., Berends, M., & LePore, P. C. (1995). An organizational analysis of the effects of ability grouping. *American Educational Research Journal, 32,* 687–715.

Garber, H. L. (1988). *The Milwaukee Project: Preventing mental retardation in children at risk.* Washington, DC: American Association on Mental Retardation.

Garcia, E., Jensen, B., & Scribner, K. (2009). The demographic imperative. *Educational Leadership, 66*(7), 8–13.

Garcy, A. (2009). The longitudinal link between student health and math achievement scores. *Journal of Education for Students Placed at Risk, 14*(4), 283–310.

Gardner, H. (2000). *Intelligence reframed: Multiple intelligences for the 21st century.* New York, NY: Basic Books.

Gardner, H. (2004). *Multiple intelligences: New horizons, in theory and practice.* New York, NY: Basic Books.

Gardner, H., & Moran, S. (2006). The science of multiple intelligences theory: A response to Lynn Waterhouse. *Educational Psychologist, 41*(4), 227–232.

Gardner, M., & Steinberg, L. (2005). Peer influence on risk taking, risk preference, and risky decision making in adolescence and adulthood: An experimental study. *Developmental Psychology, 41,* 625–635.

Gathercole, S. E., Pickering, S. J., Ambridge, B., & Wearing, H. (2004). The structure of working memory from 4 to 15 years of age. *Developmental Psychology, 40,* 177–190.

Gay, Lesbian, and Straight Education Network (GLSEN) (2011). *2011 National School Climate Survey.* Retrieved from www.glsen.org

Gaydos, M. (2015). Seriously considering design in educational games. *Educational Researcher, 44*(9), 478–483.

Gee, J., & Levine, M. (2009). Welcome to our virtual worlds. *Educational Leadership, 66*(6), 48–53.

Gelman, R. (2000). Domain specificity and variability in cognitive development. *Child Development, 71,* 854–856.

Gelzheiser, L., Scanlon, D., Vellutino, F., Hallgren-Flynn, L., & Schatschneider, C. (2011). Effects of the interactive strategies approach-extended. *The Elementary School Journal, 112*(2), 280–306.

Gentner, D., Loewenstein, J., & Thompson, L. (2002). Learning and transfer: A general role for analogical encoding. *Journal of Educational Psychology, 94*(2), 393–408.

Gerard, L., Ryoo, K., McElhaney, K., Liu, O., Rafferty, A., & Linn, M. (2016). Automated guidance for student inquiry. *Educational Psychology, 108*(1), 60–81.

Gerdes, D., & Ljung, E. J. (2009). The students have the answers. *Educational Leadership, 67*(1), 71–75.

Germeroth, C., & Day-Hess, C. (2013). *Self-regulated learning for academic success: How do I help students manage their thoughts, behaviors, and emotions?* Alexandria, VA: ASCD.

Gersten, R., Baker, S., Shahahan, T., Linan-Thompson, S., Collins, P., & Scarcella, R. (2007). *Effective literacy and English language instruction for English learners in the elementary grades* (NCEE 2007–4011). Washington, DC: Institute of Education Sciences, U.S. Department of Education.

Gersten, R., Chard, D., Jayanthi, M., & Baker, S. (2006). *Experimental and quasi-experimental research on instructional approaches for teaching mathematics to students with learning disabilities: A research synthesis.* Signal Hill, CA: Center on Instruction/RG Research Group.

Gersten, R., Chard, D., Jayanthi, M., Baker, S., Morphy, P., & Flojo, J. (2009). Mathematics instruction for students with learning disabilities: A meta-analysis of instructional components. *Review of Educational Research, 79*(3), 1202–1242.

Gersten, R., Fuchs, L. S., Williams, J. P., & Baker, S. (2001). Teaching reading comprehension strategies to students with learning disabilities: A review of research. *Review of Educational Research, 71*(2), 279–320.

Gersten, R., Rolfhus, E., Clarke, B., Decker, L, Wilkins, C., & Dimino, J. (2015). Intervention for first graders with limited number knowledge: Large-scale replication of a randomized controlled trial. *American Educational Research Journal, 52*(3), 516–546.

Gess-Newsome, J. (2012). Pedagogical content knowledge. In J. Hattie & E. Anderman (Eds.), *International handbook of student achievement.* New York, NY: Routledge.

Gettinger, M., Brodhagen, E., Butler, M., & Schienebeck, C. (2013). School psychology. In W. Reynolds, G. Miller, & I. Weiner (Eds.) *Handbook of psychology* (Vol. 7, 2nd ed., pp. 365–388). Hoboken, NJ: Wiley.

Gewertz, C. (2013, March 13). Common-Core tests to take students up to 10 hours. *Education Week, 32*(24), 10.

Gewertz, C. (2015, November 11). Searching for clarity on formative assessment. Retrieved August 24, 2016 from http://www.edweek.org/ew/articles/2015/11/11/searching-for-clarity-on-formative-assessment.html.

Giangreco, M. (2007). Extending inclusive opportunities. *Educational Leadership, 64*(5), 34–38.

Gibbs, L. (2009). Stimulating evidence-based reform. *Better: Evidence-based Education, 1*(1) 22–23.

Giedd, J. N. (2004). Structural magnetic resonance imaging of the adolescent brain. In R. E. Dahl & L. P. Spear (Eds.), *Adolescent brain development. Vulnerabilities and opportunities. Annals of the New York Academy of Sciences* (Vol. 1021). New York, NY: New York Academy of Science.

Gilligan, C. (1982). *In a different voice: Sex differences in the expression of moral judgment.* Cambridge, MA: Harvard University Press.

Gilligan, C., & Attanucci, J. (1988). Two moral orientations: Gender differences and similarities. *Merrill-Palmer Quarterly, 34,* 223–237.

Ginsburg-Block, M., Rohrbeck, C., & Fantuzzo, J. (2006). A meta-analytic review of social, self-concept, and behavioral outcomes of peer-assisted learning. *Journal of Educational Psychology, 98*(4), 732–749.

Giorgis, C., & Glazer, J. I. (2009). *Literature for young children: Supporting emergent literacy, ages 0–8* (6th ed.). Boston, MA: Allyn & Bacon.

Glantz, M. D., Johnson, J., & Huffman, L. (Eds.). (2002). *Resilience and development: Positive life adaptations.* New York, NY: Kluwer.

Glaser, C., & Brunstein, J. (2007). Improving fourth-grade students' composition skills: Effects of strategy instruction and self-regulation procedures. *Journal of Educational Psychology, 99*(2), 297–310.

Glazer, J. L. (2009). External efforts at district-level reform: The case of the National Alliance for Restructuring Education. *Journal of Educational Change, 4,* 295–314.

Gleason, J. B., & Ratner, N. B. (Eds.). (2009). *The development of language* (7th ed.). Boston, MA: Pearson.

Goddard, R. D., Hoy, W. K., & Woolfolk Hoy, A. (2004). Collective efficacy beliefs: Theoretical developments, empirical evidence, and future directions. *Educational Researcher, 33*(3), 1–13.

Goldman, R., Black, J., Maxwell, J., Plass, J., & Keitges, M. (2013). Engaged learning with digital media: The points of viewing theory. In W. Reynolds, G. Miller, & I. Weiner (Eds.) *Handbook of psychology* (Vol. 7, 2nd ed., pp. 321–364.). Hoboken, NJ: Wiley.

Goldsmith, P. R. (2011). Coleman revisited: School segregation, peers, and frog ponds. *American Educational Research Journal, 48*(3), 508–535.

Gollnick, D. M., & Chinn, P. C. (2017). *Multicultural education in a pluralistic society* (10th ed.). Boston, MA: Pearson.

Good, T., & Brophy, J. (2008). *Looking in classrooms* (10th ed.). Boston, MA: Allyn & Bacon.

Good, T., Grouws, D., & Ebmeier, H. (1983). *Active mathematics teaching.* New York, NY: Longman.

Goode, E. (2011). *Deviant behavior* (9th ed.). Upper Saddle River, NJ: Pearson.

Goodman, J. (2013). *The digital divide is still leaving Americans behind.* Retrieved 2/17/16 from http://mashable.com/2013/08/18/digital-divide

Goodwin, B. (2011a). Bullying is common—and subtle. *Educational Leadership, 69*(1), 82–83.

Goodwin, B. (2011b). Grade inflation: Killing with kindness. *Educational Leadership, 69*(3), 80–81.

Goodwin, B. (2011c). *Simply better: Doing what matters most to change the odds for student success.* Alexandria, VA: ASCD.

Goodwin, B. (2012a). Address reading problems early. *Educational Leadership, 69*(5), 80–81.

Goodwin, B. (2012b). For positive behavior, involve peers. *Educational Leadership, 70*(2), 82–83.

Goodwin, B. (2014). Curiosity is fleeting, but teachable. *Educational Leadership, 72*(1), 73–74.

Goodwin, B. (2015). Simple interventions boost self-esteem. *Educational Leadership, 72*(6), 74–75.

Goodwin, B., & Miller, K. (2013). Creativity requires a mix of skills. *Educational Leadership, 70*(5), 80–83.

Goodwin, B., & Miller, K. (2013). Teaching self-regulation has long-term benefits. *Educational Leadership, 70*(8), 80–81.

Gordon, P. (1957). *The social system of the high school: A study in the sociology of adolescence.* Glencoe, IL: Free Press.

Gorski, P. (2013). Building a pedagogy of engagement for students in poverty. *Phi Delta Kappan, 95*(1), 48–52.

Goslin, D. (2003). *Engaging minds: Motivation and learning in America's schools.* Lanham, MD: Scarecrow.

Gottfried, A. E., & Fleming, J. S. (2001). Continuity of academic intrinsic motivation from childhood through late adolescence: A longitudinal study. *Journal of Educational Psychology, 93*(1), 3–13.

Gottfried, A. E., & Gottfried, A. W. (2004). Toward the development of a conceptualization of gifted motivation. *Gifted Child Quarterly, 48*(2), 121–132.

Gottfried, M. (2009). Excused versus unexcused: How student absences in elementary school affect academic achievement. *Educational Evaluation and Policy Analysis, 31*(4), 392–415.

Gottlieb, J., & Weinberg, S. (1999). Comparison of students referred and not referred for special education. *The Elementary School Journal, 99*(3), 187–200.

Gould, M., & Gould, H. (2003). A clear vision for equity and opportunity. *Phi Delta Kappan, 85*(4), 324–328.

Graham, S. (2006). Strategy instruction and the teaching of writing: A meta-analysis. In C. MacArthur, S. Graham, & J. Fitzgerald (Eds.), *Handbook of writing research* (pp. 187–207). New York, NY: Guilford Press.

Graham, S., Harris, K., & Chambers, A. B. (2015). Evidence-based practice in writing instruction: A review of reviews. In C.A. MacArthur, S. Graham, & J. Fitzgerald (Eds.), *Handbook of writing research* (2nd ed.). New York: Guilford Press.

Graham, S., MacArthur, C., & Schwartz, S. (1995). Effects of goal setting and procedural facilitation on the revising behavior and writing performance of students with writing and learning problems. *Journal of Educational Psychology, 87*(2), 230–240.

Grant, P., & Basye, D. (2014). *Personalized learning.* Arlington, VA: ISTE.

Graseck, S. (2009). Teaching with controversy. *Educational Leadership, 67*(1), 45–49.

Graves, M. (2007). Conceptual and empirical bases for providing struggling readers with multifaceted and long-term vocabulary instruction. In B. M. Taylor & J. E. Ysseldyke (Eds.), *Effective instruction for struggling readers, K–6* (pp. 55–83). New York, NY: Teachers College Press.

Graves, M., August, D., & Carlo, M. (2011). Teaching 50,000 words. *Better: Evidence-based Education, 3*(2), 6–7.

Gredler, M. E. (2009). Hiding in plain sight: The stages of mastery/self-regulation in Vygotsky's cultural-historical theory. *Educational Psychologist, 44,* 1–19.

Gredler, M. E., & Shields, C. (2008). *Vygotsky's legacy. A foundation for research and practice.* New York, NY: Guilford Press.

Greenberg, M. T., Weissberg, R., O'Brien, M., Zins, J., Fredericks, L., Resnick, H., & Elias, M. (2003). Enhancing school-based prevention and youth development through coordinated social, emotional, and academic learning. *American Psychologist, 58,* 466–474.

Greene, B. A., Miller, R. B., Crowson, M., Duke, B. L., & Akey, K. L. (2004). Predicting high school students' cognitive engagement and achievement: Contributions of classroom perceptions and motivation. *Contemporary Educational Psychology, 29*(4), 462–482.

Greene, D., & Lepper, M. R. (1974). How to turn play into work. *Psychology Today, 8,* 49–54.

Greene, J. P. (1997). A meta-analysis of the Rossell & Baker review of bilingual education research. *Bilingual Research Journal, 21,* 2–3.

Greene, J., & Azevedo, R. (2007). A theoretical review of Winne and Hadwin's model of self-regulated learning: New perspectives and directions. *Review of Educational Research, 77*(3), 334–372.

Greene, R. (2011). Collaborative problem solving can transform school discipline. *Phi Delta Kappan, 93*(2), 25–29.

Greene, R. L. (2008). Repetition and spacing effects. In J. Byrne (Ed.), *Learning and memory* (pp. 65–78). Oxford, England: Elsevier.

Greenfield, P. M. (2004). Culture and learning. In C. Casey & R. Edgerton (Eds.), *A companion to psychological anthropology: Modernity and psychocultural change.* Oxford, England: Blackwell.

Greenstein, L. (2012). *Assessing 21st century skills: A guide to evaluating mastery and authentic learning.* Thousand Oaks, CA: Corwin.

Greenwood, C. R., Terry, B., Utley, C. A., Montagna, D., & Walker, D. (1993). Achievement, placement, and services: Middle school benefits of Classwide Peer Tutoring used at the elementary level. *School Psychology Review, 22*(3), 497–516.

Gregory, G., & Kaufeldt, M. (2015). *The motivated brain: Improving student attention, engagement, and perseverance.* Alexandria, VA: ASCD.

Griffin, K., & Botvin, G. (2012). LifeSkills training and educational performance. *Better: Evidence-based Education, 4*(3), 18–19.

Grimes, S., & Fields, D. (2012*). Kids online: A new research agenda for understanding social networking forums.* New York, NY: Joan Ganz Cooney Center.

Gronlund, N. (1993). *How to make achievement tests and assessments* (5th ed.). Boston, MA: Pearson.

Gronlund, N., & Brookhart, S. (2009). *Writing instructional objectives* (8th ed.). Upper Saddle River, NJ: Pearson.

Guay, F., Marsh, H. W., & Boivin, M. (2003). Academic self-concept and academic achievement: Developmental perspectives on their causal ordering. *Journal of Educational Psychology, 95*(1), 124–136.

Guernsey, L., & Levine, M. (2015). *Tap, click, read: Growing readers in a world of screens.* San Francisco, CA: Jossey-Bass.

Guillaume, A. (2016). *K-12 classroom teaching: A primer for new professionals.* Boston, MA: Pearson.

Gullen, K. (2014). Are our kids ready for computerized tests? *Educational Leadership, 71*(6), 68–72.

Gunn, A. (2013). Caring encounters. *Phi Delta Kappan, 94*(4), 21–23.

Gunter, M. A., Estes, T. H., & Schwab, J. (2003). *Instruction: A models approach* (4th ed.). Boston, MA: Allyn & Bacon.

Gura, M. (2016). *Make, learn, succeed.* Arlington, VA: ISTE.

Gura, M. (Ed.). (2014). *Teaching literacy in the digital age.* Arlington, VA: ISTE.

Gureasko-Moore, S., DuPaul, G., & White, G. (2006). The effects of self-management in general education classrooms on the organizational skills of adolescents with ADHD. *Behavior Modification, 30,* 159–183.

Guskey, T. (2005). Mapping the road to proficiency. *Educational Leadership, 63*(3), 32–37.

Guskey, T. (2010). Lessons of mastery learning. *Educational Leadership, 68*(2), 53–57.

Guskey, T. (2011). Five obstacles to grading reform. *Educational Leadership, 69*(3), 16–21.

Guskey, T. R. (2014). *On your mark: Challenging the conventions of grading and reporting.* Bloomington, IN: Solution Tree.

Guskey, T., & Anderman, E. (2008). Students at bat. *Educational Leadership, 66*(3), 8–15.

Guthrie, J. T. (Ed.). (2008). *Engaging adolescents in reading.* Thousand Oaks, CA: Corwin.

Guthrie, J. T., & Cox, K. (2001). Classroom conditions for motivation and engagement in reading. *Educational Psychology Review, 13*(3), 283–302.

Gutiérrez, L. (2013). Student-centered in a 21st century classroom. In G. Solomon & L. Schrum (Eds.), *Web 2.0: How to for educators* (pp. 22–24). Washington, DC: International Society for Technology in Education.

Gutiérrez, R., & Slavin, R. E. (1992). Achievement effects of the nongraded elementary school: A best evidence synthesis. *Review of Educational Research, 62*(4), 333–376.

Hadwin, A. F. (2008). Self-regulated learning. In T. L. Good (Ed.), *21st century learning* (Vol. 1, pp. 175–183). Thousand Oaks, CA: Sage.

Haggerty, K., & Kosterman, R. (2012). Helping parents prevent problem behavior. *Better: Evidence-based Education, 4*(3), 22–23.

Hakuta, K. (2011). Educating language minority students and affirming their equal rights: Research and practical perspectives. *Educational Researcher, 40*(4), 163–174.

Hakuta, K., Butler, Y. G., & Witt, D. (2000). *How long does it take English learners to attain proficiency?* University of California Linguistic Minority Research Institute, Policy Report 2000/1.

Halford, G., & Andrews, G. (2006). Reasoning and problem solving. In D. Kuhn & R. Siegler (Eds.), *Handbook of child psychology* (Vol. 2, 6th ed., pp. 557–608). Hoboken, NJ: Wiley.

Halford, G., Baker, R., McCredden, J., & Bain, J. (2005). How many variables can your mind process? *Psychological Science, 16*(1), 70–76.

Hall, L. J. (2013). *Autism spectrum disorders: From theory to practice* (2nd ed.). Upper Saddle River, NJ: Pearson.

Hall, R., & Greeno, J. (2008). Conceptual learning. In T. L. Good (Ed.), *21st century learning* (Vol. 1, pp. 212–224). Thousand Oaks, CA: Sage.

Hallahan, D., Kauffman, J., & Pullen, P. (2015). *Exceptional learners: An introduction to special education* (13th ed.). Boston, MA: Pearson.

Hallinan, M. T. (2004). *The detracking movement.* Palo Alto, CA: Stanford University, Hoover Institute.

Halpern, D. F., Hansen, C., & Riefer, D. (1990). Analogies as an aid to understanding and memory. *Journal of Educational Psychology, 82,* 298–305.

Halpern, D., Aronson, J., Reimer, N., Simpkins, S., Star, J., & Wentzel, K. (2007). *Encouraging girls in math and science: IES practice guide* (NCER 2007–2003). Washington, DC: Institute of Education Sciences, U.S. Department of Education.

Halpern, J. M., & Schulz, K. P. (2006). Revisiting the role of the prefrontal cortex in the pathophysiology of ADHD. *Psychological Bulletin, 132,* 560–581.

Hamilton, L., Halverson, R., Jackson, S., Mandinach, E., Supovitz, J., & Wayman, J. (2009). Using student achievement data to support instructional decision making (NCEE 2009-4067). Washington, DC: NCES, USDOE.

Hamilton, L., Stecher, B., & Yuan, K. (2008). *Standards-based reform in the United States: History, research, and future directions.* Washington, DC: Center on Education Policy.

Hamm, J., & Zhang, L. (2010). School contexts and the development of adolescents' peer relations. In J. Meece & J. Eccles (Eds.), *Handbook of research on schools, schooling, and human development* (pp. 128–145). New York, NY: Routledge.

Hamman, D., Berthelot, J., Saia, J., & Crowley, E. (2000). Teachers' coaching of learning and its relation to students' strategic learning. *Journal of Educational Psychology, 92*(2), 342–348.

Hamre, B., & Pianta, R. (2010). Classroom environments and developmental processes: Conceptualization and measurement. In J. Meece & J. Eccles (Eds.), *Handbook of research on schools, schooling, and human development* (pp. 25–41). New York, NY: Routledge.

Harackiewicz, J., Barron, K., Tauer, J., & Carter, S. (2000). Short-term and long-term consequences of achievement goals: Predicting interest and performance over time. *Journal of Educational Psychology, 92*(2), 316–330.

Hardin, C. (2012). *Effective classroom management: Models and strategies for today's classrooms* (3rd ed.). Boston, MA: Allyn & Bacon.

Hareli, S., & Weiner, B. (2002). Social emotions and personality inferences: A scaffold for a new direction in the study of achievement motivation. *Educational Psychologist, 37*(3), 183–189.

Harmon, K., & Marzano, R. (2015). *Practicing skills, strategies, and processes: Classroom techniques to help students develop proficiency.* West Palm Beach, FL: Learning Sciences International.

Harn, B., Chard, D., Biancarosa, G., & Kame'enui, E. (2012). Coordinating instructional supports to accelerate at-risk first-grade readers' performance. *The Elementary School Journal, 112*(2), 332–355.

Harris, C., & Marx, R. (2014). Teaching practices that matter in middle school science. In R. E. Slavin (Ed.), *Science, technology, & mathematics (STEM)* (pp. 83–91). Thousand Oaks, CA: Corwin.

Harris, D., Ingle, W., & Rutledge, S. (2014). How teacher evaluation methods matter for accountability: A comparative analysis of teacher effectiveness ratings by principals and teacher value-added measures. *American Educational Research Journal, 51*(1), 73–112.

Harris, K. R., Graham, S., & Mason, L. (2006). Improving the writing, knowledge, and motivation of struggling young writers: Effects of self-regulated strategy development with and without peer support. *American Educational Research Journal, 43*(2), 295–340.

Harris, K. R., Graham, S., & Pressley, M. (2001). Cognitive strategies in reading and written language. In N. N. Singh & I. Beale (Eds.), *Current perspectives in learning disabilities: Nature, theory and treatment.* New York, NY: Springer-Verlag.

Harrison, J. R., Bunford, N., Evans, S. W., and Owens, J. S. (2013). Educational accommodations for students with behavioral challenges: A systematic review of the literature. *Review of Education Research, 83*(4), 551–597. doi:10.3102/0034654313497517

Harry, B., & Klingner, J. (2014). *Why are so many minority students in special education?* (2nd ed.). New York, NY: Teachers College Press.

Hart, B., & Risley, R. T. (1995). *Meaningful differences in the everyday experience of young American children.* Baltimore, MD: Brookes.

Harter, S. (1998). The development of self-representations. In W. Damon (Ed.), *Handbook of child psychology* (Vol. 3, pp. 553–618). New York, NY: Wiley.

Hartup, W. W. (2005). Peer interaction: What causes what? *Journal of Abnormal Child Psychology, 33,* 387–394.

Haspe, H., & Baddeley, J. (1991). Moral theory and culture: The case of gender. In W. Kurtines & J. L. Gewirtz (Eds.), *Handbook of moral behavior and development* (Vol. 1, pp. 223–250). Mahwah, NJ: Erlbaum.

Hauser, R. (2010). Causes and consequences of cognitive functioning across the life course. *Educational Researcher, 39*(2), 95–109.

Hauser-Cram, P., Sirin, S. R., & Stipek, D. (2003). When teachers' and parents' values differ: Teachers' ratings of academic competence in children from low-income families. *Journal of Educational Psychology, 95*(4), 813–820.

Hawkins, J. D., Guo, J., Hill, K., Battin-Pearson, S., & Abbott, R. (2001). Long-term effects of the Seattle social development intervention on school bonding trajectories. *Applied Developmental Sciences, 5,* 225–236.

Hawkins, J. D., Herrenkohl, T. I., Farrington, D. P., Brewer, D., Catalano, R. F., Harachi, T. W., & Cothern, L. (2000). *Predictors of youth violence.* Washington, DC: Office of Juvenile Justice and Delinquency Prevention.

Hawkins, J., Kosterman, R., Catalano, R., Hill, K., & Abbott, R. (2008). Effects of social development intervention in childhood fifteen years later. *Archives of Pediatrics and Adolescent Medicine, 162,* 1133–1141.

Hawkins, J., Kuklinski, M., & Fagan, A. (2012). Reducing barriers to learning with Communities That Care. *Better: Evidence-based Education, 4*(2) 8–9.

Hawley, W., & Nieto, S. (2010). Another inconvenient truth: Race and ethnicity matter. *Educational Leadership, 68*(3), 66–71.

Hay, D., Payne, A., & Chadwick, A. (2004). Peer relations in childhood. *Journal of Child Psychology and Psychiatry, 45,* 84–108.

Haycock, K. (2001). Closing the achievement gap. *Educational Leadership, 58*(6), 6–11.

Haynie, W., III, & Haynie, G. (2008). *Effects of test taking on retention learning: A meta-analysis of eight quasi-experiments.* Paper presented at the annual meeting of the American Educational Research Association, San Diego, CA.

Headley, K. (2008). Improving reading comprehension through writing. In C. Block & S. Parris (Eds.), *Comprehension instruction: Research-based best practices* (2nd ed., pp. 214–225). New York, NY: Guilford Press.

Hehir, T. (2007). Confronting ableism. *Educational Leadership, 64*(5), 8–15.

Heilig, J., & Darling-Hammond, L. (2008). Accountability Texas-style: The progress and learning of urban minority students in a high-stakes testing context. *Educational Evaluation and Policy Analysis, 30*(2), 75–110.

Hempenstall, K. (2008). Corrective reading: An evidence-based remedial reading intervention. *Australasian Journal of Special Education, 32*(1), 23–54.

Henson, K. T. (2004). *Constructivist teaching strategies for diverse middle-level classrooms.* Boston, MA: Pearson.

Herbert, J., & Stipek, D. (2005). The emergence of gender differences in children's perceptions of their academic competence. *Applied Developmental Psychology, 26,* 276–295.

Heritage, M. (2011). Formative assessment: An enabler of learning. *Better: Evidence-based Education, 3*(3), 18–19.

Heritage, M. (2014). Formative assessment: An enabler of learning. In R. E. Slavin (Ed.), *Classroom management and assessment* (pp. 35–38). Thousand Oaks, CA: Corwin.

Heritage, M., & Chen, E. (2005). Why data skills matter in school improvement. *Phi Delta Kappan, 86*(9), 707–710.

Herman, J., & Linn, R. (2014). New assessments, new rigor. *Educational Leadership, 71*(6), 34–38.

Hernandez, D. (2012). *Double jeopardy: How third-grade reading skills and poverty influence high school graduation.* Baltimore, MD: Annie E. Casey Foundation.

Herold, B. (2016). Seven studies comparing paper and computer test scores. *Education Week, 35*(22), 8.

Herrell, A., & Jordan M. (2016). *50 strategies for teaching English language learners* (5th ed.). Boston, MA: Pearson.

Herrenkohl, T. I., Maguin, E., Hill, K. G., Hawkins, J. D., & Abbott, R. D. (2001). Developmental risk factors for youth violence. *Journal of Adolescent Health, 26,* 176–186.

Herrera, S. G., Cabral, R. M., & Murry, K. G. (2013). *Assessment accommodations for classroom teachers of culturally and linguistically diverse students* (2nd ed.). Upper Saddle River, NJ: Pearson.

Hersh, R. (2009). A well-rounded education for a flat world. *Educational Leadership, 67*(1), 50–53.

Hess, F., & McShane, M. (2013). Common Core in the real world. *Phi Delta Kappan, 95*(3), 61–66.

Hess, F., & Mehta, J. (2013). Data: No deus ex machine. *Educational Leadership, 70*(5), 71–75.

Hetland, L. (2013). Connecting creativity to understanding. *Educational Leadership, 70*(5), 65–70.

Heward, W. L. (2013). *Exceptional children: An introduction to special education* (10th ed.). Columbus, OH: Merrill.

Heymann, S. J., & Earle, A. (2000). Low-income parents: How do working conditions affect their opportunity to help school-age children at risk? *American Educational Research Journal, 37*(3), 833–848.

Heyns, B. (2002). Summer learning. In D. L. Levinson, P. W. Cookson, Jr., & A. R. Sadovnik (Eds.), *Education and sociology: An encyclopedia* (pp. 645–650). New York, NY: Routledge.

Hicks, T. (2015). *Assessing students' digital writing.* New York, NY: Teachers College Press.

Hicks-Bartlett, S. (2004). Forging the chain: "Hands across the campus" in action. In W. G. Stephan & W. P. Vogt (Eds.), *Education programs for improving intergroup relations.* New York, NY: Teachers College Press.

Hidi, S., & Harackiewicz, J. M. (2000). Motivating the academically unmotivated: A critical issue for the 21st century. *Review of Educational Research, 70*(2), 151–179.

Hiebert, E. (1983). An examination of ability groupings for reading instruction. *Reading Research Quarterly, 18,* 231–255.

Hiebert, E. H. (1996). Revisiting the question: What difference does Reading Recovery make to an age cohort? *Educational Researcher, 25*(7), 26–28.

Hiebert, E., & Reutzel, R. (Eds.). (2010). *Revising silent reading.* Newark, DE: International Reading Association.

Hiebert, J., & Grouws, D. A. (2014). Which instructional methods are most effective for mathematics? In *Proven practices in education: STEM* (pp. 14–17). Corwin. [Reprinted from Hiebert, J., & Grouws, D. (2009). Which teaching methods are most effective for maths? *Better: Evidence-based Education, 2*(1), 10–11.]

Higgins, S. (2014). Formative assessment and feedback to learners. In R. E. Slavin (Ed.), *Classroom management and assessment* (pp. 11–15). Thousand Oaks, CA: Corwin.

Hill, J., & Miller, K. (2013). *Classroom instruction that works with English language learners* (2nd ed.). Alexandria, VA: ASCD.

Hill, N. E. (2001). Parenting and academic socialization as they relate to school readiness: The roles of ethnicity and family income. *Journal of Educational Psychology, 93*(4), 686–697.

Hindman, A., & Wasik, B. (2012). Unpacking an effective language and literacy coaching intervention in Head Start. *The Elementary School Journal, 113*(1), 131–154.

Hinduja, S., & Patchin, J. (2011). High-tech cruelty. *Educational Leadership, 68*(5), 48–52.

Hinnant, J., O'Brien, M., & Ghazarian, S. (2009). The longitudinal relations of teacher expectations to achievement in the early school years. *Journal of Educational Psychology, 101*(3), 662–670.

Hirsh, S. A., & Hord, S. M. (2008). Role of professional learning in advancing quality teaching and student learning. In T. L. Good (Ed.), *21st century learning* (Vol. 2, pp. 337–350). Thousand Oaks, CA: Sage.

Hoachlander, G., & Yanofsky, D. (2011). Making STEM real. *Educational Leadership, 68*(6), 60–65.

Hodgkinson, H. (2008). *Demographic trends and the federal role in education.* Washington, DC: Center on Education Policy.

Höffler, T., & Leutner, D. (2006). *Instructional animation versus static picture: A meta-analysis.* Poster presented at the annual meeting of the American Educational Research Association, San Francisco, CA.

Hoerr, T. (2009). How book groups bring change. *Educational Leadership, 66*(5), 80–84.

Hoerr, T. (2012). Got grit? *Educational Leadership, 69*(5), 84–85.

Hoerr, T. (2013). *Fostering grit: How do I prepare my students for the real world?* Alexandria, VA: ASCD.

Hoffman, D. (2009). Reflecting on social emotional learning: A critical perspective on trends in the United States. *Review of Educational Research, 79*(2), 533–556.

Hogan, T., Rabinowitz, M., & Craven, J. A., III. (2003). Representation in teaching: Inferences from research of expert and novice teachers. *Educational Psychologist, 38*(4), 235–247.

Hollingsworth, J., & Ybarra, S. (2009). *Explicit Direct Instruction (EDI): The power of the well-crafted, well-taught lesson.* Thousand Oaks, CA: Corwin.

Holloway, J. H. (2001). Inclusion and students with learning disabilities. *Educational Leadership, 58*(6), 88–89.

Holmes, J., & Kiernan, K. (2013). Persistent poverty and children's development in the early years of childhood. *Policy and Politics, 41*(1), 19–41.

Holt, D. G., & Willard-Holt, C. (2000). Let's get real: Students solving authentic corporate problems. *Phi Delta Kappan, 82*(3), 243–246.

Hong, G., & Raudenbush, S. (2005). Effects of kindergarten retention policy on children's cognitive growth in reading and mathematics. *Evaluation and Policy Analysis, 27*(3), 205–244.

Hong, G., & Yu, B. (2007). Early-grade retention and children's reading and math learning in elementary years. *Educational Evaluation and Policy Analysis, 29*(4), 239–261.

Hong, L. K. (2001). Too many intrusions on instructional time. *Phi Delta Kappan, 82*(9), 712–714.

Hood, M., Conlon, E., & Andrews, G. (2008). Preschool home literacy practices and children's literacy development: A longitudinal analysis. *Journal of Educational Psychology, 100*(2), 252–271.

Hook, C., & Farah, M. (2012). Neuroscience for educators: What are they seeking, and what are they finding? *Neuroethics.* doi: 10.1007/512152-012-9159-3

Horn, S. S., Drill, K. L., Hochberg, M. J., Heinze, J., & Frank, T. (2008). Development: 6–8. In T. L. Good (Ed.), *21st century learning* (Vol. 1, pp. 93–102). Thousand Oaks, CA: Sage.

Horner, R., Sugai, G., & Anderson, C. (2010). Examining the evidence base for Positive Schoolwide Behavioral Support. *Focus on Exceptional Children, 42*(8), 1–16.

Howard, T. C. (2014). *Black male(d): Peril and promise in the education of African American males.* New York, NY: Teachers College Press.

Howard-Jones, P. (2014a). *Neuroscience and education: A review of educational interventions and approaches informed by neuroscience.* Milbank, England: EEF.

Howard-Jones, P. A. (2014b). Neuroscience and education: Myths and messages. *Nature Reviews Neuroscience, 15,* 817–824.

Hruby, G., & Hynd, G. (2006). Decoding Shaywitz: The modular brain and its discontents. [Review of the book *Overcoming dyslexia: A new and complete science-based program for reading problems at any level.*] *Reading Research Quarterly, 41*(4), 544–566.

Hsueh, J., Lowenstein, A., Morris, P., Mattea, S., & Bangser, M. (2014). *Impacts of social-emotional curricula on three-year-olds.* New York, NY: MDRC.

Huang, C. (2012). Discriminant and criterion-related validity of achievement goals in predicting academic achievement: A meta-analysis. *Journal of Educational Psychology, 104*(1), 48–73.

Hubbard, L., & Mehan, H. (1998). Scaling up an untracking program: A co-constructed process. *Journal of Education for Students Placed at Risk, 4*(1), 83–100.

Huber, C. (2010). Professional learning 2.0. *Educational Leadership, 67*(8), 41–46.

Huebner, T. (2008). Balancing the concrete and the abstract. *Educational Leadership, 66*(3), 86–88.

Huebner, T. (2009). Encouraging girls to pursue math and science. *Educational Leadership, 67*(1), 90–92.

Hughes, F. (2010). *Children, play, and development.* Thousand Oaks, CA: Sage.

Hughes, J., Kwok, O., & Im, M. (2013). Effect of retention in first grade on parents' educational expectations and children's academic outcomes. *American Educational Research Journal, 50*(6), 1336–1359.

Huguet, P., & Regner, I. (2007). Stereotype threat among schoolgirls in quasi-ordinary classroom circumstances. *Journal of Educational Psychology, 99,* 345–360.

Hulett, K. E. (2009). *Legal aspects of special education.* Upper Saddle River, NJ: Pearson.

Hulleman, C., Durik, A., Schweigert, S., & Harackiewicz, J. (2008). Task values, achievement goals, and interest: An integrative analysis. *Journal of Educational Psychology, 100*(2), 398–416.

Hunter, P. (2012). *It's not complicated! What I know for sure about helping our students of color become successful readers.* New York, NY: Scholastic.

Hurley, E. (2000, April). *The interaction of culture with math achievement and group processes among African American and European American children.* Paper presented at the annual meeting of the American Educational Research Association, New Orleans, LA.

Hurn, C. J. (2002). IQ. In D. L. Levinson, P. W. Cookson, Jr., & A. R. Sadovnik (Eds.), *Education and sociology: An encyclopedia* (pp. 399–402). New York, NY: Routledge.

Hurry, J., & Sylva, K. (2007). Long-term outcomes of early reading intervention. *Journal of Research in Reading, 30*(3), 227–248.

Husman, J., & Lens, W. (1999). The role of the future in student motivation. *Educational Psychologist, 34*(2), 113–125.

Hustedt, J., Epstein, D., & Barnett, W. (2013). Early childhood education programs in the public schools. *Handbook of research on the education of young children* (pp. 403–413). New York, NY: Routledge.

Hutchings, J. (2012). Support for teachers around the world. *Better: Evidence-based education, 5*(1), 18–19.

Hyde, J., & Mertz, J. (2009). Gender, culture, and mathematics performance. *Proceedings of the National Academy of Sciences, 106*(8), 801–807.

Hyman, I. A., & Snook, P. A. (2000). Dangerous schools and what you can do about them. *Phi Delta Kappan, 81*(7), 488–501.

Ialongo, N., Poduska, J., Wethamer, L., & Keller, S. (2001). The digital impact of two first-grade preventive interventions on conduct problems and disorder in early adolescence. *Journal of Emotional and Behavioral Disorders, 9*(3), 146–160.

Igo, L. B., Bruning, R., & McCrudden, M. (2005). Exploring differences in students' copy-and-paste decision making and processing: A mixed-methods study. *Journal of Educational Psychology, 72*(3), 165–178.

IMPAQ International (2016). *The impact of the Institute for Student Achievement on African American male students' high school outcomes.* Retrieved 2/17/16 from www.studentachievement.org

Inhelder, B., & Piaget, J. (1958). *The growth of logical thinking from childhood to adolescence.* New York, NY: Basic Books.

Internet World Statistics. (2015). *Internet users in the world by regions, November 2015.* Retrieved February 11, 2016 from www.internetworldstats.com

Iran-Nejad, A., & Stewart, W. (2007, April). *What's wrong with Bloom's cognitive taxonomy of educational objectives?* Paper presented at the annual meeting of the American Educational Research Association, Chicago, IL.

Ireson, J., & Hallam, S. (2001). *Ability grouping in education.* London, England: Sage.

Ivey, G., & Fisher, D. (2006). Then thinking skills trump reading skills. *Educational Leadership, 64*(2), 16–21.

Jackson, L. A., Witt, E.-A., Games, A., Fitzgerald, H., VanEye, E., & Zhao, Y. (2012). Information technology use and creativity: Findings from the Children and Technology Project. *Computers in Human Behavior, 28*(2), 370–376.

Jackson, R. (2009). *Never work harder than your students and other principles of great teaching.* Alexandria, VA: ASCD.

Jackson, R. (2011). *How to motivate reluctant learners.* Alexandria, VA: ASCD.

Jackson, R. (2011). *How to plan rigorous instruction.* Alexandria, VA: ASCD.

Jackson, R., & Lambert, C. (2010). *How to support struggling students.* Alexandria, VA: ASCD.

Jackson, R., & Zmuda, A. (2014). 4 (secret) keys to student engagement. *Educational Leadership, 72*(1), 18–24.

Jacob, R. T., Armstrong, C., & Willard, J. (2015). *Mobilizing volunteer tutors to improve student literacy.* New York, NY: MDRC.

Jacobs, J., Lanza S., Osgood, D., Eccles, J., & Wigfield, A. (2002). Changes in children's self-competence and values: Gender and domain differences across grades one through twelve. *Child Development, 73,* 509–527.

Jaffee, S., & Hyde, J. S. (2000). Gender differences in moral orientation: A meta-analysis. *Psychological Bulletin, 126,* 703–726.

Jagers, R. J., & Carroll, G. (2002). Issues in educating African American children and youth. In S. Stringfield & D. Land (Eds.), *Educating at-risk students* (pp. 48–65). Chicago, IL: National Society for the Study of Education.

James, A. (2007). *Teaching the male brain: How boys think, feel, and learn in school.* Thousand Oaks, CA: Corwin.

James, A. (2009). *Teaching the female brain: How girls learn math and science.* Thousand Oaks, CA: Corwin.

James, W. (1912). *Talks to teachers on psychology: And to students on some of life's ideals.* New York, NY: Holt.

James-Ward, C., Fisher, D., Frey, N., & Lapp, D. (2013). *Using data to focus instructional improvement.* Alexandria, VA: ASCD.

Janzen, J. (2008). Teaching English language learners in the content areas. *Review of Educational Research, 78*(4), 1010–1038.

Jenkins, J. R., Peyton, J. A., Sanders, E. A., & Vadasy, P. F. (2004). Effects of reading decodable texts in supplemental first-grade tutoring. *Scientific Studies of Reading, 8,* 53–85.

Jennings, P., & Greenberg, M. (2009). The prosocial classroom: Teacher social and emotional competence in relation to student and classroom outcomes. *Review of Educational Research, 79*(1), 491–525.

Jensen, E. (2000). Brain-based learning: A reality check. *Educational Leadership, 57*(7), 76–80.

Jensen, E. (2013). *Engaging students with poverty in mind: Practical strategies for raising achievement.* Alexandria, VA: ASCD.

Jensen, E. P. (2009). *Teaching with poverty in mind: What being poor does to kids' brains and what schools can do about it.* Alexandria, VA: ASCD.

Jensen, E., & Nickelsen, L. (2008). *Deeper learning: Seven powerful strategies for in-depth and longer-lasting learning.* Thousand Oaks, CA: Corwin.

Jensen, E., & Nickelson, L. (2013). *Bringing the Common Core to life in K-8 classrooms: 30 strategies to build literacy skills.* Bloomington, IN: Solution Tree.

Jetton, T. L., & Alexander, P. A. (2001). Interest assessment and the content area literacy environment: Challenges for research and practice. *Educational Psychology Review, 13*(3), 303–318.

Jeynes, W. (2012). A meta-analysis of the efficacy of different types of parental involvement programs for urban students. *Urban Education, 47*(4), 706–742.

Jimerson, S. R., Anderson, G. E., & Whipple, A. D. (2002). Winning the battle and losing the war: Examining the relation between grade retention and dropping out of high school. *Psychology in the Schools, 39,* 441–457.

Jitendra, A., Edwards, L., Sacks, G., & Jacobson, L. (2004, April). *What research says about vocabulary instruction for students with learning disabilities.* Paper presented at the annual meeting of the American Educational Research Association, San Diego, CA.

Jitendra, A., Star, J., Starosta, K., Leh, J., Sood, S., Caskie, G., Hughes, C., & Mack, T. (2009). Improving seventh grade students' learning of ratio and proportion: The role of schema-based instruction. *Contemporary Educational Psychology, 34*(3), 250–264.

Joe, S., Joe, E., & Rowley, L. (2009). Consequences of physical health and mental illness risks for academic achievement in grades K–12. *Review of Research in Education, 33,* 283–309.

Joët, G., Usher, E., & Bressoux, P. (2011). Sources of self-efficacy: An investigation of elementary school students in France. *Journal of Educational Psychology, 103*(3), 649–663.

Johnson, D. (2012). On board with BYOD. *Educational Leadership, 70*(2), 84–85.

Johnson, D. (2015). Helping to close the digital divide. *Educational Leadership, 72*(5), 81–82.

Johnson, D. W., & Johnson, R. T. (1999). *Learning together and alone: Cooperative, competitive, and individualistic learning.* Boston, MA: Allyn & Bacon.

Johnson, J., Sevimli-Celik, S., & Al-Mansour, M. (2013). Play in early childhood education. *Handbook of research on the education of young children* (pp. 265–274). New York, NY: Routledge.

Johnson, P. (2009). The 21st century skills movement. *Educational Leadership, 67*(1), 8–15.

Johnson, S., Riley, A., Granger, A., & Riis, J. (2012). The science of early life toxic stress for pediatric practice and advocacy. *Pediatrics, 131*(2), 319–327.

John-Steiner, V., & Mahn, H. (1996). Sociocultural approaches to learning and development: A Vygotskian framework. *Educational Psychologist, 31*(3 & 4), 191–206.

John-Steiner, V., & Mahn, H. (2003). Sociocultural contexts for teaching and learning. In W. M. Reynolds & G. E. Miller (Eds.), *Handbook of psychology: Vol. 7. Educational psychology* (pp. 125–151). Hoboken, NJ: Wiley.

Johnston, P. (2011). Response to intervention in literacy: Problems and possibilities. *The Elementary School Journal, 111*(4), 511–534.

Jonas, P. M. (2010.) *Laughing and learning: An alternative to shut up and listen.* Lanham, MD: Rowman & Littlefield.

Jones, M., Levin, M., Levin, J., & Beitzel, B. (2000). Can vocabulary-learning strategies and pair-learning formats be profitably combined? *Journal of Educational Psychology, 92*(2), 256–262.

Jones, S., & Dindia, K. (2004). A meta-analytic perspective on sex equity in the classroom. *Review of Educational Research, 74*(4), 443–472.

Jones, V., & Jones, L. (2016). *Comprehensive classroom management* (11th ed.). Boston, MA: Pearson.

Jordan-Young, R. M. (2010). *Brainstorm: The flaws in the sicence of sex differences.* Cambridge, MA: Harvard University Press.

Jorgenson, O. (2012). What we lose in winning the test score race. *Principal, 91*(5), 13–15.

Journell, W. (2012). Walk, don't run—to online learning. *Phi Delta Kappan, 93*(7), 46–50.

Joyce, B. R., Weil, M., & Calhoun, E. (2004). *Models of teaching* (7th ed.). Boston, MA: Allyn & Bacon.

Jung, J. (2010). *Alcohol, other drugs, and behavior* (2nd ed.). Thousand Oaks, CA: Sage.

Jussim, L., & Harber, K. D. (2005). Teacher expectations and self-fulfilling prophecies: Knowns and unknowns, resolved and unresolved controversies. *Personality and Social Psychology Review, 9,* 131–155.

Juvonen, J. (2000). The social functions of attributional face-saving tactics among early adolescents. *Educational Psychology Review, 12*(1), 15–32.

Juvonen, J., & Gross, E. (2008). Extending the school grounds? Bullying experiences in cyberspace. *Journal of School Health, 78,* 496–505.

Kafele, B. (2013). *Closing the attitude gap: How to fire up your students to strive for success.* Alexandria, VA: ASCD.

Kafele, B. (2009). *Motivating black males to achieve in school and in life.* Alexandria, VA: ASCD.

Kagan, S., & Kagan, M. (2012). *Kagan cooperative learning* (2nd ed.). San Clemente, CA: Kagan.

Kagan, S., Kyle, P., & Scott, S. (2004). *Win-win discipline.* San Clemente, CA: Kagan.

Kahneman, D. (2011). *Thinking fast and slow.* New York, NY: Penguin.

Kallick, B., & Colosimo, J. (2009). *Using curriculum mapping and assessment data to improve learning.* Thousand Oaks, CA: Corwin.

Kallison, J. M. (1986). Effects of lesson organization on achievement. *American Educational Research Journal, 23,* 337–347.

Kalogrides, D., & Loeb, S. (2013). Different teachers, different peers: The magnitude of student sorting within schools. *Educational Researcher, 42*(6), 304–316.

Kamhi, A. G., & Catts, H. W. (2012). Language and reading disabilities (3rd ed.). Boston, MA: Allyn & Bacon.

Kamil, M. L., Borman, G. D., Dole, J., Kral, C. C., & Salinger, T. (2008). *Improving adolescent literacy: Effective classroom and intervention practices* (NCEE 2008-4027). Washington, DC: Institute of Education Sciences, U.S. Department of Education.

Kamil, M. L., Intrator, S. M., & Kim, H. S. (2000). The effects of other technologies on literacy and literacy learning. In M. L. Kamil, P. B. Mosenthal, P. D. Pearson, & R. Barr (Eds.), *Handbook of reading research* (Vol. 3, pp. 771–788). Mahwah, NJ: Erlbaum.

Kampwirth, T. J., & Powers, K. M. (2016). *Collaborative consultation in the schools* (5th ed.). Boston, MA: Pearson.

Kane, M. S., Hambrick, D. Z., & Conway, A. R. A. (2005). Working memory capacity and fluid intelligence are strongly related concepts: Comment on Ackerman, Beier, & Boyle (2005). *Psychological Bulletin, 131*(1), 66–71.

Kaplan, R., & Saccuzzo, D. (2013). *Psychological testing: Principles, applications, and issues* (8th ed.). Wadsworth.

Kapur, S., Craik, F. I. M., Tulving, E., Wilson, A. A., Hoyle, S., & Brown, G. M. (1994). Neuroanatomical correlates of encoding in episodic memory: Levels of processing effect. *Proceedings of the National Academy of Sciences, 91,* 2008–2011.

Karpicke, J. D., & Roediger, H. L. (2007). Repetition during retrieval is the key to long-term retention. *Journal of Memory and Language, 43,* 508–529.

Karten, T. J. (2016). *Inclusion & CCSS supports.* West Palm Beach, FL: Learning Sciences International.

Karweit, N. L., & Slavin, R. E. (1981). Measurement and modeling choices in studies of time and learning. *American Educational Research Journal, 18,* 157–171.

Katz, L. (2015). Reducing inequality: Neighborhood and social interventions. *Focus, 31*(2), 12–17.

Katzir, T., & Paré-Blagoev, J. (2006). Applying cognitive neuroscience research to education: The case of literacy. *Educational Psychologist, 41*(1), 53–74.

Kauffman, J. M., Mostert, M. P., Trent, S. C., & Pullen, P. L. (2006). *Managing classroom behavior: A reflective case-based approach* (4th ed.). Boston, MA: Allyn & Bacon.

Kauffman, J., & Landrum, T. J. (2013). *Characteristics of emotional and behavioral disorders of children* (10th ed.). Upper Saddle River, NJ: Pearson.

Kauffman, J., McGee, K., & Brigham, M. (2004). Enabling or disabling? Observations on changes in special education. *Phi Delta Kappan, 85*(8), 613–620.

Kauffman, J., Pullen, P., Mostert, M., & Trent, S. (2011). *Managing classroom behavior: A reflective case-based approach* (5th ed.). New York, NY: Merrill.

Kaufman, J., Gottlieb, J., Agard, J., & Kukic, M. (1975). *Project PRIME: Mainstreaming toward an explication of the construct. Project No IM-71-001.* Washington, DC: U.S. Office of Education, Bureau of Education for the Handicapped.

Kazdin, A. E. (2001). *Behavior modification in applied settings* (6th ed.). Belmont, CA: Wadsworth.

Keen, L. (2011, April 26). LGBTs comprise 3.5% of US adult population. *Gay San Diego.* Retrieved from http://gay-sd.com/lgbts-comprise-3-5-percent-of-u-s-adult-population/

Keenan, T., & Evans, S. (2010). *An introduction to child development.* Thousand Oaks, CA: Sage.

Kelly, N., & Norwich, B. (2004). Pupils' perceptions of self and of labels: Moderate learning difficulties in mainstream and special schools. *British Journal of Educational Psychology, 74*(3), 411–435.

Kelly, S., & Monczunski, L. (2007). Overcoming the volatility in school-level gain scores: A new approach to identifying value added with cross-sectional data. *Educational Researcher, 36*(5), 279–287.

Kemple, J. J. (1997). *Career academies: Communities of support for students and teachers: Further findings from a 10-site evaluation.* New York, NY: MDRC.

Kendall, J. (2011). *Understanding Common Core State Standards.* Alexandria, VA: ASCD.

Kenkel, S., Hoelscher, S., & West, T. (2006). Leading adolescents to mastery. *Educational Leadership, 63*(7), 33–37.

Kennedy, M. M. (2008). Teachers thinking about their practice. In T. L. Good (Ed.), *21st century learning* (Vol. 1, pp. 21–30). Thousand Oaks, CA: Sage.

Kerr, M., Stattin, H., Biesecker, G., & Ferrer-Wreder, L. (2003). Relationships with parents and peers in adolescence. In R. M. Lerner, M. A. Easterbrooks, & J. Mistry (Eds.), *Handbook of psychology: Vol. 6. Developmental psychology* (pp. 395–419). Hoboken, NJ: Wiley.

Khan, S. (2012). *The one world school house: Education reimagined.* New York, NY: The Hachette Book Group.

Khan, S., & Slavitt, E. (2013). A bold new math class. *Educational Leadership, 70*(6), 28–31.

Kidron, Y., & Darwin, M. (2007). A systematic review of whole-school improvement models. *Journal of Education for Students Placed at Risk, 12*(1), 9–35.

Kidron, Y., & Fleischman, S. (2006). Promoting adolescents' prosocial behavior. *Educational Leadership, 63*(7), 90–91.

Kidron, Y., & Lindsay, J. (2014). *What does the research say about increased learning time and student outcomes?* Washington, DC: USDOE.

Kieffer, M. (2011). Converging trajectories: Reading growth in language minority learners and their classmates, kindergarten to grade 8. *American Educational Research Journal, 48*(5), 1187–1225.

Kieffer, M., Lesaux, N., Rivera, M., & Francis, D. (2009). Accommodations for English language learners taking large-scale assessments: A meta-analysis on effectiveness and validity. *Review of Educational Research, 79*(3), 1168–1201.

Kim, J. (2006). Effects of a voluntary summer reading intervention on reading achievement: Results from a randomized field trial. *Educational Evaluation and Policy Analysis, 28*(4), 335–355.

Kim, J. S., & Quinn, D. M. (2013). The effects of summer reading on low-income children's literacy achievement from kindergarten to grade 8: A meta-analysis of classroom and home interventions, *Review of Educational Research, 83*(3), 386-431.

Kim, S. E. (2001, April). *Meta-analysis of gender differences in test performance using HLM.* Paper presented at the annual meeting of the American Educational Research Association, Seattle, WA.

Kim, S., & Hill, N. (2015). Including fathers in the picture: A meta-analysis of parental involvement and students' academic achievement. *Journal of Educational Psychology, 107*(4), 919–934.

King, A. (1992). Facilitating elaborative learning through guided student-generated questioning. *Educational Psychologist, 27,* 111–126.

King, A. (1999). Teaching effective discourse patterns for small-group learning. In R. J. Stevens (Ed.), *Teaching in American schools.* Upper Saddle River, NJ: Merrill/Prentice-Hall.

King, E. W. (2002). Ethnicity. In D. L. Levinson, P. W. Cookson, Jr., & A. R. Sadovnik (Eds.), *Education and sociology: An encyclopedia* (pp. 247–253). New York, NY: Routledge.

King, K., Gurian, M., & Stevens, K. (2010). Gender-friendly schools. *Educational Leadership, 68*(3), 38–42.

King, R., & McInerney, D. (2014). Culture's consequences on student motivation: Capturing cross-cultural universality and variability through personal investment theory. *Educational Psychologist, 49*(3), 175–198.

Kirschner, P., & van Merrienboer, J. J. G. (2008). In T. L. Good (Ed.), *21st century learning* (Vol. 1, pp. 244–253). Thousand Oaks, CA: Sage.

Kirschner, P., & van Merrienboer, J. (2013). Do learners really know best? Urban legends in education. *Educational Psychologist, 48*(3), 169–183.

Kirschner, P., Sweller, J., & Clark, R. (2006). Why minimal guidance during instruction does not work: An analysis of the failure of constructivist, discovery, problem-based, experiential, and inquiry-based teaching. *Educational Psychologist, 41*(2), 75–86.

Kist, W. (2015). *Getting started with blended Learning: How do I integrate online and face-to-face instruction?* Alexandria, VA: ASCD.

Klahr, D., & Nigam, M. (2004). The equivalence of learning paths in early science instruction: Effects of direct instruction and discovery learning. *Psychological Science, 15*(10), 661–667.

Klein, A. (2016). Path to accountability taking bold new turns. *Education Week, 35*(16), 4–6.

Klein, J. D., & Schnackenberg, H. L. (2000). Effects of informal cooperative learning and the affiliation motive on achievement, attitude, and student interactions. *Contemporary Educational Psychology, 25*(1), 332–341.

Klein, P. D. (1999). Reopening inquiry into cognitive processes in writing-to-learn. *Educational Psychology Review, 11*(3), 203–270.

Kleinert, H. L., & Kearns, J. F. (2001). *Alternate assessment: Measuring outcomes and supports for students with disabilities.* Baltimore, MD: Brookes.

Knapp, M. S., & Woolverton, S. (1995). Social class and schooling. In J. A. Banks & C. A. M. Banks (Eds.), *Handbook of research on multicultural education.* New York, NY: Macmillan.

Knobel, M., & Wilber, D. (2009). Let's talk 2.0. *Educational Leadership, 66*(6), 20–25.

Kobayashi, K. (2005). What limits the encoding effect of note-taking? A meta-analytic examination. *Contemporary Educational Psychology, 30*(2), 242–262.

Koch, J. (2003). Gender issues in the classroom. In W. M. Reynolds & G. E. Miller (Eds.), *Handbook of psychology: Vol. 7. Educational psychology* (pp. 259–281). Hoboken, NJ: Wiley.

Kohlberg, L. (1963). The development of children's orientations toward moral order. I: Sequence in the development of human thought. *Vita Humana, 6,* 11–33.

Kohlberg, L. (1969). Stage and sequence: The cognitive–developmental approach to socialization. In D. A. Golsin (Ed.), *Handbook of socialization theory and research* (pp. 347–380). Chicago, IL: Rand McNally.

Kohlberg, L. (1978). Revisions in the theory and practice of moral development. In W. Damon (Ed.), *New directions for child development* (No. 2, pp. 83–87). San Francisco, CA: Jossey-Bass.

Kohlberg, L. (1980). High school democracy and educating for a just society. In M. L. Mosher (Ed.), *Moral education: A first generation of research and development* (pp. 20–57). New York, NY: Praeger.

Kolb, B., & Whishaw, I. (2011). *An introduction to brain and behavior* (3rd ed.). New York, NY: Worth.

Kolbe, T., Partridge, M., & O'Reilly, F. (2013). Time and learning in schools: A national profile. Retrieved from www.timeandlearning.org

Konstantopoulos, S., & Chung, V. (2009). What are the long-term effects of small classes on the achievement gap? Evidence from the lasting benefits study. *American Journal of Education, 116* (1), 125–154.

Konstantopoulos, S., Miller, S., & van der Ploeg, A. (2013). The impact of Indiana's system of interim assessments on mathematics and reading achievement. *Educational Evaluation and Policy Analysis, 35*(4), 481–499.

Koppelman, K., & Goodhart, L. (2008). *Understanding human differences: Multicultural education for a diverse America* (2nd ed.). Boston, MA: Pearson.

Kornhaber, M., Fierros, E., & Veenema, S. (2004). *Multiple intelligences: Best ideas from research and practice.* Boston, MA: Allyn & Bacon.

Korpershoek, H., Harms, T., de Boer, H., van Jukik, M., & Doorlaard, S. (2016). A meta-analysis of the effects of classroom management strategies and classroom managementprograms on students' academic, behavioral, emotional, and motivational outcomes. *Review of Educational Research, 86* (3), 643-680.

Kosterman, R., Haggerty, K., & Hawkins, J. (2010). Long-term effects of social development intervention. *Better: Evidence-based Education, 2* (2), 6–7.

Kraft, M., & Dougherty, S. (2013). The effect of teacher-family communication on student engagement: Evidence from a randomized field experiment. *Journal of Research on Educational Effectiveness, 6*(3), 199–222.

Kramarski, B., & Mevarech, Z. R. (2003). Enhancing mathematical reasoning in the classroom: The effects of cooperative learning and metacognitive training. *American Educational Research Journal, 40*(1), 281–310.

Kratochwill, T. (2012). What works in classroom management. *Better: Evidence-based education, 5*(1), 10–11.

Krinsky, R., & Krinsky, S. G. (1996). Pegword mnemonic instruction: Retrieval times and long-term memory performance among fifth grade children. *Contemporary Educational Psychology, 21*(2), 193–207.

Kristof, N. D. (2009, April 15). How to raise our I.Q. *New York Times.* Retrieved from www.nytimes.com/2009/04/16/opinion/16kristof.html

Kroesbergen, E. H., Van Luit, J. E. H., & Maas, C. J. M. (2004). Effectiveness of explicit and constructivist mathematics instruction for low-achieving students in the Netherlands. *The Elementary School Journal, 104*(3), 233–251.

Kubiszyn, T., & Borich, G. (2010). *Educational testing and measurement: Classroom application and practice* (9th ed.). New York, NY: Wiley.

Kugler, E., & Albright, E. (2005). Increasing diversity in challenging classes. *Educational Leadership, 62*(5), 42–45.

Kuhara-Kojima, K., & Hatano, G. (1991). Contribution of content knowledge and learning ability to the learning of facts. *Journal of Educational Psychology, 83*(2), 253–263.

Kuhn, D. (2006). Do cognitive changes accompany developments in the adolescent brain? *Perspectives on Psychological Science, 1*(1), 59–67.

Kulik, J., & Fletcher, J. (2016). Effectiveness of intelligent tutoring systems: A meta-analytic review. *Review of Educational Research, 86* (1), 42-78.

Kumar, R., & Maehr, M. (2010). Schooling, cultural diversity, and student motivation. In J. Meece & J. Eccles (Eds.), *Handbook of research on schools, schooling, and human development* (pp. 308–324). New York, NY: Routledge.

Kutnick, P., Ota, C., & Berdondini, L. (2008). Improving the effects of group working in classrooms with young school-aged children: Facilitating attainment, interaction and classroom activity. *Learning and Instruction, 18*(1), 83–95.

Kyle, P., & Rogien, L. (2004). *Opportunities and options in classroom management.* Boston, MA: Pearson.

Ladd, G. W., & Troop-Gordon, W. (2003). The role of chronic peer difficulties in the development of children's psychological adjustment problems. *Child Development, 55,* 1958–1965.

Ladd, G., & Sechler, C. (2013). Young children's peer relations and social competence. *Handbook of research on the education of young children* (pp. 33–66). New York, NY: Routledge.

Ladson-Billings, G. (2006). From the achievement gap to the education debt: Understanding achievement in U.S. schools. *Educational Researcher, 35*(7), 3–12.

Lampert, M. (1986). Knowing, doing, and teaching multiplication. *Cognition and Instruction, 3,* 305–342.

Land, D., & Legters, N. (2002). The extent and consequences of risk in U.S. education. In S. Stringfield & D. Land (Eds.), *Educating at-risk students* (pp. 1–28). Chicago, IL: National Society for the Study of Education.

Landrum, T. J., & McDuffie, K. A. (2008). Learning: Behavioral. In T. L. Good (Ed.), *21st century learning* (Vol. 1, pp. 161–167). Thousand Oaks, CA: Sage.

Landrum, T., Scott, T., & Lingo, A. (2011). Classroom misbehavior is predictable and preventable. *Phi Delta Kappan, 93*(2), 30–34.

Lane, K., Harris, K., Graham, S., Driscoll, S., Sandmel, K., Morphy, P., ... & Schatschneider, C. (2011). Self-regulated strategy development at Tier 2 for second-grade students with writing and behavioral difficulties: A randomized controlled trial. *Journal of Journal of Research on Educational Effectiveness, 4*(4), 322–353.

Langer, G., & Colton, A. (2005). Looking at student work. *Educational Leadership, 62*(5), 22–27.

Lapkoff, S., & Li, R. (2007). Five trends for schools. *Educational Leadership, 64*(6), 8–17.

Larmer, J. (2014). Boosting the power of projects. *Educational Leadership, 72*(1), 42–46.

Larmer, J., Mergendoller, J., & Boss, S. (2015). *Setting the standard for project-based learning.* Alexandria, VA: ASCD.

Larson, L. (2015). The learning potential of e-books. *Educational Leadership, 72*(8), 42–46.

Lauer, P. A., Akiba, M., Wilkerson, S., Apthorp, H., Snow, D., & Martin-Glenn, M. L. (2006). Out-of-school-time programs: A meta-analysis of effects for at-risk students. *Review of Educational Research, 76*(2), 275–313.

Lave, J. (1988). *Cognition in practice.* Boston, MA: Cambridge Press.

Lawner, E., & Terzian, M. (2013). *What works for bullying programs: Lessons from experimental evaluations of programs and interventions.* Bethesda, MD: ChildTrends.

Lawson, M., & Alameda-Lawson, T. (2012). A case study of school-linked, collective parent engagement. *American Educational Research Journal, 49*(4), 651–684.

Learning First Alliance. (2001). *Every child learning: Safe and supportive schools.* Washington, DC: Author.

Lee, C. (2008). Synthesis of research on the role of culture in learning among African American youth: The contributions of Asa G. Hillard, III. *Review of Educational Research, 78*(4), 797–827.

Lee, C. D. (2000, April). *The state of knowledge about the education of African Americans.* Paper presented at the annual meeting of the American Educational Research Association, New Orleans, LA.

Lee, J. (2004). Multiple facets of inequity in racial and ethnic achievement gaps. *Peabody Journal of Education, 79*(2), 51–73.

Lee, J., & Bowen, N. (2006). Parent involvement, cultural capital, and the achievement gap among elementary school children. *American Educational Research Journal, 43*(2), 193–218.

Lee, O. (2014). Diversity and equity in science education. In R. E. Slavin (Ed.), *Science, technology, & mathematics (STEM)* (pp. 98–102). Thousand Oaks, CA: Corwin.

Lee, V. E., & Burkam, D. T. (2003). Dropping out of high school: The role of school organization and structure. *American Educational Research Journal, 40*(2), 353–393.

Lehr, C. A., Hansen, A., Sinclair, M. F., & Christenson, S. L. (2003). Moving beyond dropout prevention to school completion: An integrative review of data-based interventions. *School Psychology Review, 32,* 342–364.

Lehr, C. A., Sinclair, M. F., & Christenson, S. L. (2004). Addressing student engagement and truancy prevention during the elementary school years: A replication study of the Check & Connect model. *Journal of Education for Students Placed at Risk, 9*(3), 279–301.

Leinhardt, G., & Steele, M. D. (2005). Seeing the complexity of standing to the side: Instructional dialogues. *Cognition and Instruction, 23,* 87–163.

Lemov, D. (2010). *Teach like a champion.* San Francisco, CA: Jossey-Bass.

Lepper, M. R. (1983). Extrinsic reward and intrinsic motivation: Implications for the classroom. In J. M. Levine & M. C. Wang (Eds.), *Teacher and student perceptions: Implications for learning* (pp. 281–317). Hillsdale, NJ: Erlbaum.

Lepper, M. R. (1998). A whole much less than the sum of its parts. *American Psychologist, 53*(6), 675–676.

Lepper, M. R., Greene, D., & Nisbett, R. E. (1973). Undermining children's intrinsic interest with extrinsic rewards: A test of the overjustification hypothesis. *Journal of Personality and Social Psychology, 28,* 129–137.

Lereya, S., Samara, M., & Wolke, D. (2013) Parenting behavior and the risk of becoming a bully/victim: A meta-analysis study. *Child Abuse and Neglect, 37*(12), 1091–1108.

Lesaux, N., Kieffer, M., Kelley, J., & Harris, J. (2014). Effects of academic vocabulary instruction for linguistically diverse adolescents: Evidence from a randomized field trial. *American Educational Research Journal, 51*(6), 1159–1194.

Lesnick, J., Goerge, R., Smithgall, C., & Gwynne J. (2010). *Reading on grade level in third grade: How is it related to high school performance and college enrollment?* Chicago, IL: Chapin Hall at the University of Chicago.

Lessow-Hurley, J. (2005). *The foundations of dual language instruction.* Boston, MA: Pearson.

Levenstein, P., Levenstein, S., & Oliver, D. (2002). First grade school readiness of former participants in a South Carolina replication of the Parent-Child Home Program. *Journal of Applied Developmental Psychology, 23,* 331–353.

Lever-Duffy, J., & McDonald, J. (2015). *Teaching and learning with technology.* Boston, MA: Pearson.

Levin, J. R., O'Donnell, A. M., & Kratochwill, T. R. (2003). Educational/psychological intervention research. In W. M. Reynolds & G. E. Miller (Eds.), *Handbook of psychology: Vol. 7. Educational psychology* (pp. 557–581). Hoboken, NJ: Wiley.

Levin, J., & Nolan, J. (2010). *Principles of classroom management: A professional decision-making model* (6th ed.). Upper Saddle River, NJ: Pearson.

Levin, J., Nolan, J., Kerr, J., Elliott, A., & Bajovic, M. (2016). *Principles of classroom management: A professional decision-making model.* Ontario, CN: Pearson.

Levine, C., Kohlberg, L., & Hewer, A. (1985). The current formulation of Kohlberg's theory and a response to critics. *Human Development, 28,* 94–100.

Levine, M. (2004). Celebrating diverse minds. *Educational Leadership, 61* (2), 12.

Levine, M., & Gershenfeld, A. (2011, November 9). The video game-learning link. *Education Week,* 24–25.

Levitt, S., List, J., Neckermann, S., & Sadoff, S. (2012). *The behaviorist goes to school: Leveraging behavioral economics to improve educational performance.* Cambridge, MA: NBER.

Levy, S. (2008). The power of audience. *Educational Leadership, 66*(3), 75–79.

Lewin, L., & Shoemaker, B. J. (2011). *Great performances: Creating classroom-based assessment tasks* (2nd ed.). Alexandria, VA: ASCD.

Li, G., & Wang, W. (2008). English language learners. In T. L. Good (Ed.), *21st century learning* (Vol. 2, pp. 97–104). Thousand Oaks, CA: Sage.

Lin, T., & Anderson, R. (2008). Reflections on collaborative discourse, argumentation, and learning. *Contemporary Educational Psychology, 33*(3), 443–448.

Lin-Siegler, X., Dweck, C., & Cohen, G. (2016). Instructional interventions that motivate classroom learning. *Educational Psychology, 108*(3), 295-299.

Lindeman, B. (2001). Reaching out to immigrant parents. *Educational Leadership, 58*(6), 62–66.

Lindholm-Leary, K. (2004/2005). The rich promise of two-way immersion. *Educational Leadership, 62*(4), 56–59.

Lindsey, L. L. (2015). *Gender rules* (6th ed.). Boston, MA: Pearson.

Linebarger, D., Kosanic, A., Greenwood, C., & Doku, N. (2004). Effects of viewing the television program *Between the Lions* on the emergent literacy skills of young children. *Journal of Educational Psychology, 96,* 297–308.

Linn, R. L. (1994). Performance assessment: Policy promises and technical measurement standards. *Educational Researcher, 23*(9), 4–14.

Linn, R. L. (2000). Assessments and accountability. *Educational Researcher, 29*(2), 4–15.

Lissitz, R., & Schafer, W. (2002). *Assessment in educational reform: Both means and ends.* Boston, MA: Allyn & Bacon.

Lloyd, J. W., Landrum, T. J., Cook, B. G., & Tankersley, M. (2013). *Research-based approaches for assessment.* Upper Saddle River, NJ: Pearson.

Lomawaima, K. T., & McCarty, T. L. (2002). When tribal sovereignty challenges democracy: American Indian education and the democratic ideal. *American Educational Research Journal, 39*(2), 279–305.

Lomawaima, T., & McCarty, T. (2006). *To remain an Indian: Lessons in democracy from a century of Native American education.* New York, NY: Teachers College Press.

Losen, D. J. (Ed.) (2015). *Closing the school discipline gap.* New York, NY: Teachers College Press.

Lou, Y., Abrami, P. C., & d'Apollonia, S. (2001). Small group and individual learning with technology: A meta-analysis. *Review of Educational Research, 71*(3), 449–521.

Loury, G. C. (2002). *The anatomy of racial inequality.* Cambridge, MA: Harvard University Press.

Loveless, T. (2012, April 18). Does the common core matter? *Education Week,* 32.

Lovett, B. (2010). Extended time testing accommodations for students with disabilities: Answers to five fundamental questions. *Review of Educational Research, 80*(4), 611–638.

Lowe, J. (2011, December 7). Want to boost learning? Start with emotional health. *Education Week,* 40.

Lowther, D., Ross, S., & Morrison, G. (2003). *When each one has one: The influences on teaching strategies and student achievement of using laptops in the classroom.* Paper presented at the annual meeting of the American Educational Research Association, Seattle, WA.

Loyens, S., & Rikers, R. (2011). Instruction based on inquiry. In R. Mayer & P. Alexander (Eds.), *Handbook of research on learning and instruction* (pp. 361–381). New York, NY: Routledge.

Lucas, S. R., & Gamoran, A. (2002). Tracking and the achievement gap. In J. E. Chubb & T. Loveless (Eds.), *Bridging the achievement gap* (pp. 171–198). Washinton, DC: Brookings.

Lyons, C. A., Pinnell, G. S., & DeFord, D. E. (1993). *Partners in learning: Teachers and children in reading recovery*. New York, NY: Teachers College Press.

Lyytinen, H., Guttorm, T. K., Huttunen, T., Hamalainen, J., Leppanen, P. H. T., & Vesterinen, M. (2005). Psychophysiology of developmental dyslexic: A review of findings including studies of children at risk for dyslexia. *Journal of Neurolinguistics, 18,* 167–195.

Maag, J. (2001). Rewarded by punishment: Reflections on the disuse of positive reinforcement in schools. *Exceptional Children, 67,* 173–186.

MacArthur, C., Ferretti, R., Okolo, C., & Cavalier, A. (2001). Technology applications for students with literacy problems: A critical review. *The Elementary School Journal, 101*(3), 273–302.

MacArthur, C. A., Graham, S., & Fitzgerald, J. (Eds.). (2015). *Handbook of writing research* (2nd ed.). New York, NY: Guilford Press.

MacIver, D., Ruby, A., Balfanz, R., Jones, L., Sion, F., Garriott, M., & Brynes, V. (2010). The Talent Development Middle Grades model: A design for improving early adolescents' developmental trajectories in high-poverty schools. In J. Meece & J. Eccles (Eds.), *Handbook of research on schools, schooling, and human development* (pp. 446–462). New York, NY: Routledge.

MacKenzie, A. A., & White, R. T. (1982). Fieldwork in geography and long-term memory. *American Educational Research Journal, 19,* 623–632.

Madden, N. A., & Slavin, R. E. (2015). *Evaluations of technology-assisted small-group tutoring for struggling readers.* Baltimore, MD: Success for All Foundation.

Maehara, Y., & Saito, S. (2007). The relationship between processing and storage in working memory span. *Journal of Memory and Language, 56*(2), 212–228.

Magaño, S., & Marzano, R. (2014). Using polling technologies to close feedback gaps. *Educational Leadership, 71*(6), 82–84.

Mager, R. F. (1997). *Preparing instructional objectives.* Atlanta, GA: CEP.

Maguire, E. A., Gadian, D. G., Johnsrude, I. S., Good, C. D., Ashburner, J., Frackowiak, R. S. J., & Frith, C. D. (2000). Navigation-related structural change in the hippocampi of taxi drivers. *Proceedings of the National Academy of Sciences, 97*(8), 4398–4403.

Maher, F. A., & Ward, J. V. (2002). *Gender and teaching.* Mahwah, NJ: Erlbaum.

Mahn, H., & John-Steiner, V. (2013). Vygotsky and sociocultural approaches to teaching and learning. In W. Reynolds, G. Miller, & I. Weiner (Eds.), *Handbook of psychology* (Vol. 7, 2nd ed., pp. 117–146.). Hoboken, NJ: Wiley.

Maloy, R., Verock-O'Loughlin, R-E., Edwards S., & Woolf, B. (2014). *Transforming learning with new technologies.* Boston, MA: Pearson.

Mandinach, E. (2012). A perfect time for data use: Using data-driven decision making to inform practice. *Educational Psychologist, 47*(2), 71–85.

Mandinach, E., & Gummer, E. (2016). Every teacher should succeed with data literacy. *Phi Delta Kappan, 97* (8), 43–46.

Manna, P. (2008). *Federal aid to elementary and secondary education: Premises, effects, and major lessons learned.* Washington, DC: Center on Education Policy.

Manning, B. H. (1988). Application of cognitive behavior modification: First and third graders' self-management of classroom behaviors. *American Educational Research Journal, 25,* 193–212.

Manning, M. A., Bear, G. G., & Minke, K. M. (2001, April). *The self-concept of students with learning disabilities: Does educational placement matter?* Paper presented at the annual meeting of the American Educational Research Association, Seattle, WA.

Manning, M. L., & Baruth, L. G. (2009). *Multicultural education of children and adolescents* (5th ed.). Boston, MA: Pearson.

Manning, M. L., & Bucher, K. T. (2013). *Classroom management: Models, applications, and cases* (3rd ed.). Saddle River, NJ: Pearson.

March, J., Gershwin, D., Kirby, S., & Xia, N. (2009). *Retaining students in grade: Lessons learned regarding policy design and implementation.* Arlington, VA: RAND.

Marchez, M. A., Fischer, T. A., & Clark, D. M. (2015). *Assistive technology for children and youth with disabilities.* Boston, MA: Pearson.

Marcia, J. E. (1991). Identity and self-development. In R. M. Lerner, A. C. Petersen, & E. J. Brooks-Gunn (Eds.), *Encyclopedia of adolescence* (Vol. 1, pp. 527–531). New York, NY: Garland.

Mares, M-L, & Pan, Z. (2013). The effects of Sesame Street: A meta-analysis of children's learning in 15 countries. *Journal of Applied Developmental Psychology, 34*(3), 140–151.

Markovitz, C. E., Hernandez, M. W., Hedberg, E. C., & Silberglitt, B. (2014). *Impact evaluation of the Minnesota Reading Corps K-3 program.* Chicago, IL: NORC.

Marks, H., Doane, K., & Secada, W. (1998). Support for student achievement. In F. Newmann & Associates (Eds.), *Restructuring for student achievement: The impact of structure and culture in 24 schools.* San Francisco, CA: Jossey-Bass.

Marsh, H. W. (1993). The multidimensional structure of academic self-concept: Invariance over gender and age. *American Educational Research Journal, 30,* 841–860.

Martella, R., Nelson, J., Marchand-Martella, N., & O'Reilley, M. (2012). *Comprehensive behavior management.* Thousand Oaks, CA: Sage.

Martin, A. J., Marsh, H. W., & Debus, R. L. (2001). Self-handicapping and defensive pessimism: Exploring a model of predictors and outcomes from a self-protection perspective. *Journal of Educational Psychology, 93*(1), 87–102.

Martin, A., & Dowson, M. (2009). Interpersonal relationships, motivation, engagement, and achievement: Yields for theory, current issues, and educational practice. *Review of Educational Research, 79*(1), 327–365.

Martin, G., & Pear, J. (2011). *Behavior modification: What it is and how to do it* (9th ed). Upper Saddle River, NJ: Pearson.

Martin, K., Sharp, C., & Mehta, P. (2013). *The impact of the summer schools programme on pupils.* London, England: Department for Education.

Martone, A., & Sireci, S. G. (2009). Evaluating alignment between curriculum, assessment, and instruction. *Review of Educational Research, 79*(4), 1332–1361.

Marulis, L., & Neuman, S. (2013). How vocabulary interventions affect young children at risk: A meta-analytic review. *Journal of Research on Educational Effectiveness, 6*(3), 223–262.

Marx, R., & Harris, C. (2006). No Child Left Behind and science education: Opportunities, challenges, and risks. *The Elementary School Journal, 106*(5), 467–478.

Marzano, R. (2009). *Teaching basic and advanced vocabulary: A framework for Direct Instruction.* Alexandria, VA: ASCD.

Marzano, R. (2010a). *Formative assessment & standards-based grading.* Bloomington, IN: Marzano Research Laboratory.

Marzano, R. (2010b). Summarizing to comprehend. *Educational Leadership, 67*(6), 83–84.

Marzano, R. (2010c). Using games to enhance student achievement. *Educational Leadership, 67*(5), 71–72.

Marzano, R. (2010d). When students track their progress. *Educational Leadership, 67*(4), 87–88.

Marzano, R. (2011). Objectives that students understand. *Educational Leadership, 68*(8), 86–87.

Marzano, R. (2011). The inner world of teaching. *Educational Leadership, 68*(7), 90–93.

Marzano, R. (2011). The perils and promises of Discovery Learning. *Educational Leadership, 69*(1), 86–87.

Marzano, R. (2013). Asking questions–at four different levels. *Educational Leadership, 70*(5), 76–77.

Marzano, R. J., Pickering, D. J., & Pollock, J. E. (2001). *Classroom instruction that works: Research-based strategies for increasing student achievement.* Alexandria, VA: ASCD.

Marzano, R. J., Yanoski, D. C., Hoegh, J. K., & Simms, J. A. (2013). *Using Common Core Standards to enhance classroom instruction and assessment.* Bloomington, IN: Solution Tree.

Marzano, R., & Heflebower, T. (2011). Grades that show what students know. *Educational Leadership, 69*(3), 34–39.

Marzano, R., & Heflebower, T. (2012). *Teaching and assessing 21st century skills.* Bloomington, IN: Marzano Research Laboratory.

Marzano, R., & Kendall, J. (2007). *The new taxonomy of educational objectives* (2nd ed.). Thousand Oaks, CA: Corwin.

Marzano, R., & Pickering, D. (2007). The case for and against homework. *Educational Leadership, 64*(6), 74–79.

Mash, E. J., & Wolfe, D. A. (2003). Disorders of childhood and adolescence. In G. Stricker & T. A. Widiger (Eds.), *Handbook of psychology: Vol. 8. Clinical psychology* (pp. 27–64). Hoboken, NJ: Wiley.

Maslow, A. H. (1954). *Motivation and personality.* New York, NY: Harper & Row.

Mason, D. A., & Good, T. L. (1993). Effects of two-group and whole-class teaching on regrouped elementary students' mathematics achievement. *American Educational Research Journal, 30*(2), 328–360.

Mason, L. H. (2004). Explicit self-regulated strategy development versus reciprocal questioning: Effects on expository reading comprehension among struggling readers. *Journal of Educational Psychology, 96*(2), 283–296.

Massey, C. (2008). Development: PreK–2. In T. L. Good (Ed.), *21st century learning* (Vol. 1, pp. 73–81). Thousand Oaks, CA: Sage.

Master, A., Cheryan, S., & Meltzoff, A. (2016). Computing whether she belongs: Stereotypes undermine girls' interest and sense of belonging in computer science. *Educational Psychology, 108*(3), 424–437.

Mastropieri, M. A. (2016). *The inclusive classroom* (5th ed.). Boston, MA: Pearson.

Mathes, P. G., Denton, C. A., Fletcher, J. M., Anthony, J. L., Francis, D. J., & Schatschneider, C. (2005). The effects of theoretically different instruction and student characteristics on the skills of struggling readers. *Reading Research Quarterly, 40*(2), 148–182.

Mathes, P. G., Torgesen, J. K., Clancy-Menchetti, J., Santi, K., Nicholas, K., Robinson, C., & Grek, M. (2003). A comparison of teacher-directed versus peer-assisted instruction to struggling first-grade readers. *The Elementary School Journal, 103*(5), 461–479.

Mathes, P. G., Torgeson, J. K., & Allor, J. H. (2001). The effects of peer-assisted literacy strategies for first-grade readers with and without additional computer-assisted instruction in phonological awareness. *American Educational Research Journal, 38*(2), 371–410.

Mathes, P., & Babyak, A. (2001). The effects of peer-assisted literacy strategies for first-grade readers with and without additional mini-skills lessons. *Learning Disabilities Research & Practice, 16*(1), 28–44.

Matthews, J., Ponitz, C., & Morrison, F. (2009). Early gender differences in self-regulation and academic achievement. *Journal of Educational Psychology, 101*(3), 689–704.

Mattingly, D. J., Prislin, R., McKenzie, T. L., Rodriguez, J. L., & Kayzar, B. (2002). Evaluating evaluations: The case of parent involvement programs. *Review of Educational Research, 72*(4), 549–576.

Maxwell, L. (2012, March 28). 'Dual' classes see growth in popularity. *Education Week,* pp. 1, 16.

Maxwell, L., & Shah, N. (2012, August 29). Evaluating ELLs for special needs a challenge. *Education Week, 32*(2), 1, 12.

May, H., Goldsworthy, H., Armijo, M., Gray, A., Sirinides, P., Blalock, T., … & Sam, C. (2015). *Evaluation of the i3 scale-up of Reading Recovery: Year 2 report.* Philadelphia, PA: CPRE.

Mayer, R. (2008a). Applying the science of learning: Evidence-based principles for the design of multimedia instruction. *American Psychologist, 63*(8), 757–769.

Mayer, R. (2008b). Information processing. In T. L. Good (Ed.), *21st century learning* (Vol. 1, pp. 168–174). Thousand Oaks, CA: Sage.

Mayer, R. (2011a). *Applying the science of learning.* Boston, MA: Pearson.

Mayer, R. (2011b). Instruction based on visualizations. In R. Mayer & P. Alexander (Eds.), *Handbook of research on learning and instruction* (pp. 427–445). New York, NY: Routledge.

Mayer, R. E. (2009). *Multimedia learning* (2nd ed). New York, NY: Cambridge University Press.

Maynard, A. E. (2008). What we thought we knew and how we came to know it: Four decades of cross-cultural research from a Piagetian point of view. *Human Development, 51*(1), 56–65.

Mazur, J. E. (2013). *Learning and behavior* (7th ed.). Upper Saddle River, NJ: Pearson.

Mbwana, K., Terzian, M., & Moore, K. (2009). What works for parent involvement programs for children: Lessons from experimental evaluations of social interventions. Retrieved from www.childtrends.org

McAfee, O., Leong, D., & Bodrova, E. (2016). *Assessing and guiding young children's development and learning.* Boston, MA: Pearson.

McCaffrey, D. F., Lockwood, J. R., Koretz, D., Louis, T. A., & Hamilton, L. (2004). Models for value-added modeling of teacher effects. *Journal of Educational and Behavioral Statistics, 29*(1), 67–101.

McClarty, K., Way, W., Porter, A., Beimers, J., & Miles, J. (2013). Evidence based standard setting: Establishing a validity framework for cut scores. *Educational Researcher, 42*(2), 78–88.

McComb, E. M., & Scott-Little, C. (2003). *After-school programs: Evaluations and outcomes.* Greensboro, NC: SERVE.

McCombs, B. (2010). Learner-centered practices: Providing the context for positive learner development, motivation, and achievement. In J. Meece & J. Eccles (Eds.), *Handbook of research on schools, schooling, and human development* (pp. 60–74). New York, NY: Routledge.

McCombs, J. S., Kirby, S. N., & Mariano, L. T. (2009). *Ending social promotion without leaving children behind: The case of New York City.* Arlington, VA: RAND.

McCormick, C. B. (2003). Metacognition and learning. In W. M. Reynolds & G. E. Miller (Eds.), *Handbook of psychology: Vol. 7. Educational psychology* (pp. 79–102). Hoboken, NJ: Wiley.

McCormick, C. B., Dimmitt, C., & Sullivan, F. (2013). Metacognition, learning, and instruction. In W. Reynolds, G. Miller, & I. Weiner (Eds.) *Handbook of psychology* (Vol. 7, 2nd ed., pp. 69–98). Hoboken, NJ: Wiley.

McDaniel, M., Roediger, H., & McDermott, K. (2007). Generalized test-enhanced learning from the laboratory to the classroom. *Psychonomic Bulletin and Review, 14,* 200–206.

McDermott, K. (2007). "Expanding the moral community" or "Blaming the victim"? The politics of state education accountability policy. *American Educational Research Journal, 44*(1), 77–111.

McDevitt, T., & Ormrod, J. (2016). *Child development and education.* Boston, MA: Pearson.

McElvany, N., & Artelt, C. (2009). Systematic reading training in the family: Development, implementation, and initial evaluation of the Berlin Parent-Child Reading Program. *Learning and Instruction, 19*(1), 79–95.

McGarry, R. (2013). Build a curriculum that includes everyone. *Phi Delta Kappan, 94*(5), 27–31.

McGill-Franzen, A., & Allington, R. (2006). Contamination of current accountability systems. *Phi Delta Kappan, 87*(10), 762–766.

McHale, S. M., Dariotis, J. K., & Kauh, T. J. (2003). Social development and social relationships in middle childhood. In R. M. Lerner, M. A. Easterbrooks, & J. Mistry (Eds.), *Handbook of psychology: Vol. 6. Developmental psychology* (pp. 241–265). Hoboken, NJ: Wiley.

McKenna, M., & Walpole, S. (2007). Assistive technology in the reading clinic: Its emerging potential. *Reading Research Quarterly, 42*(1), 140–145.

McKeown, M. G., & Beck, I. L. (2004). Transforming knowledge into professional development resources: Six teachers implement a model of teaching for understanding text. *The Elementary School Journal, 104*(5), 391–408.

McLeskey, J., Rosenberg, M. S., & Westling, D. L. (2013). *Inclusion: Effective practices for all students* (2nd ed.). Upper Saddle River, NJ: Pearson.

McLoyd, V. C. (1998). Economic disadvantage and child development. *American Psychologist, 53*(2), 185–204.

McMillan, J. H. (2011). *Classroom assessment principles and practice for effective standards-based instruction* (5th ed.). Upper Saddle River, NJ: Pearson.

McNally, S. (2014). England vs. Wales: Education performance and accountability. In R. E. Slavin (Ed.), *Classroom management and assessment* (pp. 45–49). Thousand Oaks, CA: Corwin.

McPartland, J. M., Balfanz, R., Jordan, W. J., & Legters, N. (2002). Promising solutions for the least productive American high schools. In S. Stringfield & D. Land (Eds.), *Educating at-risk students* (pp. 148–170). Chicago, IL: National Society for the Study of Education.

McTighe, J., & Curtis, G. (2015). *A blueprint for vision-driven schools.* Bloomington, IN: Solution Tree.

McTighe, J., & March, T. (2015). Choosing apps by design. *Educational Leadership, 72*(8), 36–41.

McTighe, J., & Wiggins, G. (2013). *Essential questions: Opening doors to student understanding.* Alexandria, VA: ASCD.

McVee, M., Dunsmore, K., & Gavelek, J. (2005). Schema theory revisited. *Review of Educational Research, 75*(4), 531–566.

MDRC (2013). *Reforming underperforming high schools.* New York, NY: Author.

Mead, S. (2006). *The truth about boys and girls.* Washington, DC: Education Sector.

Means, B., Toyama, Y., Murpny, R., Bakia, M., & Jones, K. (2010). *Evaluation of evidence-based practices in on-line learning studies.* Washington, DC: U.S. Department of Education, Office of Planning, Evaluation, and Policy Development.

Meece, J. L., & Daniels, D. H. (2008). *Child and adolescent development for educators* (3rd ed.). New York, NY: McGraw-Hill.

Meek, C. (2003). Classroom crisis: It's about time. *Phi Delta Kappan, 84*(8), 592–595.

Meichenbaum, D. (1977). *Cognitive behavior modification: An integrative approach.* New York, NY: Plenum.

Mendler, A. (2012). *When teaching gets tough: Smart ways to reclaim your game.* Alexandria, VA: ASCD.

Mendler, A. N., & Mendler, B. D. (2011). *Power struggles: Successful techniques for educators.* Bloomington, IN: Solution Tree.

Mercer, C. D., & Pullen, P. C. (2009). *Students with learning disabilities* (7th ed.). Upper Saddle River, NJ: Pearson.

Merickel, A., Linquanti, R., Parrish, T. B., Pérez, M., Eaton, M., & Esra, P. (2003). *Effects of the implementation of Proposition 227 on the education of English language learners, K–12: Year 3 report.* San Francisco, CA: WestEd.

Mertler, C. (2014). *The data-driven classroom: How do I use data to improve my instruction?* Alexandria, VA: ASCD.

Meyer, A., & Rose, D. H. (2000). Universal design for individual differences. *Educational Leadership, 58*(3), 39–43.

Meyer, E., & Van Klaveren, C. (2013). The effectiveness of extended day programs: Evidence from a randomized field experiment in the Netherlands. *Economics of Education Review, 36,* 1–11.

Mickelson, R. (2015). The cumulative disadvantages of first- and second-generation segregation for middle school achievement. *American Educational Research Journal, 52*(4), 657–692.

Mickelson, R. A. (2002). Race and education. In D. L. Levinson, P. W. Cookson, Jr., & A. R. Sadovnik (Eds.), *Education and sociology: An encyclopedia* (pp. 485–494). New York, NY: Routledge.

Midkiff, B., & Cohen-Vogel, L. (2015). Understanding local instructional responses to federal and state accountability mandates: A typology of extended learning time. *Peabody Journal of Education, 90*(1), 9–26.

Miller, D. (2013). Got it wrong? Think again. And again. *Phi Delta Kappan, 94*(5), 50–52.

Miller, D., Partelow, L., & Sen, A. (2004, April). *Self-regulatory reading processes in relation to fourth-graders' reading literacy.* Paper presented at the annual meeting of the American Educational Research Association, San Diego, CA.

Miller, M. D., Linn, R. L., & Gronlund, N. E. (2013). *Measurement and assessment in teaching* (11th ed.). Upper Saddle River, NJ: Pearson.

Miller, P. H. (2011). Piaget's theory. In U. Goswami (Ed.), *The Wiley-Blackwell handbook of childhood cognitive development* (2nd ed.). Oxford, England: Wiley-Blackwell.

Miller, S., Connolly, P., & Macguire, L. (2013). Well-being, academic buoyancy, and educational achievement in primary school students. *International Journal of Educational Research, 62,* 239–248.

Miller, T. R. (2015). Project outcomes of nurse-family partnership home visitation during 1996–2013, USA. *Prevention Science, 16*(6), 765–777.

Miltenberger, R. G. (2012). *Behavior modification: Principles and procedures* (5th ed.). Belmont, CA: Wadsworth.

Mirsky, L. (2011). Building safer, saner schools. *Educational Leadership, 69*(1), 45–49.

Mitchell, K. J., & Johnson, M. K. (2009). Source monitoring 15 years later: What have we learned from fMRI about the neural mechanisms of source memory? *Psychological Bulletin, 135*(4), 638–677.

Moore, W. (2010). *The other Wes Moore: One name, two fates.* New York, NY: Spiegel & Grau.

Moors, A., & De Houwer, J. (2006). Automaticity: A theoretical and conceptual analysis. *Psychological Bulletin, 132*(2), 297–326.

Mora, J. (2009). From the ballot box to the classroom. *Educational Leadership, 66*(7), 14–19.

Moran, C., & Young, C. (2015). Questions to consider before flipping. *Phi Delta Kappan, 97*(2), 42–46.

Moran, S., Kornhaber, M., & Gardner, H. (2006). Orchestrating multiple intelligences. *Educational Leadership, 64*(1), 22–29.

Morris, D., Tyner, B., & Perney, J. (2000). Early steps: Replicating the effects of a first-grade reading intervention program. *Journal of Educational Psychology, 92,* 681–693.

Morrow, L. M. (2009). *Literacy development in the early years: Helping children read and write* (6th ed.). Boston, MA: Pearson.

Morrow, L. M., Roskos, K. A., & Gambrell, L. B. (2015). *Oral language and comprehension in preschool.* New York, NY: Guilford Press.

Morrow-Howell, N., et al. 2009. *Evaluation of Experience Corps: Student reading outcomes.* St. Louis, MO: Washington University in St. Louis.

Mosenthal, J., Lipson, M., Torncello, S., Russ, B., & Mekkelsen, J. (2004). Contexts and practices of six schools successful in obtaining reading achievement. *The Elementary School Journal, 104*(5), 343–368.

Moser, S., West, S., & Hughes, H. (2012). Trajectories of math and reading achievement in low-achieving children in elementary school: Effects of early and later retention in grade. *Journal of Educational Psychology, 104*(3), 603–621.

Moss, C., & Brookhart, S. (2012). *Learning targets: Helping students aim for understanding in today's lesson.* Alexandria, VA: ASCD.

Moss, C., Brookhart, S., & Long, B. (2011). Knowing your learning target. *Educational Leadership, 68*(6), 66–69.

Munakata, Y. (2006). Information processing approaches to development. In W. Damon & R. Lerner (Series Eds.) & D. Kuhn & R. S. Siegler (Vol. Eds.), *Handbook of child psychology: Vol 2: Cognition, perception, and language* (6th ed., pp. 426–463). New York, NY: Wiley.

Muñoz, M. A., Dossett, D., & Judy-Gullans, K. (2004). Educating students placed at risk: Evaluating the impact of Success for All in urban settings. *Journal of Education for Students Placed at Risk, 9*(3), 261–277.

Munoz, M., Chang, F., & Ross, S. (2012). No Child Left Behind and tutoring in reading and mathematics: Impact of supplemental educational services on large-scale assessment. *Journal of Education for Students Placed at Risk, 17*(3), 186–200.

Murawski, W., Lockwood, J., Khalili, A., & Johnston, A. (2010). A bully-free school. *Educational Leadership, 67*(4), 75–78.

Murayama, K., & Elliot, A. (2009). The joint influence of personal achievement goals and classroom goal structures on achievement-relevant outcomes. *Journal of Educational Psychology, 101*(2), 432–447.

Murdock, T. B., & Anderman, E. (2006). Motivational perspectives on student cheating: Toward an integrated model of academic dishonesty. *Educational Psychologist, 41*(3), 129–145.

Murdock, T. B., Hale, N. M., & Weber, M. J. (2001). Predictors of cheating among early adolescents: Academic and social motivations. *Contemporary Educational Psychology, 26*(1), 96–115.

Murphey, D. (2014). *The academic achievement of English language learners.* Bethesda, MD: ChildTrends.

Murphey, D., & Redd, Z. (2014). *Five ways poverty harms children.* Bethesda, MD: ChildTrends.

Murphy, J. (2011). Homeless children and youth at risk: The educational impact of displacement. *Journal of Education for Students Placed at Risk, 16*(1), 38–55.

Murphy, S., & Smith, M. A. (2015). *Uncommonly good ideas: Teaching writing in the Common Core era.* New York, NY: Teachers College Press.

Murphy, S., & Underwood, T. (2000). *Portfolio practices: Lessons from schools, districts, and states.* Norwood, MA: Christopher-Gordon.

Nansel T. R., Overpeck M., Pilla R. S., Ruan W., Simons-Morton B., & Scheidt P. (2001). Bullying behaviors among U. S. youth: Prevalence and association with psychosocial adjustment. *JAMA.* 285 (16):2094-2100. doi:10.1001/jama.285.16.2094.

Nasir, N., & Hand, V. (2006). Exploring sociocultural perspectives on race, culture, and learning. *Review of Educational Research, 76*(4), 449–476.

National Association of State Boards of Education (1992). *Winners All: A call for inclusive schools.* Alexandria, VA: Author.

National Center for Education Statistics (NCES). (2013). *The condition of education.* Washington, DC: Author.

National Center for Education Statistics (NCES). (2015). *National assessment of educational progress.* Washington, DC: Author.

National Center for Education Statistics (NCES). (2004). *Language minorities and their educational and labor market indicators—recent trends.* Washington, DC: U.S. Department of Education.

National Center for Education Statistics (NCES). (2011). *National assessment of educational progress.* Washington, DC: U.S. Department of Education.

National Center on Universal Design for Learning. (2011). *UDL principles and practice.* Wakefield, MA: Author. Available at www.udlcenter.org

National Information Center for Children and Youth with Disabilities. (1998). *Office of Special Education Programs' IDEA amendments of 1997 curriculum.* Retrieved from www.nichcy.org/Trainpkg/trainpkg.htm

National Institute for Literacy. (2008). *Developing early literacy.* Jessup, MD: Author.

National Institute of Allergy and Infectious Diseases. (2002). *HIV infection in adolescents: Fact sheet.* Rockville, MD: National Institutes of Health.

National Institute on Drug Abuse. (2005). *Marijuana abuse.* Bethesda, MD: Author.

National Joint Committee on Learning Disabilities. (1988). (Letter to NJCLD member organization). Washington, DC: Author.

National Reading Panel. (2000). *Teaching children to read: An evidence-based assessment of the scientific research literature on reading and its implications for reading instruction.* Rockville, MD: National Institute of Child Health and Human Development.

National Research Council. (2000). *Improving intergroup relations among youth.* Washington, DC: Author.

National Research Council. (2001). *Educating children with autism.* Washington, DC: National Academies Press.

Natriello, G. (2002). At-risk students. In D. L. Levinson, P. W. Cookson, Jr., & A. R. Sadovnik (Eds.), *Education and sociology: An encyclopedia* (pp. 49–54). New York, NY: Routledge.

Neill, M. (2003). Leaving children behind: How No Child Left Behind will fail our children. *Phi Delta Kappan, 85*(3), 225–228.

Neill, M., & Gaylor, K. (2001). Do high-stakes graduation tests improve learning outcomes? Using state-level NAEP data to evaluate the effects of mandatory graduation tests. In G. Orfield & M. L. Kornhaber (Eds.), *Raising standards or raising barriers? Inequality and high-stakes testing in public education* (pp. 107–126). New York, NY: Century Foundation Press.

Neisser, U., Boodoo, G., Bouchard, T. J., Boykin, A. W., Brody, N., Ceci, S. J., … Urbina, S. (1996). Intelligence: Knowns and unknowns. *American Psychologist, 51,* 77–101.

Nesbit, J., & Adesope, O. (2006). Learning with concept and knowledge maps: A meta-analysis. *Review of Educational Research, 76*(3), 413–448.

Neufield, B., & Roper, D. (2003). *Coaching: A strategy for developing instructional capacity.* Providence, RI: Annenberg Institute.

Neuman, S. (2007). Changing the odds. *Educational Leadership, 65*(2), 16–21.

Neuman, S. (2008). *Educating the other America: Top experts tackle poverty, literacy, and achievement in our schools.* Baltimore, MD: Brookes.

Neuman, S. (2010). Empowered—after school. *Educational Leadership, 67*(7), 30–36.

Neuman, S. (2014). Content-rich instruction in preschool. *Educational Leadership, 72*(2), 36–41.

Nevin, A. (1998). Curriculum and instructional adaptations for including students with disabilities in cooperative groups. In J. W. Putnam (Ed.), *Cooperative learning and strategies for inclusion* (pp. 49–66). Baltimore, MD: Brookes.

Ng, J., Lee, S., & Park, Y. (2007). Contesting the model minority and perpetual foreigner stereotypes: A critical review of literature on Asian Americans in education. *Review of Research in Education, 31,* 95–130.

Niaz, M. (1997). How early can children understand some form of "scientific reasoning"? *Perceptual and motor skills, 85,* 1272–1274.

Nicoll, D., Lu, C., Pignone, M., & McPhee, S. (2012). *Pocket guide to diagnostic tests* (6th ed.). New York, NY: McGraw-Hill.

Nieto, S. (2009). From surviving to thriving. *Educational Leadership, 66*(5), 8–13.

Nieto, S., & Bode, P. (2008). *Affirming diversity: The sociopolitical context of multicultural education* (5th ed.). Boston, MA: Pearson.

Niguidula, D. (2005). Documenting learning with digital portfolios. *Educational Leadership, 63*(3), 44–47.

Nitsch, K. E. (1977). *Structuring decontextualized forms of knowledge.* Unpublished doctoral dissertation, Vanderbilt University.

Noddings, N. (2008). All our students thinking. *Educational Leadership, 65*(5), 8–13.

Noguera, P. (2012). Saving black and Latino boys. *Phi Delta Kappan, 93*(5), 8–11.

Nolan, J., Preston, M., & Finkelstein, J. (2012). Can you DIG/IT? *Phi Delta Kappan, 94*(2), 42–46.

Nomi, T., & Allensworth, E. (2013). Sorting and supporting: Why double-dose algebra led to better test scores but more course failures. *American Educational Research Journal, 50*(4), 756–788.

Nomi, T., (2010). The effects of within-class ability grouping on academic achievement in early elementary years. *Journal of Research on Educational Effectiveness, 3*(1),56–92.

Noonan, M. J., & McCormick, L. (1993). *Early intervention in natural environments.* Pacific Grove, CA: Brooks/Cole.

Novak, S. (2014). *Student-led discussions: How do I promote rich conversations about books, videos, and other media?* Alexandria, VA: ASCD.

Nucci, L. P. (2009). *Nice is not enough: Facilitating moral development.* Columbus, OH: Merrill Pearson.

Nussbaum, E. (2008). Collaborative discourse, argumentation, and learning: Preface and literature review. *Contemporary Educational Psychology, 33*(3), 345–359.

Nzinga-Johnson, S., Baker, J., & Aupperlee, J. (2009). Teacher–parent relationships and school involvement among racially and educationally diverse parents of kindergartners. *The Elementary School Journal, 110*(1), 81–91.

O'Connor, C., & Fernandez, S. D. (2006). Race, class, and disproportionality: Reevaluating the relationship between poverty and special education placement. *Educational Researcher, 35*(6), 6–11.

O'Connor, C., Hill, L., & Robinson, S. (2009). Who's at risk in school and what's race got to do with it? *Review of Research in Education, 33,* 1–34.

O'Connor, K. (2009). *How to grade for learning, K–12* (3rd ed.). Thousand Oaks, CA: Corwin.

O'Connor, K., & Wormeli, R. (2011). Reporting student learning. *Educational Leadership, 69*(3), 40–44.

O'Donnell, A. M. (2006). The role of peers and group learning. In P. A. Alexander & P. H. Winne (Eds.), *Handbook of Educational Psychology* (2nd ed., pp. 781–802). Mahway, NJ: Erlbaum.

O'Donnell, A. M., Dansereau, D. F., & Hall, R. H. (2002). Knowledge maps as scaffolds for cognitive processing. *Educational Psychology Review, 14*(1), 71–86.

O'Donnell, J., Hawkins, J. D., Catalano, R. F., Abbott, R. D., & Day, L. E. (1995). Preventing school failure, drug use, and delinquency among low-income children: Long-term intervention in elementary schools. *American Journal of Orthopsychiatry, 65*(1), 87–100.

O'Leary, K. D., & O'Leary, S. G. (1972). *Classroom management: The successful use of behavior modification.* New York, NY: Pergamon.

Oakes, J. (2005). *Keeping track: How schools structure inequality* (2nd ed.). New Haven, CT: Yale University.

Oakes, J., & Lipton, M. (2006). *Teaching to change the world* (3rd ed.). New York, NY: McGraw-Hill.

Oakes, J., Quartz, K., Ryan, S., & Lipton, M. (2000). *Becoming good American schools: The struggle for civic virtue in school reform.* San Francisco, CA: Jossey-Bass.

Odden, A. (2009). *IO strategies for doubling student performance.* Thousand Oaks, CA: Sage.

Odden, A., & Archibald, S. J. (2009). *Doubling student performance and finding the resources to do it.* Thousand Oaks, CA: Corwin.

Ogbu, J. (2004). Collective identity and the burden of "acting white" in black history, community, and education. *The Urban Review, 36*(1), 1–35.

Ohler, J. (2006). The world of digital storytelling. *Educational Leadership, 63*(4), 44–47.

Ohler, J. (2013). The uncommon core. *Educational Leadership, 70*(5), 42–46.

Olds, D. L., et al. (2007). Effect of nurse home visiting on maternal and child functioning: Age nine follow-up of a randomized trial. *Pediatrics, 120,* 832–845.

Oliver, R. (2012). Classroom management: What teachers should know. *Better: Evidence-based Education, 5*(1), 8–9.

Olson, A. (2005). Improving schools one student at a time. *Educational Leadership, 62*(5), 37–41.

Olson, J., & Mokhtari, K. (2010). Making science real. *Educational Leadership, 67*(6), 56–62.

Olszewski-Kubilius, P., & Thomson, D. (2013). Gifted education programs and procedures. In W. Reynolds, G. Miller, & I. Weiner (Eds.) *Handbook of psychology* (Vol. 7, 2nd ed., pp. 389–410). Hoboken, NJ: Wiley.

Online Safety and Technology Working Group. (2010). *Youth safety on a living Internet.* Retrieved from http://www.ntia.doc.gov/legacy/reports/2010/OSTWG_Final_Report_070610.pdf

Oosterhof, A. (2009). *Developing and using classroom assessments* (4th ed.). Upper Saddle River, NJ: Pearson.

Orfield, G. (2014). Tenth annual Brown Lecture in education research: A new civil rights agenda for American education. *Educational Researcher, 43*(6), 273–292.

Orfield, G., & Frankenberg, E. (2007). The integration decision. *Education Week, 26*(43), 34, 44.

Orfield, G., & Kornhaber, M. L. (Eds.). (2001). *Raising standards or raising barriers? Inequality and high-stakes testing in public education.* New York, NY: Century Foundation Press.

Orfield, G., Frankenberg, E., & Siegel-Hawley, G. (2010). Integrated schools finding a new path. *Educational Leadership, 68*(3), 22–27.

Ormrod, J. (2016). *Human learning.* Boston, MA: Pearson.

Osher, D., Bear, G., Sprague, J., & Doyle, W. (2010). How can we improve school discipline? *Educational Researcher, 39*(1), 48–58.

Osher, D., Dwyer, K., & Jackson, S. (2004). *Safe, supportive and successful schools step by step.* Longmont, CO: Sopris West.

Ostroff, W. (2012). *Understanding how young children learn: Bringing the science of child development to the classroom.* Alexandria, VA: ASCD.

Overton, T. (2016). *Assessing learners with special needs: An applied approach.* (8th ed.). Boston, MA: Pearson.

Owens, R. (2016). *Language development: An introduction* (9th ed). Boston, MA: Pearson.

Packard, B., & Babineau, M. E. (2008). Development: 9–12. In T. L. Good (Ed.), *21st century learning* (Vol. 1, pp. 103–112). Thousand Oaks, CA: Sage.

Padrón, Y. N., Waxman, H. C., & Rivera, H. H. (2002). Issues in educating Hispanic students. In S. Stringfield & D. Land (Eds.), *Educating at-risk students* (pp. 66–88). Chicago, IL: National Society for the Study of Education.

Page, R. M., & Page, T. S. (2011). *Promoting health and emotional well-being in your classroom.* Columbus, OH: Jones & Bartlett Learning.

Page-Voth, V., & Graham, S. (1999). Effects of goal setting and strategy use on the writing performance and self-efficacy of students with writing and learning problems. *Journal of Educational Psychology, 91*(2), 230–240.

Pahomov, L. (2014). *Authentic learning in the digital age: Engaging students through inquiry.* Alexandria, VA: ASCD.

Pajares, F., Britner, S. L., & Valiante, G. (2000). Relation between achievement goals and self-beliefs of middle school students in writing and science. *Contemporary Educational Psychology, 25*(4), 406–422.

Palincsar, A. S., & Herrenkohl, L. (2002). Designing collaborative learning environments. *Theory into Practice, 41*(1), 26–32.

Palm, M. (2013). First, do no harm. *Phi Delta Kappan, 94*(4), 13–15.

Palmer, E. (2015). *Researching in a digital world: How do I teach my students to conduct quality online research?* Alexandria, VA: ASCD.

Pang, V., Han, P., & Pang, J. (2011). Asian American and Pacific Islander students: Equity and the achievement gap. *Educational Researcher, 40*(8), 378–389.

Parillo, V. N. (2008). *Understanding race and ethnic relations* (3rd ed.). Boston, MA: Allyn & Bacon.

Paris, S., Cross, D., & Lipson, M. (1984). Informal strategies for learning: A program to improve children's reading awareness and comprehension. *Journal of Educational Psychology, 76,* 1239–1252.

Parkay, F. W. (2006). *Social foundations for becoming a teacher.* Boston, MA: Allyn & Bacon.

Parke, R. D., & Clarke-Stewart, C. (2011). *Social development.* Hoboken, NJ: Wiley.

Parrett, W., & Budge, K. (2012). *Turning high-poverty schools into high-performing schools.* Alexandria, VA: ASCD.

Parsons, S., Dodman, S., & Burrowbridge, S. (2013). Broadening the view of differentiated instruction. *Phi Delta Kappan, 95*(1), 38–42.

Parten, M. (1932). Social participation among preschool children. *Journal of Abnormal and Social Psychology, 27,* 243–269.

Partnership for 21st Century Skills. (2009). *Framework for 21st century learning.* Retrieved from www.21stcenturyskills.org

Pasquinelli, E. (2012). Neuromyths: Why do they exist and persist? *Mind Brain Education, 6,* 89–96.

Patall, E. A., Cooper, H., & Allen, A. B. (2010). Extending the school day or school year: A systematic review of research (1985–2009). *Review of Educational Research, 80*(3), 401–436.

Patall, E., Cooper, H., & Robinson, J. (2008). Parent involvement in homework: A research synthesis. *Review of Educational Research, 78*(4), 1039–1101.

Patrick, B., Hisley, J., & Kempler, T. (2000). "What's everybody so excited about?": The effects of teacher enthusiasm on student intrinsic motivation and vitality. *Journal of Experimental Education, 68,* 217–236.

Patterson, G. (2012). An interview with Michael Horn: Blending education for high-octane motivation. *Phi Delta Kappan, 94*(2), 14–18.

Pattison, E., Grodsky, E., & Muller, C. (2013). Is the sky falling? Grade inflation and the signaling power of grades. *Educational Researcher, 42*(5), 259–265.

Paul, P. V., & Whitelaw, G. M. (2011). *Hearing and deafness.* Columbus, OH: Jones & Bartlett Learning.

Pearson, P. D., & Hiebert, E. H. (Eds.) (2015). *Research-based practices for teaching Common Core literacy.* New York, NY: Teachers College Press.

Pellegrini, A. D. (2002). Bullying, victimization, and sexual harassment during the transition to middle school. *Educational Psychologist, 37*(3), 151–163.

Pellegrini, A. D., & Bartini, M. (2000). A longitudinal study of bullying, victimization, and peer affiliation during the transition from primary school to middle school. *American Educational Research Journal, 37*(3), 699–725.

Penfield, R. (2010). Test-based grade retention: Does it stand up to professional standards for fair and appropriate test use? *Educational Researcher, 39*(2), 110–119.

Penuel, W., & Shepard, L. (2016). Assessment and teaching. In D. Gitomer & C. Bell (Eds.), *Handbook of research on teaching* (5th ed.). (pp. 851–916). Washington, DC: AERA.

Perfetti, C. A. (2003). The universal grammar of reading. *Scientific Studies of Reading, 7*(1), 3–24.

Perfetto, G. A., Bransford, J. D., & Franks, J. J. (1983). Constraints on access in a problem solving context. *Memory and Cognition, 11,* 24–31.

Perkins, D. F., & Borden, L. M. (2003). Positive behaviors, problem behaviors, and resiliency in adolescence. In R. M. Lerner, M. A. Easterbrooks, & J. Mistry (Eds.), *Handbook of psychology: Vol. 6. Developmental psychology* (pp. 373–394). Hoboken, NJ: Wiley.

Perkins, D., & Salomon, G. (2012). Knowledge to go: A motivational and dispositional view of transfer. *Educational Psychologist, 47*(3), 248–258.

Perks, K., & Middleton, M. (2014). Navigating the classroom current. *Educational Leadership, 72*(1), 48–52.

Peterson, L. R., & Peterson, M. J. (1959). Short-term retention of individual verbal items. *Journal of Experimental Psychology, 58,* 193–198.

Petrill, S. A., & Wilkerson, B. (2000). Intelligence and achievement: A behavioral genetic perspective. *Educational Psychology Review, 12*(2), 185–199.

Peverly, S., Ramaswamy, V., Brown, C., Sumouski, J., Alidoust, M., & Garner, J. (2007). What predicts skill in lecture note taking? *Journal of Educational Psychology, 99*(1), 167–180.

Pew Research Center. (2015). *Teen relationships survey.* Washington, DC: Author.

Pew Research Center. (2015). *Modern immigration wave brings 59 million to U.S., driving population growth and change through 2065: Views of immigration's impact on U.S. society mixed.* Washington, D.C.: September.

Phillips, V., & Popovic, Z. (2012). More than child's play: Games have potential learning and assessment tools. *Phi Delta Kappan, 94*(2), 26–30.

Phillips, V., & Wong, C. (2012). Teaching to the Common Core by design, not accident. *Phi Delta Kappan, 93*(7), 31–37.

Piaget, J. (1952a). *The language and thought of the child.* London, England: Routledge and Kegan-Paul.

Piaget, J. (1964). *The moral judgment of the child.* New York, NY: Free Press.

Pianta, R. C., Barnett, W. S., Justice, L. M., & Sheridan, S. M. (Eds.). (2015). *Handbook of early childhood education.* New York, NY: Guilford Press.

Pietsch, J., Walker, R., & Chapman, E. (2003). The relationship among self-concept, self-efficacy, and performance in mathematics during secondary school. *Journal of Educational Psychology, 95*(3), 589–603.

Pine, J., & Aschbacher, P. (2006). Students' learning of inquiry in "inquiry" curricula. *Phi Delta Kappan, 88*(4), 308–313.

Pink, D. (2009). *Drive: The surprising truth to what motivates us.* New York, NY: Riverhead.

Pinnell, G. S., Lyons, C. A., DeFord, D. E., Bryk, A. S., & Seltzer, M. (1994). Comparing instructional models for the literacy education of high risk first graders. *Reading Research Quarterly, 29,* 8–38.

Pinquart, M., & Teubert, D. (2010). Effects of parenting education with expectant and new parents: A meta-analysis. *Journal of Family Psychology, 24*(3), 316–327.

Pintrich, P. R. (2003). A motivational science perspective on the role of student motivation in learning and teaching contexts. *Journal of Educational Psychology, 95*(4), 667–686.

Pintrich, P. R., & Schunk, D. H. (2002). *Motivation in education: Theory, research, and applications* (2nd ed.). Upper Saddle River, NJ: Merrill/Prentice-Hall.

Pitler, H., Hubbell, E., & Kuhn, M. (2012). *Using technology with classroom instruction that works.* Alexandria, VA: ASCD.

Pittard, V., Bannister, P., & Dunn, J. (2003). *The big picture: The impact of ICT on attainment, motivation, and learning.* London, England: Department for Education and Skills.

Plucker, J. A., Beghetto, R. A., & Dow, G. T. (2004). Why isn't creativity more important to educational psychologists? Potential, pitfalls, and future directions in creativity research. *Educational Psychologist, 39*(2), 83–96.

Plucker, J., & Callahan, C. M. (Eds.). (2014). *Critical issues and practices in gifted education: What the research says.* (2nd ed.). Waco, TX: Prufrock Press.

Plucker, J., & Esping, A. (2014). *Intelligence 101.* New York, NY: Springer.

Poel, E. (2007). Enhancing what students can do. *Educational Leadership, 64*(5), 64–67.

Pohl, A., & Storm, K. (2014). Promoting engagement with Check & Connect. In R. E. Slavin (Ed.), *Classroom management and assessment* (pp. 85–89). Thousand Oaks, CA: Corwin.

Polite, L., & Saenger, E. B. (2003). A pernicious silence: Confronting race in the elementary classroom. *Phi Delta Kappan, 85*(4), 274–278.

Pollock, J., Ford, S., & Black, M. (2012). *Minding the achievement gap one classroom at a time.* Alexandria, VA: ASCD.

Pomerantz, E. M., Altermatt, E. R., & Saxon, J. L. (2002). Making the grade but feeling distressed: Gender differences in academic performance and internal distress. *Journal of Educational Psychology, 94*(2), 396–404.

Pomerantz, E., Moorman, E., & Litwack, S. (2007). The how, whom, and why of parents' involvement in children's academic lives: More is not always better. *Review of Educational Research, 77*(3), 373–410.

Poole, I., & Evertson, C. (2012). Am I the only one struggling with classroom management? *Better: Evidence-based education, 5*(1), 6–7.

Popham, W. J. (2014a). *Classroom assessment: What teachers need to know* (7th ed.). Upper Saddle River, NJ: Pearson.

Popham, J. (2014b). Criterion-referenced measurement: Half a century wasted? *Educational Leadership, 71*(6), 62–67.

Popham, W. J. (2004). "Teaching to the test": An expression to eliminate. *Educational Leadership, 62*(3), 82–83.

Porowski, A., & Passa, A. (2011). The effect of communities in schools on high school dropout and graduation rates: Results from a multiyear, school-level quasi-experimental study. *Journal of Education for Students Placed at Risk, 16*(1), 24–37.

Porter, A., McMaken, J., Hwang, J., & Yang, R. (2011). Assessing the common core standards: Opportunities for improving measures of instruction. *Educational Researcher, 40*(4), 186–188.

Powell, W., & Kusuma-Powell, O. (2011). *How to teach now: Five keys to personalized learning in the global classroom.* Alexandria, VA: ASCD.

Preckel, F., Baudson, T., Krolak-Schwerdt, S., & Glock, S. (2015). Gifted and maladjusted? Implicit attitudes and automatic associations related to gifted children. *American Educational Research Journal, 52*(6), 1160–1184.

Premack, D. (1965). Reinforcement theory. In D. Levine (Ed.), *Nebraska symposium on motivation.* Lincoln, NE: University of Nebraska Press.

Pressley, M., Harris, K. R., & Marks, M. B. (1992). But good strategy instructors are constructivists! *Educational Psychology Review, 4,* 3–31.

Pressley, M., Raphael, L., & Gallagher, J. (2004). Providence St. Mel School: How a school that works for African American students works. *Journal of Educational Psychology, 96*(2), 216–235.

Pressley, M., Roehrig, A. D., Raphael, L., Dolezal, S., Bohn, C., Mohan, L., … Hogan, K. (2003). Teaching processes in elementary and secondary education. In W. M. Reynolds & G. E. Miller (Eds.), *Handbook of psychology: Vol. 7. Educational psychology* (pp. 153–175). Hoboken, NJ: Wiley.

Pressley, M., Tannenbaum, R., McDaniel, M. A., & Wood, E. (1990). What happens when university students try to answer prequestions that accompany textbook material? *Contemporary Educational Psychology, 15,* 27–35.

Price, H. (2008). Mobilizing the community to help students succeed. Alexandria, VA: ASCD.

Prichard, J., Bizo, L., & Stratford, R. (2006). The educational impact of team skills training: Preparing students to work in groups. *British Journal of Educational Psychology, 76,* 119–148.

Pugh, K., & Bergin, D. (2006). Motivational influences on transfer. *Educational Psychologist, 41*(3), 147–160.

Puma, M. J., Jones, C. C., Rock, D., & Fernandez, R. (1993). *Prospects: The congressionally mandated study of educational growth and opportunity* (Interim Report). Bethesda, MD: Abt Associates.

Purves, D. (2010). *Brains: How they seem to work.* Upper Saddle River, NJ: Pearson.

Quinn, T. (2012). A crash course on giving grades. *Phi Delta Kappan, 93*(6), 57–59.

Quint, J. C., Zhu, P., Balu, R., Rappaport, S., & DeLaurentis, M. (2015). *Scaling up the Success for All model of school reform.* New York, NY: MDRC.

Quiroga, C., Janosz, M., Bisset, S., & Morin, A. (2013). Early adolescent depression symptoms and school dropout: Mediating processes involving self-reported academic competence and achievement. *Journal of Educational Psychology, 105*(2), 552–560.

Rakow, S. (2012). Helping gifted learners soar. *Educational Leadership, 69*(5), 34–39.

Ramey, C. T., & Ramey, S. L. (1992). *At risk does not mean doomed.* Birmingham, AL: Civitan International Research Center, University of Alabama.

Ramey, C. T., & Ramey, S. L. (1998). Early intervention and early experience. *American Psychologist, 53*(2), 109–120.

Ramirez, A., & Soto-Hinman, I. (2009). A place for all families. *Educational Leadership, 66*(7), 79–82.

Rappaport, N., & Minahan, H. (2012a). *The behavior code: A practical guide to understanding and teaching the most challenging students.* Cambridge, MA: Harvard Education Press.

Rappaport, N., & Minahan, J. (2012b). Cracking the behavior code. *Educational Leadership, 70*(2), 18–25.

Rasinski, T., & Zutell, J. (2010). *Essential strategies for word study.* New York, NY: Scholastic.

Raudenbush, S. W., Rowan, B., & Cheong, Y. F. (1993). Higher order instructional goals in secondary schools: Class, teacher, and school influences. *American Educational Research Journal, 30*(3), 523–553.

Redd, Z., Boccanfuso, C., Walker, K., Princiotta, D., Knewstub, D., & Moore, K. (2012). *Expanding time for learning both inside and outside the classroom: A review of the evidence base.* Bethesda, MD: ChildTrends.

Reed, S. (2006). Cognitive architectures for multimedia learning. *Educational Psychologist, 41*(2), 87–98.

Reeves, A. (2011). *Where great teaching begins: Planning for student thinking and learning.* Alexandria, VA: ASCD.

Reeves, D. (2006). Preventing 1,000 failures. *Educational Leadership, 64*(3), 88–89.

Reeves, D. (2009). Three challenges of Web 2.0. *Educational Leadership, 66*(6), 87–88.

Reeves, D. (2015). *Elements of grading.* Bloomington, IN: Solution Tree.

Reich, J., Murnane, R., & Willett, J. (2012). The state of wiki usage in U. S. K–12 schools: Leveraging Web 2.0 data warehouses to assess quality and equity in online learning environments. *Educational Researcher, 41*(1), 7–15.

Reichow, B., Barton, E. E., Boyd, B. A., & Hume, K. (2014). Early intensive behavioral intervention (EIBI) for young children with autism spectrum disorders (ASD): A systematic review. *Campbell Systematic Reviews 2014*:9. doi:10.4073/csr.2014.9

Reid, D., & Knight, M. (2006). Disability justifies exclusion of minority students: A critical history grounded in disability studies. *Educational Researcher, 35*(6), 18–23.

Reid, R., & Lienemann, T. O. (2006). Self-regulated strategy development for written expression with students with attention deficit hyperactivity disorder. *Exceptional Children, 73,* 53–68.

Rekrut, M. D. (1992, April). *Teaching to learn: Cross-age tutoring to enhance strategy acquisition.* Paper presented at the annual meeting of the American Educational Research Association, San Francisco, CA.

Relijic, G., Ferring, D., & Martin, R. (2014). A meta-analysis on the effectiveness of bilingual programs in Europe. *Review of Educational Research.* Retrieved from rer.sagepub.com/content/early/2014/09/05/0034654314548514.abstract

Renkl, A. (2011). Instruction based on examples. In R. Mayer & P. Alexander (Eds.), *Handbook of research on learning and instruction* (pp. 272–295). New York, NY: Routledge.

Renninger, K., & Hidi, S. (2011). Revisiting the conceptualization, measurement, and generation of interest. *Educational Psychologist, 46*(3), 168–184.

Renzetti, C. M., Curran, D. J., & Maier, S. L. (2012). *Women, men, and society.* Boston, MA: Pearson.

Renzulli, J. S., & Reis, S. M. (2000). The schoolwide enrichment model. In K. A. Heller, F. J. Mönks, R. Subotnik, & R. J. Sternberg (Eds.), *International handbook of giftedness and talent* (2nd ed., pp. 367–382). New York, NY: Pergamon.

Reschly, D. J. (2003). School psychology. In W. M. Reynolds & G. E. Miller (Eds.), *Handbook of psychology: Vol. 7. Educational psychology* (pp. 431–453). Hoboken, NJ: Wiley.

Reynolds, A. (2009). Why every student needs critical friends. *Educational Leadership, 67*(3), 54–57.

Reynolds, A., & Wolfe, B. (1999). Special education and school achievement: An exploratory analysis with a central-city sample. *Educational Evaluation and Policy Analysis, 21*(3), 249–269.

Reynolds, A., Magnuson, K., & Ou, S. (2010). Preschool-to-third grade programs and practices: A review of research. *Children and Youth Services Review, 32,* 1121–1131.

Reynolds, A., Temple, J., Robertson, D., & Mann, E. (2002). Age 21 cost-benefit analysis of the Title I Chicago child–parent centers. *Educational Evaluation and Policy Analysis, 24*(4), 267–303.

Reynolds, C., & Livingston, R. (2012). *Mastering modern psychological testing: Theory and methods.* Upper Saddle River, NJ: Pearson.

Rice, F. P., & Dolgin, K. G. (Eds.). (2008). *The adolescent: Development, relationships, and culture* (12th ed.). Boston, MA: Pearson Education Group.

Richardson, W. (2009). Becoming network-wise. *Educational Leadership, 66*(6), 26–31.

Richardson, W. (2012). Preparing students to learn without us. *Educational Leadership, 69*(5), 22–26.

Richardson, W. (2013). Students first, not stuff. *Educational Leadership, 70*(6), 10–14.

Rideout, V. (2014). *Learning at home: Families' educational media use in America.* New York, NY: The Joan Ganz Cooney Center.

Rideout, V., & Katz, V. (2016). *Opportunity for all? Technology and learning in lower-income families.* New York, NY: The Joan Ganz Cooney Center at Sesame Workshop.

Ridnouer, K. (2011). *Everyday engagement: Making students and parents your partners in learning.* Alexandria, VA: ASCD.

Riehl, C. (2006). Feeling better: A comparison of medical research and education research. *Educational Researcher, 35*(5), 24–29.

Riehl, C. J. (2000). The principal's role in creating inclusive schools for diverse students: A review of normative, empirical, and critical literature on the practice of educational administration. *Review of Educational Research, 70*(1), 55–81.

Rifkin, J. (1998). The sociology of the gene. *Phi Delta Kappan, 79*(9), 649–657.

Rijlaarsdam, G., Van den Bergh, H., Couzijn, M., Janssen, T., Braaksma, M., Tillema, M., Van Steendam, E., & Raedts, M. (2010). Writing. In S. Graham, A. Bus, S. Major, & L. Swanson (Eds.). *Application of educational psychology to learning and teaching.* APA Handbook. Vol. 3 (pp. 189–228). Washington, DC: American Psychological Association.

Rimm-Kaufman, S. (2010). The responsive classroom approach for improving interactions with children. *Better: Evidence-based Education, 2*(2) 10–11.

Ritchhart, R., & Perkins, D. (2008). Making thinking visible. *Educational Leadership, 65*(5), 57–63.

Rix, J., Sheehy, K., Fletcher-Campbell, F., Crisp, M., & Harper, A. (2015). Moving from a continuum to a community: Reconceptualizing the provision of support. *Review of Educational Research, 85*(3), 319–352.

Roach, A., & Elliott, S. (2006). The influence of access to general education curriculum on alternate assessment performance of students with significant cognitive disabilities. *Educational Evaluation and Policy Analysis, 28*(2), 181–194.

Robelen, E. (2012, March 28). More states retaining 3rd graders. *Education Week, 1,* 15.

Robelen, E., Adams, C., & Shah, N. (2012, March 7). Data show retention disparities, *Education Week, 1,* 18–19.

Robinson, D. H., Katayama, A. D., Beth, A., Odom, S., & Hsieh, Y. P. (2004). *Training students to take more graphic notes: A partial approach.* Austin, TX: University of Texas.

Robinson, D. H., Robinson, S. L., & Katayama, A. D. (1999). When words are represented in memory like pictures: Evidence for spatial encoding of study materials. *Contemporary Educational Psychology, 24*(1), 38–54.

Robinson, F. P. (1961). *Effective study.* New York, NY: Harper & Row.

Robinson, J. P., & Lubienski, S. T. (2011). The development of gender achievement gaps in mathematics and reading during elementary and middle school: Examining direct cognitive assessments and teacher ratings. *American Educational Research Journal, 48*(2), 268–302.

Robinson, J., & Espelage, D. (2011). Inequities in educational and psychological outcomes between LGBTQ and straight students in middle and high school. *Educational Researcher, 40*(7), 315–330.

Robinson, J., & Espelage, D. (2012). Bullying explains only part of LGBTQ–heterosexual risk disparities: Implications for policy and practice. *Educational Researcher, 41*(8), 309–319.

Robison, J. (2012). Call me different, not difficult. *Educational Leadership, 70*(2), 40–44.

Roblyer, M. (2016). *Integrating educational technology into teaching* (7th ed.). Boston, MA: Pearson.

Roblyer, M. D., & Doering, A. H. (2012). *Integrating educational technology into teaching* (6th ed.). Boston, MA: Allyn & Bacon.

Roderick, M., & Nagaoka, J. (2005). Retention under Chicago's high-stakes testing program: Helpful, harmful, or harmless? *Evaluation and Policy Analysis, 27*(4), 309–340.

Roderick, M., & Stoker, G. (2010). Bringing rigor to the study of rigor: Are advanced placement courses a useful approach to increasing college access and success for urban and minority youths? In J. Meece & J. Eccles (Eds.), *Handbook of research on schools, schooling, and human development* (pp. 216–234). New York, NY: Routledge.

Rodkin, P. (2011). Bullying—and the power of peers. *Educational Leadership, 69*(1), 10–17.

Roeser, R., Eccles, J., & Sameroff, A. (2000). School as a context of early adolescents' academic and social-emotional development: A summary of research findings. *The Elementary School Journal, 100*(5), 443–472.

Rogers, K. B. (2009, April). *Academic acceleration and giftedness: The research from 1990 to the present: A best-evidence synthesis.* Paper presented at the annual meeting of the American Educational Research Association, San Diego, CA.

Rogoff, B. (2003). *The cultural nature of human development.* London, England: Oxford University Press.

Rohrbeck, C. A., Ginsburg-Block, M. D., Fantuzzo, J. W., & Miller, T. R. (2003). Peer-assisted learning interventions with elementary school students: A meta-analytic review. *Journal of Educational Psychology, 94*(2), 240–257.

Rohrer, D., & Pashler, H. (2010). Recent research on human learning challenges conventional instructional strategies. *Educational Researcher, 39*(5), 406–412.

Rolfhus, E., Gersten, R., Clarke, B., Decker, L., Wilkins, C., and Dimino, J. (2012). *An evaluation of Number Rockets: A Tier-2 intervention for Grade 1 students at risk for difficulties in mathematics.* Washington, DC: NCES, USDOE.

Rolland, R. (2012). Synthesizing the evidence on classroom goal structures in middle and secondary schools: A meta-analysis and narrative review. *Review of Educational Research, 82*(4), 396–435.

Roscoe, R., & McNamara, D. (2013). Writing pal: Feasibility of an intelligent writing strategy tutor in the high school classroom. *Journal of Educational Psychology, 105,* 110–125.

Rose, A., & Rudolph, K. (2006). A review of sex differences in peer relationship processes: Potential tradeoffs for the emotional and behavioral development of girls and boys. *Psychological Bulletin, 132*(1), 98–131.

Rose, D. H., & Rappolt-Schlichtmann, G. (2008). Applying universal design for learning with children living in poverty. In S. B. Neumann (Ed.), *Educating the other America.* Baltimore, MD: Brookes.

Rose, M. (2010). Reform: To what end? *Educational Leadership, 67*(7), 6–11.

Rosen, L. (2011). Teaching the igeneration. *Educational Leadership, 68*(5), 10–15.

Rosenberg, M. S., Westling, D. L., & McLeskey, J. (2011). *Special education for today's teachers: An introduction.* Columbus, OH: Merrill.

Rosenfield, D., Folger, R., & Adelman, H. F. (1980). When rewards reflect competence: A qualification of the overjustification effect. *Journal of Personality and Social Psychology, 39,* 368–376.

Rosenshine, B. (2008). Systematic instruction. In T. L. Good (Ed.), *21st century learning* (Vol. 1, pp. 235–243). Thousand Oaks, CA: Sage.

Roseth, C., Johnson, D., & Johnson, R. (2008). Promoting early adolescents' achievement and peer relationships: The effects of cooperative, competitive, and individualistic goal structures. *Psychological Bulletin, 134*(2), 223–246.

Roseth, C., Saltarelli, A., & Glass, C. (2011). Effects of face-to-face and computer-mediated constructive controversy on social interdependence, motivation, and achievement. *Journal of Educational Psychology, 103*(4), 804–820.

Roskosky, J. (2010). Targeted tutoring. *Educational Leadership, 68*(2), 68.

Ross, S. M., Smith, L. J., Casey, J., & Slavin, R. E. (1995). Increasing the academic success of disadvantaged children: An examination of alternative early intervention programs. *American Educational Research Journal, 32,* 773–800.

Ross, S. M., Smith, L. J., Lohr, L., & McNelis, M. (1994). Math and reading instruction in tracked first grade classes. *The Elementary School Journal, 95*(2), 105–119.

Rotberg, I. C. (2001). A self-fulfilling prophecy. *Phi Delta Kappan, 83*(2), 170–171.

Roth, W.-M., & Lee, Y.-J. (2007). "Vygotsky's neglected legacy": Cultural-historical activity theory. *Review of Educational Research, 77*(2), 186–232.

Rotherham, A., & Willingham, D. (2009). 21st century skills: The challenges ahead. *Educational Leadership, 67*(1), 16–21.

Rothstein, R. (Ed.). (2004). *Class and schools: Using social, economic, and educational reform to close the black–white achievement gap.* Washington, DC: Economic Policy Institute.

Rothstein, R., & Jacobsen, R. (2009). Measuring social responsibility. *Educational Leadership, 66*(8), 14–19.

Rotter, J. (1954). *Social learning and clinical psychology.* Englewood Cliffs, NJ: Prentice-Hall.

Rowan, B. & Correnti, R. (2009). Studying reading instruction with teacher logs: Lessons from the Study of Instructional Improvement. *Educational Researcher, 38*(2), 120–131.

Rowan, B., Correnti, R., & Miller, R. (2002). *What large-scale, survey research tells us about teacher effects on student achievement: Insights from the Prospects study of elementary schools.* Philadelphia, PA: Consortium for Policy Research in Education, University of Pennsylvania.

Rowan, B., Correnti, R., Miller, R. J., & Camburn, E. M. (2009). *School improvement by design: Lessons from a study of comprehensive school reform programs.* Ann Arbor, MI: Consortium for Policy Research in Education.

Rowley, S., Kurtz-Costes, B., & Cooper, S. (2010). The schooling of African American children. In J. Meece & J. Eccles (Eds.), *Handbook of research on schools, schooling, and human development* (pp. 275–292). New York, NY: Routledge.

Rubie-Davies, C. (2008). Teacher expectations. In T. L. Good (Ed.), *21st century learning* (Vol. 1, pp. 254–264). Thousand Oaks, CA: Sage.

Rubie-Davies, C. M. (2007, September). *Teacher expectations, student achievement, and perceptions of student attitudes.* Paper presented at the Biennial Conference of the Educational Association for Research in Learning and Instruction, Budapest, Hungary.

Rubin, B. C. (2003). Unpacking detracking: When progressive pedagogy meets students' social worlds. *American Educational Research Journal, 40*(2), 539–573.

Rumberger, R. (2011, October 26). Solving the nation's dropout crisis. *Education Week,* p. 28.

Rummel, N., Levin, J. R., & Woodward, M. M. (2002). Do pictorial mnemonic text-learning aids give students something worth writing about? *Journal of Educational Psychology, 94*(2), 327–334.

Russell, M., & Airasian, P. (2012). *Classroom assessment* (7th ed.). New York, NY: McGraw-Hill.

Ryan, K., & Ryan, A. (2005). Psychological processes underlying stereotype threat and standardized math test performance. *Educational Psychologist, 40*(1), 53–63.

Ryan, K., & Shepard, L. (2008). *The future of test-based educational accountability.* New York, NY: Routledge.

Ryan, R. M., & Deci, E. L. (2000). Intrinsic and extrinsic motivations: Classic definitions and new directions. *Contemporary Educational Psychology, 25*(1), 54–67.

Ryan, R., Fauth, R., & Brooks-Gunn, J. (2013). Childhood poverty: Implications for school readiness and early childhood education. *Handbook of research on the education of young children* (pp. 301–321). New York, NY: Routledge.

Sachs, J. (2000). The activist professional. *Journal of Educational Change, 1*(1), 77–95.

Sackett, P., Kuncel, N., Arneson, J., Cooper, S., & Waters, S. (2009). Does socioeconomic status explain the relationship between admissions tests and post-secondary academic performance? *Psychological Bulletin, 135*(1), 1–22.

Sadker, D., & Zittleman, K. (2009). *Still failing at fairness: How gender bias cheats girls and boys and what we can do about it.* New York, NY: Charles Scribner.

Sadker, D.M., Zittleman, K., & Sadker, M.P. (2013). *Teachers, schools, and society* (10th ed.). New York, NY: McGraw-Hill.

Safer, N., & Fleischman, S. (2005). How student progress monitoring improves instruction. *Educational Leadership, 62*(5), 81–83.

Sahadeo-Turner, T., & Marzano, R. (2015). *Processing new information: Classroom techniques to help students engage with content.* West Palm Beach, FL: Learning Sciences International.

Sahlberg, P. (2012, January 12). Finland's success is no miracle. *Education Week,* 41.

Saleh, M., Lazonder, A., & De Jong, T. (2007). Structuring collaboration in mixed-ability groups to promote verbal interaction, learning, and motivation of average-ability students. *Contemporary Educational Psychology, 32*(3), 314–331.

Salend, S. (2011). Creating student-friendly tests. *Educational Leadership, 69*(3), 52–58.

Salend, S. (2016). *Creating inclusive classrooms: Effective, differentiated, and reflective practices.* Boston, MA: Pearson.

Saleno, S., & Garrick-Duhaney, L. (1999). The impact of inclusion on students with and without disabilities and their educators. *Remedial and Special Education, 20*(2), 114–126.

Salganik, M. W. (1980, January 27). Teachers busy teaching make city's 16 "best" schools stand out. *Baltimore Sun,* p. A4.

Salinger, T., & Fleischman, S. (2005). Teaching students to interact with text. *Educational Leadership, 64*(1), 90–93.

Salkind, N. J. (2013). *Tests and measurement for people who (think they) hate tests and measurement* (2nd ed.). Thousand Oaks, CA: Sage.

Sampson, R. (2002). *Bullying in schools.* Washington, DC: U.S. Department of Justice.

Sams, A., & Bergmann, J. (2013). Flip your students' learning. *Educational Leadership, 70*(6), 16–20.

Sanburn, J. (2016). The toxic tap. *Time, 187*(3), 32–39.

Sanders, M. G., Allen-Jones, G. L., & Abel, Y. (2002). Involving families and communities in the education of children and youth placed at risk. In S. Stringfield & D. Land (Eds.), *Educating at-risk students* (pp. 171–188). Chicago, IL: National Society for the Study of Education.

Sansone, C., & Harackiewicz, J. M. (Eds.). (2000). *Intrinsic and extrinsic motivation.* Orlando, FL: Academic Press.

Sarafino, E. (2012). *Applied behavior analysis: Principles and procedures in behavior modification.* Boston, MA: Wiley.

Savage, T. V., & Savage, M. K. (2010). *Successful classroom management and discipline: Teaching self-control and responsibility* (3rd ed.). Thousand Oaks, CA: Sage.

Savage, T., & Harley, D. (2009). A place at the blackboard: LGBTIQ. *Multicultural Education, 16*(4), 2–9.

Sawchuk, S. (2012, January 12). Among top-performing nations, teacher quality, status entwined. *Education Week,* 12–14.

Scalise, K., & Felde, M. (2017). *Why neuroscience matters in the classroom: Principles of brain-based instructional design for teachers.* Boston, MA: Pearson.

Schaaf, R. L. (2015). *Using digital games as assessment and instruction tools.* Bloomington, IN: Solution Tree.

Schacter, J. (2000). Does individual tutoring produce optimal learning? *American Educational Research Journal, 37*(3), 801–829.

Schad, L. (2014). *Bring your own learning.* Arlington, VA: ISTE.

Schafer, W. D., Swanson, G., Bené, N., & Newberry, G. (2001). Effects of teacher knowledge of rubrics on student achievement in four content areas. *Applied Measurement in Education, 14,* 151–170.

Scharf, M., & Hertz-Lazarowitz, R. (2003). Social networks in the school context: Effects of culture and gender. *Journal of Personal Relationships, 20*(6), 843–859.

Scheetz, N. A. (2012). *Deaf education in the 21st century: Topics and trends.* Boston, MA: Allyn & Bacon.

Scherrer, J. (2012). What's the value of VAM? *Principal, 91*(5), 58–60.

Scheuermann, B. K., & Hall, J. A. (2016). *Positive behavioral supports for the classroom* (3rd ed.). Boston, MA: Pearson.

Scheurich, J., Skrla, L., & Johnson, J. (2000). Thinking carefully about equity and accountability. *Phi Delta Kappan, 82*(4), 293–299.

Schimmer, T. (2014). *Ten things that matter from assessment to grading.* Upper Saddle River, NJ: Pearson.

Schimmer, T. (2016). *Grading from the inside out.* Bloomington, IN: Solution Tree.

Schirmer, B., & McGough, S. (2005). Teaching reading to children who are deaf: Do the conclusions of the National Reading Panel apply? *Review of Educational Research, 75*(1), 84–117.

Schlechty, P. (2011). The threat of accountabilism. *Educational Leadership, 69*(1), 80–81.

Schmidt, R., & Marzano, R. (2015). *Recording and representing knowledge: Classroom techniques to help students accurately organize and summarize content.* West Palm Beach, FL: Learning Sciences International.

Schmidt, W. H., & Houang, R. (2012). Curricular coherence and the Common Core State Standards for Mathematics. *Educational Researcher, 41,* 294–308.

Schmidt, W., & Cogan, L. (2009). The myth of equal content. *Educational Leadership, 67*(3), 44–47.

Schmoker, M. (2011). *Focus: Elevating the essentials to radically improve student learning.* Alexandria, VA: ASCD.

Schmoker, M. (2012a). The madness of teacher evaluation frameworks. *Principal, 91*(5), 70–71.

Schmoker, M. (2012b). The stunning power of good, traditional lessons. *Phi Delta Kappan, 93*(6), 70–71.

Schneider, B. (2002). Social capital: A ubiquitous emerging conception. In D. L. Levinson, P. W. Cookson, Jr., & A. R. Sadovnik (Eds.), *Education and sociology: An encyclopedia* (pp. 545–550). New York, NY: Routledge.

Schneider, B. (2015). The college ambition program: A realistic transition strategy for traditionally disadvantaged students. *Educational Researcher, 44*(7), 394–403.

Schneider, J. (2011, October 5). Tech for all? *Education Week,* 24.

Schnotz, W. (2002). Towards an integrated view of learning from text and visual displays. *Educational Psychology Review, 14*(1), 101–120.

Schoenfeld, A. (2014). What makes for powerful classrooms, and how can we support teachers in creating them? A story of research and practice, productively intertwined. *Educational Researcher, 43*(8), 404–412.

Schott Foundation. (2010). *Yes, we can: The 2010 Schott 50-state report on public education of black males.* Cambridge, MA: Author. Retrieved from www.blackboysreport.org

Schraw, G., Flowerday, T., & Lehman, S. (2001). Increasing situational interest in the classroom. *Educational Psychology Review, 13*(3), 211–224.

Schultz, F. (2012, March 7). New technologies engage students with disabilities. *Education Week,* 14.

Schunk, D. (2016). *Learning theories: An educational perspective* (7th ed.). Boston, MA: Pearson.

Schunk, D. H., & Pajares, F. (2004, April). *Self-efficacy in education: Issues and future directions.* Paper presented at the annual meeting of the American Educational Research Association, San Diego, CA.

Schunk, D., & Zimmerman, B. (2013). Self-regulation and learning. In W. Reynolds, G. Miller, & I. Weiner (Eds.), *Handbook of psychology* (Vol. 7, 2nd ed. pp. 45–69). Hoboken, NJ: Wiley.

Schunk, D., Pintrich, P., & Meece, J. (2008). *Motivation in education: Theory, research, and applications* (3rd ed.). Columbus, OH: Merrill.

Schutz, A. (2006). Home is a prison in a global city: The tragic failure of school-based community engagement strategies. *Review of Educational Research, 76*(4), 691–744.

Schwanenflugel, P. J., & Knapp, N. F. (2015). *The psychology of reading.* New York, NY: Guilford Press.

Schwartz, D., Chase, C., & Bransford, J. (2012). Resisting overzealous transfer: Coordinating previously successful routines with needs for new learning. *Educational Psychologist, 47*(3), 204–214.

Schwartz, D., Chase, C., Oppezzo, M., & Chin, D. (2011). Practicing vs. inventing with contrasting cases: The effects of telling first on learning and transfer. *Journal of Educational Psychology, 103*(4), 759–775.

Schwartz, N. H., Ellsworth, L. S., Graham, L., & Knight, B. (1998). Assessing prior knowledge to remember text: A comparison of advance organizers and maps. *Contemporary Educational Psychology, 23*(1), 65–89.

Schweinhart, L. J., & Weikart, D. P. (1998). High/Scope Perry Preschool Program effects at age twenty-seven. In J. Crane (Ed.), *Social programs that work* (pp. 148–162). New York, NY: Russell Sage Foundation.

Scott, J., Skobel, B., & Wells, J. (2008). *The word-conscious classroom: Building the vocabulary readers and writers need.* New York, NY: Scholastic.

Scott, T., Anderson, C., & Alter, P. (2012). *Managing classroom behavior using positive behavior supports.* New York, NY: Merrill.

Scriffiny, P. (2008). Seven reasons for standards-based grading. *Educational Leadership, 66*(2), 70–74.

See, B., & Gorard, S. (2003). *What do rigorous evaluations tell us about the most promising parental involvement interventions?* London, England: Nuffield Foundation.

Seifert, K. (2013). Cognitive development and the education of young children. In O. Saracho & B. Spodek (Eds.), *Handbook of research on the education of young children* (pp. 19–32). New York, NY: Routledge.

Sénéchal, M., & Young, L. (2008). The effect of family literacy interventions on children's acquisition of reading from kindergarten to grade 3: A meta-analytic review. *Review of Educational Research, 78*(4), 880–907.

Senko, C., & Miles, K. (2008). Pursuing their own learning agenda: How master-oriented students jeopardize their class performance. *Contemporary Educational Psychology, 33*(4), 561–583.

Senko, C., Hulleman, C., & Harackiewicz, J. (2011). Achievement goal theory at the crossroads: Old controversies, current challenges, and new directions. *Educational Psychologist, 46*(1), 26–47.

Senn, D., & Marzano, R. (2015). *Organizing for learning: Classroom techniques to help students interact within small groups.* West Palm Beach, FL: Learning Sciences International.

Sethi, S., Drake, M., Dialdin, D. A., & Lepper, M. R. (1995, April). *Developmental patterns of intrinsic and extrinsic motivation: A new look.* Paper presented at the annual meeting of the American Educational Research Association, San Francisco, CA.

Shah, N. (2012, June 6). Challenges seen in testing special ed. pupils on Common Core. *Education Week, 7.*

Shanahan, T. (1998). On the effectiveness and limitations of tutoring reading. In P. D. Pearson & A. Iran-Nejad (Eds.), *Review of research in education* (pp. 217–234). Washington, DC: American Educational Research Association.

Sharan, S., & Shachar, C. (1988). *Language and learning in the cooperative classroom.* New York, NY: Springer.

Shavelson, R. (2013). An approach to testing and modeling competence. *Educational Psychologist, 48*(2), 73–86.

Shavelson, R. J., Baxter, G. P., & Pine, J. (1992). Performance assessments: Political rhetoric and measurement reality. *Educational Researcher, 21*(4), 22–27.

Shaywitz, S. (2003). *Overcoming dyslexia: A new and complete science-based program for reading problems at any level.* New York, NY: Knopf.

Shaywitz, S., & Shaywitz, B. (2004). Reading disability and the brain. *Educational Leadership, 61*(3), 7–11.

Shaywitz, S., & Shaywitz, B. (2007). What neuroscience really tells us about reading instruction: A response to Judy Willis. *Educational Leadership, 64*(5), 74–78.

Shea, T., & Bauer, A. (2012). *Behavior management: A practical approach for educators* (10th ed.). Upper Saddle River, NJ: Pearson.

Sheard, M., & Chambers, B. (2011). *Self-paced learning: Effective technology-supported formative assessment.* Retrieved from www.york.ac.uk/iee/news/2011/self-paced-learning.htm

Sheard, M., & Ross, S. (2012). Improving social-emotional learning. *Better: Evidence-based Education, 4*(2),14–15.

Sheard, M., Chambers, B., Slavin, R., & Elliott, L. (2012). *Effects of self-paced learning devices on achievement in elementary grammer.* York, England: IEE, University of York.

Shepard, L. (2005). Linking formative assessment to scaffolding. *Educational Leadership, 63*(3), 66–71.

Shepard, L. A. (2000). The role of assessment in a learning culture. *Educational Researcher, 29*(7), 4–14.

Shih, M., & Sanchez, D. (2005). Perspectives and research on the positive and negative implications of having multiple racial identities. *Psychological Bulletin, 131*(4), 569–591.

Shih, S., & Alexander, J. (2000). Interacting effects of goal setting and self- or other-referenced feedback on children's development of self-efficacy and cognitive skill within the Taiwanese classroom. *Journal of Educational Psychology, 92*(3), 536–543.

Shin, H. B., & Kominski, R. (2010). *Language use in the United States: 2007, American Community Survey Reports, ACS-12.* U.S. Census Bureau, Washington, DC.

Shonkoff, J., et al. (2012). The lifelong effects of early childhood adversity and toxic stress. *Pediatrics, 129,* 232–246.

Shore, R. (2008). *The power of pow! Wham!* New York, NY: Sesame Workshop.

Shuler, C. (2007). *D is for digital.* New York, NY: Sesame Workshop.

Shulman, L. S. (2000). Teacher development: Roles of domain expertise and pedagogical development. *Journal of Applied Developmental Psychology, 21,* 129–135.

Shute, V. J. (2008). Focus on formative feedback. *Review of Educational Research, 78*(1), 153–189.

Siegel, L. S. (2003). Learning disabilities. In W. M. Reynolds & G. E. Miller (Eds.), *Handbook of psychology: Vol. 7. Educational psychology* (pp. 455–486). Hoboken, NJ: Wiley.

Siegler, R. (2006). Microgenetic analyses of learning. In D. Kuhn & R. Siegler (Eds.), *Handbook of child psychology* (Vol. 2, 6th ed., pp. 464–510). Hoboken, NJ: Wiley.

Siegler, R. S., & Svetina, M. (2006). What leads children to adopt new strategies? A microgenetic/cross-sectional study of class inclusion. *Child Development, 77,* 997–1015.

Silver, H. (2010). *Compare & contrast: Teaching comparative thinking to strengthen student learning.* Alexandria, VA: ASCD.

Silver, H., Dewing, R., & Perini, M. (2012). *Inference: Teaching students to develop hypotheses, evaluate evidence, and draw logical conclusions.* Alexandria, VA: ASCD.

Silver, H., Jackson, J., & Moirao, D. (2011). *Task rotation: Strategies for differentiating activities and assessments by learning style.* Alexandria, VA: ASCD.

Silver, H., Perini, M., & Dewing, R. (2012). *The core six: Essential strategies for achieving excellence with the Common Core.* Alexandria, VA: ASCD.

Silver, H., Strong, R., & Perini, M. (2007). *The strategic teacher: Selecting the right research-based strategy for every lesson.* Alexandria, VA: ASCD.

Silvia, S., Blitstein, J., Williams, J., Ringwalkt, C., Dusenbury, L., & Hansen, W. (2011). *Impacts of a violence prevention program for middle schools: Findings after 3 years of implementation.* Washington, DC: NCES, USDOE.

Sinclair, M. F., Christenson, S. L., Evelo, D. L., & Hurley, C. (1998). Dropout prevention for high-risk youth with disabilities: Efficacy of a sustained school engagement procedure. *Exceptional Children, 65*(1), 7–21.

Singer, J., Marx, R. W., Krajcik, J., & Chambers, J. C. (2000). Constructing extended inquiry projects: Curriculum materials for science education reform. *Educational Psychologist, 35*(4), 165–178.

Sins, P., van Joolingnen, W., Savelsbergh, E., & van Hout-Wolters, B. (2008). Motivation and performance within a collaborative computer-based modeling task: Relations between students' achievement goal orientation, self-efficacy, cognitive processing, and achievement. *Contemporary Educational Psychology, 33*(1), 58–77.

Sio, U., & Ormerod, T. (2009). Does incubation enhance problem solving? A meta-analytic review. *Psychological Bulletin, 135*(1), 94–120.

Sireci, S., Scarpati, S., & Li, S. (2005). Test accommodations for students with disabilities: An analysis of the interaction hypothesis. *Review of Educational Research, 75*(4), 457–490.

Sirin, S. (2005). Socioeconomic status and academic achievement: A meta-analytic review of research. *Review of Educational Research, 75*(3), 417–453.

Skinner, E., & Greene, T. (2008). Perceived control, coping, and engagement. In T. L. Good (Ed.), *21st century learning* (Vol. 1, pp. 121–130). Thousand Oaks, CA: Sage.

Slama, R. (2014). Investigating whether and when English learners are reclassified into mainstream classrooms in the United States: A discrete-time survival analysis. *American Educational Research Journal, 51*(2), 220–252.

Slates, S., Alexander, K., Entwisle, D., & Olson, L. (2012). Counteracting summer slide: Social capital resources within socioeconomically disadvantaged families. *Journal of Education for Students Placed at Risk, 17*(3), 165–185.

Slavich, G., & Zimbardo, P. (2012). Transformational teaching: Theoretical underpinnings, basic principles, and core methods. *Educational Psychology Review.* doi:10.1007/s10648-012-9199-6

Slavin, R. (2011). Instruction based on cooperative learning. In R. Mayer & P. Alexander (Eds.), *Handbook of research on learning and instruction* (pp. 344–360). New York, NY: Routledge.

Slavin, R. (2013). Cooperative learning and achievement: Theory and research. In W. Reynolds, G. Miller, & I. Weiner (Eds.), *Handbook of psychology* (Vol. 7, 2nd ed., pp.199–212.). Hoboken, NJ: Wiley.

Slavin, R. (2014). Making cooperative learning powerful. *Educational Leadership, 72*(2), 22–27.

Slavin, R. E. (1986). The Napa evaluation of Madeline Hunter's ITIP: Lessons learned. *Elementary School Journal, 87*, 165–171.

Slavin, R. E. (1987b). Grouping for instruction in the elementary school. *Educational Psychologist, 22*, 109–127.

Slavin, R. E. (1990). Ability grouping and student achievement in secondary schools: A best-evidence synthesis. *Review of Educational Research, 60*, 471–499.

Slavin, R. E. (1995a). *Cooperative learning: Theory, research, and practice* (2nd ed.). Boston, MA: Allyn & Bacon.

Slavin, R. E. (1994). *Using student team learning* (4th ed.). Baltimore, MD: Johns Hopkins University, Center for Research on Elementary and Middle Schools.

Slavin, R. E. (1995b). Cooperative learning and intergroup relations. In J. Banks (Ed.), *Handbook of research on multicultural education.* New York, NY: Macmillan.

Slavin, R. E. (1997/1998). Can education reduce social inequality? *Educational Leadership, 55*(4), 6–10.

Slavin, R. E. (2002). The intentional school: Effective elementary education for all children. In S. Stringfield & D. Land (Eds.), *Educating at-risk students* (pp. 111–127). Chicago, IL: National Society for the Study of Education.

Slavin, R. E. (2008). Comprehensive school reform. In C. Ames, D. Berliner, J. Brophy, L. Corno, & M. McCaslin (Eds.), *21st century education: A reference handbook* (pp. 259–266). Thousand Oaks, CA: Sage.

Slavin, R. E. (2010). Cooperative learning. In P. Peterson, E. Baker, & B. McGaw (Eds.), *International encyclopedia of education* (3rd ed.). Oxford, England: Elsevier.

Slavin, R. E. (2011). Instruction based on cooperative learning (pp. 344–360). In R. Mayer & P. A. Alexander (Eds.), *Handbook of research on learning and instruction.* New York, NY: Routledge.

Slavin, R. E., & Cheung, A. (2005). A synthesis of research on language of reading instruction. *Review of Educational Research, 75*(2), 247–284.

Slavin, R. E., & Karweit, N. L. (1982, August). *School organizational vs. developmental effects on attendance among young adolescents.* Paper presented at the annual convention of the American Psychological Association, Washington, DC.

Slavin, R. E., & Karweit, N. L. (1984, April). *Within-class ability groupings and student achievement: Two field experiments.* Paper presented at the annual convention of the American Educational Research Association, New Orleans, LA.

Slavin, R. E., & Madden, N. A. (2015). Success for All: Design and implementation of whole school reform at scale. In C. Meyers & W. C. Brandt (Eds.), *Implementation fidelity in education research: Designer and evaluator considerations.* (pp. 132–153.). New York, NY: Routledge.

Slavin, R. E., & Madden, N. A. (Eds.). (2001). *One million children: Success for All.* Thousand Oaks, CA: Corwin.

Slavin, R. E., Cheung, A., Groff, C., & Lake, C. (2008). Effective reading programs for middle and high schools: A best-evidence synthesis. *Reading Research Quarterly, 43*(3), 290–322.

Slavin, R. E., Lake, C., & Groff, C. (2009). Effective programs in middle and high school mathematics: A best-evidence synthesis. *Review of Educational Research, 79*(2), 839–911.

Slavin, R. E., Lake, C., Chambers, B., Cheung, A., & Davis, S. (2009). Effective reading programs for the elementary grades: A best-evidence synthesis. *Review of Educational Research, 79*(4), 1391–1465.

Slavin, R. E., Lake, C., Davis, S., & Madden, N. (2011). Effective programs for struggling readers: A best-evidence synthesis. *Educational Research Review, 6*, 1–26.

Slavin, R. E., Lake, C., Hanley, P., & Thurston, P. (2012). *Effective programs for elementary science: A best-evidence synthesis.* Baltimore, MD: Johns Hopkins University, Center for Research and Reform in Education.

Slavin, R. E., Madden, N. A., Chambers, B., & Haxby, B. (Eds.). (2009). *Two million children: Success for All.* Thousand Oaks, CA: Corwin.

Slavin, R., & Lake, C. (2008). Effective programs in elementary mathematics; A best-evidence synthesis. *Review of Educational Research, 78*(3), 427–515.

Slavin, R., Cheung, A., Holmes, G., Madden, N., & Chamberlain, A. (2013). Effects of a data-driven district reform model on state assessment outcomes. *American Educational Research Journal, 50*(2), 371–396.

Slavin, R., Madden, N., Calderon, M., Chamberlain, A., & Hennessy, M. (2011). Reading and language outocmes of a multiyear randomized evaluation of transitional bilingual education. *Educational Evaluation and Policy Analysis, 33*(1), 47–58.

Slavin, R. E. (2013). Overcoming the four barriers to evidence-based education. *Education Week, 32*(29), 24.

Slesaransky-Poe, G. (2013). Adults set the tone for welcoming all students. *Phi Delta Kappan, 94*(5), 40–44.

Smaldino, S., Lowther, D., Mims, C., & Russell, J. (2015). *Instructional technology and media for learning.* Boston, MA: Pearson.

Small, M. (2010). Beyond one right answer. *Educational Leadership, 68*(1), 28–32.

Smith, D. D. (2001). *Introduction to special education: Teaching in an age of opportunity.* Boston, MA: Allyn & Bacon.

Smith, D. D., & Tyler, N. C. (2010). *Introduction to special education: Making a difference* (7th ed.). Columbus, OH: Merrill.

Smith, D., Fisher, D., & Frey, N. (2015). *Better than carrots or sticks: Restorative practices for positive classroom management.* Alexandria, VA: ASCD.

Smith, H., Higgins, S., Wall, K., & Miller, J. (2005). Interactive whiteboards: Boon or bandwagon? A critical review of the literature. *Journal of Computer-Assisted Learning, 21,* 91–101.

Smith, K. (2009). From test takers to test makers. *Educational Leadership, 67*(3), 26–31.

Smith, L. (2011/2012). Slowing the summer slide. *Educational Leadership, 69*(4), 60–63.

Smith, L. J., Ross, S. M., & Casey, J. P. (1994). *Special education analyses for Success for All in four cities.* Memphis, TN: University of Memphis, Center for Research in Educational Policy.

Smith, R., Johnson, M., & Thompson, K. (2012). Data, our GPS. *Educational Leadership, 69*(5), 56–59.

Smith, S. (2013). Would you step through my door? *Educational Leadership, 70*(8), 76–78.

Smith, S. S. (2002). Desegregation. In D. L. Levinson, P. W. Cookson, Jr., & A. R. Sadovnik (Eds.), *Education and sociology: An encyclopedia* (pp. 141–149). New York, NY: Routledge.

Smith, T., Polloway, E., Doughty, T., Patton, J., & Dowdy, C. (2016). *Teaching students with special needs in inclusive settings* (7th ed.). Boston, MA: Pearson.

Snipes, J., Fancali, C., & Stoker, G. (2012). *Student academic mindset interventions: A review of the current landscape.* Sausalito, CA: Stupski Foundation.

Snow, C. (2006). Cross-cutting themes and future research directions. In D. August & T. Shanahan (Eds.), *Developing literacy in second-language learners* (pp. 631–652). Mahwah, NJ: Erlbaum.

Snow, C. E., Burns, S. M., & Griffin, P. (Eds.). (1998). *Preventing reading difficulties in young children.* Washington, DC: National Academies Press.

Snyder, F., Flay, B., Vuchinich, S., Acock, A., Washburn, I., Beete, M., & Li, K-K. (2010). Impact of a social-emotional and character development program on school-level indicators of academic achievement, absenteeism, and disciplinary outcomes: A matched-pair, cluster-randomized, controlled trial. *Journal of Research on Educational Effectiveness, 3*(1), 26–55.

Solso, R. L., Maclin, O. H., & Maclin, M. K. (2007). *Cognitive Psychology* (6th ed.). Allyn and Bacon.

Sornson, N. (2001). Vision and learning. In B. Sornson (Ed.), *Preventing early learning failure.* Alexandria, VA: ASCD.

Sousa, D. (2011). *How the brain learns* (4th ed.). Thousand Oaks, CA: Corwin.

Sousa, D. A. (2016). *Engaging the rewired brain.* West Palm Beach, FL: Learning Sciences International.

Sparks, S. (2011a, December 7). Learning declines linked to moving to middle school. *Education Week,* 1, 23.

Sparks, S. (2011a, June 8). Panel finds few learning benefits in high-stakes exams. *Education Week,* 1, 6.

Sparks, S. (2011b, September 28). Schools "flip" for lesson model promoted by Khan Academy. *Education Week,* 1, 14.

Sparks, S. (2012, August 8). Study suggests timing is key in rewarding students. *Education Week,* 18.

Specht, L. B., & Sandling, P. K. (1991). The differential effects of experiential learning activities and traditional lecture classes in accounting. *Simulation and Games, 2,* 196–210.

Spencer, M. B., Noll, E., Stoltzfus, J., & Harpalani, V. (2001). Identity and school adjustment: Revisiting the "acting white" assumption. *Educational Psychologist, 36*(1), 21–30.

Spiegel, D. L. (2005). *Classroom discussion: Strategies for enhancing all students, building higher-level thinking skills, and strengthening reading and writing across the curriculum.* New York, NY: Scholastic.

Spielberger, C., & Vagg, P. (Eds.). (1995). *Test anxiety: Theory, assessment, and treatment.* Washington, DC: Taylor & Francis.

Spinelli, C. G. (2011). *Linking assessment to instructional strategies: A guide for teachers.* Boston, MA: Allyn & Bacon.

Sporer, N., Brunstein, J., & Kieschke, U. (2009). Improving students' reading comprehension skills: Effects of strategy instruction and reciprocal teaching. *Learning and Instruction, 19*(3), 272–286.

Sprenger, M. (2009). Focusing the digital brain. *Educational Leadership, 67*(1), 34–39.

Squires, D. A. (2009). *Curriculum alignment: Research-based strategies for increasing student achievement.* Thousand Oaks, CA: Corwin.

Squires, J., Pribble, L., Chen, C., & Pomes, M. (2013). Early childhood education: Improving outcomes for young children and families. In W. Reynolds, G. Miller, & I. Weiner (Eds.), *Handbook of psychology* (Vol. 7, 2nd ed., pp. 99–116.). Hoboken, NJ: Wiley.

Staker, H., & Horn, M. B. (2012). *Classifying K–12 blended learning.* Retrieved from www.innosightinstitute.org

Stallings, J., & Krasavage, E. M. (1986). Program implementation and student achievement in a four-year Madeline Hunter follow-through project. *Elementary School Journal, 87,* 117–138.

Stansbury, M. (2009, July 21). *What educators can learn from brain research.* Retrieved from www.eschoolnews.com

Starnes, B. (2011). Superstars, cheating, and surprises. *Phi Delta Kappan, 93*(1), 70–71.

Starnes, B. A. (2006). Montana's Indian education for all: Toward an education worthy of American ideals. *Phi Delta Kappan, 88*(3), 184–189.

Starratt, R. (2003). Opportunity to learn and the accountability agenda. *Phi Delta Kappan, 85*(4), 298–303.

Steel, P. (2007). The nature of procrastination: A meta-analytic and theoretical review of quintessential self-regulatory failure. *Psychological Bulletin, 133*(1), 65–94.

Steele, C. (2010). Inspired responses. *Educational Leadership, 68*(4), 64–68.

Stein, B. S., Littlefield, J., Bransford, J. D., & Persampieri, M. (1984). Elaboration and knowledge acquisition. *Memory and Cognition, 12,* 522–529.

Stein, N. (2000). Listening to—and learning from—girls. *Educational Leadership, 57*(4), 18–20.

Steinberg, L. (2011). Demystifying the adolescent brain. *Educational Leadership, 68*(7), 42–46.

Steiner, H. H., & Carr, M. (2003). Cognitive development in gifted children: Toward a more precise understanding of emerging differences in intelligence. *Educational Psychology Review, 15*(3), 215–246.

Steinfeld, E., & Maisel, J. (2011). *Universal design: Creating inclusive environments.* Boston, MA: Wiley.

Stephan, W. G., & Vogt, W. P. (Eds.). (2004). *Education programs for improving intergroup relations.* New York, NY: Teachers College.

Sternberg, R. (2008). Applying psychological theories to educational practice. *American Educational Research Journal, 45*(1), 150–165.

Sternberg, R. (2011). Ethics from thought to action. *Educational Leadership, 68*(6), 34–39.

Sternberg, R. J. (2002). Raising the achievement of all students: Teaching for successful intelligence. *Educational Psychology Review, 14*(4), 383–393.

Sternberg, R. J. (2007). Who are the bright children? The cultural context of being and acting intelligent. *Educational Researcher, 36*(3), 148–155.

Sternberg, R., Jarvin, L., & Grigorenko, E. (2009). *Teaching for wisdom, intelligence, creativity, and success.* Thousand Oaks, CA: Corwin.

Steubing, K., Barth, A., Trahan, L., Reddy, R., Miciak, J., & Fletcher, J. (2015). Are child cognitive characteristics strong predictors of responses to intervention? A meta-analysis. *Review of Educational Research, 85*(3), 395–429.

Stevens, R. J., & Slavin, R. E. (1995a). The cooperative elementary school: Effects on students' achievement, attitudes, and social relations. *American Educational Research Journal, 32,* 321–351.

Stevens, R. J., & Slavin, R. E. (1995b). The effects of Cooperative Integrated Reading and Composition (CIRC) on academically handicapped and non-handicapped students' achievement, attitudes, and metacognition in reading and writing. *Elementary School Journal, 95*(3), 241–262.

Stewart, V. (2010). Raising teacher quality around the world. *Educational Leadership, 68*(4), 16–20.

Stiefel, L., Schwartz, A., & Wiswall, M. (2015). Does small high school reform lift urban districts? Evidence from New York City. *Educational Researcher, 44*(3), 161–172.

Stiggins, R., & Chappuis, J. (2012). *An introduction to student-involved assessment for learning* (6th ed.). Upper Saddle River, NJ: Pearson.

Stinson, D. (2006). African American male adolescents, schooling (and mathematics): Deficiency, rejection, and achievement. *Review of Educational Research, 76*(4), 477–506.

Stipek, D. (2002). *Motivation to learn: Integrating theory and practice* (4th ed.). Boston, MA: Allyn & Bacon.

Stipek, D., de la Sota, A., & Weishaupt, L. (1999). Life lessons: An embedded classroom approach to preventing high-risk behaviors among preadolescents. *The Elementary School Journal, 99*(5), 433–452.

Stoet, G., & Geary, D. (2013). Sex differences in mathematics and reading achievement are inversely related: Within- and across-nation assessment of 10 years of PISA data. *PLOS One.*

Stout, K., & Pohl, A. (2012). Promoting engagement with Check & Connect. *Better: Evidence-based education, 5*(1), 14–15.

Strand, S., Deary, I. J., & Smith, P. (2006). Sex differences in cognitive abilities test scores: A UK national picture. *British Journal of Educational Psychology, 76,* 463–480.

Strout, M. (2005). Positive behavioral support on the classroom level: Considerations and strategies. *Beyond Behavior, 14,* 3–8.

Stuebing, K. K., Fletcher, J. M., LeDoux, J. M., Lyon, G. R., Shaywitz, S. E., & Shaywitz, B. A. (2002). Validity of IQ discrepancy classifications of reading disabilities: A meta-analysis. *American Educational Research Journal, 39*(2), 469–518.

Stumbo, C., & McWalters, P. (2010). Measuring effectiveness: What will it take? *Educational Leadership, 68*(4), 10–15.

Stumpf, H., & Stanley, J. C. (1996). Gender-related differences on the College Board's advanced placement achievement tests 1982–1992. *Journal of Educational Psychology, 88*(2), 353–364.

Summers, J. (2006). Effects of collaborative learning in math on sixth graders' individual goal orientations from a socioconstructivist perspective. *The Elementary School Journal, 106*(3), 273–290.

Superfine, B. (2010). Court-driven reform and equal educational opportunity: Centralization, decentralization, and the shifting judicial role. *Review of Educational Research, 80*(1), 108–137.

Supovitz, J. A., & Brennan, R. T. (1997). Mirror, mirror on the wall, which is the fairest test of all? An examination of the equitability of portfolio assessment relative to standardized tests. *Harvard Educational Review, 67*(3), 474–505.

Susman, E. J., Dorn, L. D., & Schiefelbein, V. L. (2003). Puberty, sexuality, and health. In R. M. Lerner, M. A. Easterbrooks, & J. Mistry (Eds.), *Handbook of psychology: Vol. 6. Developmental psychology* (pp. 295–324). Hoboken, NJ: Wiley.

Sutherland, K., Wehby, J., & Copeland, S. (2000). Effect of rates of varying behavior-specific praise on the on-task behavior of students with EBD. *Journal of Emotional and Behavioral Disorders, 8,* 2–8, 26.

Suzuki, L. A., Ponterotto, J. G., & Meller, P. J. (Eds.). (2000). *Handbook of multicultural assessment* (2nd ed.). San Francisco, CA: Jossey-Bass.

Swann, W., Chang-Schneider, C., & McClarty, K. (2007). Do people's self-views matter? *American Psychologist, 62*(2), 84–94.

Swanson, C. (2012). *Diplomas count.* Retrieved from http://www.edweek.org/media/diplomascount2012_presspacket_final.pdf

Swanson, H. (2001). Research on interventions for adolescents with learning disabilities: A meta-analysis of outcomes related to higher-order processing. *The Elementary School Journal, 101*(3), 331–348.

Swanson, H., & Jerman, O. (2006). Math disabilities: A selective meta-analysis of the literature. *Review of Educational Research, 76*(2), 249–274.

Swartz, E. (2009). Diversity: Gatekeeping knowledge and maintaining inequalities. *Review of Educational Research, 79*(2), 1044–1083.

Swearer, S., Espelage, D., Vaillancourt, T., & Hymel, S. (2010). What can be done about school bullying? Linking research to educational practice. *Educational Researcher, 39*(1), 38–47.

Swisher, K., & Schoorman, D. (2001). Learning styles: Implications for teachers. In C. F. Diaz (Ed.), *Multicultural education in the 21st century.* New York, NY: Longman.

Sykes, G., & Wilson, S. (2016). Can policy (re)form instruction? In D. Gitomer & C. Bell (Eds.), *Handbook of research on teaching* (5th ed.). (pp. 917–950). Washington, DC: AERA.

Takacs, Z., Swart, E., & Bus, A. (2015). Benefits and pitfalls of multimedia and interactive features in technology-enhanced storybooks: A meta-analysis. *Review of Educational Research, 85*(4), 698–739.

Tangney, J., & Dearing, R. (2002). Gender differences in morality. In R. Bornstein & J. Masling (Eds.), *The psychodynamics of gender and gender role.* Washington, DC: American Psychological Association.

Tate, W., IV. (2008). "Geography of opportunity": Poverty, place, and educational outcomes. *Educational Researcher, 37*(7), 397–411.

Taylor, C. (1994). Assessment for measurement or standards: The peril and promise of large-scale assessment reform. *American Educational Research Journal, 31*(2), 231–262.

Taylor, E. (2014). *Spending more of the school day in math class: Evidence from a regression discontinuity in middle school.* Stanford, CA: Center for Education Policy Analysis, Stanford University.

Temple, C., Ogle, D., Crawford, A., & Freppon, P. (2016). *All children read: Teaching for literacy in today's diverse classrooms.* Boston, MA: Pearson.

Temple, E., Deutsch, G., Poldrack, P., Miller, S., Tallal, P., Merzenech, M., & Gabrielli, J. (2003). Neural deficits in children with dyslexia ameliorated by behavioral remediation: Evidence from functional MRI. *Proceedings of the National Academy of Sciences, 100*, 2860–2865.

Tenenbaum, H., & Ruck, M. (2007). Are teachers' expectations different for racial minority than for European American students? A meta-analysis. *Journal of Educational Psychology, 99*(2), 253–273.

Terman, L. M., & Oden, M. H. (1959). The gifted group in midlife. In *Genetic studies of genius* (Vol. 5). Stanford, CA: Stanford University Press.

Terzian, M., Hamilton, K., & Ericson, S. (2011). *What works to prevent or reduce internalizing problems or social-emotional difficulties in adolescents: Lessons from experimental evaluations of social interventions.* Retrieved from www.childtrends.org/Files//Child_%20 Trends-2011_12_01_FS_%20WWInternalizing.pdf

Texas Center for Educational Research. (2007). *Evaluation of the Texas technology immersion pilot: Findings from the second year.* Austin, TX: Author.

Thio, A. (2010). *Deviant behavior* (10th ed.). Upper Saddle River, NJ: Pearson.

Thomas, D., & Stevenson, H. (2009). Gender risks and education: The particular classroom challenges for urban low-income African American boys. *Review of Research in Education, 33,* 160–180.

Thomas, E. L., & Robinson, H. A. (1972). *Improving reading in every class: A sourcebook for teachers.* Boston, MA: Allyn & Bacon.

Thomas, M. D., & Bainbridge, W. L. (2001). "All children can learn": Facts and fallacies. *Phi Delta Kappan, 82*(9), 660–662.

Thompson, R. A., Easterbrooks, M. A., & Padilla-Walker, L. M. (2003). Social and emotional development in infancy. In R. M. Lerner, M. A. Easterbrooks, & J. Mistry (Eds.), *Handbook of psychology: Vol. 6. Developmental psychology* (pp. 91–112). Hoboken, NJ: Wiley.

Thompson, W., & Hickey, J. (2011). *Society in focus.* Boston, MA: Pearson.

Thorndike, R., & Thorndike-Christ, T. (2010). Measurement and evaluation in psychology and education (8th ed.). Upper Saddle River, NJ: Pearson.

Thorsen, C. (2009). *Tech tactics: Technology for teachers* (3rd ed). Boston, MA: Pearson.

Thousand, J. S., & Villa, R. A. (1994). *Creativity and collaborative learning: A practical guide to empowering students and teachers.* Baltimore, MD: Brookes.

Thurlings, M., Evers, A., & Vermeulen, M. (2015). Toward a model of explaining teachers' innovative behavior: A literature review. *Review of Educational Research, 85*(3), 430–471.

Thurston, A. (2010). Engaging students in science with cooperative learning. *Better: Evidence-based Education, 2*(3), 14–15.

Thurston, A. (2014). Using cooperative learning to engage students in science. In R. E. Slavin (Ed.), *Science, technology, & mathematics (STEM)* (pp. 79–82). Thousand Oaks, CA: Corwin.

Thurston, A., Tymms, P., Merrell, C., & Conlin, N. (2012). Improving achievement across a whole district with peer tutoring. *Better: Evidence-based Education, 4*(2) 18–19.

Tibbals, C. Z., & Bernhardt, V. L. (2015). *Shifting to Common Core literacy.* Bloomington, IN: Solution Tree.

Tileston, D., & Darling, S. (2008). *Teaching strategies that prepare students for high-stakes tests.* Thousand Oaks, CA: Corwin.

Tingley, J. (2001). Volunteer programs: When good intentions are not enough. *Educational Leadership, 68*(7), 53–55.

Tishman, S., Perkins, D. N., & Jay, E. (1995). *The thinking classroom.* Boston, MA: Allyn & Bacon.

Tobias, S. (1992). The impact of test anxiety cognition in school learning. In K. A. Hagtvet & T. B. Johnsen (Eds.), *Advances in test anxiety research* (Vol. 7, pp. 18–31). Amsterdam, Netherlands: Swets & Zeitlinger.

Toga, A. W., & Thompson, P. M. (2005). Genetics of brain structure and intelligence. *Annual Review of Neuroscience, 28,* 1–23.

Tolan, P., Henry, D., Schoeny, M., Bass, A., Lovegrove, P., & Nichols, E. (2013). *Mentoring interventions to affect juvenile delinquency and associated problems: A systematic review.* Oslo, Norway: The Campbell Collection.

Tolchinsky, L. (2015). From text to language and back: The emergence of written language. In C. A. MacArthur, S. Graham, & J. Fitzgerald (Eds.), *Handbook of writing research* (2nd ed.). New York, NY: Guilford Press.

Tollefson, N. (2000). Classroom applications of cognitive theories of motivation. *Educational Psychology Review, 12*(1), 63–84.

Tomassini, J. (2012, May 9). Educators weight e-textbook cost comparisons. *Education Week, 1,* 18–19.

Tomlinson, C, & Imbeau, M. (2014). *A differential approach to the Common Core: How do I help a broad range of learners succeed with challenging curriculum?* Alexandria, VA: ASCD.

Tomlinson, C. (2008). The goals of differentiation. *Educational Leadership, 66*(3), 26–31.

Tomlinson, C. (2014a). The bridge between today's lesson and tomorrow's. *Educational Leadership, 71*(6),10–15.

Tomlinson, C. (2014b). *The differentiated classroom: Responding to the needs of all learners* (2nd ed.). Alexandria, VA: ASCD.

Tomlinson, C. A. & Moon, T. R. (2013). *Assessment and student success in a differentiated classroom.* Alexandria, VA: ASCD.

Tomlinson, C., & Javius, E. (2012). Teach up for excellence. *Educational Leadership, 69*(5), 28–33.

Tomlinson, C., & Moon, T. (2014). Assessment in a differentiated classroom. In R. E. Slavin (Ed.), *Classroom management and assessment* (pp. 1–5). Thousand Oaks, CA: Corwin.

Tong, F., Lara-Alecio, R., Irby, B., Mathes, P., & Kwok, O. (2008). Accelerating early academic oral English development in transitional bilingual and structured English immersion programs. *American Educational Research Journal, 45*(4), 1011–1044.

Toppo, G. (2015). *The game believes in you: How digital play can make our kids smarter.* New York, NY: St. Martin's Press.

Topping, K., Duran, D., & Van Keer, H. (Eds.). (2015). *Using peer tutoring to improve reading skills.* New York, NY: Routledge.

Topping, K., Samuels, J., & Paul, T. (2007). Does practice make perfect? Independent reading quantity, quality, and student achievement. *Learning and Instruction, 17*(3), 253–264.

Torrance, M., & Fidalgo, R. (2011). Learning writing strategies. *Better: Evidence-based Education, 4*(4), 18–19.

Torrance, M., Fidalgo, R., & Garcia, J.-N. (2007). The teachability and effectiveness of cognitive self-regulation in sixth-grade writers. *Learning and Instruction, 17*(3), 265–285.

Tough, P. (2011, September 14). What if the secret to success is failure? *New York Times.*

Towne, L., Wise, L., & Winters, T. (2005). *Advancing scientific research in education.* Washington, DC: National Academies Press.

Trammel, D. L., Schloss, P. J., & Alper, S. (1994). Using self-recording evaluation and graphing to increase completion of homework assignments. *Journal of Learning Disabilities, 27,* 75–81.

Trautwein, U. (2007). The homework-achievement relation reconsidered: Differentiating homework time, homework frequency, and homework effort. *Learning and Instruction, 17*(3), 372–388.

Trautwein, U., Marsh, H., Nagengast, B., Ludtke, O., Nagy, G., & Konkmann, K. (2012). Probing for the multiplicative term in modern expenctancy–value theory: A latent interaction modeling study. *Journal of Educational Psychology, 104*(3), 763-777.

Trawick-Smith, J. (2014). *Early childhood development: A multicultural perspective* (6th ed.). Boston, MA: Pearson.

Traylor, F. (2012). Bringing early childhood into the education system: Pre-K to 3rd. In S. Kagan & K. Kauerz (Eds.), *Early childhood systems: Transforming early learning.* New York, NY: Teachers College Press.

Trefil, J., & O'Brien-Trefil, W. (2009). The science students need to know. *Educational Leadership, 67*(1), 28–33.

Troop, W. R., & Asher, S. R. (1999). Teaching peer relationship competence in schools. In R. J. Stevens (Ed.), *Teaching in American schools.* Upper Saddle River, NJ: Merrill/Prentice-Hall.

Trotter, A. (2009, January 6). Students turn their cellphones on for classroom lessons. *Education Daily.* Retrieved from www.csun .edu/~krowlands/Content/Academic_Resources/Technology/ cell%20phones%20in%20classroom.pdf

Tucker, M. (2012). Teacher quality: What's wrong with U.S. strategy? *Educational Leadership, 69*(4), 42–46.

Tulving, E., & Craik, F. I. M. (Eds.). (2000). *The Oxford handbook of memory.* New York, NY: Oxford University Press.

Turiel, E. (2006). The development of morality. In N. Eisenberg (Ed.), *Handbook of Child Psychology* (Vol. 3, 6th ed., pp. 789–857). Hoboken, NJ: Wiley.

Turkeltaub, P. E., Gareau, L., Flowers, D. L., Zeffiro, T. A., & Eden, G. F. (2003). Development of neural mechanisms for reading. *Nature Neuroscience, 6,* 767–773.

Turnbull, A., Turnbull, R., Wehmeyer, M., & Shogren, K. (2016). *Exceptional lives: Special education in today's schools* (8th ed.). Boston, MA: Pearson.

Turner, L. A., & Johnson, B. (2003). A model of mastery motivation for at-risk preschoolers. *Journal of Educational Psychology, 95*(3), 495–505.

Turner, S., & Alborz, A. (2003). Academic attainments of children with Down's syndrome: A longitudinal study. *British Journal of Educational Psychology, 73*(4), 563–583.

Tyson, K., Darity, J., & Castellino, D. (2005). It's not a "black thing": Understanding the burden of acting white and other dilemmas of high achievement. *American Sociological Review, 70*(4), 582–605.

U.S. Administration for Children and Families Office of Planning, Research, and Evaluation (2014). *Home visiting programs: Reviewing evidence of effectiveness.* OPRE Report.

U.S. Census Bureau. (2013). *Annual social and economic supplement to the current population survey.* Retrieved from www.census.gov

U.S. Census Bureau. (2014). *Projected 2020-2060 data.* Retrieved January 12, 2015, from http://www.census.gov/population/ projections/data/national/2014/summarytables.html

U.S. Department of Education, Office of Special Education and Rehabilitation Services. (1998, September). *IDEA '97 general information.* Retrieved May 2, 2010, from www.ed.gov/offices/ OSERS/IDEA/overview.html

U.S. Department of Education. (2000). *The 22nd annual report to Congress on the implementation of the Indivials with Disabilities Education Act.* Washington, DC: U.S. Government Printing Office.

U.S. Department of Education. (2005). *Annual report to Congress on the implementation of the Individuals with Disabilities Education Act.* Washington, DC: Author.

U.S. Department of Education (2015). *College- and career-ready standards.* Retrieved July 28, 2016 from http://www. ed.gov/k-12reforms/standards.

U.S. Department of Education. (2015). *Digest of education statistics.* Washington, DC: Author.

Udelhofen, S. (2014). *Building a Common Core-based curriculum.* Bloomington, IN: Solution Tree.

University of Wisconsin-Madison. (2009, June 2). Culture, not biology, underpins math gender gap. *Science Daily.* Retrieved from www.sciencedaily.com/releases/2009/090601182655.htm

Unsworth, N., & Engle, R. (2007). On the division of short-term and working memory: An examination of simple and complex span and their relation to higher order abilities. *Psychological Bulletin, 133*(6), 1038–1066.

Urdan, T., & Mestas, M. (2006). The goals behind performance goals. *Journal of Educational Psychology, 98*(2), 354–365.

Usher, A., & Kober, N. (2012). *Student motivation: An overlooked piece of school reform.* Washington, DC: CEP.

Vacca, R. (2006). They can because they think they can. *Educational Leadership, 63*(5), 56–59.

Vadasy, P. F., Sanders, E. A., & Tudor, S. (2007). Effectiveness of paraeducator-supplemented individual instruction: Beyond basic decoding skills. *Journal of Learning Disabilities, 40*(6), 508–525.

Vagle, N. D. (2014). *Design in five: Essential phases to create engaging assessment practice.* Bloomington, IN: Solution Tree.

Valentino, R., & Reardon, S. (2015). Efectiveness of four instructional programs designed to serve English learners: Variation by ethnicity and initial English proficiency. *Educational Evaluation and Policy Analysis, 37*(4), 612-637.

Valenza, J., & Stephens, W. (2012). Reading remixed. *Educational Leadership, 69*(5), 75–78.

Vamosi, R. (2005, February 18). *Alarm over pharming attacks: Identity theft made even easier.* Retrieved from http://reviews.cnet .com/4520-3513_7-5670780-1.html

van Goozen, S., Fairchild, G., Snoek, H., & Harold, G. (2007). The evidence for a neurobiological model of childhood antisocial behavior. *Psychological Bulletin, 133*(1), 149–182.

van IJzendoorn, M. H., Juffer, F., & Klein Poelhuis, C. W. (2005). Adoption and cognitive development: A meta-analytic comparison of adopted and nonadopted children's IQ and school performance. *Psychological Bulletin, 131*(2), 301–316.

Van Keer, H., & Vanderlinde, R. (2013). A book for two. *Phi Delta Kappan, 94*(8), 54–58.

Van Laar, C. (2001). Understanding the impact of disadvantage on academic achievement. In F. Salili & R. Hoosain (Eds.), *Multicultural education: Issues, policies, and practices.* Greenwich, CT: Information Age.

Van Meter, P. (2001). Drawing construction as a strategy for learning from text. *Journal of Educational Psychology, 93*(1), 129–140.

VanTassel-Baska, J., & Brown, E. (2007). Towards best practice: An analysis of the efficacy of curriculum models in gifted education. *Gifted Child Quarterly.* Fall, Volume 51, No. 4, 342-358.

Van Voorhis, F., Maier, M., Epstein, J., & Lloyd, C. (2013). *The impact of family involvement on the education of children 3–8.* New York, NY: MDRC.

Vander Ark, T. (2012). *Getting smart: How digital learning is changing the world.* San Francisco: Jossey-Bass.

VanLehn, K. (2011). The relative effectiveness of human tutoring, intelligent tutoring systems, and other tutoring systems. *Educational Psychologist, 46,* 197–221.

Vansteenkiste, M., Lens, W., & Deci, E. (2006). Intrinsic vs. extrinsic goal contents in self-determination theory: Another look at the quality of academic motivation. *Educational Psychologist, 41*(1), 19–31.

Varma, S., McCandliss, B., & Schwartz, D. (2008). Scientific and pragmatic challenges for bridging education and neuroscience. *Educational Researcher, 37*(3), 140–152.

Vatterott, C. (2014). Student-owned homework. *Educational Leadership, 71*(6), 39–43.

Vatterott, C. (2015). *Rethinking grading: Meaningful assessment for standards-based learning.* Alexandria, VA: ASCD.

Vaughn, S., & Fletcher, J. (2011). Reading interventions for secondary students. *Better: Evidence-based Education, 4*(1), 8–9.

Vaughn, S., Bos, C., & Schumm, J. (2014). *Teaching students who are exceptional, diverse, and at risk in the general education classroom.* Boston, MA: Pearson.

Vaughn, S., Cirino, P., Tolar, T., Fletcher, J., Cardenas-Hagan, E., Carlson, C., & Francis, D. (2008). Long-term follow-up of Spanish and English interventions for first-grade English language learners at risk for reading problems. *Journal of Research on Educational Effectiveness, 3*(2), 179–214.

Vaughn, S., Levy, S., Coleman, M., & Bos, C. S. (2002). Reading instruction for students with LD and EBD: A synthesis of observation studies. *Journal of Special Education, 36*(1), 2–13.

Vavrus, M. (2008). Culturally responsive teaching. In T. L. Good (Ed.), *21st century learning* (Vol. 2, pp. 49–57). Thousand Oaks, CA: Sage.

Veenman, M. (2011). Learning to self-monitor and self-regulate. In R. Mayer & P. Alexander (Eds.), *Handbook of research on learning and instruction* (pp. 197–218). New York, NY: Routledge.

Vekiri, I. (2002). What is the value of graphical displays in learning? *Educational Psychology Review, 14*(3), 261–312.

Vellutino, F. R., Scanlon, D. M., Sipay, E. R., Small, S. G., Chen, R., Pratt, A., & Denckla, M. B. (1996). Cognitive profiles of difficult-to-remediate and readily remediated poor readers: Early intervention as a vehicle for distinguishing between cognitive and experiential deficits as basic causes of specific reading disability. *Journal of Educational Psychology, 88*(4), 601–638.

Venables, D. (2014). *How teachers can turn data into action.* Alexandria, VA: ASCD.

Vernon-Feagans, L., & Ginsberg, M. (2011). Teaching struggling readers in the classroom. *Better: Evidence-based Education, 4*(1), 6–7.

Villa, R., & Thousand, J. (2003). Making inclusive education work. *Educational Leadership, 61*(2), 19–23.

Villanueva, A. B., Rudd, P., Elliot, L., Chambers, B., & Blower, S. (2016). *Flipped learning evaluation.* York, England: University of York.

Villegas, A., & Lucas, T. (2007). The culturally responsive teacher. *Educational Leadership, 64*(6), 28–33.

Vinson, B. P. (2012). *Preschool and school-age language disorders.* Stamford, CT: Cengage.

Voight, A., Shinn, M., & Nation, M. (2012). The longitudinal effects of residential mobility on the academic achievement of urban elementary and middle school students. *Educational Researcher, 41*(9), 385–392.

Vokoun, M., & Bigelow, T. (2008). Dude, what choice do I have? *Educational Leadership, 66*(3), 70–74.

Volkmar, F., & Pauls, D. (2003). Autism. *Lancet, 362,* 1133–1141.

Voltz, D., Sims, M., & Nelson, B. (2010). *Connecting teachers, students, and standards.* Arlington, VA: ASCD.

Vuilleumeir, P. (2005). How brains beware: Neural mechanisms of emotional attention. *Trends in Cognitive Sciences, 9,* 585–594.

Vygotsky, L. S. (1978). *Mind in society.* (M. Cole, V. John-Steiner, S. Scribner, & E. Souberman, Eds.). Cambridge, MA: Harvard University Press.

Wade, S. E. (2001). Research on importance and interest: Implications for curriculum development and future research. *Educational Psychology Review, 13*(3), 243–261.

Wadsworth, B. (2004). *Piaget's theory of cognitive and affective development* (5th ed.). Boston, MA: Pearson.

Wagmeister, J., & Shifrin, B. (2000). Thinking differently, learning differently. *Educational Leadership, 58*(3), 45–48.

Waitoller, F., Artiles, A., & Cheney, D. (2010). The miner's canary: A review of overrepresentation research and explanations. *Journal of Special Education, 44*(1), 29–49.

Walker, H. M., & Gresham, F. M. (2003). School-related behavior disorders. In W. M. Reynolds & G. E. Miller (Eds.), *Handbook of psychology: Vol. 7. Educational psychology* (pp. 511–530). Hoboken, NJ: Wiley.

Walker, H., & Gresham, F. (2013). The school-related behavior disorders field: A source of innovation and best practices for school personnel who serve students with emotional and behavioral disorders. In W. Reynolds, G. Miller, & I. Weiner (Eds.), *Handbook of psychology* (Vol. 7, 2nd ed., pp. 411–440). Hoboken, NJ: Wiley.

Walker, J. E., Shea, T. M., & Bauer, A. M. (2011). *Behavior management: A practical approach for educators* (10th ed.). Upper Saddle River, NJ: Pearson.

Walker, J. M. T., & Hoover-Dempsey, K. V. (2001, April). *Age-related patterns in student invitations to parental involvement in homework.* Paper presented at the annual meeting of the American Educational Research Association, Seattle, WA.

Walker, J., & Hoover-Dempsey, K. V. (2008). Parent involvement. In T. L. Good (Ed.), *21st century learning* (Vol. 2, pp. 382–391). Thousand Oaks, CA: Sage.

Walker, L. J. (2004). Progress and prospects in the psychology of moral development. *Merrill-Palmer Quarterly, 50,* 546–557.

Wallace-Broscious, A., Serafica, F. C., & Osipow, S. H. (1994). Adolescent career development: Relationships to self-concept and identity status. *Journal of Research on Adolescence, 4*(1), 122–149.

Walsh, J. A., & Sattes, B. D. (2005). *Quality questioning: Research-based practice to engage every learner.* Thousand Oaks, CA: Corwin.

Wang, A. Y., & Thomas, M. H. (1995). Effect of keywords on long-term retention: Help or hindrance? *Journal of Educational Psychology, 87,* 468–475.

Wanzek, J., Vaughn, S., Scammacca, N., Metz, K, Murray, C., Roberts, G., & Danielson, L. (2013). Extensive reading interventions for students with reading difficulties after grade 3. *Review of Educational Research, 83*(2), 163–195.

Warikoo, N., & Carter, P. (2009). Cultural explanations for racial and ethnic stratification in academic achievement: A call for a new and improved theory. *Review of Educational Research, 79*(1), 366–394.

Warner, J. (2013, March 21). Is there really a "boy crisis"? *Time Magazine.* Retrieved 08/31/2016 from http://ideas.time.com/2013/03/21/the-boy-crisis-is-it-fictional/

Warren, J., & Saliba, J. (2012). First through eighth grade retention rates for all 50 states: A new method and initial results. *Educational Researcher, 41*(8), 320–329.

Warren, J., Hoffman, E., & Andrew, M. (2014). Patterns and trends in grade retention rates in the United States, 1995–2010. *Educational Researcher, 43*(9), 433–443.

Wasley, P. A. (2002). Small classes, small schools: The time is now. *Educational Leadership, 59*(3), 6–10.

Waterhouse, L. (2006). Multiple intelligences, the Mozart Effect, and emotional intelligence: A critical review. *Educational Psychologist, 4*(4), 207–225.

Watkins, D., & Wentzel, K. (2008). Training boys with ADHD to work collaboratively: Social and learning outcomes. *Contemporary Educational Psychology, 33*(4), 625–646.

Watkins, M., & Canivez, G. (2004). Temporal stability of WISC-III composite strengths and weaknesses. *Psychological Assessment, 16,* 6–16.

Watson, J. (1930). *Behaviorism.* New York, NY: Norton.

Watson, J., Murin, A., Vashaw, L., Gemin, B., & Rapp, C. (2011). *Keeping pace with K–12 online learning: An annual review of policy and practice.* Evergreen, CO: Evergreen Education Group.

Watson, N., & Breedlove, S. (2012). The mind's machine: Foundations of brain and behavior. Sunderland, MA: Sinauer.

Watt, K. M., Powell, C. A., & Mendiola, I. D. (2004). Implications of one comprehensive school reform model for secondary school students underrepresented in higher education. *Journal of Education for Students Placed at Risk, 9*(3), 241–259.

Waugh, C. K., & Gronlund, N. E. (2013). *Assessment of student achievement* (10th ed.). Upper Saddle River, NJ: Pearson.

Waxman, H. C., Gray, J. P., & Padron, N. (2002). Resiliency among students at risk of academic failure. In S. Stringfield & D. Land (Eds.), *Educating at-risk students* (pp. 29–48). Chicago, IL: National Society for the Study of Education.

Weaver-Hightower, M. (2003). The "boy turn" in research on gender education. *Review of Educational Research, 73*(4), 471–498.

Webb, N. M. (2008). Learning in small groups. In T. L. Good (Ed.), *21st century learning* (Vol. 1, pp. 203–211). Thousand Oaks, CA: Sage.

Webb, N., & Mastergeorge, A. (2003). Promoting effective helping behavior in peer-directed groups. *International Journal of Educational Research, 39,* 73–97.

Webber, J., & Wilson, M. (2012). Do grades tell parents what they want and need to know? *Phi Delta Kappan, 94*(1), 30–35.

Webster-Stratton, C. (2012). Incredible years: Nurturing children's social, emotional, and academic competence. Retrieved at www.incredibleyears.com

Weinberger, E., & McCombs, B. L. (2001, April). *The impact of learner-centered practices on the academic and non-academic outcomes of upper elementary and middle school students.* Paper presented at the annual convention of the American Educational Research Association, Seattle, WA.

Weiner, B. (2000). Intrapersonal and interpersonal theories of motivation from an attributional perspective. *Educational Psychology Review, 12*(1), 1–14.

Weiner, B. (2010). The development of an attribution-based theory of motivation: A history of ideas. *Educational Psychologist, 45*(1), 28–36.

Weinstein, C. S. (2007). *Middle and secondary classroom management: Lessons from research and practice* (3rd ed.). New York, NY: McGraw-Hill.

Weinstein, C., & Mignano, A. (1993). *Organizing the elementary school classroom: Lessons from research and practice.* New York, NY: McGraw-Hill.

Weinstein, C., & Mignano, A. (2007). *Elementary classroom management: Lessons from research and practice* (4th ed.). New York, NY: McGraw-Hill.

Weinstein, R. S. (1996). High standards in a tracked system of schooling: For which students and with what educational supports? *Educational Researcher, 25*(8), 16–19.

Weinstein, R. S., Madison, S. M., & Kuklinski, M. R. (1995). Raising expectations in schooling: Obstacles and opportunities for change. *American Educational Research Journal, 32,* 121–159.

Weisberg, D., Hirsh-Pasek, K., & Golinkoff, R. (2013). Guided play: Where curricular goals meet a playful pedagogy. *Mind, Brain, and Education, 7* (2), 104–113.

Weissberg, R., & Cascarino, J. (2013). Academic learning + social-emotional learning = national priority. *Phi Delta Kappan, 95*(2), 8–13.

Weissbourd, R., & Dodge, T. (2012). Senseless extravagance, shocking gaps. *Educational Leadership, 69*(5), 74–78.

Weissbourd, R., & Jones, S. (2012). Joining hands against bullying. *Educational Leadership, 70*(2), 26–31.

Wells, A. S., Hirshberg, D., Lipton, M., & Oakes, J. (1995). Bounding the case within its context: A constructivist approach to studying detracking reform. *Educational Researcher, 24*(5), 18–24.

Welner, K. (2006). K–12 race-conscious student assignment policies: Law, social science, and diversity. *Review of Educational Research, 76*(3), 349–382.

Wentzel, K. (2010). Students' relationships with teachers. In J. Meece & J. Eccles (Eds.), *Handbook of research on schools, schooling, and human development* (pp. 75–91). New York, NY: Routledge.

Wentzel, K. R. (2003). School adjustment. In W. M. Reynolds & G. E. Miller (Eds.), *Handbook of psychology: Vol. 7. Educational psychology* (pp. 235–258). Hoboken, NJ: Wiley.

Wentzel, K. R., & Brophy, J. (2014). *Motivating students to learn* (4th ed.). New York, NY: Routledge.

Wentzel, K. R., & Wigfield, A. (Eds.) (2009). *Handbook of motivation at school.* New York, NY: Routledge.

Wentzel, K. R., Barry, C. M., & Caldwell, K. A. (2004). Friendships in middle school: Influences on motivation and school adjustment. *Journal of Educational Psychology, 96*(2), 195–203.

Wentzel, K., & Watkins, D. (2011). Instruction based on peer interactions. In R. Mayer & P. Alexander (Eds.), *Handbook of research on learning and instruction* (pp. 322–343). New York, NY: Routledge.

Wertsch, J. V. (2007). Mediation. In H. Daniels, M. Cole, & J. V. Wertsch (Eds.), *The Cambridge companion to Vygotsky* (pp. 178–192). New York, NY: Cambridge University Press.

Wessler, S. (2011). Confronting racial and religious tensions. *Educational Leadership, 69*(1), 36–39.

Westwater, A., & Wolfe, P. (2000). The brain-compatible curriculum. *Educational Leadership, 58*(3), 49–52.

Wheeler, J. J., & Richey, D. D. (2014). *Behavior management: Principles and practices of positive behavior supports* (3rd ed). Boston, MA: Pearson.

Wheeler, J. J., Mayton, M. R., & Carter, S. L. (2015). *Methods for teaching students with autism spectrum disorders.* Boston, MA: Pearson.

White, A. G., & Bailey, J. S. (1990). Reducing disruptive behaviors of elementary physical education students with sit and watch. *Journal of Applied Behavior Analysis, 3,* 353–359.

Whitehurst, G., Crone, D., Zevenbergen, A., Schultz, M., Velting, O., & Fischel, J. (1999). Outcomes of an emergent literacy intervention from Head Start through second grade. *Journal of Educational Psychology, 91*(2), 261–272.

Whitman, S., Williams, C., & Shah, A. (2004). *Sinai Health System's community health survey: Report 1.* Chicago, IL: Sinai Health System.

Wigfield, A., & Eccles, J. (1989). Test anxiety in elementary and secondary students. *Educational Psychologist, 24,* 159–183.

Wigfield, A., & Eccles, J. (2000). Expectancy-value theory of achievement motivation. *Contemporary Educational Psychology, 25*(1), 68–81.

Wigfield, A., & Guthrie, J. (2010). The impact of concept-oriented reading instruction on students' reading motivation, reading engagement, and reading comprehension. In J. Meece & J. Eccles (Eds.), *Handbook of research on schools, schooling, and human development* (pp. 463–477). New York, NY: Routledge.

Wigfield, A., Byrnes, J., & Eccles, J. (2006). Development during early and middle adolescence. In P. Alexander & P. Winne (Eds.), *Handbook of educational psychology* (2nd ed., pp. 87–114). Mahwah, NJ: Erlbaum.

Wigfield, A., Tonks, S., & Klauda, S. (2009). Expectancy-value theory. In K. R. Wentzel & A. Wigfield (Eds.), *Handbook of motivation at school.* (pp. 55–75). New York, NY: Routledge.

Wiggan, G. (2007). Race, school achievement, and educational inequality: Toward a student-based inquiry perspective. *Review of Educational Research, 77*(3), 310–333.

Wiggins, G. (1993). Assessment: Authenticity, context, and validity. *Phi Delta Kappan, 75*(3), 200–214.

Wiggins, G. (1994). Toward better report cards. *Educational Leadership, 52*(2), 28–37.

Wiggins, G. (2012). Seven keys to effective feedback. *Educational Leadership, 70*(1), 10–16.

Wiggins, G., & McTighe, J. (2007). *Schooling by design: Mission, action, and achievement.* Alexandria, VA: ASCD.

Wijekumar, K., Meyer, B., Lei, P., Lin, Y., Johnson, L., Spielvogel, J., Shurmatz, K., … & Cook, M. (2014). Multisite randomized controlled trial examining intelligent tutoring of structure strategy for fifth-grade readers. *Journal of Research on Educational Effectiveness, 7*(4), 331–357.

Wiles, J., & Bondi, J. (2015). *Curriculum development: A guide to practice*. Boston, MA: Pearson.

Wiliam, D. (2007). Content then process: Teacher learning communities in the service of formative assessment. In D. B. Reeves (Ed.), *Ahead of the curve: The power of assessment to transform teaching and learning*. Bloomington, IN: Solution Tree.

Wiliam, D. (2007/2008, December/January). Informative assessment. *Educational Leadership, 65*(4), 36–42.

Wiliam, D. (2009). *Assessment for learning: Why, what, and how?* London, England: University of London, Institute of Education.

Wiliam, D. (2010). Standardized testing and school accountability. *Educational Psychologist, 45*(2), 107–122.

Wiliam, D. (2014). The right questions, the right way. *Educational Leadership, 71*(6), 16–19.

Wiliam, D., & Leahy, S. (2015). *Embedding formative assessment: Practical techniques for K–12 classrooms*. West Palm Beach, FL: Learning Sciences Intenrational.

Wilkins, C., Gersten, R., Decker, L., Grunden, L., Brasiel, S., Brunnert, K., & Jayanthi, M. (2012). *Does a summer reading program based on lexiles affect reading comprehension?* (NCEE 2012-4006). Washington, DC: NCEER, IES, USDOE.

Wilkins, J. (2000). *Group activities to include students with special needs*. Thousand Oaks, CA: Corwin.

Williams, D., & Dixon, P. (2013). Impact of garden-based learning on academic outcomes in schools: Synthesis of research between 1990 and 2010. *Review of Educational Research, 83*(2), 211–235.

Williams, R. (2009). Black-white biracial students in American schools: A review of the literature. *Review of Educational Research, 79*(2), 776–804.

Willingham, D. (2003). Students remember what they think about. *American Educator, 27*(2), 37–41.

Willingham, D. T. (2004). Practice makes perfect—but only if you practice beyond the point of perfection. *American Educator, 28*(1), 31–33.

Willingham, D. T. (2006). Brain-based learning: More fiction than fact. *American Educator, 30*(3), 30–37.

Willingham, D., & Daniel, D. (2012). Teaching to what student have in common. *Educational Leadership, 69*(5), 16–21.

Willis, J. (2007). *Brain-friendly strategies for the inclusion classroom*. Alexandria, VA: ASCD.

Willis, J. A. (2006). Research-based teaching strategies for improving learning success. California Association of Independent Schools (CAIS) Faculty Newsletter.

Willoughby, T., Porter, L., Belsito, L., & Yearsley, T. (1999). Use of elaboration strategies by students in grades two, four, and six. *The Elementary School Journal, 99*(3), 221–232.

Wilson, G., & Blednick, J. (2011). *Teaching in tandem: Effective co-teaching in the inclusive classroom*. Alexandria, VA: ASCD.

Winsler, A. (2003). Vygotskian perspectives in early childhood education. *Early Education and Development, 14*(3), 253–270.

Witte, R. (2012). Classroom assessment for teachers. New York, NY: McGraw-Hill.

Wittwer, J., & Renkl, A. (2008). Why instructional explanations often do not work: A framework for understanding the effectiveness of instructional explanations. *Educational Psychologist, 43*(1), 49–64.

Wixson, K. (2011). A systemic view of RTI research. *Elementary School Journal, 111*(4), 503–510.

Wolfe, P. (2010). *Brain matters: Translating research into classroom practice* (2nd ed.). Alexandria, VA: ASCD.

Wolk, R. (2010). Education: The case for making it personal. *Educational Leadership, 67*(7), 16–21.

Wonder-McDowell, C., Reutzel, D., & Smith, J. (2011). Does instructional alignment matter? *The Elementary School Journal, 112*(2), 259–279.

Wong, B., & Butler, D. L. (2013). *Learning about learning disabilities* (4th ed.). New York, NY: Elsevier.

Wong, H., & Wong, R. (2004). *The first days of school: How to be an effective teacher*. Mountain View, CA: Wong.

Woolfolk, A., & Perry, N. (2015). *Child and adolescent development*. Boston, MA: Pearson.

Woolfolk, A., Winne, P., & Perry, N. (2015). *Educational Psychology* (6th ed.). Upper Saddle River, NJ: Pearson.

Woolfolk-Hoy, A., Hoy, W. K., & Davis, H. (2009). Teachers' self-efficacy beliefs. In K. Wentzel & A. Wigfield (Eds.), *Handbook of motivation in school*. Mahwah, NJ: Erlbaum.

Woolley, M., Rose, R., Orthner, D., Akos, P., & Jones-Sanpei, H. (2013). Advancing academic achievement through career relevance in the middle grades: A longitudinal evaluation of Career-Start. *American Educational Research Journal, 50*(6), 1309–1335.

Worden, J., Hinton, C., & Fischer, K. (2011). What does the brain have to do with learning? *Phi Delta Kappan, 92*(8), 8–13.

Wormeli, R. (2011). Redos and retakes done right. *Educational Leadership, 69*(3), 22–26.

Wormeli, R. (2014). Motivating young adolescents. *Educational Leadership, 72*(1), 26–31.

Wright, J. C., Huston, A. C., Murphy, C., St. Peters, M., Pinon, M., Scantlin, R. M., & Kotler, J. A. (2001). The relations of early television viewing to school readiness and vocabulary of children from low-income families: The Early Window Project. *Child Development, 72,* 1347–1366.

Wulczyn, F., Smithgall, C., & Chen, L. (2009). Child well-being: The intersection of schools and child welfare. *Review of Research in Education, 33,* 35–62.

WWC (2014a). *Energize instruction to maintain or increase academic engagement*. Retrieved from ies.ed.gov/ncee/wwc/news.aspx?sid=10

WWC (2014b). *Preventing and addressing behavior problems: Tips from the What Works Clearinghouse*. Retrieved from ies.ed.gov/ncee/wwc/news.aspx?sid=8

WWC (2015). *Check and Connect: WWC intervention report*. Washington, DC: Author.

Wyra, M., Lawson, M., & Hungi, N. (2007). The mnemonic keyword method: The effects of bidirectional retrieval training and of ability to image on foreign language vocabulary recall. *Learning and Instruction, 17*(3), 360–371.

Xu, J., & Corno, L. (2003). Family help and homework management reported by middle school students. *The Elementary School Journal, 103*(5), 503–517.

Yeager, D., Walton, G., & Cohen, G. (2013). Addressing achievement gaps with psychological interventions. *Phi Delta Kappan, 94*(5), 62–65.

Yeager, S., & Dweck, C. (2012). Mindsets that promote resilience: When students believe that personal characteristics can be developed. *Educational Psychologist, 47*(4), 302–314.

Yeager, D., Romero, C., Paunesku, D., Hulleman, C., Schneider, B., Hinojosa, C., … & Dweck, C. (2016). Using design thinking ot improve psychological interventions: The case of the growth mindset during the transition to high school. *Educational Psychology, 108*(3), 374–391.

Yeager, D.S., & Walton, G.M. (2011). Social-psychological interventions in education: They're not magic. *Review of Educational Research, 81*(2), 267–301.

Yell, M. L., Meadows, N. B., Drasgow, E., & Shriner, J. G. (2014). *Evidence-based practices for educating students with emotional and behavioral disorders* (2nd ed.). Upper Saddle River, NJ: Pearson.

Yeung, J., Linver, M., & Brooks-Gunn, J. (2002). How money matters for young children's development: Human capital and family process. *Child Development, 73,* 1861–1879.

Yoder, N. (2014). *Teaching the whole child: Instructional practices that support social-emotional learning in three teacher evaluation frameworks.* Washington, DC: AIR.

Yonezawa, S., Wells, A. S., & Serna, I. (2002). Choosing tracks: "Freedom of choice" in detracking schools. *American Educational Research Journal, 39*(1), 37–67.

York-Barr, J., Sommerness, J., & Hur, J. (2008). Teacher leadership. In T. L. Good (Ed.), *21st century learning* (Vol. 1, pp. 12–20). Thousand Oaks, CA: Sage.

Yoshikawa, H., Weiland, C., Brooks-Gunn, J., Burchinal, M., Espinosa, L.,…& Zaslow, M. (2013). *Investing in our future: The evidence base on preschool education (Vol 9).* Society for Research in Child Development and Foundation for Child Development.

Zettergren, P. (2003). School adjustment in adolescence for previously rejected, average and popular children. *British Journal of Educational Psychology, 72*(3), 207–221.

Zhao, Y. (2009). Needed: Global villagers. *Educational Leadership, 67*(1), 60–65.

Zhao, Y. (2015). (Ed.). *Counting what counts: Reframing education outcomes.* Bloomington, IN: Solution Tree.

Zigler, E., Pfannenstiel, J., & Seitz, V. (2008). The Parents as Teachers program and school success: A replication and extension. *Journal of Primary Prevention, 29*(2), 103–120.

Zimmerman, B. (2013). From cognitive modeling to self-regulation: A social cognitive career path. *Educational Psychologist, 48*(3), 135–147.

Zimmerman, B. J., & Schunk, D. H. (Eds.) (2011). *Handbook of self-regulation of learning and performance.* New York, NY: Routledge.

Zimmerman, S., Rodriguez, M., Rewey, K., & Heidemann, S. (2008). The impact of an early literacy initiative on the long-term academic success of diverse students. *Journal of Education for Students Placed at Risk, 13*(4), 452–481.

Zirpoli, T. (2016). *Behavior management: Positive application for teachers* (7th ed.). Boston, MA: Pearson.

Zittleman, K., & Sadker, D. (2003). The unfinished gender revolution. *Educational Leadership, 60*(4), 59–62.

Zmuda, A. (2008). Springing into active learning. *Educational Leadership, 66*(3), 38–43.

Zmuda, A. (2010). *Breaking free from myths about teaching and learning: Innovation as an engine for student success.* Alexandria, VA: ASCD.

Zohar, A., & Peled, B. (2008). The effects of explicit teaching of metastrategic knowledge on low- and high-achieving students. *Learning and Instruction, 18*(4), 337–353.

Zvoch, K., & Stevens, J. (2013). Summer school effects in a randomized field trial. *Early Childhood Research Quarterly, 28*(1), 24–32.

NAME INDEX

A

Abbott, R., 56, 58, 294
Abbott, R. D., 278, 292
Abdul Jabbar, A., 233
Abel, Y., 71
Aber, J. L., 261
Aber, L., 56, 58, 227
Abilock, D., 235
Abrami, P. C., 72, 168, 202, 208, 224, 231
Achilles, C. M., 14
Ackerman, P., 125
Acock, A., 293
Adams, A., 148
Adams, C., 221
Adams, J. L., 205
Addison, P., 326
Adelman, H. F., 261
Adesope, O., 80, 148, 153
Agard, J., 327
Agodini, R., 229, 236
Aikens, N., 70, 72
Airasian, P., 345, 354
Akey, K. L., 256
Akiba, M., 228
Akos, P., 264
Al-Mansour, M., 53
Al-Namlah, A. S., 34
Al-Otaiba, S., 201, 305
Alameda-Lawson, T., 83
Alberto, P. A., 99, 101, 102, 104, 105, 107, 108, 111, 221, 283, 284, 285, 286, 288, 308
Alborz, A., 304
Albright, E., 219
Alexander, J., 264
Alexander, K., 67, 68, 69
Alexander, P., 197
Alexander, P. A., 248, 263
Algozzine, B., 331
Alicea, S., 227
Alidoust, M., 147
Allen, A. B., 264
Allen, C., 221, 263
Allen, J., 263
Allen, L., 69
Allen, L. K., 231
Allen, R., 292
Allen-Jones, G. L., 71
Allensworth, E., 221
Allington, R., 40, 69, 72, 221, 228
Allor, J. H., 223, 305
Allspach, J., 85
Allyn, P., 403
Alper, S., 115
Altenderfer, L., 309
Alter, P., 283, 285, 288
Altermatt, E. R., 85

Ambridge, B., 125
Amendum, S., 331
Amico, M., 88
Amrein, A., 400
Amrein-Beardsley, A., 8, 408
Anagnostopoulos, D., 221
Ancess, J., 61
Ancheta, A., 78
Anderman, E. M., 59, 188, 192, 248, 256, 259, 263
Anderman, L. H., 259
Anderson, C., 283, 285, 288
Anderson, G. E., 221
Anderson, J., 375
Anderson, J. R., 129, 139, 142, 145, 179, 188, 189
Anderson, K., 56
Anderson, L. M., 147
Anderson, R., 204
Anderson, R. C., 151
Anderson-Inman, L., 331
Andrew, M., 221
Andrews, D., 15
Andrews, G., 32, 38, 68, 71
Anglemeyer, K., 74
Ansary, N., 295
Anstrom, K. A., 81, 82
Anthony, H. M., 147
Anthony, J. L., 38, 39, 224
Antil, L., 202, 204
Antonetti, J. V., 160
Apthorp, H., 228
Archer, J., 241
Archibald, S. J., 406, 408
Arends, R. I., 176
Arici, A., 9
Armijo, M., 72, 223, 308
Armony, J., 125
Armstrong, C., 224
Armstrong, T., 91, 329
Arneson, J., 67
Arnold, M. L., 51
Aronson, E., 201
Aronson, J., 77, 87
Artelt, C., 71
Arter, J., 349, 369
Artiles, A., 307, 328
Arzubiaga, A., 81
Aschbacher, P., 197
Ash, K., 233, 235, 238
Ashburner, J., 134
Ashcraft, M. H., 123, 125, 127, 141, 147, 173
Asher, N., 67
Asher, S. R., 333
Assouline, S., 316
Atkins, J., 217

Atkinson, J. W., 254
Atkinson, L., 154
Atkinson, R., 154
Atkinson, R. C., 123, 130, 143, 154
Atkinson, R. K., 167
Attanucci, J., 51
August, D., 41, 80, 82, 83, 167
Aupperlee, J., 67
Austin, V. L., 56, 60
Ausubel, D. P., 150
Avalos, A., 201
Axelrod, S., 283, 284
Axford, N., 71
Azano, A., 316
Azevedo, R., 192
Azzam, A., 9, 263

B

Babineau, M. E., 29, 31
Babyak, A., 201
Baddeley, J., 51
Badgett, J., 346, 356, 358, 364
Badke, W., 235
Badli, T., 168
Bailey, F., 127, 137, 141, 146, 147, 148, 149
Bailey, J. S., 103, 105, 106, 287
Baillargeon, R., 31
Bain, J., 24
Bainbridge, W. L., 225
Baines, C., 329
Baines, E., 197
Baines, L., 329
Bajovic, M., 272, 273, 277, 281, 283, 295, 312
Baker, J., 67
Baker, L. L., 81, 82
Baker, R., 24
Baker, S., 40, 81, 83, 198, 203, 308, 331
Bakia, M., 238
Balfanz, R., 60, 61, 72, 227
Bali, V., 221
Ball, D., 6, 10
Ball, E. W., 40
Balu, R., 227
Bandalos, D. L., 259
Bandura, A., 112–114, 116, 118, 192, 249, 252, 253, 256, 261
Bandy, T., 58
Banerjee, R., 53
Bangert-Drowns, R. L., 195, 402
Bangser, M., 58
Banko, K., 261
Banks, J. A., 66, 77, 79, 80, 84
Banks, S., 339, 350, 354
Bankson, N. W., 310
Bannister, P., 230

SUBJECT INDEX